The Bibl
in One Year

A Commentary

The Bible in One Year

A Commentary

Nicky Gumbel

First published in Great Britain in 2019 by Hodder & Stoughton
An Hachette UK company

In association with Alpha International

This edition first published in 2021

1

Some scriptural references have been italised by the author for emphasis.

A CIP catalogue record for this title is available from the British Library

Trade Paperback ISBN 978 1 473 67707 4
eBook ISBN 978 1 473 68436 2

Typeset in Circular Std 9/10 pts by MPS Limited

Printed and bound in Great Britain by Clays Ltd, Elcograf S.p.A

Hodder & Stoughton policy is to use papers that are natural, renewable and recyclable products and made from wood grown in sustainable forests. The logging and manufacturing processes are expected to conform to the environmental regulations of the country of origin.

Hodder & Stoughton Ltd
Carmelite House
50 Victoria Embankment
London EC4Y 0DZ

Alpha.org
www.hodderfaith.com

Contents

Preface

For much of my life I was not interested in Christianity. My father was a secular Jew and my mother rarely went to church. I was at times an atheist and at times unsure of what I believed. I had studied the Bible in religion classes at school but had ended up rejecting it all and arguing against the Christian faith.

On Valentine's Night 1974 my convictions were challenged by my closest friend at university. I had just returned from a party when he and his girlfriend arrived home and told me that they had become Christians. I was horrified! I knew I had to help my friends so I thought that I would embark on some thorough research of the subject. I happened to have a rather dusty copy of the Bible on my shelves, so that night I picked it up and started reading. I read all the way through Matthew, Mark and Luke, and halfway through John's Gospel. I fell asleep. When I woke up, I finished John's Gospel and carried on through Acts, Romans, and 1 and 2 Corinthians. I was completely gripped by what I read. Previously it had meant virtually nothing to me. This time it came alive and I could not put it down. It had a ring of truth about it. I knew as I read it I had to respond because it spoke so powerfully to me. Very shortly afterwards I put my faith in Jesus Christ.

Most days since then I have tried to start the day by reading the Bible and praying. In 1990, Sandy Millar gave me a Christmas present of the *Bible in One Year* – which I have used ever since. The *Bible in One Year* is a special arrangement of the Bible designed to let you get the most out of reading the whole Bible methodically in the space of one year. For every day in the year, starting on 1 January, readings are given from Psalms or Proverbs, the New Testament, and the Old Testament. The New Testament is presented in traditional Bible order and the Old Testament books are placed in broadly chronological order. Psalms and Proverbs have been divided evenly over the whole year.

Each day, the Psalm or Proverb is printed first to act as a call to worship God and help us to focus on him. Next is the New Testament passage which often most directly points to Jesus. The Old Testament passage is last, not because the Old Testament is unimportant, but because reading the Old Testament passage after the New Testament reminds us to read it through the lens of Christ. Jesus is the fulfilment of the Old Testament, and it helps us to make that connection more readily if we have already been reading from the New Testament.

In January 2009, I started to write comments on each day's readings as I read the passages and looked to apply them to my life. Pippa joined me and wrote her own short reflection each day which became 'Pippa Adds' in the digital version of this volume. At Holy Trinity Brompton, we have also begun using this format of daily Bible reading as a church family. It has given added impetus to all of us in the church to read the Bible every day, and it has created a deeper level of community because we are all reading the same thing at the same time. Now that commentary is in the form of an app and the passages are read by millions of people around the world.

There appears to be a huge hunger for spirituality today. As Jesus said, 'People do not live on bread alone, but on every word that comes from the mouth of God' (Matthew 4:4). Recently, we had a reunion of our small group at the end of an Alpha course. As we went around the group at the end of the evening asking how people were getting on, one of the things that surprised me was that all of them were studying the Bible in One Year on the app and reading the notes that Pippa and I circulate each day. This included not only those who had recently come to faith in Christ, but also those who would not yet have considered themselves to be Christians. All of them seemed to be finding it helpful in their exploration of faith.

At the end of the course, many people who have done Alpha ask the question, 'What next?'. Joining a church and developing a prayer life are key next steps, but so too is reading the Bible. If all those on the course are studying the same passages, it means that we are able to discuss and exchange thoughts on similar biblical themes, get excited about what we discover together, and also encourage and support each other when the reading is feeling more of a struggle.

There are parts of the Bible, especially parts of the Old Testament, which are extremely difficult to understand and interpret. There are moral and historical difficulties. It is encouraging in some ways that even the apostle Peter found some of St Paul's letters 'hard to understand' (2 Peter 3:16).

Might I encourage you, if you are new to reading the Bible, to approach it in some ways as you would a crossword puzzle. If you are stuck on one clue, don't give up. Move onto the next one and if you can deal with that it may help with resolving the other clues. In other words, don't get bogged down with the difficult passages in the Bible. Try to find bits that you do understand and can apply to your own life. You can always come back to the difficult parts later and hopefully what you have learnt from the passages that you can understand may help you to resolve some of the previous difficulties, just like what happens with a crossword puzzle.

If you miss a day, or even a few days, please don't give up. I would encourage you to do it as often as you can and come back to the days that you've missed next time round. The aim is not to become legalistic but to encourage us all to establish a regular habit of reading the Bible.

The American pastor, Rick Warren, has written that 'reading the Bible generates life, it produces change, it heals hurts, it builds character, it transforms circumstances, it imparts joy, it overcomes adversity, it defeats temptation, it infuses hope, it releases power, it cleanses the mind.'[1] I hope and pray that reading the *Bible in One Year* brings much benefit to your life, just as it has done to mine.

I cannot claim that anything I've written is original. Over the last forty-five years in my journey as a Christian I have listened to so many talks and read numerous inspiring books. I owe a massive dept to numerous people. Among others who have greatly influenced me over the years are Sandy Millar, Father Raniero Cantalamessa, Jackie Pullinger, Bishop Lesslie Newbigin, John Stott, Joyce Meyer, Rick Warren, C. S. Lewis, Billy Graham, Jean Vanier and many, many more. I am also hugely grateful to all those who have contributed to the editing, Jo Soda, Stephen Foster, David Ingall, Mark Knight, Henry Gumbel, Jonny Gumbel, Nicky Lee, Jago Wynne, Mark Elsdon-Dew, Tim Matthews, Pete Bellenger, Sophie Matthews, Ros Suni, Sarah O'Sullivan, Stephanie Fons, Tilly Bacon, Sarah Toulmin, Serena Wynter, Erin Clifford, James Borrows, Stewart Sylvester, Alice Milner, Helen Kirkland, Philly Dobbin, Victoria Brewer, Julia Evans, Alice Goodwin-Hudson, Rebecca Cotter, Susie Diver, Kate Crossland-Page, Amy Watkins, Lucy Simpson, Max Perkin, Louise Fowkes, Mollie Nicholson and I don't know how many other people over the years. I have gleaned wisdom from so many of them and even this is a quote from Bishop Lesslie Newbigin, who wrote in the preface to *The Gospel in a Pluralist Society*, 'I make no claim, either to originality or to scholarship. I am a pastor and a preacher, trying to make available to my fellow pastors and others such thinking as I have gleaned in my unsystematic reading, bearing on the topic I am trying to address. A scholarly work would contain references to all the relevant literature and evidence that the writer had taken in to account of all the various arguments. To have dignified my text with a proper apparatus of footnotes would have been to pretend to a kind of scholarship which I do not possess. It is better in this foreword simply to acknowledge some massive debts to writers from whom I have borrowed without always acknowledging the fact.'[2] This gathering together of some of the thoughts I have been so encouraged by over the years is intended to be passed on as an encouragement and inspiration to those who read it.

Nicky

1 January | Day 1
New Year's Resolutions

I belong to a squash club, which is also a gym. Each year on 1 January they bring in extra gym equipment. The place is packed out. By about 7 January, they move all the extra equipment out again, as most people have given up their New Year's resolution, and the club returns to normal!

- Get fit
- Lose weight
- Reduce drinking
- Stop smoking
- Get out of debt

There is nothing wrong with making these common New Year's resolutions. Of course, all of us make resolutions that we fail to keep.

The good news is that each year is an *opportunity* for a fresh start. But then so is each week. Every Sunday is the first day of the week – a new beginning. Actually, every day is an opportunity for a new beginning.

The first three words in the Bible are, 'In *the beginning...*' (Genesis 1:1). Each of the passages for today tells us something about new beginnings and new opportunities, and suggests some possible New Year's resolutions.

READING FROM PSALMS

Psalm 1:1–6
'Delight' in the Bible

If you are beginning the challenge to read the *Bible in One Year*, this psalm has encouraging words for you.

The promise is that if you 'delight' in God's word and 'meditate' on Scripture 'day and night' (v.2), your life will be blessed. *Happiness* comes from what *happens* to you. *Blessing* is what happens to you through knowing God and meditating on his words.

God promises you *fruitfulness* ('which yields its fruit in season', v.3b), *vitality* ('whose leaves do not wither', v.3c) and *prosperity* ('whatever they do prospers', v.3d), though not necessarily material prosperity!

This message is backed up by a glance across at the ultimate fate of 'the wicked'. The psalmist does not try to pretend that the wicked don't sometimes prosper. He simply reminds us of the transitory nature of that prosperity – 'they are like chaff that the wind blows away ... [they] will perish' (vv.4, 6).

The key to lasting – and ultimately eternal – fruitfulness and vitality lies in your relationship with God. As you seek to follow 'the way of the righteous', you are assured that the Lord himself will watch over you (v.6).

PRAYER

Lord, thank you for your wonderful promises as I resolve to make a regular habit of delighting in your word and meditating on it.

NEW TESTAMENT READING

Matthew 1:1–25
Focus on Jesus

Resolve to focus your life on Jesus. The Bible is all about Jesus. The New Testament opens with his family tree.

As we read the list of Jesus' ancestors it is encouraging to see that they include Tamar (the adulteress), Rahab (the prostitute), Ruth (the non-Jewish Moabite), Solomon (who was conceived after King David's adulterous affair with Bathsheba), as well as many others. Thankfully, God uses sinful human beings and, therefore, can use us. Whatever your past, however broken your life may seem right now, God can use you to do something great with your life.

The very name 'Jesus' means, 'he will save his people from their sins' (v.21). Every time we use the name Jesus it reminds us that our greatest need is not for happiness or contentment (although these may both be by-products). Our greatest need, as with Jesus' ancestors, is for forgiveness. Therefore, we need a Saviour.

The beginning of Matthew shows us that Jesus is the completion of all that is recorded in the Old Testament:

• Jesus is the climax of history
Matthew opens his Gospel by summarising the Old Testament story in terms of Jesus' ancestry (vv.1–17). The Old Testament tells the story that Jesus completes. Matthew sets out the history of the people of God in terms of three equal periods: fourteen generations from Abraham to David, fourteen from David to the exile and fourteen from the exile to Christ (v.17).

In the genealogy, biological generations are skipped over (as was quite common in Old Testament family trees). Matthew was pointing out that Old Testament history falls into three approximately equal spans of time between crucial events. Jesus is the end of the line as far as the Old Testament story goes – the climax has been reached.

• In Jesus, all the promises of God are fulfilled
Jesus is not only the completion of the Old Testament story at a historical level, he is also the fulfilment of the Old Testament prophecies and all of God's promises.

Matthew concludes each of five scenes from the conception, birth and early childhood of Jesus by quoting the Hebrew Scriptures that have been 'fulfilled' by the events described (Matthew 1:22–3; 2:5–6, 17–18, 23; 4:14–16).

The first one is the fulfilment in the conception of Jesus: 'All this took place *to fulfil* what the Lord had said through the prophet: "The virgin will be with child and will give birth to a son and they will call him Immanuel" (which means "God with us")' (1:22–3).

All of history, prophecy and promise, is completed in Jesus. Your whole life is completed in Jesus. Every part of your life: your work, family, relationships, friends, memories and dreams are completed in Jesus.

PRAYER

Lord, thank you for this promise for the new year – that, in Jesus, you are with me. Help me to focus my life on you in the year ahead.

OLD TESTAMENT READING

Genesis 1:1–2:17
Enjoy God's creation

You are not here by chance. This universe is God's creation. You are made in his image.

Genesis gives an account of the beginning of the universe. It goes way beyond the scientific theories of '*how?*' and '*when?*' It answers the questions of '*who*' and '*why?*' Scientific theories do not prove or disprove this explanation. Rather, they are complementary.

Reading this passage through the lens of the New Testament we see the whole Trinity involved in creation. The Hebrew noun for God (*Elohim*) is a plural noun. The Holy Spirit was involved in creation (1:2). It was through Jesus that creation came into being: 'And God said…' (v.3a). Jesus is God's Word and through him the universe was created (see John 1:1–3).

In the midst of this account of the creation, there is an amazing throwaway line showing the immense power of God: '*He also made the stars*' (Genesis 1:16). We now know there are probably between 100 and 400 billion stars in our galaxy alone, and our galaxy is but one of around 100 billion galaxies. He made them all, *just like that*!

The pinnacle of his creation was human beings. You are made in the image of God (v.27). If we want to know what God is like, it is men and women together ('male and female', v.27b) who reflect his image.

Every human being is created in his image and should be treated with dignity, respect and love. Your ability to communicate with God is a reflection of the fact that you are made in his image.

God approves of all that he created. He said, 'It is good.' Many people feel worthless, insecure and of no value. But God did not create rubbish. God created you. He loves you and approves of you. He may not approve of everything you do, but he loves you unconditionally, wholeheartedly and continually.

We see in this passage that *work* is a *blessing:* 'The LORD God took the man and put him in the Garden of Eden *to work it* and *take care of it*' (2:15). Work is part of God's good creation – not a result of the fall. This passage also reminds us that taking care of the environment is right at the heart of God's plan for human beings.

Rest is not an optional extra. It is what God did ('he rested', v.2). These days of rest are days of special blessing: 'God blessed the seventh day and made it holy' (v.3). Holidays are holy days. They point to the fact that life is primarily about *being* rather than doing. Don't feel guilty about taking time off. Holidays are good in themselves. They are also a time to recharge spiritually.

Don't work too hard. God took time to rest and enjoy what he had made. You are not supposed to work constantly. You are created with a need for relaxation and rest – taking the time to enjoy your work and the fruit of your work.

In Genesis 2:16–17 we see that God gave Adam and Eve far-reaching *permission* ('you are free to eat from any tree in the garden', v.16), with one *prohibition* – 'but you must not eat from the tree of the knowledge of good and evil' (v.17a). He warned them of the *penalty* if they disobeyed ('when you eat of it you will surely die', v.17b). You do not need to know and experience evil. God wanted you to know only good.

PRAYER

Lord, thank you for this universe that you have made. Help me to keep well away from evil and to enjoy all the good things you have given us to enjoy.

2 January | Day 2

Your First Question

'What is your first question going to be?' I was preparing my cross-examination for one of the first criminal trials in which I was involved when I worked as a barrister. A senior and experienced lawyer was helping me prepare. He showed me the significance of a first question.

READING FROM PSALMS

Psalm 2:1–12

1. The first question in the *Psalms* is about Jesus

It is all about Jesus. The safest place to be in life is close to Jesus.

Paul, preaching the gospel in Antioch, quotes this psalm. He says, 'We tell you the *good news*: What God promised our ancestors he has fulfilled for us, their children, by raising up *Jesus*. As it is written in the second Psalm: "You are my Son; today I have become your Father"' (Acts 13:32–3, quoting Psalm 2:7).

It is Jesus who is his *'anointed'* (Psalm 2:2). The Hebrew word here is *mashiach* ('messiah'). He is the Christ, the Son of God, whom we are to love: 'Kiss his son' (v.12).

The psalm's original context probably concerned a particular situation involving a human king of Israel. Yet, as we read it with a larger horizon in mind, we see that the first question asked in the Psalms points forward in anticipation to Jesus. Why do people 'conspire' and 'plot' against him (vv.1–2)?

This is exactly what we see happening in the New Testament, even in today's passage, in relation to Jesus. Right from the start of Jesus' life, we see rulers *gathering together* and *conspiring and plotting in vain* (Matthew 2:3–4).

Yet the psalm ends, 'Blessed (happy, fortunate, and to be envied) are all those who seek refuge and put their trust in him!' (v.12b, AMP). With all the storms of life, and supremely the storm of Jesus' coming in final judgment, the only safe place to be is *'in Him'*.

PRAYER

Lord, thank you that as I look to the year ahead and all the potential challenges, opportunities and possibilities, the safest place to be is in you.

NEW TESTAMENT READING

Matthew 2:1–18

2. The first question in the *New Testament* is about *Jesus*

Appropriately, the first question in the New Testament is also about Jesus. The whole of the Old Testament is fulfilled in Jesus.

The Magi (often referred to as 'the wise men') sensed the significance of Jesus' birth. They asked, '*Where is the one who has been born king of the Jews?*' (v.2). They sought and found him. When 'they saw the child ... they bowed down and worshipped him' (v.11). They recognised that Jesus was the fulfilment of all the hopes and dreams of the people up to his birth.

Jesus is the one who *fulfils* all God's promises. In yesterday's reading we looked at one example of such a fulfilment. Today we see three more examples:

1. Place of his birth

Matthew saw that even the place of Jesus' birth was prophesied in Micah 5:2. It was out of *Bethlehem* that the 'ruler' and 'shepherd' would arise, '*for this is what the prophet has written*' (Matthew 2:5–6).

2. Exile in Egypt

When Herod tried to kill Jesus, the family escaped to Egypt (v.13). Matthew writes, 'So was *fulfilled* what the Lord had said through the prophet: "Out of *Egypt* I called my son"' (v.15; see also Hosea 11:1).

3. Slaughter of the children
When Herod ordered the murder of all boys under the age of two (Matthew 2:16), this *fulfilled* the prophecy of Jeremiah 31:15 (Matthew 2:17–18).

PRAYER

Lord Jesus, today I want to bow down and worship you. I want to offer you everything I have – my life, my all.

OLD TESTAMENT READING

Genesis 2:18–4:16

3. The first question in the *Bible* is about *God's goodness*

Do you ever find yourself doubting whether God's way really is the best? Do you find yourself wondering whether, even though God says it is wrong, something is worth trying anyway?

God gave to humankind everything they could possibly want. The whole created world was made for us to enjoy. Every possible need was catered for. The pinnacle of God's creation was humankind. The need for community was solved by the creation of other human beings: 'It is not good for the man to be alone' (2:18).

It started with the beautiful gift of marriage: 'For this reason a man will leave his father and mother and be united to his wife, and they will become one flesh' (v.24). Marriage is the lifelong union of a man and a woman in which sex, another of God's beautiful gifts, is to be enjoyed with intimacy and freedom, without guilt or 'shame' (vv.24–5).

Yet despite this abundant provision of everything good, human beings looked for something more and they succumbed to the temptation to take forbidden fruit.

The temptation started with doubts about God. Here is the first question in the Bible: '*Did God really say, "You must not eat from any tree in the garden"?*' (3:1). Behind this question is the demonic lie that God is withholding from you something that is really exciting.

Eve's first mistake was to engage with the snake in conversation. We are created to converse with God, not the devil.

The devil, in the form of the snake, fools Eve into thinking that there will be no consequences to her sin – 'You will not certainly die' (v.4). He imputes bad motives to God: 'For God knows that when you eat from it your eyes will be opened, and you will be like God, knowing good and evil' (v.5). It is often the case that you swallow a lie about God, before you swallow forbidden fruit.

The fruit looked 'good' and 'pleasing to the eye' and 'desirable for gaining wisdom' (v.6). This is often how temptation appears. Adam and Eve sinned and, as so frequently happens, cover-up followed the sin: 'So they sewed fig leaves together and made *coverings* for themselves' (v.7).

4. The first question *God* asks in the Bible is about *you*

Adam and Eve's friendship with God was broken. When they heard God coming, they *hid* (v.8). But God immediately came looking for them, and we find his first question in the Bible: '*Where are you?*' (v.9). God did not give up on them.

Whenever you fall away from him, God comes searching for you, wanting the relationship to be restored.

He says to the snake that one of Eve's descendants 'will crush your head, and you will strike his heel' (v.15b). Jesus is the one who will crush the head of the snake. But there will be a cost – 'you will strike his heel'. We see here the first hint of what it will cost to restore the relationship. On the cross Jesus crushed Satan, but it cost him his life. His blood was shed so that you and I could be forgiven and our relationship with God restored.

5. The first question *human beings* ask is about *responsibility*

'Am I my brother's keeper?' (4:9b). This is the crucial question for today. Do you have responsibility for others?

The result of the fall is a broken relationship with God. Adam and Eve blamed each other (3:11–12), and in chapter 4 we read that their children also fell out with each other. Arguments, quarrelling and falling out with one another began here. It has blighted the human race ever since. Try to avoid arguments. You will rarely win one and they are so destructive.

Cain was angry with his brother Abel. God's questioning continued: 'Why are you angry? Why is your face downcast? If you do what is right, will you not be accepted? But if you do not do what is right, sin is crouching at your door; it desires to have you, but you must master it' (4:6–7).

You will either master sin (now through the power of the cross and resurrection and with the help of the Spirit), or else sin will master you. In Cain's case, it did. He killed his brother (v.8). God asked him yet another question: 'Where is your brother Abel?' (v.9a).

In response, Cain asked the first question by a human being in the Bible: *'Am I my brother's keeper?'* (v.9b). Cain wanted to avoid responsibility. He was saying, 'Do I really have responsibility for anyone other than myself?'

The biblical answer is that you *do* have responsibility for others. We cannot exempt ourselves from responsibility for what is happening around us – in our city, nation and the world. For example, we cannot accept that thousands of children die every day as a result of extreme poverty and simply say, 'It's not our responsibility.'

Not only do you have responsibility towards your fellow human beings, but it is your privilege to bring blessing and joy to your friends, family and all those around you, and to make a difference in the lives of as many people as possible.

PRAYER

Lord, thank you that you have created this wonderful universe for us to enjoy in relationship with you. Help me this year to fulfil the potential I have to make a difference in other people's lives.

3 January | Day 3
Talk as You Walk

I love walking. Apparently, it is one of the best forms of physical exercise. Of course, walking is also a means, and for some people their only means, of transport.

Walking for whatever reason is more enjoyable with someone else. Walking and talking is a great way to communicate with family, friends and also with God.

The point is that we are doing two things at the same time. We are not just taking exercise or travelling. As we walk together we are in communion with one another. Both Enoch and Noah 'walked ... with God' (Genesis 5:24; 6:9). They didn't just sit, kneel or stand with God (the kind of actions we would often associate with spending time with God), but they were also in *communion* with God when doing something else. While you are doing other things – working, eating, exercising or relaxing – you can be in communion with God at the same time.

Personally, I also find it the best way to pray. This has been my pattern for the last few years. After reading the Bible each day, I go out and walk around our local park – which is almost deserted early in the morning. I note down anything I sense the Holy Spirit saying as I pray. You can pray as you walk to the bus stop or walk between meetings during the day. Talk as you walk.

The Bible has a great deal to say about walking with God. It is how you were intended to live. God's desire for you is that you *walk humbly* in a relationship with him (Micah 6:8). This is what Jesus has made possible – for you to *walk as Jesus did* (1 John 2:6). You may stumble from time to time, but one day you will *walk with him* 'dressed in white' (Revelation 3:4).

READING FROM PSALMS

Psalm 3:1–8
Walk with your head held high

David walked with God. But this does not mean that everything was perfect.

This psalm was written during a rebellion by David's son Absalom that had been partly caused by David's adultery (see 2 Samuel 12:11). Yet David repented of what he had done, and God forgave him and restored his relationship.

David did not have an easy life: 'LORD, how many are my foes! How many rise up against me! Many are saying of me, "God will not deliver him"' (Psalm 3:1–2). David cries out to God, 'But you, GOD, shield me on all sides; you ground my feet, you lift my head high…' (v.3, MSG). Like David, bring your fears and requests to God: 'To the LORD I cry aloud, and he answers me from his holy hill' (v.4).

In spite of his distressing situation God lifted up David's head. God does not want you to be downcast. Don't keep looking at the regrets behind you, the problems around you and the sin within you. Rather, lift up your head and see the help above you – walk with your head held high, and your eyes fixed on him.

David was able to say, 'I lie down and sleep; I wake again, because the LORD sustains me. *I will not fear* the tens of thousands drawn up against me on every side' (vv.5–6). In spite of all the troubles, he seems to have a deep peace – like a lake, where there may be rough waves on the surface, but deeper down there is a great stillness.

PRAYER

Lord, I pray for the year ahead that you would help me to walk with you daily in the way of peace, with my head held high, trusting you to supply all I need for the day ahead.

NEW TESTAMENT READING

Matthew 2:19–3:17
Walk in step with the Holy Spirit

John the Baptist prepared the way for Jesus. Whereas John's baptism was symbolic, Jesus would 'baptise you *with the Holy Spirit*' (3:11). This prophecy is then dramatically affirmed when the Holy Spirit descends on Jesus as he is baptised (v.16), showing that he is the one John is speaking about and that Jesus is able to pour out this same Holy Spirit on you and me.

In many ways Jesus' baptism was different from ours. He did not need to be baptised 'for repentance', and he was already filled with the Holy Spirit. John the Baptist was hesitant about baptising him (v.14) but Jesus said, 'Let it be so now; it is proper for us to do this to fulfil all righteousness' (v.15).

Jesus identified with us, sinful human beings, right from the start. He did this so that he could bear our sin on the cross for us. As a result, you are able to experience the Holy Spirit in a similar way and walk 'in step with the Spirit' (Galatians 5:25). We see here something of what it means to walk 'in step with the Spirit':

1. Get refined in the fire

John said that whereas he baptised with water, Jesus would baptise 'with the Holy Spirit and fire' (Matthew 3:11). The Holy Spirit will come like a refining fire to bring power and purity in your life. Knowing the refining fire of the Spirit in this life means that you can be free from the fear of the fire of judgment when Jesus returns (v.12).

2. Be filled with peace

When Jesus was baptised and came out of the water, 'heaven was opened, and he saw the Spirit of God descending like a dove and alighting on him' (v.16). The dove is a symbol of peace that the Holy Spirit brings to your life. The 'fruit of the Spirit is ... peace' (Galatians 5:22).

3. Be assured of your adoption

A voice from heaven said, 'This is my Son' (Matthew 3:17). Jesus is *the* Son of God in a unique way. However, the Holy Spirit assures *all of us* that through what Jesus has done for us, we too are sons and daughters of God: You receive the spirit of adoption. And by him you cry, '*Abba*, Father'. The Holy Spirit himself testifies with your spirit that *you* are a child of God (see Romans 8:15–16).

4. Know that you are loved by God

The voice from heaven said '...whom I love...' (Matthew 3:17). The apostle Paul writes that God's love for you is poured into your heart by the Holy Spirit (Romans 5:5).

5. Feel his pleasure

The voice from heaven says, 'with him I am *well pleased*' (Matthew 3:17). Again, it was supremely true of Jesus but as you walk in step with the Spirit, you too can experience this sense of God's delight and pleasure. I love the moment in the film *Chariots of Fire* when the Olympic runner Eric Liddell says, 'When I run, I *feel his pleasure*.'[1]

PRAYER

Lord, thank you that you give me your Holy Spirit to refine me, to give me peace, to assure me that I am a child of God, to know your love and to feel your pleasure. Help me to walk 'in step with the Spirit'.

OLD TESTAMENT READING

Genesis 4:17–6:22
Walk in relationship with God

Human beings are the pinnacle of God's creation. God created us to walk in relationship with him. 'When God created the human race, he made it godlike, with a nature akin to God. He created both male and female and blessed them, the whole human race' (5:1–2, MSG).

However, sadly the human race went astray: 'Human evil was out of control. People thought evil, imagined evil – evil, evil, evil from morning to night ... it broke [God's] heart' (6:5–6, MSG).

Evil starts in our thinking and imagination – that is, in our hearts. It is a case of 'garbage in, garbage out'. We need to watch not just our actions but also our thoughts, attitudes, motives and imagination.

In the midst of corruption and evil, it is possible to be different and to make a difference. Enoch and Noah are two examples of those who did not go along with the crowd but '*walked with God*'.

It appears that 'after he became the father of Methuselah' (5:22), Enoch *walked faithfully with God* for the rest of his life. There is something so powerful, amazing and almost miraculous about seeing the birth of our own children. One of my very close friends became a Christian through experiencing the birth of *his* first child.

'Enoch walked steadily with God. And then one day he was simply gone: God took him' (v.24, MSG).

Noah also walked with God. He found 'grace (favor) in the eyes of the Lord' (6:8, AMP). In spite of all the evil going on around him, 'Noah was a good man, a man of integrity in his community. Noah *walked with God*' (v.9, MSG). Noah believed God and built a boat, even though it was not raining and there was no water in sight. Noah did exactly what God told him to do (v.22).

PRAYER

Lord, help me to be righteous and blameless in my thoughts, words and deeds, walking with you in a close relationship. Help me to do everything you tell me to do.

4 January | Day 4
Battles and Blessings

I have never forgotten a talk I heard over thirty years ago. The speaker started by saying that the Christian life is 'battle and blessing, battle and blessing, battle and blessing, battle and blessing, battle and blessing ... battle and blessing...'

At the time I thought, 'Why is he going on like this? Will it never end?' But he was making a memorable and profound point. When we are in the battle it is hard to believe that it will ever come to an end. When we are in a period of blessing we sometimes expect it will go on for ever. But life is not like that. There are battles *and* blessings.

Pastor Rick Warren says that he used to think that the Christian life was a succession of battles and blessings, whereas now he thinks of life as being on two tracks. At any given moment in life there are usually blessings, but also battles to face.

He gives the example of the huge blessing that came to him through the publication of *The Purpose Driven Life,* which became the fastest-selling Christian book of all time. It gave him enormous influence. But at the same time he found out that his wife, Kay, had cancer. On one track of his life there was great blessing; on the other track there was a massive battle to face.

READING FROM PROVERBS

Proverbs 1:1–7
Learn to steer through battles and blessings

The purpose of the book of Proverbs is stated right from the start: 'These are the *wise* sayings ... Written down so we'll know how to live well and right ... A manual for living, for learning what's right and just and fair' (vv.1–3, MSG). It provides practical wisdom for everyone – both the 'inexperienced' and the 'experienced' (vv.4–6, MSG).

These Proverbs tell you how life usually works. They provide pragmatic and wise advice learnt from a lifetime of experience. They help you attain 'wisdom and discipline' (vv.2, 7) – two vital aspects of life, which do not happen overnight.

The purpose of the book is to enable you 'to steer [your] course rightly' (v.5, AMP). Wisdom is the 'art of steering' through the battles and blessings of life, and living skilfully in whatever conditions you find yourself. 'Wisdom', as Bible teacher Joyce Meyer says, 'is choosing to do now what you will be happy with later on'.[1]

Wisdom starts with the 'fear of the LORD', which 'is the beginning of knowledge' (v.7a). The 'fear' of the Lord can be translated 'reverence'. It means to respect and honour the Lord as God. The most important lesson you can learn about life is to 'start with GOD' (v.7a, MSG).

PRAYER

Lord, help me to learn the art of steering through the battles and blessings that lie ahead.

NEW TESTAMENT READING

Matthew 4:1–22
Learn how Jesus dealt with battles and blessings

Jesus' ministry begins with the *blessing* of the Holy Spirit at his baptism but, as so often happens after great experiences of the Holy Spirit, *battles* immediately follow.

'Next Jesus was taken into the wild by the Spirit for the Test' (4:1, MSG). The temptations start with the words, '*If* you are the Son of God...' (vv.3, 6). The devil is tempting Jesus to presume on his identity, and thus to test his Father. Sometimes the devil comes to us and says, 'If you are a Christian, then you are better than others.' Or, 'If God forgives everything, it doesn't matter how you live.' Respond by following Jesus' example.

Jesus faced three powerful temptations:

1. Instant gratification (economic)
There are some things that provide instant gratification but leave you feeling hollow afterwards.

Jesus had prepared by fasting for forty days and forty nights. 'That left him, of course, in a state of extreme hunger, which the Devil took advantage of in the first test' (vv.2b–3a, MSG). He says to Jesus, 'If you are the Son of God, tell these stones to become bread' (v.3b).

Jesus answers, 'It is written: "People do not live on bread alone, but on every word that comes from the mouth of God"' (v.4). Although 'bread' is necessary it is not enough on its own. Material things can never fully satisfy.

There is a deeper spiritual hunger that can only be satisfied by 'every word that comes from the mouth of God' (v.4). We need regular spiritual food even more than regular physical food.

2. Testing God (religious)
Next, the devil puts before Jesus the challenge to throw himself off the highest point of the temple. This is a temptation for Jesus to take his Father's loving protection for granted, and to test it.

The devil goaded Jesus by quoting Psalm 91, but it is a verse taken *out of context*. Jesus countered with a verse that is *in context*: 'Do not put the Lord your God to the test' (Matthew 4:7).

3. Wrong means (political)
Third, the devil shows Jesus all the kingdoms of the world and offers them, 'if you will bow down and worship me' (vv.8–9). This is the temptation to be dissatisfied with God himself and to embark on a programme of unscrupulous manipulation to achieve his ends by the wrong means. Jesus responds: 'Away from me, Satan!' He backed his rebuke with a third quotation from Deuteronomy: 'Worship the Lord your God, and serve him only' (v.10).

To each temptation Jesus responds with a verse from Deuteronomy chapters 6–8. Perhaps he had been studying these chapters at that time. As you study the Bible it reveals God's character and loving care for you, and deepens your relationship with him. This protects you against the devil's lies, and helps and equips you to resist temptation when it comes.

At the end of these battles, Jesus enjoyed the blessing of angels who 'came and took care of Jesus' needs' (v.11, MSG). The period of blessing did not last long. Jesus heard that John had been put in prison (v.12). It must have been devastating for Jesus to find out that his cousin had been imprisoned for his preaching.

Jesus was not daunted. He began to preach the very message that had caused John's arrest: 'Repent, for the kingdom of heaven is near' (v.17). He was fearless and courageous in the face of his battles.

Life is not just a matter of defensively seeing off the attacks; there are also positive advances to make. Jesus was on a mission. He began to build his team for that mission calling his first disciples: 'Jesus said to them, "Come with me. I'll make a new kind of fisherman out of you. I'll show you how to catch men and women..." They ... dropped their nets and followed' (vv.19–20, MSG). These were exciting times. The beginning of the ministry of Jesus was a period of great blessing.

PRAYER

Lord, help me to follow the example of Jesus in battles and blessings. May I learn your word so I can respond to temptation and be courageous in proclaiming the message of Jesus.

OLD TESTAMENT READING

Genesis 7:1–9:17
Learn how others have coped with battles and blessings

Christians should be positive people. We see in this passage that the blessings outweigh the battles. Of the four great themes that run through this passage (and the entire Bible) only one is negative (the fall that leads to the battles). The other three are all about positive blessing.

1. Creation

Human beings are created in the image of God (9:6b). There is a nobility and dignity about all human life. Every human being is of immense value. That is why taking another person's life has such serious consequences (vv.5, 6). Treat every human being with respect and dignity.

2. Fall

Noah faced a major battle – the flood and the destruction of almost *the entire human race*! It rained for forty days and forty nights (7:4) (exactly the same period as the temptation of Jesus). God's judgment came because of the seriousness of sin: 'Every inclination of the human heart is evil from childhood' (8:21).

3. Redemption

Despite the *battle* of the flood, Noah enjoyed the *blessing* of God's love, even though only Noah and those with him in the ark were left (7:23). Through the lens of the New Testament we see that the ark is a picture of being baptised into Christ (see 1 Peter 3:18 onwards). Those who were in the ark were safe. Those who are in Christ are safe.

God *blessed* Noah and his sons. He said 'Prosper! Reproduce! Fill the Earth!' (Genesis 9:1, MSG).

4. Glorification

God made a covenant with them (v.9). Every time you see a rainbow (v.13) it is a reminder of God's commitment to you, which led ultimately to the cross – the blood of the new covenant. It is an 'everlasting covenant' into eternity (v.16).

PRAYER

Lord, thank you that ultimately your blessings far outweigh the battles. Help me to remember that my light and momentary battles are achieving for me an eternal glory that far outweighs them all (see 2 Corinthians 4:17).

5 January | Day 5

God Will Give You Good Things

We all seek happiness. We are all searching for love. We are all desperate for peace. But so often, we look in the wrong places.

St Augustine prayed, 'Lord ... you have made us for yourself and our hearts are restless until they find their rest in you.'[1] God is the source of *all good things*.

READING FROM PSALMS

Psalm 4:1–8
The source of joy and peace

So often we seek joy and peace in the wrong places: 'How long will you love *delusions* and seek *false gods*?' (v.2). We think that money, possessions or success will be the answer. But these are delusions and false gods. True joy and peace, as David tells us, are to be found in a relationship with God (v.3).

We are not promised a problem-free life – the psalm starts with a cry: 'Give me *relief* from my *distress*; be merciful to me and hear my prayer' (v.1b). David is confident that God will hear: 'He listens the split second I call to him' (v.3b, MSG).

God alone is the true source of joy and peace: 'Let the light of your face shine upon us, O LORD. You have filled my heart with greater *joy* than when their grain and new wine abound. I will lie down and *sleep in peace*, for you alone, LORD, make me dwell in safety' (vv.6b–8).

There is greater joy in the presence of God than there is in material prosperity and luxury. Prosperity, despite the apparent security it brings, does not necessarily lead to peaceful sleep. Only in God's will can we truly 'dwell in safety' (v.8).

PRAYER

Lord, let the light of your face shine on me. Fill my heart with the joy of your presence and grant me peaceful sleep.

NEW TESTAMENT READING

Matthew 4:23–5:20
The source of God's favour and true happiness

According to Jesus, true happiness does not come from all the things that society suggests. It does not come from celebrity, beauty, wealth and possessions. It is not about how you feel. It is not about what you have or even about what you do.

The Greek word *makarios* (used in 5:3–11) means 'blessed', 'fortunate', 'happy' – the privileged recipient of *God's favour*. Or, as the Amplified version puts it, 'happy, to be envied, and spiritually prosperous, that is, with life-joy and satisfaction ... regardless of their outward conditions.'

In the Beatitudes ('beautiful attitudes'!) Jesus highlights eight unexpected situations in which you receive God's favour and blessings.

1. Be spiritually desperate for God

'Blessed are the poor in spirit' (v.3a). The word for 'poor' means 'begging ... dependent on others for support'. Here, it means being brought low or weakened to the point of realising the need to depend on Jesus: 'You're blessed when you're at the end of your rope' (v.3a, MSG). The poor in spirit are blessed because, through what Jesus has made possible, 'theirs is the kingdom of heaven' (v.3b).

2. Weep over your condition

'Blessed are those who mourn' (v.4a). Mourn your own sin and the mess in the world around you. Weep with those who weep. It is not wrong to weep and to mourn the loss of those you love. Jesus' promise is that those who mourn 'will be comforted' (v.4b). God's comfort goes way beyond any kind of ordinary comfort. As Joyce Meyer writes, 'It's almost worth having a problem just to be able to experience [God's comfort].'[2]

3. Be content with who you are

'Blessed are the meek' (v.5a). 'You're blessed when you're content with just who you are – no more, no less' (v.5a, MSG).

The Greek word for 'meek' means 'gentle', 'considerate', 'unassuming'. It is showing kindness and love for others. It is the opposite of arrogance and self-seeking. It means 'broken', not in the sense of a broken glass that is shattered, but in the way that a horse is broken – tamed, strength under control. Through Jesus the meek are blessed – 'they will inherit the earth' (v.5b).

4. Be hungry for God

'Blessed are those who hunger and thirst for righteousness' (v.6a). 'You're blessed when you've worked up a good appetite for God' (v.6a, MSG). Pursue a relationship with God as your number one priority in life. Pursuing anything else for its own sake ultimately leaves you empty. But the blessing of a hunger for God and his righteousness is that you 'will be filled' (v.6b).

5. Receive forgiveness and be merciful

'Blessed are the merciful, for they will be shown mercy' (v.7a). Don't give people what they 'deserve'; give them what they don't deserve. As C. S. Lewis put it, 'To be a Christian means to forgive the inexcusable, because God has forgiven the inexcusable in you.'[3] The merciful are blessed because 'they will be shown mercy' (v.7b).

6. Be completely sincere

'You're blessed when you get your inside world – your mind and heart – put right' (v.8a, MSG). 'Blessed are the pure in heart' (v.8a). This is not just outward purity but integrity, openness, sincerity and authenticity. It is a purity that truly allows you to 'see God' (v.8b). A pure heart starts with your thoughts because your thoughts become your words, your actions and your character.

A key step to being pure in heart is allowing others to see us as we are – in all our brokenness and vulnerability.

7. Strive to bring peace

'Blessed are the peacemakers' (v.9a). Don't stir up conflict, but make peace. Jesus, the Son of God, came to make peace for you on the cross (Colossians 1:20). Blessed are the peacemakers 'for they will be called children of God' (Matthew 5:9b).

'You're blessed when you can show people how to cooperate instead of compete or fight' (v.9a, MSG).

8. Expect nothing in return except persecution

'Blessed are those who are persecuted because of righteousness' (v.10a). Don't expect anything from the world in return except criticism. But God is with the persecuted church: 'theirs is the kingdom of heaven' (v.10b).

'You're blessed when your commitment to God provokes persecution' (v.10, MSG).

We see here the third way in which Jesus fulfils the Old Testament. We have already seen that Jesus fulfils the Old Testament *history* (1:1–17) and how he fulfils the promises of the Old Testament *prophecies* (1:18–4:16). Now, in the Sermon on the Mount, Jesus fulfils the Old Testament *Law* by revealing its full depth and meaning: 'Don't suppose for a minute that I have come to demolish the Scriptures – either God's Law or the Prophets. I'm not here to demolish but to *complete*' (5:17, MSG).

The American rock singer turned pastor, John Wimber, said, 'Jesus is insatiable. Everything we do pleases him but nothing satisfies him. I have been satisfied with Jesus. He has not been satisfied with me. *He keeps raising the standards.* He walks in high places.'

In the Sermon on the Mount, Jesus 'raised the bar' to the sky, not to bring us down but to lift us up: 'I've put you there on a hilltop, on a light stand – shine!' (5:16, MSG).[4]

PRAYER

Lord, help me this year to live by the values of the Sermon on the Mount and to be characterised by the Beatitudes, so I might be a light to the world around me.

OLD TESTAMENT READING

Genesis 9:18–11:9
The source of love and unity

Love covers and protects. It does not seek to expose other people's weaknesses and faults. It does not delight in other's misfortunes.

Today's passage begins with the rather strange account of Noah getting drunk. The fact that he was a righteous man did not mean that he was perfect. Shem and Japheth are commended for '*cover[ing]* their father's nakedness' (9:23).

Love and unity go hand in hand. The Tower of Babel is the symbol of disunity (11:1–9). The people said, 'Come, let us build ourselves a city, with a tower that reaches to the heavens, so that we may make *a name for ourselves*' (v.4). This act of pride and power-seeking led to disunity, symbolised in the confusion of different languages in the world. 'The LORD confused the language of the whole world. From there the LORD scattered them over the face of the whole earth' (v.9).

The day of Pentecost was the reversal of Babel. The Holy Spirit enables people to say: 'each of us hears them [speaking] in our native language' (Acts 2:8). The gift of tongues symbolises the fact that the Holy Spirit reverses the disunity of Babel and unites all peoples and languages.

This is a common experience today as we see the Holy Spirit bringing love and unity across churches, languages and nations.

PRAYER

Lord, may we never seek to make a name for ourselves or our own church, denomination or movement. Rather, may we seek to glorify your name. Pour out your Spirit, O Lord, on the church as on the day of Pentecost. May there be a reversal of Babel. May there be an end to disunity. May your Spirit and the values of the kingdom of God bring love, joy, peace, true happiness and unity.

6 January | Day 6
Directions for Life

Pippa and I are often in a hurry. We are not good at planning our car journeys. We often set off in the wrong direction and frequently get lost (even with a satnav!). I don't know why it has taken me so long to learn the importance of getting good directions and following them.

Many of us are like this in life. We charge off in a hurry. We don't realise the importance of getting good directions for life. If you follow God's directions for life, you will enjoy his blessing and bring blessing to others.

READING FROM PSALMS

Psalm 5:1–12
Start each day waiting for directions

When embarking on a journey the best time to get good directions is before you begin.

In this psalm, we have a wonderful example of how to begin each day: 'Listen to my cry for help, my King and my God, for to you I pray. *In the morning*, O LORD, you hear my voice; *in the morning* I lay my requests before you and wait expectantly' (vv.2–3). David is 'waiting for directions' (v.8, MSG).

There is something special about beginning your day by laying your requests before God. The whole day has a different dimension as you 'wait expectantly' (v.3).

PRAYER

Lord, today I lay my requests before you and wait for directions. Lead me, O Lord. Spread your protection over me. Surround me with your favour as with a shield (vv.8, 11, 12).

NEW TESTAMENT READING

Matthew 5:21–42
Follow Jesus' directions for life

There are some general directions that apply to every car journey. They are the rules of the road. Jesus' directions in the Sermon on the Mount are like a 'highway code' for a life of blessing.

Following Jesus' directions involves a radical lifestyle. He challenges us to be ruthless in dealing with every wrong attitude, thought, word and action.

Our words should be words of blessing, not anger. Do not speak *angry words* against your brothers and sisters (vv.21–22). 'The simple moral fact is that words kill' (v.22, MSG). But, words can also give life. Choose today to speak life-giving words of wisdom, encouragement and blessing.

We are called to do everything within our power to bless those we have fallen out with (vv.23–26). If we remember a 'grudge' a friend has against us, we should go to the friend and try to 'make things right' (vv.23–24, MSG). If we encounter an 'old enemy' we should 'make the first move; make things right' with them (v.25, MSG).

We need to guard what we do with our eyes and our heart. If we allow them to become corrupted then, far from being a blessing to others, we will be rotten ourselves.

Take radical action. When teaching on adultery, Jesus says it is not simply about the physical act: 'Don't think you've preserved your virtue simply by staying out of bed. Your *heart* can be corrupted by lust even quicker than your *body*. Those leering looks you think nobody notices – they also corrupt' (v.28, MSG).

Jesus speaks of the eye as the starting point of adultery. Take radical steps to avoid such a course (vv.29–30). As Job said, 'I made a covenant with my eyes not to look lustfully at a girl' (Job 31:1).

Marriage is intended to be a place of blessing one another and a source of blessing for others. This means a life of radical faithfulness within marriage (Matthew 5:31–32). Jesus speaks against using divorce as 'a cover for selfishness and whim' (v.32a, MSG).

We are to live lives of radical integrity in which we say what we mean, and mean what we say: 'Simply let your "Yes" be "Yes", and your "No", "No"; anything beyond this comes from the evil one' (v.37).

Blessing others means blessing even those who do bad things to us (vv.38–42). 'Don't hit back at all ... No more tit-for-tat stuff. Live generously' (vv.39, 42, MSG). To return evil for good is demonic. To return good for good is human. To return good for evil is the way of Jesus.

PRAYER

Lord, help me this year to follow your directions for life and to spread blessing wherever I go.

OLD TESTAMENT READING

Genesis 11:10–13:18
Trust God to direct you one step at a time

What I love more than anything when I set out on a long car journey (even better than a satnav), is to have someone in the car with me who knows the directions and tells me, one step at a time, where I should go. In the journey of life God offers to accompany you and direct you one step at a time into a life of blessing.

This is one of the key moments in the Bible, as God initiates his rescue plan for humanity. The previous chapters have been a tale of ever increasing sinfulness and separation from God. In these verses suddenly everything shifts as God reveals his solution – Abraham!

God promises Abraham: 'I will make you into a great nation and I will *bless* you; I will make your *name great*, and *you will be a blessing*. I will *bless* those who *bless* you ... and all peoples on earth will be *blessed* through you' (12:2–3).

God chooses one individual and blesses him, and then one nation and blesses them – but his plan is always that they will *pass the blessing on* (v.3b). This is key for our understanding of the Old Testament, as it explains *why* God chose Israel – so that through them the whole world might be blessed.

Ultimately this promise is fulfilled in Jesus. He is the fulfilment of all the promises and hopes of Israel and through him 'all people' can be blessed.

This is now God's purpose for you. The apostle Paul writes, 'Those who *have faith* are children of Abraham. Scripture foresaw that God would justify the Gentiles by faith, and announced the gospel in advance to Abraham:

"All nations will be *blessed through you*." So those who rely on faith are *blessed along with Abraham*, the man of faith' (Galatians 3:7–9).

The church is blessed, like Abraham and Israel, not for its own sake but in order to bring blessing to the whole world. If you have been blessed by God, it is not for your own selfish indulgence or self-congratulation; it is in order that you can be a blessing to others.

God calls Abraham to leave his country, his people and his father's household and go to the land God is going to show him (Genesis 12:1). Abraham did exactly as the Lord *directed* him (v.4, AMP). He trusted God to direct him one step at a time. He could not have seen the next steps at this time but he trusted God's promises.

This has been my experience in life. God may give us a general picture of what he wants us to do – but as far as the details are concerned he leads us *one step at a time*. The life of faith involves following his directions one step at a time.

The journey is not always entirely smooth. Abraham was very much a flawed human being just like us. God blessed him with great wealth (13:1, MSG) and a 'stunningly beautiful' wife (12:14, MSG). Nevertheless, in an act of weakness and deception, he allows Pharaoh to take her as *his* wife (vv.10–20).

Then, after 'quarrelling arose between Abram's herdsmen and Lot's' (13:7), Abraham decides that there has to be a parting of the ways between himself and his nephew (vv.8–11). Actually, it was not Abraham and Lot who fell out – it was, as so often happens, their followers. The reality of friction in human relationships is very evident.

Lot chose the best land and left Abraham with what looked less good. But, again, God gives Abraham directions. He tells him: 'look around from where you are' (v.14).

God said, 'I'll make your descendants like dust – counting your descendants will be as impossible as counting the dust of the Earth. So – on your feet, get moving! Walk through the country, its length and breadth; I'm giving it all to you' (vv.16–17, MSG).

When you are disappointed by someone or something, resist the urge to give in to feeling angry or bitter. Instead, 'look around from where you are' (v.14); fix your eyes on God and see things from his perspective, not the enemy's. Trust him to help you in these difficult situations, rather than trusting in yourself. His plan is to bless you. It is only because of the grace of God that Abraham is promised these amazing blessings. The intention was that he would be a blessing to the whole world. Likewise, for you. You are called to live under God's blessing and bring blessing to those around you.

PRAYER

Lord, help me this year to follow your directions, one step at a time, to live under your blessing, and bring as much blessing as I can to everyone around.

7 January | Day 7
Your Double Blessing

I love the word '*mercy*'. I am so thankful that God is a God of mercy. William Shakespeare captured something of the wonder of mercy in Portia's speech in *The Merchant of Venice*.

> 'The quality of mercy is not strain'd,
> It droppeth as the gentle rain from heaven
> Upon the place beneath: it is *twice blest*;
> It blesseth him that gives and him that takes.'
> Act IV Scene I

You are blessed when you receive mercy and you are blessed when you are merciful to others.

READING FROM PSALMS

Psalm 6:1–10
Cry out for mercy

Are there times in your life when you are really struggling and nothing seems to go right? Do you feel 'faint' (v.2), 'in agony' (v.2), 'anguish' (v.3), 'worn out' (v.6), 'groaning' (v.6), 'weeping' (v.6), in 'tears' (v.6), and 'weak with sorrow' (v.7)?

At times this may be caused by our own sin. At other times, it may be due to bereavement, sudden loss, relationship difficulties, family break-up, sickness, work issues, unemployment or opposition.

David also experienced difficult times but, in the midst of them, he cried out to God for mercy: '*Be merciful to me, Lord*' (v.2). He knew that God is a God of mercy. He prayed: 'Save me for the sake of Your steadfast love and *mercy*' (v.4, AMP).

Sometimes it seems that our difficulties will never come to an end. They seem to go on and on. When we are in a season of battle we cry out like David, 'How long, Lord, how long?' (v.3). We cry out for mercy and it does not seem as if God is listening. But he is. There will come a point when you can say with David: 'The Lord has heard my weeping. The Lord has heard *my cry for mercy*' (vv.8–9).

PRAYER

Lord, thank you for 'your unfailing love' (v.4) and mercy. Thank you that you hear my cry and accept my prayers. Be merciful to me, O Lord.

NEW TESTAMENT READING

Matthew 5:43–6:24
Be merciful to others

Having mercy on others is right at the heart of Jesus' teaching. 'Love your enemies and pray for those who persecute you, that you may be children of your Father in heaven' (5:44–45a). Love is more than showing mercy, but mercy is an essential part of love.

Jesus gives three reasons in the passage why you should be merciful towards those who have wronged you:

1. To have mercy on your enemies is to imitate your Father in heaven – 'that you may be children of your Father in heaven' (v.45a). God's mercy extends to those who are hostile towards him: 'He causes his sun to rise on the evil and the good, and sends rain on the righteous and the unrighteous' (v.45b).
2. To have mercy like this marks you out from the world: 'If you love those who love you, what reward will you get? Are not even the tax collectors doing that?' (v.46). We tend only to love people who are like us, or whom we like. But you are called to be different. You are called to what Dietrich Bonhoeffer referred to as 'the "extraordinary" ... the hallmark of the Christian'.[1]
3. There is a connection between forgiving and receiving forgiveness. We cannot receive God's mercy ourselves and then show no mercy to others. We do not earn forgiveness by forgiving others, but Jesus says that our forgiveness of others is essential to receiving forgiveness from God. 'You can't get forgiveness from God, for instance, without also forgiving others. If you refuse to do your part, you cut yourself off from God's part' (6:14b–15, MSG). Daily, receive mercy and forgiveness, and daily have mercy and forgive others.

Jesus also explains *how* you can express this mercy practically in what you do. He highlights the importance of *prayer*. He tells you to 'pray for those who persecute you' (5:44). Praying for your enemies helps you to see them as God sees them. In prayer you stand side by side with them, take their guilt and distress on yourself, and plead to God for them. Prayer is the acid-test of love. Coming into the light of God's presence reveals the true feelings in the depths of our hearts.

The theme of mercy is also at the heart of the Lord's Prayer: 'Forgive us our debts, as we also have forgiven our debtors' (6:12). (Of course, there is much besides mercy in this prayer, which we will look at later when we encounter it in the other Gospels.)

When we pray, Jesus teaches us to:

1. Keep it quiet
'Find a *quiet*, secluded place so you won't be tempted to role-play before God' (v.6a, MSG).

2. Keep it honest
'Just be there as simply and *honestly* as you can manage' (v.6b, MSG).

3. Keep it simple
'With a God like this loving you, you can pray very *simply*' (v.9a, MSG).

Finally, mercy should also be at the heart of our giving. Generosity is a form of having mercy on others. 'When you help someone out, don't think about how it looks. Just do it – quietly and unobtrusively. That is the way your God, who conceived you in love, working behind the scenes, helps you out' (vv.3–4, MSG).

Every time I read the Sermon on the Mount, I see how far short I fall and I am very aware of my own need for mercy.

PRAYER

Lord, thank you that you are merciful to me. Thank you that you forgive my sins. Lord, help me always to be merciful to others.

OLD TESTAMENT READING

Genesis 14:1–16:16
Receive God's mercy

Two crucial passages in the Old Testament reading for today point to the way in which God's mercy is made possible.

1. Receive God's mercy through Jesus
It starts with what appears to be a rather strange and disconnected account of four kings defeating five kings. Then the connection is made with Abraham's nephew Lot being captured by the four kings (14:12) and then rescued by Abraham (v.16). Then mysteriously Abraham, returning from his victory, is *blessed by Melchizedek* (vv.18–20).

This is expounded in the New Testament by the writer of the book of Hebrews (Hebrews 7), who explains that it all points forward to Jesus. Melchizedek's priesthood is superior to all the other priests in the Old Testament (the Levitical priesthood). Abraham, who was the great-grandfather of Levi (who was therefore 'in his loins') gave a tithe to Melchizedek (Genesis 14:20). In other words, *Levi* recognised the *superiority* of Melchizedek.

Melchizedek foreshadows Jesus, the great high priest, whose one perfect sacrifice on the cross made it possible for all our sins to be totally forgiven. Therefore, this brought to an end the need for the old priesthood and sacrificial system.

The 'bread and wine' (v.18) foreshadow the bread and wine of the communion service. They point to the one perfect sacrifice of Jesus, whose body was broken and whose blood was shed so that you and I could be *totally forgiven* and *receive God's mercy*.

2. Receive God's mercy by faith
The account then moves on to God's promises to Abraham – in spite of the fact that he and Sarah are old and childless, their descendants are going to be as many as the stars they can count. 'Abram *believed the LORD*, and he *credited* it to him *as righteousness*' (15:6).

Not only are you forgiven, God in his mercy declared you 'Set-Right-with-God' (v.6, MSG). The New Testament often refers to this verse because it shows that mercy, forgiveness and righteousness are obtained by faith – that is, believing God (see, for example, Romans 4:1–5; Galatians 3:6).

It is encouraging to see that in the New Testament, Abraham is listed by the writer of Hebrews as one of the great people of faith, even though his faith was not entirely unwavering.

When their prayers for a child do not seem to be answered, Abraham and Sarah hatch a plot to achieve God's ends by human means (Genesis 16:1–2). They agree that Abraham should sleep with Hagar and Ishmael is conceived (vv.2–4). One sin leads to another and Sarah ill-treats Hagar (vv.5–6).

This is the first time that God is called *El Roi*, the 'God Who Sees' (16:13). It is easy to feel that you have been forgotten by God, particularly at moments when, like Hagar, you feel unjustly treated. But knowing God is the 'God Who Sees' can help you to live by faith. God is a God who finds you in the midst of the wilderness and *sees* you.

The 'God Who Sees' is a God of mercy. The New Testament suggests that God overlooks the sin of Sarah and Abraham and only remembers their faith (Hebrews 11:11–12).

PRAYER

Lord, thank you for your amazing mercy made possible through the one perfect sacrifice of Jesus, our great high priest, dying for me. Thank you that I can never earn your mercy but I receive it as a gift by faith.

8 January | Day 8
Nothing Is Too Hard for the Lord

Are you facing a seemingly impossible situation in your life? Is there an apparently irretrievable breakdown in a relationship? A serious health issue? An almost impossible challenge in your job? Is there a habit or addiction that you are finding hard to break?

Whatever challenges you may face in the year ahead, *nothing is too hard for the Lord*.

Abraham was a hundred years old. His wife Sarah was ninety. God promised them a son. They said, in effect, '*That is impossible.*' This is the context of the great rhetorical question: '*Is anything too hard for the LORD*?' (Genesis 18:14). The answer is 'No'. If Sarah could conceive when 'already very old, and ... past the age of childbearing' (v.11), then *nothing is too hard for the Lord*.

In each of the three great challenges we see in today's passages we need to remember that *nothing is too hard for the Lord*.

READING FROM PROVERBS

Proverbs 1:8–19
Resist the temptations

Jesus never tells us to withdraw from the world. The challenge is to be '*in* the world' but not '*of* the world'. You are called to resist the temptations of the world around you.

The book of Proverbs gives practical advice on how to achieve that balance. Don't let others entice you into sin: 'If bad companions *tempt you*, don't go along with them' (v.10, MSG). 'If they say, "*Come along with us...*"' (v.11), do not to give in to them. When I was practising as a barrister I noticed how many people were led into crime by others saying to them, '*Come along with us.*' Don't be enticed into sin by the fact that everybody else seems to be doing something – evading tax or travel fares, getting drunk or being promiscuous. Don't follow the crowd: 'Do not set foot on *their* paths' (v.15). Something is not acceptable just because others are doing it. I can't justify my actions on the basis that it is the way in which the world works.

In the end, if your 'feet rush into sin' (v.16), or you go after 'ill-gotten gain' (v.19a), it takes away your life. 'When you grab all you can get, that's what happens: the more you get, the less you are' (v.19, MSG).

The enticement of the world is very strong. Yet, nothing is too hard for the Lord.

PRAYER

Lord, I pray that in the year ahead you will give me the strength to resist all the temptations of the world and not to be enticed into sin.

NEW TESTAMENT READING

Matthew 6:25–7:23
Live the Jesus lifestyle

Jesus' words are the greatest words ever spoken. They are so challenging. For example, he says, 'do to others what you would have them to do you' (7:12). This golden rule is beautifully simple but seems almost impossibly hard to live out. 'Ask yourself what you want people to do for you, then grab the initiative and do it for them' (v.12, MSG).

The great challenge is putting Jesus' words into practice. His instructions are clear, but the standards seem impossibly high. Yet, nothing is too hard for the Lord.

• Stop worrying and start living

Jesus commands you not to worry about your life or material things (6:25, 28–31). Think ahead, plan ahead, but don't worry ahead. Trust in your Heavenly Father to provide (v.26). He knows your every need (v.32). Faith is the antidote to worry.

You cannot add a single hour to your life by worrying (v.27). As Corrie ten Boom put it: 'Worry does not empty tomorrow of sorrow; but it empties today of strength.'[1]

Live in day-tight compartments. Live one day at a time. Don't borrow trouble from tomorrow: 'each day has enough trouble of its own' (v.34b). Make a decision today not to worry about tomorrow. Trust God to provide for you one day at a time.

• Sort out your priorities

Jesus tells you to change your ambitions and priorities. Seek God for *who* he is and not for what he can do for you. Like us, God does not want his friends only to be interested in what they can get out of him. He wants you to seek his 'presence' not just his 'presents'.

Take on a new set of responsibilities that are both exciting and challenging: 'seek first [the kingdom of God] and his righteousness and all these things will be given to you as well' (v.33).

• Do not be judgmental

We are not to take pleasure in judging others, not to enjoy seeking out other people's failings or presuming their actions spring from bad motives. If we knew what people had been through, their sorrow and their suffering, we would not be so quick to judge. Jesus tells us to get our own lives sorted out first. We are to change ourselves before we try and change other people (7:1–5). Rather than sowing harsh criticism and judgment, sow mercy, kindness and love.

• Persist in prayer

Don't be repetitious, but be persistent. Jesus makes wonderful promises of answered prayer (vv.7–8). He promises 'good gifts' as you pray (vv.9–11).

• Choose to live a radical life
Stay on the narrow road that leads to life (vv.13–14). On the narrow road there is no room for pride, dishonesty, anger, hatred of enemies or unforgiveness.

Humility is the order of the day. You have to give, pray, exercise self-control and seek first the kingdom of God. It is a road of purity, integrity, honesty and forgiveness. It is a road where you are required to 'do to others what you would have them do to you' (v.12). You are to show good fruit – by your character, lifestyle, teaching, actions, impact and relationships (vv.15–23).

PRAYER

Lord, as I face the challenge of living the Jesus lifestyle this year, thank you that nothing is impossible with you. Fill me today with your Holy Spirit and help me to live the kind of life that deep down I long to live.

OLD TESTAMENT READING

Genesis 17:1–18:33
Trust the Lord in difficult times

The Lord appears to Abraham and sets before him a huge challenge: 'I am God Almighty; walk before me faithfully and be *blameless'* (17:1). Then he makes a wonderful promise: 'I will confirm my covenant between me and you and will greatly increase your numbers' (v.2). No wonder Abraham 'fell face down' (v.3).

God makes a covenant with Abraham. He promises him the land of Canaan, and also that many descendants and nations will come from him (vv.4–8). This promise is highlighted by God in the name change from Abram to Abraham, as Abraham means 'father of many nations' (v.5). God also changes Sarai's name to Sarah – who was to be 'the mother of nations' (v.16). The sign of the covenant was circumcision (v.9 onwards).

God did not just say once to Abraham that he would have a son. He confirmed it time and time again (15:4; 17:16; 18:10). You can expect God to speak to you about major matters in your life and confirm them many times over.

Abraham's relationship with God is very intimate. God engages in conversation with Abraham. Abraham pleads with him about Ishmael. God's response is 'Yes, but...' (17:19). He says he is not only going to answer Abraham's prayer for Ishmael, he is also going to do more than Abraham could have ever asked or even imagined (vv.19–21).

The third time that God made this promise to Abraham he sent the 'three visitors' (18:1–15). As we read this through New Testament eyes, we can see an image of the Trinity here. It is clear that there are three of them (v.2) and yet it seems they speak as one: 'Then the LORD said...' (v.13).

Indeed, this is famously illustrated by Andrei Rublev's 1410 painting, 'Holy Trinity' which reflects the communion of the three angels who visited Abraham and symbolises the tri-unity of God (one God in three persons), and the fellowship of love at the heart of God's being.

God promises, 'I will surely return to you about this time next year, and Sarah your wife will have a son' (v.10). Sarah laughs. She thinks, 'After I am worn out and my lord is old, will I now have this pleasure?' (v.12).

It is encouraging that Sarah also had the usual human weaknesses. The Lord says to Abraham, 'Why did Sarah laugh and say, "Will I really have a child, now that I am old?"' (v.13). 'Sarah was afraid, so she lied and said, "I did not laugh"' (v.15). We all are tempted sometimes to lie to get ourselves out of trouble. With the exception of Jesus, the Bible never presents the great men and women of God as faultless.

The Lord's response is to repeat his promise and ask rhetorically: *'Is anything too hard for the Lord?'*

PRAYER

Lord, help me this year to continue to trust in you. Thank you that, whatever the issues I am facing in my life, nothing is too hard for you.

9 January | Day 9
Trust God to Put Things Right

Pippa and I enjoy doing crosswords together. When we are stuck on one clue we don't give up, we move on to the next clue. Every time we find an answer it helps us in resolving some of the other clues. In the end, we are sometimes able to solve most of the puzzle.

In a way, reading some of the difficult parts of the Bible is like trying to solve a crossword puzzle. Rather than getting bogged down in a tricky section, you can use the passages you do understand to help you resolve some of the more difficult ones.

Often I find it hard not only to understand some of the difficult passages in the Bible, but also to understand why certain things are happening in our world. There seems to be so much injustice. There are no easy answers.

I love the second great rhetorical question from yesterday's passage, 'Will not the Judge of all the earth do right?' (Genesis 18:25). One thing that you can be sure about is that on the last day, when all is revealed, you will see God's perfect judgment – and everyone will say, 'That is absolutely right.' Each of today's passages tells us something about the fact that, in the end, *God will put things right*.

READING FROM PSALMS

Psalm 7:1–9
Trust that there will be a just judgment

Some people might think that belief in a God who judges would lead to more violence in the world today. In fact, it is the opposite. When people stop believing in God's just judgment, they may be tempted to take it into their own hands and seek revenge against their enemies.

David trusted that there will be a judgment – that God will be the judge and he will judge justly. 'My accusers have packed the courtroom; it's judgment time. Take your place on the bench, reach for your gavel, throw out the false charges against me. I'm ready, confident in your verdict' (vv.7–8, MSG). In other words, David trusted that God would deal with his enemies.

If you believe in a God who is going to execute judgment with perfect justice, then you can leave it in his hands and do what Jesus told you to do: *love your enemies* (see Matthew 5:43–48; Luke 6:27–36).

In fact, as Miroslav Volf put it, 'The practice of non-violence *requires* a belief in divine vengeance.'[1] So many of the world's problems today would be solved if people believed in the fact that there is a God who judges justly and that we can trust him to put things right in the end.

PRAYER

Lord, I take refuge in you (Psalm 7:1). Thank you that as I can be confident in your perfect judgment, I need never seek revenge but rather love my enemies and pray for those who persecute me (Matthew 5:44).

NEW TESTAMENT READING

Matthew 7:24–8:22
Trust in Jesus, to whom God has entrusted all judgment

Jesus knew all about building houses. He was a craftsman by trade and had worked as a carpenter. The illustration he uses is down-to-earth and practical: two men who each decide to build a house (7:24–26). No doubt they intended to live in and enjoy them, perhaps with their families. Both were building something of long-lasting significance. Our lives are like these houses, yet their significance is for all eternity.

The most important feature of any house is its foundations. These houses differed little in appearance. But only one had 'its foundation on the rock' (v.25). Similarly, two lives can look alike, but the difference in the foundations is evident when, inevitably, the storms of life come.

You will face challenges in life. They will come in many forms: misunderstandings, disappointments, unfulfilled longings, doubts, trials, temptations, setbacks and satanic attacks. Success, too, can be a test. There is also pressure, suffering, sickness, bereavement, sorrow, trauma, tragedy, persecution and failure.

Ultimately, all of us will face death and God's judgment. The image of 'rain... torrents... winds' is used in Ezekiel to refer to God's judgment (Ezekiel 13:11), but the language of judgment is not confined to the Old Testament. Here, and elsewhere, Jesus warns of the coming judgment, as do the other New Testament writers.

When 'the rain came down, the streams rose, and the winds blew and beat against that house' (Matthew 7:25, 27), the house built on the rock 'did not fall' (v.25), but the one built on the sand 'fell with a great crash' (v.27). These are solemn words of warning. The trial may be during this life or it may come on the day of judgment. What is certain, according to Jesus, is that it will come.

However, you need not live in fear. It is not easy, but there is a way to be sure that, when *the foundations* of your house are tested, they stand firm. It is possible to know that your future is secure.

Jesus tells us that the key difference is that the wise man not only hears the words of Jesus, but he also 'puts them into practice' (v.24). The foolish man, on the other hand, although he hears Jesus' words 'does not put them into practice' (v.26).

Knowledge must lead to action – our theology must affect our lives or else we are building our lives on sand.

The words of Jesus are, first of all, a call to believe in him (John 6:28–29). Our salvation is by faith in Jesus, lived out in obedience.

You can have absolute confidence in Jesus' judgment, because he has the *authority* of God himself. Jesus was amazed at the centurion's faith in him. He said, 'Truly I tell you, I have not found anyone in Israel with such great faith' (Matthew 8:10).

The evidence for this faith came because the centurion believed that Jesus' word alone was sufficient to heal his servant (v.8). His rationale for believing this is profound. The centurion recognised that, as in the army, authority comes from being under authority – so Jesus' *authority* comes from being *under the authority* of his Father. The centurion saw that when Jesus spoke, God spoke.

Furthermore, this perfect Judge is not aloof from human suffering. We know Jesus experienced injustice, imprisonment, torture and crucifixion. But, in this passage, we see that he also experienced sickness (on our behalf, v.17) and even homelessness (v.20). There is little in human suffering that Jesus himself did not experience.

PRAYER

Father, thank you that not only is Jesus able to sympathise with my weaknesses, but he also died for my sins bearing the judgment for me so that I need not be afraid.

OLD TESTAMENT READING

Genesis 19:1–20:18
Trust that, in the end, the Judge of all the earth will do right

Yesterday, we saw how Abraham pleaded for Sodom and Gomorrah. We do not know exactly what their sin was, but, 'the LORD said, "The outcry against Sodom and Gomorrah is so great and their sin so grievous"' (18:20).

It appears from today's passage that their sin included a horrific culture of group rape (19:3, 5). We read in Ezekiel 16 that their sins also included being 'arrogant, overfed and unconcerned; they did not help the poor and needy' (Ezekiel 16:49). This could be a description of our own society in the West.

God says that if there had been ten righteous people in Sodom and Gomorrah he would have spared it for their sake: 'For the sake of ten, I will not destroy it' (Genesis 18:32). He gave every opportunity for the only 'righteous' people to leave. When Lot hesitated, the angels 'grasped his hand and the hands of his wife and of his two daughters and led them safely out of the city, for the LORD was *merciful* to them' (19:16).

The judgment on Lot's wife seems very severe (v.26). Whatever the reasons for it (and I am not confident I know the answer) it certainly stands as an example. Jesus said, 'Remember Lot's wife!' (Luke 17:32). We are not to look back. If we have left a life of sin, then we must not turn back to it. They were told, 'Flee for your lives!' (Genesis 19:17). In the same way, we are told to flee from evil desires (2 Timothy 2:22).

Even Abraham was not without sin. Indeed, he repeated the same sin over again – trying to pass off Sarah as his sister and almost causing her to commit adultery. The message of the Bible is that not only does God save sinners, he also uses sinners. He blessed Abraham and answered his prayer (Genesis 20:7). God uses us despite our sin because he is merciful and God, in Jesus, has taken the judgment upon himself.

PRAYER

Lord, thank you so much for the difference the cross of Christ makes to the day of judgment. Thank you that I can be confident that, in the end, the Judge of all the earth will do right.

10 January | Day 10
Facing the Storms of Life

On 31 July 2003, the adventurer Bear Grylls led a team of five across the North Atlantic Ocean in an inflatable rigid dinghy. They set out from Halifax, Nova Scotia, heading for John o' Groats, Scotland. On 5 August, a great storm arose. There were 100-foot waves. They lost satellite contact. They (and we) feared for their lives. Thankfully they survived to tell the tale (see *Facing the Frozen Ocean* by Bear Grylls).

Not all of us will have to face physical storms of this kind. But Jesus said that we would all face the storms of life (Matthew 7:25–27). Life is not easy. These storms are many and varied. Abraham, David and Jesus' disciples all faced storms in their lives. What can we learn from their example?

READING FROM PSALMS

Psalm 7:10–17
Take up the shield of faith

In the midst of the storms David says, '*My shield* is God Most High ... I will give thanks to the LORD because of his righteousness and will sing praise to the name of *the LORD Most High*' (vv.10a, 17).

If we fall for temptation and start to enjoy and nurture it, David warns, 'Whoever is pregnant with evil and conceives trouble gives birth to disillusionment' (v.14). In another image, he likens it to digging a hole, scooping it out, and then falling into the pit we have made (v.15).

The apostle Paul says that you are to take up a *shield* with which you can extinguish all the flaming arrows of the evil one (Ephesians 6:16). The shield is the 'shield of faith' or, as David puts it here, his shield is 'God Most High' (Psalm 7:10). This is the best protection you could ever have against the attacks of the enemy.

PRAYER

Lord, thank you that I, too, am able to say, 'My shield is God Most High.'

NEW TESTAMENT READING

Matthew 8:23–9:13
Trust in Jesus the Saviour

Sometimes the storms in our lives appear without warning. Jesus was in the boat with his disciples sleeping when '*without warning*, a *furious storm* came up on the lake, so that the waves swept over the boat' (8:24).

Presumably the disciples were used to storms on the Sea of Galilee; it was renowned for sudden flash storms, stirring the water into twenty-foot waves. However, this storm must have been a particularly serious one because the disciples woke Jesus up and said, 'We're going to drown!' (v.25).

During the storms of life, it is natural to panic (certainly, I tend to). Sometimes it appears that Jesus is 'sleeping' (v.24). He does not appear to be doing anything about our problems. Thankfully, we can all cry out, as they did, 'Lord, *save* us!' (v.25).

The natural response to the storms is *doubt* and *fear*. Jesus tells them that the response to storms should be *trust* ('You of little faith', v.26a) and that you should *not be afraid* ('Why are you so afraid?' v.26a). Jesus is quite capable of calming the storm and that is exactly what he did. Trust God and fear not.

Having shown his authority over the elements ('Even the winds and the waves obey him!' v.27), he goes on to demonstrate his authority over evil powers by freeing the two demon-possessed men (vv.28–34). Jesus was far more concerned about people than possessions, unlike those who pleaded with him to leave their region (v.34).

Jesus goes on to make the point that forgiveness is more important than healing. But healing is not unimportant. Jesus does both. He shows his power over sickness and disability by healing a paralysed man (9:1–2). 'The crowd was awestruck, amazed and pleased that God had authorized Jesus to work among them this way' (v.8, MSG).

In the midst of the storms there are moments of calm. Today's passage ends with such a moment as Jesus calls Matthew to follow him. Jesus is invited to dinner at Mathew's house.

The Pharisees are surprised to see Jesus eating with 'a lot of disreputable characters' (v.10, MSG) and say, 'What kind of example is this from your Teacher, acting cozy with crooks and riffraff?' (v.11, MSG).

'Jesus, overhearing, shot back, "Who needs a doctor: the healthy or the sick? Go figure out what this Scripture means: '*I'm after mercy*, not religion.' I'm here to invite outsiders, not coddle insiders"' (vv.12–13, MSG).

God's 'mercy' is his kindness and forgiveness towards people who do not deserve it. Today, receive and enjoy his mercy yourself and be merciful to others.

PRAYER

Lord, thank you that in all the storms of life I can cry out, 'Lord, save us.' Help me to trust you and not to be afraid.

OLD TESTAMENT READING

Genesis 21:1–23:20
Thank God for his provision

Abraham certainly faced storms in his life. The passage for today is full of struggles, but it starts with a wonderful moment of calm in the midst of these storms. 'The Lord was gracious to Sarah ... and ... did for Sarah what he had promised' (21:1). Like us sometimes, they had had to wait a long time, but eventually God's promise was fulfilled. During the waiting period, the challenge is to keep on trusting God.

'Sarah became pregnant and bore a son to Abraham in his old age, at the very time God had promised him' (v.2). It was a moment of great joy. Sarah said, 'God has brought me laughter, and everyone who hears about this will laugh with me' (v.6).

But very soon Abraham faced a storm in his own household. Ishmael mocked Isaac (v.9), and this led to deeper divisions in the family (v.10). Tragically Hagar and Ishmael left (v.14). These divisions were ultimately the consequences of Abraham's previous sin in making Hagar his mistress, following his lack of faith in believing that Sarah would have a son.

Sometimes the hardest situations in life to face can be those of our own making. Even so, God is still with Abraham (vv.12–13), and he watches over and blesses Hagar and Ishmael (vv.17–18). We see God's grace at work in the midst of a sinful situation.

Abraham was about to face the biggest storm of his life: 'God *tested* Abraham' (22:1).

God sometimes allows us to be tested. Personally, I don't think God ever intended for a moment that Abraham should actually sacrifice his son Isaac. The sacrifice of children was always an abomination to the Lord. But, he wanted to establish Abraham's priorities.

The New Testament reminds us that this test came after God's promises to Abraham about Isaac (Hebrews 11:17–19), and was therefore a test of both Abraham's *faith* and his *priorities*.

The test was of his *faith*, because it challenged him to trust that God could fulfil his promises about Isaac, even if Abraham was willing to sacrifice him. Abraham had to trust that no matter what happened, Isaac would be restored to him (Hebrews 11:19).

Yet it was also a test of Abraham's *priorities*. Your relationship with God is meant to be the number one priority of your life – above all other loves, the vision God has given you for your life and even above your closest human relationships. Abraham was willing to obey God whatever the cost. His great strength was that he loved God more than anything or anyone else.

Thankfully, God provided the sacrifice that was necessary ('God himself will provide *the lamb*', Genesis 22:8). This foreshadows the great sacrifice God was to make on our behalf. As you think about how Abraham must have felt at the thought of sacrificing his son, you get a glimpse of what it cost God to give his one and only Son for you and me (John 3:16).

Jesus is '*the Lamb* of God, who takes away the sin of the world' (John 1:29). If God provided the ultimate sacrifice to meet your greatest need, will he not also provide for all your other needs? Here Abraham calls God *Jehovah-Jireh*, or 'The Lord Will Provide' (Genesis 22:14). He is acknowledging that God providing is part of his character.

God is the great provider. So often, I have found this to be true in my own life and in our community. God is true to his promise. As the apostle Paul put it, 'My God will meet all your needs according to his glorious riches in Christ Jesus' (Philippians 4:19).

Our task is to obey God (to 'seek first his kingdom and his righteousness', Matthew 6:33a) and he promises that if we do that, he will provide for all our needs ('All these things will be given to you as well', v.33b).

God's provision and blessing is almost unbelievably great (Genesis 22:16–18). It included this: 'And in your Seed [Christ] shall all the nations of the earth be blessed' (v.18, AMP).

PRAYER

Lord, thank you that you are my shield, my Saviour and my provider. Help me to keep trusting in you and to not be afraid. Help me to keep you as the number one priority in my life.

11 January | Day 11
'Lord ... Give Me Success Today'

How to Be a Huge Success is a little book of quotations and tips from a variety of well-known 'successful' people. The back cover asks, 'Are you on a collision course with *fame*, *fortune* or *greatness*?'[1] This is so often how '*success'* is perceived in our society.

Perhaps because of some of its negative connotations, sometimes in the church we are a little wary of the word 'success'. However, 'success' is not a dirty word in the Bible. It occurs at least five times in our Old Testament passage for today (Genesis 24:12, 21, 40, 42, 56) – each time in a very positive light.

Success is a blessing from the Lord (Genesis 24:31, 50). Success is a good thing. However, the ministry of Jesus and the message of the Bible *redefine success*.

READING FROM PSALMS

Psalm 8:1–9
Praise God for the success of his creation

In our galaxy there are probably over a hundred billion stars like our sun. Our galaxy is one of a hundred billion galaxies. When we consider the vastness of the universe it is easy to feel small and insignificant.

David starts and ends this psalm by worshipping God for the success of his creation (vv.1–2a, 9).

As he stares into the night sky, David says, 'I look up at your macro-skies, dark and enormous, your handmade sky-jewelry, Moon and stars mounted in their settings. Then I look at my micro-self and wonder, Why do you bother with us? Why take a second look our way?' (vv.3–4, MSG).

David marvels at the fact that human beings are the pinnacle of God's creation – a masterpiece – made in his image. Not only does God love you and care about you (v.4), but he has given you extraordinary privileges: 'You made them a little lower than the heavenly beings and crowned them with glory and honour. You made them rulers over the works of your hands; you put everything under their feet' (vv.5–6).

We have been put in charge of everything God has made. Knowing this, Christians should be at the forefront of the protection, preservation and care of God's amazing creation.

Of course, God's original plan for our dominion over creation has been distorted. However, in the New Testament, we see these verses are also applied directly to Jesus (Hebrews 2:8). In Christ, creation is restored (Ephesians 1:19–23; 2:5–6), and one day it will be complete and we will see everything under his feet (1 Corinthians 15:24–26).

PRAYER

Lord, I see the vastness, beauty and success of your creation and proclaim: 'O Lord, our Lord, how majestic is your name in all the earth!' (Psalm 8:9).

NEW TESTAMENT READING

Matthew 9:14–38
Pursue success modelled on Jesus

Jesus redefines success. If you want to know what true success looks like, study the model of Jesus – his vision, life and teaching. It is the kind of success that is not universally recognised as such.

Jesus was both *admired* and *hated*. Success does not necessarily mean popularity. Some *admired* him: 'There's never been anything like this' (v.33, MSG). Others *hated* him. The Pharisees said, 'It's nothing but hocus-pocus. He's probably made a pact with the Devil' (v.34, MSG).

As followers of Jesus, you also may be both admired and hated. For example, because of his campaign to end the slave trade, it was said of William Wilberforce that he was the *most admired* and the *most hated* man in England.

In his Gospel, Matthew sets out the *success* of Jesus' ministry (chapters 5–9). He summarises, 'Jesus went through all the towns and villages, *teaching* in their synagogues, *proclaiming* the good news of the kingdom and *healing* every disease and illness' (9:35).

In word and action Jesus ushered in the kingdom of God, bringing the reality of God's rule and presence into the lives of those around him. This is what Jesus-style success looks like and this is what you and I are called to emulate.

To achieve Jesus-style success you, like the twelve disciples, need to model your life on Jesus and share his vision:

1. The need is urgent
Jesus saw that 'they were harassed and helpless, like sheep without a shepherd' (v.36). Today, we see millions who don't know Jesus and are spiritually lost. In addition, we see millions who are starving, homeless, suffering from preventable diseases and without even the most basic education.

2. The motive is love
Jesus had *compassion* (v.36). This is the strongest word for love in the Greek language (derived from the Greek word for 'guts'). It is used only of Jesus. It could be translated 'he was gutted' – his heart broke.

Jesus was unconcerned about worldly categories of importance or success. Here we see him helping two very different classes of people – an important 'ruler' (v.18) and a woman whose menstrual bleeding would have made her unclean and left her on the fringes of society (v.20). Yet Jesus had *compassion* on them both.

3. The trigger is prayer
Jesus said to his disciples, 'Ask the Lord of the harvest, therefore, to send out workers into his harvest field' (v.38). Pray for more people to be raised up who will follow Jesus and reap the harvest.

4. The potential is vast
Jesus said, 'The harvest is plentiful' (v.37). Jesus has modelled what success looks like – *proclaiming* the kingdom and *demonstrating* its in-breaking into history. Now he calls you to follow his model – to share in his mission, multiplying its reach.

PRAYER

Lord, there is so much need in our world yet it seems that the workers are few. I pray that you would raise up and send out more workers to go out into the harvest field and change the world.

OLD TESTAMENT READING

Genesis 24:1–67
Pray for success in guidance

Abraham's servant was not embarrassed to pray for success. He prayed a prayer that we can all emulate: *'Give me success today'* (v.12). It was not a selfish prayer. It was a prayer that God would bless someone else, 'show kindness to my master Abraham' (v.12). He asked to be guided by God.

This is one of the most remarkable stories of God's guidance. On Alpha,[2] we talk about five ways in which God guides us, under the heading of 'the five CSs'. In this passage, we can see an example of all these working together and especially the fifth one, 'Circumstantial Signs'.

1. Commanding Scripture
Obviously, Abraham did not have the Scriptures that we have – but he did have the commands of God that later became part of the Scriptures. God commanded his people to only marry other believers in him. Abraham told his servant he must not get a wife for his son from the Canaanites, but from his own people (vv.3–4).

2. Compelling Spirit
The Holy Spirit leads us as we pray. Although the words 'Holy Spirit' are not used in this passage, it is clear that all the participants are in a position to be guided by God, listening to him and being led by the Spirit. Abraham's servant prayed from his heart (vv.12, 45), Rebekah appeared 'before he had finished praying' (v.15), and when Rebekah appeared, Isaac was out in the field where he had gone to meditate (v.63).

3. Common Sense
The choice of Rebekah made sense. She was clearly someone who was appropriate for Isaac. It so happened that she was 'very beautiful' (v.16). She was also 'a virgin; no man had ever lain with her' (v.16). Most importantly, she was clearly generous, gracious and kind. Her immediate response to the request for water was not only to offer it, but also to say, 'I'll draw water for your camels too, until they have finished drinking' (v.19).

4. Counsel of the Saints
One of the ways in which God guides us is through godly advice ('saints' is used here in the New Testament sense to describe all God's people). Although Isaac and Rebekah's marriage was very different from the modern western marriage, in that it involved a large element of arrangement, there was also an element of choice. Rebekah was asked, '"Will you go with this man?" "I will go," she replied' (v.57). Isaac chose to marry her and 'loved her' (v.67). They were following the *counsel of the saints* in the sense that everyone around, especially their parents, recognised, 'This is from the LORD' (v.50).

5. Circumstantial Signs
This is one of the clearest cases in the Bible of God guiding through circumstantial signs. The servant asks for a sign and was given exactly what he asked for (vv.12–26). However, as we have seen, the sign was not random. It was a test of Rebekah's character, which she fulfilled.

As a result of being guided by God, not only was their meeting a great success, but more importantly, so was their marriage.

PRAYER

Lord, I pray that you would multiply this wonderful example of successful guidance among us. May there be more and more couples coming together and being able to say, 'This is from the Lord' (v.50).

12 January | Day 12
No Fear

At one level, fear is healthy. 'Fear' is an emotion induced by a perceived threat. It is a natural human emotion. It is God-given. It is a basic survival mechanism. It keeps us alive. It protects us from danger.

However, there is also such a thing as unhealthy fear. The Greek word commonly used in the New Testament is *phobos* – from which we get the word 'phobia'. This is unhealthy fear. It is disproportionate to the danger posed. It is '**F**alse **E**vidence **A**ppearing **R**eal'. It is when I catastrophise – overestimating the danger and underestimating my ability to cope.

Common phobias include fears in relation to health, finances, failure, growing old, death, loneliness, rejection, messing up, public speaking, flying, heights, snakes and spiders. They also include things such as, what is now called, FOMO – the Fear Of Missing Out, the fear of not being special.

In my own life, I have experienced many fears – from a fear of heights to panic attacks and other irrational fears, fears about preaching and a fear of doing anything that might bring dishonour to the name of Jesus.

Whereas the Spirit of God does not produce negative fear, there is a kind of healthy fear – the *fear of God*. This does not mean being frightened of God. In fact, it means the opposite. It is an understanding of who God is in relation to us. It means respect, reverence, awe, honour, adoration and worship; it could even be translated as *love for God*. It recognises the power, majesty and holiness of God Almighty. It leads to a healthy respect of God and is the antidote to all other fears and phobias we experience in life. Fear God and you need not fear anything else or anyone else.

It is no coincidence that as the fear of God has decreased in our society, all the other fears have increased. We need to return to a right relationship with God.

The expression *'do not be afraid'* is one of the most frequent commands in the Bible. Four of the occurrences are in our passages for today.

READING FROM PROVERBS

Proverbs 1:20–33
No fear of harm

This passage gives you the key to avoiding 'terror and panic' (v.26, AMP) and living 'without fear or dread of evil' (v.33, AMP).

The idea of the 'fear of the Lord' is one of the key themes of Proverbs and appears twenty-one times throughout the book. It is a *choice* that you make. If you are wise, you will '*choose to fear the Lord*' (v.29) and 'listen' to him. He promises that you 'will live in safety and be *at ease*, *without fear* of harm' (v.33).

Wisdom is personified in the book of Proverbs (v.20). As we read it through the lens of the New Testament, we know that it is Jesus who is 'the wisdom of God' (1 Corinthians 1:24).

This passage (Proverbs 1:20–32) is a warning against ignoring the Lord's voice and following a path of 'waywardness' and 'complacency' (v.32).

Instead, *choose* to fear God, listen to him and repent when he corrects you. If you do, God will reveal to you more than you could ever imagine. 'I [Wisdom] will pour out my spirit upon you, I will make my words known to you' (v.23a, AMP). He will reveal to you the hidden treasures of wisdom in his words. Choose this fear of God and you will be 'in good hands' (v.33, MSG) and can be free from the fear of harm.

PRAYER

Lord, I choose to fear you – to live a life in reverence and awe of your power, majesty and holiness. Help me to live life fearing you alone.

NEW TESTAMENT READING

Matthew 10:1–31
No fear of people

Three times in this passage Jesus says, 'Do not be afraid' (vv.26, 28, 31).

The context is Jesus sending out his disciples to preach the gospel and heal the sick. The moment Jesus calls his twelve disciples, he sends them out on mission (theological training should be intensely practical!).

He sends them (and us) to follow his example:

- To *proclaim*: 'The kingdom of heaven is near' (v.7)
- To *demonstrate*: 'Heal the sick' (v.8).

As Jesus sends us out, he warns us that we will face a lot of opposition: 'I am sending you out like sheep among wolves' (10:16a). We need pure wisdom ('be as shrewd as snakes and as innocent as doves', v.16b).

We may be opposed by 'local councils' (v.17), face hatred (v.22), be persecuted (v.23) and be called demonic (v.25). It is in this context that Jesus says three times, 'Do not be afraid' (vv.26, 28, 31).

- **Do not be afraid about what to say**
Jesus says, 'Do not be afraid *of them*' (v.26). You do not need to be afraid of other people, however powerful they may be (for example local councils, governors and kings, vv.17–18): 'Without knowing it, they've done you – and me – a favor, giving you a platform for preaching the kingdom news! And don't worry about what you'll say or how you'll say it. The right words will be there; *the Spirit of your Father will supply the words*' (vv.17–18, MSG).

- **Do not be afraid of what others will do to you**
Jesus says that rather than fearing those who can 'kill the body but cannot kill the soul', you should fear God, 'who can destroy both soul and body in hell' (v.28). Have a healthy respect for an all-powerful, as well as all-loving God. 'Save your fear for God, who holds your entire life – body and soul – in his hands' (v.28, MSG).

- **Do not be afraid of what will happen to you**
Jesus says that if you fear God, you need fear no one and nothing else. God is in ultimate control: 'Are not two sparrows sold for a penny? Yet not one of them will fall to the ground apart from the will of your Father' (v.29). Not only is he in control but he also loves you deeply: 'Even the very hairs of your head are all numbered. Fear not, then; you are of more value than many sparrows' (vv.30–31, AMP). Jesus cares about what happens to you even more than you do (v.30, MSG).

PRAYER

Lord, thank you that you value and love me so much. Help me to know your love, to trust in you and not to be afraid.

OLD TESTAMENT READING

Genesis 25:1–26:35
No fear of death

Life is never easy. It was not easy for Isaac. Among other difficulties, he waited twenty years for the birth of a child (25:20–26). Then there was sibling rivalry when the twins were born. He lived among hostile Philistines and one of his sons became a 'source of grief' (26:35), 'thorns in the side of Isaac and Rebekah' (v.35, MSG).

Isaac committed the very same sin as his father – trying to pass off his wife as his sister (vv.7–11). However, it seems that Isaac did learn from some of his father's mistakes. When Rebekah was unable to have a baby – unlike Abraham's disastrous attempt to solve things himself through his relationship with Hagar – Isaac's response was to pray to God for a miracle (25:21).

The Lord had appeared to Isaac and promised, 'I will be with you and will bless you... Through your offspring all nations on earth will be blessed' (26:3–4).

Nevertheless, Isaac was afraid. He feared that he might die: 'The men of this place might *kill me* on account of Rebekah, because she is beautiful ... I thought I might *lose my life* on account of her' (vv.7, 9b).

God said to Isaac, 'Do not be afraid, for I am with you' (v.24). Isaac feared people more than he feared God, and yet he is reminded that he need not fear others because God is with him. Remember the same truth when you are tempted to fear: God is with you. If God is with you, you need not be afraid of anyone or anything.

In spite of Isaac's fear of others, God blessed him. God says, 'I will bless you and will increase the number of your descendants...' (v.24). God's blessing meant growth, reaping many times over. This is what he wants for your life too.

'Isaac reopened the wells that had been dug in the time of his father Abraham, which the Philistines had stopped up' (v.18). (Perhaps the equivalent for us is to reopen churches that have been closed to be a source of living water!) When Isaac met opposition and was stopped, he moved on until he found another well he could reopen. In this way, the Lord gave him room to flourish (v.22).

None of this is easy, but remember what the Lord says to you: 'Do not be afraid, for I am with you' (v.24).

PRAYER

Lord, thank for your promise to be with me. Thank you that you tell me over and over again that if I fear you, I do not need to be afraid of anything or anyone else.

13 January | Day 13
Divine Acceleration

A few years ago, Pippa and I were asked to speak at a conference in Somerset, southwest England. The journey from London should have taken about three hours. However, it was a really hot day and ahead of us a hay wagon had caught fire and spilled its load across the motorway, which had melted as a result. We were stuck, almost stationary, for five hours. It was such a relief when, finally, it was *time to accelerate*.

There are times in our own personal lives, church life and ministry when it feels like we are stuck and unable to move at any pace. At other times, openings begin to appear and it is 'time to accelerate'.

God is the God of acceleration. He is able to speed things up at a much faster rate than is humanly possible.

READING FROM PSALMS

Psalm 9:1–6; Matthew 10:32–36
Expect opposition

Acceleration may lead to increased opposition. The higher the profile you have, the more criticism you can expect. God's people have always faced opposition. David faced many 'enemies' (Psalm 9:3–6). Opposition and enmity are extremely painful and difficult. However, in Christ you are promised that ultimately you will overcome.

We see a foretaste of this in the psalm for today. David praises God for the victory: 'I will praise you, O Lord, with all my heart; I will tell of all your wonders. I will be glad and rejoice in you; I will sing the praises of your name, O Most High. My enemies turn back…' (vv.1–3).

We still live in a hostile world. Jesus warned, 'Don't think I've come to make life cozy' (Matthew 10:34, MSG). Jesus is saying, 'don't be surprised by opposition'.

Be peacemakers (5:9, 38–48). You are called to break the cycle of retaliation. Nevertheless, opposition may come even from those who are very close to you (10:34–36).

Millions of followers of Jesus around the world are facing physical persecution today simply because of what they believe. Some face opposition, repression and discrimination from governments at a local or national level.

You may not face opposition like this in your life, but you should expect some opposition – whether from the media, friends and family who do not understand your faith, or work colleagues who disagree with what you stand for.

PRAYER

Lord, in the face of opposition, I will praise you with all my heart. I will tell of all your wonders. I will be glad and rejoice in you (Psalm 9:1–2a).

NEW TESTAMENT READING

Matthew 10:32–11:15
Embrace sacrifice

Jesus calls on his disciples to be willing to sacrifice everything for his sake: 'Anyone who loves father or mother more than me is not worthy of me; anyone who loves son or daughter more than me is not worthy of me' (10:37). Your love for Jesus should exceed even the greatest love you have for those closest to you.

Jesus continues, 'Whoever does not *take up their cross* and follow me is not worthy of me. Whoever finds their life will lose it, and whoever loses their life for my sake will find it' (vv.38–39). Perhaps this is what the apostle Paul means when he urges us 'to offer [our] bodies as a *living sacrifice*' (Romans 12:1).

This is the way in which you discover God's will for your life, 'his good, pleasing and perfect will' (v.2). If you want God to use you more, if you want to accelerate, you must be willing to embrace this kind of sacrifice.

Nothing you do in the service of Jesus is wasted. Jesus says, 'Give a cool cup of water to someone who is thirsty, for instance. The smallest act of giving or receiving makes you a true apprentice. You won't lose out on a thing' (Matthew 10:42, MSG).

Martin of Tours (AD 316–97) was Bishop of Tours, France, from AD 371. One very cold night, riding on horseback, he passed a beggar. Martin got off his horse, tore his robe in two and gave half of it to the beggar. That night, Martin had a dream in which he saw Jesus wearing the robe that had been torn in two on his shoulders. When asked where it had come from, Jesus replied, 'My servant Martin gave it to me.'

In the immediate context in Matthew, the *sacrifice* Jesus is referring to may be simply being identified with him in a hostile world. He says, 'Whoever acknowledges me before others, I will also acknowledge before my Father in heaven. But whoever disowns me before others, I will disown before my Father in heaven' (vv.32–33).

'Acknowledging' Jesus can lead to opposition and difficulties. For many of the first disciples it literally meant taking up their cross and following him (v.38), even to death. For us the cost may be different but we are called to the same radical commitment to Jesus.

PRAYER

Lord, help me to be willing to take up my cross and follow you. Today I offer you my body as a living sacrifice.

OLD TESTAMENT READING

Matthew 11:1–15; Genesis 27:1–28:22
Enjoy the challenge

Apparently, Formula 1 racing drivers have to be exceptionally fit and physically strong because of the forces exerted on their bodies during the race.

If we want to see acceleration in the advancement of the kingdom of God, Jesus says it will need *forceful people* (Matthew 11:12). (Some translations use the word 'violent' instead of 'forceful'. However, most commentators prefer this translation and positive interpretation.) These are people who are not put off by opposition or the need for sacrifice. In fact, they enjoy the challenge.

As we look back in church history there are many examples of men and women who inspire us by their passionate, dynamic and proactive lives. They have been used to change the world. Throughout history, the kingdom of heaven has been advancing as forceful, Spirit-filled people lay hold of it.

Jesus says, 'From the days of John the Baptist until now, the kingdom of heaven has been *forcefully* advancing, and *forceful* people lay hold of it' (Matthew 11:12). The context of these words is that John the Baptist, in prison, is asking if Jesus is the one prophesied about. In effect, Jesus replies by saying, effectively, 'Look at the evidence' (vv.4–5).

Jesus goes on to say that John the Baptist was the greatest person who ever lived before Jesus and his church (v.11). John the Baptist was the last of the old covenant prophets (v.13). We see many examples in the Old Testament of these 'forceful' men and women (v.12).

Jacob was a forceful man. Later we will read of how he was forceful in a good way, determined to know God's blessing (see Genesis 32:22–32). However, in this passage, we see how his forceful nature led him into wrongdoing. He was absolutely determined to get his father's blessing. He knew how important it was, but he ended up using deception in order to get it (chapter 27).

Jacob's mother, Rebekah, was also a *forceful* woman. Not only did she show favouritism to Jacob, but she was also involved in the conspiracy to deceive Isaac. The end result is a spectacular family feud, the consequences of which lasted for centuries.

It is a fairly unedifying tale and we can be left wondering what to make of it – it certainly does not present itself as a good example to follow!

Despite everything, God's plans and purposes continue to be worked out. His promises to Abraham and his descendants continue. They are passed on to Jacob (28:13–15), exactly as God had promised before the brothers were born (25:23). If everyone had acted openly and honourably a lot of grief and heartache might have been avoided.

Almost everything about these stories and these people is flawed – and yet God *still* manages to work through them. I find it such a relief to know that a perfect God can use imperfect people.

God blessed Jacob. His father, Isaac, gave him his blessing (28:3–4). Later on, God spoke to Jacob in a dream. He sees a ladder that reaches from earth to heaven, with the angels of God ascending and descending it (v.12). There is an open way between heaven and earth for all of us. God tells him, 'All peoples on earth will be blessed through you and your offspring. *I am with you* and will *watch over you* wherever you go' (vv.14b–15a).

God used these forceful men and women: Abraham and Sarah, Isaac and Rebekah,

Jacob and Rachel. But Jesus says none of them were as great as John the Baptist. And John the Baptist is not as great as the least of the followers of Jesus in the days of the kingdom of heaven – and that includes you!

PRAYER

Lord, thank you that you are with me and watch over me wherever I go. Help me to be counted among those forceful people enjoying the exhilaration, excitement and challenge of a life spent following Jesus.

14 January | Day 14

Just Relax and Let God Be God

Joyce Meyer tweeted, 'Just relax and let God be God.'[1] It is a great comfort to know that a loving God is ultimately in control of everything that happens.

Bishop Sandy Millar often says in the face of some tragedy or when things have gone badly wrong: 'The Lord reigns.'

Many times throughout the Bible, God is referred to as the *Sovereign Lord*. Both Joyce Meyer and Sandy Millar are expressing, in different ways, absolute confidence in the sovereignty of God.

If God is sovereign and ultimately in control, does that mean that you are absolved of responsibility for your actions? Does it mean that you do not have 'free will'? The Bible teaches both – the ultimate sovereignty of God at the same time as human responsibility and free will.

READING FROM PSALMS

Psalm 9:7–12
Confidently trust in the sovereign Lord

God is in ultimate control of the universe: 'the LORD reigns' (v.7). God 'will judge the world in righteousness (rightness and equity); He will minister justice to the peoples in uprightness' (v.8, AMP). This knowledge is an enormous comfort. We may never know in this life why God allows some horrendous things to happen.

Trust in the sovereignty of God and keep on believing that he will never forsake you: 'And they who know Your name ... will lean on and *confidently* put their trust in You, for You, LORD, have not forsaken those who seek ... You' (v.10, AMP).

In the meantime, keep doing three things:

1. Praising

'Sing the *praises* of the Lord' (v.11a).

2. Proclaiming

'*Proclaim* among the nations what he has done' (v.11b).

3. Praying

'The LORD is a refuge for the oppressed, a stronghold in times of trouble' (v.9); 'He does not ignore *the cry of the afflicted*' (v.12b).

PRAYER

Lord, thank you that you do not ignore my cries and that I can confidently trust in you. Thank you that I can relax and let you be God.

NEW TESTAMENT READING

Matthew 11:16–30
Accept the invitation to walk with Jesus

The teaching of Jesus is fascinating. In the first section of today's passage he seems to be saying, 'You can't win.' On the one hand, John the Baptist was an ascetic and was accused of being demon-possessed. On the other hand, Jesus went to parties with all kinds of people and made friends with those who were regarded as unsavoury characters. He was accused of being 'a glutton and a drunkard' and 'a friend of tax collectors and sinners' (v.18).

Whatever you do may be misinterpreted. Yet Jesus adds, 'But wisdom is proved right by her actions' (v.19). I take this to mean that all we can do is the *right* thing and not worry about what anybody else thinks. 'Opinion polls don't count for much, do they? The proof of the pudding is in the eating' (v.19, MSG).

Jesus then denounces the cities that he has visited and performed miracles in, where people have neither repented nor believed. He suggests that their sin is worse than the sin of Sodom (v.24). The sin of unbelief is perhaps the most serious of all.

Jesus goes on to teach in such a way that it is clear that he believed in both predestination (that God has already determined everything that will happen) and free will. He teaches both alongside one another. It is a paradox. The two seemingly contradictory things are both true at the same time.

It is not 50 per cent 'predestination' and 50 per cent 'free will'. Jesus says we are 100 per cent predestined and we have 100 per cent free will. This may seem impossible, but God is able to transcend and yet not distort human freedom. We ultimately see this in the incarnation: Jesus is 100 per cent God and 100 per cent human; he is fully God and fully human.

- **Predestination**
'All things have been committed to me by my Father. No one knows the Son except the Father, and no one knows the Father except the Son and those to whom the Son *chooses to reveal him*' (v.27).
Why God chooses to reveal himself to some and not to others is a mystery. It is certainly not based on wisdom and learning. Sometimes the great intellectuals simply cannot see it: 'you have hidden these things from the wise and learned' (v.25). And yet sometimes people of little or no education, or those who are very young ('little children', v.25), seem to have a very profound understanding of Jesus. 'You've concealed your way from sophisticates and know-it-alls, but spelled them out clearly to ordinary people' (v.25, MSG).

- **Free will**
Jesus says, '*Come to me*, *all* you who are weary and burdened, and I will give you rest' (v.28). The invitation to come to Jesus is for everyone. No one is excluded. We are all invited. We all have a choice whether to accept the invitation of Jesus or to refuse it.

I find it difficult to get my mind around this paradox. However, I have found the following illustration helpful. Imagine a room with an arched doorway. The outside of the arch is inscribed with the words, 'Come to me, all you…' (v.28). Everyone is invited into the room. When you get into the room, on the inside of the same arch is written, 'No one knows the Father except the Son and those to whom the Son chooses to reveal him' (v.27b).

In other words, free will is a doctrine for everyone. No one can say, 'I am not going to become a Christian because I have not been chosen.' The invitation is to all. On the other hand, predestination is a doctrine of assurance for those who *are* Christians. Once you have accepted the invitation and entered, you can know that God has chosen you and therefore he will not let you go.

I love the fact that in a stressful world, where so many are 'weary and burdened', Jesus promises you rest. He offers to take your burdens and replace them with his own.

The yoke (something that Jesus would have made in the carpenter's shop) was a wooden frame joining two animals (usually oxen) at the neck, enabling them to pull a plough or wagon together. The function of the yoke is to make burdens easier to carry. I love this image of walking in step with Jesus, sharing our burdens, making the trials to be endured and the battles to be faced 'easy' and 'light' by comparison.

Jesus is not a slave driver. When you pursue his agenda for your life you carry a burden but it is 'not harsh, hard, sharp, or pressing, but comfortable, gracious, and pleasant' (v.30, AMP). When you do what Jesus asks you to do, he gives you the strength and wisdom to do it and you carry his burden with him. There will, of course, be many challenges and difficulties, but there will also be a lightness and ease.

Jesus says to you: 'Are you tired? Worn out? Burned out on religion? Come to me. Get away with me and you'll recover your life. I'll show you how to take a real rest. Walk with me and work with me – watch how I do it. Learn *the unforced rhythms of grace*. I won't lay anything heavy or ill-fitting on you. Keep company with me and you'll learn to live freely and lightly' (vv.28–29, MSG). Just relax and let God be God.

PRAYER

Lord, thank you that you promise me rest for my soul. I come to you today. I give to you my burdens.

OLD TESTAMENT READING

Genesis 29:1–30:43
Watch God work his purposes out

God works his purposes out in spite of our weakness, vulnerability and sin. Jacob was a deceiver. What we sow, we reap. He sowed deception and he reaped deception from Laban (29:25b). He then continued the cycle of deception (30:37–43). This is an extraordinary story of deception, unfaithfulness and disloyalty.

Yet somehow, in all of this, God worked his purposes out for the individuals involved, for Israel, for the birth of his Son Jesus and for the future of the people of God.

A lot of human sin and disappointment was involved in the birth of Jacob's children (29:31–30:21). Yet, through it all, God was working out his purposes for the twelve tribes of Israel. Rachel's prayer was finally answered with the birth of Joseph (30:22).

As God was in control of *their* lives, you can trust that he is ultimately in control of *yours* as well and that 'in all things God works for the good of those who love him, who have been called according to his purpose' (Romans 8:28). So, just relax and let God be God.

PRAYER

Lord, thank you that you use even weak, vulnerable and sinful people like me. Thank you that although you love me as I am, you love me too much to leave me as I am. Help me to take responsibility for my life and at the same time confidently trust in your sovereignty.

15 January | Day 15
God Is Just and God is Merciful

Media headlines frequently express outrage at judges who are 'soft on crime' and fail to impose the appropriate penalty for the offence committed.

When I worked as a barrister, I noticed that the legal profession did not respect judges who were regarded as too lenient. We expect judges to execute justice. We do not expect them simply to be merciful.

On the other hand, we do expect mercy in our personal relationships. A loving parent will be merciful to their child. We expect friends to be merciful to one another. Justice and mercy do not normally go together. We tend to see them as alternatives. We expect *either* justice or mercy, but not both at the same time.

Yet God is *both* a God who *judges with justice*, and also a *God of mercy*. How can he combine these two apparently contradictory characteristics? The answer is that the sacrifice of Jesus has made it possible for God to combine both justice and mercy.

When I first encountered Jesus, the following illustration helped me to understand what Jesus achieved for you and me on the cross. Two people went through school and university together and developed a close friendship. Life went on and they went their separate ways and lost contact. One went on to become a judge, while the other's life spiralled downwards and he ended up as a criminal. One day the criminal appeared before the judge. He had committed a crime to which he pleaded guilty. The judge recognised his old friend and faced the dilemma, which, in effect, God faces.

He was a judge so he had to be just; he couldn't simply let the man off. On the other hand, he wanted to be merciful, because he loved his friend. So he fined him the correct penalty for the offence. That was *justice*. Then he came down from his position as judge and wrote a cheque for the amount of the fine. He gave it to his friend, saying that he would pay the penalty for him. That was an act of *mercy*, love and sacrifice.

The illustration is not an exact one. Our plight is worse – the penalty we face is death. The relationship is closer – your Father in heaven loves you more than any earthly parent loves their child. And the cost is greater. It cost God far more than money – he came himself, in the person of Jesus, and paid the penalty of sin.

God is not soft on crime. In his *justice*, God judges us because we are guilty. Then in his *mercy* and love he comes down in the person of his Son, Jesus Christ, and pays the penalty for us. Through the sacrifice of Jesus on the cross, God is both just and merciful.

READING FROM PSALMS

Psalm 9:13–20
Rely on the justice of God

David knows that God is a God of *justice:* 'The Lord is known by his *justice*' (v.16).
He also cries out for *mercy*: 'Have *mercy* … that I may declare your praises' (vv.13–14).

In this psalm, the desire for justice and the desire for mercy come together. David prays that God will have *mercy* on him by executing *judgment* on his enemies: 'Arise, O Lord … let the nations be *judged* in your presence' (v.19).

We sometimes think of justice in a negative way, as primarily about punishment. But justice is also profoundly positive. In Hebrew, the word for justice (*mishpat*) carries the sense of putting things right. It is because of God's justice that David can be confident that 'the needy will not always be forgotten, nor the hope of the afflicted perish' (v.18).

PRAYER

Thank you, Lord, that you are a God of justice. Thank you that one day there will

be justice for all those who face injustice in our world today. Thank you that one day there will be justice for the poor and the oppressed.

NEW TESTAMENT READING

Matthew 12:1–21
Receive the mercy of Jesus

We sometimes send parcels with the words 'Fragile – Handle with Care' stuck on them. Have you ever felt in need of one of these stickers yourself? Jesus is there for you when you feel like this.

Jesus utterly rejected the legalism of the Pharisees (vv.1–12), quoting and fulfilling the prophecy of Hosea: 'I desire *mercy* not sacrifice' (Matthew 12:7; Hosea 6:6). Justice and legalism are not the same – indeed they can be opposites. Jesus breaks the legalistic pharisaical laws by healing a man on the Sabbath in an act of great *mercy*, love and compassion (Matthew 12:13–14).

Jesus combines *justice* and *mercy*. He fulfilled all the promises of the Old Testament about God bringing justice to the nations. Here Matthew quotes Isaiah's prophecy (Isaiah 42:1–4), which Jesus fulfilled (Matthew 12:18–21). He would bring '*justice* to the nations' (v.18c) and lead '*justice* to victory' (v.20c).

Yet he is full of mercy, love and compassion: 'A bruised reed he will not break, and a smouldering wick he will not snuff out' (v.20). There are times in life when we are physically, emotionally or spiritually fragile – like a 'bruised reed' or a 'smouldering wick'.

Jesus continues to show us mercy, love and compassion when we are weak and fragile. When you are fragile, Jesus handles you with care.

Jesus is quoting one of the 'servant songs' from Isaiah 40–55. These songs are all about a suffering servant who will sacrifice his life in order to bring forgiveness of sins (Isaiah 52:13–53:12).

In these 'servant songs', God's mercy and justice come together. The world is set right; injustice and oppression are ended, and the needy and broken are set free. Yet it is God himself who makes the sacrifice, who bears the punishment and consequences of our sins. Rather than being crushed by God's justice, you are set free by it. At the cross, justice and mercy meet.

PRAYER

Thank you, Jesus, that you came as the suffering servant. Thank you that you enable justice and mercy to come together through your sacrifice on the cross.

OLD TESTAMENT READING

Genesis 31:1–55
Rejoice in the sacrifice of God

Have you ever experienced a promise of promotion that never came, or spent countless wasted hours working late to complete some thankless task? Have you ever been the victim of envy, false accusation or downright deception?

So much in this passage resonates with our day-to-day lives. In our everyday situations of frustration and pain, it is reassuring to know that the Lord always has the last word.

We see a breakdown in what was essentially a family business. Perhaps Laban took his son-in-law for granted. Certainly Jacob felt his goodwill had been abused. He felt Laban's 'attitude to him was not what it had been' (v.2). He had given his job 100 per cent effort – he had worked with all his strength: 'I have served ... with all my might and power' (v.6, AMP).

Jacob's terms of employment had been very tough. His father-in-law had been a fairly draconian boss. He had made Jacob pay for any loss that occurred due to accident or theft by others (v.39). His working conditions were very unsatisfactory (v.40).

Further, he felt cheated. Instead of putting his salary up, Laban appears to have put it down ten times (v.7). Rachel and Leah also felt they had been hard done by. They had been sold off to Jacob and then watched as their father envied their husband's success (vv.14–16).

It is understandable that they all felt resentment towards Laban. However, their response was not very gracious. They all ran off when Laban was out at work. They did not give him the opportunity to say goodbye to his children and grandchildren (vv.26, 28). On top of all that, for some incomprehensible reason, Rachel steals from her father without telling her husband.

In spite of all this, God blesses Jacob: 'But God did not allow [Laban] to hurt me' (v.7, AMP). He becomes more prosperous than Laban. It was actually God who had called Jacob to return home to Isaac and promised him 'I will be with you' (v.3). Although Jacob was doing the right thing, the way it was done was not right. Nevertheless, God intervened on his behalf by speaking to Laban in a dream (v.24). But for that, Jacob might have been sent away empty-handed (v.42).

In the end, they negotiate a satisfactory settlement. In the midst of this passage we see hints of the foreshadowing of what was to come. Both Jacob and Laban look to God for justice (v.53). Then there is sacrifice (v.54).

As they seek God's justice and offer this sacrifice, we are reminded once more of the cross, where God's justice and mercy come together.

PRAYER

Father, thank you that you are just and merciful. Thank you for the sacrifice of Jesus. Thank you that, in times of injustice, I can look to you for protection and mercy. Help me to be merciful, as you are merciful to me.

16 January | Day 16
The Overflow of the Heart

For many years I wanted to meet the great evangelist Billy Graham (1918–2018). I felt deeply honoured when I discovered he was following me on Twitter! Of course, I followed back! He is one of my heroes of the faith. He spoke to more people about Jesus than anyone else in human history.

I heard Billy Graham speak many, many times. Every single time I listened to him, I felt inspired. He said that before he spoke he liked to fill his heart. He would prepare enough material for five talks so that he could speak '*out of the overflow*'.

According to Jesus, the heart really matters: '*For out of the overflow of the heart the mouth speaks*' (Matthew 12:34). How do you store up good things in your heart?

READING FROM PROVERBS

Proverbs 2:1–11
Store up God's word in your heart

Do you long to know God better? Would you like to be wiser, more skilful and to have more knowledge and understanding?

I encourage you to make a lifelong, daily habit of reading God's word. The writer of Proverbs urges, '*store up* my commands within you, turning your ear to wisdom and applying *your heart* to understanding ... For wisdom will enter *your heart*' (vv.1–2, 10).

- **What do you need to do?**
'Store up' God's words within you (v.1). You need to 'accept' (v.1), listen and apply (v.2), 'call out' (v.3) and 'search' (v.4). 'Searching for it like a prospector panning for gold, like an adventurer on a treasure hunt' (v.4, MSG). This takes time and commitment. Don't just prioritise your schedule; schedule your priorities. Set aside a regular time to read the Bible and schedule it as a top priority.

- **What does God promise if you do this?**
You will 'find the knowledge of God' (v.5). 'God gives out Wisdom free' (v.6, MSG). Because of God's character he 'gives wisdom' and 'understanding' (v.6), 'victory' (v.7), protection (v.8) and 'discretion' (v.11). He promises that God will 'keep his eye on' you (v.8, MSG) and 'protect you, and ... guard you' (vv.8, 11).

PRAYER

Lord, help me to continue to spend time with you each day and to apply the teachings of the Bible to my life.

NEW TESTAMENT READING

Matthew 12:22–45
Go on being filled with the Holy Spirit

The words you speak really matter. Joyce Meyer writes, 'Every word we speak can either be a brick to build or a bulldozer to destroy'.[1] Whatever is stored up in your heart will sooner or later be expressed by your words. Be careful what you look at, read and think about. Fill your heart with good things and you will think good thoughts, speak good words and bear good fruit (v.33).

Jesus says, '...out of the overflow of the heart the mouth speaks. Good people bring good things out of the good stored up in them, and evil people bring evil things out of the evil stored up in them' (vv.34–35).

You cannot change your thought patterns on your own. You need the help of the Holy Spirit – filling your heart with his love and good fruit.

Jesus says that every sin will be forgiven except for blasphemy against the Holy Spirit (vv.30–32). Sometimes people worry that they have committed the 'unforgivable sin'. However, if you are worried about it, it is almost certain you have not committed it. There is no sin that cannot be forgiven if you repent and ask God's forgiveness. The only 'unforgivable sin' is to refuse to repent and turn to Christ, resisting his Holy Spirit throughout your life.

The Pharisees and teachers of the law may have been in danger, since they attribute Jesus' healing power to the prince of demons (vv.22–24). They have already seen plenty of miraculous signs from Jesus, but they refuse to acknowledge that Jesus' power is the work of the Holy Spirit. When they say to Jesus, 'How about a miracle?' (v.38, MSG), it is as though they are putting Jesus under cross-examination.

However, Jesus' reply turns the tables on them. Comparing himself with the Old Testament prophet Jonah, Jesus is referring to what would soon take place – his death and resurrection three days later (vv.39–40). The resurrection of Jesus is the ultimate sign of his identity.

Jesus gives two case studies from the Old Testament to show that the Pharisees already have enough evidence. First, when Jonah preached to the Ninevites they changed their lives. Jesus is greater than Jonah. Second, the Queen of Sheba recognised the wisdom of Solomon. Jesus' wisdom is greater than that of Solomon. They, and we, need no more evidence.

Jesus uses a description of how evil spirits work to warn of the danger of turning back to our old lives having cleaned up 'the house'. Jesus warns that when people return to their old sin, they often do so even more excessively (v.43 onwards), and that 'the final condition – is worse than the first' (v.45).

It is the Holy Spirit who gets rid of the demonic powers (v.28). Fight a daily battle to resist evil and ask to be filled with the Holy Spirit. The test of whether your heart is good is what comes out of your mouth. It is out of the 'overflow of the heart that the mouth speaks' (v.34).

Jesus says to them, 'You have minds like a snake pit! How do you suppose what you say is worth anything when you are so foul-minded? It's your heart, not the dictionary, that gives meaning to your words' (v.34, MSG). The way to make sure that you say the right things is to make sure your heart is full of the Holy Spirit.

PRAYER

Lord, help me to fill my heart constantly with good things and guard it from evil. I pray today that you would again fill me with the Holy Spirit.

OLD TESTAMENT READING

Genesis 32:1–33:20
Wrestle with God in prayer

Are you facing a major fear or worry in your life?

Jacob faced a very worrying situation. He had fallen out with his brother Esau, and feared that Esau might be out to get him. He was in 'great *fear* and *distress*' (32:7).

Jacob was a man of prayer – in spite of all his sin, he knew God. He recognised his own unworthiness: 'I am *unworthy* of all the kindness and faithfulness you have shown your servant' (v.10).

He prayed, believed and claimed the promise of God: 'Save me, *I pray*, from the hand of my brother Esau – you have said, "I will surely make you prosper and will make your descendants like the sand of the sea which cannot be counted"' (vv.11–12). His prayer was answered – more than he could have even imagined.

Prayer is not always straightforward. Sometimes it seems, like Jacob, that we have to wrestle with God (32:22–32; Colossians 4:12). It can be costly in terms of time and energy. This requires determination. Jacob said to God, 'I will not let you go unless you bless me' (Genesis 32:26), and we are told that from then on he walked with a limp (v.31).

Probably the nearest New Testament equivalent is the apostle Paul's 'thorn in the flesh' (2 Corinthians 12:7), which he asked God to remove three times. Your weaknesses and vulnerabilities do not stop God using you. In fact, God often uses our weaknesses *more* than our strengths. God did not remove Paul's thorn in the flesh. Rather he said, 'my power is made perfect in weakness' (v.8).

Perhaps you feel you have a 'thorn in the flesh' or you seem to be 'walking with a limp': you have some vulnerability or apparent handicap. Jackie Pullinger says she never trusts anyone who doesn't walk with a limp! It is often through the difficulties, disappointments and struggles that our hearts are changed. We see a transformation in Jacob after he has wrestled with God. His attitude to his brother is totally transformed (Genesis 33).

After the victory had been achieved in prayer, everything seemed to fall into place. There was a wonderful reunion and reconciliation: 'Esau ran to meet Jacob and embraced him; he threw his arms around his neck and kissed him. And they wept' (v.4).

Their attitude to each other had totally changed. Esau says, 'I already have plenty, my brother. Keep what you have for yourself' (v.9).

Jacob replies, 'No, please! ... If I have found favour in your eyes, accept this gift from me. For to see your face is like seeing the face of God, now that you have received me favourably. Please accept the present that was brought to you, for God has been gracious to me and I have all I need' (vv.10–11).

PRAYER

Lord, thank you that you are a God who answers prayer. Help us to wrestle in prayer like Jacob. Lord, I pray that you would bring reconciliation in all my relationships with my brothers and sisters in Christ. May my mouth speak out of the overflow of my heart.

---

17 January | Day 17
Five Ways to Fulfil Your Potential

In life, many people do not reach their full potential. We can become so caught up in the every-day that it is easy to continue in old patterns rather than change. Yet, we all have a God-given desire to live to our full potential. Perhaps you remember this celebrated biography:

> 'Solomon Grundy ... Born on a Monday...
> Christened on Tuesday ... Married on Wednesday...
> Took ill on Thursday ... Grew worse on Friday...
> Died on Saturday ... Buried on Sunday...
> And that was the end of Solomon Grundy.'

For some people, that just about sums up their life. And yet, all of us feel deep down 'there must be more to life than that'. Jesus says, in effect, 'Yes, there is!' The potential for every human being is great.

Jesus wants you to live a highly productive life. He wants you to produce 'a crop – a hundred, sixty or thirty times what was sown' (Matthew 13:8). The minimum is a thirty-times multiplication. The key to that potential lies in your relationship with Jesus – a relationship that can be as close as that of a brother or sister or mother (12:50). You can live a life of real purpose that will make a difference to the world, because of what you receive from him (13:11, 12, 16).

Your potential is not about being driven by ambition or success; it is about recognising who you are in God. As you seek him and live your life according to his purposes, you will bear much fruit. The more you begin to fulfil your God-given potential, the more he entrusts to you. He wants you to live a life of abundance (v.12).

The potential for Israel was very great (Genesis 35:11). God intended that Israel would not only be blessed, but also be a blessing to other nations. You have the potential to live a life of even greater blessing than those you read about in the Old Testament. Jesus says, 'Blessed are your eyes because they see, and your ears because they hear. For I tell you the truth, many prophets and righteous people longed to see what you see but did not see it, and to hear what you hear but did not hear it' (Matthew 13:16–17).

Jesus warns that although there is great *potential* in each of us, there are *pitfalls* ahead. How can you avoid the pitfalls and fulfil your potential?

READING FROM PSALMS

Psalm 10:1–11
1. Possess humility

In his book, *Finding Happiness: Monastic Steps for a Fulfilling Life*, Abbot Christopher Jamison defines pride as 'self-importance'. He writes, 'Humility is an honest approach to the reality of our own lives and acknowledges that we are *not* more important than other people.'[1]

The psalmist goes on a journey from feeling that God is 'far off ... in times of trouble' (v.1 onwards), to a realisation (as we will read tomorrow) that God certainly does '*see* trouble and grief', does '*listen*' to the 'cry' of the 'afflicted' and does *defend* 'the fatherless and oppressed' (v.14 onwards).

In fact, it is the 'wicked' (v.2) who seek to make themselves distant – 'your laws are rejected by him' (v.5). They think of themselves as more important than others – especially the poor, whom they 'draw into their net and crush' (vv.9–10, AMP). These verses tell us about the pitfall of 'pride' (v.4).

When things go well it is tempting to say, 'Nothing will ever shake me... No one will ever do me harm' (v.6). We can be tempted to feel that we have no need of God: 'In his pride the wicked man does not seek him; in all his thoughts there is no room for God' (v.4). It's easy to become arrogant (v.2) and boastful (v.3). This psalm warns us against doing so, and reminds us of our need for God.

PRAYER

Lord, keep me from pride, arrogance and self-importance. May I seek you with all my heart, remembering that I need you and that you never forget me.

NEW TESTAMENT READING

Matthew 12:46–13:17
2. Pursue intimacy

Some dangerous cults have twisted the words of Jesus (12:50) to teach that becoming a Christian means severing relations with your family. This is not only dangerous, but also unbiblical. The fifth commandment is 'honour your father and your mother' (Exodus 20:12). In the New Testament, we are told that, 'Anyone who does not provide for relatives, and especially for immediate family members, has denied the faith and is worse than an unbeliever' (1 Timothy 5:8).

Yet Jesus shows here that there is something *even more important* than your relationship with your own family. Your supreme calling is to an intimate relationship with Jesus, doing 'the will of the Father' (Matthew 12:50).

Jesus says, 'Whoever does the will of my Father in heaven is my brother and sister and mother' (v.50). His words speak of intimacy, permanence and acceptance – a relationship at the deepest possible level. You can have this amazing closeness to Jesus. Stay close to him each day and you will fulfil your potential.

3. Put down roots

The highs of spiritual experiences are very important, but if they are not combined with deep spiritual roots there is the danger of shallowness, which can lead to falling away. Be aware of this pitfall. We can all fall away in our hearts even while we are doing the right things.

Jesus talks about the seed that falls on shallow ground. It springs up quickly but withers because it has *no root* (13:6). Later on, he will explain that the person who has *no roots* lasts only a short time because they fall away when trouble or persecution come (v.21).

Your spiritual roots are the parts of your life that no one else sees – your secret life with God. This includes your prayers, your giving and your thought life. If you want to fulfil your potential make sure you develop *deep, strong* and *healthy roots* in your relationship with God.

4. Protect your heart

It is so easy for people to be distracted by the busyness of life. Many things can fill your life and push out time for God, church and other ways in which your spiritual roots could be developed. Again, this is a danger for us all.

Jesus warned about thorns that choke the plant (v.7). Later on, he explains that the thorns are 'the worries of this life' and the 'deceitfulness of wealth' (v.22).

PRAYER

Father, thank you that you call me into this intimate relationship with Jesus. Help me to put my roots down deep and to keep my eyes fixed on you. Help me to guard this relationship and never allow other things, even good things, to crowd in and choke my life.

OLD TESTAMENT READING

Genesis 34:1–35:29
5. Purify yourself

In this passage, we read a warning of the danger of escalating revenge (cf. 1 Corinthians 10:11). One terrible crime (the rape of Dinah, Genesis 34:2) led to another. The retribution was not proportionate. The people of God 'attacked the unsuspecting city, killing *every* male ... They carried off ... *all* their women and children' (vv.25–29).

The result was a disaster. Jacob says, 'You have brought trouble on me by making me a stench to ... the people living in this land. We are few in number, and if they join forces against me and attack me, I and my household will be destroyed' (v.30). The actions of Simeon and Levi are roundly condemned for their violence, ferocity and cruelty (see 49:5–7).

Revenge was not just a pitfall for Simeon and Levi; it is a temptation for all of us. When I am offended, I want revenge. In the Old Testament, retribution was limited by proportionality – 'life for life, eye for eye, tooth for tooth' and so on (Exodus 21:23–24). Jesus sets (and by his death and resurrection makes possible) an even higher standard in your relationships today. Forgive and love your enemies.

Joyce Meyer, who often speaks of the terrible abuse that she suffered as a child, writes: 'Have you, like Dinah, ever been an innocent victim? I can assure you that even in the worst circumstances, God gives us grace to forgive so that we can go on with our lives.'[2]

Jacob said to his household, 'Get rid of the foreign gods you have with you, and purify yourselves' (Genesis 35:2). God appeared to Jacob (renamed Israel, v.10) and said, 'I am God Almighty; be fruitful and increase in number. A nation and a *community of nations* will come from you' (v.11).

The potential is great. As Rick Warren says, 'In ministry, private *purity* is the source of public *power*.'[3] This is true for all of us, whether we are operating in the family, the workplace, the community or the church. If we want to have a powerful impact for Christ in the world, we need to be people of purity.

PRAYER

Lord, thank you that the potential for my life is vast. May I produce a crop thirty, sixty or even a hundred times what was sown.

---

18 January | Day 18
Your Kingdom Come

Her Majesty the Queen, Elizabeth II, has ruled the United Kingdom for over sixty-five years. She is now by far the longest reigning British monarch. Each year, on Christmas Day, the Queen gives a message to the nation. In her 2018 address she said, 'Only a few acknowledged Jesus when he was born. Now billions follow him. The message of Jesus is never out of date and is needed as much as ever.'[1]

In a previous year, she said of Jesus, 'Billions of people now follow his teaching and find in him the guiding light for their lives. I am one of them.'[2]

The Queen of the United Kingdom was pointing to another kingdom, a kingdom that Jesus came to establish, and which he will come again to rule. Jesus taught us to pray, 'Your *kingdom* come' (Matthew 6:10). The kingdom of God is the rule and reign of God.

READING FROM PSALMS

Psalm 10:12–18
Cry out for the transformation of society

'*The Lord is King* for ever and ever' (v.16a). God is in ultimate control of the universe. Yet the psalmist also cries out to God: 'Time to get up, GOD – get moving' (v.12a, MSG). He prays, in effect, that God's kingdom will come on earth. When God gets moving, 'The reign of terror is over, the rule of the gang lords is ended' (v.18b, MSG).

The psalmist prays in particular for various groups of people. He prays for those who are:

- helpless (v.12)
- troubled (v.14)
- grieving (v.14)
- victims (v.14)
- fatherless (v.14, 18)
- homeless (v.18, MSG)
- oppressed (v.18).

If you want to see God's kingdom come and society transformed, these are the people you must be concerned about.

PRAYER

Lord, thank you that you're my King. I lift up to you those who are in need ... May your kingdom come.

NEW TESTAMENT READING

Matthew 13:18–35
Keep telling people about Jesus

Every time you have told someone about Jesus and the gospel, you have 'planted' a seed in their heart. Not every seed you plant will bear fruit, as we see in the parable of the sower. Some seed never takes root (v.19). Other seed produces only temporary results. We can be drawn away from God by 'trouble' or 'the worries of this life and the deceitfulness of wealth' (vv.21–22).

Yet if the seed grows well, each of these parables shows us that you can have a huge impact. 'The seed cast on good earth is the person who hears and takes in the News, and then produces a harvest beyond his wildest dreams' (v.23, MSG).

When I look at the lives of some of those who did Alpha five, ten or fifteen years ago, they have had a massive impact. Some have even started ministries that have had a global influence.

Jesus tells many parables about the *kingdom of God* (the '*kingdom of heaven*' is Matthew's preferred form, following the regular Jewish practice of reverentially saying 'heaven' rather than 'God').

The kingdom is both 'now' and 'not yet'. Jesus' parable about the weeds tells us that there is a future aspect of the kingdom. At the moment, the wheat and the weeds grow together. One day there will be a harvest and a judgment. When Jesus returns the kingdom of God will come in all its fullness (vv.24–30).

Jesus goes on to say: 'The *kingdom of heaven* is like a *mustard seed* that a man took and planted in a field. Although it is the smallest of all seeds, yet when it grows it is the largest of garden plants and becomes a tree so that the birds come and perch in its branches' (vv.31–32).

The image of birds in branches appears quite a few times in the Old Testament, where it symbolises people from all nations becoming part of God's family (see Ezekiel 17:22–24; 31:3–14; Daniel 4:9–23). Jesus was reminding his listeners that the kingdom of heaven was not just for one nation but for the whole world.

There are many different types of planting. For example, one small group plants another and 'it grows' (Matthew 13:32). Then there is 'church planting'. What is planted is often quite small – like a mustard seed. But when '*planted ... it grows*' (vv.31–32).

I look around at some of the 'church plants' from our local church and see the huge impact they are having on the area – 'The birds of the air come and perch in its branches' (v.32) – with people coming into God's kingdom who are as unexpected as Gentile believers were to the Jewish nation. All over the world today we see the impact of 'church planting'. As the church growth expert, Peter Wagner, has said that church *planting* is the most effective form of evangelism known under heaven.[3]

Jesus goes on to talk about the kingdom of heaven being like yeast that works its way all through the dough (v.33). Your influence can be enormous – in your home, family, school, university, factory or office. This is how the transformation of society takes place.

PRAYER

Lord, help me to plant as many seeds as possible as I seek to bring the good news of Jesus to our world. May your kingdom come in my city, nation and throughout the world.

OLD TESTAMENT READING

Genesis 36:1–37:36
Bow down before the King of kings

Today we begin the story of Joseph. He was loved more than any of the other sons of Israel (37:3) and his brothers were jealous (v.4). Joseph was famous for his dreams, in one of which he saw his brothers bowing down to him (vv.7, 9).

There is no doubt that God does sometimes speak to us through dreams – he certainly spoke to Joseph this way (vv.5, 9). Through these dreams Joseph caught a glimpse of what the future held and what God was going to do with his life.

However, it is not always wise to tell everybody about the dreams and visions that you have for your own life. Joseph was aged seventeen (v.2). He was inexperienced. His mistake was to tell everyone about his dreams. This led to further hatred (vv.5, 8) and to greater jealousy (v.11). His brothers said, '"Do you intend to *reign* over us? Will you actually *rule* us?"' (v.8a). They hated the idea of Joseph being their king.

Then he had another dream in which he saw them all, in effect, '*bowing down* to [him]' (v.9). His father, wisely, simply 'observed' and 'pondered' over what Joseph had said (v.11, AMP). If you are unsure how to respond to a dream or a vision that you think may have come from God, the wisest response is simply to ponder it in your heart (see Luke 2:19).

However, Joseph again unwisely told his whole family. His brothers were even more jealous of him (Genesis 37:11). They plotted to kill him (v.18). Joseph was sold to the Midianites who sold him in Egypt to Potiphar, one of Pharaoh's officials, the captain of the guard (v.36). Joseph came under another *king* of Egypt.

As a result of Joseph unwisely telling his brothers his dreams, he had to go through years of hardship and difficulty. God used all this to develop his character and prepare him for his life's work.

The kingship we read about in the Old Testament is an anticipation of the kingdom of God in the New Testament. In today's passage we see a variety of human rulers – from the kings and chiefs of Edom (36:31–43), to the Pharaoh of Egypt (37:36). One of the key messages in these closing chapters of Genesis is that God is ultimately above and behind all human rulers. This comes out particularly in the story of Joseph.

The twists and turns of the story can sometimes seem bizarre and random. Yet, throughout, we read of God's involvement (such as in Joseph's dreams), and we eventually discover that everything was working towards God's purposes (50:20).

Joseph is a 'type' of Christ. In other words, his life foreshadows the life of Jesus (as we will see in the days ahead). But here at the start we see a contrast. Jesus also knew how God was going to use him, but he was very discreet about whom he told.

We also see in this passage the beginning of the similarities between Joseph and Jesus. One day, people were going to bow down before Joseph (37:7, 9), and one day every knee will bow before King Jesus (Philippians 2:10; Revelation 19:4, 6).

It is when you voluntarily bow the knee to Jesus now, and hold him as supreme King in your life, that you are less concerned about the outcomes of various power plays with other human beings that exist in your life (for example, the teacher, the boss and the government).

PRAYER

Lord Jesus Christ, King of kings, thank you that when I follow you I come under your kingship. I bow before you today and confess that you are Lord. May your kingdom come.

---

19 January | Day 19
Your Most Valuable Possession

Raj was one of six children born into a wealthy Brahmin family – the highest caste in the Indian caste system.

At the age of twenty-three, Raj encountered Jesus. His family disinherited him. They cut him off. As far as they were concerned he was dead. They even held a funeral service for him. Neither his parents, nor his brothers and sisters have ever spoken to him again.

For several weeks he wandered around the streets of Bangalore. He had virtually no food to eat. He walked all day and slept in the park at night.

He started a new life. He began to speak about his new-found faith. Through him, many other people encountered Jesus. For several years he was the National Director of Alpha in India. He says that he has had a blessed life and that God has more than compensated for his losses. Although he left '*everything*', in Jesus Christ he found *the 'pearl … of great value*' (Matthew 13:45–46).

Relationships are our most valuable possession. But there is one special relationship for which you were created. This is the most valuable pearl of all. It is worth selling 'everything' in order to get hold of it.

READING FROM PSALMS

Psalm 11:1–7
The intimate presence of God

Even at the most difficult time of your life you can experience the intimate presence of God. David was in a crisis. He was advised to run away and hide in the mountains. His response was to say, 'I've already run for dear life straight to the arms of GOD. So why would I run away now?' (v.1, MSG).

David starts by saying, 'In the LORD I take refuge' (v.1). He also finishes by focusing on a relationship with God, with the promise that the upright '*will see his face*' (v.7). David uses metaphorical language to paint a picture of the *intimate presence of the Lord*.

His experience and desire for a relationship with God brackets the beginning and end of the psalm. There is no safer place, nothing more valuable in life and nothing that this world offers that can compare with the intimate presence of God – seeing his face.

PRAYER

Lord, today I want to see your face. I ask you to satisfy the deepest longings of my heart with your intimate presence.

NEW TESTAMENT READING

Matthew 13:36–58
Knowing God's Son

Some people are desperately *searching* and then find Jesus. Others, like me, almost *stumble* into finding him. But once you have found the treasure it is worth giving up everything else.

In between the parable of the weeds and the parable of the net, Jesus tells two very short parables about discovering the kingdom (vv.44–46). The only difference between the two is that in one case the person was *actively searching* (v.45) and in the other he seemed to *stumble across it* (v.44). In both, there is something of enormous value ('treasure' v.44, 'fine pearls' v.45). In *both* cases it was *worth selling everything to get it* (vv.44, 46).

This is where true 'joy' (v.44), real 'treasure' (v.44) and 'great value' (v.46) are to be found. The kingdom of heaven is all about knowing the King. It is all about Jesus and how you respond to him. How everyone responds to Jesus really matters both for this life and beyond.

When you consider all the evil in the world, do you ever wonder why God does not deal with it straight away and get rid of it? In the parable of the weeds the servant wants to pull up the weeds, but his master refuses (vv.28–29). A judgment will come (vv.36–43, 47–50).

He warns about the fate of those who cause sin and all who do evil (vv.41, 49–50). He says of the weeds that God will 'pitch them in the trash' (v.41, MSG) and that he will 'cull the bad fish and throw them in the garbage' (vv.49–50, MSG). He promises on that day that you 'the righteous' (made right with God through Jesus) 'will shine like the sun in the kingdom of [your] Father' (v.43). It is your relationship with God that causes you to shine and it means that one day you will shine like the sun in the kingdom of God.

But God won't allow the destruction of all that is evil yet. He wants to gather all the wheat into his barn. He deliberately allows a delay until 'the end of the age' (v.39), so that more people have time to respond to the good news about Jesus.

PRAYER

Lord, thank you that a relationship with you is the pearl of great value. Keep me close to you and help me to avoid anything that draws me away from our relationship.

OLD TESTAMENT READING

Genesis 38:1–39:23
Experiencing God's blessing

Are your circumstances far from ideal at the moment? Do you feel confined by them? Do you wish you were in a different job, a different place, or a different relationship? Whatever your circumstances, this passage shows that if you stay faithful to God you can experience his presence, his favour and his blessing right where you are.

We see here a contrast between Judah's unfaithfulness and hypocrisy and Joseph's faithfulness when faced with sexual temptation.

Judah, vulnerable after the death of his wife, fell into sin. His own daughter-in-law, Tamar, posed as a prostitute and he slept with her. As a pledge, he left his seal and its cord and a staff. She became pregnant by him (38:1–18).

When he heard that his daughter-in-law was guilty of prostitution and as a result had become pregnant, Judah said, 'Bring her out and have her burned to death!' (v.24). She then produced what he had left behind: the 'seal and cord and staff' (v.25). Judah was caught out. He realised his own hypocrisy and sin (v.26).

The grace of God is extraordinary. Perez, one of the sons born as a result of this incident, is listed in the genealogy of Jesus (see Matthew 1:3). In his grace, God takes what the devil intended for evil and uses it for good.

Judah's sin is contrasted with Joseph's righteousness: 'The Lord was with Joseph and he prospered' (Genesis 39:2). Potiphar, who saw that the Lord was with him and had given him success in everything he did, put him in charge of his entire household (v.4). As a result, the Lord *blessed* his household (v.5).

The expression, 'The LORD was with [Joseph]' appears four times in this passage (39:2, 3, 21, 23). However, the fact that the Lord is with you does not stop you facing temptation. Joseph faced great temptation. Potiphar's wife tried to entice him to come to bed with her. He absolutely refused.

He saw that giving in to this temptation would be a sin against God and against his employer, Potiphar: 'How could I violate his trust and sin against God?' (v.9, MSG). Not only did he refuse to go to bed with her, he refused even to be anywhere near that temptation (v.10).

Joseph shows us a great example of how to deal with temptation. The best way to resist temptation is to flee from it (2 Timothy 2:22). If you are facing great temptation, take radical action. Like Joseph, run from it.

Potiphar's wife grabbed Joseph by his cloak and said again, '"Come to bed with me!" But he left his cloak in her hand and ran out of the house' (Genesis 39:12).

Look at the contrast with Judah. Judah left his seal, cord and staff in Tamar's hands. It was the evidence of *his guilt*. Joseph left his cloak in Potiphar's wife's hands. She used it to prove his guilt, although in fact it was the evidence of *his innocence*.

In spite of the fact that 'the LORD was with Joseph', having resisted temptation, he then suffered terrible injustice (v.19 onwards) and ended up confined in prison (v.20). He lost his liberty but not his freedom.

Even in prison, the Lord was with him. He 'showed him kindness and granted him favour in the eyes of the prison warden' (v.21). 'The head jailer put Joseph in charge of all the prisoners – he ended up managing the whole operation' (v.22, MSG) – 'Because the LORD was with Joseph and gave him success in whatever he did' (v.23).

Your circumstances may not be ideal. You might feel like you are in prison – literally in prison, or confined like a prisoner in your job, a health issue, a difficult relationship or other circumstances. Yet in the midst of all this, if you stay faithful to God, you can experience his presence with you, his favour in the sight of others, and his blessing on your life. This is the 'pearl ... of great value' (Matthew 13:45–46). This is your most valuable possession.

PRAYER

Lord, thank you that even when things seem to be going wrong and there are trials and temptations, I can know that you are with me and experience your blessing on my life.

20 January | Day 20
How to Navigate Life

Our car has many scratches on both sides. I suspect (although my memory is conveniently vague about this) that I am responsible for most of them. They come as a result of the difficulty of steering through the very narrow entrance on one side of the grounds of our church.

Wisdom has been defined as '*the art of steering*'. As you go through life, you will need to navigate many tight situations that require great wisdom in order to avoid damaging yourself or others.

READING FROM PROVERBS

Proverbs 2:12–22
Avoid wrong turns

Unfaithfulness (vv.16–18) is an example of a wrong turn. Wisdom will 'keep you from making wrong turns, or following the bad directions' (v.12, MSG). Wisdom will stop you veering off course. It will stop you 'travelling paths that go nowhere, wandering in a maze of detours and dead ends' (v.15, MSG). Evil may look attractive, but it is perverse and leads to darkness.

Marriage is a '*covenant* ... made before God' (v.17). 'Covenant' is an important word describing Israel's relationship with God – the *old covenant*; and our relationship with him under the *new covenant*. A covenant is a *binding agreement that should not be broken*.

To be involved in an adulterous relationship is wrong for both parties. In this case, it is the woman who has 'left the partner of her youth' and thereby 'ignored the *covenant* she made before God' (v.17). The man who commits adultery with her has fallen into the temptation to be seduced off the right path onto a path that ultimately 'leads down to death' (v.18).

Wisdom will keep you steering along the right paths (v.16a). It will 'keep your feet on the tried-and-true paths' (v.20, MSG). It will keep you walking with those who 'walk straight' (v.21, MSG).

PRAYER

Lord, give me wisdom. Help me to steer my life on the straight paths that lead to life.

NEW TESTAMENT READING

Matthew 14:1–21
Choose the good path

Difficult times in your life can take you off course in the wrong direction. But if you stay on the right course it will lead to greater compassion and wisdom.

The book of Proverbs presents us with a choice between the way of wisdom and the way of evil. Here, we read what these two paths look like in practice, in the lives of Jesus and Herod.

1. The path of evil
Herod the Tetrarch was Herod Antipas (21 BC–AD 39). This was the man who rejected Jesus to his face (when Pilate sent Jesus to Herod), just before Jesus' death (see Luke 23:8–12).

Herod had done what the writer of Proverbs warned against: he had committed adultery with his brother's wife, Herodias. When confronted with his actions he had John the Baptist 'bound ... and put ... in prison' (Matthew 14:3) because of his own guilty conscience.

Herod's life seemed to revolve around self-gratification. He had discarded one wife and acquired another. His focus was on his own personal pleasure, rather than the misery that his actions would have caused others – not least his own brother, Philip. Beware when your own pleasure matters more to you than the needs of others.

The fear of rejection can also lead us into trouble. Herod 'was afraid of the people' (v.5) if he were to have John put to death. And yet he was also afraid of *rejection* by the guests at his dinner party and therefore granted Herodias's daughter's request for the head of John the Baptist (vv.8–10). Make sure you do not allow what others think of you to matter more than what is right.

Because John the Baptist courageously spoke out, Herod wanted to kill him (v.4). In fact, evil seems to have run in the family: Herod's niece, Herodias's daughter, plotted with her mother to have John beheaded (vv.6–10). They were so hardened to evil that they were not even sickened by the sight of John the Baptist's head brought in on a platter (v.11).

2. The path of good
Jesus was clearly deeply shocked by the news of his cousin's death (v.12). His response to bad news was to withdraw 'privately to a solitary place' (v.13). He needed to be alone with God.

Yet when his plans were interrupted, Jesus did not get irritated (as I often do). It is good to make plans; but also, to allow God to interrupt your plans. Because of his compassion (v.14), Jesus had the wisdom not only to 'go with the flow', but also to respond actively – he 'healed their sick' (v.14). Even after all that, he did not take the opportunity to get away from the crowds. Instead, he fed them – or rather, he taught his disciples how to feed them miraculously (vv.16, 19–20). He mobilised *them*.

We see the extraordinary wisdom of Jesus as he navigated through this day. It was a day that started very badly, but Jesus managed to heal many sick people and miraculously feed 'five thousand men, besides women and children' (v.21). That day would be remembered throughout history and has affected millions of lives.

PRAYER

Lord, may the difficult times in my life not lead me off the right paths, but rather lead me to greater compassion and wisdom.

OLD TESTAMENT READING

Genesis 40:1–41:40
Navigate through the challenges of life

Have you ever been rejected, treated unjustly, let down by a friend or found yourself in some other frustrating situation?

'Great faith is a product of great fights. Great testimonies are the outcome of great tests. Great triumphs can only come out of great trials,'[1] said Smith Wigglesworth. We see this exemplified in the life of Joseph.

At the age of thirty (41:46), Joseph was put in charge of the entire country of Egypt. Pharaoh was looking for a wise and experienced person and he recognised that there was no one as qualified as Joseph (vv.33, 39).

But first Joseph went through a very tough time. It was all part of his training. He had been rejected by his brothers, treated unjustly and put in prison. Yet his suffering was still not at an end.

God gave him the interpretation of the dreams of his fellow prisoners, the cupbearer and the baker. He was given a clear and accurate interpretation. The baker was executed but the chief cupbearer was released and restored to his position. All Joseph had asked of him was that when he was released, he would remember to mention him to Pharaoh and get him out of prison (40:14).

However, the chief cupbearer forgot all about Joseph (v.23). This must have been so difficult and discouraging for him. It is never easy when friends let you down. In Joseph's case, it meant two more years languishing in a dungeon (41:1).

Prison must have been an extraordinarily frustrating place for a man of Joseph's talents. He was in his twenties, in the prime of his life. He did not know whether he would ever be released. I am not a very patient person. I think I would have gone mad with frustration.

Yet, in fact, God was preparing Joseph for something great. It probably did not feel like that at the time. By feeding fellow prisoners in a jail, God prepared Joseph to feed the nations from a palace.

Finally, when Pharaoh had dreams that he was unable to interpret, the chief cupbearer said, 'Today I am reminded of my shortcomings' (v.9). Joseph was called in to interpret Pharaoh's dreams.

Joseph said, '*I cannot do it ... but God will* give Pharaoh the answer he desires' (v.16). We see how Joseph has grown in wisdom. The self-confidence and swagger of his youth have been replaced by a reliance on God. He acts here with an extraordinary mixture of humility and confidence (two qualities that do not often go together). This is the humility and confidence we need when faced with the challenges of life: '*I can't ... but God can and will*.'

Joseph interprets Pharaoh's dreams (vv.25–32) and tells him how he should respond to them (vv.33–36). Even Pharaoh recognises the great wisdom that has grown in Joseph. He asks his officials, 'Can we find anyone like this man, one in whom is the spirit of God?' (v.38). Because he recognised that there was no one as 'discerning' and 'wise' as Joseph, Pharaoh put him in charge of his whole empire (vv.39–40).

Through all *your* suffering, trials and tribulations, God is preparing *you*. Joseph had grown in wisdom. As a result, he came up with a plan that enabled the people to navigate through a period of great economic recession and turmoil. Many of us will face all kinds of economic difficulties in life. God's help and wisdom may not always change the situation, but they will help you navigate through the struggles you face.

PRAYER

Lord, thank you for the way in which you use the difficult times in my life. Help me to grow in wisdom, be confident in you and navigate through the challenges of life.

---

21 January | Day 21
Be Honest with God

After much discussion, debate and research, the Oxford dictionaries word of the year for 2016 was 'post-truth'. It had shown a 2,000 per cent increase in usage during the year, spiking during the Brexit and US Presidential debates. In a 'post-truth' era, objective facts appear less influential than appeals to emotion. There is a tolerance for dishonest, inaccurate allegations and outright denial of facts. Blatant lies become routine.

But if you buy a car, you want to know the truth about that car. In a relationship, you want to know the truth. We hunger for honesty and truth.

We see in our passages for today that God hates lies and deception. David says, 'People all lie to their neighbours; their flattering lips speak with *deception*' (Psalm 12:2). Jesus quoted Isaiah, 'These people honour me with their lips, but *their hearts* are far from me' (Matthew 15:8). Although Joseph's brothers had deceived their father about the fate of Joseph (Genesis 37:31–35), they knew *in their hearts* that they could not deceive God: 'Surely we are being punished because of our brother' (42:21).

God wants you to be honest with him. He likes candour. He wants to hear what is on your heart today.

READING FROM PSALMS

Psalm 12:1–8
Ask God for help

The cry of David's heart is, 'Help, LORD' (v.1). He laments over the state of society in his day – a society that was not dissimilar to our own today. He describes lies, deceit, arrogance, greed and selfishness.

'Everyone talks in lie language;
Lies slide off their oily lips.
They doubletalk with forked tongues' (v.2, MSG).

God is not impressed by people who are clever with words. David's opening cry for help is answered as God promises aid to the weak and needy: 'I will arise ... I will protect them from those who malign them' (v.5).

David then contrasts God's trustworthiness with the emptiness of the lies of those around him: 'The words and promises of the Lord are pure words, like silver refined in an earthen furnace, purified seven times over' (v.6, AMP). This gives him confidence that the Lord will keep him safe and protect him in spite of all the deception around. 'O Lord, you will keep us safe and protect us from such people for ever' (v.7).

'Help, Lord' is a great prayer at the start of a day as you ask God to guide you in all that you are involved in.

PRAYER

Lord, help me ... (bring to God all the things that you are involved in today).

NEW TESTAMENT READING

Matthew 14:22–15:9
Keep speaking to God in the storm

Jesus loved to get away on his own to pray – 'he went up on a mountainside *by himself to pray*' (14:23). When you are completely on your own with God, you can speak to him honestly and from the depths of your heart.

It is this closeness to God that enables Jesus to walk on water. He encourages Peter to do the same. But when Peter sees 'the wind' (v.30) he starts to panic. I know that feeling exactly. Sometimes, when things start to go wrong, I take my eyes off Jesus. As I focus on the circumstances around me, I begin to 'sink'. In the middle of all this, Peter prays a panic prayer: 'Lord, save me!' (v.30).

Even though it is a panic prayer, it is also a cry from the heart. 'Immediately Jesus reached out his hand and caught him' (v.31). As I look back at panic prayers I have prayed, it is wonderful to see the ways in which some of them have been answered.

As Jesus and Peter climb back into the boat, the wind dies down and 'then those who were in the boat *worshipped* [Jesus], saying, "Truly you are *the Son of God*."' (v.33).

The incident finishes with all the disciples giving a cry of the heart in *worship*. This is quite extraordinary. Monotheistic Jews, who knew the commandment that they should worship *God* alone, worship *Jesus*. They recognise that Jesus is '*the Son of God*'.

In fact, Jesus' first words to the disciples as he is walking on water are literally, 'Take courage! I AM. Don't be afraid' (v.27). 'I AM' is the name for God in the Old Testament (Exodus 3:14). Jesus is telling the disciples, and us, that he is the great 'I AM', so there is no need to fear. In whatever situations you are in today, this is a huge reassurance that Jesus is in control.

You may not always have the comfort of understanding what Jesus is doing or why he is letting life be the way it is, but you do have the comfort of knowing that he is in control.

They brought to Jesus all who were sick and cried out for healing. They 'begged him to let the sick just touch the edge of his cloak, and all who touched him were healed' (Matthew 14:36).

In the next section (15:1–9), Jesus challenges the Pharisees about what is really going on in '*their hearts*' (v.8). It starts with them challenging Jesus about his disciples breaking traditions. But Jesus turns the tables on them.

The Scriptures make it clear that we should make it a high priority to look after our families – especially our parents. The Pharisees had come up with spurious reasons why the money that would have been used to help them was dedicated to God, and therefore could not be used to honour and help their own parents (v.5).

Jesus accuses them of hypocrisy. The word 'hypocrite' literally means 'someone who puts on a mask in a play'. Their mask is honouring God with their lips, but in reality, 'their hearts are far from [him]' (v.8). God is far more concerned about your heart than your lips.

PRAYER

Lord, I worship you today as the Son of God. Thank you that I do not need to be afraid – when things go wrong, I can speak to you and you hear my prayers.

OLD TESTAMENT READING

Genesis 41:41–42:38
Speak to God from the depths of your heart

Joseph finished well – but he started out badly. He had been in a '*pit*' (37:24, KJV), and in '*prison*' (39:20), but he ended up in a '*palace*' (45:16).

Like so many people in the Bible (Jesus, John the Baptist, Ezekiel, and the priests and Levites serving in the temple – see Numbers 4) Joseph started his life's work at the age of thirty (41:46). Up to that time Joseph had been in training. Now he is put 'in charge of the whole land of Egypt' (v.41).

God had seen Joseph's *heart* in the midst of all his trouble. For the thirteen years between the ages of seventeen and thirty Joseph must have wondered what God was doing. He had been through so much rejection, suffering, injustice, imprisonment, disappointment and other trials. But through it all God was preparing him to be put in charge of 'the whole land of Egypt' (v.41).

God knew he could be trusted because his *heart* was right. He had stayed close to the Lord through all the trials. This is what matters – not whether you are in a period of battle or a period of blessing, but whether you are staying close to the Lord and communicating with him from your heart.

Joseph named his two children Manasseh ('God has made me forget all my trouble', v.51) and Ephraim ('God has made me fruitful', v.52). The common thread in these two names is the four-word phrase 'God has made me'. In both the times of suffering (Manasseh) and the times of success (Ephraim), Joseph acknowledges that it is God who is in control.

Don't let your heart be bitter in times of suffering, nor boastful in times of success. Recognise that God is sovereign over your life and your situation.

In contrast to Joseph, his brothers had had to live with their deception and guilt (42:21 onwards): 'Now we're paying for what we did to our brother ... and now we're the ones in trouble' (v.21, MSG). 'Their *hearts* sank' (v.28), but with their lips they said, 'we are honest men' (v.31).

In all this Joseph's original dreams were being fulfilled. In spite of all he had been through, he kept trusting God and being faithful to him. It started out badly but it finished well.

Never let go of your God-given dreams. Even if you start off in a 'pit' or a 'prison', like Joseph, you may end up in a 'palace'. As Joyce Meyer writes, 'No matter where you started, you can have a great finish ... Even if you are in a pit today, God can still raise you up and do great things in you and through you!'[1]

PRAYER

Lord, help me to lead a life of integrity. May my lips and my heart be at one with each other. I want to speak to you honestly from the depths of my heart. Thank you that you hear the cry of my heart.

22 January | Day 22
How Long, O Lord?

Have there ever been times in your life when you have found yourself wondering, 'How long, O Lord?' *How long* will these struggles and disappointments last? *How long* will we have these financial difficulties? *How long* will these health issues persist? *How long* will the difficulties in this relationship last? *How long* will I struggle with this addiction? *How long* will these intense temptations last? *How long* will it take me to get over this loss?

Pippa and I sometimes visit St Peter's Brighton, one of our church plants. At the end of one service, a woman came up to us and told us that for thirty-seven years she had been praying for her husband to find faith in Christ. For all those thirty-seven long years, she had cried out, '*How long, O Lord, how long?*' (Psalm 13:1).

When St Peter's reopened in 2009, her husband decided he would like to start coming to church with her. The moment he walked into St Peter's, he felt he had come home and had been 'reborn'. Now he loves the church and comes every week. Throughout our conversation she kept repeating, with a huge expression of joy on her face: '*How long, O Lord, how long?*' God had heard. At last, her prayers were answered.

Four times in quick succession David cries out, 'How long...?' (vv.1–2).

There are periods when it appears that God has *forgotten us* (v.1a). It seems that he has *hidden his face* (v.1b). For some inexplicable reason, we don't sense his presence with us. Every day seems to be a struggle – *wrestling with our thoughts* (v.2a). Every day brings *sorrow* (v.2b). We seem to be losing the battle and the enemy seems to be *triumphing over us* (v.2c). How should you respond in times like these?

READING FROM PSALMS

Psalm 13:1–6
Keep going

David's example suggests four things that you should *continue to do* during difficult times:

1. Keep praying
David continues to cry out to God, 'Look on me and answer, O LORD my God. Give light to my eyes' (v.3). He *pours out his heart* to God. Don't give up praying even when God seems far away.

2. Keep trusting
'But I *trust* in your unfailing love' (v.5a). 'I've thrown myself headlong into your arms' (v.5a, MSG). It is relatively easy to have faith when things are going well, but the test of faith is when things do not appear to be going well.

3. Keep rejoicing
He does not rejoice in the trials, but in God's salvation. He says, 'my heart *rejoices* in *your salvation*' (v.5b). 'I'm celebrating your rescue' (v.5b, MSG).

4. Keep worshipping
In spite of everything he has been through, David is able to see the goodness of God: 'I will *sing* to the LORD, for he has been good to me' (v.6). He remembers all that God has done for him.

As you begin to praise and worship God, it brings perspective to your problems. Sometimes, I find it helpful to look back on my life and thank the Lord for bringing me through so many of my own personal struggles, disappointments and bereavements, and to remember how, through it all, 'he has been good to me' (v.6).

PRAYER
Lord, I worship you today. Thank you for your goodness to me. For all the battles ahead, I trust in your unfailing love.

NEW TESTAMENT READING

Matthew 15:10–39
Keep following Jesus

Delay does not negate the promises of God. God does not always change our situations immediately. Sickness and suffering will not finally be eradicated until Jesus returns. These stories, and our experiences of miracles and healings, are a foretaste of what will happen then.

The goodness of God is revealed supremely in Jesus. Once again, in this passage, we see the amazing goodness of Jesus and how to deal with sin, sickness and suffering.

1. Keep renewing your mind
Jesus says that our problem is not about superficial things, such as what we eat (v.11). Food goes in and out of your body (v.17). The things that harm you come from inside – 'what comes out of the mouth gets its *start in the heart*' (v.17 MSG). The real issue is sin in the heart: 'For *out of the heart* come evil thoughts – murder, adultery, sexual immorality, theft, false testimony, slander. These are what make you "unclean"' (vv.19–20a).

The challenge of Jesus' words is that while we may not have committed murder or adultery, all of us fall at the first hurdle. The very first attribute that Jesus mentions is 'evil *thoughts*'. The solution to our sin is not external rituals, as the Pharisees were suggesting. Only God can change my heart. I need the help of his Holy Spirit to transform and purify me.

2. Keep praying for healing
There are few things more painful than seeing your own children suffering. The Canaanite woman's daughter was 'suffering terribly' (v.22). This mother must have cried out in her heart, 'How long, O Lord?' But she kept on asking for healing and refused to be discouraged by the fact that Jesus did not seem to be answering her request. 'She came and, kneeling, worshipped him and kept praying, Lord, help me!' (v.25, AMP).

Jesus saw that she had 'great faith' and he healed her daughter (v.28). He went on to heal 'the lame, the blind, the crippled, the mute and many others' (v.30).

3. Keep acting on behalf of the hungry
Not only does Jesus deal with the issue of sickness (v.22 onwards), he also cares deeply about suffering caused by hunger. He says, 'I have compassion for these people; they have already been with me three days and have nothing to eat. *I do not want to send them away hungry*' (v.32).

Jesus is able to do a lot with a very little. With the small amount of food given to him, he feeds the crowds. If you give him your life and resources, however small they may seem to you, he is able to multiply them and use them greatly.

If Jesus cared so much about temporary hunger, how much more must he care about the hundreds of millions of people in the world today who are suffering from hunger and malnutrition. As followers of Jesus we are called to act on their behalf.

Surely everybody would approve of Jesus. But no. The Pharisees were offended (v.12) when they heard him. If even Jesus offended people by what he said, do not be surprised if some people are offended by what you say in his name.

PRAYER

Lord, give me your compassion for suffering people. Come, Holy Spirit.

OLD TESTAMENT READING

Genesis 43:1–44:34
Keep hoping

Jacob could have cried out, like David: 'How long, O LORD?' (Psalm 13:1a). His sufferings seemed to go on and on. He had been grieving for his lost son for over twenty years. Now there was a severe famine (Genesis 43:1) and he faced the prospect of losing his much-loved Benjamin. He asked, 'Why did you bring this trouble on me...?' (v.6). He says, almost in resignation, 'As for me, if I am bereaved, I am bereaved' (v.14).

Eventually, Jacob simply had to trust God and let go of his son Benjamin. When he did so, things worked out. Very often it is not until we let go and commit a situation into the Lord's hands – perhaps fearing the worst – that God works it all out.

The writer of this section of Genesis is a brilliant storyteller. He draws out the agony. Judah knows that if his father loses Benjamin – as well as Joseph – it would probably kill him. He speaks of the '*misery* that would come upon my father' (44:34). All the while, we – the readers – know that Joseph is actually still alive and that through it all his dreams are being fulfilled (43:26–28). Joseph is 'deeply moved' and has to look for 'a place to weep' (v.30).

Joseph puts his brothers to the test. Judah is a changed man. Earlier he had callously sold his brother into slavery (37:26–27). Now he is willing to give his life to save his brother: 'Let your servant remain here as my lord's slave in place of the boy' (44:33).

Through all the unexpected twists and turns of these events, God is at work, bringing about his purpose. He is always working on your character and enabling you one day to look back and say, 'the LORD ... has been good to me' (Psalm 13:6).

Jacob had to send his 'only' ('he is the *only* one left', Genesis 42:38) son Benjamin to save the whole family. As we read this through the eyes of the New Testament we are reminded that God sent his only Son, Jesus, to save us.

PRAYER

Lord, thank you for sending Jesus to save me. In the difficult times, when I am crying out, 'How long, O Lord?', help me to keep going, following Jesus, praying, trusting, rejoicing, worshipping and putting my hope in you.

23 January | Day 23
You Have the Keys

On 15 January 2009, US Airways flight 1549 hit a flock of geese. Both engines failed. The plane was flying over New York. Potential disaster loomed. Not only were the 155 occupants on board in danger, but thousands more could have been killed had the plane hit one of New York's skyscrapers. Captain Chesley Burnett 'Sully' Sullenberger III guided the crippled US Airways plane with immense skill and courage. He performed a successful emergency landing on the Hudson River. Not a single passenger died, nor were there any serious injuries. The Mayor of New York City gave to the heroic pilot, who had saved them, *the keys* to the city.

To give someone the keys to a city is an immense privilege. They symbolise access and authority. Keys are usually given in recognition of some great service to the city. In the New Testament, we see that Jesus is *the* key holder. The risen Christ says, '*I hold the keys* of death and Hades' (Revelation 1:18). Jesus has brought about a far greater salvation than any other person could achieve. The authority he holds is also the greatest there could ever be – *he holds the keys of life and death*.

Amazingly, Jesus gives to Peter and the church (that is, to us) '*the keys of the kingdom*' (Matthew 16:19). Many Christians feel powerless, lacking in any kind of spiritual authority. They do not seem to realise what Jesus has given to them. You are not powerless. You have the immense privilege of having been given 'the keys of the kingdom'.

READING FROM PSALMS

Psalm 14:1–7
Enjoy access to God

To be given 'the keys of the kingdom' (Matthew 16:19) means to be given *access* to God. This is what Jesus achieved for us. God has always looked for those 'who seek' him (Psalm 14:2). You can enjoy access to God.

But no one is righteous. The whole human race has sinned. Every single one of us has become corrupt (vv.1, 3; quoted in Romans 3:9–12).

David describes this corruption in general terms (v.1b), but he also gives two specific examples:

1. Denying the existence of God
'Fools say in their hearts, "There is no God"' (v.1).

2. Failing to help the poor
'You evildoers frustrate the plans of the poor' (v.6).

The kingdom of God involves seeking God and seeking justice for the poor, and that is exactly the note on which this psalm ends. David cries out to God, asking, 'Oh, that salvation for Israel would come out of Zion!' (v.7a).

Thank God it did. Salvation for Israel came out of Zion in the person of Jesus. He lived, died and rose again to make it possible for you to be forgiven, made righteous by his blood, and given access to the Father (Ephesians 2:18). Now Jesus gives *you* the keys to the kingdom of God.

PRAYER
Lord, thank you that you give me a righteousness that is not my own. Thank you that you give me access to the Father. Lord, I seek you today.

NEW TESTAMENT READING

Matthew 16:1–20
Receive the keys by faith

The context of Jesus' teaching about the keys of the kingdom is *understanding* and acknowledging who Jesus is. Just as we read in the psalm for today, God is looking for 'any who *understand*' (Psalm 14:2b), so Jesus is quite amazed at the lack of *understanding* of his disciples: 'Do you still not *understand*?... How is it you don't *understand*?' (Matthew 16:9, 11).

Then the penny drops for Peter that Jesus is 'the Christ, the Son of the living God' (v.16). It is within this context that Jesus gives Peter 'the keys' saying, 'On this rock I will build my church, and the gates of Hades will not overcome it. *I will give you the keys of the kingdom* of heaven; whatever you bind on earth will be bound in heaven, and whatever you loose on earth will be loosed in heaven' (vv.18–19).

The words of Jesus are addressed to Peter. On the rock-like faith Peter has displayed, Jesus is going to build his church. Peter receives the keys of the kingdom. On the day of Pentecost, Peter opened the door for 3,000 people (Acts 2:41). He opened the door for the Gentile centurion, Cornelius, and thereby to the whole Gentile world (Acts 10).

But it is not only Peter who has the keys of the kingdom. Later on, Jesus gives the disciples a similar authority: 'I tell you the truth, whatever you bind on earth will be bound in heaven, and whatever you loose on earth will be loosed in heaven' (Matthew 18:18).

This is the extraordinary responsibility and privilege that Jesus gives to us, his church. He gives us the keys of the kingdom. 'You will have complete and free access to God's kingdom, keys to open any and every door: no more barriers between heaven and earth, earth and heaven. A yes on earth is a yes in heaven. A no on earth is a no in heaven' (16:19, MSG).

Jesus says, in effect, that the powers of hell will 'not overcome' the person who has faith in him (v.18). Rather, the church, armed with the keys of the kingdom, can storm the gates of hell and set the prisoners free.

The 'gates of Hades' will not hold out against the church. Gates are defensive, not offensive, it is the church that is on the offensive and you can be assured of victory against the defences of the enemy.

You can have the amazing privilege of seeing people set free through the preaching of the good news of the kingdom. You can have the joy of seeing people set free from drug addiction, alcoholism, crime and every other bondage. You can approach challenges with confidence, fearing no evil, knowing that you share in a remarkable spiritual authority.

PRAYER

Lord, thank you for your promise that whatever we bind on earth will be bound in heaven, and whatever we loose on earth will be loosed in heaven.

OLD TESTAMENT READING

Genesis 45:1–47:12
Unlock doors and see lives changed

'He who has felt the deepest grief is best able to experience supreme happiness,'[1] wrote Alexandre Dumas. Jacob (Israel) and his family had been through deep grief. Now they experience supreme happiness.

Sometimes I try to hide my emotions. Yet Joseph was a man of intense emotion. When he identified himself to his brothers, 'his sobbing was so violent that the Egyptians couldn't help but hear him' (45:2, MSG). He then 'kissed all his brothers and wept over them' (v.15, MSG). Emotions are as much a part of our 'createdness' as hands and lungs. Don't fear showing your emotions. Jesus wept and showed compassion openly.

Joseph *totally forgave* his brothers (v.5). In his book *Total Forgiveness,* R. T. Kendall describes this as one of the hardest, yet greatest, things he had ever been asked to do: 'An unexpected blessing emerged as I began to forgive: a peace came into my heart that I hadn't felt for years.'[2]

Joseph is able to see that despite all the hardships he has been through, he has been used by God to 'save lives' (v.5). Three times he says it was *God* who sent him (vv.5, 7–8).

Joseph says, 'Don't blame yourself for selling me. God was behind it. God sent me here ahead of you to save lives' (v.5, MSG).

As I look back on my life I realise how many times I have worried unnecessarily. If only I had trusted God completely I would have saved myself so much turmoil. Think of how much Jacob must have suffered over Joseph when actually God had it all totally under control.

Jesus said he came to fulfil the Old Testament (Matthew 5:17–20). The story of Joseph is a good example of this: Jesus fulfilled what was foreshadowed by Joseph. Joseph's suffering was part of God's plan to save his people. In saving his people, God made Joseph a lord and ruler over all Egypt (Genesis 45:8–9).

One of the keys of the kingdom is to understand that Jesus is the Saviour of the world – to see that behind the cross was the hand of God saving lives through the suffering of Jesus 'by a great deliverance' (v.7). Now God has made Jesus not just 'lord of all Egypt' but Lord of all creation.

The hero of flight 1549 saved the lives of 155 people and was given the keys of New York. Joseph saved the lives of the people of God and was made lord of all Egypt. Jesus saved the world and is given the keys of the kingdom, which he hands on to his church. What an amazing privilege you have.

PRAYER

Thank you, Lord, that through Jesus, I can receive total forgiveness. Help me to forgive others totally. Thank you that this is one of the keys of the kingdom. May we, the church, use those keys to unlock the gates of Hades and set people free.

24 January | Day 24
How to Listen to God

Suppose I go to the doctor and say, 'Doctor, I have a lot of problems: I twisted my knee... my eyes itch... my finger is swollen... I have backache...' Then, having got through my list of complaints, I look at my watch and say, 'Goodness me, time is getting on. I must be off.' The doctor might say, 'Hang on, do you not want to hear what I have to say?'

If we only speak to God and never take time to listen, we make the same mistake. We do all the talking and we don't actually listen to him. But our relationship with God is meant to be a two-way conversation. When I'm praying, I find it helpful to write down thoughts that come into my mind that may come from the Spirit of God.

In a media-saturated age we have many voices that come to us on TV, radio, the Internet, Twitter, Facebook, Instagram, email and text message. We have the voices of family, friends and colleagues. And sometimes we have the voice of Satan tempting us to disbelieve God's word and to doubt that God has our best interests at heart.

How do you hear the voice of God in the midst of the noise and distractions of life?

READING FROM PROVERBS

Proverbs 3:1–10
Listen to God's voice in the Scriptures

The main way in which God speaks to us is through what he has already spoken in the Scriptures – his 'teaching' and 'commands' (v.1). As you read the Bible, pray that God will speak to you and that you will hear his voice.

'Don't try to figure out everything on your own. *Listen for God's voice in everything* you do, everywhere you go; he's the one who will keep you on track' (vv.5–6, MSG).

Learning verses in the Bible is one of the ways you can write God's word on the 'tablet of your heart' (v.3). Pippa and I learnt these verses on our honeymoon and have tried to live by them.

- **Be guided by 'Love and Loyalty'**
These should be our guiding principles in every decision we take. 'Love and Loyalty' (v.3, MSG) should be deeply embedded in our hearts. Loyalty means, for example, speaking about others as if they were present. We establish trust in those who are present by our loyalty to those who are not present. If you live like this, God promises you a good reputation 'in God's eyes and the eyes of the people' (v.4, MSG).

- **Run to God! Run from evil!**
We are to trust in God rather than becoming arrogant and thinking that we are clever. Fear of God, in the sense of healthy respect for him, should lead us to 'Run to God! Run from evil!' (v.7, MSG). God promises that 'this will bring health to your body and nourishment to your bones' (v.8). In other words, there is a connection between the spiritual and the physical.

- **Become a generous giver**
It really matters what you do with your money. Give God 'the first and the best' (v.9, MSG) (that is, the first part of your income not the last). I have found this to be an extraordinary principle; that if you get your giving right, you discover the truth of the promise that God will supply all your needs: 'your barns will be filled to overflowing, and your vats will brim over with new wine' (v.10).

PRAYER

Lord, help me not just to read your words, but to learn them, live by them and to bring honour to your name.

NEW TESTAMENT READING

Matthew 16:21–17:13
Listen to God through the words of Jesus

The words of Jesus are the words of God. God says, 'Listen to him' (17:5). When you read Jesus' words and take them to heart, you are listening to God.

Jesus warns his disciples to expect attack. We are never going to avoid criticism (16:21). Twice in this passage Jesus talks to his disciples about the suffering he is going to experience – explaining to them about the cross and resurrection (16:21; 17:9–12).

However, rather than listening to Jesus, Peter argues with him (16:22). Jesus' rebuke to Peter is of profound importance. In every key decision we take, we must ask ourselves whether we have in mind the concerns of God or human concerns (v.23). What Jesus is saying to Peter is the heart of his mission and it has huge implications for all of his followers (vv.24–28).

We are not to seek a life of comfort and security. Jesus said to his disciples, 'Anyone who intends to come with me has to let me lead. You're not in the driver's seat; I am. Don't run from suffering; embrace it. Follow me and I'll show you how. Self-help is no help at all. Self-sacrifice is the way, my way, to finding yourself, your true self. What kind of deal is it to get everything you want but lose yourself? What could you ever trade your soul for?' (vv.24–26, MSG).

Following Jesus involves denying yourself, taking up your cross and following him (v.24). This is the way to find life in all its fullness.

Wealth, in one sense, is utterly pointless. Purpose in life is far more important than property or possessions. All the money in the world, all the success in the world, all the fame in the world, all the power in the world is nothing if you lose your soul (v.26) and miss out on what life is all about.

On the other hand, if you follow Jesus and surrender your life to him, you find the very purpose of life. The words of Jesus are extraordinarily powerful. There has never been a time when it is more important to 'listen to him' than now!

Jesus took Peter, James and John up a high mountain. Jesus' appearance changed right before their eyes. 'Sunlight poured from his face. His clothes were filled with light. Then they realised that Moses and Elijah were also there *in deep conversation with him*' (17:1–3, MSG). They heard God say, 'This is my Son, marked by my love, focus of my delight. *Listen to him*' (v.5, MSG).

As Moses and Elijah talked with Jesus, so you too can live a life 'talking with Jesus'. Your experience may not be as visual or auditory as that of the disciples on the Mount of Transfiguration, but you too can know the presence of Jesus in your life. Through reading his words and meditating on them, you can experience a conversation with Jesus through the Holy Spirit.

You can, in a sense, look into his face, which shines 'like the sun' (v.2). You can fall down in worship (v.6). It can feel as if Jesus is actually touching you and saying to you 'do not be afraid' (v.7). And there are times when you may look up and see 'no one except Jesus' (v.8).

PRAYER

Lord, thank you that when I lose my life for you, I find it. Help me to listen to your voice and to follow you, daily.

OLD TESTAMENT READING

Genesis 47:13–48:22
Listen to God throughout your life

As Jacob came to the end of his life and looked back at all God's blessings (in spite of all the trials and difficulties), he 'worshipped as he leaned on the top of his staff' (47:31). He recognised that God had led him *throughout his life*. It is an evocative picture of a person who has lived a life in close relationship with God, listening to him and his wisdom. He recalled how God spoke to him and gave him a vision for his life (48:3–4). He is able to say 'God ... has been my *shepherd all my life*' (v.15).

Jacob also recognised that God had led his son Joseph in an extraordinary way. Because Joseph had learned to listen to God, he was able to interpret Pharaoh's dreams and, as a result, he saw great blessing. Not only did he save the lives of God's people, he also saved the lives of all Egypt (47:25). As Jacob's life draws to a close he blesses Joseph's sons, expressing his trust in God's promises and blessings for the future.

When the writer of Hebrews comments on Jacob's life of faith, he focuses on this incident: 'By faith Jacob, when he was dying, blessed each of Joseph's sons, and worshipped as he leaned on the top of his staff' (Hebrews 11:21). As he came to the end of his life, Jacob's trust in God did not peter out. He ended with a flourish of faith.

Remain faithful in worship and listen to God throughout your life. Trust God to lead and guide the next generation – that they too will listen to the voice of the Shepherd (see John 10:3–4).

PRAYER

Lord, thank you that you promise to lead me and speak to me. Help me to listen to you daily and throughout my life.

25 January | Day 25
'God Intended It for Good'

In 1947, a young New Yorker named Glenn Chambers had a lifelong dream to work for God in Ecuador. At the airport on the day of departure, he wanted to send a note to his mother but he didn't have time to buy a card. He noticed a piece of paper on the terminal floor and picked it up. It turned out to be an advertisement with '*Why*?' spread across it. He scribbled his note around the word 'Why?' and put it in the post box. That night his aeroplane exploded as it hit the 14,000-foot Colombian peak El Tablazo. When his mother received the note after the news of his death the question burned up at her from the page ... '*Why*?'

Why does God allow such suffering? This question is the single greatest challenge to the Christian faith. The amount of suffering and its distribution seem to be random and unfair. It outrages and bewilders us.

Theologians and philosophers have wrestled for centuries with the mystery of undeserved suffering, and no one has ever come up with a simple and complete solution. Today and tomorrow's passages are only part of the answer, but each of them gives us some insight.

We see that although suffering is never good in itself, God is able to use it for good in a number of ways. God loves you. Your suffering is also God's suffering. He suffers alongside you. Yet he does not always simply remove suffering from your life; he sometimes uses the bad things that happen to bring about his good purposes.

READING FROM PSALMS

Psalm 15:1–5
God uses suffering to transform you

Have there been times in your life when, because of circumstances, you have felt shaken? Times when you have lost your bearings and felt tempted to give up?

Today's psalm reminds us that you need 'never be shaken' (v.5), even in times of suffering. David describes the kind of life that God intends you to lead. The guidelines he gives are things you can hold on to during the difficult times:

1. Act right
Seek to walk blamelessly and to do what is right (v.2a).

2. Tell the truth
'...speak the truth' from your heart (v.2b).

3. Do not gossip
Let 'no slander' come from your tongue (v.3).

4. Do not hurt your neighbour
Do your 'neighbours no wrong' (v.3).

5. Keep your word
Keep your promises 'even when it hurts' (v.4b). This means doing whatever you have committed to do even when it does not suit you (a particular challenge for our generation, when a simple text message can cancel an arrangement at any moment).

6. Be generous
If you lend money, don't charge excessive interest (v.5a).

7. Be honest
Never take 'bribes' (v.5b).

As our character begins to transform in these ways, difficult circumstances and suffering have less of a destabilising impact upon us. As the psalmist notes, 'Those who do these things will never be shaken' (v.5c) and you will dwell in the sanctuary of the Lord (v.1a).

As times of suffering lead to character formation, so character formation leads to knowledge of secure hope and experience of God's love (Romans 5:3–5). Hope and love are the greatest stabilising forces that you can know in the face of suffering and uncertainty.

PRAYER

Lord, thank you that you accept me as I am, but you do not want me to remain that way. Help me to live a holy life. Help me to see the trials and difficulties I face as part of my character formation.

NEW TESTAMENT READING

Matthew 17:14–18:9
God used suffering to save you

Jesus came to deal with suffering (17:22–23) and ultimately to remove all suffering, through the cross and resurrection.

At the heart of the universe is the suffering of God on the cross: '"The Son of Man is about to be betrayed to some people who want nothing to do with God. They will *murder him* – and three days later he will be raised alive." The disciples felt terrible' (vv.22–23, MSG). They did not understand that what human beings (and all the demonic powers) intended for evil, God intended for good – the saving of many lives.

What the devil meant for evil, God meant for good. He was able to take the greatest evil ever committed (the killing of the Son of God) and use it for the greatest good (the salvation of humankind).

The healing of the boy with epilepsy (v.18) is a foretaste of a time when there will be no more sickness or suffering. The death and resurrection of Jesus means that no one need 'be thrown into the fire of hell' (18:9).

How should you respond?

1. Have faith
In this passage we see the terrible suffering (17:15, MSG) of a child with sickness and the resulting suffering of a parent. In this particular case, the disciples' inability to heal came from their lack of faith (although this is not always the case – some people have prayed for healing with enormous faith but without obvious results). Jesus says that if you have even a tiny bit of faith you can move mountains. 'Nothing will be impossible for you' (v.20).

2. Don't cause unnecessary offence
Jesus explains that though he is exempt from paying the tax for the temple (God's house) because he is God's own Son, he makes a miraculous payment for both himself and Peter, 'So that we may not offend them' (v.27). Although Jesus was willing to cause offence if necessary, he did not want to cause unnecessary offence.

3. Humble yourself
Greatness in the kingdom of heaven is not about achievement; it is about humbling yourself like a child (18:4).

4. Be radical
Jesus calls us to be ruthless in cutting sin out of our lives (vv.7–9).

PRAYER

Lord, thank you that at the heart of the universe is the event where you turned evil into good. I put my trust in you. I depend on you.

OLD TESTAMENT READING

Genesis 49:1–50:26
God uses suffering for his good purposes

Whatever evil other people – or even the devil – plan against you, God is able to use it for his own good purposes: for your own good and the benefit of others who will be blessed through your life and ministry.

As Jacob came to the end of his life, he blessed his sons. He blessed Judah with victory, prosperity and leadership. Judah was to become the most powerful southern tribe of Israel and, in the person of David, provided the king of the whole nation.

We see here a foreshadowing of Jesus: 'The sceptre will not depart from Judah, nor the ruler's staff from between his feet' (49:10). Later on, we will read that 'A star will come out of Jacob; a sceptre will rise out of Israel' (Numbers 24:17). Jacob uses the image of the lion (Genesis 49:9). Jesus is described as the 'Lion of the tribe of Judah, the Root of David' (Revelation 5:5).

Jacob went on to bless Joseph, 'a fruitful vine' (Genesis 49:22). He had been through difficulties and attacks, but God used it all for good. Joseph was successful because God's hand was upon him and turned the evil into blessing (50:20).

When Jacob died, Joseph's brothers were worried that Joseph would take revenge for all the wrongs they had done to him (v.15). But Joseph said to them, '"Don't be afraid. Am I in the place of God? You intended to harm me, but God *intended it for good* to accomplish what is now being done, the saving of many lives. So then, don't be afraid. I will provide for you and your children." And he reassured them and spoke kindly to them' (vv.19–21).

R. T. Kendall writes, 'For Joseph, vindication on the spot might have done something for him in that moment; but it wouldn't have done anything for the kingdom of God. When we are mistreated in any way, we must realise that our suffering has profound and vast implications for the greater kingdom of God. There are unseen reasons for continued suffering. Who knows what God will do with your life if you take mistreatment with dignity?'[1]

See God's hand in everything that happens to you – good and bad. See it all with the eyes of faith. Understand it all as part of God's plan to bring good out of evil (just as he did through Jesus' death on the cross).

The promise of the New Testament is that God will use everything that happens to you for good. As you face trials, temptation, struggles and difficulty, the New Testament assures you that 'in all things God works for the good of those who love him, who have been called according to his purpose' (Romans 8:28).[2]

PRAYER

Lord, help me to forgive totally those who have harmed me in any way. Help me to see your hand in everything that happens to me – whether good or bad. Thank you that in all things you are working for the good of those who love you.

26 January | Day 26
Why Does God Allow Suffering?

A one-year-old boy shattered his back falling down a flight of stairs. He spent his childhood and youth in and out of hospital. Gavin Reid, the former Bishop of Maidstone, interviewed him in church. The boy remarked, 'God is fair.' Gavin asked, 'How old are you?' 'Seventeen,' the boy replied. 'How many years have you spent in hospital?' The boy answered, 'Thirteen years.' Gavin asked, 'Do you think that is fair?' He replied, '*God has got all of eternity to make it up to me*.'

We live in a world of instant gratification that has almost entirely lost its eternal perspective. The New Testament is full of wonderful promises about the future: all creation will be restored. Jesus will return to establish 'a new heaven and a new earth' (Revelation 21:1). There will be no more crying, for there will be no more pain and suffering. Our frail, decaying mortal bodies will be changed for a body like that of Jesus' glorious resurrected body.

Suffering is not part of God's original created order (see Genesis 1–2). *There was no suffering* in the world before rebellion against God. *There will be no suffering* when God creates a new heaven and a new earth (Revelation 21:3–4). Suffering is, therefore, *an alien intrusion* into God's world.

This, of course, is not a complete answer to the question 'Why does God allow suffering?' As we saw yesterday there is no simple or complete solution, but each of today's passages gives us some further insight.

READING FROM PSALMS

Psalm 16:1–11
See the suffering of this life in the context of eternity

Today's psalm is one of the few Old Testament passages that foresees the hope of *eternity* in the presence of God. David writes, 'because you will not abandon me to the grave, nor will you let your Holy One see decay. You have made known to me the path of life; you will fill me with joy in your presence, with eternal pleasures at your right hand (vv.10–11).

This is our future hope. These verses show that the resurrection of Jesus was foretold in the Scriptures (see Acts 2:25–28). This life is not the end. You can look forward to an eternity in the presence of God, fullness of joy and pleasures for evermore. 'Our present sufferings are not worth comparing with the glory that will be revealed in us' (Romans 8:18).

PRAYER

Lord, thank you that I can, in Christ, look forward to a resurrected body and an eternity in the presence of God, where there is fullness of joy and pleasures for evermore.

NEW TESTAMENT READING

Matthew 18:10–35
Understand the relationship between human freedom and suffering

God loves you. Love is not love if it is forced; it can only be love if there is a real choice. God gave human beings a choice and the freedom to love or not to love. So much suffering is caused by us choosing not to love God or others: 'The sorrows of those will increase who run after other gods' (Psalm 16:4).

However, Jesus expressly repudiates the automatic link between sin and suffering (John 9:1–3). He also points out that natural disasters are not necessarily a form of punishment from God (Luke 13:1–5). But *some* suffering *is* a direct result either of *our own sin or the sin of others*. In this passage we see three examples:

1. Wandering away

Jesus speaks about a sheep that 'wanders away' (Matthew 18:12).

When we wander away from the protection of the Shepherd we become vulnerable. But God will never stop searching for us because he 'is not willing that any of these little ones should be lost' (v.14).

2. Sin of others

Jesus says, 'If your brother or sister sins against you ...' (v.15). So much suffering in the world is the result of other people's sin – both at a global and community level, and also at an individual one. In this passage, Jesus sets out a way of reconciliation.

He calls his disciples to *unlimited* forgiveness. Jesus says that when people sin against us we are to forgive them – not just seven times, but seventy-seven times (vv.21–22).

Forgiveness is not easy. The cross reminds us how costly and painful it is. Forgiveness does not mean approving of what the other person did, nor excusing it, nor denying it, nor pretending that you are not hurt. Rather, you are aware of what the other person has done and yet you are called to forgive. In your personal relationships lay aside all malice, revenge and retribution and show mercy and grace to the person who has hurt you.

3. Unforgiveness

Sometimes forgiving can be extremely hard. As C. S. Lewis wrote: 'Everyone thinks forgiveness is a lovely idea until they have something to forgive.'[1]

In the final parable, we can see the destructive nature of unforgiveness. The first servant's unwillingness to forgive a comparatively minor debt (around three-and-a-half month's wages compared to around 160,000 years' wages for an average person) destroys his relationship with the other servants, and leads to the second servant being cast into prison. So often unforgiveness destroys relationships between people, and results in them lashing out against those they think have sinned against them. We see the results of this in marriage breakdowns, broken relationships, or in conflicts between different communities.

We do not earn our forgiveness; Jesus achieved that for you on the cross. But your willingness to forgive is evidence that you know God's forgiveness. Forgiven people forgive. All of us have been forgiven so much by God that we must keep on forgiving the comparatively small offences committed against us.

I'm so thankful that God does not put a limit on how often he forgives me. Yet when I look at others I am tempted to think, 'I'm happy to forgive once, or even twice, but if they keep on doing this surely I'm not expected to keep on forgiving.'

Cultivate in your heart the same attitude towards others as God has towards you.

PRAYER

Lord, help me to use my freedom to love, to search for the lost and to have mercy. Help me not to cause suffering but rather to give my life, following the example of Jesus, for the relief of suffering.

OLD TESTAMENT READING

Job 1:1–3:26
Always respond to suffering with compassion

The book of Job is all about suffering. It is primarily about the question, '*How should we respond* to suffering?'

Perhaps we also see a hint about the origin of suffering. When the angels assembled before God, '*Satan* also came with them' (1:6). He had been 'roaming through the earth' (v.7). It is clear that Satan's objective is to cause as much suffering as he can.

It appears that Satan was a fallen angel. It seems that before God created human beings he created other free, imaginative and intelligent beings and that there was a rebellion within the spiritual realm before human beings even emerged.

A great deal of suffering can be explained as being the result of the fact that we live in a fallen world: a world where all creation has been affected, not only by the sin of human beings, but also before that by Satan's sin. The serpent existed before Adam and Eve sinned. As a result of Adam and Eve's sin, 'thorns and thistles' entered the world (Genesis 3:18). Ever since that time 'the creation was subjected to frustration' (Romans 8:20). 'Natural' disasters are a result of this disorder in creation.

Satan was allowed to bring several major tragedies into the life of a man who was blameless and upright, who feared God and shunned evil (Job 1:1). Job suffered loss in the areas of money, material possessions (vv.13–17), family life (vv.18–19), personal health (2:1–10) and, eventually, the support of his friends.

When we face unexplained suffering it can be very easy to blame God. Although Job did not know why he was suffering, he responded by continuing to trust and worship God in his pain, just as he had in his good fortune (1:21, 2:10). The writer tells us admiringly, 'In all this, Job did not sin in what he said' (v.10b). He remained faithful in the most difficult of circumstances.

Initially Job's friends respond in the right way: 'No one said a word to him, because they saw *how great his suffering was*' (v.13). In the face of great suffering, attempts to rationalise can be counterproductive. Usually the most positive thing you can do is to put an arm around the person and 'mourn with those who mourn' (Romans 12:15), entering their suffering and participating as far as you are able.

In the end, God restored Job's fortunes and gave him twice as much as he had before. Now we know that, through Jesus, God has all eternity to more than compensate for all your sufferings in this life.[2]

PRAYER

Lord, when I see suffering, help me to show compassion and weep with those who weep.

27 January | Day 27
How to Stay on Track

Pippa and I love to go for walks. Not so long ago, we went for quite a long walk on the South Downs. Neither of us has a very good sense of direction and we had forgotten to take the map. Somehow, we managed to wander off the track and we ended up on someone's farm.

It was one of the shortest days of the year and soon the light started to fade. It seemed that the only way to get back to where we had parked the car was to cross a field occupied by a large herd of cows. As we approached them, some surrounded us in an overly friendly fashion, blocking our way, while others took off in fright and started charging around the field.

Fearing that we were going to be mown down into the mud by terrified cows charging at us, we decided to make a rather speedy exit up a very steep and slippery bank. Pippa had exceeded her desired length of walk, darkness was falling and we seemed to be nowhere near a track. Things were not looking good.

Thankfully, we managed to find a path leading us back. It was such a relief. For future walks we decided we would definitely take a map and stick to the route. Staying on the track proves much better for being able to relax, talk together and for our relationship generally!

In the Bible, the image of God's tracks is frequently used: tracks that lead to life.

READING FROM PSALMS

Psalm 17:1–5
Determine to stay on God's tracks

David says, 'My steps have held closely to Your paths [to the tracks of the One Who has gone on before]' (v.5a, AMP). The Hebrew word for paths literally means 'wheel-tracks'. David is absolutely determined to stay on God's tracks. In order to stay on God's tracks, you need to watch:

- **Your heart (what you *think* about)**
'Though you probe *my heart, though you* examine me at night and test me, you will find that I have planned no evil' (v.3a).

- **Your words (what you *say*)**
'I have resolved that *my mouth* will not sin' (v.3c).

- **Your feet (the places that you *go*)**
'*My feet* have not slipped' (v.5b).

PRAYER

Lord, help me to stay on *your tracks*. May my feet not slip. Help me to guard my thoughts day and night. Help me not to sin against you through anything I say or do.

NEW TESTAMENT READING

Matthew 19:1–15
Stay on God's tracks in your relationships

Jesus' teaching on relationships is of vital importance for your own life and for society. In this passage, he sets out God's tracks for family life.

- **Importance of marriage**
The Pharisees ask Jesus about divorce, but he replies by speaking about *marriage*. He goes back to the creation account. Jesus quotes from Genesis 2:24, stating, 'For this reason a man will leave his father and mother and be united to his wife, and the two will become one flesh' (Matthew 19:5). This verse from Genesis is seen as the blueprint verse for marriage – not only in the Old Testament and by Paul (Ephesians 5:31) but also by Jesus himself.

  Marriage involves the public act of leaving – making a lifelong commitment to your partner that takes priority even over your parental relationships. It involves being 'united' with one's partner – the Hebrew word means literally 'glued' together – not just physically and biologically but emotionally, psychologically, socially and spiritually. This is the Christian context of the 'one-flesh' union. The biblical doctrine of marriage is the most exciting and positive one that exists. It is also the most romantic view. It sets before us God's perfect plan.

- **Concession of divorce**
The Pharisees persist with their questions about divorce. They speak of Moses' command (Matthew 19:7). Jesus replies by saying Moses permitted it 'because your hearts were hard' (v.8) and robustly confronts those men who (in a society in which women had far fewer rights) used the provision of the law to walk away from their wives (v.9).

  Moses' provision for divorce reminds us of God's grace and compassion in situations where we fall short of his ideals. But Jesus is saying that divorce is never ideal.

  Many of those who have experienced the pain of a broken marriage will identify with Job's description of his suffering in today's Old Testament passage. We need to do all we can to guard marriages (ours and others) and do all we can to comfort those who have been divorced (not by casting blame like Eliphaz).

- **Calling to singleness**

Jesus speaks of three types of singleness. First, some 'were born that way' (v.12a) and 'never give marriage a thought' (MSG). Second, there is involuntary singleness (v.12b) – those who 'never get asked – or accepted' (MSG). Third, there is voluntary singleness – those who 'decide not to get married for kingdom reasons' (v.12c, MSG). Singleness can be temporary or permanent, but it is never regarded in the New Testament as second best. Both marriage and singleness are high callings and, according to the New Testament, there are advantages and disadvantages to both.

- **Priority of children**

The words of Jesus challenged the attitude of many of his contemporaries towards children. In ancient societies children were often kept on the periphery of society – to use an old-fashioned British saying, they were to be 'seen but not heard'.

God's tracks are very different. Jesus places his hands on the little children and prays for them (v.13a). When the disciples feel that Jesus should not be distract ed by them, Jesus replies, 'Let the little children come to me, and do not hinder them, for the kingdom of heaven belongs to such as these' (v.14). He demonstrates the high priority children should have in our lives.

As parents, it is very important to prioritise our children and not to see them as distracting us from our work or ministry. As a church, we need to see that our children and youth have priority in terms of resources and facilities because the kingdom of heaven belongs to them as much as anyone else. They are not only the future of the church, they are the church.

PRAYER

Lord, help us, both in our own personal lives and as a society, not to wander off your tracks for family life. I pray for your blessing on all those working to strengthen family life.

OLD TESTAMENT READING

Job 4:1–7:21
Help others stay on God's tracks

I am so thankful for my friends who have helped me stay on track. However, sometimes it is possible even for our friends to misunderstand or get things wrong. In this passage we see a contrast between Job who helped others stay on God's tracks (4:3–4) and Eliphaz who was 'no help' to Job (6:21).

Sometimes people ask, 'Is every word in the Bible true?' I reply, 'Yes, but like every other book it needs to be interpreted.' One of the rules of interpretation is that we have to interpret according to the context.

We have to read the words of Eliphaz in the light of the fact that, in the end, the Lord says to Eliphaz the Temanite, 'I am angry with you and your two friends, because you have not spoken the truth about me, as my servant Job has' (42:7). The words that we read in this passage are not all true. Job's friends give far too simplistic an answer to the issue of suffering. Their diagnosis is often naïve, pious and unrealistic.

Job, on the other hand, is realistic and honest as he struggles with pain, sleepless nights, grief and suffering. His suffering is not as a result of his own sin, as Eliphaz and his friends suggest. Job rightly asks, 'Show me where I have been wrong' (6:24). God's Spirit will always convict us of specific sins whereas Eliphaz and his friends say to him in effect, 'You must have done something wrong to be suffering like this.' Those who are suffering have not necessarily caused their suffering by their own sin. If we have, then God will show us the specific sin.

Eliphaz and his friends give advice that is a mixture of truth and falsehood and their words need to be interpreted as such. One thing Eliphaz says that is probably true is that Job was a man who helped people stay on God's tracks: 'Think how you have instructed many, how you have strengthened feeble hands. Your words have supported those who stumbled; you have strengthened faltering knees' (4:3–4).

Your task is not just to stay on track yourself but, like Job, to help others as well by your actions and by your words.

PRAYER

Lord, thank you for all my friends who help me stay on track. Help me to be a genuine comfort to those who are suffering, to support those who stumble and strengthen those with faltering knees. Help us all to help each other to stay on your tracks.

28 January | Day 28
With God, All Things Are Possible

'When life hands you a lemon, make lemonade,'[1] wrote Norman Vincent Peale, who published his best-known book, *The Power of Positive Thinking*, in 1952. It stayed in *The New York Times* bestseller list for 186 consecutive weeks. Much of what he had to say was extremely good and helpful. But, the words of Jesus go way beyond the power of positive thinking.

Norman Vincent Peale said, 'A positive mental attitude is a belief that things are going to turn out well, and that *you* can overcome any kind of trouble or difficulty.' Jesus said, 'With *God* all things are possible' (Matthew 19:26). This is far more than the power of positive thinking. It is *the power of God* that makes what seems impossible possible. Nothing is impossible with God (Luke 1:37).

READING FROM PROVERBS

Proverbs 3:11–20
Through Jesus, the universe was created

The fact that with God 'all things are possible' is proven by the fact that God created the entire universe out of nothing: 'By wisdom the Lord laid the earth's foundations, by understanding he set the heavens in place; by his knowledge the deeps were divided, and the clouds let drop the dew' (vv.19–20).

The writer of Proverbs sees wisdom as a person (vv.13–18). Through the lens of the New Testament, we see that that person is Jesus. St Paul tells us that '*Christ* [is] the *power of God* and the *wisdom of God*' (1 Corinthians 1:24).

Until you find a relationship with *Jesus*, life will not really make sense. The entire universe was created through Jesus (John 1:3). He loves you. In a relationship with him you find *God's wisdom* and *God's power*.

When you find Jesus, you find the source of all wisdom. This is the way of blessing (Proverbs 3:13a). It is also the way to *understanding* (v.13b). It is far more profitable than all the material blessings (vv.14–15a). In fact, 'nothing you desire can compare with her' (v.15b).

This is the path to long life (v.16, which is 'eternal life' in the New Testament, see John 3:16). Here you find true 'riches and honour' (Proverbs 3:16). This is the way to a *peace* beyond understanding (v.17). Here you find the 'tree of life' (v.18).

PRAYER

Lord, I seek you today. Give me wisdom, peace and power to live the kind of life you want me to lead.

NEW TESTAMENT READING

Matthew 19:16–30
What is impossible in human terms is possible with God

Do you sometimes find yourself facing a seemingly impossible situation? It might be a relationship that seems to have broken down irretrievably, or an issue to do with health, finances or something else where change seems impossible. With God there is always hope, no matter how bad things look. Nothing is impossible with God. His power makes all things possible.

The context of Jesus' words that 'with God all things are possible' (v.26) is the account of the rich young man to whom Jesus calls, 'Come, follow me' (v.21b). He tells him, 'Go, sell your possessions and give to the poor' (v.21a). But it is too much for him to give up and the young man goes away 'sad' (v.22). Jesus points out how hard it is for the rich to enter the kingdom of heaven (vv.23–24). Yet, with God 'all things are possible' (v.26).

Jesus says that, humanly speaking, it is impossible for anyone to enter the kingdom of God (v.26). Worldly riches are of no help. In fact, they are more of a hindrance. Jesus says, 'It is easier for a camel to go through the eye of a needle than for the rich to enter the kingdom of God' (v.24).

Some people have suggested that this is a reference to a gate in Jerusalem that was called 'the needle's eye'. A camel would need to unload all it was carrying on its back to go through it. Other people have pointed out that a word very similar to 'camel' means a sort of rope. Maybe he was talking of threading rope through the eye of a needle.

These attempts to rationalise the words of Jesus miss the point. The point is that it is totally unthinkable for a camel to go through the eye of a needle. But what is impossible in human terms is possible with God (v.26).

In answer to the disciples' question, '"Then who has any chance at all?" Jesus looked hard at them and said, "No chance at all if you think you can pull it off *yourself*. Every chance in the world if you trust *God to do it*"' (vv.25–26, MSG).

In this world the rich, the powerful and the famous are the ones who people look up to as 'first'. The poor are looked down on, ignored and seen as 'last'. But in the kingdom of heaven the reverse is the case. Jesus says, 'But many who are first will be last, and many who are last will be first' (v.30).

This is God's powerful upside-down kingdom. Jesus asks the rich young man to give to the poor because he wants the man to place his trust in him *and* because the poor are such a high priority in the kingdom. They should be for us too: the thousands of children dying each day through desperate poverty and starvation, the oppressed people of so many countries, the homeless on our streets, the voiceless and the vulnerable.

Jesus rarely told people to give away everything but in this case, he did. For everyone, there is a 'cost' to following Jesus. There is the *cost* of being willing to fly his flag in a hostile world. There is what may seem to be a cost of giving up things that we know to be wrong.

Whatever 'the cost', it is nothing compared to what it cost Jesus to make 'eternal life' (v.29) possible for you and me. And it is nothing compared to the cost of *not* following Jesus. The rich young ruler missed out on so much.

Furthermore, it is nothing compared to what you receive: 'And everyone who has left houses or brothers or sisters or father or mother or wife or children or fields for my sake will receive a *hundred times* as much and will inherit eternal life' (v.29). Jesus promises that for everything you give up, you will receive far more – in this life and, even more significantly, into eternity with Jesus.

PRAYER

Lord, help me to be willing to give everything I have for the sake of the kingdom of God. Thank you that the greatest and most enduring riches come from following Jesus.

OLD TESTAMENT READING

Job 8:1–10:22
In your life, nothing is impossible with God

Sometimes when we see the suffering of others it is tempting to come up with glib explanations. In the advice of Job's friend, Bildad, we see an extraordinary mixture of truth, half-truth and falsehood (8:1–22).

When Job replies, he says, 'Indeed, I know that this is *true. But*...' (9:2). In other words, he points out that some of what Bildad said was *true, but* not all. He rejects his glib explanation of why he is suffering.

Job's words are far more authentic. They come from the heart. He cries out to God, 'I could only plead with my Judge for mercy' (v.15). He wishes he had never been born (10:18–19). He admits his struggles and doubts, and even his anger at what is happening to him. He says, 'I loathe my life; therefore I will give free rein to my complaint and speak out in the bitterness of my soul' (v.1).

Yet in the midst of all this he recognises that nothing is impossible with God. Job says, 'God's wisdom is so deep, *God's power so immense*... He moves mountains before they know what's happened, flips them on their heads on a whim... We'll never comprehend all the great things he does; his miracle-surprises can't be counted' (9:4–5, 10, MSG). 'You gave me life itself, and incredible love. You watched and guarded every breath I took' (10:12, MSG).

There is an extraordinary mixture here of honest struggles and faith. Job does not try and pretend that everything is all right, or that he can explain it, yet through it all he clings to what he knows of God.

God was able to do in Job's life what was impossible by human effort. God restored Job's fortunes and 'blessed the latter part of Job's life more than the first' (42:12).

Whatever struggles you are facing at the moment, however difficult life looks, however impossible the situation seems, it is important to remember his love for you and trust that 'with God all things are possible' (Matthew 19:26).

PRAYER

Lord, thank you for the example of Job – his faithfulness and trust in you even during the struggles of life. My life is in your hands and at your disposal. Thank you for your amazing love. Thank you that with you nothing is impossible.

29 January | Day 29
You Are Loved

Shane Taylor was considered one of the most dangerous men in the UK prison system. Originally jailed for attempted murder, he had his sentence extended by four years when he attacked a prison officer with a broken glass, setting off a riot.

He was put in a segregation unit inside a maximum-security prison. He was given his food through a hatch. His door was not opened unless there were six officers armed with riot shields waiting outside.

Later, he was transferred to Long Lartin maximum-security prison where he was invited on Alpha. During the course he prayed, 'Jesus Christ, I know you died on a cross for me. I hate who I am; who I've become. Please forgive me and come into my life.' At that moment he was filled with the Holy Spirit. He went running out onto the wing, telling everyone he could find, 'Jesus is real!'

His behaviour changed so much that he went from living in total segregation to getting a trusted job in the prison chaplaincy. He prayed for the prison officers and for his enemies and, when he came out of prison, he got involved in a church. He met a young woman called Sam, who had also had a tough life and had been involved with drugs and criminal activity. She also came to faith in Jesus. Now, they are married and have five children.

Talking to Shane now, it is hard to imagine that he is the same person who terrified so many people in the past. He has experienced *'the wonder of [God's] great love'* (Psalm 17:7). He says, 'Jesus has shown me how to love and how to forgive. He has saved me. He has forgiven me for what I have done. He has turned my life around.'

READING FROM PSALMS

Psalm 17:6–12
Know that you are loved and treasured by God

God's love for you is so great because it is so intimate. David calls on God and asks him to 'show *the wonder of your great love*' (v.7). He prays, 'Keep me as *the apple of your eye'* (v.8a). The *apple of the eye* is the pupil (the opening of the iris in the eye through which light passes to reach the retina), and so signifies the thing *most treasured*. Meditate today on just how much you are treasured by God.

Then he prays, 'Hide me in *the shadow of your wings*' (v.8b). Again, this tells of God's love, intimacy and protection. Jesus picked up this image as he looked over the people of Jerusalem in the days leading up to his crucifixion and longed for them to come and hide under *his wings* (Matthew 23:37).

David is surrounded by 'enemies' (Psalm 17:9), people with 'callous hearts' who speak arrogantly against him (v.10). There may be times in your life when you literally face 'enemies', but whatever struggles or difficulties you may face, you can rely on God's intimate love for you.

PRAYER

Lord, I call on you today. Keep me as the apple of your eye; hide me in the shadow of your wings.

NEW TESTAMENT READING

Matthew 20:1–19
Experience God's love, generosity and grace

Jesus tells a parable that demonstrates again the wonder of his great love. The parable of the workers in the vineyard shows the extraordinary generosity and grace of God, who gives to those who enter the kingdom *last* the same blessings that he gives to everybody else. This sometimes makes us 'envious' (v.15b). We are happy with our situation until we hear of someone else doing even better. Then, we are tempted to envy them.

The landowner in this parable overturns all the normal commercial practices. He does this, not to make extra profit for himself, but for the very opposite reason. He wants to be generous and pay *more* than justice demands. God is like that landowner, and his blessings and forgiveness are always *more* than we could ever deserve.

We sometimes hear testimonies from people like Shane Taylor who have lived terrible lives. Then, at the 'eleventh hour' (v.9), they repent and believe in Jesus. They are totally forgiven and receive all the benefits of Jesus' death and resurrection (v.19). Some people complain that this is unfair, or that those like Shane are given too high a profile. Yet God uses their testimonies greatly, often seemingly more than those who have borne 'the heat of the day' (v.12b).

As we saw yesterday, God's kingdom is an upside-down kingdom: 'So the last will be first, and the first will be last' (v.16). Jesus is saying this is not a reason to be envious. Rather, it is a reason to marvel at the generosity of God. In his great love, he is generous to all. It is all grace. It is all undeserved. It is all a result of what Jesus foretold (vv.17–20).

The reality is that it is not just other people like Shane to whom God is generous. He is generous to you and me. If God gave us only what we earned, we would be far worse off. Yet if you accept the generosity that God showers on you, the result is staggering.

Through his death and resurrection (vv.18–19), Jesus makes it possible for you and me to be forgiven and to enjoy his great love into eternity.

PRAYER

Lord, thank you for your extraordinary generosity to me. May I never be envious of those you seem to be blessing even more than me. Thank you that I can know that I am loved now and into eternity.

OLD TESTAMENT READING

Job 11:1–14:22

Hold on to his wonderful love through the difficult days

Job, in the middle of a long period of intense suffering, holds on to God's wonderful love. He says, 'Though he slay me, yet will I hope in him' (13:15).

Although Job had lived a blameless and upright life, fearing God and shunning evil (1:1), he was not perfect. He speaks here of 'the sins of my youth' (13:26) and says, 'My offences will be sealed up in a bag; you will cover over my sin' (14:17).

The mistake that Job's friends made was to think that his suffering was linked to his sin. In this passage we see Job's increasing frustration with his friends. They go on about 'sin' (11:6, 14) and effectively heap condemnation on Job (v.5). They talk in platitudes, which do not offer any real comfort.

Eventually Job turns around and replies, 'But I have a mind as well as you; I am not inferior to you. Who does not know all these things?' (12:3). 'What you know, I also know' (13:2). He points out to them that their best policy would be to say nothing: 'If only you would be altogether silent! For you, that would be wisdom' (v.5).

We need such wisdom when people are suffering, not to speak in glib platitudes but to ensure we demonstrate God's wonderful love by our actions and are very careful in what we say.

Job has a far healthier attitude than his friends. In his intense suffering he experiences that awful feeling of aloneness and cries out to God, 'Why do you hide your face?' (v.24). After C. S. Lewis's wife died, he wrote *A Grief Observed,* likening this kind of experience to 'a door slammed in your face'.[1]

Yet, in the midst of all this, Job is able to say to God, 'Even if he killed me, I'd keep on hoping' (v.15, MSG). He knows God and trusts him enough, even in the very depth of despair.

Know and trust that the length of your life is ultimately determined by God and that 'the number of [your] months is wholly in [God's] control' and that no one can 'pass the bounds of his allotted time' (14:5, AMP).

At the same time, Job seems to get a glimpse of life beyond the grave – that nothing, not even death, can separate you from God's great love: 'If we humans die, will we live again? That's my question. All through these difficult days I keep hoping, waiting for the final change – for resurrection!' (v.14, MSG; see also 19:25 onwards).

You and I are so much better off than Job because we know about the cross and resurrection of Jesus and we have the sure hope of eternity in the presence of God – wondering at his great love for ever.

As the story of Job unfolds, we see that he is right to keep trusting in God. God never explains to Job why he allowed him to go through so much, but Job's confidence in God's love is vindicated. In the midst of suffering, somehow we have to hold on to 'the wonders of [God's] great love' (Psalm 17:7).

PRAYER

Lord, thank you that although there is so much that I do not understand in this world, I can trust in your wonderful love. Help me today, and every day, to continue to wonder at your great love for me.

30 January | Day 30
Does God Answer All Your Prayers?

I love cricket. At least, I love watching it; I was never any good at playing it. But I know many people don't like cricket and don't even understand the rules of it (especially if they come from a country where it isn't a popular sport). So I hope you will forgive me for using a cricketing analogy.

When two batsmen are running between the wickets on a cricket pitch, they need to co-ordinate the decision about whether to run or not. One will shout to the other 'Yes' (that is, 'Let's run'), or 'No' (that is, 'Stay where you are'), or 'Wait' (that is, 'Let's see what happens before we decide whether to run').

God hears *all* your prayers (Psalm 139:4, 1 John 5:14–15, 1 Peter 3:12) and, in one sense, he answers all your prayers. But we do not always receive what we ask for. When we ask God for something, the response will be 'Yes' or 'No' or 'Wait'.

John Stott wrote that God will answer 'No' if the things we ask for 'are either not good in themselves, or not good for us or for others, directly or indirectly, immediately or ultimately'.[1]

We don't always get to know the reason why the answer is 'No'. We need to remember that God sees things from an eternal perspective and that there are some things we may never understand in this life.

In the passages for today we see examples of all three types of response from God.

READING FROM PSALMS

Psalm 17:13–15
God says 'yes'

What is the first thing you do when you wake up in the morning? David sets us a great example: 'As for me ... I shall be fully satisfied when I awake to find myself beholding Your form and having sweet communion with You' (v.15, AMP). Start each day seeking God's presence and finding satisfaction in him.

This is the heart of what prayer is all about. It is not just about asking for things; it is about seeking God's face and enjoying 'sweet communion with him'.

This is the context of David's request. He cried out to God for help in the face of his enemies (vv.13–14). God heard and answered his prayers with a positive response, 'Yes'.

PRAYER

Lord, each day, when I awake, may I enjoy sweet communion with you and 'be satisfied with seeing your likeness' (v.15b).

NEW TESTAMENT READING

Matthew 20:20–34
God says 'no' to one request, 'yes' to another

Rick Warren writes, 'When the request is not right, God says "No". When the timing is not right, God says "Slow". When you are not right, God says "Grow". But when the request is right and the timing is right and you are right, God says "Go".'[2]

In this passage we see two requests. The first receives the answer 'No' (vv.20–28) and the second the answer 'Yes' (vv.29–34).

1. Two requests

In both cases Jesus asked, 'What do you want?' He said to the mother of Zebedee's sons, '*What is it you want*?' (v.21). He said to the two blind men, '*What do you want* me to do for you?' (v.32).

In a way it must have been obvious what they wanted (in the second instance they were blind, so they must have wanted to see), but God wants us to be actively involved. The apostle James says, 'You do not have, because you do not ask God' (James 4:2). Jesus says, 'Ask and it will be given to you ... For everyone who asks receives' (Matthew 7:7–8). It may seem an obvious point, but the starting point of answered prayer is actually asking.

2. Two responses

In the case of the request of the blind men, Jesus' response was 'Yes'. 'Jesus had *compassion* on them and touched their eyes. Immediately they received their sight and followed him' (v.34).

On the other hand, Jesus, in effect, said 'No' to the mother of Zebedee's sons. This response also stemmed from *compassion*. Her request was for glory, power and promotion for her boys. He points out that she does not seem to understand all the implications of her request.

He said, 'Can you drink the cup I am going to drink?' (v.22). The Old Testament prophets spoke in several passages of the 'cup of his (God's) wrath' (for example, Isaiah 51:17–22; Jeremiah 25:15–29).

Shockingly, Jesus speaks of drinking this cup himself. He is going to 'give his life as a ransom for many' (Matthew 20:28). The Greek word for 'for' ('anti'), means '*instead of*'. This is the clearest example in the whole New Testament of Jesus explaining his death in terms of *substitution*.

3. Two reasons

The apostle James writes, 'When you ask, you do not receive, because you ask with *wrong motives*' (James 4:3). Behind the requests here lay different motives. Both requests were to do with lordship. The request of the blind men came from the recognition that Jesus is Lord, and a desire for something good (Matthew 20:30–33). On the other hand, Jesus points out that the mother's request came from a desire to '*lord it over*' others (v.25).

True greatness does not come from *lording it* over others or from what the world regards as success (wealth, position, fame or having a 'successful' ministry). Rather, Jesus says that true greatness comes from becoming 'a *servant*' – following his example in choosing '*to serve, not be served*' (vv.26–28). This is an example of where the disciples were wrong and God said '*Grow*'.

I think I have learnt more in my own life from the times when my prayers have not seemed to be answered than from the times when they have been answered with a 'Yes'. Certainly the disciples must have learnt a huge amount from this 'unanswered' prayer.

PRAYER

Lord, thank you for the lessons that we learn from 'unanswered' prayer. Thank you that you showed us true greatness. Help me to devote my life to your service and to the service of others.

OLD TESTAMENT READING

Job 15:1–18:21
God says 'wait'

Do you realise that, whatever difficulties you are facing, right now Jesus is praying for *you*?

Poor Job had to put up with increasingly irritating speeches from his friends in which they condemned him more and more, wrongly accusing him. Job described them as '*miserable comforters*' (16:2), with their 'long-winded speeches' (v.3a). They were absolutely no help to him at all (v.4).

Some people wrongly believe – as Job's so-called 'friends' did – that our suffering in this life is always caused by our own sin, or even by sin in a former life. So, if people are born in poverty or with some genetic disorder, it must be their fault. This blame must be a terrible additional unnecessary suffering (the idea of reincarnation is totally repudiated in the Bible, see Hebrews 9:27).

When your friends are suffering, avoid being a '*miserable*' comforter (Job 16:2). Rather, as Job suggests, 'encourage', 'comfort' and 'strengthen' them and 'soothe their suffering' (v.5, NIV and AMP).

One thing you can always do is to intercede (pray on their behalf) for them. Job said:

> 'My intercessor is my friend
> as my eyes pour out tears to God;
> on behalf of a human being he pleads
> with God
> as one pleads for a friend' (vv.20–21).

We are not told who the intercessor was, but whoever it was, he was a real friend to Job because he was pleading to God for him.

The prayers of the intercessor may not seem to have been answered immediately, but they were eventually when God restored Job's fortunes. His answer to Job's intercessor and to Job was '*Wait*'. Later it was Job's intercession for others that was the immediate cause of his restoration (42:8–10).

Who is Job's intercessor? Job says, 'Even now my witness is in heaven; my *advocate* is on high' (16:19). In the New Testament we see that the one 'who represents mortals before God' (16:21, MSG) is Jesus. He is your '*advocate* with the Father' (1 John 2:1, RSV). He is interceding for you (Hebrews 7:24–25).

Jesus was Job's advocate. He was interceding for him. Jesus was pleading with God 'as one pleads for a friend' (Job 16:21). There is a similarity between Job's experience and that of Peter. Jesus said to Simon Peter, 'Simon, Simon, Satan has asked to sift all of you as wheat. But *I have prayed for you*, Simon, that your faith may not fail' (Luke 22:31–32).

As John Wimber used to say, 'The good news is that Jesus is praying for you. The bad news is that you are going to need it!'

PRAYER

Lord, thank you so much that you promise to be my advocate. Thank you that in the times when, like Job or Peter, it seems that Satan is sifting me like wheat, you are praying for me. Thank you that I know that, even if it seems like I am having to wait, the answer to my advocate-in-heaven's prayer will always ultimately be 'Yes'.

31 January | Day 31
How to Lead Like Jesus

Few people have shaped the day-to-day management of people and companies more than Ken Blanchard, author of *The One Minute Manager*, which has sold more than 13 million copies. The book was so successful in such a short period of time that he had trouble taking credit for its success. He began to think about God. He started to read the Bible. He went straight to the Gospels. He wanted to know what Jesus did.

He became fascinated with how Jesus transformed twelve ordinary, and unlikely, people into the first generation of leaders of a movement that continues to affect the course of world history 2,000 years later. He became aware that everything he had ever taught or written about effective leadership, Jesus had done to perfection way beyond Ken's ability to portray or describe.

Jesus is more than just a spiritual leader. He gives a practical and effective leadership model for *all* organisations, for *all* people, for *all* situations. You may not think of yourself as a leader, but leadership is about influence. You do have influence, therefore, in a sense, all of us are leaders.

Jesus is the greatest leader of all time. In the passages for today, we see some of the characteristics of Jesus' leadership together with those of two other great influencers in the Bible – David and Job.

READING FROM PSALMS

Psalm 18:1–6
A leader's worship

David was one of the greatest leaders in the history of Israel. He also wrote some of the most beautiful songs of worship ever written. Thousands of years later, his psalms continue to be used in worship by God's people.

In this psalm we see that David's worship and prayer was the bedrock on which his leadership was founded. In the midst of difficulties and opposition he says, 'I called to the Lord, I cried to my God for help' (v.6). The result was a great reversal in circumstances followed by success, which led David to express his thanksgiving in song.

Whether in difficulty or success, follow David's example by seeking to build your life on the foundation of prayer and worship.

The starting point of worship is love for God: 'I love You fervently and devotedly, O Lord, my Strength' (v.1, AMP). David goes on to express his love, praise and thanksgiving to God. He faced enemies (v.3b), death and destruction (vv.4–5) and distress (v.6a). When he looks back he can see how God heard his cry and saved him from his enemies (vv.3–6).

For the last few years I have written down a list of cries 'for help' (v.6a) in the margins of my *Bible in One Year*. It is amazing to see the ways in which God has heard my cry. So many of the prayers (although not all quite yet) have been answered. Keeping a record helps me not to forget to thank God.

PRAYER

O Lord, my strength, thank you so much for the many times when I have called to you for help and you have heard my voice. With all the challenges ahead, again I cry to you for help...

NEW TESTAMENT READING

Matthew 21:1–17
A leader's characteristics

What does it mean, in practice, to 'lead like Jesus'?

1. Lead from who you are more than your position

Who you are is far more important than what you *do* or what you *have*, in terms of possessions or position. Jesus' *authority* did not come from having a high position in some hierarchy. It came from who he was as a person. He had a natural authority. He had total confidence that all he needed to say was, '*the Lord needs them*' (v.3). No threats or promises were required.

2. Be gentle and unassuming

'Your king comes to you, *gentle*...' (v.5). This is not a characteristic of leadership that the world expects. Yet it was right at the heart of Jesus' leadership. The Greek word for 'gentle' means considerate, unassuming. It is the opposite of aggressive or self-seeking.

3. Avoid arrogance and ostentation

Jesus entered Jerusalem on a donkey. What a contrast to so many other leaders in history, secular and religious, who have travelled with pomp and ceremony and ostentatious entourages. Jesus' mode of transport was a sign of great humility. It is the opposite of pride and arrogance, which can so easily creep into human leadership.

4. Have the courage to confront
People sometimes think that gentleness and humility mean giving way in every situation, but Jesus was not afraid of confrontation. He 'entered the temple area and drove out all who were buying and selling there. He overturned the tables of the money-changers' (v.12). One of the hardest aspects of leadership is to know the right moment for confrontation.

Failure to confront is in itself a decision with consequences. Conflict and confrontation are never easy but, wisely applied, they are a necessary part of good and courageous leadership.

5. Seek spiritual, not worldly power
The power of Jesus was so different from many of the leaders in the world. 'The blind and the lame came to him at the temple, and he healed them' (v.14). Spiritual power is far more important than earthly power. It cannot be manufactured. It can only come from the kind of relationship Jesus had with God.

6. Make prayer your number one priority
In Jesus' confrontation with the money-changers we see how passionate he was about prayer (v.13). And throughout the Gospels, we read of Jesus withdrawing (v.17) to be on his own with God. This was the source of his strength. Like with David, prayer was at the heart of Jesus' leadership.

PRAYER

Lord, help me to lead like Jesus with authority, gentleness, humility, courage and power. Like Jesus, may my strength come from my personal relationship with you.

OLD TESTAMENT READING

Job 19:1–21:34
A leader's perspective

Job's friends continue talking 'nonsense' and 'a tissue of lies' (21:34, MSG). They attempt to comfort Job with 'empty and futile words' (v.34, AMP).

On the other hand, we see Job's real struggle with his own suffering. As opposed to the simplistic analysis of his friends, he sees that the world is very complex. In this life there are many injustices. He cries out, 'Why do the wicked live on, growing old and increasing in power? ... They spend their years in prosperity and go down to the grave in peace' (vv.7, 13).

Don't be surprised that sometimes there are those who completely reject God. They say to him: 'Leave us alone! We have no desire to know your ways. Who is the Almighty, that we should serve him? What would we gain by praying to him?' (vv.14–15). Yet they appear to live lives of prosperity and peace.

The Bible never says that 'the wicked' will receive justice *in this life*. Sometimes they do, but at other times they seem to get away with it. Don't be surprised if you see 'the wicked' spending their years in prosperity. Don't be surprised if you see 'the innocent' suffering. God seems to allow both in this life. (This is not to say that we should ever be complacent about injustice or the suffering of the innocent, but rather do all in our power to combat both.)

However, this life is not the end. God has all eternity to put things right. Job glimpses – in a way almost unique in the Old Testament – our future hope:

> 'I know that my redeemer lives,
> and that in the end he will stand upon the earth.
> And after my skin has been destroyed,
> yet in my flesh I will see God' (19:25–26).

Job's insight foreshadows the New Testament hope of resurrection and eternal life. A godly leader has an eternal perspective, which gives a totally different dimension to Christian leadership.

Imagine someone important coming to visit your home. You would probably do a number of things to get ready. You would get *yourself* ready. You would ensure *others* in the house were ready, and you would ensure that the *house itself* was ready, looking clean and tidy.

A Christian leader has an eternal perspective and hope that, 'In the end [my redeemer] will stand upon the earth' (v.25). Focus on getting yourself ready, getting others ready (evangelisation, discipleship and pastoral care) and getting the house ready (the revitalisation of the church and the transformation of society). These concerns are not just confined to church leaders. Christian leaders in all spheres of work and society should have these three underlying dimensions embedded in their thoughts, their decisions and their actions.

Furthermore, this perspective should transform your attitude towards your plans and goals. When situations do not work out as hoped, due to the injustice of individuals or organisations or systems, you can still trust in the fact that one day, total justice will prevail.

PRAYER

Lord, thank you that one day I will 'see God myself, with my very own eyes' (v.27, MSG). Help me to live each day with this eternal perspective. Help me to become like Jesus and to lead like Jesus.

1 February | Day 32
You Can Trust God

During World War II, in the terrible days of the Blitz, a father, holding his small son by the hand, ran from a building that had been struck by a bomb. In the front yard was a shell hole. Seeking shelter as quickly as possible, the father jumped into the hole and held up his arms for his son to follow. Terrified, yet hearing his father's voice telling him to jump, the boy replied, 'I can't see you!' The father called to the silhouette of his son, 'But I can see you. Jump!' The boy jumped, because he trusted his father. In other words, he loved him, he believed in him, he trusted him and he had confidence in him.

'Faith', in the Bible, is primarily about putting our trust in a person. In that sense it is more akin to love. All loving relationships involve some element of trust. Faith is trust in God that transforms all your other relationships.

READING FROM PROVERBS

Proverbs 3:21–35
Be confident in the Lord

Are you a confident person? If so, where does that confidence come from? Does it come from what you do or what you possess? Does it come from your education, looks, sporting ability or some other skill you have? Does it come from what other people think about you?

There is nothing wrong with these things. Be confident, but ultimately your confidence should come from 'the Lord'. It is possible to have none of the other things and still be confident.

The writer of Proverbs says, 'The Lord shall be your confidence' (v.26a, AMP). The object of your faith is a person, 'the Lord'. God is the one person you can totally trust in everything. This 'confident trust' (v.23, AMP) transforms the way you live your life. It gives you:

1. Wisdom
The fool is 'self-confident' (v.35, AMP). But those who are confident in the Lord are wise: 'Preserve sound judgment and discretion; they will be life for you' (v.21). Wisdom, good judgment and discernment come from walking closely with God.

2. Peace
Success at work, wealth and fame are of little value if you do not have peace. Peace comes from a right relationship with God. There is no pillow as soft as a clear conscience: 'When you lie down, you will not be afraid; when you lie down, your sleep will be sweet. Have no fear of sudden disaster' (vv.24–25a). Whatever happens, you can trust that God is with you and in control.

3. Goodness
'Never walk away from someone who deserves help; your hand is *God's* hand for that person' (v.27, MSG). Take every opportunity to do good; if you have the ability to help someone, do not delay (v.28).

4. Love
'Do not contrive or dig up or cultivate evil against your neighbour, who dwells *trustingly* and *confidently* beside you' (v.29, AMP). Trust in God leads to a love for your neighbour.

5. Intimacy
'The LORD ... takes the upright into his confidence' (v.32). When the Lord is *our* confidence, he takes us into *his* confidence. This is a wonderful image of what intimacy with God looks like: 'His confidential communion and secret counsel' (v.32a, AMP).

6. Humility
God 'gives grace to the humble' (v.34b). If your confidence comes from trusting the Lord you will have no cause for pride. God promises to give you grace, blessing and honour (vv.33–35).

PRAYER
Lord, help me to live the life of faith – walking closely with you and putting my trust and confidence in you.

NEW TESTAMENT READING

Matthew 21:18–32
Believe in Jesus

Jesus says, 'If you have faith and do not doubt ... it will be done' (v.21). The answer is to 'believe ... believe ... believe' (vv.22, 25, 32). This is the one word that holds together the three otherwise seemingly disparate passages.

1. Feed your faith and your doubts will starve to death

Jesus says, 'If you *believe*, you will receive whatever you ask for in prayer' (v.22). 'If you embrace this kingdom life and *don't doubt God*, you'll not only do minor feats like I did to the fig tree, but also triumph over huge obstacles ... Absolutely everything, ranging from small to large, as you make it a part of your *believing prayer*, gets included as you lay hold of God' (vv.21–22, MSG).

Try it today. Ask, believe, then trust God.

2. Demonstrate your faith by your actions

The fig-tree does not do what it is supposed to do – bear fruit (vv.18–20). The second son in the parable does not do what he is supposed to do – obey his father's instructions (vv.28–31). Similarly, the religious leaders do not do what they are supposed to do – believe in Jesus.

Rather than put their faith in Jesus, they question Jesus' authority and ask him, 'By what authority are you doing these things? ... And who gave you this authority?' (v.23). Jesus answers with a question about the origin of John's baptism, which shows that the religious leaders have also failed to trust John the Baptist. They discuss between themselves, 'If we say, "From heaven", he will ask, "Then why didn't you *believe him*?"' (v.25).

The religious leaders' faith is all about ideas and discussions, and so they miss *the person* that faith is all about: Jesus.

3. Enter the kingdom of God by faith

Jesus contrasts the religious leaders who do not believe with the tax collectors and prostitutes who 'repent and *believe*' (v.32).

The tax collectors and prostitutes were seen as the lowest of the low ('crooks and whores', v.32, MSG), and yet Jesus said that because many of them had believed in him, they were entering the kingdom of God first.

Have you noticed how often seemingly 'upright' people seem uninterested in Jesus? They simply do not see any need. On the other hand, I have often been astonished by the openness and spiritual hunger of those in prison and ex-offenders. It is through going into the prisons that I have realised why Jesus loved to spend his time with the marginalised. They are the ones who are often most responsive to Jesus.

No one is beyond hope. Even if the past has been full of wrongdoing, nothing you have thought or said or done puts you beyond the reach of entering the kingdom of God. Like the first son in the parable, all that is needed is a change of heart and mind and to do what the father says (v.29). Only repent and *believe* in Jesus.

PRAYER

Lord, thank you that you say: 'If you believe, you will receive whatever you ask for in prayer' (v.22). Lord, today I ask...

OLD TESTAMENT READING

Job 22:1–24:25
Keep trusting when tested

Job learnt to *trust God* even though he did not understand what was going on in his life. Faith involves *trusting God* even when you don't have all the answers.

Faith is often tested when we go through difficult times. Again, there is a striking contrast between Job and his friends. Eliphaz falsely accuses Job of mistreating the poor, the hungry and widows. He said, *'That is why'* (22:10) Job was suffering. It must have been so galling for him to be falsely accused in this way. Nothing could have been further from the truth.

Eliphaz's theology was simplistic and defective: 'Submit to God and be at peace with him; in this way *prosperity* will come to you' (v.21). But life is more complex than that.

By contrast, Job was struggling with the real world of often inexplicable, innocent suffering. Yet he was full of faith in the midst of 'groaning' (23:2). Everything had gone wrong in Job's life. God seemed miles away ('If only I knew where to find him', v.3a).

Sometimes nothing seems to make sense in our lives. God may be using our circumstances to test us. Choose to trust him anyway.

Job said, 'When he has *tested me*, I shall come forth as gold' (v.10b). Gold was refined and tested by heating it and skimming off the dross over and over again until the reflection of the goldsmith could be seen in it. In the midst of his terrible suffering, Job trusted that God would use it all for good and he would emerge purer and holier. Somehow he managed to cling on to God:

> 'My feet have closely followed his steps;
> I have kept to his way without turning aside.
> I have not departed from the commands of his lips;

I have treasured the words of his mouth
more than my daily bread' (vv.11–12).

As we look at Job's life we see that strength grows through struggles, courage develops in challenges and wisdom matures from wounds. When God tested Job, his faith emerged as pure gold.

PRAYER

Lord, in those difficult times when I seem to be in the refiner's fire, help me to put my faith and trust in you and to 'come forth as gold' (v.10b). Help me every day to live a life of trust and confidence in you.

2 February | Day 33

Intimate Friendship

Nick Hills is one of the cleverest people I have ever met. He is a scholar and an intellectual. He has a brilliant mind. We were at school and university together. About three months after my first encounter with Jesus Christ (as a first-year student), he too had an experience of Jesus. (In fact, he went on to help Justin Welby, who is now Archbishop of Canterbury, find faith in Jesus). *Immediately*, Nick started reading massive theological books.

I remember asking him what he was reading about. He replied that he was reading about the 'transcendence and immanence' of God. I had no idea what he meant. I had to look up both words in the dictionary.

'Transcendence' and 'immanence' describe the almost paradoxical nature of our relationship with God. The transcendence of God means that God exists apart from, and is not subject to the limitations of, the material universe. He is above and beyond, surpassing and excelling, greatly superior to us.

On the other hand, the immanence of God means that it is possible to experience his immediate friendship. In our Old Testament passage for today, Job speaks of 'God's *intimate friendship*' (Job 29:4).

It is only when you understand the transcendence of God that you see how amazing his immanence is, and what a huge privilege it is to be able to enjoy intimate friendship with God.

READING FROM PSALMS

Psalm 18:7–15
Worship the transcendent God and love his awesome presence

David speaks of the awesome presence of God: 'The earth trembled and quaked, and the foundations of the mountains shook ... Out of *the brightness of his presence* ... The LORD thundered from heaven; the voice of the Most High resounded' (vv.7, 12–13).

In this psalm we see both the power and the anger of the transcendent God: 'They trembled because he was angry' (v.7). God's anger (though never malicious) is his personal reaction against sin.

If we look at human trafficking, the abuse of children, institutional torture or some other terrible injustice without feeling any anger, we are failing to love. Indignation against evil is an essential element of goodness. In this psalm we see that God's anger is the reverse side of his love.

Yet, this is a psalm in which David expresses his intimate friendship with God. It begins, 'I love you, O LORD, my strength' (v.1). David did not take it for granted. He understood the immense privilege of having an intimate friendship with the transcendent God.

PRAYER

Lord, thank you that I can have an intimate friendship with the one who created the entire universe. I love you, O Lord, my strength.

NEW TESTAMENT READING

Matthew 21:33–22:14
Accept God's invitation and enjoy his intimate friendship

In the last decade, we have celebrated two major Royal Weddings in the UK: Prince William to Catherine Middleton and Prince Harry to

Meghan Markle. Imagine what it would have been like if you had opened your post and found a personal invitation to their wedding. Jesus says that all of us receive an invitation to the greatest royal wedding of all time.

Jesus describes the kingdom of God as being like a vineyard and like a wedding banquet. Both of these pictures speak again of God's generosity and his amazing love for you.

But God's love is not sentimental. Again, we see the reverse side of God's love and mercy, which is his judgment on those who reject his love and do evil (21:35 onwards). When the tenants 'seized his servants ... beat one, killed another, and stoned a third' (v.35), and in a final act of rebellion, when they took his son 'and threw him out of the vineyard and *killed him*' (v.39), there was a judgment (v.41).

Jesus is prophesying about his own death. He is the 'son' and 'heir' (vv.37–38) whom God sent. Yet, they 'killed him' (v.39). He is the stone 'the builders rejected [who] has become the capstone' (v.42). He is the one who executes judgment (v.44). The judgment was to come about because of their rejection of Jesus (they were looking for a way to arrest Jesus, v.46).

Likewise, in the case of the wedding banquet, God issues an open invitation for an intimate friendship with him. It is such a great privilege to be invited to this royal wedding. It is a costly invitation (v.4) and an open invitation (vv.9–10). Everyone is invited. The invitation is repeated over and over again (vv.1–4).

I find it fascinating that Jesus compares the kingdom of God to a party. This is the opposite of how many people think about God, church and faith. They think it is something sombre, dull and boring. But Jesus says the kingdom of God is a party. It is a celebration with lots of laughter, joy and feasting.

However, there were some who, when reminded of their invitation, 'only shrugged their shoulders and went off, one to weed his garden, another to work in his shop' (22:5, MSG). Their possessions and their jobs were higher priorities than a relationship with Jesus. Some were extraordinarily rude and hostile – they 'seized his servants, ill-treated them and killed them' (v.6). Jesus says, 'The king was enraged' (v.7).

God's amazing and wonderful invitation is not something you should take lightly or flippantly. It is a huge privilege that a transcendent God invites you to have an intimate friendship with him. However, it is not enough simply to go along. You need the right wedding clothes (vv.11–13). You cannot enter the kingdom of heaven on your own terms – only on Jesus' terms. Thankfully, through his death and resurrection and the gift of the Holy Spirit, Jesus has provided the clothes you need.

PRAYER

Lord, thank you that in your love, you lay on a banquet for me. Lord, I accept your invitation and come to you today to enjoy your intimate friendship.

OLD TESTAMENT READING

Job 25:1–29:25

Understand the transcendence of God and know his immanence

Do you ever feel overwhelmed by the problems and difficulties you are facing? Do you doubt whether God has the power or the desire to help you?

Job understood the transcendence of God. He says, 'I will teach you about *the power of God*' (27:11a). He points out that everything we see of God's power in the natural world around is only 'the outer fringe of his works' (v.12).

God *is* powerful enough to help you.

God is not only powerful enough to help you; he also loves you enough to do so. Job knew all about the immanence of God. He had experienced '*God's intimate friendship*' (29:4) where true wisdom is to be found.

'Fear-of-the-Lord – that's Wisdom, and Insight means shunning evil' (28:28, MSG). The 'fear-of-the-Lord' means respect for God. It is in this respectful relationship with God that you find wisdom. Now we know that Jesus Christ *is* the wisdom of God. It is in an intimate friendship with Jesus that you find true wisdom.

Job describes the immense value of this wisdom: 'Where can wisdom be found? ... It cannot be bought with the finest gold, nor can its price be weighed in silver ... God understands the way to it and he alone knows where it dwells ... "The fear of the Lord – that is wisdom, and to shun evil is understanding"' (28:12, 15–28).

What kind of life does this lead to? It will lead to shunning evil (v.28) and serving the poor (29:12). Job describes a truly righteous life as helping 'the poor ... the fatherless ... [the] dying ... the widow ... the blind ... the lame ... the needy ... the stranger' (vv.12–16). Job was concerned not only with poverty but also with justice: 'I put on righteousness as my clothing; *justice* was my robe and my turban...

I broke the fangs of the wicked and snatched the victims from their teeth' (vv.14, 17).

As you draw close to God in intimate friendship, his concerns become your concerns. Like Job, you will desire to help the poor, the fatherless, the homeless and the widows. You want to rescue victims of injustice. You will seek to look after the blind, the lame, the needy and the refugees in your land.

Job had not actually lost his intimate friendship with God. But he had lost any tangible feeling of it. He was going through the most appalling suffering. It seemed to him that God was miles away. You may be experiencing something like this at the moment. If you are, be encouraged by the story of Job.

When we come to the end of the book of Job, we understand that God had never left him. God was going to bless him more than he could ever ask or even imagine. God would restore to him the sense of his intimate friendship.

Now, through Jesus, all of us can experience an intimate friendship with the transcendent God and know his ultimate blessing on our lives.

PRAYER

Lord, thank you for Job's example. In times of suffering, may I hold on to the promise of your intimate friendship and blessing on my life.

3 February | Day 34
Three Types of Victory in Your Life

José Henriquez was one of the thirty-three miners trapped 2,300 feet underground when a section of the San José copper mine in Northern Chile collapsed. It was 5 August 2010. For seventeen days all rescue attempts failed. There was no sign of life in the copper mine. The trapped miners had enough food for three days and a little drinking water. They faced the prospect of an agonising death through starvation.

I interviewed José Henriquez and his wife Bianca at Holy Trinity Brompton (HTB). He told how they had prayed to God for a miracle. He described the moment, on 22 August, when a drill broke through into the tunnel where the men were trapped. They hammered the drill with iron rods. They sprayed paint on it. They sent up many messages on it. Only one stayed on the drill as it went back up to the surface. The message read, 'We're fine. The 33 in the shelter.'

In total, the men survived a record sixty-nine days underground before they were brought to the surface. More than a billion people watched the rescue live on television. There were extraordinary scenes as everyone celebrated *a wonderful victory*.

The life of faith is full of challenges, difficulties and trials. But there are also *times of victory*. In the passages for today we see three different types of victory.

READING FROM PSALMS

Psalm 18:16–24
1. Victory over your enemies

David faced many battles in life. He was surrounded by enemies. They were 'too strong' for him (v.17b). However, they are not too strong for God. God rescued him from those that were too strong for him and brought him into a 'spacious place' (v.19). 'I stood there saved – surprised to be loved!' (v.19b, MSG).

If you are in a 'spacious place' at the moment, remember to thank God for it. If not, cry out to God to rescue you. And if any of your family or friends are struggling at the moment, pray that God will bring them too into a 'spacious place'.

PRAYER

Lord, thank you for the times when you brought me out into a spacious place. Today I pray for...

NEW TESTAMENT READING

Matthew 22:15–46
2. Victory over your critics

Jesus' opponents interrogate him with three questions: a trap, a trick and a test (vv.17, 23, 35). Each time, he is victorious and gives an answer that not only amazes (v.22) and astonishes (v.33), but also influences the whole of human history. What can we learn from Jesus' answers?

• Don't divide your life into sacred and secular

The Pharisees planned to *trap* Jesus with his words. They said to Jesus, 'Tell us then, what is your opinion? Is it right to pay taxes to Caesar or not?' (v.17). The taxes they referred to were extremely unpopular. If Jesus had said 'Yes', he would have been discredited in the eyes of the people. Everyone would have hated him and seen him as a traitor wanting to help the Romans.

Yet if he had said, 'No', he would have been guilty of sedition and been liable to arrest and execution.

Jesus, in his unique wisdom, did not lay down rules and regulations but expounded principles that are timeless. He gives an amazing answer: *'Give to Caesar what is Caesar's, and to God what is God's'* (v.21).

Every follower of Jesus has a double citizenship. You have a responsibility to play your part as a good citizen involved in the structures of your society on earth.

You are also a citizen of heaven with a responsibility to God. In principle, the two – Caesar and God – need not be in conflict. You are called to be a good citizen of both. Get involved in the life of your society, don't withdraw from it.

It is not that God is in charge of the 'sacred' area of your life and the government is in charge of the 'secular' area of your life. Rather, your whole life is under God's authority. Part of your commitment to God is to honour and obey the demands that the government legitimately makes on you. In the same way that a coin would have born Caesar's image, you bear God's image (Genesis 1:26). God wants you to give him the whole of your life.

• Know that there *is* life after death

Next, the Sadducees come along with a *trick* question about a woman with seven husbands. Because the Sadducees didn't believe in the resurrection they designed a complicated trick question to show how absurd it was (Matthew 22:23–28).

Jesus replies, 'You are in error because you do not know the *Scriptures* or the *power of God*' (v.29). Jesus uses the Pentateuch (the first five books of the Bible – which are the only ones the Sadducees trusted) to show that God is 'not the God of the dead but of the living' (v.32b).

He does this by quoting God's words to Moses at the burning bush in Exodus 3:6: 'I *am* the God of Abraham, Isaac, and Jacob' (Matthew 22:32a). Although Abraham, Isaac and Jacob had been dead for hundreds of years, God did *not* say 'I *was* their God' but 'I *am* their God.' They are still alive.

Jesus is showing that this life is not all there is. Furthermore, there will be continuity between this life and the life to come. There is a *physical* resurrection. Yet, there is discontinuity too for we 'will be like the *angels in heaven*' (v.30). Above all, the Scriptures show that there will be a resurrection and if God is all-powerful, why shouldn't there be?

• Prioritise love for God and others

Then, the Pharisees come up with a *test* question to which Jesus gives a brilliant answer, which goes to the heart of the whole of the Old Testament: love God ('with all your passion and prayer and intelligence', v.37, MSG) and love people ('love others as well as you love yourself', v.39, MSG). Everything else is a detailed working out of these two commands (vv.34–40).

Having silenced his critics, Jesus then asks *them* a question about his identity. He shows from the Scriptures that the Christ is not just David's son – he is David's Lord (vv.41–46). He demonstrates that the Messiah is far more than simply a great human king. This not only challenges their assumptions about the Messiah, it is also a veiled indication to them of Jesus' identity.

This is a moment of victory for Jesus: 'That stumped them, literalists that they were. Unwilling to risk losing face again in one of these public verbal exchanges, they quit asking questions for good' (v.46, MSG).

PRAYER

Father, please give me wisdom like Jesus to avoid the traps, to deal with the trick questions and to answer the testing ones.

OLD TESTAMENT READING

Job 30:1–32:22

3. Victory over your temptation

The book of Job demonstrates once and for all that sin and suffering are not necessarily directly connected to an individual's sin or lack of sin. The whole point of the book of Job is that, although Job is not perfect (13:26; 14:17), it was *not* Job's sin that caused his suffering. Job was 'blameless and upright; he feared God and shunned evil' (1:1).

Job knew that in spite of the accusations of his friends he had a totally clear conscience. It is as if he had been put on trial, facing his 'accuser' in the dock with an 'indictment' (31:35) against him. In today's passage he gives his *defence* (v.35).

Job's life was an example, an inspiration and a challenge. This is a wonderful picture of holy and righteous living.

• Keep yourself pure
He said, 'I made a covenant with my eyes not to look lustfully at a girl' (v.1). He was not enticed (v.9) in his heart into adultery. He realised that 'adultery is a fire that burns the house down' (v.12, MSG).

• Avoid materialism
He did not put his trust in riches (v.24) in spite of the great wealth he had. Nor did he put his hope in pure gold by saying, 'You are my security' (v.24). Again, his heart had not been 'secretly enticed' (v.27).

• Love your enemy
He had resisted the temptation to hate his enemies. He didn't gloat when his enemies were in trouble (v.29b) – which is such a powerful temptation. There is a great temptation to speak words of anger, but Job did not allow his 'mouth to sin by invoking a curse' (v.30) against his enemies.

• Be generous
It was not just in his personal life that he avoided sin. He was fair to his employees (v.13). He did not deny 'the desires of the poor' (v.16a). His 'door was always open to the traveller' (v.32).

PRAYER

Lord, help me to live with a clear conscience, to keep myself pure and to put my trust in you alone. Thank you that through the cross of Jesus, you make forgiveness for my past failures possible, and through the power of the Holy Spirit I can be victorious over temptation.

4 February | Day 35
Seven Characteristics of a Good Leader

'Leadership is influence,'[1] writes John C. Maxwell, whose organisations have trained more than one million leaders worldwide. He points out that, according to sociologists, even the most isolated individual will *influence* 10,000 other people during his or her lifetime!

In one sense there is only one leader. In our New Testament reading today, Jesus says, 'There is only one Life-Leader for you ... Christ' (Matthew 23:10, MSG). On the other hand, every Christian is called to be a leader in the sense that other people will look to you as an example. You have *influence* over others in different ways. To be called by God to influence others is an enormous privilege, but it carries with it great responsibility.

READING FROM PSALMS

Psalm 18:25–36
Confidence

David was a leader who had confidence. However, it was not self-confidence but *confidence in God*: 'With *your* help I can advance against a troop; *with my God* I can scale a wall' (v.29). David recognised that he needed God for:

1. Protection
'He is a *shield* for all who take refuge in him' (v.30b). 'You protect me with salvation-armour' (v.35, MSG).

2. Strength
'It is *God* who arms me with *strength* and makes my way perfect. *He* makes my feet like the feet of a deer; *he* enables me to stand on the heights' (vv.32–33).

3. Training
'*He trains* my hands for battle' (v.34a). It was as I was reading this verse back in 1992, that I realised the need to train our small group hosts and helpers before each Alpha began.

4. Guidance
'You, O LORD, *keep my lamp burning*; my God turns my darkness into light' (v.28). 'As for God, his way is perfect: the word of the LORD is flawless' (v.30).

PRAYER
Lord, I need your help. I pray for your protection, strength and guidance. Lead me in your perfect way.

NEW TESTAMENT READING

Matthew 23:1–39
Character

Jesus attacks the religious leaders of his day with strong language: 'You *snakes*! You brood of *vipers*!' (v.33). This language would have come as a complete shock. They were highly regarded, respectable people.

The scribes were lawyers. They preserved and interpreted the law. They were authorised to act as judges. They had been ordained after a course of study. They were experts in the Scriptures. They were teachers who gathered pupils around them.

The Pharisees were laypeople. They tended to come from the middle classes (unlike the Sadducees who were more aristocratic). They were much respected for their piety. They prayed and fasted often. They attended the services. They gave regularly. They led 'upright, moral lives'. They had a big influence in society. They were much admired by ordinary people.

Yet, Jesus criticises them for being hypocrites: 'They talk a good line, but they don't live it. They don't take it into their hearts and live it out in their behaviour. It's all spit-and-polish veneer' (v.3, MSG).

Jesus' 'Seven Woes' challenge me to aspire to seven characteristics of a good leader:

1. Integrity
Jesus attacks the hypocrisy of the religious leaders (vv.3–4). He says, 'They do not practise what they preach. They tie up heavy loads and put them on other people's shoulders, but they themselves are not willing to lift a finger to move them' (vv.3b–4). Integrity is the opposite of this, it means practising what you preach and making sure that your words lift people up, rather than weighing them down with guilt or other burdens.

2. Authenticity
Jesus attacks their superficiality (vv.5–7). He says to them, 'Everything they do is done for *others to see*' (v.5a). But what matters is who you are when nobody is looking. Jesus speaks about your 'secret' life with God. Seek to develop an authentic private life with God.

3. Humility
Jesus warns against loving titles and recognition (vv.8–11). Be on your guard so that you are not enticed by 'prominent positions', 'public flattery', and being given titles of one sort or another (vv.6–7, MSG). Jesus warns, 'Don't let people do that to you, put you on a pedestal like that' (v.8, MSG). This is such a temptation but Jesus says, 'For those who exalt themselves will be humbled, and those who humble themselves will be exalted' (v.12). Always seek to exalt *Jesus*, rather than yourself.

4. Compassion
Jesus attacks the religious leaders for putting stumbling-blocks in the way of others (vv.13–15). He says, 'You shut the kingdom of heaven in people's faces. You yourselves do not enter, nor will you let those enter who are trying to' (v.13). Leaders need to have the opposite spirit – one that is open and welcoming to everyone.

Jesus himself sets an example of compassion. He says, 'O Jerusalem, Jerusalem ... how often I have longed to gather your children together, as a hen gathers her chicks under her wings' (v.37).

5. Vision
Leaders should have big vision. Jesus attacks the small-mindedness and pettiness of the religious leaders (vv.16–22). The 'ridiculous hairsplitting!' (v.19, MSG). They could not see the wood for the trees. Concentrate on the important issues, pray for God's vision, and don't be sidetracked. Ask God to give you a vision that is so big that without him it is impossible.

6. Focus
Focus on what really matters (vv.23–24). Avoid getting caught up with minor details and becoming legalistic. Jesus says, 'You strain out a gnat but swallow a camel' (v.24). Rather focus on, 'The more important matters ... justice, mercy and faithfulness' (v.23). Fight against injustice, champion the poor,

and demonstrate 'faithfulness' in your relationships with your family and others.

7. Generosity

This is the opposite of the greed and self-indulgence, which Jesus decries (vv.25–28). Their inner life is so different from the outer life. Jesus calls you to be yourself – for the inside to be like the outside (vv.27–28).

These are extremely high standards and very hard to attain. Jesus' words here, as the 'woes' come to a climax (vv.29–36), are some of the strongest to come from his mouth. It is important to note that they were not addressed to ordinary people. Jesus was criticising powerful leaders who were seeking to 'exalt themselves' (v.12), and who 'shut the door of the kingdom of heaven in people's faces' (v.13).

Don't use the words of Jesus as an excuse to berate ordinary people, or even leaders who are genuinely seeking to point people to Jesus. You need to direct them at yourself. I know I do. These are challenging words – but the challenge should not be directed at the wrong people!

What is so amazing about Jesus' words is that humanly speaking he was in a position of great weakness, and yet he was not afraid to take on the powers of his day.

PRAYER

Lord, forgive me for the times when I have failed in these areas. Help me to lead a life of integrity, authenticity, humility, compassion, vision, focus and generosity. Help me to have the same concern for my city as Jesus had for his.

OLD TESTAMENT READING

Job 33:1–34:37

Criticism

As Rick Warren has pointed out, 'Criticism is the cost of influence. As long as you don't influence anybody, nobody is going to say a peep about you. But the greater your influence ... the more critics you are going to have.'

Poor Job, who was in a prominent position of leadership (see chapter 1), has to put up with a constant tirade of abuse from his so-called 'friends'. Criticism is always hardest when it comes from those who should be our friends. It is sad when unjustified criticism of Christian leaders comes from within the church itself – from the so-called 'friends'.

It must have been extremely galling for Job to have to listen to Elihu, who was much younger and yet convinced of his own experience, arrogantly saying to Job, 'I will teach you wisdom' (33:33) and 'Job speaks without knowledge; his words lack insight' (34:35). And to suggest that, because he disagreed with his critics, 'To his sin he adds rebellion [against God]' (v.37).

Elihu, like so many critics, claims to be 'carefully thought out' and to 'have no ulterior motives' (33:2–3, MSG). He claims that others agree with him: 'All right-thinking people say – and the wise who have listened to me concur – "Job is an ignoramus. He talks utter nonsense"' (34:34–35, MSG).

I too can easily fall into the trap of judging God's people on a superficial basis, just as Elihu does. Beware of the dangers of criticising others.

Although it has been pointed out that no one ever built a monument to a critic, it does not stop us all wanting to be critics. Be very careful of what you say about other people. And if you are on the receiving end of criticism, don't be surprised.

PRAYER

Lord, help me to avoid passing superficial judgments on other people. Give me wisdom and sensitivity towards those who are struggling with life. Help me to fix my eyes on the one true leader, Jesus, to come under his Lordship and follow his example.

5 February | Day 36

How to Use Your Words for Good

If you include scientific words, there are over 1,000,000 words in the English language. The average person knows about 20,000 words and uses 2,000 different words a week. Women and men both speak about 16,000 words a day on average.

Your words matter. However, what matters most is not the number of words you speak but the kind of words you choose and the purpose for which you use them. The apostle James tells us that although 'the tongue is a small part of the body' it is extremely powerful (James 3:5). In the passages for today, we see how your words can be used, just as the apostle James describes, for good or evil. Each day you have great potential: either to destroy or to build.

In our passages for today we see *six keys* to using your words for good.

READING FROM PROVERBS

Proverbs 4:1–9

1. Listen to wise words

I do not want to get to the end of my life and look back with regret at the decisions I have made. Wisdom helps you to make decisions now that you will be happy with later.

In this passage we see the value of learning from the wise words and teaching of others: 'Lay hold of my *words* with all your heart ... Get wisdom, get understanding; do not forget my *words* or swerve from them' (vv.4–5). A willingness to learn is at the heart of wisdom. Although it requires hard work, it is of immense value: 'Wisdom is supreme: therefore get wisdom. Though it cost all you have, get understanding' (v.7b).

Here the focus is on the young learning from the old. A father teaches his sons, 'Listen, my sons, to a father's instruction...' (v.1). Children are encouraged to learn as much as they can from their parents. Parents have a responsibility to pass on as much wisdom as possible to their children.

All the way through your life, value learning, esteem it and embrace it (v.8). As my grandmother used to say, 'The day I stop learning, I wish to die.'

It is not enough to listen to wise words; live them out (vv.2, 4, 5b). Put God's words into practice and you will acquire wisdom.

If you gain this wisdom and understanding, 'She'll make your life *glorious*. She'll garland your life with *grace*. She'll festoon your days with *beauty*' (vv.8–9, MSG).

PRAYER

Lord, help me to grow in wisdom and understanding by reading and listening to wise words – and putting your teaching into practice in my life.

NEW TESTAMENT READING

Matthew 24:1–31

2. Hold on to the words of Jesus

When will the world end? How will it end? Jesus' words here to his disciples are about the future. He answers their questions about the fall of Jerusalem (which took place in AD 70), and about the end times (the question is in Matthew 24:2). The passage can seem confusing, as it is difficult to disentangle the two themes. Jesus' purpose was not to give a specific schedule for the future, but to help his disciples not to worry or be distracted by what will happen.

Jesus says, at the end of this section (which starts today and ends tomorrow), that 'Heaven and earth will pass away, but *my words* will never pass away' (v.35). There is a lot of uncertainty about the end times. However, some things are clear:

- There will be lots of false claims (vv.4–5, 23–26).
- There will be upheaval, persecution, division and even falling away (vv.6–12).
- The love of the great body of people will grow cold (v.12, AMP).
- When it does actually happen, *it will be obvious to everyone* (vv.27–31).

The first time, Jesus came in weakness. The second time he comes, he will return in power (vv.27, 30–31).

As you wait for Jesus to return, hold onto his words and refuse to allow your love to *'grow cold'* (v.12). It is so important to keep your heart on fire with love for him, remembering your first love (Revelation 2:4). As Joyce Meyer writes, 'Stir up love in your life – towards your spouse and towards your family, friends, neighbours and co-workers. Reach out to others who are hurting and in need. Pray for people and bless them. Grow to the point that one of your first thoughts each morning in your heart is about how you can bless someone else that day.'[1]

3. Discern prophetic words

'Prophecy' is a gift of the Holy Spirit. Listen carefully to the words of the 'prophet'. This passage reminds us of the importance of genuine prophecy (although no modern-day prophecies will have the same level of authority as those in Scripture).

We need to distinguish between true and false prophecy. Jesus warns against false prophets who 'will appear and deceive many people' (Matthew 24:11). He warns that the false prophets will try to deceive people by claiming, 'I am the Christ' (vv.4–5). People will say, '"Look, here is the Christ!" or, "There he is!"' (v.23). Jesus warns us not to believe them. They are 'Fake Messiahs and lying preachers [who] are going to pop up everywhere' (v.24, MSG).

On the other hand, Jesus affirms the words of the true prophets. He announces that the words 'spoken of through the prophet Daniel' (v.15) will be fulfilled (see Daniel 9:27; 11:31; 12:11). He quotes from the prophet Isaiah (see Isaiah 13:10; 34:4): 'the sun will be darkened, and the moon will not give its light; the stars will fall from the sky, and the heavenly bodies will be shaken' (Matthew 24:29).

In fact, in his description of his return (v.27 onwards; see especially v.30), he is making an implicit claim to be the messianic Son of Man prophesied by Daniel (see Daniel 7:13).

4. Speak life-changing words

The words of Jesus totally changed my life when I was eighteen years old. Since then I have watched with joy, and often astonishment, the power of his message to transform the lives of other people.

Between the first coming of Jesus and his second coming, we have been given the task of taking this life-changing message of the gospel to the whole world. 'And this *gospel* of the kingdom will be preached in the whole world as a testimony to all nations, and then the end will come' (Matthew 24:14).

The words of the gospel are powerful and life-changing. The apostle Paul wrote, 'I am not ashamed of the *gospel,* because it is the *power* of God for the salvation of everyone who believes' (Romans 1:16). Never give up on the proclamation of the gospel. You have the great privilege of being entrusted with words that have the potential to change people's lives in a radical way – for this life and into eternity.

PRAYER

Lord, thank you that your words are eternal. Thank you for the immense privilege of being able to use the most powerful words in the world to see people's lives transformed by Jesus. Help me to take every opportunity to get this message out to as many people as possible.

OLD TESTAMENT READING

Job 35:1–37:24

5. Avoid speaking empty words

Elihu's verbal attack continued with his usual mixture of falsehood and half-truths. He said, 'Be assured that my words are *not false*' (36:4). Actually, they were. He suggested that our sins do not affect God (35:6). In fact, our sins do have an effect on God as we see supremely in the cross of Christ.

Ironically, he said something about Job that, although not true of Job, was actually true of *himself*. He said, 'So Job opens his mouth with *empty talk*; *without knowledge he multiplies words*' (v.16). ('Job, you talk sheer nonsense – nonstop nonsense!' v.16, MSG). This is a perfect description of Elihu's own speech. It is empty talk without knowledge. Elihu 'multiplies words', criticising Job.

The fact that we are all capable of talking nonsense does not mean that we should be silent. Rather, we should realise the enormous potential that every human being has to affect the lives of others through their tongues. You may or may not have the power that comes from money, fame or position, but you have the power and the potential that come from being able to communicate with words.

6. Put God's words into practice

Elihu said a number of things in this passage about God's words (37:4–13). Thankfully, the Lord is about to speak himself. What a relief! We have had chapter after chapter of false comfort and empty words. We live in a world like this. It is such a relief when God speaks. The words of God are like manna from heaven, and water in a desert.

PRAYER

Lord, may the words I speak today be guided by the Holy Spirit. Put a guard over my lips and a watch over my tongue.

Thank you that you speak to me and that your words are so powerful and life-changing. Help me to hear your words, speak them and put them into practice.

6 February | Day 37
The Secret Things

When I first encountered Jesus, I thought I had to know the answer to every question about faith. However, the more I have studied the Bible, the more I have realised that we do not need to know the answer to *everything*. There is such a thing as *healthy* agnosticism, or what might be described as *biblical* agnosticism.

There are some questions to which we *do know* the answer. But there are other questions to which the best answer we can give is, '*I don't know*.' 'The *secret things* belong to the LORD our God, but the *things revealed* belong to us' (Deuteronomy 29:29a).

We need to be clear about what the Bible is clear about. Don't be agnostic about what you *can* know. Equally, don't be dogmatic about the things that the Bible is agnostic about.

In today's passages, we see three examples of big questions that are frequently asked. In answer to each of these questions there are some things we know ('the things revealed') and some things we don't know ('the secret things').

READING FROM PSALMS

Psalm 18:37–42
What does the future hold for me?

At one point in my life I developed a tendency to catastrophise – especially about my health. If I experienced the slightest pain or symptom I would assume the worst. I was really helped by someone who pointed this out to me and said that to catastrophise means to 'overestimate the danger and underestimate your ability to cope'.

Catastrophising leads to fear and is the opposite of faith. Fear tells you that you will not be able to cope. Faith tells you that your Father in heaven knows when you will need strength to cope and he will supply all you need just in time. God will arm you with the strength that you need for whatever lies ahead.

God had given David victory over all his enemies. As David looks back at these battles he says, 'You *armed me with strength* for the battle' (v.39). These were not the last enemies that David would have to fight. Plenty of battles lay ahead.

1. What you *don't* know

Like David, what you don't know is which battles lie ahead. However, for most of us, it would probably be very unhelpful to know exactly what the battles will be.

2. What you *do* know

As the saying goes, 'We don't know what the future holds, but we know who holds the future.' What David knew was that since God had 'armed [him] with strength' (v.39) in the past, he would do so in the future. You can know that *God will supply you with the strength you need when you need it.*

PRAYER

Lord, thank you that I can be confident that your Holy Spirit will arm me with strength *just in time* for whatever battles lie ahead.

NEW TESTAMENT READING

Matthew 24:32–25:13
When will Jesus return?

Jesus speaks about his return – the second coming. He says that there are certain things about this that you are supposed *to know* and certain things that *you do not know*. ('You have *no idea* what day your Master will show up. But you *do know*...', 24:42–43, MSG.)

1. What you *don't* know

Jesus makes it absolutely clear that *no one knows when* he will return. He says, '*No one knows* about that day or hour, not even the angels in heaven, *nor the Son*, but only the Father' (v.36). There were certain questions to which *even Jesus* (while he was on earth) had to say, '*I don't know*.'

So much time and energy has been wasted speculating about the exact time that Jesus will return. You are not meant to know *when* Jesus will come back because you are supposed to 'keep watch' (v.42) and be ready for him to return *at any moment*.

2. What you *do* know

Jesus tells us to learn from the fig-tree. When the leaves come out '*you know* that summer is near' (Matthew 24:32). Jesus says if you look at the signs then '*you know*' that Jesus' coming '*is near*'. Therefore, you are to '*keep watch*' (v.42; 25:13) and '*be ready*' (24:44).

You know too that although his coming is near, it may be *a long time* before he comes (25:5). And you also know that he will come at an hour 'when you *do not expect him*' (24:44). Whenever he comes it is going to be a surprise and the key is to *be ready* for him to come *at any moment*.

To enable you to see what it means to be ready for his return, Jesus paints a picture of the difference between a servant being *wise* or *wicked*. The *wise* servant remains ready for their master's return by remaining faithful to their master's instructions and honourable in the way they treat others. The *wicked* servant is faithless to their master's instructions and destructive in *how they treat others*. The conclusion is markedly different (compare v.47 with v.51). In other words, you are ready for Jesus' return if you live a life where you *love God* and *love others*.

However, underneath this love for God and love for others is the key component of what it means to be ready for Jesus' return. In the parable of the ten virgins, the bridegroom says to those virgins who have been asleep and are not ready, '*I don't know you*' (25:12). We see here that the key lies in a different type of '*knowing*'. It is not *intellectual* knowledge but *personal* knowledge.

Ultimately, it is not about *what* you know, but about *whom* you know. It is about having a personal relationship with the bridegroom. In the end, this is what matters more than anything else – *knowing Jesus* (John 17:3).

PRAYER

Lord, thank you that all that matters in the end is that I know you. Help me each day to get to *know you* better.

OLD TESTAMENT READING

Job 38:1–40:2
Why does God allow suffering?

As we reach the climax of the book of Job, after many chapters of Job and his friends asking questions of God, the tables are turned and God starts asking questions. This passage might be described as 'Job's final examination'. In his exam paper there are numerous questions to which he does not know the answer.

We see that in answer to the question that is so often asked, 'Why does God allow suffering?' there are some things we know, and some things we don't know. The Lord's complaint about Job's friends was that they had spoken 'words *without knowledge*' (38:2). Instead of saying, '*I don't know,*' they had tried to explain Job's suffering, but without really knowing the answers.

1. What you *don't* know

God asks him forty-nine questions (in poetic language) about the natural universe to which Job, if given the chance, would surely respond, '*I don't know*.' Many of the questions start, '*Do you know…?*' (v.33; 39:1–2). It is almost as if God is lovingly teasing Job. He says to him, 'Surely *you know*!' (38:5) and, 'Tell Me, if you *know it all*' (v.18b, AMP).

The point of God's questioning is to demonstrate the fact that there are certain things that we do not know as human beings – the '*secret things*' belong to the Lord our God. This is especially true in relation to the issue of suffering. Theologians and philosophers have wrestled for centuries with the problem of suffering and no one has ever come up with a simple and complete solution.

When you are suffering you will not always be able to work out why. God never told Job why he was suffering (even though *we* know part of the answer from the start of the book), but he did tell him that there *was* a good reason. He pointed out to Job that he really knew very little about the universe and asked him to trust God.

The book of Job is not so much about *why* God allows suffering (theodicy) as it is about the appearance of God in the midst of suffering (theophany), and *how* we should respond to suffering.

2. What you *do* know

In tomorrow's passage we will see that Job recognised that there are some things 'too wonderful for me *to know*' (42:3). In other words, there are some things that you are never going to know in this life. On the other hand, there are some things that you can know, '*I know* that you can do all things; no plan of yours can be thwarted' (v.2).

You can *know* that God is ultimately in control and therefore you can live at peace and confidently trust that, in everything, God will work for the good of those who love him (Romans 8:28).

PRAYER

Lord, I know that you can do all things and no purpose of yours can be thwarted. Help me to have humility about the secret things that I cannot know and to be confident about the things that I can know.

7 February | Day 38

Use It or Lose It

Myra Hindley was one of the most notorious murderers of the twentieth century. Her crimes were almost unbelievably horrific. Yet one person took it upon himself to visit her regularly while she was in prison.

Lord Longford (1905–2001) was a controversial figure who spent much of his life visiting prisoners, including Myra Hindley. Yet, no one can doubt his compassion and his *faithfulness*, both to God and to those he visited.

When he died, former prisoners joined hundreds of mourners to say farewell to the man who had spent his life *faithfully* fighting for society's outcasts.

He found inspiration in the words of Jesus from today's passage. On his deathbed he asked his wife, 'You know what the most important quotation from the Bible is?' He spoke his last words by answering his own question, quoting the words of Jesus: '*I was in prison and you came to visit me*' (Matthew 25:36).

Life is not a competition that you have to win. It is not supposed to be a rat race. Life is a huge privilege and an opportunity. God has trusted you with gifts and abilities, which he wants you to use. Use them or lose them. He is faithful to us and he expects us to be faithful to him.

READING FROM PSALMS

Psalm 18:43–50
God's faithfulness

'Be kind,' said the philosopher Plato, 'for everyone you meet is fighting a hard battle.' The Bible gives us an even stronger reason to always be kind. God is *always* kind to us. In his faithfulness, he shows us '*unfailing kindness*' (v.50).

David is able to look back at his life and see how God has shown '*unfailing kindness*' to him and his children and grandchildren, ('his descendants', v.50). God had delivered him from all 'the attacks of the people' around (v.43a). He had put him in a position of leadership with great responsibility (v.43b).

He had given David 'great victories' (v.50a) and had saved him and exalted him (v.48). David responded in worship ('I will sing praises to your name', v.49b), thanking God for his *faithfulness* to his 'anointed' (v.50b).

You also are 'anointed' (2 Corinthians 1:21–22; 1 John 2:20). God will show *you* his 'unfailing kindness' (Psalm 18:50). He is kind *all the time*. And, if you want to be like him, try to be kind to others *all the time*.

PRAYER

Thank you, Lord, for your faithfulness to me, that you show me unfailing kindness. Help me to be kind to everyone I meet.

NEW TESTAMENT READING

Matthew 25:14–46
A life of faithfulness

How can you be 'faithful' (vv.21, 23)?

1. Use it or lose it

God is generous and kind. He gives us so much. A 'talent' was a huge sum of money – probably equivalent to twenty years' wages. Even the person with one talent was given much. In the parable, the talent (this is the origin of the English word 'talent') represents not only your money but your gifts, skills, time, energy, education, intellect, strength, influence and opportunities.

Be faithful with whatever you have been given. It is no good wishing that you had been given more. You are simply called to do the best you can with what you have.

To be faithful means to use the gifts and abilities that God has given you. I am sometimes tempted to be like the third servant who said, 'I was afraid' (v.25). We hide our talents because we are afraid of failure and what others may think of us, or of the hard work and responsibility that may be involved.

It has been said that, 'The greatest mistake you could make in life is to be continually fearing you will make one.'

The servant who received five talents and the one who received two talents must both have had to risk losing it all. Step out in faith, use your gifts and risk failure.

Jesus says, in effect, 'use them or lose them' (vv.28–30). If you do the very best with what you have, God will give you more and say, 'Well done, good and *faithful* servant! You have been faithful with a few things; I will put you in charge of many things. Come and share your master's happiness!' (vv.21, 23).

2. See the least and the last as Jesus in disguise

Jesus said, 'Whatever you did for one of the least of these brothers and sisters of mine, you did for me' (v.40). He tells us that faithfulness to him is shown in what we do for the most vulnerable and most needy in our world (vv.35–36, 42–43):

- **The hungry**
  Millions of people are dying of starvation. Every time you feed the hungry, you encounter Jesus. Mother Teresa said, 'The dying, the unwanted, the unloved – they are Jesus in disguise.'

- **The stranger**
  To be homeless, a refugee or an asylum seeker must be one of the most painful experiences of life. When you encounter people who are 'strangers' and when you look after the homeless, provide them with shelter and invite them into the heart of your community, you encounter Jesus (vv.35b,38).

- **The sick**
  Another way in which you can meet Jesus is through ministering to those who are sick, whether they are in hospital, at home or at church. Every time you pray for the sick you have the opportunity to encounter Jesus.

- **The prisoners**
  Those in prison often come from the category of 'the last and the least' of our society. Jesus challenges us to imitate his grace and acceptance of 'sinners'. We need to remember that we too are forgiven sinners.

  It is a huge privilege to go into the prisons or to care for and mentor ex-offenders. I remember the chaplain general to the prison service saying that when he first went into the prisons he thought he would take Jesus in with him. He soon realised that Jesus was already there. He said that from then on he went into the prisons in order to encounter Jesus.

In all these areas Jesus says, 'Whatever you did for one of the least of these brothers and sisters of mine, *you did for me*' (v.40). Jesus tells us that when he comes again in glory there will be a judgment (vv.31–33), and it will involve a separation that will surprise people (v.37, 44). How we respond to Jesus has eternal consequences (vv.30, 46).

PRAYER

Lord, thank you that when I reach out to the least and the last, I encounter you.

OLD TESTAMENT READING

Job 40:3–42:17
Job's faithfulness

God has had a good plan for you from the moment you were conceived. He also had a good plan for Job. Right from the start he had planned Job's restoration and blessing.

Job is remembered throughout history for his faithfulness. The apostle James says, 'You have heard of Job's perseverance and have seen what the Lord finally brought about' (James 5:11).

Once again God fires questions at Job making him realise that there are simply some things 'too wonderful for [Job] to know' (Job 42:3b). Job holds on to the faithfulness of God, 'I know that you can do all things; no plan of yours can be thwarted' (v.2). This is a wonderful promise to hold on to when things in your life are not going according to your plans. God has a good plan for you and it will not be thwarted.

God does not give us trouble-free lives. He does not answer all our questions. But he does reassure us that *he is with us* in our troubles.

God tells Job to pray for his friends who had hurt him, let him down, wrongly accused him, judged him and criticised him (vv.7–8). Job forgave them and showed his total forgiveness by praying for them. As he interceded for them, God not only accepted Job's prayer for his friends but also, 'The LORD made him prosperous again and gave him *twice as much as he had before*' (v.10).

Joyce Meyer writes, 'If you do things God's way, he will give you *double for your trouble*.'[1] 'The LORD blessed the latter part of Job's life more than the first' (v.12). As with David, God showed his kindness to him *and his descendants* (v.16).

Job is commended for his perseverance in the face of suffering (James 5:10–11). Satan believed that suffering would cause Job to turn away from God. Job's perseverance demonstrated that Satan was wrong. With brutal honesty at times, Job was nonetheless able to maintain his worship of God in good times and times of great trial.

His perseverance is an example to us of how to respond to suffering. When you respond with *faithful* perseverance, Satan is defeated. Job is a 'type' of Christ. Through Jesus' *faithful* perseverance in response to his suffering on the cross, Satan has been totally defeated, once and for all.

PRAYER

Lord, help me to be faithful with my talents, in praying for my friends and to persevere like Job.

8 February | Day 39

How to Live in a Hostile Environment

Hundreds of thousands of Christians are among those who have fled Iraq and Syria in the midst of Islamic extremism and conflict. Christians face the threat of systematic torture and mass executions. Isis has declared Christianity as the number one enemy.

Millions of Christians live in countries where they are persecuted for their faith. Many governments try to control the growth of the church. Even in traditionally Christian countries, sometimes there is hostility towards vibrant Christianity. Hostility to the people of God is not something new. People are often threatened by success, growth and large numbers.

Perhaps you are facing hostility in your workplace or even in your family because of your faith. The passages today not only highlight the reality of living in a hostile environment, but they also point out how you can survive and thrive in the midst of such hostility.

READING FROM PSALMS

Psalm 19:1–6
Study God's revelation

God has revealed himself to the whole world through creation. David says that when you look at the universe it is obvious that *there is a God*: 'The heavens declare the glory of God; the skies proclaim the work of his hands. Day after day they pour forth speech; night after night they display knowledge' (vv.1–2).

Francis Collins, director of the Human Genome Project, led a team of over 2,000 scientists who collaborated to determine the three billion letters in the human genome – our own DNA instruction book. He said, 'I cannot see how nature could have created itself. Only a supernatural force that is outside of space and time could have done that.'[1]

God's revelation in creation is available to everyone. No one is excluded from this. 'There is no speech or language where their voice is not heard. Their voice goes out into all the earth, their words to the ends of the world' (vv.3–4).

As we look at the world we see God's footprint – 'his eternal power and divine nature' (Romans 1:20). Yet, although God has revealed himself to the entire world, much of it remains hostile to him.

Take time to study God's creation and thank him for who he is and enjoy all the beautiful things God has made.

PRAYER

Lord, thank you that you speak every day and every night through creation, and that there is no speech or language where your voice is not heard.

NEW TESTAMENT READING

Matthew 26:1–30
Understand God's solution

Have you ever been *falsely accused* or *betrayed* by a friend? Have you had people *plotting* against you? Or have you ever experienced some other form of personal *hostility*? Jesus experienced all these things.

God has revealed himself in creation. However, his supreme revelation is in the person of his Son, Jesus Christ.

God himself has come to be part of this hostile world, to do something about it. In this passage we see a glimpse of God's solution, which he achieved through coming in the person of his Son Jesus. Yet the world was hostile *even to Jesus*.

1. Plotting

We should not be surprised by the world's hostility to Jesus and to Christians today. Jesus knew he would be 'handed over to be crucified' (v.2). The chief priests and elders '*plotted* to arrest Jesus in some sly way and kill him' (v.4).

Jesus says to the Twelve, 'One of you is going to hand me over to the *conspirators*' (v.21, MSG).

2. Accusations

When a woman came to Jesus 'with an alabaster jar of very expensive perfume, which she poured on his head' (v.7), even the disciples regarded what was done for Jesus as a 'waste' (v.8).

There is something deeply moving about this incident. Jesus is given for us. The cost is beyond anything we can ever imagine, and his death is imminent. A jar of expensive perfume is only fitting, and yet the disciples are fussing about waste.

Most people understand your *works* of social action (for example, in response to poverty) but they find it harder to understand your *worship* of Jesus and all the things associated with it. They regard these things as a '*waste*' and think that surely there is a better use of your time and money (v.9), but Jesus sees things differently: 'She has done a beautiful thing *to me*' (v.10). She showed her extravagant love for Jesus.

3. Betrayal

What people will do for money! Judas waited for an opportunity to hand Jesus over for 'thirty silver coins' (v.15). How painful this must have been for Jesus! Judas was one of his closest 'friends'; one of the inner circle of twelve he had chosen. He knew – 'one of you will *betray* me' (v.21).

Yet Jesus in his extraordinary love, dies for them all. During a meal together, he begins to explain the meaning of his death. He explains through the breaking of the bread and drinking of wine that his blood is to be 'poured out for many *for the forgiveness of sins*' (v.28). Jesus' answer to a hostile world was to be crucified in order to make forgiveness and redemption possible.

Every time you receive communion, you are reminded both of the hostility of the world towards Jesus and of his love for that same world.

PRAYER

Lord Jesus, thank you that you died for me and demonstrated how to love a hostile world.

OLD TESTAMENT READING

Exodus 1:1–3:22
Know who God is

Moses asked God, '*Who am I*, that I should go?' God replied by telling him *who He is*. In the end, the answer to all our questions and problems is *not* to be found in *who we are* but in *who God is*.

If you asked a Jew in the first century who was the greatest person who ever lived, they would have replied, without doubt: 'Moses'. He was the supreme figure in their history. He rescued them from slavery into a life of freedom. He gave them the law. The book of Exodus presents us with the constitution of a new nation and introduces us to the man who was responsible for it.

A 'new king' came to power who 'did not know about Joseph' (1:8). The 'new king' was ignorant of the fact that Joseph had saved Egypt. The government quickly forgot the good that the people of God had done in the past. They started to oppress them 'ruthlessly' with forced labour (vv.11–14). They cried for help and 'God heard their groaning' (2:24).

People have tried throughout history to get rid of God's people – but it has never worked. 'The more they were oppressed, the more they multiplied and spread' (1:12). Even today, when the church is persecuted and oppressed, it often multiplies and spreads.

Moses was Pharaoh's adopted grandson – a powerful prince. Money, sex and power would have been at Moses' disposal in abundance. But he chose to endure hostility instead. He obeyed God's call and chose to identify himself with God's people – a group of people whom those with an upbringing like Moses' would have regarded with contempt, a slave nation.

Through the lens of the New Testament, we see that Moses 'chose to be ill-treated along with the people of God rather than to enjoy the pleasures of sin for a short time. He regarded disgrace for the sake of Christ as of greater value than the treasures of Egypt, because he was looking ahead to his reward' (Hebrews 11:25–26).

It was not an easy choice to make. However, in the end he obeyed God's call and took on a hostile world.

At the heart of his obedience was the recognition of who God is. God revealed himself in various ways to Moses, and promised, '*I will be with you*' (Exodus 3:12). The revelation of his name was particularly significant, as names were understood as a declaration of a person's character or nature: God reveals himself as, 'I AM WHO I AM' (v.14). The only way in which God can be fully described is with reference to himself.

This name declares the unique greatness and eternal nature of our God. This name (in a contracted form) then becomes the name by which God is known throughout the rest of the Old Testament. In Hebrew it is *Yahweh*, normally translated into English as 'the Lord'. Moses' subsequent obedience to God was rooted in his understanding of who God is.

In effect, God tells Moses not to worry about the hostility he will face. All that matters is that 'I AM WHO I AM' is with him. He is sufficient for all your fears, anxieties and challenges.

Jesus said, 'Before Abraham was born, I am!' (John 8:58). The great, eternal and sufficient 'I AM', has drawn near to us in Jesus and he has promised to be with you (Matthew 28:20). When you know 'I AM WHO I AM' is with you, you can relax and be at peace.

PRAYER

Lord Jesus, thank you that you are with me in this hostile world and that you are sufficient for all my fears, anxieties and challenges.

9 February | Day 40
Five Excuses

It is the song most frequently played at British funeral services. It is the most remade song in history. It was popularised by Frank Sinatra on his 1969 album, *My Way*. In the Philippines, 'My Way' is so popular in karaoke bars that it has been declared responsible for a number of deaths where arguments over performance degenerated into violence!

'*And did it my way*!'[1]

'I did it my way' is the way of the world. It is not the way of Jesus. Jesus said, 'Yet *not as I will*, but *as you will*' (Matthew 26:39). He prays, 'May *your will* be done' (v.42). He made no excuses. Jesus did it God's way. Moses, on the other hand, as we will see today, made five excuses before eventually agreeing to follow God's way.

READING FROM PROVERBS

Proverbs 4:10–19
'Wisdom Way'

Spiritual growth is like a journey. You progress one step at a time. What matters is not so much how far you have got – but that you are heading in the right direction and that you keep going.

The book of Proverbs tells us that there are two ways: 'The *path* of the *wicked* ... the *way* of evildoers' (v.14) and 'The *way* of wisdom...' (v.11); 'The *path* of the *righteous*' (v.18). We are not told to avoid wicked people (that would mean withdrawal from the world). Rather, we are told to avoid their ways – to avoid doing what they do. If you follow God's guidance he promises to lead you on the 'Wisdom Way' (v.11, MSG).

God's way may not be easy, but there is great joy and excitement in following his way: 'The path of the righteous is like the first gleam of dawn, shining ever brighter till the full light of day' (v.18). '*The longer they live*, the brighter they shine' (v.18, MSG).

PRAYER

Lord, thank you that you promise to lead me along straight paths. Help me to follow the way of wisdom today.

NEW TESTAMENT READING

Matthew 26:31–46
Your way

The way of Jesus is to say to God, 'not *my* way but *your* way'. Jesus not only taught us to pray 'your will be done', he also prayed it himself: 'My Father, if there is *any way*, get me out of this. But please, *not what I want*. You, what do *you want*?' (v.39, MSG). A second time he prayed, 'My father, if there is no other way than this, drinking this cup to the dregs, I'm ready. Do it *your way*' (v.42, MSG).

These are not prayers of resignation, but prayers of great courage – being willing to follow God's ways, no matter what.

In this passage we see Jesus' humanity: 'He began to show grief and distress and was *deeply depressed*' (v.37, AMP). He has his three closest friends with him. The same three who saw Jesus in divine glory at the transfiguration now see Jesus in the depths of human sorrow. He prays for God the Father to show him if there is any alternative. Nevertheless, he is willing to do the Father's will whatever the cost.

For Jesus, the cost was of a totally different order to anything we face. He took the sins of the whole world on his shoulders. Hence his soul was 'overwhelmed with sorrow' (v.38). Three times, Jesus prays for 'this cup' to be taken away from him (vv.39, 42, 44). The cup refers to his impending suffering and death.

Just before going to the Garden of Gethsemane, Jesus spoke of the cup at the Passover meal representing his blood 'poured out for many for the forgiveness of sins' (v.28). More than that, as is often the case in the Old Testament, this cup includes reference to God's wrath (for example Isaiah 51:22; Habakkuk 2:16). On the cross Jesus took the cup in your place.

When you are deeply depressed, overwhelmed with sorrow, troubled or in the middle of tough times, it is such an encouragement to know that Jesus has experienced all that you face, and far more. He knows what you are going through and you can follow his example by submitting your ways to God.

There is an amazing contrast between what took place in the Garden of Gethsemane and in the Garden of Eden. 'Not your way, but mine', was the essence of the response of Adam and Eve to God in the first garden. However, in the second garden, 'Not my way, but yours' was Jesus' prayer to the Father. Doing it God's way meant suffering and death. But, it brought the redemption of the whole world.

PRAYER

Lord, help me to follow your example and pray, 'Yet not as I will, but as you will ... May your will be done.'

OLD TESTAMENT READING

Exodus 4:1–6:12
God's way

I find great comfort and encouragement in this passage. I am quite shy and introverted. I am, by nature, a reluctant leader. I find it enormously encouraging that even the great leader Moses was a reluctant leader and that he tried to make excuses as to why he should not do what God was calling him to do.

In yesterday's and today's passage, we see his *five excuses* (all of which I can identify with):

1. 'You have got the wrong person'

Moses says, 'Who am I?' (3:11). He felt inadequate. I feel, 'I am not good enough.' 'I am not holy enough.' Moses said to God, you've got the wrong person. Why me?

God's reply is, '*I will be with you*' (v.12a). That is all that matters.

2. 'I am not ready yet'

Moses says, 'What shall I tell them?' (v.13). He felt ill-informed. He did not think he would be able to answer all the questions. He thought he would have nothing to say.

God said, 'This is what you are to say' (v.14). God will give you the message at the right time.

3. 'I might fail'

Moses says, 'What happens if it all goes wrong?' 'It might not work out.' 'What if they do not believe me or listen to me and say, "The LORD did not appear to you"?' (4:1).

In answer, God showed Moses his power (vv.2–9).

4. 'I do not have the skills'

'Moses says, 'I do not have the right gifts': 'O Lord, I have never been eloquent ... I am slow of speech and tongue' (v.10). It seems that Moses may have had a stutter or some other form of speech impediment. ('I speak with faltering lips', 6:12).

God said, 'I will help you speak and will teach you what to say' (4:12). God's strength is made perfect in weakness.

5. 'Someone else will do it'

Moses says, 'Please send someone else to do it' (v.13). It is easy to think, 'someone else will do it better than me'.

God was not best pleased with Moses but said he would send Aaron to be with him: 'I will help both of you speak and will teach you what to do' (v.15b).

Eventually Moses agreed to go God's way and followed God's call. Then all the battles started and things got worse rather than better. Pharaoh's '*way*' (5:15) was certainly not God's way. The people of God were required to make bricks without straw. Moses and Aaron faced criticism and opposition from their own people (v.21). Moses complained to God that he had not yet done what he promised to do (v.23).

God responded to Moses' complaint by giving him a clearer vision of who he is. God said, 'I am the LORD. I appeared to Abraham, to Isaac and to Jacob as God Almighty, but by my name the LORD I did not make myself known to them' (6:2–3).

In a few sentences, God reveals more of his character to Moses. His character has not changed; he is faithful and keeps his word (vv.4–5). He suffers with you and feels your pain (v.5). He guarantees deliverance and freedom (v.6). He brings you into an intimate relationship with himself (v.7). He leads you to your inheritance and takes you home (v.8).

But when Moses told the people all this, 'They refused to listen to Moses because of their *impatience* and *anguish of spirit* and because of their *cruel bondage*' (v.9, AMP). Moses complains to God that the very thing he fears has happened. He says, 'My own people won't listen to me anymore. How can I expect Pharaoh to listen? I'm such a clumsy speaker!' (v.12, NLT).

This is so often the biblical pattern. First comes God's call and vision; then follows all the challenges and difficulties before you see the promise fulfilled. God's way is not always easy – it is extraordinarily challenging but, at the end of the day, wonderfully fulfilling.

PRAYER

Lord, thank you that you say, 'I will be with you' (3:12). Thank you for the immense privilege of hearing your call and walking in your ways. Even when sometimes things seem to be getting worse rather than better, help me to keep going your way.

10 February | Day 41
Life-Changing Words

My father wanted to go to Russia before he died. We went there on holiday as a family. At that time Bibles were strictly illegal there. I took with me some Russian Bibles. While I was there I went to churches and looked for people who seemed to be genuine Christians. (Church meetings were often infiltrated by the KGB.)

On one occasion, I followed a man down the street after a service. I went up to him and tapped him on the shoulder. There was nobody about. I took out one of my Bibles and handed it to him. For a moment, he had an expression of utmost disbelief. Then he took from his pocket a New Testament, which was probably 100 years old. The pages were so threadbare they were virtually transparent. When he realised that he had received a whole Bible, he was elated. He didn't speak any English and I didn't speak any Russian. But we hugged each other and he started to run up and down the street jumping for joy.

The words of God are 'more precious than gold, than much pure gold; they are sweeter than honey, than honey from the comb' (Psalm 19:10).

Why are the words of God so precious? Jesus said: 'People do not live on bread alone, but on every word that comes from the mouth of God' (Matthew 4:4). The original expression means 'is continually coming out of the mouth of God'; it is like a stream pouring forth and, like the stream of a fountain, it is never static. God is continually communicating with us. He does so, primarily, through the life-changing words of the Bible.

READING FROM PSALMS

Psalm 19:7–14
Let the words of God transform you

We all need the transforming power of God's word in so many ways. Whether you are seeking wisdom in stressful and complex situations, encouragement when you are downhearted, or guidance on the way forward, you can find help in the pages of the Bible.

David did not have nearly as much of the Bible as you have. But he did have 'the law', 'the statutes', 'the precepts' and 'the ordinances' of the Lord (vv.7a-9b).

He describes these words as being 'perfect' (v.7a), 'pure' (v.9a) and 'precious' (v.10a).

In this psalm, we see some of the life-changing effects of reading the Bible. It:

1. *revives* your soul (v.7a)
2. brings you *wisdom* (v.7b)

3. gives *joy* to your heart (v.8a)
4. gives *light* to your eyes (v.8b)
5. *warns* you of danger (v.11a)
6. brings you great *reward* (v.11b).

Reading the Bible and praying are very closely associated. Don't simply read the Bible for information, but to hear God speaking to you. The natural response to that is prayer. It is a two-way process. That is why we finish each section of this *Bible in One Year* commentary with a prayer, responding to what God has shown us through his word. David goes straight from extolling the virtues of the word of God into a wonderful prayer. David's prayer is my prayer (vv.12–14):

PRAYER

Lord, 'forgive my hidden faults. Keep your servant also from wilful sins; may they not rule over me ... May the words of my mouth and the meditation of my heart be pleasing in your sight, O LORD, my Rock and my Redeemer'.

NEW TESTAMENT READING

Matthew 26:47–68
Be guided by the words of God

Jesus clearly studied the Scriptures very carefully. His whole life was shaped by what he read. It was from his reading of the Scriptures that he understood what was happening to him when he was arrested. His companions try to resist but Jesus says, '...how then would the *Scriptures be fulfilled* that say it must happen in this way?' (v.54). He explains to the crowd that, '...this has all taken place that *the writings of the prophets might be fulfilled*' (v.56).

It was the Scriptures that gave him the ability to deal with disloyalty, abandonment and false accusation. He set an example of how you can deal with these things in your own life:

1. Disloyalty

Judas appears to be expressing his love for Jesus with a kiss, when actually he is betraying him: '*The betrayer*... embraced Him and kissed Him with [pretended] warmth and devotion' (vv.48–49, AMP). It was the ultimate two-faced act.

Jesus knew exactly what Judas was doing. Nevertheless, he calls him 'friend' (v.50). However disloyal we are, Jesus remains loyal to us.

2. Abandonment

All his friends 'deserted him and fled' (v.56b). In the moments of triumph – when people get engaged, have a baby or do well in their exams – it is natural to want to make contact and be around them. When people are down, it is much harder to know what to say and the temptation is, in effect, to abandon them.

It is said, 'When you are up in life, your friends get to know who you are. When you are down in life, you get to know who your friends are!'

3. False accusation

Have you ever been falsely accused? It is a horrible experience. Jesus faced the terrible injustice of false witnesses testifying against him in order that they might *put him to death* (v.59).

He exercised extraordinary restraint. He did not answer back (v.63), but he allowed himself to be attacked physically (v.67), and he chose not to win the argument but rather to win the war (something for small group hosts on Alpha to remember!). He understood from the Scriptures that all of this had a purpose and would lead, ultimately, to a great victory.

Jesus' understanding of his own identity and of his mission clearly came from his reading of the word of God. At his trial before the Sanhedrin, where Jesus appears to be a helpless victim, he is actually progressively revealed as the builder of a new temple (v.61), the Messiah (v.63), the Son of God (v.63) and the Son of Man who was to be enthroned at God's right hand (v.64). In reality, the helpless victim is the one with all the authority and power.

The reference to being the 'Son of Man' is a quotation from Daniel 7:13. Jesus understood this as a messianic promise about himself, pointing to his coming suffering, his vindication and his God-given authority.

The irony is that it is the judges who are actually the ones on trial. Like them, we all have to decide what we think about Jesus (Matthew 26:66).

PRAYER

Lord, help me to follow the example of Jesus, studying the Scriptures and applying them to my own life.

OLD TESTAMENT READING

Exodus 6:13–8:32
Obey the words of God

Moses and Aaron listened to God's words and did exactly what God commanded them to do

(Exodus 7:6). They obeyed the word of God. On the other hand, in stark contrast, Pharaoh constantly refused to obey. He stubbornly disobeyed the word of God.

At this stage in history, Moses may not have had any written words from God. But the Lord spoke to Moses. He heard the word of God over and over again (6:13, 28; 7:1, 14, 19; 8:5, 16, 20, and so on) and did what God commanded. The heart of God's word was, 'Let my people go, so that they may worship me' (for example 7:16; 8:1; 9:1, 13; 10:3).

We should not be surprised that the magicians and sorcerers 'by their enchantments and secret arts' (7:11, AMP) were able to perform some of the same miracles as Moses (7:22; 8:7). The devil is an imitator. He is able to perform destructive signs and even some that might appear constructive. His aim is always to deceive.

Today, God often works through the gifts of the Spirit, such as prophecy, healing, speaking in tongues and words of knowledge. The fact that the devil may attempt to imitate such gifts through telepathy, spiritualised 'healing' or even speaking in tongues, does not mean that you should avoid such things – but rather be discerning about them.

Look to the fruit. The Egyptian magicians imitated Moses' miracles 'by their secret arts'. The effect of these magicians was not neutral. They were evil and had the effect of hardening 'Pharaoh's heart' against God (7:22).

It is clear that Pharaoh hardened his own heart against God, '*He hardened his heart* and *would not listen* to Moses and Aaron' (8:15; see also v.32). At the same time, he reaped what he had sown. God hardened his heart (7:3). The two are complementary. God's hardening of the heart follows Pharaoh's own hardening.

God gives people so many opportunities. Through Moses, God repeatedly spoke to Pharaoh. Pharaoh had plenty of opportunity to respond and ultimately, he refused to do so. Moses, on the other hand, walked in a very close relationship with God; praying to him often (8:12, 30) and listening to his words.

PRAYER

Lord, thank you that in *obeying* your words there is great reward. Help me today not only to listen to your life-changing words but also to put them into practice.

11 February | Day 42
Freedom

Steve McQueen's film *Twelve Years a Slave* is based on the memoirs of Solomon Northup, born free in New York state but kidnapped in Washington DC in 1841, sold into slavery and kept in bondage for twelve years in Louisiana. He describes at length the horrors of slavery on the cotton and sugar plantations.

Eventually, in 1853, he was rescued from slavery and reunited with his family. He wrote, 'They embraced me, and with tears flowing down their cheeks, hung upon my neck. But I draw a veil over a scene that can better be imagined than described … I have been restored to happiness and *liberty*.'[1]

Slavery, in any form, is a horrific evil. Freedom is a wonderful blessing.

Moses is the liberator of God's people in the Old Testament. He foreshadows Jesus – the supreme liberator. As Moses set God's people free from slavery, so Jesus sets you free from slavery to sin.

'Freedom' is probably the best contemporary word to define what the Bible means by 'salvation'. The whole Bible could be summed up as the 'history of salvation'. It is the story of God's desire and purpose to free his people. You are set free.

READING FROM PSALMS

Psalm 20:1–9
Enjoy the freedom that comes through faith

Are you in a time of trouble, distress or difficulty? David was in such a time, most likely connected to an impending battle. He called out to God for help. The first line of the psalm is a request for God to '*answer* you when you are in *distress*' (v.1a) and the final line of the psalm is a request for God to '*answer us* when we call' (v.9b). God *answers* prayer.

When you have '*days of distress*', call out to God in prayer, asking him to bring salvation and freedom in the midst of struggle (vv.6–8). It is not a matter of foolhardy optimism, but rather one of realistic faith.

David recognises God's 'saving power' – his power to bring freedom (v.6c). He says, 'Now I know that the LORD *saves* his anointed' (v.6a). He speaks of six things that you can ask for yourself, your family, your friends and your community:

1. Protection
'May the LORD... *protect you*' (v.1). 'Put you out of harm's reach' (v.1b, MSG)

2. Help
'May he send you *help* from the sanctuary' (v.2a)

3. Support
'May he... grant you *support* from Zion' (v.2b)

4. Acceptance
'May he remember... and *accept*' (v.3)

5. Success
'May he give you the desire of your heart and make all your plans succeed' (v.4)

6. Victory
'When you *win*, we plan to raise the roof... May all your wishes come true!' (v.5, MSG). Success, victory and freedom do not come from trusting in 'chariots' and 'horses' (v.7a). Rather, they come through faith – we '*trust* in the name of the LORD our God' (v.7b).

PRAYER

Lord, thank you that you set me free. I put my trust in your name. Today I bring to you my plans and lay before you the desires of my heart...

NEW TESTAMENT READING

Matthew 26:69–27:10
Marvel at how your freedom was achieved

Jesus is the supreme liberator. Salvation history reaches its climax in the life, death and resurrection of Jesus Christ. We see here a glimpse of how much that cost Jesus: he is *denied* by one of his closest friends (26:69–75); he is *betrayed* by one of his disciples (27:1–10); he is *handed over* to the Roman authorities (v.2) and *condemned* (v.3a). Yet, Matthew sees that all this was *to fulfil God's plan* (v.9).

Jesus was taken captive in order that you might go free. *He was bound* (v.2) *to set you free from the things that bind you*. Jesus came to set you free from your sin, guilt, shame, addictions and fears.

Have you ever really messed up in your Christian life? Have you ever felt a failure and that you have badly let the Lord down? Have you ever 'wept bitterly' (26:75) as a result? I certainly have.

Two of Jesus' closest friends let him down badly. Sadly, we will all let Jesus down at points in our lives. These two examples help us learn how we should respond to such failures and disappointments.

There are many similarities between Judas and Peter. Both were disciples of Jesus. Both were told they would let him down (vv.24–25, 34). Both fulfilled Old Testament prophecies through their actions (26:31; 27:9). Both deeply regret their actions (27:5; 26:75).

Yet there are also crucial differences between the two men. Peter responded to failure in the right way. Judas did not. As St Paul writes, '*Godly sorrow* brings repentance that leads to salvation and leaves no regret, but *worldly sorrow* brings death' (2 Corinthians 7:10).

Judas is an example of '*worldly sorrow*'. He went to the religious leaders and confessed his sin, but they just weighed him down with more guilt (Matthew 27:4). He was seized with *remorse* but sadly he was not able to throw himself on God's mercy and receive his forgiveness.

On the other hand, Peter is an example of '*godly sorrow*'.

Peter must have been so frightened to deny and disown Jesus three times. Perhaps, understandably, he feared being crucified with Jesus or perhaps he had doubts before this about whether Jesus really was who he claimed to be. But the cock crowing must have removed all his doubts. It left him feeling distraught: 'He went outside and wept bitterly' (26:75).

There is no more terrible feeling than the knowledge that we have let Jesus down. Thankfully, this is not the end of the story for Peter (see John 21). 'Godly sorrow' brought 'repentance', and his relationship with Jesus was restored. He was freed from his guilt and shame, and went on to become a great, holy, powerful and anointed leader of Jesus' church.

You do not need to go around weighed down by guilt or shame about past sins and mistakes. Those whom Jesus sets free are free indeed (John 8:36). However much you have messed up and failed, it is never too late. Respond as Peter did and you can have a great future ahead of you in the service of Jesus.

PRAYER

Lord, thank you that you were bound in order to liberate me from my sins. When I fail, help me always to turn back to you in 'godly sorrow ... that leads to salvation and leaves no regret'.

OLD TESTAMENT READING

Exodus 9:1–10:29
Use your freedom to worship God

In the service of God we find perfect freedom. You were created to worship and serve God. This is your purpose.

Pope Benedict XVI (when he was still Cardinal Ratzinger) wrote, 'The only goal of the Exodus is shown to be *worship* ... The land is given to the people to be a place for *worship* of the true God ... *the freedom to give right worship* to God, appears, in the encounter with Pharaoh, to be the *sole purpose* of the Exodus, indeed, its *very essence*.'[2]

Once again, in the history of the people of Israel, we see God's salvation plan foreshadowed. We see his plan to free his people from slavery through Moses. Time and again God says words along these lines to Moses: 'Go to Pharaoh and say to him, "This is what the Lord, the God of the Hebrews, says: 'Let my people go, so that they may *worship me*'" (9:1).

He gives Pharaoh so many opportunities. Again and again Moses speaks the words of God to him: 'Let my people go, so that they may *worship me*' (9:13; 10:3, 7). 'Release my people so that they can *worship me*' (MSG).

The world may understand your 'good *works*' but does not see the importance of your *worship*. Pharaoh accuses them of being lazy and sees worship as an alternative to work (5:17–18). But worship is your supreme purpose and work – in fact, the Hebrew word for 'worship' in this passage ('*avad*'), can be translated as both worship and work.

God loves you. He does not want anyone to perish, but everyone to come to repentance (2 Peter 3:9). The only way we will perish is if, like Pharaoh, we harden our hearts and ignore all the warning signs that God puts in the way. Pride was at the root of Pharaoh's sin. The more he refused, the harder it became to change his mind without losing face.

Be prepared to admit to making mistakes rather than going on in the wrong direction regardless. No matter how long you have travelled in the wrong direction, you can always turn around.

God's desire is for his people to be set free to worship him throughout the whole of life. He wants to set you free from guilt, shame, sin, addiction and fear. He wants to set you free to love, serve and worship him.

PRAYER

Lord, thank you that you said, 'if the Son sets you free, you will be free indeed' (John 8:36). May I use my freedom to worship and serve you.

12 February | Day 43
He Saved You

On 13 January 1982, Air Florida Flight 90 taking off from Washington, DC, crashed into the Potomac River. It was winter and the river was full of ice. The crash happened near a bridge going over the river. The TV cameras could see everything. Millions of viewers, sitting in their living rooms, watched as a helicopter overhead let down a life-belt on a line to a man struggling in the water. He grabbed the line, swam to another survivor just by him, clipped the woman in and they hoisted her up to safety. The helicopter let down the line again, and again the man did the same thing. He swam to someone else, and rescued them. He saved others, before finally, exhausted, he himself drowned.

Why did this man not save himself? The answer is that he was out to save others. In an even more amazing way, Jesus did not save himself because he was out to save you and me.

Today, focus your thoughts on Jesus, the Saviour of the world, and meditate on how he saved you.

READING FROM PSALMS

Psalm 21:1–7
Saved by God

You cannot save yourself. Only God can save you. He saved you because of his 'unfailing love'. Therefore, like David, put your trust in him today (v.7).

This psalm begins with David praising God for his salvation:

'O Lord the king [David] will delight in Your strength,

And in Your *salvation* how greatly will he rejoice!' (v.1, AMP).

In this passage we see some of the many blessings that salvation includes:

1. Answered prayer
'You have given him *his heart's desire* and have not withheld *the request of his lips*' (v.2, AMP).

2. Unending blessings
'You send *blessings* of good things ... You set a crown of pure gold on his head ... You make him *to be blessed* and *a blessing* for ever' (vv.3, 6a, AMP).

3. Eternal life
'He asked life of You, and You gave it to him – *long life for ever and ever more*' (v.4, AMP).

4. Victorious living
'Through the *victories You gave*, his *glory is great*; You have bestowed on him *splendour* and *majesty*' (v.5).

5. Joy and gladness
'You make him *exceedingly glad* with the *joy of Your presence*' (v.6b, AMP).

PRAYER

Thank you, Lord, that you saved me. Thank you for your unfailing love and many blessings. I put my trust in you today.

NEW TESTAMENT READING

Matthew 27:11–44
Saved by self-sacrifice

The people of God in the Old Testament expected a *Messiah* (Christ). This Messiah would '*reign on David's throne* and over his *kingdom*, establishing and upholding it with justice and righteousness' (Isaiah 9:7).

However, in the Old Testament there was another stream of messianic expectation. This is seen in the '*suffering servant*' of Isaiah 40–55 who 'was led like a lamb to the slaughter' (Isaiah 53:7), who would take the sin of the world on himself and die on behalf of the guilty (vv.5–6).

Nobody expected the *messianic king* and the *suffering servant* to be *the same person*. Yet, in a breathtaking way Jesus brought these great messianic themes together. Jesus is both the *King* and also the *suffering servant*.

1. Messianic king
When Pilate asked Jesus, 'Are you *the king* of the Jews?' (Matthew 27:11a) he replied, 'Yes, it is as you say' (v.11b). The soldiers mocked Jesus, dressing him up as a king and pretending to salute him and kneel down before him, hailing him '*king of the Jews*!' (v.29b).

'Above his head they placed the written charge against him: This is Jesus, the *King of the Jews*' (v.37). The religious leaders also mocked him, saying, 'He's the *King* of Israel!' (v.42).

Matthew makes clear that the only crime of which Jesus is 'guilty' is being '*the King*' (v.11), *the 'Christ'* (Messiah) (v.22) and '*Son of God*' (v.43).

2. Suffering servant
Jesus also fulfilled these prophecies. 'He was led *like a lamb to the slaughter*, and as a sheep before its shearers *is silent*, so he *did not open his mouth*' (Isaiah 53:7).

When he is accused by the chiefs and elders, '*he gave no answer*' (Matthew 27:12). When Pilate asked him, 'Don't you hear the testimony they are bringing against you?' (v.13), Jesus '*made no reply, not even to a single charge* – to the great amazement of the governor' (v.14).

Jesus, the innocent suffering servant, died in your place so that you may go free. In this sense Barabbas represents you and me, the guilty. He is 'a notorious criminal' (v.16). It is a question of 'Barabbas or Jesus' (v.17). The people asked for Barabbas and put Jesus to death (v.20). Barabbas is set free (v.26). The prophecy of Isaiah about the suffering servant is fulfilled: '*He* was pierced for *our* transgressions, *he* was crushed for *our* iniquities' (Isaiah 53:5).

Although Jesus was the long-awaited king, he was not the kind of king that the people expected – such as one who would go from one great victory to another. Rather, Jesus had to deal with envy, false accusations, unjust criticism, unfairness, misunderstanding, weak authorities, mockery and insults from religious people and the secular world – even the robbers. It came from all sides.

Pilate knew that Jesus was innocent. He realised that it was 'out of *envy* that they had handed Jesus over to him' (Matthew 27:18). (Envy is often the sin of the religious. There is a temptation to envy those whom God appears to be using more than he is using us.) Pilate knew that Jesus was innocent for another reason also. His wife had been warned in a dream and confirmed that Jesus was an 'innocent man' (v.19). He foolishly ignored her advice.

Ironically, the man who was to be remembered throughout history as the one responsible for the death of Jesus ('crucified under Pontius Pilate' – recited in the creed for hundreds of years throughout the world) tried to avoid responsibility by blaming others: '*I am innocent ...* It is *your responsibility*!' (v.24).

Jesus' blood was shed as he was flogged and handed over to be crucified (vv.24–26b). Again, ironically those who passed by said, 'Come down from the cross, if you are the Son of God!' (v.40b), but Jesus died as the Lamb of God who came to take away the sin of the world. The onlookers didn't understand that Jesus' self-sacrifice was voluntary. They said, 'He saved others ... but he can't save himself!' (v.42a).

He saved you and me because he was willing *not* to save himself.

PRAYER

Lord, thank you that you went through all this for me. Thank you that you chose not to save yourself, in order to save me.

OLD TESTAMENT READING

Exodus 11:1–12:51
Saved by the Lamb of God

Jesus says to his disciples, 'As you know, *the Passover* is two days away – and the Son of Man will be handed over to be crucified' (Matthew 26:2). St Paul writes, 'For Christ, *our Passover lamb*, has been sacrificed' (1 Corinthians 5:7b).

The blood of a lamb protected the people of God under the old covenant at the first Passover (Exodus 12:1–30). You are far better off now under the new covenant. The blood of Jesus (the Lamb of God) cleanses and protects you *permanently* (Hebrews 9:12–26).

At the first Passover, a lamb had to be sacrificed. The lamb had to be '*without defect*' (Exodus 12:5), pointing forward to the innocent Jesus. There is great emphasis on '*the blood*' *of the lamb* (vv.7, 13, 22–23). The blood of the lamb without defect was to be shed as a sacrifice (v.27). When John the Baptist saw Jesus he said, 'Look, *the lamb of God, who takes away the sin of the world*!' (John 1:29).

The *blood of the lamb* gave the people protection from God's judgment. It was the 'Passover *sacrifice*' (Exodus 12:27). This foreshadowed the sacrifice of Jesus.

God's instruction about the Passover lamb, '*Do not break any of the bones*' (v.46), was specifically fulfilled at Jesus' death. Breaking a person's legs was a way of speeding up death through crucifixion. They broke the legs of two men crucified with Jesus, 'but when they came to Jesus and found that he was already dead, *they did not break his legs*' (John 19:33).

Where there was blood on the door-frames of a house, it indicated that death had already taken place in the household. Those who obeyed God's word by putting blood on the door-frames were spared. The blood of Jesus, the Lamb of God, has been shed for you and me. The Passover points forward to how Jesus died as a sacrifice on our behalf. He saved you.

PRAYER

Father, thank you for the blood of Jesus shed for me. I offer the whole of my life to you: my body and my mind; my will and all my decisions; my family and all of my relationships; my finances and all you have given to me; my work and service to you. In Jesus' Name, I receive the protection that comes through the blood of the lamb over my life.

13 February | Day 44
God Works for Your Good

Lord Radstock was staying in a hotel in Norway in the mid-nineteenth century. He heard a little child playing the piano downstairs in the hallway. She was making a terrible noise: 'Plink ... plonk ... plink...' It was driving him mad! A man came and sat beside her and began playing alongside her, filling in the gaps. The result was the most beautiful music. He later discovered that the man playing alongside was the girl's father, Alexander Borodin, composer of the opera *Prince Igor*.

God calls you into a relationship that involves co-operation with him. The Christian faith is primarily about what has been done for you by God in Christ. However, we are not mere spectators. You are called to respond. God involves you in his plans. God comes and sits alongside you and 'in all things ... works for the good' (Romans 8:28). He takes our 'plink ... plonk ... plink ...' and makes something beautiful out of our lives.

READING FROM PROVERBS

Proverbs 4:20–27
Walk wisely

You have a part to play in responding to God's call, staying on his paths, living wisely and thereby making something beautiful out of your life. In this passage we see four areas in particular that you need to watch if you want to enjoy victory over temptation:

1. What you think about
You can choose what you think about. The life you lead will flow from your heart. 'Above all else, guard *your heart*, for it is the wellspring of life' (v.23). You are to fill *your heart* with good things – especially the words of God (vv.20–21). They bring 'life' and 'health' (v.22). Think about 'things that are true, noble, right, pure, lovely, admirable, excellent or praiseworthy' (Philippians 4:8).

2. What you say
Your words are powerful. Use them carefully. 'Put away perversity from *your mouth*; keep corrupt talk far from *your lips*' (Proverbs 4:24). It is said that the words of the tongue should have three gatekeepers: 'Is it true? Is it kind? Is it necessary?'

3. What you look at
Guard your eyes. Be careful what you look at (especially in this age of TV and internet). 'Let *your eyes* look straight ahead, fix *your gaze* directly before you' (v.25). Jesus warned that if you look at the wrong things, your 'whole body will be full of darkness'. But he also said, 'If your eyes are good, your whole body will be full of light' (Matthew 6:22–23).

4. Where you go
You will avoid a lot of temptation if you are careful about where you go. 'Make level paths for *your feet* ... keep *your foot* from evil' (Proverbs 4:26–27). The writer of Hebrews quotes from this verse. He urges us to 'run with perseverance the race marked out' for you with your eyes fixed 'on Jesus... "Make level paths for your *feet*"' (Hebrews 12:1–2, 12).

PRAYER
Lord, put a watch over my tongue and a guard over my heart. Help me to walk wisely today.

NEW TESTAMENT READING

Matthew 27:45–66
Give generously

Supremely, through the cross and resurrection of Jesus, God works for your good. Jesus experienced appalling suffering and real separation from God in order that you could *enjoy the presence of God*.

Jesus was abandoned by the religious leaders, by his own family, by the crowds, by his disciples and finally, 'Jesus groaned out of the depths, crying loudly, "*Eli, Eli, lama sabachthani*?" which means, "My God, my God, why have you abandoned me?"' (v.46, MSG).

Jesus' words of agony express a real sense of alienation from God. He is quoting from Psalm 22:1, which is a cry of suffering, lament and alienation from God. In the book of Job, we saw how Scripture engages with the difficulties and complexities of human suffering. At the cross though we see God's ultimate answer to our suffering – he chooses to enter into it and take it upon himself.

John Stott reflects on suffering and the cross: 'I could never myself believe in God if it were not for the cross ... in the real world of pain, how could one worship a God who was immune to it?'[1]

Yet Jesus' embrace of our suffering on the cross goes beyond mere solidarity. His words reflect how he came 'to give his life as a ransom for many' (Matthew 20:28). He died so that you could go free. Jesus was abandoned so that you and I might be accepted by God.

We see the reality of this acceptance by what happens at the moment of Jesus' death: 'the curtain of the temple was torn in two from top to bottom' (27:51). The symbolism of this is explained in the book of Hebrews. The curtain separated the people from the 'Most Holy Place' – that is the presence of God (Hebrews 9:3).

Now, through Jesus, you can experience God's presence and an intimate friendship with him. Even the very detail that the curtain was torn *from the top* to the bottom reminds us that it was the work of God, and not of humans, that enabled your acceptance into God's presence. You can know God's acceptance and presence because of Jesus' abandonment and suffering. God was working for your good.

Even at the moment God acted decisively in human history through the cross and resurrection of Jesus Christ, he included human beings in his plans. He used a rich man called Joseph of Arimathea, who had become a disciple of Jesus, to buy the tomb where Jesus was to be buried and then resurrected (Matthew 27:57–60).

What matters is not so much whether you are rich or poor; but how you respond to what Jesus has done for you and what you do with what you have. Joseph gave generously and God made something beautiful out of his life that has been remembered for all time.

PRAYER

Lord, thank you that you went through all this for me. Thank you that not only do you forgive me, but you also allow me to be part of your plans.

OLD TESTAMENT READING

Exodus 13:1–14:31
Trust totally

God's deliverance through Jesus is foreshadowed in the Old Testament. As God opened the way into his presence through the tearing of the curtain, so God opened a way through the sea by the parting of the waters.

All the way through, we see *God's initiative* in delivering his people out of Egypt: '*The LORD brought you out*... Tell your children, "I do this because of what *the LORD did for me*"... *The LORD brings you into the land*... with a mighty hand *the LORD brought us out of Egypt*, out of the land of slavery' (13:3–16).

God led his people all the way – although, interestingly, he did not take them the shortest route (v.17). Sometimes, instead of taking us the easy way, God takes us a longer and more difficult way to prepare us for the battles ahead. Even though they were now out of Egypt they were going to have to fight one battle after another. They needed to learn to rely totally on God's strength and guidance.

He guided them constantly – in a pillar of cloud by day and a pillar of fire by night (v.21). This is what we need individually and as the community of the people of God – his constant guidance.

Sometimes we get into situations where there seems to be no way out. The Egyptians were behind them and the sea was in front of them, 'they were exceedingly frightened' (14:10, AMP). Yet Moses totally trusted in God to deliver them. He said, '*Do not be afraid*. Stand firm and you will see the deliverance the LORD will bring you today ... The LORD will fight for you; you need only to be still' (vv.13–14). I often come back to these verses when I find myself in a situation where I cannot, humanly speaking, see a way out.

Moses had to play his part ('Raise your staff and stretch out your hand over the sea', v.16a), God's part was rather harder; he divided the waters. When we pray, for example, for someone to be filled with the Holy Spirit, God uses us. You have to stretch out your hands and pray. But God fills people with his Spirit – he does the hard part. Nevertheless, he involves you in his plans.

God's part was to bring rescue and salvation: 'The LORD saved Israel' (v.30). Your part is to trust God: 'the people put their *trust* in him and in Moses his servant' (v.31).

God is working for your good. He wants you to co-operate with him. This is the way that he has designed his creation – whether it is the natural world (where we plant and God gives the growth) or the kingdom of God (where God brings about his kingdom, yet you have a part to play).

PRAYER

Lord, thank you that, in all things, you work for my good and that you give me a role to play. Please take my 'plink ... plonk ... plink ...' and turn it into something beautiful.

14 February | Day 45

The Most Important Question in the World

The brilliant professor of philosophy at London University, C. E. M. Joad, was not a Christian. He was asked on a radio programme, 'If you could meet any person from the past and ask them just one question, whom would you meet and what question would you ask?'

Professor Joad answered without hesitation: 'I would meet Jesus Christ and ask him *the most important question in the world – "Did you or did you not rise from the dead?"*'

There came a day in Professor Joad's life when he assessed the evidence, encountered Jesus himself and wrote a book called *Recovery of Belief*. If Jesus Christ is risen from the dead, this changes everything.

When the New Testament writers speak of God's love they point to the cross. When they speak of God's power they point to the resurrection. God's 'incomparably great power' was 'exerted in Christ when he raised him from the dead' (Ephesians 1:19–20). The risen Jesus says to his disciples, 'All authority (*all power to rule*) in heaven and on earth has been given to Me' (Matthew 28:18, AMP).

The resurrection means that the risen Jesus is present with you now. Jesus continues, 'I am with you always' (v.20).

The result of the resurrection is not only his power and his presence but also his provision.

READING FROM PSALMS

Psalm 21:8–13
His power

According to the New Testament it is Jesus who is '*the power of God*' (1 Corinthians 1:24).

David praises God for his 'strength' and '*power*' (Psalm 21:13, AMP). He speaks of his confidence in God's 'hand' (v.8a) and in particular his 'right hand' (v.8b). In the Bible, the hand, especially the right hand, is used as a symbol of might and power (Exodus 15:6, 12). David is speaking of God's powerful hand in judgment.

In the New Testament, the resurrected *Jesus* is frequently described as being *at 'the right hand of God*' (for example, Acts 2:33a). When you see those who 'plot evil' and 'devise wicked schemes' (Psalm 21:11) succeed in life, remember that their power is temporary because Jesus sits at the place of ultimate authority and power at God's right hand. There will come a time when God will intervene. Jesus is risen and will come again to judge the living and the dead.

PRAYER

Lord, thank you for your great strength and power. 'Be exalted, Lord, in your strength; we will sing and praise your power' (v.13, AMP).

NEW TESTAMENT READING

Matthew 28:1–20
His presence

I have found that there is nothing greater in life than to experience the sense of the *presence of the resurrected Jesus*.

The risen Jesus commissions his followers to '*go and make disciples of all nations*' (v.19a). This is our calling as individuals and as a church community. The vision statement of our church is 'to play our part in the evangelisation of the nations, the revitalisation of the church and the transformation of society'. It is based on this command of Jesus.

Together with the command comes a promise: '*I am with you always*' (v.20b). The resurrection isn't just an historical fact or religious idea; it is a life-changing reality. God promises that as you go about fulfilling his commission, *the presence of the resurrected Jesus goes with you*.

When the women see the empty tomb the angel tells them, 'He is not here; he has risen ... you will see him' (vv.6–7).

Filled with 'great joy' they ran to tell the disciples. As they did so, 'Jesus met them' (v.9). They experienced *the presence of the risen Jesus* (vv.8–10), 'clasped his feet' (v.9) and worshipped him as God (vv.9b, 17a).

The attempts of others to explain away the empty tomb began very early on (v.13) and, in spite of all the evidence, not everyone believed (v.17b). It was suggested that 'his disciples ... stole him away while [the soldiers] were asleep' (v.13). Some people still postulate this explanation. But it does not fit the evidence:

1. The disciples were discouraged and frightened. Only the miracle of the resurrection could have transformed them.
2. They did not expect Jesus to rise from the dead. They had no motive to steal the body.
3. The tomb was heavily guarded (27:62–66).
4. They were not the only ones who saw Jesus. Many others saw him after the resurrection and interacted with him over a period of forty days (Acts 1:3; 1 Corinthians 15:6).
5. If the disciples did steal the body, their whole lives thereafter were based on a lie. My friend Ian Walker, a Cambridge scientist, became a Christian because he could not believe that the disciples would have been willing to be tortured and put to death for something they would have known was not true.

It really is true. Jesus is risen. Death and burial are not the end. In Christ, you too will be raised from the dead.

It was women who were the first to be entrusted with the message of the resurrection. This is particularly noteworthy since women at the time were not considered valid witnesses in court. They are one of many examples in the Bible of women in leadership (Miriam in our Old Testament passage for today is another example).

Matthew's Gospel starts by stating that Jesus is 'God with us' (Matthew 1:23). In the very last verse of the Gospel, Jesus affirms his eternal ongoing presence with all of his followers. To those who believe and obey Jesus' command, he promises, '*I am with you always*' (28:20b).

PRAYER

Lord, thank you that you send me out to go and make disciples of all nations and you promise that the presence of Jesus will go with me.

OLD TESTAMENT READING

Exodus 15:1–16:36
His provision

Are you worrying about the future – your health, your job, your family or your finances? Make a decision today not to worry. Corrie ten Boom said, 'Worrying is carrying tomorrow's load with today's strength – carrying two days at once. It is moving into tomorrow ahead of time.' Trust God and learn to live one day at a time.'

We see in this passage that God promises to provide, but only *one day at a time*. Jesus taught us to pray 'Give us *this day* our *daily* bread' (Matthew 6:11). Trust God that he will provide for you just when you need it.

The song of Moses and Miriam in chapter 15 is a great example of this trust in God expressed in worship. They praised God for his character (Exodus 15:1–5), then they praised God for what he had done in the past – salvation, rescue and *provision* (vv.6–12), and finally they praised him for what he would do in the future – guidance, salvation, protection and *provision* (vv.13–18).

God promises his provision for their material needs. He promises to rain down '*bread from heaven*' (16:4a) called 'manna' (v.31). Each day he provides them with all they need in terms of their '*daily bread*'. Each one gathered as much as they needed (vv.18c, 21a). But they were told not to store it up for the future: 'No one is to keep any of it until morning' (v.19).

This is something that we have experienced as a church community over the years. God supplies all our material needs but he does not give us more than we need. We do not store up reserves for the future, rather we trust God constantly that he will provide month by month and year by year.

It is always a temptation to want to store up everything we receive as security for the future – rather than trusting God to provide what we need when we need it. This also applies to our spiritual needs – we cannot just rely on past blessings.

It is sad to see in this passage how quickly the people of God seem to forget about God's goodness and provision in the past and begin to grumble about problems in the present. So often I am tempted to do the same. This passage is a reminder of the need to trust in God's provision in the good times and the hard times.

Jesus himself tells us that he is the ultimate provision of God. He says, 'I am the bread of life. Your ancestors ate the manna in the desert, yet they died. But here is the bread that comes down from heaven, which people may eat and not die. I am the living bread that came down from heaven. Whoever eats of this bread *will live for ever*.' (John 6:48–51).

It is *the resurrection of Jesus* that gives an eternal quality to this provision. *Because Jesus has been raised to life, those who eat this bread will live for ever*.

PRAYER

Thank you, Lord, that you promise that '[you] will meet all [our] needs according to [your] glorious riches in Christ Jesus' (Philippians 4:19). As I look back with thanksgiving, I look forward with anticipation and trust that you will continue to supply all my needs according to your riches in the resurrected Jesus Christ.

15 February | Day 46
The Highs and Lows of Life

As I look back on the past forty-five years as a Christian, there have been times of great spiritual highs – experiences of the Holy Spirit, God's love, the joy of seeing people encounter Jesus for the first time, amazing answers to prayer and seeing the kingdom of God advancing. On the other hand, there have also been spiritual lows – desert experiences, bereavements, disappointments, failures, temptations, opposition, health issues and exhaustion. In the passages for today we see how spiritual highs and lows are closely connected.

READING FROM PSALMS

Psalm 22:1–11
Trust that ultimately, suffering will end in victory

This psalm forms the background to Jesus' cry on the cross, 'My God, my God, why have you forsaken me?' (v.1a). It is not a coincidence that Jesus quoted this psalm (Matthew 27:46).

Psalm 22 lays out a prophetic background to the cross and resurrection, which we see fulfilled in Jesus. He was 'scorned by everyone, and despised by the people' (v.6); mocked and insulted (v.7). They hurled insults at him, shaking their heads (v.7b). 'He trusts in the LORD; let the LORD rescue him' (v.8a).

This accurately describes the suffering of Jesus (see Matthew 27:31–46) and *yet* it ends in victory.

The message of the psalm is about the importance of trust at our very low points (Psalm 22:4–5, 9). Jesus, at the very lowest point of his life – crucified and God forsaken – trusted in God to deliver him. The apparent defeat of the cross turned out to be the greatest victory of all time.

If you are at a low point, remember that suffering does not have the last word. In Jesus, the resurrection and the victory of God have the last word. Keep trusting him.

PRAYER

Lord, thank you so much for the times when I have cried out to you and been saved; trusted in you and not been disappointed. Help me in times of suffering to keep trusting in you.

NEW TESTAMENT READING

Mark 1:1–28
Grow in authority through the battles and blessings

Pippa and I watched a video of Billy Graham preaching in Los Angeles in 1963. The film is in black and white. He preaches from the Authorised Version of the Bible. But even after more than half a century there is power in the message. What is most striking of all is the *authority* with which he speaks. This kind of authority is a reflection of the *supreme authority* of Jesus.

In this passage, we see that God prepared Jesus through the spiritual highs and lows in the blessings and battles he experienced.

Mark is the shortest Gospel. It covers three weeks of Jesus' actions and twenty minutes of his words. It is the liveliest Gospel; it races from event to event with an air of breathless excitement. It is the urgent announcement of the good news of Jesus Christ.

Mark's favourite word is 'immediately'. Jesus knew all about a pressurised life. He experienced both spiritual highs and lows. At his baptism Jesus experienced a great spiritual high. He saw a vision: 'He saw heaven being torn open' (v.10b). He experienced the Holy Spirit: 'The Spirit descending on him like a dove' (v.10b). He heard God's voice: 'A voice came from heaven' (v.11a). He received an assurance of sonship: 'You are my Son' (v.11b). He knew deep down God's love for him: '...whom I love' (v.11c). He enjoyed God's pleasure: 'With you I am well pleased' (v.11d).

From there he went straight into a spiritual low out in the desert where he was tempted by Satan for forty days (v.12).

Do not be surprised by the spiritual attack that follows great spiritual experiences. We always try to warn people about this. If, for example, on the Alpha Weekend,[1] you have been filled with the Holy Spirit, receiving a deep assurance of God's love for you and knowing that you are a child of God, do not be surprised by the enemy's attacks – in the form of doubts and temptations – that often follow.

As I look back on my own life, I can see that, although these times of testing seemed very painful at the time, I now recognise how significant they were in preparing me for what lay ahead.

This is all part of God's economy – it was 'the Spirit' who sent Jesus into the desert (v.12) to 'be tempted by Satan' (v.13). In some ways, the 'desert' times and fierce temptations give an assurance that it really is true. The experience of the Holy Spirit is real but at the same time the spiritual battle and testing may be intense.

Jesus emerged from this period of testing with an extraordinary authority:

1. Authority to evangelise

Jesus preached the gospel and called people to *follow him*. Your number one priority is to cultivate a relationship with Jesus.

2. Authority to lead

When Jesus wanted someone to leave their job and work directly for the kingdom, he went up to them and asked (vv.17, 20). The earliest disciples' lives were changed completely from being centred on fish to being centred on people.

3. Authority to teach

People were amazed at Jesus' teaching because 'he taught them *as one who had authority'* (v.22). All the people were so astonished that they asked each other, 'What is this? A new teaching – and *with authority*!' (v.27).

4. Authority to heal

Jesus heals the man possessed by an evil spirit. He has authority to say to the evil spirit, 'Come out of him!' (v.25). People are amazed not only at his teaching, but also at the way in which he 'gives orders to evil spirits and they obey him' (v.27).

Whatever you are going through, believe that God is preparing you and giving you an increasing authority for whatever it is that he is calling you to do.

Ask him to fill you again with the Holy Spirit. Know that God looks at you with pleasure. Listen to his voice saying to you: 'You are my [child], whom I love; with you I am well pleased' (v.11).

PRAYER

Lord, fill me again with your Holy Spirit ... Help me to grow in authority in my words and actions.

OLD TESTAMENT READING

Exodus 17:1–18:27
Pray and act to turn the lows into highs

Moses had moments of great spiritual lows. The people 'quarrelled with Moses' (17:2); they 'grumbled' (v.3); they were 'almost ready to stone [him]' (v.4); the 'Amalekites came and attacked' them (v.8). Yet God turned the lows into highs. How?

1. Support and encourage one another

First, Moses prayed for himself. He 'cried out to the LORD, "What am I to do" ... [and] the LORD answered' (vv.4–5). Second, he interceded for Joshua and the people: 'As long as Moses held up his hands, the Israelites were winning, but whenever he lowered his hands, the Amalekites were winning' (v.11).

'When Moses' hands grew tired ... Aaron and Hur held his hands up – one on one side and one on the other ... So Joshua overcame the Amalekite army with the sword ... "For hands were lifted up to the throne of the Lord"' (vv.12–13, 16).

This passage reminds us of the power and necessity of intercessory prayer. It also reminds us of the importance of the loving support and encouragement that we can give to one another when we are weary.

2. Learn how to delegate

Moses' father-in-law, Jethro, gave Moses some excellent advice (18:19). He pointed out that if he didn't delegate, he would wear himself out: 'The work is too heavy for you; you cannot handle it alone' (v.18b). Moses was humble and wise enough to listen to his father-in-law.

Trying to do everything yourself is 'not good' (v.17). It is a bad form of leadership and leads to exhaustion: 'You'll burn out' (v.18, MSG). It also results in the underutilisation of other people's gifts, time and ability. They are likely to get frustrated and so are you.

However, delegation in itself will not solve the problem. We need the *right* leaders. If you delegate to the wrong people, no amount of micromanaging will solve the problems. If you get the right leaders you can trust them, release them and empower them.

Follow Jethro's advice. Use, at least, these three criteria when selecting and appointing leaders. First, choose *capable* people (v.21a). You need people of ability in order to have confidence as you delegate. Second, choose leaders on the basis of their *spirituality* – those who 'fear God' (v.21b). The third criterion was *character*. You need people who are 'trustworthy' (v.21c) – loyal, discreet and reliable.

Moses gave leaders a variety of responsibilities ('thousands, hundreds, fifties and tens', v.21c), presumably depending on their ability. He delegated a certain amount of the decision making but not all. The simple decisions were delegated but not the difficult ones (v.26). The result was that Moses was able 'to stand the strain' and the people went home 'satisfied' (v.23).

PRAYER

Lord, help me to make my relationship with you my number one priority and, through the highs and lows of life, to stay close to you.

16 February | Day 47
Put First Things First

Shortly after we were married, Pippa and I went to a conference about marriage. One of the sessions I will never forget was about *priorities*. We were given five cards – each with a word on it: 'work', 'God', 'ministry', 'husband/wife' and 'children'. We were asked to rank these in *order of priority*. With hindsight, I can see I got them in completely the wrong order.

I put 'God' first (at least I got that one right – but it was fairly obvious!), followed by ministry, wife, work, and, finally, children (we didn't have any children at that stage so they didn't seem very important!)

As the leaders of the conference took us through these priorities, it became clear to me that my order should be: first of all God, then my wife (my primary calling), our children, my job (my primary ministry), and finally my ministry – which, though obviously very important, should not be allowed to displace the primary responsibilities of my life. As the philosopher Goethe put it, 'Things which matter most must never be at the mercy of things which matter least.'

Put first things first. The things which matter most to God should take first place in our lives.

Psalm 22:12–21
The priority of relationship

Your relationship with God should be your number one priority. In this psalm we see that the psalmist's first priority (and prophetically Jesus' first priority) was his relationship with God.

The gateway through which we pass into a restored relationship with God is the cross. As with the first part of the psalm, we see a continuation of the prophecies about Jesus' death that are fulfilled in the New Testament.

It is as though this psalm is written in the first-person singular by someone hanging on a cross, hundreds of years before the Romans even invented crucifixion. It is an extraordinarily accurate prophecy about the suffering of Jesus – describing the cruelty of crucifixion.

1. 'All my bones are out of joint ... My tongue sticks to the roof of my mouth' (vv.14a,15b; John 19:28).
2. 'They pierced my hands and my feet' (Psalm 22:16c; John 19:37).
3. 'A band of evil people has encircled me. I can count all my bones, the people stare and gloat over me' (Psalm 22:16b–17b; Luke 23:17, 35).
4. 'They divide my garments among them and cast lots for my clothing' (Psalm 22:18; John 19:23–24).

As we saw yesterday, the suffering of Jesus on the cross was far greater than even the horror of crucifixion. He bore our guilt and was God-forsaken on our behalf (Psalm 22:1). Jesus died for you so that you could be restored to a relationship with God.

PRAYER

Thank you, Jesus, that you went through the agony of crucifixion for me in order that my relationship with God could be restored and become the number one priority in my life.

NEW TESTAMENT READING

Mark 1:29–2:17
The priorities of Jesus

I love Jesus. He is absolutely amazing and wonderfully attractive. He loved the people: he was filled with 'compassion' for them (1:41). The people loved him: 'The people ... came to him from everywhere' (v.45). Everyone wanted to *see Jesus*: 'Everyone is looking for you!' (v.37).

They would do anything to get other people to see Jesus (2:4). The crowds came to him (v.13). When he said to people, 'Follow *me*', they followed him (v.14). They brought all the sick to Jesus and he healed them (1:32–34), including Simon's mother-in-law (vv.30–31). He loved tax collectors and sinners and was quite happy to go and have dinner with them (v.15). He came for us 'sinners' (v.17).

You can tell people's priorities by how they spend their time. In this passage we see how Jesus spent his time.

1. Praying to God

Most people do not get up very early unless they have something important to do. Jesus' first priority was his relationship with God the Father: '*Very early in the morning*, while it was still dark, *Jesus got up*, left the house and went off *to a solitary place*, where *he prayed*' (v.35). This challenges us all to get up early, find 'a secluded spot' (MSG) and pray.

Personally, I have found the only way to get up early on a regular basis is to go to bed early on a regular basis!

2. Proclaiming the kingdom

Jesus said, 'Let us go somewhere else – to the nearby villages – so that I can preach there also. *That is why I have come*' (v.38). The message he preached was good news about the kingdom of God and the need for people to 'repent and believe the good news!' (vv.14–15). It was a message all about forgiveness (2:5, 10) and it was good news especially for 'sinners' (v.17), which everyone needed to hear. For Jesus, forgiveness was an even higher priority than healing.

3. Power evangelism

Jesus was 'filled with compassion' (1:41). Out of love for the people he wanted to bring them first the good news of forgiveness. But it was not just words. He also acted to heal the sick (vv.40–42; 2:8–12) and to drive out demons (1:39). Through the healing of the paralytic, Jesus demonstrated that he is the one who has the authority and power to forgive sins (2:9–11).

Jesus' priorities were clear. It was God first and then people second – and everything else was about acting out those two great priorities.

PRAYER

Lord, help me to prioritise my relationship with you. Thank you that I am able to proclaim the good news of forgiveness to others. May I be filled with compassion as I pray for the sick and seek to see people set free.

OLD TESTAMENT READING

Exodus 19:1–20:26
The priority of love

Although God invites you into intimacy with him, never forget the wonder of his holiness and power. God has such a passion for you, and therefore he will not let you be less than you can be. He wants us to learn holiness from him.

From Exodus 19 to Numbers 10:10 the people of God stay in the same place learning how to be God's people. They begin by learning the holiness and power of God. They cannot even touch the mountain on which his presence rests. Then he speaks to them about *their priorities* through the Ten Commandments.

1. God loves you

The context is in 20:2: 'I am the LORD your God, who brought you out of Egypt, out of the land of slavery.' God is a God who shows '*love* to a thousand generations' (v.6). We see pictures of his love earlier in the passage. God says, 'I *carried you on eagles' wings* and *brought you to myself'* (19:4). He says, 'You will be *my treasured possession*...' (v.5). Our love is a response to God's love.

The context of the Ten Commandments is God's love for you. Some people miss this fact and see them merely as a set of rules. God gives the commandments as an act of love for you. Seek to obey them as an act of love for God.

2. Love God

The first four commandments are about how we respond to God's love by loving him: 'We love because he first loved us' (1 John 4:19). Our love is to be exclusive (Exodus 20:3–4), respectful (v.7) and is demonstrated by setting aside time to be with him (v.10).

3. Love others

The last six commands are all about our love for others – our families (v.12), our husbands/wives (v.14) and our neighbours: 'No murder. No adultery. No stealing. No lies about your neighbour. No lusting after your neighbour's house – or wife or servant' (vv.13–17, MSG).

Jesus summarised it like this, '"Love the Lord your God with all your heart and with all your soul and with all your mind." This is the first and greatest commandment. And the second is like it: "Love your neighbour as yourself." All the Law and the Prophets hang on these two commandments' (Matthew 22:37–40).

The Ten Commandments were not given as a ladder that people had to climb up to get into God's presence. Rather they were a God-given pattern of life for those who had already known God's grace and redemption. They are not given to restrict your freedom, but to safeguard it. They help you enjoy the freedom of living in a relationship with God, showing you how to live a holy life just as God is holy. Your love for God flows out from, and is a response to, God's love for you.

PRAYER

Heavenly Father, I worship you today with reverence and awe. Thank you that you carry me on eagles' wings and bring me to yourself. Thank you that you say that I am your treasured possession. Help me to make it my first priority to worship and to love you with all of my heart and with all my soul and with all my mind. Help me to love other people unconditionally in the way that you love me.

17 February | Day 48
Sharpen Your Conscience

Jesus asks the question in today's passage, 'Which is lawful ... to do *good* or to do *evil*...?' (Mark 3:4).

I used to be an atheist. I believed that our bodies and minds and the circumstances into which we were born determined all our actions. Logically, it seemed to me, if there is no God there is no absolute basis for morality. Therefore, following this logic, there is no absolute 'good' or 'evil'.

Yet, deep down, I knew that there *was* such a thing as 'good' and 'evil'. Even though I did not believe in God, I used those words. However, it was not until I encountered Jesus that I understood that there is a God who has created a moral universe. In the Scriptures, and in particular in the person of Jesus Christ, the nature of *good* and *evil* are revealed.

God has given us *a conscience* so that we know that some things are 'good' and others are 'evil'. But our consciences can be dulled and they need to be sharpened by objective truth.

READING FROM PROVERBS

Proverbs 5:1–14
Beware of evil disguised as good

All sin involves a kind of deception. It often involves the disguising of evil as good. There is a superficial attraction – 'For the lips of an adulteress *drip honey*, and her speech is *smoother than oil*' (v.3). But in the end she is 'bitter as gall' (v.4) and following that path leads to 'death' (v.5a) and 'the grave' (v.5b).

These verses capture both the appeal and the danger of sexual temptation. We live in an increasingly sexualised society, with internet pornography readily available, sexual images all around us and a culture that encourages us to seek sexual 'fulfilment'.

Our sexuality is a God-given blessing (see Genesis 2:24), but when used wrongly it can be destructive and damaging. These verses alert us to the attractiveness of sexual sin, but warn us not to be deceived by it.[1]

Keep away from the path you will regret. 'Keep your distance ... stay out of her neighbourhood' (v.8, MSG). If we ignore this advice we may waste our lives and end our lives 'full of regrets' (Proverbs 5:11, MSG). Don't flirt with temptation; flee temptation.

Joyce Meyer writes, 'Wisdom is our friend; it helps us not to live in regret. I think the saddest thing in the world would be to reach old age and look back at my life and feel nothing but regret about what I did or did not do. Wisdom helps us make choices now that we will be happy with later.'[2]

PRAYER

Lord, help me to take wise precautions in order to stay far away from anything that could lead me into sin. 'Lead us not into temptation, but deliver us from the evil one' (Matthew 6:13).

NEW TESTAMENT READING

Mark 2:18–3:30
Decide about Jesus: good or evil?

Who is Jesus? All of us have to make up our minds about Jesus: Was he evil? Was he insane? Or was he God? This is not a new question. The people in Jesus' time also had to decide between these three options.

Jesus was not just a great religious teacher. He clearly regarded himself as far more than that. Jesus made astonishing claims about himself. Even in this relatively short part of Mark's Gospel we see a number of such claims.

There really are only three options: either he was evil or insane or else the claims were true.

1. Was he evil?

The teachers of the law said, 'He is possessed by Beelzebul! By the prince of demons he is driving out demons' (3:22). They were saying, 'He has an *evil* spirit' (v.30b, NIV).

2. Was he insane?

People were saying about Jesus, 'He is *out of his mind*' (v.21b).

3. Is he God?

Jesus is implicitly saying that he is *the bridegroom* (see 2:18–19). He describes himself as '*Lord* even of the Sabbath' (v.28), and when the evil spirits cry out, 'You are the *Son of God*'

(3:11), Jesus did not deny it but 'gave them strict orders not to tell others about him' (v.12).

Our decision about whether Jesus is evil, insane or God has huge consequences.

C. S. Lewis sums it up like this: 'We are faced, then, with a frightening alternative. The man we are talking about was (and is) just what he said or else [insane] or something worse. Now it seems to be obvious that he was neither [insane] nor a fiend: and consequently, however strange or terrifying or unlikely it may seem, I have to accept the view that he was and is God. God has landed on this enemy-occupied world in human form.'[3]

After spending three years with him, his disciples came to the conclusion that he really was the unique Son of God, the Word made flesh, a man whose identity was God (2:21–22). Jesus called them, as he calls us, first to be 'with him' and then to take his message to the world (3:14–15).

Jesus says to those who are describing him as evil, 'Whoever blasphemes against the Holy Spirit will never be forgiven' (v.29). Many people have become anxious about this verse, but anyone who is worried about it will not have committed the sin. The fact people are troubled (and willing to repent) is sure proof that they have not committed it. Those who are repentant will be forgiven.

What is referred to here is not the uttering of a sentence but a fixed attitude of mind. Jesus does not say that they have committed a sin – but warns them of the danger they are in. These are not ordinary people. The scribes were duly accredited theological teachers of God's people. They were in daily contact with the word of God.

This sin is an attitude that regards good as evil and evil as good. Such a person has sunk to a point where they cannot repent and be forgiven. Also, in this category is 'Judas Iscariot, who betrayed him' (v.19).

The New Testament assures us that *anyone* who does repent and turn to Jesus *will be forgiven*.

PRAYER

Jesus, I worship you today as the bridegroom, my Lord and the Son of God.

OLD TESTAMENT READING

Exodus 21:1–22:31
Promote good and prevent evil

The people of God drew up rules for their society. Some of the laws may appear very strange or harsh to us. However, if we compare them to the laws of other ancient people they are remarkably humane and some of the principles are still relevant today.

These laws were designed to *limit* evil. For example, there is a right to self-defence, but not to use excessive force in self-defence (22:2–3). There is also the prohibition against escalating violence and the provision of an equivalent penalty – 'life for life, eye for eye...' and so on (21:23–25).

The law was clearly designed for judges and not for private individuals (see Deuteronomy 19:18–21). It was a guide for judges and sentencing. It was never intended that individuals should exact such revenge. In fact, it was almost certainly never taken literally, except in the case of capital offences. The laws were seen as giving the maximum possible sentence. Penalties were generally replaced by financial fines and damages.

To an ancient reader, the emphasis on slaves' rights would have been revolutionary. Masters had to release their slaves after a maximum of six years (Exodus 21:2) and there were strict controls to limit the mistreatment of slaves (vv.20, 26–27). There seems to have been a particular concern for the rights of female slaves, who would have been especially vulnerable in the ancient world. They are not to be treated the same as male slaves (v.7) but must either be married or allowed to be redeemed (vv.8–11).

At the same time, the laws of Ancient Israel sought *to promote good*. God said, 'You are to be my *holy people*' (22:31a). So there were laws *to protect the 'foreigners'* (v.21), as well as *widows* and *orphans* (v.22). In tomorrow's passage we will see that there were also laws to ensure *'justice' for the poor* (23:6). Individuals were taught not to seek revenge and not to bear grudges. Rather, they were taught, *'Love your neighbour as yourself'* (Leviticus 19:18).

The law helped to build a community that had interdependence and mutual accountability as its basis. Each regulation, however strange, helped the people to learn how to belong together and care for each other. This is a lesson we all need to learn, particularly in the independent and isolated environment of twenty-first-century living. We do not follow rules and regulations just because we have to, but because they help us to treat each person as someone made in the image of God.

PRAYER

Lord, help me in my life to avoid evil and to do good. Help me to treat each person that I am in contact with today as someone made in the image of God – with love, dignity and respect.

18 February | Day 49
Your Love Letter

Thankfully, there have been very few times since our relationship began that I have been apart from my wife Pippa. However, before we were married, there was a period of three weeks when I was away. In those days, without email or mobile phones, our only way of communication was by letter.

I wrote every day. She wrote every day. I remember so well the feeling of intense excitement and joy when I saw the handwriting on the envelope and knew that a letter from Pippa was inside.

I would quickly take the letter and go off to a quiet place by myself to study it! The actual letter wasn't valuable, but the fact that it was written by the person I love made it so precious to me.

The Bible is a love letter from God to you. What makes the Bible so exciting is not the book itself, but the fact that through it we encounter the person we love. The whole Bible is about Jesus. The New Testament is obviously about Jesus. However, Jesus said of the Scriptures that were available in his lifetime (that is, the Old Testament): 'These are the very Scriptures that testify *about me*' (John 5:39).

READING FROM PSALMS

Psalm 22:22–31
Proclaim the victory of Jesus

This psalm, which starts off with despair and suffering (v.1) describing, prophetically, the death of Jesus, ends with a great cry of victory: 'He has done it!' (v.31). God 'has not despised or scorned the suffering of the afflicted one; he has not hidden his face from him but has listened to his cry for help' (v.24).

This victory will lead to people all over the world turning 'to the LORD' (v.27). All the nations will bow down before him (v.27b). This victory will be proclaimed: 'They shall come and shall declare His righteousness to a people yet to be born – that He has done it [that it is finished]!' (v.31, AMP; John 19:30).

Not only does the resurrection of Jesus bring great victory, it also brings about a familial intimacy. The word translated 'my people' (in Psalm 22:22) is an intimate one, referring to close companions, and it is usually translated as 'brother' or 'relative'. In the New Testament, the writer to the Hebrews specifically relates this to our relationship with Jesus (Hebrews 2:11–12). Jesus declares to us, his people, that he is in our midst, and sees us as his brothers and sisters, part of his family.

PRAYER

Lord, thank you so much that you have listened to my cry for help (v.24). Today again I cry for help...

NEW TESTAMENT READING

Mark 3:31–4:29
Embrace the words of Jesus

Jesus sees you as part of his close family. He wants all of us to have the closest possible intimate relationship with him – like a brother or sister or mother (3:31–35).

In this passage we see that this relationship is nurtured through the word of God, both by hearing the word and by putting it into practice: 'Whoever *does God's will* is my brother and sister and mother' (v.35).

Jesus speaks about the power of his own words, which are the words of God. Much of his teaching comes to us in stories. Everybody enjoys a good story. The meaning of a 'parable' is contained within the story. People go to sleep during abstract preaching but wake up for a good story. A story has the power to get through to us before our defences come up.

The parable of the sower shows the power of words to change lives. If you 'hear the Word [and] embrace it' (4:20, MSG), you will be like 'seed sown on good soil, [who] hear the word, [and] accept it, and produce a crop – some thirty, some sixty, some a hundred times what was sown' (v.20). You will 'produce *a harvest beyond [your] wildest dreams*' (v.20, MSG).

We see again and again on Alpha the extraordinary power of the words of Jesus to totally transform lives and make them fruitful. There is a multiplication as people bring their friends to hear the words of Jesus.

If the words of Jesus do not have any effect, then the fault lies with the hearer. At times, my life is so shallow that his words do not take root (vv.4–6). At other times, problems in my life or opposition ('trouble or persecution', v.17) take me away from a close relationship with Jesus. At other times still, 'the worries of this life, the deceitfulness of wealth and the desires for other things come in and choke the word, making it unfruitful' (v.19).

There is great power in vulnerability. Jesus says, 'For whatever is hidden is meant to be disclosed, and whatever is concealed is meant to be brought out into the open' (v.22). We are not meant to keep things hidden or concealed in our lives. It is far healthier to bring them out into the open. We may impress people by our strengths, but we connect with them through our vulnerabilities.

Jesus goes on to stress over and over again the importance of words and of hearing *his* words: 'Be careful what you are hearing. The measure [of thought and study] you give [to the truth you hear] will be the measure [of virtue and knowledge] that comes back to you – and more [besides] will be given to you *who hear*' (v.24, AMP).

The more time you invest in studying and applying God's word to your life, the greater benefit you will experience. Make this a high priority. Give time to embracing the words of Jesus and you will not regret it.

The parable of the growing seed shows that once the words of Jesus have been planted in your life, you can expect to bear fruit. You reap later. You may need to be patient while you wait for the harvest. But you can be sure that if you keep on sowing the seed, you will reap far, far more than what you have sown. The harvest will come (v.29).

PRAYER

Lord, help me not only to hear your words but also to speak them to others and see the extraordinary power of the word of God to transform my life and those around me.

OLD TESTAMENT READING

Exodus 23:1–24:18
Be a minister of the covenant of Jesus

God's relationship with his people was defined by the covenant (the agreement between God and the people) on Mount Sinai. In the covenant relationship, God committed himself to his people and asked them to respond by committing themselves to him. He called them to live lives that would keep them close to him in this covenant relationship.

In particular, we see how high on God's agenda are the issues of justice and poverty (23:1–12). In many parts of the world it is almost impossible for the poor to get justice. People are often thrown in prison on false charges with little or no redress. Some legal systems are dominated by bribery. If only these words were adhered to: 'Do not deny justice to your poor ... Have nothing to do with a false charge ... Do not accept a bribe' (vv.6, 8).

It is really hard to go against the crowd and the culture. But it is no defence to say, 'Well, that's the culture – everybody does it – so there's no alternative.' God says, '*Do not follow the crowd in doing wrong* ... Do not pervert justice by siding with the crowd' (v.2).

Covenants in the ancient world were frequently ratified by the eating of a meal ('they ate and drank', 24:11). The covenant is sealed by the shedding of blood. Moses took the blood and sprinkled it on the people saying, 'This is the blood of the covenant' (v.8).

The prophets foretold that one day there would be a new covenant written *not* on tablets of *stone* (v.12) but on our *hearts* (for example, Jeremiah 31:31–34). Jesus explained to his disciples how this new covenant was going to be made possible through his blood (Mark 14:24). You celebrate this new covenant through a meal each time you receive Holy Communion and hear the words: 'This cup is the new covenant in my blood' (Luke 22:20; 1 Corinthians 11:25).

Under this covenant all of your sins are forgiven (Hebrews 9:15) and you have a relationship with Jesus that goes on for ever (13:20).

Through Jesus you are a minister of the new covenant (2 Corinthians 3:6). The old covenant 'came with glory' (v.7). The 'glory of the Lord settled on Mount Sinai ... a consuming fire' (Exodus 24:16–17). St Paul writes, 'Will not the ministry of the Spirit be even more glorious? ... And we all, who with unveiled faces contemplate the Lord's glory, are being transformed into his image with ever-increasing glory' (2 Corinthians 3:8, 18).

PRAYER

Lord, thank you that as I read the Scriptures I encounter Jesus. Lord, help me each day, as I listen to your words and meet with you, to grow in my love relationship and to reflect your glory.

19 February | Day 50
God Loves *Me*

High on the moors in the Welsh highlands, two ministers met a young shepherd boy who had impaired hearing and was illiterate. They explained that Jesus wanted to be *his shepherd*, who would always look after him as he, the boy, looked after his sheep. They taught him to repeat the words, 'The Lord is *my* shepherd' (Psalm 23:1), using the fingers and thumb of his right hand to help him remember, starting with his thumb and then a finger for each word. They told him to pause at the fourth word '*my*', and remember, 'this psalm was meant for *me*'.

Some years later, one of them was passing through that same village and asked after the shepherd boy. The previous winter there had been terrible storms and the boy had died on the hills, buried in a snowdrift. The villager who was telling the story said, 'There was one thing, however, that we didn't understand. When his body was discovered he was holding *the fourth finger of his right hand*.'

The story illustrates the nature of *God's personal love for each one of us*.

Many people today think of God as some great impersonal force. However, the God of the Bible is very different. His relationship with us is personal. St Paul wrote, 'The Son of God, who loved *me* and gave himself for *me*' (Galatians 2:20). He is '*My* God' (Philippians 4:19). God loves *me*.

READING FROM PSALMS

Psalm 23:1–6
1. *My* Shepherd

God cares for us like a shepherd cares for their sheep. There are times when I have felt spiritually drained. I love the fact that 'He refreshes my soul' (v.3a). Many times, I have written down situations in which I have needed guidance, and later I have been able to thank God because 'He guides me along the right paths for his name's sake' (v.3b). God has a great purpose for your life. Let him guide you along the right path for you. You don't have to go through life full of fear, because he is with you (v.4).

2. *My* Host

The scene changes from a shepherd with his sheep to a host with his guest. This is a wonderful picture of what it is like to get alone with God in the midst of all the hassles of life: 'You prepare a table before me in the presence of my enemies' (v.5a). He satisfies the hunger in your soul with a feast. Accept his invitation and spend time each day feeding your soul in his presence.

All of us will at some stage 'walk through the valley of the shadow of death' (v.4), facing our own death or the death of someone we love. Even then we need not be afraid because the Lord is with us (v.4).

I have often read this psalm to people who are very sick or dying. It is a great comfort to know that the Lord is near to us at all times: 'Surely your goodness and love will follow me all the days of my life, and I will dwell in the house of the LORD for ever' (v.6).

PRAYER

Lord, thank you for the way you have led me and protected me. Thank you that you satisfy my spiritual hunger and thirst with your presence and your love.

NEW TESTAMENT READING

Mark 4:30–5:20
3. *My* Lord

Have you ever been in a situation when suddenly, without warning, your life seems to be hit by a storm of hurricane proportions (4:37, AMP)?

The Sea of Galilee was notorious for sudden storms. The disciples knew that waves of that size could overturn their boat and take their lives.

Yet, Jesus was asleep (v.38). Sometimes when the storms come it appears that God is not doing anything. He does not seem to be answering your prayers or even listening to you. In times like this, your faith is being tested.

Eventually, Jesus calms the storm. He addresses the power behind the storms with words someone might use to a puppy: 'Quiet! Be still!' (v.39), showing he is *Lord over nature*. For the disciples, the passage starts with fear and ends with faith. A crisis tests your faith.

Jesus wants you to learn to conquer your fears and trust him even in the middle of the storms of life.

Next, Jesus demonstrates that he is *Lord over the powers that try to destroy our lives*. Somehow this demon-possessed man (nicknamed Legion, 5:9) had ended up in a hellish place, self-harming (v.5) and chained by society (v.4), whose only answer was to lock him up. That was all they could do. The power of politicians, the state and the police is limited. However, Jesus did not judge or condemn the man. Rather he saw his potential to live in wholeness. In restoring the man to 'his right mind' Jesus gave an authoritative command and demonstrated his Lordship and power to set us free and heal us.

There were two distinct reactions from the people to the lordship of Jesus. The first was hostile (v.17). Commercial interests had been damaged. It can be rather uncomfortable when we see real power operating. On the other hand, some were interested (v.20).

One of the fascinating aspects of this story is that after Jesus had healed the demon-possessed man and set him free, the man begged to go with him (v.18), but Jesus did not let him (v.19).

I would have thought that this man would have benefited from some intensive follow-up with Jesus! However, Jesus gets him involved in evangelism straight away. He says, 'Go home to your own people and tell them how much the Lord has done for you' (v.19). And that is exactly what he did (v.20).

Don't be overprotective of people who have recently come to faith. It's sometimes good to get them speaking publicly about their new faith straight away. The next time Jesus came to the Decapolis, 4,000 people came to listen. This man's testimony seems to have had a big impact.

Maybe this is why Mark places the story shortly after the parable of the mustard seed. The demoniac may have felt he had little to offer, but his life had a huge impact. Jesus says that God can do a lot with a very small seed – a mustard seed (4:31). 'When planted, it grows' (v.32).

The issue is not how much you have, but what you do with it. A mustard seed needs to be planted in the ground straight away or else it is lost. If it is planted, the growth is so strong it can go through concrete. The lesson is simple: use it or lose it. Use what you have and God will multiply it many times over.

PRAYER

Thank you that you are Lord over all. Thank you that I can trust you in times of crisis and I do not need to fear.

OLD TESTAMENT READING

Exodus 25:1–26:37

4. *My* Guide

Generosity is an act of the will. If you are passionate about God, you will give generously in order to see his name honoured. The people of God were able to raise the money they needed for the work of God from all 'whose *hearts* [prompted] them to give' (25:2b). They gave 'willingly and ungrudgingly' (v.2b, AMP). God's love never forces you. He wants you to respond freely from your heart.

The tabernacle ('tent of meeting') was a provisional meeting place of God and his people. Theologically, the tabernacle as *the dwelling place of God on earth* is of immense importance. It is the first in the series of the dwelling places of God: tabernacle, temple, Jesus himself, the body of the individual believer, the church.

God promises to guide even about the fine details: 'Make this tabernacle and all its furnishing *exactly* like the pattern *I will show you*' (v.9). God is my guide, even in the details of life.

5. *My* Saviour

The writer of Hebrews explains that the sanctuary described here (Exodus 25:10–26:37) is 'a copy and shadow of what is in heaven. This is why Moses was warned when he was about to build the tabernacle: "See to it that you make everything according to the pattern shown you on the mountain"' (Hebrews 8:5–6).

All these instructions for the Holy Place and the Most Holy Place were preparation for the saving work of Christ: 'When Christ came as high priest of the good things that are now already here, he went through the greater and more perfect tabernacle that is not made with human hands, that is to say, is not a part of this creation. He did not enter by means of the blood of goats and calves; but he entered the Most Holy Place once for all by his own blood, so obtaining eternal redemption' (9:11–12).

Through the atoning sacrifice of Jesus, you and I have access to the Most Holy Place. Jesus is my Saviour.

PRAYER

Lord, thank you that you are my Shepherd, my Host, my Lord, my Guide and my Saviour. Thank you that you love me.

20 February | Day 51
How to Meet with God

In 1949, one of the greatest revivals in the history of the United Kingdom took place in the Hebrides. Duncan Campbell, the preacher at the centre of the revival, later described how it began.[1]

Seven men and two women had decided to pray earnestly for revival. One night, at a prayer meeting held in a barn, a young man took his Bible and read from Psalm 24 (the psalm for today): *'Who may ascend the mountain of the LORD? Who may stand in his holy place? The one who has clean hands and a pure heart*' (vv.3–4a).

He shut his Bible and said: 'It seems to me just so much sentimental humbug to be praying as we are praying, to be waiting as we are waiting here, if we ourselves are not rightly related to God.' He asked God to reveal if his own hands were clean and his own heart was pure.

That night God met with them in a powerful way. As they waited on God 'his awesome presence swept the barn'. They came to understand that revival is always related to holiness. A power was let loose that shook the parish from centre to circumference.

'Three men were lying on the straw having fallen under the power of God. They were lifted out of the ordinary into the extraordinary. They knew that God had visited them and neither they nor their parish could ever be the same again.'

Four miles away, two sisters aged eighty-two and eighty-four had a vision of God. They saw the churches crowded and the youth and the community flocking into the churches. They had 'a glorious assurance that God was coming in revival power'.

Duncan Campbell was invited to come and speak to them. When he arrived in the parish church, it was packed out with hundreds waiting outside. No one could explain where they had come from. Within ten minutes of the service starting, men and woman were crying out to God. They were meeting with God in all his holiness.

There was such a sense of the presence of God on the island that a businessman visiting said, 'The moment I stepped ashore I was suddenly conscious of the presence of God.' God was *meeting* with his people.

How do you and I *meet with God?*

READING FROM PSALMS

Psalm 24:1–10
Awesome privilege

David *starts* this psalm with a reminder that God is a *mighty creator*: 'The earth is the LORD's, and everything in it, the world, and all who live in it' (v.1). He *ends* with a reminder that God is a *glorious King*. Five times he is referred to as 'the King of glory' (vv.7b, 8a, 9b, 10a, 10b). He is 'The LORD Almighty – he is the King of glory' (v.10b).

In light of the awesome nature of God, David asks the question, 'Who may ascend the mountain of the LORD? Who may stand in his holy place?' (v.3). The answer is only those who are totally pure: 'The one who has *clean hands* and a *pure heart*, who does not trust in an idol' (v.4).

Yet, we know that no one lives like this. It is only through Jesus that we can be made holy and approach God with confidence, 'For by one sacrifice he has made perfect for ever those who are being made holy' (Hebrews 10:14).

PRAYER

Lord, I want to meet with you today. Show me whether my hands are clean and my heart is pure. Thank you that through the blood of Jesus I can be made holy. Forgive me, cleanse me and fill me again with your Spirit.

NEW TESTAMENT READING

Mark 5:21–6:6a
Act of faith

Are you struggling with a long-term problem in your life that does not seem to be getting any better (5:26)? Have you ever been 'seized with alarm' and 'struck with fear' (Matthew 5:36)? We see in this passage how Jesus responded to people in these situations.

In the New Testament, we have the extraordinary sense of people meeting God through Jesus. St John (1 John 1:1) writes about 'the Word of life' whom 'we have *heard*' (Mark 5:27), 'we have *seen* with our own eyes' (v.22) and 'our hands have *touched*' (vv.27, 30–31).

People who came into contact with Jesus seemed to have a sense of coming into the presence of a holy God. Jairus 'prostrated himself at His feet' (v.22, AMP). The sick woman 'fell at his feet' (v.33).

This woman had suffered from a chronic disease for twelve years, which was incurable at that time (v.26). 'She heard about Jesus' (v.27) and she responded with *faith*. She 'touched his cloak' because she thought, 'If I just touch his clothes, I will be healed' (vv.27–28). 'Immediately, her bleeding stopped and she felt in her body that she was freed from her suffering' (v.29).

Contact with Jesus had a profound impact on people. Jesus says to the sick woman, 'Go in peace and be freed from your suffering' (v.34). The pain of the past twelve years is replaced by peace and freedom. Whatever you are struggling with in your life and however long it has been going on, like this woman, reach out to Jesus for help.

Jairus's daughter experiences the ultimate impact of meeting with Jesus as she is brought back to life. When Jesus arrived, there was anything but an atmosphere of faith. There was a commotion and wailing. They said, don't 'bother' Jesus (v.35). But Jesus said, 'Do not be seized with alarm and struck with fear; only keep on believing' (v.36, AMP).

Jesus said, 'The child is not dead but asleep' (v.39). Since Jesus was going to raise her up, her death was no more permanent than falling asleep. The apostle Paul, like Jesus, used the term 'falling asleep'. When you fall into a deep sleep, the next thing you know it is morning. When you die in Christ, the next thing you know you will be with the Lord.

Jesus took with him just three of the disciples whose faith he could trust (in addition to the parents). He appears to have wanted there to be an atmosphere of faith as he prayed for her to be raised from the dead.

There was nothing 'super-spiritual' about Jesus. He is very practical. He told them to 'give her something to eat' (v.43). Again, the account starts with fear and ends with faith.

When people saw what Jesus did they were 'completely astonished' (v.42b) and 'amazed' (6:2b). Of course, as today, not everyone had that reaction. Some 'laughed at him' (5:40) and some 'took offence at him' (6:3). In his *hometown* Jesus was 'a prophet ... without honour' (6:4). Those closest to him failed to recognise him. Sometimes we find it harder to take things from those we know best.

As today, some recognised Jesus and some totally missed out. The key distinction was whether or not they had 'faith'. He said to the sick woman, '*Your faith* has healed you' (5:34). He said to Jairus, 'Don't be afraid; just *believe*' (v.36b). In his hometown he was 'amazed at their *lack of faith*' (6:6).

Through his death on the cross, Jesus fulfilled the criteria for meeting God. Now it is by faith that you and I encounter Jesus and, through him, meet with God.

PRAYER

Lord, thank you that it is by faith that I encounter you. Lord, increase my faith. When I am 'seized with alarm' or 'struck with fear', help me to 'keep on believing'.

OLD TESTAMENT READING

Exodus 27:1–28:43
Access through Jesus

We cannot fully understand what an amazing privilege it is to be able to meet with God without seeing the Old Testament background. Here we see a description of the Tent of *Meeting* (27:21), (where God meets with Moses and the priests: 30:36; 28:30). It was an awesome thing to enter into the '*presence of the Lord*' (28:30a). Aaron was entering the 'Holy Place before the Lord' (v.35).

The writer of Hebrews explains how all this points to Jesus. The tabernacle was just '*a copy* and *shadow* of what is in heaven' (Hebrews 8:5a). Even so, the priests were only allowed to enter the Holy Place, and not the Most Holy Place. 'The Holy Spirit was showing by this that the way into the Most Holy Place had not yet been disclosed as long as the first tabernacle was still functioning' (9:8). This was an *illustration* (v.9a).

As the writer of Hebrews shows, this passage forms the background to Jesus' sacrifice on our behalf – making it possible for you and me *to meet with a holy God* through the blood of Jesus, offered 'once for all' (v.26).

PRAYER

Lord, thank you that you have made it possible, through the blood of Jesus, for me to enter the Most Holy Place and to come into the presence of the Lord. Thank you that I have access through Jesus 'to the Father by one Spirit' (Ephesians 2:18). Thank you that I can meet with you.

21 February | Day 52
Better Together

I have never been very good at using visual aids. I am not a very practical person. On the other hand, my great friend, Nicky Lee (who, together with his wife Sila, has pioneered The Marriage Course[1] and other courses for couples and parents), is extremely practical and often uses visual aids.

When he is speaking at weddings he sometimes uses a visual aid to illustrate the passage in Ecclesiastes 4, where the writer says, '*Two are better than one* ... A cord of three strands is not quickly broken' (vv.9, 12).

As a picture of marriage, Nicky Lee takes two strands of different coloured wool and weaves them together. Together they are stronger and yet they can quite easily be broken. Then he takes a third strand of nearly invisible fishing line. With this third strand, it is almost impossible to break the two pieces of wool. (I did try to use this illustration once but, for reasons I cannot remember, it went horribly wrong!)

The point that he makes so well, and that comes out of the passage in Ecclesiastes, is that while friendships and marriages are wonderful gifts, having God at the centre of a friendship or marriage provides an invisible thread of enormous strength.

In today's passages, we see how two are stronger than one in marriage, mission and ministry.

READING FROM PROVERBS

Proverbs 5:15–23
Marriage: two become one

This is a wonderful picture of marriage as a source of blessing (v.18a), rejoicing (v.18b), love (v.19a), grace (v.19a), satisfaction (v.19b) and romance (v.19c).

It is a beautiful description of marriage in which two people 'become one flesh' (Genesis 2:24). Part of its beauty lies in its exclusiveness. The writer uses the evocative image of a spring, well or fountain to describe the delight of sexual union. However, it is a delight that is grounded in exclusiveness though, and he stresses this four times (Proverbs 5:15–18).

The greatness of the emotional and physical love between a husband and wife ('enduring intimacies', v.19, MSG) is contrasted with the 'cheap thrills' of 'dalliance with a promiscuous stranger' (v.20, MSG).

That is why the writer warns so strongly against adultery. Be aware, he says, that God is watching (v.21). And the path that leads to adultery is 'evil', 'wicked', sinful, foolish and *leads to death* (vv.22–23). We see an example of this in the New Testament passage where it was Herod's adultery that led to him murdering John the Baptist (Mark 6:14–29).

While the fact that our 'ways are in full view of the LORD' (Proverbs 5:21) is a warning against adultery, it is also a reminder of the strength that comes from having 'the Lord' involved in a marriage, as the third strand of the cord.

God's love for us is the best example and central guiding principle of how we should love our spouse.

PRAYER

Thank you, Lord, for the difference that the third strand, the presence of Jesus, makes to a marriage. Thank you that two are better than one and that a cord of three strands is not quickly broken.

NEW TESTAMENT READING

Mark 6:6b–29
Mission: two by two

Marriage is *not* the *only* answer to aloneness. Although marriage is a great blessing, we are reminded here that we do not need to be married to know community or completeness. Jesus was not married and he was the most complete human to have ever walked this earth. He modelled another way of wholeness.

Jesus went around 'doing the stuff' (to coin a phrase used by John Wimber). Then he sent his disciples out to do the same. They went out and preached, drove out demons and healed the sick (vv.12–13).

It is significant that he sent them out in pairs: '*two by two*' (v.7). This kind of mission can be very lonely if you are on your own. It is so much better to go out in pairs.

It must have been great fun and deeply satisfying to go out together and preach the gospel, drive out demons and anoint the sick with oil and see them healed as a result (v.13).

'They preached with joyful urgency that life can be radically different; right and left they sent the demons packing; they brought wellness to the sick, anointing their bodies, healing their spirits' (vv.13–14, MSG).

They did it together. By contrast with these disciples, poor John the Baptist had been on his own in prison. We see in him a striking example of moral courage in speaking truth to power. He had been saying to Herod, 'It is not lawful for you to have your brother's wife' (v.18). He did not hesitate to incur the wrath of the great and powerful as often as was found necessary.

Herod liked to listen to John (v.20). He felt better after a good sermon! But there was one thing in Herod's life that he refused to give up: his adulterous relationship with Herodias. This made him morally weak, and it stopped him from enjoying a relationship with God.

Herod, like Pilate with Jesus, was not keen to order the death of John the Baptist. But Herod made a foolish offer and found himself in a position where he would have lost face had he not gone ahead and ordered John the Baptist's execution.

While John the Baptist had followers (John 1:35), he had to face prison and execution alone. Jesus sent his disciples out 'two by two'.

Jago Wynne, author of the book *Working Without Wilting*, talks about pastoring mid-week gatherings for people working in London. He says that those who came by themselves from their workplace as isolated Christians generally looked weary, struggling with the pressures of working life.

On the other hand, those who had found other Christian colleagues and who came to the services in groups of two or more were almost universally far more upbeat and radiant.

Jago writes, 'If we are isolated Christians in our day-to-day environments, whether that is the workplace or school or university or home, it is good to pray for the Lord to provide us with another brother or sister in Christ. Even their mere presence can be a source of encouragement to keep going in serving the Lord in life and in mission.'[2]

As the writer of Ecclesiastes says, 'Two are better than one ... If either of them falls down, one can help the other up. But pity anyone who falls and has no one to help them up! ... Though one may be overpowered, two can defend themselves. A cord of three strands is not quickly broken' (Ecclesiastes 4:9–12). This verse is often used to illustrate the importance of friendship and unity in marriage – but the original context of this verse is actually that of friendship.

PRAYER

Thank you, Lord, for friendship. Thank you that you do not send us out on our own. Thank you that as we go out, two by two, we know that there is a third cord also. You said, 'Go and make disciples of all nations ... and surely *I am with you always*' (Matthew 28:19–20).

OLD TESTAMENT READING

Exodus 29:1–30:38
Ministry: two lambs

The elaborate ceremonies we read about in this passage emphasise the meticulous care with which a holy God was to be approached. It was the outward adorning that gave the priests glory, beauty and holiness. In the New Testament, the garments that lead to inner beauty and holiness come from God's Spirit in your heart.

In these Old Testament ceremonies, everything had to be multiplied. That is why they needed *two* rams (29:1, 3), *two* gold rings (30:4) and, most significantly, *two* lambs (29:38). The multiplication of implements and sacrifices was a sign of God's greatness. They pointed to the inadequacies of any animal sacrifice or ritual to truly bring us to God. Two is better than one – but it is still not enough.

The writer of Hebrews tells us that all these regulations have been set aside: 'The former regulation is set aside because it was weak and useless' (Hebrews 7:18). Instead of two lambs, *one perfect lamb* was sacrificed for us – Jesus. '*He sacrificed for their sins once for all when he offered himself*' (v.27). We no longer need a multiplication of sacrifices.

Atonement was necessary (Exodus 29:33, 37; 30:10, 16) and required '*the blood of the atoning sin offering*' (30:10).

Jesus shed his own blood for us. Paul describes his death on the cross as a 'sacrifice of *atonement*' (Romans 3:25).

It was only through sacrifice that the priests could approach the altar '*to minister*' (Exodus 30:20). 'Ministry' means service to God. It is the one sacrifice of Jesus on the cross that enables you to be involved in ministry (service of God and of others).

PRAYER

Thank you, Jesus, that you are the one perfect lamb who was sacrificed for my sins once and for all. Thank you that I no longer need a multiplication of sacrifices. Thank you that, as the great hymn puts it, I am 'ransomed, healed, restored, forgiven'.[3]

22 February | Day 53
How to Spend Time with Jesus

I first encountered Jesus in February 1974. I am so grateful to those who taught me, right from the start, the importance of what they called 'the quiet time'.

The old-fashioned expression 'the quiet time' (meaning time set aside to read the Bible and pray) probably has its origin in the words of Jesus in today's New Testament passage, 'Come *with me by yourselves to a quiet place*' (Mark 6:31). Practically every morning since I was eighteen years of age, I have begun the day in this way. I try to spend time with Jesus, by myself, in a quiet place. Sometimes it is very brief, sometimes it is longer. But just as I do not like beginning the day without breakfast, I cannot imagine beginning the day without spiritual food.

Nearly always, I start by reading the Bible, as I believe it's more important that Jesus speaks to me than I speak to him. My thoughts from each day are now the basis of these notes that accompany the *Bible in One Year*.

READING FROM PSALMS

Psalm 25:1–7
Time to look to God

Do you ever feel daunted by your circumstances? Do you ever fear that you might fail and end up disappointed or even ashamed?

David clearly had such fears and gives us an example of how to start a quiet time. He begins by saying, 'Unto You, O Lord, do I bring my life' (v.1, AMP). He is determined to trust God despite all the challenges that lie ahead. He goes on, 'O my God, I trust, lean on, rely on, and am confident in You. Let me not be put to shame or [my hope in You] be disappointed; let not my enemies triumph over me' (v.2, AMP).

He says, in effect, 'I am looking to you, God' (v.1, MSG). He was obviously under attack, but he trusted that God would never let him be put to shame (v.3). His hope was in God 'all day long' (v.5).

Take time each day to look to God in preparation for what lies ahead. Ask for God's mercy, forgiveness, help, guidance and deliverance.

PRAYER

Lord, I pray for your guidance in everything I'm involved in today: 'Take me by the hand; Lead me down the paths of truth ... plan only the best for me, God!' (vv.5, 7, MSG).

NEW TESTAMENT READING

Mark 6:30–56
Time alone with Jesus

Jesus taught his disciples the priority of time alone with him. He said to them, 'Come *with me by yourselves* to a *quiet place*' (v.31b) and they went off by themselves 'to *a solitary place*' (v.32).

There was so much action going on in Jesus' life that it must have been very hard for him to escape and get some rest (v.31). God was using him in amazing ways – feeding the 5,000 and walking on water for a start! He saw the vast needs of all the people ('He had compassion on them, because they were like sheep without a shepherd', v.34).

They were desperate for him and were literally running towards him (vv.33, 55). Nevertheless, Jesus found it necessary to send them all off. He needed some solitude. He climbed a mountain to pray (vv.45–46). He prioritised his time alone with God.

Prayer and action go hand in hand. The activity comes out of the relationship. Jesus 'had compassion on them' (v.34). The word used is the strongest word in the Greek language for 'pity'. 'His heart broke' (v.34, MSG).

Jesus was constantly developing and encouraging the disciples in their ministry. He did not merely feed the 5,000 miraculously by himself. He said to them, '*You* give them something to eat' (v.37).

Sometimes I feel daunted by the ministry God has given to me. Often, I feel I have little to offer the people I am called to serve. I take great comfort from this passage. *Jesus can do a lot with a little.* If you offer to Jesus the little you have, he can multiply it and meet the needs of all the people.

Jesus was efficient, organised and practical. He 'told them to make all the people sit down in groups on the green grass. So they sat down in groups of hundreds and fifties' (vv.39–40).

After the disciples had fed the 5,000, Jesus sent them off again by themselves. He made his disciples get into a boat and go on ahead of him, while he went up on a mountainside to pray.

Even when we are doing what Jesus tells us to do, it is sometimes very difficult and hard work. There are times when I feel 'agitated (troubled and filled with fear and dread)' (v.50, AMP). The disciples were 'straining at the oars, because the wind was against them' (v.48). When Jesus joined them he said, 'Take courage! It is I. Don't be afraid' (v.50).

As Jesus climbed into the boat with them, 'the wind died down' (v.51). We see a picture of the difference Jesus makes to our lives. It is an uphill struggle unless you are conscious of Jesus' presence with you.

Only those who recognise Jesus (v.54) can enjoy this relationship. Those who did recognise him ran towards him (v.55) and – I love these words – 'all who touched him were healed' (v.56).

PRAYER

Lord, thank you that in the storms of life you say to me, 'Take courage! It is I. Don't be afraid' (v.50).

OLD TESTAMENT READING

Exodus 31:1–33:6
Time to receive help from God

Part of the reason Jesus wanted his disciples to come away was to get some *rest* (Mark 6:31). We see in this passage the importance of rest and refreshment (Exodus 31:13–17). Look ahead at your schedule and make sure that you put these times in as a priority.

Time alone with Jesus includes listening to him. The main way in which we hear Jesus speak to us is through the Bible. It is often when I fail to spend time alone with Jesus that I more easily succumb to temptation or feel afraid.

In Exodus 32, we see that however much God has done for us in the past, we so quickly forget and doubt him and, as a result, fall into sin: 'They have been *quick to turn away* from what I commanded them' (32:8).

The initial cause of their idolatry was a lack of patience. They did not wait for God's timing. The fact that God takes what we consider to be a long time does not mean that he is not at work.

After the people had made the golden calf as an idol, it was the prayer of Moses that averted total disaster (vv.11–14). By the power of prayer it is possible to change the course of history.

Aaron was held responsible for the idolatry: 'What did these people do to you, that *you* led them into such a great sin?' (v.21). Actually, Aaron simply followed popular opinion. It was the people's idea, which he had put into action. Yet in God's sight he was still the leader. He should have stood against them, rather than allowing himself to be persuaded to lead them into sin.

Aaron replied, 'You know how prone these people are to evil ... they gave me the gold and I threw it into the fire, and out came this calf!' (vv.22–24). This is obviously nonsense but it is easy to distort the truth slightly to justify ourselves.

Today's passage can be more fully understood in the light of St Paul's exposition of it in the New Testament. He writes, 'Now these things occurred as examples to keep us from setting our hearts on evil things as they did' (1 Corinthians 10:6). This passage warns us about four things:

1. Self-indulgence (1 Corinthians 10:7; Exodus 32:6)
2. Promiscuity (1 Corinthians 10:8, MSG)
3. Self-worship (v.9)
4. Grumbling (v.10).

The severity of the punishments the people of God faced is a mark of how serious and destructive these sins are, 'and were written down as *warnings* for us' (v.11). This shows us God's unwillingness simply to let things fester.

Yet Paul does not just leave it there, he tells us how to deal with temptation: 'No test or temptation that comes your way is beyond the course of what others have had to face. All you need to remember is that God will never let you down; he'll never let you be pushed past your limit; he'll always be there to help you come through it' (v.13, MSG).

These final words remind us of God's extraordinary grace towards us, helping us through temptation. However, even when we fall down in these areas we can be forgiven through Jesus.

PRAYER

Lord, thank you for the amazing privilege that we have of being able to spend time in your presence. Thank you that I can listen to your voice and that you speak to me. Help me to be careful not to fall into temptation. Keep me walking in a close relationship with you each day.

23 February | Day 54
How to Hear God

When I saw him coming down the street I would cross the road in order to avoid him. I had met him in my first week at university. He had a shiny, smiley face. I had also met one or two others like him who had that same look on their face. It made me very suspicious.

A few months later, I encountered Jesus and realised that these people's faces were shining because they had been spending time with Jesus. Like Moses, when he came down from the mountain after *hearing God* speak to him, their faces were 'radiant' (Exodus 34:29, 35).

Jesus said that 'people do not live on bread alone, but on every word that comes from the mouth of God' (Matthew 4:4). Just as we need physical food, so we also need spiritual food. Spiritual food comes from *hearing the words of God*.

READING FROM PSALMS

Psalm 25:8–15
Hear the guidance of God

When we try to force our own agenda or strive to do what we want to do, there is a sense of spiritual discomfort. Joyce Meyer uses the analogy of the discomfort that comes from wearing a pair of shoes that don't fit.

When we are living a life of worship and obedience and following God's way, he promises that we will be 'at ease' (v.13, AMP). That does not mean that life will be easy. But when we start following God's plans for our lives, it is like finding a pair of shoes that fit comfortably.

Again and again in this psalm we are reminded of how God guides us. He 'instructs' (vv.8, 12), he 'guides' (v.9a), he 'teaches' (v.9b), he 'confides' in his people (v.14).

1. The people he guides

Amazingly, David explains that God's goodness leads him to want to teach *even* sinful people; 'therefore he instructs *sinners* in his ways' (v.8). Even though David's 'iniquity' is 'great', he knows that he can be forgiven and put right by God (v.11).

Thankfully, you do not need to be perfect in order to hear God's guidance but you do need an attitude of humility: 'He guides the *humble* in what is right and teaches them his way' (v.9). 'God-friendship is for God-worshipers; They are the ones he confides in' (v.14, MSG).

2. The purpose of his guidance

You can be sure that God will only ask you to do 'what is right' (v.9a). The test of whether the guidance comes from God is whether what you are being asked to do is 'loving and faithful' (v.10a). God will never ask you to do something that is unloving or unfaithful. '*All* the ways of the Lord are loving and faithful' (v.10a).

PRAYER

Lord, I pray for your guidance – that you will instruct, teach and confide in me today.

NEW TESTAMENT READING

Mark 7:1–30
Hear the word of God

Jesus says that the word of God takes priority over all our traditions (v.8). There is nothing wrong with tradition. Traditions can be very important and valuable. However, tradition should never take precedence over the word of God. Jesus attacks the Pharisees for using tradition to avoid obeying the word of God: 'You get rid of God's command so you won't be *inconvenienced* in following the religious fashions' (v.9, MSG).

For example, supporting elderly parents can sometimes be *inconvenient*. It can be tempting to find excuses why we should not need to do so. The Pharisees said it was permissible not to support your parents financially if you had given the money as a gift to God (v.11). Jesus said that in doing this they were disobeying the command to 'Honour your father and mother' (v.10a). 'Thus', he says, 'you nullify the word of God by your tradition that you have handed down' (v.13).

The Pharisees honoured God by what they did outwardly (vv.1–5). It is relatively easy to do the right things or even say the right things. We can obey all the rules of the community and yet *our hearts* can be far away from God (vv.6–8).

God is not so concerned about the outward appearance but about the heart. Jesus says, 'For it is from within, out of a person's *heart*, that evil thoughts come – sexual immorality, theft, murder, adultery, greed, malice, deceit, lewdness, envy, slander, arrogance and folly. All these evils come from inside and defile a person' (vv.21–23). These are the things that pollute our lives and spoil our relationship with God.

Jesus says, 'listen to me' (v.14). This is the key to life – listening to Jesus.

Jesus goes on to draw out what is in the heart of the Syro-Phoenician woman. As John Calvin put it, Jesus intends 'not to extinguish the woman's faith' by his apparent coldness 'but rather to whet her zeal and inflame her ardour'.[1]

Jesus came for the Jews first, then the Gentiles (vv.27–29; see Isaiah 49:6; Romans 1:16). The greatness of the woman's faith is shown by the fact that she not only recognised who he was and his heavenly power, but, as Calvin goes on to say, she 'pursued her course steadily through formidable opposition'.[2] She is a great example for us of uncynical and persevering faith.

PRAYER

Lord, thank you for the power of the word of God to challenge the attitudes of my heart. Cleanse my heart today, I pray, and give me a passionate, uncynical and persevering faith.

OLD TESTAMENT READING

Exodus 33:7–34:35
Hear the plans of God

You can be a friend of God. Jesus regards those who follow him as his friends (John 15:15). Moses was God's friend. If it was possible for Moses then, the New Testament tells us, it is possible for you now.

God revealed his plans to Moses. Moses had an extraordinary relationship with God. He would go into the Tent of Meeting to enquire of the Lord. A pillar of cloud would come down 'while the Lord spoke with Moses' (Exodus 33:9). 'The Lord would speak to Moses face to face, *as one speaks to a friend*' (v.11a). This describes the closeness of God to Moses and the immediacy of hearing his voice. Moses prayed, 'Let me in on your plans' (v.13, MSG).

It is clear that they were not *physically* face-to-face (v.20). God's presence was so glorious and holy that no one could see him face-to-face and live. It is a metaphor denoting very close contact and communion. This is what we need daily; to hear God speak 'face-to-face' and grow in our friendship with him.

What Moses wanted more than anything else was the 'Presence of God'. This is what we all need so much in our lives – his presence and his peace. The Lord promises him, 'My Presence will go with you and I will give you rest' (v.14). This is what God promises to you as well.

Moses says, 'If your Presence does not go with us, do not send us up from here' (v.15). It was the *presence* of God that distinguished the people of God from everybody else (v.16b). It is this above all else that distinguishes you from the world around you.

When Moses had spent time in the *presence* of the Lord, 'his face was radiant because he had spoken with the Lord' (34:29). This is the background to Paul's extraordinary words in 2 Corinthians 3. He says that we can enjoy something far greater than Moses experienced.

'What was glorious has no glory now in comparison with the surpassing glory. And if what was transitory came with glory, how much greater is the glory of that which lasts!' (2 Corinthians 3:10–11).

You can be even bolder than Moses, 'who would put a veil over his face to prevent the Israelites from seeing the end of what was passing away' (v.13). Paul writes, 'Whenever anyone turns to the Lord, the veil is taken away. Now the Lord is the Spirit, and where the Spirit of the Lord is, there is freedom. And we all, who with unveiled faces contemplate the Lord's glory, are being transformed into his image with ever-increasing glory, which comes from the Lord, who is the Spirit' (vv.16–18).

It is an extraordinary privilege to be involved in the ministry of the Spirit. On every Alpha Weekend we watch people experiencing the presence of God and being filled with the Holy Spirit. I have often noticed the radiance on people's faces at the end of the weekend. But this is not meant to be a one-off experience that fades like Moses' radiance.

Through the Holy Spirit you can experience the 'Presence of God': 'Our lives gradually becoming brighter and more beautiful as God enters our lives and we become like him' (v.18, MSG).

PRAYER

Lord, thank you that you promise, 'My Presence will go with you, and I will give you rest' (Exodus 33:14). Help me to hear your voice, speak to you face to face as a friend, to reflect your glory and be transformed into your likeness with ever-increasing glory.

24 February | Day 55
What You Give to God, He Multiplies

Hattie May Wiatt, a six-year-old girl, lived near Grace Baptist Church in Philadelphia, USA. The Sunday school was very crowded. Russell H. Conwell, the minister, told her that one day they would have buildings big enough to allow everyone to attend. She said, 'I hope you will. It is so crowded I am afraid to go there alone.' He replied, 'When we get the money we will construct one large enough to get all the children in.'

Two years later, in 1886, Hattie May died. After the funeral Hattie's mother gave the minister a little bag they had found under their daughter's pillow containing 57 cents in change that she had saved up. Alongside it was a note in her handwriting: 'To help build bigger so that more children can go to Sunday school.'

The minister changed all the money into pennies and offered each one for sale. He received $250 – and 54 of the cents were given back. The $250 was itself changed into pennies and sold by the newly formed 'Wiatt Mite Society'. In this way, her 57 cents *kept on multiplying*.

Twenty-six years later, in a talk entitled, 'The history of the 57 cents', the minister explained the results of her 57-cent donation: a church with a membership of over 5,600 people, a hospital where tens of thousands of people had been treated, 80,000 young people going through university, 2,000 people going out to preach the gospel – all this happened 'because Hattie May Wiatt invested her 57 cents'.[1]

The theme of multiplication runs throughout the Bible. What cannot be achieved by addition, God does by multiplication. You reap what you sow, only many times more. What you give to the Lord, he multiplies.

READING FROM PSALMS

Psalm 25:16–22
Multiplication of blessings ... and troubles

Jesus promised his followers a multiplication of blessings. But he also warned them that alongside the blessings there would be trouble. He said that whoever followed him would receive a hundredfold in this life – with persecutions (Mark 10:30).

David expresses how '*the troubles* of my heart have *multiplied* ... See how *my enemies* have *increased*' (Psalm 25:17, 19). He speaks of loneliness, 'affliction', 'anguish' and 'distress'.

Wherever God blesses, troubles and persecutions tend also to increase. Any kind of leadership will involve opposition. The greater the responsibility, the more your troubles will multiply and your critics increase.

David prays to the Lord for his help in guarding and rescuing him (v.20). When under attack, always try to act with integrity, uprightness and faith (v.21). Do the right thing regardless of what people say or think.

PRAYER

Lord, as I face opposition, help me to do the right thing whatever the cost or consequences may be.

NEW TESTAMENT READING

Mark 7:31–8:13
Multiplication of resources

With seven loaves and a few small fish, Jesus fed the 4,000 and the disciples picked up seven basketfuls of broken pieces that were left over – the extraordinary multiplication of God's provision!

Interestingly though, Jesus doesn't just do a miracle, he first involves the disciples. He calls them over to explain what he wants to do (8:1–3). He allows them to think their way towards a solution (v.4), perhaps hoping that they will remember the feeding of the 5,000 (6:30–44).

He then enlists their help, by asking them for the food that they have (8:5). It is only at that point that Jesus performs a miracle, multiplying the food that they have given him. Even then he gets the disciples to help with the distribution of the food (v.6). Jesus loves to involve you in his plans and work.

The disciples' role seems fairly small in comparison to what Jesus is able to do. God is able to do a lot with a very small amount. Whatever you give to God, he multiplies.

Today's passage starts with Jesus healing a man 'who was deaf and could hardly talk' (7:32). He prayed for him 'with a deep sigh' (v.34). Perhaps this is the kind of prayer that Paul is describing as 'wordless groans' (Romans 8:26). It represents the Holy Spirit struggling in prayer through us. Jesus 'said to [the man], "*Ephphatha!*" (which means, "Be opened")' (Mark 7:34). Jesus not only opens ears – he releases and opens up your whole being – your heart, mind, emotions, finances and every other part of your life.

Aware of the multiplication of opposition, Jesus commanded people 'not to tell anyone' (v.36). However, 'overwhelmed with amazement' (v.37), they 'kept talking about it' (v.36).

After the miracle of multiplication, Jesus sent the crowds away so that he could concentrate on a smaller group of his disciples (8:9–10). The needs of the crowd were enormous – for evangelism and healing. Nevertheless, Jesus prioritised time with a small group of leaders.

In spite of all the miracles, not everyone believed. 'The Pharisees came and began to question Jesus. To test him, they asked him for a sign from heaven' (v.11). They wanted compelling outward proof of his authority.

They were spiritually blind and unable to recognise the signs God had given. They wanted to choose signs of their own – which Jesus refused to do. It is still true today that miracles do not always lead to faith – people often dismiss miracles, thinking there must be some other explanation.

PRAYER

Lord, thank you that you are able to do a lot with a little and that whatever we give to you, you multiply. Lord, today I give you my life, my time, and all I have.

OLD TESTAMENT READING

Exodus 35:1–36:38
Multiplication of volunteers

I have observed over the years the astonishing achievements that are possible when every member of even a small congregation gets involved in praying, serving and giving.

The people of God faced a massive task in the building of the tabernacle. They achieved it through a multiplication of involvement of volunteers. Moses assembled 'the entire congregation' (35:1, MSG). This is what is needed in every church today:

1. Everyone praying

We saw in yesterday's passage how 'they all stood and worshipped' (33:10). The Sabbath was not just a day of rest, it was a '*holy* day' of 'rest *to the Lord*' (35:2). It was a day when people could devote more time to prayer and worship. The whole community prayed and worshipped.

2. Everyone giving

They took up 'an offering for the Lord' (v.5a). Everyone was urged to give: 'Everyone who is willing is to bring to the Lord an offering of gold, silver and bronze' (v.5b).

The task was not achieved by one generous donor alone. 'And everyone who was *willing* and whose *heart moved* them came and *brought an offering* to the Lord for the work ... All who were *willing*, men and women alike' (vv.21–22). Like Hattie May Wiatt, each one brought their '57 cents'.

If your community is to achieve everything that God is calling you to do, you will need everyone giving – not under compulsion but *willingly* (2 Corinthians 8 and 9).

As everyone got involved in giving, they had 'more than enough' (Exodus 36:5). 'The people were ordered to stop bringing offerings! There was plenty of material for all the work to be done. Enough and more than enough' (vv.6–7, MSG).

3. Everyone serving

Everybody got involved in serving. The words 'everyone' and 'all' appear many times in this passage. It was entirely voluntary: 'All who are skilled among you are to come and make everything the Lord has commanded' (35:10). For example, '*everyone* who had acacia wood ... brought it' (v.24); '*Every* skilled woman spun with her hands' (v.25).

A key role was played by the artists, Bezalel and Oholiab. They were filled with the Spirit to make artistic designs and to teach others to do the same. Together they used their skills and ability to do the work: 'Every skilled person to whom the Lord has given skill and ability to know how to carry out all the work of constructing the sanctuary are to do the work' (36:1).

All this was entirely voluntary. The people of God were 'stirred up for God' (35:21, 26, AMP). The task was achieved by 'everyone whose heart was roused, whose spirit was freely responsive' (v.21, MSG). If we are to achieve what God is calling us to do as a community we need this multiplication of volunteers.

Enthusiasm is infectious. Don't waste your time hanging around people who try to belittle your dreams. Associate with people who inspire and challenge you, lift you higher and make you better. Walk with the visionaries, the believers, the doers and the courageous. Great people make you feel that you too can become great.

Stir one another up to pray, serve and give. You will be astonished by how God is able to multiply your 57 cents and do more than you could ever ask or even imagine.

PRAYER

Lord, thank you for what is possible when everyone gets involved in praying, serving and giving. Thank you that you multiply more than we could ever ask or even imagine.

25 February | Day 56
How to Make the Most of Your Life

'People often ask me what Mother Teresa was like,' writes Shane Claiborne in his book *The Irresistible Revolution*. 'Sometimes it's like they wonder if she glowed in the dark or had a halo. She was short, wrinkled, and precious, maybe even a little ornery, like a beautiful, wise old granny. But there is one thing I will never forget – her feet. Her feet were deformed.

'Each morning I would stare at them. I wondered if she had contracted leprosy. One day a Sister explained, "Her feet are deformed because we get just enough donated shoes for everyone, and Mother does not want anyone to get stuck with the worst pair, so she digs through and finds them. And years of doing that have deformed her feet." Years of loving her neighbour as herself deformed her feet.'[1]

When people are asked about the person whose life they most admire, so often the answer is 'Mother Teresa'. She made the most of her life. It is a paradox, because her life was a life of self-denial, taking up her cross and following Jesus.

Life is an extraordinary and wonderful gift. In the Bible we are constantly urged not to waste this gift, but instead to make the most of our lives.

READING FROM PROVERBS

Proverbs 6:1–11
Master self-discipline

The book of Proverbs gives you practical wisdom on how to make the most of your life and how to avoid wasting it by falling into various traps. In the passage for today we see two examples:

1. Master your finances

One of the areas of life that requires self-discipline is our finances. There are always plenty of financial traps and snares – such as unmanageable debt, unwise investment and foolish pledges. The writer urges you that, if you have got yourself into a financial muddle (vv.2–5), you should do everything in your power to get out of it as soon as possible: 'Don't waste a minute' (v.3, MSG).

You may have to humble yourself (v.3b). You may have to plead your case (v.3c). Do everything in your power to free yourself from these snares (v.5). If we don't get our finances sorted out it can have a very detrimental effect on our lives and on our families.

2. Master your time

We can waste our lives through a lack of self-discipline. Without accountability we can easily become lazy, and this can have disastrous consequences (vv.9–11). We can learn self-leadership from the ant; nobody tells it what to do. 'It has no commander, no overseer or ruler' (v.7), yet it works extremely hard: 'It stores its provisions in summer and gathers its food at harvest' (v.8).

Of course, it is important to get enough sleep. Our bodies need rest. But we need to be careful not to waste our time in unproductive activity.

PRAYER

Lord, give me wisdom in the handling of my finances and my time.

NEW TESTAMENT READING

Mark 8:14–9:1
Give your life away

Jesus warns his disciples against the 'yeast' (8:15) of the Pharisees and of Herod. 'Yeast' was a common metaphor for the evil tendency in human beings, which, although it might seem only a small thing, nevertheless corrupts the whole person. The disciples still did not understand because they were so caught up with the physical that they could not see the spiritual.

Not that there is anything wrong with physical things in themselves. The blind man wanted to *touch Jesus* (v.22). Jesus did something very physical – *he spat on the man's eyes* and *put his hands on him* twice (vv.23–25). He prayed twice before the man was totally healed. This encourages us to keep on praying more than once for those who are sick.

Finally, the disciples understand who Jesus is: 'You are the Christ' (v.29). 'Christos' means '*the Anointed One, the Messiah*'. In the time of Jesus the term was particularly associated with the expectation of a new Davidic King. In the Old Testament, however, kings, priests and prophets were all anointed. Jesus is the fulfilment of them all. He is *the* King, *the* Great High Priest, *the* Prophet.

Yet this title, 'Messiah', was not adequate. Jesus preferred to use the title 'Son of Man' (v.31). 'Son of Man' was an even more majestic, and therefore more suitable, title. It contained the idea of suffering (Daniel 7:21). The 'Son of Man' was also a *representative* figure identifying himself with human beings.

Then Jesus begins to speak about the cross (Mark 8:31). We can't understand the cross unless we understand who Jesus is. His teaching is so paradoxical, counterintuitive and surprising that Peter takes him aside to rebuke him (v.32).

There is a parallel here with the healing of the blind man, which acts as a visual parable of the gradual eye-opening of the disciples. First, Peter's eyes are opened about Jesus' identity (v.29). However, he only half-understood. He did not yet see Jesus' mission (vv.31–32). Peter can 'see', but he can't fully 'see'.

Jesus has to explain to his disciples the extraordinary paradox involved in making the most of our lives – of which he is to show the supreme example. He says if you want to make the most of your life, you have to give it away. You have to abandon your life to his service and the gospel – 'whoever wants to save their life will lose it, but whoever loses their life for me and for the gospel will save it' (v.35).

In contrast, he then says that it is possible to 'gain the whole world, yet forfeit [your] soul' (v.36). The actor Jim Carrey said, 'I think everyone should get rich and famous and do everything they dreamed of so they can see that it is not the answer.'

Even the biggest multi-billionaires only own a proportion of the world. Jesus warns us that if we are tempted to set out in that direction, even if we topped their success and gained *the whole world*, we could still totally waste our lives and forfeit our souls (v.36). He says the way to find life is to *deny yourself*, take up your cross and follow him (v.34).

The words 'deny yourself' mean *saying no to* yourself. The Christian life involves the challenge of daily denial. The world thinks that the way to life is to deny yourself nothing. Jesus says that the opposite is true. The way to *find life* is to deny yourself, take up your cross and follow him.

You are called to love. You are to live for God and for other people. And as you give yourself away, God will take care of your life.

The teaching of Jesus is radical and revolutionary. It is exactly the opposite of what we would expect, yet we see how it works out in practice. Those who seek their own satisfaction end up disillusioned and dissatisfied having wasted their lives; those who follow Jesus' teaching find life in all its fullness.

PRAYER

Lord, your words are so challenging. Help me each day to learn to deny myself in little things as well as big and to take up my cross and follow you. Thank you that as I give my life to you, I find life in all its fullness.

OLD TESTAMENT READING

Exodus 37:1–38:31
Serve God at work

You do not need to leave your job in order to serve God wholeheartedly. In the life of Bezalel, we see an example of someone who made the most of his life by serving God in his place of work. His daily job was his primary ministry.

God fills his people with his Spirit for the workplace: 'I've filled him with the Spirit of God, giving him skill and know-how and expertise in every kind of craft to create designs … he's an all-around craftsman' (31:3–5, MSG).

Bezalel was a sculptor. He was chosen by God to build the tabernacle (37:1; see also

31:1–5). He responded to God's call and 'made everything the LORD commanded Moses' (38:22). He worked in a team, which included a designer called Oholiab (v.23) and accomplished great things for God. The key to his success was that he was a man filled 'with the Spirit of God' (31:3; 35:31).

It is possible to be a talented musician, writer, or artist without being filled with the Spirit. But when the Spirit of God fills people for these tasks their work often takes on a new dimension. It has a far greater spiritual impact. This can be true even where the natural ability of the musician or artist is not particularly outstanding. Hearts can be touched and lives changed. No doubt something like this happened through Bezalel.

PRAYER

Lord, thank you for all those who serve you wholeheartedly – with their artistic abilities, in healthcare, education, business, retail, law, banking and every other area of the workplace. May we all be filled with the Spirit of God, like Bezalel, and do everything you command us. Help me to make the most of my life.

26 February | Day 57
Better Than Fame and Celebrity

In a survey of millennials, 50 per cent of young adults said that a major life goal was to become famous. In the past people wanted to be famous for *doing* something. Now, celebrity has become an end in itself. It has attained god-like characteristics. Not only do people want to be famous, they idolise those who have achieved celebrity status. This widespread interest in famous individuals has been described as 'the cult of celebrity'.

Fame to the ambitious is like salt water to the thirsty. The more you get, the more you want. Madonna, who at one stage was probably the most famous woman on the planet, said, 'I won't be happy until I am as famous as God.'

Celebrity and fame are only a pale reflection of true glory. 'Glory' is used in the Bible to denote the manifestation of God's presence. Glory is one of the most common words in the Bible. God's 'glory' means his importance, reputation, majesty and honour.

Perhaps it is not surprising that as society moves away from worshipping *the glory of God*, it turns towards the worship of the 'glory' of celebrity and fame. We are called to worship God's glory and reflect it, however imperfectly, in our lives.

READING FROM PSALMS

Psalm 26:1–12
Seek God's glory

David writes, 'GOD, I love living with you: your house glows with *your glory*' (v.8, MSG). King David was a 'celebrity' in his own right (see 1 Samuel 18:7). Yet he did not seek glory for himself, rather he led the people in giving glory to God: 'My feet stand on level ground; in the great congregation I will praise the LORD' (Psalm 26:12).

If you want to reflect the Lord's glory, follow David's example. Try to lead a blameless life (v.1). Trust in the Lord without wavering (v.1b). Try to keep your heart and mind pure (v.2). Be guided by God's love and truth (v.3). Avoid getting too close to people who might bring you down: 'tricksters'; 'thugs'; 'gangsters'; 'double-dealers' (vv.4–5, MSG).

Although David says, 'I lead a blameless life' (v.11a), he goes on to say, 'Deliver me and be merciful to me' (v.11b). He must have been conscious that, although he was trying to live a sinless life, he did not succeed and needed God's redemption and mercy. Rather than claiming to be sinless, David is declaring that he is living a life of 'integrity' (vv.1, 11, AMP), that is sincere and wholehearted for God.

Other kings at the time might have expected the people to worship them at the 'cult of their celebrity'. But David was a worshipper of the Lord. He writes, 'I ... go about your altar, LORD, proclaiming aloud *your* praise and telling of all *your* wonderful deeds. LORD I love the house where *you* live, the place where *your glory dwells*' (vv.6–8).

For the people of God in the Old Testament, the temple in Jerusalem was the place where God's glory could be found. But the glory of

God is supremely revealed in Jesus (John 1:14). Jesus is the new temple (2:10, 21).

Further, the amazing truth is that God's glory also dwells in all people who are trusting in Jesus. Both individually (see 1 Corinthians 6:19) and together (see 1 Corinthians 3:16), followers of Jesus are seen as God's temple in whom the Spirit dwells: 'Being built together to become *a dwelling* in which *God lives by his Spirit*' (Ephesians 2:22).

PRAYER

Lord, thank you that your glory dwells among your people. I will proclaim aloud your praise and tell of all your wonderful deeds.

NEW TESTAMENT READING

Mark 9:2–32
Reflect Jesus' glory

Peter, James and John caught a glimpse of the glory of God when Jesus was transfigured before them. The transfiguration came, not coincidentally, just after Jesus had asked the disciples, 'Who do people say I am?' (8:27). It revealed Jesus' divine nature as the Son of God.

The curtain of time was drawn aside and the disciples saw Moses (representing the Law) and Elijah (representing the prophets) clearly alive and alongside Jesus. The disciples would have known all about Moses and Elijah. In the Judaic world, these men were the ultimate celebrities. But God is saying that Jesus is *even greater* than these two revered men.

When the disciples looked again, they saw only Jesus (9:8). Peter, James and John saw Jesus as we will see him when he comes again, with his glory revealed.

The word used for 'transfigured' is the same word as is translated 'transformed' when the apostle Paul writes, 'And we all, who with unveiled faces contemplate the Lord's *glory*, are being *transformed* [transfigured] into his image with ever-increasing *glory*, which comes from the Lord, who is the Spirit' (2 Corinthians 3:18).

Celebrity today is often about fame and seeking publicity. Jesus did not seek publicity; rather the opposite. He 'swore them to secrecy. "Don't tell a soul what you saw"' (Mark 9:9, MSG).

Celebrity is also often associated with wealth and a luxurious lifestyle. In the life of Jesus, *suffering* and *glory* are inextricably linked. The moment he comes down from the mountain he explains to his disciples that 'the Son of Man must *suffer* much and be rejected' (v.12). Jesus' 'glory' was of a different kind to that which the world expects, then and now.

One thing Jesus does share with today's 'celebrities' is that he drew a crowd (v.14): 'As soon as all the people saw Jesus, they were *overwhelmed with wonder* and *ran to greet him*' (v.15).

The disciples who had not gone up the mountain did not have the faith necessary to heal the boy with an evil spirit. Jesus said, 'Everything is possible for him who believes' (v.23). The world says, 'I need to see first, then I will believe.' Jesus says, 'Believe first, then you will see.' St Augustine wrote, 'Faith is to believe what we do not see. The reward of faith is to see what we believe.'

The boy's father exclaims a tension we all feel from time to time: 'I do believe; help me overcome my unbelief!' (v.24).

Jesus heals the boy without any great ceremony or even, in this case, the laying on of hands. There is no drawn out battle but the simple power of the command of Jesus. The battle is already won through his prayer life (v.29). Again, we have seen a glimpse of the glory of Jesus.

Jesus goes straight on to speak about his suffering: 'The Son of Man is going to be delivered into the hands of men. They will kill him, and after three days he will rise' (v.31).

PRAYER

Lord, help me today to spend time in your presence and to reflect your glory in everything I do and say.

OLD TESTAMENT READING

Exodus 39:1–40:38
Await an eternity of glory

David caught a glimpse of God's glory when he entered the temple. The disciples caught a glimpse of God's glory when Jesus was transfigured before them. When you gather together with the people of God you should get a glimpse of God's glory.

When they had finished building the tabernacle ('The Dwelling', MSG) (which precedes the temple) the cloud covered the Tent of Meeting and '*the Glory of God* filled The Dwelling' (40:34, MSG). Moses could not enter the Tent of Meeting because the cloud had settled upon it and '*the Glory of God* filled The Dwelling' (v.35, MSG).

The glory of God was tangibly powerful at that moment. It could actually be seen 'settling' in the tabernacle. The Hebrew word for settling (*shekinah*) is sometimes used today to describe a particularly powerful or tangible sense of the presence and glory of God.

The *cloud* above the tabernacle, which represented the *glory of God*, accompanied the people of God in their travels and led them by day and by night (vv.36–38) as the Holy Spirit of God now leads you. This is the Old Testament background to the *cloud* in the story of the transfiguration. What Peter, James and John experienced on that occasion was a glimpse of the glory of the Lord (Mark 9:7).

Through 'the gospel that displays the *glory of Christ*' (2 Corinthians 4:4) you can get a glimpse of the glory of God. 'For God, who said, "Let light shine out of darkness," made his light shine in our hearts to give us the light of the knowledge of *God's glory displayed in the face of Christ*' (v.6).

It is only a glimpse and one day you will see the reality itself. The apostle Paul said that this is why you should not lose heart even when you are going through difficult times: 'For our light and momentary troubles are achieving for us an *eternal glory* that far outweighs them all' (v.17).

PRAYER

Lord, thank you that you are preparing us for the moment when you will reveal your full glory. Help me to see the struggles of life in the perspective of 'an eternal glory that far outweighs them all'.

27 February | Day 58
Six Characteristics of a Holy Life

Do you try to fit Jesus into your schedule? Or do you work your schedule around Jesus?

'God cannot fit into our plans, we must fit into his,' writes Eugene Peterson. 'We can't use God – God is not a tool or appliance or credit card. Holy is the word that sets God apart and above our attempts to enlist him in our wish-fulfilment fantasies or our utopian schemes for making our mark in the world. Holy means that God is alive on God's terms, alive in a way that exceeds our experience and imagination. Holy refers to life burning with an intense purity that transforms everything it touches into itself.'[1]

The Hebrew word 'holy' (*qadosh*) probably originally meant 'separate' or 'set apart'. It came to be used to describe the 'otherness' of God, and how his character and nature are so much greater and more wonderful than any other person or thing. For something else to be 'holy' simply means for it to be dedicated to God. You are holy to the extent that your life is devoted to him and your actions reflect his character. Holiness and *wholeness* are closely related, and God wants the *whole* of your life.

READING FROM PSALMS

Psalm 27:1–6
Worship the Lord in the beauty of holiness

How do you live a life without fear?

David had plenty of reasons to be afraid. He was surrounded by 'vandals', 'bullies' and 'toughs' (v.2, MSG). Yet he said, 'I'm fearless, afraid of no one and nothing' (v.1, MSG). 'I'm calm as a baby ... I'm collected and cool' (v.3, MSG). How can you be confident in the face of opposition and attack?

The focus of his life was *worship*. He focused on '*one thing*' (v.4). This was his number one priority. Don't try to fit God into your plans. Make your plans around the priority of worship.

David gives a wonderful description of worship. What he wants to do more than anything is 'to gaze upon *the beauty of the Lord* and to seek him in his temple' (v.4b). There he will 'sacrifice with shouts of joy; [he] will sing and make music to the Lord' (v.6b).

I love the expression 'the beauty of the Lord' (v.4b). The Greek word for 'beauty' (*kalos*) is the word used to describe everything that Jesus did (Mark 7:37). Dostoevsky described Jesus as 'positively beautiful'.[2] Jesus had no *outward* beauty (Isaiah 53:2–3); he had a different kind of beauty – the *beauty of holiness*.

As you seek the Lord and gaze upon the beauty of the Lord in worship, he lifts you above all the distractions, fears and temptations. As David puts it, 'That's the only quiet, secure place in a noisy world ... God holds me head and shoulders above those who try to pull me down' (Psalm 27:5–6, MSG).

PRAYER

Lord one thing I ask, that I may dwell in your house all the days of my life, to gaze on your beauty.

NEW TESTAMENT READING

Mark 9:33–10:12
Serve the Lord in a life of holiness

What should our attitude be to other Christian ministries and other Christian churches?

Divisions among followers of Jesus started very early on! The disciples started arguing about who was the greatest (9:33–34). In this context, Jesus speaks to them about the characteristics of a life of holiness.

1. Humility

Jesus tells them not to compete to be number one. It is always a temptation to compare. Envy and rivalry are great dangers. Jesus says if you are going to compete it should be to get the last place. If anyone wants to be first, they 'must be the very last, and the servant of all' (v.35). Leaders are called to humble service.

2. Love

'He took a little child whom he placed among them. Taking the child in his arms, he said to them, "Whoever welcomes one of these little children in my name welcomes me"' (vv.36–37). Love and welcome everyone, even those who are unable to do anything for you – the very young, the weak, the poor – in doing so you are loving and welcoming Jesus.

3. Tolerance

Jesus tells the disciples not to dismiss or judge others who do things 'in Jesus' name' just because they are not part of your group (vv.38–39, 41) or do things in a different manner to how you do them. It is a mistake to dismiss other Christians, other denominations or other organisations because they are *not 'one of us'* (v.38).

4. Discipline

We sometimes tolerate sin in our own lives but are intolerant towards other people's sin. Jesus teaches us to be tolerant towards others, but intolerant about sin in our own lives (vv.42–49).

Of course, Jesus is not speaking about literal maiming. Rather, he uses figurative language about what we do (with our hands, v.43), places we go (with our feet, v.45) and what we look at (with our eyes, v.47). Be disciplined, uncompromising and radical about sin. It is often sin that leads to division. Jesus calls us to be ruthless about living a life of holiness.

5. Peace

Jesus tells them not to argue but to be at peace. Jesus longed for his disciples to get along with one another, to stop arguing and to 'be at peace with each other' (v.50). Later, he prayed that we may be one in order that the world would believe (John 17:21).

6. Faithfulness

Jesus calls us to faithfulness in marriage. He points out that Moses' permission of divorce was a *concession* and not a *command*. God's intention for marriage is life-long faithfulness. Husband and wife are so closely united that they become one flesh: 'So they are no longer two, but one flesh' (Mark 10:8). This is the origin of the wonderful words in the marriage service, which follow the joining of hands and the exchange of vows: 'Therefore, what God has joined together, let no one separate' (v.9).

PRAYER

Lord, help me through the power of your Holy Spirit to live a holy life and to develop the characteristics of humility, love, tolerance, discipline, peace and faithfulness.

OLD TESTAMENT READING

Leviticus 1:1–3:17
Be holy as the Lord is holy

How can you live a holy life when the world around is unholy?

As the people of God are about to enter the promised land, there is what Eugene Peterson describes as a 'narrative pause'; an 'extended time-out of instruction, a detailed and meticulous preparation for living "holy" in a culture that doesn't have the faintest idea what "holy" is.'

'First', he writes, 'every detail of our lives is affected by the presence of this holy God.' You are called to holiness in *every* aspect of your day-to-day life. Second, he continues, 'God provides a way (the sacrifices and feasts and Sabbaths) to bring everything in and about us into his holy presence, transformed in the fiery blaze of the holy.'[3]

The language of Leviticus sounds very strange to our modern ears. The law required that the sacrifice be perfect – 'without defect' (1:3). Through the sacrifice, 'atonement' was made (v.4). Symbolically, through the laying on of hands on the head of the bulls, goats and lambs (for example 3:2, 8) the sin passed to a substitute who would be sacrificed on behalf of human beings. The blood of the sacrifice was extremely important (1:5; 3:2, 8, 13).

All this can only be understood fully in the light of the New Testament. The writer of Hebrews tells us that '*without the shedding of blood there is no forgiveness*' (Hebrews 9:22). He tells us that the law is a 'copy' (v.23) and a 'shadow' (10:1). In other words, this is just a foreshadowing and a picture of something far greater and more wonderful.

He writes, 'The law is only a shadow of the good things that are coming – not the realities themselves ... It *is impossible for the blood of bulls and goats to take away sins*' (vv.1, 4).

All this was leading up to 'the sacrifice of the body of Jesus Christ *once for all*' (v.10). 'By one sacrifice he has *made perfect* for ever those who are being *made holy*' (v.14). We receive total forgiveness; '*sacrifice for sin is no longer necessary*' (v.18).

So, the New Testament tells us none of these sacrifices are needed anymore. However, they form the background to the sacrifice of Jesus and help us to understand just how amazing it is. Holiness starts by putting your faith in what Jesus has done for you and asking his Holy Spirit to come into your life to help you to begin to live a holy life.

In gratitude for all that God has done for you, by the sacrifice of Jesus on your behalf, offer your body as 'a living sacrifice, *holy* and pleasing to God – this is your true and proper *worship*' (Romans 12:1–2).

PRAYER

Lord, full of thankfulness and praise, I offer you my body as a living sacrifice. Help me, through your Holy Spirit who lives in me, to be holy as you are holy.

---

28 February | Day 59
Rich in Mercy

A man was having his portrait painted by a successful artist. When the portrait was finished it was unveiled. The man was most unhappy with the result. When asked whether he liked it, he replied, 'I don't think it does me *justice*.' To which the artist replied, 'Sir, it is *not justice* you need, but *mercy*!'

At the end of the day we all need mercy even more than justice. God is '*rich in mercy*' (Ephesians 2:4). The theme of the 'mercy *of God*' runs throughout the Bible. In the original Greek, '*eleos*' (mercy) also means 'compassion, pity, clemency'. The mercy of God is available for you. In our passages for today we see some examples of people who are recipients of God's mercy.

READING FROM PSALMS

Psalm 27:7–14
The struggling

No matter what struggles you are facing in your life, hold on to God's promises. Expect to see God's goodness, not just in heaven when you die, but in the ordinary activities of your life here on earth ('in the land of the living', v.13).

David cries out to God, '*Be merciful to me*' (v.7b). Being falsely accused is a horrible experience. David faces 'oppressors' (v.11b) and 'false witnesses' (v.12b). Going through this very painful experience he cries out to God for mercy, and in the middle of all the accusations he is able to say, 'I *remain confident* of this: I will see *the goodness of the* LORD *in the land of the living*' (v.13).

The reason that David has this confidence is because he recognises that God is his Saviour (v.9b) and *a perfect parent*. 'Though my *father and mother* forsake me, the LORD will receive me' (v.10).

Many people today struggle as a result of a lack of love from their parents. But whatever your relationship with your parents, you can still begin to picture what a relationship with a perfect parent would look like.

God is such a parent. His faithfulness is without question. His generosity is perfect. His affection is tender and loving. His presence is permanent. His acceptance of you is unconditional. His communication is up-building and for your best interest. His authority is right and true.

When David writes that 'the LORD will receive me' (v.10b), he is thinking of those kinds of perfect parental attributes.

God is not going to fail you, especially when you are struggling. Some earthly parents only provide love and protection when they feel their children deserve it. Not God. The amazing truth is that our Father is merciful and gives us love and protection, even when we don't deserve it.

PRAYER

'Hear my voice when I call, LORD; *be merciful to me* and answer me. My heart says of you, "Seek his face!" Your face, LORD, I will seek ... Teach me your way, LORD' (vv.7–8, 11).

NEW TESTAMENT READING

Mark 10:13–31
The children

In a society that did not hold 'little children' (v.13) in high regard, Jesus had *compassion* on them (vv.13–16). He said, 'The kingdom of God *belongs to such as these*' (v.14b). He took them '*in his arms*, put his hands on them and *blessed them*' (v.16). We must make sure that as a church community we give children the same love, protection and priority that Jesus gave them – in terms of time, energy and resource.

In fact, Jesus tells us, whoever we are, however old we are, we all need to *learn from children* when it comes to being a part of the kingdom of God: 'I tell you the truth, anyone who will not receive the kingdom of God like *a little child* will never enter it' (v.15).

Jesus is not suggesting that we become like children in every aspect. We are not to give in to every childish whim or assume no responsibility for our actions. But, like children, we are to be open and receptive, to be honest about our feelings – acknowledging how fragile and vulnerable we are and how much we need others. Like children, be quick to forgive and quick to move on in trust.

Children are usually enthusiastic, appreciative and excited when given gifts. When it comes to God's kingdom, we are to be exactly the same – dependent on Jesus' gift to us and ready to accept it as a gift which we do not deserve, but which Jesus, in his mercy, offers to us.

PRAYER

Lord, help me to learn from children, to become like them in the right ways and to give them the same priority that you give them.

The poor

Jesus tells the rich young man to 'give to the poor' (v.21b). This surely is not just for his own benefit but because the poor were another high priority in Jesus' life and ministry.

PRAYER

Lord, help me to have the same love and compassion for the poor as you do.

The rich

The compassion of Jesus reached not just the poor but also the rich. Jesus looked at this rich young man and 'loved him' (v.21a). It is extremely hard for the rich to enter the kingdom of God (vv.24–25).

Rich people and even rich nations are sometimes more resistant to the gospel. Wealth can lead to arrogance and a wrong kind of self-reliance. Yet Jesus says it is not impossible for the rich to be saved: 'All things are possible with God' (v.27).

PRAYER

Lord, thank you that you are so merciful – not only to the poor but also to the rich.

The persecuted

Jesus says that *all* his followers will be persecuted (v.30). For some of us the 'persecutions' are very minor and trivial. People may laugh at you, ridicule you and oppose you. However, for millions of Christians around the world the persecutions are very real and physical.

This is part of the cost to following Jesus – persecution. There is always a cost to following Jesus. It may be that we lose friends or that Jesus calls us to leave a situation or a relationship. But the cost comes in a sandwich of blessing – in this life there is a hundredfold return (vv.29–30), 'and then the bonus of eternal life!' (v.30, MSG). God will be merciful to the persecuted.

PRAYER

Lord, thank you for the courage, example and inspiration of those who bear real hardship for you. Give me boldness to follow you whatever the cost.

OLD TESTAMENT READING

Leviticus 4:1–5:13
The guilty

We are all *guilty* of sin (James 2:10). The word '*guilt*' appears over and over again in this passage (Leviticus 4:3, 13, 22, 27; 5:2, 3, 4, 5). There is a *penalty* for sin (5:5–6). The apostle Paul tells us that the penalty for sin is death (Romans 6:23).

The elaborate sacrifices described in this passage were preparing the people for the *one perfect sacrifice of Jesus* who died for you and me (*the guilty*) so that *we might receive the mercy of God*.

- **Jesus made *atonement* for your sins**
Forgiveness does not come without *atonement* for sin (Leviticus 4:31, 35; 5:10, 13). One definition of atonement is 'the action of making amends for a wrong or injury that brings two parties together as one' – hence the word 'at-*one*-ment'. Ultimately, it is only Jesus who made the *perfect atonement* for our sins (Hebrews 2:17).

- **Jesus died as a *sacrifice* of atonement**
We read here of the elaborate sacrificial system of 'sin offerings' (Leviticus 4:3, 29, 33, 34; 5:9, 11, 12). Jesus died as the '*sacrifice of atonement*' (Romans 3:25) for your sin and mine.

- **Jesus was the *perfect* sacrifice**
The sacrifice had to be '*without defect*' (Leviticus 4:3, 28, 32). Ultimately, it was only Jesus – who was without sin – who could be the *perfect* sacrifice (Hebrews 5:9).

- **Jesus is *the Lamb* of God**
A *lamb* was brought as a sin offering (Leviticus 4:32). The guilty person had to lay their hands on its head. The lamb died as a sin offering to take away sin. Jesus is '*The Lamb of God*, who takes away the sin of the world!' (John 1:29).

- **Jesus' *blood* was shed for you**
The priest had to take some of 'the *blood* of the sin offering ... and pour out the rest of the blood' (Leviticus 4:34). The blood represented the life of the animal (17:11). Pouring out the blood was symbolic of the fact that the animal had died. This was in the place of the person making the sacrifice. The *blood* of Jesus was *poured out* for you and me (Matthew 26:28).

- **Jesus has made God's mercy available to all**
The words 'forgiveness' and 'forgiven' appear over and over again (Leviticus 4:20, 26, 31, 35; 5:10, 13). 'Without the shedding of blood there is no forgiveness' (Hebrews 9:22). Through Jesus' blood, forgiveness of sins is possible (Ephesians 1:7). As a result, God's mercy is available for you and me.

PRAYER

Lord, thank you so much that I no longer have to go through these elaborate processes to obtain mercy and forgiveness. Thank you that total forgiveness is available for me through Jesus. Thank you that in your great love for me you are 'rich in mercy' (2:4).

1 March | Day 60
My Eyes Were Opened

It was as if I was blind. I must have heard many times that Jesus died for our sins. But I simply did not see it. I was spiritually blind. But when I understood the cross, my eyes were opened.

Since then, I have noticed that as I have attempted to pass on the message of 'Christ crucified', there are different responses. Sometimes very intelligent people simply cannot see it (see 1 Corinthians 1:23–25). On the other hand, I am often amazed at the understanding of others, including very young children. For all who see it, it is life-changing: 'to us who are being *saved* it is the power of God' (1 Corinthians 1:18).

I think it is fascinating that in today's New Testament passage, after Jesus has explained his death, we have the story of blind Bartimaeus having his eyes opened (Mark 10:46–52). He says to Jesus, 'I want to see' (v.51). Jesus replies, '"Go ... your faith has *healed* you." Immediately he received his sight and followed Jesus' (v.52). The word used for *healed* is the same Greek word as *saved* (*sozo*).

Do you see it? The passages for today help us to see the significance of Jesus' death.

READING FROM PROVERBS

Proverbs 6:12–19
See God's *reaction* to evil

You cannot fully understand the cross unless you understand why it was necessary.

See God's hostile reaction to sin. The writer of Proverbs lists things that 'the Lord *hates*' and that are '*detestable* to him' (v.16a) – arrogance, lies, murder, evil plots, 'feet that race down a wicked track, a mouth that lies under oath, a troublemaker in the family' (vv.16–19, MSG).

God is love. God is also just and holy. The kind of sin listed here causes enormous damage to our lives, the lives of others and to society. Take, for example, a person 'who stirs up dissention' (v.19). Think how much damage can be done by one person bringing division in a family or in the church, neighbourhood or nation.

God's hatred is not like ours: it contains no element of spite, pettiness or hypocrisy – but it is the reaction of the altogether holy and loving God to sin. His anger is his loving and holy hostility to evil.

When we realise the extent of God's hostility to sin that led to the cross, the only real response we can make is to turn to God in prayer to ask for forgiveness and help.

PRAYER

Merciful Lord, you know our struggle to serve you: when sin spoils our lives and overshadows our hearts, come to our aid and turn us back to you again; through Jesus Christ our Lord.[1]

NEW TESTAMENT READING

Mark 10:32–52
See the *results* of the cross

If Jesus asked you, 'What do you want me to do for you?', how would you reply? In this passage Jesus asks this question twice (vv.36, 51). The disciples give the wrong answer (v.37). Bartimaeus gives the right answer: '*I want to see*' (v.51).

Some people simply do not see it. Some have described the death of Jesus as 'unexpected and tragic'. But, in fact, it was planned, prophesied and predicted.

This passage in Mark's Gospel (vv.32–34) is the third and most detailed prediction Jesus gave about his death. It shows us that Jesus *expected* his own death and even his resurrection (vv.33–34). His death was *not unexpected*. It was *a deliberate choice*. It would end *not in tragedy*, but in *triumph*.

Further, he had a clear understanding of the *purpose* of his death and the results: 'For even the Son of Man did not come to be served, *but to serve, and to give his life as a ransom for many*' (v.45).

The background to Jesus' understanding of his own death includes Isaiah 53 – one of the 'suffering servant' passages. We see here clear evidence that Jesus saw his own death in terms of this 'suffering servant'.

1. Suffering

Why did Jesus come into this world? He understood that the whole purpose of his mission was *to suffer*. This is the reason he '*came*' (Mark 10:45b). He came to give his life for you and me.

2. Servant

Jesus uses the expression 'to *serve*' (v.45a). He saw himself as '*the servant*'. He came not to be served, but '*to serve*'. The expression '*to give his life*' (v.45b) echoes the words of the servant in Isaiah 53:10 ('makes his life *an offering for sin*') and Isaiah 53:12 ('he *poured out* his life unto death').

3. Saviour

The word 'ransom' (Mark 10:45b) is used of prisoners of war and slaves. It means the price paid for *redemption* (Numbers 18:15–16). It is paid to set the captives free. Jesus' death on the cross saves you and me by setting us free.

4. Substitute

The word translated '*for*' in Mark 10:45 is the Greek word *anti* which means '*in place of*', and it suggests the idea of substitution. It is this idea of suffering in our place that so strongly underlies Isaiah 53. By using these words Jesus showed that he believed that his death was not accidental or for his own sin, but suffering '*in the place of*' others who would otherwise have had to suffer.

Further, Jesus understood his own death in the light of the metaphor of *the cup* (Mark 10:38). The Old Testament speaks of the cup of God's 'wrath' against sin. Jesus speaks of 'the cup I drink' (v.38). He saw himself as drinking the cup of God's hostile reaction to sin on our behalf.

By his death and resurrection Jesus defeated sin, evil and death. As a result, you can be forgiven, set free from guilt, shame and addictions. You can be sure of the ultimate triumph of good over evil. You need not fear the future. Death itself has been defeated.

When Jesus asked his disciples, 'What do you want me to do for you?', they gave the wrong answer. They wanted *position* (v.37). It's always a temptation for Christian leaders to compete with one another for the most prominent position.

We are called to follow Jesus, serving him and each other. Spiritual ambition is not wrong, but it is possible to have the wrong sort of spiritual ambition. This could be as subtle as seeking our own glory rather than being ambitious for Jesus. Jesus says, 'Whoever wants to become great among you must be your servant' (v.43).

Of course, for most of us, most of the time, our motives are mixed. Where we, like the disciples, are tempted to seek our own position, prospects, promotion, pay and popularity, Jesus says four words to us: '*Not so with you*' (v.43). You are called to serve because it is the pattern of Jesus to serve.

The clothes of authentic discipleship are not the purple robes of an emperor, but the crown of thorns of our Saviour. It is about a cross, not a throne. It is a life laid down for others.

Let's follow the example of Bartimaeus who cried out to Jesus for mercy (v.47). Jesus always responds when you cry for mercy. Bartimaeus asked for his sight. His eyes were opened and he saw Jesus.

Ask God today to open your eyes to see Jesus and understand all that he has done for you through his death on the cross *for you*.

PRAYER

Lord, open my eyes to see you more clearly, love you more dearly and follow you more nearly.[2]

OLD TESTAMENT READING

Leviticus 5:14–7:10
See the *reason* for his death

Here again we see the background to Jesus' understanding of his own death. The 'guilt offering' provided a 'penalty' (5:15) for sin. It leads to forgiveness (v.16) and involves blood being shed (7:2). This foreshadows what Jesus was going to do on the cross for you and me.

As I began to understand the Old Testament background and the seriousness of my own sin, I began to understand more and more the enormity of the sacrifice that Jesus made on my behalf. When Jesus bore with his own body God's hostile reaction to my sin, he made it possible for me to be forgiven and to experience life in all its fullness.

My experience was similar to that of blind Bartimaeus. My blindness had not been physical but spiritual. Like him I cried out, 'Jesus ... have *mercy* on me' (Mark 10:47–48). I received my sight and followed Jesus. It was not something I earned. It was a gift I received by faith, just as Jesus said to Bartimaeus, 'Go ... your faith has healed [saved] you' (v.52).

PRAYER

Lord, thank you for opening my eyes to understand the enormity of your sacrifice on my behalf. Thank you that I can never earn forgiveness but can only receive it as a gift by faith. Help me, like Bartimaeus, to follow you and to give my life in service to you and other people.

2 March | Day 61
A Loving, Ongoing Relationship

In spite of the fact that he had amassed a huge fortune and had attracted thousands of fans, Freddie Mercury, the lead singer of the rock group Queen, admitted in an interview shortly before his death in 1991 that he was *desperately lonely*. He said, 'You can have everything in the world and still be the loneliest man, and that is the most bitter type of loneliness. Success has brought me *world idolisation* and *millions of pounds*, but it's prevented me from having the one thing we all need – *a loving, ongoing relationship*.'[1]

There is only one relationship that is completely loving and ongoing, and for which we were created. Without that relationship there will always be a deep sense of aloneness and a lack of ultimate meaning and purpose.

At the heart of the Christian faith is this relationship with God where we find meaning and purpose and the answer to loneliness.

How can you and I have a relationship with the Creator of the universe? How in practice can we begin to communicate with God? What is the basis of this relationship?

READING FROM PSALMS

Psalm 28:1–9
Develop a pattern of *prayer*

Prayer is a key way to develop a relationship with God by speaking with him. There is no set way to do this. There are hundreds of different prayers in the Bible. Sometimes, it is helpful to follow a pattern (such as the Lord's Prayer). Another pattern that I have found helpful is using the mnemonic 'ACTS'. These elements are often found in the prayers we see in Scripture.

The context of this psalm is fear – possibly the fear of premature death. David may be facing illness or deep despair. He fears that he might die in disgrace and go down 'to the pit' (v.1).

His prayer to God includes the following:

1. A: Lord I *adore* you

'*Praise* be to the Lord' (v.6a); even in the midst of a difficult situation, David chose to praise God. Whatever the circumstances, praise God for *who* he is and *what* he has done. We see another example of this in the New Testament passage as the people worship Jesus (Mark 11:9–10).

2. C: I *confess*

'Hear my cry for *mercy*' (Psalm 28:2a); ask God's forgiveness for anything that you have done wrong. This is also a moment to forgive anyone you need to forgive. As Jesus says in todays' New Testament passage, 'When you stand praying, if you hold anything against anyone, forgive them, so that your Father in heaven may forgive you your sins' (Mark 11:25).

3. T: I will give you *thanks*

'My heart leaps for joy, and with my song I praise him' (Psalm 28:7c). Thank God for health, family, friends and so on. The importance of thanksgiving can also be seen in the Old Testament reading for today (see Leviticus 7:12–15).

4. S: Hear my *supplication*

'...as I *call* to you *for help*' (Psalm 28:2a). Pray for yourself, for your friends and for others. Interestingly David says, 'I lift up my hands' (v.2b). This seems to be almost synonymous with prayer. Hands raised in worship is not a modern idea; it is actually one of the most ancient forms of prayer.

PRAYER

Lord, I *adore* you. I worship you today. Praise be to the Lord...
I *confess* my sins to you ... Hear my cry for mercy and forgive my sins.
I will give *thanks* to you for you are good. Thank you, Lord, for...
Hear my *supplication*. Today I call on you for help...

NEW TESTAMENT READING

Mark 11:1–25
Pray in faith

The great emphasis of the New Testament is that we relate to God by faith. We cannot earn the right to a relationship with God; it is a gift to be received by faith. In this passage we see the importance that Jesus placed on faith. He said, 'Have faith in God' (v.22). He says that by faith you can move mountains if you do not doubt in your heart but instead *believe* (v.23).

Jesus' relationship with God, particularly through prayer, lies at the heart of each of the incidents we read about today. As Jesus approaches Jerusalem the people worship him. They cry out 'Hosanna' (vv.9–10), which was originally both a cry of happiness and a cry for help, meaning 'save, we *pray'* or 'save now'.

On reaching Jerusalem, Jesus drives out the money-changers because of his passion for the purity of God's house. He says, 'Is it not written: "My house will be called a *house of prayer* for all nations?"' (v.17).

The passage ends with Jesus teaching his disciples that *lack of forgiveness* can be *a barrier to prayer* and to your relationship with God. He says, 'And when you stand *praying*, if you hold *anything* against *anyone*, forgive them, so that your Father in heaven may forgive you your sins' (v.25).

Jesus says we are not to hold '*anything against anyone*'. There are no limits to forgiveness. Lack of forgiveness destroys relationships.

Forgiveness sometimes takes great courage but it restores relationships and brings great joy. It is said that, 'The first to apologise is the bravest. The first to forgive is the strongest. The first to forget is the happiest.'

Intertwined in these events, Jesus demonstrates the power of prayer in the acted parable of the fig-tree. From this he teaches his disciples about the importance of faith and fruit in our relationship with God.

The fig-tree had leaves but no fruit. Jesus said to it: 'May no one ever eat fruit from you again' (v.14). I love the way Joyce Meyer applies this parable: 'If our lives revolve around the church but we have no fruit, we are not living our faith.' We can read our Bibles, listen to Christian podcasts and go to prayer meetings, but 'if we do not have time to help anyone else or even show kindness, we are like the fig- tree with leaves but no fruit ... if we have leaves, we need to also have fruit'.[2]

Jesus uses hyperbole to explain that we must be absolutely confident in God's readiness to respond to faith. In Rabbinic literature, 'mountain' is sometimes used figuratively to denote an obstacle. Jesus seems to be saying that God will come in response to faith to remove *seemingly impossible obstacles*. He says, 'Therefore I tell you, whatever you ask for in prayer, believe that you have received it, and it will be yours' (v.24).

PRAYER

Lord, please help me never to hold any lack of forgiveness in my heart. Help me to forgive. Thank you for your amazing promise that 'whatever you ask for in prayer, believe that you have received it, and it will be yours' (v.24). Lord, today I ask...

OLD TESTAMENT READING

Leviticus 7:11–8:36
Approach God through Jesus

The way to relate to God in the Old Testament was through the priesthood. Because of sin, human beings could not relate directly to God. They needed to go through a priest, and in particular they needed a high priest.

In this passage, we see how Aaron was anointed for this task. Moses 'poured some of the anointing oil on Aaron's head and anointed him to consecrate him' (8:12). Aaron was a forerunner of Jesus Christ. The word Christ means 'the anointed one'. Aaron's priesthood was fallible; he had to offer sacrifices for his own sins as well as the people's. Jesus is the great high priest. Through Jesus you can relate to God with confidence and have a direct relationship with him.

As the writer of Hebrews puts it, 'Therefore, since we have a great high priest who has ascended into heaven, Jesus the Son of God, let us hold firmly to the faith we profess. For we do not have a high priest who is unable to feel sympathy for our weaknesses, but we have one who has been tempted in every way, just as we are – yet he did not sin. Let us then approach God's throne of grace with *confidence*, so that we may receive mercy and find grace to help us in our time of need' (Hebrews 4:14–16).

In fact, because of Jesus' sacrifice for your sins, you are in an even better position than the Old Testament priests (compare Hebrews 10:22 with Leviticus 8:30). Through repentance and forgiveness your relationship with God is utterly transformed and you can come directly into God's presence, just as the Old Testament priests did when they entered the Tent of Meeting. 'Let us draw near to God with a sincere heart and with the full assurance that faith brings, having our hearts sprinkled to cleanse us from a guilty conscience' (Hebrews 10:22).

PRAYER

Lord, thank you that through Jesus I can approach the throne of grace with confidence and receive mercy and grace. Help me to stay close to you and walk in a *loving, ongoing relationship* with you.

3 March | Day 62
How to Exercise Spiritual Authority

I first met him when he came to speak at a student weekend while I was studying at Cambridge University. Although he was the guest speaker, he was very gracious and I sensed a deep humility.

When he spoke, he did so with real authority. His message was simple and focused on telling people about Jesus. A few years later he came to be the vicar of Holy Trinity Brompton.

This modest and deeply spiritual man not only led our church (and others) at a key moment in its growth, but also trained some of the most influential Christian leaders in the UK over the last 40 years. David Watson, David MacInnes, Sandy Millar and John Irvine were all curates to *John Collins*, a clergyman who has never sought prominence or platform, but who has invested his whole life in serving others.

His authority does not come from his position in life or from worldly power. Rather, his authority comes from his relationship with Jesus Christ. It is self-authenticating.

Today people are very wary of authority. Of course, it can be abused. However, godly, spiritual authority is a source of great blessing.

READING FROM PSALMS

Psalm 29:1–11
Voice of authority

There is a huge spiritual hunger and need in our society. People are searching for spiritual knowledge and experience. This psalm points us towards '*the voice of the Lord*' (v.3). David describes the awesome power, majesty and *authority* of God's voice (vv.4–5a,7–9a).

Today, the supreme way we hear the voice of the Lord is through the words of the Bible. The word of God is authoritative, powerful and majestic: 'We fall to our knees – we call out, "Glory!"' (v.9, MSG). Being on our knees is an appropriate way to listen to the voice of the Lord. I love to start each day on my knees, reading the Bible, trying to hear God's voice – asking, 'Lord, what are you saying to me today?'

David starts by saying, 'Ascribe to the Lord, you heavenly beings, ascribe to the Lord glory and *strength*' (v.1). All authority, power and strength belong to God. However, he does not keep it all to himself. As you listen to his voice he shares with you his authority, power and strength. David ends with, 'The Lord gives *strength* to his people' and 'blesses his people with *peace*' (v.11).

These are two things that we desperately need as we face the battles of life (internal and external). We need God's 'strength' and his 'peace'.

PRAYER

Lord, thank you that you share with us your authority, power and strength. Please strengthen me for the battles of today and give me peace in the midst of the storms of life.

NEW TESTAMENT READING

Mark 11:27–12:12
God-given authority

Jesus spoke and acted with God-given authority. He listened to the voice of the Lord and spoke the very words of God. This is the key. If you want to speak with authority, spend time with God, listening to his voice.

It was perfectly obvious to everyone that Jesus had authority. The only question his opponents asked was *where that authority came from* (11:28). Jesus responded with a brilliant question about John the Baptist.

He asked them whether John's authority was from God ('heaven') or of 'human origin' (v.30). They could not answer the question because they did not want to admit it came from God (as they had not believed him) (v.31). Nor did they want to say that it came from human origin because the people recognised that John was a true prophet (v.32).

I once heard a preacher, who believed that the supernatural gifts of the Holy Spirit ended with the apostolic age, being asked the question, 'Is the Pentecostal movement a move of God?' It provoked a similar response to the one in today's passage – he could not answer the question.

To say that 'it came from God' would mean recognising the outpouring of the supernatural gifts of the Holy Spirit in our contemporary world. To deny that it came from God would be to deny the experience of over 600 million

Christians around the world who have experienced God's power through the Pentecostal movement.

Because Jesus' interrogators refuse to answer his question about John the Baptist, Jesus refuses to answer their question about his authority. 'Jesus said, "Neither will I tell you by what authority I am doing these things"' (v.33b).

Jesus then tells a parable, which is intended to reveal *the source of his authority*. His opponents certainly recognise Jesus' aim, for Mark tells us that they 'looked for a way to arrest [Jesus] because they knew he had spoken the parable against them' (12:12).

Jesus' parable is about a man who 'planted a vineyard ... put a wall around it, dug a pit for the winepress and built a watchtower' (v.1). The parable is based on Isaiah 5:1–7 in which God is the owner and his people (particularly the leaders) are the vineyard. In Jesus' parable, the servants who are sent and killed are God's prophets, including John the Baptist. Jesus then *introduces himself* into his own parable: God 'had one left to send, *a son*, whom he loved. He sent him last of all, saying, "They will respect *my son*."' (Mark 12:6).

Jesus shows he has a *unique authority* because he is the *unique Son of God*. There is a very clear distinction made between the unique beloved son and heir and the different servants who are sent first. Yet, with amazing foresight, Jesus declares that he, the unique Son of God, *will be killed* (vv.7–8).

He then explains that the leadership of God's people will be transferred to a new leadership (the early leaders of the church) with Jesus as their cornerstone: 'The stone the builders rejected [that] has become *the cornerstone*' (v.10; see also Psalm 118:22).

The unique Son of God has unique authority as the unique cornerstone of God's people. Listen to him and you too will speak with the authority that derives from his authority.

PRAYER

Lord, thank you that you are the unique Son of God who spoke with the authority of God himself. Help me to walk in a close relationship with you, hear your voice and speak your words with authority.

OLD TESTAMENT READING

Leviticus 9:1–10:20
Authority of Jesus

It is an awesome thing to enter into the presence of God – 'The Glory of God appeared to all the people. Fire blazed out from God ... When all the people saw it happen they cheered loudly and then fell down, bowing in reverence' (9:23–24, MSG).

The example of Nadab and Abihu (10:1–2) shows that access to God's presence should never be taken for granted. People today often want a relationship with God on their own terms and in their own way. However, it is only because of Jesus that you can enter God's presence with confidence and without fear.

Access to the presence of God was made possible, in the Old Testament, through the complex sacrificial system. The high priest had to offer sacrifices for himself and the people (9:7–8). Because the high priest was a human being and, like us, was weak and sinful, he had to go on offering sacrifices for his own sin as well as the sins of the people.

Jesus has a unique authority. He is the sinless high priest. As the writer of Hebrews puts it: 'Such a high priest truly meets our need – one who is *holy, blameless, pure, set apart from sinners, exalted above the heavens*. Unlike the other high priests, he does not need to offer sacrifices day after day, first for his own sins, and then for the sins of the people. He sacrificed for their sins *once for all* when he offered himself' (Hebrews 7:26–27).

As a result, through Jesus you have access to the holy presence of God: 'Therefore, brothers and sisters, since we have *confidence* to enter the Most Holy Place by the blood of Jesus, by a new and living way opened for us through the curtain, that is, his body, and since we have a great priest over the house of God, let us draw near to God with a sincere heart and with the *full assurance that faith brings*, having our hearts sprinkled to cleanse us from a guilty conscience and having our bodies washed with pure water' (10:19–22).

You can come into the presence of God today and hear the voice of the Lord, receive his strength and peace, and speak with the authority that comes from having heard the voice of God.

PRAYER

Lord, thank you that I now have access to the Most Holy Place by the blood of Jesus. Today I want to draw near to God with a sincere heart in full assurance of faith to hear the voice of the Lord, receive his strength and peace, and speak with the authority that comes from having heard the voice of God.

4 March | Day 63

How to Enjoy a Lifetime of Favour

When I was at university I was taken to a talk entitled, 'Where will you be in ten years' time?' It was intended to be an encouragement to us to persevere in our faith in spite of all the challenges that life would hold after university. All that I can remember is thinking at the time, 'Ten years! That is a lifetime away.' I could not even begin to imagine that far ahead.

Now, by contrast, I look back at my life and ten years ago seems like yesterday. Life has flown past. It seems to be accelerating at an alarming rate. I now understand the wisdom of those who encouraged us early on to take the long view.

We live in a society of instant gratification. Instant meals. Instant messaging. Instant cash. Instant loans. Instant fake tans. Instant fortunes won. There is a great danger of short-termism. The passages for today remind us that God is the 'everlasting God' (Isaiah 40:28). God views things through a wide-angled lens: he takes a long view and he wants you to enjoy a lifetime of his favour (Psalm 30:5).

READING FROM PSALMS

Psalm 30:1–7
The long view of life

Are you going through a difficult time? Do you wonder whether it will last for ever?

God's 'favour lasts a lifetime' (v.5). As David looked back on his life, he was filled with thankfulness and 'praise' (v.4). Yes, he had been through some very difficult times. But God 'lifted [him] out of the depths and did not let [his] enemies gloat over [him]' (v.1). When he called to God for help, God 'healed' him (v.2).

> 'GOD, my God, I yelled for help
> and you put me together.
> GOD, you pulled me out of the grave,
> gave me another chance at life
> when I was down-and-out' (vv.2–3, MSG).

David had times when God was angry with him (v.5) and where God hid his face from him (v.7b). (After all, David did commit adultery and murder.) Yet, as he looked back on his life he was able to see that the moments of trial and testing were in the context of a lifetime of God's favour.

PRAYER

Father, thank you that your anger lasts only a moment but your favour lasts a lifetime. Thank you that you are the same yesterday, today and for ever and I can trust you.

NEW TESTAMENT READING

Mark 12:13–27
The long view of eternity

What happens to people when they die? Is death really the end? You may have lost a family member or close friend and you wonder whether you will ever see them again. Where are they now? Are they gone for ever? Are they just asleep? Or are they, in some way, alive?

Jesus' opponents were constantly trying to catch him out with their questions (v.13).

First, they tried to trap him over money. However, even they recognised that Jesus was 'a man of integrity'. They knew that Jesus spoke the truth whether or not it was popular (v.14). Jesus avoided the trap and gave an amazing answer (vv.15–17).

Next, they asked Jesus a hypothetical question to test him. This one was about life after death. There was an internal debate in Judaism between the Pharisees and the Sadducees about whether or not there was life after death. [The way I remember the distinction is that it was the Pharisees ('far I see') who did believe in the resurrection, whereas the Sadducees ('sad you see') did not.]

Jesus pointed out that the Sadducees were wrong for two reasons: First, they did 'not know *the Scriptures*', and second, they did not know '*the power of God*' (v.24).

1. The Scriptures

Jesus affirms the absolute certainty of the resurrection of the dead. Since the Sadducees only really believed in the authority of the Pentateuch (the first five books of the Bible) Jesus bases his argument on them and quotes from Exodus 3:6: 'Now about the dead rising – have you not read in the Book of Moses, in the account of the burning bush, how God said to him, "I am the God of Abraham, the God of Isaac, and the God of Jacob"? He is not the God of the dead, but of the living' (Mark 12:26–27). In other words, Abraham, Isaac and Jacob are still living now!

2. The Power of God

In 1 Corinthians 15, there is the most sustained and in-depth argument of the New Testament on the subject of the resurrection of the dead. Paul emphasises again and again *the power of God,* which the Sadducees denied. He writes that the body is sown 'in weakness', yet it is raised as a resurrection body after death, '*in power*' (1 Corinthians 15:43). God 'gives us the victory through our Lord Jesus Christ' (vv.56–57).

The wonderful truth is that the same power that was at work in raising Christ from the dead is at work in you *now,* bringing you more into the likeness of Christ (see Ephesians 1:19–20), and also *in the future,* in bringing your body to be a resurrection body in the new creation.

Therefore, everyone who has died in Christ is still *living now*. You will see them again. Even though the separation is so hard, all the struggles of this life have to be seen in terms of eternity. God takes the long view.

PRAYER

Thank you so much, Lord, that this life is not the end. Thank you that the dead will rise. Help me to see all the struggles of this life in the light of eternity.

OLD TESTAMENT READING

Leviticus 11:1–12:8
The long view of history

What on earth is the point of all these regulations in Leviticus? Why are they in the Bible?

As always, we understand the Old Testament in the light of the New Testament and, in particular, through the lens of Jesus. God had a long-term plan. He was preparing the world for the coming of Christ.

The New Testament tells us that all these seemingly strange regulations that we read about in today's passage are only 'a shadow of the things that were to come; the reality, however, is found in Christ' (Colossians 2:17). The purpose of the regulations was to teach about holiness – 'I am the Lord your God; consecrate yourselves and be holy, because I am holy' (Leviticus 11:44).

Peter quotes this verse in his first letter when encouraging holy living among the early Christians. He writes, 'As obedient children, do not conform to the evil desires you had when you lived in ignorance. But just as he who called you is holy, so be holy in all you do; for it is written: "Be holy, because I am holy"' (1 Peter 1:14–16).

Yet the New Testament also tells us that God has now made us holy through Christ. Therefore, the apostle Paul also says, 'Do not let anyone judge you by what you eat or drink' (Colossians 2:16). All these regulations have now been superseded through the coming of Jesus.

Many of the regulations were probably there for very practical reasons. For example, the eating of pigs (as carriers of disease) may well have been banned chiefly as a danger to health. Similarly, the rules of decontamination, strict as they are, take account of practical necessities. God wants you to eat wisely and healthily!

Purification after childbirth was not about moral uncleanness but ceremonial uncleanness (Leviticus 12:2). The cleansing was from the 'flow of blood' (v.7), not from any guilt attached to marital intercourse or childbirth. These regulations may actually have been a great blessing to women who had recently given birth. The extended period of separation from wider society would have protected her from having to return to the hustle and bustle of normal life too quickly after childbirth.

This passage also gives us a clue to Jesus' background. It shows the poverty from which he came; Mary could not 'afford a lamb' (v.8). When Mary and Joseph went to Jerusalem '*for the purification rites required by the Law* of Moses' they offered 'a pair of doves or two young pigeons' (v.8; Luke 2:22–24).

God had a long-term plan for the birth of his Son under these laws. God was working all the way through history to prepare the ground for Jesus. Jesus was born under the law. He fulfilled the law and brought all these regulations to an end on the cross. He rose from the dead and made it possible for us too, one day, to rise from the dead and to become, along with Jesus, heirs of God (Galatians 4:4–7).

PRAYER

Lord, thank you that I am no longer under law. Thank you that I have received adoption as your child and that you have sent the Spirit of Jesus into my heart. Thank you that I will spend all eternity with you. Help me to take the long view and to enjoy a lifetime of your favour.

5 March | Day 64
How to Keep Healthy

According to the American Heart Association, these are the seven things that you should do to keep your physical heart healthy:

1. Avoid smoking and using tobacco products
2. Be physically active every day
3. Eat a heart-healthy diet
4. Maintain a healthy weight
5. Manage your blood pressure
6. Control your total cholesterol
7. Keep your blood sugar healthy.[1]

The human heart weighs less than a pound (450g). It beats 100,000 times a day and over 2.5 billion times in the average lifetime. Your system of blood vessels – arteries, veins and capillaries – is over 60,000 miles long – enough to go around the world more than twice.

This is not just an amazing spectacle; it is the 'heart' of human life. Without your heart your body would quickly cease to work. Heart disease is the number one cause of death in the Western world.

Jesus spoke a great deal about the heart. The heart is a metaphor for the inner life. The word Jesus used means the seat of the physical, spiritual and mental life. The heart is the centre and the source of the whole inner life – thinking, feeling, and willing.

God is concerned, primarily, about your heart. He wants you to have a healthy heart. He said to Samuel, 'The Lord does not look at the things people look at. People look at the outward appearance, but the Lord looks at the heart' (1 Samuel 16:7).

Even more important than a healthy physical heart is the condition of your spiritual heart. In the passages for today we see five key ways to keep your spiritual heart healthy.

READING FROM PROVERBS

Proverbs 6:20–29
1. Guard your heart

Jesus taught that adultery starts in the heart. He said, 'I tell you that anyone who looks at a woman lustfully has already committed adultery with her *in his heart*' (Matthew 5:28). His teaching goes back to the book of Proverbs where the writer emphasises the importance of the heart – 'do not lust in *your heart*' (Proverbs 6:25).

He warns of the terrible dangers of adultery. We are dealing with something so powerful it is like a fire. In its right place (just like fire in the fireplace) sex, within marriage, is a source of great blessing. However, if you allow your sexual desires to go in the wrong direction then it is like fire in your lap: 'Can a man scoop fire into his lap without his clothes being burned? Can a man walk on hot coals without his feet being scorched? So is he who sleeps with another man's wife' (vv.27–29a).

Adultery does not usually just appear from nowhere. The unfaithfulness starts with the heart. This is where we have to exercise self-discipline. Take these words of wisdom and 'bind them upon *your heart*' (v.21).

PRAYER

Lord, help me to take your words and bind them upon my heart. When I walk, may they guide me. When I sleep, may they watch over me. When I awake, may they speak to me. May they be like a lamp and a light keeping me on the way to life. Guard my heart, Lord.

NEW TESTAMENT READING

Mark 12:28–44
2. Love Jesus with your whole heart

Mark 12:28–37

There is something *delightful* about the *teaching of Jesus*: 'The large crowd listened to him *with delight*' (v.37b). If I were asked to summarise this teaching in one word, I would use the word *'love'*.

When Jesus is asked by a lawyer which of all the commandments is the most important, he replies, '"*Love* the Lord your God with all your *heart* and with all your soul and with all your mind and with all your strength." The second is this: "*Love* your neighbour as yourself"' (vv.30–31). At the centre of the message of Jesus is a love relationship with the Lord your God, which starts with your heart and overflows into a love for other people.

Who is 'the Lord'? The question underlying all this quizzing of Jesus is, 'Who does this man think he is?' In the temple courts, Jesus turns the tables on them by challenging their assumptions about the coming Messiah ('the Christ', v.35).

He asks them a question quoting Psalm 110. He challenges the idea that the Christ will simply be a king from David's line. He will not only be a son of David, he will be David's *Lord* (Mark 12:35–37a).

We now know that Jesus is '*the Lord*'. The command to *love the Lord* with all your heart is a command to *love Jesus* with all your heart. Make this the number one priority of your life.

Jesus is concerned, not with legalistic literalism, but with the *spirit* of the law. He is concerned not with outward appearances *but with the heart*.

3. Focus on your heart

Mark 12:38–40

Speaking for myself, I find that hypocrisy is always a danger in my own life. It is a temptation to be concerned about position, platforms, titles and honours. And we have to be careful about praying prayers to impress, rather than from the heart.

Jesus criticises the leaders of his day because their hearts are not right. They are far more concerned about outward appearances than about their own hearts. He says, 'They love to walk around in academic gowns, preening in the radiance of public flattery, basking in prominent positions, sitting at the head table at every church function. And all the time they are exploiting the weak and helpless. The longer their prayers, the worse they get' (vv.38–40, MSG).

All the things mentioned indicate their love of being shown deference and of receiving honour from other people. But God is not concerned about status and 'show' (v.40). He is concerned about our hearts.

4. Give from your heart

Mark 12:41–44

Jesus is not concerned about the size of your wallet. He is concerned about the size of your heart.

Jesus challenged the conventional assumption that large gifts are worth more to God than small ones. He encourages us that it is not only the rich who can please God through their giving – the poor can do so as well. He challenges the rich that it is not enough simply to give sums that greatly surpass that of the poor. Jesus was looking for generous and sacrificial hearts.

What we give, and the way in which we give, reflects our hearts. Jesus does not actually criticise the rich people who throw in large amounts of money. But he does say that the poor widow who gives 'two very small copper coins, worth only a few pence' (v.42) has put in more than all the others.

Jesus sees her heart and the fact that 'this poor widow gave more to the [offering] than all the others put together. All the others gave what they'll never miss; she gave extravagantly what she couldn't afford – she gave her all' (vv.43–44, MSG). Others look at the outward appearance; Jesus looks at the heart. It is not the amount, but the attitude of the heart that matters to God.

PRAYER

Lord, help me to love you with all of my heart and with all of my soul and with all of my mind and with all of my strength. Forgive me for the times that I have been concerned about status or show, and help me to focus not on outward appearance but on the heart. Lord, help me to be generous and sacrificial in my giving. Give me a generous heart.

OLD TESTAMENT READING

Leviticus 13:1–59

5. Keep your heart holy

The Old Testament laws covered every aspect of life, including cleanliness, health and hygiene. As a result, we read a great deal in the Old Testament about the kinds of regulations set out in this chapter, in addition to all the burnt offerings and sacrifices. These rules and regulations were all concerned with *holiness* though, and their motivation was supposed to stem from a desire to please and emulate God (Leviticus 11:44). In other words, the outward rituals were supposed to reflect the inner attitudes of the heart.

At the time of Jesus, many of the teachers were putting the emphasis in the wrong place. They thought that holiness could be attained simply by obeying a whole lot of rules that concerned outward behaviour and actions, rather than heartfelt obedience towards God.

Jesus pointed out that there is something far more important than all of this. As we see in today's New Testament passage, 'To love [God] with all your heart, with all your understanding and with all your strength, and to love your neighbour as yourself is *more important* than all burnt offerings and sacrifices' (Mark 12:33). Holiness is not a matter of outward appearance. It is a matter of the heart.

PRAYER

Lord, help me to guard my heart from spiritual heart disease. May we be a community of love – loving you and loving one another. Please fill my heart today with your Holy Spirit and keep my heart holy and healthy.

6 March | Day 65
Turn Your Life Around

'Big John' had been living on the streets of London for over ten years. Before that he had spent over nine years in prison. Most of his teeth were missing. He was addicted to methadone. His nickname on the streets of London was 'Big John' because he was a big guy who had once boxed for the Army.

'Big John' walked into our night shelter for the homeless at Holy Trinity Brompton. He came with his friend 'Little John'. 'Big John' loved it and appreciated all the young people who cared for him. He started coming to church. He came on Alpha. He encountered Jesus. He was filled with the Holy Spirit on the Alpha Weekend. He came off the drugs. *God turned his life right around – from despair to joy*.

He started telling his friends on the streets about Jesus. Each week he would turn up at church with more friends. His nickname, on the streets, changed from 'Big John' to 'John the Baptist'!

One of the guys he had met on the Alpha weekend was in the property business and found him accommodation. A dentist in our congregation volunteered to replace all his missing teeth. He has been reconciled with his mother and his daughter and he now has a relationship with his grandchildren, whom he had never met before.

Following Jesus is life-changing. He constantly turns people's lives around. He turns despair into joy (Psalm 30:11).

READING FROM PSALMS

Psalm 30:8–12
Call out to God who turns lives around

God can turn your life right around. God *turns* 'wailing into dancing' (v.11a). He *removes* our 'sackcloth' and replaces it with 'joy' (v.11b). All this happens when you cry 'mercy' (vv.8, 10).

David called out to God, 'Help me out of this!' (v.10, MSG). God did: 'You have turned my mourning into joyful dancing. You have taken away my clothes of mourning and clothed me with joy' (v.11, NLT)

It is amazing and wonderful to hear story after story of Jesus *turning people's lives around*, bringing them out of despair, setting them free from drugs, restoring marriages and changing lives – turning 'mourning into dancing' and sackcloth into 'gladness'.

No wonder David ends this psalm by saying, 'I can't thank you enough' (v.12, MSG).

PRAYER

Thank you, Lord, that when I cried out to you for help you answered me. Thank you for turning my life right around!

NEW TESTAMENT READING

Mark 13:1–31
Watch out for God's great turnaround

Everything you experience now in terms of God turning things around is only a foretaste of the great turnaround that will occur when Jesus returns.

The Jerusalem temple at the time of Jesus was one of the most impressive sights in the ancient world. Yet Jesus saw beyond the earthly splendour of the buildings and knew that its glory was momentary. He points the disciples beyond the architectural splendour and makes a series of prophecies about the future.

1. Turnaround of the temple

As they leave the temple, one of the disciples says to Jesus, 'Look, Teacher! What massive stones! What magnificent buildings!' (v.1). Jesus says all this is going *to be turned right around*. He says, 'You're impressed by this grandiose architecture? There's not a stone in the whole works that is not going to end up in a heap of rubble' (v.2, MSG).

Jesus prophesied the destruction of the temple, which occurred in AD 70. This may be what he is referring to when he says, 'Don't take this lightly. I'm not just saying this for some future generation, but for this one, too – these things will happen' (v.30, MSG).

2. Turnaround when Jesus returns

Jesus' prophecies about the destruction of the temple are not just about an isolated event. They are also indicative of the whole period until Jesus' second coming and they foreshadow what will happen at the end. He therefore doesn't limit his words to the immediate future but continues on with prophecies about the end itself.

Jesus prophesies about the events surrounding his return. Jesus warns us that as we approach the end times, things are going to get about as bad as they can get. There will be 'wars and rumours of wars' (v.7), 'earthquakes' and 'famines' (v.8b). And these are only the 'beginning of birth-pains' (v.8c). Worse is to come: 'The sun will be darkened, and the moon will not give its light; the stars will fall from the sky, and the heavenly bodies will be shaken' (vv.24–25).

Just before the dawn is the darkest hour. But after the darkest hour comes the new dawn. God is going to turn things right around with the return of Jesus: 'And then they'll see the Son of Man enter in grand style, his Arrival filling the sky – no one will miss it! He'll dispatch the angels; they will pull in the chosen from the four winds, from pole to pole' (vv.26–27, MSG).

As Jesus speaks of *the great turnaround* that will take place in the events of the future, he also urges his followers to make a *turnaround now in their own lives*. Three times he encourages his disciples to '*watch out*' and 'be on your guard' (vv.5, 9, 23). Jesus wants us to turn around from focusing on the wrong things, and to watch out for three things:

1. *Deception*

He warns his disciples to watch out for false messiahs who will be particularly active during times of war, earthquake and famine (v.5).

2. *Persecution*

Jesus says that there will be an intensification of persecution (v.9) where 'everyone will hate you because of me' (v.13).

3. *Distress*

As well as deception and persecution, the last days 'will be days of *distress* unequalled from the beginning' (v.19).

In the face of all this, Jesus says 'do not worry beforehand about what to say. Just say whatever is given you at the time, for it is not you speaking but the Holy Spirit' (v.11). Jesus' people are encouraged to watch out and be assured that God is in control of these events and Jesus is coming back to turn things right around.

PRAYER

Thank you, Jesus, that you are coming back. Thank you that although you came the first time in weakness and dishonour, you will return 'with great power and glory' (v.26).

OLD TESTAMENT READING

Leviticus 14:1–57

Thank God for the greatest turnaround in history

Can God revitalise the church? Can he transform a nation? Can he reduce the crime rate and empty the prisons? Can he turn around the state of marriage and family life?

The *greatest turnaround in history* took place on the cross through the blood of Jesus that was shed for us. What looked like an utter defeat, God turned around into the greatest victory of all time. In doing so he made it possible for you and me to be part of God's 'turning the world around' today in our communities.

All this is foreshadowed in the Old Testament passage for today. Again and again in the book of Leviticus we read of the need for cleansing because of sin and guilt. Sacrifice is required (14:19). Atonement is necessary (vv.18, 19, 31). The blood (vv.14, 25, 28) of a lamb (vv.10, 12, 23–24) without defect (v.10) that brings atonement and cleansing from sin (vv.11, 19, 20, 23, 29, 31).

The apostle Paul explains how this all points to Jesus' *great turnaround* 'to which the Law and the Prophets *testify*' (Romans 3:21). Everything we read about in Leviticus today is designed to '*testify*' *about Jesus*. Paul continues, 'This righteousness is given through faith in Jesus Christ to all who believe ... by his grace through the redemption that came by Christ Jesus' (vv.22–24).

As a result, you can approach God today with confidence. In this passage in Leviticus, we read of cleansing taking place through water (Leviticus 14:7, 8) as well as blood (vv.14, 25, 28). This is picked up in the New Testament as a foreshadowing of how Jesus cleanses us. So, the writer of Hebrews says, 'Let us *draw near to God* with a sincere heart and with the *full assurance that faith brings*, having our hearts sprinkled to cleanse us from a guilty conscience and having our bodies washed with pure water' (Hebrews 10:22; see also 1 John 5:6).

He then finishes his explanation by explicitly drawing on the sacrificial imagery we see in today's passage to explain how this is all achieved: 'God presented Christ as a *sacrifice of atonement*, through the shedding of his *blood*' (Romans 3:25).

This is how history is turned around. This is how 'Big John's' life was turned around. This is how my life was turned around. This is how your life is turned around. This is how despair is turned to joy. Thank God for Jesus.

PRAYER

Lord, thank you that you have already turned history around. Lord, I pray that you will turn our nation around. Pour out your Spirit. Revive your church. Turn around the state of marriage and family life. May the crime rate fall. May the prisons begin to empty. May our cities, towns and villages be transformed. May your kingdom come.

7 March | Day 66
God Has Rescued Me

Tony Bullimore, aged fifty-six, was one of Britain's most experienced transatlantic yachtsmen. He was feared dead after his sixty-foot yacht, *Exide Challenger*, capsized amid the icy vastness of the Southern Ocean, two months into the Vendée Globe round-the-world race.

The keel came off in fifty-foot waves. The boat went over. In his book, *Saved,* Tony Bullimore described it as being like the Niagara Falls upside down. For four days he was entombed in a dark, noisy, wet and cold upside-down world with fifty-foot swells and a temperature hovering around freezing.

He suffered the discomfort of seasickness and drawing breath from a few feet of air between the water level and what was once the bottom of the boat. He was more than a thousand miles from land. As the air supply diminished he prayed that he would be *rescued*.

It was the Royal Australian Navy that came to the rescue. With modern satellite and surveillance technology the Australian government had pinpointed the progress of all the yachts and sent out a rescue team.

After four days, Bullimore heard banging on the side of his yacht. He said afterwards, 'I can never thank the Australian Navy enough for what they have done because they have genuinely *saved my life*, there is no question.' The first words when he emerged were, 'Thank God, it is a miracle.' He said, 'I felt like I had been born all over again. I felt like a new man. I felt I had been brought to life again.'

As one journalist put it at the time, 'A *rescue* that succeeds against all odds and every expectation is the best of all stories. It is pure and spontaneous joy.' Supremely Jesus 'gave himself for our sins to *rescue* us' (Galatians 1:4a).

As I look back on my life I can see many occasions when God has rescued me. As you face difficult situations you can trust that God will rescue you.

READING FROM PSALMS

Psalm 31:1–8
Trust God to rescue you

It is sometimes very hard to keep trusting in God, especially if things seem to go wrong in your life – with your relationships, work, finances, health or some other situation. David's prayer here is an encouragement to cry out to God to rescue you and then to put your trust in God.

As Tony Bullimore prayed for rescue, so David prayed, 'Turn your ear to me, come quickly to *my rescue*' (v.2a), '*I trust in, rely on,* and *confidently lean on the Lord*' (v.6b, AMP).

David said, 'Into your hands I commit my spirit' (v.5). Just before he died, Jesus echoed these words. He called out with a loud voice, '*Father, into your hands I commit my spirit*' (Luke 23:46). These are the ultimate words of trust.

In this psalm we see the results of God's love for you shown supremely through the death of Jesus. The Lord is:

1. Your *refuge*

The psalm starts with the words, 'In you, LORD, I have taken *refuge*' (Psalm 31:1a). Later he says, 'Keep me free from the trap that is set for me, for you are *my refuge*' (v.4). There are many trials, tests, traps and temptations in this life. In all this, the Lord is your *refuge*.

2. Your *rock*

David writes, Lord 'be my rock' (v.2b) and 'since you are *my rock* and my fortress, for the sake of your name lead and guide me' (v.3). You can know God's guiding and leading, by his Spirit. He is your security on which you can depend.

3. Your *rescuer*

He prays, 'Turn your ear to me, come quickly to *my rescue*' (v.2a). He goes on to describe how God saw the 'affliction and ... anguish of [his] soul' (v.7b). Yet God did not hand him over to the enemy (v.8a). He rescued him and has 'set [his] feet in a spacious place' (v.8b). In Jesus you receive the ultimate rescue. He will set your feet in a spacious place.

PRAYER

Lord, thank you that you have *rescued* me. In all the trials of life, help me to keep trusting in you.

NEW TESTAMENT READING

Mark 13:32–14:16
Love your rescuer passionately

Love for Jesus is even more important than love for the poor. Indeed, it is our very love for Jesus that overflows into love for others, especially the poor.

Love like this lies behind the anointing of Jesus' body. This woman acted out of gratitude and love for Jesus. In light of this, her extravagance with very expensive perfume (probably a year's wages) was not a 'waste' (14:4). Of course, Jesus was not unmindful of the needs of the poor. However, he said the money she gave was not wasted: 'She poured perfume on my body beforehand to prepare for my burial' (v.8).

That act of generosity would be remembered for all time (v.9). In Jesus' eyes, nothing you give out of love for him is ever wasted (vv.7–8) or ever forgotten by him (v.9). Rather, he sees everything you give out of love for him as 'a beautiful thing' (v.6). There is something beautiful about every act of generosity.

Jesus' reference to his burial draws attention to the fact that the events of Jesus' life are coming to a climax. As they do, it is clear that the Passover was the setting that Jesus chose for the final events of his life.

Five times, in this passage alone, the Passover is mentioned (vv.1, 12, 14, 16). Jesus clearly understood his death in terms of the Passover lamb that was to be sacrificed (v.12). It was the blood of the Passover lamb that rescued God's people from judgment and death. 'For Christ, our Passover lamb, has been sacrificed' (1 Corinthians 5:7b).

We see here further evidence that Jesus thought of himself as the unique Son of God. As he speaks about his coming again he says, 'About that day or hour no one knows, not even the angels in heaven, *nor the Son*, but only the Father' (Mark 13:32).

What gratitude Tony Bullimore felt for those who rescued him! He said that he could never thank them enough. How much more gratitude and love should we have for the one who has given his life to rescue us from eternal death.

PRAYER

Lord, thank you that you gave your life as a Passover sacrifice to rescue me from judgment and death. Thank you that every time I eat the 'Lord's Supper' I am reminded of your sacrifice and my rescue.

OLD TESTAMENT READING

Leviticus 15:1–16:34
Marvel at God's amazing rescue plan

Because of his great love for you, God meticulously planned your rescue. The rescue of Tony Bullimore took days of planning and preparation. Of course, God's great rescue plan for humanity took far more planning, preparation and prefiguring.

The regulations about 'uncleanness' seem very strange to our modern ears. This is because they no longer apply to us. They were fulfilled and superseded by Jesus.

The Day of Atonement (chapter 16) lays the background to the death of Jesus. St Paul writes, 'God presented Christ as a sacrifice of *atonement*' (Romans 3:25). The writer of Hebrews says that Jesus 'had to be made like them, fully human in every way, in order that he might become a merciful and faithful high priest in service to God, and that he might make *atonement* for the sins of the people' (Hebrews 2:17).

The fact that the high priest's own access had to be won by sacrifice was proof enough of the priesthood's inadequacy (Hebrews 5:3; 7:27; 9:7; 9:11–15).

In the sacrifice on the Day of Atonement we see an astonishing foreshadowing of the cross: 'He is to lay both hands on the head of the live goat and confess over it all the wickedness and rebellion of the Israelites – all their sins – and put them on the goat's head. He shall send the goat away into the wilderness ... the goat will carry on itself all their sins' (Leviticus 16:21–22a). This is the origin of the English word 'scapegoat' ('the goat of removal', v.8).

This prefigures your sin and my sin being 'laid' on Jesus (see Isaiah 53:4–6). The apostle Peter writes of Jesus, '"He himself bore our sins" in his body on the cross' (1 Peter 2:24a). He is the one who sends our sins away 'as far as the east is from the west' (Psalm 103:12). When John the Baptist saw Jesus he said, 'Look, the Lamb of God, who *takes away* the sin of the world!' (John 1:29).

As a result, an amazing change has taken place in your relationship with God. Through Jesus, you can now enter into the Holy of Holies everyday (Hebrews 10:19–20). You can come boldly to the throne of grace (4:16) and know that you will always be welcome.

PRAYER

Lord, thank you that you have rescued me by your blood and you died as a ransom to set me free. Thank you that I can now come boldly into your presence every day.

8 March | Day 67
'...BUT'

During one of the severe potato famines in Ireland, a number of families wrote letters to their landlord saying they had absolutely no money at all to pay their rent and begged to be let off all their debts. The Irish landlord was Canon Andrew Robert Fausset, born near Enniskillen, County Fermanagh, Ireland, in 1821.

Canon Fausset wrote back to his tenants. He said it was quite impossible to let them off their debts. It would set a bad precedent. They had to pay every single penny.

'*But*,' he wrote, 'I enclose something that might help you.' In contrast to so many of the other landlords at the time, he sent a cheque for a very large sum of money – which far more than covered all their debts.

Their hearts must have leapt with joy when they saw the word '*but*'. '*But*' is a powerful word when facing trouble, tests and temptations.

READING FROM PSALMS

Psalm 31:9–18
In trouble ... 'BUT I trust in you'

No one can go through life without facing troubles. If David's example is anything to go by, anyone in a position of leadership will face more than most.

David was *in trouble*: 'with grief my eye is weakened, also my inner self and my body' (v.9b, AMP). He was facing spiritual, mental and physical challenges.

He faced 'distress', 'sorrow', 'grief', 'anguish', 'groaning', 'affliction', illness, 'enemies', 'contempt' from his neighbours, brokenness, 'terror', conspiracy and plots (vv.9–13).

Yet, in the midst of all this, he is able to say, '*But* I trust in you, LORD; I say, "You are my God." My times are in your hands' (vv.14–15a). He trusts in God's 'unfailing love' (v.16). Sometimes, when things are going wrong, it is hard to believe that God really does love you. *But* he does. David cries out for help because he trusts that God will deliver him.

It is in the tough times that the object in which you trust is really put to the test. *But,* as Henry Ford wrote, 'When everything seems to be going against you, remember that the airplane takes off against the wind, not with it.'

Trust that 'in all things, God works for the good of those who love him, who have been called according to his purpose' (Romans 8:28).

PRAYER

Lord, in all the challenges that lie ahead, help me to trust in you. My times are in your hands ... Let your face shine on your servant; save me in your unfailing love. Let me not be put to shame, Lord, for I have cried out to you' (Psalm 31:14b–17a).

NEW TESTAMENT READING

Mark 14:17–42
In tests ... 'Yet not what I will, BUT what you will'

Sometimes you may face difficulties in life not because you are doing something wrong but because you are doing something right. All of us will face tests, trials and temptations in life. You are not alone. Jesus himself never did anything wrong, yet he faced greater tests, trials and temptations than anyone in human history.

1. Disloyalty

Loyalty is a wonderful quality. Loyalty of friends and colleagues is encouraging, upbuilding and reassuring in times of troubles, trials and temptations. Disloyalty is gutting.

Jesus had spent three years with twelve people he loved, lived with and had trained. Yet he had to say to them, 'One of you will betray me' (v.18). It is horrible to be betrayed by an enemy or an acquaintance. But to be betrayed by a friend is almost unbearable.

2. Disappointment

Not only did one of the disciples betray him, all the rest fell away (v.27). Again, this must have been a huge disappointment to Jesus. These were his closest friends yet in the time of trial they all fell away – even the one who was such a strong leader, Peter. Although Peter was absolutely determined not to deny Jesus, he did eventually disown him.

3. Distress

As Jesus approaches the terrible moment, he is 'deeply *distressed* and troubled' (v.33b). His soul is 'overwhelmed with sorrow to the point of death' (v.34a).

4. Death

We looked previously (see Day 60) at the Old Testament background to the cup of God's wrath against sin. As he passes around the cup he says, 'This is my blood of the covenant, which is poured out for many' (v.24). Later on in Gethsemane he prays, 'Take this cup from me' (v.36a).

In addition, 'poured out for many' (Mark 14:24b) echoes Isaiah 53; 'because he poured out his life unto death' (Isaiah 53:12c). Jesus knew he was facing unimaginable suffering, taking the sin of the world on his own shoulders and shedding his blood for us.

Again, to understand this fully, we need to refer to the Old Testament background. In our Old Testament passage for today, twice we read that 'the life of a creature is in the blood' (Leviticus 17:11, 14). 'It is the blood that makes atonement for one's life' (v.11). In other words, it is 'life for life' (Exodus 21:23). Jesus gave his life for us.

Every time you take the bread and the wine in communion, meditate on his great love, his sacrifice and his death for you. Receive again his forgiveness, mercy, grace and favour. Dedicate your life again to him and say, 'Yet not my will *but* yours be done.'

Jesus, facing disloyalty, disappointment, distress and death, puts his trust in his loving heavenly Father and says, 'Yet not what I will, *but* what you will' (Mark 14:36c). He knows that God is his perfect Father, whom he can address as 'Abba, Father' (v.36a) – an intimate way of addressing him, almost like 'Daddy' or 'Papa'.

He knows that God is all-powerful. In many ways, he wants to escape 'this cup' (v.36b). However, he trusts that God knows best and is willing to submit to his will. It is the supreme example for us when we are fearful of what lies ahead.

The contrast between Jesus and his disciples would be amusing, were it not for the context. They are not facing anything like what he is facing. But they cannot even keep awake to support him in prayer; they keep falling asleep. I must say, I sympathise with them. I often find it hard to stay awake!

Jesus says, 'Watch and pray so that you will not fall into temptation. The spirit is willing, but the flesh is weak' (v.38). I have to confess this is often true of me in the face of the challenge to pray more, my spirit is willing, but my body is weak.

PRAYER

Thank you, Father, that I too can address you as 'Abba' and put my trust in you. For all the plans that lie ahead I pray, 'not what I

will, *but* what you will' (v.36). Help me to put your will above my own.

OLD TESTAMENT READING

Leviticus 17:1–18:30
In temptation ... 'BUT you...'

The Israelites were facing great temptation because of the sexual immorality and activities of the people around them. However, God spoke to his people about the way that they were to live: '*But you* must keep *my* decrees and *my* laws' (Leviticus 18:26a).

I heard this true story: A woman was asked 'What is the best thing about being 104 years old?' She replied: 'No peer pressure!'

There is often a temptation to conform to peer pressure and follow the standards of those around us. One area where there is a great pressure to conform is sexual morality.

In this context God says to his people, 'Don't live like the people of Egypt where you used to live, and don't live like the people of Canaan where I'm bringing you. *Don't do what they do.* Obey my laws and live by my decrees. I am your GOD' (vv.2–4, MSG).

Like the ancient Israelites we live in a culture that has very different sexual ethics to God's. God wants you to safeguard his wonderful gift of sex, and not get enticed into following those around you. Be careful to follow God's ways. If you do, far from missing out, you will actually find *life*; 'the person who obeys [God's decrees and laws] will *live* by them' (v.5).

God's people are called to be different. St Paul wrote, '*Do not conform* to the pattern of this world' (Romans 12:2). This call to be different goes right back to the earliest days of God's people (Leviticus 18).

In the New Testament, the apostle Paul lists some of the activities (including sexual activities) that Christians had been involved in before their conversion. Again, he uses this powerful word, '*but*': '*But you,*' he says, 'were washed, you were sanctified, you were justified in the name of the Lord Jesus Christ and by the Spirit of our God' (1 Corinthians 6:11). Therefore, you are to live differently.

PRAYER

Lord, help me not to conform to the standards of those around me. Rather, help me to keep your decrees and your laws. Help me to honour you with my whole being – with my body, mind and heart.

9 March | Day 68
What's in Your Heart?

The Nobel Prize winner and most important Russian literary artist of the second half of the twentieth century, Aleksandr Solzhenitsyn (1918–2008), who was imprisoned for eight years for criticising Stalin, wrote, 'The line separating good and evil passes, not through states, nor through classes, nor between political parties ... but right through every human heart – and through all human hearts.'[1]

We are all created in the image of God. Human beings are capable of acts of great love, courage and heroism. Yet, not one of us (apart from Jesus) is without sin. Do you know what's in your heart?

READING FROM PROVERBS

Proverbs 6:30–35
Your heart and its weakness

All sin breaks God's law and is therefore serious. But there *are* gradations of sin. Some sins are far worse than others.

The writer of Proverbs makes this point by using the example of a person who steals because he is starving. Yes, even this is wrong and there is a price to pay (vv.30–31).

But the writer says the consequences of adultery are *far more serious*. It leads to 'shame' (v.33b), 'jealousy' (v.34a), 'revenge' (v.34b) and to the destruction of lives, particularly the adulterers themselves: 'Soul-destroying, self-destructive... a reputation ruined for good' (vv.32–33, MSG).

The writer says, 'jealousy arouses a husband's fury, and he will show no mercy when he takes revenge' (v.34). Human nature has not changed in thousands of years.

There is nothing wrong with sex or money. But there are many temptations that surround them both. Several of the laws in the Old Testament passage for today were developed to put boundaries around them, safeguarding their proper use.

PRAYER

Lord, thank you for the gifts you give us and the boundaries that you have provided for their proper use. Lead me not into temptation but deliver me from evil.

NEW TESTAMENT READING

Mark 14:43–72
Your heart and its results

Sinful human nature led to the death of Jesus. The challenge is to live differently:

1. Be authentic

Judas betrayed Jesus with a kiss. He said, 'The one I kiss is the man' (v.44a). He went up to Jesus and 'kissed him' (v.45).

In the Greek, the word for hypocrisy is the same word as the word for mask (masks were used in Ancient Greece for acting). On the outside Judas was wearing a mask of love for Jesus. In reality, he was betraying him to be crucified. The kiss was the ultimate act of hypocrisy.

Joyce Meyer writes about what she calls the 'Judas kiss test' – the test of being betrayed by friends we have loved, respected and trusted. Most people in positions of leadership for any length of time are likely to experience this. You need to 'forgive the offender and not allow him or her to cause you to fail or delay in doing what God has called you to do'.[2]

2. Speak the truth

Because there was no evidence against Jesus they had to rely on false testimony. Yet it appears that many were prepared to testify against him (v.56). Having worked as a barrister I have observed first hand that some are still prepared to give 'false testimony' in a court of law.

3. Fight corruption

Corrupt judges are still a feature of the world today. They knew, or ought to have known, that Jesus was entirely innocent yet 'they all condemned him as worthy of death' (v.64b). It must be terrible to live in a society without the rule of law, where judges cannot be trusted.

4. Identify with Jesus

I can sympathise totally with Peter's denial of Jesus. He was really determined not to do it, yet he failed. I know how weak my own human nature is.

The account of Peter's denial can only have come from Peter himself – who with extraordinary openness and vulnerability reveals his own weakness and failure.

When Jesus was in serious trouble, *'Everyone deserted him and fled'* (v.50).

However, Peter is brave and committed enough to make his way 'right into the courtyard of the High Priest' (v.54), albeit following *at a distance*, in sight of Jesus and the trial. I suspect that by this point I would have been with the rest of the disciples – halfway to Galilee!

Yet, there are haunting words about the self-indulgence of the great apostle Peter. While Jesus, his friend and leader, was taken to trial, Peter 'sat with the guards and *warmed himself* at the fire' (vv.54, 67).

As Peter saw what was happening to Jesus and what he was going to have to suffer, Peter increasingly distanced himself from Jesus (v.54a). Having started in that direction the next step was to deny him. Having set out on a course that involved lying, he ended up saying, 'I don't know this man you're talking about' (v.71b).

I am sure Peter didn't intend to go so far when keeping his distance from Jesus, but as it is for all of us, one sin can easily lead to another and, before we realise it, we end up doing things that we deeply regret. When Peter realised what he had done 'he broke down and wept' (v.72c).

PRAYER

Lord, thank you for the encouragement that although even the great apostle Peter failed and messed up, you forgave him, restored him, and used him so powerfully. Thank you for your amazing grace.

OLD TESTAMENT READING

Leviticus 19:1–20:27
Your heart and God's law

God wants us to live lives that are pure and clean. We are to reflect who he is and, thereby, point people towards him. This part of Leviticus has been called 'the holiness code' – 'Be holy because I, the LORD your God, am holy' (19:2).

Because human nature has a wayward side there is a need for law. As in any society there are *civil* and *criminal* laws. Some of these laws are specific and directed at the problems of Ancient Israel. Others are broad and generally applicable to most societies.

The *ceremonial* laws are now obsolete, the dietary laws having been superseded by Jesus and the sacrifices fulfilled in his death. The *civil* laws are not necessarily appropriate to other nations. Some were humane, and others severe. They seem to have been necessary for the earlier stages of Israel's history, but they are not all of permanent or universal validity.

The *moral* law, as expanded and deepened by Jesus, and as illustrated in the apostolic letters – especially in their positive parallels to the law's prohibitions – is still in force as a revelation of God's will for his people.

The moral law is summed up by Jesus as 'Love the Lord your God ... and ... love your neighbour as yourself' (Luke 10:27). This goes back to our passage for today, 'Love your neighbour as yourself' (Leviticus 19:18b). The moral law was that God's people should be holy (v.2b). The rest of the law instructs us *how* to love our neighbour as ourselves and *how* to be holy.

The moral laws applicable to us now would include the laws to protect the poor (v.10), the laws against racial discrimination (for example vv.33–34), as well as the more obvious ones about theft (v.11), fraud and robbery (v.13a) and so on.

There are often important principles that have very real applications today. For example, 'do not hold back the wages of a hired worker overnight' (v.13b) is a challenge to us to pay all our bills on time. There is an increasing tendency to delay the payment of bills until the final reminder. God's people are called to be different. This is but one tiny example of what it means to be a holy people.

To keep your heart pure, you need to turn away from the things that spoil your life. Among the more obvious sins listed here (vv.3–31) is one about being a 'dispenser of gossip' (v.16, AMP) and 'holding grudges' (v.18, AMP). Keep confidences and try not to hold anything against anyone. Holding a grudge is like allowing someone else to live rent free in your head.

There are also warnings about the dangers of 'witchcraft' (v.26b). Avoid reading horoscopes, consulting psychics, fortune-telling, palm reading, tarot cards and every other kind of occult activity (vv.31). If you have meddled in any of these things, you can be forgiven. Repent and get rid of the things associated with that activity such as books, charms, DVDs and magazines (Acts 19:19).

Another aspect of the law is that it brings sin to light and leads to repentance and reliance on the grace of God. As I read all these laws I see how hard they are to live up to, how far short I fall of God's standards and how much I need his forgiveness and the help of his Holy Spirit.

PRAYER

Lord, thank you that you died to set us free from the law. Thank you that there is now no condemnation for those who are in Christ Jesus. Fill me with your Holy Spirit today and help me to lead a holy life.

10 March | Day 69
Crucified

In the days of slavery in the United States, southern slaves were living under brutal conditions. They composed some deeply moving songs with haunting melodies, rich with emotion. These 'spirituals' were songs of hope and anticipation. They were the soul-cry of the slave longing for freedom.

They embraced Jesus as their Saviour and *Lord* and, in the midst of almost unbearable suffering, they experienced his grace, peace and hope for the future. From this relationship they were able to sing:

Were you there when they crucified my Lord?[1]

In the New Testament passage for today, we see the background to the extraordinary claim of the New Testament that the one '*they crucified*' is in fact *my Lord*. God is described in the Old Testament as '*The Lord*'.

The original Hebrew word for 'Lord' (*YHWH*) had no vowels and was not vocalised. It was considered too sacred to pronounce. For that reason, when vowels were added to the original Hebrew texts they weren't added to 'the name' (*YHWH*). There has been much debate in modern times as to what vowels should be used – it used to be thought it should be 'Jehovah', but most scholars now think 'Yahweh' is more accurate.

In the Greek translation of the Old Testament, the Septuagint, this sacred name (*YHWH*) is translated *Kyrios* ('Lord'). It really is quite extraordinary, therefore, that the New Testament writers (who were Jewish monotheists) made this fundamental Christian affirmation that '*Jesus is Lord*' (*Kyrios*) (Romans 10:9; 2 Corinthians 4:5; Acts 2:36) and that *our Lord* has been *crucified for us*.

READING FROM PSALMS

Psalm 31:19–24
Love the Lord

David urges, '*Love the Lord*, all his faithful people!' (v.23a). To love the Lord is the first commandment. This is a two-way relationship of love. We love because he first loved us (1 John 4:19). Our love is a response to his love.

David writes, 'Praise be to *the Lord*, for he showed his wonderful love to me' (Psalm 31:21a). Meditate on *how much God loves you*. 'What a *stack of blessing* you have piled up for those who worship you' (v.19, MSG).

He hides you in the 'shelter of [his] presence' (v.20a), *he keeps you safe* in his dwelling (v.20b). He *protects you* from 'accusing tongues' (v.20b). He *hears your 'cry* for mercy' when you call 'for help' (v.22b). 'God takes care of all who stay close to him' (v.23, MSG). Therefore, you can 'be strong and take heart' (v.24a), even when things seem difficult. 'Be brave. Be strong. Don't give up' (v.24, MSG).

PRAYER

Lord, I praise you for the wonders of your love. Thank you that you hear my cry for mercy when I call to you for help. Lord, help...

NEW TESTAMENT READING

Mark 15:1–32
Jesus is Lord

'Were you there when they crucified *my Lord?*' I find it heart-rending to read the account of the abuse, torture and crucifixion of Jesus. They crucified my *friend and my Lord*. Jesus is:

1. My King

Jesus accepts the title of 'king of the Jews' (Mark 15:2). The soldiers use it as a term of abuse (v.18) and it is the name written on the cross as the charge against him (v.26). However, Jesus is the fulfilment of the great longing of Israel and the many promises of a Davidic king (see Isaiah 9 and 11). He is a king with a difference.

He is handed over to Pilate out of envy ('Sheer spite', Mark 15:10, MSG) by the religious leaders. Be careful of envy. It is sometimes described as the 'religious sin'.

Jesus is subject to insults and false accusation. If you are slandered or bad-mouthed be thankful that God allows you, in a tiny way, to enter into the sufferings of Jesus and pray that God will help you to respond as he did – with love and forgiveness.

2. My Messiah

It is ironic that the religious leaders mocked him and described him as 'this Christ' (vv.31–32), because that is exactly what he was and is. The English term 'Christ' is derived from the Greek *Christos,* which translates the Hebrew *Mashiach* or *Messiah*. Both the Greek and the Hebrew literally mean 'anointed'. We have seen Jesus as *the anointed* High Priest of God. Here we see him as *the anointed* King.

3. My Saviour

Again we see the extraordinary irony of the mocking words of both the passers-by, 'Come down from the cross and save yourself!' (v.30), and the religious leaders, '*He saved others ... but he can't save himself!*' (v.31). This was exactly true – in order to be the Saviour of the world he could not save himself. He had to go through the agony of the crucifixion in order to save you and me.

The incident with Barabbas provides us with a picture of what Jesus has done as Saviour of the world. Barabbas, like me, was guilty and deserved punishment. He was 'in prison with the rebels who had committed murder in the uprising' (v.7). Jesus, on the other hand, was totally innocent. As Pilate remarked, 'What crime has he committed?' (v.14). Yet Barabbas was 'released' and set free, while Jesus was 'handed ... over to be crucified' (v.15). The innocent one faced the punishment of death so that I, the guilty one, could go free. We may not be murderers like Barabbas, but all of us need rescuing by the Saviour of the world.

4. My Lord

In yesterday's passage we saw how when Jesus was asked by the High Priest, 'are you the Messiah, the Son of the blessed one?' he answered, 'I am' (14:61–62). The high priest's response was to accuse Jesus of blasphemy – that is claiming to be God. Why was this? When God revealed his name *YHWH* to Moses (Exodus 3:14–15), he also explained its meaning. It comes from the Hebrew phrase 'I AM WHO I AM' or simply 'I Am'. The high priest's response to Jesus' statement suggests that Jesus was declaring himself to be none other than *YHWH* ('the Lord').

This amazing truth is the background behind St Paul's extraordinary soul-cry in Philippians 2:5–11 (which forms the basis of the prayer below).

PRAYER

Lord, help me to have the same attitude as Jesus, who humbled himself and became obedient to death. Thank you that you exalted him to the highest place and gave him the name that is above every name, that at the name of Jesus every knee shall bow in heaven and on earth and under the earth and every tongue acknowledge that *Jesus Christ is Lord*.

OLD TESTAMENT READING

Leviticus 21:1–22:33
Worship the Lord

There is a great emphasis in this passage on the 'holy name' (22:2) of God. In chapter 22 God says to his people *'I am the LORD'* nine times (vv.2–3, 8–9, 16, 30–33). Why does God emphasise his name in these verses?

Names were very significant in the ancient times. They were believed to tell you something important about the person in question. As we have seen, God's name was no exception. The name *YHWH* declared the uniqueness and greatness of God.

God's name also reminded the people of his unique relationship with them. It was a name that had been revealed to Moses as a sign of God's promise to be with his people (Exodus 3).

Each time God declares 'I am the LORD' it reminds the people both of his greatness and of their relationship with him. Each of the laws in the chapter is built upon these truths and is designed to point towards them.

The theme of Leviticus 21 is God's holiness and the need for the priesthood in order for the people to be able to approach God. In the New Testament we see that *Jesus is* the Great High Priest and it is through him that we approach God. *Jesus is*:

1. Completely holy

The high priest had to be *ceremonially clean* (21:11b). Jesus was morally perfect. Jesus is 'completely holy, uncompromised by sin' (Hebrews 7:26, MSG).

2. Dedicated to God

The high priest had to be *dedicated to God* (Leviticus 21:12), as Jesus was (Luke 2:22).

3. The anointed one

The high priest had to be *anointed* with oil (Leviticus 21:12) as a symbol of the Holy Spirit. Jesus was anointed by the Holy Spirit at his baptism. He is the anointed one: the Christ.

If we are reminded of the need for a perfect priest in chapter 21, we are also reminded of the need for a perfect sacrifice in chapter 22. The sacrifice has to be 'without defect' (22:19, 21). Jesus was both the perfect priest and the perfect sacrifice.

Take these three passages together and meditate on the extraordinary soul-cry: 'Jesus Christ is Lord' (Philippians 2:11) and on his wonderful love for us demonstrated by his crucifixion on our behalf, and our appropriate response to 'Love the Lord' (Psalm 31:23a).

PRAYER

Lord, I want to worship you. It is you who makes me holy. It is you who rescues me from captivity. You are the Lord. I love you Lord.

11 March | Day 70
Forgive Yourself

Bishop Sandy Millar speaks of a time when he was walking along the beach and he noticed how the sand had been churned up by the footprints of those who had gone before him. The next morning the footprints were all wiped away by the sea. He sensed Jesus saying to him, 'That is a picture of forgiveness.'

Or, to use another analogy, forgiveness from Jesus Christ is like deleting the file of all the bad stuff in our lives.

Forgiveness is never easy. We all know how hard it is to forgive others. However, we often assume that forgiveness from God is almost automatic. On her deathbed, the Empress Catherine the Great of Russia (1729–1796), said, 'I shall be an autocrat: that's my trade. The good Lord will forgive me: that's his.'

In the passages for today we see the very high cost and huge blessing of God's forgiveness. As P. T. Forsyth (1848–1921) pointed out, first, you have to know the 'despair of guilt'. Then you can appreciate 'the breathless wonder of forgiveness'.

READING FROM PSALMS

Psalm 32:1–11
Experience the relief of forgiveness

Do you ever find it difficult to forgive other people or even to forgive yourself for something you have done? The key to forgiving others and yourself is, knowing how much God has forgiven you. Forgiven people forgive.

As C. S. Lewis pointed out, 'To be a Christian means to forgive the inexcusable because God has forgiven the inexcusable in you.'[1] As far as forgiving yourself is concerned, he wrote, 'If God forgives us we must forgive ourselves. Otherwise, it is almost like setting up ourselves as a higher tribunal than him.'[2]

Through Jesus, God has made *total forgiveness* available to you and me. In this psalm, we see the huge difference that God's forgiveness makes.

1. Release from the hand of judgment
David describes the spiritual agony of not being forgiven: 'My bones wasted away through my groaning all day long. For day and night your hand was heavy on me; my strength was sapped as in the heat of summer' (vv.3–4).

2. Transparency with God
The route to forgiveness is simply to come to the Lord with no mask or pretence: 'Then I *acknowledged my sin* to you and did not cover up my iniquity. I said, "I will *confess* my transgressions to the LORD" – and *you forgave* the guilt of my sin' (v.5).

3. A fresh start
David describes the enormous blessing of knowing you are forgiven: 'Blessed is the one whose transgressions are *forgiven*, whose sins are *covered*. Blessed is the one whose sin the LORD does *not count against them* and in whose spirit is *no deceit*' (vv.1–2).

Imagine that in our diaries were recorded, not just our engagements and meetings, but also all our sins. The first two verses of this psalm give us three pictures of what God does with your sins. First, 'the LORD does not count' your sins against you (v.2). He acts as though they do not exist.

Second, they are 'covered' (v.1). It is as if God gets out his heavenly eraser and rubs out the sinful entries in your records: 'Your slate's wiped clean' (v.1, MSG). Third, they are 'forgiven' (v.1a). Literally that word means 'removed' or 'taken away'. The pages relating to your sins are ripped out and destroyed. 'You get a fresh start' (v.1, MSG).

The apostle Paul quotes this psalm as evidence that through the death of Jesus for you, God credits you with righteousness by faith and that forgiveness is not something that you can earn by good works (see Romans 4:6–8). Through the cross, God restores you to a right relationship with him. Therefore, you can pray to him (Psalm 32:6a). He becomes your 'hiding-place' (v.7a). He protects you from trouble (v.7b). He guides you (v.8) and his 'unfailing love surrounds' you (v.10).

This is not earned by good works. It comes to the person who trusts in him by faith (v.10). A proper understanding of the Old Testament shows that the path to forgiveness is repentance and faith.

Forgiveness is not a reason to sin – it is an incentive *not* to sin. We want to stay on God's paths. He promises that he will guide you: 'I will instruct you and teach you in the way you should go; I will counsel you and watch over you' (v.8).

He does not want you to be difficult to guide like a horse or a mule that must be controlled by bit and bridle (v.9). He wants you to avoid the pain of resisting the Holy Spirit. Follow the promptings of God's Spirit. He wants you to hear his voice daily, listen to his instruction, walk in his ways and trust in his love.

PRAYER

Lord, thank you that you died for me on the cross so that I can know the relief of forgiveness. I am sorry for the things I have done wrong in my life ... Please forgive me.

NEW TESTAMENT READING

Mark 15:33–47
Thank Jesus for paying the price of forgiveness

Take time today to thank Jesus for dying for you. Jesus paid a very high price for our forgiveness. Forgiveness is not easy, but Jesus made it possible.

1. Jesus *did die* on the cross for you
Sometimes people suggest that Jesus did not really die on the cross but recovered in the cool of the tomb.

However, Pilate checked that he was indeed 'already dead' (v.44a). The centurion who had overseen the crucifixion confirmed that Jesus was actually dead. Roman soldiers were experts at carrying out crucifixions. The centurion would also have faced severe punishment himself if he let a living prisoner go.

Joseph of Arimathea 'took down the body, wrapped it in the linen, and placed it in a tomb cut out of rock' (v.46). Joseph would have noticed if Jesus was still alive and breathing. He would not have buried a living Jesus.

2. Jesus was 'God-forsaken' because of our sins
'...darkness came over the whole land' (v.33). Jesus cried out, '*Eloi, Eloi, lama sabachthani*?' (v.34a). Mark retains the original Aramaic words of Jesus, which mean, 'My God, my God, why have you forsaken me?' (v.34b). As we have seen, this is a quote from Psalm 22, which ends with a great victory (see Day 46).

3. Jesus opened the way for forgiveness and entry into the presence of God
The curtain of the temple (see in today's Old Testament passage, Leviticus 24:3), which was what separated people from the presence of God, was torn in two supernaturally by God from *top* to *bottom*. It was sixty feet high and at least, one inch thick. The fact that it was torn from top down (where humans could not reach it) emphasises that it was God who caused it to be torn.

This symbolised the fact that through the death of Jesus you are given access to God, because your sins are forgiven. God credits you with righteousness and allows you and me the immense privilege of an intimate relationship with him.

PRAYER

Lord Jesus, thank you that 'you loved me and gave [yourself] for me' (Galatians 2:20). Thank you that I can now enter the presence of God with boldness and confidence in your name.

OLD TESTAMENT READING

Leviticus 23:1–24:23
Understand that forgiveness is earned not by us but for us

We see in the Old Testament how seriously sin is taken. It is not a trivial matter. And forgiveness is not to be taken for granted.

Justice required an equivalence: 'Life for life' (24:18); 'fracture for fracture, eye for eye, tooth for tooth' (v.20). This was never intended for personal relationships but for the law courts to prevent escalating violence.

It showed the need of the appropriateness of a penalty for sin (incidentally, it was under this law of blasphemy, vv.10–16, that Jesus himself was condemned to death as we saw in Mark 14:64).

Again, we see Jesus' death foreshadowed. Forgiveness of sins requires sacrifice; it requires a lamb. The lamb must be perfect, 'without defect' (Leviticus 23:12). St Paul describes Jesus as 'our Passover lamb [who] has been sacrificed' (1 Corinthians 5:7).

Forgiveness cannot be earned. On the Day of Atonement, 'atonement is made *for you*' (Leviticus 23:28). It is not made *by* you but *for* you. This is the radical and revolutionary teaching of the whole Bible. When you understand how forgiveness is made possible through Jesus, it takes your breath away and it totally transforms your life. And when you know that you have received total forgiveness from God, you have to forgive others and you have to forgive yourself.

PRAYER

Lord Jesus, thank you that you have set me free from all these Old Testament laws. Thank you that you are 'the Lamb of God, who takes away the sin of the world!' (John 1:29). Thank you that you made atonement for me. Thank you for the breathless wonder of your forgiveness that transforms my life and eternity.

12 March | Day 71
Be Confident About Your Future

What does the future hold in store for you? Futurologists predict what will happen in the future. For example, it has been predicted that some babies born today will live to the age of 150. Some of their predictions may come true. Others may not. For example,

- in 1962 Decca Recording Company rejected the Beatles. They said, 'We don't like their sound, and *guitar music is on the way out*.'[1] And, amusingly,
- in 1977 Ken Olson, Chairman of Digital Equipment Co., said, 'There is *no reason anyone would want a computer in their home*.'[2]

There are certain things about the future that *we don't know* and that we are not *supposed to know*. However, there are other things that *you can know* about the future and that makes a real difference to your life now. In the passages today we see three reasons why, if you put your trust in the Lord, *you can be confident about your future*.

READING FROM PSALMS

Psalm 33:1–11
1. The plans of the Lord

'*The plans of the Lord* stand firm for ever' (v.11). God has plans. God has a good plan for your life. He has 'plans to prosper you and not to harm you, plans to give you hope and a future' (Jeremiah 29:11).

The psalmist's confidence about the future comes from looking back on the past. He reflects on what God has done through 'the word of the Lord' (Psalm 33:6a).

As we read this psalm through the lens of the New Testament, we see that it was through Jesus (the Word of God) that the whole world came into being (vv.6–9). He is the one who is the source of all that is 'right and true' (v.4a). He is 'faithful' (v.4b). He 'loves righteousness and justice; the earth is full of his unfailing love' (v.5).

It is on this basis that the psalmist can be confident that 'The *plans of the Lord stand firm for ever*, the purposes of his heart through all generations' (v.11). Governments and people make plans. These may fail (v.10). Yet you can be confident in God's good plans for you and for your life.

The appropriate response to all this is worship – to sing joyfully to the Lord and to praise him with different instruments, to write new songs, to use every musical skill and ability, and even make lots of noise ('shout for joy', v.3b)!

PRAYER

Lord, thank you that you have good plans for me. Thank you that you are in ultimate control of history, the future and my life.

NEW TESTAMENT READING

Mark 16:1–20
2. The power of the resurrection

The resurrection of Jesus did actually happen. When the women arrived at the tomb they found the huge stone, which had been blocking the entrance, rolled back. Jesus had been raised up. He was no longer there. They saw for themselves that the tomb was empty (vv.6–8).

Jesus repeatedly liberated and affirmed women – treating men and women as equals. Women were the last at the cross and the first at the tomb – the first to be entrusted with the news of the resurrection of Jesus.

It is significant that the first witnesses of the resurrection recorded in all the Gospels were women. Women's testimonies were widely seen as unreliable (in most Jewish courts it was not even allowed). Yet in appearing first to them, Jesus affirms the importance and role of women in his new community.

This also gives the story the ring of truth of an eyewitness account. The early church would never have invented this feature of the story.

The fact is that the resurrection was, initially, as unbelievable for the first disciples as it is for many today. When other disciples were told of Jesus' resurrection, they did not believe (vv.11, 13) until they saw the risen Jesus for themselves. Yet when they witnessed his resurrection, either at the tomb or in one of the many subsequent resurrection appearances of Jesus (vv.12, 14), *their lives were transformed*. They moved from fear to faith, from alarm to action and from despair to hope.

As a result of the resurrection you can face the future with confidence:

1. Confident about your eternal future
This life is not the end. There is life beyond the grave. As Jesus was raised from the dead, so in Christ you will be raised with him (see 1 Corinthians 15).

As Tim Keller writes, 'Why is it so hard to do the right thing if you know it's going to cost your money, reputation, maybe even your life? Why is it so hard to face your own death or the death of loved ones? It's so hard because we think this broken world is the only world we're ever going to have ... But if Jesus is risen, then your future is so much more beautiful, and so much more certain, than that.'[13]

2. Confident about your future life
Jesus is alive. He is with you as you 'go into all the world and preach the gospel to all creation' (Mark 16:15). You, like the disciples, are commissioned to go out and preach the good news to the whole world. You can be confident that God's power will be with you. You can expect powerful signs to accompany your message – driving out demons, speaking in tongues and healing the sick. This is what occurred (v.20) and this is what we should expect today.

Healing, for example, is not confined to those who have the special gift of healing but is for all 'who believe' (v.17). It is God who heals, but he involves you in his plans: 'The Lord worked with them and confirmed his word by the signs that accompanied it' (v.20).

There are a variety of models in the New Testament, but they are always simple. Healing comes 'in [Jesus'] name' (v.17). The most common model is the one Jesus speaks of here – the laying on of hands: 'They will place their *hands* on people who are ill and they will get well' (v.18).

PRAYER

Thank you, Lord, for the resurrection of Jesus. Thank you that I can face the future with hope and confidence because you are alive and with me.

OLD TESTAMENT READING

Leviticus 25:1–26:13
3. The promises of God

Although you cannot know the details of the future, you can be assured of God's blessing on your future. In chapter 26, God promises that *if* you obey him you will enjoy fruit (v.4), satisfaction, safety (v.5), peace (v.6), no fear (v.6), growth (v.9), the presence of the Lord (v.12) and confidence 'to walk with heads held high' (v.13).

God says, '*If* you live by my decrees ... you'll have ... a place of peace – you'll be able to go to sleep at night without fear ... I'll make sure you prosper ... grow in numbers ... I am God, your personal God ... I ripped off the harness of your slavery so that you can move about freely' (vv.3–13, MSG).

This is *God's long-term plan for your future*. You will face trials and difficulties in this life as you seek to obey God, but through Jesus you can enjoy some of these blessings even now.

In chapter 25, we see some of the things we need to do in order to obey God. Some of these, of course, are specific to Ancient Israel but some apply for all time.

I love what Joyce Meyer writes about the year of Jubilee (Leviticus 25) in which all debts were forgiven and all debtors were pardoned and set free: 'In Christ, *every day* can be *a year of Jubilee*. We can have our own sins forgiven continually through repentance and faith in Jesus Christ. We can enjoy a continual year of Jubilee. Our trouble is either that we are trying to pay our debt to the Lord, or that we are still trying to collect debts from others. Just as God cancelled our debt and forgave us so we can cancel the debts of others and forgive them what they owe us.'[14]

The key to this chapter is 'do not take advantage of each other' (vv.14, 17). It is not enough to be honest – we must also be considerate.

This is radically different from the world's view. The world admires a person who makes money – however ruthlessly. They may be successful in one sense. But God cares about how we treat others more than how much we own and he cares especially about how we treat the poor (vv.25, 35, 39).

We are only stewards. The Lord says, 'The land is mine ... you reside ... as foreigners and strangers' (v.23). This is how we should regard property and possessions. They belong to God. They are on loan to you. God was teaching his people that there is no such thing as permanent wealth. You own what you own for a season. It is only God who owns them permanently.

PRAYER

Thank you, Lord, for all your promises of blessing. Thank you that you have a long-term plan for my future. Thank you that, one day, I will be raised with Christ to full and eternal life.

13 March | Day 72
Love Boundaries

I remember, years ago, a football match that had been arranged involving twenty-two young boys (including one of my sons, aged eight at the time). A friend of mine, Andy, was going to referee. Unfortunately, by 2.30 p.m. he had not turned up. The boys could wait no longer.

I was press-ganged into being the substitute referee. But, I had no whistle, there were no markings for the boundaries of the pitch and I did not know the rules nearly as well as some of the boys.

The game soon descended into complete chaos. Some shouted that the ball was in. Others said that it was out. I wasn't at all sure, so I let things run. Then the fouls started. Some cried, 'Foul.' Others said, 'No foul.' I didn't know who was right. So I let them play on. Then people began to get hurt. By the time Andy arrived, there were three boys lying 'injured' on the ground and all the rest were shouting, mainly at me!

But the moment Andy arrived, he blew his whistle, arranged the teams, told them where the *boundaries* were and had them under complete control. The boys then enjoyed a great game of football.

Were the boys freer without the rules, or were they in fact *less* free? Without any effective authority, they could do exactly what they wanted. But people were confused and hurt. They much preferred it when the game was played according to the rules. Then they were free to enjoy the game. The rules of football are not designed to take away the fun of the game. They are designed to enable the game to be enjoyed to the full.

God's 'rules' are his boundaries for life, given out of his love for us. His boundaries are not designed to restrict our freedom but rather to *give* us freedom. Like the rules of football, they do not stop the enjoyment of the game. Rather, they enable the game of life to be enjoyed to the full.

READING FROM PROVERBS

Proverbs 7:1–5
God's loving boundaries

God does not invite us to follow his laws; he commands. But these are not the commandments of a dictator, they are the commands of a loving Father, designed to ensure justice, peace and fullness of life.

The writer of Proverbs is like a parent encouraging their children and passing on God's commands to them. He urges his children: 'Store up my commands within you' (v.1); 'Keep my commands and you will live' (v.2a); 'Keep my law … as the apple (the pupil) of your eye' (v.2b, AMP); 'Write them on the tablet of your heart' (v.3b). This is what the Holy Spirit does. He writes God's laws on your heart and gives you the ability to keep them (Jeremiah 31:33–34).

God's commands bring 'wisdom' – and wisdom should be our 'intimate friend' (Proverbs 7:4, AMP). They bring 'insight' (v.4), and they keep us out of trouble (v.5).

PRAYER

Loving Spirit of God, you have written your rules in my heart. Help me to keep your boundaries and live life in all its fullness.

NEW TESTAMENT READING

Luke 1:1–25
The example of others

One of the things that has helped me most in my life is the inspiring example of others. Sometimes it has been older people who, like Zechariah and Elizabeth, have lived their life 'walking blamelessly in all the commandments and requirements of the Lord' (v.6, AMP). Other times it has been young people who, like John the Baptist, had been filled with the Holy Spirit and power. Anyone, at any age, can be an inspiring example.

Luke was an educated man, a historian and traditionally thought to have been a doctor. He is the only Gentile in an all-Jewish cast of New Testament writers. This is the first volume of his two-volume work, 'Luke-Acts'.

Luke made a careful investigation of the events surrounding Jesus (v.3). He wrote 'an account' based on 'eyewitnesses' (vv.1, 2) so that you 'may know the *certainty* of the things you have been taught' (v.4). You can have a *certain* confidence about the life, death and resurrection of Jesus.

He starts his account with the birth of John the Baptist. In particular, he begins with John's parents, Zechariah and Elizabeth:

'Both of them were righteous in the sight of God, observing *all the Lord's commands* and *decrees blamelessly'* (v.6). (It is worth noting in passing that there is absolutely no suggestion that Elizabeth was barren because of some sin in their lives – quite the contrary.)

Finally, their prayer was heard (v.13). When we pray, God hears more than we say, answers more than we ask, gives more than we imagine – in his own time and in his own way. They waited a long time for their prayer to be answered. If God makes you wait you are in good company.

God granted their request for a child – who brought them joy and delight. God gave Zechariah 'a vision' (v.22) of what would happen. John the Baptist was 'filled with the Holy Spirit even before he [was] born' (v.15). He was 'to turn the hearts of the parents to their children and the disobedient to the wisdom of the righteous' (v.17).

God's desire is to set the world back to wise ways of living and away from the chaos that comes from disobeying his commands. Jesus is the one who makes this possible. John the Baptist came to prepare the way for Jesus.

PRAYER

Thank you, Lord, for the inspiring examples from the Bible and in society today of those who live within your boundaries. Lord, transform our society. Restore marriage and good parenting. Fill me today with the Holy Spirit.

OLD TESTAMENT READING

Leviticus 26:14–27:34
The blessing of boundaries

God loves you. He does not want you to get hurt and mess up your life and the lives of other people. That is why he gives you his instruction manual and warns of the dangers of living outside of his loving boundaries.

The last verse of Leviticus summarises what the whole book is about: 'These are the commandments that God gave to Moses on Mount Sinai for the People of Israel' (27:34, MSG). His boundaries were intended to bring blessing.

Today's passage describes the disastrous results when God's people 'will not listen to [him] and carry out all these commands' (26:14): 'If you *reject my decrees* and *abhor my laws* and *fail to carry out all my commands* and so *violate my covenant*, then I will do this to you…' (v.15).

We see the chaotic world that results from 'stubborn pride' (v.19). The relationship with God is broken. Prayers do not get through. God says, 'I will … make the sky above you like iron' (v.19). Disobedience is draining, 'Your strength will be spent in vain' (v.20). However successful you are materially, it does not satisfy: 'You will eat, but you will not be satisfied' (v.26b). These are described literally as 'the *curses* of disobedience'.

God gives every possible opportunity to repent. He puts all kind of obstacles in our way to persuade us to turn back to him (vv.18, 21, 23, 27). In his faithfulness, and in spite of continual rejection, God is always ready to receive us back if we confess and humble ourselves (vv.40–42).

This all points forward to Jesus. The sad thing about all these commands is that no one is able to keep them. It is clear in these verses that God knows that the people will break them and bring all these curses upon themselves. Yet that is not the end of the story, God promises that even then he will act to save and redeem his people (vv.42–45). Ultimately God did this by taking the curses of the law upon himself.

It is only as we see the background to all this that we understand quite how amazing the cross is and how much Jesus took upon himself by becoming *a curse for us*, and the extraordinary blessing of being justified by faith and receiving the promise of the Spirit (Galatians 3:10–14).

God's Holy Spirit changes us as he writes his boundaries on the tablets of our hearts. As Paul says, 'Live by the Spirit, and you will not gratify the desires of the flesh' (5:16). God's Spirit produces within you the fruit of 'love, joy, peace' and much more besides (v.22).

The boundaries were given out of love. Jesus summarises the commandments, '*Love* the Lord your God … and … *love* your neighbour as yourself' (Matthew 22:37–40). 'We *love* because he first *loved* us' (1 John 4:19). In love, he died for you and now he gives you his Holy Spirit to enable you to follow his commandments by living a life of love.

PRAYER

Lord, thank you that, through Jesus, you forgive my failure to keep within your boundaries. Thank you that now you give me your Holy Spirit to help me to keep your commands and to live a life of love.

14 March | Day 73
The Battles of Life

The Christian life is a battle. I have been following Jesus for four decades. As I look back at these years, they have been years of great blessing – more than I could have asked or even imagined. At the same time, there have been many challenges and obstacles. There have been very few periods when I have not been facing some kind of battle.

The nature of these battles has varied enormously. There have been internal battles – times of intense temptation, doubt, fear and anxiety. There have been times of deep sadness, great loss and bereavement. There have been battles over health, sleep, finances, work and relationships. There have been periods of great opposition and criticism.

Fr Raniero Cantalamessa, preacher to the Papal household, speaks of our battle being against a triple alliance: the world ('the enemy around us'), the flesh ('the enemy within us'), and the devil ('the enemy above us').[1]

How can you navigate these spiritual battles of life?

READING FROM PSALMS

Psalm 33:12–22
Trust in God

The key to winning your battles, according to David, is not to rely on your own strength but to put your trust in God. This goes against the grain, but at the end of the day human strength and power is not enough: 'No king succeeds with a big army alone, no warrior wins by brute strength. Horsepower is not the answer; no one gets by on muscle alone' (vv.16–17, MSG).

Rather, God gives victory to those who trust in him: 'Watch this: God's eye is on those who respect him, the ones who are looking for his love. He's ready to come to their rescue in bad times; in lean times he keeps body and soul together. We're depending on GOD; he's everything we need' (vv.18–20, MSG).

PRAYER

Merciful Lord, grant your people grace to withstand the temptations of the world, the flesh and the devil, and with pure hearts and minds to follow you, the only God; through Jesus Christ our Lord.[2]

NEW TESTAMENT READING

Luke 1:26–38
Unite around the King

Raniero Cantalamessa points out, 'In the tales of medieval battles, there always comes a moment when the orderly ranks of archers and cavalry and all the rest are broken and the fighting concentrates *around the king*. That is where the final outcome of the battle will be decided. For us too, *the battle today is taking place around the King*: it is the person of Jesus Christ himself that is the real point at issue.'[3]

The theological battles of the twenty-first century are not those of the eleventh century, which divided Catholic and Orthodox churches. Nor are the battles those of the sixteenth-century Reformation. The battle today is the same as the battle of the first century: *is Jesus the universal Saviour?*

Luke sets out right at the start of the Gospel a number of claims about Jesus (vv.31–35):

1. Saviour
The angel says to Mary, 'You are to call him Jesus' (v.31). The name 'Jesus' means '*saviour*'.

2. Messiah
He is the long-awaited Messiah in the line of David. The angel says, 'The Lord God will give him the throne of his father David, and he will reign over Jacob's descendants for ever; his kingdom will never end' (vv.32–33).

3. Son of God
The angel goes on, 'He will be great and will be called the Son of the Most High' (v.32). Jesus' birth was unique, as is explained by the angel in these verses. Mary was a virgin, and so a 'normal' conception was clearly impossible (v.34). Instead she was told, 'The Holy Spirit will come on you, and the power of the Most High will overshadow you' (v.35a). The angel then immediately explains why this is so significant: 'the holy one to be born will be called the *Son of God*' (v.35b). We see here how Jesus is both fully human

(born in the normal way), and yet also fully God (conceived by the Holy Spirit).

Christians from all churches – Catholic, Orthodox, Protestant and Pentecostal – believe in Jesus as our Saviour, the Messiah and the Son of God. To be a Christian is to be a follower *of Christ*. All followers of Jesus are children of God (John 1:12). This makes us brothers and sisters. Furthermore, if we belong to Christ, the Holy Spirit lives in each of us (Romans 8:9).

What unites us is infinitely more important than what divides us. Therefore, the battle should never be with our brothers and sisters in Christ. In-fighting distracts and destroys. Focus on the real battle, which is around the King.

Mary sets a wonderful example of the right attitude. For Mary, the Lord is *with* her (Luke 1:28), *within* her (v.35) and *over* her (v.38). While, of course, Mary is unique as the mother of Jesus, all believers can know this same connection with the Lord.

The way we fight the triple alliance of the enemy is with the *triple alliance of the Lord*.

First, just as the angel tells Mary that '*the Lord is with you*' (v.28), so Jesus' last words to his disciples were, 'I am with you always' (Matthew 28:20). Whatever circumstances you face, you need not fear. *The King is with you* and 'nothing is impossible with God' (Luke 1:37).

Second, the Holy Spirit is *within you* (1 Corinthians 3:16). As the Holy Spirit came upon Mary (Luke 1:35), to bring about a physical birth, so the Holy Spirit comes upon you, to bring about a spiritual birth (John 1:13).

Third, the King is *over you*. You are called to be the Lord's servant – strong and courageous. Mary is our model of trust. In the greatest and most decisive act of faith in history she offered herself to God as a clean page on which he could write what he wanted. Her response is the model for us: 'I am the Lord's servant, and I am willing to do whatever he wants' (Luke 1:38, TLB).

PRAYER

Lord, help us to focus on the real battle and unite around Jesus. I want to say, like Mary, 'I am the Lord's servant, and I am willing to accept whatever he wants.'

OLD TESTAMENT READING

Numbers 1:1–2:9
Listen to God

The battles of life need not intimidate you. All the way through history, God's people have faced obstacles and challenges. The book of Numbers is about how God's people prepare for battle.

In Exodus we see the people of God as *a liberated people*. In Leviticus we see them as *a holy people*. In Numbers we see them as *a fighting force*. In the chapters for today we see a military emphasis that sets the tone for the whole book.

When we read this through the lens of Jesus, we see that the Christian life is a spiritual battle. The apostle Paul describes this as a battle against the spiritual forces of evil in the heavenly realm (Ephesians 6:12). You are *liberated* by the cross. You have been *made holy* but you have *a battle on your hands*. As the people of God in the Old Testament prepared for their battles, be prepared.

Here, we see three keys:

1. Take instructions from God

'The Lord spoke to Moses in the Tent of Meeting *in the Desert* of Sinai' (Numbers 1:1). God can speak to you even in the very dry periods of your life, or in a place that seems completely godless. Of course, it is *not enough* simply *to hear* God's instructions – *act* on them too. This initial set of instructions ends with the report that the people of God 'did all this *just as the Lord commanded Moses*' (v.54).

2. Raise up good leadership

The leaders were appointed from the community (v.16), and represented it (v.4) but, ultimately, they were chosen by God.

Leadership is key in every level and section of society. Parents are leaders in the home. Teachers are leaders in schools. We need good leadership in the church, market-place, judiciary, government, media, arts and so on.

3. Mobilise the people

Everyone had to be listed ('by name, one by one', v.2). This expression occurs over and over again in the passage. Each individual matters to God and has an important part to play in his plans. What at first seems to be dry statistics is in fact a key tool in mobilising and equipping the entire people of God.

Eugene Peterson writes in his introduction to the book of Numbers, 'We need organisational help. When people live together in community, jobs have to be assigned, leaders appointed, inventories kept. Counting and list-making and rosters are as much a part of being a community of God as prayer and instruction and justice. Accurate arithmetic is an aspect of becoming a people of God.'[14]

PRAYER

Lord, I pray that you would raise up good leadership, both in the church and in society, and that you would mobilise your people for the battles ahead.

15 March | Day 74
You Have the Favour of God

In my first year at university, aged eighteen, I read the entire New Testament in a week – from Matthew to Revelation – and became convinced, 'it is true'. But I was reluctant to follow Jesus, as I thought my life would be very dull and that I would have to give up all enjoyment. In fact, it was the exact opposite. I found something even better than happiness.

We all want to live happy lives. 'Happiness,' wrote Aristotle, 'is the meaning and purpose of life, the whole aim and end of human existence.' But there is something even better, greater and deeper than happiness. Happiness is dependent on what happens – our circumstances. Joy is far deeper and is not so dependent on our outward circumstances. It is a blessing from God. Joy is the characteristic of an encounter with Jesus even in his mother's womb (Luke 1:44).

Today's New Testament passage uses a Greek word that we translate 'blessed'. It means to be the privileged recipient of *God's favour*, and to be fortunate and happy because of it. The Amplified Bible describes it as being 'happy, to be envied, and spiritually prosperous – with life-joy and satisfaction in God's favor and salvation, regardless of their outward conditions' (Matthew 5:3, AMP).

READING FROM PSALMS

Psalm 34:1–10
Praise God for all his favour

In the last thirty years, Pippa and I have travelled all over the world. Sometimes we are offered some quite unusual looking food that we have never eaten or even seen before. Often it turns out to be delicious. There is only one way to find out – to 'taste and see'.

David says, '*Taste and see* that the LORD is good; *blessed* is the one who takes refuge in him' (v.8). That is what I experienced as I began to follow Jesus. Ever since, it has been my desire to get that message out to as many people as I can, and say to them, 'Join me in spreading the news; together let's get the word out' (v.3, MSG).

Like David, praise God for all the *favour* your relationship with God has brought to your life. Praise God 'at all times' (v.1) not just when things are going well or it is convenient to do so: 'I *bless* GOD every chance I get; my lungs expand with his praise. I live and breathe GOD; if things aren't going well, hear this and be happy' (vv.1–2, MSG).

Praise God for:

1. Answered prayer

David writes, 'I sought the LORD, and he *answered me*' (v.4a). God helped him in times of trouble, 'When I was desperate, I called out, and GOD got me out of a tight spot' (v.6, MSG).

2. Freedom from fear

David continues by explaining exactly how God had answered his prayers in this instance: 'he delivered me from all my fears' (v.4b).

Those who *fear* God are delivered from all their *fears*. 'Fear [of] the LORD' (v.9a) is the equivalent of 'seeking the Lord' (compare verse 9b, 'those who *fear him* lack nothing' with verse 10b, 'those who *seek the LORD* lack no good thing').

David does not say we will lack nothing, but he does say, 'Those who seek the LORD lack *no good thing*' (v.10b). Or as *The Message* puts it, 'Worship opens doors to all his goodness' (v.9b, MSG).

3. Radiant faces

One of the things I noticed, even before I was a Christian, was the radiant expression on the faces of many Christians. 'Those who look to him are radiant; their faces are never covered with shame' (v.5).

4. Angelic protection
'GOD's angel sets up a circle of protection around us while we pray' (v.7, MSG). It's an amazing thought that as you pray and worship God you experience angelic protection.

'All enjoyment spontaneously overflows into praise,' wrote C. S. Lewis. '...delight is incomplete till it is expressed.'[1]

PRAYER

Lord, thank you that you promise to deliver me from all my fears. Thank you that your angel sets up a circle of protection around me as I pray. Lord, I thank, praise and worship you today.

NEW TESTAMENT READING

Luke 1:39–56
Believe God's promises of favour

Mary was '*highly favoured*' (1:28). The angel said to her 'you have found *favour* with God' (v.30).

This passage is full of celebration, as Elizabeth and Mary recognise the ways in which God has *favoured* them.

Elizabeth, filled with the Holy Spirit, sings of Mary: 'Blessed are you among women, and blessed is the child you will bear! But why am I so favoured, that the mother of my Lord should come to me? ... Blessed is she who has believed that what the Lord has said to her will be accomplished!' (vv.42–45).

The emphasis on Mary's faith is significant, as many people would have responded very differently to the situation. God's favour did not mean that all Mary's problems disappeared – she was pregnant and unmarried in a culture where that would have caused all kinds of difficulties.

Yet she chooses to recognise the ways that God has *blessed her*. She picks up on Elizabeth's greeting and sings the song that has become known as the 'Magnificat'. In it she 'rejoices in God my Saviour' (v.47) for all the ways in which he has 'done great things for me' (v.49).

In some ways the favour on Mary is unique: 'Blessed are you among women' (v.42a). Mary is:

1. The mother of the Lord
Mary carried in her womb the Son of God, Jesus the blessed one (v.42b). When Elizabeth comes into the presence of the foetal Jesus she is 'filled with the Holy Spirit' (v.41). 'Joy' is the characteristic response to Jesus – even the baby 'leapt with joy' in the womb (v.44).

2. Recognised for all future generations
'From now on all generations will *call me blessed*' (v.48). Mary has been known as 'the *Blessed* Virgin Mary' ever since.

Jesus' DNA came from a combination of Mary and the Holy Spirit. He was the genetic son of Mary. He must have looked like her. He must have had some of her physical features. She brought him up. She trained and taught him. For thirty years she was the dominant female influence on his life.

3. The pinnacle of faith
'*Blessed* is she who has believed that the Lord would fulfil his promises to her!' (v.45). Mary believed that what the Lord said to her – something unique and *humanly impossible* – would happen. As the angel had said to Mary, 'Nothing is impossible with God' (v.37).

For Mary, what God had promised was as good as done: 'For the Mighty One *has* done great things for me' (v.49). Corrie ten Boom said, 'Faith sees the invisible, believes the unbelievable, and receives the impossible.'[2]

Of course, in many ways, Mary was unique. Yet in some ways the favour she talks about can apply to you and me. You are blessed by a Saviour ('God my Saviour', v.47). The promise to fill the hungry with good things (v.53) – the promise of God's favour to satisfy your spiritual hunger with his provision – applies to you and me.

PRAYER

Lord, thank you for Mary's extraordinary faith: that she believed you could do what was humanly impossible. Like Mary, I want your favour to lead me to worship you.

OLD TESTAMENT READING

Numbers 2:10–3:51
Experience now the favour of God's presence

These events took place 'at the time the LORD talked with Moses' (3:1). What was once a special favour for Moses is now open to us all. You can experience the favour of God talking with you.

Enormous care had to be taken because of the huge responsibility and great blessing of God's presence being in the midst of his people. The 'Tent of *Meeting*' (where God's presence dwelt) was 'set out in the middle of the camps' (2:17). Everyone was given a role and a responsibility. In particular, a certain group of people were ordained (the Levites) to full-time ministry. They were 'ordained to serve' (3:3); they were 'given wholly' to God (v.9).

The life of God's people literally revolved around the presence of God. It was the key to their identity, their successes and their favour.

But here we see that God's presence with his people was also limited. The people were barred from the sanctuary (v.10), the heart of God's presence. The extraordinary message of the New Testament is that this separation has now been removed.

You can now experience the full favour of God's presence with you. This theme of the blessing of God's presence is a recurring one throughout the Scriptures. Jesus brings God's presence to us (John 1:14a). Jesus has given you the Holy Spirit, who is God's empowering presence dwelling within you (1 Corinthians 6:19). We experience God's presence especially when we gather together (Matthew 18:20). One day you will know God's presence face to face (Revelation 21:3, 22:4).

PRAYER

Lord, thank you so much for the blessing of your presence and your favour. As you did with Moses, please talk with me today.

16 March | Day 75

What God Has in Store for You

Sam, aged twenty-three, was a militant atheist. He associated himself with the teachings of fervent opponents of faith and religion. One evening, he went online and discovered that Alpha was about to start within easy access of his home. He turned up to our church thinking, 'I'm going to take down a few irrational Christians here.'

But his encounter with the teachings and person of Jesus Christ was not what he expected.

On his questionnaire at the end of the course, he wrote, 'I found the draw of Jesus irresistible and have gone from [being] someone with no faith to someone with an immense hope. To live in a state of non-truth to living in truth is, to me, the difference between *being bound to complete freedom*.'

Three months later, he was baptised. He told me, 'I'm free of my previous life. I was a slave to a lot of things. I was a slave to society, a slave to my peers ... But now I'm free to live my life. I'm excited to see what God's got in store for me.' Salvation means freedom. Sam had an experience of how Jesus Christ sets us free.

READING FROM PSALMS

Psalm 34:11–22
Live a life of freedom

Are you facing major challenges in your life – perhaps to do with your finances, relationships, health, family or some other difficult situation? This psalm is full of guidance and wonderful promises to those who face 'many troubles' (v.19).

The apostle Peter quotes this psalm in one of his letters as evidence of the kind of life we should lead – a life that reflects our new freedom as children of God.

Peter introduces David's call to righteous living with the explanation that it is 'to this you were called' (1 Peter 3:9): 'Whoever among you loves life and desires to see many good days, keep your tongue from evil and your lips from speaking lies. Turn from evil and do good; seek peace and pursue it. The eyes of the LORD are on the righteous and his ears attentive to their cry; the face of the LORD is against those who do evil' (Psalm 34:12–16a; 1 Peter 3:10–12).

'The LORD ... saves' (Psalm 34:18). You cannot save yourself. It is the Lord who sets you free.

Our God rescues us. He watches over you, waiting to hear your prayer: 'His ears are attentive to [your] cry' (v.15b). When we do cry out, 'the LORD hears' (v.17a), and delivers us from all our 'troubles' (v.17b). I find it so helpful to look back over the years at various 'troubles' I have written in the margins of my Bible and to see how God has delivered me. It encourages me to cry out again.

God does not say that there won't be any troubles (v.19a), but he does promise to deliver you from them all (v.19b). He is especially close in the tough times, 'The LORD is close to the broken-hearted and saves those who are crushed in spirit' (v.18). When you are going through a difficult time, you may not necessarily *feel* God is close, but he is: 'God is there every time' (v.19, MSG).

'God pays for each slave's *freedom*' (v.22a, MSG). He promises that there is no condemnation for those who take 'refuge in him' (v.22b, see Romans 8:1). You have a righteousness from God through Christ, hence, you can include yourself in the category of 'the righteous' (Psalm 34:17, 19, 21).

PRAYER

Lord, thank you for the many times I have cried out to you and you have heard me and set me free. Help me today to keep my tongue from evil, to do good and to seek peace. Help me to live in harmony with others: not to repay anyone evil with evil or insult with insult but rather with blessing. Thank you that it is for a life of freedom that Christ has set me free.

NEW TESTAMENT READING

Luke 1:57–80
Think about the greatness of your freedom

God's people at this time were suffering from the oppression of Roman rule. They felt surrounded by darkness and death. They longed for a liberator to *set them free* from the pain and the sorrow of their situation. They were looking for someone who would come and put things right. They had waited for a long time.

Zechariah was John the Baptist's father. His nine months of silence may be symbolic of the longer period of prophetic silence that was about to come to an end. As Zechariah's 'mouth was opened and his tongue *set free*' (v.64), he 'was filled with the Holy Spirit and prophesied' (v.67).

The birth of John the Baptist was an occasion of great celebration, joy and expectation (vv.57–66). When Zechariah (unable to speak) wrote, '"His name is to be John"... it took everybody by surprise. Surprise followed surprise – Zechariah's mouth was now open, his tongue loose, and he was talking, praising God!' (vv.63–64, MSG).

Even John's name was an expression of God's blessings – it means 'the Lord is a gracious giver'.

It was said of John the Baptist, 'The Lord's hand was with him' (v.66). That is a good prayer to pray for yourself, your family and your community: that the Lord's hand will be with you.

Zechariah was filled with the Spirit and prophesied that salvation was coming. He said, 'He set the power of salvation in the centre of our lives' (v.69, MSG). John the Baptist was to 'present the offer of salvation to his people, the forgiveness of their sins' (v.77, MSG).

Zechariah sees that God is coming to bring salvation to his people. But his prophecy goes well beyond political salvation. Something far deeper and wider is about to happen, fulfilling the great promises of the Old Testament. It will involve 'redemption' (v.68b), rescue from enemies (v.74a) and forgiveness of sins (v.77b). Salvation is the 'path of peace' (v.79). Zechariah, in this description of salvation, summed up so many of the freedoms that Jesus would bring to us:

- freedom from fear (v.74b)
- freedom to serve God (v.74b)
- freedom to be holy (v.75)
- freedom to be righteous (v.75)
- freedom from death (v.79b).

PRAYER

Praise you, Lord, that you have rescued me from slavery and shown me mercy. Thank you for forgiving my sins. Thank you that you give me freedom from death and fear. Thank you that you set me free to serve you. Help me today to serve you without fear, in holiness and righteousness, and guide my feet into the path of peace. May your hand be with me.

OLD TESTAMENT READING

Numbers 4:1–5:10
Never take your freedom for granted

Are you serving in some way in your local church? Are you a contributor or merely a consumer? God has a role and responsibility for you.

We see in this Old Testament passage an anticipation and foreshadowing of the church, with *each member* having a different part to play (Ephesians 4:7, 11–13). As we read of the Kohathites, Gershonites and Merarites, aged between thirty and fifty years old, who came 'to serve', we see that God assigned each individual specific tasks (Numbers 4:3–4, 24–25, 31–32), just as today God has assigned to you specific work to do in the church.

For the Israelites, ministry was centred on the Tent of Meeting – the place of God's presence. Now, God's presence is among his people in the body of Christ. The work and ministry to which you are called is to build up the body of Christ. This is one of the ways that you will experience the presence of God today. God's presence is not confined to a particular place, but rather is experienced wherever his people are.

In this passage, we see that we cannot take our freedom for granted. We are reminded of the holiness of God and the fact that it required something amazing to allow you to have the kind of relationship with God that you are now able to enjoy.

God reminds Moses that any kind of sin is actually an act of unfaithfulness to God: 'Any man or woman who wrongs another in any way and so is unfaithful to the LORD is guilty' (5:6). The guilty person is required to confess their sin, make restitution for it and offer a sacrifice of *atonement* (vv.6–8).

We cannot make atonement for ourselves. Atonement had to be made for us. That is what Jesus did on the cross. A simplified definition of atonement is 'at-one-ment' – in other words, God enabled you to be at one with him. The barrier of sin was removed through Jesus so that you and I can say, 'I was a slave. Now I'm free'.

PRAYER

Thank you, Lord, for setting me free to live a life of freedom. May I never take that freedom for granted. Help me to use my freedom to serve you and to serve others. Help me to fulfil my responsibilities in a way that pleases you.

17 March | Day 76

If the Grass Looks Greener, It Is Probably AstroTurf

A campaign by one online agency offered a dating service for married men and women who wanted to have an affair. The agency is by no means alone in this market. What was different was that they executed an extensive advertising campaign specifically on massive billboards next to motorways with the slogan, 'The grass is always greener.'

Essentially, they were making money feeding on people's weaknesses and helping them to be unfaithful. This may seem attractive, but the reality is that it can ruin the lives of the individuals involved, as well as the lives of their partners, their families and their children.

Jesus puts *faithfulness* alongside justice and mercy (Matthew 23:23). Faithfulness is a fruit of the Holy Spirit (Galatians 5:22). Mother Teresa said, 'I am not called to be successful but to be *faithful*.'[1]

God's faithfulness towards us gives us an example to follow in our own relationships. Faithfulness is something we should strive for in marriage, friendships and in our relationship with God.

READING FROM PROVERBS

Proverbs 7:6–20
Be faithful in relationships

The book of Proverbs warns of the dangers of unfaithfulness. We see in this passage the foolishness of both the man and woman involved in a sexual relationship outside of marriage.

There is a contrast throughout the book of Proverbs between the ways of two very different women. On the one hand, there is 'Lady Wisdom' (see chapter 8) and on the other hand, there is 'the adulteress' (in this chapter). Much of the teaching is presented as the advice of a father to his son (although it is relevant to us all). The father urges his son to embrace 'Lady Wisdom', but to avoid 'the adulteress' at all costs.

It has been said that, 'Opportunity knocks. But temptation leans on the doorbell.' Sexual temptation is pervasive, 'at every corner she lurks' (7:12). It offers instant gratification but it is deceptive. She says, 'Let's drink deeply of *love'* (v.18a).

Sometimes people try to justify unfaithfulness by using the word 'love'. Yet, there is really no love here. It is certainly not deep or long-lasting. It only lasts 'till morning' (v.18a). Worst of all, giving in to these temptations is unfaithful: 'My husband is not at home; he has gone on a long journey' (v.19).

The person who follows this path lacks judgment (v.7). The mistake was not staying well away; but going 'near her corner ... in the direction of her house' (v.8). To live a life of faithfulness, start not just with avoiding *acts* of unfaithfulness, but with your *thoughts* and in your *heart*. Part of the deceptiveness of unfaithfulness lies in its secrecy – 'As the dark of night set in' (v.9).

Unfaithfulness has the potential to destroy a marriage, or a future marriage, and to ruin lives. That is why on a wedding day, the bride and groom promise to *be faithful* to each other, as long as they both shall live. As has often been said, 'The grass is not greener on the other side of the fence – it is greener where we water it.' In fact, 'If the grass looks greener, it's probably AstroTurf!'

PRAYER

Lord, help me to be faithful in all my relationships. Help those who are married to be faithful to their marriage vows. Please guard and protect the marriages in our church and in our society.

NEW TESTAMENT READING

Luke 2:1–20
Be faithful to God's calling, his promises and his message

The faithfulness of those who played a part in the birth of Jesus is inspirational.

1. Be faithful to God's calling

In this understated account, we read how Joseph went to Bethlehem, 'to register with Mary, who was pledged to be married to him and was expecting a child' (v.5).

It can't have looked good. Joseph knew that Mary had not been unfaithful. However, he must have known that to everyone else around, it looked as if she had. The temptation must have been to dissociate himself from her (the account found in Matthew 1:19 even says he considered divorcing her quietly until an angel of the Lord spoke to him).

However, he was utterly faithful to God's calling and to Mary, no matter how it looked from the outside.

2. Be faithful to God's promises

Mary must have been bewildered by what was going on. Yet, she believed what she had been told – she was faithful to the promises she had received. She 'treasured up all these things and pondered them in her heart' (Luke 2:19).

This is a wonderful example of what to do with prophecy and other words that you sense may be from God. Sometimes, you need to keep them to yourself. Like Mary, keep your mouth closed and, at the same time, keep your heart open. Treasure up God's promises to you and ponder them in your heart.

3. Be faithful to God's message

The shepherds' message was very different however. It was 'good news ... for *all* the people' (v.10). Once they had found the baby in the manger as the angel had described, 'they spread the word concerning what had been told them' (v.17). You too have been entrusted with this amazing message about Jesus and are called to faithfully 'spread the word'.

4. Trust that God is faithful

Above all, this is an account of *God's* faithfulness. Everything that God had promised to Mary, Joseph and the shepherds, took place 'just as they had been told' (v.20). Yet God's faithfulness to them was part of something even greater.

We begin to see how Jesus is the fulfilment of all God's promises in the Old Testament. He is born in 'the town of David' (v.11), and his earthly father is 'of the house and line of David' (v.4). He is the promised king to whom the whole Old Testament points, 'he is the Messiah' (v.11).

This is 'good news ... for *all* the people' (v.10). We see here a glimpse of what that means for us. Jesus is your 'saviour' (v.11), through whom you can know the peace and favour of God (v.14). You no longer need to carry a burden of fear ('Do not be afraid', v.10a). In knowing Christ, you know God. He himself is God; he is 'the Lord' (v.11). God's faithfulness and love are the bedrock on which everything else is built.

PRAYER

Thank you, Lord, for your faithfulness to me in Christ Jesus. Thank you that you give me hope, joy, freedom and purpose. Help me to be faithful in getting this message out to 'all the people' (v.10).

OLD TESTAMENT READING

Numbers 5:11–6:27
Be faithful in response to God's faithfulness

1. Be faithful to your marriage partner

The elaborate instructions here (5:11–31) are an indication of how destructive unfaithfulness can be in a marriage. Whereas our passage in Proverbs was a warning against adultery, this passage deals with the consequences of adultery.

However, the law recognised that suspicion of sexual unfaithfulness was not enough. It might have arisen simply out of jealousy. There might have been false accusations. It was particularly important to protect women from false accusations, as their position in ancient societies was more vulnerable.

If the woman was innocent, this test meant that she had nothing to fear. The water was not harmful in itself. The law required a demonstration of guilt rather than one of innocence. Whether the husband chose to use this test depended on the kind of person he was. Joseph did not use it (Matthew 1:19).

2. Be faithful to your promises

The Nazirite vow (Numbers 6:1–21) could be lifelong (for example Samson, Samuel and John the Baptist) or temporary. It was a particular expression of holiness not required of everyone. It was not a matter of extra merit. Jesus himself was not a Nazirite (although he was a Nazarene – which is slightly different!). The important point of this passage is that if you do make promises to God, you should be faithful to them.

3. Be faithful in response to God's faithfulness

Aaron and his sons were told by God how to pronounce God's blessing on his people (vv.24–27). This is how God wants to bless you and me.

He wants to bless you with his presence, his face shining on you: 'God smile on you' (v.25, MSG). He wants to be gracious to you (v.25b). He is kind, merciful, forgiving and full of love.

He gives you his peace (v.26b) in the midst of the troubles of life and his protection (v.24). He wants to keep you from evil and falling away from him. God's desire from first to last is to bless you (vv.24, 27).

As you experience God's faithfulness to you, your response should be to be faithful to him in all your relationships.

I pray this blessing over you today:
'The Lord bless you and keep you;
the Lord make his face shine upon you
and be gracious to you;
the Lord turn his face toward you and give
you peace.'
(Numbers 6:24–26)

18 March | Day 77
Saviour

The world is looking for a saviour. The Canadian musician, Lights, expresses this in the lyrics of her song, 'Saviour': '... I know that *something is missing*... Sooner than later, *I'll need a saviour*.'

Bear Grylls said in an interview, 'I am no longer too proud to admit that I need my saviour beside me.'

'Lecrae' (Moore), is a rapper, entrepreneur, record-producer and actor. He speaks for many of us when he says, 'I'm not a Christian because I'm strong and have it all together. I'm a Christian because I'm weak and admit *I need a saviour*.'[1]

The amazing truth of Christianity is that in Jesus *you do have a saviour*. How should you respond to this extraordinary good news?

READING FROM PSALMS

Psalm 35:1–10
Call out to God your Saviour

At any time, you can call out to God for help.

Life is a battle. If we fly God's flag, there are bound to be those who will be out to get us. David prays that God would contend with those who contend against him (v.1a).

He prays, 'Fight against those who fight against me ... arise and come to my aid ... Say to me, "I am your *salvation*"' (vv.1b–3). Or as *The Message* puts it, 'Reassure me; let me hear you say, "*I'll save you*."' (v.3, MSG).

When you are under attack it is easy to feel that it must be your fault. But twice David repeats that their desire to trap him is 'without cause' (v.7). Sometimes you may face opposition not because you are doing something wrong but because you are doing something right. David prays to God to rescue him: 'then my soul will rejoice in the LORD and delight in his *salvation*' (v.9).

Your enemies may be stronger than you. David faced 'hecklers', 'bullies' and 'thugs try[ing] to knife [him] in the back' (vv.1, 4, MSG). But God is the Saviour who rescues and 'protects the unprotected' (v.10b, MSG).

God's ultimate rescue is the salvation that is in Jesus. I love the song written by Ben Fielding and Reuben Morgan that celebrates this salvation. Let's use these words as prayer and worship:

> Saviour,
> He can move the mountains,
> My God is mighty to save,
> He is mighty to save.
> Forever,
> Author of salvation,
> He rose and conquered the grave,
> Jesus conquered the grave.[2]

NEW TESTAMENT READING

Luke 2:21–40
Look to Jesus as your Saviour

Jesus is the Saviour of the world. The angel had announced the birth of a '*Saviour*' (2:11). In this passage we see how on the eighth day he was named 'Jesus' which means '*the Lord saves*'.

His parents take him to Jerusalem 'to present him to the Lord' and 'to offer a sacrifice in keeping with what is said in the Law of the Lord' (vv.22–24). Jesus is the ultimate fulfilment of all the offerings and sacrifices we read about in the Old Testament.

1. Look to Jesus to receive peace
Simeon takes Jesus in his arms and says to the Lord, 'My eyes have seen *your salvation*' (v.30). To see Jesus is to see salvation. Seeing Jesus gives Simeon 'peace' (v.29b).

2. Look to Jesus to see what God is like
Jesus is a light that reveals God. He is 'a light for revelation to the Gentiles' (v.32a). It is impossible to know God unless he reveals himself to us. Yet God has done just that in Jesus. Jesus shows us what God is like. Jesus said, 'Anyone who has seen me has seen the father' (John 14:9). Jesus fully reveals God for everyone.

3. Look to Jesus for grace and truth
Jesus is a light who brings glory: 'the glory of your people Israel' (Luke 2:32b). The word 'glory' speaks of God's excellence, beauty, greatness and perfection. God is glorious. Israel had glory because God had lived among them, first in the tabernacle in the desert (as written about in today's Old Testament passage), and then in the temple in Jerusalem.

With Jesus, Israel came to see God's glory in its truest and fullest sense. As John writes of Jesus, 'We have seen his glory, the glory of the one and only Son, who came from the Father, *full of grace and truth*' (John 1:14b). Jesus brings glory to Israel and to us, because Jesus is God coming to live among us.

Tragically though, many people reject the revelation and glory of God that we see in Jesus. Simeon prophesies about this, 'This child is destined to cause the falling and rising of many in Israel and to be a sign that will be spoken against, so that the thoughts of many hearts will be revealed' (Luke 2:34–35).

Being so closely associated with Jesus brings great blessing but also suffering. Maybe you have a family member, close friend, or someone else you really care about who is either antagonistic to Jesus or simply not interested. When we see people reject Jesus we get a tiny glimpse of what Mary must have experienced: 'And a sword will pierce your own soul too' (v.35).

This great suffering of Mary lay in the future. In the meantime, she had the joy of seeing Jesus growing up and becoming 'strong'. 'He was filled with wisdom, and the grace of God was on him' (v.40). 'Wisdom' and 'grace' are characteristics of the Saviour that we should seek to imitate in our own lives.

PRAYER

Lord, give me eyes like Simeon to see your salvation in the world today. Give me grace and wisdom today for all my decisions, meetings and conversations.

OLD TESTAMENT READING

Numbers 7:1–65
Worship the Saviour of the world

Many new parents have a deep sense that God has given them their baby, but it must have been even more so for Mary and Joseph that day in the temple as they gave back to God the miracle baby he had given them.

The birth of Jesus the Saviour was the most momentous event in history. Simeon takes Jesus in his arms and says, 'For my eyes have seen your salvation, which *you have prepared* in the sight of all nations' (Luke 2:30–31). Perhaps it is not surprising that the prophecies and preparations for the coming of Jesus were so extraordinarily detailed and elaborate.

In this section of the book of Numbers we discover how the Tabernacle service was inaugurated (Numbers 7:1 – 10:10). We read of each of the tribes making a voluntary offering. Each gave an equal share. They were given to God (through his servant Moses). The whole people of God were involved in the inauguration of the tabernacle.

At first this passage might seem like needless technicalities for the modern reader. Yet, the presentation of extravagant gifts to God in the Tabernacle (Numbers 7) is so beautifully mirrored by the presentation of Jesus in the temple (Luke 2:22). This Old Testament passage is not merely a bit of ancient accountancy.

The occasion for these extravagant gifts is the completion and dedication of the tabernacle. The tabernacle was the symbolic place of God's presence with his people. The people give as a response to God's grace and presence among them. Their gifts are an expression of *worship and thanksgiving to the Saviour*.

At the same time, though, these gifts are also part of the preparations for the final dedication of the tabernacle. They are making it fit for the presence of God. The elaborate preparations, the extravagance of the gifts, and the detail with which the writer records them, all point to what an amazing blessing it was for the Israelites to have the presence of God in their midst.

All the offerings and sacrifices in the Law of Moses were but preparation and a foreshadowing of the birth and death of the Saviour. The tabernacle pointed forward to something even greater. No longer does God dwell in a tent in our midst, he has come to live among us as one of us. Jesus is consecrated according to the Law, but he would go on to fulfil the Law's very purpose (vv.22–24a): 'When Joseph and Mary had done everything required by *the Law of the Lord...*' (v.39a).

Many years later, Jesus the Saviour abolished the need for all the offerings and sacrifices of the Old Testament through the sacrifice of his body 'once for all' (see Hebrews 10:1–10).

No wonder that when Simeon realised the baby in his arms was the Saviour of the world, he 'praised God' (Luke 2:28). Anna likewise 'gave thanks to God' (v.38). Jesus the Saviour is the focus of all our praise and thanksgiving.

I love the words of another song, this one written by Ben Cantelon, which are an appropriate response in prayer and worship to everything we have read today about Jesus the Saviour:

> For He made us a way, by which we have been saved,
> He's the Saviour of the world.
> So we lift up a shout for his fame and renown,
> Praise the Lord, Praise the Lord,
> Jesus, Saviour of the world.[3]

19 March | Day 78

How to Develop Intimacy with God

The life and ministry of the American pastor, John Wimber, has had a great influence on my own life, our church and many other churches around the world.

He said, 'The ability to hear what God is saying, to see what God is doing, and to move in the realm of the miraculous comes as an individual develops *the same intimacy with* and *dependence upon the Father* [as Jesus had].'[1] How did Jesus do what he did? The answer is found in his relationship with the Father. How will we do the 'greater things than these' which Jesus promised (John 14:12)? By discovering the same relationship of *intimacy*, *simplicity* and *obedience*.

God loves you with an intimacy that surpasses all your dreams. He wants you to have a close, personal relationship with him of intimacy, simplicity and obedience. This is an extraordinary honour and privilege. Moses, David and, of course, Jesus had an intimate relationship with God. But how do you develop intimacy with God?

READING FROM PSALMS

Psalm 35:11–18
Openness, vulnerability and honesty

There were times when David was down; his soul felt empty (v.12, MSG). He was honest and open enough to talk about the challenges:

1. Opposition
David faced great opposition from those who repaid evil for good and attacked him. You also may face great opposition from those who repay evil for good and attack you (vv.12, 15b). They may slander (v.15c), or maliciously mock (v.16a). Opposition does not only come through the world – it can even come from God's people (v.16).

2. 'Unanswered' prayer
There may be times when your prayers do not seem to be heard. 'My prayers returned to me unanswered' (v.13). He says to God, 'How long are you going to stand there doing nothing?' (v.17, MSG).

3. Failure
We all stumble (v.15a). We can feel we are walking with the Lord quite happily and then suddenly we stumble. There may be times when we fail to meet our own standards, let alone God's.

Like David, speak to God about all these challenges. Do not pretend that all is well. Speak from the depth of your heart. He will not be surprised or shocked by anything you say. It is this openness, vulnerability and honesty that draws you into an intimate relationship with God.

PRAYER

Lord, thank you that you listen to the cries of my heart. Thank you that you rescue me and enable me to say, 'I will give you thanks in the great assembly; among the throngs I will praise you' (v.18).

NEW TESTAMENT READING

Luke 2:41–52
Grow in wisdom

Even as a child Jesus had astonishing wisdom: 'And all who heard Him were *astonished* and overwhelmed with bewildered wonder at His intelligence and understanding and His replies' (v.47, AMP).

As someone has said, 'Knowledge is knowing that a tomato is a fruit. Wisdom is not putting it in a fruit salad!' Knowledge is horizontal. Wisdom is vertical. It comes down from above. It is far more important to grow in wisdom than to grow in wealth. Wisdom outweighs wealth. Intimacy with the Father leads to growth in wisdom.

After Jesus' parents find him in the temple courts he says to them, 'Didn't you know I had to be in my Father's house?' (v.49b). Or as *The Message* translation puts it, 'Dealing with the things of my Father' (v.49b, MSG).

On the one hand, Jesus' relationship with his 'Father' was unique. On the other hand, he also enables you to call God 'Father'. He prayed to God as '*Abba*' (the Aramaic word used by children on intimate terms with their father), and he taught his disciples to do the same (11:2). St Paul, writing about the Holy Spirit, says, 'For you did not receive a spirit that makes you a slave again to fear, but you received the Spirit of adoption. And by him we cry, "*Abba*, Father"' (Romans 8:15).

We can learn four things about the wisdom that comes from intimacy with the Father by examining Jesus' example in these verses.

1. Wisdom comes from listening
Wisdom is willingness to listen to and learn from others. Jesus was 'sitting among the teachers, listening to them and asking them questions' (Luke 2:46).

Sir Isaac Newton said, 'I find intelligence is better spotted when analysing the questions asked rather than the answers given.'

Often, those who know most speak least. When we are talking, we are usually merely repeating what we already know. When we are listening, we may learn something new.

Asking good questions is the key to being a good conversationalist. It was said of President J. F. Kennedy that he made you think he had nothing else to do except *ask you questions and listen*, with extraordinary concentration, to your answer. You knew that, for the time being, he had blotted out both the past and the future for you.

2. Wisdom leads to simplicity
Wisdom brings clarity. Jesus knew where he should be and what he should do. He declared, 'Didn't you know I had to be in my Father's house?' (v.49). Knowledge leads us from the simple to the complex; wisdom leads us from the complex to the simple.

3. Wisdom is holistic
Wisdom is shown not only in what we say, but also in how we live: 'Then he went down

to Nazareth with them and was obedient to them' (v.51). Wisdom is about the whole of life, rather than just our intellect or our words.

4. Wisdom should grow

Through his intimate relationship with God, 'Jesus *grew in wisdom* and stature, and in favour with God and people' (v.52) – a very similar description to that used of Samuel (1 Samuel 2:26).

Wisdom should grow as we get older. Not that Jesus' wisdom was flawed or imperfect, but it grew as he matured, as it should with us.

This is a prayer Pippa and I often pray for our children – that they would grow in wisdom and stature and in favour with God and people.

Above all, Jesus' wisdom came from his intimate relationship with God. God was his Father. He knew he had to be in his Father's house, and his intimacy with his Father was the foundation of his wisdom.

PRAYER

Father, thank you that you have given me the Spirit of adoption by which I can cry, '*Abba*, Father'. Thank you that you call me into the same relationship of intimacy that Jesus had with you. Help me to grow in this relationship of intimacy, simplicity and obedience. Through your Spirit may I grow in wisdom and stature, in favour with God and people.

OLD TESTAMENT READING

Numbers 7:66–9:14
Stand still and listen

You cannot develop an intimate relationship with God without setting aside time to communicate with him. 'When Moses entered the Tent of Meeting to speak with the LORD, he heard the voice speaking to him ... and he spoke with him. The LORD said to Moses...' (7:89 – 8:1).

God spoke to Moses (8:1; 9:1). Moses spoke with God (7:89). It was a two-way conversation. God spoke to Moses face-to-face, as a person speaks with a friend (12:8) – talking and listening at the same time, watching for each other's reaction.

In the age of the Holy Spirit you are in an even better position than Moses. You no longer have to go to a particular place, like Moses did, but can be with God wherever you are. By the Spirit of adoption you are brought into an intimate and eternal conversation with God the Father (Romans 8:15–17, 26–27).

This was the pattern: 'The LORD spoke to Moses ... So Moses told the Israelites ... The Israelites did everything just as the LORD commanded Moses' (Numbers 9:1–5). The Israelites' whole way of life was built upon obedience to what God had said to Moses in the place of intimacy. Your intimacy with God needs to overflow into the way in which you live your life. Put into practice the things that God shows you in the place of intimacy.

There are times when it is not always clear how God is guiding us. Again, Moses' example is a good one. When the people asked Moses a difficult question to which he did not know the answer, he replied, '*Wait* until I find out what the LORD commands concerning you' (v.8). If you don't know the right answer it is wise to ask people to '*wait*'. This gives you time to pray and to find out from God the right way forward.

Eugene Peterson translates, 'Give me some time; I'll find out what GOD says in your circumstances' (v.8, MSG). The *Amplified Bible* says, '*Stand still* and I will hear what the LORD will command concerning you.' In the busyness of life stand still and listen to what God wants you to do.

PRAYER

Lord, thank you that I can meet with you each day, speak with you and listen to you. Help me to hear what you are saying to me and to live today in this relationship of intimacy, simplicity and obedience.

20 March | Day 79
God is Good – All the Time

Of all the prisons Pippa and I have visited around the world, this was the worst. It is in Lusaka, Zambia. The prison was built in 1950 for 250 men. Today it holds over 1,300. The cells, which were built to hold 50, are now home to over 150 men. They are locked in these cells from eight o'clock at night until eight o'clock in the morning. There isn't enough room for all of them to lie down at the same time. They have to take it in turns. The stench and the heat in those cells must be almost unbearable. If the prisoners do not have AIDS or tuberculosis when they enter the prison, they are likely to become infected soon after.

The cells surround a courtyard, which is at the centre of the prison. We held a service there. Maybe because there was nothing else to do, virtually every one of the inmates attended. The service was led by a man who had been awaiting trial for four years. He was a Christian pastor who was accused of some minor offence (for which the penalty in England would probably have been a small fine, had he been convicted). Though he may well have been innocent, this man had been languishing in a prison for four years, unconvicted, without trial, not knowing when he would be released – if ever.

I will never forget his opening words as he began to lead the service: '*God is good – all the time*.' Here was a man who had absolute confidence in the *goodness* of God, not because of his circumstances but in spite of them. He knew and had experienced *the goodness of God* in the midst of great suffering. As a result, even though he found himself in the appalling conditions of this prison, he followed Jesus' example and 'went around *doing good'* (Acts 10:38).

As John Wesley said, '*Do all the good you can*, by all the means you can, in all the ways you can, in all the places you can, at all the times you can, to all the people you can, as long as ever you can.'[1]

READING FROM PSALMS

Psalm 35:19–28
In all things God works for your good

Let's be honest. Not everyone is good. Some people hate without reason and act maliciously (v.19).

There is a great contrast running through this passage between the difficulties that David is facing from those around him, and the goodness of God. *The Message* version brings out this contrast by using the word 'good' four times, but in very different contexts:

1. Beware the 'no good' crowd
There will be times in your life and in the life of your community when you come under attack from those who are 'cooking up gossip' (v.20, MSG). 'They do not speak peaceably, but devise false accusations' (v.20). David says, '*No good* is going to come from that crowd' (v.20, MSG).

2. Having a 'good time' is not always good
David speaks of this crowd's '*good* time' (v.24, MSG). These people are having 'a party at [David's] expense' (v.19, MSG). They hate him for no reason: 'winking and rolling their eyes' (v.19, MSG). They think they are having 'a *good* time' but, actually, what they are doing is not good.

3. God works everything for good
'God is great – everything works together *for good* for his servant' (v.27, MSG). God takes even the bad things that are done to you and are said about you and uses them for good: 'In all things God works for the *good* of those who love him' (Romans 8:28).

4. Tell the world how good God is
David ends this psalm by celebrating God's goodness. He writes, 'I'll tell the world how great and *good* you are, I'll shout Hallelujah all day, every day' (Psalm 35:28, MSG).

PRAYER

Lord, help me to remember your goodness and trust in the 'good things' that you have stored up for me.

NEW TESTAMENT READING

Luke 3:1–22
Goodness comes from repentance and the Holy Spirit

The good news is based on solid historical facts. This is no fairy story or myth. 'In the fifteenth year of the reign of Tiberius Caesar when Pontius Pilate was governor of Judea ... the word of God came to John...' (v.1–3)

People are sometimes surprised to see John's message described as '*good news'* (v.18) – it can seem very negative to us! Yet the word of God is *always* 'good news'. The word of God came to John the Baptist in the desert (v.2b). It is a message of 'repentance for the forgiveness of sins' (v.3b). Repentance means changing your mind – turning away from sin and towards God. Repentance is *good*; it is liberating. It leads to freedom and forgiveness.

Repentance should lead to '*good* fruit' (v.9). John the Baptist says, 'Produce fruit in keeping with repentance' (v.8). What is this '*good* fruit'? '*Good fruit'* includes both social justice and personal morality. Interestingly the examples given all relate in some way to work and money. What does goodness look like?

1. ***Generosity***
Those who can afford it should support those who can't: 'Anyone who has two shirts should *share* with the one who has none, and anyone who has food should do the same' (v.11).

2. ***Honesty***
John tells the tax collector, 'Don't collect any more than you are required to' (v.13).

3. ***Contentment***
John tells the soldiers, 'Don't extort money and don't accuse people falsely – *be content* with your pay' (v.14b).

John is not just a preacher of social righteousness. He says of Jesus, 'He will baptise you with the Holy Spirit and fire' (v.16b). Fire symbolises purity (Numbers 11:1–3), power and passion. As Jesus prayed, 'the Holy Spirit descended on him in bodily form like a dove. And a voice came from heaven: "You are my Son, whom I love; with you I am well pleased"' (Luke 3:21–22).

Goodness is one of the characteristics listed by St Paul as the fruit of the Spirit (Galatians 5:22). Through the Holy Spirit we experience God's *goodness*. What God said to Jesus, he says to you:

1. Enjoy being a child of God
God says to Jesus, 'You are my Son' (Luke 3:22). Through Jesus you can call God 'Father'. While Jesus' sonship is unique, the apostle Paul writes that God 'sent the Spirit of his *Son* into our hearts' (Galatians 4:6). You are given this same experience of being a child of God – by adoption. This experience is vital for your identity, confidence and security.

2. Experience God's love
God says to Jesus, 'You are my Son, *whom I love*' (Luke 3:22). Now, as Paul writes, 'God's love has been poured out into *our* hearts through the Holy Spirit, who has been given to us' (Romans 5:5). The Holy Spirit gives you an experience of God's goodness and love for you.

3. Expect God's pleasure
God says to his son Jesus, 'With you I am well pleased' (Luke 3:22). When the Spirit of God dwells in you, your life becomes pleasing to him (Romans 8:8–9).

As you experience God's love and goodness poured into your heart by the Holy Spirit, the good fruit of the Holy Spirit will grow.

PRAYER

Lord, thank you that you love me as your child and that you take pleasure in me. Help me to live a life of generosity, honesty, contentment, and to bear good fruit.

OLD TESTAMENT READING

Numbers 9:15–11:3
God has promised to give you good things

Moses told his father-in-law, 'The LORD has promised *good things*' (10:29). He urged him to come with them, 'We will share with you whatever *good things* the LORD gives us' (v.32).

Moses, together with God's people, had experienced so much of God's goodness. God had guided them with 'cloud' and 'fire' – symbolising his presence (9:16). This is but one example of the goodness that is seen throughout the history of the people of God.

Despite God's goodness to them, his people 'complained about their hardships in the hearing of the LORD' (11:1). On another occasion in the wilderness they also grumbled about their leaders – Moses and Aaron (Exodus 16:2). Sometimes, when we forget the goodness God has shown us, we complain about our situation and can even blame our leaders. But wherever possible, leaders need our support and encouragement.

Remember God's goodness to you, especially in Christ, who is the 'high priest of the good things' God gives (Hebrews 9:11). *Complaining* keeps you *captive*, while remembering *God's faithfulness* sets you *free*. Praise, thanksgiving and worship are the antidote to complaining and grumbling.

PRAYER

I praise you, God, for all your goodness to me – for the good news of Jesus, for your forgiveness, for your love for me, for the Holy Spirit and the love of God poured into my heart, for the fact that you delight in me and rescue me. Thank you, Lord, for all your blessings, for your provision, freedom, friends, family and every spiritual blessing in the heavenly realms. 'God is good – all the time.'

21 March | Day 80
How to Resist Temptation

The Sirens were three mysterious women who, according to Homer's *Odyssey,* lived on an island. Whenever a ship passed by, they would stand on the cliffs and sing. Their beautiful song would tempt sailors closer and closer, until eventually they were shipwrecked on the rocks below.

Odysseus was curious to hear the Sirens' song, but was well aware of the dangers. He ordered his men to tie him to the mast as they approached the island and then to plug their own ears with beeswax. When Odysseus heard the Siren call he demanded to be untied, but his shipmates bound him tighter, releasing him only when then the danger had passed.

The story explores the powerful pull we all feel at times to flirt with choices that we know are bad, and even destructive. No one can go through life without being tempted. Temptation is not sin; Jesus was 'without sin', yet even he was 'tempted in every way, just as we are' (Hebrews 4:15).

READING FROM PROVERBS

Proverbs 7:21–27
Tempted to cheat

This passage describes the power and the dangers of sexual temptation.

1. Beware persuasive *words*
Be careful about what you listen to and what you read: 'With persuasive *words* she led him astray; she seduced him with her smooth talk' (v.21).

2. Avoid foolish *actions*
Thoughts and words lead eventually to *actions*: 'All at once *he followed her*... little knowing it will cost him his life' (vv.22–23).

3. Control straying *thoughts*
Temptation often starts in our hearts: 'Do not let your *heart* turn to her ways [the adulteress]' (v.25; see Matthew 5:28).

Heed this warning: 'Listen ... take these words of mine most seriously. Don't fool around ... don't even stroll through her neighborhood' (Proverbs 7:24–25, MSG). Following this path is a 'highway to the grave, leading down to the chambers of death' (v.27).

PRAYER
Lord, lead me not into temptation, but deliver me from the evil one. Guard my heart, give me discernment and guide my feet.

NEW TESTAMENT READING

Luke 3:23–4:13
Tempted over control

God allows temptation in your life. As you go through these tests your faith is strengthened.

Jesus knows all about temptation. Jesus was tempted for forty days (4:2). Although it was the devil doing the tempting (v.3), God allowed it (he 'was *led by the Spirit* into the wilderness', v.1).

This period of temptation followed Jesus' powerful experience of the Holy Spirit at his baptism. This sequence of events is common, which is why we warn people on Alpha that they may experience increased temptation after the weekend away (where the focus is on the work and experience of the Holy Spirit).

Luke emphasises Jesus' identity as the Son of God (3:23–38) but the temptations that Jesus faced are often similar to the ones we face.

All these temptations revolve around control – control of our *appetites*, control of our *ambitions*, and control of our *lives*. The devil wants to control your life. In contrast, God wants you to know the freedom that comes from being led by the Holy Spirit.

1. Instant gratification
The devil appeals to Jesus' physical appetite (v.3) and offers instant gratification. Jesus answers, 'It is written: "People do not live on bread alone"' (v.4).

In the long run instant gratification leads to disillusion, emptiness and despair. Listening to God and building a relationship with him leads to deep spiritual satisfaction, joy and purpose.

2. Selfish ambition
The devil showed Jesus in an instant all the kingdoms of the world. 'He said to him, "I will give *you* all their authority and splendour ... If you worship me, it will all be *yours*"' (vv.6–7).

The temptation to accumulate things for ourselves is very powerful. Material prosperity may lead to 'authority' and 'splendour' (v.6) in this lifetime, but the danger is that financial security becomes our ambition and we put our trust in wealth and not in God.

Jesus responded to this temptation by saying, '*It is written*: "Worship the Lord your God and serve him only"' (v.8). Ultimately, there is only one thing that can be totally secure and that is your relationship with God. This must be your primary ambition.

3. Presumptuous power

The devil takes Jesus to the highest point in the temple and says, 'If you are the Son of God ... throw yourself down from here' (v.9). He then quotes the Bible at him (out of context, of course). Jesus answered this scripture with *scripture,* 'It is said: "Do not put the Lord your God to the test"' (v.12).

You are called to a life of obedience and service to God. Jesus performed some dramatic miracles during his ministry. In doing so, however, he was obeying God and following the Holy Spirit's leading. This is quite different from testing God and then asking him to back you up. Rather than coming up with *your own* plans and asking God to bless them, seek to find out *God's* plans and obey his calling. Jesus saw off the devil and his temptations with God's word. He repeatedly said, 'It is written...' and then quoted scriptures that directly answered the devil's lies and temptations.

The devil 'left him'. But he only 'retreated temporarily, lying in wait for another opportunity' (v.13, MSG). It is a relief to have periods in life when temptations are not so strong – but you can be sure that the devil will try to lure you astray again.

PRAYER

Lord, I want to follow the leading of your Holy Spirit. Help me to stay close to you, to know your words and to resist temptation.

OLD TESTAMENT READING

Numbers 11:4–13:25
Tempted to compare

Just as Jesus was tempted in 'the wilderness' (Luke 4:1), the people of God were tempted during their wilderness years. The examples in this passage were written down as warnings for us (see 1 Corinthians 10:6).

1. Discontent

God had supplied them with food but they craved '*other* food' (Numbers 11:4). Rather than thanking God for his miraculous provision they said, 'If only we had meat to eat!' (v.4b). They kept 'whining' (vv.10, 13, MSG) and complaining.

They were tempted to make comparisons with the old life back in Egypt and turn back to where they had come from. It is easy to fall into this trap. There is always something to complain about. Yet, if we have eyes to see it, we are constantly surrounded by God's goodness, mercy, forgiveness, love and grace.

'...be content with what you have, because God has said,
Never will I leave you;
never will I forsake you' (Hebrews 13:5).

The antidote to discontent is thanksgiving. Cultivate an attitude of gratitude.

2. Jealousy

We see an example of jealousy with Miriam and Aaron asking, 'Has the LORD spoken only through Moses? Hasn't he also spoken through us?' (12:2). When Joshua had been upset about others prophesying in the camp, Moses asked in response, 'Are you *jealous* for my sake?' (11:29). The context here is spiritual leadership and gifting.

Moses' leadership structure involved a group of three at the centre (Aaron, Miriam and Joshua). Then, there were the twelve leaders of the tribes of Israel (13:4–15), then the seventy leaders and officials (11:16 onwards). This is very similar to Jesus' inner circle of three, the twelve apostles, and then the seventy-two others (see Luke 10). When the Holy Spirit rested on the seventy of Moses, 'they prophesied' (Numbers 11:25).

Like Moses, try to avoid the temptation to compare and to be jealous when you see God using other people in a powerful way. Moses recognised that he needed all the help he could get. He replied, 'I wish that all the LORD's people were prophets and that the LORD would put his Spirit on them!' (v.29). He did not feel he had to be the only one God used. The Lord had said, 'I will take some of the power of the Spirit that is on you and put it on them. They will share the burden of the people with you so that you will not have to carry it alone' (v.17).

3. Pride

Jealousy comes from comparing ourselves with others and thinking that we are less well off. Pride comes from thinking too much of ourselves, comparing with others and thinking we are better.

Moses also resisted the temptation of pride. Pride is the biggest barrier between God and human beings. God loves the humble.

As C. S. Lewis put it, 'True humility is not thinking less of yourself. It is thinking of yourself less.'[1]

'Now Moses was a very humble man, more humble than anyone else on the face of the earth' (12:3). Perhaps that is why God used Moses in such a powerful way.

Moses was 'humble' (v.3), 'faithful' (v.7), compassionate and forgiving (v.13). All this stemmed from the very close relationship he had with God in which God spoke to him intimately in person ('With him I speak face to face', v.8).

PRAYER

Lord, help me to resist the temptations of discontent, jealousy and pride. Help me to be trustworthy, faithful and humble.

22 March | Day 81

Always Be Generous

Generosity is a beautiful characteristic in people. We love and admire generosity. My mother used to urge us as children, 'Always be generous.'

How do you think of God? Do you think of him as a little bit mean or tight-fisted? Or do you think of him as extraordinarily generous?

God's generosity is seen in the natural world. For example, there are over 25,000 varieties of orchids. The orchid is just one of 350,000[1] species of flowers. God does not do things by halves. In our galaxy there are over 100 billion stars like our sun. Our galaxy is one of over 100 billion galaxies. It is thought that for every grain of sand there are a million stars. In a throwaway line in Genesis, the writer tells us, 'He also made the stars' (Genesis 1:16).

God is extraordinarily, extravagantly generous. David speaks of God's '...river of delights' (Psalm 36:8b)'. He 'gives generously to all' (James 1:5). If God is so generous to us, we also should 'always be generous'.

READING FROM PSALMS

Psalm 36:1–12
God's generous river of delights

David pictures God as a rich and generous host who gives indiscriminately to all people (v.7).

David was surrounded by people with 'no regard for God' and who were 'eager to sin' (v.1, MSG). They were 'wicked and deceitful' (v.3a) and constantly plotting evil (v.4a). They had 'ceased to be wise and to do good' (v.3b). By committing themselves to a sinful path (v.4b), they had spurned God's generosity.

Yet even in the middle of all this, David knew God (v.10) and drank from his 'river of delights' (v.8b). These delights include knowing and experiencing the extent of God's love (see *The Message* translation):

1. God's love is 'meteoric'
His love 'reaches to the heavens' (v.5a).

2. God's faithfulness is 'astronomic'
His faithfulness reaches 'to the skies' (v.5b).

3. God's purpose is 'titanic'
His righteousness is 'like the highest mountains' (v.6a).

4. God's justice is 'oceanic'
His justice is 'like the great deep' (v.6b).

You can find 'refuge' in the shadow of his wings (v.7b). You can 'feast' in the *abundance* of his house (v.8a). Abundance is a synonym for generosity. The 'fountain of life' is found in him (v.9a). In his light you 'see light' (v.9b).

These are some of the 'delights' that he generously gives you in your relationship with him.

PRAYER

Lord, thank you that you invite me to feast in the abundance of your house and to drink from your river of delights. I pray that you would continue to generously pour out your love on me, on the church and on your people.

NEW TESTAMENT READING

Luke 4:14–37
God's generous outpouring of his Holy Spirit

Jesus returned to Galilee 'in the power of the Spirit' (v.14a). He went into the synagogue at

Nazareth and revealed his manifesto. Reading from Isaiah 61 he said,

'The Spirit of the Lord is on me,
because he has anointed me to preach good news to the poor.
He has sent me to proclaim freedom for the prisoners
and recovery of sight for the blind,
to release the oppressed,
to proclaim the year of the Lord's favour' (Luke 4:18–19).

He announced, 'You've just heard Scripture make history. It came true just now in this place' (v.21, MSG).

The 'Spirit of the Lord' is the same as the Holy Spirit 'whom he poured out on us *generously* through Jesus Christ our Saviour' (Titus 3:6). In Jesus we see the fruit of a life filled with the Holy Spirit that is available to all who follow him:

1. Anointing of the Spirit

The word 'Christ' literally means 'anointed one' (it is the Greek form of the Hebrew, '*messiah*'). Here we see how Jesus was anointed by the Holy Spirit in his ministry. That same anointing was given to his followers at Pentecost: 'He anointed us ... and put his Spirit in *our* hearts as a deposit' (2 Corinthians 1:21–22). St Theophilus of Antioch (the second-century theologian) wrote, 'We are called Christians (*christianoi*) because we have been anointed (*chrisometha*) with the oil of God.'

The Holy Spirit anoints you to 'proclaim good news to the poor ... proclaim freedom for the prisoners and recovery of sight for the blind, to set the oppressed free' (Luke 4:18). There is nothing more exciting or fulfilling than ministry in the power of the Holy Spirit.

2. Gracious words

People were 'amazed at the *gracious words*' that came from the lips of Jesus (v.22). Love is never rude (1 Corinthians 13:5). Jesus was always gracious. Gracious words are evidence of the power of the Spirit in your life.

3. Amazing teaching

'They were *amazed* at his *teaching*, because his words had authority' (Luke 4:32). 'His teaching was so forthright, so confident, so authoritative, not the quibbling and quoting they were used to' (v.32, MSG). Authority comes from the power of the Spirit. Without the Holy Spirit, teaching is mere words.

4. Authority and power

Through the power of the Holy Spirit Jesus dealt with demonic powers (vv.33–35). Again, 'All the people were amazed' (v.36), because, 'with *authority and power* he gives orders to impure spirits and they come out!' (v.36).

5. Praise and fury

Ministry in the power of the Holy Spirit provokes two opposite reactions – praise and fury. In verse 15 we read that Jesus 'was teaching in their synagogues, and everyone *praised* him'. Then a few verses on we read, 'All the people in the synagogue were *furious*' (v.28). Today, you can expect the same reaction. The message of Jesus and the ministry of the Holy Spirit produce both praise and fury.

PRAYER

Thank you, Lord, that the same Holy Spirit who filled Jesus and anointed him now fills and anoints me. Lord, I pray today that you will anoint me with the power of your Holy Spirit. Help me to speak gracious words with the authority that comes from you.

OLD TESTAMENT READING

Numbers 13:26–14:45
God's generous provision

God is so generous to his people. In this passage, we see how he had provided them with 'a land flowing with milk and honey'. Joshua and Caleb reported that 'the land we passed through and explored is *exceedingly good*. If the LORD is pleased with us, he will lead us into that land, *a land flowing with milk and honey*, and will give it to us' (14:7–8).

God's generosity is extraordinary. Some things are stored up for the future when you will be face-to-face with him (see Ephesians 1:13–14; Hebrews 4:8–11; 1 Peter 1:4–5), but there is much that God gives to his people here on earth now. If you want to enjoy all God's generosity, here are four things you could focus on today:

1. Take possession

Caleb said, 'We should go up and *take possession* of the land, for we can certainly do it' (Numbers 13.30b). But others objected, 'They're way stronger than we are. They spread scary rumors' (vv.31–32, MSG). There is always going to be opposition but do not be put off by the giants.

The people did not think that they could defeat the giants. Only four individuals (Moses, Aaron, Caleb and Joshua) believed God was greater than the problem. Joyce

Meyer comments, 'Sadly, we often stare at our giant-sized problems instead of at our God ... I believe that more time spent worshipping and praising God would help us keep a clear focus and enable us to go forward with a strong, positive attitude, believing we can do anything God tells us to do.'[2]

2. Believe God's promises

The Lord said to Moses, 'How long will they refuse *to believe in me*?' (14:11). The people of God started grumbling against their leaders and saying, 'Why didn't we die in Egypt? ... Let's pick a new leader; let's head *back to Egypt*' (vv.2–4, MSG). In the face of opposition and a few problems, are you sometimes tempted into self-pity and wanting to return to your old life – thinking that you were better off before you started following Jesus? This is a temptation to be avoided at all costs.

3. Watch for his guidance

God is so kind and generous to us. He promises to go before us 'in a pillar of cloud by day and a pillar of fire by night' (v.14). If you want to enjoy all the good things God has for you, keep your eyes fixed on his guidance.

4. Follow him passionately

The majority were put off by the giants. Only Joshua and Caleb were different: 'Caleb has a different spirit and *follows me wholeheartedly*' (v.24). In the end, only those who followed the Lord 'passionately' (v.24, MSG) enjoyed the land flowing with milk and honey.

PRAYER

Lord, I thank you for your amazing generosity and all the good things you have in store for your people. Help me to take possession of all the gifts that you have for me, to believe your promises, to listen to your guidance, to follow you passionately and to constantly drink from your 'river of delights'.

23 March | Day 82
Your Hotline to God

In October 1962, there was a standoff between President Kennedy of the United States and Premier Khrushchev of the Soviet Union over planting missiles in Cuba. The Cuban Missile Crisis was probably the closest we have ever been to World War III, but it was averted because communication was established.

In the days before mobile phones and contemporary ways of instant messaging, it was decided to put one red telephone on the desk of the President of the United States, and another on the desk of the Premier of Soviet Russia. The communication link was called the '*hotline*'. If at any time there was a danger of misunderstanding they could simply lift up the phone and communicate.

Communication is vital to all relationships. Setting aside time to build and nurture communication is essential. Jesus has given you a 'hotline' to God, but it is not just for emergency use – it is to be used all the time.

READING FROM PSALMS

Psalm 37:1–9
Open up before God

How can your desires be fulfilled? The psalmist, David, says, '*Take delight in the Lord*, and he will *give you the desires of your heart*' (v.4). Rather than pursuing the things you desire, if you delight in God he will give you the desires of your heart. Letting God give you things is so much better than trying to get them for yourself. He promises:

1. Faith in the midst of your fears

There may be lots going on that could make you afraid and even panic. But three times David repeats, 'Do not fret' (vv.1, 7b, 8b). Nor are we to be envious (v.1b). Rather, turn to the Lord, bring him your fears, and 'trust in the Lord' (v.3). Faith is trust. It is the opposite of fear and panic.

2. Guidance in your decisions

'Commit your way to the Lord' (v.5). This is the key to guidance: bring the decision to God, ask him to act and trust in him. Over and over again, I have used this verse in my own life. I have also used it when praying with others who are struggling with decisions, especially about their jobs or potential marriage partners.

It is a simple three-part process. First, to commit the decision to God in prayer, asking him to open the doors that are right for you, and to close the ones that are not right. Second, thereafter trust that he is in control. Third, watch in faith for him to act as you continue on your 'way', in the expectation that God will act.

3. Peace in your heart

Make use of your hotline to God. Set aside time to 'be still before the LORD and wait patiently for him' (v.7). This is the source that makes your 'righteous reward shine like the dawn' (v.6). This is the way to avoid fretting and anger and to find peace and hope (vv.8–9).

PRAYER

Lord, keep me from fear, envy and anger as I trust in you. Today I want to commit my way to you. I will be still before you God. I will delight in you.

NEW TESTAMENT READING

Luke 4:38–5:16
Listen to the word of God

Your hotline to God involves two-way communication. It involves both *speaking* to God in prayer and *listening* to his words. This was the secret of Jesus' own ministry. No one has ever had a more powerful ministry than Jesus. No one has ever had more demands on his time and energy than Jesus.

Everyone wanted his help. When they asked for Jesus' help to heal Simon's mother-in-law, he healed her. He laid hands on all who were brought to him and healed them. He kept on preaching the gospel (4:44). He healed the lepers. The crowds increased; 'crowds of people came to hear him and to be healed of their illnesses' (5:15).

How could he do it? What was his secret? What was the source of his power? 'At daybreak, Jesus went out to a solitary place' (4:42). 'Jesus often withdrew to lonely places and prayed' (5:16). You will never cope with the demands of life in the kingdom of God unless you are being recharged through your hotline to God.

The crowd was pushing in on Jesus 'to better hear the Word of God' (v.1, MSG). Using the boat for a pulpit, Jesus taught the crowd (v.3). Hearing the word of God through Jesus transformed Peter's life.

Peter not only caught a big catch of fish, he also caught a big vision of what God could do with his life. Three years later, he preached a sermon in which 3,000 people were converted in one day. He laid the foundations whereby 2,000 years later over two billion people profess the name of Jesus. What lessons can we learn from this acted-out parable?

1. The potential is vast

They had not caught any fish but there were plenty to catch. In the Sea of Galilee there were phenomenal shoals of fish that covered the sea as if it were solid for as much as an acre.

Although cleaning nets is important for fishermen, the primary purpose is to catch fish. The primary task of the church is mission. Jesus says, 'Put out into deep water, and let down the nets for a catch' (v.4). There are so many people who need to hear the message about Jesus.

2. Nothing is impossible with Jesus

Peter's first reaction was negative and pessimistic. He didn't think it would work, 'We've worked hard all night and haven't caught anything' (v.5a). However, possibly after a long pause, he says, 'But *because you say so*, I will let down the nets' (v.5b). Jesus made what seemed impossible possible. 'When they had done so, they caught such a large number of fish that their nets began to break' (v.6).

3. It cannot be done alone but only in partnership

'So they signalled to their partners in the other boat to come and help them, and they came and filled both boats so full that they began to sink' (v.7). Partnership is the key to mission. Disunity is so off-putting to those outside the church. Partnership and unity are very attractive.

4. It is a vision worth going for

Peter's first reaction was to sense his own unworthiness: 'Go away from me, Lord; I am a sinful man!' (v.8). At the same time, he and the others were astonished at the catch of fish (v.9). They must have been very daunted but Jesus said, 'Don't be afraid; from now on you will fish for people' (v.10). They saw it was a vision worth going for: 'So they pulled their boats up on shore, left everything and followed him' (v.11).

PRAYER

Lord, thank you that you have given me a hotline to you. Help me, like Jesus, to seek solitude with you, to withdraw to lonely places, pray and hear your words.

OLD TESTAMENT READING

Numbers 15:1–16:35
Prioritise communication with God

As you read the Old Testament and particularly some of the passages for today, you may find them quite shocking. There are no easy answers or glib explanations. There are many things that are hard to understand. Perhaps it is better to focus on what we *can* understand.

What is clear in this passage is the vital importance of your relationship with God and spending time with him. The expression 'pleasing to the LORD' appears several times (15:7, 10, 13, 24). Offerings were required to make 'atonement' (v.25). 'At-one-ment' leads to us being *at one with God*. For this, forgiveness is required (vv.25–26, 28). All this was preparing us for Jesus' offering of himself, which brings total forgiveness and atonement so that you can have a hotline to God.

Jesus transformed our understanding of the Sabbath. The people of God placed huge importance on the Sabbath as a day set aside to spend time with God. The Sabbath rules may not still apply, but the Sabbath principle of taking time out to rest and spend time with God still stands.

The purpose of Sabbath rest is to force us to pause and stop 'the lusts of [our] own hearts and eyes' (v.39) becoming our idols. You are supposed to be consecrated to God (v.40) and God wants to bring you near to himself (16:9). It is because of the importance of this relationship that any threat to it, caused by insolence or rebellion (vv.1–2), is taken so seriously (vv.1–35).

We are so privileged to live in the age of the Holy Spirit and to be able to enjoy the freedom that Jesus has brought through the cross and resurrection. This enables you to enjoy a hotline to God without fear. These passages encourage you to make the most of this extraordinary privilege and to spend time alone with him, delighting in his presence and bringing your requests before him.

PRAYER

Lord, help me to lead a life that is pleasing to you, to stay close to you each day and to find time to spend alone with you.

24 March | Day 83
God Wants to Amaze You

'The Eagle has landed,' said Neil Armstrong. President Nixon, watching the events on television, described it as 'one of the greatest moments of our time'. The Pope greeted the news by exclaiming, 'Glory to God in the highest and peace on earth to men of good will!'

At 3:56 a.m. on 20 July 1969, Armstrong stepped off the ladder from the Eagle and onto the moon's surface. 'That's one small step for a man, one giant leap for mankind,' he said, as he became the first man to walk on the moon.

Due to the recent invention of television, this remarkable event was the first of such historic significance to be seen so widely and known so immediately. The whole world watched with *awe and amazement*.

James Irwin, another astronaut who walked on the moon, said, 'Jesus walking on the earth is *more important* than man walking on the moon.' When people saw what Jesus did, their response was awe and amazement: 'Everyone was *amazed* ... They were filled with *awe*' (Luke 5:26).

READING FROM PSALMS

Psalm 37:10–20
Stand in awe and amazement at the choice of God

Do you ever stand in *awe* and *amazement* at the sort of people God chooses? Whereas the world tends to be impressed by people of 'wealth' (v.16) and 'power' (v.17), it is not so with God. 'God chose the foolish ... the weak ... the lowly ... the despised things – and the things that are not – to nullify the things that are, so that no one may boast before him' (1 Corinthians 1:27–29). God chooses:

1. The unassuming

'*The meek* will inherit the land and enjoy peace' (Psalm 37:11). Meek does not mean weak, spineless or feeble. It is the word used of Moses (Numbers 12:3, RSV). Jesus described himself as meek (Matthew 11:29, RSV). It means gentle, considerate and unassuming.

It is the opposite of being arrogant and self-seeking. It is the word used of a horse that has been 'broken', that is, tamed. It means strength under control. Jesus seems to be quoting this verse when he said, '*Blessed are the meek*, for they will inherit the earth' (Matthew 5:5).

2. The poor and needy

God is concerned for 'the poor and the needy' (Psalm 37:14). Those who treat them badly are 'wicked' in God's eyes: 'Better the little that the righteous have than the wealth of many wicked; for the power of the wicked will be broken, but the LORD upholds the righteous' (vv.16–17).

3. The persecuted

The theme of these verses in Psalm 37 is that the wicked plot against the righteous. As the psalmist contrasts the 'righteous' and the 'wicked', it is not that they are merely two separate categories of people, but one is proactive in its hostility to the other: 'Bad guys have it in for the good guys' (v.12, MSG).

These verses remind us that it is not for us to retaliate if we are persecuted because God has it all under control and he will ensure that justice is done in the end. We do not need to take revenge into our own hands (see Romans 12:17–21).

PRAYER

Lord, I stand in awe and amazement at the people you choose. Help me to see people as you see them – not by the world's standards but with your eyes.

NEW TESTAMENT READING

Luke 5:17–32

Look with awe and amazement at the ministry of Jesus

Have you wondered how people must have felt when they saw Jesus perform a miracle? His ministry led to amazement and awe: 'Everyone was *amazed* ... They were filled with *awe*' (v.26). The Amplified version captures this sense of excitement: 'And overwhelming astonishment and ecstasy seized them all, and they recognised and praised and thanked God; and they were filled with and controlled by reverential fear and kept saying, We have seen wonderful and strange and incredible and unthinkable things today!' (v.26, AMP).

1. Healing the sick

Even in the ministry of Jesus there seemed to be ebbs and flows in terms of healing. Sometimes, when there was unbelief, Jesus healed fewer people (Matthew 13:58). At other times, as we read here, 'The power of the Lord was with Jesus to heal those who were ill' (Luke 5:17).

2. Forgiving sins

We tend to find healings amazing. But we can take the forgiveness of sins rather for granted. Jesus demonstrates here that forgiveness is even more amazing and awesome than healing. He first forgives the man's sin (v.20) and then shows that he has the authority to do so by healing him (v.24). Forgiveness was the priority.

3. Reading people

Jesus read their minds. He knew what they were thinking in their hearts (v.22). To forgive those who have sinned against others is something only God can do. When Jesus claimed the authority to forgive the sins of those who had sinned against others, in their hearts they accused him of 'blasphemy' (v.21a), 'Who can forgive sins but God alone?' (v.21b).

In a sense they were right; Jesus was claiming the authority of God to forgive sins. No wonder 'the people rubbed their eyes, incredulous – and then also gave glory to God. *Awestruck*, they said, "We've never seen anything like that!"' (v.26, MSG).

4. Choosing outcasts

Jesus' choice of Levi the tax collector as his follower was *amazing*. He chose an outcast. But he made the right choice. Levi 'got up, left everything and followed him' (v.28). He then gave a great banquet for Jesus at his house and a large crowd came. Levi was clearly an influential leader. People were fascinated by what had happened to him and wanted to meet Jesus.

Jesus' choice was shocking and startling. Whenever I go into prisons, I see that Jesus is still calling as his followers people who are rejected by society, and I am filled with *awe* and *amazement*.

5. Befriending sinners

Once again Jesus amazed people. They asked, 'Why do you eat and drink with tax collectors and "sinners"?' (v.30). Jesus replied, 'It is not the healthy who need a doctor, but those who are ill. I have not come to call the righteous, but sinners to repentance' (vv.31–32).

This is the heart of the good news for all of us. Joyce Meyer writes about this passage; 'So often we feel we must hide our weaknesses and always pretend we are strong and in need of nothing ... [but] we *all* have weaknesses and inabilities ... Jesus came for those who were sick (needy) not those who were healthy (not needy) ... Go ahead and be needy. Tell God everything you need. He already knows anyway and is waiting for you to ask for help.'[1]

PRAYER

Lord, thank you that you are the same yesterday, today and for ever. I ask that your power would be present to heal the sick. May people be struck with awe and amazement as they see you continuing to do remarkable things.

OLD TESTAMENT READING

Numbers 16:36–18:32

Meditate in awe and amazement at the wonder of forgiveness

We have a tendency to take forgiveness for granted. The poet Heinrich Heine once said, '*Dieu me pardonnera. C'est son métier*.'[2] ('God will forgive me. It is his job.') In one sense, nothing could be further from the truth. Sin has a very high cost (16:38). Many of the things we read about in the Old Testament strike us as 'awful' in the sense that they seem to be appalling.

However, another sense of the word 'awful' is 'filled with awe'. One dictionary definition of 'awful' is 'worthy of or commanding profound respect or reverential fear or wonder ... solemnly impressive, sublimely majestic'.[3]

The language in this passage shows the seriousness of sin – its cost and the reaction of God to it: 'Wrath has come out from the Lord' (v.46). God is not pleased at, for example, 'constant grumbling' (17:5).

Sin required atonement (16:46). There was a need for redemption (18:15–16). Sprinkling of blood was required (v.17). The setting up of the Levitical priesthood was necessary to foreshadow and prepare the way for Jesus, the great high priest, whose blood was sprinkled and who made atonement to redeem us from our sins (Hebrews 4:14; 12:24; 2:17).

Unless you understand the seriousness of sin and the Old Testament background, which shows the difficulty and complication of receiving forgiveness, you will not understand how wonderful, awesome and amazing God's forgiveness is. Forgiveness is not automatic, but it is made possible by Jesus. As you meditate on what God has done you should be filled with wonder, *awe* and *amazement*.

PRAYER

Lord, thank you that through Jesus' death and resurrection I can know that I am forgiven. Thank you that I live in the age of the Holy Spirit. Thank you for how the events of the life, death and resurrection of Jesus and the outpouring of the Holy Spirit have transformed my life and transformed this world. May the eyes of the whole world be opened to see these remarkable events with *awe* and *amazement*.

25 March | Day 84

Seven Titles of Jesus

Prince Charles has many titles. He is the Heir Apparent to the Crown, His Royal Highness, The Prince of Wales, Knight of the Garter, Duke of Cornwall, Colonel in Chief of the Royal Regiment of Wales, Duke of Rothesay, Knight of the Thistle, Rear Admiral, Grand Master of the Order of Bath, Earl of Chester, Earl of Carrick, Baron of Renfrew, Lord of the Isles and Prince and Great Steward of Scotland.

Titles are attached to people by virtue of rank, office or attainment. In the Bible, Jesus is given far more titles than a royal prince. In fact, there are well over a hundred titles ascribed to Jesus.

The whole Bible revolves around Jesus (John 5:39). Seven titles of Jesus emerge from the passages for today and each reveal something distinct about Jesus. They help you to see what it means to put Jesus in the centre of your life.

READING FROM PROVERBS

Proverbs 8:1–11
1. Wisdom of God

Many people today have no idea how to live. They make a mess of their marriages and other relationships. Often, they wreck their own lives and the lives of others. We all need wisdom in order to live well.

Where is wisdom to be found? The New Testament answer is that, ultimately, it is found in Jesus Christ. St Paul writes, '*Christ ... the wisdom of God*' (1 Corinthians 1:24). The 'wisdom of God' is one of Jesus' titles.

Wisdom in the book of Proverbs is personified and female ('Lady Wisdom'; 'Madam Insight', Proverbs 8:1, MSG). She is contrasted with an adulterous woman who lurks at street corners when darkness falls and who speaks in secretive, seductive whispers (7:6ff.). Wisdom openly competes against her 'right in the city square where the traffic is thickest' (8:2, MSG) and offers herself as a counter-attraction – a pure bride rather than a fatal seductress.

This shows us that wisdom is not just about knowledge, but that to be wise is to live well. The first step in living well is to set the right goals and ambitions. Seek wisdom, rather than the sensual pleasures represented by the adulteress.

Wisdom is highly desirable. It, or rather she, is better than silver, gold or jewels: 'Choose my instruction instead of silver, knowledge rather than choice gold, for wisdom is more precious than rubies, and nothing you desire can compare with her' (vv.10–11).

If you want true wisdom, it starts with a relationship with Jesus Christ. This is far more valuable than anything the world can offer.

That relationship will have an effect on the way you live out your life. An example of this wisdom is excellence in your speech (vv.6–9) – honest, truthful communication with words that are righteous and true (compare and contrast the words spoken in Numbers 20:3–5, which reveal a lack of trust in God).

PRAYER

Lord Jesus, thank you that true wisdom is found in a relationship with you. You are more precious than rubies and nothing I desire can compare with knowing you. Help me today to act wisely and to speak words of wisdom that bring blessing to others.

NEW TESTAMENT READING

Luke 5:33–6:11
2. Bridegroom

The title of the 'bridegroom' is used in the Old Testament to refer to God himself, 'as a *bridegroom* rejoices over his bride, so will *your God* rejoice over you' (Isaiah 62:5).

Jesus, in the use of this image (Luke 5:34), puts himself in the place of God, not ostentatiously, but almost incidentally. It was, for him, a perfectly natural substitution. Jesus' assumption of the divine role is all the more impressive.

The image of Jesus as the bridegroom and us as the bride is one of greatest possible intimacy (see Ephesians 5:23). It is also an image which points forward to the ultimate consummation of your relationship with Jesus when he returns. You are called to prepare yourself with the same care and love as a bride on her wedding day, particularly focusing on 'righteous' living (see Revelation 19:6–9).

Jesus' teaching is radically new. It cannot be fitted into the thought-forms or behaviour-patterns of the Pharisees. New wine requires new wine skins (Luke 5:36–39).

PRAYER

Lord, thank you that you call me to an intimate relationship with you and rejoice over me as a bridegroom rejoices over his bride. I want to respond with my love and intimate worship.

3. Son of Man

This was Jesus' favourite way of referring to himself (see, for example, Luke 6:5). This is a messianic title. Daniel 7 speaks of 'one like a son of man' (Daniel 7:13) and it is likely that this aspect of Jesus' understanding of his identity and mission stems from that passage. It is a title that combines authority and power with humility and suffering.

We are reminded both of Jesus' love for us and his authority over us. Often we can focus on the first without paying enough attention to the second. Submit to Jesus' authority, obeying his teaching and following where he leads you.

PRAYER

Lord, thank you that you are the representative Son of Man who suffered for me.

4. Lord

Jesus reinterprets the Old Testament. The Pharisees ask, 'Why are you doing what is unlawful on the Sabbath?' (Luke 6:2). Jesus replies by quoting an example in the Old Testament (vv.3–4). He shows from a wider reading of the Old Testament that the Pharisees' understanding of the Sabbath was far too narrow.

He heals a man on the Sabbath and asks this question, 'Which is lawful on the Sabbath: to do good or to do evil, to save life or to destroy it?' (v.9). In other words, he looks behind the *letter* of the law to the *spirit* of the law and shows that as '*Lord of the Sabbath*' (v.5), he is not bound by the letter of the law.

Jesus is radical in his reinterpretation of the Old Testament and we need to read the Old Testament through this lens. We need to understand it in the light of the fact that Jesus says, 'These are the very Scriptures that testify about me' (John 5:39). We see this in our Old Testament passage in three particular ways.

PRAYER

Thank you, Lord, that you are the key that unlocks our understanding of the Old Testament.

OLD TESTAMENT READING

Numbers 19:1–21:3

5. Mediator

These passages about the blood of goats and bulls and the 'ashes of the heifer' (19:9) foreshadow Jesus' death in our place on the cross.

The writer of Hebrews draws attention to these sacrifices, but then explains: 'How much more, then, will the blood of Christ, who through the eternal Spirit offered himself unblemished to God, cleanse our consciences from acts that lead to death, so that we may serve the living God! For this reason, Christ is *the mediator*' (Hebrews 9:14–15a).

PRAYER

Thank you, Lord, that there is 'one God and one mediator between God and human beings, Jesus Christ, himself human, who gave himself a ransom for all' (1 Timothy 2:5–6).

6. Rock

God tells Moses to bring water out of the rock. Moses strikes the rock twice and water gushes out for everyone to drink (Numbers 20:1–11). 'Water came out *abundantly*' (v.11, AMP).

The apostle Paul also tells us how to interpret the water coming out of the rock. He says, 'They ... drank the same spiritual drink; for they drank from the spiritual rock that accompanied them, and that *rock was Christ*' (1 Corinthians 10:3–4). He is the one who quenches our thirst. Material things alone do not satisfy.

God is so generous to us. Water did not come out in a trickle – it came out *abundantly*. Jesus came to give you *abundant* life (John 10:10, RSV). He promises to satisfy your spiritual thirst with 'rivers of living water' (John 7:37–38).

PRAYER

Lord, my rock, thank you that you satisfy my spiritual thirst. May I, through the Holy Spirit within me, bring the water of life to others.

7. Great high priest

Jesus is the 'great high priest' (Hebrews 4:14) who lives for ever to intercede for us. The death of Aaron (Numbers 20:28–29) reminds us that one of the weaknesses of the Levitical priesthood was that these priests died.

The writer of Hebrews contrasts these priests like Aaron whose '*death* prevented them from continuing in office' with Jesus who '*lives for ever*' and 'has a permanent priesthood. Therefore, he is able to save completely those who come to God through him, because *he always lives* to intercede for them' (Hebrews 7:23–25).

This reminds us of the certainty that you can have in your faith. You do not have to worry about whether you will be 'good enough', you can be totally confident in the salvation that you have in Jesus.

PRAYER

Thank you, Lord, my Great High Priest who lives for ever, that you are able to save me completely. Thank you that you rose from the dead and live to intercede for me. Thank you that you are interceding for me right now.

26 March | Day 85
The Fullness of the Blessing

Mother Teresa once gave an interview to *Hello!* magazine. She was asked the question, 'Is it only the affluent who give?'

She replied, 'No, even the poorest of the poor give. The other day a very poor beggar came up to me and said, "Everyone gives to you and I also want to give you twenty paisa" – which is about 2p. I thought to myself, what do I do? If I take it he won't have anything to eat, but if I don't take it I would hurt him so much. So I took, and he was *so happy* because he had given to Mother Teresa of Calcutta to help the poor . . . Giving cleans the heart and helps you get closer to God. *But you also get so much back in return*.'[1]

Generosity is not just a nice character trait that people have. It is right at the heart of what our faith is all about. C. S. Lewis defined Christianity as *'a kind of giving'*.[2] God has poured out his generosity to you in Jesus (John 3:16), and you are called to respond in faith and generosity to others. Each of the passages today is about blessings and curses. The key to the fullness of the blessing is generosity – 'the righteous give generously' (Psalm 37:21).

READING FROM PSALMS

Psalm 37:21–31
Be generous, *always*

Some people in life are 'givers' and some are 'takers'. According to David, this is a key difference between the 'righteous' and the 'wicked': 'Wicked borrows and never returns; Righteous gives and gives. Generous gets it all in the end' (vv.21–22a, MSG).

Generosity is not an occasional act; it is a way of living. The generous are *'always generous* and lend freely' (v.26). The Lord delights in those who live like this (v.23). You may hit problems and stumble but you will not fall (v.24). God's promise is to *bless you* and your children (vv.25–26).

In today's world, we are confronted by many 'children begging bread' (v.25). The bigger picture of this psalm is a vision of the entire people of God upheld by the practice of mutual generosity: giving and receiving. It was the people who followed God in generous giving to the poor that would find that their own needs were met when things took a turn for the worse. Whether financially, or otherwise, the rest of the community would support them in their need.

Today we are aware of great need both locally and further afield. God's will for all his people is to uphold one another by '[giving] generously' (v.21). Take every opportunity to give generously and you will experience the fullness of God's blessing.

PRAYER

Lord, thank you for the amazing promises you make to those who give generously. Help me never to be satisfied with the level of my giving but always to seek to become more generous.

NEW TESTAMENT READING

Luke 6:12–36
Be generous *to everyone*

Jesus spent the night praying to God. He was filled with insight as he chose his disciples. He was also filled with power to heal the sick: 'and the people all tried to touch him, because power was coming from him and healing them all' (v.19).

Jesus contrasts those who accumulate for themselves (the takers) and those who have *generosity* of spirit (the givers).

There is an emptiness about the way of life which involves becoming 'rich', being 'well fed', with lots of superficial laughter and gaining a good reputation (vv.24–26). It leaves people feeling ultimately dissatisfied and 'hungry' (v.25).

The way of blessing is totally different. It is the way of generosity. It may involve poverty, hunger, weeping, being hated, excluded, insulted and rejected (vv.20–22) – but it is a way of satisfaction ('You will be satisfied', v.21) and joy ('You will laugh', v.21).

Jesus calls us to be generous towards our enemies: 'Love your enemies ... If someone grabs your shirt, gift wrap your best coat and make a present of it ... No more tit-for-tat stuff. Live *generously'* (vv.27–29, MSG).

Be generous to everyone; 'Give to everyone' (v.30). This is an attitude of generosity, 'without expecting to get anything back' (v.35).

As always, Jesus is only calling us to imitate the generosity of God: 'Help and give without expecting a return. You'll never – I promise – regret it. Live out this God-created identity the way our Father lives toward us, generously and graciously, even when we're at our worst. Our Father is kind; you be kind' (vv.35–36, MSG).

Generosity towards your enemies means not only to forgive them but also to bless them. You must not speak evil of them even if you think they deserve it. You are to pray for them, bless them and speak well of them. As Nelson Mandela put it, 'Resentment is like drinking poison and waiting for your enemy to die.'[3] Instead, like God, be generous to everyone (v.36).

PRAYER

Father, help me to love my enemies, to do good to those who hate me, to bless those who curse me and to pray for those who ill-treat me. Help me to be merciful, just as you are merciful.

OLD TESTAMENT READING

Numbers 21:4–22:20
Be generous – *like God*

Again in this passage we see the theme of blessings and curses (22:6), and the contrast between 'taking' and 'giving'. We see God's continuing generosity to his people. Their life was not easy. If you have been a Christian for any length of time you have probably experienced times like these. They went through the 'desert', the 'valley' and 'wasteland' (21:18–20). This could be seen as a picture of life's trials; dry patches, low spots and seeming fruitlessness.

But God gives water (v.16). Jesus said, 'whoever drinks the water I give them will never thirst. Indeed, the water I give them will become in them a spring of water welling up to eternal life' (John 4:13–14).

By contrast, Sihon was not a giver. He was mean: 'Sihon would not let Israel pass through his territory' (Numbers 21:23).

Balaam was also a taker. He was after 'the fee for divination' (22:7). He is condemned in the New Testament because he 'loved the wages of wickedness' (2 Peter 2:15). Balaam's 'error' was to 'rush for profit' (Jude 11).

The Israelites themselves grumbled against God and against Moses (Numbers 21:4–5). Despite all that God had done for them, they were not satisfied and rebelled against him. Their rebellion could not go unchecked, and so God initially sent judgment on the people (v.6). God's ultimate plan though was to redeem and bless his people, restoring their relationship with him.

They confessed their sin and 'the Lord said to Moses, "Make a snake and put it up on a pole; anyone who is bitten can look at it and live." So Moses made a bronze snake and put it up on a pole. Then when anyone was bitten by a snake and *looked at* the bronze snake, they lived' (vv.8–9).

Speaking of this incident in the desert Jesus said, 'Just *as Moses lifted up the snake* in the wilderness, so *the Son of Man must be lifted up*, that *everyone who believes may have eternal life in him*' (John 3:14–15). Jesus is referring, of course, to his death on the cross (12:32–33).

God, in his generosity, provides the sacrifice that enables you to know forgiveness. The uplifted snake in Moses' day brought *physical* life to those who looked in faith. The uplifted crucified Christ brings *eternal* life to anyone who looks in faith and believes in him. You cannot earn forgiveness. Eternal life is a free gift, but you still have to choose to accept that gift. Believing is an act of the will that accepts the free gift of God (3:15).

Charles Haddon Spurgeon was one of the greatest and most influential speakers of the nineteenth century. He described his own conversion when, as a teenager, he heard a speaker say, 'Look to Jesus Christ. Look! Look! Look! You have nothing to do but to *look and live*.'

'Like as when the brazen serpent was lifted up, the people only looked and were healed, so it was with me ... When I heard that word, "Look!" what a charming word it seemed to me! Oh! I looked until I could almost have looked my eyes away ... and I could have risen that instant, and sung with the most enthusiastic of them, of the precious blood of Christ, and the simple faith which looks alone to him.'[4]

This is the generosity of God. Your call to be generous stems from God's generosity to you. As the apostle Paul writes, 'Thanks be to God for his indescribable gift!' (2 Corinthians 9:15).

PRAYER

God, thank you for your generosity to me, in providing a way back to you. Help me to look to you daily for forgiveness. Help me to drink in deeply your water of life that sustains me. Thanks be to God for his indescribable gift!

27 March | Day 86
Ten Top Tips for God's Messengers

Billy Graham died on 21 February 2018 at the age of ninety-nine. As a messenger of God, he had planned his own funeral very carefully to be a call for people to put their faith in Jesus.

He had said beforehand, 'Someday you will read or hear that Billy Graham is dead. Don't believe a word of it. I shall be more alive than I am now. I will just have changed my address. I will have gone into the presence of God.'

In 1934, at the age of sixteen, he'd heard God's call and became a faithful messenger of the gospel. He spoke about Jesus to over 210 million people in person and to almost half the population of the world on TV or radio. He was determined to make the most of every opportunity, including his own funeral, to pass on God's message to the world.

'*My messenger*' is the way John the Baptist is described by God (Luke 7:27). You too can be God's messenger. Jesus speaks of '*the message* about the kingdom' (Matthew 13:19). In the New Testament, '*the message*' is a synonym for '*the gospel*' (see Acts 2:41; 4:4; 10:44 and so on). Our task is both *to hear* this message and *to declare* it to others (1 John 1:5).

READING FROM PSALMS

Psalm 37:32–40

1. Stay close to God

If you want to hear God's message, you need to 'wait passionately for GOD, don't leave the path' (v.34a, MSG). 'The spacious, free life is from GOD, it's also protected and safe. GOD-strengthened, we're delivered from evil – when we run to him, he saves us' (vv.39–40, MSG).

PRAYER

Lord, help me to stay close to you, staying on your path and hoping in you.

2. Seek peace

God's messengers must be messengers of peace; 'For there is a happy end for the man of peace' (v.37b, AMP). God's messengers should not be stirrers or seek to bring unnecessary division. Rather, be a person of peace. Jesus said, 'Blessed are the peacemakers' (Matthew 5:9).

PRAYER

Lord, make me an instrument of your peace. Where there is hatred, let me sow love.[1]

NEW TESTAMENT READING

Luke 6:37–7:10

3. Do not judge

Jesus says, 'Do not judge' and 'Do not condemn' (6:37). 'Don't pick on people, jump on their failures, criticise their faults' (v.37, MSG). Jesus' famous story about trying to take a 'speck of dust' out of someone else's eye when we have a 'plank' in our own eye is a challenging one (vv.41–42). It is far easier to see the faults in those around me than to see my own shortfalls and weaknesses. If we live this way, we will always be falling out with others.

I need to pay more attention to my own faults and the areas where I need to grow. Only then can I help reconcile others to God in their struggles. When you treat others with the same patience God shows you, you are much more likely to get on with everybody else and recognise the validity of other people's ministries.

PRAYER

Lord, help me to remove the 'planks' from my life and to extend grace to those around me.

4. Forgive others

Jesus said, 'Forgive, and you will be forgiven' (v.37b). Forgive people even if they are not sorry. Forgiveness saves the expense of anger, the cost of hatred and the waste of energy. The forgiveness that God gives you should be a virtuous circle that overflows into your relationships with others.

PRAYER

Lord, thank you that you have forgiven me. Help me to forgive others, regardless of whether they are sorry or not.

5. Give away your life

As we saw yesterday, generosity is at the heart of Christianity. In this passage Jesus reiterates that message: 'Give away your life; you'll find life given back, but not merely given back – given back with bonus and blessing. Giving, not getting, is the way. Generosity begets generosity' (v.38, MSG).

PRAYER

Lord, help me to reflect your generosity in my attitude to others. Help me to look for the good in others, to forgive, and to give.

6. Hitch your wagon to a star

'Hitch your wagon to a star' was the best piece of advice I was given when I was looking for a place to train as a pastor. Jesus says, 'The student is not above the teacher, but everyone who is fully trained will be like their teacher' (v.40). As I looked at Sandy Millar, I knew that he was the 'star' that I wanted to be like. Therefore, I wanted to train under him because even though I felt I would never equal the wisdom and gifting of my teacher, at least I knew what I was aiming for.

That is why I often read biographies of people like William Wilberforce, Corrie ten Boom, Pope John Paul II, Mother Teresa and Billy Graham. Their examples enrich us and inspire us to aim higher. Of course, Jesus ultimately is the only star. Hitch your wagon to him.

PRAYER

Lord, thank you for the heroes of the faith who have gone before me, and for the leaders that you have put in my life. Help me to learn from them and to aim higher in my walk with you.

7. Guard your heart

Jesus says, 'Good people bring good things out of the good stored up in their hearts, and an evil person brings evil things out of the evil stored up in their hearts. For out of the overflow of one's heart the mouth speaks' (v.45). If you want to be God's messenger you have to fill your heart with his message, his presence and his love. Billy Graham always used to say he liked to speak 'out of the overflow'.

PRAYER

Lord, help me to guard my heart and store up good within it. As David prayed, 'create in me a pure heart, O God' (Psalm 51:10).

8. Obey God's Word

Superficially the two houses in the parable looked the same. But the one that collapsed had no foundation (Luke 6:49). Jesus said, 'If you just use my words in Bible studies and don't work them into your life, you are like a dumb carpenter who built a house but skipped the foundation' (v.49, MSG).

The difference between the two is that the wise person hears the message and puts it into practice (v.47). It is not enough to study God's message. Live it out. Knowing God's word and obeying it should be the foundation of your life.

PRAYER

Lord Jesus, help me to listen to your words and to put them into practice in my life.

9. Be under authority

All authority comes from being *under* authority. The centurion recognised that Jesus' authority came from being *under authority*, just as his own authority as a centurion to give commands came from being '*under authority*' (7:8).

Your message today will have authority if you are under God's authority and are led by his Holy Spirit. This authority does not belong to you: you are authorised by God to be his messenger. The apostle Paul spoke of being an 'ambassador' of the gospel (2 Corinthians 5:20).

PRAYER

Lord Jesus, thank you that you have authorised me to be your messenger. Help me to be a faithful ambassador of the gospel to those around me.

OLD TESTAMENT READING

Numbers 22:21–23:26

10. Finish well

According to the New Testament, Balaam's life is a counterexample. He is cited as an example of a false prophet: 'They have left the straight way and wandered off to follow the way of Balaam son of Bezer, who loved the wages of wickedness. But he was rebuked for his wrongdoing by a donkey – an animal without speech – who spoke with a human voice and restrained the prophet's madness' (2 Peter 2:15–16).

It is a warning against ignoring the guidance of the Holy Spirit. Three times the angel of the Lord tried to stop Balaam going with Balak. But Balaam was determined to go in spite of the fact that the angel of the Lord was trying to stand in his way and said to him, 'I have come here to oppose you because your path is a reckless one before me' (Numbers 22:32).

Balaam had set out to accept a fee for giving Balak the oracle he wanted to hear. Yet, we see in the passage for today that at one stage in Balaam's life he had tried to do the right thing. He said, 'I must speak only what God puts in my mouth' (22:38; see also 23:8, 12, 26).

Balaam's life is a warning that even those who are used by God can get themselves into a mess. It is an encouragement to keep on doing what Balaam, at one point, set out to do – to hear God's message and pass it on to others. Be faithful and finish well.

PRAYER

Lord, help me to be your faithful messenger. I want to be sensitive to the guidance of your Holy Spirit, to follow where you are leading and to stay faithful to the end.

28 March | Day 87

In the Day of Trouble

Ajay was brought up as a Hindu and worked for the family business in a newsagent in North London. At the age of twenty-one he contracted erythrodermic psoriasis, a chronic skin disease. His weight dropped from 11.5 stone (73kg) to 7.5 stone (47.6kg). The disease was all over his body from head to toe. He lost all his friends. His wife and son left him. He wanted to die.

As Ajay lay dying in hospital he cried out to God. He looked in his locker and found a Bible there. He opened it at Psalm 38 – the psalm for today. Each and every verse seemed relevant to him. He prayed for God to heal him. He fell into a deep sleep. By the next morning he was totally healed. His skin was new like a baby's and his life was turned around. He was reunited with his son. I interviewed him in one of the services at Holy Trinity Brompton. He said, 'Every day I live for Jesus.'

Life is not all plain sailing. We will all face troubles. Whatever you are facing today, God is able to rescue you. In the passages for today we see examples of traps, tests and temptations – and how to handle them.

READING FROM PSALMS

Psalm 38:1–12
Traps

David knew what it was like to experience ill-health: 'my back is filled with searing pain; there is no health in my body' (v.7). These are some of the words that struck a chord with Ajay as he read this psalm on his hospital bed.

David also knew what it was like to fail. God convinced him of his sin: 'Your hand has come down on me ... because of my sin. My guilt has overwhelmed me like a burden too heavy to bear ... because of my sinful folly ... the light has gone from my eyes' (vv.2–5, 8, 10).

On top of all this, David had to cope with opposition. He was surrounded by people who wanted to see his downfall. He wrote, 'Those who want to kill me set their *traps*, those who would harm me talk of my ruin; all day long they scheme and lie' (v.12).

Yet, in the midst of these traps and his own failings and difficulties, David cried out to God. He knew that God was able to forgive him, rescue him, and heal him. Whatever your failings or whatever difficulties you may face, you too can bring them to God in prayer.

PRAYER

Lord, I cry to you today – forgive my sin, heal my body and rescue me from the traps set for me.

NEW TESTAMENT READING

Luke 7:11–35
Tests

Each person you meet and every situation that confronts you is, in a sense, a test. How are you going to respond to the needs of the people around you, and the situations you find yourself in?

1. Needs of others

I took the funeral of a young man who died of cancer aged thirty. I saw his mother (a friend of ours for over thirty years) standing by the coffin of her only son. I understand how, when Jesus saw the woman in today's passage in a similar situation, 'his heart went out to her' (v.13).

Jesus had the power and authority to raise her son from the dead, but he still had to have the courage to step out in faith and do it.

We all have to operate within the limits of our own faith. Responding to this kind of situation can be really testing. To get it wrong would be pastorally disastrous. Certainly, I do not recommend doing what Jesus did unless you have his authority, power, faith and a direct instruction from God. But we must seek the right words and the right responses to all those in need. Whatever we do must be motivated by 'compassion' (v.13, AMP).

Jesus is able to say, 'Go back and report to John what you have seen and heard: The blind receive sight, the lame walk, those who have leprosy are cleansed, the deaf hear, the dead are raised, and the good news is proclaimed to the poor' (v.22). You may not be able to say *all* these things, but you *can* pray for the sick and you can certainly proclaim good news to the poor.

2. Criticism

In spite of the fact that Jesus was doing so much that was extraordinary, wonderful and life-changing, he was not universally accepted. The religious leaders of the time 'rejected God's purpose for themselves' (v.30) and brought false accusations against John the Baptist and Jesus.

How you respond to criticism is another test. Jesus said, 'For John the Baptist came neither eating bread nor drinking wine, and you say, "He has a demon." The Son of Man came eating and drinking, and you say, "Here is a glutton and a drunkard, a friend of tax collectors and 'sinners'"' (vv.33–34).

Jesus is saying it is almost impossible to avoid criticism. As Aristotle said, 'The only way to avoid criticism is to do nothing, say nothing and be nothing.' Whatever you do, some people will find fault, but Jesus was not put off by criticism. He says, 'But wisdom is proved right by all her children' (v.35). Perhaps he means that, in the end, wisdom (and Jesus' actions) will be proved by the results, or as we would say, 'the proof of the pudding is in the eating' (v.35, MSG). Jesus and John the Baptist were very different but they were both 'wisdom's children'.

PRAYER

Lord, help me today, with every person I encounter, to have the right words, to bring good news, to have a heart of compassion and to seek to minister to others, as Jesus did.

OLD TESTAMENT READING

Numbers 23:27–26:11
Temptations

The events we read about today are '*a warning sign*' (26:10). As we have seen, when Paul writes about temptations (1 Corinthians 10) he refers back to this section in the book of Numbers and says that what is written here stands as a '*warning*'.

'These are all *warning* markers – DANGER! – in our history books, written down so that we don't repeat their mistakes ... we are just as capable of messing it up as they were ... You could fall flat on your face as easily as anyone else. Forget about self-confidence; it's useless. Cultivate God-confidence' (1 Corinthians 10:11–12, MSG).

What are we being warned about? What are these temptations?

1. Witchcraft

'Sorcery' (sometimes translated divination) means turning to supernatural, magical powers, which do not come from God, to find out something, or to make something happen. Today, we see the use of horoscopes, tarot cards, fortune tellers, Ouija boards, palm reading, and so on. People want to know what is going to happen. Especially in times of trouble, they sometimes turn to these wrong methods.

Balaam's life was a curious mixture. At times he was capable of acting under the inspiration of the 'Spirit of God' (Numbers 24:2). He uttered one of the great messianic prophecies: '*A star* will come out of Jacob; a sceptre will rise out of Israel ... A ruler will come out of Jacob' (vv.17–19; see also Matthew 2:1–10). Jesus describes himself as 'the bright Morning *Star*' (Revelation 22:16).

Yet, Balaam is condemned in the New Testament. We see the reason here. He was a sorcerer. He would normally have received a 'fee for divination' (Numbers 22:7) and been rewarded handsomely for his sorcery (24:11). The moments when he operated under the Spirit of God were exceptions. There were occasions when, 'he did not resort to sorcery as at other times' (v.1).

2. Immorality

The people fell into sexual immorality: 'the men began to indulge in sexual *immorality* with Moabite women (25:1). They were all deceived (v.18). God's judgment came on them and especially on one of their leaders, Zimri, 'the leader of a Simeonite family' (v.14). Sexual immorality is not a temptation from which the leaders of the church are exempt. If leaders fail it is even more serious and damaging, partly because of their influence.

3. God-substitutes

The people were unfaithful to God. They worshipped and bowed down to other gods. They 'joined in worshipping the Baal of Peor' (vv.3, 5). Idols are far broader than statues to other gods. Idols are God-substitutes. They are created things that we are serving as number one in our lives rather than serving the creator (see Romans 1:25).

The apostle Paul warns us of the dangers of falling into the same temptations but ends with these encouraging words:

'No test or temptation that comes your way is beyond the course of what others have had to face ... God will never let you down; he'll never let you be pushed past your limit; he'll always be there to help you come through it' (1 Corinthians 10:13, MSG).

PRAYER

Father, help me to stand against the temptations of the enemy. May I never do anything that brings dishonour to the name of Jesus. May your name be glorified in everything I do.

29 March | Day 88
How to Become Wise

Oprah Winfrey says, 'Follow your instincts. That's where true wisdom manifests itself.'[1] In other words, wisdom comes from within and is a kind of intuition. Since you are created in the image of God, there is truth in this. However, as we see in today's passages, true wisdom comes from God and it is supremely acquired through your relationship with him. As we have seen, knowledge is horizontal. But wisdom is vertical. It comes down from above. You will grow in wisdom as you learn, reflect and live in relationship with God.

We all desperately need wisdom. In the Old Testament there are several books of 'Wisdom': Proverbs, Job, Ecclesiastes and Song of Songs. In addition, sprinkled throughout the Bible are various writings which might loosely be described as 'Wisdom Literature', dealing with such diverse areas as the power of the tongue, the blessings of faithfulness, the dangers of adultery, the hazards of strong drink, the inequalities of life, the sufferings of the righteous, the skill of leadership and the art of parenting.

This wisdom is a kind of sanctified common sense. It leads to greater self-understanding. It gives you the ability to cope in life and to steer through and master its challenges. It is the sort of legacy good parents want to hand on to their children. Ultimately, wisdom is found in Jesus Christ, who is the 'wisdom of God' (1 Corinthians 1:24).

READING FROM PROVERBS

Proverbs 8:12–21
Seek wisdom from God

Wisdom is immensely valuable: 'My benefits are worth more than a big salary, even a very big salary; the returns on me exceed any imaginable bonus' (vv.18–19, MSG). This wisdom is worth more than all the material wealth in the world. Apart from anything else, unlike material wealth, it lasts for ever (v.18).

In this passage, we see *why* wisdom is so valuable and *how* we should seek God for such wisdom:

1. Wisdom comes from God

Wisdom begins with a relationship with God. It starts with the 'fear of the Lord' (v.13). 'Fear' means 'respect' and a deep awareness of God that is the foundation of all wisdom.

2. Wisdom is pure and beautiful

The writer of Proverbs says, 'To fear the LORD is to hate evil; I hate pride and arrogance, evil behaviour and perverse speech ... I walk in the way of righteousness, along the paths of justice' (vv.13, 20). This is the test of true wisdom that comes from God. As the apostle James writes, 'Wisdom that comes from heaven is first of all pure; then peace-loving, considerate, submissive, full of mercy and good fruit, impartial and sincere' (James 3:17).

3. Wisdom helps you lead well
Wisdom is of particular importance for leaders. If you want to be a good leader you need wisdom and common sense: 'With my help, leaders rule, and lawmakers legislate fairly; With my help, governors govern, along with all in legitimate authority' (Proverbs 8:15–16, MSG).

4. Wisdom is available to you
God promises wisdom to all who seek after it: 'I love those who love me, and *those who seek me find me*' (v.17). As the apostle James puts it, 'If *any of you* lacks wisdom, you should ask God, who gives generously to all without finding fault, and it will be given to you' (James 1:5). This is a prayer you can be sure will be answered.

PRAYER

Lord, I desperately need your wisdom today. Please give me wisdom that is pure, peace-loving, considerate, submissive, full of mercy and good fruit, impartial and sincere.

NEW TESTAMENT READING

Luke 7:36–50
See people with wise eyes

Have you ever made a misjudgement about somebody based only on outward appearances?

In today's passage we see a woman with a past, who sold her love by the hour as the town prostitute, washing Jesus' feet with her hair, kissing them and pouring perfume on them. The Pharisee's reaction was the natural one: 'If this man were a prophet, he would know who is touching him and what kind of woman she is – that she is a sinner' (7:39).

But Jesus, '*filled with wisdom*' (2:40) right from his earliest days, could see beneath the surface. He saw the fact that the woman was expressing her immense love for him because she knew how much she had been forgiven. You may have had a negative past but you can have a positive and blessed future.

We see the wisdom of Jesus both in his insight into people and in the way he chose to teach. He tells a parable about an eccentric bank manager. He has two customers. One owes £5,000, another £50,000. He lets both of them off completely. No human bank manager is likely to act like that. But that is exactly what Jesus' love is like. All your sins are wiped out. You receive total forgiveness. The greater the debt, the more grateful you will be and the greater your love for Jesus.

This parable enabled Simon the Pharisee, unwittingly, to answer his own concern (7:43). Jesus wisely and gently points out that Simon had not given him a very warm welcome, nor shown a great deal of love. Simon's problem was that he didn't realise how much he needed forgiveness.

On the other hand, the woman loved Jesus much because she knew she had been forgiven much (v.47). She was willing to risk rejection and give of herself practically, emotionally and financially.

She wept so much that she 'wet his feet with her tears' (v.38). In order to wipe his feet, she let her hair down in public (something regarded as shameful). She was in the grip of her emotions and oblivious to what others thought. She did not stop kissing his feet out of deep reverence.

Then she poured rare and expensive perfume (normally reserved for the head) on his feet. She loved Jesus with all of her heart. Jesus sees your heart, rather than your past. He said to her, '*Your faith* has saved you; go in peace' (v.50). Your love is a result of your faith. As the apostle Paul wrote, 'The only thing that counts is *faith expressing itself through love*' (Galatians 5:6).

You may not have had a good beginning in life but this does not mean you cannot have a great finish. Whatever your past life was like, with Jesus you can make a completely new start and have a great future. You do not need to go around burdened by guilt – from previous relationships or from incidents in your past. The moment you repent and put your faith in Jesus, all your sins are wiped out. It is important that what you know in your head drops to your heart.

Jesus wants you to acknowledge that you are a sinner. You can't pay off your debts. But Jesus forgives you. Ask the Holy Spirit to fill you today with an overflowing love for God and love for others.

PRAYER

Lord, give me wisdom like Jesus not to judge by outward appearances but to see the heart. Fill me with the Holy Spirit today. May I overflow with love for you and for others.

OLD TESTAMENT READING

Numbers 26:12–27:11
Show wisdom in practical decisions

Moses shows very practical wisdom, allotting the size of land according to the size of the group (26:54).

Sadly, not everyone was as wise as Moses. When they were in the desert they rebelled and grumbled against God. As a result, God said that they would not enter the promised land. This is exactly what happened. Of those counted in the desert of Sinai, 'not one of them was left except Caleb son of Jephunneh and Joshua son of Nun' (vv.64–65).

There is an old ditty that goes:

> *Joshua*, the son of Nun
> And *Caleb*
> The son of Jephunneh
> Were the *only two*
> Who ever got through
> To the land of milk and honey.

Zelophehad's daughters also showed great wisdom in being courageous and speaking out. They stood up for women's rights (27:1–11). Had these women not done so, the results might have been very different. They were right to have the courage to speak out.

Moses dealt with the situation with great wisdom. He did not simply follow the customs of his day; he was remarkably open-minded. He had the wisdom not to make a hasty decision in his own strength, or automatically equate God's will with ancient custom.

Yet the heart of Moses' wisdom lay in his recognition that true wisdom comes from God. Again and again, Moses brought the problems and challenges of the people to God. He sought God's help and guidance, and it was this that made him wise.

PRAYER

Lord, I need your wisdom for all the decisions I have to make each day. Help me not just to look within at my own instincts but to seek your wisdom that comes from above, to follow the example of Jesus' wisdom and to be guided by the Holy Spirit, who gives me wisdom in my heart.

30 March | Day 89
A Hundredfold Return

He was brought up on one of the roughest estates in Manchester. His father was an alcoholic. He left school at fifteen. He ran away from home. He lived on the streets. He joined a gang. He got involved in crime and ended up in prison. When he came out he joined the army. He went through two divorces.

In 1994, he walked into our church and did Alpha. He encountered Jesus and was filled with the Holy Spirit. He started visiting prisoners. He joined the Holy Trinity Brompton staff team to head up the work in prisons. He started an organisation to care for ex-offenders. He set up a homeless project. He started a course to help those with addictions and courses to help those struggling with depression and debt.

Under his leadership, Alpha for Prisons has spread through the prisons in the UK and seventy-six countries around the world. Thousands have come to faith in Jesus Christ. Hundreds of men and women have been placed in churches through the ministry of Caring for Ex-Offenders.

This man is Paul Cowley – an example of someone who was the good soil on which the seed fell. He has a noble and good heart. He heard the word, retained it and by persevering has produced a crop hundreds of times more than was sown (Luke 8:8, 15). He encountered Jesus as his Saviour, Sower and Shepherd.

READING FROM PSALMS

Psalm 38:13–22
Personal Saviour

David, in the midst of all his troubles, suffering and persecution, turns to the Lord as his personal Saviour: '*my* Saviour' (v.22). You may or may not be facing the extreme difficulties David faced, but you can still follow this pattern today:

1. Ask
Cry out for help: 'I wait for you, O LORD; you will answer, O LORD my God. For I said, "Do

not let them gloat or exalt themselves over me when my foot slips'" (vv.15–16).

2. Confess

Confess your sin: 'I'm ready to tell my story of failure, I'm no longer smug in my sin' (v.18, MSG).

3. Trust

'For in You, O Lord, do I hope' (v.15, AMP). Trust God to save you: 'O Lord, do not forsake me; be not far from me, O my God. Come quickly to help me, O Lord *my Saviour*' (vv.21–22).

PRAYER

Lord, I ask you for your help to ACT today. Forgive my sin. O Lord, do not forsake me; be not far from me, O my God. Come quickly to help me, O Lord my Saviour.

NEW TESTAMENT READING

Luke 8:1–18
Great Sower

A great deal of Jesus' ministry was about sowing seeds. Jesus went about 'proclaiming the good news of the kingdom of God' (v.1) wherever he went. Our ministry today is often about simply sowing seeds.

Sometimes this involves *travelling* (v.1) to sow seed (for example, on a mission trip). At other times, Jesus *gathered* people together and then sowed seeds: '*A large crowd was gathering* and people were coming to Jesus from town after town' (v.4). Every year I am excited about the Leadership Conference[1] which takes place at the Royal Albert Hall in May. Thousands of people gather together, 'from town after town', around Jesus.

Jesus did not do all of this sowing on his own. He had a team, at the heart of which were twelve men and 'also some women' (v.2). Women played a very important role in Jesus' ministry. Among other things, they helped 'to support' the team 'out of their own means' (v.3).

Jesus then describes what they are all doing in terms of the parable of the sower. They, like us, are all sowing the seed of the word of God (v.11). Don't be disappointed if not everyone responds equally.

1. Hard-hearted

Some won't believe: 'The seeds on the road are those who hear the Word, but no sooner do they hear it than the Devil snatches it from them so *they won't believe* and be saved' (v.12, MSG).

2. Faint-hearted

I have never met a strong person with an easy past. Faith is tested. 'Trouble' in life is almost inevitable. Some seem to respond very enthusiastically, but it does not last. They have 'no root'. They 'hear with enthusiasm, but the enthusiasm doesn't go very deep. It's only another fad, and the moment there's *trouble* it's gone' (v.13, MSG).

3. Half-hearted

Others seem to be very responsive but later they drop out due to 'the thorns of life': 'anxieties', 'cares', 'riches', and 'pleasures' (v.14, AMP). 'These are the ones who hear, but then the seed is crowded out and nothing comes of it as they go about their lives worrying about tomorrow, making money, and having fun' (v.14, MSG).

4. Wholehearted

The first three categories lead to great disappointment and sadness. However, Jesus says *some* will be responsive and 'steadily bring forth fruit with patience' (v.15, AMP). Or as *The Message* puts it: 'These are the good-hearts who seize the Word and hold on no matter what, sticking with it until there's a harvest (v.15, MSG). Earlier, he had said that this crop might reap 'a hundred times more than was sown' (v.8).

I often say that running Alpha is *the most disappointing thing I have ever been involved in*. It is disappointing when people respond negatively or drop out. But as we read the words of Jesus we should not be surprised by this.

On the other hand, Alpha has also been *the most exciting thing I have ever been involved in*. Those who do respond wholeheartedly to the seed that has been sown, like Paul Cowley, have a huge impact – a hundred times what was sown. We see this time and again in the lives of those who come to know Jesus – they are filled with the Holy Spirit, go out and tell their friends, and make a great impact on society.

These words of Jesus are not just about other people. It is about you and me, every time we hear the word of God – for example when we are reading the Bible or listening to a talk. Be careful how you listen to the word of God. In one sense the whole of your life is a response to the word of God. The more responsive you are, the more you will be given (v.18).

PRAYER

Lord, thank you for the power of your word to change lives. Help me not to be discouraged by the disappointments but to keep on sowing the seed. Thank you for the great joy there is when we see seed take root in a person's life and produce a crop a hundred times what was sown.

OLD TESTAMENT READING

Numbers 27:12–29:11
Chief Shepherd

As Moses comes to the end of his life he sees the desperate need that God's people have for a leader. He prays to the Lord: 'May the LORD, the God who gives breath to all living things, appoint someone over this community to go out and come in before them, one who will *lead them* out and bring them in, so that the LORD's people will not be *like sheep without a shepherd*' (27:16–17).

God heard Moses' prayer and appointed Joshua as his successor. God said of Joshua, 'The Spirit is in him!' (v.18, MSG). Hands were laid on him, he was commissioned, he was given authority, and he became a *shepherd* of God's people. *'Shepherd'* was a common term for kings and rulers at the time.

Moses' concern for the Lord's people foreshadows Jesus' concern for his people. When Jesus saw crowds of people in his ministry, 'he had compassion on them, because they were harassed and helpless, *like sheep without a shepherd*' (Matthew 9:36).

This image of the Christian leader as a shepherd is picked up in a number of places in the New Testament. Peter writes, 'Be shepherds of God's flock that is under your care ... not lording it over those entrusted to you, but being examples to the flock' (1 Peter 5:2–3). Jesus is the 'Chief Shepherd' (v.4).

Jesus said, 'I am the good shepherd. The good shepherd lays down his life for the sheep ... I know my sheep' (John 10:11–14). He says that one day there will be 'one flock and one shepherd' (v.16). The writer of Hebrews describes Jesus as 'that great Shepherd of the sheep' (Hebrews 13:20).

The rest of the passage in Numbers, with its regulations for eating and drinking, religious festivals and the Sabbath, again points us ultimately to Jesus (Numbers 28–29). St Paul writes, 'These are a shadow of the things that were to come; the reality, however, is found *in Christ*' (Colossians 2:17). Jesus is the Chief Shepherd, the Great Sower and the Saviour of the world.

PRAYER

Lord, I worship you today as the Chief Shepherd, the Great Sower and the Saviour of the world. May I, in turn, be a good shepherd, sow the seed of your word and produce a hundredfold return.

31 March | Day 90
How to Overcome Your Fears

Millennials (those born between 1981 and 2000) are sometimes known as *'generation fear'*. In one of her most popular songs, Lily Allen sings about *'being taken over by the fear'*.[1]

'Fear' carries two meanings in the Bible – one healthy, one unhealthy. In the good sense of the word, it is usually used in the context of respect for God and sometimes of respect for people (especially those in authority).

In the bad sense, it means to be frightened. We are supposed to fear God (in the good sense) and not be frightened of anyone or anything else. Many people today live with the opposite. They do not fear God but their lives are full of the wrong kinds of fear.

How can you overcome your fears?

READING FROM PSALMS

Psalm 39:1–13
Be honest about your fears

All of us experience fear. You can try to suppress and deny your fears or you can be honest and open about them.

David comes before God with some burning questions. He has tried being 'silent and still' but found that his 'anguish increased' when he wasn't communicating with God (v.2).

He has realised how much of human life is spent in anxiety and fear. However, the brevity of life gives perspective to our anxieties. Life is fleeting (v.4). Our lives are 'but a breath' (v.5). Fear often concerns money: 'Human beings ... bustle about, but only in vain; they heap up wealth, not knowing who will get it' (v.6).

David is particularly concerned about the suffering that he sees around him and in his own life. He cannot understand how God can allow it. He is so incensed by God's actions that he even prays, 'Look away from me, that I may rejoice again' (v.13).

In the midst of desperation, it is healthy to voice your concerns and grievances to God. God understands that suffering will cause us confusion and grief – he went through the worst of it for us.

This psalm does not provide the full answer to these fears about suffering. Yet, right at the heart of the psalm, as David lays his fears, anguish and frustration before God, we see that he finds the answer in his relationship with God. David declares to God: 'My hope is *in you*' (v.7). And his prayer at the end is a recognition that he depends completely on God for an answer.

Life is too short to worry about stupid things. Pray. Trust God. Enjoy life. Don't let the little things get you down.

PRAYER

'Hear my prayer, O Lord, listen to my cry for help; be not deaf to my weeping' (vv.8, 12).

NEW TESTAMENT READING

Luke 8:19–39
Keep trusting in Jesus

There may be times in your life when fear seems overwhelming. Sometimes it comes like the unexpected storm that the disciples experienced (vv.22–25).

This section starts with an extraordinary combination of intimacy and awe. Jesus says of his followers that 'those who hear God's word and put it into practice' (v.21) will have an intimate relationship with him. They are his 'mother and brothers' (v.21).

Intimacy and 'fear' (in the good sense) are not opposites – they complement one another. This is true of the best relationships – whether in marriage, in close friendships or with parents and children. Extraordinary intimacy is combined with healthy respect.

The disciples experienced two different types of fear when they were on the lake with Jesus. When a storm came, they were in 'great danger' (v.23) and the disciples were afraid. They woke Jesus and said, 'Master, Master, we're going to drown!' (v.24a).

Jesus 'got up and rebuked the wind and the raging waters; the storm subsided, and all was calm' (v.24b). He said to his disciples, 'Where is your faith?' (v.25a). Again we see the contrast between unhealthy fear and faith. Jesus said to them, '*Why can't you trust me*?' (v.25a, MSG).

The answer to their fear is so simple and yet so hard to put into practice. I have found it is a lesson I have had to keep re-learning. In the midst of your fears, keep trusting Jesus – keep putting your confidence in him. Sometimes Jesus calms the storm as he did here. Sometimes he lets the storm rage and he calms you.

The disciples' response to Jesus is one of healthy fear – absolute awe (v.25b, MSG), amazement and humility in the presence of Jesus. They ask each other: 'Who is this?' (v.25).

Their question is answered by the demon-possessed man whom Jesus heals. Jesus is the 'Son of the Most High God' (v.28).

When those tending the pigs saw the man healed, 'sitting at Jesus' feet, dressed and in his right mind', they 'were *afraid'* (v.35) – 'scared to death' (v.34, MSG). They asked Jesus to leave because they were '*overcome with fear*' (v.37) – 'too much change, too fast and they were scared' (v.37, MSG).

This was again the wrong kind of fear. They were afraid because they had lost valuable pigs. What would it be next? They could not see the immense value of one person's life. They rejected Jesus out of fear, but Jesus had no fear of them or anything else.

Jesus had an interesting approach to follow-up. The man who had been demon-possessed wanted 'to go with him' (v.38). However, Jesus' approach is to get him involved in telling others straight away. He says, '"Return home and tell how much God has done for you." So the man went away and told all over the town how much Jesus had done for him' (v.39).

In encountering Jesus, he had encountered God. Luke interchanges, 'how much *God* has done for you' (v.39a) and 'how much *Jesus* had done for him' (v.39b). Jesus is God. This is why ultimately Jesus is the answer to all our unhealthy fears. Don't be overcome by fear but overcome your fear with Jesus.

PRAYER

Lord, give me a healthy fear – awe, amazement and humility in the presence of Jesus and a faith in him that delivers me from all my unhealthy fears.

OLD TESTAMENT READING

Numbers 29:12–31:24
Fear God and nothing else

The episodes in this Old Testament passage are deeply shocking to our modern ears. Some parts of the Old Testament seem to be very difficult (for example, Numbers 31:15–18). There are no easy answers to these issues. Sometimes all we can do is hold on to what we know about God's love and goodness, and trust that there is an answer – even if we do not fully understand it.

The people of God in the Old Testament had a very healthy fear of God. They did not take access into his presence for granted. They knew that their God of love was a God of justice who takes sin and rebellion very seriously (Numbers 31).

The key for us, as Christians, is to interpret all this in the light of Jesus:

1. Jesus is the one perfect sacrifice
The decreasing numbers of bulls sacrificed each day (Numbers 29), from thirteen, to seven, to one, points ahead to a time where no sacrifice would be needed any longer. Jesus, the one perfect sacrifice, abolished the need for any further sacrifices.

2. In Jesus there is neither male nor female
These regulations about vows (Numbers 30) seem both to try and protect women and discriminate against them. We need to remember that most ancient societies were patriarchal, and men were considered the leaders of the family. These regulations were probably therefore designed to protect women in situations where they were prevented from fulfilling a vow they had made.

However, we need to read this through the eyes of the New Testament, and in particular through the words of the apostle Paul – that in Christ there is neither male nor female (Galatians 3:28). This passage in Numbers is responding to a cultural context, not establishing a principle about gender.

3. Jesus said 'love your enemies'
As we read of the vengeance on the Midianites, it is a reminder how seriously God views those who try to lead people away from following him. It appears that the Midianites had deliberately tried to do this, first through sex, and then through military opposition (Numbers 31:16; see also v.18).

Nonetheless, we must also read this act of judgment through the lens of Jesus who said, 'Love your enemies' (Matthew 5:44). The key to all this is the cross. At the cross we see again how seriously God views sin, and the full extent of his judgment. Yet we also see that his ultimate desire is to bless and redeem us all.

This transforms our response to passages like this. Paul writes, 'Do not take revenge' (Romans 12:19). Rather, we are to live lives of love. As St John writes, 'There is no fear in love. But perfect love drives out fear' (1 John 4:18). This is the way to overcome your fears.

PRAYER

Lord, thank you that there is no fear in love but perfect love drives out all fear. Help me to love you and not to be frightened of anyone or anything else.

1 April | Day 91
Follow Jesus

Curious to know what all the fuss was about, Pippa and I, eventually, entered the world of Twitter and Instagram. It is a world where you 'follow' other people and are yourselves 'followed'.

Many celebrities have huge followings. People become avid spectators of their lives, relationships and lifestyle, diets and fashion choices. They want to know all about them, interact with them and be like them. There is nothing inherently wrong with this. It is natural to want to follow those we admire. Following celebrities on social media can be fun and even enlightening.

However, following people on Instagram or Twitter is one thing; being a *true follower* of someone is quite another. It means fully devoting yourself to their cause, living by their example and even doing what they tell you to do. Choose the right people to follow. It really does matter whom you follow. Millions, for example, followed Hitler, Stalin and Pol Pot. Still today, millions follow evil dictators, terrorists and gang leaders.

Some people are sceptical about tradition and institutions and do not know whom to follow. The traditional models, which often came from or were championed by our families, institutions and political leaders, have, to some extent, broken down. This leaves many people unsure of whom to follow.

Jesus said many times, 'Follow me.' Of all the people who have ever lived, Jesus has the largest number of followers. Over 2.4 billion people in the world today profess to follow Jesus. Jesus' followers are called 'disciples'. They want to be with him, to know him, to be like him and to do everything that Jesus asks them to do.

READING FROM PSALMS

Psalm 40:1–8
Follow Jesus' example

When you are going through difficult times you will be strengthened as you remember past blessings and the times that God has delivered you.

David writes about the time when he was in '*the slimy pit*', full of 'mud and mire' (v.2a). He may be describing some experience of sin, sickness or the depth of depression. Corrie ten Boom said, 'There is *no pit* so deep that God's love is not deeper still.'[1]

'The pit' of depression can be a terrible place. In these times we remember all our failures and disappointments. We start to believe that nothing good could ever happen to us. We feel miserable and helpless. We start to think that we will never rise above our problems and fulfil God's call in our lives.

In his helplessness David says, 'I waited and waited and waited for God. At last he looked; finally he listened. He lifted me out of the ditch, pulled me from deep mud' (vv.1–2a, MSG).

After God lifted him out of the slimy pit, 'He stood me up on a solid rock to make sure I wouldn't slip' (v.2b, MSG). God put a new song of worship in David's mouth and his witness led many others to 'put their trust in [the Lord]' (v.3).

David describes the great blessing of ignoring 'what the world worships' (v.4, MSG) and following the Lord. 'Blessed are those who make the Lord their trust ... The things you planned for us no one can recount to you; were I to speak and tell of them, they would be too many to declare' (vv.4–5).

David writes, 'You have given me the capacity to hear and obey' (v.6, AMP). The secret of his success was praying and obeying.

David offers himself to follow God's will in its entirety. He says, 'Here I am, I have come – it is written about me in the scroll. *I desire to do your will*, O my God; your law is within my heart' (vv.7–8).

This too was Jesus' secret of success. According to the writer of Hebrews these verses found perfect fulfilment in Jesus. He tells us that Jesus himself quoted verses 6–8 in this psalm (see Hebrews 10:5–10). Jesus prayed and he obeyed. He said, 'I have come to do your will, O God' (v.7). The writer of Hebrews continues, 'And by that will, we have been made holy through the sacrifice of the body of Jesus Christ once for all' (v.10).

Follow Jesus' example and offer yourself to do God's will. David says that those who make the Lord their trust will be blessed. You will see all kinds of 'wonders' (Psalm 40:5) and 'things you planned for us no one can recount ... they would be too many to declare' (v.5).

PRAYER

Lord, thank you for the times when you have lifted me out of the slimy pit, out of the mud and mire, set my feet on a rock, given me a firm place to stand, put a new song in my mouth and enabled me to testify so that others put their trust in the Lord. Help me today to pray and to obey.

NEW TESTAMENT READING

Luke 8:40–9:9
Follow Jesus' instructions

Jesus did not have social media, broadcast capacity, big screens or even a simple microphone with which to get the message out. He did not need them. He had 'power and authority', which he gives to his followers (29:1).

While it is fine to use every available means to get the message of Jesus out, we must not get so caught up with modern means of communication that we forget what is at the heart of it all. Follow Jesus' example and his instructions, which we read about in this passage.

Jesus healed a woman who had been subject to bleeding and raised Jairus's daughter back to life. Jairus and the woman are two very different characters: one male, the other female; one an individual, the other part of a crowd; one influential, the other seemingly insignificant; one told Jesus about his daughter, the other was called 'daughter' by Jesus; one was healthy and the other was sick.

Yet both were dependent on Jesus' power and authority, and both reacted in the same way on approaching Jesus. Jairus 'came and fell at Jesus' feet' (8:41) and the woman 'came trembling and fell at his feet' (v.47).

Both had the right response to Jesus. They recognised his power and were prepared to follow his instructions and believe that Jesus had the power to heal. Jesus said to the woman: 'Daughter, your faith has healed you. Go in peace' (v.48). And he said to Jairus: 'Don't be afraid; just believe, and she will be healed' (v.50). These are stories of both extraordinary power, and extraordinary compassion.

It was said of Jesus, 'All who *touched him* were healed' (Mark 6:56). When the woman who had been subject to bleeding for twelve years *touched him*, he said, 'Someone *touched me*; I know that *power* has gone out from me' (Luke 8:46). She was 'instantly healed' (v.47). Jesus then raised Jairus's daughter from the dead. People were 'astonished' (v.56). Jesus ministered with great power and authority.

It is even more astonishing that he passes this on to you. *Power* and *authority* are words we rightly associate with Jesus' ministry. However, they are not unique to Jesus. Jesus called his disciples together and 'gave *them power* and *authority* ... to *preach the kingdom* of God and to *heal the sick*' (9:1–2). This is the ministry to which every one of Jesus' disciples is called (Matthew 28:18–20). His power and authority are available to you today.

PRAYER

Lord, help me to follow your instructions – to preach the kingdom of God and to heal the sick. Help me to follow your example closely and to learn to minister with power and authority.

OLD TESTAMENT READING

Numbers 31:25–32:42
Follow Jesus wholeheartedly

God's power and authority are given to those who follow the Lord *wholeheartedly* (32:22). Caleb and Joshua are picked out as the exceptions from the Israelites because only the two of them 'followed the LORD *wholeheartedly*' (v.12). This is what God's people are called to do.

Moses warned the people not to 'turn away from *following* him' (v.15). He warned them not to sin against the Law: 'you may be sure that your sin will find you out' (v.23). The constant challenge of the Scriptures is to follow the Lord with all our hearts and not to dabble with sin.

Reading this through the lens of the New Testament, to 'follow the Lord' is to follow Jesus. '*Jesus is Lord*' is the central claim of the New Testament. (See for example Romans 10:9.)

We see in these passages how much is available to those who follow Jesus *wholeheartedly*, put their faith and trust in him and offer themselves to do his will. *This* is what you are called to. As you do this, Jesus sends you out into the world with power and authority to *proclaim the gospel* and *heal the sick*.

PRAYER

Lord, I want to be like Caleb and Joshua and follow you wholeheartedly. Today I want to follow your example and offer myself to do your will. Help me to minister with power and authority, to proclaim the gospel and heal the sick.

2 April | Day 92
It Is All Yours

The Chelsea Flower Show may well be the most famous flower show in the world. It attracts visitors from all continents.

There are four grades of award presented, Gold, Silver-Gilt, Silver and Bronze. As well as awards for gardens and flowers, the Knightian award is for exhibits of vegetables.

I once heard a man being interviewed about the fact that he was retiring after winning the gold medal for his vegetables for ten years in a row. Asked for the secret of his success, he said, '*I aim for perfection. But I settle for excellence*.'

'Aim for perfection' (2 Corinthians 13:11), writes the apostle Paul. This is very different from 'perfectionism'. Perfectionism is a personality trait characterised by striving for flawlessness. It leads to setting excessively high performance standards.[1] Perfectionists are overly critical of themselves and constantly concerned about what others think of them. It leads to a fear of failure and making mistakes. It can lead to depression, anxiety and missed opportunities.

God's people have always been called to aim high (while avoiding the dangers of perfectionism). God gave to his people in the Old Testament a wonderful vision of their potential *inheritance*. It is all yours in Christ Jesus.

READING FROM PROVERBS

Proverbs 8:22–31
Aim to be full of joy

Jesus wants you to be full of joy. He wants you to experience complete joy. He said, 'I have told you this so that *my joy may be in you* and that *your joy may be complete*' (John 15:11).

The description of personified Wisdom in today's passage is echoed in the way the New Testament talks about Jesus. Jesus 'was with God in the beginning' (John 1:2) (compare Proverbs 8:23, 30).

Wisdom is seen to be full of joy: 'Day after day I was there, with my *joyful* applause, always *enjoying* his company, *delighted* with the world of things and creatures, *happily celebrating* the human family' (Proverbs 8:30b–31, MSG).

This joy is overflowing – 'filled with delight' (v.30). It is constant – 'day after day' (v.30). Where does this joy come from?

First, it comes from God's presence ('in his presence', v.30). Second, it comes from relationships with other people ('the human family', v.31, MSG). Third, it comes from God's creation ('world of things and creatures', v.31, MSG). God has given us all good things richly to enjoy (1 Timothy 6:17). It is all yours in Christ Jesus.

The joy that Jesus experienced in his relationship with God the Father strengthened him in his life on earth. Fix your 'eyes on Jesus ... who for *the joy* set before him endured the cross' (Hebrews 12:2–3). Jesus teaches us to aim high with our own lives, never just 'making do' but enduring hardships and always seeking the joy of God's presence.

PRAYER

Lord, thank you that you want your joy to be in me and my joy to be complete. May I never settle for anything less.

NEW TESTAMENT READING

Luke 9:10–27
Aim to be full of love

Jesus is the supreme example of love. Even the secular world often recognises this. *TIME* Magazine said this: 'Jesus, the most persistent symbol of purity, selflessness and *love* in the history of western humanity.'[2]

Jesus loves you. He cares about your physical needs. Rather than sending the crowd away hungry to find food for themselves, he gets his disciples to feed them – miraculously.

We come back again to the feeding of the five thousand – the only miracle (apart from the resurrection) recorded in all four Gospels. We are reminded of how much Jesus can do with the very little that we offer him, and of the fact that Jesus involves us in his miracles. This is a huge privilege and it is all yours in and through Jesus.

The disciples begin to understand who Jesus really is when he asks: '"Who do you say I am?" and Peter answers, "The Christ of God."' (v.20). Jesus begins to explain to them about his death (the greatest act of love in history) and resurrection. He challenges his disciples to aim high. He calls you to aim at three things, which together comprise love for others and love for Jesus.

1. No sin

Sin is the opposite of love. In the middle of the word SIN is the letter 'I'. Jesus says, 'Those who would come after me must deny themselves' (v.23). God may ask you to make different sacrifices in your life, but the only thing we are *all* required to give up is sin.

Every day the challenge of love requires little acts of self-denial.

2. No self

Jesus says, 'Those who would come after me must ... take up their cross daily and follow me, for those who want to save their lives will lose them, but those who lose their lives for me will save them' (vv.23–24).

Effectively, Jesus invites us to 'come ... and die'. The cross today is a symbol of hope. However, then it was a symbol of pain, shame, disgrace and ultimately death.

Jesus said that if you live a life of selfish ambition – even if you are the most successful person of all time and 'gain the whole world' (v.25) – it will do you no good at all. The way to find life in all its fullness is to abandon your life to the love of Jesus and of others. Take up your cross *daily* and follow him (v.23).

Being willing to give up your life is the ultimate act of love. This is the example that Jesus set first. He calls you and me to follow his example: 'cleave steadfastly to Me, conform wholly to My example in living and, if need be, in dying' (v.23, AMP).

3. No secrecy

Jesus says, 'All who are ashamed of *me* and *my words*, the Son of Man will be ashamed of them when he comes in his glory and in the glory of the Father and of the holy angels' (v.26).

If you love Jesus don't be ashamed of him. Sometimes even taking his name on our lips is a challenge. Don't be ashamed of his teaching (his 'words'). If you want Jesus to be proud of you, you must be proud of him. If you love people you will want everyone to know about Jesus.

Speaking for myself, I know how often I fall short in these areas. But the fact that our lives fall very far short of perfection should not stop us aiming high.

PRAYER

Lord, help me to aim high. Help me today to deny myself and take up my cross and follow you. May I never be ashamed of you or your words but rather boldly declare the good news of your death and resurrection for us.

OLD TESTAMENT READING

Numbers 33:1–34:29
Aim to be full of the Spirit

You have an amazing inheritance. It is all yours in Jesus. This passage describes *the inheritance* that God assigned to his people (34:29). Although they set out 'boldly' (33:3), they had wandered around in the desert for forty years (v.38). They never fully enjoyed their inheritance.

Paul, preaching in the book of Acts, explains that God gave the land to his people as their inheritance (Acts 13:17–20). He goes on, 'We tell you the good news: *What God promised our ancestors he has fulfilled for us*, their children, by raising up Jesus' (vv.32–33). This is now your inheritance.

God's promise to give his people the land of Canaan was always about more than simply good real estate. It was a promise of flourishing, as God's people enjoyed relationship with God, under the security of God's protection, in God's promised place. This points forward to the New Testament concept of the 'kingdom of God', the sphere of God's presence and rule. It is this that is fulfilled in Jesus, and it is yours now.

In Christ, your inheritance is 'the promised *eternal inheritance*' (Hebrews 9:15). It is 'an *inheritance* that can never perish, spoil or fade – kept in heaven for you' (1 Peter 1:4).

Not only do you have this inheritance to look forward to in the future but you can experience something of this inheritance right now: 'Having believed, you were marked in him with a seal, the promised Holy Spirit, who is a deposit guaranteeing *our inheritance*' (Ephesians 1:13–14).

The Greek word for deposit (*arabone*) is a word that means 'down payment'. In other words, you experience here and now a foretaste of that inheritance through the Holy Spirit. As you live in the Spirit, your life will be changed to produce the fruit of 'love, joy, peace, patience, kindness, goodness, faithfulness, gentleness and self-control' (Galatians 5:22). Don't settle for second best; aim to be full of the Holy Spirit. Receive your inheritance.

PRAYER

Lord, help us in the Spirit to be ruthless with sin so that we do not allow anything to become 'barbs in [our] eyes and thorns in [our] sides' (Numbers 33:55). Help me to aim high, to receive my inheritance and be filled with the Holy Spirit.

3 April | Day 93
How to Love

Four bullets hit Pope John Paul II – two of them lodging in his lower intestine, the others hitting his left hand and right arm. This assassination attempt on the Pope in May 1981 left him severely wounded and with considerable blood loss – his health was never the same again. In July 1981, the perpetrator, Ali Ağca, was sentenced to life imprisonment. Pope John Paul II asked people to pray 'for my brother Ağca, whom I have sincerely forgiven'.

Two years later, he was to take the hand of Ali Ağca, then in prison, and quietly tell him that he had forgiven him for what he had done (even though his would-be killer had not asked for forgiveness). He developed a friendship over the years, meeting Ağca's mother in 1987 and his brother a decade later. In June 2000 Ağca was pardoned by the Italian President at the Pope's request. In February 2005 Ağca sent a letter to the Pope wishing him well. When the Pope died on 2 April 2005, Ağca's brother, Adrian, gave an interview saying that Ağca and his entire family were grieving and that the Pope had been a great friend to them.

Pope John Paul II's response of love and mercy is exemplary. God's love and mercy is even more extraordinary because 'At the cross of Jesus, pardon is complete. *Love* and *justice* mingle, *truth* and *mercy* meet.'[1]

READING FROM PSALMS

Psalm 40:9–17
Love and truth

Jesus personified God's *love* but he also said, 'I am ... the *truth*' (John 14:6). The Holy Spirit pours God's *love* into your heart (Romans 5:5) but is also the Spirit of *truth* (John 15:26). Truth becomes hard if it is not softened by love; love becomes soft if it is not strengthened by truth.

David says, 'I do not conceal *your love* and *your truth*' (Psalm 40:10c). He prays, 'may *your love* and *your truth* always protect me' (v.11b). He does not see love and truth as mutually exclusive in any sense, but rather as complementary. The truth about God is that he loves you, he is righteous and faithful and he brings justice upon the earth.

As love and truth go together, so do justice and mercy. The concepts of righteousness (as in v.10) and justice are very closely related in Scripture. In this passage, it is on the basis of his knowledge of God's righteousness that David pleads for God's mercy: 'Do not withhold your mercy from me, O Lord ... my sins have overtaken me, and *I cannot see*' (vv.11a,12b). Sin blinds us. We need God's mercy and forgiveness so that we can see clearly.

PRAYER

Lord, may your love and your truth always protect me.

NEW TESTAMENT READING

Luke 9:28–56
Love and mercy

Have there been mountaintop experiences of the presence of God in your life when you have felt extraordinarily close to Jesus? This passage begins with such an experience.

Jesus takes Peter, John and James on to a mountain to pray. As Jesus is praying, they see him transfigured before them. They see his glory (v.32). Peter says to Jesus, 'Master, this is a great moment!' (v.33, MSG). They become 'deeply aware of God' (v.34, MSG). They hear God say, 'This is my Son, whom I have chosen; listen to him' (v.35).

However, like the disciples, who 'came down from the mountain', there comes a time when you too must descend (v.37). Mountaintops inspire us, but valleys mature us.

The tough realities of life awaited the disciples at the bottom – failure in their ministry, lack of understanding and rivalry. But the experience of the mountain can help you to see your life down below in a new and different way.

Jesus calls his followers to a love that is all embracing. He calls you to welcome people: 'Whoever welcomes this little child in my name welcomes me; and whoever welcomes me welcomes the one who sent me' (v.48). Welcome people regardless of what they can do for you.

How you welcome people really matters. Some people are warm and welcoming, others are not. Some churches are warm and welcoming, others are not. I have been hugely inspired by Hillsong Church and the welcome they give to every person who arrives at their services and conferences. They seem to have a profound understanding that in welcoming people, they welcome Jesus. And in welcoming Jesus, they welcome the one who sent him.

John said, 'We saw someone driving out demons in your name and we tried to stop him, because he is not *one of us*' (v.49). Jesus replied, 'Do not stop him ... for whoever is not against you is for you' (v.50; cf. Luke 11:23). Accept people beyond your own immediate circles, denomination and traditions. If they are not against Jesus they are for him. Welcome them as such.

On the other hand, do not be surprised if you are not always welcomed. Even Jesus was not always welcome. As Jesus resolutely set out for Jerusalem he sent messengers ahead of him who went into the Samaritan village to get things ready for him, but the people there did not welcome him (9:51–53).

My immediate response to not being welcomed would be similar to that of James and John – to seek revenge. When the disciples saw how Jesus was treated they asked, 'Lord, do you want us to call fire down from heaven to destroy them?' (v.54). However, revenge is not the right response: 'Jesus turned and rebuked them' (v.55).

Jesus, who is the truth and who was to take God's justice on himself on the cross, shows us what it means to love even our enemies and have mercy on them.

PRAYER

Lord, help me to love, like Jesus, in an all-embracing way. Help me never to seek revenge but to extend mercy and love even to my enemies.

OLD TESTAMENT READING

Numbers 35:1–36:13
Love and justice

The whole of Israel's national life was directly governed by God. It was operating in a very different world to our own. Some of the laws do have a universal application. Others were specific to Ancient Israel. Here we see the beginnings of a code of legal practice that was specific to Ancient Israel.

Capital punishment for murder was an expression of the sanctity of human life (Genesis 9:6). It was because the taking of a human life was so *serious* that the penalty needed to be so *severe*. This was a society in which the alternative – life imprisonment, for example – was not really practical.

We see that a distinction was made between murder 'with malice aforethought' (Numbers 35:20) and what was effectively manslaughter ('without hostility' and 'unintentionally', v.22). We see the beginnings of the right of trial by jury – that is by the people. Those accused of a crime are to 'appear before the community in court' (v.12, MSG). 'The community is to judge' (v.24, MSG).

'The avenger of blood' (v.19) was not taking private vengeance. The matter had to be brought before the court ('the assembly', v.12) by more than one witness and the decision was made by the court. There had to be really good evidence (v.30). There must be no bribery (v.31).

The New Testament makes a distinction between the dealings of the state and personal morality. Governing authorities are established by God and 'the one in authority is God's servant to do you good ... They are God's servants, agents of wrath to bring punishment on the wrongdoer' (Romans 13:4). The state is concerned with the protection of others. To stand by and allow injustice would actually be unloving and unchristian. It would be to allow evil to go unchecked, and to ignore the pain of the victims.

Yet, in personal morality we are told, both by Jesus and the apostle Paul, not to take revenge (Matthew 5:38–42; Romans 12:17–19). This attitude of love and forgiveness is not to deny justice, but rather it is an expression of trust in *God's* ultimate justice (see Romans 12:19). As we trust in God's justice, we are empowered to imitate his love. As Miroslav Volf writes, 'The practice of non-violence requires a belief in divine vengeance.'[2] He explains that when we know that the torturer will not eternally triumph over the victim, we are free to rediscover that person's humanity and imitate God's love for them.

The distinction between our own morality and that of the state creates a tension within us all. We are all individuals with a command from Jesus not to retaliate or take revenge. We are also citizens of the state with a duty to prevent crime and bring wrongdoers to justice. It is not easy to hold this tension, but an attitude of love requires that we do. Our motive should always be love and justice, not retaliation or revenge. In every situation, we need to act with an attitude of love.

PRAYER

Lord, help me to combine a passion for truth and justice with an attitude of love and mercy.

4 April | Day 94

No Blessing Goes Uncontested

'*No blessing goes uncontested*' is one of Bishop Sandy Millar's many original aphorisms, with which he would encourage us all. During his time as vicar of Holy Trinity Brompton he taught us not to be discouraged by the difficulties we faced because, as he liked to reassure us, 'No blessing goes uncontested.'

God will bless you in amazing and wonderful ways. In the passages for today we read about the promise, the extent and the privilege of God's blessing.

However, it was true of the people of God in the Old Testament and of the disciples of Jesus, and it will also be true in your life that '*No blessing goes uncontested*.'

READING FROM PSALMS

Psalm 41:1–6
Blessings contested by trouble, sickness and slander

1. Blessings on those who care for the poor

Blessings follow those 'who have regard for the weak' (v.1) – those who care, for example, about the poor, the hungry, the sick, the addicts and those in prison. This should be a characteristic of those who follow the Lord. If you care for the poor, God promises to deliver you in times of trouble, to protect you, to preserve your life and to *bless* you (v.2). He promises to sustain you and to heal you (v.3). But these blessings from God do not go uncontested.

2. Contested by trouble, sickness and slander

There may be 'times of trouble' (v.1b). There may be 'foes' (v.2b). There may be periods of 'illness' (v.3). There may be enemies: 'they speak falsely, while their hearts gather slander; then they go out and spread it abroad' (v.6).

Being aware that there are enemies around should put you on guard. There are some, for example, who come to '*gather slander*'. They are on a fishing expedition to find gossip against you so that they can go out and '*spread it abroad*'. But God promises his blessing and that he will 'not surrender' you (v.2b).

One of the encouraging things about the psalm is that this blessing of protection does not seem to be dependent on you always getting it right. David is very aware of his own sin, crying out to God for mercy and healing where he has fallen short (v.4).

PRAYER

Lord, thank you for all the blessings you have poured out on me. Thank you for your promise to deliver me in times of trouble, sickness and slander.

NEW TESTAMENT READING

Luke 9:57–10:24
Blessings contested by Satan and demonic powers

1. Blessings of following Jesus

As a follower of Jesus, you are more blessed than any human being in history who lived before Jesus. Jesus says, '*Blessed* are the eyes that see what you see. For I tell you that many prophets and kings wanted to see what you see but did not see it, and to hear what you hear but did not hear it' (10:23–24).

The blessings are so great that they far outweigh any apparent cost. At times, you may have to say farewell to comfort (9:58), compromise (v.60) and even company (vv.61–62).

Like the 'seventy-two', you have the great blessing of being sent out by Jesus into a huge harvest (10:2). You have the privilege of healing the sick and of telling people, 'God's kingdom is right on your doorstep' (v.9, MSG).

It is not just the Twelve who were sent out to heal the sick and proclaim the kingdom.

The seventy-two went out and did exactly that. They returned 'with joy' (v.17). Jesus is 'full of joy through the Holy Spirit' (v.21) as he sees the wonderful blessings that come to his disciples.

2. Contested by Satan and demonic powers

Jesus sends us out as 'lambs among wolves' (v.3). But our ultimate enemy in the New Testament is spiritual ('our struggle is not against flesh and blood,' Ephesians 6:12). When 'the seventy-two returned with joy and said, "Lord, even the demons submit to us in your name." [Jesus] replied, "I saw Satan fall like lightning from heaven. I have given you authority to trample on snakes and scorpions and to overcome all the power of the enemy..."' (Luke 10:17–19). The enemy is Satan and his demons.

It is remarkable that, almost as an aside, Jesus says he was there at the moment, before the creation of the world, when Satan fell.

Again, you are promised victory. The demons have to submit to the name of Jesus (vv.17, 20). But Jesus says there is an even greater blessing and that is that 'your names are written in heaven' (v.20).

PRAYER

Lord Jesus, thank you that my name is written in heaven. Help me not to be put off by attacks, because you have given me 'authority ... to overcome all the power of the enemy' (v.19).

OLD TESTAMENT READING

Deuteronomy 1:1–2:23
Blessings contested by problems, burdens and disputes

1. Blessings in the wilderness years

Are you going through hard times at the moment? Do you feel like you are in a wilderness period of your life?

Sometimes there seems to be a long delay between the promise of God and the fulfilment of that promise. What do we do while we are waiting for God to do what he has promised to do?

During these times, your faith is tested. Learn to trust God, seek his presence and worship him when life is hard.

Deuteronomy is one of the longest sermons ever preached. It is certainly the longest sermon in the Bible and the last preached by Moses.

In the book of Deuteronomy we read of Moses' parting instructions to the people. Here Moses reiterates the law God had given the people, re-transmitting God's ways for a new generation. A key theme is 'the land', which is perhaps paralleled in the New Testament by the blessings of the 'kingdom of God', which come through being in Christ and living under God's rule and reign.

The Bible is the story of God's people, God's blessing and God's rule. You experience God's blessing when you are living under God's rule. At the start of Deuteronomy, we are reminded about God's blessings to his people in the past, present and future.

First, regarding the past, Moses said, 'The LORD your God carried you, as a father carries his son ... The LORD your God has blessed you in all the work of your hands. He has watched over your journey through this vast desert. These forty years the LORD your God has been with you, and you have not lacked anything' (1:31; 2:7).

Second, concerning the present, Moses reminds them of the ways in which God has been faithful to his promises to Abraham: 'The LORD your God has increased your numbers so that today you are as many as the stars in the sky' (1:10). Four times in the opening chapter we discover that God is giving his people the land of Canaan (vv.8, 20, 21, 25). It is a gift of undeserved grace to God's people – much as it is pure grace that you and I can have a relationship with God through Jesus.

Third, in relation to the future, Moses spoke of all the blessings God will give to his people. He prayed, 'May the LORD, the God of your ancestors, increase you a thousand times and bless you as he has promised!' (v.11). You will increasingly experience God's blessing as you continue to live under God's rule.

2. Contested by problems, burdens and disputes

Yet alongside all these blessings Moses also highlights a series of problems, burdens and disputes (v.12). God said, 'You have stayed long enough at this mountain ... See, I have given you this land. Go in and take possession of the land' (vv.6–8). It was only eleven days' journey, but it had taken them forty years! They had developed a wilderness mentality and allowed themselves to be overcome by fear and discouragement (v.21), grumbling (v.27), loss of heart (v.28) and opposition (v.26 onwards).

Now the time had come to 'get moving' (v.7, MSG). Yet Moses did not promise that they would be free of problems. In fact, Moses talked about 'your enemies' (v.42). They were going to have many battles ahead and much opposition. The key is to follow the Lord wholeheartedly (v.36b).

We also need leadership and organisation. Moses told them to choose 'wise, understanding and respected' people (v.13) and then to delegate. Choosing the right people is the key to delegation and will avoid the need to micromanage. As General George Patton said, 'Never tell people how to do things. Tell them what to do and they will surprise you with their ingenuity.'[1] Delegation involves putting others in charge but being willing to take ultimate responsibility (vv.9–18).

Never allow opposition to put you off. Moses said, 'Do not be terrified; do not be afraid of them. The Lord your God, who is going before you, will fight for you' (vv.29–30).

PRAYER

Lord, help me not to be put off by problems, burdens and disputes, fear, discouragement or opposition, but to follow you wholeheartedly and to enjoy your blessings to the full.

5 April | Day 95
One Thing is Needed

I first encountered Jesus in a personal way in 1974. Soon afterwards, I heard a talk and, all these years later, I still remember it. It was given by an eighty-year-old man. The title was, 'The Five "One Things"'. His talk highlighted five significant occurrences of the expression 'one thing' in the Bible (Psalm 27:4; Mark 10:21; Luke 10:42; John 9:25; Philippians 3:13). Each one speaks about our priorities. One of those five occurrences is in our New Testament passage for today (Luke 10:42).

I have great empathy with Martha. Jesus said to her, 'You are worried and upset about many things' (v.41). There are so many things in life, but Jesus says, 'only *one thing* is needed' (v.42). It was Mary who had her priorities right.

READING FROM PSALMS

Psalm 41:7–13
The priority of his presence

You can know God's presence and his pleasure in the midst of all the challenges of life.

David had his worries and distractions. He had his enemies and, like Jesus, he says, 'Even *my close friend*, *whom I trusted*, he who shared my bread, has lifted up his heel against me' (v.9; see also John 13:18).

Be confident, as David was, in the ultimate triumph of good over evil (Psalm 41:11b). Know that God is pleased with you (v.11a). David's overwhelming desire is that God would set him *in his presence* (v.12). Make this your highest priority. This is what you were created for. The presence of God satisfies your deepest need.

PRAYER

Father, help me today to enjoy your pleasure and your presence in the midst of all the challenges and difficulties of life.

NEW TESTAMENT READING

Luke 10:25–11:4
The priorities of Jesus

What are your priorities? Is time with Jesus something you try and squeeze into your busy schedule? Or do you schedule your relationship with him as your number one priority?

A learned theologian and lawyer asks Jesus, a layman, the billion-dollar question about the way to eternal life.

Jesus gives us a model way to respond – and one that we try to follow in small group discussions on Alpha. In effect, Jesus asks the question, 'What do *you* think?' (10:26, 36).

The lawyer gives the correct answer: 'Love the Lord your God with all your heart and with all your soul and with all your strength and with all your mind' (v.27). This should be your highest priority. Your next priority is to love your neighbour as yourself.

The lawyer then asks a question, which shows he is looking for a loophole (v.29). He wants to make 'neighbour' a term of limited liability – family, friends, relatives, members of the same people and religious community.

Jesus responds with a story about injustice. A man was travelling on a notoriously dangerous road, 17 miles long with a 3,000-foot descent from Jerusalem to Jericho. He was carrying goods and valuables. He became a victim of injustice. He was robbed, stripped, beaten and left for dead (v.30).

The religious leaders came along. First, the priest (who had probably just been running the services in the temple in Jerusalem) and then the Levite (the assistant responsible for the liturgy and music). Both '*saw*' the victim (vv.31–32) but neither of them stopped. There are at least three possible reasons why they, and we, don't get involved:

1. We are too busy
Possibly they were in a hurry. They didn't want to get involved in a time-consuming activity.

2. We don't want to pollute ourselves
Touching a dead body would have made them unclean for seven days (Numbers 19:11). They would not have been able to enter the temple during this period (Leviticus 21:1). They might have lost their turn of duty at the temple.

3. We don't want to take a risk
Obviously there were robbers around. This could have been a decoy for a possible ambush.

The audience listening to Jesus would have been shocked by the eventual hero of the story. Jesus chooses their least favourite person. The Samaritans were a race despised by Jews socially, politically and religiously. This is a story about a person of a different race and religion having compassion (Luke 10:33). The Samaritan provided practical help. It cost him time, energy and money (vv.34–35).

The story Jesus told shows that the lawyer asked the wrong question (v.29). The right question is not, 'Who is my neighbour?' but, '*To whom can I be a neighbour?*' Jesus teaches the absolute and unlimited nature of the duty of love. Jesus came to destroy all the barriers. The whole human race is our neighbour.

Queen Elizabeth II said in one of her Christmas Day messages: 'For me, as a Christian, when Jesus answers the question, "Who is my neighbour?" the implication drawn by Jesus is clear. Everyone is our neighbour, no matter what race, creed or colour.'

'[He] passed by on the other side' (v.31b) is such an evocative expression. There are so many hurting people around us. Once you have seen, don't be like the priest and the Levite in Jesus' parable and pass by on the other side. The Samaritan 'took pity' (v.33b), he took care of him (v.34b) and he gave his money (v.35). Jesus says at the end of this story, 'Go and do likewise' (v.37b).

Draw near to people who are in need – get involved and help them. You are never more like God than when you are helping hurting people, lifting up the fallen and restoring the broken. Try to make this a high priority in your life. Yet the next story shows that your ability to do this stems from an even higher priority.

Mary had her priorities right. She 'sat at the Lord's feet, listening to what he said' (v.39). She realised that, although there were many distractions and worries around, there was nothing more important than simply sitting at Jesus' feet and listening to him. This should be your number one priority.

Martha was too busy to take time to enjoy her friendship with Jesus when he came to her home. Not spending time with Jesus is the biggest mistake you can make in your spiritual life. Nobody on their death bed ever said, 'I wish I had spent more time at the office.' Many regret not spending more time on their most important relationships.

It is probably no accident that the next story Luke tells is about Jesus teaching his disciples how to pray. We see Jesus himself modelling the importance of spending time with God in prayer, and the interest that sparks in his disciples (11:1). That is then the context for him to teach them the 'Lord's Prayer'.

The prayer starts with extraordinary intimacy with God, as you are encouraged to call him 'Father'. But a relationship with God should impact the rest of your life as well. Pray for daily provision (v.3). Pray 'your kingdom come' (v.2) and think about the sins you need to forgive in others, or be forgiven in yourself (v.4).

There are many different ways to develop a relationship with Jesus. Whatever way you do it, it needs to be your number one priority.

PRAYER

Lord, help me to enjoy your presence. May I have the love and courage to lift up the fallen, restore the broken and help hurting people.

OLD TESTAMENT READING

Deuteronomy 2:24–4:14
The priority of relationship

Moses recorded how God had given them the land and had also given them the commands.

Yet the greatest privilege for the people of God is not the land or the law but the love of God: '*The Lord our God is near us whenever we pray to him*' (4:7).

Furthermore, there seems to be an intentional connection between the way God's people were instructed to live and the impact they would have on the other nations (v.6). God intended them to be a highly visible example both as to the nature of the God they worshipped, and as to the quality of social justice embodied in their community. In other words, following the example of the Good Samaritan has an evangelistic consequence.

The law is an expression of God's love and desire to be close to his people. That is why they are urged, 'Watch yourselves closely so that you do not forget the things your eyes have seen or let them slip from your heart as long as you live. Teach them to your children and to their children after them' (v.9). The law was given in the context of the covenant (v.13). It starts with God's commitment to us and his love for us.

Likewise, the new covenant starts with God's commitment through the death and resurrection of Jesus and through God's love being poured into your heart by the Holy Spirit. You have permanent access to the presence of God (Ephesians 2:18).

PRAYER

Father, help me to stay close to you, to live in your presence, sitting at the feet of Jesus, hearing your words and going out and acting on them.

6 April | Day 96
Press Through

'Can you see anything?' his assistant asked as Carter's eyes adjusted to the semi-darkness. Carter could see well enough, but he had difficulty speaking because of the dazzling array of treasure spread out before him.

For more than two thousand years, tourists, grave robbers and archaeologists had searched for the burial places of Egypt's Pharaohs. Armed with only a few scraps of evidence, British archaeologist Howard Carter's search, after many years, seemed doomed to failure.

But, Carter pressed through and finally unlocked an ancient Egyptian tomb. No one in the modern world had ever seen anything like it. The king's embalmed body lay within a nest of three coffins, the inner one of solid gold. On the king's head was a magnificent golden portrait mask and numerous pieces of jewellery lay on the body and in its wrappings.

Other rooms were crammed with statues, a chariot, weapons, chests, vases, daggers, jewels and a throne. It was the priceless tomb and treasure of King Tutankhamun, who reigned from 1352 to 1343 BC. It was 3,265 years later, on 26 November 1922, that Carter made this discovery.

Howard Carter made the world's most exciting archaeological *find* because he did not give up *seeking*. He pressed through. He persevered. A river cuts through rock not because of its power but because of its persistence.

God loves you. God does not force himself upon you, but he promises to reveal himself to you if you persistently *seek* him.

READING FROM PROVERBS

Proverbs 8:32–36
Seek God's wisdom daily

We see here a wonderful picture of what you are doing each day as you open your Bible and seek to hear from God. You are 'watching *daily* at [his] *door*, *waiting* at [his] doorway' (v.34). This is the way to life in all its fullness. This is the way to 'receive favour from the Lord' (v.35). It is so important it is a matter of life and death (vv.35–36).

We have seen that the wisdom of the book of Proverbs foreshadows Christ, who is the wisdom of God. It is not just a matter of learning some 'top tips for life', but learning *from* the source of wisdom himself.

Seeking God requires discipline and patience – you have to learn to *wait* on God. You can miss out if you are in too much of a hurry.

PRAYER

Lord, thank you that when I find you I find life. Help me to seek you daily, to wait

patiently for you and to listen to your instructions.

NEW TESTAMENT READING

Luke 11:5–32
Seek God's Spirit persistently

Jesus encourages you not to be put off easily. He tells a story to show the power of 'persistence' (v.8, AMP) in even imperfect *human* relationships (vv.5–8).

He then goes on to explain how *persistence* is just as important in your relationship with *God*. '*Keep on asking* … *keep on seeking* … *keep on knocking* … For everyone who asks and *keeps on asking* receives; and he who seeks and *keeps on seeking* finds; and to him who knocks and *keeps on knocking*, the door shall be opened' (vv.9–10, AMP).

Jesus particularly relates this to receiving the Holy Spirit (v.13). *Keep on seeking* for more of the Holy Spirit and his wisdom and power in your life.

Jesus deals with some of the principal difficulties you may have in receiving from God.

1. Doubt

People have many doubts in this whole area. They wonder, 'If I ask will I receive?' Jesus says simply: 'I say to you: Ask and it will be given to you' (v.9).

Jesus must have seen that they were a little sceptical because he repeats it in a different way: 'Keep on seeking and you will find.' And again, he says a third time: 'Keep on knocking and the door will be opened to you.'

He knows human nature so he goes on a fourth time: 'For everyone who asks receives' (v.10). They are not convinced so he says it a fifth time: 'Everyone who keeps on seeking finds.' Again a sixth time: 'To everyone who keeps on knocking, the door will be opened.'

Why does he say it six times? Because he knows our tendency to doubt. You may find it very difficult to believe that God would give you anything – let alone something as wonderful as his Holy Spirit and the gifts that come from the Spirit.

2. Fear

Even if you have cleared the first hurdle of doubt, you may trip up on the next hurdle of fear. The fear is about what you will receive. Will it be something good?

Jesus uses the analogy of a human father. If a child asks for a fish, no father would give them a snake. If a child asks for an egg, no father would give them a scorpion (vv.11–12). It is unthinkable that we would treat our children like that.

Jesus goes on to say that in comparison with God we are evil! If we would not treat our children like that, it is inconceivable that God would treat us like that. God will not let you down. If you ask for the Holy Spirit and all the wonderful gifts he brings, that is exactly what you will receive (v.13).

3. Inadequacy

Of course, it is important to ask for forgiveness and turn your back on all that you know is wrong. However, even after you have done that, you may have a vague feeling of unworthiness and inadequacy. You may not believe that God would give you anything.

It is sometimes easier to believe that he will give gifts to very advanced Christians, but not to us. But Jesus does not say, 'How much more will your Father in heaven give the Holy Spirit to all very advanced Christians.' He says, 'How much more will your Father in heaven give the Holy Spirit to *those who ask him!*' (v.13).

The second part of the passage teaches us to make sure we are seeking the right things. Some people were seeking, 'for a sign from heaven' (v.16). These same people were attributing the work that Jesus was doing through the Holy Spirit to the devil (v.15).

Jesus points out that the devil does not drive out demons (vv.17–20) as Jesus did. Then he tells them not to seek 'signs'. The only sign we need is the sign of the resurrection (vv.29–30). This is the sign that Jesus is greater than both Solomon and Jonah (vv.31–32).

Don't seek the wrong things. But never give up seeking God, his kingdom, his righteousness and his Holy Spirit.

PRAYER

Lord, today I ask you to refill me with the love, power and wisdom that come from your Spirit.

OLD TESTAMENT READING

Deuteronomy 4:15–5:33
Seek God's presence wholeheartedly

You can have a *personal* relationship with God. God says to his people, 'To you it was shown, that you might realise and have *personal knowledge* that the Lord is God' (4:35, AMP).

Moses tells the people of God that they will be scattered among the nations (v.27). But he said, 'If from there you *seek* the LORD your God, you will find him if you look for him *with all your heart* and with all your soul' (v.29).

We see this same emphasis on our relationship with God at the start of the Ten Commandments. We live in a world that thinks the only thing that matters is how we relate to other people. How we relate to others is hugely important and it is the subject of commandments six to ten (5:16–21). However, there is something even more important than how you relate to others. Your relationship with God is the most important aspect of your life.

It is out of this relationship that your love for others should flow. God is not an optional extra in your life. Moses says, 'The LORD your God is a consuming fire' (4:24). He loves you. He chose you and wants to bless you with *his presence* (v.37). He is a 'merciful God' (v.31). He has set you free from captivity, as he freed the Israelites: 'I am the LORD your God, who brought you out of Egypt, out of the land of slavery' (5:6).

It is in this context that he tells you to put your relationship with him above everything else (commandments one to four, vv.6–15). The next priority is your relationships in the family (v.16). Then your relationship with others (commandments six to nine, vv.17–20). Finally, commandment number ten addresses your thought-life (v.21).

Moses tells the people to *'listen'* to these instructions, *'learn* them', *'live* them' (v.1, MSG). Like Howard Carter, press through. Seek God daily, persistently and wholeheartedly, you will find life in all its fullness, and it will transform the way that you love and serve others.

PRAYER

Lord, I seek your presence today wholeheartedly. Help me to experience personally your love and great strength, to listen to your commandments, to obey them and to live under your favour.

7 April | Day 97
Love from the Inside Out

Celine, a young woman who came on Alpha because of what she described as her 'spiritual search', wrote, 'I am not entirely sure what happened! Over the course I have grown more and more thirsty for God's presence like when on a hot, dry summer's day one gets a sip of cold fresh water, just the right temperature, one wants to drink and drink, and one can never get enough.

'I am now constantly skipping and laughing and wanting to tell everyone how amazing God is ... plus I *seem to love everybody*! I was seeking to forgive someone, but just seemed to grow more and more bitter and resentful, until I came on Alpha ... It's gone, I have totally forgiven that person and *love* them too!'

She says that she is now 'passionately *in love with Christ*!' Her *inner thirst* is being satisfied. She has a new *inner light* and a new *inner love*.

READING FROM PSALMS

Psalm 42:1–6a
Inner thirst

Are there times when you have a nebulous feeling and you don't know quite what it is that is causing you to be *'downcast'*? You are not alone. The psalmist knew this feeling: 'Why are you downcast, O *my soul*? Why so disturbed *within me*?' (v.5a). God does not want you to stay in this place – he loves you and he wants to encourage you.

The psalmist speaks of an *inner thirst*: 'As the deer pants for streams of water, so my soul pants for you' (v.1). He continues, *'My inner self thirsts for God'* (v.2, AMP).

Only God himself can satisfy this *thirst*. Knowledge about God will not satisfy your inner thirst. Cry out for God's presence. Meet with God (v.2) and pour out your soul (v.4).

Worship is key: 'I was always at the head of the worshiping crowd, right out in front, leading them all, eager to arrive and worship, shouting praises, singing thanksgiving – celebrating, all of us, God's feast!' (v.4, MSG). Remember past experiences of God's favour and his blessings. This will inspire you to keep trusting in God and gives you strength to worship him again (v.5b-6a).

PRAYER

Lord, my soul thirsts for you. Only your presence can satisfy my deep inner thirst. I hope in you and praise you, my Saviour and my God.

NEW TESTAMENT READING

Luke 11:33–54
Inner light

A clean heart and conscience is far more important than clean hands. What goes on in your heart and thoughts really matters. Your eyes are key – they are the gate to the inner life. That is why what you look at matters so much. You let things into your inner life through your eyes. Your eyes also reflect what is going on in your heart.

Jesus calls you to fill your inner being with light: 'Your eye is a lamp, lighting up your whole body. If you live wide-eyed in wonder and belief, your body fills up with light. If you live squinty-eyed in greed and distrust, your body is a dank cellar. Keep your eyes open, your lamp burning, so you don't get musty and murky. Keep your life as well-lighted as your best-lighted room' (vv.34–36, MSG).

Jesus calls you to an intimate and loving relationship with God – to that secret place, the heart, where true contact with God takes place. He calls you to be clean on the *inside*, not just on the outside (v.39). It is no good appearing clean outwardly if *inside* you are full of 'greed and wickedness' (v.39).

The focus of the *inner life,* according to Jesus, is the poor: 'Give as donations to the poor ... and behold, everything is purified and clean for you' (v.41, AMP). Giving cleanses the heart.

Jesus goes on to say that outward giving in itself is not enough if you neglect '*justice* and the love of God' (v.42).

As Father Raniero Cantalamessa writes, 'It would be a mistake to think that insistence on the *inner life* could harm our energetic commitment to the kingdom and to *justice*. Far from diminishing the importance of acting for God, interior life lays its foundation and keeps it going.'[1]

Jesus warns these religious leaders about wrong attitudes of the heart into which we can so easily fall. These words are a challenge to those of us in any kind of leadership. Jesus warns against:

1. Self-importance
'You love the most important seats' (v.43).

2. Love of recognition
'Greetings in the market-place' (v.43).

3. Hypocrisy
There is a danger of teaching a standard that we ourselves fail to live up to: 'You load people down with burdens they can hardly carry and you will not lift one finger to help them' (v.46).

Jesus was not afraid to confront people about their inner lives. He was not afraid of confrontation nor was he afraid of making enemies. It is not surprising that the object of his attack, the religious leaders, began to oppose him fiercely (v.54).

PRAYER

Lord, may my eyes only look at things that light up the inside. Fill me today with your Holy Spirit. May my heart be filled with generosity, justice and the love of God.

OLD TESTAMENT READING

Deuteronomy 6:1–8:20
Inner love

At the heart of the Old Testament, as of the New Testament, is *love*. '*Love* the LORD your God with all your heart and with all your soul and with all your strength' (6:5). The Hebrew words here are much broader than any translation can fully capture, something that is probably reflected in the New Testament using a fourfold translation (heart, soul, strength, mind). The phrase is meant to sum up the *whole of life*, including both mind and will.

God always intended that the law of love should be internal – in the heart: 'Write these commandments that I've given you today on your *hearts.* Get them *inside of you* and then get them *inside* your children' (v.6, MSG).

Your *love* for God flows out of *his love for you*. His love for you is not dependent on any innate moral quality that you possess. It is the grace of God – loving us in *spite of* our sins, weaknesses and failures. 'The LORD did not set his affection on you and choose you because you were more numerous than other peoples, for you were the fewest of all peoples. But it was because *the LORD loved you*' (7:7–8a). He loves you because he loves you!

God showers his love upon you because of his loving character and his faithfulness: 'The LORD your God will keep his covenant of *love* with you ... He will *love* you and bless you and increase your numbers' (vv.12–13).

You are called to this intimate and loving relationship with God. However, there are three warnings given in chapter 6:

1. The danger of abandoning God because of the surrounding idolatry – 'do not follow other gods' (6:14)

There is the temptation to fit in with the surrounding culture and adopt the beliefs of the people around us. However, God wants you to remain faithful to him rather than merely seeking to fit in with those around you. (Deuteronomy 7 expands on this.)

2. The danger of doubting God because of hardship – 'do not test the Lord' (6:16)

When hardship comes, the temptation is to think that God no longer cares about you, but you need to hold on to the faithfulness and word of God. (Deuteronomy 8:1–5 unpacks this challenge further.)

God allows you to go through tests and trials so you can learn by experience that doing things his way is the best way. If you will not serve and worship him in the hard times of life (the valleys), you may not consistently serve and worship him in the good times (the mountaintops). Remember that mountaintops encourage you, but valleys mature you.

3. The danger of forgetting God because of affluence – 'do not forget the Lord' (6:12)

In the enjoyment of the gift, you can sometimes forget the giver. (See Deuteronomy 8:6–20 for more on this) 'But remember the LORD your God, for it is he who gives you the ability to produce wealth' (8:18).

Underlying these three warnings is the realisation that material things alone – whether personal possessions or 'idols' – do not satisfy: 'human beings do not live on bread alone but on every word that comes from the mouth of the LORD' (8:3).

Jesus quoted this verse when he was being tempted in the desert by the devil to satisfy his physical hunger in the wrong way. His response to the devil was that it is the inner life – the inner hunger – that is far more important than the material things. This inner hunger can only be satisfied by every word that comes from the mouth of the Lord.

Whether you are materially well-off or not, the focus of your life should be on the inner life which alone can satisfy the deep inner longing which God has put in every human heart.

PRAYER

Lord, thank you for your amazing love for me. Thank you that you promise to love me and bless me. Help me to love you with all my heart and soul and strength.

8 April | Day 98
How to Stop Worrying

I can't even remember his name and I didn't think much of his talk. We were both eighteen years of age. He had just joined the army. As he stood up to give the talk he produced his army boots as a visual aid. He called one of the boots '*trust*' and the other one '*obey*'. He described them as the left and right boot of the Christian life. He only spoke for seven minutes, but his illustration hit home and I have never forgotten it.

'*Trust*' and '*obey*' are, as he said, a very good summary of the Christian life. We see in the passages for today that they are the answer to trials, temptation, worry, anxiety, fear, failure and all the other struggles of life. In particular, Jesus shows us how to stop worrying and start living.

READING FROM PSALMS

Psalm 42:6b–11
Trials and temptation

It is often in times of difficulty that we put down deep roots. The psalmist uses the evocative expression '*deep calls to deep*' (v.7). Anything that is not from the depth in us will not reach the depth in others.

The psalmist is 'downcast' (v.6b). He feels as if God has forgotten him (v.9). He is 'mourning, oppressed by the enemy' (v.9b). He is in 'agony' (v.10a). People are taunting him, saying, 'Where is your God?' (v.10b) – rather like the way some people taunt Christians today.

The trials and temptations of life have overcome him like a mighty waterfall (v.7). Yet he knows deep down that despite being submerged by the waves of life, he can trust in God: 'GOD promises to love me all day' (v.8, MSG).

Continuing with the image of a torrential river, he refers to God as 'my Rock' (v.9). Though he *feels* that God has forgotten him, he *knows the reality* that God is the greatest security on which he can stand.

In the middle of all this he speaks to himself: 'Why are you downcast, O my soul? Why so disturbed within me? Put your hope in God, for I will yet praise him, my Saviour and my God' (v.11). Through all the struggles, trials and temptation, fix your eyes on God and keep trusting and obeying him.

PRAYER

Lord, thank you that you direct your love towards me. Help me to keep trusting and obeying you, 'my Saviour and my God' (v.11).

NEW TESTAMENT READING

Luke 12:1–34
Worry and anxiety

Do you worry a lot? Are you ever 'struck with fear' or 'seized with alarm' (vv.7, 32, AMP)? Are you ever 'anxious and troubled' (v.22, AMP)?

Jesus never said, 'Don't worry because there is nothing to worry about.' He said, 'Don't worry in spite of the fact that there is so much to worry about.' Many times Jesus says to his followers, 'Do not be afraid' (vv.4, 7, 32) and 'Do not worry' (vv.11, 22, 29). The answer to fear and worry is to trust and obey. Jesus gives us *seven ways to deal with* worry, anxiety and fear.

1. Fear God and nothing else

If you have a right and healthy fear of God, you *need fear nothing else* (v.5). 'Don't be bluffed into silence or insincerity by the threats of religious bullies... There's nothing they can do to your soul, your core being. Save your fear for God, who holds your entire life – body and soul – in his hands' (v.5, MSG).

2. Know your value to God

Jesus tells you not to worry or be afraid because you are of *infinite value to God*. He loves you; 'You are worth more than many sparrows' (v.7b). He knows you intimately: 'The very hairs of your head are all numbered' (v.7a).

3. Trust the Holy Spirit

He tells you not to worry because you can *trust the Holy Spirit* to help you. As you face opposition, difficult situations, meetings, and so on, Jesus says, '*Do not worry* about how you will defend yourselves or what you will say, for *the Holy Spirit will teach you at that time what you should say*' (vv.11–12).

4. Don't miss the point of life

Jesus says that by worrying you *miss the whole point of life*: 'Life is not defined by what you have, even when you have a lot' (v.15, MSG).

He tells the story of a businessman, who had built up a highly successful enterprise and made a considerable amount of money. The world probably admired him. However, Jesus describes him as a fool and a failure (v.20). He had made the false assumption that he had many years to live (vv.19–20). He had never seen beyond this life (v.20).

His life was focused on himself. The word 'I' or 'my' appears eleven times (vv.17–19). As has been pointed out, 'A person wrapped up in themselves makes a very small package.' He thought he was worth what his possessions were worth. He failed to understand the way to be truly rich. He was not 'rich towards God' (v.21). Who you are as a person is far more important than what you do for a living.

5. Realise that fussing is futile

Jesus encourages you to look beyond material possessions and physical needs, 'don't fuss about what's on the table at mealtimes or if the clothes in your closet are in fashion' (v.22, MSG). There is nothing wrong with these things, but they should not be your focus – 'life is more than food, and the body more than clothes' (v.23).

6. Trust God's care and provision

Jesus points out that *worry is the opposite of faith* (v.28). If you trust you will not worry. 'If that is how God clothes the grass of the field, which is here today, and tomorrow is thrown into the fire, how much more will he clothe you, O you of little faith!' (v.28). Faith involves *trust* in God's care and provision.

7. Seek God's kingdom

Trust and obedience go hand in hand. Rather than storing up things for yourself you need to be 'rich towards God' (v.21). Rather than worrying about material things you should '*seek his kingdom*' (v.31) – which God in his good pleasure has given to you (v.32). This should be the focus of your life. 'For where your treasure is, there your heart will be also' (v.34).

PRAYER

Lord, thank you that you tell me over and over again not to worry and not to be afraid. Help me to seek your kingdom and trust that all 'these things will be given to [me] as well' (v.31).

OLD TESTAMENT READING

Deuteronomy 9:1–10:22
Fear and failure

God's blessing is pure grace: 'It is not because of your righteousness or your integrity' (9:5). Moses reminds the people of God of all the things that went wrong for them in the past. He tells them that the reason was, 'You did not *trust* him or *obey* him' (v.23).

Moses urges them that now they are to *trust* and *obey God.* 'What does the Lord your God ask of you but to fear the Lord your God, to walk in *obedience* to him, to love him, to serve the Lord your God with all your heart and with all your soul, and to observe the Lord's commands and decrees that I am giving you today *for your own good*?' (10:12–13).

When we are tempted to disobey God, it is because we do not *trust* that he has our best interests at heart. We like to think that we know better than God as to what is best for us. However, the reality is that all God's commands are '*for your own good*'. God loves you, cares for you and knows you, and that is why he wants you to obey him.

The truth is that you can trust God, even when you find his commands difficult or restrictive. The omnipotent God, to whom belong 'the heavens, even the highest heavens, the earth and everything in it' has 'set his affection' on you 'and loved' you, 'and he chose you' (vv.14–15).

This faith is inward, not just outward: 'Circumcise your hearts' (v.16). Yet, it is a faith that leads to action. You are called to follow God's example and defend the cause of the fatherless and the widow, and love the alien, giving them food and clothing (v.18). There is to be no racial discrimination. We should have a special love and service for the poor and the marginalised.

God promises that if you *trust* and *obey* him you will see growth and multiplication. 'Your ancestors who went down into Egypt were seventy in all, and now the Lord your God has made you as numerous as the stars in the sky' (v.22).

PRAYER

Lord, thank you that you have set your affection on me, loved me and chosen me. Help me today to fear you, to walk in all your ways, to love you and to serve you with all my heart and all my soul. I pray that you would make your church as numerous as the stars in the sky.

9 April | Day 99
See His Goodness

When we were children, my sister and I went on a picnic with our parents. The two of us were playing on what we all assumed was a disused railway track. Suddenly my mother shouted, 'Jump! Get off the track!' She had seen an express train coming down the track. Thankfully, we didn't shout back, 'Don't threaten us. You can't scare us.' If we had done, I would not be in a position to write this now. We both jumped off the track.

The command arose out of a mother's love for her children. God's commands arise out of his goodness and his love for you. They are given for '*your own good*' (Deuteronomy 10:13). See his goodness. The warnings of Jesus about the coming judgment and how to be ready for it come out of his love for you. In all the passages for today we see that obedience is the way to experience his goodness and be a magnet for his blessing.

READING FROM PSALMS

Psalm 43:1–5
The presence of God

Like many of the great men and women of God down the ages, the writer is struggling with spiritual depression. He is 'downcast' (v.5). His soul is 'disturbed' within him (v.5). Jesus himself cried out, 'Now my heart is troubled' and 'My soul is overwhelmed with sorrow' (John 12:27; Mark 14:34).

The psalmist is surrounded by an 'ungodly nation' (Psalm 43:1a), a 'deceitful and wicked' people (v.1b). He is 'oppressed by the enemy' (v.2b). There is something very real and authentic about the Psalms. Life is not easy. We may face battles, opposition and even depression.

The right response is to turn to God. Pray for God's guidance, and his presence, his 'joy and delight' (vv.3–4). The focal point of God's presence with his people at that time was the temple in Jerusalem. Built on a 'mountain', it was 'the place where you dwell' (v.3). In the

New Testament Jesus is the temple in whom God dwelt in all his fullness (see John 2:19–21; Colossians 1:19).

On the day of Pentecost, Jesus sent his Holy Spirit as the way in which God now dwells in his 'holy temple' – both in the individual and in the gathered community. 'Church' should never be boring. It should be a place of joy, delight and praise.

At its heart, obedience is all about turning to God, trusting his goodness, no matter what the situation. What we need in our darkness is the presence of God – and you can trust that is ultimately what you will find.

PRAYER

Lord, please send your light and your truth; let them lead me into your presence (Psalm 43:3a).

NEW TESTAMENT READING

Luke 12:35–59
The reward of Jesus

Life is a wonderful gift. You have been 'entrusted' (v.48) with talents and responsibilities. It really matters how you use these. The warnings that run throughout this passage about how you use your life are given out of love. Jesus warns of the coming judgment and how to be ready.

Jesus calls you to be 'ready for service' (v.35). Expect Jesus to return today. What a wonderful reward is offered to those who are ready: 'It will be *good* for those servants whose master finds them watching when he comes' (v.37a). You will sit and eat with Jesus and he will serve you (v.37b). The goodness and grace of Jesus is almost unbelievable. He reverses the roles in a way that most human beings would never even contemplate.

Be ready for when he returns (v.40). Be like the 'faithful and wise manager' (v.42). You will be richly rewarded 'It will be *good*' for you (v.43). He will put you 'in charge of all his possessions' (v.44).

There is a danger in thinking that Jesus won't come yet (v.45), that we can carry on doing exactly what we like and that there will be plenty of time to put things right.

It is the fact that the master 'is taking a long time in coming' that deceives the unwise servant into neglecting his task and not acting as the master would want (v.45). To many people today, God seems a distant or irrelevant figure with little impact on their lives. This story is a warning to remind us that there will one day be a reckoning for all that we do, and we would be wise to act on that now.

Jesus says that if you know something is wrong and you do it anyway, that is worse than doing something wrong when you didn't realise. But the latter is still wrong (vv.47–48).

Jesus calls you to obey and to serve him with faithfulness and wisdom. If you use what God has given you wisely, he blesses you by giving you more responsibility. The more that God has given you, the greater the responsibility to use it well. Jesus says, 'From everyone who has been given much, much will be demanded; and from the one who has been entrusted with much, much more will be asked' (v.48b).

If you have a happy home, a good education, health, friends, job, food, clothes, holidays; if you have access to the Bible, freedom to meet together and pray, and so on, then you are one of those to whom much has been given. And much will be expected.

Jesus himself did not have an easy life. He says, 'I have a baptism to undergo, and how distressed I am until it is completed!' (v.50). Jesus lived under the shadow of the cross. He knew that he was going to have to suffer. When we know we are facing some difficulty or challenge in our lives, we often feel 'constrained until it is accomplished' (v.50, RSV). If we feel this with relatively small things, how terrible it must have been for Jesus as he saw ahead the horrors of crucifixion, bearing the sin of the whole world.

This would be the means by which Jesus would bring us peace with God. Yet Jesus says that at one level we will not always experience an outward peace. Rather, there will be division: 'Do you think I came to bring peace on earth? No, I tell you, but division' (v.51). This division can even be with those who are most closely related to us. There may be division between those who are for Jesus and those who are against him.

Yet you are called to be a peacemaker. Always 'try hard to be reconciled' (v.58).

PRAYER

Lord, help me to be always ready for service and to make the most of everything that you have entrusted to me.

OLD TESTAMENT READING

Deuteronomy 11:1–12:32
The strength of God

Jesus was not the first to connect love and obedience. The Law of Moses was given by God out of love. This calls for a response of love: 'So *love* God, your God; guard well his rules and regulations; *obey* his commandments for the rest of time' (11:1, MSG).

Ensure that the words of God permeate your entire being. 'Place these words on your hearts. Get them deep inside you ... Teach them to your children. Talk about them wherever you are, sitting at home or walking in the street; talk about them from the time you get up in the morning until you fall into bed at night' (vv.18–19, MSG).

Know, learn and teach God's word and put it into practice in your life. Great blessing comes from living openly and honestly, walking in the light of God's truth as he reveals it in his word.

He promises his blessings to those who faithfully *obey* the commands he gives – 'to *love* the LORD your God and to serve him with all your heart and with all your soul' (v.13; see also vv.22, 27).

Disobedience is very draining and destructive. I know that in my own life deliberate sin leads to guilt and saps energy. Ultimately, we end up miserable. Moses said in effect, 'See his goodness': 'it was your own eyes that saw all these *great things* the LORD has done. Observe therefore all the commands I am giving you today, so that you may have the *strength...*' (vv.7, 8). Obedience brings *the blessing of strength*.

Make good choices. God says, 'I've brought you today to the crossroads of Blessing and Curse' (v.26, MSG). If you choose obedience you will be blessed by God; you will be a magnet for his blessings. Wisdom is choosing to do now what you will be satisfied with later.

The temptation is to disobey God because we see everyone around us doing that. Moses says, 'Be careful not to be ensnared by enquiring about their gods, saying, "How do these nations serve their gods? We will do the same"' (12:30). He goes on to say, 'Do all I command you; do not add to it or take away from it' (v.32).

PRAYER

Lord, thank you for all your goodness. Please fill me today with your love and strength, joy and delight, faithfulness and wisdom.

10 April | Day 100

Seven Ways to Grow in Wisdom

Lawrence of Arabia is one of the most successful films of all time. Much of the film is drawn from T. E. Lawrence's own account of his time in Arabia. He was a British archaeological scholar, military strategist (colonel by the age of thirty), best known for his activities in the Middle East during World War I. Lawrence explores the theme of *wisdom* in his memoirs, written in 1926, with the title, *The Seven Pillars of Wisdom*.

Presumably, Lawrence had in mind today's passage, '*Wisdom* has built her house; she has hewn out *its seven pillars*' (Proverbs 9:1). In Scripture, the number seven is often used to represent completion or perfection. In the book of Proverbs, the teaching of Jesus and the Bible in general, we find many ways to acquire and grow in wisdom. Seven of these can be seen in today's passages.

READING FROM PROVERBS

Proverbs 9:1–12

1. Handling criticism

When we are criticised, there is no point in replying to those who are merely mocking us (v.7). If we do, they will hate us even more. But it is worth replying to the 'wise'.

Our response to criticism should never be to 'insult', 'abuse' or 'hate' (vv.7–8). Rather, we must learn from it in order to become 'wiser' and to 'add to [our] learning' (v.9). Indeed, our response to a rebuke should be increased 'love' (v.8b).

This is far from easy – my natural reaction to criticism is often to be tempted to lash out verbally or try and justify myself. Yet the wise path is to seek to learn from the rebuke or instruction, however difficult that may be.

For example, I have noticed over the years that those speakers who do not like their talks criticised seldom improve. Those who invite constructive criticism and are not threatened by it often improve rapidly and become far more effective. A right relationship with God will increase your wisdom (v.10) and enable you to hear constructive criticism and grow through it.

PRAYER

Lord, give me wisdom to be constructive when I give criticism and gracious when I receive it.

NEW TESTAMENT READING

Luke 13:1–30

2. Responding to suffering

In this passage we see Jesus responding in two different ways to suffering. Jesus' response to *people* who were suffering was always one of *compassion*, as we see in his healing of the crippled woman (vv.10–16). Yet here we also see his response to the *questions* raised about 'suffering'.

'Pilate had killed some Galileans while they were at worship, mixing their blood with the blood of the sacrifices on the altar' (v.1, MSG). Some people came to ask Jesus, in effect, 'Why does God allow suffering?' 'Was their suffering the result of their sin?'

Jesus, of course, shows extraordinary wisdom in his response. So much suffering in the world is caused by human sin, and we are all guilty. Yet Jesus makes it very clear that there is *no automatic link* between sin and suffering. They were *not* suffering because they were worse sinners than all the other Galileans (vv.1–2). Jesus also points out that natural disasters are not necessarily a form of punishment from God (vv.1–5).

While it may be appropriate for us to examine our own hearts when we are suffering, we need to be very careful about making judgments about why others are suffering. Jesus was not so interested in philosophical explanations for suffering. Rather, he was interested in our response. He warns of the dangers: 'unless you repent…' (v.3).

3. Pruning and planting

The parables of the fig-tree (vv.6–9), mustard seed and yeast (vv.18–20) give us wisdom on how things grow in the kingdom of God. We see when things should be nurtured, when activities should be stopped and when projects should be started.

God is patient, giving as much time as possible for people to repent. In response to the desire to cut the fig-tree down, the man gives it one more chance: 'If it *bears fruit* next year, fine! If not, then cut it down' (v.9).

The key is to 'look for fruit' (v.6). For example, as we look at the numerous ministries in the church, some are extremely fruitful. Others are less so. The temptation is to cut back on the less fruitful ones straight away. However, Jesus encourages us to be patient: 'If it bears fruit next year, fine!' (v.9a). Yet this patience doesn't last for ever – sometimes the moment will come to stop an unfruitful ministry, to 'cut it down' (v.9b).

The parables of the mustard seed (vv.18–19) and of the yeast (v.20) remind us that, while the kingdom of God starts small, over time there is vast potential for growth. When the seed was planted it 'grew and became a tree, and the birds of the air perched in its branches' (v.19). This shows the enormous value in planting seeds of the kingdom (church planting included). It also suggests that we need to wait patiently to see this potential fulfilled.

4. Knowing when to confront

Personally, I find confrontation extremely difficult. Jesus had the wisdom of knowing when to confront. He exposed the hypocrisy and double standards of those who criticised him for healing a woman who had been crippled for eighteen years, simply because he did so on the Sabbath. He reminds them of the importance of compassion over legalism. If that is a principle they follow in caring for animals, how much more should they follow it in caring for people (vv.15–16)!

Jesus' answer was brilliantly wise. It 'delighted' the people (v.17).

5. Turning to Jesus

When someone asks Jesus a question: 'Lord, are only a few people going to be saved?' (v.23), he gives an intensely practical answer. He says, 'Make every effort to enter through the narrow door' (v.24). In other words, don't focus first on others, but make sure you yourself have entered the kingdom of God. You cannot know about everybody else but you can be sure about yourself.

In this parable, many find themselves unable to enter the house, which represents the kingdom of God. The reason for this is because of the lack of a personal relationship with Jesus. Twice the owner of the house, who represents Jesus, says to those shut out of his house, 'I don't know you or where you come from' (vv.25, 27). Being part of God's kingdom is all about turning to and knowing Jesus.

It appears that some who expected to be included are excluded, but it also appears that more people will get in than expected: 'People will come from east and west and north and south, and will take their places at the feast of the kingdom of God' (v.29). Turning to and following Jesus is the wise thing to do, even if it feels like we are in a minority.

PRAYER

Lord, I pray for wisdom today in all the conversations that I have and all the decisions I make. Please fill me with your Holy Spirit and give me the wisdom of Jesus.

OLD TESTAMENT READING

Deuteronomy 13:1–14:29
6. Testing prophecy

We need wisdom in discerning between true and false prophets. 'Prophets' today might include not only those with the 'gift of prophecy', but also anyone who speaks 'in the name of the Lord' – such as pastors, preachers, teachers and evangelists. In all these cases, we need to distinguish the true from the false.

One of the Old Testament tests of the true prophet comes in this passage. Even if a prophet performs signs and wonders, if he says 'Let us follow other gods' the people were warned: 'You must not listen to the words of that prophet' (13:2–3). In other words, the people were to test the prophet by *his teaching* – whether he led people to God or away from him. Jesus says, 'we will recognise them by their fruit' (Matthew 7:15–23).

7. Revering God

You are a child 'of the Lord your God' (Deuteronomy 14:1) and God's people are called to be holy to the Lord (v.2a). You have been chosen to be his '*treasured possession*' (v.2b). Under the old covenant this involved strict rules as to what could and could not be eaten. Under the new covenant, Jesus declared all food clean (Mark 7:19).

Under both the old and new covenant, one of the ways in which you 'revere' the Lord is through your giving (Deuteronomy 14:22–23). It is a blessing to give. God blesses you as you bless others, and so that you *can* bless others (v.29c). In particular, God promises here to bless us in our work (v.29). God's vision for his people is as a community, upheld in mutual giving. As we saw in today's reading in Proverbs, reverence for the Lord is 'the beginning of wisdom' (Proverbs 9:10). And 'if you are *wise*, *your wisdom* will reward you' (v.12).

PRAYER

Lord, thank you that I am your treasured possession. Please help me to grow daily in wisdom.

11 April | Day 101
Eight Things That Really Matter to God

My mother and father were great parents. They had strong values. My sister and I were left in no doubt about what mattered to them.

What mattered most to my father was *honesty*. I remember how my father used to say, 'I expect to be believed.' He regarded honesty as the highest possible value and sometimes went to absurd lengths to retain that standard.

On one occasion, when they were engaged, but not yet married, he and my mother got on the wrong bus. The bus conductor refused to accept any money as they had only travelled a few yards. My father was unhappy to have been unable to pay what he felt he owed. He sent the money for the fare to the bus company. They sent it back. This resulted in a long correspondence, which my mother found hard to understand (she joked that she almost broke off the engagement).

I remember, in my childhood, many similar incidents. My father may have been a little extreme, but my sister and I were in no doubt about what mattered to him: honesty. In our passages today we see some of the things that *really matter to God*.

READING FROM PSALMS

Psalm 44:1–12
1. Trust

What do you place your trust in?

It is vital to put your trust in the right place. Your trust should not ultimately be in your own strength ('It was not by their sword that they won ... I do not trust in my bow', vv.3, 6). Rather, you are to trust the Lord: 'It's *you*, *you* who saved us' (v.7, MSG).

The psalmist looks both backwards and forwards. As he looks back he says, 'It was your right hand, your arm, and the light of your face, for you loved them' (v.3b). As he looks forwards he says, 'You are *my* King and *my* God ... Through you we push back our enemies; through your name we trample our foes ... you give us victory over our enemies' (vv.4–5, 7).

PRAYER

Lord, as I face the challenges of today and of the future, I thank you for the victories you

have given us. I do not rely on my own strength for the future but instead put my trust in you.

NEW TESTAMENT READING

Luke 13:31–14:14

2. Courage

Do you find that you sometimes take decisions based on fear?

Nelson Mandela said, 'I learned that courage was not the absence of fear, but the triumph over it. The brave man is not he who does not feel afraid, but he who conquers that fear.'[1]

It is not surprising, humanly speaking, that Jesus was crucified after three years of ministry. He was a man of great courage. When Jesus was told 'run for your life! Herod's on the hunt. He's out to kill you!' (13:31, MSG) he replied, 'Go tell that fox…' (v.32). Here, we see that Jesus had the courage to take on one of the most powerful (and evil) men of the day.

Nor was Jesus afraid of confrontation with the scribes and Pharisees. He did not avoid them. He often spent time in their company. It must have been tempting simply 'to eat' (14:1) with those who liked him and accepted him rather than with those who were suspicious and critical – those who watched his every move.

He also had the courage to heal the man 'hugely swollen in his joints' (v.2, MSG) on the Sabbath and then to confront the Pharisees about their views on this subject.

3. Compassion

Is your heart moved by the people you come across?

Jesus not only had compassion for individuals (for example, healing the sick man, v.4), he also had compassion for the city. In this passage, he uses maternal imagery to describe his love for God's city: 'How often I have longed to gather your children together, as a hen gathers her chicks under her wings' (13:34). (Interestingly, he quite naturally puts himself in the place of God, to whom both male and female imagery is applied in the Bible.)

Supremely, Jesus showed his compassion in going to his death on the cross for us.

The story is told of a fire in Yellowstone National Park in the USA. When a forest ranger went to assess the damage, he discovered a bird that was lying dead, black and carbonised, at the bottom of a tree. It was a rather unnerving sight, so he pushed the bird over with a stick. Suddenly, three little chicks scurried out from under the wing of the dead mother. Because the mother had been willing to die out of compassion for her chicks, the chicks under her wing had lived. So too with Jesus, our mother hen – he died to protect us.

4. Humility

Do you worry about your status compared to others?

Jesus speaks about humility. He tells us to 'take the lowest place' (14:10). He says, 'do not take the place of honour … For all those who exalt themselves will be humbled, and those who humble themselves will be exalted' (vv.8, 11).

As *The Message* version puts it, 'If you walk around with your nose in the air, you're going to end up flat on your face. But if you're content to be simply yourself, you will become more than yourself' (v.11, MSG).

5. Poverty

Are you tempted to spend time with people of influence and wealth who will be able to pay you back?

Again and again the Scriptures come back to 'the poor'. We see this in both the New Testament and the Old Testament readings for today. What matters to God is your attitude to the poor.

Jesus said, 'When you give a banquet, invite the poor, the crippled, the lame, the blind, and you will be blessed' (vv.13–14). Jean Vanier, founder of L'Arche, a community for and with people with disabilities, has done this every day for over fifty years.

Jesus is encouraging us to seek out those who are poor in our own community. We are to spend our time serving those who 'won't be able to return the favor' (v.14, MSG).

Moses said, 'There should be *no poor* among you' (Deuteronomy 15:4). He also said, 'There will always be poor people in the land' (v.11). Jesus said something similar: 'The poor you will always have with you' (Matthew 26:11). The fact that the poor will always be with us does not mean that we should not seek to eradicate poverty.

PRAYER

Lord Jesus, help me to be more like you – more courageous, more compassionate and more humble. Give me your heart for the poor, your eyes to see them and your heart to serve them.

OLD TESTAMENT READING

Deuteronomy 15:1–16:20

6. Generosity

Do you ever find yourself being a little mean or penny-pinching?

The principle of generosity runs throughout the Bible. Don't be 'hard-hearted' (15:7) when you see poverty and need. Don't be 'tight-fisted' (v.7). Rather be 'open-handed' (v.8) – giving to all those who are in need. If people need to borrow from you, you should 'freely lend' (v.8) without interest. Always give generously without a grudging heart. We should '*always* be *generous*, open purse and hands' (v.11, MSG).

Your giving is a response to God's generosity to you: 'Give to them as the Lord your God has blessed you' (v.14).

7. Remembrance

Do you easily forget what God has done for you?

The people of God were called to '*Remember* that you were slaves in Egypt' (v.15; 16:12). '*Remember* the time of your departure from Egypt' (v.3). Part of the great festivals of Passover (vv.1–8), Weeks (vv.9–12) and Tabernacles (vv.13–17) was to do with remembrance (see v.3, '*Remember...*').

One of the aspects of Holy Communion is that it is a constant reminder of the death and resurrection of Jesus – rescuing you from the slavery of sin and death, and setting you free to know God and to receive life in all its fullness – indeed, eternal life.

8. Justice

Do you care about justice?

Justice is of high value to God. Honesty matters to God (my father was right!). 'Appoint judges ... to judge the people fairly and *honestly*. Don't twist the law. Don't play favorites' (vv.18–19a, MSG). Follow *justice* and *justice* alone' (v.20).

The rule of law really matters. We see all around the world the terrible injustice and suffering that results in places where either there are no judges or the judges do not judge the people fairly. There are many parts of the world where the police and judges accept bribes. Hence the importance of this command, 'Do not accept a bribe, for a bribe blinds the eyes of the wise and twists the words of the righteous' (v.19). Where the rule of law is not strong, the innocent can be arrested and imprisoned simply because someone has been dishonest and taken a bribe.

PRAYER

Lord, may my values be more like your values. May my thoughts and my ways become more like your thoughts and your ways. May what matters to me be what matters to you.

12 April | Day 102
It's a Party!

One day, I received a message that the Queen of England had invited me to lunch. At first, I thought it was a practical joke. But it wasn't. I turned up at Buckingham Palace on my bicycle, which an amused policeman looked after for me. I sat next to the Queen as we ate some amazing food. Then she turned and began to talk to me as the 'Parfait de Rhubarbe et Chocolat Blanc' arrived.

It looked delicious. But I did not want to talk with my mouth full – nor did I want to seem rude by cutting into it while the Queen was speaking to me. Eventually she asked me whether I did not like the food. 'No, no, no,' I said, 'I love it' (as I quickly began to eat). I did not say it to her, but the real reason I had not eaten was that I was overwhelmed by the privilege of being invited to lunch with the Queen of England.

Jesus likens the kingdom of God to a great party with the King, one to which we are all invited. It is an even greater privilege than lunch with the Queen of England, and it is extraordinary that anyone would refuse this invitation.

READING FROM PSALMS

Psalm 44:13–26
Cry out to God as King

Have there been times when you have found yourself 'a reproach' to your neighbours because of your faith (v.13a)? Have you faced 'scorn and derision' from those around you (v.13b)? I certainly have. Sometimes you may face difficulties in your life, not because you are doing something wrong but because you are doing something right.

This psalm is addressed to God as King (v.4). That God is the King (and real leader) of Israel is a common idea in the psalms. Suffering is not necessarily a result of disobedience to the King. Rather it may be a result of following him.

Opposition is not necessarily a sign of failure on the part of God's people: 'All this came down on us, and we've done nothing to deserve it. We never betrayed your Covenant:

our hearts were never false, our feet never left your path' (vv.17–18, MSG).

Paul quotes this psalm (v.22) in Romans when he asks if anything can separate us from Christ's love: '"*For your sake we face death all day long; we are considered as sheep to be slaughtered.*" No, in all these things we are more than conquerors through him who loved us' (Romans 8:35–37).

As I have seen so often in my own life, the King is faithful. He answers our cry for help and his love never fails (Psalm 44:26).

PRAYER

O Lord, my King and my God, 'Rise up and help us; redeem us because of your unfailing love' (v.26).

NEW TESTAMENT READING

Luke 14:15–35
Accept the invitation of the King

The kingdom of God is *a party*. It is a feast. '*Blessed* is the one who will eat at the *feast* in the kingdom of God' (v.15). Jesus is the host of this party. The Son of God invites you to experience the lavish hospitality and love of God. You are not on your own with the host. It is the presence of other guests that turns it into a celebratory party.

The food that Jesus supplies satisfies the hunger in your heart. It fills the spiritual vacuum. It satisfies your hunger for meaning and purpose in life, for forgiveness and for life beyond death. The drink at the banquet satisfies the spiritual thirst in every human heart.

The sad thing is that many people do not see it as a banquet but as a bore. They make excuses as to why they should not come. 'All alike began to make excuses' (v.18). One person's excuse is *property*: 'I have just bought a field, and I must go and see it. Please excuse me' (v.18). The second excuse is *possessions*: 'I have just bought five yoke of oxen, and I'm on my way to try them out. Please excuse me' (v.19). The third is to do with other *people*: 'I have just got married, so I can't come' (v.20).

When analysed, these are pathetic excuses. Each is utterly irrational and perfectly absurd. There is no urgency about going to see a field that has already been bought or trying out five yoke of oxen. There is no shortage of space at this party and the recently married man could have been accompanied by his wife.

Yet, Jesus' words ring true today: when people are invited to the great party of the kingdom of God, 'all alike [begin] to make excuses' (v.18).

Jesus also talks to the crowds about the cost of following him. He urges them to 'sit down and estimate *the cost*' (v.28) and later to 'sit down and consider' *the cost* (v.31). He says, 'If anyone comes to me and does not hate father and mother, wife and children, brothers and sisters – yes, even life itself – such a person cannot be my disciple' (v.26). The word for 'hate' is a Semitic idiom that means 'love less'. It is a relative term meaning not to honour or privilege something above something else. In other words, Jesus must be the number one priority in your life above even family and your own life.

He goes on, 'And those who do not carry their cross and follow me cannot be my disciples' (v.27). The image of the cross clearly suggests that there will be suffering. Finally he says, 'Those of you who do not give up everything you have cannot be my disciples' (v.33). You have to open your hands and put everything you have at his disposal.

It is worth remembering the cost of following Jesus is nothing compared to:

1. What you receive

God has prepared a party for you, a feast, which nothing else on this earth can match.

2. The cost of not following Jesus

Jesus said those who made excuses will not get 'a taste of my banquet' (v.24). There could be no higher cost than missing out on all the blessings that God has prepared for you.

3. What it cost him to make it possible

Jesus calls you to carry your cross (v.27). But the small cross you carry is nothing in comparison to the cross Jesus carried for you.

Don't miss out on all that Jesus has made possible for you. Accept his invitation to the party of the kingdom of God. And invite others to it as well as you respond to Jesus' command to 'go out quickly into the streets and alleys of the town and bring in the poor, the crippled, the blind and the lame' (v.21).

PRAYER

Lord, thank you for the privilege of being invited to your party in the kingdom of God. Today, I open my hands and put everything I have at your disposal.

OLD TESTAMENT READING

Deuteronomy 16:21–18:22
Worship Jesus as your God and King

Jesus is the only true king. Worship him and him alone. There is a warning in this passage against worshipping 'other gods' (16:21–17:7).

There is also a severe warning here for everyone to avoid fortune-tellers, psychics, horoscopes, tarot cards, palm reading, Ouija boards and other such activities (18:10–11).

There is no need to worship the stars when you can worship the one who made them. Don't waste your time, energy or money on those who purport to tell you about your future. Let God be your guide as far as the future is concerned.

There would come a point in Israel's history when they would say, 'Let us set a king over us' (17:14). Unlike God, of course, the king would not be perfect. He would be subject to the temptations to which so many of the kings of Israel and Judah fell and into which many leaders today still fall. These temptations include immorality (v.17a), greed (vv.16, 17b) and pride (v.20).

The passage sets out the ideal king (vv.18–20). This high ideal of the monarchy came closest to fulfilment in David. But it was never fully realised. In later years, it provided a basis for the hope of a coming King who would 'reign on David's throne and over his kingdom' (Isaiah 9:7).

Jesus is not only the ideal King, he is also the ideal prophet. Moses prophesied that there would be a prophet like him who would speak the words of God (Deuteronomy 18:15). Both the apostle Peter and Stephen, the first Christian martyr, quote this passage and see Jesus as the fulfilment of it (Acts 3:21–22; 7:37).

What an amazing privilege it is to live in a time when the kingdom of God has been inaugurated by Jesus. The great prophet has arisen. All the Old Testament prophecies are fulfilled. Jesus is King.

PRAYER

Lord Jesus, you are my God and my King. I love you and I thank you that you love me and invite me to your eternal party.

13 April | Day 103

What is God Like?

A six-year-old girl was drawing a picture one day. Her teacher said, 'What are you drawing?' The little girl answered, 'I am drawing a picture of God.' The teacher was surprised and said, 'But nobody knows what God looks like!' The little girl carried on drawing and replied, 'They will in a minute.'

One of the advantages of reading through the Bible in a year is that we get a rounded picture of the nature and character of God, and a greater understanding of what God is like.

READING FROM PSALMS

Psalm 45:1–9
King Jesus

The writer of Hebrews sees this psalm as a prophetic description of Jesus. He writes, 'But about *the Son* he says, "Your throne, *O God*, will last for ever and ever..."' (See Hebrews 1:8–9, quoting verses 6–7 of this psalm).

This is one of the clearest cases in the New Testament of Jesus being addressed as 'God' – as the legitimate object of worship. Jesus is the fulfilment of the expected 'anointed King', known as the Messiah. Jesus fulfils these prophecies.

Jesus said, 'Anyone who has seen me has seen the Father' (John 14:9). In other words, if you want to know what God is like, look at Jesus.

He is 'anointed with grace' (Psalm 45:2). We see in these verses hints of the whole Trinity: God the Father ('God, your God', Psalm 45:7), Jesus the Son ('Your throne, O God', v.6a), and the Holy Spirit ('the oil of joy', v.7b, see also Isaiah 61:1, 3).

PRAYER

Jesus, my King, 'in your majesty ride forth victoriously on behalf of truth, humility, and righteousness; let your right hand display awesome deeds' (Psalm 45:4a).

NEW TESTAMENT READING

Luke 15:1–32
Loving Father

God loves you passionately, wholeheartedly and unconditionally. However much you may have messed up in your life, whatever your regrets, it is never too late to turn to God. He will accept you and embrace you as a loving father embraces a lost child.

Jesus shocked and offended the religious leaders: 'They growled, "He takes in sinners and eats meals with them, treating them like old friends." Their grumbling triggered this story' (vv.2–3, MSG).

Jesus then tells three parables to show that God cares desperately about the lost. If you have ever lost anything of value, searched frantically and then found it, you will remember your joy when you found what was lost. Jesus says that that joy pales into insignificance compared to the joy of heaven.

The story of the lost sheep shows that 'there's more joy in heaven over one sinner's rescued life than over ninety-nine good people in no need of rescue' (v.7, MSG). The story of the lost coin shows 'the kind of party God's angels throw every time one lost soul turns to God' (v.10, MSG).

Then, in probably the greatest short story ever told, Jesus gives us another astonishing revelation of what God is like: a *loving father*.

The younger son requests his inheritance while the father is still alive and in good health. In traditional Middle Eastern culture this is equivalent to saying, 'Father, I am eager for you to die!' A traditional Middle Eastern father would drive him out of the house. It is an outrageous request, which a father is expected to refuse.

But, in an act of extraordinary love, the father breaks tradition and gives his son the freedom to sell his portion of the estate (this would have brought shame on the family before the entire community). The son 'turned it into cash' (v.13). Then he set off and left the town as quickly as possible.

So many people today, myself included, have experienced what the younger son found while away from his father. He was *wasting his life* ('squandered his wealth in wild living', v.13). 'He began to *hurt*' (v.14, MSG). He was *enslaved* ('hired himself out', v.15). He felt *empty inside* ('he longed to fill his stomach with the pods that the pigs were eating', v.16). He felt *alone in this world* ('no one gave him anything', v.16).

Turning to God is *not an irrational act*. It is the opposite – 'he came to his *senses*' (v.17). The son realised that he needed help. He decided to swallow his pride and go back to his father (v.18). He knew that he needed to go home. He was prepared to admit his sin. He planned to say to his father, 'I have sinned ... I am no longer worthy to be called your son; make me like one of your hired servants' (vv.18–19).

We need to take a step of faith: 'So he got up and went to his father' (v.20). He did not know what would happen. At the time of Jesus, a Jewish boy who lost the family inheritance to Gentiles could be punished by his village, and they would have nothing to do with the wayward son.

God's love is extraordinary, and goes beyond anything that you could ever expect or imagine. Rather than the disgrace we deserve, we receive forgiveness and love. While the boy was still a long way off, his father saw him. It appears that the father had been waiting and watching, and had never forgotten his son. 'His heart pounding, he ran out, embraced him, and kissed him' (v.20, MSG). The word used implies that he *kissed him over and over again*. This is how God receives you.

As you begin your prepared speech of repentance, the father interrupts. He treats you as *an honoured guest*, giving you the best robe (v.22). He gives you a sign of confidence by putting the family ring on your finger (v.22, MSG). He puts sandals, reserved not for slaves but for sons, on your feet (v.22). He plans a lavish celebration party (vv.23–24).

We get a glimpse here of what God is like and how much he loves us. Again, we see the picture of the kingdom of heaven being like a party. This is the opposite of what many people think. They do not associate God with music and dancing, feasting and celebrating.

God's love extends also to the older son, who goes into 'an angry sulk' (v.28, MSG) and is begrudging of his brother's forgiveness and acceptance. You can imagine the father putting his arm around him and saying, 'Son, you don't understand. You're with me all the time, and everything that is mine is yours – but this is a wonderful time, and we had to celebrate. This brother of yours was dead, and he's alive! He was lost, and he's found!' (vv.31–32, MSG).

The story (told to the religious leaders) ends on a cliff-hanger – how will the elder son respond to the father's love?

PRAYER

Father, thank you that you love me so much and when I mess up, you don't reject me. The moment I repent and come back to you, you accept me and say, 'Let's have a feast and celebrate' (v.23).

OLD TESTAMENT READING

Deuteronomy 19:1–20:20
Holy Judge

It is vital to read the Old Testament through the lens of Jesus. We cannot simply apply the laws of the Old Testament to our society today. Nor can we take the concept of the 'holy war' (20:1–20) and turn it into a 'crusade'.

What we see throughout the Bible is that God is a holy God and a God of justice. Some of the principles of the legal system of Ancient Israel were specific to the time. Others are more generally applicable.

Murder is clearly a more serious crime than manslaughter (19:1–13). Good evidence is required before anyone is convicted of a crime (v.15). Perjury is a very serious offence (vv.16–18). Retribution should be deserved and proportionate (v.21 – this was never taken literally, except in the case of the death penalty). A secondary purpose of imposing a just retribution is deterrence (v.20).

But not everything in Ancient Israel is applicable to us. In Jesus Christ a new way has been established. The wrath of God that broke out upon the offender in the community has been visited once and for all upon the righteous representative, the Son of Man.

We cannot accept Israel as a model for our study of the punishment of crime. As former Oxford Professor of Theology, Professor Oliver O'Donovan writes, 'not because it would be illiberal but because it would be unchristian to do so. "Israel", in the strong sense in which it claimed to be God's unique dwelling-place on earth, has been superseded in Christ.'[1]

For example, when Jesus quoted from this passage he said, 'You have heard that it was said, "Eye for eye, and tooth for tooth." [Deuteronomy 19:21]. But I tell you, Do not resist an evil person. If someone strikes you on the right cheek, turn the other cheek also' (Matthew 5:38–39).

PRAYER

Lord, thank you that you are the God of love, justice and truth. Thank you that you reveal yourself to me as I study your word and spend time in your presence.

14 April | Day 104

How to Avoid the *Titanic* Mistake

James Cameron, director of the movie *Titanic,* describes the *Titanic* as a 'metaphor' of life: 'We are all living on ... [the] *Titanic*.'[1]

When the *Titanic* set sail in 1912, it was declared to be 'unsinkable' because it was constructed using a new technology. The ship's hull was divided into sixteen watertight compartments. Up to four of these compartments could be damaged or even flooded, and still the ship would float.

Tragically, the *Titanic* sank on 15 April 1912 at 2.20 a.m. and 1,513 people lost their lives. At the time, it was thought that five of its watertight compartments had been ruptured in a collision with an iceberg.

However, on 1 September 1985, when the wreck of the *Titanic* was found lying upright on the ocean floor, there was no sign of the long gash previously thought to have been ripped in the ship's hull. What they discovered was that damage to one compartment affected all the rest.

Many people make the *Titanic* mistake. They think they can divide their lives into different 'compartments' and that what they do in one will not affect the rest. However, as Rick Warren (from whom I have taken this illustration) says, '*A life of integrity is one that is not divided into compartments.*'[2]

David prayed for '*an undivided heart*' (Psalm 86:11). He led the people with '*integrity of heart*' (78:72). Supremely, Jesus was a '*man of integrity*' (Matthew 22:16; Mark 12:14). How can you and I avoid the *Titanic* mistake and live lives of integrity?

READING FROM PROVERBS

Proverbs 9:13–18
Integrity in relationships

It is not easy to lead a life of integrity in relationships. Temptations abound and the lure is strong: 'The woman Folly is *loud*' (v.13a), '*calling out*' (v.15a), '*come in here*!' (v.16a). She says, '*Stolen* water is *sweet*; food eaten in *secret* is *delicious*!' (v.17).

Yet this is a total deception. Why should '*stolen*' water be sweet or food eaten '*in secret*' be delicious? In fact, unfaithfulness leads to a deadening of the spirit: 'But little do they know that the dead are there, that her guests are in the depths of the grave' (v.18).

The apostle Paul writes that if you set your mind on what your sinful nature desires it leads to death, 'but the mind governed by the Spirit is life and peace' (Romans 8:6).

PRAYER

Lord, by your Spirit, help me to live a life of integrity, rooting out the secret sin and living a life that is authentic and faithful.

NEW TESTAMENT READING

Luke 16:1–18
Integrity with money

Jesus spoke about money more than virtually any other subject (including prayer and heaven). Twelve out of his thirty-eight parables are about money or possessions. As Billy Graham put it, 'If a person gets their attitude towards money straight, it will help straighten out almost every other area in their life.'

In today's passage, Jesus teaches us how to get a right view of money. He starts with the rather strange parable of the dishonest manager, who is commended for his shrewdness.

1. Money is a tool

The people of this world are often more sensible, thoughtful, prudent and wise than the people of God in understanding that money is *a tool*. The dishonest manager is commended for his shrewdness in seeing this. The reality is that money can be a tool for eternal benefit. 'I tell you, use worldly wealth to gain friends for yourselves, so that when it is gone, you will be welcomed into *eternal* dwellings' (v.9).

Jesus taught on the wonder of being with him for eternity in the parables of the great banquet (14:15–24) and the prodigal son (15:11–32). Here, we are reminded that the use of our money on earth can have eternal consequences. One of Jesus' primary concerns was to see the good news of the kingdom of God being preached (16:16). Your money can be used to see God's rule and reign coming in to people's lives – with eternal consequences.

2. Money is a test

Jesus is not commending the dishonest manager for his dishonesty. Indeed, the opposite is the case. He goes on to say, 'Whoever can be *trusted* with very little can also be *trusted* with much, and whoever is dishonest with very little will also be dishonest with much. So if you have not been *trustworthy* in handling worldly wealth, who will *trust* you with true riches?' (vv.10–11).

Be an honest and trustworthy steward of everything God has given you, including your money. The more trustworthy you are with money, the more God will give you 'true riches'.

3. Money is a threat

Jesus says, 'No one can be a slave to two masters. Either you will hate the one and love the other, or you will be devoted to the one and despise the other. You cannot be a slave to both God and Money' (v.13). As Dietrich Bonhoeffer put it, 'Our hearts have room for only one all-embracing devotion, and we can only cleave to one Lord.'[3]

Money is to be used, but not loved. Don't love money and use people. Love people and use money.

The threat is that love of money leads to hatred of God (v.13). The Pharisees loved money (they were 'money-obsessed', MSG) and sneered at Jesus (v.14). Have the opposite attitude to money. 'Despise' it (v.13). In other words, treat it with contempt by giving generously and focusing your love not on money, but on God who 'knows your hearts' (v.15).

PRAYER

Lord, help me to be a good steward of everything that you have entrusted to me, to be honest and trustworthy. Help me to give generously and focus my thoughts not on money but on you.

OLD TESTAMENT READING

Deuteronomy 21:1–22:30
Integrity of lifestyle

Many of these laws were temporary in purpose. For example, the food laws and so on were symbolic. They educated the people of God in the pursuit of purity.

Others, however shocking they may seem to us, are surprisingly advanced for the standards of the time. For example, there are limits put on how a captive woman can be treated (21:10–14); she must not be dishonoured or humiliated (v.14).

There is to be honour in sexual relationships. God is concerned about premarital sex, promiscuity (22:21), adultery (v.22), rape (vv.25–27), and incest (v.30). As we saw in today's New Testament passage, Jesus himself spoke strongly about the need for marriage vows to be honoured (Luke 16:18).

God is also concerned about protecting the vulnerable. Rape is always a horrible crime, but in ancient societies it could also lessen a woman's chances of marrying. This is the context behind the obligation for a rapist to pay compensation, and to marry the woman in question (Deuteronomy 22:29). However, in the equivalent passage in Exodus 22:17 it is made clear that this does *not* mean that the woman *has* to marry the man. This law is designed *to protect* rape victims – not add forced marriage to their suffering.

Consideration is to be shown to neighbours (Deuteronomy 22:1–3). It is not enough to do no harm to your neighbour. Positively do them good. Ignoring those in need is wrong. 'Don't look the other way as if you didn't see it' (v.3, MSG).

We see the beginnings here of what our English law came to describe as 'a *duty of care*' towards our neighbour. Make sure that your property (home, car, bike and so on) is safe and not likely to cause harm to your neighbour. '*Make it safe*' (v.8, MSG).

I find all of today's passages very challenging. I know I fall short in many of these areas. I have often failed. Is there any hope?

In the middle of all these laws comes a clue: 'Anyone who is hung on a tree is under God's *curse*' (21:23). Paul quotes this verse in Galatians and explains its significance to us. Everyone who fails to keep *all* the law of God is under a curse – this is the curse of the law (Galatians 3:10). However, the wonderful news is that Jesus took the curse on himself on our behalf on the cross ('the tree').

'He became a curse, and at the same time dissolved the curse' (v.13, MSG). As a result, all of us are now able to receive, by faith, the promise of the Holy Spirit (v.14).

My failure to live a life of total integrity means that I have failed to keep the law. I would therefore be under God's curse. But Jesus became a curse for me on the cross. Hanging on the tree he took God's curse upon himself for you and me so that we can be redeemed, set free and receive the promise of the Spirit to enable us to begin to lead lives of complete integrity.

PRAYER

Lord, thank you that you died for me so that I might be forgiven and receive the gift of your Holy Spirit. By your Spirit help me to live a life of integrity of heart.

15 April | Day 105
Choose What You Remember

Memory is strange. There are some things I would prefer not to remember but find difficult to forget. There are other things that I would love to remember that are all too easily forgotten.

There are some things that are important for societies as a whole not to forget. All over the world, we see war *memorials* with the names of those who have died for their country. Often in Britain these memorials feature the words *'Lest We Forget'*. A plaque at Auschwitz Concentration Camp reads, 'The one who does not remember history is bound to live through it again' (George Santayana).

We do have some control over our memory. There are *some things* we are told in the Bible to *'forget'*. There are *other things* we are repeatedly called to *'remember'*. You can make choices about what you *choose to 'forget'* and what you *choose to 'remember'*.

The word 'remember' in its various Hebrew and Greek forms occurs over 250 times in the Bible. It is so easy to forget all that God has done for you. It is important to look back at your own life as well as the history of the church, both local and global, to remember all that God has done.

At the Last Supper, Jesus instituted the service of communion so that we would not forget the central events of world history – the death and resurrection of Jesus.

READING FROM PSALMS

Psalm 45:10–17
Remember Jesus always

Generations come and go but the name of Jesus will be remembered for ever.

The New Testament applied this psalm to Jesus (Hebrews 1:8ff). The early church saw its own relationship with Christ reflected in the relations between the bridegroom and the bride as they are described here.

Jesus loves the church: 'The king is enthralled by your beauty' (Psalm 45:11a).

We are to honour Jesus; he is our Lord (v.11b): 'I will perpetuate your *memory* through all generations; therefore the nations will praise you for ever and ever' (v.17). Jesus the King will be remembered for all time. Every nation will worship him for ever and ever (Revelation 5:13).

PRAYER

Lord Jesus, I worship you today. Help us to perpetuate your memory through all generations, that all the nations might praise you for ever and ever.

NEW TESTAMENT READING

Luke 16:19–17:10
Remember the poor

If you have food to eat every day, own a pair of shoes and have a roof over your head you are *rich* in comparison to most of the rest of the world. And if you own a car, or even a bicycle, you are *very rich* in comparison to the rest of the world.

This passage is a challenge to me personally as I look at our situation compared with much of the poverty around the world. It is also a challenge to our society, as we look at our global neighbours, for example in Africa, who as a result of television and other forms of global communication are now 'at [our] gate' (16:20).

The great nineteenth-century preacher D. L. Moody often took as the title of his talks the words: 'Son, *remember*...' (v.25). This parable is a warning. (It is a parable and therefore it is not a complete teaching about life after death.)

The words of Abraham to the rich man, who had '[wasted] his days in conspicuous consumption' (v.19, MSG), are haunting: '*Son, remember* that in your lifetime you received your good things, while Lazarus received bad things' (v.25). The rich man was judged for his failure to act on behalf of the poor. I live in Western Europe, which is one of the wealthiest parts of the world. Relative to most of the world I live 'in luxury every day' (v.19).

The rich man was aware of the poverty of Lazarus because he was laid at his gate 'covered with sores and longing to eat what fell from the rich man's table' (vv.20–21a). Modern media makes us increasingly aware of global poverty. Now is the time to act. I have even less of an excuse than the rich man. In the Old Testament the people were called to act upon the word of Moses and the Prophets (v.29). We are called to *remember* and to live out of the death and resurrection of Jesus (v.31).

Yet this parable is not merely an attack on being rich. After all, Abraham was exceedingly wealthy and he is pictured in heaven (v.22). The rich man's love of money reveals his spiritual state and lack of relationship with God based on repentance and faith.

When he realises his mistake, he says to Abraham, 'If someone from the dead goes to [my five brothers] they will *repent*' (v.30). Abraham replies, 'If they do not listen to Moses and the Prophets, they will not be convinced even if someone *rises from the dead*' (v.31).

If the rich man had listened to Moses and the Prophets, he would have repented and put his faith in God. Luke, in recording this parable of Jesus, is of course confronting the reader with the fact that we have even less of an excuse now that we have the evidence of *Jesus* rising from the dead. We are challenged to repent and put our faith in Jesus.

Underlying all the sections of today's New Testament passage is the common theme of a relationship with God based on repentance and faith.

This continues in the next section (17:1–4). Jesus calls us to watch our lives carefully to avoid either causing others to sin or falling into the traps set by others. Live a life of constant forgiveness. Forgive even those who sin against you seven times a day (v.4).

The disciples realise that this is only possible with great faith. They say to Jesus, 'Increase our *faith*!' (v.5). Jesus replies, 'If you have *faith* as small as a mustard seed, you can say to this mulberry tree, "be uprooted and planted in the sea," and it will obey you' (v.6).

It is this faith that leads to humility. Whatever you do in service of God, you can never put God in your debt. Everything we do is simply out of gratitude for what he has done for us. All we can say, at the end of the day, is, 'We are unworthy servants; we have only done our duty' (v.10).

Faith is a muscle that grows by stretching. One of the ways you increase your faith is by doing something God asks you to do.

If you want to avoid hearing those haunting words, 'Son, *remember*...' in the future, *now is the time* to respond in repentance, put your faith in Jesus and live out your faith, especially in your response to the poor.

PRAYER

Lord, have mercy. Forgive my sin. Help me always to forgive. Increase my faith. Open my eyes to see the needs of those around me and to act now.

OLD TESTAMENT READING

Deuteronomy 23:1–25:19
Remember what God has done for you

Throughout this passage the people of God are told to '*remember*' (24:9, 18, 22; 25:17). In particular, they are to *remember* that they were slaves in Egypt and the Lord their God redeemed them (24:18–22). Indeed, the passage for today ends with the words, '*do not forget!*' (25:19).

Again, there is a link with the poor. Because they were slaves in Egypt, they should remember those who are suffering: the lonely, the fatherless and the widow (24:21). They are to look after the poor and needy (v.14).

Generosity towards the poor was not a matter left to each individual's conscience – it was a matter of law. It is surely right for a society to have laws to provide for the needs of the poor. But it should not stop there. It is also the calling of every Christian.

As the people of God in the Old Testament were called to remember that they had been slaves in Egypt and that God had redeemed them, we remember that at one time we also were enslaved to sin. Jesus redeemed you from that slavery.

Constantly *remember* what Jesus has done for you. That is one of the reasons the service of Holy Communion is so important. Jesus said, 'do this in *remembrance* of me' (Luke 22:19).

The purpose of the Christian calendar is to *remember*. At *Christmas* we *remember* and celebrate the *incarnation*. At *Pentecost* we *remember* and celebrate the *outpouring of the Holy Spirit*.

Supremely, at *Easter* we *remember* and celebrate the *death and resurrection of Jesus*. The resurrection is the peak of the Christian calendar. From the very earliest days, Christians have remembered the death and resurrection of Jesus in a service of celebration involving bread and wine taken in *remembrance* of Jesus.

PRAYER

Lord, thank you for the body of Jesus that was given for me and his blood that was shed for me. Through the power of the Holy Spirit, your word and sacrament, may my thoughts and memories be focused on you.

16 April | Day 106
His Presence

If you love somebody, what you long for more than anything else is that person's presence with you. Photos are a comfort. Telephone calls, emails and texts are nice. Letters are good. Skype and FaceTime are great ways to communicate. Yet nothing can compare to actually spending time with them in person.

What Adam and Eve lost in the Garden of Eden when they sinned was *the presence of God*. Even more than possessing the law, the distinguishing feature of Israel was *God's presence with them*. The temple was not primarily a place of sacrifice but *a place of God's presence*. The exile was such a disaster for the people of God because they were *away from God's presence*.

God promised to be in the midst of his people again. This promise was fulfilled with the coming of Jesus and the Holy Spirit. He promises to be with you.

READING FROM PSALMS

Psalm 46:1–11
'The Lord Almighty is with us'

The presence of God in the Old Testament was associated with Jerusalem – the city of God. 'God lives here' (v.5, MSG). In particular, it was associated with the temple – 'the holy place where the Most High dwells' (v.4b); 'God is within her' (v.5a); 'The Lord Almighty is with us' (vv.7, 11).

When Jesus was on earth, he declared that his body was the temple where God was present (see John 2:19–22). On the day of Pentecost, God's presence came to dwell with his people through the Holy Spirit, the Spirit of Christ. In the New Testament, God's presence is not in a physical temple but with his people – 'a holy temple' (Ephesians 2:19–22).

In life, it seems there is always so much that needs to be done and it is tempting to want to be active and get on and do it. But the Lord encourages you to 'Be still, and know that I am God' (Psalm 46:10). If you take time to be still and to listen to him, you see in this psalm some of the blessings that come from knowing his presence with you.

1. Peace

'God is our refuge and strength, an ever-present help in trouble. Therefore we will *not fear*' (vv.1–2a).

2. Joy

'There is a river whose streams *make glad* the city of God' (v.4a). Jesus spoke of the Holy Spirit bringing 'streams of living water' (John 7:38). This river is now not in a physical city but in your heart.

3. Security

'God is within her, she will not fall; God will help her at break of day' (Psalm 46:5).

4. Protection

'The LORD Almighty is with us; the God of Jacob is our fortress' (vv.7, 11). 'God fights for us' and 'protects us' (v.11, MSG).

PRAYER

Lord, today I want to 'Be still, and know that [you are] God' (v.10). I bring to you my fears, worries and anxieties. Thank you that I can trust you. Thank you for your presence and the peace, joy, security and protection you bring.

NEW TESTAMENT READING

Luke 17:11–37
'The kingdom of God is among you'

With the coming of Jesus and the coming of the kingdom of God, God has come to dwell among his people. Jesus is 'Immanuel ... God with us' (Matthew 1:23). Jesus taught that the kingdom of God is *both 'now'* and *'not yet'*:

1. God's presence: *'Now'*

The Pharisees asked Jesus when the kingdom of God would come. Jesus answered, 'The kingdom of God doesn't come by counting the days on the calendar. Nor when someone says, "Look here!" or, "There it is!" And why? Because God's kingdom is already *among you*' (Luke 17:20–21, MSG).

The kingdom of God is God's rule and reign. Jesus *inaugurated* the kingdom of God, preaching the good news of the kingdom and healing the sick (for example, vv.15–18), and through his death and resurrection. With the coming of Jesus and the Holy Spirit, God is present among his people. However, his presence is not always visible. People today will not always be able to say, 'Here it is,' or 'There it is' (v.21), but a time is coming when his presence will be visible.

2. God's presence: *'Not yet'*

One day Jesus will return. This will be the day of *consummation* for the kingdom of God. Then everyone will see, 'For the Son of Man in his day will be like the lightning, which flashes and lights up the sky from one end to the other' (v.24).

This will be the day when the Son of Man is revealed in all his glory (v.30), then we will see him *face to face* (1 Corinthians 13:12); and 'we will be with the Lord for ever' (1 Thessalonians 4:17). We will experience the visible presence of God for ever.

Right now God's presence is not visible. People focus on eating, drinking, marrying, buying, selling, planting and building (see Luke 17:27–28). None of these things is wrong in itself. They are part of regular, ordinary life. The problem in both Noah's time and Lot's time was that most people did not listen to the warnings. Jesus urges you to be ready.

Paradoxically, whoever tries to keep their life will lose it and whoever loses their life will preserve it (v.33). If you are always trying to find ways of getting the most out of life for yourself – the most money, highest position, best reputation, most popular – you will miss out. If you lose your life in denying yourself and serving Jesus, you will actually find life in all its fullness.

As you live in this time between the first and second coming of Jesus, don't forget to thank God for all his blessings. Of the ten lepers whom Jesus cured, only one came back 'praising God in a loud voice. He threw himself at Jesus' feet and thanked him' (Luke 17:15–16).

It is easy to be like the nine lepers who forgot to thank Jesus. Cultivate an attitude of gratitude – taking time to thank Jesus for answers to prayer, his constant love, his forgiveness, his kindness and especially for the promise of God's presence with you. Recently, while praying in Hyde Park, I decided to try and think of a hundred things for which to thank God. I got there very quickly and realised that I'd hardly begun to list all the things for which to give thanks.

PRAYER

Lord, forgive me for forgetting so often to thank you. Thank you so much for all your blessings...

OLD TESTAMENT READING

Deuteronomy 26:1–28:14
'The presence of the Lord'

In this passage, we see part of the Old Testament background to the understanding of 'the presence of the Lord'. The land that God had given as an inheritance was the place that he chose as 'a *dwelling for his Name*' (26:2).

They were to recite their history 'in the *Presence of God*' (v.5, MSG). They were to prostrate themselves 'in the *Presence of God*' (v.10, MSG). In the '*Presence of God*' they were to pray for God's blessing on his people (vv.9–16, MSG). They were to rejoice in 'the *Presence of God*' (27:7, MSG).

God had rescued his people from 'misery, toil and oppression' (26:7). This is a good description of life without the presence of God. He called his people to be 'his treasured possession' (v.18). He tells them to build a place of worship where they can rejoice 'in the *presence* of the LORD your God' (27:7).

Sin is what takes us away from the presence of God. Therefore, God warns his people to avoid idol worship, dishonouring families, theft, leading the blind astray, injustice, sexual immorality, murder and bribery (vv.14–26).

By contrast, if his people fully obey they will enjoy all his blessings (28:1–14). God promises to bless their homes, families, work and other activities. As Joyce Meyer writes, 'Obedience is not to be an occasional event; it is to be a way of life. There is a big difference between people who are willing to obey God daily and those who are willing to obey only in order to get out of trouble. God certainly shows people how to get out of trouble, but He showers blessings on those who decide to live wholeheartedly for Him and make obedience to Him their lifestyle.'[1]

Of course, none of us have fully obeyed the Lord, except Jesus. His death and resurrection have made it possible for you to be forgiven and to enjoy the presence of God and a foretaste of all the blessings that are promised in this passage. And one day, when Jesus returns, you will experience them in all their fullness in the visible presence of God: Father, Son and Holy Spirit.

PRAYER

Father, thank you for all the blessings that you promise. Thank you for the forgiveness that is available in Jesus Christ. Thank you that I experience a foretaste of these blessings in this life and one day I will experience them fully, in the visible presence of God.

17 April | Day 107

Six Steps to a God-Centred Life

William Temple, like his father before him, was Archbishop of Canterbury (1942–1944). Among his many remarkable achievements, he wrote a superb commentary on the Gospel of John. He wrote the entire commentary, entitled *Readings in St John's Gospel*, while praying on his knees before God.

About worship, he wrote: 'Worship is a submission of all our nature to God. It is the quickening of conscience by his holiness; the nourishment of mind with his truth; the purifying of imagination by his beauty; the opening of the heart to his love; the surrender of will to his purpose – and all this gathered up in adoration.'[1]

Worship saves us from being self-centred and makes us *God-centred*. You were created to live in a relationship with God. That should be your number one priority. If you put God first in your life all kinds of blessings follow. Because God loves you he warns you of the dangers of disregarding the design for your life.

But what does it mean to lead a God-centred life and what steps do you need to take in order to get there?

READING FROM PSALMS

Psalm 47:1–9
Worship God

You are invited to worship God.

Worship in this psalm sounds quite emotional and noisy: '*Clap your hands*, all you nations; *shout* to God with *cries* of joy ... God has ascended amid *shouts of joy*, the LORD amid the *sounding of trumpets*' (vv.1, 5). It also includes lots of singing (vv.6–7).

There is great exuberance in worship, as adoration and amazement of God bubbles over in extravagant action.

These are all outward ways of expressing your worship of the Lord. Worship includes the use of emotions to express your love and gratitude to God and to bring him honour.

All relationships involve emotions. I don't say to Pippa, 'I love you with my mind.' What I say is, 'I love you with my whole being, my mind, my heart, my will…'

We are good at expressing our emotions in other contexts such as football matches or other sporting events – then why should it be any different in our worship to God?

PRAYER

Lord, today I submit myself to you. Quicken my conscience with your holiness. Nourish my mind with your truth. Purify my imagination with your beauty. Open my heart to your love. I surrender my all to your purpose. I worship and adore you.

NEW TESTAMENT READING

Luke 18:1–30

Pray consistently

The God-centred life is a life of consistent prayer. Jesus taught his disciples to 'always pray and not give up' (v.1). You can talk to God not just in church or in set times of prayer, but anywhere and at any time. I was taught very early in my Christian life to 'talk as you walk' through the day.

Jesus tells the parable of the widow and the unjust judge who eventually gives in to her demands in order to stop her bothering him and wearing him out (vv.4–5). Jesus says that if an unjust judge will listen to a widow's plea, how much more will God listen to those who 'cry out to him *day and night*?' (v.7b). Never give up praying and pray hardest when it is hardest to pray.

Humble yourself

Humility is not something that happens to you. It is something that you are supposed to do to yourself. Rather than exalting yourself, you are supposed to 'humble [your]self'. God promises that he will exalt you (v.14).

If we compare ourselves with others, we may become like the Pharisee, thanking God that we are not like other people – 'robbers, evildoers, adulterers' (v.11). The Pharisee was 'confident of his own righteousness' (v.9). He fell into the trap of trusting himself. If our lives are truly God-centred (our consciences quickened by his holiness), we compare ourselves with him and all we can say is, 'God, have mercy on me, a sinner' (v.13). The truth is that we are all sinners, and we are all in need of God's mercy.

I find it very easy to read this passage and to thank God that I am not like the Pharisee. But by doing so I fall into the very trap that Jesus is describing – thinking I am more righteous than others, rather than recognising my sin and need for God. This is exactly the sin of the Pharisee.

Be childlike

Sometimes the 'babies' (v.15), children or young people in a church are described as 'the church of the future'. But, according to Jesus, they are *not* just the church of the *future*, they are the church of *today:* 'The kingdom of God belongs to such as these' (v.16).

Jesus calls us to become like children. He never tells us to be childish (in the sense of being simplistic), but he does tell us to be *childlike*.

To be childlike is the opposite of being independent and 'grown up'. Children tend to be open, receptive, trusting, humble, loving and forgiving. The God-centred life is a life of childlike dependence on him.

You become childlike when you show and share your honest feelings, acknowledge how fragile and vulnerable you are and how much you need God and other people.

Children are instinctively driven to explore and discover. They neither dwell in the past nor settle for the present, but look forward – with an unquenchable curiosity – to the future, fuelled by wonder and an immense capacity for enjoyment.

Cultivate this freedom to respond instinctively, like a child, and to feel and express wonder, awe, love and joy – to rush in and eagerly explore, probe and discover things for yourself.

Follow Jesus

There is nothing more rewarding than following Jesus. Peter said to Jesus, 'We have left all we had to follow you!' (v.28). Jesus replies, 'I tell you the truth … no one who has left home or wife or brothers or sisters or parents or children for the sake of the kingdom of God will fail to receive *many times as much* in this age *and*, in the age to come, *eternal life*' (vv.29–30)

Jesus calls the rich young ruler to the God-centred life. He calls him to give up everything else and follow him (v.22). Perhaps Jesus saw in him the potential to be like the apostle Peter, or Matthew, or one of the others who responded positively when Jesus said, 'follow me'.

The more we accumulate the harder it is to live God-centred lives. The rich young ruler 'became very sad, because he was very wealthy' (v.23). It is not impossible for the rich to enter the kingdom of God (v.27), but it is very hard (vv.24–25) – not because the standards are higher, but because the risk appears greater.

In fact, it is impossible for any one of us, including the rich, to enter the kingdom of God on the strength of our own performance (vv.24–25). Yet with God it is possible for anyone, including the rich, to enter the kingdom of God. Jesus said, 'What is humanly impossible is possible with God' (v.27). Neither your past failings nor your present circumstances need determine your future. With God all things are possible.

PRAYER

Lord, have mercy on me, a sinner, give me a childlike faith and dependence on you and help me to be willing to give up everything else in order to follow you wholeheartedly.

OLD TESTAMENT READING

Deuteronomy 28:15–68
Serve God

In this passage we see the disastrous consequences of not living the God-centred life, not obeying the law, not carefully following his command (v.45) and not serving the Lord (v.47). We also see the disastrous consequences of this within Israel's own history.

In my own life, I have seen a glimpse of some of the things described, especially in the years before I experienced a relationship with God: 'The sky over your head will be bronze' (v.23). I have experienced the sense of what seems to be a great separation from God.

We see how 'the Lord will give you an anxious mind, eyes weary with longing, and a despairing heart. You will live in constant suspense, filled with dread, both night and day, never sure of your life' (vv.65–66). 'Worry is a cycle of inefficient thoughts whirling around a centre of fear' (Corrie ten Boom).[2] This is the opposite of the peace and joy that Jesus offers.

Of course, sometimes I have failed to serve, obey and follow his command wholeheartedly. The wonderful news of the New Testament is that Jesus has rescued us from the deserved punishment and curses that would have otherwise followed: 'Christ redeemed us from the curse of the law by becoming a curse for us' (Galatians 3:13).

PRAYER

Lord, thank you so much that you died in my place so I can be forgiven and set free from the consequences that I deserve. Thank you that you call me to a God-centred life. Help me to worship you wholeheartedly, to serve you joyfully and gladly, and to obey and follow you always.

18 April | Day 108
It's Never Too Late

I like to think of myself as young. Recently, I heard that middle age runs from thirty-five to fifty-eight years of age. On that basis, not only am I not *young*, I am not even middle-aged!

People often speak of being middle-aged as a time of 'midlife crisis'. A midlife crisis can be caused by ageing itself, or ageing in combination with changes, problems, or regrets over work, career, relationships, children and physical changes associated with ageing.

Individuals experiencing a midlife crisis are often searching for an undefined dream or goal. We may have a deep sense of remorse for goals not yet accomplished. We may fear humiliation among more successful colleagues. We often desire to achieve a feeling of youthfulness.

At the root of all these things is a sense of something being missing. There is often a tragic wisdom in mid-life crises, as individuals realise the emptiness of much of what they used to strive for (even if what they replace it with is not always particularly wise).

I have often wondered whether Zacchaeus, whom we read about in today's New Testament passage, was going through a midlife crisis. Whether he was or not, he found the answer that so many people are searching for in his encounter with Jesus.

No matter how long you have travelled in the wrong direction, you can always turn around. With Jesus it's never too late to make a new start and ensure that your life is set in the right direction.

READING FROM PROVERBS

Proverbs 10:1–10
Apply 'the rocking chair test'

A successful businessman, who is well known to be a man of extraordinary integrity, told me that he applies the 'rocking chair test' to all his decisions. He pictures himself one day, in his retirement, sitting in his rocking chair and looking back on the decisions that he has made. What will he decide was a good decision and what will he decide was a bad decision? He wants to ensure that the decisions he makes now he will not regret later.

This passage shows us the things we need to avoid, such as malice (v.10), foolish gossip (vv.8, 10) and laziness (v.4).

Honesty and integrity are key to a life lived without regret. 'Ill-gotten gain gets you nowhere; an *honest life* is immortal' (v.2, MSG). 'A good and honest life is a blessed memorial; a wicked life leaves a rotten stench' (v.7, MSG).

If you live honestly and with integrity you can be 'confident and carefree' (v.9a, MSG). But the dishonest will be caught: (v.9b, GNB).

PRAYER

Lord, help me today to be wise and righteous (vv.3, 7), to avoid malice (v.10) and foolish gossip (vv.8, 10), to live a life of diligence (v.4), honesty and integrity (v.9).

NEW TESTAMENT READING

Luke 18:31–19:10
Set your life in the right direction

Jesus came to make it possible for our lives to be redeemed and transformed.

He takes the Twelve aside (18:31) and explains that the purpose for which he has come will involve being mocked, insulted, spat on, flogged and killed (v.32). But, 'on the third day he will rise again' (v.33). It is the crucifixion and resurrection of Jesus that provides hope for every human being.

The blind man is an example of someone whose life is totally transformed by an encounter with Jesus. A man, whose life had ended up with him sitting by the roadside begging, is transformed when he cries out for mercy. Jesus says to him: '"Go ahead – see again! Your faith has saved and healed you!" The healing was instant: He looked up, seeing – and then followed Jesus, glorifying God' (vv.42–43a, MSG).

Next, Zacchaeus encounters Jesus. Zacchaeus was probably not young. As 'a chief tax collector', he had reached the top of his profession (19:2). He was still able to run and climb a tree at least (v.4) – but he wasn't getting any younger. He had become wealthy (v.2) and his work was probably his priority. As a chief tax collector Zacchaeus would have had people working under him.

He would have been promoted many times, and could look back with satisfaction upon his achievements. Yet, as a tax collector the personal cost of this work was ostracism and unpopularity. People in Zacchaeus's situation often resent their job and feel trapped in their chosen life.

He would most likely have had a family, and we read of his 'house' (v.9). Perhaps he worked very hard for them. A midlife crisis can be devastating to family life. A person in midlife crisis can become angry, depressed and resentful to those closest to them – feeling that no matter how hard they work, their family require more than they can earn.

Zacchaeus was almost certainly from a religious home. His parents called him Zacchaeus: 'the righteous one'. But now religious people regarded him as a 'sinner' (v.7) because he was collecting taxes from his own people to give to the Romans and taking a lot of it for himself.

Still, 'He wanted to see who Jesus was' (v.3). He must have realised he had a need. For all his money, success, family life and 'religion', there was still something missing. Zacchaeus wanted to see Jesus without Jesus seeing him (v.4).

Many people feel that because of their sin and imperfections, God will turn away from them. But God loves imperfect people and, instead of turning away from you, he turns towards you.

Zacchaeus did not realise that you cannot hide from God. Jesus knew him and he even knew his name. Zacchaeus did not realise that Jesus *loved him* and wanted to know him (v.5). Whatever you have done in your life and whatever your imperfection, Jesus loves you and wants to be in a relationship with you. But he requires a response. In a dramatic moment of encounter, Jesus said, 'Come down immediately' (v.5).

Zacchaeus humbled himself and obeyed Jesus. He did not put it off. He came down 'at once and welcomed him gladly' (v.6). Jesus was not put off by the negative response of the crowd (v.7).

The result was a total transformation in Zacchaeus's life (v.8 onwards). He decided to 'give half of my possessions to the poor, and if I have cheated anybody out of anything, I will pay back four times the amount' (v.8). His attitude to possessions changed completely. The question for us should not be, 'How much can I get?' but, 'How much can I give?' (v.8).

His whole family was transformed. Jesus said to him, 'Today salvation has come to this *house*' (v.9). Salvation came to his household in the arrival of Jesus. Salvation means freedom. It means a relationship with Jesus that goes on for ever. This puts even a midlife crisis in perspective.

Finally, you, like Zacchaeus, can be part of God's transformation of society. The transformation in Zacchaeus and his household brought benefits for the poor and justice for those who had been cheated.

His crucial decision to follow Jesus certainly passes the rocking chair test.

PRAYER

Lord, thank you that you love me and that you often use a crisis to transform my life for the better. Help me to encounter you afresh today.

OLD TESTAMENT READING

Deuteronomy 29:1–30:10
Live a wholehearted life

Recently, I sat next to an eighty-six-year-old woman at lunch. She was in a wheelchair. I soon realised that although her body was failing, her mind was not. She raised some very difficult theological issues. When I asked her what she thought the answer was to these questions, she replied with a verse from this passage: 'The secret things belong to the LORD our God, but the things revealed belong to us and to our children for ever' (29:29).

She said she had come to realise that some things we did know the answer to, but others (such as the kind of questions she had been raising!) we would probably not know the answer to in this life. They were part of the 'secret things' that 'belong to the LORD'.

There are some things, however, that do belong to us. God has revealed to us how to 'live well and wisely' (v.9, MSG). We need to avoid getting 'sidetracked from God' (v.18), thinking 'I'll live just the way I please, thank you' and end up 'ruining life for everybody' (v.19, MSG)

The way to know you will be at peace in your rocking chair is to listen to and obey God *wholeheartedly* (30:2–10): 'Obey him with your whole heart and soul ... He'll have compassion on you; he'll come back and pick up the pieces ... And you will make a new start, listening obediently to GOD ... Nothing half-hearted here; you must return to GOD, your God, totally, heart and soul, holding nothing back' (vv.2–10, MSG).

It's never too late to start living a wholehearted life.

PRAYER

Lord, help me from now on to live a life of wholehearted obedience to you. May today be a new start. Help me to obey you wholeheartedly.

19 April | Day 109
God's Strategic Plan

I live in London. With a population of over 8 million, it is the largest city in Europe and one of the largest in the world. It receives over 18 million visitors a year. It is a city where over 300 languages are spoken.

Cities are strategic places for the spread of the gospel. They always have been. The apostle Paul took the gospel from city to city. As early as AD 100, more than 40 Christian communities existed in cities around the Mediterranean world, including North Africa and parts of Italy. By AD 300 half the citizens of that region were Christian while 90 per cent of the countryside was still pagan. Most of Paul's letters were written to cities.

Cities tend to be places where culture is formed. Many of the spheres of influence emanate from the city, including government, politicians and law-makers; arts and entertainment; business and the market-place; universities and other places of education; media and communication centres. The river of influence tends to flow from the city to the suburbs and rural areas. The way to transform a culture is to transform the city.

It is not surprising, therefore, that cities have always had an important role in the purposes of God. In particular, one city has been at the heart of God's strategy for the world.

READING FROM PSALMS

Psalm 48:1–8
The power of the city

This psalm is all about the '*City of God*' (Jerusalem). '*The city*' is mentioned in different ways seven times in the passage. It celebrates the *beauty* (v.2) and *security* of the city (v.8). Most of all though, it celebrates the fact that it is the 'city *of our God*' (vv.1, 8), the place where God's temple had been built and *his presence* could be found (v.3), and a place that was under his *protection* (vv.3, 8). It was intended to be *a source of blessing for the whole world*: 'the joy of *all the earth*' (v.2).

Paul contrasts the physical city of Jerusalem with the even greater 'Jerusalem that is above' (Galatians 4:26). He sees the Christian church as the new Jerusalem.

In the book of Revelation, John sees '*the Holy City*, the *new Jerusalem*, coming down out of heaven from God, prepared as *a bride beautifully dressed* for her husband' (Revelation 21:2). The new Jerusalem is the church, the bride of Christ. This is the place where God will dwell for ever (v.3).

The church should be amazing: 'beautiful in its loftiness, the joy of the whole earth' (Psalm 48:2). We should sense the presence of God there, know his security and protection and be a blessing to the world around us.

PRAYER

Lord, thank you for the power of your presence in the church. May we be a source of blessing to the world.

NEW TESTAMENT READING

Luke 19:11–44
The passion for the city

As Jesus approaches the city of Jerusalem (v.11) he tells the parable of the minas. It is a parable that challenges his hearer's assumptions about the kingdom of God and God's plans for the earthly city. A mina is worth three months' wages – a large sum of money. It really matters how you use all that God has entrusted to you.

You are supposed to use not only your money, but all the gifts God has given you – including your time, education, job, skills and opportunities for the benefit of the king and his kingdom.

It is interesting that the reward for trustworthiness in looking after minas was to 'take charge of ten *cities*' or 'of five *cities*' (vv.17, 19).

When Jesus makes the triumphal entry into the *city* of Jerusalem, 'the whole crowd of disciples began joyfully to praise God in loud voices for all the miracles they had seen: "Blessed is the king who comes in the name of the Lord!" "Peace in heaven and glory in the highest!"' (vv.37–38).

They see Jesus as the coming Messiah who will *reign in the city* of Jerusalem, fulfilling all the promises of a Davidic king, *freeing the city* from its Roman captors.

However, Jesus has a different agenda. As he approaches Jerusalem he *weeps over the city* (v.41). Jesus was *passionate about the city* and had *compassion* on it. He foresees the destruction of Jerusalem, which was to occur in the year AD 70. The temple has never again been rebuilt and the city of Jerusalem remains a place over which many tears are shed.

The tragedy was that Jerusalem 'did not recognise the time of God's coming' (v.44). God had come in the person of Jesus. Yet by his death and resurrection in Jerusalem, he made possible a new Jerusalem.

PRAYER

Lord, give me that same passion and compassion for the people in the place where I live.

OLD TESTAMENT READING

Deuteronomy 30:11–31:29
The person of the city

Do you ever find yourself bombarded with thoughts of doubt, fear, or even depression, dismay and 'unnerved with alarm' (31:8, AMP)?

These are common human emotions. Moses faced them and he knew that his successor, Joshua, and all the people would have to face not only physical battles but also battles of the mind.

As we come to the end of Moses' life, he urges the people to follow God's word (30:14, MSG). He urges them to love God and walk in his ways (v.16, MSG). He warns them against having a change of heart and refusing to obey God. He encourages them to 'choose life' (v.19, MSG).

This choice starts with your thoughts. Your thoughts become your words. Your words become your actions. Each day, choose life-giving thoughts.

Moses' successor is Joshua. He is the new leader of the people of God. He is going to face many battles ahead. He is told, 'Be strong and courageous … The LORD himself goes before you and will be with you; he will never leave you nor forsake you. Do not be afraid; do not be discouraged' (31:6, 8).

Moses would not have said this if there had been nothing to fear and no cause for discouragement. Rather he knew that there would be *causes* for fear and lots of discouragement. All leadership requires courage to cling tenaciously to a vision and toughness to endure the blame for every difficulty along the way. Both then and now, the people of God need strong leadership that is courageous and not frightened or discouraged by all the opposition and resistance that there is bound to be.

The answer to fear is this: God promises that he would always go with him ('The LORD your God goes with you', v.6). God makes the same promise to you and me today. When you are assailed by doubts, discouragement and difficulties remember that wherever you go, whatever your circumstances, you can ask God to go before you and prepare the way. Therefore, you can be *confident* and need *not be afraid*.

Then Moses tells them, '*During the Feast of Tabernacles*, when all Israel comes to appear before the LORD your God at *the place he will choose*, you shall read this law…' (vv.10–11).

Of course, 'the place he will choose' turns out to be the *city* of Jerusalem. At the Feast of Tabernacles, the people would go to Jerusalem to celebrate the time when God, through Moses, brought water from a rock in the desert. They would thank God for providing water in the past year and pray that he would do the same in the coming year. The water was also seen as a sign of God's favour and a symbol of spiritual refreshment (see, for instance, 1 Corinthians 10:3–4).

It was on the last and greatest day of the Feast of Tabernacles that 'Jesus stood up and proclaimed, "If any one thirst, let him come to me and drink. He who believes in me, as the scripture has said, 'Out of his [innermost being] shall flow rivers of living water'" (John 7:37–38, RSV). He was saying that these promises would *not be fulfilled in a place, but in a person*.

It is *out of the innermost being of Jesus* that the river of life will flow. Also, in a derivative sense, the streams of living water will flow from *every Christian*! ('Whoever believes in me', v.38). From you, Jesus says, this river will flow, bringing life, fruitfulness and healing to others.

This picture is picked up again in the book of Revelation, where we see fulfilment of the *city of Jerusalem* (Revelation 22:1–3). Just as a river had flowed out of Eden at the very beginning of the Bible story (Genesis 2:10), so now at the end, in the new heaven and the earth, a river flows from this *city of God*, where God makes his home with humanity for ever.

PRAYER

Lord, thank you that you promise to be with me wherever I go and that you will never leave me nor forsake me. Fill me with your Holy Spirit so that rivers of living water may flow out of my heart today.

20 April | Day 110

Five Ways God Guides You

God designed you with a purpose in mind. God loves you. He has a specific, unique and glorious destiny for you. He promises to guide you.

God's purpose for you is bigger than your mistakes. I have made many mistakes in my life, but God has not stopped guiding me.

When we go on a journey by car we use a GPS. When we take a wrong turn, it reroutes us. But it never gives up until we reach our destination. You can ignore it or switch it off but if you follow it, it makes your journey more enjoyable and peaceful. Eventually, it will say 'You have reached your destination.'

Of course, this is not a perfect analogy. God is not a machine but a person who is with us on the journey. God wants to communicate with you and has promised to guide you.

There are five main ways in which God guides us (the five CSs):

- **C**ommanding **S**cripture (the Bible)
- **C**ompelling **S**pirit (the Holy Spirit)
- **C**ounsel of the **S**aints (the church)
- **C**ommon **S**ense (reason)
- **C**ircumstantial **S**igns (providence).

In each of today's passages, we see first something general about the way in which God guides us, and then specific examples of each of these 'five CSs'.

READING FROM PSALMS

Psalm 48:9–14
Promise of guidance

God promises to guide us all the way through our lives: '*he will be our guide* even to the end' (v.14). But how do you receive this guidance?

The secret is a close relationship with God. It involves spending time in his presence *meditating* on his 'unfailing love' (v.9).

1. Counsel of the Saints

Guidance is not an individual activity. It is significant that the psalmist says, 'Within your *temple* ... *we* meditate on your unfailing love' (v.9). The temple was where the people of God came together to worship God. We receive guidance in the context of community. On our own, we can sometimes get things very wrong (Proverbs 12:15). God can speak to others, as well as to us, and it is always wise to seek advice about major decisions.

PRAYER

Lord, thank you for your promise to be my guide and that you guide me in the context of the community of your people.

NEW TESTAMENT READING

Luke 19:45–20:26
Model of guidance

As in every other area of life, Jesus is our model for how to be guided by God.

Living under God's guidance does not lead to a trouble-free life. Jesus was constantly under attack from the 'religious police' of his day. He did not shy away from controversy and confrontation.

Indeed, in the parable of the tenants Jesus shows that God's servants can expect trouble. The servants were beaten, sent away empty-handed, treated shamefully, wounded and thrown out (20:9–12). When the son was sent they 'killed him' (v.15).

Divine guidance led Jesus to the cross. However, it also led to the resurrection. Behind it all was God's purpose and his victory. What Jesus did had the appearance of failure but Jesus accomplished more in his life, death and resurrection than any other person in history.

Of course, much is said in the New Testament about the way in which God guided Jesus. In the passage for today we see:

2. Commanding Scripture

Be extremely careful to avoid any situation in which ministry is being used for personal gain.

Jesus sees people who are trying to make money off the back of spiritual activity. He confronts the activity with the *word of God*. He says, '*It's written in Scripture*, My house is a house of prayer; You have turned it into a religious bazaar' (19:46, MSG).

Jesus' understanding of the will of God came from studying the Scriptures very carefully. This is the supreme way in which God guides us all.

3. Compelling Spirit

When Jesus is questioned about his authority he challenges the 'religious police' with a question about John's authority. Jesus is suggesting that John received his authority 'from heaven', that is, from God himself. The clear implication is that Jesus' own authority also came 'from heaven'. It came from his close relationship with God.

Even his opponents recognised 'the truth' (20:21) in Jesus' teaching. Jesus was not willing to curry favour or to show partiality. He was guided by what he knew to be *the truth*. He spoke *the truth* fearlessly.

Jesus challenges the premise behind their question: to what earthly power should we give our primary allegiance? The key issue, he explains, is whether we give *God* the primary allegiance we owe him – whether we count ourselves as citizens of his kingdom before any earthly one. We should 'give to Caesar what is Caesar's, and to God what is God's' (v.25). They were astonished by Jesus' answer and became silent (v.26).

Luke tells us that Jesus was 'led by the Spirit' (Luke 4:1). Presumably it was the Holy Spirit who gave Jesus his answer. As Jesus walked in this close relationship with God, studying the Scriptures and teaching the truth, the Holy Spirit ('the Spirit of truth', John 15:26) prompted him with words of extraordinary wisdom.

PRAYER

Father, help me to follow the example of Jesus, to stay close to you and to hear your voice as I read the Bible and seek to be led by the Spirit.

OLD TESTAMENT READING

Deuteronomy 31:30–32:52
Example of guidance

A century or so ago, a ship in a storm was dashed against the rocks in Cornwall, at the South West corner of England. A fifteen-year-old sailor swam to safety on an offshore rock. He climbed up and waited all night until he was rescued the next morning. A reporter interviewed him and commented, 'You must have been shaking all night as you clung to that rock.' 'Yes,' the young sailor replied, 'I trembled all night with fear and cold.' Then he added, 'But *the rock* never trembled once.'[1]

As Moses comes to the end of his life he reflects on the way that God has guided his people throughout his life, and has been their rock (32:4a,15, 18, 30, 37). He is your rock. He is solid, stable, dependable, always the same and totally reliable; he does not have his 'ups' and 'downs' as we do. You can trust in his unwavering faithfulness. He will always be there for you.

God is not only 'the rock', he is also 'your Father' (v.6b).

Moses described how God guided and led his people (Israel) with a father's love: 'In a desert land he found him, in a barren and howling waste. He *shielded him* and *cared for him*; he *guarded him* as the apple of his eye, like an eagle that stirs up its nest and hovers over its young, that spreads its wings to catch them and carries them on its pinions. The LORD alone *led him*' (vv.10–12a).

4. Circumstantial Signs

He goes on to describe how God, in his providence, looked after his people. He 'fed him ... nourished him with honey ... oil ... curds and milk ... lambs and goats ... the finest grains of wheat ... the foaming blood of the grape' (vv.13–14). These were the providential signs of his presence with them on the road.

However, God's people, here described as 'Jeshurun' (meaning 'the upright one', that is, Israel), 'abandoned the God who made [Jeshurun] and rejected the Rock his Saviour' (v.15c). It was this rejection that led to God saying, 'I will hide my face from them' (v.20).

Sometimes, it is sin that prevents us from hearing God's voice. Sin can lead to disaster (vv.23–27). Now we have a remedy in the death and resurrection of Jesus: 'the blood of Jesus, his Son, purifies us from all sin... If we confess our sins, he is faithful and just and will forgive us our sins and purify us from all unrighteousness' (1 John 1:7, 9).

5. Common Sense

When we fall, as we all do, the sensible thing is to get up quickly. Part of guidance generally is doing the sensible thing. This was Moses' complaint: 'They are a nation *without sense*, there is no *discernment* in them. If only they were *wise* and would *understand* this and *discern* what their end will be!' (Deuteronomy 32:28–29). God made us thinking beings. He guides your mind as you walk in a close relationship with him. Avoid a *super*-spirituality that expects an inward voice to guide every little detail of your life.

Moses returned at the end of his song to the word of God, 'Take to heart all these *words* to which I give witness today and urgently command your children to put them into practice, *every single word of this Revelation*. Yes. This is no small matter for you; it's your life' (vv.46–47, MSG).

PRAYER

Lord, thank you for the way that you have led me through all these different ways at different times. Thank you that you have had compassion on me. Help me to take to heart all the words you have spoken and to obey them carefully. Help me to reach my destination.

21 April | Day 111
Hello God!

The Vicar of Dibley, a UK TV sitcom featuring a woman vicar played by Dawn French, is based on the life of one of the first women vicars – Joy Carroll Wallis. A few years ago, Pippa and I met Joy. She told us a story about when she was an Anglican priest in London.

One of the congregation members was a very godly eighty-seven-year-old woman, called Flory Shore, who underwent serious surgery. Flory had been told that her prospects of recovery were very slim.

Thankfully, she survived the surgery. As she opened her eyes, one of the first things she saw was the blurred image of her doctor, dressed in his white jacket.

She smiled and said, 'Hello God! I'm Flory Shore.'

Joy commented that this demonstrated two things. First, it showed Flory's humility. She did not expect God to know who she was. Second, it showed her absolute certainty about the resurrection and where she was going.

Her certainty about the resurrection was based on the cornerstone of Christianity: the resurrection of Jesus Christ on the first Easter day. The same power that raised Jesus from the dead now lives in you through the Holy Spirit (see Ephesians 1:18–23). One day, you too will be raised and be able to say, 'Hello God!'

READING FROM PSALMS

Psalm 49:1–20
Life beyond the grave

There is a stark contrast between life without God, and life with God.

1. Life without God

Those who live without God tend to end up trusting in either wealth (v.6a) or themselves (v.13a). This trust is characterised by a search for status. The wealthy may 'boast of their great riches' (v.6b) and use money to impress others with their possessions (v.16). They may even name lands after themselves (v.11a).

They enjoy the praise of others (v.18b) and they count 'themselves blessed' (v.18a). They may try to use their wealth to 'buy off' their own death (v.7). Yet no amount of money is ever enough (v.8). In the end, it is all futile as wealth gets left to others (v.10b). 'So don't be impressed with those who get rich and pile up fame and fortune. *They can't take it with them*' (vv.16–17a, MSG). What is this all worth if we '*decay* in the grave?' (v.14).

2. Life with God

By contrast, if you live a life with God there is no need to search for status. This is because your status is determined not by your success in accumulating wealth, but in knowing to whom you belong and how precious you are to him.

Your ransom has been paid (v.7b) and you have been redeemed – your future is secure: 'But me? God snatches me from the clutch of death, he reaches down and grabs me' (v.15, MSG).

A life with God means you will 'live on for ever and *not see decay*' (v.9). The psalmist says, 'Why should I fear?' (v.5). Fear is a natural human emotion. But, with God you can face your fears with confidence because you are able to have complete trust in God for this life *and the life to come*.

Here is one of the few hints in the Old Testament of life after death. The writer is confident that 'God will redeem my life from the grave; he will surely *take me to himself*' (v.15). Life with God does not end with death but continues on into eternity. The psalmist was confident in this, even though he did not know *how* it was possible. The answer is revealed through Jesus' resurrection.

PRAYER

Lord, thank you for the power of your resurrection, which now lives in me. Thank you that you will snatch me from the clutch of death and take me to yourself.

NEW TESTAMENT READING

Luke 20:27–21:4
The dead will rise

When we start to think about the resurrection and life after death, it is hard to imagine what it will be like. What will people look like? What kind of body will you have? How will we relate to one another?

Sometimes, people use these kinds of questions to suggest that the idea of the resurrection is fanciful or even absurd. The Sadducees belonged to a 'party that denies any possibility of resurrection' (20:27, MSG). They came to Jesus with this kind of trick question about a woman who had had seven husbands, asking mockingly how it would all work out with the resurrection.

Jesus answered by explaining that their question is flawed because they are working with a this-worldly mindset. The resurrection will transform all our human relationships and the need for marriage as a means of continuing a family line will be removed (vv.34–36).

Jesus answers the question, but then goes on to address the real issue. The Sadducees were unimpressed by the hints of the resurrection in the Old Testament because they placed far greater weight on the first five books of the Bible (the Pentateuch).

Jesus takes them on, on their own territory, by quoting from one of these books: 'Moses showed that the dead rise, for he calls the Lord "the God of Abraham, and the God of Isaac, and the God of Jacob". He is not the God of the dead, but of the living, for *to him all are alive*' (vv.37–38).

Jesus is absolutely clear that he believed, not only in his own resurrection, but also in a much wider 'resurrection from the dead' (v.35). Those who rise 'can no longer die; for they are like the angels. They are God's children, since they are *children of the resurrection*' (v.36).

Of course, it all depends on Jesus being who he claimed to be. Jesus points out that he is not only a son of David, he is David's Lord (vv.41–44). If Jesus is Lord, you can be confident in his assurance that 'the dead rise' (v.37).

If you really believe in the resurrection it changes your attitude to everything in life, including your possessions. Like the widow (21:1–4) you are challenged to give generously, hold your possessions lightly and, ultimately, to be willing to give up everything you have in this life.

Furthermore, you have a whole different perspective on this life. There is real hope in the face of the tragedy of death. This life is only the beginning.

PRAYER

Lord, thank you so much for dying for me and thank you for the amazing hope that I have through your resurrection. Thank you that the same power that raised Jesus from the dead will raise us also.

OLD TESTAMENT READING

Deuteronomy 33:1–34:12
The everlasting arms

If ever a person had a good end to their life it was Moses: 'Moses was 120 years old when he died. His eyesight was sharp; he still walked with a spring in his step' (34:7, MSG). He had lived a life of knowing the Lord 'face to face' (v.10).

Moses had been greatly used by God: 'For no one has ever shown the mighty power or performed the awesome deeds that Moses did' (v.12).

One of the great challenges in life is to finish well. Part of finishing well is planning succession.

Moses finished well. He had planned for Joshua to be his successor: 'Now Joshua son of Nun was filled with the spirit of wisdom because Moses had laid his hands on him. So the Israelites listened to him and did what the Lord commanded Moses' (v.9). This is one of the few examples of the anointing of God passing from one generation to the next.

Before he died, Moses blessed all the different tribes with some extraordinary words. For example, about Benjamin he said, 'Let the beloved of the Lord rest secure in him, for he shields him all day long, and *the one the Lord loves rests between his shoulders*' (33:12).

As he comes to the end, having blessed each tribe, he says, 'There is no one like the God of Jeshurun, who rides on the heavens to help you and on the clouds in his majesty. *The eternal God is your refuge, and underneath are the everlasting arms*' (vv.26–27a).

Moses perhaps realised that death was not the end. He trusted the eternal God and he knew his arms were everlasting.

This does not entirely remove the pain and sadness of death. The people wept and mourned when Moses died (34:8a). It is natural and important to grieve and vital that we do so. Your emotions are God-given and should not be repressed.

However, there is a difference between grief with no hope, and the grief of the believer who has hope in the resurrection (1 Thessalonians 4:13).

I have been to many funerals and memorial services over the years and often the opening words are these great, reassuring, comforting and powerful words: 'The eternal God is your refuge, and underneath are the everlasting arms' (Deuteronomy 33:27a).

PRAYER

Lord, may I, like Moses, live in a close relationship with you, and know that the eternal God is my refuge and underneath are the everlasting arms.

22 April | Day 112
Your Words Are Powerful

Sir Winston Churchill's impact on the twentieth century is difficult to overestimate. A master orator and writer, Churchill knew the power of words. Martin Gilbert, Churchill's official biographer, wrote a book called *Churchill: The Power of Words*. Churchill's words sing in a way that English-language leaders and politicians have tried unsuccessfully to match ever since.

Nevertheless, for all of us, words are powerful. *Your* words are powerful. With kind and encouraging words, you can change a person's day – or even their entire life.

READING FROM PROVERBS

Proverbs 10:11–20
Speak words of love

Your words have the power to bring great blessing: 'The mouth of the good person is a deep, life giving well' (v.11a, MSG). But words can also do a great deal of harm: 'The mouth of the wicked is a dark cave of abuse' (v.11b, MSG).

Words have the power to destroy relationships: 'Hatred starts fights' (v.12a, MSG). On the other hand, they have the power to heal relationships: 'But love covers over all wrongs' (v.12b). 'Love pulls a quilt over the bickering' (v.12b, MSG).

Control of the tongue is vital. 'When *words* are many, sin is not absent, but the wise hold their *tongues*' (v.19). Abraham Lincoln said, 'It is better to be silent and thought a fool, than to speak and remove all doubt!'

Throughout this passage, the writer of Proverbs contrasts 'the *mouth* of a fool' (v.14b) with 'the *mouth* of the righteous' (v.11a). One speaks *words of hatred* (v.12a). The other speaks *words of love* (v.12b) and wisdom (v.13).

Words of hatred (v.12a) lead to violence (v.11b), dissension (v.12a), ruin (v.14b) and spreading slander (v.18b).

Words of love (v.12b) are a fountain of life (v.11a); they cover over 'all wrongs' (v.12b) and are 'choice silver' (v.20a). If someone has offended you, don't return the offence. It is said that holding a grudge is like letting someone live rent-free in your head. Instead, return hatred with love. Speak well of the other person even behind their back and you may find that your love puts an end to the bickering and heals the relationship.

PRAYER

Lord, help me today to control my tongue – to speak only words of love and life. Help me always to respond to any wrong committed against me with words of love.

NEW TESTAMENT READING

Luke 21:5–38
Speak words given by Jesus

Jesus did not have a degree or any formal training. Although he knew the Scriptures back to front, he never went to theological college. Yet his words and language about God were so powerful that, in his early thirties, he was able to teach every day in the temple and draw in the crowds.

The words of Jesus are the most powerful words ever uttered. 'He spent his days in the Temple teaching ... All the people were up at the crack of dawn to come to the Temple and listen to him' (vv.37–38, MSG).

The words of Jesus are eternal. Jesus contrasted his own words with the temporary things that the disciples could see around them. Jesus prophesied about the coming destruction of the temple (vv.5–6) and of Jerusalem (v.8 onwards), which occurred in AD 70. He said, 'Heaven and earth will pass away, but *my words* will never pass away' (vv.24, 33). Two thousand years later more and more people around the world are affected by the words of Jesus.

The teaching of Jesus is widely acknowledged to be the greatest teaching of all time. We have advanced so much in science and technology. Yet in the last two thousand years, no one has ever improved on the moral teaching of Jesus. They are the greatest words ever spoken. They are the kind of words you would expect God to speak.

Jesus warns about deceptive words. He says, 'Watch out that you are not deceived. For many will come in my name, claiming, "I am he," and "The time is near." Do not follow them' (v.8).

Jesus has told us to love everyone – our neighbours and even our enemies. Now he warns us that although we are to love everyone, we will also be hated *by all* (v.17).

If you are persecuted, you are to see this as an opportunity to be a 'witness' (v.13). On these occasions Jesus says, 'Make up your mind not to worry beforehand how you will defend yourselves. For I will give you *words* and wisdom that none of your adversaries will be able to resist or contradict' (vv.14–15). Not only are the words of Jesus powerful, but he also promises to put powerful words in *your* mouth.

So much of the language Jesus uses is the language of love and relationship. It has to do with your heart and your prayer life. He says, 'But be on your guard. Don't let the sharp edge of your expectation get dulled by parties and drinking and shopping' (v.34, MSG). Don't be 'weighed down with ... the anxieties of life' (v.34). 'Be always on the watch, and *pray...'* (v.36).

PRAYER

Lord, please give me words and wisdom for every occasion. Help me to develop the language of love and prayer and to speak powerful words in your name.

OLD TESTAMENT READING

Joshua 1:1–2:24
Speak the words of God

Joshua succeeds Moses. Moses was described as 'the servant of the LORD' (1:1), and Joshua takes up the same title from God. It is a title that was also borne by the prophets (Amos 3:7), Paul (Romans 1:1) and Jesus himself (Isaiah 52:13). To be a 'servant of the Lord' is now a blessing that all Christians enjoy. But every blessing God gives you comes with a measure of responsibility. Take that responsibility seriously.

Joshua is to pay particular attention to the *words* God has spoken (Joshua 1:7). He is to obey them (v.7), speak them (v.8a), meditate on them day *and night* (v.8b) and put them into practice (v.8b). Fill your mind with God's truth even in those wakeful moments of the night. This will affect your thinking – your thoughts will be thoughts of truth, freedom, love, victory and peace. God also underlines this by speaking to Joshua directly (v.1), encouraging and strengthening him with two key promises.

First, there is the promise of *God's peace*: 'I will give you every place where you set your foot' (v.3). 'No one will be able to stand up against you all the days of your life' (v.5a). 'The LORD your God is *giving you* rest' (v.13). For us now, that rest comes through Jesus. Rest is not just putting your feet up and relaxing but unburdening your troubles and having a deep sense of peace and security in your identity because of who Jesus is.

The writer of Hebrews states that, 'If Joshua had given them rest, God would not have spoken later about another day' (Hebrews 4:8) – and that 'day' is a day made possible through Jesus. As Jesus himself promised, 'Come to me, all you who are weary and burdened, and *I will give you rest'* (Matthew 11:28).

Second, there is the promise of God's *personal presence*: 'As I was with Moses, so *I will be with you*; I will never leave you nor forsake you' (Joshua 1:5b). This brings strength and courage: 'Do not be terrified' (v.9b). God does not tell us not to feel fear. But he does tell us not to give into it. Do not allow fear to rob you of the blessings God wants to give you. He goes on, 'Do not be discouraged, for the LORD your God will be with you wherever you go' (v.9b).

Again, you now experience that promise through Jesus, by the work of the Spirit. Jesus' last words before ascending to heaven were, 'Surely *I am with you* always, to the very end of the age' (Matthew 28:20).

As Joshua comes under the authority of God's words, his own words carry power and authority. The people replied, 'Whatever you have *commanded* us we will do ... Just as we fully obeyed Moses, so we will obey you' (Joshua 1:16–17). If you hear and speak God's words, 'your words' (v.18), like those of Joshua, will be powerful words.

In case all this should lead to intensity, super spirituality or self-righteousness, today's passage ends with the wonderful account of how God uses a prostitute called Rahab. It is so like God to choose a sinner, a prostitute, to be an ancestor of Jesus (Matthew 1:5) and a hero of faith (Hebrews 11:31). This is an encouragement to us not to be weighed down by our past. As Joyce Meyer says, 'We all have a past. No matter how bad your past is, you can get past your past. God can give you a new beginning; he can use you greatly and give you a future.'[1]

PRAYER

Lord, help me each day to meditate on your words, obey them, put them into practice and pass them on to others in the power of the Holy Spirit.

23 April | Day 113
The Gracious Hand of God

Things happen to us. So much of life is simply the set of circumstances we find ourselves in – things *happen to us*. For example, our parents, our genetic design, the weather, much of our education and our government are all things that we experience as 'happening *to* us'. In Greek grammar, these things are expressed in what we call the '*passive voice*'. However, we also *make things happen*. When I initiate an action and do something, this is expressed in the '*active voice*'.

But Greek grammar also has *a third voice – the 'middle voice'*. This is neither wholly active nor wholly passive. When I use the middle voice, I am participating in the results of an action.

Christian prayer is spoken in the middle voice. It cannot be in the active voice because it is not an action I control, as in the ritualistic pagan prayers where the gods do our bidding. Prayer is not in the passive voice either, in which I'm at the mercy of the will of gods and goddesses. In Christian prayer, as Eugene Peterson puts it, 'I enter into an action begun by another, my creating and saving Lord, and find myself participating in the results of his [gracious] action.'[1]

In one sense, the whole of the Christian life is prayer. We welcome God's gracious hand in our lives, and we participate in what he is doing in the world. God involves you in his plans. Of course, he could do it all on his own, but he chooses to involve you. He gives you freedom, yet he remains in control.

READING FROM PSALMS

Psalm 50:1–15
God will deliver you

Are you facing trouble in your life? A stressful situation at work? A difficult relationship? A worrying health issue? A financial challenge?

God is in utter control of his universe: 'God, the LORD, speaks and summons the earth from the rising of the sun to the place where it sets' (v.1).

He owns everything. We may fight and struggle for our little corner and our possessions but, in the end, God owns it all: 'Every animal of the forest is mine, and the cattle on a thousand hills' (v.10).

He is not dependent on human beings: 'If I were hungry I would not tell you, for the world is mine, and all that is in it' (v.12).

Nevertheless, he graciously gives you a part to play.

1. Thank God

'Sacrifice *thank-offerings* to God' (v.14a).

2. Call on God

'*Call upon me* in the day of trouble' (v.15a).

3. Honour God

'I will deliver you, and *you will honour me*' (v.15b).

I have come back many times to Psalm 50:15. I have called out to the Lord 'in the day of trouble'. It is amazing to look back and see how often his gracious hand has delivered me.

PRAYER

Lord, thank you so much for all the wonderful answers to prayer. Now, Lord, I call upon you again to deliver me...

NEW TESTAMENT READING

Luke 22:1–38
Your prayers make a difference

Are you sometimes tempted to compare yourself with other people?

It is encouraging to see that Jesus' disciples struggled with many of the same things that we do. There is bickering among the disciples over which of them would end up the greatest (v.24). It is always a temptation to compare ourselves with others. This either leads to pride (if we think we are doing better) or jealousy, envy and insecurity (if we think we are not doing as well).

Jesus points out that the values of the kingdom are the polar opposite to the world: 'Kings like to throw their weight around and people in authority like to give themselves fancy titles. It's not going to be that way with you. Let the senior among you become like the junior; let the leader act the part of the servant ... I've taken my place among you as the one who serves' (vv.25–27, MSG).

As we look at the parts played by each of the people in this drama, we see, once again, that the Bible teaches both predestination (that God has planned everything in advance) and free will. This is a mystery that the Scriptures hold in tension and we are rightly suspicious when any human system attempts to explain it away one way or the other. In this passage we see three examples of how this tension operates in practice.

1. Judas

We see here a terrifying description of how evil works. No one is immune from temptation. Judas is one of Jesus' chosen twelve, yet Satan enters him (v.3).

Jesus says that all this was foreknown and indeed predestined: 'The Son of Man will go *as has been decreed*' (v.22a). But the fact that it is foreknown and predestined does not absolve Judas of responsibility: 'But woe to that man who betrays him' (v.22b).

The paradox is that although 'it has been decreed', Judas is a free agent. Judas's 'will' was involved. When he was offered money to betray Jesus, Judas '*consented*, and watched for an opportunity to hand Jesus over' (v.6).

2. Simon Peter

The same 'Satan' who entered Judas (v.3) wanted to 'sift' Peter 'as wheat' (v.31).

Peter was very confident that he would not let Jesus down: 'Lord, I am ready to go with you to prison and to death' (v.33). Jesus knew that Peter would fail: 'I tell you, Peter, before the cock crows today, you will deny three times that you know me' (v.34).

But ultimately his faith did not fail. Jesus said, 'But I have prayed for you, Simon, that your faith may not fail' (v.32). This shows that in the midst of this extraordinary paradox of predestination and free will, prayer really does make a difference. Why and how it works we may never understand. However, the example of Jesus shows that it really does count. Your prayers *do make a difference*.

3. Jesus

Supremely, in the life and death of Jesus we see this paradox of predestination and free will. Jesus says, 'The Son of Man will go as it *has been decreed*' (v.22a). He says, '*It is written*: "And he was numbered with the transgressors"; and I tell you that this *must be* fulfilled in me. Yes, what is written about me is reaching *its fulfilment*' (v.37). There could not be a stronger statement that Jesus' death was preordained, pre-planned and predestined. Yet Jesus went willingly to his death; he *chose* to die. He gave his body for us (v.19).

We see the balance between God's part and our part. We are reminded of it every time we take communion. Jesus said, 'This is my body *given for you* ... This cup is the new covenant in my blood, which is poured out for you' (vv.19, 20). That was the hard part – the sacrifice of his life voluntarily given for us. Our part is relatively simple: '*do this in remembrance of me*' (v.19).

PRAYER

Lord, thank you that you have done all this for me. Thank you that you gave your body and shed your blood for me. Thank you for your gracious hand in my life.

OLD TESTAMENT READING

Joshua 3:1–5:12
God will do amazing things

Do you realise that God is with you? And if God is with you then you can face every challenge that lies ahead. God says to Joshua, '*I am with you* as I was with Moses' (3:7).

Again, we see here the balance between our part and God's part.

1. Prepare yourselves

God was about to act in a miraculous way on behalf of his people. But the people themselves had a part to play. Joshua tells the people to prepare themselves: 'Sanctify yourselves. Tomorrow God will work miracle-wonders among you' (3:5, MSG).

They were also given the task of choosing people to play particular roles in preparation for the crossing of the Jordan (4:1–4).

2. Provision of God

We see again the gracious hand of God. The Lord did 'amazing things' (3:5). One of these amazing things was the crossing of the Jordan (Joshua 3).

God promised to exalt Joshua (v.7). Joshua did not exalt himself. But 'That day the Lord exalted Joshua in the sight of all Israel' (4:14).

He provided for all the people's needs: 'The manna stopped the day after they ate this food from the land; there was no longer any manna for the Israelites, but that year they ate of the produce of Canaan' (5:12). God provided as much as they needed and no more.

This kept them from material security and self-sufficiency and, perhaps, from not trusting in God. Your security and trust must be in God alone. He has always provided enough, but no more.

PRAYER

Thank you, Lord, for the astounding way in which you involve me in your plans. I consecrate myself to you today. Thank you that you promise that you will do amazing things in me and provide for all my needs.

24 April | Day 114
Two Ways to Live

Albert Einstein said, 'There are *only two ways to live your life*. One is as though nothing is a miracle. The other is as though everything is a miracle.'

Jesus himself said that – ultimately – there are only two ways to live: there are two paths; there are two gates; there are two destinations and there are two groups of people (see Matthew 7:13–14). In the passages for today we see starkly contrasting ways of life.

READING FROM PSALMS

Psalm 50:16–23
Two attitudes to God: hate or honour

When it comes down to it, there are only two possible attitudes to God. We can *honour him* or we can *hate him*. For God says, 'Those who sacrifice thank-offerings *honour* me' (v.23). He contrasts those who '*hate* my instruction' (v.17a).

Those who 'hate' God ignore him and '*forget God'* (v.22). The twentieth century saw the terrible consequences of the actions of those who forgot him and *hated* his instruction.

As the great Russian novelist, Aleksandr Solzhenitsyn, considered the great disasters 'that swallowed up some 60 million' Russians, he saw the principal trait of the twentieth century was that '*people have forgotten God*'.[1]

This does not just apply to other people; it applies to us all. Do you find that sometimes, possibly because everything seems to be going well in your life, you forget to pray, read the Bible or give thanks to God for all his blessings? It is almost as if you have forgotten about God? There are times in all our lives when we forget God and mess things up.

The contrast to forgetting God is a life honouring him – one full of thankfulness and praise: 'It's the praising life that honours me. As soon as you set your foot on the *Way*, I'll show you my salvation' (v.23, MSG).

PRAYER

Lord, today I want to honour you by offering a sacrifice of thanks. Thank you for all the blessings that you have given to me...

NEW TESTAMENT READING

Luke 22:39–62
Two paths to choose from: God's will or your own

Do you ever find yourself in a situation where you know the right thing to do, but you also know that the right thing is very difficult and costly? Are you sometimes tempted to take the easy way out?

In this passage, we see that Jesus, as well as being fully God, was *fully human*. First, he faced the terrible suffering of the cross. He 'knelt down and prayed' (v.41), 'Father, if you are willing, take this cup from me; yet *not my will*, but *yours be done*' (v.42).

Jesus' humanity is seen in his anguish and his sweat 'like drops of blood falling to the ground' (v.44). Despite all the difficulties, he chose *God's will* over his own, and 'an angel from heaven appeared to him and strengthened him' (v.43).

You will never face as great a challenge as Jesus faced. But there will be times in your life when God asks you to choose his will over what you want to do. In every sacrifice, great or small, ask for God's strength to choose his will over your own, as Jesus did.

Judas, on the other hand, chose his own way. With a kiss he betrayed the one who had loved him. We see a stark contrast between Jesus and Judas. On the one hand, as Jesus prayed, 'an angel *from heaven* appeared to him and strengthened him' (v.43). On the other hand, we see that the result of Judas' act of betrayal – 'when darkness reigns' (v.53) – is *hellish*.

If you feel, as I do, that you could never be quite like Jesus, but desperately don't want to be like Judas, then Peter gives us all hope. Peter messed up, as we all do, and yet God used him.

Peter's first mistake was to follow 'at a distance' (v.54). When others are hostile towards Jesus it is tempting to put a bit of distance between us and him – not to align ourselves too closely with Jesus. This path, in the end, led to straight out denials (vv.57–58, 60).

When Jesus turned and looked straight at Peter (v.61), Peter knew he had blown it and 'wept bitterly' (v.62). Like Judas, Peter had failed. Yet his future was very different from Judas's. God went on to use Peter, perhaps more than anyone else in the entire history of the Christian church.

The difference between Peter and Judas was their reaction to failure. Peter was deeply repentant and received forgiveness and restoration from Jesus (see John 21). This gives us all hope. However far you have gone in the wrong direction, it is never too late to turn around. Turn back to Jesus, receive forgiveness and restore the relationship.

For all of us, like Peter, yesterday's mess can become today's message. Your test can become your testimony.

PRAYER

Father, fill me today with your Spirit and help me to say, like Jesus, 'not my will, but yours be done' (v.42).

OLD TESTAMENT READING

Joshua 5:13–7:26

Two types of ground to stand on: holy or hidden

Is there any area of your life that you keep hidden because it is a place of secret sin?

In this passage we see two contrasting kinds of ground. We see Joshua standing on *holy ground* (5:15). On the other hand, we see Achan standing on *the ground of hidden sin* (7:21–22).

God's messenger appears to Joshua. Whether it was an angel of the Lord or the second person of the Trinity (Jesus), we do not know. What we do know is that Joshua 'fell face down to the ground in reverence' (5:14) and was told, 'Take off your sandals, for the place where you are standing is *holy*' (v.15).

There are times in life when the presence of God seems to be so strong that we sense we are standing on holy ground. All we can do is fall down to the ground and worship.

God gave Joshua success (6:1–26): 'The Lord was with Joshua, and his fame spread throughout the land' (v.27). His success did not come from the size of his army, the power of his weapons or his skill as a leader; it came from his *faith* in God, which led him to follow God's instructions.

Likewise, the prostitute Rahab, her family and all who belonged to her were spared because of her *faith*, which led to an act of kindness towards God's servants (v.25).

In the New Testament, both Joshua and Rahab are recognised as heroes of faith: 'By *faith* the walls of Jericho fell ... By *faith* the prostitute Rahab, because she welcomed the spies, was not killed with those who were disobedient' (Hebrews 11:30–31).

The book of Joshua raises many difficult questions to which we may struggle to find answers. As Christians, again we have to remember to read it through the lens of Jesus and the New Testament.

The book of Hebrews suggests that the promised land is a picture of the blessings you receive by obedience, that is, by faith in Jesus: 'For if Joshua had given them rest, God would not have spoken later about another day ... Let us, therefore, make every effort to enter that rest, so that no one will fall by following their example of *disobedience*' (4:8–11).

One incident of such '*disobedience*' is seen in Achan, whose coveting led to him disobeying God and taking silver and gold, which he eventually admits 'are *hidden in the ground* inside my tent' (Joshua 7:21). Sure enough, Joshua's messengers 'ran to the tent, and there it was, *hidden* in his tent, with the silver *underneath*' (v.22).

We need to be aware of the danger of compartmentalising our lives. Like Achan's tent, everything can look respectable on the surface, but underneath, *hidden away*, there lurks sin. Other people cannot see the compartments of our lives where sin resides, but God can.

Achan's sin did not just affect him. It affected the whole camp. God wanted a holy people who were consecrated to him (v.13). Sin and disobedience in the camp affected their purity. The Lord said, 'You cannot stand against your enemies until you remove it' (v.13).

It is a good question to ask: Is there some area that is not consecrated to God, which is stopping me from receiving the blessings and victory God wants to give to his people?

My experience has been that the Holy Spirit continues to shine his light on the 'hidden' areas of my life that I need to deal with. The process will probably never be complete this side of heaven.

The good news for us is that we need no longer fear the punishment of sin that Achan faced. Through Jesus, no matter what your failings have been, you are forgiven and restored.

PRAYER

Lord, I consecrate my life to you again today. Thank you that you go with me as you went with Joshua. I choose today the path of your will for my life – holiness and honour.

25 April | Day 115
Your Loving Substitute

A little girl named Liz was suffering from a rare and serious disease. Her only chance of recovery appeared to be a blood transfusion from her five-year-old brother, who had miraculously survived the same disease and had developed the antibodies needed. The doctor explained the situation and asked the little boy if he would be willing to give his blood to his sister. He hesitated for only a moment before taking a deep breath and saying, 'Yes, I'll do it if it will save her.'

As the transfusion progressed, he lay in bed next to his sister, and smiled, as they all did, seeing the colour returning to her cheeks. Then his face grew pale and his smile faded. He looked up at the doctor and asked with a trembling voice, 'Will I start to die right away?'

The little boy had misunderstood the doctor. He thought he was going to have to give his sister *all* of his blood in order to save her. This boy loved his sister so much that he was willing to die *instead* of her – as her substitute. This story (possibly fictional) is simply an illustration of what loving substitution means.[1]

God loves you. The amazing and wonderful message of the Bible is that God came to this earth in the person of his Son, Jesus Christ, and died in your place. Words, images, metaphors, pictures and illustrations (such as that of the five-year-old boy) can help our understanding, but they can never perfectly describe the indescribable love of God. Jesus died to remove all the bad stuff. He died instead of you and me (Mark 10:45).

READING FROM PSALMS

Psalm 51:1–9
My *sin*

David cried out, 'Have mercy on me, O God' (v.1). I have often used this psalm as a prayer of confession. David wrote this psalm when the prophet Nathan came to challenge him after David had committed adultery with Bathsheba (and then sinned greatly in trying to cover up his initial act).

1. To whom do you pray?

This prayer for God's mercy and forgiveness is rooted in David's understanding of God's character. He prays, 'Have mercy on me, O God, *according to your unfailing love; according to your great compassion*' (v.1).

2. What do you confess?

David confesses his iniquity (v.2), transgressions (vv.1b,3a) and his sin (vv.2b,3b). He says, 'Surely I was sinful at birth, sinful from the time my mother conceived me' (v.5). This prayer is in response to a specific sin, but David recognises there is a deeper problem as well. Sin is not just an occasional act. It is something deeply ingrained within all human beings from our very earliest moments.

God desires truth 'in the inner parts' and 'in the inmost place' (v.6). He wants you to be honest, open and real with him about yourself and your sins.

3. What do you ask for?
David cries out for *mercy*. Ask to be *washed*: 'Soak out my sins in your laundry' (v.2a, MSG). Ask for *cleansing*: 'Cleanse me from my sin' (v.2b), 'cleanse me with hyssop, and I shall be clean' (v.7a). Ask for your sins to be *wiped out*: 'wipe out my bad record' (v.1c, MSG), 'blot out all my iniquity' (v.9b).

Pray that your sin will be completely removed, so that God will not see any sin: 'Hide your face from my sins' (v.9a).

4. What will the result be?
David says, 'Let me hear joy and gladness; let the bones you have crushed rejoice' (v.8). There is nothing like the joy, gladness and rejoicing that follow total forgiveness. David knew that God, in his mercy, love and compassion, would forgive. What he did not see clearly, and what only the New Testament reveals to the full, is how God made that possible.

PRAYER

Thank you, Lord, that when I confess my sins, you wash me clean and forgive me because Jesus died for me.

NEW TESTAMENT READING

Luke 22:63–23:25
Jesus' *sacrifice*

Luke's account is not just about recording the facts about Jesus' death. He also seeks to show us the amazing truth of *why* Jesus died. Unlike that five-year-old boy, Jesus did *actually* give his life to save you and me. Luke helps us to understand this act of substitution:

1. What did Jesus endure for you?
Jesus was mocked (22:63; 23:11), beaten (22:63), insulted (v.65), falsely accused (23:10), ridiculed (v.11) and eventually crucified (v.23). Luke sums it up with the chilling words that Pilate 'surrendered Jesus to their will' (v.25).

2. Who was responsible?
Luke makes it clear that *everyone* is responsible. The council, chief priests, teachers of the law (22:66), the whole assembly (23:1) and Herod and Pilate (22:66 – 23:25) all played their part. (The death of Jesus was what made Herod and Pilate friends – 'as thick as thieves' (v.12, MSG) – before that, they had been enemies. Sharing a common enemy can result in unlikely bedfellows!) Luke says the chief priests, rulers and people (v.13) were of one mind: '*With one voice* they cried' (v.18). We cannot blame the Jews or the Romans or anyone else. Ultimately, we are *all* responsible.

3. Who is it that died in your place?
This was not some innocent 'third party' whom God punished instead of us. Rather, God himself came in the person of his son Jesus to die for you and me. God was doing what was completely unexpected. The Jews hoped for a messiah and saviour, but *no one* imagined it would be *God himself*.

The New Testament church, filled with the Holy Spirit, came to realise just who Jesus is. We see the *uniqueness* of Jesus in the *titles* he used of himself.

He is the *Son of Man*. The Son of Man who will be seated at the right hand of the mighty God (22:69) is clearly used here by Jesus as a messianic title.

He is *Christ the King* (23:2) – the 'king of the Jews' (v.3) – the long-awaited Messiah.

Most remarkably of all, he is the *Son of God*: When they asked, '"Are you then the Son of God?" [Jesus] replied, "You are right in saying I am"' (22:70). It seems likely that Jesus was actually using the name of God here ('*I AM*') – a direct claim that Jesus is God – which may be why the elders are so angered by his response (v.71).

4. What is substitution?
The innocent dies *instead of* the guilty. Jesus is innocent; we are guilty.

Even Pilate, who condemned him to death, said, 'I find *no basis for a charge against this man*' (23:4). Again he repeats, 'I have examined him in your presence and have found *no basis for your charges against him* ... he has done *nothing to deserve death*' (vv.14–15). A third time he says, 'What crime has this man committed? I have found in him *no grounds* for the death penalty' (v.22). Luke makes it clear that Jesus died precisely because he was the *innocent son of God* (22:70–71).

On the other hand, Barabbas, *like us*, was guilty. In his case, Barabbas was guilty of insurrection and murder (23:19, 25). Luke hints at substitution: 'Away with this man [Jesus]! Release Barabbas to us!' (v.18). 'He *released the man* who had been thrown into prison for insurrection and murder, the one they asked for, and *surrendered Jesus to their will*' (v.25).

PRAYER

Lord Jesus Christ, how can I ever thank you enough that you, the Son of God, died in my place – the innocent on behalf of the guilty.

OLD TESTAMENT READING

Joshua 8:1–9:15
God's *sovereignty*

God has a purpose for your life. He is in control of the universe. He is able to take even bad things you have done or have been done to you and turn them for good (Romans 8:28).

In this passage, we see an example of this. The people of God had failed in the past to take the city of Ai (Joshua 7:4). Now God uses their past failure as part of the victory plan (8:6–7). Sometimes God uses even your past sins and mistakes for good (although this is not an excuse for repeating them, as Israel did by not asking God about the Gibeonites, 9:14).

Supremely, of course, God turned the sinfulness and the failures of humanity that led to the crucifixion of Jesus into the greatest victory of all time. The cross was not a mistake. It was part of God's sovereign purpose to make possible our forgiveness and the cleansing, washing and covering of our sins through Jesus' death on the cross for us. God is a God of love. 'This is how we know what love is: Jesus Christ laid down his life for us' (1 John 3:16).

PRAYER

Lord, thank you that in all things you work for the good of those who love you. Thank you that you can even use the bad things for good. Thank you for your amazing love revealed to me in Jesus Christ, who laid down his life for me and died in my place as my substitute.

26 April | Day 116
Right Relationships

At an Alpha Conference we held in East Malaysia, there were people from all over Asia. Many had been persecuted because of their faith. One man told me that his father had been imprisoned for six years for the simple fact that he was a Christian pastor. He himself was imprisoned for a year, aged nineteen, for speaking out on behalf of his father.

It is a terrible injustice when the innocent are convicted and imprisoned – even worse when they are executed.

In the New Testament passage for today we read of one of the greatest injustices in human history. Jesus was totally innocent. He was 'a *righteous man*' (Luke 23:47). Yet he was executed by crucifixion. The apostle Peter explains it like this: 'For Christ died for sins once for all, the *righteous* for the *unrighteous*, to bring you to God' (1 Peter 3:18).

The word 'righteous' is often associated with the 'self-righteous', and has almost become a term of abuse. However, 'righteous' in the Bible is a wonderful word. It is also extremely important for our understanding of the whole Bible. 'Righteousness' is ultimately about *right relationships* – a right relationship with God and right relationships with others. In the New Testament, we come to understand that this righteousness is only possible through faith in Jesus Christ (see Romans 3:21 – 4:25).

READING FROM PROVERBS

Proverbs 10:21–30
Blessings of the righteous

The book of Proverbs contrasts the life of the 'fool' with the life of the 'wise'. It also contrasts the life of the 'righteous' with the life of the 'wicked'. Here are some of the many blessings that are promised to 'the righteous':

1. Difference to others

'The lips of the righteous nourish many' (v.21a). We cannot be righteous in isolation. Righteousness is about our relationships – it is about bringing blessing to others. Who could you 'nourish' (feed, guide, encourage) with your words today?

2. Delight in wisdom
'Those who have insight *delight in wisdom*' (v.23b). One of the things that come from a relationship with God is a hunger for knowledge and wisdom. Ask for wisdom today. God promises to give wisdom when you ask (James 1:5).

3. Desires fulfilled
'What the righteous desire will be granted' (Proverbs 10:24b). God's Spirit begins to change your will to align it with his (Philippians 2:13) and, as it becomes aligned with his will, God promises to give you the desires of your heart (Psalm 37:4).

4. Destiny of joy
'The prospect of the *righteous* is *joy*' (Proverbs 10:28a). 'The *righteous* stand firm forever' (v.25b); 'The fear of the LORD adds length to life' (v.27a) and 'The *righteous* will never be uprooted' (v.30a). Right relationships are a source of great joy. Your joy is made 'complete' in a relationship with Jesus (John 15:11). Your destiny is eternal joy.

PRAYER

Lord, I pray for wisdom today and that you would put a guard over my lips so that my words may be used to feed and guide others.

NEW TESTAMENT READING

Luke 23:26–56
The righteous for the unrighteous

This passage gives hope to us all. We see from the example of one of the criminals who were executed with Jesus, that the moment you recognise your sin and turn to Jesus, you receive total forgiveness and are put in a '*right relationship*' with God. This man did absolutely nothing to earn this gift. He did not even have the opportunity to be baptised. Yet, instantly, this criminal received the promise that on that same day he would be with Jesus in paradise (v.43). How is this possible?

1. The righteousness of Jesus
Is there someone who has hurt you whom you need to forgive today?

Jesus sets the bar very high in terms of the challenge to love our enemies – our critics, those who sneer and mock us. The test of our character is how we respond when we are suffering and in pain. Jesus, as he is being tortured on the cross, prays for his torturers: 'Father, forgive them, for they do not know what they are doing' (v.34).

Jesus was living in a right relationship with God. His very last words recorded in Luke's Gospel are: '*Father, into your hands I commit my spirit*' (v.46).

Even the Roman centurion, 'seeing what had happened, praised God and said, "Surely this was a *righteous man*"' (v.47).

2. The unrighteousness of us all
The righteousness of Jesus is contrasted with the people who stood watching, the rulers who *sneered* at Jesus (v.35), the soldiers who *mocked* him (v.36) and the criminals who were '*punished justly*' and were getting what their 'deeds deserved' (v.41).

One of them hurled insults at Jesus. The other rebuked his fellow criminal and, turning to Jesus, he recognised his own sin ('We are punished *justly*, for we are getting what our deeds deserve', v.41a) and the *righteousness of Jesus* ('This man has done nothing wrong', v.41b). Then he said, 'Jesus, remember me when you come into your kingdom' (v.42). Jesus answered him, 'I tell you the truth, today you will be *with me in paradise*' (v.43).

3. The righteous died for the unrighteous
This passage is full of irony. As the rulers sneer at Jesus, saying, 'He saved others; let him save himself if he is the Christ of God, the Chosen One' (v.35). The soldiers mock, 'If you are the king of the Jews, *save yourself*' (v.37).

One of the criminals calls on him: 'Aren't you the Christ? Save yourself and us!' (v.39). Actually, he is dying in order to save *them and us*. But in doing so he cannot save himself. He is dying as 'the *righteous for the unrighteous*, to bring you to God' (1 Peter 3:18).

The curtain of the temple is torn in two (Luke 23:45) symbolising that through the death of Jesus, access to the presence of God is made possible for everyone. Jesus has made it possible for you and me to have a right relationship with God.

4. 'Righteous' or 'unrighteous'?
In the contrast between the two criminals and the difference in their reaction to Jesus, Luke lays before us the decision we all need to make. You can reject Jesus, as one of them did. Or you can put your faith in him, as the other one did when he turned to Jesus and said, 'Jesus, remember me' (v.42).

Although many at the time rejected Jesus, others put their faith in him. For example, Joseph of Arimathea, 'a good and *upright* man' (v.50), came to believe in Jesus. He had not consented to the decision of the council (v.51), was waiting for the kingdom of God (v.51) and arranged a dignified burial for Jesus.

The women who had come with Jesus also put their faith in him. They 'followed Joseph and saw the tomb and how his body was laid in it. Then they went home and prepared spices and perfumes. But they rested on the Sabbath in *obedience* to the commandment' (vv.55–56).

You too get to choose. When you put your faith in Jesus, he promises that, like the criminal who turned to him, you too will be with him in paradise.

If you ever feel the burden to try to earn God's love, you can be comforted by this passage that there is nothing you can do to make God love you more and there is nothing you can do to make God love you less.

PRAYER

Thank you, Lord, that by faith, you give me the gift of righteousness and put me in a right relationship with God.

OLD TESTAMENT READING

Joshua 9:16–10:43
Righteous by faith

Joshua says to his leaders exactly the words the Lord had spoken to Joshua himself at the start of his own leadership (Joshua 1:6,9,18), 'Do not be afraid; do not be discouraged. Be strong and courageous' (10:25). Hear these words for yourself today and then pass them on to others.

The name of the king of Jerusalem was Adoni-Zedek (v.1). 'Zedek' means 'righteous'. However, in all probability he was far from righteous. It is likely that the people living in Canaan at that time were involved in all kinds of child sacrifices and other evil practices.

On the other hand, Joshua was living a life in a right relationship with God. The New Testament makes clear that the righteousness of Joshua, like Abraham and others in the Old Testament, came by 'faith' (Romans 3:21 – 4:25). Joshua was a man of faith (Hebrews 11:30).

The results of the death of Jesus are not confined to those who lived after him. The death of Jesus affected those who lived before him as well. Jesus died for Abraham, Moses and Joshua. He died for the criminal on the cross. He died for me. He died for you. We are made righteous: '*This righteousness from God* comes through *faith in Jesus Christ to all who believe*' (Romans 3:22).

PRAYER

Lord, thank you that you died, the righteous for the unrighteous. Help me to live today in a right relationship with you and a right relationship with others.

27 April | Day 117
How to Live a Life of Victory

Years ago, a young member of our congregation at Holy Trinity Brompton had a job working in the library of a major national newspaper. This newspaper kept files of old cuttings about every well-known person. The files were kept in rows of long shelves and were separated into 'living people' and 'dead people'.

One day, the young man was looking through the files of dead people and came across a large file marked 'Jesus Christ'. He glanced over his shoulder to check that no one was looking and quickly moved the file from the 'dead people' section to the 'living people' section.

Jesus Christ is alive. He is risen from the dead. To anyone looking for him among files of dead people, the angels would say, '*Why do you look for the living among the dead*? He is not here; he has risen!' (Luke 24:5–6).

Victory is not a dirty word. Jesus is the great victor. As Bishop Lesslie Newbigin often said, 'The resurrection is not the reversal of a defeat but the manifestation of a victory.'[1] The cross was *not* a defeat. On the cross, Jesus won a great victory for us over sin, death and the powers of evil.

READING FROM PSALMS

Psalm 51:10–19
Receive the benefits of his victory

I love this prayer of David and have often prayed it myself. David, like us all, had messed up. He had cried out for forgiveness and now he *cries out for victory*. When we sin we do not lose our salvation but we may lose the *joy* of our salvation (v.12a). David does not want to be defeated by sin again.

All this starts with 'a broken and contrite heart' (v.17b). You can be absolutely certain that if you come to God in this way you will not be rejected: 'A broken and contrite heart, O God, you will not despise' (v.17b).

David prays that he might live a life of victory. It is worth noting that David's prayer is not purely personal. He prays that he might also have an impact on the city (v.18).

PRAYER

Lord, I pray for a pure heart (v.10a), a persevering spirit (v.10b), the presence of God (v.11a), the power of the Spirit (v.11b) and the pleasure of salvation to be restored to me (v.12a).

I pray for a trusting spirit (v.12b) and that I would be able to teach the ways of God (v.13a), turning people back to God (v.13b). I pray for a tongue that worships you. 'O Lord, open my lips, and my mouth will declare your praise' (vv. 14b–15). I pray for the transformation of our society (v.18).

NEW TESTAMENT READING

Luke 24:1–35
Recognise Jesus and his victory

How can you and I encounter Jesus today?

The resurrection of Jesus is a historical event. It actually happened. But it is not just a historical event. As people experienced the risen Jesus at the time, you too can experience his presence today. This passage tells you how.

This was the day the world changed for ever. Jesus was raised on 'the first day of the week' (v.1). Thereafter, the first day of the week (Sunday) was to become the day of rest and worship.

In this passage we see two key pieces of evidence of Jesus' victory over death:

1. Jesus' body was *absent*

'They found *the stone rolled away* from the tomb, but when they entered, they *did not find the body* of the Lord Jesus' (vv.2–3).

The angels said to them, 'Why do you look for the living among the dead? *He is not here; he has risen*!' (vv.5–6). Indeed, as he predicted, on the third day he would be '*raised again*' (v.7). (Sometimes the New Testament states that Jesus 'rose' from the dead. More often it is in the passive; 'he was raised'.)

When the disciples are told by the women 'they did not believe' (v.11). However, we can picture Peter's excitement – he 'got up and ran to the tomb' (v.12). He too saw that the body of Jesus was gone. He 'saw the strips of linen lying by themselves' (v.12b) – the tomb itself was *not empty* but *the body of Jesus was absent*.

Peter must have begun to realise at that moment that Jesus had won a great victory. Jesus had died, but death was not the end. Death is *not cancelled* but it is *definitively conquered*.

2. Jesus himself was *present*

Jesus himself was seen. This was not just a 'spiritual' presence. His physical, resurrected, transformed body was present with his disciples. The first appearance we read of in Luke's Gospel is on the road to Emmaus. Jesus *reveals himself* to the two disciples in two ways.

First, he *reveals himself through the Scriptures*: 'And beginning with Moses and all the Prophets, he explained to them what was said in all the Scriptures concerning himself' (v.27). This must have been the most amazing Bible study in the history of the world. Jesus went through the Bible explaining that it was all about him.

Have you ever had a sense of your heart 'burning within' as you have been listening to the Bible being explained, or as you have been reading it yourself? Sometimes, when I am reading the Bible or listening to a talk explaining the Bible, the words suddenly seem so relevant to me and to my life that it feels as if God is speaking directly to me. At that moment it seems like my heart is burning within me. A young woman who was in our Alpha small group recently had just started reading the Bible for the first time in her life. She said it is as if the words were jumping off the page towards her.

The disciples said, 'Were not our hearts *burning within us* while he talked with us on the road and *opened the Scriptures to us*?' (v.32). We get a taste of this every time we hear the Bible explained in such a way as to *reveal Jesus*.

Second, he *reveals himself through the bread*: 'When he was at the table with them, he took bread, gave thanks, broke it and began to give it to them. Then *their eyes were opened* and they recognised him' (vv.30–31). Later on they explained 'how Jesus was *recognised by them when he broke the bread*' (v.35).

Luke's description of this encounter is probably deliberately told in a way that echoes the account of Jesus' last supper with his disciples. It is supposed to encourage us that we too can encounter Jesus in the 'breaking of bread' when we celebrate Communion together.

The Scriptures and the sacraments are two of the ways in which we can encounter Jesus today. Jesus will continue to *reveal himself* to us as we study the Scriptures and as we break bread together. If you want to experience the presence of Jesus – make sure that you do these things on a regular basis.

PRAYER

Father, thank you that Jesus is alive right now. As I study the Scriptures, may my heart burn within me as I encounter Jesus through them. As I receive the bread and the wine, may my eyes be opened to recognise Jesus.

OLD TESTAMENT READING

Joshua 11:1–12:24
Reflect the victory of Jesus

I would love to know what Jesus said about this passage when he was going through *all the Scriptures* and explaining what they said '*concerning himself*' (Luke 24:27).

This passage continues the theme of Joshua's victories ('great victory', Joshua 10:10). Here we read of how the kings joined forces to fight against Israel (11:5). But the Lord says, '*Do not be afraid of them*' (v.6). The Lord 'gave them into the hand of Israel' (v.8). God gives them *victory* wherever they go: 'So Joshua took the entire land, just as the LORD had directed Moses, and he gave it as an inheritance to Israel' (v.23).

I imagine that Jesus would have explained that Joshua's military tactics are not the model for anyone today. Nevertheless, one aspect, the victory itself, prefigured and foreshadowed the great and very different type of victory that God was to bring about through the death and resurrection of Jesus. Joshua was a 'type' of Christ; indeed, Jesus is actually the Greek form of the name Joshua, meaning 'the Lord saves'.

As we will read tomorrow, the victory of Joshua was never complete. The Lord said to him, 'You are very old, and there are still very large areas of land to be taken over' (13:1). It is Jesus alone who brings a complete victory. He is the one to whom all the Scriptures point. He is the great victor and the source of every possible victory in our own lives.

PRAYER

Lord, thank you for your great victory over sin and death and all the powers of evil. May my life today reflect this great victory. May I see it more, not only in my own personal life but also in our community, city and nation.

28 April | Day 118
It's Not Over

You could have heard a pin drop. It was mesmerising. We were spellbound. An eighty-five-year-old man, almost totally blind, got up to speak to 1,500 people of all ages on our church holiday. He had no notes, of course, because he could no longer read. He gave two talks, each of them an hour long.

In the first talk, he gave a breathtaking summary of the entire Old Testament. In the second, which was equally brilliant, he gave a summary of the whole of the New Testament. There was no hesitation, no stumbling and not a word was out of place. It was the distilled wisdom of a man who had followed the Lord wholeheartedly all his life.

Bishop Lesslie Newbigin had one of the most remarkable ministries of the twentieth century. At the age of thirty-six he was elected as one of the first bishops of the new Church of South India. When he returned from India, later on in life, he wrote several books that aimed to help the church in the West fulfil its mission in a world that was rapidly changing and felt no need for God.

His writing and speaking influenced thousands of Christian leaders around the world. Yet for this astonishing man, who had achieved so much in his life, it was not over. He entitled his autobiography *Unfinished Agenda*. For him, there was always still so much to hope for and so much more to be done.

READING FROM PSALMS

Psalm 52:1–9
It is never over for a visionary

How do you react in the midst of tragedy and opposition? It is tempting to panic, withdraw, lose hope or even give up.

David was a visionary. Vision has been defined as a combination of 'a deep dissatisfaction with what *is* and a clear grasp of what *could be*'. If you have vision, you will always be able to say, '*It's not over*.'[1]

David achieved so much in his lifetime. Yet, he had to deal with the reality of opposition. This psalm was written after a devastating setback. David had been on the run from Saul, but his location had been betrayed by 'Doeg the Edomite'. Although David had moved on by the time Saul's men arrived, his friend Ahimelek, and almost all of Ahimelek's family, had been killed (see 1 Samuel 21–22).

In this psalm we see how he had to deal with those who were trying to destroy him by 'deceit' (Psalm 52:2c), 'falsehood' (v.3b) and 'harmful word[s]' (v.4a). David may be describing Doeg. He was like the man described in verse 7 'who did not make God their stronghold but trusted in his great wealth and grew strong by destroying others!' This has a very contemporary ring to it.

Yet, even in the midst of such tragedy and opposition, David did not despair or give up. He sees that, with God, *it is not over*. It is not over for Doeg: 'God will bring you down to everlasting ruin' (v.5a). And *it is not over* for David: 'I am like an olive tree flourishing in the house of God' (v.8a). David turns to God. What can we learn from his response?

1. Trust in God's love
'I *trust* in God's unfailing love for ever and ever' (v.8b). God's love will never fail.

2. Praise God's deeds
'I will *praise* you for ever for what you have done ... I will praise you in the presence of your saints' (v.9a). Until God opens the door, praise him in the hallway.

3. Hope in God's name
'In your name I will *hope*, for your name is good (v.9b). With God, however bad your circumstances look, it is not over. Put your hope in God's name.

PRAYER

Lord, thank you for the dreams and visions that you put into my heart. As I face all the challenges ahead and the opposition, may I trust in your unfailing love and put my hope in you for the future.

NEW TESTAMENT READING

Luke 24:36–53
It is not over for Jesus

When Jesus died on the cross, it looked as bad as it could possibly be. It looked like it was all over for him and his followers.

But it was *not over*. God had not finished. He raised Jesus to life again. In this passage we see that Jesus appears to his disciples and says, 'Peace be with you' (v.36). They *still* seem '*troubled*' and have their '*doubts*' (v.38). Jesus gives them very *solid* proof that he really is alive.

'Look at my hands; look at my feet – it's really me. Touch me. Look me over from head to toe. A ghost doesn't have muscle and bone like this' (v.39, MSG).

Jesus is more than a historical figure who was born and died 2,000 years ago. He is alive. He is here and present today.

When the disciples realise that Jesus really is alive, they are overcome with 'joy' and 'amazement' (v.41). Having eaten a piece of leftover fish (v.42) he says to them, 'Everything I told you while I was with you comes to this: All the things written about me in the Law of Moses, in the Prophets, and in the Psalms have to be fulfilled' (v.44–47, MSG).

When Jesus showed them 'how to read their Bibles this way' (v.45, MSG), he set the pattern for us. This is why you should always try to read the Old Testament Scriptures through the lens of Jesus.

Jesus had totally fulfilled this part of his mission, which had been foretold in the Old Testament. Yet, the agenda of Jesus was unfinished.

His disciples had a task: 'Repentance and forgiveness of sins will be preached *in his name* to all nations, beginning in Jerusalem' (v.47). Now, you and I, his disciples, have the task of telling 'all nations' about Jesus – speaking about repentance and forgiveness of sins (v.47). For this part of his agenda you are going to need the power of the Holy Spirit. Jesus promises that you will be 'clothed with power from on high' (v.49).

Having set out his new agenda, Jesus 'lifted up his hands and blessed them. While he was blessing them, he left them and was taken up into heaven' (vv.50–51). It is interesting that after he had been taken up to heaven and he was not physically present they then *worshipped him* (v.52a), knowing that he was still with them. They then returned to Jerusalem, 'bursting with great joy' (v.52b, MSG). The end of Jesus' time with them was also a very exciting beginning.

On the day of Pentecost, they received what Jesus had promised. They were filled with the Holy Spirit and began to take on this new agenda of Jesus. All over the world today, Jesus' agenda is being carried out by his disciples. It is far from finished. You and I can play a part in completing Jesus' unfinished agenda. It's not over yet. One day it will be finished and then Jesus will return.

PRAYER

Lord, may I give my life to serve your great, unfinished agenda. Thank you that the Holy Spirit equips me and empowers me for this task.

OLD TESTAMENT READING

Joshua 13:1–14:15
It is never over for those who 'finish well'

Those who finish well will always have an unfinished agenda. You will be able to say, 'It's not over.'

Again, we see this theme of the 'unfinished agenda' in the life of Joshua: 'When Joshua had reached a venerable age, God said to him, "You've had a good, long life, but *there is a lot of land still to be taken*"' (13:1, MSG).

Be inspired by Joshua's example. He followed the Lord wholeheartedly. So did Caleb, who was able to say, 'I, however, followed the LORD my God wholeheartedly' (14:8). 'He gave himself totally to God' (v.14, MSG).

Not only did Caleb follow God wholeheartedly at the age of forty (v.7), he still did so at the age of eighty-five (v.10 – the same age that Lesslie Newbigin was when he gave those astonishing talks). This is the challenge – to finish well, not to lose your first love but to keep your eyes on Jesus.

The result for Caleb was 'strength' – Caleb was able to say, 'I'm still as strong today as the day Moses sent me out' (v.11). For him it was physical strength as well as inward strength of character (v.11). But for all who give themselves totally to God there is the inward strength of the Holy Spirit, which Jesus promises to you and me. You need this inner strength of the Holy Spirit if you are to finish well and fulfil your calling to seek the fulfilment of Jesus' new agenda.

PRAYER

Lord, help me to finish well. May I be able to say at the end of my life, 'I have followed the Lord my God wholeheartedly.' Please fill me with the inner strength of the Holy Spirit as I seek to see Jesus' new agenda fulfilled and the gospel preached in his name to all nations.

29 April | Day 119
The Battle Today Is Around Jesus

I have been involved in helping or leading a small group on Alpha for over twenty-five years. During this time, I have noticed a shift in our culture. There is a change in the attitude towards Jesus, especially among young people. Many will say that they believe in God and are even open to the idea of the Holy Spirit. But increasingly, Jesus has become the stumbling-block. They say things like, 'I don't get the *Jesus* bit.'

As Father Raniero Cantalamessa has often said, 'The battle today is around Jesus.'[1]

Is Jesus the universal Saviour? This is the same battle as the first century. People today are happy to accept Jesus as 'one of many'. It is the uniqueness of Jesus that causes offence. In the passages for today we see that while we meet some exceptional people throughout the Bible, like Moses, Joshua, Elijah and John the Baptist, there was no one like Jesus. Jesus is unique. He is the *universal Saviour*.

READING FROM PSALMS

Psalm 53:1–6
There is no one like Jesus

Napoleon Bonaparte said, 'I know men and I tell you that Jesus Christ is no mere man. Between him and every other person in the world there is no possible term of comparison.'[2] Jesus is different from every other human being who has ever lived.

David says, 'There is *no one* who does good' (v.1). As God looks down from heaven on the human race, he sees that '*there is no one* who does good, *not even one*' (v.3).

David looks in hope for a saviour: 'Is there anyone around to save Israel?' (v.6a, MSG). His longing was, of course, fulfilled in Jesus. Jesus was unique in his complete goodness. The apostle Paul quotes from this psalm to show the need of every human being for a saviour (Romans 3:10–12).

As Paul examines different people in this world – Jew and Gentile, moral and immoral – he comes to the conclusion that there is *no one* whom God can classify as good and righteous. He writes, 'Therefore *no one* will be *declared righteous* in [God's] sight...' (v.20).

The wonder of the gospel is that we, who are not righteous, can be *declared righteous* through Jesus' perfect righteousness. 'This *righteousness from God* comes through *faith in Jesus Christ* to *all who believe*' (v.22).

PRAYER

Lord, thank you that now it is possible for me to have the righteousness from God that comes through faith in Jesus to all who believe.

NEW TESTAMENT READING

John 1:1–28
Jesus is the one and only[3]

Jesus Christ is the one and only. He 'remains, to say the least of it, *unique*. If God is like Jesus, God is worth believing in,' wrote the journalist Anthony Burgess.

The whole of John's Gospel from start to finish is an answer to the question, 'Who is Jesus?' John's answer is that God *is* like Jesus and he *is* worth believing in. Jesus is totally unique. He is the '*One and Only*' (vv.14, 18). He is the 'one-of-a-kind God-expression' (v.18, MSG). The purpose of John's Gospel is to lead you into an experience of communion with God through friendship with Jesus.

You are a friend of Jesus. But who is Jesus?

1. Unique Word of God

John's Gospel opens with a brilliant description of Jesus as '*the Word*'. To us this seems like a strange concept, but to John's original readers it would have been much more familiar. The idea of the 'word of God' would have been important to *Jewish readers*. They would have remembered the *words of God* in *creation* (Genesis 1), and all that the prophets had to say about the '*word of the Lord*' (for instance Isaiah 40:6–8 and Jeremiah 23:29).

For *Greek readers* the idea of 'the Word' would have been associated with the search for the meaning of life. Philosophers often used '*the Word*' as a shorthand way of referring to the unknowable *meaning and purpose* behind the universe.

John's opening words would have been electrifying to *both* groups. He was in effect saying, 'I am going to tell you about what you've been searching for all this time.'

It is absolutely clear that 'the Word' that John is writing about is Jesus: 'The Word became flesh and blood, and moved into the neighborhood' (John 1:14a, MSG). Jesus was not only with God at the very beginning: 'The Word *was God*' (v.1, MSG). *Jesus was and is God*.

2. Unique Creator of all

'*Everything was created through him*; nothing – not one thing! – came into being without him' (v.3, MSG).

It is through Jesus that the entire universe came into being. 'For by him all things were created: things in heaven and on earth, visible and invisible, whether thrones or powers or rulers or authorities; *all things were created by him and for him*' (Colossians 1:16).

3. Unique light of the world

'In him was life, and that life was the *light* of all the people. The light shines in the darkness, but the darkness has not understood it' (John 1:4).

Light is a synonym of goodness and truth. Darkness is a synonym of evil and falsehood. Light and darkness are opposite, but *not* equal. A little candle can light a whole room full of darkness and will not be dimmed by it. Light is stronger than darkness; darkness cannot prevail against light.

4. Unique transformer of lives

'Yet to all who received him, to those who believed in his name, he gave the right to become children of God – children born not of natural descent, nor of human decision or a husband's will, but born of God' (vv.12–13).

Belief in Jesus brings about the biggest and most significant transformation possible. As you receive Jesus into your own life, so God receives you into his own family.

5. Unique revelation of God

'No one has ever seen God, but God the One and Only, who is at the Father's side, has made him known' (v.18).

Everything in the Old Testament was leading up to God's supreme revelation in Jesus. 'We got the basics from Moses, and then this exuberant giving and receiving, this endless knowing and understanding – all this came through Jesus the Messiah' (vv.16–17, MSG). This is why everything we read about in the Old Testament needs to be understood in light of Jesus.

Jesus is contrasted with John the Baptist. The emphasis is on what John the Baptist is *not*. He is *not* 'the light' (v.8). He is *not* eternal (v.15). He is *not* the Christ (v.20). He is *not* Elijah (v.21). He is *not* the Prophet (v.21).

Although Jesus says of John, 'There has not risen anyone greater than John the Baptist' (Matthew 11:11), John the Baptist says of Jesus, 'He is the one who comes after me, the thongs of whose sandals I am not worthy to untie' (John 1:27). John the Baptist's task, like us all, is to point away from ourselves and to the one and only Jesus, the unique Word of God, creator of all, light of the world, transformer of lives and revealer of God.

PRAYER

Jesus, I worship you, the unique Word of God. I pray today for fresh revelation of who you are and a deeper understanding of what it means to be a child of God.

OLD TESTAMENT READING

Joshua 15:1–16:10
Jesus is the unique Saviour

Joshua and Caleb were the *only two* of the original group to enter the promised land because they were the only ones who obeyed God and followed him wholeheartedly. (Joshua's name means 'Yah Saves', or 'The Lord Saves'. (*Joshua* is the Hebrew form of 'Jesus'.) Joshua foreshadows Jesus. Joshua and Caleb were *exceptional but, unlike Jesus, they were not unique*.

Hebron, a portion of land in Judah, was given to Caleb by Joshua (15:13) but he still had to go in and take it (v.14). Similarly, salvation, the greatest blessing of all, comes to us by grace as a gift, yet we still have to receive it and take hold of it for ourselves by faith. 'Grace and truth came through Jesus Christ' (John 1:17) – it is a gift given to us.

All the way through the Bible, God is looking for your response. He is looking for you to 'seek God' (Psalm 53:2) and 'call on God' (v.4). You have to take hold of the gift given to you and believe in Jesus. As you do, you are given the right to become a child of God (John 1:12).

Jesus is the unique Saviour. There is nothing more wonderful than taking hold of salvation through faith in him and becoming a friend of Jesus.

PRAYER

Lord, today I want to seek you. Thank you that you have revealed yourself in Jesus Christ – full of grace and truth. Help me to live a life that is full of grace and truth. I call on you for help in all the tasks I undertake and all the words that I speak – may I be full of grace and truth.

30 April | Day 120
It's Already Yours

My maternal grandparents lived in the small fishing village of Pittenweem near Edinburgh in Scotland. They owned a house there. In 1939, at the start of World War II, they let their home to tenants. When the war ended, they wanted to return to their home but they were unable to. The law at the time allowed the tenants to remain in the house for as long as they lived, at approximately the same rent (with no adjustment for inflation!).

For fifty years my grandparents were unable to get *possession* of the house they *owned*. My uncle inherited the house from my grandparents. By the time he got possession, the condition of the house had deteriorated greatly. He sold it for a very small sum.

Although my family *owned* this house in Pittenweem, they never took *possession* of it. There is a big difference between *ownership* and *possession*.

The people of Israel had been given *ownership* of Canaan, the promised land. Now Joshua says to the Israelites, 'How long will you wait before you begin to take *possession* of the land...?' (Joshua 18:3). The New Testament presents the 'land' as a picture of the Christian life (Hebrews 4). Realise what is already yours in Christ Jesus and then take possession of it.

READING FROM PROVERBS

Proverbs 10:31–11:8
Gift of righteousness

Do you realise that God has already given to you the gift of righteousness? Have you taken possession of this gift?

The writer of Proverbs contrasts 'the wicked' with 'the righteous'. Wickedness will lead to destruction – 'the unfaithful are *destroyed* by their duplicity ... the wicked are brought down by their own wickedness' (11:3b, 5b). Most significantly of all, wickedness is undone by death: 'When the wicked die, their hope perishes; all they expected from their power comes to nothing' (v.7).

On the other hand, 'righteousness delivers from death' (v.4b). This is one of the arguments the apostle Peter uses about Jesus on the Day of Pentecost – righteousness cannot rot: '*It was impossible for death to keep its hold on him*' (Acts 2:24).

No one is totally righteous except Jesus. Righteousness means right relationships, both with God and with other people. You receive this *righteousness from God* as a gift *by faith* (Romans 3:22; Philippians 3:9) but you have to take possession of it. You have to live it out.

In this passage we see some examples of what this means.

1. Wisdom
'A good person's mouth is a clear fountain of *wisdom*; a foul mouth is a stagnant swamp. The speech of a good person clears the air; the words of the wicked pollute it' (Proverbs 10:31a, 32a, MSG).

2. Humility
'The stuck-up fall flat on their faces, but down-to-earth people stand firm' (11:2, MSG).

3. Integrity
'The integrity of the honest keeps them on track ... a principled life can stand up to the worst' (v.3a, 4b, MSG).

4. Character
'Moral character makes for smooth travelling ... Good character is the best insurance' (v.5a, 6a, MSG).

PRAYER
Lord, I take possession of your gift of righteousness by faith. Help me to live a life of wisdom, humility, integrity and faithfulness.

NEW TESTAMENT READING

John 1:29–51
Gift of the Holy Spirit

Are you enjoying everything Jesus has made possible for you? Or are you still feeling guilty and powerless? Jesus came to bring forgiveness, new life and the power of the Holy Spirit to you. Make sure you take possession of what is already yours, today.

In this passage we see a remarkable sequence of the titles given to Jesus. Jesus is the 'Son of God' (vv.34, 49), 'Messiah' (v.41), 'King of Israel' (v.49) and 'Son of Man' (v.51).

I want to focus particularly on two titles in this passage that describe the *ministry* of Jesus.

1. Sin remover
The blood of the lamb saved the Israelites from slavery and allowed them to walk in freedom to the promised land (Exodus 11–15). John says of Jesus, 'Look, the Lamb of God, who takes away the sin of the world!' (John 1:29). As you come to Jesus, he takes away your sins. Claim, trust, believe in the forgiveness bought for you. Actively reject feelings of guilt, shame or unworthiness. It is a proactive, practical, daily choice to take possession of the forgiveness that Jesus has made possible for you.

2. Spirit baptiser
John the Baptist describes Jesus as 'the one who will baptise with the Holy Spirit' (v.33). Jesus fills you with his Holy Spirit. This

is what Jesus has made possible for you. However, you have to take possession of this wonderful gift that God has made available for you.

Jesus invited Philip, 'follow me' (v.43). The Greek word for 'to follow' means not only 'to walk in the footsteps' but also to accompany, to be with. When they ask Jesus, 'Where are you staying?', the Greek for 'staying' is the same word Jesus uses in John 15 – 'remain in me as I remain in you'. They see where Jesus is staying and remain with him. Jesus invites you, too, to a deep, personal friendship with him.

Jesus also gives you the opportunity to do what John the Baptist did – to point others to him. Of course, God does not need a human agent. Jesus could continue his ministry without our help. However, we see in this passage how God uses his *disciples* to call people.

They bring their friends to Jesus: John the Baptist introduces Andrew (vv.35–36); Andrew introduces Peter (v.41) and Philip introduces Nathanael (v.45). Nathanael was suspicious at first, but then he came and immediately found that Jesus really was the Son of God (v.49).

The former Archbishop of Canterbury, William Temple, wrote a commentary on John's Gospel. When he came to the words 'and he [Andrew] brought him [Simon Peter] to Jesus' (v.42a), Temple wrote a short but momentous sentence: 'The greatest service that one [person] can [do] to another.'[1]

Simon Peter went on to be one of the most significant influences in the history of Christianity. You may not be able to do what Peter did, but you can do what his brother Andrew did – you can bring someone to Jesus.

Or, just like Philip, you can say 'come and see' (v.46) to your friends, family and work colleagues. You can be a part of God's plan for people to hear about and respond to Jesus as you invite them to 'come and see'.

I have found that there is nothing more exciting in life than being involved in the ministry of Jesus. It is so gracious of God to involve us, imperfect human beings, in his perfect plan.

PRAYER

Lord, help me today to enjoy this gift of forgiveness and the fullness of life in the Holy Spirit. Help me also to introduce others to you – to invite people to 'come and see' (v.46).

OLD TESTAMENT READING

Joshua 17:1–18:28
Gift of your inheritance

Is there some area of your life where you are still not enjoying your inheritance in Christ?

The land was the inheritance of the people of God (17:4, 7; 18:7, 20, 27). 'Joshua addressed the People of Israel: "How long are you going to sit around on your hands, putting off taking *possession* of the land that God, the God of your ancestors, has *given you*?"' (18:3, MSG).

Here, once again, we see the great difference between ownership and possession and enjoyment of the land. Israel was given the ownership of the land before they took possession and enjoyment.

When you follow Jesus you become his friend. You receive forgiveness, justification, the righteousness of God and the Holy Spirit. You become a child of God. You have power over sin and access to God. You have victory over demonic powers. You have peace with God. You have authority over evil in your life and the lives of others. *All* the promises of God belong to you. This is your inheritance in Christ.

But you may not always, necessarily, *take possession* and fully enjoy the blessing of all these things in your life. Here God says, in effect, to his people: 'Don't you realise I have given all of this to you? What are you waiting for?'

You may have given your life to Jesus, but have you allowed him to possess every aspect of how you live – your finances, work, prayer life, friends and family. In my experience this is a lifetime task.

St Paul writes that you need to take every thought captive to obey Christ (2 Corinthians 10:5). In some areas the victory may be immediate. In others it may be more gradual. You have to drive out even the little pockets of resistance.

As Israel received the land as a gift from the Lord (Joshua 18:3), so you and I have received, in Jesus, every spiritual blessing (Ephesians 1:3). The question is, 'How long will you wait before you begin to take possession' of these gifts? (Joshua 18:3).

PRAYER

Lord, thank you that you have blessed me in Christ with every spiritual blessing. Help me today to take possession of what is already mine by faith through Jesus.

1 May | Day 121
God Wants to Surprise You

At the age of eighteen I set out to read the entire New Testament in order to disprove Christianity. As I read, I was surprised to find that I became convinced that it was true. The last thing that I wanted to do was to 'become a Christian'. I thought that would ruin my life and make it boring by stopping me having any fun. Yet, knowing in my heart that it was true, I felt I had no option but to say 'yes' to Jesus.

The moment I did so – to use the words that C. S. Lewis chose to describe his own experience of encountering Jesus – I was 'surprised by joy'.[1] Ever since, Jesus has never ceased to surprise me.

God is the God of surprises. Jesus constantly surprised his followers and he wants to continue to surprise you.

READING FROM PSALMS

Psalm 54:1–7
Surprised by God's help

Even if the attacks are justified or partly justified, it is always surprising when we come under attack from people we do not know. David says, '*strangers* are attacking me' (v.3a). I remember how surprised I was when I first started to read articles by people I had never met attacking Alpha, Holy Trinity Brompton and, sometimes, me personally. Surprise attacks can come from neighbours, work colleagues or other sources.

What I have found even more surprising is how God intervenes to help us: 'Oh, look! God's right here helping!' (v.4a, MSG), 'God is my helper and ally' (v.4a, AMP); he sustains us (v.4b) and he brings deliverance from our troubles (v.7).

As I look back over my own experience, deliverance has not always been instantaneous; it has sometimes taken months or even years. Yet, I am challenged by David's response. In the midst of the attacks, he says, 'I will sacrifice a freewill offering to you; I will praise your name, O Lord, for it is good' (v.6).

The point of a 'freewill offering' was that there was no condition placed on the sacrifice. David did not say that he would only offer a sacrifice if God rescued him. Regardless of the outcome, he resolved to praise the Lord for his goodness.

If you are facing an attack right now put your trust in God, believe that he wants to help you and praise him in advance.

PRAYER

Lord, thank you that one day I will be able to look back and see that you have delivered me from *all* my troubles.

NEW TESTAMENT READING

John 2:1–25
Surprised by Jesus

The ministry of Jesus was full of surprises. Jesus is constantly calling you to go deeper in your life with him. He wants to *surprise* you in new ways.

1. Surprising abundance

Some might be surprised that not only were Jesus and his disciples invited to parties (like this wedding banquet), they actually accepted and went along. At that time, wedding feasts lasted about a week. They were times of great revelry and rejoicing – where people put on their best clothes, rejoiced, sang, danced, joked, laughed and had fun. Perhaps what is even more surprising is that rather than condemning those drinking wine, Jesus transformed over 120 gallons of bath water into the very best wine (v.10). Jesus does things abundantly. He wants to give you more and more life and joy.

Simply letting Jesus know what the problem was ('They have no more wine', v.3) and then following his instructions ('do whatever he tells you', v.5) led to this surprising miracle. Jesus not only answered the need, but he answered it beyond anything they could have expected or even imagined. The master of the banquet was surprised when he 'tasted the water that had been turned into wine' (v.9).

This is also true in our own lives; Jesus turns the water of life without him into the wine of life with him. I thought that following Jesus would mean a life that was 'watered down'. In fact, it is the very opposite. Jesus constantly surprises us by how he enriches our lives. In particular, we see here how he enriches weddings and, indeed, marriages. He can turn the water of an ordinary marriage into the wine of an enriched one.

Jesus transforms drudgery and dreariness into fullness of joy.

Through this miracle Jesus 'revealed his glory, and his disciples put their faith in him' (v.11). For many this must have been a very surprising revelation.

2. Surprising passion

Jesus amazed everybody when he went into the temple courts and found people selling cattle, sheep and doves and others at tables exchanging money: 'The loan sharks were also there in full strength' (v.14, MSG).

He made a whip of cords and drove them all out of the temple area. He said, 'Get your things out of here! Stop turning my Father's house into a shopping mall' (v.16, MSG). His disciples remembered the words, 'Zeal for your house will consume me' (v.17).

We are surrounded by commercialism and seductive images. Huge shopping centres are replacing churches. There is a danger of worshipping money and commerce.

There was a terrible temptation then, as there is now, for money-making to interfere with the worship of God. Of course, there is a practical side of worship, both in the temple and in churches today. However, when the object of our focus becomes money, we are in serious trouble. Jesus surprised people by how passionate he was about this.

3. Surprising dwelling

Jesus redefines the temple. Jesus' body is the true temple. Jesus says to them, 'Destroy this temple, and I will raise it again in three days' (v.19). The true temple will be destroyed, but God will rebuild it again in three days, through the resurrection. They are surprised and cannot understand this – they ask Jesus how on earth he thinks he can rebuild this temple in a mere three days. But John adds, 'the temple he had spoken of was his body' (v.21).

The temple was important because it was the symbolic dwelling place of God. It was where God and humanity met. These surprising words of Jesus show us that he himself is the new temple. He is the dwelling place of God on earth.

Through Jesus, you are now called to be the home, the dwelling place of God. Your body is a temple of the Holy Spirit (1 Corinthians 6:19).

4. Surprising wisdom

When people saw the miracles Jesus performed and what he was doing, many 'believed in his name' (John 2:23). 'But,' John tells us, 'Jesus would not entrust himself to them, for he knew all people. He did not need human testimony about them, for he knew what was in people' (vv.24–25).

It is surprising to read that Jesus did not immediately trust these people – especially when we read that love 'always trusts' (1 Corinthians 13:7). Jesus is realistic about human nature. We tend to look for the perfect spouse, perfect parents, perfect children, perfect friends, perfect leaders and the perfect church. But these don't exist. All of us are flawed human beings.

Recognising this helps us to be more realistic and less disappointed – and more forgiving in our relationships.

We need the wisdom of Jesus in our dealings and in our relationships. We need to balance openness and loving trust with the wisdom and understanding of the human heart.

PRAYER

Lord, thank you for Jesus. Help me to fix my eyes on him today, so he can surprise me afresh with his wisdom, passion, love and abundance.

OLD TESTAMENT READING

Joshua 19:1–21:19
Surprised by humaneness

We are often surprised, even shocked, by parts of the Old Testament law. The Israelites would also have been surprised, though in a different way, because these laws were *surprisingly humane* by the standards of the time.

If a situation arose that seemed to be an accidental homicide, a person could be admitted to a city of refuge. Thereafter they could stay if, after the trial, the avenger failed to prove it was murder. The city had a duty to protect them until it was time for them to return (Joshua 20).

These laws preserved the sanctity of human life. Every human life is of infinite value to God. When a person's life is taken, even if accidentally, it is a very serious matter. On the other hand, there is a humaneness about these laws that protects the person who has killed accidentally. This humaneness would probably have surprised people at the time.

As Pippa and I have travelled around the world, we have often visited the local prisons. In some countries the justice system seems to be relatively humane. In other places the prison conditions and penalties imposed seem inhumane.

As God's people today, we should, of course, seek to ensure justice, just laws, deterring and reducing crime. But we should also be passionate about ensuring that our justice systems are humane.

PRAYER

Lord, help me in my own life, and also in society, to work towards just and humane laws. Thank you for your love, compassion and mercy.

2 May | Day 122

How to Handle Confrontation

Confrontation is not something that I find easy. It is a delicate operation. It is crucial to find the right approach, the right words for the job. Or, to use a golfing analogy, it is about knowing which club to use.

Those who are skilled at confrontation have a great variety of approaches and words, and know when and how to use the appropriate one.

Confrontation is not always the right course. Not every critic has to be confronted. Not every wrong statement needs to be refuted.

I greatly admire the skill of those who know when to confront and are good at confronting in a loving way. They have learnt how to speak the truth in love (Ephesians 4:15).

When confrontation is necessary, how should you go about it?

READING FROM PSALMS

Psalm 55:1–11
Confront evil prayerfully

There are forces of evil at work in our 'cities' today. Terrorist attacks take place in cities all over the world – from Baghdad to Brussels, and recently in the heart of London.

David also faced violent and destructive forces of evil at work in the city (vv.9b,11a).

As David faces his 'enemy' as they 'revile' him 'in their anger' (v.3), he says, 'Oh, that I had the wings of a dove! I would fly away and be at rest – I would flee far away and stay in the desert; I would hurry to my place of shelter, far from the tempest and storm' (vv.6–8).

Escapism is a temptation – to shy away from confrontation. But evil must be confronted. Don't run away. Don't be overwhelmed. Rather do what you can. You can make a difference. As St Paul writes, 'Do not be overcome by evil, but overcome evil with good' (Romans 12:21).

David's response to the violence and destruction is to ask God to intervene. He prays, 'Lord, *confuse* the wicked, *confound* their words' (Psalm 55:9). Prayer is an important part of our response to 'destructive forces' (v.11).

Prayer and action go hand in hand. Even when you cannot help physically, you can always pray. God acts in response to your prayers.

PRAYER

'Listen to my prayer, O God, do not ignore my plea; hear me and answer me' (v.1). Help me not to be overcome by evil but to overcome evil with good.

NEW TESTAMENT READING

John 3:1–21
Confront people lovingly

Confronting those who are in a position of weakness is relatively easy and sometimes cowardly. Confronting those in positions of power over us, through their job, status or wealth, takes great courage.

Jesus was the master at confrontation. He never shied away from it. On the other hand, he never acted out of any motive but love.

Nicodemus was a very powerful man; a moral and upright Pharisee and 'a member of the Jewish ruling council' (v.1). Jesus was undaunted by his position. He lovingly confronts Nicodemus with his need to be 'born again' (v.3) – to start anew, leave behind past hurts, habits and old ways. The message of Jesus is about transformation.

Nicodemus needs to be born again of water and the Spirit (v.5). The outward washing must be accompanied by the inward dwelling of the Holy Spirit.

We do not see God physically now. But we see *evidence* of God. Like the wind, we cannot see it but we can see its effect on the trees and the leaves – 'the invisible moving the visible' (v.5, MSG).

Likewise, Jesus says you cannot see the Holy Spirit but you can see the *impact on people's lives*: 'The person who takes shape within is formed by something you can't see and touch – the Spirit – and becomes a living spirit' (v.6, MSG).

Jesus lovingly challenges Nicodemus about his beliefs. Using the image of the snake in the desert (from Numbers 21), Jesus predicts that he himself will be lifted up on the cross so 'that everyone who *believes* in him may have eternal life' (v.15).

'Believes' means 'trusts'. Every time we enter a relationship we take a risk. All relationships require trust. Trust in a dynamic relationship grows and endures.

Jesus teaches about God's love. The Greek word used for 'love' in verse 16, *agape*, appears forty-four times in John's Gospel alone. This verse sums up John's Gospel and, indeed, the whole of the New Testament: 'God so *loved* the world that he gave his one and only Son, that whoever *believes in him* shall not perish but have eternal life' (v.16).

There is a God and his love is wide enough to embrace all humankind without distinction or exception. It is not a vague or sentimental love. God's love is of immeasurable intensity, demonstrated by his willingness to sacrifice his only son for you and me.

The world is in such a mess. People often ask, 'Why doesn't God do something?' The answer is that he has. He came in the person of his Son, Jesus, to die on a cross and rise again for you. Jesus understands about suffering. He suffered for us and he suffers alongside us.

Many people have ceased to believe in life after death. But Jesus promised that we would 'have eternal life and [actually] live for ever!' (v.15, AMP). This life is not the end. There is hope beyond the grave. Jesus offers you eternal life.

There is a big difference between confrontation and condemnation. Jesus confronted people, but he did not condemn them. Jesus did not come to condemn you but to save you from condemnation (vv.17–18). Like Jesus, you and I need to bring a message – not of condemnation, but the good news of salvation. To save means to pull a person out of danger, to liberate, to open the doors of a prison, to heal, to make whole.

Next, Jesus speaks of how light exposes and *confronts darkness* (vv.19–21). Jesus seems to be suggesting that the reason some people reject him is because 'their deeds [are] evil' (v.19). We do not want to come into the light because we do not want to give up the things that we know are wrong.

We do not want people to see the shadow areas in us. We hide all the dark inside us behind our apparent goodness. Sin hates light. When we sin, we want to avoid the light of Jesus. We do not want our evil deeds to be exposed. But Jesus came *to confront the darkness*. We may be afraid or ashamed. It may be extremely difficult for us. But we too must confront darkness in our lives and seek to live in the light of Christ – who loves you just as you are.

Martin Luther King said, 'Darkness cannot drive out darkness; only light can do that. Hate cannot drive out hate; only love can do that.'[1]

PRAYER

Lord, thank you for the example of Jesus. Help me to live in the light and to have the courage to speak the truth in love.

OLD TESTAMENT READING

Joshua 21:20–22:34
Confront opposition wisely

Many conflicts could be avoided if people would talk *to* each other, rather than just talk *about* each other.

As a result of a genuine misunderstanding, the rest of Israel looked at the two and a half tribes (the Reubenites, the Gadites and the half-tribe of Manasseh) and thought they were doing the wrong thing and disobeying God (22:12).

However, instead of going to war straight away they were wise enough *to confront them* and challenge them verbally. Once they had done that it became clear that their fears were groundless.

They were right to want to interfere rather than ignore because what one part of the body does affects the whole body. They could not simply say, 'It's up to them what they do.'

When the two and a half tribes were confronted they gave their explanation: 'We did it because we cared' (v.24, MSG). They wanted to ensure their children kept the faith.

The explanation was satisfactory: 'Now we're convinced that God is present with us since you haven't been disloyal to God in this matter' (v.31, MSG).

This was one of the occasions when it was a good idea to have a meeting (vv.32–33). After the meeting 'they talked no more about going to war' (v.33).

Be careful not to jump to hasty adverse conclusions about other Christians and other churches. Do not attack them verbally behind their backs. If necessary, arrange a meeting, confront and hear the explanation. If we all do this, much needless division and ill-feeling will be avoided.

In this case, when they heard the explanation, instead of being sceptical or cynical, they accepted it and 'praised God' (v.33). When you make mistakes about people, be generous in admitting your mistakes. It takes a 'big' person to admit that they are wrong.

PRAYER

Lord, give me the wisdom to know when it is important to meet, to confront and to hear explanations. Help us to avoid unnecessary divisions and disunity. Help me to learn the skills of loving confrontation.

3 May | Day 123
How to Make Good Choices

Charles Finney, lawyer and evangelist, was speaking in a New York church in the 1830s. At the end of each evening, he gave people the opportunity to come to the front of the room and commit their life to Jesus. A great many lawyers came to hear him. One night, the Chief Justice of New York was sitting way up in the gallery. As he listened to Finney proclaiming the gospel he became convinced it was true.

Then this question came into his mind: 'Will you go forward like the other ordinary people?' Something within him made him think that it would be inappropriate to do so, because of his prestigious social position (at the top of the legal hierarchy of New York State). He sat there pondering *the choice he had to make*. Then he thought, 'Why not? I am convinced of the truth ... why should I not do it like any other person?'

He got up from his seat in the gallery, went down the staircase and came up the stairs at the back to where Finney was preaching. Finney, in the middle of his sermon, felt someone tugging at his jacket. He turned around. The Chief Justice said, 'Mr Finney, if you will call people forward I will come.' Finney stopped his talk and said, 'The Chief Justice says that if I call people forward he will come. I ask you to come forward now.'

The Chief Justice went forward. Almost every lawyer in Rochester, New York, followed him! It is said that 100,000 people were converted in the next twelve months in that area. One person's choice affected the lives of numerous others.

Life is full of choices. We make choices every day of our lives. You can make bad choices or you can make good choices. Your choices matter. Some choices have life-changing consequences.

READING FROM PSALMS

Psalm 55:12–23
Choose trust over worry

As has been said, 'Worrying is like a rocking chair. It gives you something to do but it gets you nowhere.' No one goes through life without facing problems, battles and causes for worry.

David faced many difficulties in his life. Here David speaks of one of the most painful battles of his life (v.18b). His 'close friend' (v.13b) with whom he 'used to share' his 'secrets' (v.14, ERV) has turned against him and joined the many who oppose him (v.18c). David, of course, found this more difficult than if 'an enemy were insulting [him]' (v.12a), as we all would.

As in any battle, we have a 'choice' about how we respond. David *chose* to turn to the Lord and cry out to him 'evening, morning and noon' (vv.16–17). If you are involved in a confrontation with a close friend or family member, turn to God for comfort and strength. David did so and as a result he experienced God's *peace*. He wrote, 'He has redeemed my life *in peace* from the battle that was against me' (v.18, AMP).

From David's own experience he is able to give this advice: 'Cast your cares on the LORD and he will sustain you' (v.22a). Each year, I have written in the margins of my Bible the 'cares' that I have 'cast upon the Lord' in response to this verse. Most of them (though not quite all) have been more than resolved.

As you face the worries, battles and disappointments of life, don't allow them to overwhelm you. Like David, turn to the Lord, cast your burdens on him and then say, 'as for me, I trust in you (v.23b).

PRAYER

Lord, today I want to bring to you my cares... I cast all these things on you and trust in you.

NEW TESTAMENT READING

John 3:22–36
Choose Jesus

John the Baptist had become a celebrity. He had a remarkable ministry. People 'were constantly coming [to him] to be baptised' (v.23). John's followers were very competitive. They became envious of Jesus' success. They came to John and said about Jesus, 'He's now competing with us... everyone's going to him instead of us' (v.26, MSG).

John had *to choose* how he responded. He began by pointing out to his disciples that 'it's not possible for a person to succeed – I'm talking about eternal success – without heaven's help' (v.27, MSG). He chose to point people to Jesus rather than to himself: 'You yourselves can testify that I said, "I am not the Christ but am sent ahead of him."' (v.28).

John likens his own position to 'the friend who attends the bridegroom' (whom we might call the 'best man'). Far from being threatened by the arrival of the groom, it is the very thing he has been waiting for, and he is delighted by it. Likewise, John explains that he has been waiting for Jesus, and is 'full of joy' at Jesus' ministry. Jesus was John the Baptist's successor. John says of Jesus: 'He must become greater; I must become less' (v.30).

At times, all of us may be driven to become greater, more important, more honoured, more highly promoted or better qualified. These are not all bad aims in themselves, but our daily choices will be swayed by these ambitions. You have to choose how you live your life. Are you focused on your promotion or on exalting Jesus? Is your ambition more for yourself or for Jesus?

Sometimes, we even see different Christian ministries competing with each other. This should never happen.

Echo these words in your heart: 'He must become greater; I must become less' (v.30). Ultimately, the focus is not on yourself – it is always on Jesus. Our ambition must always be to point people to Jesus.

John highlights the real issue: 'Whoever accepts and trusts the Son gets in on everything, life complete and forever! And that is also why the person who avoids and distrusts the Son is in the dark and doesn't see life. All he experiences of God is darkness, and an angry darkness at that' (v.36, MSG).

That is the most vital choice of all – do I choose Jesus or reject him?

PRAYER

Lord, I choose that you 'must become greater; I must become less' (v.30). Fill me with the Holy Spirit so that I may speak the words of God, enabling others to believe in the Son.

OLD TESTAMENT READING

Joshua 23:1–24:33
Choose to serve the Lord

Worshipping and serving God is the way to a fulfilling life. Don't waste your life chasing after false 'gods'. As St Cyprian wrote, 'Whatever man prefers to God, that he makes a *god* to himself.' There are numerous *other gods* around today – perhaps the most common could be summed up as 'money, sex and power'.

Israel had enjoyed a long period of rest after all the battles (23:1). Joshua, 'a venerable old man' (v.1, MSG) at the end of his life, called all the people together and spoke to them. He told them that they had to *choose* how to spend the rest of their lives.

He reminds them of everything that God has done for them and all the ways in which he has blessed them (23:14; 24:10). Now Joshua urges them to worship the Lord, their God, 'in total commitment' (v.10b, MSG).

In response to all that the Lord has done for you, you are also called 'to love the LORD' (23:11), to worship and to serve him. Joshua says, '*choose* for yourselves this day whom you will serve' (24:15). He lays out the options (vv.14–15):

1. False 'gods' ('gods' of their ancestors or 'gods' of the conquered people), or
2. The God of Israel, who is the one true God.

The gods of the conquered people claimed to be modern and 'scientific' – with true control over agriculture, fertility and sex. The people of Canaan felt themselves intellectually and culturally miles ahead of the Israelites. But Joshua stresses the shortcomings of the 'other gods' as against the goodness and the power of God (vv.3–13).

You have to make a choice. You cannot just drift. Many people just drift through life, never making a conscious decision.

Joshua, like all good leaders, leads by example. He makes a deliberate, personal choice to worship and serve the Lord. He says, 'But *as for me and my household, we will serve the Lord'* (v.15).

The people answered, '*We too will serve the Lord*, because he is our God' (vv.18, 21, 24). Joshua said, 'You have *chosen* to serve the Lord' (v.22). As a result, 'Israel served the Lord throughout the lifetime of Joshua' (v.31). While Joshua and the elders – trained presumably by him – were leading Israel, Israel served the Lord. Leadership is key.

Joshua called the people to repentance and faith. This is always what God requires. First, repentance: 'throw away the foreign gods' (v.23a). Get rid of the bad stuff. Second, faith: 'yield your hearts to the Lord' (v.23b) – put your whole life into the hands of the Lord.

PRAYER

Lord, I choose to yield my heart to you. Help me to make good choices in my life.

4 May | Day 124

Three Ways to Transform Your World

Martin Luther King Jr (1929–1968) lived and died to see society transformed. In 1964, he became the youngest person ever to receive the Nobel Peace Prize – for his work to end social segregation and discrimination.

He spoke powerfully and memorably of his dream that, one day, he would live in a nation where his children would 'not be judged by the colour of their skin but by the content of their character'.

He dreamt of a transformed world where everyone would be able to join hands and say, 'Free at last! Thank God Almighty, we are free at last!'

Martin Luther King Jr was a follower of Jesus. His agenda was the kingdom of God. The kingdom of God is not just about the conversion of individuals – important though that is – but about the transformation of society.

READING FROM PROVERBS

Proverbs 11:9–18
Be a blessing to your nation

Your life can have an influence, not only on your own family and local community, but also on your city, and even on the whole nation.

The writer of Proverbs makes the point that how we live as individuals affects not only ourselves, but also the world around us – for good or for evil.

On the one hand, 'when the righteous prosper, *the city* rejoices' (v.10). And 'by the *blessing of the influence* of the upright and God's favour [because of them] the city is exalted' (v.11a, AMP). On the other hand, 'the mouth of the wicked' can destroy a city (v.11b). And, 'for lack of guidance a *nation* falls' (v.14).

How then should you live? Don't slander your neighbours, but rather exercise restraint and hold your tongue (v.12). Don't gossip but be trustworthy in keeping secrets (v.13).

We all need wise, godly people around us to provide good advice: 'Where no wise guidance is, the people fall, but in the multitude of counsellors there is safety' (v.14, AMP). If you have wise counsellors consult them often. If you don't have them, ask God to provide you with such advisers.

Be kind-hearted (v.16) and sow righteousness (v.18). If you live like this, the whole world around you will be affected.

PRAYER

Lord, help me to be a good influence in my city and in my nation so that I may see the whole world around me transformed.

NEW TESTAMENT READING

John 4:1–26
Break down divisions of every kind

Every church should be an inclusive church because God's love is radically inclusive. The church should be famous for its love. We should welcome people regardless of their gender, race or lifestyle. Jesus came to break down every barrier in our society.

Jesus' fame was increasing. 'The Pharisees were keeping count of the baptisms that he and John performed ... They had posted the score that Jesus was ahead, turning him and John into rivals' (vv.1–2, MSG).

Jesus was not interested in rivalry, fame or competition: 'When the Lord learned of this, he left Judea and went back once more to Galilee' (v.3). He was very interested in helping one individual Samaritan. He takes time to minister to her. Mother Teresa said, 'Never worry about numbers. Help one person at a time, and always start with the person nearest you.'

In this encounter, Jesus demonstrated that one of the ways in which society will be transformed is by the breaking down of divisions.

1. End the war between the sexes

Jesus had a prolonged conversation with a woman in public. This flew in the face of the conventions of the time. The strict rabbis forbade a rabbi even to greet a woman in public, let alone have a long conversation. When the disciples returned, they were 'surprised to find him talking with a woman' (v.27).

As John Stott wrote, 'Without any fuss or publicity Jesus terminated the curse of the Fall, reinvested woman with her partially lost nobility and reclaimed for his new kingdom community the original creation blessing of sexual equality.'[1]

The sexes should not be at war. As Pope Benedict XVI put it, 'In Christ the rivalry, enmity and violence which disfigured the relationship between men and women can be overcome and have been overcome.'[2]

2. End racism, discrimination and apartheid

The division between Jews and Samaritans went back a long way. Samaritans were a despised and powerless minority – pushed down and without value. John explains that 'Jews in those days wouldn't be caught dead talking to Samaritans' (v.9, MSG).

Jesus does not compromise on the truth: 'Salvation is from the Jews' (v.22). Nevertheless, he reaches out to this Samaritan woman. In doing so he breaks the curse of racial discrimination and apartheid. The transformation of society requires the breaking down of the walls of division of race and ethnicity.

3. End class war and social division

God loves you regardless of your previous life or present lifestyle. Thank God, he loves imperfect people.

In asking her for water, Jesus is showing us how to approach people who are broken and wounded – not patronisingly as someone superior but humbly like a beggar.

This woman would have been a social outcast. With a history of broken relationships, rejected and mocked by her own people, she comes to draw water all alone at midday.

Not only did Jesus speak to a woman who was a Samaritan, he spoke with a 'sinner'. This woman had led an immoral life. 'You have had five husbands, and the man you now have is not your husband' (v.18). She has been divorced several times and is now living with a man to whom she is not married. Jesus does not compromise on the truth, but neither does he judge, condemn or reject the Samaritan woman because of her lifestyle or social position (cf. Mark 2:17; John 8:10–11).

The religious did not mix with 'sinners'. By his interaction with this sexually promiscuous woman, Jesus breaks down yet another barrier. His love reaches to all sections of society – across the barriers of class, lifestyle and social position.

Ultimately, it is only the Holy Spirit who can bring about the transformation of society. It is the Holy Spirit who brings unity, breaking down the divisions of gender, race and social position. Those indwelt by the Holy Spirit should be at the forefront of the fight for gender, racial and social equality.

Jesus' conversation with this woman was all about the Holy Spirit. She doesn't need a lecture; she needs living water. He says to her, 'All who drink this water will be thirsty again, but those who drink the water I give them will never thirst. Indeed, the water I give them will become in them a spring of water welling up to eternal life' (vv.13–14).

Jesus came to quench our thirst for acceptance, relationship and meaning. The life we receive is the life we give. We become a source of life for others.

The transformation of society starts with the Holy Spirit transforming our lives. It starts with drinking the water of life, which Jesus gives to everyone who believes in him. When the Holy Spirit comes to live within you he becomes a permanent spring of overflowing water throughout your life and into eternity.

You are transformed by the Holy Spirit and by your personal relationship with God. The word used for 'worship' here means 'to go down on our knees, to draw close in an intimate relationship of love' – we 'must worship in spirit and in truth' (v.24).

PRAYER

Lord, today I come to you and drink your living water. May this water flow out of my heart and transform all my relationships.

OLD TESTAMENT READING

Judges 1:1–2:5
Cry out to God for good leadership

We live in a disordered and chaotic world – in some ways not very different to the world described in the book of Judges.

Entering the book of Judges is quite a shock. We find a mix of violence, rape, massacre, brutality, deceit and mayhem. We see how the people failed to get a grip on idolatry and sin when they settled in the promised land. Despite God's warnings, they compromised with the religious and ethical practices of the people around them (2:1–2). Who then became 'thorns in [their] sides and... a snare to [them]' (v.3).

God calls you to be utterly ruthless about the bad stuff. He does not want us to compromise. He does not want you simply to cut down the areas of your life that you know are wrong, but to cut them out completely and ruthlessly.

The people found themselves in a cycle of disobedience, being oppressed by their enemies, then crying out to God for help.

God answered by sending them judges (leaders). He used all kinds of rather unlikely people as leaders – which gives great encouragement to us all. Empowered by the Holy Spirit, these leaders delivered them and transformed their world.

PRAYER

Lord, please raise up good leaders in our city and in our culture who will transform our world and bring honour to the name of Jesus.

5 May | Day 125
Jesus Always Delivers

Pippa and I met Ah Yin when we visited Jackie Pullinger[1] in Hong Kong. He had become a drug addict as a teenager. His father was an addict. He was brought up in the notorious Walled City. He joined a gang at the age of eleven. They ate, stole, fought and took heroin together. At the age of fourteen, he got caught doing a robbery and spent his first time in detention.

Over the years he tried everything to get off drugs. Nothing worked. Then he met Jackie and, through the power of Jesus, came off drugs with no pain at all. Since then he has become one of the leaders of Jackie's work in Hong Kong. He has trained many people to pray for the sick and to work with the poor. He is one example of the millions of people whom Jesus has delivered from addiction and set free. Ah Yin has spent the rest of his life testifying about the Saviour who always delivers.

READING FROM PSALMS

Psalm 56:1–13
Trust God to deliver you

I have found that sometimes fear can be overwhelming. David feared for his life (v.6). He discovered that the answer to fear is trust in God (vv.6, 11).

David had been captured by the Philistines in Gath. It must have been a terrible experience. He was 'kicked around', 'stomped on every day' and beaten up (v.1, MSG). Yet in the midst of it all he trusted in God: 'When I get really afraid I come to you in *trust*. I'm proud to praise God; fearless now, *I trust in God*' (vv.3–4, MSG),

There are times in life when we come under attack. It could be spiritual attack or attack from other people – at work, from neighbours, or from further afield.

Whatever the cause of the fear, like David, put your trust in God: 'In God I have put my *trust* and confident reliance; I will not be afraid' (v.11a, AMP).

This psalm ends on a note of triumph and deliverance ('you have *delivered me*', v.13). David thanks God for setting him free: 'God, you did everything you promised, and I'm thanking you with all my heart. You pulled me from the brink of death, my feet from the cliff-edge of doom. Now I stroll at leisure with God in the sunlit fields of life' (vv. 12–13, MSG).

PRAYER

Lord, thank you for the many times in my life when I have been afraid and have called on you for help and you have delivered me. Today I call on you for help and trust in you to deliver me.

NEW TESTAMENT READING

John 4:27–42
Testify about the Saviour

Every Christian has a testimony. The most powerful way of passing on the message of Jesus is to tell people your story. If they are interested then you can say, like the woman in this incident, 'come, see...' (v.29a).

The population of a whole town come to the conclusion that Jesus 'really is *the Saviour of the world*' (v.42). The Samaritan woman had been transformed by her encounter with Jesus. She immediately began to testify about her Saviour. She went back to her village and told the people, '*Come see* a man who knew all about the things I did, who knows me inside and out. Do you think this could be the Messiah?' (v.29, MSG).

There really is great power in a testimony. This woman had no theological training or even understanding of Christian doctrine. She was not even totally convinced about Jesus herself. She does not say with great conviction, 'Jesus is the Christ'. Rather, she has reached the position of saying, '*Could* this be the Christ?' (v.29b). Yet she was powerfully used by God in evangelisation.

In this sense, she is like so many of the testimonies we hear on Alpha. People are not even sure themselves of what they have discovered, but they speak powerfully at the end when they give their testimonies and often bring their friends to the next course.

All they know is that Jesus has revealed himself in some way to them. They have experienced some kind of 'deliverance' from the empty way of life. They have discovered a new well of water welling up to eternal life. They say to their friends, 'Come, see...' (v.29a).

'Many of the Samaritans from that town believed in him because of the woman's testimony' (v.39). Jesus had changed her life. The waters of life were pouring out of her as Jesus had promised. The people were amazed and astonished by her transformation. They came and saw, and 'because of [Jesus'] words many more became believers' (v.41).

'They said to the woman, "We no longer believe just because of what you said; now we have heard for ourselves, and we know that this man really is the Saviour of the world"' (v.42). The *teaching* of Jesus and the *testimony* about Jesus both powerfully point to his identity as Saviour of the world.

He said, 'My food... is to do the will of him who sent me' (v.34). Jesus shows by the example of his ministry that our spiritual hunger, a life of emptiness and lack of purpose, can only be satisfied by doing God's will. Nothing is more satisfying than doing God's will – being where he wants you to be and doing what he wants you to do.

Jesus says, 'I tell you, open your eyes and look at the fields! They are ripe for harvest' (v.35). This was fulfilled by the coming of Jesus. The disciples can see that the time is right because people everywhere need to know this message about Jesus.

Jesus said, 'I sent you to reap what you have not worked for. Others have done the hard work, and you have reaped the benefits of their labour' (v.38). This, of course, originally applied to the coming of Jesus. However, again it is fulfilled at a different level in many ways.

For example, I feel that we are reaping now as a local church – and also with Alpha – what others have sown. For many years, people have prayed for an outpouring of the Holy Spirit at HTB. Many worked hard in developing Alpha . We are reaping what others have sown. Now we must sow so that others can reap.

PRAYER

Lord, I pray that you would use my testimony so that many others may believe in you.

OLD TESTAMENT READING

Judges 2:6–3:31
Thank God for leaders who deliver

We see in this passage a recurring pattern that runs throughout the book of Judges:

1. Disobedience

'Another generation grew up, who knew neither the LORD nor what he had done for Israel ... they forsook the LORD ... they followed and worshipped various gods of the peoples around them' (2:10, 12).

2. Disaster
God's response was to allow disaster, so that they might turn back to him: 'The LORD handed them over... He sold them to their enemies' (v.14).

3. Distress
This understandably left the people 'in great distress' (v.15).

4. Deliverance
When they got into trouble they cried out to the Lord and he raised up judges 'who saved them' (v.16). The word translated 'judge' (*shophet*) has a wide meaning in Hebrew. It can also mean '*deliverer*' – anyone who brings about justice or sets things right.

The first of these 'deliverers' is Othniel. 'The Spirit of the LORD came upon him' (3:10). Othniel was anointed by the Spirit of God, and it was this anointing that enabled him to deliver the people and establish forty years of peace (v.11).

Once again though, the people slipped into disobedience and disaster (vv.12–14) and cried out to God for a *deliverer* (v.15).

God delivered the people in a fascinating, if rather unpleasant, way (v.21). Ehud must have been an extremely courageous and brave man to walk right into enemy territory alone, with a sword hidden on him. It was a crazy thing to do, but for the fact that God was with him. And it was remarkably successful. Once again, the land had peace. This time for eighty years (v.30).

God sometimes uses people who are not part of the people of God to deliver his people. Shamgar may have been a Canaanite (see 5:6). He was a powerful man: he 'struck down six hundred Philistines with an ox-goad. He too *saved* Israel' (3:31).

These leaders only brought temporary peace, 'as long as the judge lived' (2:18).

All this only foreshadows, in rather a murky and inadequate way, the great work of Jesus, the Saviour of the world. Jesus is the great deliverer. Through his death and resurrection, he has delivered you. He is your Saviour. The Holy Spirit now lives within you (Romans 8:9). He gives you power and wisdom so that you too can make a difference with your life.

PRAYER

Lord, today I cry out to you for deliverance from all the difficulties, troubles and fears that I face today. I praise and thank you for your great deliverance through my Saviour Jesus Christ.

6 May | Day 126
Pray God-Sized Prayers

I remember so well praying for a baby called Craig. I had been asked to visit a woman in the Brompton Hospital. Vivienne had three children and was pregnant with a fourth. Her third child, who was eighteen months old, had Down's syndrome. He had a hole in his heart that had been operated on. The operation had not been a success and, not unnaturally, the medical staff wanted to turn the machines off. Many times they asked Vivienne if they could turn the machines off and let the baby die. She said no, as she wanted to try one last thing. She wanted someone to pray for him. So I went.

Craig had tubes all over him. His body was bruised and swollen. She said that the doctors had indicated that even if he recovered he would have brain damage because his heart had stopped for such a long time. She told me she didn't believe in God but she said, 'Will you pray?'

I prayed in the name of Jesus for God to heal him. Then I explained to her how she could give her life to Jesus Christ and she did. I left, but returned two days later. Vivienne came running out the moment she saw me. She said, 'I've been trying to get hold of you; something amazing has happened. The night after you prayed he completely turned the corner. He has recovered.' Within a few days Craig had gone home.

Vivienne went around all her relatives and friends saying, 'I didn't believe, but now I do believe.'

This was over thirty years ago. I'm still in touch with the family. Craig still had Down's syndrome but a remarkable healing had occured. He became the glue in that family. This healing was not autosuggestion; he was a baby at the time. It was not positive thinking. It was not the placebo effect. It was a God-sized answer to a God-sized prayer.

READING FROM PSALMS

Psalm 57:1–6
Pray for mercy

Have you ever cried out to God for mercy? I certainly have, many times. David cried out 'to God Most High' (v.2). He prayed, 'Have *mercy* on me, O God, have *mercy* on me' (v.1a).

There is a God-sized prayer for mercy that God *always* answers. That is the prayer for forgiveness through Jesus. Through his death on the cross, Jesus has made it possible that 'everyone who calls on the name of the Lord will be saved' (Romans 10:13).

The context for David's prayer for mercy is probably when he had fled from Saul and into the cave (see 1 Samuel 22; 24). He cried out to God, and God heard and answered his prayer. David says, 'I cry out to God Most High, to God, who fulfils his purpose for me' (Psalm 57:2).

David knew that God had a purpose for his life and that he would fulfil that purpose. God has a God-sized purpose for your life. Respond, like David, to God's call and obey him.

God answers God-sized prayers in a God-sized way: 'He sends from heaven and saves me ... God sends his love and his faithfulness' (v.3).

PRAYER

O God, thank you for your love and your faithfulness (v.3). My soul will take refuge in the shadow of your wings.

NEW TESTAMENT READING

John 4:43–5:15
Pray for healing

There are times in our lives when we are desperate for healing – either for others, or for ourselves. In this life our prayers for healing will not always be answered. Unanswered prayer can be a difficult and painful thing to wrestle with.[1] But sometimes God *does* intervene miraculously to bring healing. We see here two examples of this, both coming about as a result of God-sized prayers:

1. Healing for others

The royal official *begged Jesus* to heal his son (4.47), who was on the brink of death.

'Jesus put him off: "Unless you people are dazzled by a miracle, you refuse to believe"' (v.48, MSG). But the official would not be put off: 'Come down! It's life or death for my son' (v.49, MSG).

Jesus responded to the man's faith. The man believed that if Jesus came he could heal his son. Jesus asked him to go one step further and believe that his words from miles away could heal his son. The man did believe. And Jesus performed the miracle – he heard the man's God-sized prayer and healed his son. As a result, his whole household *believed* (v.53).

2. Healing for ourselves

Jesus went to a place where there were a multitude of people with disabilities; lame, blind and paralysed (5:3). This was a culture that saw disability as a punishment from God. Such people were hidden away. But God has chosen the weak and the foolish of the world in order to confound the wise (1 Corinthians 1:27–28).

Jesus healed a man who had been an invalid for thirty-eight years (John 5:5). The man must have been desperate: he had been putting his hope in the healing powers of the waters of Bethesda, which would bubble up periodically, and it was thought that the first person in after the waters bubbled up would be healed. But this man had no one to help him get in first (v.7).

He had no friends, no close family. Nobody cared for him. He was alone and abandoned. Nobody loved him, but Jesus loved him.

Jesus says to him, as he says to each one of us, 'Do you want to get well?' (v.6). For thirty-eight years, this man had learned to survive as he was. Now he has to rise up, make choices, find new friends, find work and become responsible for his life.

Joyce Meyer writes of this incident that, in effect, Jesus said to the man, 'Don't just lie there, do something!' She continues, 'Being sexually abused for approximately fifteen years and growing up in a dysfunctional home left me lacking confidence and filled with shame. I wanted to have good things in my life, but I was stuck in emotional torment and despair.

'Like the man in John 5, Jesus did not give me pity either. Jesus was actually very firm with me and He applied a lot of tough love, but His refusal to let me wallow in self-pity was a turning point in my life. I am not in the pit any longer. I now have a great life. If you will reject self-pity, actively look to God and do what He instructs you to do, you can have a great life too.'[2]

PRAYER

Thank you, Lord, that you hear our prayers for healing for ourselves and others. Today I cry out to you for healing for...

OLD TESTAMENT READING

Judges 4:1–5:31
Pray for leadership

Everything rises and falls on leadership. If a business is well-led it tends to do well. If a church is well-led it usually flourishes. If a nation is well-led it will most often prosper.

After Sisera had 'cruelly oppressed the Israelites for twenty years, they cried to the LORD for *help*' (4:3). Sisera's mother looked out of the window waiting for Sisera to return. She cried out, 'Are they not finding and dividing the spoils: a woman or two for each man' (5:30). We get a hint here of how Sisera treated the people of God.

In answer to their God-sized prayer God raised up an outstanding leader. Deborah was both a spiritual leader (a 'prophetess') and also a political leader. She was 'leading Israel at that time' (4:4). She was a charismatic leader whose presence was so valued that Barak says to her, 'If you go with me, I will go; but if you don't go with me, I won't go' (v.8).

Interestingly, it is another woman, Jael, who finally finishes off Israel's oppressor (v.21).

Both women and men can make outstanding leaders. What matters is not gender but that leaders actively *lead*: 'When the princes in Israel *take the lead*, when the people willingly offer themselves – praise the LORD!' (5:2, 9).

Deborah and Barak gave God the glory (vv.1–5). Again, Joyce Meyer points out that God 'chooses to use and promote those who know they are nothing without him and who give him the glory and the credit for all their accomplishments. Every time you have a success in your life, remember to give God the glory'.[3]

The way in which God answered the prayer of his people was to raise up wise and humble leadership. As a result, 'the land had peace for forty years' (v.31c).

Deborah prayed that those who loved the Lord would be 'like the sun when it rises in its strength' (v.31b) – bringing warmth and energy; strong, bold and fearless.

PRAYER

Lord, I pray today that I would be 'like the sun when it rises in its strength' (v.31b). May I bring light in a dark world; may I show people the way.

7 May | Day 127
Twelve Ways to Be Useful to God

A water-bearer in India had two large pots, both hung on the ends of a pole, which he carried across his neck. One of the pots had a crack in it while the other pot was perfect and always delivered a full portion of water. At the end of the long walk from the stream to the house, the cracked pot always arrived half full.

The poor cracked pot was ashamed of its own imperfection, and miserable that it was able to accomplish only half of what it had been made to do. After two years of what it perceived to be a bitter failure, it spoke to the water-bearer one day by the stream:

'I am ashamed of myself, and I want to apologise to you. I have been able to deliver only half my load because this crack in my side causes water to leak out all the way back to your house. Because of my flaws, you have to do all of this work, and you don't get full value from your efforts.'

The bearer said to the pot, 'Did you notice that there were flowers only on your side of the path, but not on the other pot's side? That's because I have always known about your flaw, and I planted flower seeds on your side of the path, and every day while we walk back, you've watered them. For two years I have been able to pick these beautiful flowers to decorate the table. Without you being just the way you are, there would not be this beauty to grace the house.'

Thankfully, God uses cracked pots! You do not need to be perfect for God to use you. We want our lives to count for something. If you want to be useful to God, here are twelve keys:

READING FROM PSALMS

Psalm 57:7–11
1. Know that you are loved

God uses you because he loves you. David says, 'For *great is your love*, reaching to the heavens; your faithfulness reaches to the skies' (v.10). This is where it all starts – knowing that you are loved by God.

2. Worship the Lord whatever

God is looking for worshippers. David says, 'My heart is *steadfast*, O God... I will sing and make music... I will *praise you*, O Lord' (vv.7–9). Respond to the experience of God's love by worshipping him with every gift that you have – not just privately but also in public (v.9) – not just when you feel like it but '*steadfastly*' – in difficult times as well.

3. Honour God in your life

God honours those who honour him. David writes, 'Be exalted, O God, above the heavens; let your glory be over all the earth' (v.11). This is David's ultimate desire. It is the same desire that is expressed in the prayer that Jesus taught us to pray, 'hallowed be your name' (Matthew 6:9).

PRAYER
Lord, thank you for your great love for me that reaches to the heavens and for your faithfulness that reaches to the skies. I pray today that your name will be honoured through everything I do and say.

NEW TESTAMENT READING

John 5:16–30
4. Do what 'the Father' is doing

The Pharisees, who were deeply religious, had become corrupted, legalistic and rigid. They criticised Jesus because a man paralysed for thirty-eight years had carried his bed on the Sabbath.

Jesus is in communion with God and is the beloved Son of God who does everything the Father wants him to do. He cannot be separated from his Father. He is one with the Father.

Jesus is God: 'he was even calling God his own Father, making himself equal with God' (v.18). Yet Jesus is also the obedient Son of his Father. He said in response to those who wanted to kill him: 'I tell you the truth, the Son can do nothing by himself; he can do only what he *sees his Father doing*, because whatever *the Father does the Son also does*' (v.19).

Rather than initiating your own plans and asking God to bless them, try to see what God's plans are and join in.

5. Listen to God

The people of God got themselves into trouble, as we see in today's Old Testament passage, because they did not listen to God (Judges 6:10). Jesus says the key to life is to listen to him and believe: 'I tell you the truth, those who hear my word and believe him who sent me have eternal life and will not be condemned; they have crossed over from death to life' (John 5:24).

Even Jesus says, 'I can't do a solitary thing on my own: I *listen*, then I decide' (v.30, MSG).

6. Do all the good you can

You cannot earn your salvation by 'doing good'. However, the evidence of a life of faith is a life of doing good. Jesus himself, we are told, 'went around *doing good*' (Acts 10.38). Jesus says, 'For a time is coming when all who are in their graves will hear his voice and come out – those who have *done good* will rise to live, and those who have done evil will rise to be condemned' (John 5:28–29).

As Barack Obama said, 'Don't wait for good things to happen to you. If you go out and make some good things happen, you will fill the world with hope, you will fill yourself with hope.'

7. Seek to please God

I find this one of the hardest things to even begin to put into practice. It seems so natural to seek to please myself. Jesus said, 'I seek *not* to please myself but him who sent me' (v.30). To live a life seeking to please God involves a complete U-turn. It is not only a one-off U-turn but it is something that you have to try to put into practice every day. It is not easy!

PRAYER
Father, help me to listen to your voice, to discern what you are doing and join in – not seeking to please myself but rather seeking to please you.

OLD TESTAMENT READING

Judges 6:1–7:8a
8. Cry out to the Lord for help

The people of God were in trouble once again. They had done 'evil in the eyes of the LORD' (6:1). As a result they were oppressed (v.2) and 'reduced to grinding poverty' (v.6, MSG).

The turning point came for them, as it so often does for us, when they 'cried out to the LORD for help' (v.6). I am so thankful for the many times in my life when God has answered my cry for help. Whatever difficulties and challenges you are facing today, cry out to the Lord for help.

9. Know that God is with you

God raised up Gideon and said to him, '*The LORD is with you*, mighty warrior' (v.12). Gideon said to God, 'But Lord... How can I save Israel? My clan is the weakest in Manasseh, and I am the least in my family' (v.15). The Lord answered, '*I will be with you*' (v.16).

Jesus, has promised that *he will be with you always,* until the very end of the age (Matthew 28:20).

10. Know your weaknesses

Gideon is another example of God using cracked pots! Gideon said, 'How can I save Israel? My clan is the *weakest* in Manasseh, and I am the *least* in my family' (Judges 6:15). I often feel that God cannot use me because of my weaknesses. But sometimes God works through our weaknesses better than through our strengths.

Personally, I draw great comfort from the words of the apostle Paul: 'Therefore I will boast all the more gladly about my *weaknesses*, so that Christ's power may rest on me ... For when I am *weak*, then I am strong' (2 Corinthians 12:9–10).

11. Obey God fearlessly

Gideon 'did as the LORD told him' (Judges 6:27), even though he risked death (v.30). I find that I am often timid in the face of opposition. However, the opposition we face is nothing compared to what Gideon and, certainly, what Jesus faced. When fear knocks on the door of your life, let faith answer!

12. Be God-confident

The secret of Gideon's power was that 'the Spirit of the LORD came upon [him]' (v.34). Don't be self-confident; be God-confident.

God does not need large numbers. In fact he said to Gideon, 'you have *too many* men' (7:2). He does not want the people to think it was their own strength that saved them. He reduced the numbers from 32,000 to 300 (vv.1–7).

We do not need large numbers to see a nation transformed but we do need the power of the Holy Spirit. If you are confident in God, he can work through you as he did through Gideon.

PRAYER

Lord, I need your Holy Spirit if I am going to fulfil the calling you have given me. Please send your Holy Spirit upon me today. Come, Holy Spirit.

8 May | Day 128
How to Live in High Definition

It was back in 1966 when England last won the football World Cup, yet I can still remember the moment. As children, we were watching the match on a black and white television set. We could never get a very good picture; it was always fuzzy and going into lines. We were quite happy with it since we did not know anything different. One day, we discovered all it needed was an aerial! Suddenly, we found that we could get clear and distinct pictures. Our enjoyment was transformed.

Now, not only do we have colour television, we can get high definition (HD). There are no fuzzy lines or distortions, and it produces a richer, bolder and more vibrant picture than ever before.

Rather than black and white, or even colour, Jesus offers you high-definition life. There are two Greek words for 'life'. The word 'bios', from which we get the word 'biological' means the condition of being *alive* rather than dead – mere existence. The other word 'zoe' means the full, abundant, spacious, open-hearted, richness of life that Jesus speaks about – a life of fulfilment and purpose. This is life in high definition.

READING FROM PROVERBS

Proverbs 11:19–28
Enjoy the high-definition life

The book of Proverbs sets out two paths: one leads to 'death' (v.19b); the other leads to '*life*' (v.19a). The path that leads to death is the path of evil (v.19b), perversity (v.20a), wickedness (v.21a), meanness (v.24b), hoarding (v.26a) and trusting in wealth (v.28a).

The path that leads to *life* is for those who are righteous (vv.19, 21). *You* are 'righteous' through your faith in Jesus Christ (Romans 3:22).

In this passage we see a description of what this *life* is like. It is not mere existence. It is high-definition living. It means enjoying God's *delight* (Proverbs 11:20b). It is a life of *freedom* (v.21b). It 'ends only in *good*' (v.23).

When you are generous, you are 'enriched'. When you 'refresh' others, you are 'refreshed' (v.25).

This does not mean that life is without its difficulties, challenges and suffering. But ultimately, you will be *crowned with blessing* (v.26b). You will find *goodwill* (v.27a) and will '*thrive* like a green leaf' (v.28b).

PRAYER

Lord, thank you that you give me the righteousness of Christ by faith and put me on a path that leads to life.

NEW TESTAMENT READING

John 5:31–47
Encounter Jesus daily

If we fail to see that the Bible is about Jesus and a relationship with him, reading it can easily become a dry, academic and arid activity. Once you understand that it is all about Jesus, and you see that studying the Bible is a way to grow in your relationship with him, it becomes the source of life (v.40).

The way to find life is to come to Jesus. On numerous occasions, especially in John's Gospel, Jesus refers to this life as 'eternal life' (for example, v.39). Eternal life comes from this relationship (v.40). It starts now and goes on for ever. It is the high-definition life.

How can you know that Jesus really is who he says he is? As if in a court of law, Jesus calls *four witnesses,* as evidence, to support his case.

1. The *first witness* Jesus calls is *other people* – in particular, John the Baptist (vv.31–35). John came as 'a witness to testify' (1:7). Today, there are more witnesses than ever before (over 2 billion) pointing to Jesus.
2. The *second witness* Jesus calls is his *own life work*. This is a 'weightier' witness than the first one – it is the 'very work the Father has given me to *finish*' (5:35), which culminates in the resurrection of the crucified Christ who cries out on the cross, 'It is *finished*' (19:30).
3. The *third witness* Jesus calls is the *Father's direct testimony* (5:37). You too can experience his direct testimony today through his Spirit in your heart (15:26).
4. The *fourth witness* Jesus calls is the *Scriptures*. The whole Bible is about Jesus and about coming into a relationship with him. Jesus says, 'These are the Scriptures that *testify about me*' (5:39). He says, 'Moses ... *wrote about me*' (v.46).

It is possible to 'study the Scriptures' but miss the whole point. Jesus says to religious leaders, 'You diligently study the Scriptures because you think that by them you possess eternal life. These are *the Scriptures that testify about me*, yet you refuse to *come to me to have life*' (vv.39–40). Every time you study the Bible, expect to encounter Jesus.

Even though there is ample evidence about Jesus, ultimately coming to him is an act of the will. And some, Jesus says, 'refuse to come to me to have life' (v.40). Why would anyone refuse?

Some are not willing to put God first in their lives (v.42). Others are more concerned about what people think than about what God thinks (v.44). Still others simply refuse to believe in spite of the evidence (v.47). 'If you believed, really believed, what Moses said, you would believe me. He wrote of me' (v.46, MSG).

Jesus touches our fundamental sin. We are continually seeking honour, glory and admiration from one another – seeking our own glory (v.44).

Do not worry about what other people think. What God thinks is what matters. Encounter Jesus again today and enjoy the full, abundant, spacious, open-hearted, high-definition life which Jesus offers.

PRAYER

Lord Jesus, today I come to you – the source of life. As I study the Scriptures, may my heart burn within me as I encounter you.

OLD TESTAMENT READING

Judges 7:8b–8:35
Examine the biblical examples

Gideon is listed in the New Testament as an example of someone who lived 'by faith' (Hebrews 11:32–33). He, therefore, received a foretaste of this 'high–definition' life.

Gideon knew the Lord, who spoke to him and told him he was going to give him victory over the Midianites (Judges 7:9). Gideon 'worshipped God' (v.15) even *before* he had won the battle. This demonstrated his faith and inspired the others.

Such was Gideon's faith that he went into battle with only 300 men – each with a torch in one hand and a trumpet in the other ('leaving no chance to use swords', v.20, AMP). Faith and confidence was not in themselves but in God, who gave them a great victory.

Whatever battles you are facing today, put all of your confidence and trust in God instead of in your own ability to cope. Like Gideon, resolve in faith to worship God ahead of the battle and walk with the boldness that comes from God-confidence. Whatever God has asked you to do may seem impossible for you, but it is not impossible for him.

Learn from studying the example of Gideon:

1. Wisdom in dealing with criticism
When 'the Ephraimites asked Gideon, "Why didn't you call us when you went to fight Midian?" they criticised him sharply' (8:1). Gideon dealt with this criticism with great charm and tact. He said to them, 'What have I accomplished compared to you? ... What was I able to do compared to you?' (vv.2–3a). And we are told, 'At this, their resentment against him subsided' (v.3b).

On the whole, people want to be valued for what they do. They want to be included in God's plans. Criticism may flow from a person who is feeling underused or undervalued. Once the Ephraimites realised that Gideon valued them and rated them highly, their criticism subsided.

Sometimes, I forget the wisdom of this example. I respond to criticism in the wrong way. But I have been struck by how often, if we go to people and say, 'I need your help' (in effect, 'what have I accomplished compared to you?'), their criticism subsides.

2. Determination when exhausted
'Gideon and his 300 men, *exhausted yet keeping up the pursuit...*' (v.4). There are times in life when we feel exhausted. Most often it is wise to stop, rest and get refreshed. But there are some occasions when you just have to keep going. Presumably, Gideon's strength came from the fact that the Spirit of the Lord had come upon him (6:34).

The life of Gideon is an inspiration. But there is also a warning. After his great victory, he became overconfident and failed to consult God. He thought of a nice idea and went ahead. It turned out to be a disaster. He made a golden ephod that became 'a snare to Gideon and his family' (8:27).

Although Gideon, like us all, was a fallible human being, he is listed in Hebrews as one of the great people of faith. Yet, you are better off than Gideon: 'God had planned something *better for us...*' (Hebrews 11:40). You can enjoy an even better life than Gideon. You can enjoy full, abundant, spacious, high-definition living by faith in Jesus.

PRAYER

Lord, thank you that I can enjoy 'high-definition living', life in all its fullness, through faith in Jesus. Please give me, today, wisdom and energy through the power of your Holy Spirit within me.

9 May | Day 129
How to Reap Far More Than You Sow

Walter Nishioka knew that the service was good at the Hawaiian hotel where he ate brunch on Wednesdays. But he found out just how good it was when he was offered something that was definitely not on the menu – one of the waiter's own kidneys.

Mr Nishioka, aged seventy, was a local businessman. He was seriously ill with kidney disease and had been told by doctors that he needed a transplant urgently. He had almost given up hope of finding a matching donor until the waiter, Jose Rocasa, fifty-two, volunteered one of his own. Nishioka said, 'I didn't have long to survive and the doctors said that it was unlikely that they could find a match in time. But with this good man here and a lot of help from above, now I am alive and well.'

In the twenty-two years that Mr Nishioka had frequented the hotel, Jose Rocasa had been his waiter, and recalled that he had always been kind and affable – and had tipped generously. 'I just wanted to help him,' he said. 'For years, we have this friendship in which he comes to lunch and I do my best to make him very happy, and he is always good to me in return. So of course I say, "Don't worry – I can give you a kidney."'[1]

Mr Nishioka sowed generosity and he reaped generosity!

Today, we see that:

- You reap *what* you sow
- You reap *later* than you sow
- You reap *more* than you sow.

READING FROM PSALMS

Psalm 58:1–11
Sow justice

Hundreds of thousands of people (mainly women and children) are trafficked for sex every year in this almost unbelievably evil trade. There are millions of people in modern day slavery. Almost every day we read of atrocities carried out by ruthless tyrants and evil regimes.

The psalmist speaks out against this kind of injustice: 'Is this any way to run a country? Is there an honest politician in the house?' (v.1, MSG).

He cries out against rulers who do not speak justly (v.1), whose hearts devise injustice and whose hands 'mete out violence' (v.2). They are 'cauldrons of evil', doing 'deals with demons' (v.2, MSG) and they speak out lies (v.3). They ignore the cries of those who desire justice – both humans and God himself – for they are like 'a cobra that has stopped its ears, that will not heed the tune of the charmer, however skilful the enchanter may be' (vv.4b–5).

Leadership is key in any society. A leader who sows injustice will reap terrible consequences. They are sowing poison: 'Their venom is like the venom of a snake' (v.4). They create an unstable society and will eventually be 'swept away' (v.9). When this happens there will be great relief all round. They reap what they sow. Likewise, 'the righteous … are rewarded' (v.11a). When we see this principle at work we say, 'there is a God' (v.11).

Often, the reaping will happen a lot later than the sowing. Even if we have to wait until the final judgment, this psalm reminds us that justice will take place. God's judgment is a good thing. It stems from his love. God values each one of us so much that he cares how we treat one another. Ultimately, injustice will not triumph. Justice will prevail and the righteous will 'be glad' (v.10).

PRAYER

Lord, help me to do everything I can to sow justice in this world. Help me to fight against injustice wherever I see it.

NEW TESTAMENT READING

John 6:1–24
Sow generously

There are, of course, so many lessons to be learned from events in the life of Jesus. One of these is the principle that *those who sow generously will also reap generously*.

Jesus looked up and saw a great crowd coming towards him. 'He said to Philip, "Where can we buy bread to feed these people?" He said this to *stretch* Philip's *faith*' (vv.5–6a, MSG). Faith is like a muscle, it grows by *stretching*.

In fact, although Jesus asked the question 'he already had in mind what he was going to do' (v.6b). This shows that it is alright to ask questions to which you already know the answer. (In fact, when I was practising as a barrister I was taught *only* to ask questions to which I already knew the answer!)

'Philip answered him, "Eight months' wages would not buy enough bread for each one to have a bite!" Another of his disciples … spoke up, "Here is a boy with five small barley loaves and two small fish, but how far will they go among so many?"' (vv.7–8).

This boy's act of generosity will never be forgotten. Jesus is able to do *a lot with a little*. The boy gave generously all that he had. It was not very much – it was 'a drop in the bucket for a crowd like this' (v.8, MSG).

However, it multiplied in the hands of Jesus. At least 5,000 people were fed and there was plenty left over. Jesus said, 'Gather the pieces that are left over. *Let nothing be wasted*' (v.12). If it needed a biblical basis, here is a biblical basis for not wasting food – it always seems a terrible waste if food is thrown away unnecessarily.

The world produces enough food to feed everyone. Yet, well over half a billion people are suffering from chronic undernourishment.[2] At the same time, around a third of the food produced in the world for human consumption every year gets lost or wasted. Individually and corporately we need to act urgently on Jesus' instruction: 'Let nothing be wasted' (v.12).

What you give to Jesus, he multiplies. The apostle Paul wrote, 'Remember this: Whoever sows sparingly will also reap sparingly, and whoever sows generously will also reap generously' (2 Corinthians 9:6).

Make it your aim to be the most generous person you know. Be generous with your money, your possessions, your time and your love. You cannot out-give God. The more you give the more you will harvest and the more you will enjoy the favour of God on your life.

Straight after this amazing miracle of the feeding of the 5,000, the disciples find themselves in a storm (John 6:18). Jesus calls his disciples to move from a faith based on a very visible miracle that fulfilled their physical need to a faith that is a total trust in him and his words.

Miraculously, Jesus walks on the water towards them. They were 'scared senseless' (v.19, MSG). Jesus says to them, 'It's me. It's all right. Don't be afraid' (v.20, MSG). Following Jesus is not always easy. There are storms and other challenges of life, but Jesus' presence with us is transformational. No wonder the crowd went 'in search of Jesus' (v.24).

PRAYER

Thank you, Jesus, that what I give to you, you multiply. Lord, help me to be generous with everything – with money, possessions, hospitality and time.

OLD TESTAMENT READING

Judges 9:1–57
Sow loyalty

I have noticed, over the years, how those who sow loyalty to their leaders reap a high degree of loyalty when they themselves come into positions of leadership. On the other hand, those who refuse to come under another's leadership and who stir up trouble, invariably reap the same attitude of disloyalty if they themselves come into a position of leadership.

In this passage we see the disastrous consequences of the disloyalty of Abimelech to his father and to his brothers. Abimelech was a passionate leader, a good communicator and a skilled tactician but he was also arrogant and self-promoting. He wanted no rivals. Abimelech sowed violence. 'He hired some reckless, riffraff soldiers ... and killed his half brothers ... seventy men!' (vv.4–5, MSG). The youngest managed to hide – the only survivor.

Again, we see this biblical principle at work: we reap what we sow. Abimelech sowed disloyalty and violence. He reaped disloyalty and violence. Initially, he was in cahoots with the citizens of Shechem (v.2 and following). But three years later bad feeling arose between Abimelech and the citizens of Shechem, who had acted treacherously against Abimelech.

Abimelech reaped what he had sown. Shechem's leaders 'worked treacherously behind his back. Violence boomeranged: the murderous violence that killed the seventy brothers, the sons of Jerub-Baal, was now loose among Abimelech and Shechem's leaders, who had supported the violence' (vv.23–24, MSG).

Abimelech showed no loyalty to the people of Shechem. He used them when he needed them (v.2). However, he had no hesitation in wiping them out (vv.42–49).

Ultimately, they all reaped what they had sown, and Abimelech himself was ingloriously killed soon after (vv.53–54). The writer sums it all up: 'God avenged the evil Abimelech had done to his father, murdering his seventy brothers. And God brought down on the heads of the men of Shechem all the evil that they had done' (vv.56–57, MSG).

PRAYER

Lord, help us to be loyal to one another in the church, in the workplace, in our families and in our friendships. Help us as a community to sow truth and justice, generosity and loyalty.

10 May | Day 130
God Turns Your Weakness into Strength

The great Christian leader, John Stott, was speaking on one occasion at a university mission in Sydney, Australia. On the last night of the mission, as a result of an infection, he had virtually lost his voice.

Nevertheless, he was persuaded to speak. Waiting in the side room beforehand, he whispered a request that the words of the 'thorn in the flesh' verses from 2 Corinthians 12 be read to him. The conversation between Jesus and the apostle Paul came alive.

Stott (Paul): 'I beg you to take it away from me.'

Jesus: 'My grace is sufficient for you, for my power is made perfect in weakness.'

Stott (Paul): 'I will all the more gladly boast of my weaknesses, that the power of Christ may rest upon me... for when I am weak, then I am strong.'

When the time came to speak he croaked the gospel through the microphone in a monotone, utterly unable to modulate his voice or exert his personality in any way. But all the time he was crying to the Lord to perfect *Christ's power* through *his weakness*.

He went back to Australia many times after that, and on every occasion somebody came up to him and said, 'Do you remember that final service in the University Great Hall, when you had lost your voice? I came to Christ that night.'[1]

As someone who is very aware of my own weaknesses, I find it encouraging that when I feel weak, I am not alone. As you put your *faith* in God he turns your weakness into strength.

READING FROM PSALMS

Psalm 59:1–8
Faith and opposition

God is your strength in times of difficulty. Belief in God is not the recipe for an easy life. In fact, the reverse is the case. You are likely to face all kinds of opposition.

David's life was under threat. Saul had sent men to watch David's house in order to kill him. He finds himself surrounded by 'enemies ... mutineers ... dirty tricks ... hit men ... desperadoes ... they're after me, determined to get me' (vv.1–4, MSG).

Yet, in the midst of this, David prays, 'Rescue me...' (vv.1–2, MSG) and has total confidence that the Lord can and will deliver him (v.8). Later in the psalm, twice David calls on God: '*O my Strength*' (vv.9, 17).

He is able to say, 'I did nothing to deserve this, GOD, crossed no one, wronged no one' (v.4, MSG). David was not perfect (see, for example, 2 Samuel 11). However, sometimes you may face difficulties not because you are doing something wrong but because you are doing something right.

Cry out to God for help in times of personal difficulties. 'Arise to help me; look on my plight' (Psalm 59:4b). You can also cry out to God for help at times of international crisis. The very next sentence is a prayer for the nation (v.5a). At whatever level the opposition appears, ask the Lord for his deliverance, help and intervention.

PRAYER

O my Strength, help me to trust you in times of difficulty and opposition. Deliver us from those who oppose your plans.

NEW TESTAMENT READING

John 6:25–59
Faith and emptiness

Jesus taught about the centrality of faith. When asked, '"What must we do to do the works God requires?" Jesus answered, "The work of God is this: to *believe* in the one he has sent"' (vv.28–29).

We are called, primarily, 'believers', not 'achievers'. The way we achieve is by first believing.

Jesus says, 'I am the bread of life' (v.35). When we are physically hungry we crave food. But as well as physical needs you have spiritual needs and a spiritual hunger. The bread Jesus is talking about is the Word made flesh, present with them as a friend. Jesus is offering us a personal, intimate, heart-to-heart relationship with him. It is the gift of his total person to each one of us.

Faith in Jesus fills the emptiness you experience and satisfies your spiritual hunger for purpose, permanence and pardon.

1. Purpose

Physical bread is not enough. Material things alone do not satisfy. Money, homes, cars, success and even human relationships do not satisfy our desire for ultimate purpose in life.

The bread that does satisfy is the 'bread of life'. This is not a commodity that Jesus supplies. He is the gift and the giver. The words, 'I' or 'me' appear thirty-five times in this discussion. '*I am* the bread of life. Whoever comes *to me* will never go hungry, and whoever *believes in me* will never be thirsty' (v.35).

It is easy, even once you have put your faith in Jesus, to get caught up either in material things or the trappings of religion. But it is actually only a relationship with Jesus that satisfies our spiritual hunger.

The expressions, 'Believe in me' (v.29), 'Come to me' (v.35), 'Look to the Son' (v.40), 'Eat my flesh and drink my blood' (v.53 onwards) describe living in an intimately close relationship with Jesus.

2. Permanence

We are all going to die. Death is the great unmentionable reality. Jesus says *this life is not the end*: 'I am the living bread that came down from heaven. Whoever eats of this bread *will live for ever ... I will raise them up* on the last day' (vv.51, 54).

Jesus promises to raise you up at the last day and that you will live for ever. You can have absolute assurance that your relationship with Jesus will outlast death.

There is both a present and a future dimension to this eternal life. They said, '*From now on* give us this bread' (v.34). Jesus says it can be received immediately (v.35 onwards). Yet he also made clear that it will last for ever (vv.50–51).

3. Pardon

Forgiveness is actually our greatest need. The atheist philosopher, Marghanita Laski, said, 'What I envy most about you Christians is your forgiveness. I have no one to forgive me.'[2] We all want to know that we are pardoned for all that we have done wrong.

Jesus said, 'This bread is my flesh, which I give for the life of the world' (v.51). His blood was shed for the forgiveness of sins. Every time you receive communion, you are reminded that Jesus gave his life so that you could be forgiven.

How do you receive this bread? Jesus says, 'I tell you the truth, whoever *believes* has everlasting life. I am the bread of life' (vv.47–48). While there is no separate account of Jesus' institution of Holy Communion in John's Gospel, here we see Jesus' teaching on communion set in the context of faith.

Among other things, communion is a visible sign that helps us receive Christ by faith (vv.53–58). It reveals and nourishes the friendship Jesus wants to have with you. It is a gift of his love and a sign of his desire to dwell in you all the time.

PRAYER

Lord, thank you that through faith in you I have found a lasting purpose in my life, forgiveness for my sins and the promise of eternal life. Help me today to walk in a close, intimate relationship with you.

OLD TESTAMENT READING

Judges 10:1–11:40
Faith and fallibility

As we read through the ongoing saga of the people of God sinning, crying out to the Lord and being rescued by Judges, we come across one of the most disturbing stories in the entire Bible.

Jephthah is described as a 'mighty warrior' (11:1). His mother was a prostitute (v.1). His half-brothers drove him away (v.2). He gathered a group of adventurers around him (v.3). He became a remarkable leader. The Spirit of the Lord came upon him (v.29), and he was used by God to secure victory over the Ammonites – 'the LORD gave them into his hands' (v.32).

However, there is an incident in his life that is almost unbearable to read. He made a vow to God that if God gave him victory, he would sacrifice whatever came out of the door of his house to meet him upon his return. It was his daughter, his only child. And, it appears, that is what he did (vv.29–40).

It is important to note that God never asked him to make this vow. Nor did he ask him to carry out the sacrifice. Indeed, it went against all the teaching of the Old Testament, which forbade child sacrifice. Jephthah never actually seeks God's will in this situation. It seems to be his own pride that drives him to put his reputation above the life of his daughter. This shows the fallibility of even great people of faith.

In spite of his weakness, he is listed in the book of Hebrews as one of the heroes of faith whose weakness was turned into strength (Hebrews 11:32–34).

PRAYER

Lord, thank you for the way you use people of faith and turn our weakness into strength. Help me today to live a life of faith, trusting and believing in Jesus, who is 'the bread of life' (John 6:35).

11 May | Day 131
Endless Energy, Boundless Strength

We often tell the story of when John Wimber first visited our church. We saw a remarkable outpouring of the Holy Spirit and several healings. One incident, which occurred on the second night, is indelibly printed in my memory. One of our closest friends was eight months pregnant at the time. The Holy Spirit came upon her with great power. She started to whirl around at high speed. As she did so, she exclaimed over and over again, 'I feel so *strong*!'

A few weeks later she gave birth to a son who, from his earliest days, showed not only spiritual and emotional strength but also extraordinary physical strength. He became an outstanding rugby player, a superb athlete and is now a successful model.

To some (like Samson, who we read about in today's Old Testament passage), the Holy Spirit gives extraordinary physical strength. To all of us, the Holy Spirit gives spiritual strength.

The apostle Paul describes God's 'incomparably great power for us who believe. That power is like the working of his *mighty strength*, which he exerted in Christ when he raised him from the dead' (Ephesians 1:19–20).

It was the Holy Spirit who raised Jesus from the dead (Romans 8:11a). The Holy Spirit is 'his mighty strength'. That same strength now lives in *you* and 'will give life to your mortal body through his Spirit, *who lives in you*' (v.11b).

I love Eugene Peterson's translation (of the Ephesians passage) where he speaks of God giving 'endless energy, *boundless strength*'!

READING FROM PSALMS

Psalm 59:9–17
O my strength

Are you struggling with some issue in your life? Do you feel deeply troubled?

Like David, who was in deep trouble, call out to God today: '*O my Strength*, I watch for you; you, O God, are my fortress, my loving God' (vv.9–10a).

The psalm ends in triumph: 'But I will sing of *your strength*, in the morning I will sing of your love; for you are my fortress, my refuge in times of trouble. *O my Strength*, I sing praise to you; you, O God, are my fortress, my loving God' (vv.16–17).

PRAYER

Lord, thank you that you are my '*Strength*', my loving God. Please give me your endless energy and boundless strength.

NEW TESTAMENT READING

John 6:60–7:13
A tough call

Do you ever find the teaching of Jesus very hard to live out? Do you sometimes find it difficult to be a Christian, in the workplace, for example? Do you sometimes find people seem to dislike you for no good reason? Do you ever feel like giving up following Jesus?

If you want an easy life I don't recommend following Jesus. It was not easy then. It's not easy now. Alice Cooper, the rock singer said, 'Drinking beer is easy. Trashing your hotel is easy. But being a Christian, that's *a tough call*. That's real rebellion.'[1]

Following Jesus *is a tough call*. And yet, at the same time, it is the way to life in all its fullness. This fullness of life comes, Jesus explains, from the Holy Spirit.

The teaching of Jesus is not easy. The disciples said, 'This is a hard *and* difficult *and* strange saying ... Who can stand to hear it?' (6:60, AMP). In fact, some of the teaching of Jesus was *so hard* that 'many of his disciples turned back and no longer followed him' (v.66). The chapter begins with many people following Jesus. It ends with many people turning away from him.

It is not so much that the hearers found Jesus' teaching difficult to understand, but that they did not like its content. They actually found his teaching offensive (v.61). It seems that they were particularly offended by Jesus' huge claims. He claimed to be 'the bread of life', he called them to believe in him and he offered eternal life.

Not only was this teaching 'hard', it was 'hated'. Jesus says, 'The world ... *hates* me because I testify that what it does is evil' (7:7).

He was accused of being a deceiver (v.12). There was a very high cost in following someone who was hated in this way.

When many turned back and no longer followed him, apparently, deeply wounded in his heart, Jesus asked the Twelve, 'You do not want to leave too, do you?' Simon Peter, the spokesperson for the group, answered him, 'Lord, to whom shall we go? You have the words of eternal life. We believe and know that you are the Holy One of God' (6:67–69).

This is such a powerful truth. Jesus has the words of eternal life. He is the Holy One of God. He is the only one to go to.

In this passage, we see the whole Trinity. Peter recognises Jesus as 'the Holy One of God' (v.69). Jesus is unique. He embodies the holiness of God. He is divine. He speaks about the Father (v.65). He also speaks of the Holy Spirit (v.63).

Jesus says, '*The Spirit* gives life' (v.63a). Just as physical flesh gives birth to physical life, so the Holy Spirit gives birth to spiritual life. He says, 'The words I have spoken to you are *spirit* and they are life' (v.63b).

All this takes place just before the 'Festival of Tents' (7:2, ISV). Families would leave their homes and live in tents for eight days of joyful celebrations (rather like our summer church holiday!). They would give thanks to God for water that brings life. This was the setting Jesus chose to teach them about his life-giving Holy Spirit.

When Jesus speaks of eternal life, he is speaking of a quality of life that starts now and goes on for ever: '*life in all its fullness*' (10:10). This is the kind of life that the Holy Spirit brings. That is why, although there is a cost in following Jesus, the benefits far outweigh the cost. In fact, there is no real alternative. Only Jesus can give you the Holy Spirit. Only Jesus can give you fullness of life.

PRAYER

Lord, I need your Holy Spirit to give me life. Please fill me with your Holy Spirit so that the words I speak today may be 'spirit' and 'life' to those who hear (6:63).

OLD TESTAMENT READING

Judges 12:1–13:25
His extraordinary power

Do you ever get frustrated by the length of time God seems to take to answer your prayers? God is never in a hurry, but he is always on time.

We see in this passage God's elaborate preparation for the birth of Samson, whose extraordinary power was to save the people of his day. But this only prefigured something that would take even longer. Hundreds of years later, John the Baptist arose (who was in many ways like Samson) to prepare for the ultimate Saviour of the world.

God often specially blesses the children of those who have waited a long time to have children and have thought it was an impossibility, for example: Sarah with Isaac; Elizabeth with John the Baptist.

Samson was like John the Baptist in many ways:

1. In both cases, it was thought that the mother could not have children and something of a miracle was required (Judges 13:3; Luke 1:7).
2. In both cases, the angel of the Lord spoke clearly to the parents (Judges 13:7; Luke 1:13).
3. Both children were set apart for God from birth (Judges 13:7; Luke 1:14–17).
4. Neither of them was allowed to touch any alcohol (Judges 13:7; Luke 1:15).
5. *The Spirit of the Lord* came upon both of them from a very early moment in their lives (Judges 13:25; Luke 1:15).

Again, we see a hint of the whole Trinity in this passage. We read of 'the LORD' (Judges 13:1), but we also hear about the awesome '*angel of the LORD*' who appeared to Samson's parents (vv.3, 6) and who then ascended towards heaven in a flame (v.19).

'Seeing this, Manoah and his wife fell with their faces to the ground ... Manoah realised that it was *the angel of the LORD*: "We are doomed to die!" he said to his wife. "We have seen God!"' (vv.19–22). (Thankfully he had a 'sensible wife'!, v.23, AMP.)

Could '*the angel of the LORD*' be the second person of the Trinity? Jesus uses the language of the Son of Man *ascending* (John 6:62). Earlier in John's Gospel we read of 'the angels of God *ascending* and descending on the Son of Man' (John 1:51).

The third person of the Trinity, the Holy Spirit, is clearly at work here at the birth of Samson: 'The woman gave birth to a boy and named him Samson. He grew and the Lord blessed him, and the *Spirit of the LORD* began to stir him...' (Judges 13:24–25). The Holy Spirit gave Samson endless energy and boundless strength.

PRAYER

Lord, thank you for the extraordinary strength you gave to Samson. Please fill me with your Spirit today. Give me spiritual strength and power to resist the enemy and power to live a holy life.

12 May | Day 132
The Wonderful Holy Spirit

The singer Robbie Williams once went on a shopping spree in Los Angeles. He bought seven cars, including a brand new Ferrari, a brand new Porsche and a brand new Mercedes. Within a week he wished he had not bought any of them.

I admire Robbie Williams' openness about himself. He is ruthlessly honest about his self-obsession and addictions. In his song, *Feel*, he sings:

I just want to feel real love...
There's a hole in my soul
You can see it in my face
It's a real big place.[1]

God implants this desire 'to feel real love' in humanity. This 'hole in my soul' is common to all human beings. It cannot be filled by cars, wealth, success or drugs. It is a God-shaped hole. It is a spiritual hunger and thirst for God which Jesus told us could only be filled by his wonderful Holy Spirit (John 7:37).

READING FROM PROVERBS

Proverbs 11:29–12:7
Fruitfulness

Do you want your life to make a difference? Do you realise that your life can be a source of blessing to other people *every day*?

'*The fruit* of the righteous is *a tree of life*' (11:30). As we look back at Proverbs 11, we can see all *the fruit of the Spirit* that the apostle Paul describes in Galatians 5:22:

- love (Proverbs 11:23)
- joy (v.10)
- peace (v.8)
- patience (v.16)
- kindness (v.17)
- goodness (v.17)
- faithfulness (v.6)
- gentleness (v.2b)
- self-control (v.12).

The image of a 'tree of life' (v.30) is a beautiful depiction of God's favour. It recurs again and again in Scripture, and is also closely linked to the work of the Spirit in your life (see Ezekiel 47:1–12; Revelation 22:1–2). It is the Spirit who enables and helps you to live the kind of righteous life that is described and to enjoy '*favour from the Lord*' (Proverbs 12:2).

PRAYER

Lord, I pray for more of the fruit of the Spirit in my life today: more love, joy, peace, patience, kindness, goodness, faithfulness, gentleness and self-control.

NEW TESTAMENT READING

John 7:14–44
Fullness

You know what it is like to be physically thirsty. Your mouth goes dry, your throat is parched, your strength fades and you crave water. How satisfying it is to drink when you are thirsty.

To be spiritually thirsty is to be dried up inside, to feel totally empty and in anguish. In this golden passage, Jesus describes how your *spiritual* thirst can be quenched (the hole in your soul filled) and the effect that this can have on your life.

Jesus anticipates what will happen on the day of Pentecost. He speaks about the transformation by the streams of living water that the Holy Spirit brings to your life: 'By this he meant *the Spirit*, whom those who believed in him were *later to receive*. Up to that time *the Spirit* had not been given, since Jesus had not yet been glorified' (v.39).

It was 'the last and greatest day of the Feast' (v.37). This was the day when the people anticipated that the great river prophesied in Ezekiel 47 would flow out from Jerusalem. 'Jesus stood' (John 7:37). The usual custom was to sit when teaching, but the words Jesus had to say were so significant that he wanted to be seen and heard by all the people. He cried out 'in a loud voice' (v.37). His message is only twenty-four words in the Greek language, but it is a life-changing promise that you can still experience today.

1. Who makes this promise?

The people were amazed by Jesus' teaching. He had never even been to Bible school or theological college! (v.15). He received his teaching from God (v.16). And he says anyone who 'chooses to do the will of God' (v.17) will recognise this.

Jesus calls for a response. Some thought: 'Surely this man is the Prophet' (v.40). However, as C. S. Lewis pointed out, Jesus did not leave that option open. There are really only three options: that someone who said the sort of things Jesus said would either be insane or 'the Devil of Hell'. The only other possibility is that 'this man was, and is, the Son of God'.[2] We see these three options demonstrated in today's reading:

1. Some thought him *'the Devil of Hell'*: 'You are *demon-possessed*' (v.20)
2. Some thought him *insane*: 'He is... *raving mad*' (10:19)
3. But others recognised, *'He is the Christ'* (7:41).

2. To whom is the promise made?

Jesus said, 'Let *anyone who is thirsty* come to me and drink' (v.37). It is made to every person. It applies to *all* who have never experienced the Holy Spirit. But it also applies to those who feel dissatisfied spiritually. Do you feel like a failure in your prayer life? Do you feel frustrated at your level of holiness? Do you long for a closer relationship with God? If you do, you are spiritually 'thirsty' and the promise applies to you, today.

3. What is the promise?

Jesus says, 'Whoever believes in me, as the Scripture has said, will have streams of living water flowing from within' (v.38). The Feast of Tabernacles was anticipating the river that would flow out of the temple in Jerusalem as prophesied in Ezekiel 47 (which was read and enacted at the feast). Jesus tells them that this has been fulfilled, not in a place but in a *Person*.

The river flows out of the heart of Jesus (out of his *'koilia'* – the pit of his stomach or his innermost being) and out of *every* Christian (John 7:38) through our personal, heart-to-heart relationship with Jesus.

The river flows into you and out of you. The river will flow into the little 'Dead Seas' of our hearts and out from our 'innermost being'. Superficially, life may not be easy, but deep down the Holy Spirit *constantly flows* like a 'river of living water'.

This river does not flow once in a while. It flows continuously. It is not supposed to be blocked up. It should be constantly bubbling up and flowing out of us.

As Father Raniero Cantalamessa put it, 'A Christian in whom the Holy Spirit dwells is not exempt from having to experience struggle, temptations, disorderly desires, rebellious feelings... [the difference is that all these things come] upon him against his will.' They are on the surface. Yet there is a 'peace in the depth of their hearts. That is like a deep-ocean current always flowing steadily regardless of the wind and the waves on the surface'.

4. How do you receive the promise?

Jesus says let them 'come to me and drink' (v.37). It is a promise for 'whoever believes in me' (vv.38–39). It is as simple as that. It can flow from you as you come to him and drink today.

You become like Jesus. Through your love, your words, your presence, you will transmit the Spirit you have received from Jesus. You will quench the thirst of the poor, the lonely, the needy, those in pain and anguish and will give them life, love and peace of heart.

PRAYER

Lord, I come to you today. Fill me again with your Spirit, with streams of living water to bring life to everyone I encounter.

OLD TESTAMENT READING

Judges 14:1–15:20
Freedom

Are there habits in your life from which you long to break free? Are there thought patterns you need to change? Are there spiritual bondages from which you need to be released?

If anyone was 'wild at heart' it was Samson. He had extraordinary strength, might and ability. But his life was hardly a model. The story of Samson's life is bizarre, extraordinary and perhaps a bit embarrassing.

However, Samson is highlighted in the New Testament as one of the heroes of faith (Hebrews 11:32). God uses all types of people. He uses us in spite of our sins and weaknesses.

Samson's strength and successes are the result of his being filled with the Holy Spirit. On three occasions in today's passage we read that, 'The Spirit of the LORD came upon him in power' (Judges 14:6, 19; 15:14).

It is amazing what can happen when the Spirit of the Lord comes upon people 'in power'. As so often, what God did in the Old Testament in a physical way he did in the New Testament in a spiritual way. The wonderful Holy Spirit sets us free from spiritual bondages.

On the third occasion that 'the Spirit of the LORD came upon him in power, the ropes on his arms became like charred flax, and the bindings dropped from his hands' (15:14). This can be seen as a picture of release from our bad habits, obsessions and addictions. The power of the Holy Spirit can release you and me from the things that bound us.

PRAYER

Lord, fill me with streams of living water, satisfy my thirst, break every bondage and help me like Jesus, to demonstrate not only the power of the Spirit, but also the fruit of the wonderful Holy Spirit in my daily life.

13 May | Day 133

How to Deal with Desperate Times

'I don't suppose there are many places where Alpha happens to the sound of gunfire and rockets flying, but for us the message is simple: it is about hope, light and a future because it is about Jesus.'

This is what Canon Andrew White, former Vicar of St George's, Baghdad, wrote to me in a letter describing their Alpha course. They were in a desperate situation. The church had been bombed more than once. Many people in their congregation had been killed. Some of the leaders had been kidnapped. For some, profession of faith in Jesus means almost certain death. Yet in these desperate times, Andrew White is able to say that Jesus brings hope, light and a future.

David, in the Psalms, speaks of 'desperate times' (Psalm 60:3). There are times in life when everything seems to go wrong. Maybe even now you are facing a desperate situation – perhaps with your health, a bereavement, the breakdown of a relationship, work problems, family difficulties, financial trouble or a combination of these. Even in desperate times, you can find the three great virtues of faith, hope and love.

READING FROM PSALMS

Psalm 60:1–4
Hope despite apparent defeat

Sometimes it appears God's people are being defeated. While there is a great revival in many parts of the world, such as Asia; in Western Europe, for example, church attendance has been in decline. Churches get closed. Christian faith is marginalised.

There are desperate moments in the history of the people of God. This psalm is a national lament after a conquest by their enemies. The people of God felt rejected. David says, 'You have shown your people desperate times' (v.3a).

He uses the image of an earthquake to describe the desperation and uncertainty they faced: 'You have shaken the land and torn it open; mend its fractures, for it is quaking' (v.2). The same image is used today to describe turmoil in all spheres of life. The instability of the economy, corporate institutions, marriage and community are all often portrayed as shaking and fractured.

Yet, there is hope. David writes, 'But for those who fear you, you have raised a banner to be unfurled against the bow' (v.4). The Lord has designated a place where his people may find refuge under his protection and be confident in the Lord – even in desperate times.

PRAYER

Thank you, Lord, that even in desperate times, I can take refuge under your protection.

NEW TESTAMENT READING

John 7:45–8:11
Love rather than condemnation

Is sex outside marriage acceptable? Or is it sinful? If it is, what should our attitude be to those who are guilty of sexual sin?

The debate about sexual ethics continues to fill our media today. And the teaching of Jesus is as relevant now as it was 2,000 years ago.

The words of Jesus were the greatest words ever spoken, the kind of words you would expect God to speak. The temple guards declared, 'No one ever spoke the way this man does' (7:46). (It is so sad that some religious leaders failed to recognise him and regarded those who did believe in him as 'this mob', v.49.)

This woman, caught in the act of adultery, must have felt absolutely desperate. Despair can come from defeat. It can also come from moral failure. She must have been experiencing both – filled with guilt, shame and fear of death.

The condemners tried to 'trap' Jesus with a question (8:6). Jesus gives one of the most brilliant, memorable and often quoted replies in the history of the world: 'Let any one of you who is without sin be the first to throw a stone at her' (v.7).

Jesus did not condone her adultery, nor did he regard it as the unforgivable sin. He demonstrated how easy it is to condemn others while being guilty of the same sins in our own hearts (vv.7–9). This can be applied to many areas of our lives. Before we criticise others, it is worth asking ourselves whether we are 'without sin' in that area that we are about to criticise in another.

When we judge, accuse and condemn others, we project on to them what we refuse to see in ourselves.

As is often said, 'People who live in glass houses shouldn't throw stones.' In the context of the debate about sexual ethics, as we look at our own hearts there is often a lot of glass around.

In the account of the woman caught in adultery, each of the condemners is convicted by Jesus' words until eventually 'only Jesus was left' (vv.7–9). Jesus asks her, 'Has no one condemned you?' (v.10). When she replies, 'No one, sir', he says, '*Then neither do I condemn you* ... Go now and leave your life of sin' (v.11).

Guilt is a horrible emotion. Condemnation is a terrible state to be in. How amazing it must have been to hear the words of Jesus: 'Then neither do I condemn you' (v.11). Since he was without sin, Jesus was the one person there in a position to 'throw stones', but he did not.

There is an extraordinary balance and almost unique combination in the words of Jesus – full of wisdom and grace, mercy and compassion. Jesus could not be clearer that adultery is sin. Yet he does not condemn her in any way. This is the message of the New Testament. There is no condemnation for those who are in Christ Jesus (Romans 8:1). As a result of Jesus' death for us on the cross, you and I can be totally forgiven, however far we may have fallen.

Yet, this is *not* a reason to go on sinning. Jesus does not condone her sin. He says to her, '*Leave your life of sin*' (v.11). Jesus does not condemn us. But he does say to us, as he said to her, 'Leave your life of sin.'

Jesus' words, as always, are motivated by love and compassion. Follow his example.

It is easy to fall into one of two opposite extremes. Either we condemn people or we condone sin. Love does not condemn nor does it condone sin, because sin leads to people getting hurt. If we love, like Jesus, we will neither condone sin nor condemn people, but lovingly challenge people (starting with ourselves) to leave sin behind.

The Greek word for 'to forgive' also means 'to liberate'. Jesus came to liberate you by the power of his Holy Spirit. You are liberated to love as God loves you. Forgiveness is at the heart of every relationship. It is the essence of love.

PRAYER

Lord, thank you that there is no condemnation for those who are in Christ Jesus. Thank you that you died to make it possible for me to be cleansed, forgiven and to go free. Help me to love people as you did.

OLD TESTAMENT READING

Judges 16:1–17:13
Faith in the midst of chaos

These were desperate times. There is a refrain that runs through the book of Judges: 'In those days Israel had no king; everyone did as they saw fit' (17:6). This was a time of chaos.

In these desperate times God raised up judges like Samson. He led Israel for twenty years (16:31). He was one of the heroes of faith (Hebrews 11:32).

Anointed by the Holy Spirit, God used him powerfully. However, he also had a weakness that led to immorality (sleeping with a prostitute, Judges 16:1–3) and deception (vv.4–10). Eventually, he pushed God to the limit through his persistent disobedience and 'the LORD ... left him' (v.20).

Samson received extraordinary strength from God. But it was directly related to his obedience. God had told him not to cut his hair. So long as he obeyed God he would have supernatural strength.

However great a person of God may be, it is vital to remember that strength comes from God alone. Jesus said, 'Without me you can do nothing' (John 15:5, NKJV). Never rely on past victories but rather on God who gave them.

After persistent temptation, Samson gave in and told Delilah the secret of his strength – although it must have been obvious to him by then that she would take advantage of him. She cut his hair and his strength was gone.

Not only was the society chaotic, but also Samson reached a point of utter desperation in his own life. He was in captivity, he was blind and his captors were about to make a spectacle of him (Judges 16:21–25).

In the midst of his despair, Samson prayed to the Lord: 'O Sovereign LORD, remember me. O God, please strengthen me just once more' (v.28). And God heard his prayer of faith. Even after all his failures, God still answered Samson's cry. No matter what the situation, and no matter what you have done, it is never too late to turn back to God.

PRAYER

Lord, thank you that I can find refuge in your presence, and that you always hear my desperate cries for help. Lord, help!

---

14 May | Day 134
It's Possible with God

I was eighteen years old when I first encountered Jesus. I remember distinctly a conversation I had with a Christian leader shortly afterwards. I said how glad I was that I had not become a Christian earlier, since I had been able to experience the difference between life without God and life with God. He pointed out the fallacy of this way of thinking and suggested that the sooner we experience life with God, the better.

Looking back on my life now, I see the wisdom of his words. I am so grateful to God that our children can look back on their own lives and say that there has never been a time in their life when they were 'without God'.

Over the years, I have interviewed hundreds of people who have encountered Jesus through Alpha. They contrast their life *without* God and their life *with God*. There is a sense of great joy and relief, and often regret that they did not begin their life *with God* earlier.

You are created to live in a relationship with God. Without that, life will never really make sense. Being *with* God is even more important than what you do *for* God. With God, everything is possible.

READING FROM PSALMS

Psalm 60:5–12
Gain the victory

Compared with God's help, human help is worthless. '*With God*', David says, 'we shall gain the victory' (v.12). He was speaking about physical battles. The apostle Paul writes that our main battles are not physical. They are not 'against flesh and blood, but ... against the spiritual forces of evil in the heavenly realms' (Ephesians 6:12).

David prays, 'Save us and help us with your right hand, that those you love may be delivered ... Give us aid against the enemy, for human help is worthless. *With God* we shall gain the victory' (Psalm 60:5, 11–12a).

PRAYER

Lord, thank you that *with you* I can be confident. In all the battles I am facing, I trust in you today.

NEW TESTAMENT READING

John 8:12–30
Give God pleasure

Do you realise that you can give God pleasure? Jesus says, 'I always do what pleases him' (v.29). This should be your aim in life – to please God.

Jesus models for us a life *with God*. He says, 'I am not alone. I stand with the Father, who sent me' (v.16). He says, 'The one who sent me is *with me*; he has not left me alone' (v.29a). Throughout this passage, we discover something about Jesus' relationship *with his Father*.

Jesus says, 'I know where I came from and where I am going' (v.14). So many people struggle in life because they don't know where they came from or where they are heading. They struggle with a lack of purpose and direction in their lives. In a close relationship with God, you can know where you came from and ultimately where you are heading.

Jesus' relationship with the Father was also the source of his purpose and direction day by day. He says, 'I do nothing on my own but speak just what the Father has taught me' (v.28). He says, 'The one who sent me is *with me*; he has *not left me alone*' (v.29a).

This is the model for us. God was *with* Jesus. Jesus knew he was never alone. There was not a single thing he did without God. At every moment his desire is to please God: 'I always do what pleases him' (v.29b). This is what gave his life such power and effectiveness. 'Even as he spoke, many put their faith in him' (v.30).

Not only was Jesus with God, he was God.

Twice in today's passage Jesus says, 'I am he' (8:24, 28). The words translated 'I am he' are the same words that are used in the Greek translation of Exodus 3:14–16. There, God revealed himself to Moses as 'I AM WHO I AM'. This name came to express both the identity of God *and* the closeness of God to his people.

Jesus uses this name himself. We do not possess existence. We are born and we die. We receive our existence. Jesus is existence. He is telling the people that God has once again come near to them in him. Jesus is Immanuel, *God with us*.

It is as you look to the cross that Jesus says you have the clearest demonstration of his identity: 'So Jesus said, "When you have lifted up the Son of Man, then you will know that *I am the one I claim to be*."' (John 8:28).

Jesus had complete confidence in his own identity. The key to Jesus' confidence and identity lay in his relationship with the Father. The same will also be true for you. As you spend time with the Father in prayer, in worship, or in reading the Scriptures, your sense of identity and confidence in who you are in God will grow. You can know where you have come from and where you are heading.

No matter what people say about you, you can walk confidently with head held high. Your identity is in Christ. It is rooted in what he says about you and his presence *with you*.

PRAYER

Father, thank you that you are *with me*, you have not left me alone. Help me, like Jesus, always to do what pleases you and always to speak just what you have taught me.

OLD TESTAMENT READING

Judges 18:1–19:30
Shine God's light

The shocking atrocities committed by Isis – beheading and crucifixion of innocent victims, widespread abuse of children, the terrible evil of human trafficking and modern-day slavery – we live in a dark world. But we are not without hope. With God, light can drive out darkness.

Israel was in a dark period of its history. The people were called to walk in a close relationship with God – under the direct rule and reign of God as their King. Had they lived like this they would not have needed a human king.

However, they were now living in the worst possible scenario. They were not living under the kingship of the Lord, and did not even have a human king to keep order and restrain the chaos.

These were bleak days. 'In those days Israel had no king' (18:1; 19:1). They turned to idol worship (chapter 18). We read a terrible and distressing account of the evil excesses of a lawless land. The appalling rape, abuse and dissection of a woman caused everyone who saw it to say, 'Such a thing has never been seen or done, not since the day the Israelites came up out of Egypt. Think about it! Consider it! Tell us what to do!' (19:30). This was a time of utter darkness, of life without God.

Terrible as this atrocity was, it is not unique in the history of the world. Appalling atrocities can happen when a society rejects God and his laws: it sometimes descends into utter chaos.

Lt Gen Romeo Dallaire, who, in 1994, was part of the UN mission to Rwanda and witnessed the genocide, was asked how he could still believe in God. He replied: 'I know there is a God because in Rwanda I shook hands with the devil. I have seen him, I have smelled him and I have touched him. I know the devil exists, and therefore I know that there is a God.'[1]

In biblical language, 'darkness' is not only the night but also the forces of evil that can seduce us and lead us away from walking in the right direction, towards the light of life – Jesus who brings light into this dark world.

In a staggering claim, Jesus naturally puts himself in the place of God, and says that he is 'the light of the world' (John 8:12). A world without God is a world of darkness. Yet Jesus said, 'Whoever follows me will never walk in darkness, but will have *the light of life*' (v.12).

When you turn to Jesus you come out of the darkness of life *without* God into the light of life *with* him. He leads us out of darkness, conflict and death into the light of life and love. He gives meaning and direction to your life. Not only that, but as you live *with* God, seeking to please him, you embody together with other believers the 'light of life' to bring light into our dark world.

You really can make a difference to the world around you. Your life, in Christ, can shine like light in the spiritual darkness in the world around you. As Martin Luther King put it, 'Darkness cannot drive out darkness; only light can do that. Hate cannot drive out hate; only love can do that.'[2]

PRAYER

Lord, help us to be a community that brings your light to a dark world. Help us as individuals and as a church to live with you, to please you and to bring the light of life, love and joy to those around us today.

15 May | Day 135
All He Wants Is You

In his book, *All I Want Is You*, Bishop Sandy Millar describes attending a conference in California some years ago at which he saw the Spirit of God working in powerful ways. When it was over, he went for a long walk along the coast. He writes, 'As I was walking I was caught up with the excitement of all that lay ahead and the thrill of the Spirit of God. I was saying, "Lord, I will give you anything you want ... I will do anything you want me to do."'

Sandy continues, 'I can honestly claim to have only heard the Lord speak about three times in this way, but as clearly as I have ever heard him speak, he said, "All I want is you" ... It was the most humbling thing ... He can do anything he likes. But all he wants is you.'[1]

READING FROM PSALMS

Psalm 61:1–8
Be led by God

Do you ever find yourself overwhelmed by all the issues you face in life? David was 'overwhelmed and fainting' (v.2, AMP).

He was a leader ('the King', v.6). Those who lead others need themselves to be led by God. This prayer is applicable to us all. He cried out to God to listen to his prayer and to lead him (vv.1–2).

Above all, this prayer is a prayer for protection. There are times when we want to run and hide. God provides us with '*a place to get away from it all*' (v.3, MSG). He is a '*safe-house*' (v.4, MSG). He provides us with *physical protection* of rock-like strength (v.2), the *emotional protection* of his arms around us (v.4) and the *spiritual protection* of 'your love and faithfulness' (v.7).

PRAYER

Lord, lead me into your presence today and lead me in all the decisions I make, the conversations I have and the words that I speak.

NEW TESTAMENT READING

John 8:31–59
Be liberated by Jesus

Nelson Mandela spoke about a prison guard who said to him, 'Do you know that I have the power to have you killed?' Mandela responded, 'Do you not know that I have the power to go to my death freely?'[2]

Do you want to live a life of true freedom? Jesus is the great *liberator*. If Jesus '*liberates you* then you are really and unquestionably free' (v.36, AMP).

But who is this Jesus? (vv.12–59). Indeed, Jesus is asked that very question, 'Who do you think you are?' (v.53). His answer points to his unique relationship with his Father. It culminates with the extraordinary claim, 'before Abraham was born, I am!' (v.58). This was exactly the same way that God had revealed himself to Moses at the burning bush (Exodus 3:14). Jesus uses language that only God could use. His opponents pick up stones to stone him for blasphemy (John 8:59).

Although Jesus' relationship with his Father was unique, through Jesus you, too, can know God. The relationship brings freedom to your life. But what does this freedom mean?

Jesus says that to know him is to know the truth, and that 'the truth will set you free' (v.32). In Judaism, the truth was the law; and the study of, and adherence to, the law made a person free. Jesus says, 'If you hold to *my teaching*, you are really my disciples' (v.31).

Christians are sometimes accused of being narrow-minded or anti-intellectual – as contrasted with those who call themselves 'free thinkers'. Jesus says that, in fact, the opposite is the case. Following Jesus is the way of intellectual freedom and integrity.

Truth is revealed by God. Jesus is 'the truth' (14:6). He is God's ultimate revelation. Knowing the truth is not about assenting to propositions, but about knowing a person. Knowing Jesus broadens your mind, increases your depth of insight and widens your scope of understanding. To live in truth is to live in a relationship of love with Jesus who is the truth.

This does not mean that we have all the answers but that we have a true framework of thinking. Scientific laws provide a framework that gives freedom to investigate in the physical realm. God's revelation provides the framework that gives intellectual freedom to investigate in the spiritual realm. Belief leads to understanding.

The response to Jesus' words were, 'We are Abraham's descendants and have never been slaves of anyone. How can you say that we shall be set free?' (8:33). But Jesus replied, 'I tell you the truth, *everyone who sins is a slave to sin*' (v.34). To sin is to be a slave to our compulsions, our addictions, our need for power and admiration, a slave to what others think of us, a slave to the fear of others. Without Jesus Christ, all of us are slaves to sin. But, '*if the Son liberates you, then you are really and unquestionably free*' (v.36, AMP).

1. Freedom from shame

Jesus sets you free from guilt and shame. He died so that you could be forgiven and your guilt and shame could be taken away.

2. Freedom from addiction

He sets you free from addiction – being 'a slave to sin' (v.34). On the cross the power of addiction was broken. Although you may still fall from time to time, the power of the addiction to sin is broken when Jesus sets you free. While some may receive complete freedom from a specific addiction when they come to Jesus, for others it may be a longer process.

3. Freedom from fear

Jesus sets you free from fear. He came so that 'by his death he might destroy him who holds the power of death – that is, the devil – and free those who all their lives were held in slavery by their fear of death' (Hebrews 2:14–15). Jesus says here, 'I tell you the truth, whoever keeps my word will never see death' (John 8:51).

Death is not the end for those whom Jesus has set free. Rather it is the gateway to heaven. When Jesus sets you free from the fear of death, he also sets you free potentially from all other fears.

4. Freedom to know God

Jesus sets you free to have a relationship with God like his own. Jesus is the supreme example of a person who is led by God. He says of himself, 'I *heard from God*' (v.40). But he also goes on to say, 'Whoever belongs to God *hears what God says*' (v.47). It is possible for us *all* to hear from God.

Jesus says, 'I know him' (v.55). He makes it possible for you to know God.

5. Freedom to be yourself

Rather than attempting to be a second-rate version of someone else Jesus sets you free to be your true self as God intended you to be.

6. Freedom to love

Jesus sets you free to love (the opposite of the self-centredness of sin).

He sets you free intellectually, morally and emotionally. This is true freedom: '…if the Son sets you free, you will be free indeed' (v.36).

PRAYER

Lord, thank you for the freedom that you bring to my life. Thank you that I can know you and hear your voice.

OLD TESTAMENT READING

Judges 20:1–21:25
***Be loyal* to God**

As the account of this chaotic period in Israel's history comes to an end in the book of Judges, the writer concludes: 'At that time there was no king in Israel. People did whatever they felt like doing' (21:25, MSG). God had given them a political system based on loyalty to the one God. But that *loyalty* was short-lived and the whole system began to dissolve.

As we will see when we look at the book of 1 Samuel, the provision of having a king in Israel was not seen as wholly positive. Yet it was preferable to this chaotic state of affairs where everyone did just 'whatever they felt like doing' (Judges 21:25, MSG).

Even in the midst of the chaos, there were moments when the people of God 'enquired of God' (20:18). They asked to be led by God. The lesson of staying in constant communication and consultation with God is so prevalent throughout the Old Testament. If Israel made a mistake here, it was that they did not ask God whether or not they should go into battle – they only asked how the battle was to be waged.

We also learn that even if God is behind a scheme, you may suffer great setbacks, as the people of God did here. Even though God promised victory, there were casualties along the way. If this is true of the physical battles they faced, it is certainly true of the spiritual battles that you face. Do not be surprised by setbacks. It does not necessarily mean that you are not being led by God. The lesson of the book of Judges is that, whatever happens, stay loyal to God. All he wants is you.

PRAYER

Lord, help me to stay constantly loyal to you. May I not be put off by setbacks. May I always seek your will in my life.

16 May | Day 136
Your Story Has Power

Mark Heather's parents split up when he was a child and he was brought up by his alcoholic mother who beat him. When he was fourteen years old, he stood up to her and said he would not accept the beatings any more. The next day she committed suicide.

From that moment, he was placed in care and became, in his words, 'pretty nuts really' – getting into trouble with the police, involved in drugs, and spiralling into an increasingly self-destructive lifestyle.

Mark (now in his 30s) was invited by his girlfriend to do Alpha at Holy Trinity Brompton. On the weekend away, he had a powerful encounter with God. He said, 'My group leader, Toby, prayed for me, for the Holy Spirit to come – and I knew that it was happening. The experience resulted in me crying uncontrollably.

'I ran to the pub down the road, grabbed a beer, wandered back and sat in the darkest corner outside that I could find. After sitting quietly, a total comfort enveloped me. I felt total love. I felt part of a family, which is something that I had no way of knowing until then.

'Crying, I prayed for one more sign. I asked for Toby to come out the door. As I asked, Toby walked through that very door to look for me.

'God is real and he loves me unconditionally and he is gentle. The Holy Spirit saved me. The Alpha weekend helped me find him. He knew where I was so when I got to the right place, he was waiting.'

Mark's personal story has had a powerful impact on many people's lives. Your story may not be as dramatic as Mark's, but *everyone* has a story. Whether you were brought up as a Christian or whether you have only been a Christian for a few hours, your story has power.

READING FROM PROVERBS

Proverbs 12:8–17
Tell your story authentically

The proverbs for today cover many different subjects, from taking care of animals (v.10) to overlooking insults rather than showing our annoyance at once: 'Fools have short fuses and explode all too quickly; the prudent quietly shrug off insults' (v.16, MSG).

There is one proverb that is specifically on today's theme: 'A truthful *witness* gives *honest testimony*' (v.17a). This, of course, has implications for *witnesses* in court. But also, all of us are *witnesses* in the sense that we are all in a position to testify about Jesus.

Whether you are on a night out with friends or speaking at the front of a crowd of people in church or elsewhere, there is something very powerful about a person telling their story truthfully, honestly and from the heart.

PRAYER

Lord, help me to tell my story from my heart, with honesty and authenticity.

NEW TESTAMENT READING

John 9:1–34
Tell your story persistently

I love the story in today's passage about the man born blind. First, Jesus expressly repudiates the automatic link between sin and suffering (vv.1–3). The Pharisees assumed that the man was blind because he had been 'steeped in sin at birth' (v.34).

Even Jesus' disciples asked the question that every culture asks: 'Why is someone born with disability? Whose fault is it – this man or his parents?' (v.2). Jesus tells them that they are asking the wrong question. He replies, 'Neither this man nor his parents sinned ... but this happened so that the work of God might be displayed in his life' (v.3).

Jesus heals this man through his words and his touch. He touches him with deep love and respect. The miracle causes much excitement. Those who know the blind man begin to discuss the matter.

We see how it is always possible to attempt to explain away miracles of healing. When the blind man's eyes were opened, his 'neighbours and those who had formerly seen him begging asked, "Isn't this the same man who used to sit and beg?" Some claimed that he was. Others said, "No he only looks like him"' (vv.8–9a).

We see the danger of getting caught up in religious minutiae and missing the whole point. When the man gave his testimony of healing, some responded, 'This man is not from God, for he does not keep the Sabbath' (v.16).

This man simply tells his story over and over again. He does not have the answer for all their complex questions. However, he gives the best answer that you can give when you are asked questions to which you do not know the answer. He simply says, '*I don't know*' (v.12).

What I love most is his answer when he finally gets frustrated by all their scepticism and cynical questioning. He tells them he does not know the answer to all their questions, '*But one thing I do know, that whereas I was blind before, now I see*' (v.25, AMP).

As his eyes are opened, so too are his heart and his mind. He begins by knowing 'The man they called Jesus' (v.11). Then he sees him as 'a prophet' (v.17) 'from God' (v.33). Finally, he believes he is '*the* Son of Man' and worshipped him (v.38).

This is the power of the testimony. It is an almost unanswerable way of dealing with objections: 'Before I was like this... and now I am like this... This is the difference that Jesus has made to my life.'

Telling your story is still one of the keys to communicating your faith in the modern world as it was here in the New Testament.

PRAYER

Lord, thank you for the power of the stories of those who say, 'I was blind but now I see' (v.25). May there be many more who can testify about encountering you, having their eyes opened and being healed.

OLD TESTAMENT READING

Ruth 1:1–2:23
Tell your story humbly

Real love is often hard, inconvenient and costly; but true happiness only comes to those who care about others at some cost to themselves.

The book of Ruth is a story of two widows and a farmer in a remote village. It is a wonderful contrast to the previous book of Judges. While the *context* of the two books is identical (Ruth is set 'in the days when the judges ruled', 1:1), the *content* of the two books is very different.

While Judges recounts a catalogue of evil and upheaval because 'everyone did as they saw fit' (Judges 21:25), the book of Ruth is a wonderful story of loyalty, faithfulness and kindness – all the more impressive for taking place in this period of strife. Furthermore, while Judges looks at the big picture of the nation of Israel during this period, the book of Ruth is focused on a specific family.

It is a reminder to us that the God of the universe and of history is also the God of all the little details in your life. He is not just almighty and powerful, but he is also your Father who is intimately concerned with you. Your life and all the details matter to God. Your life counts.

The book of Ruth reminds us of God's care, provision and faithfulness in the little pieces of our life.

Naomi was more concerned for Ruth than for herself. Naomi wanted Ruth to return home so that she might have a better chance of remarrying and Naomi is prepared to lose Ruth for the sake of Ruth's happiness (Ruth 1:8–13). Ruth's love for Naomi was equally unselfish and self-giving.

She is quite prepared not to get married again. She shows extraordinary loyalty to her mother-in-law. She says, 'Don't force me to leave you; don't make me go home. Where you go, I go; and where you live, I'll live. Your people are my people, your God is my god; where you die, I'll die, and that's where I'll be buried, so help me God – not even death itself is going to come between us!' (vv.16–17, MSG).

Boaz was also a God-fearing person. He had heard of Ruth's reputation. She was not only loyal and faithful – she was extremely hard working (2:7). Someone must have testified about her. Boaz says, 'I've heard all about you – heard about the way you treated your mother-in-law after the death of her husband, and how you left your father and mother and the land of your birth and have come to live among a bunch of total strangers' (v.11, MSG).

Furthermore, Ruth had obviously testified about her own faith in God, for Boaz knows that she is committed to 'God, to whom you've come seeking protection under his wings' (v.12, MSG).

Boaz then shows extraordinary kindness to Ruth. Ruth says to her mother-in-law, 'The name of the man I worked with today is Boaz' and Naomi declares, 'He has not stopped showing his kindness to the living and the dead' (vv.19–20).

PRAYER

Lord, thank you for the example of loyalty, kindness and faithfulness. Help me to be like that. Help us as a community to be a people known for our loyalty, kindness and faithfulness.

17 May | Day 137

Knowing God as a Father

- What is the best thing in life, bringing more joy, delight, and contentment, than anything else? *Knowledge of God...*
- What were you made for? *To know God.*
- What aim should you set yourself in life? *To know God.*

These are the questions J. I. Packer raises at the start of his influential book, *Knowing God*.[1] Jesus said, 'I am the good shepherd; I *know* my sheep and my sheep *know* me – just as the Father *knows* me and I *know the Father*' (John 10:14).

READING FROM PSALMS

Psalm 62:1–12
Trust him, at all times

It is easy to trust God when things are going well. David urges, 'Trust in, lean on, rely on, and have confidence in Him *at all times* (v.8a, AMP). Trusting in God *at all times* means trusting him not only when things are going well, but also when things are not going so well. You develop character by trusting him when you are facing difficulties in your life.

Knowing and trusting God leads to:

1. Soul-rest

In the midst of all your fears and anxieties you can find peace: '*My soul finds rest* in God alone ... *Find rest, O my soul*, in God alone' (vv.1, 5)

2. Salvation

Salvation comes by faith in God: 'My salvation comes from him. He alone is my rock and my salvation ... My salvation and my honour depend on God' (vv.1b–2a,7a)

3. Security
Everything else in life is uncertain, and ultimately insecure, but God 'is my fortress, I shall never be shaken ... he is my mighty rock, my refuge' (vv.2b,6b–7b)

Like Jesus, David contrasts the love of God with money: 'Though your riches increase, *do not set your heart on them*' (v.10). When I started practising as a barrister, I wrote this in the margin of my Bible: 'This is a vital message for me at this time. It was easy in student days not to think about money – but now with money starting to come in I find myself thinking about it more and more, talking about it more and more. The battle is fierce – the pull of the world is so strong. Either you set your heart on God or on money.'

PRAYER

Father, may my soul find rest in you alone. Thank you that you promise that I will never be shaken. I trust in you today.

NEW TESTAMENT READING

John 9:35–10:21
Enjoy life in all its fullness

I thought that becoming a Christian would mean the end to my enjoyment of life. In fact, I found the opposite. Jesus says he came that we might 'enjoy life, and have it in abundance (to the full, till it overflows)' (10:10, AMP).

The man healed of blindness had no trouble believing in Jesus. When Jesus finds him and says, 'Do you believe in the Son of Man?' (9:35), he asks, 'Who is he sir? ... Tell me so that I may believe in him' (v.36). Jesus replies, '"You have now seen him; in fact, he is the one speaking with you." Then the man said, "Lord, I believe," and he *worshipped him*' (vv.37–38). In Jesus, the man realised that he had encountered God himself. You too can encounter God in Jesus.

Jesus explains how, through him, you can know God. He uses two analogies. First, he speaks of himself as 'the gate' (10:1). The Greek word '*thura*' is perhaps better translated as '*the door*'. Jesus is *the door* for the sheep to come in and find salvation (v.9). He is *the door* to the Father. The door to *knowing God* is to *know Jesus*.

The second analogy Jesus uses is that he is *the good shepherd*. The Greek word for good (kalos) means 'beautiful', 'noble', 'wonderful'. The sheep *know* the shepherd: 'I am the good shepherd; I *know* my sheep and my sheep *know* me – just as the Father *knows* me and I *know* the Father' (vv.14–15). The background to this is that God himself is described as the 'shepherd' in the Old Testament (for example, see Psalm 23:1; Isaiah 40:11). To *know Jesus* is to *know God*.

1. Enjoy fullness of life
In a relationship with Jesus, you find meaning, purpose, fulfilment, peace, forgiveness, and life in all its fullness.

2. Don't let the devil rob you
Jesus contrasts himself with 'the thief' who comes to 'steal and kill and destroy' (John 10:10a). The devil wants to rob you of your peace and enjoyment of life. Don't let him.

3. Be assured of God's love for you
Jesus also contrasts the good shepherd with the 'hired hand' who, when the wolf attacked the flock, runs away because he cares nothing for the sheep (vv.12–13).

On the other hand, the good shepherd lays down his life for the sheep (vv.11, 15). This is entirely voluntary: 'The reason my Father loves me is that I lay down my life – only to take it up again. No one takes it from me, but I lay it down of my own accord' (vv.17–18).
If you ever doubt that God loves you, you simply have to look at the cross: Jesus laid down his life for you.

Jesus came to give his life on the cross to take away all the blocks that prevent you knowing and being in communion with God as your Father.

4. Learn to listen to his voice
It is in the instinctive nature of sheep to recognise the shepherd's voice. 'The sheep *listen to his voice*. He calls his own sheep by name and leads them out. When he has brought out all his own he goes on ahead of them, and his sheep follow him because *they know his voice*' (vv.3–4).

The more you get to know Jesus, the more you will get to discern whether it is his voice rather than the deceptive voice of the wolf.

5. Know that you have eternal life
The one you know not only dies for you but he also rises from the dead for you. He has the power to take his life again: 'I have authority to lay it down and authority to take it up again' (v.18b). He gives you eternal life.

Jesus later defines eternal life like this: 'Now this is eternal life: that they may *know* you, the only true God, and Jesus Christ, whom you have sent' (17:3).

PRAYER

Lord, thank you that you love me so much that you laid down your life for me. Thank you that you give me life and life in all its fullness.

OLD TESTAMENT READING

Ruth 3:1–4:22
Honour God in all circumstances

God honours those who honour him and do what is right – even when it is costly to do so and even through the trials and difficulties of life. We see how each of the main characters *honours the Lord*: Naomi (1:8–9), Ruth (v.17 and following), and Boaz (2:4, 12; 3:10, 13; 4:11). They are great models for us to follow.

The book of Ruth begins with Naomi despairing of the kindness of God (1:20–21). She then experiences many of the people around her displaying great human kindness. She experiences it in her two daughters-in-law, Ruth and Orpah (v.8), and in Boaz's treatment of Ruth. Finally, she declares, 'He has not stopped showing his kindness to the living and the dead' (2:20).

Ruth obeys her mother-in-law in every detail. Naomi's concern is wholly for Ruth's wellbeing. Boaz is self-controlled, generous and honourable. Boaz's life is obviously God-centred. His immediate reaction when he wakes up and sees Ruth is '*The Lord* bless you' and 'as the Lord lives' (3:10, 13).

Yesterday, we saw how Ruth *honoured the Lord* and did the right thing by being loyal to her mother-in-law. Today, we see how Boaz clearly wanted to marry Ruth, and felt it was the right thing, yet did not simply go ahead as he could have done on the basis of the end justifying the means. He was completely upright in the way that he approached the matter – abiding by the etiquette and traditions of the culture.

Boaz did not just rush ahead and get married. He went through the correct process. Humanly speaking he was taking a great risk and might have lost Ruth. But he trusted that the Lord was in control.

The Lord honoured this in an amazing and wonderful way. Boaz and Ruth were married and gave birth to the grandfather of King David (4:17). Indeed, Ruth, the servant girl, became an ancestor of the Lord Jesus Christ (Matthew 1:5–6). In one sense, Jesus is our kinsman-redeemer (Ruth 4:14). He calls us his brothers and sisters, understands our struggles and acts to redeem us (Hebrews 2:11–12, 17–18).

We see the kindness of God throughout the book of Ruth. Behind the human kindness of Ruth, Naomi and Boaz lies the kindness of God.

PRAYER

Father, thank you for your amazing kindness to me. Thank you for redeeming me. Give me courage to honour you always and to seek to do the right thing even when that is difficult.

18 May | Day 138
How to Satisfy Your Soul

Bernhard Langer was one of the best golfers of his generation, twice winning the US Masters and at one time topping the world golf rankings. He said, 'I had ... won seven events in five different continents; I was number one in the world and I had a beautiful young wife. Yet there was *something missing*.

'The lifestyle we all (especially us sportsmen) are leading – it is all about money and who you are and who you know and what you have and these things aren't really the most important things. I think people who have these things, they realise that ... there is *still something missing* in their life and *I believe that is Jesus Christ*.'[1]

The spiritual emptiness that Bernhard Langer is describing is common to all humanity. One young woman said to me that she felt there was 'a chunk missing in her soul'. You are not simply body and mind. You are a soul created for relationship with God. How then do you *satisfy your soul*?

READING FROM PSALMS

Psalm 63:1–11
Seek God day and night

Spiritual 'food' is just as real as physical food and it satisfies us in a way that cannot be satisfied by anything physical.

David was in the desert. He knew what physical thirst and physical hunger were like. But he also knew and experienced spiritual thirst: '*My soul thirsts for you*, my body longs for you, in a dry and weary land where there is no water' (v.1). And he knew what it was like for his spiritual hunger to be satisfied: 'My soul will be satisfied as with the richest of foods' (v.5a).

His spiritual hunger and thirst are satisfied as he worships God: 'So here I am in the place of worship, eyes open, drinking in your strength and glory' (v.2, MSG).

He lifts his hands as an expression of adoration, reverence and surrender: 'Because your love is better than life, my lips will glorify you. I will praise you as long as I live, and in your name *I will lift up my hands*' (vv.3–4). Lifting up hands is the oldest gesture of prayer. As Pope Emeritus Benedict writes, 'This gesture is the radical form of worship ... To open oneself to God, to surrender oneself completely to him.'[2]

What do you do when you can't sleep or you have wakeful moments in the night? David says that he worships and praises God, 'I remember You upon my bed and meditate on You in the night watches' (v.6, AMP).

As he pours out his heart in worship day and night to God, David discovers strength and support. He writes, 'Because you are my help, I sing in the shadow of your wings. *My soul clings to you*; your right hand upholds me' (vv.7–8).

PRAYER

Lord, I seek you today. Thank you that you satisfy my soul as with the richest of food and quench my spiritual thirst. Thank you that your love is better than life.

NEW TESTAMENT READING

John 10:22–42
Communicate with God through Jesus

How do you and I communicate with God?

Communication with Jesus is communication with God. Those who met Jesus understood he was claiming to be God (v.33). When he said, 'I and the Father are one' (v.30) and 'the Father is in me, and I in the Father' (v.38), there was no ambiguity in the ears of his hearers. His opponents understood it as blasphemy – 'because you, a mere human being, claim to be God' (v.33) – and they picked up stones to stone him (vv.31–33).

Jesus communicated with his disciples and he continues to communicate with us. He says, 'My sheep listen to my voice; I know them, and they follow me' (v.27). We see here the marks of a true Christian:

1. Believing in Jesus

There is a contrast in this passage between those who 'believed in Jesus' (v.42) and those who 'do not believe' (vv.25–26). Belief in Jesus means believing in him when he says, 'I am God's Son' (v.36) and putting your trust in him.

2. Knowing Jesus

Jesus says, 'my sheep listen to my voice. I know them...' (v.27). To be a Christian is to recognise and follow the voice of Jesus. This is what defines a Christian – not so much knowledge about Jesus, but actually *knowing him*. This is then followed up by the wonderful declaration that Jesus also knows us.

3. Following Jesus

Jesus says, 'they follow me' (v.27). It affects your life. As Jesus said elsewhere, 'By their fruit you will recognise them' (Matthew 7:16, 20). James wrote, 'Faith by itself, if it is not accompanied by action, is dead' (James 2:17). The primary evidence of faith is love. Those who follow Jesus will follow his example of love.

Jesus promises every true Christian: 'I give them eternal life' (John 10:28). This is not just about quantity of life; it is also about quality. Jesus satisfies our spiritual hunger and thirst. In a relationship with Jesus we find this deep soul satisfaction that cannot be found anywhere else.

Jesus promises that this relationship with him will go on for ever. It starts now, but it is 'eternal' (v.28). Those who follow Jesus will 'never perish' (v.28). This is a gift ('I *give* them eternal life', v.28). It cannot be earned, nor can it be lost. Jesus promises, 'no one can snatch them out of *my* hand ... no one can snatch them out of *my Father's* hand' (vv.28–29).

There may be many struggles and temptations along the way, but ultimately the hand of Jesus and the hand of the Father are engaged together in protecting you. A Christian may lose their job, their money, their family, their liberty and even their life, but they can never lose eternal life.

PRAYER

Thank you, Lord, that I can listen to your voice, that I can know you and that you give me eternal life. Thank you that you promise that I will never perish and that no one can snatch me out of your hand. Thank you that in this relationship I find soul satisfaction both now and for evermore.

OLD TESTAMENT READING

1 Samuel 1:1–2:26
Pour out your heart and soul to God

Is there something you want desperately from God?

It is almost inevitable that at times in our lives we will feel 'distress of soul' (1:10, AMP). Never allow bitterness to eat away in your heart – but, like Hannah, pour it out to the Lord. 'Crushed in soul, Hannah prayed to GOD and cried and cried – inconsolably' (v.10, MSG).

There is nothing more releasing than to pour out your soul before the Lord – to tell him what your problems are, rather than carrying them around yourself – and to ask him for the solution, and then to receive the peace of God (Philippians 4:6–7).

Relief from her anguish comes to Hannah long before she actually sees the answer to her prayer.

This is a beautiful picture of heartfelt prayer from the depth of the soul. 'As she kept on praying to the LORD, Eli observed her mouth. Hannah was praying in her heart, and her lips were moving but her voice was not heard' (1 Samuel 1:12–13a). Eli accuses her of being drunk. She replies, 'Not so, my lord ... I am a woman who is deeply troubled ... I was *pouring out my soul to the Lord* ... I have been praying here out of my great anguish and grief' (vv.15–16).

Eli tells her, 'Go in peace, and may the God of Israel grant you what you have asked of him' (v.17). And as she left her face was no longer downcast: 'She ate heartily, her face radiant' (v.18, MSG). She knew deep down that God had heard her prayer and, indeed, 'the LORD remembered her' (v.19). In fact, God more than answered her prayer. Not only did he give her the child she longed for, she gave birth to six children (2:21).

Meanwhile, 'the boy Samuel continued to grow in stature and in favour with the LORD and with people' (v.26). This is the prayer we have prayed so often for our children.

Hannah's prayer after Samuel's birth is a vivid demonstration of the soul satisfaction that she experiences through her relationship with God. She prays and thanks God that 'those who were hungry hunger no more' (v.5).

The amazing revelation in Hannah's prayer is that the supreme source of her joy is not her child, but in the Lord. She says, 'My heart rejoices in the LORD' (v.1). He is the source of soul satisfaction:

'I'm walking on air ... GOD brings life ... he rekindles burned-out lives with fresh hope, restoring dignity and respect to their lives' (vv.1, 6, 8, MSG).

PRAYER

Lord, thank you for amazing answers to prayer, which you give when I pour out my soul to you. Thank you that sometimes you answer my prayers in remarkable ways. But whether I receive what I specifically ask for or not, thank you that you promise me your peace.

19 May | Day 139

Your Hope in Times of Trouble

However difficult your situation may be – however much 'trouble' you are facing in your life, you can have hope. Hope is the confident expectation of God's ultimate blessing in this life and the life to come, based upon the goodness and promises of God. With Jesus, there is always hope.

Like Lazarus in our New Testament passage for today, some parts of the church have been prematurely declared dead. In his book, *The Death of Christian Britain,* Callum Brown writes, 'This book is about the demise of the nation's core religious moral identity. As historical changes go, this has been no lingering and drawn-out affair. It took several centuries (in what historians used to call the Dark Ages) to convert Britain to Christianity, but it has taken less than forty years for the country to forsake it.'[1]

We often read headlines such as, 'Crisis in the Church', 'Dramatic decline in attendance' and 'Church attendance figures fall again'.

At the same time, we are seeing the results of a society that is attempting to shut God out. Every day in Britain, around 300 couples are divorced.[2] Somebody calls the Samaritans every six seconds.[3] The pornographic industry is worth billions of pounds. There are 30,000 Christian clergy of all types, and more than 80,000 registered witches and fortune tellers.

Britain is not the only nation in trouble. Many other nations are going through difficult times. As well as on a national level, all of us are likely at some point to face times of trouble in our own individual lives.

'Trouble' can take many forms. What is your hope in times of trouble?

READING FROM PSALMS

Psalm 64:1–10
Hope in the ultimate triumph of good over evil

Do you ever feel terrified by something you are facing in your life? David faced '*the terror* of the enemy' (v.1b, AMP).

He went through times of real trouble, 'the conspirators out to get me' (v.2, MSG), 'evil plans' (v.5a) and 'traps' (v.5b, MSG). Yet, he is confident that God will triumph over evil. What should you do when you face similar troubles? The psalm today gives us some clues:

1. Cry out to God
David prays, 'Listen and help, O God' (v.1a, MSG). David asks God: 'protect my life from the threat of the enemy' (v.1b).

2. 'Rejoice in the Lord'
'Rejoice in the Lord' (v.10a). Or, as the apostle Paul puts it, 'Rejoice in the Lord *always*. I will say it again: Rejoice!' (Philippians 4:4).

3. Stay close to the Lord
'Take refuge in him' (Psalm 64:10b). 'Fly to God' (v.10b, MSG).

4. Keep praising God
'Let all the upright in heart praise him!' (v.10c). 'Make praise your habit' (v.10c, MSG).

PRAYER

Lord, thank you that I can be confident of the ultimate triumph of good over evil and that I am never alone. Lord, I praise you.

NEW TESTAMENT READING

John 11:1–44
Hope in the resurrection of Jesus

Do you fear death? Many people are afraid of death. But if you put your faith in Jesus, you do not need to fear death. Jesus has defeated the power of death.

I once heard the English comedian, Russell Brand, say, 'Laughter is addictive because of the inevitability of death. It gives us a temporary escape – for the moment it stops the fear of the inevitability of death.' Every human being will face the 'trouble' of death. Where does your hope lie?

In today's passage we see the full humanity of Jesus in the face of death. Lazarus was his friend (v.11). Jesus loved him and his family (vv.3, 5, 36). He was '*deeply moved*' and '*troubled*' by Lazarus's death (v.33). In the shortest verse in the Bible we read, '*Jesus wept*' (v.35).

Yet Jesus is also, uniquely, the answer to death. Jesus said to Martha, '"Your brother will be raised up." Martha replied, "I know that he will be raised up in the resurrection at the end of time."' Jesus' response was: 'You don't have to wait for the End. I am, right now, Resurrection and Life. The one who believes in me, even though he or she dies, will live. And everyone who lives believing in me does not ultimately die at all' (vv.24–26, MSG).

There is life beyond the grave. Jesus died and rose again. Everyone who believes in Jesus will rise again from the dead. As a foretaste of the future, Jesus raises Lazarus from the dead.

The story of Lazarus is the story of each one of us. Jesus calls you to rise up and become fully alive in order to give life – to bring hope to your family, friends, work colleagues and the world.

This resurrection power is within you. Paul writes to the church of Rome, 'If the Spirit of him who raised Jesus from the dead is living in you, he who raised Christ from the dead will also give life to your mortal bodies because of his Spirit who lives in you' (Romans 8:11). The resurrection of Jesus Christ is the basis of your future hope.

Christianity is the largest movement of all time. It is the only one that never loses a member through death. I remember one of my sons, when he was a little boy, saying, 'When you die, I'll be sad. Then I'll see you in heaven and I won't be sad anymore!'

Mother Teresa was asked shortly before her death, 'Are you afraid of dying?' She said, 'How can I be? Dying is going home to God. I have never been afraid. No, on the contrary,' she said, 'I look forward to it.'[1]

This passage also indirectly provides a picture of *hope for the church*. There is a sickness in parts of the church and many are declaring its death. Some parts of the church seem to have 'fallen asleep' (John 11:11). And in some cases there seems to be a 'bad odour' (v.39).

This passage reminds us of Jesus' power to bring even the dead to life. This resurrection power is still at work in the church today. The same Jesus who said over Lazarus 'this sickness will not end in death' (v.4), also promised that he would 'build [his] Church, and the gates of Hell shall not prevail against it' (Matthew 16:18, KJV).

Some parts of the church seem to have been prematurely buried. Jesus said about Lazarus, 'Take off the grave clothes and let him go' (John 11:44c). Maybe Jesus would say something similar to parts of the church today. The Brighton and Hove Argus described what has happened at one of our church plants – St Peter's, Brighton – as 'the Lazarus-like recovery of the city's "unofficial cathedral"'. We have called our church planting programme: 'Project Lazarus'!

PRAYER

Lord, I pray for your church. Forgive us where we have fallen asleep and are giving off a bad odour. We know you are deeply moved by the situation, that you weep over the church, and that you will act out of love. Please bring new life. May we see the church come alive all across the nations.

OLD TESTAMENT READING

1 Samuel 2:27–4:22
Hope in the word of the Lord

Do you realise that God wants to speak to you? You can say, like Samuel, '*Speak Lord, for your servant is listening*' (3:9).

These were times of trouble, not just for the people of God, but for everyone (4:7). It was a time when it seemed that God was almost silent. 'In those days the word of the Lord was rare; there were not many visions' (3:1).

It must have been heartbreaking for Eli to see his own sons dishonouring the Lord. They slept with the women who served at the entrance to the Tent of Meeting (2:22). They dishonoured God who has said, 'Those who honour me I will honour, but those who despise me will be disdained' (v.30).

As a result of the dishonouring of God, the people of God are defeated (4:1b–11). Eli dies heartbroken (vv.12–18). His daughter-in-law gives birth to a child with the name Ichabod: 'The glory has departed' (vv.19–22).

Yet, in the midst of these terrible times of trouble for the people of God there is hope. The Lord called Samuel (3:4). God revealed himself to Samuel and he listened to the Lord (vv.9–10). He said, 'Speak, God. I'm your servant, ready to listen' (v.9, MSG). The Lord said, 'See, I am about to do something in Israel that will make the ears of everyone who hears of it tingle' (v.11).

Samuel was prepared to pass on the message in its entirety, however unpopular, embarrassing and difficult it was (v.18). He did not hide anything. As a result, God was able to use him greatly: 'The Lord was with Samuel as he grew up, and he let none of his words fall to the ground' (v.19).

PRAYER

'Speak, Lord, for your servant is listening' (v.9). Help me to listen carefully to the word of God and then pass it on so that others too may hope in the word of the Lord.

20 May | Day 140
How to Find Peace in Adversity

For 2,000 years, followers of Jesus have faced adversity, opposition and persecution. In many places Pippa and I have visited over the years, Christians face physical persecution.

In fact, persecution of Christians around the world today is probably worse than at any time in history.

We do not, at this time, face physical persecution in the West. However, as we see some of the messages that are emerging from those with their stated intention of 'eradicating faith', it is clear that the aggression and vehemence of the attacks may increase.

Opposition is bound to come. Those who desire 'to live a godly life in Christ Jesus will be persecuted' (2 Timothy 3:12). Opposition comes both from those far away from us (the Philistines in the Old Testament passage for today), and also, sadly, sometimes from those closer to home (the Pharisees in the New Testament passage). How do you find peace in adversity?

READING FROM PROVERBS

Proverbs 12:18–27
Promote peace

The antidote to opposition and evil is to walk in the opposite spirit – to be those who 'promote peace'. The writer contrasts the 'deceit in the hearts of those who *plot evil'* (v.20a) with 'joy for those who *promote peace*' (v.20b). How can you do this?

1. Bring healing

Promote peace with your words. 'Rash language cuts and maims, but there is *healing* in the words of the wise' (v.18, MSG). Words are so powerful; they can hurt deeply but they can also heal.

2. Be truthful

'Truthful lips endure for ever, but a lying tongue lasts only a moment' (v.19). Truthful words are not only cathartic, they also have a lasting impact – they 'endure for ever' (v.19).

3. Be restrained

'Fools blurt out folly' (v.23b). But 'a prudent person is reluctant to display his knowledge' (v.23a, AMP). The mere fact that you know the answer does not mean that you should give it. I am always so impressed by the restraint of hosts and helpers on Alpha who do this so well.

4. Be kind

'Anxiety weighs down the heart' (v.25a). God wants you to enjoy life, to help others, not to be weighed down by anxiety. 'A kind word cheers' up other people's hearts (v.25b). By an encouraging word you can transform a person's day or even their life.

PRAYER

Lord, help me to be a person who promotes peace and who speaks words of healing, truth, restraint and kindness.

NEW TESTAMENT READING

John 11:45–12:11
Live in peace

God is sovereign. He uses even the worst things for good. Supremely, we see this on the cross: the very worst plot ever – torture and murder of the innocent Son of God – was used by God to bring salvation to the entire human race.

This being the case, you can live in peace, trusting that God will use even the worst things that you face in life, for good (Romans 8:28).

Jesus faced evil plots. The motive appears to be *envy* (a sin the religious are prone to). People were envious of Jesus because he had so many followers and seemed to be more 'successful' than the religious leaders. Out of envy, the chief priests and the Pharisees called a meeting of the Sanhedrin (John 11:47a).

The Sanhedrin was the supreme court of the nation. It comprised seventy-one members including the high priest. The chief priests were the majority and the Pharisees an influential minority. They asked, 'What are we accomplishing?' (v.47b). It was a very good question! They were envious of the popularity of Jesus and *plotted* to take his life (v.53).

They meant it for evil. God meant it for good. Caiaphas (who was high priest from AD 18–36) prophesied, 'It is better for you that one person die for the people than that the whole nation perish' (v.50). God is able to speak through an unwitting agent.

John comments, 'He didn't say this of his own accord, but as Chief Priest that year he unwittingly prophesied that Jesus was about to die sacrificially for the nation, and not only for the nation but so that all God's exile-scattered children might be gathered together into one people' (vv.51–52, MSG).

Perhaps because he knew of the plot against him, 'Jesus no longer moved about publicly ... Instead he withdrew ... he stayed with his disciples' (v.54). But this was not to be the end of the opposition Jesus faced.

Most painful of all must have been the opposition from Judas. When Mary pours the perfume on Jesus' feet, Judas objects, 'Why wasn't this perfume sold and the money given to the poor? It was worth a year's wages' (12:5). This, on the face of it, is a perfectly good objection, but we read, 'He did not say this because he cared about the poor' (v.6).

It must have been so distressing for Jesus that his friend and disciple, Judas, was, in fact, stealing money from the gifts made to Jesus and his disciples by generous donors (Luke 8:2–3).

Jesus simply responds to Judas's objection, 'You will always have the poor among you, but you will not always have me' (John 12:8).

Jesus was certainly not encouraging complacency about the poor. The fact that we will never obliterate poverty in the world does not mean that we should not try – after all, compassion for the poor was central to Jesus' ministry. Rather, Jesus was turning the attention of his disciples to the significance of what Mary had done.

While all this was going on, plans against Jesus were being formed (vv.9–11). Envy can lead to murder. Not only did they plot to take Jesus' life (11:53), they also made plans to kill Lazarus as well, because he was leading many people to faith (12:10–11).

Extraordinarily, we see God's hand at work through it all. Despite opposition and wrongdoing, God's ultimate plan was still fulfilled. What Jesus' opponents meant for evil, God used for good.

PRAYER

Lord, thank you that I can live in peace, knowing that in everything you work for the good of those who love you.

OLD TESTAMENT READING

1 Samuel 5:1–7:17
Pray for peace

God never forgets a single prayer you pray, even though you may forget. Things may have happened to you today as a result of prayers that you prayed years ago and you have forgotten all about them. But God is still working on them in his timing. Keep stacking up the prayers. Persevering prayer prevails.

Under the old covenant, the ark of God was the place where God was supremely present, and it was the location of God's glory. Yesterday we read that 'the glory has departed from Israel, for the ark of God has been captured' (4:22).

You may sometimes have to wait a *long time* for the Lord to act and answer your prayers. 'It was a long time, twenty years in all ... all the people of Israel mourned and sought after the LORD' (7:2). I feel we have prayed for a long time if we have prayed for a week, but they prayed for twenty years for their country before God acted.

The path to deliverance often begins when we return to the Lord with all our heart. Samuel said, '"If you are truly serious about coming back to GOD, clean house. Get rid of the foreign gods and fertility goddesses, ground yourselves firmly in GOD, worship him and him alone, and he'll save you from Philistine oppression." They did it. They got rid of the gods and goddesses, the images of Baal and Ashtoreth, and gave their exclusive attention and service to GOD' (7:3–4, MSG).

The first thing you need to do in your life when you are seeking God's presence and help is remove anything that is drawing your attention and focus away from God.

After the return to the Lord there was a need for a period of confession and repentance, which was shown by their fasting: 'On that day they fasted and there they confessed, "We have sinned against the LORD."' (v.6).

Finally, it was Samuel's intercession and persistence in prayer for twenty years that brought the people of God victory. Samuel said, 'I will intercede with the LORD for you' (v.5). They said, 'Pray with all your might! And don't let up! Pray to GOD, our God, that he'll save us from the boot of the Philistines' (v.8, MSG). Samuel 'cried out to the LORD on Israel's behalf, and the LORD answered him' (v.9).

They recognised it was an amazing answer to prayer: 'Thus far has the LORD helped us' (v.12). They were delivered from the power of the Philistines and there was *peace* in the land (v.13).

PRAYER

Lord, I commit myself to you again to serve you only. Forgive my sins and the sins of your people. I cry out to you for deliverance and peace. May we see many people in this land putting their faith in Jesus, finding peace in adversity.

21 May | Day 141

Good Government?

Government is the system or group of people governing an organised community, often a state. It usually consists of legislative, executive and judiciary. Government is the mechanism for deciding state policies and the means by which those policies are enforced. Historically, forms of government have included theocracy, autocracy (such as monarchy), oligarchy, aristocracy and democracy.[1]

Sir Winston Churchill once said that 'Democracy is the worst form of government except for all those other forms that have been tried from time to time.'[2]

Governments have their ups and downs. Our politicians are human beings with human weaknesses like our own.

There is a certain ambivalence about all human government in the Bible. There are parts where human government is affirmed as God-given (for instance, in Romans 13), and others where it is pictured as being under demonic control (for instance, in Revelation 13). Together they represent the reality of human government. Governments reflect the mix that is in us all of what is good and true alongside what is sinful and flawed.

However, be assured that one day there will be a new type of government – the kingship of Jesus (John 12:12–36).

READING FROM PSALMS

Psalm 65:1–13
Government of God

Do you realise how good God is? He loves you and wants you to enjoy his blessings today in your life. This psalm is all about the goodness of God. It paints a beautiful picture of what life can look like when lived under God's rule. Meditate, today, on his goodness.

God hears your prayers (v.2), he forgives your sins, even when you may feel 'overwhelmed by sins' (v.3). God's forgiveness is amazing.

'We are filled with the good things' (v.4) being in his presence. He gives you 'hope' (v.5b) and 'joy' (v.8b).

See his great love in the way he treats creation (the watering of the land, the provision of corn, crops, flocks, and so on, vv.9–13).

We don't live in a society directly governed by God, but through Christ you have a direct relationship with God in your own personal life. You can follow his rule and experience the blessing of God's presence. This is one of the ways in which you can experience 'the kingdom of God' in your life now.

PRAYER

Lord, thank you that one day your kingdom will come and every knee will bow before Jesus and he will rule rightly in a 'new creation'.

NEW TESTAMENT READING

John 12:12–36
Government of Jesus

Are you troubled by something you are facing? Are you distressed by some trial in your life? If you are, you have a leader who understands. Jesus said, 'My soul is troubled and distressed…' (v.27a, AMP).

Jesus gives us a model of how to respond to difficulties in our lives and to a suffering world. Then, as now, was a time of crisis. As Jesus said, 'the world is in crisis' (v.30, MSG).

At the time of the Feast of Passover, 'the great crowd' came to Jerusalem (v.12). Josephus estimated that around 2.7 million people would assemble. This may well be an exaggeration. Nevertheless, it was a massive festival and there must have been a great sense of excitement and expectation.

At the time of Jesus, people were awaiting the Messiah. They were looking for a human king, in the line of David, who would free them from their oppressors. As Jesus enters Jerusalem he is seen to be that king: 'Blessed is the *King of Israel*!' (v.13b). The crowd probably saw Jesus as a military king and were hoping for an immediate liberation from Roman rule.

Then, as now, there were different attitudes to the government. The Pharisees (v.19) took the view that Roman occupation, oppressive though it might be, must be *endured* until *God* removed it. The Sadducees favoured *co-operation* with the government. The Zealots were the most popular with the people. They wanted a *violent revolt* led by a messianic king.

Jesus is indeed the King. But he did not ride into Jerusalem triumphantly, powerfully, in a chariot or on a stallion. He is a different type of leader: 'See, your king is coming, seated on a donkey's colt' (v.15b) – humbly, gently, sitting on a baby donkey. He is the messianic King but not a military one. This acted parable was designed to correct the misguided expectations of the crowds and show the city of Jerusalem the way of peace.

He came as the victorious King – not by *doing violence* to the oppressors but by *having violence done to him*. He says, 'The hour has come for the Son of Man to be glorified' (v.23) – and yet he is talking about the cross. '"I, when I am lifted up from the earth, will draw all people to myself." He said this to show the kind of death he was going to die' (vv.32–33).

We see an insight here into the inner struggle in Jesus' heart as he faces his imminent trial, suffering and death: 'Now my heart is troubled and what shall I say? "Father, save me from this hour"? No, it was *for this very reason I came* to this hour. Father, *glorify your name*!' (vv.27–28a).

The victory of Jesus came not through military force but through his self-sacrificial death, which defeated the demonic powers (v.31). The death of Jesus signifies judgment on the world, the overthrow of evil, the glorification of Jesus and a drawing of all people to him.

Here, indeed, was a different kind of victorious king. Jesus not only fulfilled the prophecies about the messianic King, he also fulfilled the prophecies about the suffering servant. He brought the two lines of prophecy together.

One day Jesus will return as the triumphant King to rule and reign for all eternity. In the meantime, you are called to be light in the darkness. If you live under the leadership of Jesus 'then the light will be within you, and shining through your lives. You'll be children of light' (v.36, MSG), and God will honour you – Jesus says, 'My father will honour the one who serves me' (v.26).

PRAYER

Lord, help me to serve you in such a way that my life brings light to a dark world.

OLD TESTAMENT READING

1 Samuel 8:1–10:8
Government of humans

God had planned that his people would be different from others. He planned a society in which God himself was the King. But Israel wanted to be like everyone else. Direct rule of God only works when the people are wholly devoted to God. If not, it results in the chaos we saw in Judges. It is better to have a human king than no king at all. We might list the preferences like this:

1. *God as King* (theocracy): The government God wanted – his perfect will
2. *A human king* (monarchy): The government God allowed – his permissive will
3. *No king* (anarchy): The government in Judges – chaos.

The people of God rejected his rule. The Lord says, 'they have *rejected me as their king*' (8:7). The people ask for a king. They say, 'appoint a king to lead us, such as all the other nations have' (v.5).

Samuel warns them that human governments are weak and fallible. Power corrupts. Samuel warns that the king who will rule over them will take some of their families, land, possessions and employees and use them for his own benefit and that of his inner circle (vv.11–16).

In other words, he warns them about the failings and weaknesses of *all* human government. He also warns them about taxes and 'extensive bureaucracy'! (v.15, MSG).

In spite of the warning, the people say, '*We want a king over us*' (v.19). The Lord allowed 'plan B': he gave them a king (v.22). Saul is chosen to be the anointed leader of Israel to deliver his people (9:16). The moment Samuel sees Saul, in the blink of an eye he recognises that this was the man who was going to govern the people of God (v.17). Saul, who comes from a humble background (v.21), becomes the anointed king (10:1).

God graciously blesses this new plan. Three remarkable things happen to Saul (which now happen to you and every Christian). First, when he is anointed the *Spirit of the Lord comes upon him in power* (v.6b). Second, he is 'transformed'. He becomes a *new person* (v.6c, see 2 Corinthians 5:17). Third, Samuel tells him, 'Whatever job you're given to do, do it. *God is with you!*' (v.7, MSG).

This was true of Saul and it is true of you. However down you might feel about a circumstance, however far from God you may feel, however difficult you may find it to pray, whatever doubts you have, the Spirit of the Lord is upon you; you are being transformed into his likeness and God is with you.

PRAYER

Lord, give wisdom to our leaders that they may lay aside their own personal agendas and work together to maintain justice, peace and unity in the nation for the glory of your name.

22 May | Day 142
Take Time to Celebrate

'A glimpse of heaven' is how one twenty-seven-year-old woman described her experience of our annual church holiday (Focus). She also described the year she missed it in order to go on an exotic holiday: each day she could only think of how she longed to be at Focus.

This is the time when the whole community comes together in a festival of celebration, worship, thanksgiving and praise. We often experience a great outpouring of the Holy Spirit. It is a time of spiritual growth when we listen to visionary and practical teaching from the Bible on how to live our lives. It is a time of laughter and fun as we meet together for a week-long party: playing, picnicking, singing and dancing. We make new friends as well as having a great holiday. It really is 'a glimpse of heaven'.

It takes time but celebration is an important part of life.

READING FROM PSALMS

Psalm 66:1–12
Celebrate God's goodness

Do you sometimes feel like you have been 'to hell and back'? Have you found yourself 'pushed to the limit'? It may be that God is training you, like silver being refined in the fire.

God had brought his people through very difficult times:

> 'He trained us first,
> passed us like silver through refining
> fires ...
> pushed us to our very limit,
> Road-tested us inside and out,
> took us to hell and back;
> Finally he brought us
> to this well-watered place'
> (vv.10–12, MSG).

Don't let these occasions go unmarked. Celebrate. Their celebration sounds a fairly noisy affair: 'All together now – applause for God!' (v.1, MSG). They sang praise: 'How awesome are your deeds! So great is your power' (v.3). They celebrated what God had done (v.5). They rejoiced and praised God in a way that everybody around could hear: 'Bless our God, O peoples! Give him a thunderous welcome!' (v.8, MSG).

PRAYER

Lord, I celebrate your goodness. Thank you that you bring me through fire and water in order to bring me to a place of abundance.

NEW TESTAMENT READING

John 12:37–13:17
Celebrate Jesus

There will be times in your life when things go well. There may also be times when things go badly. But there is one thing you can always celebrate. Jesus died and rose again for you. Jesus said, 'For I did not come to judge the world, but to save it' (12:47). He said, 'I have come ... so that no one who believes in me should stay in darkness' (v.46).

The context of Jesus washing his disciples' feet is set just before the Passover feast (13:1). There would have been great excitement in the air as hundreds of thousands came to Jerusalem to *celebrate* the Passover. This time of *celebration* foreshadowed the death and resurrection of Jesus, which we now *celebrate* especially at Easter.

When he had finished washing their feet, he said to them, 'Do you understand what I have done for you?' (v.12). What was it all about? What were they to understand? We can see *four pictures* from the passage:

1. Love
The act of Jesus washing his disciples' feet demonstrated *'the full extent' of his love* (v.1). This is a very striking contrast to what the world thinks of when people use the word 'love'. It is far more than a feeling or an emotion; it is a decision to treat people the way that Jesus would treat them (vv.14–15).

2. Service
The roads of Palestine were unsurfaced and uncleaned. In dry weather they would have been inches deep in dust. In wet weather they would have been liquid mud.

In a wealthy household, on arrival there would be a bowl at the door. The second lowest slave of the household would untie the sandals. The lowest slave would wash the feet.

While the others are reclining, Jesus gets up, takes off his sleeveless tunic and strips down to a loincloth. Like a slave, he starts washing their feet. Jesus is taking the place of a person at the bottom of society, the last place, the place of a slave – the one who does the dirty jobs. This is *a total reversal of the world's model of leadership.*

Jesus, their 'Lord and Teacher' (v.14), reveals himself as the least one in society, the one who does the dirty jobs, the one who is in the last place.

Jesus shows us that if you love people, you will be willing to serve them and that those who serve you should always be treated with the greatest respect.

3. Humility
Jesus uniquely combined absolute love (v.1) and absolute power: 'The Father has put all things under his power' (v.3a). In love, he chose to act in humility and serve his disciples.

Those who seek their own glory (like Judas, v.2) are reduced to nothing. Those who exalt themselves are humbled. Those who humble themselves, God will exalt.

Jesus reveals a new way of exercising authority through love, service and humility. In this dramatic way, he bridges the gap between those in leadership and those under their leadership.

4. Forgiveness
The washing and cleansing is a sign of forgiveness – cleansing from sin. Foot-washing is a picture of what Jesus is about to do on the cross for them (v.7). Through Jesus' death for you, you are totally forgiven. Why then does Jesus teach us to pray regularly for forgiveness?

I find the most helpful analogy and picture is the one given here. When Jesus moved to wash Peter's feet, Peter said, '"No, you shall never wash my feet." Jesus answered, "Unless I wash you, you have no part with me"' (v.8). Peter replied, in effect, 'Well, in that case, wash my whole body.' Jesus said, 'Those who have had a bath need only to wash their feet; their whole body is clean' (v.10).

This is a picture of forgiveness. When you put your faith in Jesus you are made totally clean and you are forgiven – everything is dealt with. You do not need to repeat this one-off act of repentance and faith that leads to total forgiveness. It is the equivalent of having a bath.

However, as we go through the world we do things that tarnish our friendship with God. Your relationship is always secure but your friendship is sullied with the dirt that you pick up on your feet. Each day pray, 'Lord, forgive me, cleanse me from the dirt.' You don't need to have a bath again, Jesus has done that for you, but a measure of cleansing may be necessary each day.

In addition to our great Easter celebration, each week when we gather on the day of the resurrection (Sunday), we remember and celebrate these amazing events. Furthermore, every time you receive communion you are celebrating the death and resurrection of Jesus for you.

PRAYER

Lord, help us to follow Jesus' example, not just in words but also in actions. Thank you that you have given us so much to celebrate.

OLD TESTAMENT READING

1 Samuel 10:9–12:25
Celebrate success

Saul began his reign as king with a honeymoon period. The Spirit of God came upon him in power and he prophesied (10:9–13). God gave him great wisdom in dealing with opposition. He knew when to keep silent (v.27).

Saul soon had to deal with 'troublemakers' (v.27). God is in the business of touching human hearts (v.26). But, as always, the Bible is realistic. Troublemakers were around the corner. Wherever God is at work in power, expect to find troublemakers as well.

When the people of God were facing appalling cruelty from a man who wanted to gouge out the right eye of every person, 'the Spirit of God came upon [Saul] in power' (11:6). God gave him a great victory and he had the wisdom to say afterwards, 'No one shall be put to death today, for this day the LORD has rescued Israel' (v.13). Instead they held *'a great celebration'* (v.15).

In Samuel's farewell speech, he spoke of how often God has given success to his people when they cried to him for help (12:8, 10–11). He urged them to *'consider what great things he has done for you'* (v.24). Many of these things came about as a result of Samuel's prayer and he said, 'As for me, far be it from me that I should *sin against the LORD* by *failing to pray for you'* (v.23).

Don't get so bound up with your own needs and worries that you fail to pray for others. It's very important that we pray for one another.

The passage for today ends with Samuel telling the people to 'consider what great things he has done for you' (v.24). Whatever else is going on in your life, look back, consider and *celebrate* your forgiveness, the gift of the Holy Spirit, the promise of glory and all the other great things God has done for you.

PRAYER

Lord, today I want to look back with thanks and celebrate all the great things you have done for me...

23 May | Day 143

The Love of Your Life

In February 1977, Bishop Festo Kivengere was part of a group of church leaders who delivered a letter of protest to the dictator, Idi Amin, speaking out against the beatings, arbitrary killings and unexplained disappearances taking place across Uganda at that time. The next day, Festo Kivengere's friend and leader, Archbishop Janani Luwum was murdered by Idi Amin and Bishop Festo was driven into hiding and then exile.

Soon afterwards, Festo Kivengere published a book entitled *I Love Idi Amin*. In the book he explained the extraordinary title: 'The Holy Spirit showed me that I was getting hard in my spirit ... so I had to ask for forgiveness from the Lord, and for grace to *love* President Amin more ... this was fresh air for my tired soul. I knew I had seen the Lord and been released: love filled my heart.'[1]

Love is more than a feeling or an emotion. It is a *decision* about how we treat one another. Jesus was the supreme example of love in the history of the world. He tells us to love God, to love one another (John 13:34–35), to love our neighbour as ourselves and even to love our enemies. He demonstrates all this in his own life through loving everyone (even Judas who betrayed him as we see in today's passage), and laying down his life for us all in love.

READING FROM PSALMS

Psalm 66:13–20
Love God

When you are in trouble do you ever make a promise that if God were to answer your prayer you will do something (...or you won't do something ever again!)? The psalmist made such a promise – and when his prayer was answered he fulfilled his promise. He wrote, 'I will ... fulfil my vows to you – vows my lips promised and my mouth spoke when I was in trouble' (vv.13–14).

God loves you. He does not withhold his love from you. The psalmist praises God: 'He stayed with me, *loyal in his love'* (v.20, MSG). Your love for God and others is a response to his love for you. 'We love because he first loved us' (1 John 4:19).

God, in his love for you, hears and answers your prayers. If you want to enjoy God's love to the full, experience answered prayer and show your love for him, there is one thing you need to avoid. the psalmist writes: 'If I had cherished *sin* in my heart, the Lord would not have listened' (Psalm 66:18).

If there is sin in the past, you can confess it and repent of it and be forgiven. What really blocks our relationship with God is if we deliberately plan to sin in the future. Then we cannot come into God's presence with a clear conscience. This blocks the experience of his love.

It is because God, in his love 'has surely listened and heard my voice in prayer' (v.19), that in response the psalmist wants other people to listen to him: 'Come and listen, all you who fear God; let me tell you what he has done for me' (v.16). It is so encouraging to hear other people's testimonies about what God has done in their lives. It inspires the rest of us and increases our faith.

PRAYER

Lord, thank you for your forgiveness, mercy and love. Thank you for the many times when you have listened and heard my voice in prayer (v.19). 'Praise be to God, who has not rejected my prayer or withheld his love from me!' (v.20).

NEW TESTAMENT READING

John 13:18–38
Love one another

Nothing is more of a hindrance to the message of Jesus than a lack of love between Christians. If our nations are to be changed, if people are going to turn back to following Jesus, we must start loving one another. This means loving Christians of different churches, denominations, traditions and different views to ourselves.

It means loving one another in the local church. Disunity destroys. Love unites. Love attracts others to the person of Jesus. Loving God and loving one another in Jesus' name must be our overall ambition above all others. That is the kind of love that can change the world.

Here we have three men (Judas, Peter and John, author of John's Gospel) who have radically different relationships with Jesus. They represent each of us at different moments in our lives.

John, the beloved disciple, knew the love of Jesus in a very intimate way. Of all the disciples he was the closest friend of Jesus. He was the one dwelling next to him (v.23). Four times in this Gospel, John describes himself as 'the disciple *whom Jesus loved*': here (v.23), at the cross (19:26), at the empty tomb (20:2) and with the risen Jesus (21:20). He reveals that we are all called to be in close communion with Jesus.

Out of this intimate experience of Jesus' love, John's Gospel and letters speak so much about love. He records that Jesus told his disciples, 'A new command I give you: love one another. As I have loved you, so you must love one another. By this everyone will know that you are my disciples, if you love one another' (13:34–35).

People fail to love for different reasons. Judas betrays Jesus in spite of being so close to him: 'He who shares my bread has lifted up his heel against me' (v.18). Satan entered into him (v.27). Here we see the very opposite of love. Judas hated love. He was in revolt against Jesus. Yet Jesus continued to love Judas.

Peter loved Jesus. But he was a complex personality with a very human vision of Jesus and his mission. Peter said that he would lay down his life for Jesus (v.37), but Jesus tells him, 'You will disown me three times' (v.38). And that is what Peter did (18:15–18, 25–27). Yet Jesus continued to love Peter.

Jesus sets before you this amazing challenge: 'As I have loved you, so you must love one another' (13:34). Jesus loved you by laying down his life for you. He says that you are to follow his example and show self-sacrificial love. This is the mark of a true Christian. 'By this everyone will know that you are my disciples, if you love one another' (v.35).

Love is the most effective form of evangelism. When people see real love they see God. The best way to start to tell people about Jesus is to love them and to love other followers of Jesus.

Generally, in the world, people get into groups with people they are naturally attracted to and who think the same way as them. We are meant to be quite different. The church of Jesus Christ brings us together with a variety of people from different backgrounds, of different interests, different ages, ethnicities, races, perspectives, lifestyles, opinions and different views: all who love one another.

PRAYER

Lord, help us to love one another as you have loved us. May we see a new love between Christians of all churches, denominations and traditions in the local, national and global church. May the world be changed by our love.

OLD TESTAMENT READING

1 Samuel 13:1–14:23
Love like God

There are times in your life when you may feel outnumbered by problems – illness, temptation, attacks on your faith and so on – but God is able to save you when he acts on your behalf. However much you seem to be outnumbered by your enemies, when the Lord acts on your behalf you will be saved.

Trust God not just when things are going well, but also in the difficult times. God is looking for men and women of faith.

Samuel said, 'The LORD has sought out a man *after his own heart* and appointed him leader of his people' (13:14).

God's heart is full of love, compassion, mercy, justice and creativity. He is looking for people who are like him – like Jesus. Only the work of the Holy Spirit in your heart can make you like Jesus.

Saul failed. God had told Saul to wait until Samuel arrived. When Samuel was delayed, the people became restless. Saul cared more about what the people thought than what God thought. He became impatient and panicked (vv.6–12), just as we so often do. Learn to be more patient – to wait for God to act – and not panic if little things go wrong. Do not rush into rash decisions in the heat of the moment.

Jonathan, on the other hand, trusted ultimately in God's love. He said 'Perhaps the LORD will act on our behalf. Nothing can hinder the LORD from saving, whether by many or by few' (14:6).

PRAYER

Lord, please give me a heart like yours – a heart of love. Help me to trust in your unfailing love. Thank you that your love is poured into my heart by the Holy Spirit, who has been given to me (Romans 5:5). Lord, please pour your love into my heart today.

24 May | Day 144
How to Finish Well

You can finish well. You may have had a bad start in life. You may have messed up along the way. You may have made mistakes. You may have regrets. But you can *finish well* and that is what matters most.

Some *start* well but fall. In the recession, many of the companies that business consultant Jim Collins had profiled in his international bestseller *Good to Great,* fell. Even the 'mightiest' of companies can fall.

In his most recent book, *How the Mighty Fall*, he examines the path towards doom. The first stage of the process begins with 'hubris born of success'.[1] As with Saul in the Old Testament passage for today, it is 'arrogance' (1 Samuel 15:23) that begins the process by which the mighty fall. Saul started well but did not finish well.

It is more important to finish well than to start well. In the New Testament, Saul (of Tarsus) started off very badly (as a persecutor of Jesus) but he finished well (as the great apostle, Paul).

Jesus, as always, shows us the way. His life was relatively short. He died in his early thirties, yet he finished well. He *completed the work the Father gave him to do* (John 17:4). This is my ambition in life. I want to complete the work God has given me to do.

How can you make sure you finish well?

READING FROM PROVERBS

Proverbs 12:28–13:9
Take the long view

The writer of Proverbs encourages us to take the long view and stay in the way of 'righteousness' where 'there is life; along that path is *immortality'* (12:28). Avoid the temptation to focus just on the here and now. Act in the light of eternity.

What does a righteous life look like?

1. Listen to parental advice

'A wise child heeds a parent's instruction' (13:1). Honouring parents is high on the list of God's priorities. Family life and good parenting are so important. I recommend *The Parenting Book* by Nicky and Sila Lee.

2. Guard your lips

'Those who guard their lips *guard their lives*, but those who speak rashly *will come to ruin*' (v.3). It is impossible to overestimate the importance of your words and of controlling the tongue.

3. Work hard

'The desires of the *diligent* are fully satisfied' (v.4). Work is a blessing. Success can be hard work. It requires diligent perseverance.

Winston Churchill said, 'Success consists of going from failure to failure without loss of enthusiasm.'

4. Love the truth

'The righteous hate what is false' (v.5). We are to hate dishonesty and love the truth. Mark Twain once said, 'If you tell the truth, you don't have to remember anything.'

5. Be a person of integrity

'Righteousness guards the person of integrity' (v.6). Integrity does not mean being perfect. It means being honest, real and authentic (it is the opposite of hypocrisy). In his book, *Integrity*, the clinical psychologist Dr Henry Cloud writes that integrity 'is the key to success. A person with integrity has the – often rare – ability to pull everything together, to make it all happen no matter how challenging the circumstances.'[2]

PRAYER

Lord, help me to be wise, to honour parents, to guard my lips, to work hard, to speak the truth and to live a life of integrity.

NEW TESTAMENT READING

John 14:1–31
Trust in the legacy of Jesus

Are you troubled, distressed, agitated or afraid? Jesus does not want you to be troubled, but to have peace in your heart (vv.1, 27).

Jesus knew that his life on this earth was about to finish. He was about to leave his disciples (v.27); he was going back to the Father (v.3). Yet he said to them, 'Do not let your hearts be troubled, distressed, agitated' (v.1, AMP). 'Peace I leave with you' (v.27). Jesus does not leave you alone but passes on to you an amazing legacy.

1. Jesus has good plans for your future

Jesus says, 'There is plenty of room for you in my Father's home ... I'm on my way to get your room ready' (v.2, MSG). In Christ, your long-term future is totally secure.

2. Jesus is coming back for you

The end of earthly life is not the end. Jesus told his followers, 'I will come back and take you to be with me that you also may be where I am' (v.3). You will be with Jesus for ever.

3. Jesus has opened the way for you to know God

Thomas asks, 'How can we know the way?' Jesus replies, 'I am the way and the truth and the life. No one comes to the Father except through me' (vv.5–6).

4. Jesus reveals God for you

Philip says, 'Lord, show us the Father' (v.8). Jesus replies, 'Anyone who has seen me has seen the Father' (v.9). If you want to know what God looks like, look at Jesus.

5. Jesus will do even greater things through you

Jesus will do even greater miracles *through his disciples* than he did while he was on earth (v.12).

6. Jesus will continue to answer your prayers

'From now on, whatever you request along the lines of who I am and what I am doing, I'll do it. That's how the Father will be seen for who he is in the Son. I mean it. Whatever you request in this way, I'll do' (vv.13–14, MSG).

7. Jesus will never leave you alone

Jesus says, 'I will not leave you as orphans' (v.18). He says that he'll 'provide you another Friend so that you will always have someone *with you*. This Friend is the Spirit of Truth ... he has been staying *with you*, and will even be *in* you!' (vv.16–17, MSG).

8. Jesus will continue to love you

'Those who love me will be loved by my Father, and I too will love them and show myself to them' (v.21b).

9. Jesus and the Father will make their home *with you*

Jesus said, 'Those who love me will obey my teaching. My Father will love them, and we will come to them and make our home *with them*' (v.23).

10. Jesus leaves you with peace

'Peace I leave with you ... Do not let your hearts be troubled and do not be afraid' (v.27). Peace comes from trusting that Jesus is there with us and in us. Jesus is our peace.

How is all this possible? The way in which Jesus passes on his legacy to you is through the Holy Spirit. He has sent the Holy Spirit to live in your heart: 'The Friend, the Holy Spirit whom the Father will send at my request, will make everything plain to you' (v.26, MSG).

The Greek word for the Holy Spirit, *parakletos,* literally means 'one called alongside'. It has a multifaceted meaning – counsellor, advocate, comforter, encourager, helper, someone to stand by you, he who is to befriend you. For example, a mother is a paraclete for her child. She takes away the anguish of loneliness. She brings presence, security, peace and communion.

The Holy Spirit now lives in us to give us new strength and new love – so that we, the church, can continue the mission of Jesus to the world.

Jesus had thought it through very carefully and had made a great succession plan!

PRAYER

Lord, thank you that you give me the Holy Spirit to live in me and to be with me for ever. Thank you that you give me your peace and you promise to answer my prayers.

OLD TESTAMENT READING

1 Samuel 14:24–15:35
Honour the Lord to the end

Saul started off very well. God had given him great success. In the passage for today, we can learn from Saul's good example in the early days of his leadership. He headhunted good, 'brave' people (14:52) and mobilised them.

However, he did not finish well due to disobedience and arrogance. Partial obedience is still disobedience. Not only did he disobey God but he 'set up a victory monument in his own honor' (15:12, MSG). How different this is from Jesus who, as we see in today's passage, had only one aim in life – to bring glory to his Father (John 14:13).

Samuel tells Saul, 'When you started out in this, you were nothing – and you knew it. Then God put you at the head of Israel – made you king over Israel ... why did you not obey God? ... He wants you to listen to him! Plain listening is the thing, not staging a lavish religious production ... Getting self-important around God is far worse than making deals with your dead ancestors. Because you said No to God's command, he says No to your kingship' (1 Samuel 15:17–23, MSG).

Power is so dangerous. It has a strong tendency to corrupt. Success can so easily lead to pride and arrogance. That in turn can lead to idolatry. Keep honouring the Lord.

PRAYER

Lord, help me to follow the obedience and humility of Jesus. May the Spirit of truth lead and guide me and give me your peace.

25 May | Day 145
How to Face Giant Problems

Goliath was a giant. He was 9 feet tall, a champion, wearing heavy armour, standing and shouting, defying the people of God (1 Samuel 17:1–11). As well as physical giants, there are metaphorical ones. A 'giant' is a big, seemingly insurmountable problem or issue.

- 'Personal giants' could include giant personal challenges in relation to your health, marriage, family, relationships or lack of relationships, job or lack of job, other work issues, or some sin, temptation, addiction, fear, loneliness, discouragement or debt.
- 'National giants' in the UK include terrorism, gang violence, homelessness, the breakdown of marriage, family life and community, exploding prison populations, failing schools and the decline of church congregations. There is therefore the giant task of evangelising the country, revitalising the church and transforming our society.
- 'Global giants' include extreme poverty (as a result of which thousands of children die each day), preventable disease (millions dying of diseases for which we have a relatively easy cure), the need for universal primary education (almost one billion people unable to read) and the need for worldwide water sanitation (which could be funded by the amount of money that Europeans spend on ice-cream every year).[1]

There are two possible attitudes when facing a giant. One is to say, 'It's so big, there's nothing I can do.' The other is to say, 'It's so big, I can't miss!'

READING FROM PSALMS

Psalm 67:1–7
Think global

God loves the entire world. He wants all nations and peoples to know him, worship and love him.

The psalmist prayed for God's blessing on his people in order that 'your ways may be known on earth, your salvation among *all nations*' (v.2).

We see in this psalm that the global vision for the people of God beyond their own borders was foreshadowed in the Old Testament.

The psalmist prays for the entire globe (vv.3–5). If we are to tackle the global giants, we need a global vision. The words of this psalm are all about God. The size of your vision will be dependent on the size of your vision of God. As A. W. Tozer put it, 'What comes into our minds when we think about God is the most important thing about us.'[2]

PRAYER

Lord, be gracious to us and bless us. Make your face shine upon us. Make your ways known on earth and your salvation among all nations. May all the people praise you.

NEW TESTAMENT READING

John 15:1–16:4
Testify about Jesus

There is nothing more important and no greater privilege in life than to be a friend of Jesus. Jesus says, 'You are my friends ... I no longer call you servants ... I have called you friends' (15:14–15).

Having Jesus as your friend allows you to tackle the giants in your life, in the church and in society from a unique standpoint.

1. Personal

Jesus tells us that there are two secrets of Christian fruitfulness.

First, there is pruning (vv.1–2). The purpose of pruning is so that you can bear even more fruit. Pain, sorrow, sickness and suffering, loss, bereavement, failure, disappointment and frustrated ambition are some of the ways your life is pruned.

Pruning can seem cruel; branches are left jagged and exposed to face the harsh winter. But the purpose of pruning is to give way to newness of life. When spring and summer come, there is an abundance of fruit. The sharp pruning knife will, in the end, bring fruitfulness and blessing.

The second secret of fruitfulness is closeness to Jesus (v.4). You cannot take on the giants by yourself. Jesus says, 'When you're joined with me and I with you, the relation intimate and organic, the harvest is sure to be abundant. Separated, you can't produce a thing' (v.5, MSG). You will only succeed in tackling the giants if you stay close to Jesus.

Cultivate a growing friendship with Jesus (vv.14–15) by spending time with him, walking with him, praying and listening to him through his word, following his desires.

Jesus says that if you stay close to him ('remain in him') three things will happen in terms of fruitfulness. First, your prayers will be answered (v.7). Second, God will be glorified (v.8). Third, your joy will be complete and overflowing (v.11, AMP).

Jesus wants you to be filled with joy and fully alive. There's no greater joy than to know you are valued, precious and loved by God and to love others as you are loved. There's no greater joy than giving eternal life to others in and with Jesus.

2. Church

There are massive giants facing the church today. The biggest giant is disunity. Nothing is more of a hindrance to the message of Jesus than division between Christians. Disunity will only be overcome by love. Jesus said, 'My command is this: Love each other as I have loved you. Greater love has no one than this, to lay down one's life for one's friends ... This is my command: Love each other' (vv.12–13, 17).

3. Society

Jesus warns us that we will face the giant of a world that hates us (vv.18–19). He says, 'If they persecuted me, they will persecute you also' (v.20). He says, 'Those who kill you will think they are offering a service to God' (16:2). There are parts of the world where this is literally true today.

But there are also other more subtle forms of hidden persecution. No one likes to be rejected, looked down on, made fun of or ridiculed. Jesus warns that, wherever you are, you should expect opposition, hatred and even persecution.

On our own we would have no answers but Jesus says, 'When the Counsellor comes, whom I will send to you from the Father, the Spirit of truth who goes out from the Father, *he will testify about me*. And *you also must testify'* (15:26–27). The Holy Spirit enables you to testify about Jesus and to take on these giant challenges, to see our society transformed.

PRAYER

Lord, thank you that you call me your friend. Help me to love others as you have loved me.

OLD TESTAMENT READING

1 Samuel 16:1–17:37
Trust in God

David was extraordinarily gifted – naturally as well as supernaturally. He was handsome and in good health (16:12). He was talented musically (v.18). He was a gifted speaker (v.18). He had athletic ability (17:1–37; 18:11). He was a leader (18:13). He was successful (vv.14, 30). He was famous (v.30).

Yet it was for none of these reasons that God used him. The Lord said to Samuel, 'The LORD does not look at the things people look at. Human beings look at the outward appearance, but *the LORD looks at the heart'* (16:7).

David was outraged by Goliath's defiance of the living God (17:26). He was a courageous leader. He says, 'Let no one lose heart on account of this Philistine [Goliath]' (v.32). What lessons can we learn from the way in which David tackled this giant?

1. Reject rejection

Eliab said to David, 'What are you doing here! Why aren't you minding your own business, tending that scrawny flock of sheep? I know what you're up to. You've come down here to see the sights, hoping for a ringside seat at a bloody battle!' (v.28, MSG).

Yet David *'turned away'* from Eliab (v.30).

The lesson we learn here is not to be put off if rejected or ill-treated. As Joyce Meyer writes, 'God is not looking for someone with ability but someone with availability ... keep your heart pure by refusing to allow hatred, offense, bitterness, resentment or unforgiveness to stop you.'[2]

2. Get involved

David said to Saul, 'Let no one lose heart on account of this Philistine; your servant will go and fight him' (v.32). He volunteered his services. I am always so moved and impressed by the way in which our congregation are willing to volunteer their services: praying, serving and giving.

3. Trust God

Saul says to David, 'You are not able to go out against this Philistine and fight him; you are only a boy' (v.33). Yet David replies, 'The LORD who delivered me from the paw of the lion and the paw of the bear will deliver me from the hand of this Philistine' (v.37a). He trusts God because he knows that God is with him (see 16:18; 17:37b; 18:14).

Ultimately, the reason that David was able to tackle Goliath was that he was anointed by God: 'Samuel took his flask of oil and anointed him, with his brothers standing around watching. The Spirit of GOD entered David like a rush of wind, God vitally empowering him for the rest of his life' (16:13, MSG). The only way you will be able to tackle the giants in your life, in society and in the world, is through the anointing of the Holy Spirit.

PRAYER

Lord, as I face the giants, I need the anointing of your Holy Spirit upon me and your presence with me. Give me courage not to run away, not to lose heart and not to give up.

26 May | Day 146
His Name Has Power

Aged thirty-three, Barbara Clapham came to live in London. She decided she was going to look for a church. One Sunday morning, she arrived at Holy Trinity Brompton. The young woman who was welcoming people at the door smiled at her and asked her name. Because of that smile, Barbara came back the following week. When she walked in the next Sunday the same person said, 'Hello Barbara.'

Because the person on the door remembered her name, she decided that she was going to come back every Sunday. That was in 1947. From then on Barbara came almost every Sunday until she died, soon after celebrating her 100th birthday. She made a huge impact on the life of HTB (including running the finances of the church for many years). I wonder whether the young woman on the door had any idea of the difference she made by remembering Barbara's *name*.

There is great power in a name. Names are significant. This is true today, but it was even more so in the Hebrew culture we read about in the Bible. A Hebrew name is no mere label. *The name of the Lord* reveals who he is.

READING FROM PSALMS

Psalm 68:1–6
Praise the name of the Lord

David urges: 'sing to God, *sing praise to his name*, extol him who rides on the clouds – *his name is the Lord'* (v.4).

God *reveals* himself *through his name*. He gave *his name* to Moses ('I AM WHO I AM') when he came to liberate his people from slavery in Egypt (Exodus 3:14). Likewise, in this psalm we see that the God who bears this name has particular concern for the marginalised in society.

God is 'a father to the *fatherless'* and 'a defender of *widows'* (Psalm 68:5). 'God sets the *lonely* in families' (v.6a). 'God makes homes for the *homeless'* (v.6a, MSG). 'He leads forth the *prisoners* with singing' (v.6b).

One of the ways to honour *the name of the Lord* is to love and serve the marginalised: widows and orphans, the lonely, the homeless and those in prison.

PRAYER

Lord, I praise your holy name. May your name be honoured in my life as I love and serve the marginalised in society.

NEW TESTAMENT READING

John 16:5–17:5
Power in the name of Jesus

Do you know how much power there is in *the name of Jesus*? As Jesus leaves his disciples, he says to them, 'I tell you the truth, my Father will give you whatever you ask *in my name*. Until now you have not asked for anything *in my name*. Ask and you will receive, and your joy will be complete ... In that day you will ask *in my name*' (16:23b–26a).

When we go to God in prayer we do not ask in our own names, but in *the name of Jesus*. On our own we have no right to ask anything. But Jesus, through the cross and resurrection, has made it possible for you to have access to God in *his* name.

Praying in Jesus' name is about aligning yourself with Jesus. As you do this, your prayers harmonise with God's desires for your life and you can pray that his will be done. You cannot do this on your own. You need the Holy Spirit.

Jesus tells the disciples that it is to their *advantage* that he is going away because, 'Unless I go away the Counsellor [the 'Friend', MSG] will not come to you; but if I go, I will send him to you' (v.7). Jesus could only be in one place at a time. Now, by his Spirit, he can be with you and me as our friend and helper all the time, everywhere we go.

The Holy Spirit will convince the world about guilt (supremely because 'people do not believe in' Jesus, v.9), and 'he will guide [us] into all truth' (v.13a). Every time we go off track or in the wrong direction, the Holy Spirit convicts us. We sense in our spirit that what we are doing is not right.

The Holy Spirit never condemns us (Romans 8:1). He convicts us to repent and then to go in the right direction. He guides, sustains and strengthens you and me to become more like Jesus.

He guides you into all truth. Truth is revealed by the Spirit of truth (John 16:13a). Among other things, he reveals the truth about you. *The truth sets you free*.

Jesus promises you three things:

1. Joy – in the midst of mourning and grief

'I tell you the truth, you will weep and mourn while the world rejoices. You will grieve, but your grief will turn to *joy'* (v.20). Justice will prevail. Evil will not have the last word. When Jesus rose from the dead, the disciples' joy was so great that it completely overshadowed their grief – like a mother who has given birth to a baby and forgets the anguish of the birth (vv.21–22).

2. Love – in the midst of hate

You are loved. Even when 'the world hates you' (15:18), Jesus says to you that 'the Father himself *loves you* because you have *loved* me and have believed that I came from God' (16:27). The Spirit of Truth will reveal the Father's total love for you.

3. Peace – in the midst of trouble
Jesus never promised you a trouble free life. Indeed, he says that in the world you will experience 'tribulation and trials and distress and frustration' (v.33, AMP). But he promises you 'perfect peace and confidence in the midst of these trials' because he has 'overcome the world (I have deprived it of power to harm you and have conquered it for you)' (v.33, AMP).

The most important gift that you receive from the Holy Spirit is a relationship with God. In this prayer Jesus highlights this as the true heart and definition of 'eternal life' – 'this is eternal life that they know you, the only true God, and Jesus Christ, whom you have sent' (17:3).

This amazing description of eternal life is surrounded by Jesus' prayer that *God's name* would be glorified. Everything Jesus did while he was here on earth, and our relationship with the Father through Jesus, are all ultimately to the glory of God's name.

PRAYER

Lord, I can never thank you enough for the immense privilege of being able to pray in the name of Jesus. Today I pray... in your name.

OLD TESTAMENT READING

1 Samuel 17:38–18:30
Protection in the name of the Lord

David realised that the best *protection* was not Saul's armour but *the name of the Lord* (17:45).

At first, David tried to face Goliath in Saul's armour. Then he realised, 'I cannot go in these ... because I am not used to them' (v.39). So he took the armour off. He decided to be himself. This is such a lesson in life. It is no good putting on someone else's armour. It always looks artificial and unnatural when we try and present ourselves as if we are someone else.

There is great power in authenticity. Oscar Wilde said, 'Be yourself; everyone else is already taken!' You are at your most effective when you are being yourself. As St Catherine of Siena put it: 'Be who God meant you to be and you will set the world on fire.'

David had a concern for God's name and its vindication (v.45). He said to Goliath, 'You come against me with sword and spear and javelin, but I come against you *in the name* of the Lord Almighty' (v.45). He realised the limitations of human efforts (v.47). He was confident in his God whose name alone is sufficient to strike the strongest person to the ground (v.46). He was prepared to *trust in the name of the Lord* in the face of enormous opposition.

You may face great opposition. The world you live in can seem enormously powerful and overwhelming. You may feel weak and pathetic in contrast. But go out *in God's name* – realising your limitations and yet trusting in him to vindicate his name. Because *the Lord was with David* he was successful in everything he did (18:5, 12, 14).

David's success provoked anger and jealousy from Saul (vv.8–9). As Joyce Meyer points out, 'God always puts us around someone who is like sandpaper to smooth off our rough edges ... a testing that takes place before we get promoted. If you want to lead you must first serve in circumstances that may not be ideal and learn to behave wisely. This prepares us to be greatly used by God.'[1]

God gave David more success. Interestingly, because of his concern for God's name, David's '*name* became well known' (v.30). But that was not his aim or intention, or the focus of his life.

PRAYER

Lord, may the churches in this country be filled again with people worshipping the name of Jesus. I pray that everything we do may be focused on seeing the name of Jesus lifted up and honoured again in our society.

27 May | Day 147
The Power of Unity

In Buchenwald concentration camp, 56,000 people were put to death by a totalitarian regime that saw the Christian faith as a threat to its ideology. One block of cells in the camp was reserved for prisoners who were deemed especially dangerous or notable. Paul Schneider, a Lutheran pastor who was called 'the preacher of Buchenwald', was placed in this special block because even from the small window in his cell he loudly proclaimed the gospel of Jesus Christ – in defiance of the orders of the Gestapo guards.

Otto Neururer, a Catholic priest whose work on behalf of the Jews and other so-called 'undesirables' had made him a threat to the Nazi warlords, was also put in this block. He too ministered in Jesus' name to his fellow inmates in the concentration camp until he was crucified upside down.

In unity, these two men, one a Catholic and the other a Protestant, bore witness together to their common Lord – Jesus Christ. Unity is so powerful.

READING FROM PSALMS

Psalm 68:7–14
The people and the land

David reflects on the exodus, Mount Sinai and the conquest of Canaan. These were some of the high points of the history of the people of God when they were genuinely united.

This passage is all about recognising where that blessing and unity ultimately came from – God. It is a psalm of thanksgiving and praise to God for all the things he has done. It celebrates his leadership (v.7), his power and provision (vv.8–9), his generosity, his justice (v.10) and his victories (vv.11–14).

God had led the people to the promised land. Yet today, in this very same area, the challenge of unity is great. The search for peace in the Middle East remains one of the greatest challenges facing our world.

PRAYER

Lord, thank you for your love for everyone. I pray for peace and unity in the war-torn countries of the Middle East. Thank you that you are the source and foundation of unity.

NEW TESTAMENT READING

John 17:6–26
The church and the world

In the Gospels, we frequently read about the prayer life of Jesus. But only on rare occasions are we informed at any length of what he prayed for. In this great prayer of Jesus, before he goes out to face the cross, we see his priorities.

Jesus prays not only for his disciples, but also for those who will believe in the future – that is to say, he prays for the entire church – which includes you and me (v.20).

This prayer is dominated by the theme of unity. Jesus prays not only for unity among his disciples (v.11), but also for the church (v.20). He prays for a unity like that which unites the Trinity: 'that they may be one, *as We are one*' (v.11, AMP).

1. The *motive* for unity is the great commission of Jesus

Jesus prayed for complete unity *so that the world may believe* (v.23) and know unity with God (vv.21, 24). One of the greatest barriers to belief is disunity in the church. In politics, the moment a political party becomes disunited, it loses popularity. It happens in the secular world and even more so in the church. Jesus says that he protected his disciples and kept them safe 'so that they may be one' (v.12). Now he prays, '*protect them from the evil one*' (v.15) who will seek to divide them.

When churches fight each other, people lose interest. Conversely, when churches do unite it is so attractive. It is the source of joy. The followers of Jesus are not supposed to be miserable. Jesus prays 'that they may have *the full measure of my joy within them*' (v.13). Joy comes from unity. Disunity is a joy-stealer. Unity is powerful.

2. The *means* of unity is the Holy Spirit of Jesus

Jesus prays for your holiness. Jesus prays, '*Sanctify them by the truth*; your word is truth' (v.17). Holiness comes from the truth. The truth is found in God's word. That is why it is so important to soak yourself in God's word.

Holiness comes as you welcome the Holy One, the Spirit of Truth, who comes to dwell within you.

Jesus prays, 'that *I myself may be in them*' (v.26). This is the most extraordinary truth of the New Testament – that Jesus comes to live in you by the Holy Spirit. The same Holy Spirit lives in all Christians of whatever church or denomination. The Holy Spirit unites us.

3. The *mark* of unity is the love of Jesus
Jesus prays, 'that the love you have for me may be in them' (v.26). What higher love can you have than the love that God the Father has for Jesus his Son? Jesus' prayer for you is that you should have the same love that God the Father has for Jesus in your heart for other Christians, for other parts of the body of Christ.

4. The *measure* of unity is the visibility of Jesus
Sometimes people speak about 'invisible unity'. But Jesus didn't pray for invisible unity. Nor did he pray that we might be 'almost united'. He prayed that they may 'be brought to *complete* unity to let the world know that you sent me' (v.23). He wants the church to be completely and visibly united.

One day it will be (see Ephesians 1:9–11). In the meantime, as we build bridges, work together and come together with other Christians from different parts of the church, as hearts and minds are bonded together in communion with Jesus, we can see, as in Buchenwald, visible signs of our invisible unity.

PRAYER

Lord, thank you for the way the Holy Spirit is drawing us together. May we see increasing signs of visible unity so that the world will believe.

OLD TESTAMENT READING

1 Samuel 19:1–20:42
Friends and rivals

In politics, business or even in church life, two people who are great friends can at the same time end up competing for the same job. How should we handle the tension between our ambitions and our friendships?

The friendship between David and Jonathan was remarkable. They were rivals for the throne. They had every reason to be envious of each other and to hate each other. Yet Jonathan loved David 'as he loved himself' (20:17). This type of love, which Jesus commanded, is the highest love one person can have for another (Matthew 22:39).

On the other hand, Saul was filled with jealousy. Jealousy starts with comparing ourselves to others – comparing our achievements with those around us. Jealousy has the power to deprive someone temporarily of their senses. When Jonathan points out to his father, Saul, that David has not wronged him and has benefitted him greatly and it would be quite wrong to kill an innocent man, Saul says, 'As surely as the LORD lives, David will not be put to death' (1 Samuel 19:6).

Logic and reasonable argument may convince a person who is filled with jealousy at the time. However, jealousy is so powerful that once it gets a grip of a person, as it did with Saul, there is no stopping it. As Shakespeare put it in *Othello*, 'It is the green-ey'd monster which doth mock the meat it feeds on' (Act III Scene III).

David and Jonathan loved each other. Jonathan 'was very fond of David' (v.1) and he 'spoke well of David' (v.4). Jonathan even said to David, 'Whatever you want me to do, I'll do for you' (20:4). What a great commitment to make to a friend! Their commitment to each other took the form of a 'covenant' (v.16), which included even their descendants (v.42). And Jonathan 'made David reaffirm his oath out of love for him, because he loved him as he loved himself' (vv.16–17).

As a result of his jealousy 'Saul's anger flared up at Jonathan' (v.30). Jonathan knew that his father intended to kill David (v.33) and he 'got up from the table in fierce anger' (v.34).

The difference between Saul's anger and Jonathan's anger was that Saul's was unfounded and produced by jealousy. Jonathan's anger was righteous anger; 'He was grieved at his father's shameful treatment of David' (v.34). Anger is not always wrong – but examine your motives carefully.

David and Jonathan were not ashamed of showing their affection for each other: '… they kissed each other and wept together' (v.41). Crying can be seen by some as showing weakness, but they had no shame. In crying openly and showing their love for each other. This is a powerful model of friendship, love and unity. Marriage is one of God's answers to loneliness. Close friendship is another.

It was this love and friendship that enabled Jonathan to be totally loyal, supportive and protective in spite of the fact that he was a rival candidate to the throne.

PRAYER

Lord, help us to be willing and able to love our friends and neighbours as ourselves. May people find the answer to loneliness in the love, affection and unity of church community.

28 May | Day 148
How to Respond to Conflict

A springbok is a gazelle-like antelope. Normally they are very alert to predators. However, I remember watching a BBC wildlife programme that filmed two springboks fighting each other in the Kalahari Desert. As they became absorbed in the fight, they did not notice the lion prowling around them, waiting for his opportunity to attack.

As I watched, it struck me as a warning especially for the church. When, in the church, we fight one another, we become very vulnerable to attack. 'The devil prowls around like a roaring lion looking for someone to devour' (1 Peter 5:8).

When God calls you to follow him, he does not call you to a life of ease. Life on earth involves many battles, in all of which God promises you victory through Jesus Christ. There is never going to be a moment in your earthly life when everything is perfect. There are always going to be challenges, difficulties and problems to solve. However, there are times when these intensify and we seem to be coming under attack.

Martin Luther King said that the ultimate measure of a person is not where they stand in 'moments of convenience', but where they stand in 'moments of challenge, moments of great crisis and controversy'.

READING FROM PROVERBS

Proverbs 13:10–19
Avoid unnecessarily quarrelling

The writer of Proverbs contrasts the wise ('wisdom is found in those who take advice', v.10b) and fools ('fools detest turning from evil', v.19b). It is not surprising that we experience conflict. In particular, in this passage we see two examples:

1. Quarrels

'Pride only breeds quarrels' (v.10a). One of the most draining experiences of life is quarrelling – whether in a marriage, among friends, with colleagues or in the church. Here we see that one of the causes of quarrels can be pride. If you are willing to admit your mistakes and wrongs with humility, you can avoid a lot of quarrels.

Another key is listening carefully to one another: 'Arrogant know-it-alls stir up discord, but wise men and women listen to each other's counsel' (v.10, MSG).

2. Disappointments

'Hope deferred makes the heart sick' (v.12a). Or as *The Message* puts it, 'unrelenting disappointment leaves you heartsick'.

This is another kind of attack that is sickening. When a vision we have had for something is held up or our plans are delayed because of some attack or let down, disappointment makes the heart sick. We do battle with our own plans and our circumstances.

On the other hand, there is nothing more satisfying than persevering and seeing some part of your vision fulfilled. 'A longing fulfilled is a tree of life' (v.12a). 'A longing fulfilled is sweet to the soul' (v.19a).

In the midst of all the conflicts of life there are moments of great joy, fulfilment and satisfaction.

PRAYER

Lord, in the midst of the challenges, help me to run the race with perseverance with my eyes fixed on Jesus (Hebrews 12:1–3).

NEW TESTAMENT READING

John 18:1–24
Trust that God can bring good out of evil

Sometimes, when conflict comes in our lives, we only have ourselves to blame. However, this is not necessarily always the case. The attacks on Jesus did not come about as a result of his own sin or failure. Rather, they were the result of wrongdoing by other people. Yet God used it for good (v.14).

Having prayed for unity, Jesus now enters the world of conflict. Alone and vulnerable, filled with love and kindness, Jesus is arrested and condemned to death. He lays down his life in order to give life.

1. Betrayal
This was a terrible moment in the life of Jesus. His friend and disciple Judas, with whom he had spent three years, led a detachment of soldiers and some officials from the chief priests and Pharisees to arrest Jesus (vv.1–3).

There is nothing more painful than when an attack comes from a friend or colleague. Jesus' dignified response is exemplary. He stayed calm, refused violence and exercised extraordinary self-restraint (vv.4–12).

In order to protect his disciples, Jesus confronts the group of powerful armed men, brought by Judas. He restrains Peter's attempt to resort to violence to defend Jesus. He does not want to engage in conflict using the ways of the world.

2. Ill-treatment
The very authorities that should have been protecting the innocent joined in the attack on Jesus. They arrested Jesus. 'They bound him' (v.12). They took him first to Annas and then to Caiaphas. Standing before the high priest, still bound, Jesus is struck in the face (vv.12–14, 19–24).

If Jesus was treated in this way we should not be surprised if, from time to time, we come under attack from those in authority – whether religious or secular.

3. Denial
Peter's denial did not come from an evil heart but simply from human weakness. When asked whether he was one of Jesus' disciples he replied, 'I am not' (v.17).

I totally understand how Peter could have got himself into a position of denying Jesus in spite of all his best intentions. I have sometimes said or done things that, in hindsight, were sheer cowardice.

The reality is that Jesus is *in full control* of the situation. He knew 'all that was going to happen to him' (v.4). He acted to fulfil his own prayer in the previous chapter (v.9, see 17:12). Jesus went to his death 'to drink the cup the Father has given' him, paying the penalty for our sin and wrongdoing (18:11).

He paid the penalty for us: 'It would be good if one person died for the people' (v.14). Jesus' death is on behalf of Peter and each one of us. He faces the attack of death and judgment so that you do not have to. Jesus allows himself to be bound (vv.12, 24) so that you can be unbound and set free.

PRAYER

Father, give me courage and wisdom to know how to respond with dignity and grace when I come under attack. Help me to trust that in everything you work together for the good of those who love you and are called according to your purpose (Romans 8:28).

OLD TESTAMENT READING

1 Samuel 21:1–23:29
Strengthen one another

This was a period of intense conflict for David.

Jealousy, as we see here with Saul, never seems to ease off once it gets a grip of a person. It drove Saul to more and more cold-blooded evil acts. He thought nothing of destroying a town full of priests (22:19).

David had to resort to every ruse in order to avoid the attacks. He ate the holy Bread of the Presence (21:1–9, MSG); he pretended to go crazy (v.13) and gathered a motley crew of 'losers and vagrants and misfits of all sorts' (22:1, MSG). Yet we see in this passage the qualities of David that emerged even when he was under attack.

1. Loyalty
David had a reputation for loyalty (v.14) and was highly respected. David and Jonathan were utterly loyal to each other: 'Jonathan went to David at Horesh and helped him to find strength in God' (23:16).

Considering that he could have seen himself as heir to the throne, Jonathan's attitude to David was extraordinary: 'You shall be king over Israel, and I will be second to you' (v.17). They were utterly committed to each other: 'The two of them made a covenant before the Lord' (v.18).

There is nothing that helps more in times of conflict than the loyalty of our friends and family. They can help you in difficult times. And, when they are under attack, you can help them by your loyalty and support to find strength in God.

2. Prayer
What is your first port of call when conflict comes in your life? As Joyce Meyer puts it, when trouble comes do you 'run to the phone' or do you 'run to the throne'?[1] David had learnt at this stage of his life the vital importance of enquiring of the Lord before making decisions. When he was under attack again and

again 'David went in prayer to God' (vv.2, 4, MSG). In this way, attacks can actually draw you closer to God.

One of the tragedies of this story is that instead of fighting the real enemy (v.27), God's people, like those two springboks, were fighting one another. This gave the Philistines the opportunity to attack. Still today the church is in danger of doing this.

God can take something Satan means for evil and division and turn it into something good. God used the attack by the Philistines to rescue David: 'Then Saul broke off his pursuit of David and went to meet the Philistines' (v.28). It would be wonderful if the church would break off its infighting and in unity face the real enemies that threaten to destroy our world such as injustice, human trafficking, disease and poverty.

PRAYER

Father, help us to be loyal to one another, to stop the in-fighting in the church and to unite to face the real attacks from outside.

29 May | Day 149
Five Burdens You Need Not Carry

At the end of his life, Sir Winston Churchill said, 'When I look back on all these worries, I remember the story of the old man who said on his deathbed that he had had a lot of trouble in his life, most of which had never happened!'[1]

Churchill was speaking about the burden of worries that never materialise. However, there are many different types of 'burdens' in life, and some of them are very real. Jesus said, 'Come to me, all you who are weary and *burdened*, and I will give you rest. Take my yoke upon you ... and you will find rest for your souls. For my yoke is easy and my *burden* is light' (Matthew 11:28–30).

A yoke is something Jesus would have made in a carpenter's shop. It is a wooden frame joining two animals (usually oxen) at the neck, enabling them to pull a plough or wagon together. The function of the yoke is to make the burden easier to carry.

I love the way Eugene Peterson translates this passage in *The Message*: 'Are you tired? Worn out? Burned out on religion? Come to me. Get away with me and you'll recover your life. I will show you how to take a real rest. Walk with me and work with me – watch how I do it. Learn the unforced rhythms of grace. I won't lay anything heavy or ill-fitting on you. Keep company with me and you'll learn to live freely and lightly' (vv.28–30).

READING FROM PSALMS

Psalm 68:15–20
Anxiety

In his book *Affluenza*, the psychologist Oliver James points out that 'almost a quarter of Britain suffers serious emotional distress, such as depression and anxiety, and another quarter are on the verge thereof.'[2]

David praises God 'who daily bears our *burdens*' (v.19). Burdens here may include many things. One of the burdens that God bears for us daily is the weight of worry, stress and anxiety.

John Newton said, 'We can easily manage if we will only take, each day, the burden appointed to it. But the load will be too heavy for us if we carry yesterday's burden over again today, and then add the burden of the morrow before we are required to bear it.'

Each day, you can commit to God your fears, worries and anxieties. It makes all the difference. He daily bears your 'burdens' (v.19).

PRAYER

Thank you, Lord, that today I can come to you and bring to you all my burdens, worries and anxieties...

NEW TESTAMENT READING

John 18:25–40
Failure

The great apostle Peter is asked, '"You are not one of his disciples, are you?" He denied it, saying, "I am not"' (v.25). This is his second denial. Then a third time, Peter is challenged and denies knowing Jesus (v.26). At that moment a cock began to crow (v.27) – just as Jesus had predicted.

Peter realised, as most of us do from time to time, that he had failed Jesus. A sense of failure can be a great burden.

This passage is not the end of Peter's story. After his resurrection, Jesus met with Peter and reinstated him, forgiving him for this failure and commissioning him once more (21:15–25). With Jesus, failure is never final.

Although Peter failed him, Jesus took the burden of his failure, forgave him, reinstated him and used him as powerfully as anyone in human history.

John 18:28–38a
Injustice

One of the many things that Jesus had to bear was a totally unjust trial. It is a basic principle of every fair system of justice that it is up to the prosecution to prove the case against the defendant. It is on them that the 'burden of proof' *lies*. Therefore, every fair judicial system needs to overcome the basic prejudice that because a person is on trial they must be guilty.

When Pilate asked, 'What charges are you bringing against this man?' (v.29) they replied, 'If he were not a criminal ... we would not have handed him over to you' (v.30). In saying this, Jesus' accusers were unjustly attempting to reverse the *burden of proof*.

Pilate also unjustly denied Jesus *the right to silence*. He said, 'What is it you have done?' (v.35c). He tried to get Jesus to condemn himself out of his own mouth. Jesus says that he came into the world 'to testify to the truth' (v.37b). Pilate asked, 'What is truth?' (v.38a).

It is almost as if Pilate seems to be questioning (as our post-modern society does) whether there is such a thing as 'truth' (that is, absolute truth). However, Pilate is face-to-face with the Truth himself, Jesus Christ – who endured an unjust trial – and, far worse, the unfair penalty of crucifixion and death – for you and me.

John 18:38b–40
Sin

Despite this unjust trial, Pilate concludes, 'I find no basis for a charge against him' (v.38b). Jesus is completely innocent. Pilate wants to release him but the crowd shouts, "No, not him! Give us Barabbas!" Now Barabbas had taken part in a rebellion' (v.40). Jesus, the innocent, is condemned to crucifixion. Barabbas, the sinful, goes free.

The symbolism is clear. On the cross, Jesus, the innocent, died so that we, the sinful, may go free. He bore this burden of our sin.

PRAYER

'Praise be to the Lord, to God our Saviour... our God is a God who saves; from the Sovereign LORD comes escape from death' (Psalm 68:19–20).

OLD TESTAMENT READING

1 Samuel 24:1–25:44
Guilt

Guilt is a horrible burden. A guest in one of our Alpha small groups described the physical feeling of guilt as being like 'a very bad case of indigestion'. But guilt is more than just a physical feeling. It has even more serious emotional and spiritual consequences.

God has given us all a moral sense – a conscience. Often, we feel guilty because we have done something that we know is wrong. However, our consciences, as fallen human beings, are not perfect. Sometimes we experience false guilt. We feel guilty about things that are not actually our fault. We need our conscience to be *educated* by the word of God.

At other times we don't feel guilty about things we should feel guilty about – in which case we need our conscience to be *awakened* by the Spirit of God.

David was given an opportunity to rid himself of the person who was trying to kill him – Saul (24:1–4). Instead of taking that opportunity, David merely cut off a corner of Saul's robe in order to prove to him that he could have killed him had he wanted to.

Nevertheless, David was 'conscience-stricken for having cut off a corner of his robe' (v.5). 'He felt guilty' (v.5, MSG). David clearly had a very sensitive conscience and felt the burden of guilt for having done this to 'the LORD's anointed' (v.6). Yet he was able to declare to Saul, 'Now understand and recognise that I am *not guilty* of wrongdoing or rebellion. I have not wronged you' (v.11b).

For a moment, it seems, Saul himself was conscience-stricken, 'he wept aloud: "You are more righteous than I ... You have treated me well, but I have treated you badly"' (vv.16c–17). In the midst of his jealousy, Saul had the odd moment of sanity – where he experienced true guilt.

David avoided taking any further burden of guilt upon himself. He was about to avenge

Nabal's ill-treatment of him and his men. Abigail came to the rescue. With enormous skill and diplomacy, she brought gifts to David and said, 'Upon me alone let this *guilt* be ... The Lord has prevented you from *bloodguiltiness'* (25:24, 26, AMP).

She went on to say, '...my master [David] will not have on his conscience the staggering *burden* of needless bloodshed or of having avenged himself' (v.31).

David realised that Abigail had rescued him from the burden of guilt: 'May you be blessed for your good judgment and for keeping me from bloodshed this day and from avenging myself with my own hands' (v.33). Abigail's skill is one we all need to develop. It is good to speak with wisdom and diplomacy when advising others on how they might act, so that they avoid doing things that will lead to guilt.

David avoided taking judgment into his own hands. Then, 'the LORD struck Nabal and he died' (v.38). When David heard that Nabal was dead he said, 'Praise be to the LORD, who has upheld my cause against Nabal for treating me with contempt. He has kept his servant from doing wrong and has brought Nabal's wrongdoing down on his own head' (v.39). Eventually, it all ends well with David marrying the newly widowed Abigail.

Whether we have the feelings that accompany it or not, the burden of true guilt is real for all. Jesus died on the cross to take our guilt.

PRAYER

Thank you, Lord, that you take my guilt, my fears, my worries and my anxieties and daily bear my burdens.

30 May | Day 150
Your Trial Will Become Your Triumph

'Houston, we've had a problem,' were the words of Jim Lovell on the evening of 13 April 1970. Nearly fifty-six hours into the mission to the moon, an explosion aboard the spacecraft plunged the crew into a fight for their survival. Within less than a minute there was a cascade of systems failures throughout the spacecraft. 'It was all at one time – a monstrous failure,' said NASA's flight controller.

The spacecraft looped around the moon, using its gravity to return to earth. Millions of people followed the drama on television. Eventually, the capsule splashed down in the Pacific Ocean near Tonga.

In an article headed 'Apollo 13: From Disaster to Triumph' the BBC science reporter wrote, 'Although the mission was not a success from a conventional perspective, it was a *triumph* of ingenuity and determination'.[1] Jim Lovell said it showed the people of the world that *even if there was a great catastrophe, it could be turned into a success*.

The supreme example of triumph coming out of apparent catastrophe is the cross. What seemed to the world to be the ultimate defeat was in fact the ultimate triumph.

READING FROM PSALMS

Psalm 68:21–27
Triumph of God

As we look around at the world today we see so much evil.

This psalm celebrates God's ultimate triumph over evil and, in particular, evil nations and empires. You are invited to watch the *triumphal* entry of God into his temple. God has *triumphed*. Right will win the day. Human pride and inflated arrogance will one day be humbled before the majesty of God's just rule.

David describes a triumphal procession celebrating the victory of God over his enemies: 'Surely God will crush the heads of his enemies ... your procession has come into view, O God, the procession of my God and King' (vv.21, 24).

There follows a picture of the worshipping community as it should be, with singers, musicians, tambourines and more, all praising God – and with the princes among them (vv.24–27). Perhaps: 'They are led by 'the little tribe of Benjamin' (v.27). The last and the least will be first.'

PRAYER

Lord, I pray that we would see a revival of worship and that the leaders of our nation would be at the heart of worshipping communities, praising God in the great congregation (v.26).

NEW TESTAMENT READING

John 19:1–27
Triumph of Jesus

Have you been through hard times in your life? Perhaps you are in the middle of hard times right now and things aren't looking good in your life at this moment. Remember that at the time of his greatest triumph it did not look good for Jesus.

I remember talking to Father Raniero Cantalamessa, Preacher to the Papal Household, just before he took part in a public debate with one of the 'New Atheists'. I asked Father Raniero whether he thought he would win. He replied that he did not know. He said he might lose the debate. 'But,' he added, *'God can be glorified in defeat.'*

The crucifixion of Jesus shows that God can be glorified in what appears to be a defeat. This is the moment of Jesus' greatest triumph.

Three times Pilate protested that Jesus was innocent (18:38; 19:4–6), and on two further occasions he tried to get out of allowing Jesus' death (see also 19:12, 14). But in the end he was too weak to act as his conscience led. He 'caved in to their demand. He turned him over to be crucified' (v.16, MSG).

Jesus' death was entirely voluntary. No longer free to move, Jesus was, in fact, the only one who was totally free. Pilate said, 'Don't you realise I have power either to free you or to crucify you?' (v.10). Jesus answered, 'You haven't a shred of authority over me except what has been given you from heaven' (v.11, MSG). The irony was that Jesus had total authority over Pilate.

This was the hour of great darkness. Jesus was flogged, a crown of thorns was put on his head, he was struck in the face, he was handed over to be crucified, he was stripped of his clothes and the soldiers cast lots for his undergarments. Yet through it all, the Scriptures were being fulfilled (vv.23–24).

John emphasises the fulfilment of prophecy and the royalty of Jesus. Throughout Jesus' trial and crucifixion, there is the constant theme of whether he is a king. The soldiers dress Jesus up as a mock king and shout, 'Hail, *king* of the Jews' (v.3). Pilate declares with bitter irony, 'Here is your *king'* (v.14), and asks, 'Shall I crucify your *king*?' (v.15). The chief priests reply, 'We have no *king* but Caesar' (v.15), and so Pilate has a sign prepared stating: 'Jesus of Nazareth, the *king* of the Jews' (v.19).

As Jesus is being crucified, he looks anything but a king. He is being taunted and mocked. Yet, the irony is that as Pilate organises for the notice to be prepared (in three languages so everyone can read it, v.20), God's purposes are being fulfilled in proclaiming to the whole world that *Jesus is God's King*. He is the King of Love, hidden and silent.

During his trial, Jesus declared to Pilate, 'You are right in saying that I am a *king'* (18:37). However, unlike Caesar, his kingdom is 'not of this world' (v.36), for it is an eternal heavenly kingdom. This eternal King is *triumphing*, not through the might of Roman *triumphalism*, but through the seeming weakness of death on a cross.

Jesus is triumphing over darkness, evil and sin. Tomorrow we will read those great words, 'It is finished' (19:30). Jesus completed the task of bearing the world's sins in his own body. The greatest victory in the history of the world had been won. This is the triumph of good over evil, of life over death. His life appears to be a horrible failure. Hate seems to have conquered love. But in fact, the conquered one, who has apparently failed, has in fact triumphed and opened up a source of new life, a new vision for humankind and a new road to peace and unity.

If you are struggling at the moment with the circumstances of your life, stay close to Jesus and remember that God can be glorified in defeat. The greatest triumphs in our lives sometimes occur when the circumstances seem to be hardest.

PRAYER

Lord, thank you that because of your triumph God always leads us in triumphal procession in Christ, and 'through us spreads everywhere the fragrance of the knowledge of him' (2 Corinthians 2:14).

OLD TESTAMENT READING

1 Samuel 26:1–28:25
Triumph of David

David's triumph does not come easily. Victories in life are rarely easy. They generally come after many difficulties and failures.

Saul said to David, 'May you be blessed, my son David; you will do great things and surely *triumph*' (26:25).

It is tragic to see how far Saul had fallen. At one stage he was the Spirit-filled man of God, getting rid of evil from the land. Now he finds himself consulting the very witches he has expelled (chapter 28). Yet even in the Old Testament there were the beginnings of the knowledge of life after death, and that in spite of all he had done, the Lord saved Saul – 'tomorrow you and your sons will be *with me*' (28:19).

We also see the worst side of David's character. He joins the Philistines, lives by deceit and murders women and children (chapter 27). He has to sink to the lowest depths to hide what he is doing. The picture the Bible paints of David is far from perfect, and yet God uses him despite his failings and failures.

On the other hand, we also see David at his best. David had an opportunity to take revenge on Saul, who was trying to kill him. However, David refused to take revenge. He had great respect for Saul, because he was in a position of authority.

He says, 'Who can lay a hand on the LORD's anointed and be guiltless?... The LORD forbid that I should lay a hand on the LORD's anointed' (26:9, 11).

David stayed loyal and faithful to Saul, despite the fact that Saul was trying to murder him. Follow David's example and refuse to be led into sin in an attempt to break free of a person's authority over you.

Even Saul recognises David's 'righteousness and faithfulness' (v.23). Saul sees that he 'will do great things and surely *triumph*' (v.25).

The life of David teaches us not to expect instant success and triumph. Often, God prepares us through the years of obscurity, difficulty and even defeat or failure. It is in these times of testing that, like David, we must never act out of revenge but rather treat everyone with love, honour and respect.

PRAYER

Lord, thank you that you use us powerfully in spite of our many failings. Thank you that our triumph over evil is only possible through the triumph of Jesus on the cross and in his resurrection.

31 May | Day 151

You Have the Energy of God

The world is running out of energy – oil, coal, gas and so on. How do we ensure sufficient energy supplies to sustain life? Where will we find this energy? Now, we are searching anxiously for *power 'from above'* – trying to harness the almost limitless power of the sun.

All of us face the same problem as the physical environment, but on a spiritual level. You stand before a choice: do you look for the energy you need in yourself and the resources of your intelligence and your entrepreneurial spirit, or do you look for it '*from above*', from the risen Christ, the Sun of Righteousness?

In the passages for today we see something about the extent of God's energy, power and strength. Whereas on a physical level we struggle to harness even a fraction of the power of the sun, God has given you full access to his *endless energy* through Jesus' resurrection and the gift of the Holy Spirit.

READING FROM PSALMS

Psalm 68:28–35
Where does it come from?

Energy, power and strength come from God. This psalm ends on a note of confidence as David proclaims that 'the God of Israel gives *power* and *strength to his people*. Praise be to God!' (v.35). Amazingly, God promises to give *you his power* and *his strength*.

David prays, 'Summon your *power*, O God; show us your *strength*, O God, as you have done before' (v.28). In contrast, he is dismissive of any attempt to seek power elsewhere. He talks of the worldly power of an evil regime, 'Rapacious in her lust for silver, crushing peoples' (v.30, MSG). Yet he knows that ultimately such power 'will submit ... to God' (v.31). David knows from his own experience that God's power is more than enough for all his needs.

PRAYER

Thank you, Lord, that you will give 'power and strength' to your people. Fill me today with your energy, power and strength.

NEW TESTAMENT READING

John 19:28–20:9
What is it like?

God gives to you the same energy, strength and power that he used to raise Jesus from the dead.

I remember a time when I was speaking at a conference for church leaders. I had been speaking for several hours each day and felt completely exhausted and drained. During a break, I happened to open *The Message* Bible translation at Ephesians 1:19–20: 'The utter extravagance of his work in us who trust in him – *endless energy*, boundless strength! All this energy issues from Christ: God raised him from death'. I felt re-energised from above.

In this passage, John emphasises that Jesus had truly died. When he had 'completed' (John 19:28a) the job he had been given to do, thereby *fulfilling* the Scripture (v.28b), he cried out, '"It is finished." With that, he bowed his head and gave up (*paradoken*) his spirit' (v.30).

His last act was to give the gift of the Spirit. He breathed out his Spirit as later he would breathe on his disciples and also give them his Spirit.

Death by crucifixion could be sped up by breaking the person's legs. In Jesus' case, this was not necessary, as he was already dead (v.33). 'Instead, one of the soldiers pierced Jesus' side with a spear, bringing a sudden flow of blood and water' (v.34). At death the clot and serum of the blood separates, and this would look like blood and water. John provides good medical evidence that Jesus was truly dead.

It may be that there were already people at the time arguing that Jesus did not really die, but only *seemed* to. This view came to be known as 'docetism' from the Greek word dokew, meaning 'seen'. Mohammed was influenced by docetic views. The Quran states, 'They did not kill him, neither did they crucify him; it only seemed to be so' (Sura 4:157).

John emphasises that Jesus really did die – he gives the physiological evidence. He also shows that Jesus' death was in accordance with the will of God revealed in Scripture: 'These things happened so that the scripture would be fulfilled: "Not one of his bones will be broken," and, as another scripture says, "They will look on the one they have pierced"' (John 19:36–37).

In the blood and water flowing from the side of Jesus, we see a symbol of hope. The 'blood' symbolises his life poured out for us. Water symbolises the Spirit. The water flowing from the heart of Jesus will heal, cleanse and energise us all.

The body of Jesus was wrapped in linen cloths and seventy-five pounds (34 kg) of spices. If anyone had removed the body, surely they would have removed the lot. No thief would have left the only items of value. Jesus certainly could not have taken the grave clothes off himself (humanly speaking). Yet the disciples found 'the linen cloths lying there, and the kerchief used to cover his head not lying with the linen cloths but separate, neatly folded by itself' (vv.6–7, MSG).

As William Temple, the former Archbishop of Canterbury, pointed out that the language used is extraordinarily vivid, and 'such as no invention would devise, no freak of imagination conjure up'.[1]

On this evidence, it is hardly surprising that when the disciples saw, they *believed* (20:8). At this stage no one had even seen the risen Jesus. Yet the evidence of the state of the tomb and the absence of Jesus' body was enough in itself to convince them of the resurrection.

They had believed that Jesus was the Messiah before. But this was different. They 'saw and believed' that God's power and energy had raised Jesus from the dead. Jesus was alive again. This was unexpected sunshine. Winter was over. Spring had come.

When the New Testament speaks of God's love, the focus is the cross. When the New Testament speaks of God's energy, power and strength, the focus is the resurrection (Ephesians 1:19–20). We rightly think of power belonging to God. Yet we so easily forget that God's power is also 'for us who believe' (v.19).

The same power and energy that raised Jesus Christ from the dead now lives in you.

PRAYER

Lord, thank you for your extraordinary love; that you were willing to die for me. Thank you for your resurrection, and that the same power now lives in me. I pray you will fill me with that energy today.

OLD TESTAMENT READING

1 Samuel 29:1–31:13
How do we receive it?

Do you ever feel exhausted, at a low ebb, not knowing how you will be able to cope with all the problems you are facing?

These were terrible times for the people of God. David had reached a low ebb in his life. He had got himself in the position of being about to fight *for* the Philistines *against* Israel. But then, even the Philistines decided that they didn't want him.

He gets back to find that the Amalekites have captured his and his men's wives, sons and daughters. The result is an explosive mix of grief and anger. The whole company was distraught at what had happened, and David's followers then turned the blame on him, threatening to stone him (30:4–6).

But in the middle of all his problems, *'David strengthened himself with trust in his God'* (30:6b, MSG). This was the turning point in David's life. Those who, like David, have turned to God in their deepest distress have been repeatedly amazed at the speed with which he has been able to change their fortunes.

As the men return from battle, some of his men did not want to share what they recovered with those who were too exhausted to fight (vv.21–22). But David was wise enough to see that everyone has a part to play in God's work. He replied, 'No, my brothers, you must not do that with what the Lord has given us… The share of the man who stayed with the supplies is to be same as that of him who went down to the battle. All shall share alike' (vv.23–24). Those who do the less glamorous work are just as important as those who hit the headlines.

As we read of the death of Saul and his sons, it is clear what a brutal world they lived in. Saul takes his own life in order to avoid being abused in the way that Samson was. Faced with such dangers and barbarism it must have meant so much to David to strengthen himself 'with trust in his God'.

Follow David's example – spend time with God strengthening yourself, being re-energised and then trusting him wholeheartedly, believing that he is in you by his Spirit and believing that you are able to do whatever you need to do through him.

PRAYER

Lord, thank you that whether we are at our lowest ebb or facing great trials and challenges or just facing the ordinary struggles of life, we can all find strength and energy in the Lord our God.

1 June | Day 152
Wow!

Judah Smith is a delightful young Pentecostal pastor from Seattle, Washington. He is one of the best communicators that I have ever heard – especially to young people. When listening to others, his favourite expression is 'Wow!' For him it is an expression of respect, awe and reverence.

There are many blessings to living in Western Europe in the twenty-first century. However, we live in a society in which respect, awe and reverence do not seem to be as valued as they once were.

READING FROM PROVERBS

Proverbs 13:20–14:4
Respect

A culture of respect underlies the book of Proverbs. We see three examples in this passage:

1. Respect for the Lord

'An honest life shows *respect* for God' (14:2, MSG). The word 'fear' is probably best understood as 'respect'. Respect for the Lord is the starting point for respect in all our other relationships.

2. Respect for the wise

Choose carefully whom you spend time with. 'Whoever walks with the wise grows wise' (13:20). 'Wise speech evokes nothing but *respect*' (14:3, MSG). Our society increasingly devalues the wisdom that comes with age. Wisdom often (though not always) comes through the experience of a long life. There is a huge amount of untapped wisdom in older people.

3. Respect in the home

'A refusal to correct is a refusal to love; love your children by disciplining them' (13:24, MSG). This teaching has sometimes been abused by an over-literal interpretation. What the book of Proverbs is encouraging is a culture of respect in the family – respect for parents and also respect for children, which involves loving discipline.

PRAYER

Lord, help us to gain wisdom and to model good family life, combining love and respect.

NEW TESTAMENT READING

John 20:10–31
Awe

Jesus really was raised from the dead. The tomb really was empty on Easter morning. Jesus' followers really did meet him alive again. The resurrection did happen. The best historical explanation for the origin of Christianity is that it really is true. Jesus is alive today!

John records four resurrection appearances of Jesus – the first three of which are in this passage. In these appearances, we see not only some of the evidence but also some of the results of the resurrection.

1. Awe and amazement

There is something indefinably first-hand about the account of Jesus' appearance to Mary. There is nothing quite like it in all ancient literature.

In the culture of the day, a woman's testimony would not have been considered as weighty as that of a man. If the disciples had been making this up, they would not have devised the first appearance as being to Mary Magdalene.

Jesus does not make a triumphant appearance to signify his victory. He appears to Mary – the loved one, the forgiven one – alone in a garden, with gentle love.

This shows a huge amount about Jesus' respect for women. By this act, and others during his life on earth, he laid the foundation for a revolution in the world's attitude to women. Sadly, it has taken 2,000 years and we are still not there yet.

Jesus does not ask Mary what she is looking for. He asks, '*Who* is it you are you looking for?' (v.15).

Mary's response is one of awe and amazement. As she realised it was Jesus, she cried out in Aramaic, '"Rabboni!" (which means Teacher)' (v.16).

He explains to her that she must not try to hold on to him (v.17). She must begin a new, more internal relationship with the risen Jesus, he in her and she in him (which will be fulfilled with the gift of the Spirit).

It is not enough to know the evidence of the facts of the resurrection. We need a personal encounter with the resurrected Jesus.

2. Joy and peace

The world is desperately searching for happiness and peace of mind. The supreme source of joy and peace is a relationship with Jesus.

Mary rushed off to tell the disciples, 'I have seen the Lord!' (v.18). Jesus' appearance to the disciples brought them overwhelming joy (v.20). Three times he says to them, '*Peace* be with you!' (vv.19, 21, 26) – the inner peace that flows from his presence.

Faith in Jesus brings joy and peace to all who believe. Jesus said to Thomas, 'Blessed and *happy* and to be envied are those who have never seen Me and yet have believed' (v.29, AMP).

In this short encounter, Jesus transformed the group of frightened, confused individuals into a community of love, joy and peace.

3. Purpose and power

Jesus gives them a new sense of purpose: 'As the Father has sent me, I am sending you' (v.21). The resurrection is the message of hope for the world. Jesus Christ is risen from the dead. There is life beyond the grave. This gives your life on earth a whole new meaning and purpose. You are sent out by Jesus to proclaim this message to the world.

Finally, he also gave them power. He 'breathed on them and said, "Receive the Holy Spirit. If you forgive the sins of anyone, their sins are forgiven; if you do not forgive them, they are not forgiven"' (vv.22–23). The Holy Spirit provides the strength and authority to forgive.

The same power that raised Jesus from the dead is available to you. He gives you the power of his Holy Spirit and the power of his word to declare the message of God's forgiveness to human beings. This is the message that brings eternal life.

4. Respect and reverence

Thomas was a cynic; sceptical and full of doubt. I think I would probably have had the same response as him when he said, 'Unless I see the nail marks in his hands and put my finger where the nails were, and put my hand into his side, I will not believe it' (v.25).

He must have felt so humbled when Jesus appeared to him and said, 'Put your finger here; see my hands. Reach out your hand and put it into my side. Stop doubting and believe' (v.27).

The wounds of Jesus are there for all time to reveal the humble and forgiving love of Jesus. Jesus accepts Thomas just as he is. He accepts his challenge without complaint or criticism.

Do not feel guilty about having doubts. Like Thomas, be honest about your doubts and bring them to Jesus. When Jesus answered his doubts, Thomas's response was the pinnacle of respect, reverence and awe. He said, 'My Lord and my God!' (v.28). From a place of having doubted, Thomas makes perhaps the strongest statement of Jesus' divinity in all of the Gospels. He is the first person to look at Jesus and call him 'God'. He said, in effect, 'Wow!'

Jesus went on to tell him that belief leads to blessing (v.29). In fact, it leads to life. Belief and life go hand in hand in John's Gospel (v.31), because, if you believe in Jesus you have life. This is *real* life of high quality, an abundant life (10:10) that goes on for ever (3:16).

John's whole reason for writing his Gospel was so that 'you may believe that Jesus is the Christ, the Son of God, and that by believing you may have life in his name' (20:31). The resurrection is the basis of our hope for life *before death*, as well as beyond it.

PRAYER

Jesus, my Lord and my God, today I worship you with awe and reverence.

OLD TESTAMENT READING

2 Samuel 1:1–2:7
Reverence

David's attitude to Saul is a wonderful example of how to respond to those who try to do you harm. David did not seek revenge. He was not bitter. He treated Saul with the utmost respect. After all, God had used Saul greatly in the past. The fact that Saul had gone off the rails did not erase David's respect.

His attitude to Saul was quite extraordinary. He said to the Amalekite who claimed to have finished off Saul, 'Why were you not afraid to lift your hand to destroy the LORD's anointed?' (1:14). The Amalekite may well have been trying to benefit from what would have been a perversion of the facts. He may have been a human vulture, who took the royal insignia from Saul to gain favour with David. In any event, it did him no good because of David's reverence for Saul.

David grieved over the death of his great friend Jonathan and over Saul (vv.19–27). Grief is a natural, necessary and healthy response to the death of those we love.

Supremely, David reverenced God. He 'enquired of the LORD' (2:1). He asked, 'Shall I go up to one of the towns of Judah?' The LORD answered, 'Go up.' He then asked, 'Where shall I go?' The LORD answered, 'To Hebron.' David obeyed and was anointed king over the house of Judah.

PRAYER

Lord, help me to love and respect all those you have anointed in leadership roles, whether they support us or whether they don't. Help me to live a life of reverence, respect and awe.

2 June | Day 153
'Crazy Love'

Francis Chan's mother died giving birth to him. The only affection he can remember receiving from his father lasted about thirty seconds when he was on the way to his stepmother's funeral aged nine. When he was twelve, his father also died. Francis cried, but also felt relieved.

Francis is now a pastor. He and his wife, Lisa, have seven children. When his children were born, his own love for his children and his desire for their love was so strong that it opened his eyes to how much God desires and loves *us*. He said, 'Through this experience, I came to understand that my desire for my children is only a faint echo of God's great love for me and for every person he made ... I love my kids so much it hurts.'

Calling his first book *Crazy Love*, he wrote, 'The idea of Crazy Love has to do with our relationship with God. All my life I've heard people say, "God loves you." It's probably the most insane statement you could make to say that the eternal Creator of this universe is in love with me. There is a response that ought to take place in believers, a crazy reaction to that love. Do you really understand what God has done for you? If so, why is your response so lukewarm?'[1]

The word 'zeal' implies an *intense or passionate desire*. It can be misdirected, but as Paul writes, it is right to be zealous provided that the purpose is good (Galatians 4:18). Elsewhere he says, 'Never be lacking in zeal' (Romans 12:11). Perhaps a good modern translation of the word 'zeal' is 'crazy love'.

READING FROM PSALMS

Psalm 69:1–12
'Crazy love' for God's house

David loves God so much that it feels like anyone insulting God is insulting him. It's painful to hear people blaspheming God: 'The insults of those that insult you fall on me' (v.9b).

David writes, '... *zeal for your house consumes me*' (v.9a). He was so passionate about God's house because that was the symbolic place of God's presence with his people. *The Message* explains the zeal he expresses in this verse: 'Because I'm *madly in love* with you' (v.9a, MSG).

These words are applied by the disciples to Jesus when he cleanses the temple (John 2:17). Out of *zeal for God's house*, Jesus drove off those who were trying to profit from a place of worship, taking advantage of those who wanted to draw near to God.

David is passionate about not bringing God's name into disrepute. He does not want anyone to be disgraced because of him: 'Don't let those who look to you in hope be discouraged by what happens to me' (Psalm 69:6, MSG). He knows his folly and guilt – as I know mine: 'God, you know every sin I've committed; My life's a wide-open book before you' (v.5, MSG). David is concerned that this should not bring dishonour to God's house.

Today, God's house – the temple – is Christ and his body, his church (1 Peter 2:5). There is nothing wrong with being passionate about the church. Be zealous to see God's name honoured in his church today.

Personally, I am inspired when I see a zeal for God's house – a passion in worship, a 'leaning in' to the talks, an amazing welcome for every new person.

Passion is inspiring and infectious. We need more crazy love in the church today.

PRAYER

Lord, consume me with zeal for your name and your church.

NEW TESTAMENT READING

John 21:1–25
'Crazy love' for Jesus

This is the third time Jesus has appeared to his disciples (his fourth including Mary Magdalene) (v.14).

Jesus appears in the ordinariness of simple daily life. You do not necessarily need to do extraordinary things. Jesus meets you wherever you are. Peter is fishing. Six of the disciples join him. Jesus tells them where to catch fish and then cooks breakfast for them. Here is Jesus risen from the dead – the one through whom the whole universe came into being – saying to his friends, 'Come and have breakfast' (v.12). The God who is revealed in Jesus Christ is life-affirming and such fun!

When John recognised Jesus he exclaimed to Peter, 'It is the Lord!' (v.7a). Peter is so filled with excitement, enthusiasm and *zeal* to get to Jesus as quickly as he can that 'he wrapped his outer garment around him (for he had taken it off) and jumped into the water' (v.7b).

Sometimes in our enthusiasm and zeal we may do some rather crazy things. But what matters is a heart of love and zeal for Jesus. Peter's eyes were riveted on Jesus. All he wanted was to be with Jesus.

In Jesus' conversation with Peter after breakfast, we see what it means to have this passionate love for Jesus:

1. Supreme love

Jesus said to Simon Peter, 'Simon son of John, do you truly love me *more than these*?' (v.15). 'These' may refer to his fishing gear or the other disciples. Whatever it means, Jesus was calling him to make his love for Jesus his supreme love. Our love for Jesus should be more than our love for anything else.

Peter's zeal had not been without its obstacles. He had denied Jesus three times, so Jesus gives him the opportunity to affirm his love three times. Three times Peter tells Jesus, 'I love you' (vv.15–17).

2. Sacrificial love

Jesus hints to Peter that his love and zeal for Jesus and his church is going to be costly. Indeed, it would cost Peter his life. Jesus says to him, '"When you are old you will stretch out your hands, and someone else will dress you and lead you where you do not want to go." Jesus said this to indicate the kind of death by which Peter would glorify God' (vv.18–19). This is the earliest evidence for the martyrdom of Peter by crucifixion. To be a follower of Jesus is a dangerous undertaking.

When Peter is told this he turns, sees John and asks about *his* future. In this intimate moment with Jesus, Peter is distracted by comparison with John. Jesus politely tells him to mind his own business – something worth remembering when we are tempted to compare ourselves with others.

3. Servant love

Each time Peter tells Jesus 'I love you', Jesus tells Peter, 'Feed my lambs ... Take care of my sheep ... Feed my sheep' (vv.15–17). Peter can only guide, nourish and be responsible for people if he loves Jesus passionately.

Then Jesus says to Peter very simply, 'Follow me!' (v.19). This crazy love for Jesus means following his example of love. Jesus showed the supreme example of servant love. He said, 'Greater love has no one than this, to lay down one's life for one's friends' (15:13). He gave a very practical example of what this kind of servant love involved, when he washed the disciples' feet (John 13). It is a commitment to help people, whatever we feel about them, to grow in their love for Jesus, not seeking to control them but to liberate them.

Jesus calls you to the same kind of love. Express your passionate love for Jesus by a passionate love for other people, giving yourself to take care of his sheep.

Peter was willing to make Jesus the supreme love of his life; he was willing to pay the price and to follow in his footsteps of servant love. He loved the one who did so many things in his brief life on earth that 'if every one of them were written down ... the whole world would not have room for the books that would be written' (21:25).

PRAYER

Lord, help me to love you as Peter did – to be zealous for you. Help me to feed your lambs, take care of your sheep and be willing to pay the price, whatever it is, to follow you to the end.

OLD TESTAMENT READING

2 Samuel 2:8–3:21
'Crazy love' for unity

With the death of Saul, Israel and Judah were divided. Abner called out to Joab, 'Are we going to *keep killing each* other till doomsday? Don't you know that nothing but bitterness will come from this?' (2:26, MSG). This cry has a very modern ring as we see the continued turbulence and division in the Middle East.

'The war ... lasted a long time' (3:1). 'Then Abner sent messengers on his behalf to say to David, "*Whose land is it?*"' (v.12). Again, this is a question still asked today.

Abner went on to say, 'Make an agreement with me, and I will help you bring all Israel over to you' (v.12). Eventually this happened and for a time, at least, the land enjoyed unity.

Disunity is so destructive. We see it in the Middle East today. We see it in the church today. We should be passionate for unity.

PRAYER

Lord, I pray for a peaceful and just solution in the Middle East. Help me also to be passionate in pursuing peace, unity and reconciliation in your church.

3 June | Day 154

Even Your Weakness is Anointed

Do you ever feel too weak or inadequate to be useful to God?

A teenager from Cumbria in Northern England felt God calling him. Patrick was poorly educated, ineloquent and faced significant opposition throughout his ministry from those who felt that he wasn't up to the task. Even as an old man he still admitted, 'Today I still blush and fear more than anything to have my lack of learning brought out into the open.'

Yet despite all his disadvantages Patrick remained convinced that God had called and anointed him as an evangelist. He wrote, 'We are a letter of Christ for salvation even to the back of beyond – and what does it matter if it is not a learned letter? For it is still to be found valid and plain for all to read, written in your very hearts, not in ink but by the Spirit of the living God!'[1]

Today his more eloquent contemporaries have long been forgotten, but the impact of St Patrick's ministry and mission to Ireland 1,500 years ago is still recognised around the world. Even his weakness was anointed.

As David takes up the throne of Israel he says, '...though I am the *anointed* king, I am *weak*' (2 Samuel 3:39). The moment you put your faith in Jesus, God anoints you with the Holy Spirit. However weak and inadequate you may feel, God can use you, like David, in extraordinary ways. Even your weakness is anointed.

READING FROM PSALMS

Psalm 69:13–28
Anointed in times of trouble

Are you going through a time of trouble? David was in a time of deep trouble in his life. He felt like he was in a 'swamp', a 'Black Hole', a 'deathtrap'. He says, 'I'm ... flat on my face, reduced to a nothing' (vv.15–20, MSG).

David, the anointed leader of Israel (2 Samuel 5:3), was a person of prayer. Many of the psalms are attributed to him. In this psalm we see an example of his honest, raw and intimate prayers.

When you are in trouble or in a position of great weakness:

1. Know God's great love for you
David prays, 'In your great love, O God, answer me' (Psalm 69:13). 'Answer me, O LORD, out of the goodness of your love; in your great mercy turn to me' (v.16).

2. Cry out to God in your heart
Be honest with God. Tell him what you are really feeling: 'Rescue me from the mire, do not let me sink' (v.14). 'Do not hide your face from your servant; answer me quickly, for I am in trouble' (v.17).

PRAYER

Lord, thank you that I can pray to you in times of trouble. Lord, today I cry to you for help.

NEW TESTAMENT READING

Acts 1:1–22
Anointed by the Holy Spirit

The same power that raised Jesus from the dead now lives in you. Of the four Gospel writers, Luke is the only one who continues to tell the story of the next generation. The story of Jesus continued in 'the believers' (v.15) and now it continues in you.

The book of Acts is the History of the Church Volume I. *History* matters to Luke. He uses such words as '*eyewitnesses*', 'carefully *investigated*', 'an *orderly* account' (Luke 1:2–3) and here he talks about 'many *convincing proofs*' (Acts 1:3). He stresses that Jesus did not just appear as a fleeting impression like a ghost: 'After his death, he presented himself alive to them in *many different settings* over a period of *forty days ... as they met and ate meals together*' (vv.2–4, MSG).

This is the second volume in Luke's life of Jesus. He refers to his earlier Gospel as being about 'all that Jesus *began* to do and to teach' (v.1). Now he tells the story of what Jesus *continued* to do through the Holy Spirit.

Jesus spoke of the Holy Spirit as *the gift promised by the Father* (v.4). Now he promises that in a few days the disciples will be baptised with the Holy Spirit and receive power to be his witnesses to the city ('Jerusalem'), the nation ('all Judea and Samaria') and the world ('to the ends of the earth') (v.8).

Through the rest of the passage we see a series of examples of people who have been filled by the Holy Spirit and been his messengers across the world. The wonderful news is that *you are included* in the list!

1. David
The Holy Spirit speaks through people, including David (v.16). Peter gives examples of how the Holy Spirit spoke through David in the psalms – even predicting the replacement of Judas the betrayer (vv.15–20).

2. Jesus
Supremely, the Holy Spirit anointed Jesus. Luke tells us that Jesus gave 'instructions

through the Holy Spirit to the apostles he had chosen' (v.2).

In particular, 'On one occasion, while he was eating with them, he gave them this command: "Do not leave Jerusalem, but wait for the gift my Father promised, which you have heard me speak about. For John baptised with water, but in a few days you will be baptised with the Holy Spirit"' (vv.4–5).

3. Apostles

Though in many ways they were weak, the apostles would be anointed by the Holy Spirit for the task that lay ahead. The word 'apostle' is used in several different ways in the New Testament. In the wider sense of a person who is sent by God, it clearly applies to many people in the past and also today (see 1 Corinthians 12:28–29). In a narrower sense, there are people who have what might be described as an 'apostolic' leadership gift (Mark 3:14).

However, here it is used in the narrowest sense of the word. They were a special group of people who were uniquely qualified by Jesus. The Holy Spirit spoke through them in a unique way. These were the apostles whom Jesus had chosen and to whom he gave special instructions through the Holy Spirit (Acts 1:2).

Judas had originally been part of this group. Now they were looking for a replacement. Peter lays down the qualifications. They had to have been with Jesus throughout his ministry, witnessed his resurrection and to have received the necessary training (vv.21–22).

4. You

Jesus said, 'In a few days *you* will be baptised with the Holy Spirit ... *you* will receive power when the Holy Spirit comes on *you*; and *you* will be my witnesses in Jerusalem, and in all Judea and Samaria, and to the ends of the earth' (vv.5, 8).

On the day of Pentecost this was fulfilled and the apostle Peter made it clear that the promise was for '*all whom the Lord our God will call*' (2:39). This includes *you*!

The Holy Spirit comes to anoint and empower you – to help and guide you in every aspect of your life – not just the 'spiritual' parts. Everything you have belongs to God and he wants to be involved in all of your life. Through the Holy Spirit living within you God wants you to become like Jesus in all your thoughts, attitudes, words and actions. You are Jesus to the world.

PRAYER

Lord, thank you that your Holy Spirit now lives in me. Thank you that, though I am weak, I am anointed to be your witness. Help me to be the mouthpiece of your Holy Spirit.

OLD TESTAMENT READING

2 Samuel 3:22–5:5
Anointed for leadership

In order to be leaders, we do not need to be perfect. David said, '...though I am *the anointed king, I am weak*' (3:39). The history of David's life in the Bible is a great testimony to both the *anointing* and *weakness* of David. He knew that he was far from perfect, and yet he also knew that God could still use him. He doesn't dwell on his weakness, but rather turns the situation over to God (v.39). In spite of his weaknesses, God used him in extraordinary ways.

This passage also reminds us that God used David throughout his life. We have already seen many examples of how God had used David as a leader for many years before he became king. Yet when he became king, David was still relatively young. Thereafter he continued to be used by God throughout a long and (mostly) successful reign: 'David was thirty years old when he became king, and he reigned for forty years' (5:4).

The Lord said about David, 'You shall *shepherd* my people Israel, and you shall become their ruler' (v.2). Then, 'all the elders ... *anointed* David king over Israel' (v.3). David became a leader full of integrity. He '*shepherded them* with *integrity of heart*; with *skilful hands he led them*' (Psalm 78:72). David was the type of leader we desperately need today, in the church and in society – men and women of character and capabilities; integrity of heart and skilful hands.

PRAYER

Thank you, Lord, that the same Holy Spirit who lived in David, Jesus and in the apostles, now anoints and lives in me. Thank you that even my weakness is anointed.

4 June | Day 155
Sounds of Heaven

Have you ever noticed that the Bible is a very noisy book? Wisdom *cries out* (Proverbs 8); loud singing is encouraged (Psalm 66:8); *cymbals clash* in praise (Psalm 150); God *shouts aloud* (Isaiah 42); his voice is like *the sound of many waters* (Ezekiel 43); Jesus prays with *loud cries and tears* (Hebrews 5) and even creation *groans* (Romans 8).

On the day of Pentecost they heard 'a *sound* like the blowing of a violent wind' that 'came from *heaven*' (Acts 2:2). In today's passages we hear other sounds going to and from heaven.

READING FROM PSALMS

Psalm 69:29–36
Sounds of worship

The Bible is realistic. There are times when we are 'in pain and distress' (v.29). David doesn't try to ignore the problems he faces. Yet, he still chooses to worship God in spite of his circumstances. Even in the depths, you can still be sure of who God is and worship him.

This psalm ends with the sound of worship: 'I will praise God's name in song and glorify him with thanksgiving ... Let *heaven* and earth praise him' (vv.30, 34). Worship goes on not only on earth, but also in heaven. When you worship, you are joining in the *sounds of heaven*. Here, we see three aspects of worship:

1. Worship involves the will
David says, 'I *will* praise God's name' (v.30). You may not always feel like worshipping God but it is a decision you make; it is an act of the will.

2. Worship pleases God
'This will *please the Lord* more than an ox, more than a bull with its horns and hoofs' (v.31).

3. Worship affects others
'The poor *will see and be glad* – you who seek God, may your hearts live!' (v.32). I have noticed how those 'who seek God' on Alpha are often moved by the worship, and as a result their 'hearts live'.

PRAYER
Lord, whatever my circumstances, help me to praise your name in song and glorify you with thanksgiving.

NEW TESTAMENT READING

Acts 1:23–2:21
Sounds of the Holy Spirit

This is for you and me. The experience of the day of Pentecost is not just a historic event; it can become a present reality for you (2:29). As Joel prophesised: 'I will pour out my Spirit on *all*' – men and women, old and young, rich and poor (vv.17–21). That definitely includes you and me!

1. Seek the experience
The experience of the Holy Spirit on the day of Pentecost involved three things:

First, it involved *power from God*. They heard a gale. This was not an actual gale. It was 'a sound *like* the blowing of a violent wind' (v.2). It sounds as if it may have resembled a heavy tropical rainstorm. This is the mighty invisible power of God. It was the outward and visible sign of an inward and spiritual reality.

The Hebrew word '*Ruach*' literally means 'breath' or 'wind'. *Ruach* is used in the Old Testament for the Holy Spirit – the Spirit of God. The day of Pentecost was the fulfilment of when Jesus had *breathed* on the disciples and said, 'Receive the Holy Spirit' (John 20:22).

Supremely, the experience of the Holy Spirit is an experience of God's love for you (Romans 5:5). It is the way in which you feel God's love for you, so that you can say with the apostle Paul, 'the Son of God ... loved *me* and gave himself for *me*' (Galatians 2:20). As Rick Warren says, 'to feel loved by God ... is the starting point for every ministry, every revival, every renewal, every great awakening.'[1]

The Holy Spirit is the one who provides the power for all revivals, and he does it supremely by enabling the people of God to feel, experience and know in their hearts the love of God. It is the kind of knowledge that travels from your head to your heart.

Second, it involved *fire from God*. They saw fire. Again, this was not an actual fire: 'There appeared to them tongues resembling *fire*, which were separated and distributed and which were settled on *each one of them*' (Acts 2:3, AMP). This again was an outward and visible sign of an inward and spiritual reality. The fire of God's love represents the power, purity and passion of God.

Wherever there is an experience of the Holy Spirit, he brings a new fire and passion to your life.

Third, it involved *languages from God*: 'All of them were filled with the Holy Spirit and began to speak in other tongues as the Spirit enabled them' (v.4). These were heavenly languages they had not learnt. The apostle Paul speaks about 'heavenly tongues' as well as 'human' tongues (1 Corinthians 13:1). The languages were recognised, and the whole known world was represented (vv.5–11). This was a reversal of the chaos and disunity of Babel (Genesis 11:1–9).

The experience of God's love through the Holy Spirit brings unity to the church. As we recognise that the same Holy Spirit is at work in Catholics, Orthodox, Protestants and Pentecostals of whatever church or denomination, there is a healing of division and a visible experience of unity.

On the day of Pentecost there were three reactions (all of which we see today to the ministry of the Holy Spirit). The first reaction was *amazement*. Some were 'utterly amazed' (Acts 2:7). The second reaction was *perplexity*. 'Perplexed, they asked one another, "What does this mean?"' (v.12). The third reaction was *ridicule*. 'Some, however, made fun of them and said, "They have had too much wine"' (v.13).

2. Study the explanation

Peter explained what was happening (v.14f).

First, he countered a *false explanation* (v.15). Some were offering a *natural* explanation for something *supernatural*. It may have looked as if they were drunk because they were so exuberant and had lost their inhibitions. However, this was not intoxication with wine but the *sober intoxication of the Spirit* – the only kind of intoxication that leaves you without a hangover!

Then, he offered the *true explanation* (v.16f). Peter began his speech by pointing out that this is biblical (we will see the rest of the explanation tomorrow). Some people draw a false dichotomy between the word and the Spirit. But the Holy Spirit *is the author of the word of God*. The Old Testament – that is, the word of God – points towards this outpouring of the Holy Spirit (vv.16–20). Peter, full of the Holy Spirit, goes back to the Bible. The Holy Spirit brings a hunger for the word of God.

PRAYER

Lord, I pray for a fresh outpouring of the Holy Spirit. May the fire of God descend upon me and on the church again with power, passion and purity.

OLD TESTAMENT READING

2 Samuel 5:6–6:23
Sounds of celebration

Before we look at the sounds of celebration, it is worth noting that there is another mention of sound in this passage. When David enquired of the Lord whether he should go on the attack, the Lord first answered, 'Go' (5:19). Then, the second time he enquired of the Lord, the Lord answered, 'Do not go straight up, but ... As soon as you hear the *sound of marching in the tops of the balsam trees*, move quickly' (vv.23–24).

It is not clear exactly what this means. However, it is an evocative expression. Perhaps, it means that as soon as we hear that God is on the move, we should act quickly.

God gave David victory, and this led to a great celebration. 'David and the whole house of Israel *were celebrating with all their might before the Lord, with songs and with harps, lyres, tambourines, sistrums and cymbals*' (6:5). It must have been extremely noisy!

David danced and worshipped God in a very demonstrative way: 'David, wearing a linen ephod, *danced before the Lord with all his might...*' (v.14). David's wife, Michal, was embarrassed and 'despised him in her heart' (v.16) for his display of passion.

David replies that he will continue to worship even more passionately and boldly than before: 'David said to Michal ... "*I will celebrate before the Lord*. I will become even more undignified than this"' (vv.21–22). Here, we see a biblical example of loud and uninhibited celebration. There is a warning in this passage against looking down or despising the way others express their worship to God (v.23). Of course, we must avoid exhibitionism. But David's exuberance came from the heart and was a genuine act of celebration.

We need to be sensitive to those around us – especially, for example, in the early weeks of Alpha when there are lots of people around who are not used to exuberant worship. However, generally you should feel free to express your worship to God as passionately as you want, not worrying about what other people might think of you.

PRAYER

Lord, may the churches again be filled with the sound of worship and celebration. May every Alpha Weekend be filled with the sound of the Pentecostal outpouring of the Holy Spirit, the heavenly sounds of worship and celebration to the glory of your name.

5 June | Day 156
He Gives You Power

I play squash regularly with a group of friends. We are all about the same standard. We virtually take it in turns to win and lose. Nevertheless, winning feels good. The feelings of pleasure and satisfaction that accompany victory are quite natural.

This is, of course, a trivial example. The victory that is at the centre of today's passages is of a totally different order and significance. But even the tiniest and most insignificant victory gives us a taste of its meaning and joy.

The great victory of God that we read about in the New Testament is foreshadowed in the Old Testament. The ultimate victory of God came with the life, death, resurrection and ascension of Jesus and the outpouring of his Spirit who gives you power to live a life of victory.

READING FROM PROVERBS

Proverbs 14:5–14
Victory of goodness

The 'fool' in the book of Proverbs does not mean someone lacking intelligence. Rather it means the rebel (especially against God and the laws of decency and justice): 'the mocker ... the foolish ... the wicked ... the faithless' (vv.6, 7, 9, 11, 14) come to a sticky end (vv.11–14). Their path ends in death.

On the other hand, the book of Proverbs is full of teaching about the importance of righteousness and holiness. We read here about 'a truthful witness ... the upright ... the good' (vv.5, 9, 11, 14).

The implication is that the righteous will in some way outlast death and 'will flourish' and be 'rewarded' (vv.11–14). In other words, they will ultimately be victorious: 'a moral life is a favoured life' (v.9b, MSG).

PRAYER

Lord, help me, by the power of your Holy Spirit, to be faithful in all my ways and do the good works that you have prepared in advance for me to do (Ephesians 2:10).

NEW TESTAMENT READING

Acts 2:22–47
Victory of Jesus

The church should be a place of 'celebration, exuberant and joyful' (v.46, MSG). We should be the most positive people in the world – constantly celebrating Jesus and the victory of God.

On the day of Pentecost, Peter, full of the Holy Spirit, explains the great victory of Jesus. He speaks about his life, ministry, death and, in particular, his resurrection. He gives four reasons why you can be sure that Jesus has been raised from the dead and therefore you can be sure that, through his power within you, *you will be raised to life* with him:

1. Logical
Satan's power of death could not possibly be stronger than the power of life in God's Messiah. Peter explains, 'God raised him from the dead, freeing him from the agony of death, because *it was impossible for death to keep its hold on him*' (v.24).

2. Biblical
He points out that the resurrection was prophesied in Psalm 16:8–11 (Acts 2:25–28). Peter says, '[David] was a prophet and knew that God had promised on oath that he would place one of his descendants on his throne. Seeing what was ahead, he spoke of the resurrection of the Christ' (vv.30–31).

3. Personal
Peter gives his own testimony: 'God has raised this Jesus to life, and *we are all witnesses of the fact*' (v.32). Peter says in effect, 'We have all seen him.'

4. Experiential
The experience of the Holy Spirit is in itself evidence of the resurrection. After the life, death, resurrection and ascension of Jesus came the final act in his saving ministry: 'Exalted to the right hand of God, he has received from the Father the promised Holy Spirit and has poured out what you now see and hear' (v.33).

This experience was not confined to those who were present on the day of Pentecost. It is for *every* Christian. It is for you. 'The promise is for *you* and *your children* and for *all* who are far off – for *all* whom the Lord our God will call' (v.39). Every time someone experiences the Holy Spirit it is further evidence of the resurrection. Every time you see someone being filled with the Holy Spirit or hear their testimony of how the Holy Spirit has changed their life, it is further evidence of the resurrection.

The Holy Spirit enables us to recognise the truth of the words of Peter: 'You crucified' Jesus of Nazareth (v.36). Jesus died for my sins. I killed Jesus. My personal sin was present on the cross. The day I recognised this I, too, was 'cut to the heart' (v.37). It is this revelation that leads to true repentance.

The way you receive the promise is by repentance, faith in Jesus, baptism and receiving the gift of the Holy Spirit (vv.37–38). The evidence that you have received the Holy Spirit will be seen in a changed life and a transformed community (vv.42–47). The church is not only a place of celebration, exuberance and joy; it should also be supremely a place of *love*.

1. Love for God

The church is a place full of love for God. They had a *new love for the Bible* – 'They devoted themselves to the apostles' teaching' (v.42). Much of this teaching is now enshrined in the New Testament.

They had a *new love for the sacraments* – 'They devoted themselves to ... the breaking of bread' (v.42). 'They broke bread in their homes' (v.46).

They had a *new love for prayer* (v.42). The Spirit-filled church will be a praying church.

2. Love for one another

The church should be marked by *love for one another*. They had a new desire to meet together – 'They devoted themselves ... to the fellowship' (v.42). 'They continued to meet together' and 'ate together with glad and sincere hearts' (v.46). There was a new release of finances and generosity in giving (vv.44–45).

The Spirit-filled church will be a united church.

3. Love for the world

The church should be filled with a *love for the world*. They were an outward-focused community performing signs and wonders (v.43). 'The Lord added to their number daily those who were being saved' (v.47). The Spirit-filled church will be an outward-looking church.

PRAYER

Lord, thank you for the great victory of Jesus over sin and death. Please fill me again with the power of your Holy Spirit.

OLD TESTAMENT READING

2 Samuel 7:1–8:18
Victory everywhere you go

The *victory* of Jesus was foreshadowed in the life of David. There are over a thousand references to David in the Bible. He was an anointed (messiah) king. The Lord gave him 'rest from all his enemies around him' (7:1). Nathan the prophet said to David, 'Whatever you have in mind, go ahead and do it, for the Lord is with you' (v.3). 'The Lord gave David *victory wherever he went*' (8:6, 14).

We see in David's prayer an example to follow:

1. *Praise* for God's greatness

David has both a sense of his own unworthiness in the presence of God (7:18) and at the same time, a realisation of the greatness of God: 'How great you are, O Sovereign Lord! There is no one like you' (v.22). He praises God for his redemption of his people (v.23).

2. *Passion* for God's name

David is passionate to see God's name honoured: 'Do as you promised, so that your name will be great for ever' (vv.25–26).

3. *Promise* for God's family

David trusts in God's word (v.28). He goes on to ask for one more thing: 'Bless my family; keep your eye on them always. You've already as much as said that you would, Master God! Oh, may your blessing be on my family permanently!' (v.29, MSG).

God made a covenant with David. Whereas God had been dwelling in a tent (7:2), he promises to establish a house for David (vv.7, 10–11). He promises, 'I will raise up your offspring to succeed you ... I will establish the throne of his kingdom for ever ... Your house and your kingdom shall endure for ever before me; your throne shall be established for ever' (vv.12–13, 16).

Only in Jesus were the promises of the Davidic covenant fulfilled. The human kings failed, but there remained the hope of a future king who would fulfil the kingship ideal. Jesus was the son of David (see, for example, Matthew 1:1). As he entered Jerusalem, the people cried out, 'Blessed is the coming kingdom of our father David!' (Mark 11:10).

However, the victory of Jesus and the kingdom of Jesus were far greater than anyone had anticipated. They were achieved not by a conquering king winning physical battles, but by a dying Saviour winning the great spiritual victory over sin, guilt, addiction, fear and even death itself.

We see from the example of Jesus that victory is not always glamorous or even obvious. But God promises you, as he promises David, that his power will be with you wherever you go and that, in Christ, ultimately you will be victorious.

PRAYER

Lord, like David, I feel a sense of unworthiness in your presence. 'Who am I, O Sovereign Lord?' (7:18). Thank you that in Christ you promise to give me your power, to be with me and to help me wherever I go.

6 June | Day 157
Kindness

Steve Sjogren wrote a book called *Conspiracy of Kindness*. He started a church in Cincinnati, Ohio, that grew rapidly to an average attendance of 7,500. Their motto is, 'Small things done with great love are changing the world.' They carry out random acts of kindness like paying for a stranger's coffee or writing a 'thank you' note to a shop assistant.

Kindness is love in work clothes. Showing God's love in practical ways, they have discovered the power of kindness to effect positive change, both in their lives and in the lives of people around them. Unexpected kindness is the most powerful, least costly and most underrated agent of human change. When kindness is expressed, healthy relationships are created, community connections are nourished and people are inspired to pass on kindness.

READING FROM PSALMS

Psalm 70:1–5
Trust in the kindness of God

God is kind. He loves you. Whatever your needs are today, you can cry out to him and he will be your help and deliverer.

David prays, 'God! Please hurry to my rescue! God, come quickly to my side!' (v.1, MSG). He goes on, 'Yet I am poor and needy; come quickly to me, O God. You are *my help* and *my deliverer*; O Lord, do not delay' (v.5). As he cries out, he remembers God's kindness to him in the past.

As I look back at this passage in my Bible and see cries for help that I have written down beside it over several years, I pray:

PRAYER

Thank you so much, Lord, for your kindness and love. Today, I cry out for...

NEW TESTAMENT READING

Acts 3:1–26
Act kindly to those in need

One act of kindness can transform a person's day, or even their life. As the saying goes, '*Be kind*, for everyone you meet is fighting a hard battle.' Kindness is one of the fruits of the Holy Spirit (Galatians 5:22). Just after they had been filled with the Holy Spirit, we see in this passage what is later described as an '*act of kindness*' (Acts 4:9) performed by Peter and John (3:1–10).

This '*act of kindness*' led to a remarkable chain of events, which can perhaps best be described as 'power evangelism'. It led to astonishing church growth. It was part of the beginning of an explosion that eventually was to change the whole world.

If we were asked to start a new church, I doubt we would have done it the way they did. They had no building, no money and no resources. It began with a bunch of fisherman and tax collectors and, among other things, a whole load of people speaking in tongues! Yet the church exploded into life with astonishing growth.

People from outside were attracted because of what they saw happening *on the inside*. They were attracted by the sheer undiluted power of God released through this '*act of kindness*'.

These two guys were on their way to an evening service. When they got there they saw a person in desperate need, begging for help. This is the sort of person that we might expect to find in one of the few places they could hope to receive any kindness.

The man 'was being carried to the temple gate called Beautiful where he was put every day to beg from those going into the temple courts' (v.2). The gate was called Beautiful; yet, what they saw was not what the world sees as beautiful – a man disabled from birth, begging.

Their hearts did not sink when they saw the contrast. Rather, their faith rose. They did something. They healed him. They saw someone in need. They recognised the *inner beauty* of every human being. They didn't have any money but Peter said, 'Silver or gold I do not have, but what I have I give you. In the name of Jesus Christ of Nazareth, walk' (v.6).

There is great power in the name of Jesus. To the Hebrew mind a person's name revealed their character. This was not a magic formula or a tag-on at the end of a prayer. This was the difference between the ministry of Jesus and that of his disciples. Jesus healed on his own authority, while the disciples did it in his name. In the same way, we are dependent on him. In our weakness, you and I can continue to exercise his ministry, *in his power* and *in his name*.

Not only was this man healed (he jumped to his feet and began to walk and praise God, v.8), but many people were also converted. This one act of kindness had an astonishing effect. The people 'were filled with wonder and amazement at what happened to him ... all the people were astonished and came running to them' (vv.10–11). The demonstration of the power of God was accompanied by the proclamation of the gospel. They had the opportunity to speak about Jesus: his death and resurrection, and the need for faith (vv.14–16).

Our preaching should always be Jesus-centred. Peter's second sermon, like his first, is totally focused on Jesus. He starts by saying, 'People of Israel, why does this surprise you? Why do you stare at us as if by our own power or godliness we had made this man walk?" (v.12). Peter does not want the people to be focused on himself, but rather on Jesus.

The whole talk is about Jesus. Jesus is God's 'servant' (v.13), 'the Holy and Righteous One' (v.14), 'the author of life' (v.15) and the 'prophet' foretold by Moses (v.22). He says, 'By faith in the name of Jesus, this man whom you see and know was made strong. It is Jesus' name and the faith that comes through him that has given this complete healing to him' (v.16).

Peter gives the good news about Jesus. He speaks about sin, the cross, the resurrection and the need to repent and turn to God. He assures them of God's promise to forgive their sins and restore their relationship with God. He says, 'Repent, then, and turn to God, so that your sins may be wiped out, that times of refreshing may come from the Lord' (v.19).

'Times of refreshing' come when you spend time in God's presence. When you are weary or worn out, you can be refreshed by spending time with God. Sometimes, you need to learn to separate yourself from the busyness of life and spend time with God in the way that Jesus did. The Holy Spirit, in his kindness, wants to bring 'times of refreshing' to you.

PRAYER

Lord, thank you that there is such power in the name of Jesus. I pray for an opportunity today to show kindness to someone and help them, in Jesus' name.

OLD TESTAMENT READING

2 Samuel 9:1–10:19
Give and receive kindness

God has an endless supply of kindness. David speaks of 'God's kindness' (9:3). When you show kindness, it is a way of expressing God's kindness to you.

David asks, 'Is there anyone still left of the house of Saul to whom I can *show kindness* for Jonathan's sake?' (v.1). He then asks Ziba, 'Is there not still someone of the house of Saul to whom I may show the unfailing, unsought, *unlimited* mercy and *kindness* of God?' (v.3, AMP).

Mephibosheth was only five years old at the time of his father's death (4:4) and now had a young son (9:12). David had been reigning in Jerusalem for at least seven years and Mephibosheth was probably about twenty years of age. The kindness that David shows Mephibosheth is like the kindness of God to us – unfailing, unsought and unlimited.

Once again, it is someone who is disabled (v.3) to whom special kindness is shown. David says to Mephibosheth, 'Don't be afraid ... for I will surely *show you kindness* ... I will restore to you all the land ... and you will always eat at my table' (v.7).

Then, David looks for further opportunities to show kindness. 'I will *show kindness* to Hanun son of Nahash, just as his father *showed kindness* to me' (10:2). Sadly, as sometimes happens, this kindness was misunderstood (v.3f.). However, this should not put us off. It is natural and right to want to show kindness to the children whose parents have been particularly kind to us.

Mephibosheth said, 'Who am I that you pay attention to a stray dog like me?' (v.8, MSG). He had a poor self-image. Like many of us, he was focused on his imperfections. But God blesses us in spite of our imperfections. He wants us to know and experience his unlimited kindness. Don't focus on what is wrong – your sins, faults, weaknesses and failures. In Christ, God has given you his righteousness and wants to pour out on you the riches of his kindness to us in Christ Jesus (Ephesians 2:7).

PRAYER

Lord, thank you for the riches of your kindness to me. Help me to always be on the lookout for opportunities to show kindness to those in need.

7 June | Day 158
Trials and Temptations

John Wimber, the US pastor and pioneer of the Vineyard movement, had a huge influence on the church around the world. He died at the age of sixty-three. Life had often been extremely difficult for him.

He had been subject to an outrageous amount of criticism. I remember him once saying to me, 'Notoriety is fun for a short time, but after that it is just hassle.' But perhaps what broke his heart more than anything was the fact that three of the men who were closest to him, whom he loved and treated as his sons, all fell into temptation and moral failure.

God used John Wimber in extraordinary ways, but he and his team faced many trials and temptations. This is how life is, and the Bible is not at all naïve about it. Usually, as we emerge from one battle, there is another one around the corner. This is the challenge of life.

READING FROM PSALMS

Psalm 71:1–8
Take confidence in the Lord

This psalm is full of indications of difficulty and opposition. Yet through it all, the writer says, 'From my birth I have relied on you' (v.6). In the psalm we see three key aspects of what that reliance on God involves:

1. Prayer

Here is a prayer that you can pray: 'I run for dear life to God ... get me out of this mess' (vv.1–2, MSG).

2. Patience

Once you have cried out for help and cast your burdens on the Lord, the next step is to hope in him *with confidence* (v.5): 'You keep me going when times are tough ... I've hung on you' (vv.5–6, MSG).

3. Praise

You can praise God before, during and after battles you face: 'I'll never run out of praise' (v.8, MSG).

PRAYER

Lord, thank you that I can rely on you as I look to the future and the battles ahead.

NEW TESTAMENT READING

Acts 4:1–22
Take courage from being with Jesus

Authentic Christianity is bound to lead to opposition and trials of one sort or another. Here, the disciples have been put in jail and literally on trial. Effectively, they were charged with *the crime of being Christians* (though they didn't go by that name at the time). There has not been a single period in church history when Christians have *not* been tried for *this offence* somewhere in the world.

It was not disputed that the man had been healed. In the Gospels it is *Jesus* who does the miracles; in Acts ordinary people do miracles *in his name*. When asked, 'By what power or what *name* did you do this?' (v.7), filled with the Holy Spirit, Peter replied, 'It is by *the name of Jesus Christ of Nazareth, whom you crucified* but whom *God* raised from the dead' (v.10). Today, you can pray in this same powerful way.

Peter had the audacity to tell his judges that they were guilty of crucifying the Saviour of the world. They had rejected and crucified Jesus. Peter had been frightened to admit to a servant girl that he even knew Jesus. Now, he is a changed person. He publicly proclaims Jesus and the resurrection, in the court where Jesus was tried and 500 yards from where he was crucified.

The key was that Peter had encountered the risen Jesus and was 'filled with the Holy Spirit' (v.8). He now knew what Jesus had come to do and, through the Holy Spirit, Jesus was with him and helping him.

Peter continues, 'salvation is found in no one else, for there is no other name under heaven given to people by which we must be saved' (v.12).

It is not surprising that 'They couldn't take their eyes off them – Peter and John standing there so confident, so sure of themselves! Their fascination deepened when they realised these two were laymen with no training in Scripture or formal education. They recognised them as companions of Jesus' (v.13, MSG).

Peter and John may not have had much formal education, but they had been to '*school* with Jesus'. They were his disciples. They had been to the '*College* of God's Word'. And now they were studying at the '*University* of the Holy Spirit'. Many of the people used greatly by God have had little formal education.

Peter and John were threatened and told not to speak about Jesus. But they replied, 'We cannot help speaking about what we have seen and heard' (v.20).

As they faced their judges, they were hugely helped by the fact that everyone could see what an amazing miracle had taken place. The forty-year-old healed man was standing there as living testimony to the power of Jesus (vv.14–21).

PRAYER

Lord, fill me with your Spirit and give me the same courage that Peter and John had so that I can go on proclaiming Jesus, whatever the cost and whatever the opposition. May we see outstanding miracles like those that you performed through your first followers.

OLD TESTAMENT READING

2 Samuel 11:1–12:31
Take care to please God

In contemporary culture, the words 'You are the man!' (12:7) might be words of admiration! But these are among the most haunting words in the whole Bible. David had been found out. He had been tempted and had fallen into sin. He did it in secret and thought he had got away with it. But God sees everything. In one of the supreme understatements of the Bible we are told, 'the thing David had done *displeased the Lord*' (11:27).

Where did it all go wrong?

The point is often made that David's first mistake was to remain in Jerusalem (v.1). If he had been out there fighting the battle with his people, he would have been less prone to temptation than sitting at home with rather too little to do. John Wimber often used to say, 'It's hard to sit still and be good.' We are much less likely to fall into temptation when we are fully occupied and in the right place.

David gradually slipped. He saw a 'stunningly beautiful woman' bathing (v.2, MSG). There was no sin yet, only temptation. However, he must have given in to lustful adulterous thoughts because he made a plan, sent for her to sleep with him and sinned greatly.

Although by the standards of his day it was nothing compared to what other kings would have done, he then planned a cover-up that did not work. Eventually, it ended in the murder of Uriah. As often happens, sin led to more sin – and the cover-up was worse than the original sin.

David must have felt absolutely crushed at Nathan's words: 'You are the man! This is what the LORD, the God of Israel, says: "I anointed you … I delivered you … I gave you … And if all this had been too little, I would have given you even more. Why did you despise the word of the LORD by doing what is evil in his eyes?"' (12:7–9). Not only had David messed up badly, but he was also someone who should have known better.

Amazingly, God forgave David even this enormous sin (v.13). There is no sin or failing that is too great for God to forgive, and no situation into which God's grace cannot reach. No matter what you have done, God can forgive you.

The key to receiving that forgiveness is admitting our guilt and repenting of what we have done. This is the great difference between David (whom God forgave when he sinned) and Saul (whom God did not). Whereas Saul tried to justify himself (see 1 Samuel 15), David simply admitted everything. He said, 'I have sinned against the LORD' (2 Samuel 12:13). In effect he just said, 'I'm sorry!'

Forgiveness does not take away the consequences of our actions though. For David, the consequences were huge. His baby son died as a result (vv.13–14), and God warned him that, because of his violent actions, 'the sword shall never depart from your house' (v.10). The consequences of David's sin were long lasting.

Nevertheless, this was not the end for David. God did not abandon him. Although his son died, there is hope. One day they will be reunited: 'I will go to him, but he will not return to me' (v.23). Not only that, but God gave to David another son, Solomon, and 'The LORD loved him' (v.24).

This account is a warning and an encouragement. It is a warning to us to take responsibility for our lives, to put in boundaries, to get help early and to watch and pray that we do not fall into temptation.

If you have fallen, like David admit your sin, confess, repent, grieve if necessary and then get on with your life looking forward to what God has in store for you. We all mess up from time to time. God forgives. He restores. He blesses us again.

PRAYER

Lord, guard my heart and the hearts of all your people, that we may be faithful to you.

8 June | Day 159
No Shades of Grey

Back in the 1960s, the band The Monkees sang about how no one seemed to believe in absolute morals anymore. In *Shades of Gray* they sang: 'Today there is no black or white, only *shades of gray*.'[1]

Now the expression '*shades of grey*' has come to be associated with the notorious and controversial books and films with that name.

Many today no longer believe there is such a thing as absolute right or absolute wrong. Stark contrasts and black-and-white distinctions are not always easy to swallow in a society in which relativism is the order of the day. Everything is relative – a matter of degrees.

As followers of Jesus we cannot give in to these relativistic ideas. We must be open to the prophetic voice of Scripture, which often traces stark contrasts, urgent ethical choices and diverging paths in the midst of complex problems and situations.

The reality of right and wrong are very clear in today's passages and there are stark contrasts between the two.

READING FROM PSALMS

Psalm 71:9–18
Finishing well vs perishing in shame

The only kind of 'grey' approved of in the Bible is 'grey hair', which is seen as 'a crown of splendour ... attained by a righteous life' (Proverbs 16:31). Personally, I find this increasingly encouraging!

The psalmist is determined to finish well. He writes, 'Do not cast me away when I am old; do not forsake me when my strength is gone ... Even when I am old and *grey*, do not forsake me, O God, till I declare your power to the next generation, your might to all who are to come' (Psalm 71:9, 18).

This is in stark contrast to the fate of his enemies who he hopes will 'perish in shame' (v.13). From the New Testament perspective, this is probably not the right way to pray for one's enemies! However, it is certainly true that some people seem to 'perish in shame'. It is a tragic way for anyone's life to end.

The psalmist contrasts himself with those who perish in shame. He writes, 'but as for me...' (v.14). He wants to continue to be close to the Lord to the end of his life. In fact, he wants the end of his life to be even more fruitful than the beginning. He says, 'I will praise you *more and more*' (v.14).

Every generation has the responsibility of passing the baton 'to the next generation' (v.18). Succession planning is a key part of finishing well. It has been said that it is important to *pursue* a Paul and *train* a Timothy, be *mentored* by a Mary and *prepare* a Phoebe.

PRAYER

Lord, help me to finish well and to declare your power to the next generation. May my mouth tell of your righteousness and proclaim your mighty acts.

NEW TESTAMENT READING

Acts 4:23–5:11
Filled with the Holy Spirit vs filled by Satan

Church should never be boring. No one was ever bored in the early church. You never knew what would happen. There was such a powerful sense of God's presence. Some loved it; others were terrified.

Again, we see a stark contrast.

First, we see the results of being filled with the Holy Spirit:

1. Boldness

Peter and John are not put off by the threats made to them (4:17, 21). Rather, 'they raised their voices together in prayer to God' (v.24). They prayed, 'Now, Lord, consider their threats and enable your servants to speak your word *with great boldness*' (v.29). 'After they prayed, the place where they were meeting was shaken. And they were all filled with the Holy Spirit and spoke the word of God *boldly*' (v.31).

2. Unity

'All the believers were *one* in heart and mind' (v.32a). They were all filled with the same Holy Spirit. A mark of a Spirit-filled community is unity.

3. Generosity

They had a liberating attitude to their possessions: 'They shared everything they had ... There were no needy persons among them' (vv.32, 34). Those who could afford it helped support those who were in need (vv.34–35).

4. Power

They had prayed, 'Stretch out your hand to heal and perform miraculous signs and wonders through the name of your holy servant Jesus' (v.30). Their prayer was answered: '*With great power* the apostles continued to testify to the resurrection of the Lord Jesus' (v.33a).

5. Grace

'...much grace was upon them all' (v.33b). Experience of God's grace should lead to a community of grace and graciousness.

By stark contrast, in the second half of today's passage we see the results of being filled by Satan. Peter uses very strong language when he says, 'Ananias, how is it that *Satan* has so *filled your heart*' (5:3).

There was no necessity for Ananias and Sapphira to give away their property or money: 'Didn't it belong to you before it was sold? And after it was sold, wasn't the money at your disposal?' (v.4). They were not criticised for a lack of generosity.

Rather, the evidence that Satan had filled their hearts is not only that they *lied* (which could be a spontaneous act), but also that they *conspired* together to lie. Peter says to Ananias, 'You have lied to the Holy Spirit' (v.3) and he says to Sapphira, 'How could you *agree* to test the Spirit of the Lord?' (v.9). This conspiracy was premeditated and prepared.

God gave Peter a 'word of knowledge' (vv.3–4). This exposed their sin. The fear of God came upon the people (vv.5, 11). This type of fear was not fear of human beings or a slavish fear, but rather a holy fear. They 'had a healthy respect for God. They knew God was not to be trifled with' (v.11, MSG).

This is not an easy story to read, and many of us struggle with the severity of God's judgment in the passage. Ultimately, only God knows the secrets of our hearts, and we need to trust that his judgments are fair and just. It reminds us, though, of the awesomeness of God's presence in our midst. The sense of God's presence was so great that people feared that their sin might be exposed. But this presence of God and the Holy Spirit also brought about extraordinary conversions, healings, signs and wonders.

PRAYER

Lord, fill us with your Holy Spirit. May we be a church known for its bold proclamation, unity, generosity, power and grace.

OLD TESTAMENT READING

2 Samuel 13:1–39
Love vs hate

In this passage we see strongly contrasting emotions. Amnon '*fell in love* with Tamar' (v.1). He says, '*I'm in love* with Tamar, my brother Absalom's sister' (v.4). David had many wives and many children. The boys would probably have been separated from the girls after the age of five or six; there would not have been a sense of belonging together that exists in a normal family today.

Amnon plotted to rape Tamar, who pleaded with him: 'Don't do this wicked thing' (v.12). She even offered to marry him (v.13). The law forbade marriage to a half-sister. Possibly, this was not being practised at the time. More likely, Tamar was clutching at straws. Amnon 'refused to listen to her, and since he was stronger than she, he raped her' (v.14).

The Bible does not ignore the issue of sexual abuse. Rape has always been, and still is, a horrific crime. Tamar describes it as '*wicked*' (v.12). It is an act of a 'wicked fool' (v.13). It leads to 'desolation' (v.20) and it is a 'disgraceful' (v.21) act.

We see a glimpse of the terrible damage sexual abuse does to the victim: 'Tamar poured ashes on her head, then she ripped the long-sleeved gown, held her head in her hands, and walked away, sobbing as she went' (v.19, MSG). She became 'bitter and desolate' (v.20, MSG).

Instantly, it appears, 'Amnon hated her with intense hatred. In fact, he hated her more than he had loved her' (v.15). This led to further tragedy for David and his household. The violence is perpetuated – Amnon is killed and Absalom flees, separating him from David (vv.23–39).

Perhaps it would be more accurate to say that Amnon was 'infatuated' with Tamar. He may have been 'in love' with her, but he certainly did not love her. It is extraordinary, though true to fallen human nature and experience, that infatuation can quickly turn to hatred. Amnon's love was certainly not true love.

'Love is patient, love is kind. It does not envy, it does not boast, it is not proud. It is not rude, it is not self-seeking, it is not easily angered, it keeps no record of wrongs. Love does not delight in evil but rejoices with the truth. It always protects, always trusts, always hopes, always perseveres' (1 Corinthians 13:4–7).

PRAYER

Lord, deliver us from hatred. May we be filled, not by a superficial love, but by a love that is the fruit of the Holy Spirit.

9 June | Day 160
Stay Loyal

In 2007, a group of twenty-three South Korean missionaries were captured by the Taliban in Afghanistan. They were terrified. The Taliban separated the group, isolated them and confiscated their possessions. One of the Korean women managed to hold on to her Bible. She ripped it into twenty-three pieces and secretly gave each of them a portion so that wherever they were, each person could read a part of Scripture when no one was watching.

The group knew that the Taliban had decided to kill them, one at a time. One by one the missionaries surrendered their lives again to Jesus saying, 'Lord, if you want me to die for your sake I'll do it.' Then the pastor said, 'I've talked to [the Taliban] because they are going to start killing us and I've told their leaders that if anyone dies, I die first because I am your pastor.' Another said, 'No, because I also am a pastor and I am your *elder*. I die first.'

Then the pastor came back and said, 'You are not ordained, I have been ordained, I die first.' And sure enough, he died first. Two more were killed before the rest were eventually rescued. They had demonstrated extraordinary loyalty to God and to each other.

Loyalty is a combination of love and faithfulness. It is a quality often lacking in our society today. Disloyalty destroys families, churches, businesses, political parties and even nations.

READING FROM PROVERBS

Proverbs 14:15–24
Pursue loyalty to God in your plans

Our first loyalty is to God. His favour rests on those who are 'God-loyal' (v.19, MSG).

The book of Proverbs is full of practical wisdom. It encourages you, for example, to be discerning about what you believe: 'The gullible believe anything they're told; the prudent sift and weigh every word' (v.15, MSG). Ultimately wisdom is about how you relate to God: 'The wise fear the Lord and shun evil' (v.16).

'Fear of the Lord' is an attitude of healthy respect and loyalty. It means involving him in all your plans. Be very careful about the plans you make – that they are for good and not for evil. Eventually, even 'the wicked will respect God-*loyal* people' (v.19, MSG).

'Those who plan what is good find *love* and *faithfulness*' (v.22b). The word for 'find' is sometimes translated 'show'. Both are true. Those who plan what is good not only *find* love and faithfulness, they *show* love and faithfulness as well. This is at the heart of loyalty – to show love and faithfulness. This is contrasted with those who selfishly plot evil and go astray.

PRAYER

Lord, help me to be wise and God-loyal in my plans. May we, as a community of God-loyal people, plan what is good and find love and faithfulness.

NEW TESTAMENT READING

Acts 5:12–42
Pursue loyalty to Jesus in your words

As the apostles went out and preached the good news they performed *many* miraculous signs and wonders among the people. 'More and more men and women believed in the Lord and were added to their number' (v.14). As a result, 'Crowds gathered ... bringing their sick ... *all* of them were healed' (vv.15–16).

Sadly, their success led to 'jealousy' from religious leaders (v.17). Be warned. Envy is such a temptation for those of us who are seen as 'religious'. In their jealousy they arrested the apostles and put them in jail (v.18). But once again God performed a miracle. He sent an angel of the Lord to open the doors of the jail and bring them out.

With huge courage they obeyed the command to 'Go, stand in the temple courts ... and tell the people the full message of this new life' (v.20).

When they were caught doing exactly what they had been arrested for doing in the first place, they were re-arrested and brought before the Sanhedrin to be questioned by the high priest who said to them, 'We gave you strict orders not to teach in this name ... Yet you have filled Jerusalem with your teaching and are determined to make us guilty of this man's blood' (v.28).

Peter and the other apostles were loyal to God and to their calling. They replied, 'We must obey God rather than human beings!' (v.29).

Jesus said, 'Give to Caesar what is Caesar's, and to God what is God's' (Matthew 22:21). In saying this, he defined the limits of the authority of human beings and our loyalty to it. When it conflicts with loyalty to God, God takes precedence. Out of loyalty to God, they continued preaching the gospel – even when they were on trial.

Their brief defence (it takes only three verses – Acts 5:30–32) is a model sermon. It is all about Jesus. It is astonishing that they were able to cover so much in such a short presentation. They preach about the cross, resurrection and the exaltation of Jesus. They proclaimed Jesus as Prince and Saviour. The talk includes a description of the way of salvation: repentance and forgiveness of sins.

In addition, they managed to include the whole Trinity: God the Father ('The God of our ancestors', v.30), God the Son ('Jesus', v.30) and God 'the Holy Spirit' (v.32). This sermon produces such fury that, like the South Korean missionaries, they faced the threat of death.

However, in the providence of God, there was a wise man on the Sanhedrin, a Pharisee named Gamaliel, who pointed out to his fellow members (by giving examples from recent history) that 'if [the apostles'] purpose or activity is of human origin, it will fail. But if it is from God, you will not be able to stop these men; you will only find yourselves fighting against God' (vv.38–39).

Although his speech persuaded them, nevertheless the apostles were flogged and 'ordered ... not to speak in the name of Jesus' (v.40).

Once again, with extraordinary courage and loyalty to God and their calling, 'The apostles left the Sanhedrin, rejoicing because they had been counted worthy of suffering disgrace for the Name. Day after day, in the temple courts and from house to house, they never stopped teaching and proclaiming *the good news that Jesus is the Christ*' (vv.41–42).

PRAYER

Lord, may we be inspired by the example of the apostles and those like the South Korean missionaries who followed in their footsteps. May we never stop teaching and proclaiming the good news that Jesus is the Christ.

OLD TESTAMENT READING

2 Samuel 14:1–15:12
Pursue loyalty to each other in your heart

Loyalty is such an attractive characteristic in a person. Disloyalty is subversive and betrays trust. Disloyalty can undermine the leadership in a church, business or even a nation.

In David's case, disloyalty came from his own son. This must have been so painful for him. David loved Absalom: 'the king's heart longed for Absalom' (14:1). God speaks to David through the wise woman from Tekoa. As a result David says, 'Go, bring back the young man Absalom' (v.21). When he returned 'the king kissed Absalom' (v.33). David gave him another opportunity to be a loyal son.

Tragically, David's love and loyalty to Absalom were not returned. We see here a powerful description of how disloyalty works.

There are always opportunities for disloyalty. In any situation – whether for example in the government, workplace or the church – there are bound to be those who complain (15:2). If you are a loyal person, you will help to deal with these complaints and attempt to diffuse them.

It has been said, 'Loyalty means I am with you whether you are wrong or right. But I will tell you when you are wrong and help you get it right.'

Absalom failed the loyalty test. He would say to the complainers, '"Look, you've got a strong case; but the king isn't going to listen to you." Then he'd say, "Why doesn't someone make me a judge for this country? Anybody with a case could bring it to me and I'd settle things fair and square."' (vv.3–4, MSG).

Of course, this is absolute nonsense. But it is easy to make promises of this kind. The disloyal person says, 'If only I were in charge everything would be so much better.' In this way, Absalom *'stole the hearts of the people of Israel'* (v.6). Disloyalty begins in our hearts and in our thinking. So does loyalty. Guard your heart and your thinking and do not allow your heart to be stolen.

However, here they found a rallying point around Absalom and 'the conspiracy gained strength, and Absalom's following kept on increasing' (v.12). Those who are feeling discontented in any situation always look for a rallying point. They look for someone among the leadership team around whom they can rally. If the entire leadership team remains faithful, the discontents will be unsuccessful.

PRAYER

Lord, help us to stay loyal to our leaders – to our national leaders and governments, parents, church leaders and bosses. Lord, guard our hearts, keep us loyal, loving and faithful to you and to one another.

---

10 June | Day 161

Troubles Do Not Have the Last Word

George Matheson was born in Glasgow, the eldest of eight children. He had only partial vision as a boy. By the age of twenty he was completely blind. When his fiancée learnt he was going blind and that there was nothing the doctors could do, she told him she could not go through life with a blind man. He never married.

He was helped by a devoted sister throughout his ministry. She learnt Greek, Latin and Hebrew in order to aid him in his studies. Despite his blindness, Matheson had a brilliant career at the Glasgow Academy, University of Glasgow and the Church of Scotland Seminary.

When he was forty years old, something bittersweet happened. His sister married. Not only did this mean that he lost her companionship – it also brought a fresh reminder of his own heartbreak. In the midst of this intense sadness, on the eve of his sister's marriage, he wrote one of the most popular and best loved hymns of the Christian church – 'O Love That Wilt Not Let Me Go'. He completed the whole work in five minutes and never edited, corrected or retouched it. 'This came,' he wrote, 'like a dayspring from on high.'

O Joy that seekest me through pain,
I cannot close my heart to thee;
I trace the rainbow through the rain,
And feel the promise is not vain,
That morn shall tearless be.
George Matheson (1882)

Troubles are part of life. Jesus faced trouble and so did the apostles, David and all the people of God. However, as Matheson's hymn beautifully articulates, *troubles do not have the last word.*

READING FROM PSALMS

Psalm 71:19–24
Restored after many troubles

God does not promise you an easy path. Life can be extremely hard. The psalmist has seen 'troubles, *many and bitter*' (v.20). His troubles, pressures and worries were not occasional or trivial. They were numerous and serious. He gives you a model of how to respond in these circumstances.

1. Keep trusting
It is easy to trust God when things are going well. The challenge is to keep trusting in the midst of troubles. Do not stop *believing in the goodness of God*: 'Your righteousness reaches to the skies, O God, you who have done great things. Who, O God, is like you?' (v.19).

2. Keep hoping
Your troubles will not last for ever. In the midst of troubles, there is *hope*: 'You will *restore* my life again; from the depths of the earth you will again *bring me up*. You will *increase my honour* and *comfort me* once again' (vv.20b–21). God will use your troubles for good. He will shape your character through them. As a result, he will increase your honour. He will comfort you through them so that you can comfort others (2 Corinthians 1:4).

3. Keep worshipping
Keep on praising God in spite of the troubles: 'I will praise you with the harp for your faithfulness, O my God; I will sing praise to you with the lyre, O Holy One of Israel. My lips will shout for joy when I sing praise to you – I, whom you have redeemed' (Psalm 71:22–23). The presence of God in worship brings us peace and solace, especially in difficult times.

PRAYER
Lord, thank you that though I may see troubles many and bitter, you promise to restore my life again. I praise you for your faithfulness.'

NEW TESTAMENT READING

Acts 6:1–7:19
Rescued from all his troubles

There is sometimes a temptation to idealise the life of the early church – as if they were the perfect church and had no problems at all. We need to read the idyllic picture of the church in Acts 2 alongside the events of Acts 6 and, of course, not forget all the troubles of Paul in his letters. The early church had plenty of troubles. Do not be surprised by any of the following in the church today:

1. Complaining
Good leaders pick their battles carefully. They do not get involved in everything, but they do take responsibility for everything. The apostles faced a justified complaint that 'widows were being overlooked in the daily distribution of food' (Acts 6:1). Yet they needed to concentrate on their main task: 'prayer and the ministry of the word' (v.4). The solution lay (as it does so often) in effective delegation.

The apostles dealt with the issue by setting aside a group of people who would 'wait on tables' (v.2). They chose people 'full of the Spirit and wisdom' (v.3). As a result, they kept their focus and 'the word of God spread', and the number of disciples increased dramatically (v.7). Good leaders delegate and release others into their God-given gifts and ministries.

2. Stirring
A group of opponents of the church 'stirred up the people' (v.12) and 'produced false witnesses' (v.13). They twisted Stephen's words and said, 'This fellow never stops speaking against this holy place and against the law' (vv.13).

3. Fear of change
Some of the opposition came from a fear of change. They said, 'We have heard him say that this Jesus of Nazareth will destroy this place and *change* the customs Moses handed down to us' (v.14).

They found they could not keep their eyes off Stephen, whose 'face was like the face of an angel' (v.15). He gave his defence. He recited the history of the people of God and cited the parts of history that were particularly relevant to his own situation. He said of Joseph, 'God was with him and *rescued him* from *all his troubles*. He gave Joseph wisdom…' (7:9–10), just as God was clearly giving Stephen wisdom (see 6:10).

Stephen's own rescue came only in martyrdom. He 'saw the glory of God, and Jesus standing at the right hand of God' (7:55), and Stephen was rescued for all eternity.

PRAYER

Lord, help me not to be put off by troubles but rather, like Stephen, to be full of faith and the Holy Spirit. May we see the word of God spread and the numbers of your followers increase more and more each day.

OLD TESTAMENT READING

2 Samuel 15:13–16:14
Refreshed in the midst of troubles

David's own son Absalom has turned against him, and David is told that the 'hearts of the people of Israel are with Absalom' (15:13). This must have been devastating news. David, a great man of God, a king for God's people and a 'type' of Christ (indeed, an ancestor of Christ), faced many troubles in his life. If you face these kinds of troubles in your life, do not be surprised by them or think that you have done something wrong. Sometimes troubles come simply because you are doing something right.

1. Tears

We see just how upset David was. He 'continued up the Mount of Olives, weeping as he went; his head was covered and he was barefoot' (v.30). All the people were also 'weeping as they went up' (v.30). Indeed, 'the whole countryside wept aloud' (v.23).

2. Disappointment

Not only did David's own son turn against him but Mephibosheth was also disloyal to him even though David had gone out of his way to help him. He stayed in Jerusalem because he thought, 'Today the house of Israel will give me back my grandfather's kingdom' (16:3). Disloyalty from those we love is especially disappointing.

3. Criticism

Shimei shouted insults, threw rocks and cursed David. David does not seek revenge. Rather, he chooses to leave the matter in God's hands (vv.11–12).

4. Exhaustion

David 'and all the people with him arrived at their destination exhausted' (v.14). When we read of what David went through it is not surprising that he was genuinely 'exhausted'.

The Christian life is never without troubles, tears, sadness and disappointments. However, what distinguishes the people of God is their relationship with God.

In the midst of all his troubles, David prays, 'O LORD, turn Ahithophel's counsel into foolishness' (15:31). His prayer is answered – but not in the way he expects. Ahithophel gives good advice, but it is rejected. So God answered the spirit of the prayer (see 17:14).

In the midst of his exhaustion, David 'refreshed himself' (16:14). 'They *rested* and *were revived*' (v.14, MSG). Sometimes you just need to take a break and rest to be revived and refreshed physically, spiritually and emotionally. We are not told how David did this exactly. However, if the Psalms are anything to go by, we know it was through his close relationship with God that he found refreshment.

Also, no doubt David was *emotionally* refreshed by the loyalty of his friends Zadok (15:24 onwards), Hushai (v.37), Ziba (16:1–4) and Ittai, who said to him, 'Wherever my lord the king may be, whether it means life or death, there will your servant be' (15:21).

PRAYER

Lord, thank you that there is no trouble that this life can bring from which you do not rescue me, ultimately with eternal life in your presence. Thank you that, in the middle of my troubles, I can pray to you and be refreshed by the presence of God (Act 3:19).

11 June | Day 162
God Uses Even Your Mistakes

Handley Moule, when he was Bishop of Durham, had the task of visiting the relatives of 170 miners who had been killed in a mining accident. While he was wondering what to say to them, he picked up a little bookmark his mother had given him. As he held it up, on the reverse side of the handwoven bookmark there was a tangled web. There was no rhyme, no reason, no pattern, nothing. But on the other side it said, 'God is love'.

The world often seems to us like a tangled web. Often we cannot work out what is going on or why we are suffering in the way we are. But the claim of Jesus and the Scriptures is that behind it all is the love of God. Even though things may seem very difficult for us to understand now, God is working out his loving purposes in the world.

God can weave a pattern from the threads of our lives – including the suffering, heartaches and even our mistakes and make something beautiful. The apostle Paul tells us that 'in all things God works for the good of those who love him, who have been called according to his purpose' (Romans 8:28). Reflect today on the fact that, even though your situation may be challenging, God is weaving his purpose for your life.

Job said, 'You gave me life and showed me kindness, and in your *providence* watched over my spirit' (Job 10:12). Everything that happens in this world is within the sphere of God's working. 'Providence' means God's foresight: the way he anticipates and prepares for the future. 'Providence' is the way God guides and steers human history – he is present and active in the world – sustaining it and ruling it.

It is also the way he guides and steers your life personally and individually. God has a specific, unique destiny for you. Sometimes this thought worries people: that they might somehow mess things up and miss out on God's purpose. But that isn't the case. *Even your mistakes* he uses for good. In all the circumstances of your life and the events going on around you, you can trust in the providence of God.

READING FROM PSALMS

Psalm 72:1–20
Providence and prayer

Your prayers make a difference. Not only do they affect your own life but they can also affect the course of history.

How providence and prayer work together is a mystery. In some extraordinary way, your prayers affect the outcome of events. God is sovereign and works out his purposes through history. Yet he involves you in this process.

This psalm is David's prayer for his son and successor, King Solomon. It was a strong reminder of his high calling. Yet it goes beyond what is humanly attainable. For example, 'He will endure as long as the sun, as long as the moon, through all generations' (v.5). His reign is eternal and universal (v.8). Ultimately, it was only fulfilled in the Messiah, *God's Son*, Jesus Christ.

This psalm is a prayer for blessing on the king and through him that all the people will be blessed with 'prosperity' (v.3). The good leader will be concerned about poverty and justice: 'Please stand up for the poor, help the children of the needy, come down hard on the cruel tyrants' (v.4, MSG). It is also a prayer that in his foreign policy 'all nations will be blessed through him' (v.17).

David says, 'May people ever *pray for him* and bless him all day long' (v.15b). It is clear that God's blessing on the leader will come as people pray for him. How this works we do not know. However, it shows that praying really does make a difference. In his providence, God takes your prayers and uses them to bring blessing.

PRAYER

Lord, thank you that prayer makes a difference. I pray for our leaders whom you have set over us. Give them grace and wisdom. Enrich their lives that they may be a source of strength and inspiration, and promote your honour and glory.

NEW TESTAMENT READING

Acts 7:20–43
Providence and prophecy

We see in this passage the extraordinary way in which God planned and prepared for the coming of Jesus. God in his providence foresees the future, and so in a mysterious way anticipates, prepares for it and guides it. Therefore, you can trust God's providence in all the events and circumstances of your life.

Stephen's speech rehearses the ways in which God had guided and watched over Israel's history, and through it prepared for Jesus' coming. In this section, he focuses particularly on Moses.

Moses had said that God would raise up a prophet *like him* (Deuteronomy 18:15). Peter has already applied this to Jesus (Acts 3:22–23). Now Stephen does the same. He says, '*This is that* Moses who told the Israelites, "God will send you *a prophet like me* from your own people"' (7:37).

Moses was a 'type' of Christ. He foreshadowed and prepared the way. There are at least fifteen similarities between Moses and Jesus:

1. Like Jesus, Moses was 'no ordinary child' (v.20). The *circumstances surrounding the births* of both Moses and Jesus were appropriately *extraordinary*.
2. Like Jesus (Matthew 2:16–17), Moses was born at a time when *newborn babies were being killed off* (Acts 7:19–21).
3. Like Jesus (Luke 2:40), Moses was *noted for his wisdom* (Acts 7:22).
4. Like Jesus (John 7:46), Moses was '*powerful in speech and action*' (Acts 7:22).
5. Like Jesus, Moses had a season of *preparation*. We know little about the first thirty years of either of their lives. Both spent this time being trained for the task ahead (vv.22–23).
6. Like Jesus (John 2:16), Moses showed *righteous anger at sin* (Acts 7:24). However, unlike Jesus, Moses committed a crime. But God, in his providence, even used this mistake.
7. Like Jesus (John 1:11), Moses was sent by God to rescue his people, but was not recognised as such at the time. 'Moses thought that his own people would realise that God was using him to rescue them, but they did not' (Acts 7:25).
8. Like Jesus (2 Corinthians 5:19), Moses aimed at *reconciliation*: Moses 'tried to reconcile them' (Acts 7:26).
9. Like Jesus (John 5:22), Moses is described as *ruler and judge*. It was said to Moses, 'Who made you ruler and judge over us?' (Acts 7:27).
10. Like Jesus (Luke 3:22), Moses *heard the Lord's voice* (Acts 7:31).
11. Like Jesus (John 1:14; 2:21), Moses *recognised* that the holy place was not in a specific religious location, but *where God is present*. For Moses this was at the burning bush for God said, 'The place where you are standing is holy ground' (Acts 7:33).
12. Like Jesus (John 8:36), Moses *set the people free from oppression* (Acts 7:34).
13. Like Jesus (4:11), Moses was *misunderstood and rejected* by his own people: 'Moses whom they had rejected ... they rejected him' (7:35, 39).
14. Like Jesus (2 Corinthians 1:10), Moses succeeded in delivering his own people. Moses 'led them out of Egypt' (Acts 7:36).
15. Like Jesus (2:36), Moses' rejection brought God's judgment, but led to eventual victory (7:42). As the apostle Peter put it on the day of Pentecost, 'God has made this Jesus, whom you crucified, both Lord and Christ' (2:36).

PRAYER

Lord, thank you for the astonishing way in which you work your purposes out through history and through your prophets like Moses. Today, I trust in your providence over all the events and circumstances in my life.

OLD TESTAMENT READING

2 Samuel 16:15–18:18
Providence and protection

You can trust God with your future, your family, your church and your nation. The whole universe is in his hands and he is working his purposes out.

God is at work through all the human events that are described here.

The advice Ahithophel gave 'was like that of one who enquires of God' (16:23). If we are to give advice of any value, we have to be people who enquire of the Lord, in advance, what God is doing and what his will is.

If Absalom had followed Ahithophel's advice, it would have been disastrous for David. Instead, Absalom chose to ignore Ahithophel's wise advice and follow the bad advice of Hushai.

We see how God's providential care and protection was around David: 'For the Lord had determined to frustrate the good advice of Ahithophel' (17:14). This was an answer to the spirit of David's prayer.

Here we see that God is the hidden hand and ruler of history. David and all the other people involved in the drama had enormous power and freedom to act. But they were not free to act as though the Lord was not there.

PRAYER

Thank you, Lord, that you are in charge of human history. You reign and rule over this universe. Thank you that in all things, *including our mistakes*, you work for the good of those who love you and who have been called according to your purpose (Romans 8:28).

12 June | Day 163
You Can Change

There was a woman who lived on the streets near our church. She would ask for money and react aggressively to those who refused. When she died, I took the funeral. I discovered afterwards that this woman had inherited a large fortune. She had acquired a luxurious flat and many valuable paintings, but she chose to live on the streets with her plastic bags full of rubbish. She could not bring herself to leave behind the life she knew and she never enjoyed her inheritance.

Some people are afraid of change, while others believe change is not possible. Yet the wonderful news is that with God's help *you can change*. This change is key to spiritual life, growth and transformation. It is not just about changing our actions or appearance; we need to change on the inside – we need a change of *heart*. How can this happen?

READING FROM PSALMS

Psalm 73:1–14
Get God's perspective

Have you ever wondered whether your faith was really worthwhile? Have you ever looked around at very successful people who have no faith and wondered whether they are better off than you and even been tempted to be envious of them?

The psalmist has kept his heart pure (v.1), but he has found life extremely tough. He has had his struggles and been 'plagued' (v.5) by temptation, doubts, fears and anxiety of mind.

He looks around at an affluent society that seems to be doing very well without God. He 'almost slipped' (v.2): 'For I envied the arrogant when I saw the prosperity of the wicked' (v.3).

You may see people around who are rich and successful. In spite of their 'callous hearts' (v.7), they seem not to have struggles (v.4). They seem perfectly healthy and free from burdens (vv.4–5). They are proud and arrogant, and appear to have no need of God (vv.6–11).

If you find yourself on the slippery path of doubt and despair (v.2), wondering whether you have kept your heart pure in vain (v.13), then this psalm tells you what to do.

As we shall see, everything changes when we enter 'the sanctuary of God' (v.17) and see things from God's perspective. The psalmist had a complete change of heart. He 'understood their final destiny'. He realised the difference between their destiny and his (v.17).

The psalm starts, 'Surely God is good to Israel, to those who are pure in heart' (v.1). And it ends, 'But as for me, it is good to be near God. I have made the Sovereign LORD my refuge; I will tell of all your deeds' (v.28).

PRAYER

Lord, may I enter your sanctuary and see things from your perspective. Thank you that 'you are good to those who are pure in heart ... it is good to be near you. I have made you my refuge; I will tell of all your deeds.'

NEW TESTAMENT READING

Acts 7:44–8:3
'Circumcise' your heart

Do you ever look at someone who is very opposed to the Christian faith and wonder if they could ever change? In today's passage, we see that even the most hardened opponent can have a change of heart.

To be a Jew meant physical circumcision. Every male was circumcised on the eighth day of his life. But physical circumcision was intended to symbolise circumcision of the heart.

As Stephen's speech comes to an end, with great courage and boldness, he says to his accusers, 'You stiff-necked people, with *uncircumcised hearts* and ears! You are just like your ancestors: You always resist the Holy Spirit!' (7:51). He then accuses them of having murdered Jesus ('the Righteous One', v.52).

One main theme runs through Stephen's speech: God is not restricted to any one place: 'The Most High does not live in houses made by human hands' (v.48).

Neither the tabernacle (vv.44–45), nor the temple (vv.46–47) could ever have been viewed as God's home in a literal sense (v.48). For as God says through Isaiah, 'Heaven is my throne, and the earth is my footstool' (v.49).

Jesus came to replace the tabernacle and temple. Before Jesus, people would come to the temple to meet God. With Jesus' coming, the meeting place with God would be Jesus himself.

Now, through the Holy Spirit, God is present with his people (Matthew 18:20). It is especially in the gathered community, the church, that God lives by his Spirit (Ephesians 2:22). By his Spirit, he dwells within each of us. Our bodies are temples of the Holy Spirit (1 Corinthians 6:19). God's dwelling is now in Stephen, who is 'full of the Holy Spirit' (Acts 7:55).

Stephen is speaking to the priests of the very temple that has now been superseded by Jesus through the Holy Spirit. So it is not surprising that 'they were furious and gnashed their teeth at him' (v.54). They drag him out of the city and stone him (v.58).

One of the people with an '*uncircumcised heart*' is a young man named Saul. 'The ringleaders took off their coats and asked a young man named Saul to watch them' (v.58, MSG). He 'was right there, congratulating the killers' (8:1, MSG). This young man, Saul, 'began to destroy the church. Going from house to house, he dragged off both men and women and put them in prison' (v.3).

It would be hard to find anyone in human history who had a bigger change of heart than this young man. From being a murderer of Christians, he became a great apostle who preached all over the world that Jesus is the Son of God (9:20). Imagine if a former member of Isis ended up as the Pope and you'll be close to understanding what happened to the apostle Paul!

When did this change of heart begin? Perhaps a seed was planted when he saw Stephen's death: 'Stephen, full of the Holy Spirit, looked up to heaven and saw the glory of God, and Jesus standing at the right hand of God. "Look," he said, "I see heaven open and the Son of Man standing at the right hand of God"' (7:55–56).

Then, 'While they were stoning him, Stephen prayed, "Lord Jesus, receive my spirit." Then he fell on his knees and cried out, "Lord, do not hold this sin against them." When he had said this, he fell asleep' (vv.59–60).

Later, this same Saul, also known as Paul, would write, '...a person is a Jew who is one inwardly; *and circumcision is circumcision of the heart, by the Spirit*' (Romans 2:29).

To circumcise is to cut off. Every true Christian is circumcised by the Holy Spirit. When your heart is circumcised, you seek to cut off every wrong attitude that comes into your heart and mind. Say 'no' to anything that will stop your heart being right before God. Like Stephen, be filled with the Holy Spirit overflowing with love, courage and forgiveness.

PRAYER

Thank you, Lord, that your love has changed my heart. Thank you that through your Holy Spirit we can all change.

OLD TESTAMENT READING

2 Samuel 18:19–19:43
Mature through suffering

Are you in a period of suffering or grief? God often uses these times to change your heart and increase your compassion for others.

David's heart was purified through suffering and grief. As if he had not suffered enough up until now, he receives the news that Absalom, his son, is dead. He was 'heartbroken' (18:33, MSG). He cries out, 'O my son Absalom! My son, my son Absalom! If only I had died instead of you – O Absalom, my son, my son!' (v.33).

He is then told in no uncertain terms by Joab that he has to pull himself together and to go out and encourage his troops who have just won a great battle for him against his enemies (19:1–7). Joab tells David, 'put some heart into your servants!' (v.7, MSG).

David *changes* his attitude. He gets up and does exactly what he has been asked to do (v.8). 'He won over *the hearts* of all the men of Judah as though they were one man' (v.14).

Not only did David have a *change of heart*, Shimei did as well. He prostrates himself before the king: 'May my lord not hold me guilty. Do not remember how your servant did wrong ... For I your servant know that I have sinned, but today I have come here as the first of the whole house of Joseph to come down and meet my lord the king' (vv.19–20).

David, purified by his suffering, shines out like a brilliant light to all around him. He has mercy on Shimei. He deals wisely with Mephibosheth, Ziba and Barzillai (vv.24–39).

But David is going to face more battles ahead as a war of words breaks out between Israel and Judah (vv.41–43).

PRAYER

Lord, thank you for the ways in which you use the times of suffering and grief to bring change in my life. Purify my heart and increase my compassion for others.

13 June | Day 164
Your Nation Can Be Changed

There were 10,000 prostitutes plying their trade on the streets of London. Binge drinking and gambling were widespread. The UK had descended into decadence and immorality. This was the eighteenth century. Church congregations had declined sharply (just as they have in recent decades). Parts of the church had virtually descended into paganism.

Yet, the nation was changed. The preaching of John Wesley and George Whitefield began to take effect. Thousands of people responded to their message and encountered Jesus. Robert Raikes started his first Sunday school in 1780. The growth from this one idea reached 300,000 unchurched children within five years. By 1910, there were well over five million children in Sunday school. God raised up William Wilberforce, Lord Shaftesbury and others. Not only were individual hearts changed – but the nation was also transformed.

As we look at our world today, we see it is changing faster than ever before. In the last twenty-five years, there has been huge change – politically, economically and technologically. Massive change is taking place in many countries around the world. How can the *spiritual* climate of your nation be changed?

READING FROM PROVERBS

Proverbs 14:25–35
Peaceful people

The writer of Proverbs says, 'Righteousness exalts a nation, but sin is a disgrace to any people' (v.34). ('God-devotion makes a country strong', v.34, MSG.) Sin destroys a nation. Righteousness involves a range of right relationships:

1. Peace with God

Righteousness starts with making *peace* with God (Romans 5:1). It starts with the fear of the Lord (in the good sense of proper respect for the Lord).

'The Fear-of-God builds up confidence, and makes a world safe for your children. The Fear-of-God is a spring of living water' (Proverbs 14:26–27a, MSG).

2. Peace with others

As far as it depends on you, 'live at *peace* with everyone' (Romans 12:18). Right relationships with others are characterised by righteous words and actions. First, our words are to be truthful rather than deceitful for 'a truthful witness saves lives' (Proverbs 14:25) and patient rather than quick-tempered (v.29).

Second, our actions are to display a desire for the well-being of others. Be kind to those in need. 'You insult your Maker when you exploit the powerless; when you're kind to the poor, you honor God' (v.31, MSG). Display your delight towards those who act in wisdom (vv.33, 35).

3. Peace with ourselves

Righteousness involves a right relationship with ourselves. You can know *peace:* 'A calm and undisturbed mind and heart are the life and health of the body' (v.30a, AMP). Anger, lack of forgiveness, envy and jealousy can damage your physical body. Getting rid of the bad stuff in your life and having a 'heart at peace' is good for your health.

Ultimately, this *peace* comes from being content about both the present and the future. For, 'even in death the righteous have a refuge' (v.32b). For those who fear in the Lord, he becomes our refuge in the present (v.26) and the future (v.32b).

PRAYER

Lord, I pray that our nation will turn back to you and that the name of the Lord will be respected again in parliament, government, schools and law courts. Help us to prioritise the poor and be kind to the needy.

NEW TESTAMENT READING

Acts 8:4–40
Powerful preaching

The early church was made up of ordinary people like you and me. Yet it changed the world. The whole known world was transformed following the death and resurrection of Jesus and the outpouring of the Holy Spirit. The book of Acts tells us how this happened.

Everywhere they went they preached the message about Jesus (v.4, MSG). In this passage, we see that they preached to crowds and to individuals, like Simon the sorcerer and the Ethiopian eunuch.

Nations are comprised of cities, towns and villages. They preached the gospel in all three. Philip preached to a *city* in Samaria (v.5). Peter and John preached the gospel in many Samaritan *villages* (v.25). Philip preached the gospel in all the *towns* until he reached Caesarea (v.40).

Their preaching was accompanied – and indeed accelerated – by three factors:

1. Persecution

It began with persecution: 'Those who had been *scattered* preached the word wherever they went' (v.4). The dispersion brought great blessing. Everywhere they went they 'proclaimed the Christ' (v.5).

Again and again in the history of the church, persecution and opposition have led to unexpected fruitfulness. It is easy to lose heart when we experience setbacks, but this reminds us that God can use them in amazing ways.

2. Prayer

We see in this passage the importance of prayer. Peter and John *prayed* for the Samaritans that they might receive the Holy Spirit (vv.15–17).

Simon was a notorious magician who dazzled everyone with his wizardry and had everyone eating out of his hand (vv.9–11, MSG). He himself believed and was baptised, but following his old ways he wanted to buy the Holy Spirit (v.19).

Peter was unimpressed, 'To hell with your money! ... Ask the Master to forgive you for trying to use God to make money. I can see this is an old habit with you; you reek with money-lust' (vv.20–23, MSG).

Simon realised that only the Lord could save him and asked them to *pray for him* (v.24).

3. Power

The early church was characterised by enormous effectiveness: 'When the crowds heard Philip and saw the miraculous signs he did, they all paid close attention to what he said. With shrieks, evil spirits came out of many, and many paralytics and cripples were healed' (vv.6–7).

They were totally reliant on the Holy Spirit. Philip's encounter with the Ethiopian was not the result of a strategic planning meeting. Rather, 'the Spirit told Philip…' (v.29). The result of him following the leading of the Holy Spirit was the remarkable conversion of the Ethiopian, which has affected the whole nation of Ethiopia right down to the present day. The church that was birthed that day has never died out in that nation.

The Holy Spirit is the agent of change. He can bring about change in a nation. That change starts with the change in the lives of people. It is worth noting the factors involved in the change in this Ethiopian.

First, the Spirit of God prepared his heart. The Ethiopian is honest about his ignorance (v.31), searching for answers (v.32) and not too proud to ask for help (v.34). There is no shame in not always understanding what you read in the Bible. It is wise to get help from trusted people or Bible commentaries to help you apply it to your life.

Second, the Spirit of God is at work through the word of God. It is as the Ethiopian looks at the book of Isaiah that he begins to find answers (vv.32–33). Often, the Holy Spirit uses a human agent to help open up, explain, and apply the Scriptures. This is what happened here, beginning with Isaiah 53, Philip explains 'the good news about Jesus' (v.35). The Holy Spirit changes the heart of the Ethiopian in such a radical and complete way that he believes immediately and asks to be baptised. There is no more powerful an agent of change than the Holy Spirit.

PRAYER

Lord, help us to be more like the early church. Help us to pray more and to follow the leading of the Holy Spirit day by day. I pray that our nation would be transformed as people come to know you.

OLD TESTAMENT READING

2 Samuel 20:1–21:22
Passionate prayer

The battles in David's life never seem to come to an end. In today's passage we see two further battles.

First, there is 'a troublemaker named Sheba' (20:1). This is an echo of David's struggle with Absalom (16:22). The people of Israel seem extremely fickle: 'All the men of Israel deserted David to follow Sheba' (20:2). The Lord gave David victory over Sheba but immediately there is another battle around the corner.

There was a famine for three consecutive years (21:1a). As the nation faced disaster, 'David sought the face of the LORD' (v.1b). Sometimes it takes a real disaster to get us on our knees. God spoke to him as he prayed.

He held Israel to the promise that was made to the Gibeonites (see Joshua 9). In spite of the promise, Saul had tried to annihilate them, but the oaths that are made to God are very important and cannot be broken lightly. (The most common oaths today are in the marriage service and oaths in court.) Only after David had put things right and honoured the oath made to God did God answer prayer on behalf of the land (2 Samuel 21:14).

PRAYER

Lord, I seek your face on behalf of our nation. Have mercy upon us. Help us to be a nation that honours you with faithfulness to our marriage vows and truthfulness in our law courts. Lord, would you once again answer prayer on behalf of the land. May our nation be turned back to you. May your name be honoured. May your kingdom come.

---

14 June | Day 165

A Spacious Place

John Newton (1725–1801) was a militant atheist, bully and blasphemer. He was a wild and angry young man. He was press-ganged into the Navy at the age of eighteen where he broke the rules so recklessly that he was publicly flogged for desertion. He was hated and feared by his crew-mates and himself became a slave trader.

At the age of twenty-three, Newton's ship encountered a severe storm off the coast of Donegal and almost sank. He called out to God as the ship filled with water and on that day, 10 March 1748, God rescued him. He began a new life. He started to pray and read the Bible. Eventually he joined William Wilberforce in the campaign to abolish the slave trade and became a leading light in that campaign.

Newton is best known as the author of the hymn 'Amazing Grace':

Amazing grace! How sweet the sound
That saved a wretch like me!
I once was lost but now I'm found,
Was blind, but now I see.

To be *rescued* is to be *saved*, set free, delivered from danger, attack or harm. Jesus is the one who rescues you and brings you into 'a spacious place' (2 Samuel 22:20).

READING FROM PSALMS

Psalm 73:15–28
A spacious place for you

Have you ever experienced the slippery slope of sin? You find yourself slipping further and further down a path that you do not really want to be on.

The psalmist found himself on the slippery slope: 'As for me, my feet had almost *slipped*; I had nearly lost my foothold. For I *envied* the arrogant when I saw the prosperity of the wicked' (vv.2–3).

Your whole perspective changes when you enter 'the sanctuary of God' (v.17a): 'Then, I understood their final destiny' (v.17b). It is the arrogant and wicked who are on '*slippery ground*' (v.18). Although they may seem outwardly successful and prosperous, they are on a road that leads to destruction (vv.19–20).

It is 'senseless and ignorant' (v.22) to be envious of the 'ungodly'. When you get a proper perspective, you realise how almost unbelievably blessed you are (vv.23–26).

There is nothing that compares to walking in a relationship with God, knowing his presence, his guidance and his strength, and his promise that he will take you into glory. You are far better off than the 'ungodly', both in this life and in the future. God brings you into his 'spacious place'.

When you see what you have been rescued from, you realise how good it is to be near God (v.28), and you want to pass the good news on to others:

'But I'm in the very presence of GOD –
oh, how refreshing it is!
I've made Lord GOD my home.
GOD, I'm telling the world what you do!'
(v.28, MSG).

PRAYER

Lord, thank you that you have rescued me from the slippery slope and brought me into a spacious place.

NEW TESTAMENT READING

Acts 9:1–31
A spacious place for the church

Do you know anyone who is very antagonistic towards Christians and the Christian faith? Saul was like that. John Newton was like that. I was like that. When we read the account of Saul's conversion it gives us hope that God can change the most unexpected people.

In this passage we see a double *rescue*. The *church is rescued* from the darkness brought about by Saul's attacks, and *Saul is rescued* from his own inner darkness (13:9). God's transforming power changed Saul from a persecutor of the church into the great church leader, evangelist and apostle Paul.

Saul had a privileged background. He was a Roman citizen from Tarsus. He was a highly educated intellectual. He was a qualified lawyer. He was a deeply 'religious' man with a strong belief in God.

Yet, Saul was living in darkness on a road that led to destruction. He was 'out for the kill' (9:1, MSG). He was trying to arrest Christians and put them in prison (v.2). He had a terrible reputation among the Christians because of 'all the harm he [had] done to [them]' (v.13) and the fact that he wreaked 'havoc' among followers of Jesus (v.21).

On the road to Damascus, Saul 'was suddenly dazed by a blinding flash of *light*' (v.3, MSG). Jesus appeared to him and said, 'Saul, Saul, why do you persecute *me*?' (v.4). As Saul had never met him before, how could he be persecuting Jesus? In that moment, he must have realised that the *church* is *Jesus*. It is *his* body. In persecuting Christians, he was in fact persecuting Jesus. Later, he was to develop this understanding that the church is the body of Christ (see 1 Corinthians 12–14).

Saul's physical blindness symbolised the spiritual darkness in his life at that point. When Ananias laid hands on him, his sight was restored and he was *filled with the Spirit* (Acts 9:17): 'Immediately, something like scales fell from Saul's eyes, and he could see again' (v.18). He was rescued from physical and spiritual darkness.

Not only did Jesus rescue Saul from darkness, but he also appointed him as his 'chosen instrument'. He said to Ananias, 'Go! This man is *my chosen instrument* to carry my name before the Gentiles and their kings and before the people of Israel' (v.15).

However, God did not promise him an easy life. With great privilege would come suffering, 'for I will make it clear to him how much he will be afflicted and must endure and suffer for my name's sake' (v.16).

At once, Saul began to preach that Jesus is the Son of God (v.20). He grew 'more and more powerful ... *proving* that Jesus is the Christ' (v.22). Like a lawyer, he produced the evidence to show that something had in fact happened in history. Jesus had been crucified, raised from the dead and is the Christ.

Through the rescue of Saul, the church was also rescued: 'Things calmed down after that and the church had smooth sailing for a while. All over the country – Judea, Samaria, Galilee – the church grew. They were permeated with a deep sense of reverence for God. The Holy Spirit was with them, strengthening them. They prospered wonderfully' (v.31, MSG). God had brought the church into a spacious place and they enjoyed a time of peace and blessing.

PRAYER

Lord, I pray that you will bring the church in our nation into a spacious place, that strengthened and encouraged by the Holy Spirit, it will enjoy a time of peace and grow in numbers.

OLD TESTAMENT READING

2 Samuel 22:1–23:7
A spacious place for ever

As David comes to the end of his life, he praises God for rescuing him again and again from his enemies and from death and destruction (chapter 22 – the song is also found in Psalm 18). God is his '*rescuing knight*' (2 Samuel 22:2, MSG).

> 'A hostile world! I called to God,
> to my God I cried out.
> From his palace he heard me call;
> my cry brought me right into his
> presence –
> a private audience!' (v.7, MSG).

Many times, he called out to the Lord and the Lord heard his voice. 'He reached down from on high and took hold of me; *he drew me out of deep waters*' (v.17). 'He *rescued* me from my powerful enemy...' (v.18). '*He brought me out into a spacious place*; he *rescued* me because he delighted in me' (v.20, see also v.49).

When God rescues you, he does not want you to stay as you are: 'When I cleaned up my act, he gave me a fresh start ... GOD rewrote the text of my life' (vv.21, 25, MSG). He wants you to lead a blameless life and to keep yourself from sin (v.24). He wants you to be 'faithful' (v.26), pure (v.27) and humble (v.28).

With God's help, you can 'advance against a troop; with my God I can scale a wall' (v.30). God arms you with strength (v.33) and enables you to stand on the heights (v.34). He broadens the path beneath you so that your ankles do not turn over (v.37).

Whatever you are facing – a difficult boss, a complicated marriage, raising a problematic child – God gives you strength to stick with it.

David, in the evening of his life, summed up his experience of God and of life (chapter 23). God had rescued him and anointed him (23:1): 'The Spirit of the LORD spoke through me; his word was on my tongue' (v.2).

God had already saved him. Yet, there was more to come: 'Will he not bring to fruition my salvation and grant me my every desire?' (v.5). God's rescue plan of salvation will one day be brought to fruition. On that day, the rescue will be complete and you will enjoy a spacious place for ever.

PRAYER

Lord, thank you that you have rescued us through the cross and resurrection of Jesus. Thank you that one day the rescue will be complete, when Jesus returns and we will be in a 'spacious place' with him for ever.

15 June | Day 166
When You Don't Understand God

John Newton, whose life we looked at yesterday, mentored a man called William Cowper (1731–1800). Cowper had experienced tragedy. His mother died when he was six. His father died while he was still young. He qualified as a barrister. Outwardly he was successful. However, he suffered from serious depression. When applying for an administrative post in the House of Lords that entailed a formal examination, he was so disturbed by the prospect of the exam that he attempted suicide. For the rest of his life he suffered from mental illness.

When he was in his thirties, John Newton encouraged Cowper to begin composing hymns. He wrote powerfully of the joys and sorrows of everyday life. In 1774, he suffered such a severe episode of mental illness that he was prevented from entering into his intended marriage to Mary Unwin. He was crestfallen. Shortly afterwards, in perhaps his most famous hymn, he wrote:

God moves in a mysterious way
His wonders to perform

God is good. God is love. God loves you. God has revealed himself supremely in Jesus. All this we know. Then you read passages in the Bible that don't seem to fit with your understanding of God. You may also have experiences in life that don't seem to fit either.

You cannot put God in a box. He is far greater than you could ever conceive. Some passages in the Bible are mysterious. Jesus said on one occasion, 'You do not realise now what I am doing, but later you will understand' (John 13:7). Sometimes that understanding may come in our lifetime. Some things we will only understand when we meet the Lord.

How should you respond when you don't understand God?

READING FROM PSALMS

Psalm 74:1–9
Be honest with God

Are there times in your life when you simply do not understand why certain things are happening to you? Does it almost feel like God has rejected you? If so, your experience is common in the history of the people of God. This psalm opens with this question: 'Why have you rejected us for ever, O God?' (v.1).

Sometimes it may seem as if God is silent and not intervening to help you in any way.

As the psalmist says, 'There's not a sign or symbol of God in sight, nor anyone to speak in his name, no one who knows what's going on' (v.9, MSG).

When you go through times like this, you never know '*how long*' this will be (v.9). You might have questions about why a part of your life is working out as it is. Or perhaps you just feel that God is distant. St John of the Cross (1542–1591) referred to these times as 'the dark night of the soul'.[1]

What should you do in times like this?

1. Ask the questions

The psalmist does not beat around the bush. He pours out his heart to God. He asks God the difficult questions. 'You walked off and left us, and never looked back. God, *how could you* do that? We're your very own sheep; *how can you* stomp off in anger?' (v.1, MSG).

2. Ask for answers

'Refresh your memory of us ... you actually lived here once! Come and visit the site of disaster...' (vv.2–3, MSG).

You are not alone when you have these kinds of experiences and emotions. One of the great blessings of the Psalms is that you can turn to them in times of mysterious suffering and echo these prayers in your heart.

PRAYER

Lord, thank you that even when I can't understand what is happening to me, I can be honest with you when I pray and pour out my heart to you.

NEW TESTAMENT READING

Acts 9:32–10:23a
Be open to God

Jesus told his disciples to *heal the sick*, *raise the dead* and *preach the gospel*. The early church got on with doing exactly what Jesus told them to do. They must have been very surprised by what happened. Yet they were open to his leading.

1. The mystery of healing

They continued to see God's extraordinary power at work. Peter said to a man who was bedridden for eight years, 'Jesus Christ heals you' (9:34). He immediately 'jumped right out of bed' (v.34, MSG). 'Everybody ... woke up to the fact that God was alive and active among them' (v.35, MSG).

Yet not all are healed. Why doesn't God heal everyone? I don't know. Sometimes it is really hard to understand why God has not healed someone we have prayed for so much. It is a mystery.

2. The mystery of raising the dead

Next, Peter raised the dead! Accounts of the dead being raised are rare in the Bible. It happened twice in the Old Testament – once with Elijah and once with Elisha. Jesus raised the dead three times, Paul once, and Peter raised Dorcas from the dead. The command to raise the dead occurs only once (Matthew 10:8).

In almost every case, it was a young person who was raised from the dead. None of them lived for ever – but their lives were not cut off prematurely. Very occasionally God intervenes in this way. We don't know why. It is a mystery.

Here God did intervene. Dorcas, 'who was always doing good and helping the poor' (Acts 9:36), became sick and died. Peter got down on his knees and prayed. She opened her eyes, sat up, and Peter took her by the hand and helped her to her feet! As a result, 'many people believed in the Lord' (v.42).

3. The mystery of the gospel

The apostle Paul was later to explain, 'This *mystery* is that through the *gospel* the *Gentiles are heirs together with Israel*, members together of one body, and sharers together in the promise in Christ Jesus' (Ephesians 3:6).

Up until this point in the book of Acts, all the followers of Jesus had been Jewish. In fact, they did not think it was possible to become a Christian without being a Jew. But God surprised them. He prepared Peter with a vision. In a trance he saw heaven open and he was told to kill and eat 'impure' and 'unclean' animals and birds. His response was, 'Surely not, Lord!' (Acts 10:14).

The vision, and God's voice that accompanied it, challenged Peter not to make distinctions between clean and unclean food (vv.13–15). However, Peter also realised that this vision meant that he should not make distinctions between 'clean' and 'unclean' people – that is, Jewish and non-Jewish people. In tomorrow's reading, we discover that Peter says, 'No race is better than any other' (v.28, MSG).

At the time, it was a mystery. 'Peter, puzzled, sat there trying to figure out what it all meant' (v.17, MSG). He did not realise what God was doing. Only later did he understand. God had plans that were far bigger than theirs. The good news of Jesus was not to be confined to the Jewish people – it was for everyone in the world. Thankfully, Peter was open enough to respond to God's guidance, whether through a vision or even when 'the Spirit whispered to him' (v.19, MSG).

PRAYER

Lord, thank you that even if we do not understand some mysteries in this life, we can trust you and know that you always have a reason.

OLD TESTAMENT READING

2 Samuel 23:8–24:25
Be mystified by God

This is one of the most mysterious passages in the whole Bible. All seemed to be going well. David had good people around him. He was greatly helped and supported by his three mighty men, as well as a wider inner circle of 'the Thirty'.

Yet something terrible happened. Who incited David to count his fighting men? In this passage it appears to be God. Yet in the equivalent passage in Chronicles we are told, 'Satan rose up against Israel and incited David to take a census of Israel' (1 Chronicles 21:1). This is one of only three times in which Satan is mentioned in the Old Testament.

David apparently knew that what he was doing was wrong ('because he had counted the people, replacing trust with statistics', 2 Samuel 24:10, MSG). He was 'conscience-stricken … and he said to the LORD, "I have sinned greatly in what I have done. Now, O LORD, I beg you, take away the guilt of your servant. I have done a very foolish thing"' (v.10).

Given the various options, spoken by the prophet Gad, he chose to fall into the hands of the Lord, for 'his mercy is great' (v.14). He refused to offer a sacrifice that cost him nothing (v.24). After his sacrifice, 'the Lord answered prayer on behalf of the land' (v.25).

There is still much here that is difficult to understand. But the passage finishes on a note of hope and renewed relationship.

PRAYER

Lord, help me to trust you even in the midst of confusion and uncertainty. Thank you that, one day, your wisdom will be fully revealed. Thank you that you are good and that your love endures for ever.

16 June | Day 167
Following and Not Opposing God

I remember so well the time when Alpha started in the Catholic Church. Bishop Ambrose of Newcastle and Hexham heard what was happening with Alpha in some of the Anglican churches. He became interested and wanted to find out more. However, he did not want to let us know he was interested. So, he sent two Catholic priests to a London Alpha Conference in disguise! They went back to their parishes and started running Alpha, to great success.

As a result of that, Cardinal Hume invited us to hold a conference for Catholics at Westminster Cathedral. The place was packed out with 450 Catholic priests and laity. A few people were very critical of us doing a conference for Catholics. One or two churches even threatened to stop running Alpha if we went ahead with the conference. With hindsight it seems quite extraordinary that anybody could object, but at the time it was of some concern.

On the first night of the conference there was a great outpouring of the Holy Spirit and singing in tongues like we had never heard before. I went home that night and read the passage for today: 'If God gave them the same gift as he gave us … who was I to think that I could oppose God?' (Acts 11:17). It was the same Holy Spirit who was poured out on them as on us. I realised that if we did not continue to work together, I would be opposing God.

The most foolish thing that any human being can do is to oppose God. Jesus was opposed: 'They killed him by hanging him on a tree, but God raised him from the dead on the third day and caused him to be seen' (10:39–40). Contrastingly, the most wonderful privilege any human being can have is to be a follower of Jesus of Nazareth whom 'God anointed … with the Holy Spirit and power' (10:38).

READING FROM PSALMS

Psalm 74:10–17
The power of God

When you are facing opposition it is good to remember the power of God. The psalmist is faced by enemies who are reviling God's name (v.10). He recalls the power of God, first in his own life (v.12), and then over all of creation (vv.13–17).

These verses draw on the rich mythology of the Ancient Near East. Creation was seen as a victory of the gods over the forces of chaos and destruction, often represented by the raging sea and 'the monster', also called 'Leviathan' (vv.13–14). The sun and moon were worshipped as gods. Yet, in this psalm the writer sweeps aside those myths and declares that it was *God* who created and established the world, bringing order out of nothing and 'establishing the sun and moon' (v.16).

There is always a temptation to make 'other things' more important than your relationship with God. Devotion to 'other gods' was one of the key temptations and weaknesses of God's people in the Old Testament. This psalm reminds us of who God is and why it would be foolish to oppose God by going after other gods.

PRAYER

Lord, thank you that you are the one true God who brings salvation upon the earth. Help me to resist the temptation to make anything else more important than you in my life.

NEW TESTAMENT READING

Acts 10:23b–11:18
The Spirit of God

The Holy Spirit led Peter through a vision to the house of Cornelius. When he got there, he discovered that God had also spoken to Cornelius through another vision. On hearing this, Peter 'fairly exploded with his good news' (10:34, MSG) – the good news of *peace* through Jesus Christ who is Lord of all (v.36).

The Greek word for 'peace' takes on the meaning of the Hebrew word '*shalom*'. It means far more than an absence of hostility. It means 'completeness', 'soundness', 'well-being', 'every kind of blessing and good'. It means harmony and concord between people. It means spiritual well-being, living under the favour of God.

The good news is that you have peace with God through Jesus Christ. Jesus' death on the cross reconciled you to God. He made peace and you have received that peace as a gift.

You too should be a peacemaker as you seek to lead others to peace with God and as you bring peace into your home, place of work, community and nation.

Peter goes on to speak about 'how God anointed Jesus of Nazareth with the Holy Spirit and power, and how he went around doing good and healing all who were under the power of the devil, because God was with him' (v.38). He told them about the cross and the resurrection, about faith and the forgiveness of sins (v.43).

While Peter was still proclaiming the good news about Jesus, the Holy Spirit came on all who heard the message (v.44). 'The believing Jews who had come with Peter couldn't believe it, couldn't believe that the gift of the Holy Spirit was poured out on "outsider" non-Jews' (v.45, MSG).

They knew that this was the outpouring of the Holy Spirit, because what had happened to the apostles on the day of Pentecost was now happening to this group – 'for they heard them speaking in tongues and praising God' (v.46).

Peter's response was, 'Can anyone keep these people from being baptised with water? They have received the Holy Spirit just as we have' (v.47).

News travelled fast – the Jewish believers were worried that 'rubbing shoulders' with these 'non-Jews' would ruin their good name (11:3, MSG).

Those who had not been there at the time '*criticised* him' (v.2). But Peter *explains* (v.4). He tells the story of how he was led by the Holy Spirit – 'the Spirit told me...' (v.12).

He goes on, 'As I began to speak, the Holy Spirit came on them as he had come on us at the beginning ... So if God gave them the same gift as he gave us, who believed in the Lord Jesus Christ, who was I to think that I could *oppose God*?"' (vv.15–17).

'Hearing it all laid out like that, they quieted down. And then, as it sank in, they started praising God. "It's really happened! God has broken through to the other nations, opened them up to Life!"' (v.18, MSG). Peter's explanation was the answer to the criticism. Sometimes, when you are criticised, the answer is simply to give an explanation.

PRAYER

Lord, thank you that we see this same gift of the Holy Spirit given to all who believe in you, regardless of what part of the church or denomination they come from. May we never be found opposing you but rather following the guidance of your Holy Spirit.

OLD TESTAMENT READING

1 Kings 1–2:12
The anointing of God

Solomon was God's anointed successor for David. Zadok the priest and Nathan the prophet anointed him king over Israel (1:34).

Adonijah made the mistake of trying to set himself up as king without reference to God. 'He put himself forward and said, "I will be king"' (v.5). It is a foolish thing to ignore God, and in this case it actually meant opposing God's plans for Solomon. He did not succeed.

David gave this charge to his anointed successor: 'I'm about to go the way of all the earth, but you – be strong; show what you're made of! Do what GOD tells you. Walk in the paths he shows you: Follow the life-map absolutely, keep an eye out for the signposts, his course for life set out in the revelation to Moses; then you'll get on well in whatever you do and wherever you go' (2:2–3, MSG).

David's words are a great reminder to us. God's anointing of all believers with the Holy Spirit does not negate your need to obey God's word. Obedience of God's word (v.3a) must accompany God's anointing (v.3b). You are given the Spirit of God to empower you to obey the word of God.

Neither David, nor Solomon, nor any other king of Israel, was able to keep God's decrees and commands perfectly. It is only Jesus, the final Davidic King, who is the fully obedient, eternal, anointed King. He is the one who does 'walk faithfully before [God] ... with all [his] heart and soul' (v.4).

The book of Kings is, as Eugene Peterson puts it, 'a relentless exposition of failure'.[1] Yet God continues to work out his sovereign purposes – often silently and hidden. God's sovereignty is never cancelled out even by deeply sin-flawed leaders ('kings'). This means that you can trust his sovereignty in your life, your church and your culture.

PRAYER

Lord, help me to follow Jesus, whom God anointed with the Holy Spirit and power. As I face 'opposition and enemies', I need the power and anointing of your Holy Spirit. Help me never to find myself in the position of opposing God. Help me to be strong and to walk in your ways and to walk faithfully before you with all my heart and soul (v.4).

17 June | Day 168
Your Prayers Make a Difference

Saint John Chrysostom (349–407) wrote, 'Prayer ... is the root, the fountain, the mother of a thousand blessings ... The potency of prayer has subdued the strength of fire, it has bridled the rage of lions ... extinguished wars, appeased the elements, expelled demons, burst the chains of death, expanded the gates of heaven, assuaged diseases ... rescued cities from destruction ... and arrested the progress of the thunderbolt.'[1]

We have a 24-7 Prayer Room on our church site at Holy Trinity Brompton. It is one of the highlights of my week to go into the room and spend time alone with God. Prayer really is the root and fountain of all that we do at HTB. It is such an encouragement to know that every hour, day and night, there is someone praying in that room.

READING FROM PROVERBS

Proverbs 15:1–10
Pray and bless

The writer of Proverbs contrasts 'the wicked' with those who pray: 'The lives of God-loyal people flourish ... he delights in genuine prayers. A life frittered away disgusts GOD; he loves those who run straight for the finish line' (vv.6a,8b,9, MSG). If you live like this, you will bring great blessing to others.

One important aspect of this is what you say. Your words can transform lives. Whereas 'cutting words wound and maim', 'kind words heal and help' (v.4, MSG). Even when others are angry towards us, we are reminded that 'a gentle response defuses anger' (v.1a, MSG). Use your words to heal, help and encourage others: 'The tongue that brings healing is a tree of life' (v.4).

PRAYER

Lord, help me to pray and use my words to bring blessing to others.

NEW TESTAMENT READING

Acts 11:19–12:19a
Pray with passion

It was the equivalent of today's London, Paris or New York. The Greek city of Antioch was one of the wealthy, cosmopolitan capitals of the East. It was renowned for its buildings and culture, and for its lax moral standards and widespread corruption.

This city was transformed, and it became a distinguished Christian city and the springboard for Christian mission to the entire Gentile world. The Lord's hand was with them and 'a great number of people believed and turned to the Lord' (11:21).

God used Barnabas, whose name means 'son of encouragement'. Encouragement is not flattery or empty praise; it is like verbal sunshine. It costs nothing and warms other people's hearts and inspires them with hope and confidence in their faith. We need those around us who are like Barnabas. And you can be like Barnabas to other people.

Barnabas '*encouraged them* all to remain true to the Lord with all their hearts. He was a good man, full of the Holy Spirit and faith, and a great number of people were brought to the Lord' (vv.23–24).

It was not a hit and run visit: 'For a *whole year* Barnabas and Saul met with the church and taught great numbers of people. The disciples were called Christians first at Antioch' (v.26).

There was a release of finance. Each gave 'according to his ability ... to provide help' for those in need (v.29). This is an important principle of the Christian community – those who can afford help to pay for those who can't.

This was a period of great blessing and massive church growth. However, they also faced a rising tide of opposition.

The Judean King Herod Agrippa I (C.10 BC–AD 44) had a cruel streak. He took to persecuting Christians. He was an unscrupulous politician who wanted to gain popularity with the people (12:1–3). He had James executed. Peter was in prison and Herod planned a public lynching (v.4, MSG).

Peter was guarded by four squads of four soldiers each (v.4). He had double the usual guard and chains on both hands (v.6). Peter himself 'slept like a baby' (v.6, MSG). There is no pillow as soft as a clear conscience!

The church faced a seemingly impossible situation. The very existence of the early church seemed to be at stake. What did they do? What are you to do in situations that are seemingly impossible? We see the answer in verse 5: 'The church was *earnestly praying* to God for [Peter]'.

1. Pray *to God*

When you pray, you are not just talking to yourself or praying eloquent prayers to impress those who hear you. Prayer to God means having an audience with God. It means actually coming into the presence of God – asking and receiving.

2. Pray *together*

'The church' (v.5) joined *together* in prayer. 'Many people had gathered and were praying' (v.12). The New Testament teaches a lot about private prayer, but there is even more about praying *together*.

3. Pray *passionately*

There are two reasons why they might not have prayed at all. First, James had been executed (v.2). God had not answered their prayers for James; we don't know why. But it did not stop them praying.

Second, Peter's situation *seemed impossible*. Their choice was either to give up praying or to pray passionately. The Greek word *ektenōs* (translated here as 'earnestly') was used to describe a horse made to go at full gallop. It denotes the taut muscle of strenuous and sustained effort as of an athlete.

The imperfect tense suggests that they prayed not as a one-off, but for a considerable length of time. They persevered.

4. Pray *for others*

They prayed for Peter (v.5). There are many types of prayer: worship, praise, thanksgiving, petition, and so on – but here we read of intercessory prayer. They prayed *for him* because they loved him. Intercessory prayer is an *act of love*.

History belongs to the intercessors. You can shape your generation through prayer. You can influence the course of history.

This was an extraordinary prayer meeting and the results are evident (vv.6–15). In answer to their prayers God acted supernaturally. Peter was freed the night before his trial. God's answer involved visions, angels and chains falling off (vv.6–9). Obstacles were removed. The guards did not bar the prisoners' escape, and the iron gate to the city opened in front of them (v.10).

Peter then turned up at the prayer meeting but his release was so extraordinary that Rhoda, the girl who answered the door, forgot to let him in, and no one else believed it was actually him (vv.12–15)! They told Rhoda that she was out of her mind (v.15) but actually God had done what *seemed impossible* in answer to their *earnest prayers*.

The word of God continued to increase and spread (v.24). As John Stott wrote, 'This chapter opens with James dead, Peter in prison and Herod triumphing; it closes with Herod dead, Peter free and the word of God triumphing.'

PRAYER

Lord, help us to pray like the early church. May your hand be with us. May we too see a great number of people believing and turning to the Lord and the word of God triumphing.

OLD TESTAMENT READING

1 Kings 2:13–3:15
Pray for wisdom

Solomon ensured his long tenure by liquidating all his enemies early in his reign (chapter 2). How different was the action of this son of David compared to Jesus, '*the* Son of David', who brought life to everyone and taught us to love our enemies! He is the one who reigns eternally.

However, there was at least one thing that Solomon definitely did do right. God said to him, 'Ask for whatever you want me to give you' (3:5). His response demonstrated humility and a recognition of his need for God. Solomon prayed, 'Give your servant a discerning heart to govern your people and to distinguish between right and wrong' (v.9).

God was delighted with Solomon's response. He said to him, 'Because you have asked for this and haven't grasped after a long life, or riches, or the doom of your enemies, but you have asked for the ability to lead and govern well, I'll give you what you've asked for – I'm giving you a wise and mature heart. There's never been one like you before; and there'll be no one after. As a bonus, I'm giving you both the wealth and glory you didn't ask for ... I'll also give you a long life' (vv.10–14, MSG).

Jesus said, 'Seek first his [your heavenly Father's] kingdom and his righteousness, and all these things will be given to you as well' (Matthew 6:33). In effect, by praying for wisdom, Solomon was seeking first the kingdom of God. God said to him that as a result, all the other things would be his as well.

The offer of wisdom does not just apply to Solomon. James writes, 'If *any of you* lacks wisdom, you should ask God, who gives generously to all without finding fault, and it will be *given to you*' (James 1:5).

PRAYER

Lord, I need your wisdom. Please give me a wise and discerning heart in every situation I face. Lord, I pray for the wisdom that comes from heaven and is first of all pure, peace-loving, considerate, submissive, full of mercy and good fruit, impartial and sincere (3:17).

18 June | Day 169
Three Conversions Everyone Needs

At an Alpha Conference, someone handed me a scrap of paper with a note describing what had happened to her friend:

'Sue (who was not a Christian) was attending a rehab clinic for people with severe respiratory problems. She had a chronic condition (COPD: Chronic Obstructive Pulmonary Disease) that was getting progressively worse. The clinic meets at our church building. She arrived for her clinic, but there was no one there. (She had got the wrong date!). She waited around and had a look through flyers about our next Alpha.

'Sue turned up for our course on Wednesday evening. She soaked it all up and was full of excitement and interest. She came to church on the Sunday and was back again on the Wednesday. It suddenly clicked for Sue that Jesus is God! A huge piece of the jigsaw for her. She gave her life to the Lord – dramatic. She called her sister to tell her she had become a Christian and her sister was in the middle of a meeting with a friend to pray for Sue! She had been praying for her for twenty-five years!

'The following Sunday – Sue came to church, came forward for prayer for healing and was remarkably healed of her COPD. [She has been] running up and down stairs at home, off her medications, etc! She met with her physio at the medical clinic who was astonished at what had happened to her – remarkable difference. She has been healed and has since prayed for and seen others healed, including one of cancer!

'On 30 April Sue was baptised and brought over 150 friends and family to celebrate with her. She is having a huge impact on people – evangelising to anyone that will stand still long enough to listen!'

John Wimber often used to say that we all need three conversions: to be converted to Christ, converted to his church and converted to his cause. Sue was obviously not only converted to Christ, but also instantly converted to his church and to his cause! Today's passages focus especially on this third conversion.

READING FROM PSALMS

Psalm 74:18–23
Passion for God's cause

'Rise up, O God, and defend *your cause*', writes the psalmist (v.22). He is passionate about *God's cause* and sees, as we see today, people mocking (v.18a) and even reviling God (v.18b). He cries out to God, 'Don't forget us. Remember your promises' (vv.19b–20a, MSG).

It can be easy to become downhearted when we see people attacking God's cause. The best way to respond is with passionate prayer. Bring your frustrations to God: 'Rise up, O God, and defend *your cause*; remember how fools mock you all day long. Do not ignore the clamour of your adversaries, the uproar of your enemies, which rises continually' (vv.22–23).

PRAYER

Lord, as we look around at our society today we see many who mock and revile your name. Rise up, O God, and defend your cause. May your name be glorified. May your kingdom come.

NEW TESTAMENT READING

Acts 12:19b–13:12
Pursuit of God's cause

Ultimately, nothing can stop God's cause.

Herod had success, popularity, power and great wealth. The people flattered him and shouted, 'This is the voice of a god, not of a mere mortal' (12:22). However, 'That was the last straw. God had had enough of Herod's arrogance and sent an angel to strike him down. Herod had given God no credit for anything. Down he went. Rotten to the core, a maggoty old man if there ever was one, he died' (v.23, MSG).

This is contrasted with the word of God, which, unlike Herod's life, does not end: 'But the word of God continued to increase and spread' (v.24) – it grew in 'leaps and bounds' (v.24, MSG).

We see a similar situation as God's cause flourishes despite opposition once more. Saul ('who was also called Paul', 13:9) and Barnabas were confronted by a charlatan called Bar-Jesus who was 'as crooked as a corkscrew' (v.7, MSG). He tried to stop the proconsul being converted to Christ.

Paul, 'full of the Holy Spirit and looking him straight in the eye' (v.9, MSG), confronted him with his 'schemes to cheat people out of God' (v.10, MSG). Bar-Jesus was struck blind, and the proconsul 'became a believer, full of enthusiasm over what they were saying about the Master' (v.12, MSG). Bar-Jesus' attempts to thwart God actually achieve precisely the opposite to what he had hoped.

The early church was determined to find out what God was doing and join in. They gathered together to worship the Lord and fast (v.2). While they were doing this, the Holy Spirit spoke to them, '"Set apart for me Barnabas and Saul for *the work to which I have called them*." So after they had fasted and prayed, they placed their hands on them and sent them off' (vv.2–3).

Barnabas and Paul were 'sent on their way by the Holy Spirit' (v.4). They were *pursuing his cause*. They 'proclaimed the word of God' (v.5). They were 'filled with the Holy Spirit' (v.9). Even the proconsul, an intelligent man (v.7), was amazed at Paul's teaching 'about the Lord' (v.12).

It is so important that you seek God's guidance and help – in your ministry and in your life. With God on your side you can achieve so much more than you could ever dream of in your own strength.

PRAYER

Lord, please speak to me by your Holy Spirit. Help me to know what you are calling me to do. I want to proclaim the word of God

through the power of the Holy Spirit and pursue your cause with passion.

OLD TESTAMENT READING

1 Kings 3:16–5:18
Purpose in God's cause

Solomon was called to serve the cause of God in a special way.

David had served God's *purpose* in his own generation (Acts 13:36). However, he was not allowed to build the temple. God gave that calling to Solomon: 'Your son whom I will put on the throne in your place will build the temple for my Name' (1 Kings 5:5).

Solomon needed great wisdom in order to fulfil his calling. He had prayed for wisdom. God answered his prayer more than he could ever have asked or imagined. God promises to give *you* the same kind of wisdom if you ask for it ('If any of you lacks wisdom, you should ask God, who gives generously to all without finding fault, and it will be given to you', James 1:5). Ask for wisdom in all these areas:

1. Wisdom in decision making
God gave him wisdom to administer '*justice*' (1 Kings 3:28). When given the impossible task of deciding to which mother a baby belongs, he comes up with an ingenious idea.

The threat of the death of the surviving baby is enough to reveal who the true mother really is: 'When all Israel heard the verdict the king had given, they held the king in awe, because they saw that he had wisdom from God to administer justice' (v.28).

2. Wisdom in choosing a team
Solomon gathered around him a leadership team for his government. This included priests, managers, friends, secretaries, historians and the commander of his army. There were eleven in all, making a team of twelve. It is a similar size to Jesus' core team (the twelve disciples). It seems to be about the right size for a leadership team.

3. Wisdom in delegation
In addition to this, Solomon had another team of twelve regional managers distributed through Israel. This included two of his own sons-in-law (4:11, 15). Delegation is absolutely key to avoiding burnout and carrying out a leadership role.

4. Wisdom in peacemaking
Under his leadership there was so much growth that the people became 'densely populated' (v.20a, MSG). Nevertheless, 'All their needs were met; they ate and drank and were happy' (v.20b, MSG) and they '*had peace on all sides* ... [they] lived in safety' (vv.24–25).

5. Wisdom in insight and discernment
'God gave Solomon wisdom and very great insight, and a breadth of understanding as measureless as the sand on the seashore (v.29) ... his fame spread (v.31) ... He spoke three thousand proverbs and his songs numbered a thousand and five' (v.32). Psalm 72 and 127, Proverbs 10:1–22:16; 25:1–29:27 are attributed to him. People from all nations came to listen to his wisdom (1 Kings 4:34).

Solomon had the wisdom to know when to accept help from those who were not part of the people of God (chapter 5). 'The Lord gave Solomon wisdom, just as he had promised him' (5:12).

6. Wisdom in pursuing God's cause
Solomon had the vision to build the temple in order to see God's name honoured (vv.4–5). One of the ways in which you can pursue God's cause today is by seeking to see the church (the new temple) built up in order to bring honour to God's name.

PRAYER

Lord, please give us wisdom in order to fulfil our calling. Help us bring honour to your name and advance the cause of Jesus on earth.

19 June | Day 170
How to Find Treasures in the Bible

I first encountered Jesus through reading the Bible. Ever since, I have read it practically every day of my life. Yet, I am constantly seeing and discovering new things.

As Immanuel Kant said, 'The Bible is an inexhaustible fountain of all truths. The existence of the Bible is the greatest blessing which humanity ever experienced.' It is full of inexhaustible treasure *for you* to read and digest, and through which *you* can encounter God.

Yet, it is not always an easy book to understand. One key ingredient to understanding the Bible better is to recognise the language and genre that the writer is using – the type of literature and therefore what the writer intended.

READING FROM PSALMS

Psalm 75:1–10
Powerful metaphors

Something can be 'true' without being 'literal'. In this psalm we see examples of truth expressed in *metaphor*.

God's justice is the foundation of our universe. In today's psalm we find at least four *metaphors* about the justice of God.

1. Evil and its effects

The psalmist knew as well as we do that the earth is not held up literally by *pillars*. He is deliberately using metaphorical language that needs to be read as such. This is the language of poetry and it is every bit as true as 'literal truth'.

The quaking of the earth (v.3a) and its peoples is a metaphor for the effects of evil. Immorality undermines the stability of earth and society. The Lord proclaims that he graciously upholds his creation: 'It is I who hold its *pillars* firm' (v.3b).

2. Power and its problems

'*Horns*' (v.4) symbolise power. Again the word is used metaphorically; this is poetic language. God exalts the horn (that is to say, power) of the righteous, and cuts off the horn (the power) of the wicked (v.10). Power can so easily corrupt and lead to arrogance. God says to the arrogant, 'Boast no more' (v.4).

3. Ministry and its might

The '*hand* of the LORD' (v.8) is used as a symbol of his might and power. This is anthropomorphic language: words that are used to ascribe human form or attributes to something that is not human.

When we 'lay on hands' in ministry – our hands themselves can do little, but they *symbolise* God's mighty power working through us.

4. Judgment and Jesus

Likening God's judgment to '*a cup*' is another metaphor. 'GOD has a *cup* in his hand, a bowl of wine, full to the brim. He draws from it and pours; it's drained to the dregs. Earth's wicked ones drink it all, drink it down to the last bitter drop!' (v.8, MSG).

On the cross, Jesus bore in his own body the *cup* of God's judgment. He spoke about it beforehand (Mark 10:38; Luke 22:42; John 18:11), and took the judgment that we deserve upon himself.

PRAYER

'We give thanks to you, O God, we give thanks, for your Name is near' (Psalm 75:1). Thank you that one day you will get rid of all evil from this world, and goodness and righteousness will prevail for ever.

NEW TESTAMENT READING

Acts 13:13–41
Historical facts

How can you be sure that you have been forgiven? How can you know that death is not the end? How can you be assured that you will have eternal life?

You can be sure of all this because of the *historical facts* of the life, death and resurrection of Jesus.

Luke was writing *history*. At the beginning of his two-volume work (Luke and Acts), Luke says that the evidence of 'eyewitness' accounts have been handed down to them. He has *carefully investigated* everything and written an *orderly account* 'so that you may know the *certainty* of the things you have been taught' (Luke 1:3–4).

Today's passage describes the history of Paul's travels and reports his speech. Likewise, in his speech, Paul talks about historical facts. He retells the history of the people of God: the historical facts of the exodus, wilderness years, conquest of Canaan, the judges and the kings – all leading up to David, from whose descendants would come the historical Jesus.

Then Paul focuses on the historical facts of the death and, in particular, the resurrection of Jesus. He makes four affirmations about *the resurrection*:

1. God's action

'They took him down from the cross and buried him. And then *God raised him* from death' (Acts 13:29–30, MSG). What God had promised in the Old Testament, he fulfilled in the New Testament, by 'raising up Jesus' (v.33). It had been prophesied in the Old Testament (v.34). 'He raised Jesus, exactly as described in the second Psalm' (v.33, MSG).

2. Historical *fact*

'The *fact* that God raised him from the dead…' (v.34). The resurrection is not a metaphor. It is not something that is only experienced existentially within our hearts. It is, Paul says, a historical fact. The physical resurrection of Jesus actually happened. Jesus rose bodily from the dead.

'There is no disputing that – he appeared over and over again many times and places to those who had known him well in the Galilean years, and these same people continue to give witness that he is alive' (v.31, MSG).

3. Unique event

The resurrection of Jesus was a unique event in history. Paul contrasts Jesus with David, who 'has been in the grave, dust and ashes, a long time now' (v.36b, MSG). Others may have been resuscitated (and then later died), but Jesus was resurrected and his body never saw decay: 'When he raised him from the dead, he did it for good – no going back to that rot and decay for him' (v.34a, MSG).

4. Good news

This is the good news (v.32) that Paul preached. The resurrection means that the cross was effective, and forgiveness of sins is possible (v.38). Everyone who believes is justified (v.39). Your past has been dealt with and you can live in a right relationship with God.

The historical fact of the resurrection has huge implications for your life and your future. If Jesus died, was buried and then raised by God, it means that, one day, those who believe in him and have died will be raised by God to eternal life (see 1 Corinthians 15 and 1 Thessalonians 4:13–18).

When you have 'served God's purpose' for your 'generation', you too will 'fall asleep' (Acts 13:36) and then be raised by God to eternal life.

PRAYER

Thank you, Lord, for the amazing good news of the resurrection. Thank you that my sins are forgiven, that I am justified and I need no longer fear death. Help me, like David, to serve your purpose in my generation.

OLD TESTAMENT READING

1 Kings 6:1–7:22
Symbolic representation

Have you ever wondered whether God is really interested in the details of your life? As we read the precise instructions for the building of the temple, we see how carefully God prepared, anticipated and prefigured the far greater temple that is unveiled in the New Testament. If God is so concerned about the details of a building, you can be sure that he is even more interested in the details of your life. If something matters to you, it matters to God.

Typology is about symbolic representation. It is a key part of our understanding of the Old Testament as Christians. Some of the great New Testament truths are anticipated in the Old Testament history of salvation. For example, Adam is described as a *type* of Christ (Romans 5:14, NASB).

The temple in the Old Testament can be seen as '*a type*' of the temple in the New Testament (the people of God). In this passage, we have a description of the temple, which Solomon spent seven years building (1 Kings 6:38). It was designed to be the dwelling place for the presence of God on earth: 'I'll personally take up my residence' (v.13, MSG).

Hence, excellence was of the upmost importance because it was the place of God's presence. God's name was at stake. They did everything as well as they possibly could. It was 'dazzling' (v.22, MSG) and 'no expense was spared' (7:9, MSG). If excellence was a high value for them, it should be an even higher value for us now that God's presence is in us.

It is worth noting that God is not in a hurry! 'In the *four hundred and eightieth year* after the Israelites had come out of Egypt, in the fourth year of Solomon's reign … he began to build the temple of the LORD' (6:1).

The temple in the Old Testament points forward to the people of God. We are God's house. God lives in us individually. Your body is the *temple* of the Holy Spirit (1 Corinthians 6:19). The church today is the *holy temple* of the Lord in which God lives by his Spirit (Ephesians 2:21–22). This is God's '*house*' today.

PRAYER

Lord, open my eyes to see the inexhaustible treasures in your word. Above all, help me to see Jesus, crucified and risen from the dead – the one whom the whole Bible is about.

20 June | Day 171
Come, Holy Spirit

Spending time in the presence of God is the most important activity of your life. You need God's presence in your life more than you need anything else. But where do you find the presence of God?

I remember so well the first time I heard someone pray one of the most ancient prayers of the church, 'Come, Holy Spirit', with a real expectation that the Holy Spirit would come! It was on a Sunday night in 1982. We had a meeting in the crypt after our evening service at Holy Trinity Brompton. As we prayed, 'Come, Holy Spirit' we saw remarkable events occur. We saw people being filled with the Holy Spirit with physical manifestations similar to those described in the book of Acts on the day of Pentecost. We saw extraordinary physical healings take place the following day when again someone prayed, 'Come, Holy Spirit'.

God is always present with his people today by his Holy Spirit. When you pray, 'Come, Holy Spirit,' you are asking for an *increased sense* of the presence of God. There are times in the New Testament when the Holy Spirit filled a gathering of people sovereignly and spontaneously (Acts 2:2; 10:44). There are other times when the disciples prayed for the Holy Spirit: 'After they prayed, the place where they were meeting was shaken. And they were all filled with the Holy Spirit' (4:31). In the Old Testament passage for today we read how 'the glory of the LORD filled his temple' (1 Kings 8:11).

Each of the passages for today tells us something about how to enjoy God's empowering presence that comes through the Holy Spirit.

READING FROM PSALMS

Psalm 76:1–12
Longing for God's empowering presence

The temple in Jerusalem was not primarily a place of sacrifice, but the place of God's presence. The psalmist writes, 'In Judah God is known; his name is great in Israel. His tent is in Salem, his *dwelling-place* in Zion' (vv.1–2). 'Salem' is the old Jebusite name for Jerusalem. 'Zion' is a word often used to refer to Jerusalem as the focal point of God's *presence* (v.7, AMP), among his people in the Old Testament. This is the place of his tent ('abode', RSV). This is where God dwells.

This is why the people of God were so passionate about Jerusalem, and in particular the temple. They longed, as we all do deep inside, for the presence of God. The amazing truth is that, through Jesus, we can know the presence of God in and among us, his people, wherever we are. He dwells in you by his Spirit.

PRAYER

Lord, I long for your presence with me. Thank you that your dwelling place is with your people. Please fill us again today with your Holy Spirit and make your name great among us.

NEW TESTAMENT READING

Acts 13:42–14:7
Filled with God's empowering presence

From the day of Pentecost, God's empowering presence came upon his people. In today's passage we read that they were, once again, 'filled with joy and with the Holy Spirit' (13:52). Every Christian now has the Holy Spirit dwelling within them (Romans 8:9).

In this passage, we see the impact of God's empowering presence when you are filled with the Holy Spirit:

1. Effectiveness

In Antioch, crowds gathered to hear the word of the Lord (Acts 13:44–45). In Iconium, 'they spoke so *effectively* that a great number of Jews and Gentiles believed' (14:1).

The Lord confirmed his message by enabling them to do signs and wonders (v.3). This does not mean that everyone in the church will necessarily enjoy perfect health in this life. Rather, we see an in-breaking of the future kingdom of God so that the gospel may go forth and triumph.

2. Opposition

Do not assume that if God is with you then you will not encounter any significant opposition.

These incidents remind us that actually the opposite is often the case. Where God is at work, the enemy tries to stir up opposition and difficulty.

In Antioch, some people 'went wild with jealousy and tore into Paul, contradicting everything he was saying, making an ugly scene' (13:45, MSG). 'They stirred up persecution ... and expelled them from their region' (v.50).

In Iconium, those who refused to believe 'worked up a whispering campaign against Paul and Barnabas, sowing mistrust and suspicion in the minds of the people in the street' (14:2, MSG). They organised to 'beat them up' (v.5, MSG).

3. Joy

Your happiness does not depend on what is happening to you. There is deep joy that comes from God's presence. In the middle of all the opposition and after they had been forced to leave Antioch, they went on to the next town, Iconium, 'brimming with joy and the Holy Spirit, two happy disciples' (Acts 13:52, MSG).

4. Boldness

The Holy Spirit will give you boldness in spite of opposition. In Antioch, 'Paul and Barnabas answered them *boldly*: "We had to speak the word of God to you first"' (v.46). In Iconium, 'Paul and Barnabas spent considerable time there, speaking *boldly* for the Lord' (14:3). In spite of opposition and 'a plot afoot' (v.5) they 'continued to preach the good news' (v.7).

PRAYER

Lord, fill me today with the Holy Spirit and with joy. Help me to speak so effectively that many will believe. Help me not to be put off by opposition, stirring or plots. Give me courage to speak boldly for you. I pray that you will confirm the message of your grace with miraculous signs and wonders.

OLD TESTAMENT READING

1 Kings 7:23–8:21
The Glory of God's empowering presence

Why in the world would you not want to spend time with God? We spend hours on social media, watching TV or on our phones. As Joyce Meyer writes, 'We seem to have no problem investing our time in those pursuits. The truth is this: *The devil fights us more in the area of our spending time with God than he does in any other area of our Christian lives*. In fact, Satan would much prefer that we get involved in all kinds of religious activity rather than spend time with the Lord.'[1]

This passage helps us to understand how amazing it is to spend time in the presence of God – the extraordinary privilege that is available to you as a follower of Jesus.

This Old Testament passage – about the building of the physical temple in Jerusalem (a place for God to dwell for ever, 8:13) – takes on a whole new meaning when you read it in the light of the New Testament. The temple in Jerusalem prefigured God's dwelling place in believers' hearts in the New Testament.

In particular, the ark of the covenant represented the presence of the Lord. The climax of this temple, both in it being prepared for use (vv.3–9) and in Solomon's praise (vv.15–21), was the placing of the ark of the covenant in the temple. The ark had nothing in it 'except the two stone tablets that Moses had placed in it' (v.9) – in other words the Ten Commandments. When you, *the people of God,* live under *the word of God,* you discover *the Spirit of God* increasing your experience of *the presence of God*.

We read, 'When the priests withdrew from the Holy Place, the cloud filled the temple of the LORD. And the priests could not perform their service because of the cloud, for *the glory of the LORD filled his temple*' (vv.10–11).

Although God is present everywhere, we do not always sense his presence. Surely, what is being described here is a greatly increased sense of the presence of God. This is what Solomon was describing when he said, 'I've built this splendid Temple, O God, to mark your invisible presence for ever' (v.13, MSG).

When we pray, 'Come, Holy Spirit,' we are praying for a greatly increased sense of the presence of God to come among us. This is what we so often experience when we pray that prayer.

There can be particular moments when we experience God's presence when we are with others, but you can also experience God's presence as you spend time with him by yourself.

You don't need to be legalistic about it, but a regular time with God helps. As you read the Bible, as you talk to your Father in prayer, as you listen to Christian music or just sit in silence, you begin to experience God's presence. Indeed, sometimes the prayer 'Come Holy Spirit' can be answered with total peace, calm and stillness.

Praise you Lord that, as your glory filled the temple of Solomon, so now your glory fills your people. Thank you that all your promises are fulfilled in us (2 Corinthians 1:20).

PRAYER

Come, Holy Spirit. Fulfil your promise among us again today. Thank you that every time we pray, 'Come, Holy Spirit,' the Holy Spirit comes and we experience an increased sense of the presence of God among us. Help me to prioritise my time and enjoy your awesome presence with me.

21 June | Day 172
It's the Heart that Matters

Paul was in prison in Zambia. He was charged with treason. He was accused of being involved in a coup to overthrow the government. While in prison, he did Alpha. He encountered Jesus and cried out for God to save him. He said, 'The smile came on my face and my heart was filled with peace.'

Extraordinarily, he was the only one of the group of sixty-nine accused who was acquitted. He told his story, at our Leadership Conference at the Royal Albert Hall. His face radiated the joy of the Lord. He has now been into *every* prison in Zambia sharing the good news about Jesus Christ and how, even in the direst of situations, Jesus can bring hope and change hearts. He said, 'I've never seen a friend like Jesus.' God really has filled his heart with joy. The word 'heart' appears at least seventeen times in the passages for today. The Hebrew understanding of 'the heart' included the emotions, but it also involved the mind, the conscience and the will. It means everything that is going on inside of you.

All the men and women whom God chose to use greatly had weaknesses and made mistakes. But God saw that their hearts were turned towards him. It is your heart that matters. Your heart lies 'open before the LORD' (Proverbs 15:11). Only God sees and knows the heart of every human being (1 Kings 8:39).

READING FROM PROVERBS

Proverbs 15:11–20
Your face reflects your heart

Some people's faces radiate love and joy. Their smile puts us at ease and cheers us up. Others may have a rather more sour expression on their face and can make us feel very uncomfortable.

Your face often reflects your heart. 'A *happy heart* makes the face cheerful' (v.13). I remember a preacher saying that the life we have lived eventually shows on our face and, therefore, everybody over forty is responsible for their face!

Even where you manage to hide your heart from those around you, God can still see it: 'Even hell holds no secrets from God – do you think he can't read human hearts?' (v.11, MSG).

God is interested in your heart. This passage gives some wise advice on how you can feed your heart: 'The *discerning heart* seeks knowledge' (v.14); 'A *cheerful heart* fills the day with song' (v.15b, MSG).

The writer gives an example of how the inside is so much more important than the outside: 'Better a bread crust shared in love than a slab of prime rib served in hate' (v.17, MSG). Love and friendship are what make an evening fun.

PRAYER

Thank you, Lord, that you see beyond the outward appearance into my heart. May my face reflect the love and joy you put in my heart and bring encouragement and confidence to everyone I encounter.

NEW TESTAMENT READING

Acts 14:8–28
Your heart can be full of joy in spite of outward circumstances

Paul faced huge difficulties but was filled with joy because his heart was right, and he was making a massive difference to the world.

Joy comes from the heart and is not necessarily connected with your outward circumstances. God loves you. He approves of you. Of course, we all have weaknesses and make mistakes but God sees your heart.

Paul was conducting the first deliberate evangelistic campaign into the Gentile world. It was this that led to Christianity becoming not just a Jewish sect, but the faith with the greatest number of followers in the world today. God 'used them to throw the door of faith wide open so people of all nations could come streaming in' (v.27, MSG).

Paul speaks of 'all that God had done *through them*' (v.27). Yet outwardly the odds were stacked against him. He appeared very unimpressive (2 Corinthians 10:10). One description of Paul's physical appearance at this time (in a second-century document called 'The Acts of Paul and Thecla') describes him as 'a man little of stature, thin-haired upon the head, crooked in the legs, of good state of body, with eyebrows joining, and nose somewhat hooked, full of grace: for sometimes he appeared like a man, and sometimes he had the face of an angel'.[1]

He not only looked unimpressive but he suffered from some physical illness (Galatians 4:13). In addition to all this, his body must have been battered and bruised by all the physical persecution he had suffered. On this occasion, the crowd beat him unconscious and left him for dead (Acts 14:19).

Like so many who have followed in Paul's footsteps, in spite of all his physical suffering, *his heart was full of joy*, and God worked through him. God used Paul in his weakness. This encourages us to believe that God can also work through us in our weakness.

This heartfelt joy is one of a variety of different kinds of hearts we see in this passage:

1. Faith-filled hearts

Paul followed the Lord's example and looked at the heart. He saw 'a man crippled in his feet, who was lame from birth and had never walked' (v.8). As Paul looked at him he saw his heart and 'saw that he had *faith* to be healed' (v.9).

Sometimes God enables us to see into people's hearts – to see that they have the faith to be healed, to be filled with the Spirit or to receive some gift. Later we read of how God 'opened the door of *faith* to the Gentiles' (v.27). Faith is the key to salvation.

2. Fickle hearts

When the crowd saw the man healed they began treating Paul and Barnabas as gods. They pointed out, 'We're not gods!' and that they were only human beings, bringing good news of 'the living God' to whom the crowd needed to turn (v.15). However, the *hearts* of the crowd were fickle. They were soon won over by Paul's opponents and almost in an instant they went from trying to offer sacrifices to Paul to stoning him (vv.18–19).

3. Full-of-joy hearts

This was just one of the many 'hardships' (v.22) that Paul and his companions went through. Yet Paul can speak of how God 'fills your *hearts* with joy' (v.17). Again, he is saying that the inside is so much more important than the outside.

Paul 'strengthened' and 'encouraged' the disciples in Lystra, Iconium and Antioch (vv.21–22). The way he encouraged and strengthened them was not by saying that the Christian life was easy. Paul tells them that although their sins were behind them, their troubles were ahead of them. He says, 'Anyone signing up for the kingdom of God has to go through plenty of hard times' (v.22, MSG). Jesus did not come to make life easy; he came to make people great.

PRAYER

Lord, thank you so much for the inspiring example of those like the apostle Paul. Whatever the outward appearance or circumstance, may my heart be full of joy. May I not judge people or situations by how they look from the outside, but like you, always look to the heart.

OLD TESTAMENT READING

1 Kings 8:22–9:9
Your heart should be fully committed to the Lord

As Solomon dedicates the temple, he prays to the Lord, 'There is no God like you … You who keep your covenant of love with your servants who continue *wholeheartedly* in your way' (8:23).

God's own heart is for his people and he sees and knows the hearts of all people: 'You alone know every human heart' (v.39).

Solomon's prayer recognises the fact that we fail. We sin. He does not say 'if' they sin. Rather he says, 'When they sin against you – for there is no one who does not sin' (v.46, see also Romans 3:23).

Thankfully, there is still hope. It is possible to have 'changed hearts' (1 Kings 8:47, MSG). It is possible for our hearts to turn back to God (v.48). He prays that God will 'turn our hearts to him' (v.58). God is full of mercy and forgiveness (vv.28, 30, 34 ,36, 39, 50). He relentlessly loves and he keeps his word (v.23, MSG).

The better you get to know God – *his* heart, his character and his love for you – the easier it becomes to obey him with all *your* heart.

Never settle for second best. As Solomon puts it, 'Your *hearts* must be fully committed to the LORD our God' (v.61). God wants you to walk before him with 'integrity of *heart* and uprightness' (9:4). The people determined to live like that and went home 'joyful and glad in *heart*' (8:66). Like the disciples, their hearts were full of joy.

We all have weaknesses and make mistakes. But God sees your heart. He loves you and approves of you. Be filled with his joy today.

PRAYER

Lord, my heart is turned towards you. Yet, you know how often I fail. Please forgive and have mercy on me. Thank you that you enable me to turn back to you each day. Thank you that you fill my heart with joy. Help me to follow you wholeheartedly today.

22 June | Day 173
When Life Is Difficult

He was arrested for preaching the gospel. His wife died leaving him with four children, one of whom was blind. Yet he refused to give up telling people the good news about Jesus.

John Bunyan wrote his greatest work in a prison cell. It has been a source of spiritual inspiration and help to countless readers ever since. Translated into over 200 languages, it has never been out of print since the day it was first published in 1678.

Pilgrim's Progress is an allegory which tells the story of a person called 'Christian' on a journey from his hometown to the Celestial City. On the way he faces many difficulties, challenges and obstacles, yet he perseveres faithfully to the end.

A Christian life is not easy. You will face many difficulties along the way. But these need not derail you. In fact, as you go through difficult times staying close to Jesus, you will emerge stronger, wiser and more Christ-like.

READING FROM PSALMS

Psalm 77:1–9
Distress: How should you *respond*?

I have a friend who is a Benedictine monk. He told me that he often begins his prayers with 'a time of complaining'! This psalm also begins with the psalmist pouring out his complaints to God.

Having a relationship with God does not protect us from 'distress' (v.2). The psalmist was 'awake all night – not a wink of sleep' (v.4a, MSG). He feels as if God has rejected him and that he will never experience God's favour again (vv.7–9).

In this, the first half of Psalm 77, we begin to see how to respond to distress. You can be assured that:

1. God listens to your cry

Tell God exactly what you're feeling: 'I yell out to my God, I yell with all my might, I yell at the top of my lungs. He listens. I found myself in trouble and went looking for my Lord' (vv.1–2a, MSG).

2. God likes your honesty

There is a therapeutic effect in asking honest questions. God's people bring their doubts, difficulties and distress to God and question him. Even Jesus, on the cross, asked a question, quoting Psalm 22:1: 'My God, my God, why have you forsaken me?' (Matthew 27:46).

God wants you to be real with him. He does not want you to pretend that all is well. He wants to hear the cry of your heart. This draws you close to him, even in times of great distress.

PRAYER

Thank you, Lord, that you hear the cry of my heart. Thank you that you do not reject me, that your promises do not fail.

NEW TESTAMENT READING

Acts 15:1–21
Disputes: How should you *resolve* them?

There is nothing surprising about 'arguments', 'disputes' and 'debates' in the church. We read here of a 'sharp *dispute* and *debate*' (v.2) about what was required in order to be fully accepted as a Christian – a member of the church – and to be 'saved' (v.1). Was circumcision a requirement? (v.1).

We see here a four-step process for decision-making. This is a great model for dealing with disputes in the local, national and even global church today.

1. Call a meeting

Some were insisting that everyone be circumcised. Paul and Barnabas fiercely protested. They called a special meeting to bring the two sides of the debate together.

Do not be afraid of conflict. When people come together to talk about issues that matter, it is both natural and productive for disagreement to occur. In fact, that is what makes meetings interesting!

2. Consider and discuss

'The arguments went on and on, back and forth, getting more and more heated' (v.7, MSG). In the end, two factors swayed the debate.

First, their reasoning was based on the *experience of the Spirit*. Peter's first argument was based on what he had seen the Holy Spirit doing at Cornelius's house: 'God, who knows the heart, showed that he accepted them [the Gentiles] by giving the Holy Spirit to them, just as he did to us. He made no distinction between us and them' (vv.8–9). To make a distinction would have been to oppose God. This led him to the conclusion: 'We believe it is through the grace of our Lord Jesus that we are saved, just as they are' (v.11).

Second, their reasoning was based on the *evidence of the Scriptures*. James points out that the word of God and the Spirit of God are in alignment: 'The words of the prophets are in agreement with this' (v.15). He shows that the Scriptures foretold the inclusion of 'all the Gentiles' (v.17) and suggests a way forward consistent with following the experience of the Holy Spirit and the evidence of Scripture (vv.19–21). We can be sure that the word of God and the Spirit of God will always be in agreement. What we can*not* be sure of is that our understanding of either is correct. Those arguing that everyone should be circumcised did so on the basis of Scripture. Peter and James did not set aside the Scriptures, but they did argue that they had been misunderstood.

3. Come to a decision

In the end, *they decided* (v.22). This was an extraordinary moment in the life of the early church. 'The whole assembly became silent as they listened to Barnabas and Paul telling about the miraculous signs and wonders God had done among the Gentiles through them' (v.12). It was a spine-tingling moment, which reduced them to silence.

At the end of the day decisions require judgment. The apostle James says, 'It is my *judgment*' (v.19). The deciding factor was that they did not want to '*make it difficult* for the Gentiles who are turning to God' (v.19). All people were to be invited into the church, regardless of their background, although not all practices were allowed (v.20).

The lesson here is that we need to be very careful about putting unnecessary obstacles in front of people who are exploring faith in Jesus and we need to be careful about defining the church too narrowly.

4. Communicate the decision

They wrote it down (v.20). Minutes of a meeting are not just a formality. It is important to record decisions. Then, as we will see tomorrow, they need to be communicated (vv.23–29).

PRAYER

Lord, give us wisdom as we deal with disputes within the church. Thank you that you are pouring out your Holy Spirit again on all parts of the church today. Help us to have the same attitude as you, who 'made no distinction between us and them' (v.9).

OLD TESTAMENT READING

1 Kings 9:10–11:13
Decoys: How should you *resist* them?

Solomon's life presents us with a challenge and a warning: success can be more dangerous for us than failure.

Solomon did much that was right. He was highly successful – the richest and wisest king of his day (10:23). Everyone wanted to meet him and 'hear the wisdom God had put in his heart' (v.24).

Solomon had everything. In twenty years, he had built two great buildings: the temple and his palace (9:10). The Queen of Sheba was astonished by what she saw (10:7). She recognises it could only be God: 'making you king to keep a just order and nurture a God-pleasing people' (v.9, MSG).

Yet, the tragedy is that Solomon did not finish well. He was led astray. His 'heart was not fully devoted to the LORD his God, as the heart of David his father had been ... his heart had turned away from the LORD' (11:4, 9).

What went wrong? It started with promiscuity. King Solomon was obsessed with sex: 'He had seven hundred royal wives and three hundred concubines – a thousand women in all!' (v.3, MSG).

It ended with following detestable gods: 'As Solomon grew older, his wives beguiled him with their alien gods' (4a, MSG). He 'did evil in the eyes of the LORD; he did not follow the LORD completely, as David his father had done' (v.6). He acted contrary to the Lord's explicit command that the king 'must not take many wives, or his heart will be led astray. He must not accumulate large amounts of silver and gold' (Deuteronomy 17:17). These decoys led Solomon astray.

David messed up from time to time. When he did, he repented and turned back to the Lord and followed him wholeheartedly. Solomon shows us something different. Seven hundred wives and three hundred concubines do not happen overnight. There must have been compromise in Solomon's heart. In spite of all God's blessings, Solomon allowed sin to breed and, in the end, it ruined him.

To avoid ending up like Solomon you need to *stay close to Jesus and listen to him.* For as Jesus said, the Queen of Sheba 'came from the ends of the earth to listen to Solomon's wisdom, and now *one greater than Solomon* is here' (Matthew 12:42).

PRAYER

Lord, thank you for this warning. Guard my heart. Help me to be fully devoted to the Lord, to follow you completely to the end of my life.

---

23 June | Day 174
Three Keys to Great Friendships

The UK retail chain Topshop commissioned a survey by a team of psychologists into their key customer demographic: Millennials (those born between 1981 and the early 2000s, and also known as Generation Y). They interviewed 800 people. The results were so startling that they did not believe them. They interviewed another 800 and got the same results.

The results portrayed an alarming picture of an increasingly lonely and lost generation. More people live alone than at any other point in our recorded social history. On average, Millennials spend six-and-a-half hours a day on social media. Many who were interviewed considered work to be something they fitted in between social media and lunch! They found people had a very large number of 'friends' but an increasing sense of loneliness.

There is nothing wrong with social media, but it is no substitute for real, face-to-face friendships. We were created for friendship with God (Genesis 3:8) and with one another (2:18).

Marriage is part of the solution to aloneness. Friendship, vital also in marriage, is a crucial part of the solution too. Jesus set an example of close friendship with men and women. He demonstrated that marriage is not the *only* solution to aloneness. In one respect, friendship is even more important than marriage. Marriage is temporary; friendship is eternal. 'Friendship', as C. S. Lewis writes, is the 'crown of life and school of virtue'.[1] Friendship multiplies joy and divides sorrow.

The Bible is very realistic. We see examples of relationships at their very best, but we also see examples of their frailty and failure. Through these examples and the teaching of the Bible we see three keys.

READING FROM PSALMS

Psalm 77:10–20
Value partnerships

Mother Teresa said, 'What I can do, you cannot. What you can do, I cannot. But together we can do something beautiful for God.'[2]

We saw yesterday how the psalmist, in his distress, cried out to God. In the second half of the psalm, he recalls some of the amazing and mighty ways in which God has acted in the past (vv.11–12).

In particular, he looks back to God's great deliverance of his people in the Exodus. He prays, 'You are the God who performs miracles; you display your power among the peoples' (v.14). He meditates on the parting of the Red Sea (vv.16–19) and concludes, 'You led your people like a flock *by the hand of Moses and Aaron*' (v.20).

'*Moses and Aaron*' were the human *partnership* involved in this great work of God. It is one of the greatest success stories in the history of the people of God.

It came about because they were involved in a cause greater than themselves. They were looking outward in the same direction. Despite being brothers, they had very different skills and roles. While Moses was the leader, Aaron was responsible for the communications (Exodus 7:1–2) and for leading the people in worship (28:1).

We need good partnerships today. There are good reasons why Jesus sent his disciples out two by two. Ministry can be very lonely. Going out in pairs can make all the difference. This is how some of the greatest friendships are formed.

PRAYER

Lord, I pray today that you will raise up good partnerships in our local church and the church worldwide. Lord, may there be many who, like Moses and Aaron, complement one another and see you achieve great things through them.

NEW TESTAMENT READING

Acts 15:22–41
Guard friendships

From the very beginning of the Christian church we see examples of *friends* working together in partnership. Paul and Barnabas were *partners* in the gospel (v.22). They were sent out together to take the message of the council of Jerusalem to the Gentiles (v.23).

They are described as '*our dear friends* Barnabas and Paul – men who have risked their lives for the name of our Lord Jesus Christ' (v.26).

They were accompanied by another partnership – two other leaders, Judas (called Barsabbas) and Silas (v.22). Judas and Silas were prophets who 'said much to encourage and strengthen the believers' (v.32). Again, it is a good thing for prophets not to operate in isolation, but to work together in partnership with others.

All this is good. But as we read on, we see that division, even in the early church, was not only over doctrine (v.2), but also over personal relationships (v.39). As Sandy Millar often says, 'The *calling* is divine; but the *relationships* are human!' Paul and Barnabas fell out (vv.36–38). They had a 'sharp disagreement' and as a result they 'parted company' (v.39). They ended up going their separate ways.

In the providence of God, it all worked out well in the end. Barnabas found a new partner in Mark, who was his cousin. (See Colossians 4:10.) Paul found a new partner in Silas and 'went through Syria and Cilicia, strengthening the churches' (Acts 15:41). It may be that Paul and Barnabas were later reconciled (see 1 Corinthians 9:6).

The reality is that sometimes even Christian partnerships struggle and fail. God can bring hope into these situations: it is not the end of the world if Christians fall out and go their separate ways. This passage shows that their disagreement did not lead to the removal of God's blessing from them.

However, as John Stott points out, 'this example of God's providence should not be used as an excuse for Christian quarrelling'.[3] We should always do our best to resolve our differences and avoid such painful parting of company.

Guard your friendships. When there is a fallout, always seek reconciliation and remember that, as Martin Luther King said, 'Forgiveness is not an occasional act; it is a permanent attitude.'

PRAYER

Father, thank you for the inspiring example of Paul and Barnabas who risked their lives for the name of our Lord Jesus Christ. Help us to resolve our differences and avoid, whenever possible, painful partings of company.

OLD TESTAMENT READING

1 Kings 11:14–12:24
Prioritise loyalty

In this passage, we see human relationships at their worst. Solomon began to reap what he had sown. He had sown disloyalty to God and now he began to reap disloyalty all over the place. The first adversary was Hadad (11:14). The second was Rezon (v.23), 'the leader of a band of rebels' (v.24).

Next, Jeroboam rebelled against the king (v.26). He was one of Solomon's officials, 'a man of standing', whom Solomon had put 'in charge of the whole labour force of the house of Joseph' (v.28). Solomon ends his life surrounded by adversaries and trying to kill Jeroboam (v.40).

Rehoboam, Solomon's son, inherited a mess. He did not deal wisely with his opponents. He failed to listen. He 'turned a deaf ear to the people' (12:15, MSG). They realised that he 'hadn't listened to a word they'd said' (v.16, MSG).

He rejected the advice that the elders gave him. As a result, most of Israel rallied around Jeroboam. 'Only the tribe of Judah *remained loyal* to the house of David' (v.20). Yet again, war broke out (v.21). The result is a divided kingdom – but even that is not the end of the problems. God promised Jeroboam amazing blessings: 'if you walk in obedience to me' (v.38). Tragically (as we will see over the next few days) Jeroboam did not – and the results were disastrous.

This episode in the history of the people of God is a story of disloyalty to God, disloyalty to the king, rebellion and infighting. It is not how things are meant to be. You are called to love, unity and loyalty. Your loyalty should be a reflection of God's loyalty to you.

If you sow disloyalty, you will reap disloyalty. If you sow loyalty, you will reap loyalty. You show loyalty by your actions and your words. Be loyal to those who are not present. In doing so, you will build the trust of those who are present.

However disloyal we are, God remains faithful to his promises. He remembers his covenant with David (see 2 Samuel 7), and does not completely reject the people (1 Kings 11:32, 34, 36). Although he disciplines us – 'I will humble David's descendants because of this, but not for ever' (v.39) – his discipline is temporary, his loyalty is eternal. 'God disciplines us for our good, that we may share in his holiness' (Hebrews 12:10).

God's commitment and loyalty to you is such that nothing will be able to separate you 'from the love of God that is in Christ Jesus our Lord' (Romans 8:39).

This is not a reason to be complacent, but it is a motive to delight again at God's grace, and to give yourself to wholehearted worship. You can choose again to respond to God's call on your life – 'walk in my ways and do what is right in my eyes' (1 Kings 11:38).

PRAYER

Lord, please pour out your Spirit of love, unity and loyalty on the church. Help us to work together in partnership with one another. Guard our friendships, protect our partnerships and give us wisdom in dealing with our adversaries.

24 June | Day 175
Pass on the Baton

When I left university at the age of twenty-one, I moved to London and was looking for a church to join. I visited Holy Trinity Brompton and heard Sandy Millar speak. Afterwards, I asked if I could meet with him. Soon after, I joined the church and began to learn from this extraordinary leader, friend and role model.

After several years as a member of the congregation, I went on to train for ordination in the Church of England and ten years after our first meeting I returned to HTB as Sandy Millar's assistant minister. I continued in that role for nineteen years until 2005 when he passed on the baton to me, and I succeeded him as vicar of HTB. To this day, Sandy continues to be my role model, friend and inspiration.

There have always been people in my life from whom I am learning and others to whom I am trying to pass it on. Like runners in a relay race, we all have a responsibility to pass on the baton.

READING FROM PSALMS

Psalm 78:1–8
Tell

You have a story to tell. Every family has stories. Every church has its own stories of what God has done. Every Christian has a story – a testimony. All of us have access to the great story of what God has done in Christ. We have to 'tell the stories' (v.6, MSG).

This psalm gives us a sketch of Hebrew history leading up to King David, and stresses the importance of passing it on to the next generation. We see a contrast between the sins of Israel and the goodness of God. Jesus himself quoted this psalm (Matthew 13:35).

The psalmist says, 'We will *tell the next generation* the praiseworthy deeds of the LORD, his power, and the wonders he has done ... to teach their children, so that the *next generation* would know them ... and they in turn would tell their children. Then they would put their trust in God' (Psalm 78:4–7).

Juan Carlos Ortiz tells the story of meeting an old lady in his native Argentina who introduced him to a young girl, who was one of her great-grandchildren. She went on to tell that she had six children and thirty-six grandchildren. Her family was impressive in number and among her grandchildren were many well-educated and professional people. Carlos asked her, 'How did you manage to produce such a large, well-fed, well-dressed, well-educated extended family?' She replied, 'I didn't. I just took care of the six. And each of them took care of their six.'[1]

Each generation has a responsibility to tell the next one about the goodness of God and to warn them of the mess that we make of our lives when we turn away from God's goodness.

PRAYER

Lord, thank you for those who told us about 'the LORD, his power, and the wonders he has done' (v.4). Help us to pass it on to the next generation so that they would put their trust in you.

NEW TESTAMENT READING

Acts 16:1–15
Train

Paul recognised he had a responsibility to train up others. He found Timothy – 'a fine young man' (vv.1–2, MSG). Timothy was discipled, trained and taught by Paul. Paul was a mentor to Timothy. They are a great example of what we all should be doing. Find a Paul from whom you can learn and find a Timothy to whom you can pass it on.

As with so many, I would say that every major strategic step or decision I have made has been inspired and encouraged not from a pulpit in a crowd of thousands but rather by someone within arm's reach. There is no doubt that preaching can make a big impact, but we often overestimate the amount of truth that is assimilated between the pulpit and the pew. In my life, truth shared in proximity has been a key to my own personal growth. This seems to have been the key for Timothy.

It was through Paul that Timothy had become a Christian and they became very close friends. Paul was older than Timothy and he described their friendship as being like that of a father and son (Philippians 2:22). Paul described Timothy as 'my son whom I love' (1 Corinthians 4:17).

They went through a great deal together. 'They travelled from town to town' (Acts 16:4). They even spent time in prison together. During all this Timothy would have been watching Paul, and being trained up as his successor.

It is not enough to hope that the 'Timothys' are watching us. We must strategically position younger disciples to have significant opportunities to lead. Paul bestowed on Timothy real responsibility. He could trust him because he knew him so well.

Paul involved Timothy in the work right from the start. They took decisions together (v.4). Through their ministry together, 'Day after day the congregations became stronger in faith and larger in size' (v.5, MSG).

Timothy learnt about the guidance of the Holy Spirit. When they tried to enter Bithynia, the Holy Spirit 'blocked that route. So they went to Mysia and tried to go north to Bithynia, but the Spirit of Jesus wouldn't let them go there either' (vv.6–7, MSG). This is an important lesson in life. I can think of at least five occasions in my life where I have felt that I should go in a particular direction 'but the Spirit of Jesus would not allow' (v.7) the plan to succeed. As I look back now, I am so thankful the Spirit stopped plans which, in hindsight, were clearly not the right ones.

God then led Timothy and Paul in a new direction: 'During the night Paul had a *vision* of a man of Macedonia standing and begging him, "Come over to Macedonia and help us"' (v.9). Not surprisingly Paul took this as clear guidance that they were to go to Macedonia: 'All the pieces had come together. We knew now for sure that God had called us to preach the good news to the Europeans' (v.10, MSG).

In Philippi, Timothy would have watched Paul on the first Saturday that he was there, going down to the river where there were a group of women praying (v.13).

As Paul spoke about Jesus, Lydia, a rich merchant woman, was converted. She invited Paul and those with him to come and stay in her home. It must have been an extraordinary and wonderful experience for them both to see how the 'Lord opened her heart to respond to Paul's message' (v.14).

The final letter attributed to Paul is 2 Timothy. To the very end of his life, Paul's priority was encouraging and releasing the next generation. Let's make it ours too!

PRAYER

Lord, help every 'Paul' to find 'Timothys' who they can train up. Help every 'Timothy' to find a mentor like Paul who will pass on all their experience to them.

OLD TESTAMENT READING

1 Kings 12:25–14:20
Teach

Unless we learn the lessons of history and 'teach ... the next generation' (Psalm 78:5–6) they will repeat the mistakes of the past. The book of Kings records the history of the people of God so that the following generations may learn from them.

Sadly, the lessons we can learn from this passage are mainly negative – the account of Jeroboam is a terrifying one. He passed on a terrible legacy to the next generation.

'After seeking advice, the king made two golden calves' (1 Kings 12:28). It is not enough to 'seek advice' if we consult the wrong people! These chapters contain the account of the sin of the house of Jeroboam that 'led to its downfall and to its destruction from the face of the earth' (13:34).

Jeroboam's key sin was that he made up a form of religion and worship to suit himself. He encouraged idol worship rather than the worship of God (12:28). Jeroboam's religion is a made-up religion, created to suit his own desires and needs.

We may not worship golden calves, but the same danger is just as evident today. As Pope Francis has said, 'The most dangerous idol is our own selves when we want to occupy the place of God.'[2]

This was Jeroboam's sin, and it affected the next generation. His son Abijah became ill and died (chapter 14). He ignored the good example of the earlier generation of David who had lived with an undivided heart, pleasing God. Instead he had 'set a new record in works of evil' (14:9, MSG).

Jeroboam may have had many military, commercial and political achievements (see v.19), and yet it seems these successes are fairly irrelevant. As Jesus said, 'What good is it for you to gain the whole world, yet forfeit your soul?' (Mark 8:36). What matters most is a close relationship with the living God.

PRAYER

Lord, I pray that you will raise up leaders in industry, politics, creative arts, media and every sector of society, who will honour you and pass on your message and your standards to the next generation.

25 June | Day 176
The Power of Prayer

Archbishop Justin Welby and Pete Greig (founder of 24-7 Prayer) have launched an initiative calling hundreds of thousands of Christians, of many churches and denominations to a great wave of prayer for the evangelisation of the nations during the week before Pentecost Sunday. The week culminates in beacon events in packed cathedrals and churches around the world over the Pentecost weekend. Justin Welby, Archbishop of Canterbury, asked people to pray for three things: 'That all Christians find new life in Jesus Christ ... That all those you meet ... might see something of Jesus ... For the church to overflow with the reality of the presence of Jesus.'

Pete Grieg has described it as 'a groundswell; a movement from the grassroots up'. He said he had been very moved to hear of one boy who'd prayed for five friends, three of whom had since become Christians!

Prayer is spiritual nutrition. Just as the body needs physical food, so the soul needs spiritual food. Prayer changes us. However, the Bible goes much further than this. Prayer is powerful. It is, as Charles Haddon Spurgeon put it, 'the slender nerve that moves the muscles of omnipotence.'[1] Prayer has the power to change circumstances, other people and even the course of history.

READING FROM PROVERBS

Proverbs 15:21–30
Prayer changes circumstances

God 'closely attends to the prayers of God-loyal people' (v.29, MSG). Your prayers can make a difference to what happens. 'The LORD is far from the wicked but he *hears the prayer* of the righteous' (v.29). According to the writer of Proverbs, righteousness means keeping 'a straight course' (v.21), listening to advice (v.22) and maintaining purity in our thoughts (v.26). It means responding to people with 'prayerful answers' (v.28, MSG). Through Jesus, all who believe 'are righteous' (Romans 3:22). Therefore, God hears your prayers.

Prayer and careful planning are not opposed to each other. As well as talking with God, it is wise to get advice from others: 'Plans fail for lack of counsel but with many advisors they succeed' (v.22).

You will bring blessing wherever you go: 'The light in the eyes [of him whose heart is joyful] rejoices the hearts of others, and good news nourishes the bones' (v.30, AMP).

PRAYER

Lord, thank you for the many times you have heard and answered my prayers. Lord, today I pray...

NEW TESTAMENT READING

Acts 16:16–40
Prayer changes people

What made the early church so powerful? Surely, part of the answer is the prayer lives of those first believers.

1. Pray regularly

It appears that prayer was a regular habit. 'Once when we were going to *the place of prayer...*' (v.16). This suggests they did not only pray on their own, they met together frequently to pray.

2. Pray in the name of Jesus

Christian prayer is powerful because we pray, not in our own name, but in the name of Jesus.

Paul was followed around in the town of Philippi by a 'psychic', who was clearly under demonic influence as a result of her involvement in the occult (v.17). Finally, after several days of this, Paul could take her endless repetitions no longer. He turned around and said, '*In the name of Jesus Christ* I command you to come out of her!' (v.18). At that moment, the evil spirit came out.

The name of Jesus is so powerful. The only way to deal with demonic power is through the name of Jesus. No demon is a match for Jesus. Jesus sets us free from demonic forces. He utterly transformed this young woman's life. The demon 'was gone, just like that' (v.18, MSG).

3. Pray in all circumstances

The woman was a slave who made a lot of money for the people who owned her. Her owners were furious that she had lost her supernatural powers. They seized Paul and Silas, 'roughed them up', 'arrested them' (vv.19–20, MSG) and hauled them off to court. They whipped up the crowd against them.

The crowd joined in the 'attack' (v.22). Life is not always going to be easy if we start making a difference. Some of our views may be very unpopular or even illegal. 'Attacks' are not necessarily a mark of failure; they may be a sign of success.

The magistrates bowed to the pressure and ordered that they should be stripped, severely flogged and thrown into prison under heavy guard where they 'clamped leg irons on them' (v.24, MSG).

The prison officer would have been used to people coming into prison angry, cursing and swearing. By contrast, he sees Paul and Silas *praying*, *worshipping* and *singing hymns to God* (v.25). There is great power in this combination of prayer and worship.

An earthquake shook the prison and every door flew open. The prison officer in charge was about to commit suicide as he thought all his prisoners had escaped and he feared the consequences. Paul, faced with freedom, chose instead to stay, and bring his jailor to Christ.

When Paul assured him that all the prisoners were still there he asked, 'What must I do to be saved?' (v.30). This is what might be called 'an evangelistic opportunity'! Paul explained what the prison officer had to do and thus he, and afterwards his whole family, believed in Jesus and were baptised.

Immediately, his life began to change. He shows compassion. He washes the wounds of Paul and Silas (v.33). He feeds them (v.34). He and his whole family are 'filled with joy' (v.35). He is willing to be known publicly as a Christian. They became founding members of the church at Philippi.

These events were so clearly supernatural that Paul saw the astonishing power of God behind the human agency of his words.

This episode ends with the judges having to apologise personally to Paul and Silas as they had not realised they were Roman citizens and it was, therefore, illegal to treat them in the way they had been treated: 'The judges panicked ... apologized, personally escorted them from the jail ... Paul and Silas went straight to Lydia's house, saw their friends again, encouraged them in the faith, and only then went on their way' (vv.38–40, MSG).

Prayer has the power not just to change our own lives but also circumstances, events and the lives of others.

PRAYER

Lord, help us to be more like the early church. Help us to meet together regularly to pray. Thank you for the power of the name of Jesus. Lord, may prayer and worship undergird everything we do.

OLD TESTAMENT READING

1 Kings 14:21–16:7
Prayer changes history

Of course, prayer does not change the past, but it can change the future course of events.

The history of the people of God as set out in the book of 1 Kings is rather mixed. We read constantly of how the people of God 'did evil in the eyes of the LORD' (14:22; 15:26, 34; 16:7). They committed sins (for example, 14:22b; 15:26, 30, 34; 16:2). They had shrine-prostitutes (14:24a); they engaged in detestable practices (v.24b); there was continual warfare between Israel and Judah (v.30; 15:6, 32). The kings were often *not* 'fully devoted to the LORD' (v.3).

There were notable exceptions such as Asa (15:9–24). He 'conducted himself well before God, reviving the ways of his ancestor David. He cleaned house ...' (vv.11–12a, MSG).

In the middle of all this, there is a fascinating comment: '*Nevertheless, for David's sake* the LORD his God gave him a lamp in Jerusalem by raising up a son to succeed him and by making Jerusalem strong. For David had done what was right in the eyes of the LORD and had not failed to keep any of the LORD's commands all the days of his life – except in the case of Uriah the Hittite' (vv.4–6).

David was having an impact long after his death. God honoured his prayers for generations.

God had said to David, 'Your house and your kingdom shall endure for ever before me; your throne shall be established for ever' (2 Samuel 7:16). David had prayed, 'And now, LORD God, keep for ever the promise you have made concerning your servant and his house. Do as you promised, so that your name will be great for ever. Then people will say, "The LORD Almighty is God over Israel!" And the house of your servant David will be established before you' (vv.25–26).

The Lord heard David's prayer. The impact of David's prayer was to change the course of history. David had lived a righteous life ('except in the case of Uriah the Hittite'). However, the New Testament tells us that every person that believes in Jesus is in a *better* position than David was. Through Jesus' death and resurrection, you are righteous before God. God hears the prayers of the righteous. So, because of Jesus, your prayers also can change the course of history.

PRAYER

Lord, would you turn our city and our country back to you. I pray that you will raise up leaders and politicians, fully devoted to you, who will get rid of evil and bring peace and justice to our world.

26 June | Day 177
Three Things God Wants to Give You

Corrie ten Boom and her sister Betsie were middle-aged Christian women in Holland when World War II erupted. They resolved to conceal fleeing Jews from the Nazis. They rescued many. But they were eventually arrested and taken to Ravensbrück concentration camp. Betsie died there. Corrie miraculously survived to bear witness to the way in which God can save, heal and forgive.

When asked how to prepare for persecution, she used to tell this story about her childhood:

'When I was a little girl, I went to my father and said, "Daddy, I was afraid that I will never be strong enough to be a martyr for Jesus Christ." "Tell me," said father, "when you take a train trip to Amsterdam, when do I give you the money for the ticket? Three weeks before?" "No, Daddy, you give me the money for the ticket *just before* we get on the train." "That is right," my father said, "And so it is with God's strength. Our Father in heaven knows when you will need the strength to be a martyr for Jesus Christ. He will supply *all you need just in time*."'[1]

READING FROM PSALMS

Psalm 78:9–16
Continual guidance

God will give you all the guidance you need. As the psalmist continues to recount the history of the people of God, he recalls how, '*He guided them* with the cloud by day and with light from the fire all night' (v.14). In other words, he guided them continually.

You have the Holy Spirit dwelling within you. Expect no less. You are 'led by the Spirit of God' (Romans 8:14). The Holy Spirit will provide you with all the guidance you need.

God will also satisfy your spiritual thirst: 'He split the rocks in the desert and gave them *water as abundant as the seas*; he brought *streams* out of a rocky crag and made *water flow down like rivers*' (Psalm 78:15–16). Jesus promises you that, through the Holy Spirit, streams of living water will flow from within you (John 7:38).

PRAYER

Lord, I really need your Holy Spirit and your guidance. Please fill me today with your Holy Spirit and may streams of living water flow from within me.

NEW TESTAMENT READING

Acts 17:1–21
Good news

In a world that desperately needs good news, God has provided you with a message of good news. The word 'gospel' means 'good news'. The good news is 'about Jesus and the resurrection' (v.18). *All you need is in Jesus*. It is all about Jesus.

Every time you give your testimony or speak about your faith in other ways, ask yourself, 'Is it good news?' Every time we preach it should be good news; otherwise it is not the gospel. Your message should *always* be good news because it is about Jesus, his death and resurrection.

God will provide you with the appropriate words for every occasion. Your words are powerful and life-changing. The good news of Jesus is dynamically relevant to all generations, cultures and situations. People's needs are always the same. The message of the gospel is always the same.

1. Explain the good news

When Paul went into the synagogue in Thessalonica, he '*reasoned* with them from Scriptures, *explaining* and *proving* that the Christ had to suffer and rise from the dead. "This Jesus I am proclaiming to you is the Christ," he said' (vv.2–3). His careful explanation of the gospel resulted in a number of people being 'persuaded' (v.4).

The fact that your message comes from God does not stop you receiving *unfounded criticism*. It is often one of the costs of following Jesus. Paul's success led to jealousy (v.5). Interestingly, he was perceived already as having a global impact: 'These men who have caused trouble *all over the world* [the whole 'known world'] have now come here' (v.6b).

2. Study the good news

God gave Paul and Silas the appropriate words for the Bereans. They responded well to what they heard. They received the message with 'great eagerness' and then '*examined* the Scriptures every day to see if what Paul said was true' (v.11). Once again, the message bore fruit and a number 'believed' (v.12). I would encourage you too to set aside a regular time to study the Scriptures *every day*.

Once again, Paul and Silas's success led to opposition. Some began 'agitating the crowds and stirring them up' (v.13). Do not be surprised if you find agitators and stirrers today.

3. Reason the good news

Paul moved on to Athens. The Athenians 'spent their time doing nothing but talking about and listening to the latest ideas' (v.21). They were more interested in what was *new* than what was *true*.

Again, God provided Paul with the appropriate message for the Athenians. He '*reasoned* in the synagogue with the Jews and the God-fearing Greeks, as well as in the market-place day by day' (v.17). These were two entirely different audiences.

Speaking to the first audience would have been like preaching in a church. Speaking in a market place would have been more like speaking in the workplace. But, at its heart, Paul's message seems to have been exactly the same – 'preaching the *good news about Jesus and the resurrection*' (v.18).

PRAYER

Lord, would you give me the words I need for the conversations that are ahead of me today. Please supply the message. I ask for life-changing words in all my daily conversations. May I be led by the Spirit.

OLD TESTAMENT READING

1 Kings 16:8–18:15
Material needs

Jesus taught us to pray, 'Give us this day our daily bread' (Matthew 6:11; Luke 11:3). Look to God to provide for your daily needs. He will not necessarily give you all *you want*, but pray that he will provide you with all *you need*.

In a society that continued to sin and split into factions (1 Kings 16:8–34), God raised up a prophet who spoke with authority and power.

The New Testament tells us that Elijah was a human being 'just as we are' (James 5:17a). And yet, 'He prayed earnestly that it would not rain, and it did not rain on the land for three-and-a-half years. Again he prayed, and the heavens gave rain, and the earth produced its crops' (vv.17b–18).

Elijah's prayer resulted in problems for Elijah himself. However, God *provided for all his material needs*. Initially, '*The ravens brought him bread and meat in the morning and bread and meat in the evening, and he drank from the brook*' (1 Kings 17:6). God can be very creative in providing for you. Your part is to obey him and then trust that he will provide for all your needs.

When the brook dried up (v.7), the Lord said to him, 'Go at once to Zarephath of Sidon and stay there. I have commanded a widow in that place *to supply you with food*' (v.9). When one door closes (the brook dried up), it is usually because God is about to open another door in your life. He was relocating Elijah so that he could be the answer to someone else's prayer and need for provision.

The widow was put to the test. Elijah asks for food. She tells him that she and her son were about to eat their last meal and then die. Elijah promises that if she is generous with what she has, God will provide for all her needs. He says to her, '*The jar of flour will not run out and the bottle of oil will not become empty* before God sends rain on the land and ends this drought' (v.14, MSG).

The widow did exactly as Elijah asked. And it turned out exactly as he said (vv.15–16). The woman showed great faith. She was prepared to give all she had. She risked everything. And God supplied all her needs. They had enough, but never a surplus. They remained utterly dependent upon God to provide their daily needs. If you obey God and give generously, you will discover that you cannot out-give God. God will do amazing things for you and through you.

This does not mean life will be easy. In spite of her faith she faced further battles. Her son became ill and finally stopped breathing (v.17). Elijah exercised huge faith when he cried out to the Lord for the boy who had died (v.20). 'The Lord heard Elijah's cry, and the boy's life returned to him' (v.22).

How amazing for Elijah to be able to pick him up, carry him down from the room into the house and give him to his mother saying, 'Look, your son is alive!' (v.23).

PRAYER

Lord, thank you for your amazing love, power and provision of enough food for the entire world. Forgive us when we fail to distribute what you have provided. Give us your guidance, your words and your courage to do all we can in our generation to change this terrible injustice. Lead us by your Spirit to change our world.

27 June | Day 178

The God of Miracles

After an Alpha Weekend, a soldier called Quincy Bellot wrote to me: 'This pain started twelve years ago. After joining the Royal Marines, it became extremely bad. The cartilage below the kneecap was completely gone. Last year was the worst when the ligaments and the tendons were torn and the kneecap went in a forty-five-degree angle. It has been a long and painful journey. I could not sit or stand for too long.

'Cut a long story short, I decided to try God and try Alpha. I got back from the Alpha Weekend and agreed to come to HTB after much hesitation. I heard people testifying and I was thinking, "yeah, yeah, yeah". When someone said [a word of knowledge] about the cartilage issue, I took the sharpest breath I ever took. I agreed to be prayed for. I felt God moving in my knee. I dropped on my knees to test it and remarkably no pain. *It's just miraculous*. I went for a run last night ... it was the first time after a very long time I haven't had any pain. God is real.' The email was headed 'Brand New Knee!!'

God is a God of miracles.

READING FROM PSALMS

Psalm 78:17–31
Receive the miracle of God's provision

The psalmist continues to tell the history of the people of God's journey from Egypt to the promised land. In spite of God's miraculous provision, they 'sinned even more', rebelled and 'whined like spoiled children' (vv.17–19, MSG).

God helped them anyway. He 'rained down showers of manna to eat, he gave them the Bread of Heaven' (v.24, MSG). This prefigured the spiritual food that Jesus provides (John 6:30–35).

Likewise, 'When he struck the rock, water gushed out, and streams flowed abundantly' (Psalm 78:20). In a miraculous way, God provided water from a rock. Yet, the people still doubted God 'for they did not believe in God or trust in his deliverance' (v.22). Although miracles are wonderful, they do not always cause people to believe in God.

The miracle of water from a rock really happened, but it also prefigured and anticipated something even more amazing. St Paul writes, 'they drank from the spiritual rock that accompanied them, and that rock was Christ' (1 Corinthians 10:4).

Jesus said, '"Let anyone who is thirsty come to me and drink. Whoever believes in me, as the Scripture has said, will have streams of living water flowing from within." By this he meant the Spirit…' (John 7:37–39).

PRAYER

Lord, thank you for the 'living water' of the Holy Spirit who lives within me. Help me to be the bearer of this supernatural life to all whom I encounter today.

NEW TESTAMENT READING

Acts 17:22–18:8
Believe the miracle of the resurrection of Jesus

The message is: Jesus. When in Athens, Paul begins talking to the people on their level. He does not start with the Old Testament, as he did with the Jews – proclaiming *Jesus as Messiah*. Rather, he begins with their worship of an unknown god (17:23a), and uses that to *explain Jesus* to them.

Paul's preaching was remarkably positive. Rather than reproaching them for their idolatry, he says, 'Now what you worship as something unknown I am going to proclaim to you' (v.23b). He says three things about God: He is the creator (v.24), he is self-sufficient (he does not need us, v.25) but we all need him (vv.27–28).

Paul goes on to quote one of their poets approvingly: 'One of your poets said it well' (v.28, MSG). Christians do not have the monopoly on the truth. God has revealed himself in creation and we find remarkable insights in secular sources.

His talk climaxes with the proclamation of the greatest and *most important miracle in history*: the resurrection of Jesus (vv.30–31). Paul claims to have historical *proof* of the resurrection. He had met the risen Lord Jesus on the road to Damascus.

The implications are huge. Death was not the end for Jesus and it will not be the end for you and me. You too will be raised to life. Here, Paul says that the resurrection is evidence that God has set a day when he will judge the world with justice by the man he has appointed: Jesus. Paul gave people the opportunity to respond to this message.

The reactions to hearing a talk about Jesus and the resurrection of the dead were very similar to those we experience today.

1. Some sneered

'Some laughed at him and walked off making jokes' (v.32a, MSG). Do not be surprised if you get this reaction from some people.

2. Some were interested

'Others said, "Let's do this again. We want to hear more"' (v.32b, MSG). Many people today, as they were then, are genuinely interested but they need time to hear more and think through the issues. Courses like Alpha provide an opportunity for people to do this.

3. Some believed

'There were still others ... who were convinced then and there' (v.34, MSG). They believed straight away. It is unusual but wonderful when people accept Jesus the first time they hear about him.

When Paul went to Corinth, presumably he preached the same message of Jesus and the resurrection. He '*reasoned* in the synagogue, trying to persuade Jews and Greeks' (18:4). He was not asking them to exercise blind faith. Your faith is not irrational. The facts of the life, death and resurrection of Jesus give *reasons to believe*. It is possible to persuade people on the basis of the evidence. If Jesus was miraculously raised from the dead, that is evidence that Jesus is the Christ (v.5).

Again, as in Athens, there were different responses. Some were abusive (v.6). But some believed – 'Crispus, the synagogue ruler, and his entire household believed in the Lord; and many of the Corinthians who heard him believed and were baptised' (v.8).

PRAYER

Lord, thank you for the miracle of the resurrection of Jesus and for the power of this message to transform lives.

OLD TESTAMENT READING

1 Kings 18:16–19:21
Experience the miracle of fire from God

God performed a remarkable miracle through the human agency of Elijah. This account stresses the supernatural nature of the event.

We all have to decide how we are going to live and who we are going to follow. Elijah says, 'How long are you going to sit on the fence? If GOD is the real God, follow him; if it's Baal, follow him. Make up your minds!' (18:21, MSG).

He sets up a test for them and says, 'The god who answers by fire – he is God' (v.24).

It is futile to serve gods made by human hands. However loud they shouted, 'there was no response, no one answered, no one paid attention' (v.29). But when Elijah prayed he did not need to shout (v.36). Because he was praying to the living God.

You can have the confidence of Elijah every time you pray – knowing that you, too, are praying to the living God, who hears you and will act on your behalf.

Every time we pray, 'Come, Holy Spirit', we are asking God to repeat the miracle of Pentecost when the fire of God came on all the people. We do not need to shout or stir up emotion – we simply need to ask.

In response to Elijah's prayer, the fire of the Lord fell (v.38). When all the people saw this they fell prostrate and cried, 'The LORD – he is God! The LORD – he is God!' (v.39).

This was a wonderful miracle, but Elijah is no different from us – he was just a human being (see James 5:17). After this spiritual high, he experienced an emotional low. He was 'exhausted' (1 Kings 19:5, MSG). He became afraid, discouraged, depressed and almost suicidal: 'Enough of this, GOD! Take my life' (v.4, MSG). When we are exhausted we can easily feel abused, misunderstood and mistreated. After a good sleep and some food, he was re-energised.

Nevertheless, he felt that he was the only one left (vv.10b,14b) and that everyone was out to get him.

It was not actually true, as there were 'seven thousand in Israel – all whose knees have not bowed down to Baal' (v.18). But it is easy to feel isolated and alone in your place of work, your family or your neighbourhood. When you come together (for example on a Sunday) you are reminded that you are not alone.

The ways of the Holy Spirit are gentle. God spoke to Elijah. He was not in a 'great and powerful wind', nor in an 'earthquake', nor in a 'fire' but in a 'gentle whisper' (vv.11–12). We often need to get away from the noise and find a place and time of quiet to hear God's gentle whisper deep within our spirit.

PRAYER

Thank you, Lord, that you, the God of miracles, the God who raised Jesus from the dead, the God who answers by fire, the God who brings water from the rock – you communicate in a gentle whisper. Help me today to hear your voice.

28 June | Day 179
Power Encounters

A few years ago, David (not his real name), a young lawyer, was in our small group on Alpha. On the first night, he told us that he was an atheist and had come with a sole purpose of disrupting the small group, which he attempted to do every time he came. Unlike many who come with this attitude, he did not change at all throughout the course.

After the talk on 'How Can I Resist Evil?', one young woman, Sarah (not her real name), who was not a Christian, said that she definitely did not believe in the power of evil. This was a major stumbling-block to her becoming a Christian.

But later that evening David became extremely angry for no apparent reason and, as if he were taken over by a demonic power, he physically threatened one of the helpers in our group in a terrifying way. Sarah happened to witness the incident. She saw God's power at work in the gentle, restrained reaction of the helper. Her eyes were opened to the whole spiritual world. She put her faith in Jesus that night.

John Wimber defined 'power encounters' as the clashing of the kingdom of God and the kingdom of Satan.

The apostle Paul writes, 'Our struggle is not against flesh and blood, but … against the spiritual forces of evil' (Ephesians 6:12). God's power in you is so much greater than the power of evil.

READING FROM PSALMS

Psalm 78:32–39
Understand the nature of evil

God wants us to learn from our mistakes and not to keep on repeating the same sins over and over again. The history of the people of God is that, 'in spite of' all that God did for them, 'they *kept on sinning*' (v.32a).

God, in his love for us, respects our freedom. Although he has the power to overrule our freedom, he does not. He acted supernaturally on behalf of his people. Yet, 'In spite of his wonders, they did not believe' (v.32b).

He disciplined them and they would return to him (v.34). 'But they didn't mean a word of it; they lied through their teeth the whole time. They could not have cared less about him' (vv.36–37, MSG). Yet over and over again he was full of compassion and mercy, forgave 'their iniquities and did not destroy them' (v.38).

Why does evil seem to prevail so often in spite of God's power? Perhaps this passage gives us part of the answer. It is not simply an encounter between the supernatural power of God and the supernatural power of evil. Human beings and human freedom are part of the equation. As the apostle James writes, 'Each of you is tempted when, by your own evil desire, you are dragged away and enticed' (James 1:14).

As you read of God's power in this psalm, remember that, through the Holy Spirit, that power now lives in you.

PRAYER

Lord, thank you for your mercy and forgiveness and for the power of the Holy Spirit living in me. Help me always to be loyal to you (Psalm 78:37).

NEW TESTAMENT READING

Acts 18:9–19:13
Take authority over the power of evil

Filled with the power of the Holy Spirit, the apostle Paul took on the powers of evil. He faced 'a united attack' (18:12). 'One night the Lord spoke to Paul in a vision: "Do not be afraid; keep on speaking, do not be silent. For I am with you, and no one is going to attack and harm you"' (vv.9–10). 'That was all he needed to stick it out' (v.11, MSG).

Presumably the Lord spoke to Paul in this way because he was tempted in the face of evil (being hauled off to court again on trumped-up charges) to be afraid, to give up speaking and to be silent. Do not give up in the face of opposition.

Paul saw power encounters between good and evil: 'God did extraordinary miracles through Paul, so that even handkerchiefs and aprons that had touched him were taken to the sick, and their illnesses were cured and the *evil spirits left them*' (19:11–12).

The power of God in Paul's ministry was so impressive that even people who were not Christians tried invoking 'the name of the Lord Jesus over those who were demon-possessed. They would say, "In the name of Jesus, whom Paul preaches, I command you to come out"' (v.13). Tomorrow we will see the dangers of this approach (vv.14–16). The attempt to 'tap the power' of the name of Jesus by these Jewish exorcists had disastrous consequences.

Paul overcame the power of evil through the power of Jesus to perform miracles. This was part of the multifaceted way in which the Holy Spirit worked in his ministry along with:

1. Teaching
'He stayed another year and a half, faithfully *teaching the Word of God* to the Corinthians' (18:11, MSG).

2. Mentoring
Paul spent a great deal of time 'strengthening all the disciples' (v.23). Priscilla and Aquila were probably among those that he mentored. Often those who have been mentored well become the best mentors.

For example, Priscilla and Aquila then mentored Apollos. Apollos was 'a terrific speaker, eloquent and powerful in his preaching of the Scriptures. He was well-educated in the way of the Master and fiery in his enthusiasm' (vv.24–25, MSG).

Priscilla and Aquila took him aside. 'They invited him to their home and explained to him the way of God more adequately' (v.26). He then became even more effective. 'He was a great help to those who by grace had believed' (v.27).

3. 'Ministry'
We see an example of 'ministry' in the power of the Holy Spirit. 'Paul placed his hands on [the Ephesians], the Holy Spirit came on them, and they spoke in tongues and prophesied' (19:6). Every Alpha Weekend, we have the immense privilege of laying hands on people and praying for them to be filled with the Holy Spirit.

4. Discussion
Paul 'had *discussions* daily in the lecture hall of Tyrannus' (v.9). The small group discussion on Alpha is perhaps the most important part of the course. It gives people the opportunity to explore, to talk through issues and to begin to find some answers to their questions.

5. Apologetics
Part of the discussion involved 'apologetics'. This comes from the word '*apologia*', which Paul uses at his trial when he says, 'I make my *defence* (*apologia*)' (26:2). It means presenting a rational basis for the Christian faith against objections and misrepresentations.

Paul 'reasoned' with them (18:19). He argued 'for three months [and] spoke boldly, persuading and arguing and pleading about the kingdom of God' (19:8, AMP). He taught Apollos, who entered into public debate, 'proving from the Scriptures that Jesus was the Christ' (18:28).

We see here some of the different areas of ministry where we need training and that our theological colleges, training schools and discipleship of all church members need to cover.

PRAYER

Lord, help us to minister like Paul in the power of the Spirit by proclaiming the word of God and overcoming the powers of evil through the name of Jesus.

OLD TESTAMENT READING

1 Kings 20:1–21:29
Be prepared to confront evil

Most of us do not like confrontation. But sometimes God calls us to confront evil.

In this passage we read about Ahab who, 'pushed by his wife Jezebel and in open defiance of God, set an all-time record in making big business of evil' (21:25, MSG).

First, we read of an encounter between evil and evil. Ben-Hadad king of Aram attacked Ahab. Out of the mouth of an evil man come wise words: 'One who puts on his armour should not boast like one who takes it off' (20:11). It is never a good idea to boast about what is going to happen. It is better to report it afterwards!

Then, we see how God's power is greater than the power of Aram (chapter 20).

Next, we see just how evil Ahab and Jezebel are in the way they treated Naboth (chapter 21). In order to steal his land, they plotted to have him taken out and stoned to death. Then they stole his vineyard.

Elijah was a man of extraordinary courage. He was utterly fearless in the face of evil. God told him to go and 'confront Ahab' (v.18, MSG). Fearlessly he accused him of theft and murder and told him that he was in 'the business of evil, defying God' (v.20, MSG). He warned him that God's judgment was about to fall on him.

Elijah's words were so powerful that when Ahab heard them he repented: 'He tore his clothes, put on sackcloth and fasted ... and went around meekly' (v.27). Remarkably, God showed him mercy (v.29). No matter what we have done, it is never too late to repent and seek God's mercy.

PRAYER

Lord, help us, like Elijah and the apostle Paul, not to be afraid to take on powers of evil. Give us courage in the face of evil. Fill us with your Holy Spirit.

29 June | Day 180
How to Plan Your Life

Almost everyone makes plans. We make plans about how to spend our evenings, our weekends or our holidays. Some people plan how many children they are going to have; they make plans for their education. We need to plan our finances and our giving. Individuals have plans. Businesses have plans. Churches should have plans.

I love these pages in my own *Bible in One Year*. In June 1992, alongside the verse, 'Commit to the Lord whatever you do, and *your plans will succeed*' (Proverbs 16:3), I wrote the *plans* we had for '92/'93. God blessed these plans more than we could ever have asked or even imagined. Every year thereafter, I have written down the plans for the year ahead. I find it so encouraging and faith building to look back at how much the Lord has done for us over the years. It is so easy to forget his kindness and faithfulness.

READING FROM PROVERBS

Proverbs 15:31–16:7
Our plans

We do not always get it right (certainly I do not). But it is not wrong to make plans. Indeed, it is good to plan ahead. As has been pointed out, it wasn't raining when Noah built the ark! The writer of Proverbs says, 'To human beings belong the plans of the heart ... Commit to the Lord whatever you do, and your plans will succeed' (16:1, 3). Here, we see the key to success.

Your plans should never be made independently of the Lord. You are called into relationship with him. Your plans need to be aligned with his plans. Your vision and your plans need to be led by the Spirit. As you sense God's leading, commit your plans to the Lord. Bring them to him. Lay them before him. Then God promises '*your plans will succeed*' (v.3). What does it mean to commit to the Lord whatever you do?

1. Co-operate

One translation of the Hebrew word for commit is to 'roll towards'. There are two ways to go through life. One is to decide that we are perfectly capable of running our own lives – without God. We make plans independently of God to please ourselves. This is the way of pride (v.5) and independence. The proud cannot be told anything because they think they already know.

The other is to be willing to lay aside your own desires. This is the way of faith and humility: 'Humility comes before honour' (15:33).

God has good plans for your life (Jeremiah 29:11; Romans 12:2; Ephesians 2:10). Co-operate humbly with him, being willing to give up everything that clashes with his purpose for you.

2. Confide

To commit your plans to the Lord means to speak to him about his plans – to make plans together with him. At the start of each day you can commit your plans to him. I find that holidays are a good time to plan ahead and commit the months, or even the year ahead, to God.

I remember hearing the actor David Suchet, when he had recently become a Christian, being asked on the radio whether there were certain roles he would turn down. He replied, 'That is a very difficult question. All I can say is now when I am offered a part I go away and pray about it and if I feel it is wrong I turn it down, whereas before it would have been, "How much?"'

3. Consult

The Lord says, 'Woe ... to those who carry out *plans* that are not mine ... Who go down to Egypt without *consulting me*' (Isaiah 30:1–2a). To commit to the Lord means to consult him and discuss your plans with him and seek his wisdom and advice (Proverbs 15:33a). With major decisions, a wise person will consult others to check that they have accurately heard from the Lord (vv.31–32).

Having committed your plans to the Lord you can trust his promise of success. God is sovereign over your plans. 'Mortals make elaborate plans, but God has the last word' (16:1, MSG). 'In your heart you may plan your course, but the Lord determines your steps' (v.9).

God gives you the freedom and responsibility to make plans. It is positively right for you to do this. And yet, God relates your decisions to your destination. This is not a reason to be passive or fatalistic, but rather it is an encouragement that you can rest assured that God is in ultimate control of your life. You need not be frozen in a state of indecision.

You can trust that God will work out everything for good for those who love him (vv.6b, 7; Romans 8:28).

PRAYER

Lord, I praise and thank you for the amazing way in which you bless the plans I commit to you. This year I want to commit to you all my plans for the future.

NEW TESTAMENT READING

Acts 19:14–41
Paul's plans

Paul was a strategic thinker. He made careful plans. 'After all this had happened, Paul *decided* to go to Jerusalem, passing through Macedonia and Achaia. "After I have been there," he said, "I must visit Rome also." He sent two of his helpers, Timothy and Erastus, to Macedonia, while he stayed in the province of Asia a little longer' (vv.21–22).

Paul's vision, mission and plans revolved around the evangelisation of the whole known world. His strategy focused on cities: Jerusalem, Rome, Corinth and Ephesus.

He spent a great deal of time in these cities preaching the gospel to as many people as possible, whether in the synagogues or in the lecture halls.

He was not unopposed. Interestingly, in Ephesus the opposition was not doctrinal or ethical but economic. Demetrius thought he might lose money as a result of Paul's preaching. So, he stirred up opposition (vv.24–29).

But God also had a plan. Another proverb for today tells us that, 'The Lord works out everything for his own ends' (Proverbs 16:4). In this instance, God worked through the city clerk (Acts 19:35). Even though he didn't seem to believe in God (vv.35–36), his actions still stopped the riots. God often works through those who are not believers to achieve his plans.

PRAYER

Lord, thank you for the example of Paul's planning, strategy and courage in the face of great opposition. Thank you that you work out everything for your own ends. Please guide me in all my plans. Help me to be strategic and courageous.

OLD TESTAMENT READING

1 Kings 22:1–53
God's plans

It is not a good idea to try and outwit God! This was Ahab's problem. He tried to manipulate people and events in order to defeat God's plans.

Jehoshaphat wisely told him that before going to war with Aram he should seek the Lord's counsel: '*Before you do anything, ask God for guidance*' (v.5, MSG). This is another example of the vital principle. If you want your plans to succeed you need to ask God for his guidance in making your plans.

The 400 'puppet' prophets may have been state-employed parrots who simply did what they were paid to do – that is, say whatever the king wanted them to say.

However, Jehoshaphat knows that this is not genuine prophecy and asks, 'Is there not a prophet of the Lord here whom we can enquire of?' (v.7). The king replies, 'There is still one through whom we can enquire of the Lord, but I hate him because he never prophesies anything good about me, but always bad. He is Micaiah son of Imlah' (v.8).

Micaiah, who is a genuine prophet, speaks the word of the Lord to them. Whereas the 400 prophets put forward the popular view, Micaiah was the only one who in fact knew the mind of the Lord. We must not be swayed by popular opinion if it does not come from the Lord. The fact that we may be outnumbered is not conclusive.

Micaiah is courageous enough to speak truth to power: 'As surely as God lives, what God says, I'll say' (v.14, MSG). He warns them of the danger of going against God's plans. For his troubles, he is put in prison on nothing but bread and water (v.27).

Ahab is determined not to listen to the voice of God. He continues his manipulation. He thinks he can outwit God by disguising himself (v.30). But, as we have read, 'The Lord works out everything for his own ends' (Proverbs 16:4).

We see this principle at work as 'someone drew his bow at random and hit the king of Israel between the sections of his armour … the king died … and the dogs licked up his blood, as the word of the Lord had declared' (1 Kings 22:34, 37–38).

Lord, thank you that you are the sovereign Lord and that you control the events of history.

PRAYER

Forgive me, Lord, for the times when I have perhaps known I am on the wrong path but have tried to manipulate events. Help me always to stay in line with your plans. May my plans be your plans, and may these plans succeed.

30 June | Day 181

The Most Powerful Message in the World

At the time that Canon Andrew White was the vicar of St George's Baghdad in Iraq, he sent me an email headed, 'A Day of Tears'. He wrote, 'Well, today has been awful. For two years we have worked every day on getting the two Jasons back. They were my friends; I ate with them and lived with them. These people were not just *hostages* … they were my *friends*. Every day I prayed for them and sought their release…

'I confess that once the news was confirmed about the [killings] I *cried* ... I cannot imagine the pain of their dear families. How terrible it must be for them and how we pray for them.

'As I was *in tears* I was trying to prepare for our service ... Church was great as usual, the people are all so nice and so encouraging; together we shared our pain and love.'

As was the case with the apostle Paul (Acts 20:19, 31, 37), there were *many tears*. Yet, Andrew continues to proclaim the gospel in the power of the Spirit.

The message of Jesus is the most powerful message in the world. It is good news. It changes lives. It changes cities and cultures. Yet it is also a message that provokes opposition. God equips you to pass on this message by giving you the Holy Spirit.

READING FROM PSALMS

Psalm 78:40–55
Explain the good news of rescue from sin

You will never fully understand the good news of the gospel until you understand why you needed rescuing.

Jesus, through his life, death and resurrection and the gift of the Holy Spirit, has rescued us from sin. Here we get a glimpse of what we have been rescued from.

First, we see the *nature of sin*. Sin is rebellion against God: 'They rebelled against him' (v.40). It is not a single act. The psalmist writes, 'How often ... *again and again*' (vv.40–41). Sin comes from not trusting in God's character, God's word and God's actions (vv.41–43).

Second, we see the *consequences of sin*. It grieves God (v.40). It leads to anger, wrath, indignation and hostility (v.49). Ultimately it leads to death (v.50).

It was not only the Egyptians who sinned (vv.43–51) but also God's people (vv.40–42). Nevertheless, God rescued them. He redeemed them (v.42): 'He brought his people out like a flock; he led them like sheep through the desert' (v.52). He guided them safely, so they were unafraid (v.53). All this was preparation for God's great rescue plan in Jesus.

PRAYER

Thank you, Lord, for rescuing and forgiving me through Jesus. Thank you that you lead me and guide me so that I do not need to be afraid.

NEW TESTAMENT READING

Acts 20:1–38
Speak the good news of God's grace

Do not waste a single day of the precious life God has given you. Whatever you are called to do, however difficult your circumstances, you can enjoy your calling and complete the task with joy.

The message of the gospel is a hugely encouraging one. Everywhere Paul went he *encouraged them* to 'keep up the good work' (v.1, MSG). As he travelled around, 'he gave *constant encouragement*, lifting their spirits and charging them with fresh hope' (v.2, MSG).

Paul felt passionately about this message. It was hard to stop him speaking about it. In Troas, he 'kept on talking' (v.7). As 'Paul talked on and on' (v.9), Eutychus fell fast asleep, fell out of the window and died. Paul raised him from the dead and then 'went on telling stories of the faith until dawn!' (v.11, MSG).

It takes a lot to stop a preacher once they've started – members of the congregation dying and rising again only causes a coffee break!

Take every opportunity to get the message out. Paul said, 'I have *not hesitated to preach* to you anything that would be helpful to you ... I have not hesitated to proclaim to you the whole will of God' (vv.20, 27). He spoke both '*publicly and* from *house to house*' (v.20).

It was hard work (v.35). Paul laid his life on the line (v.19, MSG). He was not afraid to die in the process. He did not regard himself as indispensable: 'Neither do I esteem my life dear to myself, if only I may finish my course with joy' (v.24, AMP).

He knew that it would not be 'any picnic, for the Holy Spirit has let me know repeatedly and clearly that there are hard times and imprisonment ahead' (v.23, MSG). He was severely tested (v.19). There were lots of tears (vv.19, 31, 37).

Why is it worth going through all of this? We see here three reasons:

1. The Power of words

You have the most powerful message in the world. Paul went around preaching the message 'of God's grace' (v.24), the 'incredibly extravagant generosity of God' (MSG). It was 'the truth' (v.30).

It was all about Jesus. Grace is undeserved love. It is made possible through Jesus and 'his own blood' (v.28). It cannot be earned. It is a free gift.

How do you receive the gift? First, turn to God in repentance (v.21). *Repentance* is such a positive word. It means turning *away from* sin and *to* God.

Second, have *faith* in our Lord Jesus (v.21). You receive the gift by faith in Jesus Christ.

2. The Power of the Holy Spirit

You have the Holy Spirit living in you. Everyone who repents of their sins and puts their faith in Jesus Christ receives the Holy Spirit. Paul speaks about how he is '*compelled by the Spirit*' (v.22). The Holy Spirit speaks to us (v.23). It is the Holy Spirit who anoints and raises up leaders.

3. The Power of giving

You will be blessed as you give. Paul knew that money is not the key to happiness: '... keep remembering that our Master said, "*You're far happier giving than getting*"' (v.35, MSG).

Paul preaches 'the whole will of God' (v.27). That includes a lot! In this passage we only get a glimpse. But it clearly includes the word of God (v.32), prayer (v.36), a church of overseers and shepherds (v.28), the sacraments (vv.7–11), sanctification (v.32), helping the weak (v.35), and much else besides.

PRAYER

Thank you, Lord, that you have given me the power of the Holy Spirit. Give me courage to face hard work, tears and all the other obstacles in order to 'finish the race' and 'complete the task' you have given to me (v.24).

OLD TESTAMENT READING

2 Kings 1:1–2:25
Tell the good news about Jesus

Good leaders train up successors. This is one of the examples in the Bible of where succession worked really well.

A good mentor is a great gift. Elijah was a mentor to Elisha and passed on his power to him. Elisha had asked, 'Let me inherit a *double portion of your spirit*' (2:9). He wanted to be a holy man, just like his mentor.

Elijah told him he could get what he asked for if he stuck with him to the very end: 'If you're watching when I'm taken from you, you'll get what you've asked for. But only if you're watching (v.10, MSG).

'Stickability' is so important in ministry. It is easy to start off with zeal and enthusiasm, but not everyone has the 'stickability' to endure hard work, difficulties and disappointments and see things through to the end in the way that Elisha did.

Elisha did indeed receive 'a double portion'. (The book of Kings records that Elisha performed twice as many miracles as his mentor.) The mantle of Elijah fell on Elisha (v.13). It was clear to all who were watching that Elisha was the anointed successor: 'the spirit of Elijah is resting on Elisha' (v.15).

The account of Elijah and his extraordinary power to call down fire from heaven (1:12) and to divide the waters (2:8), should be read in the light of the New Testament. Elijah prefigured John the Baptist. John ministered 'in the spirit and power of Elijah' (Luke 1:14), preparing the way for Jesus.

Jesus says that you are better off than Elijah or Elisha. He says, 'Among those born of women there has not risen anyone greater than John the Baptist' (the Elijah who was to come). Yet he goes on, 'Whoever is least in the kingdom of heaven is greater than he' (Matthew 11:11). Every Christian is in a better position than Elijah and John the Baptist for at least two reasons.

First, you are in a better position to tell the good news about Jesus. Second, you have the gift of the Holy Spirit given on the day of Pentecost. Every Christian ('whoever is least in the kingdom of heaven') has the opportunity to proclaim the gospel in the power of the Holy Spirit – the most powerful message in the world.

PRAYER

Lord, thank you for the amazing privilege you have given to me and to every Christian – being able to pass on the most powerful message in the world. Thank you that this message transforms lives, communities and cultures.

1 July | Day 182
Seven Characteristics of Great Leaders

An online survey listed all the qualities that people expect from 'perfect' pastors:

They preach for exactly twelve minutes.

They are twenty-eight years of age but have been preaching for thirty years.

They work from 8 a.m. until midnight every day, and are also the caretaker.

They frequently condemn sin, but never upset anyone.

They wear good clothes, buy good books, drive a good car, give generously to the poor and have a low salary.

They make fifteen daily calls to parish families, visit the housebound and the hospitalised, spend all their time evangelising the un-churched and are always in the office when they are needed.

They are also very good-looking!

Of course, we all know that there is no such thing as a 'perfect pastor'. Nevertheless, daunted by the high expectations that people have of their church leaders, on 1 July 2004 (when I had been asked to take on the role of vicar at HTB in London), I felt both excited and a little overwhelmed by the responsibility. That day, I wrote my prayer in the margin of my *Bible in One Year*: that I, like David, would *shepherd* the people with integrity of heart and lead them with skilful hands (Psalm 78:72). This is still my prayer today.

In yesterday's passage we saw how Paul said to the Ephesian elders, 'Keep watch over yourselves and all the flock of which the Holy Spirit has made you overseers. *Be shepherds* of the church of God, which he bought with his own blood' (Acts 20:28). Pope Francis urged the spiritual leaders of the church to 'be shepherds living with the smell of sheep'.[1]

The task of an overseer is to pastor God's flock, following the example of Jesus who said, 'I am *the good shepherd*' (John 10:11). In the passages for today we see seven characteristics of good shepherds which are seen in all great Christian leaders.

READING FROM PSALMS

Psalm 78:56–72
Integrity and skill

Great leadership is rare. As we look around the world today, there are not many countries that are led well.

As the psalmist looks back at Hebrew history, there wasn't much good leadership around. It was a story of rebellion against God: 'traitors – crooked as a corkscrew' (v.57, MSG).

God was looking for a man after his own heart. God led the people *like a shepherd*: 'Then he led his people out like sheep, took his flock safely through the wilderness. He took good care of them; they had nothing to fear' (vv.52–53, MSG).

Eventually he found David, a rare example in the Old Testament of great (though not perfect) leadership: 'He chose David his servant ... to be the shepherd of his people Jacob, of Israel his inheritance. And *David shepherded them with integrity of heart; with skilful hands he led them*' (vv.70–72).

David had the experience of being a shepherd in the literal sense. God 'took him from the sheep pens; from tending the sheep' (v.70). He used these skills to be a shepherd also in the metaphorical sense of the leader and pastor of God's people:

1. Integrity of heart

'Integrity' is the opposite of 'hypocrisy'. The word integrity comes from the Latin *integer* meaning 'whole'. It describes an undivided life, a 'wholeness' that comes from qualities such as honesty and consistency of character. It means acting according to the values, beliefs and principles we claim to hold.

The pastoral care of God's people must be done with integrity of heart. This is the most important characteristic. People said of Jesus, 'we know you are a man of *integrity*' (Mark 12:14). Many leaders have reflected on the importance of integrity in their role:

Former US President Eisenhower, Supreme Commander of the Allied Forces in Western Europe during World War II said, 'The supreme quality for leadership is unquestionably *integrity*. Without it, no real success is possible, no matter whether it is ... on a football field, in an army, or in an office.'

2. Skilful hands

David was a skilful shepherd. He had learnt to protect the flock with his sling. He went on to lead the people of Israel with great skill. There are leadership skills to be learnt.

We learn these skills through watching and following good examples, listening to the wisdom of others, asking questions of those we admire, learning together with our peers and, above all, through practice.

PRAYER

Lord, help us to be good shepherds in every area of our lives, leading well in our churches, businesses, community and culture. Help us to pastor with integrity of heart and lead with skilful hands.

NEW TESTAMENT READING

Acts 21:1–26
Love, service and sensitivity

I love it when leaders, from over 100 countries around the world where Alpha is run, come together at Alpha Global Week for teaching, ministry and encouragement. When each leader reports 'in detail what God has done … through [their] ministry' (21:19) I am reminded of this passage.

We read here how 'Paul told the story, detail by detail, of what God had done among the non-Jewish people through his ministry. They listened with delight and gave God the glory. They had a story to tell, too: "And just look at what's been happening here – thousands upon thousands of God-fearing Jews have become believers in Jesus!"' (vv.19–20, MSG).

We saw yesterday that Paul said to the Ephesian elders, 'Be shepherds of the church of God' and 'keep watch over … the flock' (20:28). Today, we see examples of all this in action:

3. Love

Love and leadership go hand in hand. If you love people you will get close enough to them so that, in the words of Pope Francis, you smell of the sheep. Paul was an example of a good shepherd. Everywhere he went he met up with the disciples (21:4, 7). He prayed with them (v.5), he loved them so much that when it was time to leave he had to tear himself away from them (v.1).

In his love for them Paul had warned about savage wolves (20:29). Yet Paul also loves them through encouraging them and building up their faith. He 'reported in detail what God had done among the Gentiles through his ministry' (21:19).

4. Service

The prophet Agabus warned Paul of what awaited him in Jerusalem. They pleaded with Paul not to go to Jerusalem, but Paul answered, 'Why are you weeping and breaking my heart? I am ready not only to be bound, but also *to die* in Jerusalem for the name of the Lord Jesus' (v.13).

Jesus set the model of servant leadership (see for example Mark 10:45). Paul was willing to follow Jesus, 'The good shepherd [who] lays down his life for the sheep' (John 10:11). As Oswald Sanders wrote, 'True leadership is achieved not by reducing people to one's service, but in giving oneself in selfless service to them.'

5. Sensitivity

We often think of Paul's pioneering drive and bold approach; however, he also showed sensitivity to the culture of Jerusalem. He purified himself and his companions, in accordance with the ceremonial laws, in order that nothing would distract from what God was doing (Acts 21:24–26).

PRAYER

Lord, help us to have that same love and care for your people. Help us to protect them from the wolves. Give us the courage to be willing to make sacrifices on their behalf.

OLD TESTAMENT READING

2 Kings 3:1–4:37
Compassion and prayer

We see in this passage why the image of the shepherd was such a popular one in the Bible – there were lots of sheep around. 'Mesha king of Moab raised sheep, and he had to supply the king of Israel with a hundred thousand lambs and with the wool of a hundred thousand rams' (3:4).

The events we read of took place in the ninth century BC. Joram reigned from 852 to 841 BC. Alongside the wars there were clearly domestic problems and injustices within Israel. We see an example in the way the widow and her sons were about to be taken as slaves (4:1).

Into this situation, Elisha comes to the rescue. Like a good shepherd, he loves and cares for the people. He says, 'How can I help you?' (v.2). He rescues this widow from the terrible curse of excessive debt and the potential slavery that was about to result from it.

6. Compassion

Next, Elisha, this 'holy man of God' (v.9) has compassion for the Shunammite woman who had been unable to conceive. She discovered that God honours those who provide hospitality. He speaks the word of the Lord to her and as a result, she conceives (vv.15–17).

7. Prayer
When her son dies, he prays to the Lord (v.33). He gives him a form of supernatural mouth-to-mouth resuscitation and he revives and sneezes seven times (vv.34–35).

PRAYER
Lord, give us that same compassion for your people – especially for the marginalised, the poor and the suffering. Help us to bring your love and your healing. Help us to be more like Jesus, 'the good shepherd' (John 10:11), who loves his flock and is willing to lay down his life for them.

2 July | Day 183
Transform Your World

My new friend from Scotland, Dez, told me, 'I was a doorman; a bouncer. I was quite a violent guy. I took a lot of drugs. I was a cocaine addict. My life revolved around fighting, taking drugs, partying and living in that cycle.'

He said, 'One night I had taken a massive overdose. I felt like I was having a heart attack. My heart was jumping out of my chest. And I cried out in what I didn't know then was a prayer: to live. And I woke up the next day and I never touched coke again.'

After that, Dez kept meeting Christians. One in particular was Fiona, who really lived out her faith. He asked her out a few times, but she said 'No'. Mainly because he wasn't a Christian.

She gave him a Bible and he started reading: 'I started tearing through it trying to find something and I ended up finding Jesus. Suddenly, my whole life made sense.'

He called Fiona and asked her to take him to church. There he heard about Alpha. 'On Alpha, I met Jesus and it changed my life. I was this drug-fuelled, violent person and now I love people and love God. I just want to share my story.'

Dez has just finished his studies in Theology and is working for Alpha Scotland. And, he married Fiona. He is now a happy husband and a loving father.

Dez sums up his complete transformation: 'Jesus turned the questions I had about whether God exists into a belief that God cares about me. I have changed from a violent, loveless drug addict to a man who is happily married and full of love. I'm now running Alphas for all types of people, from gangs to grannies, and I'm seeing their lives changed.'

READING FROM PSALMS

Psalm 79:1–13
Pray for the transformation of your nation

Change is possible. God can transform individual lives. He can also transform cities and nations.

In the sixth century BC, the people of God went into exile: 'God! Barbarians have broken into your home, violated your holy temple, left Jerusalem a pile of rubble! ... We're nothing but a joke to our neighbors, graffiti scrawled on the city walls' (vv.1, 4, MSG). As the psalmist considers the destruction of the temple and the exile, he sees that God's name is dishonoured.

In the UK today, we see churches being closed and God's name dishonoured. God's people are once again the object of scorn and derision.

The psalmist prays, 'How long do we have to put up with this, GOD? ... we're at the end of our rope. You're famous for helping; God, give *us* a break. Your reputation is on the line. Pull us out of this mess, forgive us our sins – do what you're famous for doing!' (vv.5, 8–9, MSG).

This is a prayer of desperation. It is also a prayer of faith. God has the power to transform the situation. Dare to dream about a time when God answers your prayer for your nation: 'Then we your people ... will praise you for ever' (v.13).

PRAYER
Lord, as we look at our city and our nation, we cry out to you for help. May this nation be a place where, once again, your name is honoured.

NEW TESTAMENT READING

Acts 21:27–22:21
Testify to the transformation in your life

You have a testimony about the transformation Jesus has brought to your life. It may not be as dramatic as Dez's story or the apostle Paul's. Nevertheless, your story of a relationship with Jesus is powerful.

Once again, Paul was in trouble. The crowd had been 'stirred up' (Acts 21:27). People had made false assumptions about him (v.29); they were trying to 'kill him' (v.31). They beat him (v.32) and arrested him (v.33). He was 'secured with two chains' (v.33, AMP). He faced mob violence (v.35). How did he respond?

He told them about Jesus. As so often, he told his testimony, sharing what Jesus had done in his life. It is a very good model of how you should give your testimony whenever the opportunity arises. The Holy Spirit is living within you and he always brings about change in our lives as he transforms us into the likeness of Jesus (2 Corinthians 3:18). When you have an opportunity to tell your story, what should you say?

1. Tell them what you were like before

Identify with your audience. Paul identifies with his audience. He speaks in Aramaic (Acts 21:40). He stresses the parts of his life that the people of Jerusalem would identify with. Because he is speaking to Jews, he speaks only of his Jewish qualifications: 'I am a good Jew … I've always been passionately on God's side, just as you are right now' (22:3, MSG).

Paul points out that he used to persecute Christians, putting them in chains, flogging them and having them thrown in prison (vv.4–20), just as they were attempting to do to him at that moment.

When you give your testimony, find points of contact with your audience. For example, Alpha testimonies often begin with elements of their story that others can relate to, or which are likely to resonate with the guests. They start by saying things like, 'I was an atheist … I was an alcoholic … I was a drug addict … I was antagonistic to the church.'

2. Tell them what happened to you

Paul then gives a very detailed account of what happened to him when he encountered Jesus. He heard Jesus' voice when he appeared before him on the road to Damascus. Jesus asked him questions and gave him commands. Paul listened and did as Jesus instructed.

We encourage people to describe their conversion in very concrete terms, as Paul does in this passage. It is the details that make it real and powerful.

3. Describe the difference Jesus has made in your life

Ananias told Paul to be a 'key witness to everyone you meet of what you've seen and heard. So what are you waiting for? Get up and get yourself baptized, scrubbed clean of those sins and personally acquainted with God' (vv.15–16, MSG). The one who had gone around persecuting Christians was *called to preach the gospel* to the Gentiles (v.21).

Again, we encourage people who give their testimony to describe in a concrete way, the transformation Jesus has made in their lives. There is great power in the story of a changed life. Telling your story is a way you can play a part in transforming the world around you.

PRAYER

Lord, thank you for the power of a testimony. Help me never to grow tired of describing the transformation Jesus has made in my life.

OLD TESTAMENT READING

2 Kings 4:38–6:23
Recognise that transformation is an act of grace

God performed several miracles through Elisha. There were feeding miracles (4:38–44), an axe-head floating (6:1–7) and blinded Arameans (vv.8–23). Not only were miracles performed through him, but he also had an extraordinary prophetic gift: 'Elisha, the prophet who is in Israel, tells the king of Israel the very words you speak in your bedroom' (v.12). In the middle of these accounts we read of a remarkable transformation in a Syrian general's life.

Naaman was general of the army under the king of Aram. He was 'a truly great man' (5:1, MSG). But he had a problem; 'he had leprosy' (v.1). He hears about the possibility of healing through the power of God via a young servant girl (vv.2–4).

He is used to getting things by using his power and his money: 'So he went off, taking with him about 750 pounds of silver, 150 pounds of gold, and ten sets of clothes' (v.5, MSG).

When he eventually gets to meet Elisha's messenger, he is told, 'Go to the River Jordan and immerse yourself seven times. Your skin will be healed and you'll be as good as new' (v.10, MSG). Initially, he loses his temper and stomps off (vv.11–12). He expected to be healed in a grander and less humbling way. Pride can keep you from receiving everything God wants to give you.

However, encouraged by his servant, he dips himself in the Jordan seven times and 'his flesh was restored and became clean like that of a young boy' (v.14). He is utterly transformed. He says, 'Now I know that there is no God in all the world except in Israel' (v.15).

He offers to pay for his healing. Elisha refuses to accept anything. Gehazi makes the terrible mistake of trying to make money out of God's grace (vv.19–27). Healing and transformation are *a gift from God by grace*. They cannot be earned.

PRAYER

Father, thank you for your miraculous power to heal and to save. Help me to have the same attitude as Elisha and never to try to take any credit, whether material or otherwise, for myself. Thank you that transformation comes by grace. It is a gift of your undeserved love.

3 July | Day 184
God's Purposes for You

I trained as a lawyer and worked as a barrister. Then, back in 1981, Pippa and I felt that God was calling us to full-time ministry in the Church of England and for me to become an ordained minister. We also felt that we should do our training in Durham, starting in September 1982. I was at the top of the waiting list for the theological college at Durham University. I was told it was almost certain someone would drop out and I was virtually guaranteed a place. Based on this I announced our plans widely, including telling all my colleagues at work that I was leaving.

Just before I was due to start we received news that, exceptionally, no one had dropped out that year and it would not be possible for us to go. We tried everything to persuade them to change their minds. We desperately tried to find another theological college that would accept us. We prayed and pushed as hard as we could but to no avail. The door was firmly shut.

The following year was extremely difficult. I was given very little work by my workplace as people knew I was leaving and so had no incentive to build my career. It was a huge disappointment and mystifying at the time.

In the end, Pippa and I went to Oxford to study the following year and I eventually started as an assistant pastor at HTB in 1986. With hindsight, had we got the place at Durham, the timing would have meant that a job at HTB would have been out of the question and we would not be doing what we are doing today. I am so thankful to God that he blocked our plans and strategically ordered our steps.

If you are going through a setback or disappointment, remember that his purposes for you are 'good, pleasing and perfect' (Romans 12:2). Nothing happens without God's permission. God is in control and *in everything* he is working for good (8:28).

READING FROM PROVERBS

Proverbs 16:8–17
God orders your steps through human plans

It is right to plan. However, we need to do it with the necessary humility, recognising that our plans will only succeed 'if it is the Lord's will' (see James 4:13–15). The writer of Proverbs says, 'In your heart *you may plan your course*, but *the Lord determines your steps*' (Proverbs 16:9).

Sometimes we align our plans with God's purposes. At other times – certainly in my experience – God overrules our plans. We should always bear in mind that we may have got it wrong and that, ultimately, thankfully, *it is the Lord who determines our steps*.

God often works out his purposes through good leadership. Good leaders motivate others (v.10). They do not base their decisions simply on what is popular: 'Sound leadership has a moral foundation' (v.12b, MSG). They cultivate an environment of transparency: 'Good leaders cultivate honest speech; they love advisors who tell them the truth' (v.13, MSG). They 'invigorate lives; they're like spring rain and sunshine' (v.15, MSG).

PRAYER

Thank you, Lord, that although I make plans in my heart, ultimately you determine my steps.

NEW TESTAMENT READING

Acts 22:22–23:11
God orders your steps in spite of human opposition

Are you worried about your future? Are you facing difficulties and opposition or in a time of crisis? Are there plans against you?

There are a number of competing plans in this story. How do these interact with God's purposes?

1. The crowd

The crowd plan to 'rid the earth' of Paul (22:22). While it causes Paul hardship, ultimately it fails because their plans are against God's purpose.

2. The commander

The 'commander', a man of military power, plans to have Paul flogged (v.24). Paul is taken to the torture chamber but the plan failed because it was illegal to flog a Roman citizen before being convicted, and the commander had not realised that Paul was a Roman citizen.

3. The court

The religious authorities, the Sanhedrin, plan to kill Paul (23:12). Paul is taken to court and placed in the dock (22:30). He points out his innocence: 'Ananias ordered those standing near Paul to strike him on the mouth' (23:2). Paul's response is, 'God will strike you, you whitewashed wall!' (v.3).

Then Paul manages to divide the tribunal (vv.7–8), which consisted of Pharisees (who believed in the resurrection of the dead) and Sadducees (who did not). Paul decides 'to exploit their antagonism' (v.6, MSG). Paul says, in effect, 'Look, the reason I am on trial is that I am a Pharisee and believe in the resurrection of the dead' (v.6).

4. The crises

In the midst of all this, Paul seeks to align his plans with God's plans. He was guided by God. He resolved in the Spirit to go to Jerusalem and then to Rome (19:21). However, in spite of this he hit crisis after crisis.

Paul must have wondered whether he had missed out on God's purposes. But in the middle of this 'crisis', the Lord stood near Paul and said, 'Take courage! *As you have testified about me in Jerusalem, so you must also testify in Rome*' (23:11).

As with Paul, God will strategically order your steps. The sovereignty of God means we don't have to worry about the ultimate outcome. God is in complete control, even though it may not always be easy to see it at the time.

God's purpose is that you, like Paul, should be a witness. Everywhere you go, be a witness. When appropriate, give your testimony. Even when you are not speaking, your life is a testimony. Don't wait until all is going well. In fact, in times of difficulties sometimes your testimony is at its most powerful.

PRAYER

Lord, give me the same courage you gave to the apostle Paul to testify about you wherever I go.

OLD TESTAMENT READING

2 Kings 6:24–8:15
God orders your steps through human agents

God works out his purposes through human agency.

The suffering of the people of Samaria was almost unbearable: famine, food prices soaring astronomically and even cannibalism resulted (6:24–31). The king of Israel made a pathetic excuse for not helping the woman who cried to him, 'Help me, my lord the king!' (v.26). He replied, 'If the LORD does not help you, where can I get help for you?' (v.27). This is the wrong reaction.

The sovereignty of God and his plans is not meant to be an excuse for human inaction. God works through human agents. When you see needs, you are called to be God's hands responding to those needs. This is what Elisha did. God used Elisha. He prophesied, 'Listen! GOD's word! The famine's over. This time tomorrow food will be plentiful' (7:1, MSG).

God used four men with leprosy who discovered where this plentiful food was. As they ate and drank they said to each other, 'We're not doing right. This is a day of good news and we are keeping it to ourselves' (v.9). Food prices dropped over night. Every word Elisha had spoken proved true.

The world produces enough food for everyone, yet one in eight people on this planet are living with the pain of hunger. If we simply feed ourselves 'we are not doing right' (v.9). We must do everything we can to bring an end to extreme poverty in our generation.

This is also a wonderful illustration of our motive for telling others the good news about Jesus. These starving men came across a mountain of food. They realised that God had delivered them from their enemies. They could have kept the good news to themselves, but that would have been utterly selfish.

Yet they were tempted to do so. We have far better news than they had – the good news of Jesus and the gospel. Do not keep it to yourself. You are the human agent responsible for carrying out God's plans.

Similarly, the people in the city could have just stayed there in their lost condition refusing to believe the good news. Indeed, at first the king does not respond very positively. He suspects a trap (v.12). Likewise, today, some people do not respond to the offer of life Jesus makes to every human being because they suspect that there is some trap.

Not only does God work out his purposes through human agents, he sometimes reveals these plans to his prophets. Elisha prophesied at a time of famine that within twenty-four hours food would be in ample supply (v.1). It seemed totally unbelievable at the time (v.2), but God rescued his people (v.6). Elisha's prophecy came true, 'As the LORD had said' (v.16). God also revealed to Elisha what was about to happen to the king (8:8, 13, 15).

PRAYER

Lord, thank you that you have good plans for my life and your purposes will ultimately prevail. Help us to be a blessing to the world, feeding the hungry and bringing the good news of Jesus to a world that desperately needs physical and spiritual food.

4 July | Day 185

Opposition Turned into Opportunity

Stephen came to our home and told me his story. He is the oldest son of a teenage mother from a township in Zimbabwe. She was trapped in a difficult marriage to a man more than twenty years her senior. She dealt with her struggles by drinking heavily.

One day, when Stephen was three years old, his mother took him, his brother and baby sister into town. Saying she needed to go to the toilet, Stephen's mother left him holding his sister in the busy town square, while his brother John played on the ground. Two hours later she had not returned. Their mother had run away, leaving the three children in the reluctant care of an aunt. By the age of eleven, Stephen too had run away – preferring to live on the streets.

Growing up, Stephen developed a strong bitterness against God. As a teenager he was recruited into one of the urban gangs, called the Black Shadows, which carried out violence, theft and destruction on the streets of Zimbabwe.

When a travelling evangelist came to town to speak to thousands of people about Jesus in a large tent, Stephen went to firebomb the event. He carried a bag full of bombs. He wanted to attack the event because he wanted to attack God. As Stephen awaited the moment for his attack, Shadrach Maloka, a South African evangelist, took to the stage and announced that the Holy Spirit had warned him that many in the audience may die soon without Christ. Astonished, the Black Shadows thought someone had figured out their plan. Stephen Lungu was captivated by the preacher.[1]

In each of the passages for today we see attacks of various kinds and how God turns opposition into opportunity.

READING FROM PSALMS

Psalm 80:1–7
God's presence

When you face difficulties in life – opposition and attacks – there is nothing more comforting than the sense of the presence of God; knowing that he is with you, his face smiling on you.

The psalmist faced abuse and mockery from neighbours and enemies (v.6). These attacks caused a lot of grief: 'a diet of tears' (v.5, MSG). God's people had been fed with 'the bread of tears; you have made them drink tears by the bowlful' (v.5).

Whatever difficulties you are facing in your life, God can turn opposition into opportunity. Cry out to God using the prayer from this psalm:

'Restore me, O God;
make your face shine upon me,
that I may be saved' (adapted from vv.3, 7)

NEW TESTAMENT READING

Acts 23:12–35
God's protection

Gustave Flaubert once wrote, 'You can calculate the worth of a man by the number of his enemies, and the importance of a work of art by the amount that it is attacked.'[2] The reason people in the Bible, and the church today, are so embattled is because the work you do is so important. Coming under attack is not a rare event in the Bible. Nor is it a rare event in the life of any Christian. Sometimes you go through periods of relative calm. But further attacks are almost inevitable.

Whatever attacks you face, God is in control. As we saw at the end of yesterday's passage, the Lord appeared to Paul and said, 'It's going to be all right. Everything is going to turn out for the best. You've been a good witness for me here in Jerusalem. Now you're going to be my witness in Rome!' (v.11, MSG).

Paul was kept in custody despite there being no charge under Roman law that would deserve imprisonment. His enemies were determined to kill him and had a plan for his assassination (v.12) that relied, as so often occurs with violence, on lies and deception (v.15).

In fact, all the characters attacking Paul were devious. Commander Claudias Lysias himself was 'economical with the truth' (vv.26–30). He makes no mention in his letter to Felix that he himself had illegally bound Paul and was about to torture a Roman citizen who had not been convicted of any crime.

'But' is the powerful little word that now enters the story (v.16). God, in his providence, protected Paul: '*But* when the son of Paul's sister heard of this plot, he went into the barracks and told Paul' (v.16). When Paul's nephew tells him of the plot, Paul arranges for him to inform the commander who arranges protection for Paul's journey. So God protects Paul.

God seems to have used a combination of Paul's nephew, Paul's own ingenuity and a Roman commander. God's providence and protection sometimes come through those who are not necessarily Christians.

Paul is taken safely to trial with a letter of explanation from the commander. God did not step in to rescue Paul completely though, and he remained under arrest. God protected him and used him in the situation in which he found himself. God's purpose was that Paul would go and testify in Jerusalem and Rome. That is exactly what happened. Opposition turned into opportunity.

PRAYER

Lord, thank you that you can raise up people in any situation for your purposes. As you used Paul to advance your kingdom, Lord I pray that you would use me today. May your kingdom come. May your will be done.

OLD TESTAMENT READING

2 Kings 8:16–9:37
God's peace

Deep within every human heart is a longing for peace. We see this longing during a terrible period in the history of God's people. Yet another king of Judah, Jehoram, was an 'evil man living an evil life' (8:18, MSG). He is followed by Ahaziah who continued 'the same evil-in-GOD's-sight line of sin' (v.27, MSG).

For a moment there is a ray of hope. Elisha arranges for Jehu, son of Jehoshaphat, to be anointed king (9:1–3). A young prophet pours oil on Jehu's head and declares, 'This is what the LORD, the God of Israel, says: "I anoint you king over the LORD's people Israel"' (v.6). Interestingly, Jehu's fellow officers regard the prophet as a 'maniac' (v.11). Later, Jehu himself is seen driving his chariot 'like a maniac' (v.20).

When Jehu begins to carry out his instruction, Joram sends messengers to ask three times, 'Do you come in *peace*?' (vv.17, 19, 22). Jehu replies, 'How can there be *peace* … as long as all the idolatry and witchcraft of your mother Jezebel abound?' (v.22). Jezebel herself asked the same question, 'Have you come in *peace*?' (v.31). The answer was 'no'. Jezebel died a horrible death, the fulfilment of the prophecy that Elijah had given (1 Kings 21:23).

These were days of evil, death and division. Jehu's declaration that there can be no *peace* while Jezebel's wickedness continues in Israel reminds us that *true* peace can only be found in God. The turmoil of these passages is a stark reminder of the need for him to bring salvation and peace – of the need for Jesus.

Jesus said, 'Peace I leave with you; my peace I give you' (John 14:27). The early church preached 'the good news of peace through Jesus Christ' (Acts 10:36). St Paul wrote, 'we have peace with God through our Lord Jesus Christ' (Romans 5:1). 'The mind controlled by the Spirit is life and peace' (8:6). He begins many of his letters, 'Grace and peace to you' (1 Corinthians 1:3; 2 Corinthians 1:2; Galatians 1:3, and so on).

Returning to the story of Stephen Lungu, the speaker's words convinced him about his sins and drew him into an encounter with Jesus. He experienced God's presence. He heard about God's grace and peace.

Stephen staggered forward to the stage, grabbed hold of the speaker's feet and began to sob. That evening, he became a follower of Jesus Christ.

The next morning he presented himself at the local police station and confessed his crimes. The desk sergeant looked at the long charge sheet, listened to his story and released him. Boarding a bus with the morning commuters, Stephen felt so happy that he was compelled to tell others on the bus the good news. Ever since, he has been telling people about Jesus.

Stephen is now a full-time evangelist in Africa, speaking at many events. At an event a few years ago, an old lady came forward wanting to follow Jesus. That woman turned out to be his own mother who had abandoned him all those years ago!

God's presence, protection and peace are a powerful combination. As Stephen says himself, 'Because I look at myself as a miracle of God's grace, so I believe that the power of Jesus Christ to save sinners still exists. If he can change me, he can change anyone.'

In the middle of attacks, whether from neighbours or enemies or authorities, you can have peace knowing that God is in control of events and history and turns opposition into opportunity.

PRAYER

Lord, today I bring my requests to you with thanksgiving and I pray that the peace of God, which transcends all understanding, will guard my heart and my mind in Christ Jesus (see Philippians 4:6–7).

5 July | Day 186

The Light of God's Smile of Blessing Is On You

After the terrifying, appalling and deadly terrorist attack during her concert in 2017, Ariana Grande returned to the Manchester Arena for the 'One Love Manchester' concert. Marcus Mumford, lead singer of the band Mumford and Sons, opened the concert by proclaiming that 'love casts out fear'. In the middle of the concert, Justin Bieber declared, 'I'm not going to let go of love, not going to let go of God. God is good in the midst of darkness. God is in the midst. And he loves you. And he is here for you.' It was like a bright light in the midst of darkness.

St John of the Cross spoke of the 'dark night of the soul'. I have gone through dark times in my life, as have so many Christians. There were dark times for the people of God both in the Old and New Testament times. There have been dark periods in the history of the church. But the light of the gospel has never gone out. The light of Jesus will always outshine the darkness around (John 1:5). You have that light within you by the Holy Spirit and wherever you go you bring a light greater than the darkness around you.

READING FROM PSALMS

Psalm 80:8–19
The light of God's smile

Father Raniero Cantalamessa is famous, among other things, for his smile. His face shines like a light – especially when he smiles. As Mother Teresa put it, 'The smile is the beginning of love.'

How amazing to think of the light of God's smile shining on you! Not only is God with you, but you can also enjoy his favour. The psalmist prays:

'Smile your blessing smile:
That will be our salvation' (v.19, MSG).

The people of Israel were clearly facing dark times. The 'vine' (vv.8, 14) is an image for the nation of Israel. God brought the people of Israel out of Egypt. He cared for it like a vine.

But now the vineyard walls are broken down (v.12). It appears that the vine is cut down and burned with fire (v.16a). 'Trespassers pick its grapes at will ... mice nibble away at what's left' (vv.12–13, MSG). The people are perishing.

The psalmist cries out to God: 'Revive us, and we will call on your name. Restore us, O Lord God Almighty; *make your face shine upon us*, that we may be saved' (vv.18–19).

As we look at the state of the church in this country its walls have been broken down. It appears in a desperate state. Yet God has restored and revived his people in the past. He can do it again today. Cry out for revival.

PRAYER

Revive us again, O Lord, we pray. Fill your people with your Holy Spirit. May the churches again be filled with people serving Jesus with all their hearts. Smile your blessing smile on us.

NEW TESTAMENT READING

Acts 24:1–27
The light of the gospel

Everywhere Paul went he shone 'the light of the gospel'. But not everyone could see it. He wrote, 'The god of this age has blinded the minds of unbelievers, so that they cannot see *the light of the gospel* of the glory of Christ, who is the image of God' (2 Corinthians 4:4).

These were dark times in Paul's life. He was imprisoned and on trial. The prosecution lawyer, Tertullus, is an example of a sycophantic lawyer. He flattered the governor: 'We are most grateful in all times and places for your wise and gentle rule' (Acts 24:2, MSG).

His flattery was followed by false accusations about Paul, suggesting he was 'time and again disturbing the peace, stirring up riots against Jews all over the world, the ringleader of a seditious sect called Nazarenes' (v.5, MSG). The Christian faith was described as a 'sect' (v.5) – rather in the way that some people today might dismiss church as a 'cult'.

Paul makes his defence (v.10 onwards). He deals first with the specific allegations, denying what is not true and admitting what is true. He admits being a follower of Jesus ('the Way', v.14). He clarifies what happened at his hearing before the Sanhedrin (v.21). (Sometimes it is helpful to establish what the facts actually are.)

Paul shows the orthodoxy of his beliefs. He worships the God of history (v.14a). He believes everything in the Scriptures (v.14b). He shares the Jewish hope of the resurrection (v.15). He points out that he believes everything that agrees with the Law and that is written in the Prophets and that he has the same hope in God as the Pharisees, that 'there will be a resurrection of both the righteous and the wicked' (v.15). He points to his clear conscience (v.16), his 'gifts for the poor' (v.17) and his innocence (v.18).

His judge, Felix, was not necessarily evil, but he was weak, dithering, indecisive and politically motivated. He did not want to condemn an innocent man, but he did not have the courage to set him free. As a weak judge, frightened by Paul's words when he did not know what to do, he simply adjourned the proceedings (v.25).

He kept Paul in prison for two years hoping for a bribe. Then even when a new governor was appointed and there was no financial gain to be had from Paul, Felix still didn't release him for political reasons (v.27). He used delay as a device in order to avoid making a decision.

But avoiding a decision is a decision in itself. We cannot avoid responsibility by indecision. Indecision is itself a decision not to act. It is a decision to maintain the status quo. It is an action with consequences.

Paul took every opportunity to shine the light of the gospel. Whenever he could, 'he spoke about faith in Jesus Christ' (v.24).

PRAYER

Lord, help us to make the most of every opportunity. When we are opposed, falsely accused and frustrated, help us, like the apostle Paul, to take every opportunity to shine the light of the gospel in the darkness.

OLD TESTAMENT READING

2 Kings 10:1–11:21
The light of young people

Every year in the UK there are Christian summer festivals for young people. Tens of thousands attend these youth events. Pippa and I had the privilege of visiting one of them. It was so exciting to see the faith, passion and enthusiasm of these young people. It is a great sign of hope for the future. It is a bright light on the horizon. However bad things look, there is hope that the next generation will do better.

If you think you are living in a dark world, study this passage and you will see that there have been times in history that are just as bad, or even worse.

This was another dark period in the history of the people of Israel. It was a time when horrific events took place, such as the slaughter of the seventy princes whose heads were stacked in two piles at the city gates (10:7–8). And there were other massacres as well (v.17, MSG). Jehu was praised for not behaving like the worst of the kings of Israel, King Ahab. In particular, Jehu destroyed Baal worship in Israel

However, he did not turn away from the precedent set by King Jeroboam: the worship of the golden calf (v.29). He 'wasn't careful to walk in God's ways and honour the God of Israel from an undivided heart' (v.31a, MSG).

In Judah things seemed no better. Athaliah tried to massacre the whole royal family (11:1, MSG). But God protected Joash, in much the same way as he protected Moses and Jesus: Jehosheba 'hid him and his nurse in a private room away from Athaliah. He didn't get killed. He was there with her, hidden away for six years in The Temple of God. Athaliah, oblivious to his existence, ruled the country' (vv.2–3, MSG).

Later, 'Jehoiada brought out the king's son and put the crown on him; he presented him with a copy of the covenant and proclaimed him king. They anointed him, and the people clapped their hands and shouted, "Long live the king!"' (v.12). After this, the king 'took his place on the royal throne, and all the people of the land rejoiced. And the city was quiet, because Athaliah had been slain with the sword at the palace' (vv.19–20).

Joash was only seven years old when he became king (v.21) but this young man brought hope for the future (see 2 Kings 12 and 2 Chronicles 24), as so often we see hope in young people. Once again God kept a light shining even in the darkest of times.

PRAYER

Lord, thank you for the children and youth in our own church and the hope they bring. Thank you for the youth movements throughout the world and the light that shines through them. Thank you that even in the darkest of times, you always keep your light shining and that the light of your smile of blessing is on us.

6 July | Day 187

How to Cope with the Challenges of Life

President John F. Kennedy said, 'We stand today on the edge of a new frontier ... but the new frontier of which I speak is not a set of promises – it is *a set of challenges*. It sums up not what I intend to offer the American people, but what I intend to ask of them.'[1]

Life is a set of challenges, problems and hassles. We sometimes imagine that if we could just deal with the immediate challenge that we are facing, all our problems would be over. But life is not like that. If we resolve one problem, others are just around the corner.

The temptation is to see these challenges as preventing us from carrying out the ministry God has given us. In actual fact, dealing with the problems *is* the ministry. As one former Bishop of Kensington put it: 'These are not the problems associated with the ministry, they *are* the ministry.'

The Bible is true to life. The psalmist faced pain and distress. Paul faced false accusation and the frustration of being kept in prison on trumped up charges. The kings in the Old Testament faced battles and a massive building project challenge.

As I read the passages for today, I am reminded that the relatively minor challenges, problems and hassles that I face are nothing compared to what the people of God have faced in the past, and still face around the world today.

READING FROM PSALMS

Psalm 81:1–7
Talk to God about the problems

Are you in a time of testing? God sometimes allows us to be tested, as he allowed his people to be tested by the waters of Meribah (v.7, see also Numbers 20). But he does not want you to face the tests and challenges of life alone. You can talk to him about your problems.

God says, 'I removed the *burden* from their shoulders ... In your distress you called and I *rescued you*' (vv.6a–7a).

'I took the world off your shoulders,
freed you from a life of hard labor.
You called to me in your pain;
I got you out of a bad place' (vv.6–7a, MSG).

Whatever situations or difficulties you may face, you can bring them to God in prayer.

God removed their burdens and rescued them in their distress. The psalmist starts, therefore, with worship, celebration and joy: 'Sing for joy to God our strength!' (v.1).

PRAYER

Lord, thank you that you are my strength and joy as I face challenges and problems in life. Lord, I call on you today to rescue me from...

NEW TESTAMENT READING

Acts 25:1–22
Trust that God is in control

Faith means trusting God. 'Faith', as C. S. Lewis wrote, 'is the art of holding on to things your reason has once accepted, in spite of your changing moods.'[2] It is hard to trust God when everything seems to be going wrong.

Luke records Paul's trial in a very objective and unemotional way. This must have been an extraordinarily frustrating time for Paul. This great leader of the church, evangelist and teacher is locked away, apparently unable to do what he is called to do. He is in custody, enduring the physical constraints and discomfort of imprisonment.

Serious charges are brought against Paul (vv.1–7). He defends himself by pointing out that he has done 'nothing wrong' (vv.8, 10). But Festus was more interested in what people thought (v.9) than in what was right. Our first question should always be, 'What is the *right* thing to do?' But Festus was more concerned about popularity than justice. In the end, Paul appeals to Caesar (v.11).

When King Agrippa arrives, Festus discusses Paul's case with him. Festus says, 'When his accusers got up to speak, they did not charge him with any of the crimes I had expected. Instead, they had some points of dispute with him about their own religion and about *a dead man named Jesus whom Paul claimed was alive*' (vv.18–19).

The resurrection of Jesus should always be at the heart of the message we proclaim. The only accusation that could be made to stick was that Paul was preaching that Jesus was alive, yet numerous other accusations and false charges had been brought against him.

For Paul, in the midst of all these difficulties and frustrations, it must have been very hard to see what good might possibly come out of all the dishonesty, delays and dithering in his trials. Yet, as always, God was at work for good. As Paul himself wrote, 'We know that in *all things God works for the good* of those who love him, who have been called according to his purpose' (Romans 8:28).

First, in the short term, it resulted in an *opportunity* for Paul to speak to Agrippa. After hearing all about Paul, Agrippa said to Festus, 'I would like to hear this man myself' (Acts 25:22). In times of frustration and hassle you never know when opportunities may appear, but sometimes they do.

Second, in the medium term, it resulted in Paul being sent to Rome. Paul had expressed his desire to go to Rome to preach the gospel (see 19:21; Romans 1:15; 15:23), and the Lord himself had spoken to Paul saying that he would testify in Rome (Acts 23:11). It was because of what took place in Paul's defence of himself that he was eventually sent to Rome.

Third, in the long term, 2,000 years later, vast numbers of people have read Paul's story and been encouraged to know that he too faced false imprisonment, accusations and criticism. I suspect that Paul would have been astonished in the midst of all these difficulties to know how much good was going to come of them. You may never know, in this life, how God uses your faithfulness in the face of challenges.

PRAYER

Lord, thank you that you are with us whenever we face accusation and criticism. Thank you that through all of these frustrations of life you work together for the good of those who love you and are called according to your purpose (Romans 8:28).

OLD TESTAMENT READING

2 Kings 12:1–14:22
Take every opportunity that God gives you

In the middle of this rather depressing history of the kings of Israel and Judah, there is an incident in the life of Elisha that encourages you to take every opportunity that God gives you, to be persistent and never give up.

Leaders are a mixed bag. Some do 'evil in the eyes of the LORD' (13:2, 11). Some do 'right in the eyes of the LORD' (14:3).

God is extraordinarily gracious and when Jehoahaz, who did evil in the eyes of the Lord, 'sought the LORD's favour ... the LORD listened to him' (13:4). Whenever you seek the Lord's favour he listens to you.

In this list of leaders, Joash was probably the best example. He 'did what was right in the eyes of the LORD' (12:2), even if it was only for part of his reign.

Joash took on a building project. Like many projects, it took far longer than he expected: 'But by the twenty-third year of King Joash the priests still had not repaired the temple' (v.6). The king calls a meeting and asks, 'Why aren't you repairing the damage done to the temple?' (v.7).

They do eventually get on with the work. They collect the money they need (v.11). They all acted with complete honesty (v.15) and progress was made.

Of course, today, God's temple is no longer primarily a physical building but the people of God. Our money and effort should go into building up the people of God – in number (evangelism), in maturity (discipleship) and in care for the community (social transformation). However, sometimes we need buildings for this and it is not wrong to spend money on the infrastructure of church when necessary.

As well as the challenge of buildings, the people of God faced the challenge of battles. In particular, in this passage we see how they had to face Aram. Elisha says to the king of Israel, 'Get a bow and some arrows ... Take the arrows ... Strike the ground' (13:15–18). The king 'struck it three times and stopped' (v.18c). Elisha said, 'You should have struck the ground five or six times; then you would have defeated Aram and completely destroyed it. But now you will defeat it only three times' (v.19).

I remember reading these verses in 1998 after we had done the first Alpha initiative, inviting the nation to Alpha to hear the good news about Jesus. We were wondering whether to do a second initiative or wait another year or so. I sensed as I read these verses that we should keep on striking the ground again and again.

Whatever challenges you're facing today, keep praying, keep trusting, keep looking for opportunities to serve God and never, ever give up!

PRAYER

Lord, as we face challenges ahead, give us a determination not to give up but to persevere and carry through to the end.

7 July | Day 188
The Dangers of Pride

Back when I was working as a lawyer, I remember a very straightforward case that I thought I was bound to win. I was so confident I decided that it was not worth even bothering to pray about it or commit it to the Lord.

When I stood up to speak, the judge asked me whether I was aware of a case that had changed the law in the last few days. I was not. The result was a very humiliating defeat. As the passage in Proverbs today warns (Proverbs 16:18), pride had come before a fall.

In my humiliation, I cried out to God for help. I read the recent case. Then, I wrote an opinion saying I thought the decision was wrong and would be reversed on appeal. Thankfully, it was.

We were able to go back to court and win the case. The solicitor, rather than judging me for my mistake, was kind enough to be impressed by the opinion I had written and sent me many more cases. So it became a double lesson; not just about the dangers of pride but also about the extraordinary grace of God and how 'things work out when you trust in God' (Proverbs 16:20, MSG).

I try not to forget the lesson I learnt about the dangers of pride and self-reliance whenever I stand up to speak. I would like to say that I have never made the same mistake again but it is a lesson that I have had to re-learn several times.

In English, the word 'pride' can have a good sense. For example, we would not say it is wrong for a person to be proud of their children, or to take pride in their work. However, when the Bible talks about pride it means something different from this and has very negative connotations.

It means to have an excessively high opinion of one's own worth or importance; it suggests arrogant or overbearing conduct. It is the independent spirit that says, 'I have no need of God.' Arguably, therefore, it is at the root of all sin. How should we respond to the temptation and dangers of pride?

READING FROM PROVERBS

Proverbs 16:18–27
Cultivate humility

God wants you to learn to walk in humility and kindness, not arrogance and pride. Pride comes before a fall: 'First pride, then the crash – the bigger the ego, the harder the fall' (v.18, MSG).

We are reminded that 'It's better to live humbly among the poor than to live it up among the rich and famous' (v.19, MSG).

A lack of power is very frustrating at times when we think we know how best to advance the kingdom of God. However, Jesus had very little power from a human point of view. He was 'lowly in spirit and among the oppressed' (v.19).

'Lowliness of spirit', the opposite of pride, brings:

1. Prosperity

Humility means a willingness to learn: 'Those who give heed to instruction prosper' (v.20a).

2. Happiness

The humble trust in God: 'Whoever leans on, trusts in, *and* is confident in the Lord – happy, blessed, and fortunate is he' (v.20b, AMP).

3. Healing

As opposed to the arrogant words of the proud ('scoundrels plot evil, and their speech is like a scorching fire', v.27), the humble use pleasant words ('pleasant words promote instruction', v.21b). 'Pleasant words are a honeycomb, sweet to the soul and *healing* to the bones' (v.24).

PRAYER

Lord, help me always to stay dependent on you, to trust in you.

NEW TESTAMENT READING

Acts 25:23–26:23
Serve and witness

What should you do if you get the opportunity to testify about Jesus? How should you go about telling your story? We see in this passage a great example of what to do.

Paul, on trial, tells the court that Jesus gave him a commission to serve: 'I have appeared to you to appoint you as a *servant* and as a witness' (26:16). As Jesus came 'not to be served, but to serve' (Mark 10:45), all of us are called to be servants and witnesses. A witness humbly points beyond him or herself. Paul humbly points to Jesus. Here we see how he fulfils this calling.

Paul, in prison and on trial, comes face to face with pride and 'great pomp' as he is brought before Agrippa and Bernice (Acts 25:23). It must have been a very daunting experience.

Paul, once again, simply and humbly gives his testimony. He is polite and respectful to King Agrippa (26:2–3). He conforms to custom and social graces. He skilfully selects the parts of his story that are relevant to his audience.

In the first part of his testimony Paul uses 'I' messages as opposed to 'you' messages. Whereas 'you' messages can seem arrogant and patronising, 'I' messages are sometimes more effective, as well as being a more unthreatening and gracious way to make a point.

He says he used to be just like them: '*I too* was convinced that *I* ought to do all that was possible to oppose the name of Jesus of Nazareth. And that is just what *I* did in Jerusalem ... *I* put many of the saints in prison, and when they were put to death, *I* cast *my* vote against them' (vv.9–10).

The implicit message is, 'I was just like you. I was full of pride, power and pomp. I did what you are now doing. I persecuted Christians just as you are now persecuting me.'

He then tells how Jesus appeared to him and pointed out that in persecuting Christians, he was actually persecuting Jesus. '*I am Jesus*, whom you are persecuting' (v.15).

Jesus told him, 'I am sending you to them to open their eyes and turn them from darkness to light, and from the power of Satan to God, so that they may receive forgiveness of sins and a place among those who are sanctified by faith in me' (vv.17–18). Through this powerful 'I' message of his testimony, Paul is actually saying to them that *they* are in darkness and under the power of Satan, in need of forgiveness for their sins.

Not only does he point out their needs, he also points out the way to forgiveness: 'I preached that they should repent and turn to God and prove their repentance by their deeds' (v.20). In effect, he is saying to these proud and powerful people, '*You* need to repent and turn to God.'

He goes on, 'I have had God's help to this very day, and so I stand here and testify to small and great alike' (v.22). Paul was willing to speak to everyone, to the powerful and to the weak.

Paul's message was always centred on Jesus, who had appeared to him on the road to Damascus. He testifies that, '*the Christ* must suffer and ... rise from the dead' (v.23, AMP).

PRAYER

Lord, help me to take every opportunity to tell people about Jesus and to follow his example of humble service.

OLD TESTAMENT READING

2 Kings 14:23–15:38
Resist pride

If, for example, you have anyone working for you, or if you are a parent, or if you are in any position of leading as a volunteer, you are in a position of power.

Pride is a particular temptation for anyone in a position of power – whether that power comes from status, success, fame or wealth.

The history of the kings of Israel and Judah demonstrates that it is extremely difficult to become powerful and resist the temptation of pride. During this period, the kings of Judah are doing rather better than the kings of Israel. King after king in Israel did evil in the eyes of the Lord (14:24; 15:18, 24, 28), while in Judah, Azariah and his son Jotham both 'did what was right in the eyes of the LORD' (15:3, 34).

Azariah is also known as Uzziah (v.32). We know something more about him from other parts of the Old Testament (for example, Amos 1:1, Isaiah 6:1f. and 2 Chronicles 26:16–23).

Here we read that although he 'did what was right in the eyes of the LORD ... the high places ... were not removed ... The LORD afflicted the king with leprosy until the day he died' (2 Kings 15:3–5). Why did his life end in such a mess?

The book of Chronicles gives the answer: 'His fame spread far and wide, for he was greatly helped until he became powerful. But after Uzziah became powerful, *his pride led to his downfall*. He was unfaithful to the LORD his God' (2 Chronicles 26:15–16).

This warns us that if God has blessed us with success there is always a temptation to become proud.

PRAYER

Lord, thank you for all the warnings in the Bible, as well as the encouragements. Help me always to take heed of these warnings. Lord, I am utterly dependent on you. Help me to keep my eyes always fixed on Jesus who was all-powerful and yet humbled himself, made himself nothing and took the nature of a servant (Philippians 2:6–8).

8 July | Day 189
Listen to God

In all our relationships, listening is very important. As the philosopher and theologian, Paul Tillich put it, 'The first duty of love is to listen.'

Some people are very good at listening. General George Marshall said, 'Formula for handling people:

- listen to the other person's story
- listen to the other person's *full story*
- listen to the other person's full story *first*.'

Listening to God is one of the keys to your relationship with him. 'To listen', means to hear attentively, 'to pay attention to'. Prayer means giving God your *full attention first*.

READING FROM PSALMS

Psalm 81:8–16
Listen to God speak to you through the Psalms

We all experience physical hunger, which can only be satisfied by food. You also have a spiritual hunger, which can only be satisfied by listening to God. God says, 'If you would but *listen to me*...' (v.8b).

The words of God satisfy your spiritual hunger. God promises, 'Open wide your mouth and I will fill it' (v.10). If you listen to him he says, 'You would be fed with the finest of wheat; with honey from the rock I would satisfy you' (v.16).

On the one hand, he says, 'Listen, dear ones' (v.8a, MSG). God wants the best for you, and warns of the perils of ignoring him. He continues, 'But my people would *not listen to me*; Israel would not submit to me. So I *gave them over* to their stubborn hearts to follow their own devices' (vv.11–12). The result of not listening to God is that he gives us over to the consequences of our own actions (see also, Romans 1:24, 26).

On the other hand, he promises that if you do listen to him he will act on your behalf: 'If my people would but *listen to me*, if Israel would follow my ways, how quickly I would subdue their enemies' (Psalm 81:13–14a).

PRAYER

Lord, thank you that each day I can listen to you and be satisfied as with 'the finest of wheat'. Help me each day to pay attention to what you say, and then to trust you to act on my behalf.

NEW TESTAMENT READING

Acts 26:24–27:12
Listen to God speak to you through the apostles

The apostle Paul was God's messenger. God spoke through him. Those who were listening to Paul in this passage had the opportunity to listen to God.

When Paul was sailing to Rome, the centurion, 'instead of *listening to what Paul said*, followed the advice of the pilot and of the owner of the ship' (27:11). His failure to listen to Paul was almost disastrous.

In the first part of the passage we see Paul in chains before Festus and Agrippa. He was telling the good news about Jesus, his death and resurrection. Festus said, 'You are out of your mind ... your great learning is driving you insane' (26:24). He says, 'Paul, *you're crazy*!' (v.24, MSG). Some people have always thought, and still do, that Christians are just 'a little crazy'.

Paul's response was, 'I am not insane ... What I am saying is *true and reasonable*' (v.25). He did not reply, 'Yes, it is all a bit crazy but I believe it.' He refused to accept the suggestion that his beliefs were irrational.

Paul argued that there is a rational basis for faith. There are good reasons to believe that Jesus Christ rose from the dead. Our faith is '*true and reasonable*' (v.25). We should not be afraid to present logical and reasonable arguments. We need intelligent presentations of the gospel.

However, reason alone is not enough. Before I became a Christian, I had listened to the arguments and the reasons for faith. Not all of my questions had been answered. Nevertheless, I took a step of faith based on what I had heard about Jesus. The moment I took the step of faith it was as if my eyes had been opened and I understood much of what I had not seen before.

Reason will only take us so far. However, when we are trying to persuade people, as Paul was, to follow Jesus, it is important to explain that the message about Jesus is 'true and reasonable'.

Agrippa's response to Paul was, '"Do you think that in such *a short time* you can *persuade* me to be a Christian?" Paul replied, "*Short time or long* – I pray to God that not only you but all who are *listening to me* today may become what I am, except for these chains."' (vv.28–29).

Paul did not mind whether people became Christians through a crisis ('short time') or through a process ('long time'). But he did all in his power to persuade them to become Christians, as he had. Paul was not ashamed to pray that people would become what he was (Galatians 4:12).

Paul had done nothing deserving death or imprisonment (Acts 26:31), yet the civil authorities found a rather pathetic excuse for not setting him free (v.32). This was unjust and unreasonable. It must have been deeply frustrating for Paul.

Yet here we are, 2,000 years later, listening to the words that Paul spoke on that occasion, and through them having the opportunity to listen to God.

PRAYER

Lord, may we become like Paul in his faith and passion. As we tell the good news about Jesus may people have a sense that in listening to us they are listening to God.

OLD TESTAMENT READING

2 Kings 16:1–17:41
Listen to God speak to you through the prophets

God allowed Israel to be taken captive and led away into exile because they refused to *listen to him*.

The history of this period in the book of 2 Kings could be summed up in the words '*not listen*': 'They would *not listen* ... They would *not listen*' (17:14, 40). As we saw yesterday, all the problems the kings and the people of God faced were the result of *not listening* to God.

God spoke to his people through his servants the prophets. 'God had taken a stand against Israel and Judah, speaking clearly through countless holy prophets and seers time and time again ... But they *wouldn't listen*' (vv.13–14, MSG).

This was the reason they went into exile: 'The exile came about because of sin: The children of Israel sinned against GOD ... They did all kinds of things on the sly, things offensive to their GOD' (vv.7–9, MSG).

'They imitated the nations around them although the LORD had ordered them, "Do not do as they do."' (v.15). The result of not listening was that the people of Israel lost the presence of God and were sent into exile in Assyria: 'he thrust them from his presence ... the LORD removed them from his presence' (vv.20, 23).

Like us, so often, they had not been ruthless enough about sin in their lives: 'They honored and worshiped GOD, but not exclusively ... They don't really worship GOD – they don't take seriously what he says regarding how to behave and what to believe' (vv.32, 34 MSG). 'They didn't pay any attention. They kept doing what they'd always done' (v.40, MSG).

Do you sometimes find that your heart is divided between following God and following your own desires? Guard yourself against complacency or carelessness – allowing sin to creep in. Don't let the enemy lead you into disobeying God.

The truth is that God's desire is always to *bless* us. His commands and instruction are given so that you might flourish (see Deuteronomy 6:1–3).

We can see this in the fortunes of the different kings of Israel and Judah. The writer of 1 and 2 Kings gives us a thumbnail assessment of whether each king did what was right in the eyes of the Lord. Every one of the kings of Israel is described as doing 'evil in the eyes of the LORD' (2 Kings 17:2), and it leads to the early destruction of the kingdom (v.8).

In contrast, around half of the kings of Judah are described in broadly positive terms, and around half in broadly negative terms. Under the 'good' kings Judah flourished, and its history is much longer and more positive than Israel's. The reigns of the 'good' kings were generally longer than those of the 'evil' kings. The twelve evil kings reigned for a combined total of 130 years, whereas the ten good kings reigned for a total of 343 years. The 'good' kings still faced all kinds of difficulties and challenges, and following God is no guarantee of an easy life. Yet their example is a powerful reminder of the blessings and wisdom of listening to and following God.

PRAYER

Lord, help me to listen carefully to what you say. Deliver me from secret sins. May I be quick to ask for help – that I may never allow sin to creep into my life. Help me not simply to do what the people around me do. Rather, help me to listen to your voice, follow you and enjoy your presence with me.

9 July | Day 190

Trust in the Lord

One of the biggest obstacles to faith is the suffering of the innocent. It is usually one of the first questions raised in an Alpha small group: 'If there is a God who loves us, how come there is so much suffering in the world? How come there is such injustice and oppression?'

These are very important and necessary questions but there are no easy answers. Yet God is able to meet us in the midst of suffering and struggles. Extraordinarily, it is often the people who have gone through the greatest suffering who have the strongest faith. They testify to the presence of God with them, strengthening and comforting them in the midst of their pain. Betsie ten Boom, as she lay dying in Ravensbrück concentration camp, turned to her sister Corrie and said, 'We must tell them that there is no pit so deep that He is not deeper still. They will listen to us, Corrie, because we have been here.'[1]

Faith involves trusting in the Lord. The people of God in the Bible looked out on a world of suffering. But they trusted in the Lord despite what they saw.

READING FROM PSALMS

Psalm 82:1–8
Trust in the Lord in the midst of injustice and oppression

How do we respond to all the injustice in the world? The psalmist trusts that ultimately God will put things right: 'You've got the whole world in your hands!' (v.8b, MSG).

It is a great blessing to live under a good system of justice. It is a terrible curse to live under corrupt and incompetent judges. But ultimately, God will call them to account.

'God presides' over all other expressions of power ('gods') (v.1). Trust that God is 'The President' – he is in ultimate control.

'God ... puts all the judges in the dock. "Enough! You've corrupted justice long enough"' (v.2, MSG). But faith in God's 'presidency' should never lead to complacency or passivity. The psalmist is passionate to see the world changed.

We are not only to trust God but also we have a duty to do everything within our power to see that justice is done. We must act on behalf of the poor: 'Defend the cause of the weak and fatherless; maintain the rights of the poor and oppressed. Rescue the weak and needy; deliver them from the hand of the wicked' (vv.3–4).

A time will come when things will be put right; injustice will be removed and there will be deliverance from, for example, corrupt governments. He prays: 'Rise up, O God, judge the earth' (v.8a).

While we too hope in God's final judgment, we anticipate that justice by acting now on behalf of the poor and oppressed. We should raise the same challenge to those in power, 'How long will you defend the cause of the unjust?'

PRAYER

Lord, thank you that one day there will be justice for all. You will put things right. In the meantime, help me to act on behalf of the poor and oppressed in our world.

NEW TESTAMENT READING

Acts 27:13–44
Trust in the Lord in the midst of disaster and turmoil

When things go wrong in your life are you sometimes tempted to panic? I know that I am. If everything is going well in our lives, it is relatively easy to trust in the Lord. However, there are times when we face major challenges to our faith. Among his many challenges, trials and sufferings, Paul was shipwrecked three times (2 Corinthians 11:23b–25).

In today's passage, we read of one of these occasions. At first it looked as if Paul had been wrong in predicting disaster as the weather was perfect for the journey (Acts 27:13), but then a hurricane began (v.14). It must have been a terrifying experience. Luke writes, '[they] finally gave up all hope of being saved' (v.20).

Yet, Paul kept on trusting in the Lord, telling those on board to '*have faith in God*', that God was still in control and that he had promised to rescue them (vv.23–25).

It took this disaster for them to listen to Paul. Extraordinarily, Paul the prisoner appears to be completely in charge. He tells them, 'you really should have listened to me' (v.21, MSG). He is the one who stops the sailors jumping ship (v.30).

This is a great example of leadership without title or position. The best leaders are able to lead in whatever circumstances, by influence and persuasion.

The turmoil gave Paul an opportunity to speak about his faith. He takes the opportunity although he must have been suffering greatly from hunger and the effects of the storm.

Paul saw himself as belonging to God ('the God whose I am') and being his servant ('whom I serve') (v.23). But God was not *only* his owner and master; Paul trusted God and had a deep assurance of his love. He knew that God wanted the very best for him, as he does for you today.

Paul assured them, 'Not one of you will lose a single hair from his head' (v.34). And, 'after he said this, he took some bread and gave thanks to God in front of them all. Then he broke it and began to eat' (v.35).

In spite of disaster striking, God was in ultimate control: 'The soldiers planned to kill the prisoners to prevent any of them from swimming away and escaping. But the centurion wanted to spare Paul's life and kept them from carrying out their plan' (vv.42–43a).

God gave Paul favour in the eyes of people as well as in God's own eyes. As a result, 'everyone reached land in safety' (v.44).

Nothing could stop God from saving Paul and using him to work out his purposes and save lives.

PRAYER

Lord, thank you that you can protect me even when disaster strikes. When things go wrong, help me not to be afraid but rather to keep up my courage and to have faith in you.

OLD TESTAMENT READING

2 Kings 18:1–19:13
Trust in the Lord in the midst of evil and distress

It is such a relief to read, at last, about a man who 'trusted in the LORD' (18:5). Hezekiah 'trusted in, leaned on and was confident in the Lord' (v.5, AMP). He put his whole trust in the God of Israel ... And God, for his part, held fast to him through all his adventures' (vv.5–6, MSG).

When Hezekiah became king, one of his first actions was to destroy all the things that prevented the people from obeying God (vv.1–4). Perhaps there are things in your life that are a barrier to you obeying God. Although they may seem vital, there is nothing as vital as obedience to God. God wants to help us to obey him – ask him and he will honour you as he honoured Hezekiah: *'And the LORD was with him; he was successful in whatever he undertook'* (v.7).

In 701 BC, Hezekiah faced a very powerful enemy in the form of the king of Assyria who mocked and ridiculed him. This story is not fictional; you can read about these historical events not only in the Bible but also in other ancient accounts. In Sennacherib's account of these events he writes, 'As to Hezekiah, the Jew, he did not submit to my yoke.' He speaks arrogantly about Hezekiah being overwhelmed by 'the terror inspiring splendour of my lordship'.

Sennacherib scorned Hezekiah's dependence on the Lord (vv.20, 22): 'Do not let Hezekiah persuade you to *trust in the LORD* ... he is misleading you when he says, "The LORD will deliver us."' (vv.30–32).

Somehow Hezekiah must have won the respect of his people because they followed his instructions: 'But the people remained silent and said nothing in reply, because the king had commanded, "Do not answer him."' (v.36).

In the face of his powerful enemy, Hezekiah prayed. 'He tore his clothes and put on sackcloth and went into the temple of the LORD' (19:1). A delegation went to the prophet Isaiah and told him, 'This is what Hezekiah says: This day is a day of distress and rebuke and disgrace ... pray for the remnant that still survives' (vv.3–4).

Isaiah's response was, 'This is what the LORD says: Do not be afraid of what you have heard' (v.6). Not only did Hezekiah himself trust in the Lord, but he also persuaded the people to trust in the Lord.

Over the years, I have written beside this passage a list of the challenges we have faced. It is amazing to look back over the years and see the way in which God has delivered us in so many areas.

Today, whatever challenges you are facing, write them down, put your trust in God, believe that he will be with you and give you success in whatever he asks you to do.

PRAYER

Lord, thank you that I can trust in you in all circumstances. Today, I lay before you all the challenges I am facing... I put my trust in you.

10 July | Day 191
Invisible but Invaluable

Every Monday morning, he phones our offices. He asks about the events and services taking place during the week, and the people involved in them. For decades, Charles and his prayer group have faithfully supported the church in prayer. They are examples of many in our church who intercede for us. Their prayers may be *invisible* but they are also *invaluable*.

The word 'intercession' generally means praying for someone else (although, it can also be used of praying for oneself). We are *all* called to intercession. The apostle Paul writes to Timothy, 'I urge, then, first of all, that requests, prayers, *intercession* and thanksgiving be made for everyone – for kings and all those in authority' (1 Timothy 2:1–2).

Jesus is the great intercessor. He 'made *intercession* for the transgressors' (Isaiah 53:12). He 'is at the right hand of God and is also *interceding for us*' (Romans 8:34; see also Hebrews 7:25). The Holy Spirit also intercedes for us and through us: 'The Spirit himself *intercedes for us* with groans that words cannot express ... the Spirit *intercedes for the saints* in accordance with God's will' (Romans 8:26–27).

In the Old Testament passage for today, we see Isaiah's role as an *intercessor*. Interceding for others is part of the role of a prophet. Intercession was also made by kings, for example, David, Solomon, and Hezekiah. You, too, are called to this invisible but invaluable ministry.

READING FROM PSALMS

Psalm 83:1–18
Intercede for seekers

This psalm is a prayer of intercession – interceding for people to have knowledge of God's final vindication, and for this to result in conversion prior to that final day.

The surrounding nations want to destroy the people of God (v.4). Yet, the psalmist sees this more as an attack on God himself. He refers to them as 'your enemies' (v.2) who 'form an alliance against you' (v.5). This is a reminder that an attack on the people of God is ultimately an attack on God.

The prayer of the psalm is that God's enemies will be routed (vv.9–15). However, it is also intercession for conversion: 'Cover their faces with shame *so that they will seek your name, O Lord*' (v.16). There is an inherent desire that others would seek the one true God: 'Let them know that you, whose name is the Lord – that you alone are the Most High over all the earth' (v.18).

PRAYER

Lord, I pray for all those currently on Alpha, that they will seek your name. I pray that you will act; that you will not keep silent; that people know that you alone are the Most High over all the earth.

NEW TESTAMENT READING

Acts 28:1–16
Intercede for healing

I have sometimes heard it suggested that Christians should no longer pray for physical healing. It is argued that miracles of healing were particular to the ministry of Jesus and the immediate period after his death and resurrection. Some have even suggested that in the period covered by the book of Acts, miracles were already dying out. However, this is clearly *not the case*.

When a viper fastened itself on Paul's hand, he shook off the snake into the fire and suffered no ill effects (vv.3–5). Here we are in the last chapter of Acts and we read of how Paul is an example of Jesus' prophecy about those who believe in him: 'They will pick up snakes with their hands' (Mark 16:18).

When Paul and those with him were in Malta they met with Publius, the chief official of the island: 'He welcomed us to his home and for three days entertained us hospitably. His father was sick in bed, suffering from fever and dysentery. Paul went in to see him and, after prayer, *placed his hands on him and healed him*' (Acts 28:7–8).

This is such a simple model for us to follow. First, when Paul heard that Publius's father was sick, he acted in *faith*. He believed God was able to heal him so, '[He] went in to see him' (v.8).

Second, he acted with *boldness*. Publius's father was presumably not a Christian. Yet Paul was courageous enough to offer to pray for him, and to do so publicly, laying hands on him. It might have been tempting to think, 'What if he's not healed?' 'Will I look a failure?' 'Will it bring the gospel into disrepute?' But Paul took a risk. He acted in faith. He prayed, laid hands on him and God healed him. 'When this had happened, *the rest of the sick on the island came and were cured*' (vv.7–9).

Far from dying out, there is an explosion of miraculous healing as the book of Acts comes to an end. Luke clearly sees that this is something that continues in the life of the church. The real question is not, 'Does God heal today?', but, 'Does God answer prayer today?' If he does, why would we exclude something as important as health? Prayer for healing is an important part of intercession.

Pippa and I have prayed for so many people over the years. It is certainly far from the case that all have been healed. We do not pray for the sick because they *all* get healed. We pray for them because *Jesus told us to do so*. Over these years we have sometimes seen extraordinary healings. Do not be discouraged. Keep on praying with faith and boldness, love and sensitivity.

PRAYER

Lord, help us to have the courage to take every opportunity to lay hands upon those who are sick and to pray for their healing. Thank you that you are a God who heals today.

OLD TESTAMENT READING

2 Kings 19:14–20:21
Intercede for deliverance

Sometimes in your own life you may be faced with seemingly overwhelming problems. This is a great model of how to deal with them. Hezekiah did not despair. He did not panic. He did not give up. He turned to God in prayer.

This account of Hezekiah's prayer and God's deliverance is recorded three times in the Old Testament (see also Isaiah 36–39 and 2 Chronicles 32). Further, the events of this period are corroborated by Babylonian sources.

When Hezekiah received the threatening letter and was faced with a seemingly overwhelming problem, 'He went up to the temple of the LORD and *spread it out before the LORD*' (2 Kings 19:14). He prayed to the Lord, 'O LORD ... you alone are God over all the kingdoms of the earth. You have made heaven and earth. Give ear, O LORD, and hear; open your eyes, O LORD, and see ... Now, O LORD our God, deliver us from his hand, so that all kingdoms on earth may know that you alone, O LORD, are God' (vv.15–19).

Hezekiah's intercession begins by consciously recognising who God is. When we intercede we are speaking to the one who alone is, 'God over all the kingdoms of the earth' (v.15). God has the power to resolve these seemingly overwhelming problems.

Hezekiah's prayer was for God's honour and glory, 'so that all kingdoms on earth may know that you alone, O LORD, are God' (v.19). Jesus taught us to start our prayers, 'Hallowed be your name, your kingdom come' (Matthew 6:9–10).

I love the expression, 'He ... *spread it out before the LORD*' (2 Kings 19:14). Hezekiah spoke to God about the problem. The prophet Isaiah sent a message to Hezekiah saying that God had heard his prayer. He delivered the people from the threat of the Assyrians in answer to Hezekiah's intercession.

Hezekiah also prayed for his healing. He was ill, at the point of death (20:1), and he interceded on his own behalf: 'Hezekiah turned his face to the wall and prayed to the LORD' (v.2). Again, God answered his intercession: 'I have heard your prayer and seen your tears; I will heal you ... I will add fifteen years to your life' (vv.5–6).

Hezekiah experienced God's amazing blessings in answer to his intercession. However, the passage ends with a note of warning. When envoys came from Babylon, Hezekiah showed off all his treasures (vv.12–15). He appeared to be taking the glory for all that the Lord had given him. Isaiah told him that as a result, 'nothing will be left' (v.17). If we take the glory for what the Lord does for us, it is at our own peril.

PRAYER

Lord, as we look around at the state of our city, our nation and our world, we need your deliverance. You alone are God over all the kingdoms of the earth. You made heaven and earth. Give ear, O Lord, and hear; open your eyes, O Lord, and see. Pour out your Holy Spirit again. May we see people seeking your name again. May we see miracles of healing. May we see the evangelisation of our nation, the revitalisation of the church and the transformation of society, so that all kingdoms on earth may know that you alone, O Lord, are God.

11 July | Day 192
Your Words Are Powerful

'The Battle of Britain is about to begin. Upon this battle depends the survival of Christian civilisation.'[1] These words were in a speech given by Sir Winston Churchill to the House of Commons in 1940. Facing defeat, he inspired the nation to fight from the corner, urging them to brace themselves to do their duty and carry themselves in such a way that even a thousand years on people would still say, 'This was their finest hour.' The speech was powerful, the nation responded and ultimately a lasting peace was achieved.

It is one of the speeches that shaped the modern world, displaying the power of words. Speeches have affected the outcome of war, women suffrage, human rights and many other issues.

The apostle James writes that although 'the tongue is a small part of the body ... it makes great boasts' (James 3:5). This small instrument has enormous power. It can cause great damage but it can also bring extraordinary blessings. Your tongue is a powerful instrument.

READING FROM PROVERBS

Proverbs 16:28–17:4
Power to bring peace

The words you speak can be either life-giving or destructive.

Words can cause a great deal of trouble. 'The perverse stir up dissension, and gossips separate close friends' (16:28). Gossip has the power to break up friendships.

It is vital to get control over your tongue: 'Moderation is better than muscle, self-control better than political power' (v.32, MSG).

You have a responsibility, not only for the words that you speak, but also for *whose* words and the *kinds* of words you listen to. 'Evil people relish malicious conversation; the ears of liars itch for dirty gossip" (17:4, MSG). Remember that whoever gossips *to* you will probably gossip *about* you. Just as receiving stolen goods is as serious a crime in the eyes of the law as theft; so listening to gossip is as damaging as gossiping.

How you speak and how you listen will affect the whole atmosphere in your home: 'Better a dry crust with peace and quiet than a house full of feasting, with strife' (v.1).

Your words are powerful. Determine today to speak positive, encouraging words of life and blessing everywhere you go.

PRAYER

Lord, help me to avoid the temptations of gossip and malicious talk. 'Be in the heart of each to whom I speak; in the mouth of each who speaks unto me.'[2]

NEW TESTAMENT READING

Acts 28:17–31
Power to convince and convert

The greatest blessing you can bring to another person is to introduce them to Jesus. God has entrusted you with the most powerful words anyone can utter. The message of Jesus has the power to transform people's lives.

There is enormous power in listening to the words of God. Paul refers to one of the most quoted passages in the entire Old Testament, Isaiah 6:9–10: 'Go to this people and tell them this: "You're going to listen with your ears, but you won't hear a word ... They stick their fingers in their ears so they won't have to listen"' (Acts 28:26–27, MSG).

The gospel message often splits an audience in two. As Paul preached, 'Some of them were persuaded by what he said, but others refused to believe a word of it' (v.24, MSG). As Isaiah had prophesied, some people's hearts become calloused and hardened to the message, while others 'see with their eyes, hear with their ears, understand with their hearts and turn', and so God brings healing (v.27).

Paul's form of imprisonment seems now to be more like house arrest. Though he is still bound with a chain (v.20), he is able to call together the leaders of the Jews (v.17) and gather large numbers to the place where he is staying (v.23). He sets us a good example by opening his home so that as many people as possible can hear the gospel (vv.30–31).

Around the world today there is great opposition against Christians and the Christian faith. Paul was under house arrest because of his beliefs. They said, 'The only thing we know about this Christian sect is that nobody seems to have anything good to say about it' (v.22, MSG).

As many Christians face today, the charges against Paul were fabricated and didn't stick, but he was still imprisoned for a long time.

Against this background, we see the extraordinary power of Paul's words. 'Paul talked to them all day, from morning to evening, explaining everything involved in the kingdom of God, and trying to persuade them all about Jesus by pointing out what Moses and the prophets had written about him' (v.23, MSG). In fact, 'for two years ... he urgently presented all matters of the kingdom of God. He explained everything about Jesus Christ' (vv.30–31, MSG).

Paul's words were powerful because they were focused on Jesus. As we read the Gospels, we see that the central theme of the teaching of Jesus was the kingdom of God. As we read the rest of the New Testament, we see that the central theme of the apostles' teaching was the Lord Jesus Christ. In preaching Jesus, they were preaching the kingdom of God. The two become almost synonymous, as we see here.

PRAYER

Lord, thank you that we have the most powerful words in the world – the message of Jesus. Help me to find the right words to explain, declare and convince others, so that 'they might see with their eyes, hear with their ears, understand with their hearts and turn', and be healed (v.27).

OLD TESTAMENT READING

2 Kings 21:1–22:20
Power to change a nation

History shows that words have the power to change a nation. King Manasseh (696–641 BC) was an evil king. 'He reintroduced all the moral rot and spiritual corruption ... Manasseh led [the people] off the beaten path into practices of evil ... new records in evil ... he was an indiscriminate murderer. He drenched Jerusalem with the innocent blood of his victims' (21:1–16, MSG). His son Amon (641–639 BC) continued in the same vein (vv.20–22).

The book of Chronicles suggests that even for Manasseh there was hope at the end of his life. It is never too late and no sin is too great to receive forgiveness from God (see 2 Chronicles 33).

After this string of evil kings came Josiah (639–609 BC). He was a young man who led his people in great spiritual renewal, restoring worship and leading the people back into a right relationship with God. He was only eight years old when he became king (2 Kings 22:1). He 'did what was right in the eyes of the Lord and walked in the ways of his father David, not turning aside from the right or to the left' (v.2).

Words had a powerful effect on Josiah and on the nation:

1. Power of the written word
While they were working on the temple, Shaphan, the high priest found the 'Book of the Law' (v.8). It appears likely that it was the book of Deuteronomy.

Shaphan read it *for himself* (v.8). Then he read from it *in the presence of the king.* When the king heard the words of the Book of the Law, he tore his robes (in repentance). He realised that they had not obeyed the words of this book (vv.11–13). This led to a change of heart, which led to a changed nation.

This reminds us of the importance of the written word of God. Those of you who have taken up the challenge of reading the whole Bible in one year are engaged in doing something that is not only interesting and informative, but is also life-changing.

2. Power of the spoken word
Not only did God speak to Josiah and the people through his written word, he also spoke through prophecy. Interestingly, it was through a prophetess – Huldah, the wife of Shallum (v.14). This shows that the place of women in ministry has its roots in the Old Testament and in the history of the people of God.

Huldah had a powerful ministry. Indeed, it seemed to have overshadowed her husband's rather more practical role of being 'in charge of the palace wardrobe' (v.14, MSG).

Her spoken words do not contradict the written words of Scripture; rather, they complement and indeed reinforce them: 'This is what the LORD, the God of Israel, says concerning the *words you heard*: "*...I have heard you,* declares the LORD"' (vv.18–19).

She told them that because of the way they responded to the written word of God – they humbled themselves and repented – God had heard their words and responded to them. Their response to the word of God changed the course of history.

PRAYER

Lord, I pray for our nation – that we may once again rediscover the power of the word of God and listen to your prophets, who speak in accordance with your word. May there be repentance and a change of heart in our leaders and in our nation.

12 July | Day 193

How to Restore Your Relationships

Hans worked his way up from being a miner to owning a number of mines. His eldest son, Martin, was very intelligent and went to university at the age of seventeen. A respectable career as a lawyer lay ahead of him. Suddenly, to his father's dismay, he cancelled his registration for the law course and became a monk and then a priest.

Martin wanted to live a righteous life. He fasted for days and spent sleepless nights in prayer, but he was still plagued by his own unrighteousness before a righteous God. Around the age of thirty, as he was studying Romans 1:17, the penny dropped. He later wrote:

> I began to understand that in this verse the righteousness of God is that by which the righteous man lives by the *gift of God*, in other words by faith; and that this sentence, 'the righteousness of God is revealed', refers to a passive righteousness, ie, that by which the merciful God *justifies us by faith*, as it is written, 'The righteous person lives by faith.' This immediately made me feel as if I had been *born again* and *entered through open gates to paradise itself*.[1]

This experience occurred 500 years ago. It not only changed his life, it altered the course of human history. He became one of the pivotal figures of western civilisation, the founder of the Reformation – the seedbed for social, economic and political thought. His name, of course, was Martin Luther.

In essence, righteousness means a *right relationship with God*, which leads to *right relationships with others.* It is a gift made possible through the life, death and resurrection of Jesus. Here lies the secret of restored relationships – first of restored relationship with God and then all other relationships.

READING FROM PSALMS

Psalm 84:1–7
Enjoy the blessings

Dwelling in the presence of God is where the greatest blessings are found. This is one of mine and Pippa's favourite psalms. We had it read at our wedding. We love it because it describes the blessings of living in a restored relationship with God.

1. Longing for God's presence

In every human heart there is a spiritual hunger, which can only be satisfied by living in a right relationship with God. In the presence of God, the soul's longing (v.1, MSG) is satisfied and the heart's cry is answered. The psalmist writes, 'How lovely is your dwelling-place, O LORD Almighty! My soul *yearns*, even *faints*, for the courts of the LORD; *my heart and my flesh cry out* for the living God' (vv.1–2).

2. Blessing of God's presence

As you spend time praying, listening to God through the Bible and worshipping him, you will find that there is no place you would rather be than in his presence. 'Blessed are those who dwell in your house; they are ever praising you' (v.4).

God's presence is a place of blessing, praise and refreshment. It is like rain on thirsty ground (v.6).

3. Strength from God's presence

When our *strength* is in God (v.5), the difficult places, tough situations and the valleys of life can be turned into springs (v.6). As you draw your strength from God in these times, you will find yourself going from '*strength to strength*' (v.7).

Having made the tabernacle and temple the place of his presence in the Old Testament, now, through Jesus Christ, God dwells and is present by his Spirit in the church (Ephesians 2:22) and in our bodies (1 Corinthians 6:19).

PRAYER

Thank you, Lord, for all the blessings of your presence with me. Thank you for the way in which you strengthen me daily with your presence.

NEW TESTAMENT READING

Romans 1:1–17
Receive the gift

You cannot do anything to earn or deserve God's love. You receive it as a gift. Jesus has made you righteous. Through his life, death and resurrection, you can live in a right relationship with God.

How is it that in the life, death and resurrection of Jesus, world history took a new direction? How was it that the life of every man, woman and child on the planet was eternally affected?

In this ground-breaking and hugely influential document of Christian theology (written around AD 59), Paul, who had encountered the risen Jesus himself, takes the well-witnessed fact of the life, death and resurrection of Jesus of Nazareth and thinks through its implications.

It appears that the establishment of a Christian community in Rome had come about, not by any great evangelistic enterprise, but by the presence of Christians in the workplace discharging their ordinary secular duties. If you are in a secular job you can have as big an impact as any full-time evangelist.

Paul is longing to see his friends in Rome (v.11). They are inexperienced beginners, yet Paul has the humility to recognise that he will learn something from them in addition to them learning from him (vv.11–12). 'You have as much to give to me as I do to you' (v.12, MSG). I have found that in every Alpha small group, I learn as much from the guests as they do from us.

It is not only those outside of the church who need to hear the gospel. Paul is eager to preach the gospel *to the Christian community* in Rome (v.15).

He knows full well the temptation to be ashamed. It can be so easy to allow our fears and worries about what other people will think about us to stop us from speaking about Jesus. Yet Paul writes, 'I am *not ashamed* of the gospel, because it is the power of God for the salvation of everyone who believes' (v.16a). He knows also the extraordinary power of the gospel to transform the lives of both Jews and Gentiles (v.16b).

There is no greater privilege than preaching the gospel, 'for in the gospel a righteousness *from God* is revealed, a righteousness that is by faith from first to last' (v.17a). Paul does not contrast this with the Old Testament; rather, he uses the Old Testament to support his argument: 'as it is written: "The righteous will live by faith"' (v.17b, see also Habakkuk 2:4).

Paul is going to say a lot more about this 'righteousness from God'. The good news (gospel) is that God has enabled us to live in this right relationship with him. This righteousness comes from God. It is his gift to you. You cannot earn it. You receive it 'by faith'. You no longer live under guilt and condemnation. Nothing can separate you from God's love for you (Romans 8:1–39).

PRAYER

Lord, thank you that through the life, death and resurrection of Jesus Christ, you make it possible for me to have a restored relationship with you and with others. Thank you that I cannot earn it but receive it as a gift by faith.

OLD TESTAMENT READING

2 Kings 23:1–24:7
Continue to obey

God had always intended that his people should live in a right relationship with him. This relationship is described in terms of a *covenant*. God had rescued his people from Egypt. He committed himself to them totally. He then described to them how they could stay in a right relationship with him. He gave them the commandments to guard right relationship with God and one another. The purpose of these laws was to enable them to flourish.

Again and again, we read in the Old Testament how they did not obey these laws. Disaster came as a result. Occasionally there is a glimmer of hope when they recommit themselves to the covenant relationship with God.

One such glimmer of hope appears in Josiah's reign. 'The king stood by the pillar and before God solemnly committed them all to the *covenant*: to follow God believingly and *obediently*; to follow his instructions, heart and soul, on what to believe and do; *to put into practice the entire covenant*, all that was written in the book. The people stood in affirmation; their commitment was unanimous' (v.3, MSG).

Josiah did carry out a number of reforms (vv.1–25). Sadly, they did not seem to have a lasting impact on the people and after Josiah's death, things went back to the way they had been before. Josiah's life was far from easy, and ended tragically, yet he sought to follow God in all that he did – 'with all his heart and with all his soul and with all his strength' (v.25). He is remembered as one of the heroes of faith.

Thankfully, under the new covenant, the laws are written not on tablets of stone but on your heart. The moment you put your faith in Jesus all the promises of the Old Testament are fulfilled in you. You receive righteousness from God. God gives you the Holy Spirit to enable you to walk in a restored relationship with him and a restored relationship with other people.

PRAYER

Lord, I turn to you today with all my heart and soul and strength. Fill me with your Spirit and help me to obey you fully.

13 July | Day 194
How to Worship God

In his book, *The Vision and the Vow*,[1] Pete Greig tells of how a distinguished art critic was studying an exquisite painting by the Italian Renaissance master Filippino Lippi. He stood in London's National Gallery gazing at the fifteenth-century depiction of Mary holding the infant Jesus on her lap, with saints Dominic and Jerome kneeling nearby. But the painting troubled him. There could be no doubting Lippi's skill, his use of colour or composition. But the proportions of the picture seemed slightly wrong. The hills in the background seemed exaggerated, as if they might topple out of the frame at any minute onto the gallery's polished floor. The two kneeling saints looked awkward and uncomfortable.

Art critic Robert Cumming was not the first to criticise Lippi's work for its poor perspective, but he may well be the last to do so, because at that moment he had a revelation. It suddenly occurred to him that the problem might be his. The painting had never been intended to come anywhere near a gallery. Lippi's painting had been commissioned to hang in a place of prayer.

The dignified critic dropped to his knees in the public gallery before the painting. He suddenly saw what generations of art critics had missed. From his new vantage point, Robert Cumming found himself gazing up at a perfectly proportioned piece. The foreground had moved naturally to the background, while the saints seemed settled – their awkwardness, like the painting itself, having turned to grace. Mary now looked intently and kindly directly at him as he knelt at her feet between saints Dominic and Jerome.

It was not the perspective of the painting that had been wrong all these years, it was the perspective of the people looking at it. Robert Cumming, on bended knee, found a beauty that Robert Cumming the proud art critic could not. The painting only came alive to those on their knees in prayer. The right perspective is the position of worship.

READING FROM PSALMS

Psalm 84:8–12
Discover the blessings of worship

There is nothing in this world that compares to worshipping God, walking in a close relationship with him and enjoying *his favour*. This is what the psalmist prays: 'Hear my prayer, O LORD God Almighty ... look *with favour* on your anointed one' (vv.8–9).

This psalm is all about the blessings of worshipping God in his dwelling place (during this period, it was the Jerusalem temple). Those who dwell in God's house are blessed and they 'are ever praising you' (v.4).

The psalmist says he would rather spend one day in the presence of God than a thousand elsewhere: 'One day spent in your house, this beautiful place of worship, beats thousands spent on Greek island beaches. I'd rather scrub floors in the house of my God than be honored as a guest in the palace of sin' (v.10, MSG).

To worship God is to experience him as 'sunshine' (v.11, MSG), bathing us in his light and warmth, and a 'shield', defending us from evil (v.11).

He prays for this because he knows how wonderful it is: 'The LORD bestows favour and honour; no good thing does he withhold from those whose walk is blameless. O LORD Almighty, blessed are those who trust in you' (vv.11–12).

PRAYER

Lord, I worship you today. One day in your presence is better than a thousand elsewhere. Help me to keep trusting in you and worshipping you.

NEW TESTAMENT READING

Romans 1:18–32
Worship only God

You become like what you worship. If we worship worthless idols, our lives become worthless. If we worship God, eventually we will become like him.

The apostle Paul begins, in this passage, to unfold what has gone wrong in the world. The heart of the problem is that humankind has 'worshipped and served created things rather than the Creator' (v.25).

God has specifically revealed himself in the Scriptures and ultimately in Jesus Christ, who is his 'exact representation' (Hebrews 1:3). But what about those who had never heard the good news? Paul's argument here is that we are all 'without excuse' (Romans 1:20).

God has revealed himself in his creation: 'But the basic reality of God is plain enough. Open your eyes and there it is! By taking a long and thoughtful look at what God has created, people have always been able to see what their eyes as such can't see: eternal power, for instance, and the mystery of his divine being. So nobody has a good excuse' (vv.19–20, MSG).

This knowledge of God is only partial and limited. But, as the psalmist puts it, 'The heavens declare the glory of God; the skies proclaim the work of his hands' (Psalm 19:1).

We only have to look at the created world to know that there must be a God. The problem with the world is that, in spite of this revelation of God, 'they refused to worship him' (Romans 1:21, MSG). 'They neither glorified him as God nor gave thanks to him' (v.21). Instead, they 'worshipped and served created things' (v.25).

Therefore, the apostle Paul writes, 'God gave them over' (vv.24, 26, 28). God allowed us to go our own way in order that we might at last learn from the terrible consequences that follow. Life turned away from the worship of God is ultimately futile. As *The Message* puts it, it is 'godless and loveless' (v.27, MSG).

'Since they didn't bother to acknowledge God, God quit bothering them and let them run loose. And then all hell broke loose' (v.28, MSG).

As the worship of God declines, so the morality of a society declines, following in its wake. We should not be surprised that as the worship of God has declined in our nation, so many of the things described in this passage have followed in its wake.

If you want to keep the right perspective, keep your eyes fixed on Jesus and keep worshipping and serving your Creator.

PRAYER

Lord, I pray there may be a turning away in our society from the worship of created things and a restoration of worship of you, our Creator.

OLD TESTAMENT READING

2 Kings 24:8–25:30
Pray for a restoration of worship

When we look around at our society it can sometimes seem as if we are in a kind of exile. It can seem that the church is breaking down.

In this passage, we see that the people of God have been through desperate times in the past. But, we also see hope for the future.

As the book of Kings closes, we read of the terrible consequences of a nation that has done exactly what the apostle Paul describes in our New Testament passage for today. They had turned away from worshipping God to worshipping idols (created things).

As a result, we see the destruction of Jerusalem and its temple, and the people going into exile.

During the reign of Jehoiachin (597 BC), 'Nebuchadnezzar king of Babylon advanced on Jerusalem and laid siege to it' (24:10). The leaders of the people were carried off into exile (v.14).

The next king was appointed by the king of Babylon. Zedekiah (597–587 BC) was no better and things went from bad to worse, as Nebuchadnezzar once again laid siege to Jerusalem (chapter 25). This time the outcome was even more devastating. Nebuchadnezzar 'set fire to the temple of the LORD, the royal palace and all the houses of Jerusalem. Every important building he burned down' (25:9). The people were 'carried into exile' (v.11), 'Judah went into exile, orphaned from her land' (v.21, MSG).

We are told, 'it was because of the LORD's anger that all this happened to Jerusalem and Judah, and in the end he thrust them from his presence' (24:20).

All of this needs to be read alongside the books of Jeremiah and Ezekiel – two prophets who were prophesying at this time. (See especially, Jeremiah 13:18, Jeremiah 39 and 52, Ezekiel 12 and 24.) The greatest loss for the people of God was the destruction of the temple. This was the place where they worshipped God and experienced his presence. Now they were 'thrust' from his presence (2 Kings 24:20). This was the worst impact of the exile.

Yet, the book of Kings ends with a small ray of *hope*. In the thirty-seventh year of the exile of Jehoiachin king of Judah, he is released from prison (25:27). He is invited to eat regularly at the king's table (v.29). The exile is not going to last for ever. Here is a note of anticipation of better things to come. The people of God will return from exile and rebuild the temple and begin to enjoy the presence of God and the worship of God once more.

PRAYER

Lord, I cry out to you for restoration and revival. Would you restore your church in this country. Revive us again. May our nation turn back to you, begin to worship you again, enjoy your presence and, on our knees before you, see things from the right perspective.

14 July | Day 195
God of the Second Chance

'You never get a second chance at a first impression,' goes the saying, but social media profiles, online communities and virtual gaming provide, for some, an opportunity to seek a second chance in life.

Second Life is a virtual world. Over twenty million people have created a *Second Life* character, through which they can live in this new world. They are looking for another chance in life.

Second Life describes itself as a place 'to connect ... to change yourself, to change your mind, change your look ... to be different'.[1]

This virtual world is clear evidence of the longing of so many for a fresh start. Yet, in reality, God is the God of the second chance and third and many, many more. He gives us *countless* chances to turn back to him and enjoy his love again. God doesn't just give us a 'second life' – he comes to us and transforms our *real* life.

READING FROM PSALMS

Psalm 85:1–7
Make a fresh start

Like so many of us, the psalmist wants an opportunity to make a fresh start in life. He cries out to God, 'help us make a fresh start' (v.6, MSG).

God is not wishy-washy. He hates sin. There is such a thing as *righteous* anger (v.5). It is one side of God's love. But the psalmist knows that this *righteous* anger is not contrary to God's unfailing love, and in this psalm we see both side by side.

God forgives: 'You lifted the cloud of guilt from your people, you put their sins far out of sight ... you cooled your hot, righteous anger' (vv.2–3, MSG).

When you turn back to God he restores and revives you through his 'unfailing love' (v.7). The psalmist prays, 'Restore us again ... Will you not revive us again' (vv.4, 6).

PRAYER

Lord, thank you that you give me so many chances. Restore and revive me again, that I may rejoice in you.

NEW TESTAMENT READING

Romans 2:1–16
Enjoy a radical life change

God loves you. He wants the very best for your life. He does not want you to mess up your life. Sin takes us 'on a dark spiral downward' (v.1, MSG). 'God is kind, but he's not soft. In kindness he takes us firmly by the hand and leads us into a radical life-change' (v.4, MSG).

Paul speaks of the 'wrath' of God (vv.5, 8). This is God's loving, righteous anger against sin. But Paul does not begin with the 'wrath' of God. He begins with 'the riches of his kindness, tolerance and patience' (v.4). God is love. His anger is the very last resort – for those who are 'self-seeking and who reject the truth and follow evil' (v.8).

God loves everyone. He 'does not show favouritism' (v.11). He loves both Jew and Gentile alike. God is impartial. He is a righteous judge.

All of us have sinned and have no excuse: 'Every time you criticize someone, you condemn yourself. It takes one to know one. Judgmental criticism of others is a well-known way of escaping detection in your own crimes and misdemeanors' (v.1, MSG).

It is so easy to judge other people about the very things we do ourselves. We tend to look at ourselves through rose-tinted glasses and look at everyone else through a magnifying glass. A judgmental mind focuses on what is wrong with others, rather than on what is right.

The opening five books of the Old Testament establish God's relationship with his people and give instructions on how to live. But 'merely hearing God's law is a waste of your time if you don't do what he commands' (v.13, MSG). So all of us will be judged by what we know. For some, that will be God's law, for others their own consciences: 'Something deep within them that echoes God's yes and no, right and wrong' (v.15, MSG).

All of us need to repent. God's kindness is intended to lead us to repentance. The moment you repent and turn to God, you get another chance, the possibility of a new life. Repentance is not just about turning *away from* sin but turning *towards* God.

PRAYER

Lord, forgive me for the times when I judge others. Thank you that every day is an opportunity for a new start, another chance.

OLD TESTAMENT READING

Jonah 1:1–4:11
Seize a second chance

Jonah is different from all the other prophets. As Eugene Peterson writes, 'He is not a hero too high and mighty for us to identify with – he doesn't do anything great.'[2]

The book starts with Jonah disobeying God and ends with him complaining about what God has done. He is a man who suffered from severe depression. God works within and around Jonah's weaknesses to accomplish his purposes.

Each of these four short chapters tells us something about God's love:

1. *God's love will never let you go* (Chapter 1)
You cannot successfully run away from God or from his call. Jonah was a well-known preacher (2 Kings 14:25). He is told to go to Nineveh (Jonah 1:2). Instead, he runs to Tarshish – which is now the Costa Brava in southwest Spain (but Jonah was not there for a holiday!).

You can run from God, but you cannot hide. Jonah ends up in a mess. It is so easy to think that our own disobedience will not affect anyone but us. This story shows that our disobedience has consequences for other people.

Sometimes the storms we face in life are the result of our own disobedience. A storm rages, and Jonah knows it is his fault. He is prepared to die and demands to be thrown into the sea, but 'the LORD provided a great fish' (v.17). God's love would not let him go.

2. *God's love can reach you no matter how far you've fallen* (Chapter 2)
No matter how desperate or hopeless your situation may seem, it is never too late. When he hit rock bottom, from inside the fish Jonah prayed: 'In my distress I called to the LORD ... you listened to my cry' (2:2).

He recognised what we miss out on when we do not follow the Lord. 'Those who cling to worthless idols forfeit the grace that could be theirs' (v.8). It is so easy to put our trust in something other than God. We can so often put our trust in the 'idols' of money, success, fame or sex. Anything that takes you away from God prevents you from receiving the grace that can be yours.

There is no situation that God cannot rescue you from if you cry out to him.

3. *God's love means you get another chance* (Chapter 3)
God was persistent in giving Jonah a second chance and when Jonah took him up on it, the result was an eternal impact on many people's lives.

Then the word of the Lord came to Jonah a *second* time: 'Go to the great city of Nineveh and proclaim to it the message I give you' (3:2). The first time he messed up; the second time God used him powerfully.

Not only did God give *Jonah a second chance*, he also gave the city of *Nineveh a second chance*.

Nineveh was a great city (1:2; 3:2). It had more than 120,000 people (4:11). As a result of Jonah's message, the people repented; they believed (3:5). The king believed (vv.7–9). Revival came as a result of one person's preaching. Thousands were saved (v.10).

4. *God's love extends to all his creation* (Chapter 4)
God loves everyone and wants to be merciful to every person, city and nation on earth.

After all the success of his evangelistic campaign, Jonah fell into another deep depression. He was angry with God (4:1). Jonah was quick to anger, unlike God who is 'sheer grace and mercy, not easily angered, rich in love, and ready at the drop of a hat to turn your plans of punishment into a program of forgiveness!' (v.2, MSG).

We see now why Jonah ran away in the first place. He was angry that they had repented. The Ninevites were cruel oppressors. They were into witchcraft, torture, greed and prostitution. Yet, they repented and God forgave them. Still, today, some find it hard when really evil people repent and God forgives them.

God sent Jonah a visual aid. He provided a plant to give him shade. He was thrilled with it. Then God destroyed it (v.7). But God pointed out his great love for all his creation (unlike Jonah's concerns, which are rather narrow and selfish, vv.10–11).

One of God's amazing characteristics is mercy. Mercy means being kind and good to people who do not deserve it. God has extended his mercy to you and me through Jesus Christ and his mercy never runs out.

PRAYER

Lord, thank you for your great love. Thank you that even when I have messed up, you give me another chance. Help me to bring the good news of your love to others so that they too may turn back to your love.

15 July | Day 196

Soften Your Heart and Harden Your Feet

A twenty-one-year-old music college student took the cheapest ship she could find, calling at the greatest number of countries, and prayed to know where to disembark. She arrived in Hong Kong in 1966 and came to a place called the Walled City. It was a small, densely populated, lawless area controlled neither by China nor Hong Kong. It was a high-rise slum for drug addicts, gangs and prostitutes. She wrote:

> I loved this dark place. I hated what was happening in it but I wanted to be nowhere else. It was almost as if I could already see another city in its place and that city was ablaze with light. It was my dream. There was no more crying, no more death or pain. The sick were healed, addicts set free, the hungry filled. There were families for orphans, homes for the homeless, and new dignity for those who had lived in shame. I had no idea of how to bring this about but with 'visionary zeal' imagined introducing the Walled City people to the one who could change it all: Jesus.[1]

Jackie Pullinger has spent over half a century working with prostitutes, heroin addicts and gang members. I remember so well a talk she gave some years ago. She began by saying, 'God wants us to have soft hearts and hard feet. The trouble with so many of us is that we have hard hearts and soft feet.'

Jackie is a glowing example of this; going without sleep, food and comfort to serve others. God wants us to have soft hearts – hearts of love and compassion. But if we are to make any difference to the world, this will lead to hard feet as we travel along tough paths and face challenges.

READING FROM PROVERBS

Proverbs 17:5–14
Soften your heart towards others

If you have a heart softened by God, you will inevitably demonstrate love towards others. Our aim should be to live a life that 'promotes love' (v.9a).

1. Love the poor

Your attitude to the poor reflects your attitude to God: 'Whoever mocks the poor shows contempt for their Maker' (v.5a). As God's people we are called to friendship with and service of the poor.

2. Love your family

God's ideal is for you to enjoy close and loving relationships between parents, grandparents and children: 'Children's children are a crown to the aged, and parents are the pride of their children' (v.6).

3. Love your friends

Love between close friends is extremely valuable. Guard your friendships. Do not quickly take offence or bear a grudge: 'Overlook an offense and bond a friendship; fasten on to a slight and – good-bye, friend!' (v.9, MSG).

4. Love your critics

Jesus told us, 'Love your enemies' (Matthew 5:44). A soft heart is willing to take criticism, whether it comes from a friend or even from an 'enemy'. 'A rebuke impresses a discerning person more than a hundred lashes a fool' (Proverbs 17:10).

Do your utmost to avoid arguments: 'Starting a quarrel is like breaching a dam; so drop the matter before a dispute breaks out' (v.14).

PRAYER

Lord, help me to love like this. Help me to guard my relationships in my family, with my friends, and with my critics. Help me to love the poor and make a real difference in their lives.

NEW TESTAMENT READING

Romans 2:17–3:8
Soften your heart towards God

It does not matter what is happening on the outside if we do not have a 'soft heart'. Here, Paul looks at the importance of the heart. He explains that it was intended that the Jews, God's chosen people, should walk in a relationship with God. So they were given the law. They knew God's will (2:17–18). They were meant to be 'a guide for the blind, a light for those who are in the dark, an instructor of the foolish, a teacher of infants' (vv.19–20).

Physical circumcision was the outward and visible sign intended to reflect the inward and invisible attitude of the heart. Paul argues that sadly they (like us all) have failed to keep God's law (vv.21–27).

Paul then focuses on what really matters: 'You become a Jew by who you are. It's the mark of God *on your heart*, not of a knife on your skin that makes a Jew. And recognition comes from God, not legalistic critics' (v.29, MSG).

What matters to God is the *heart*. Every person who has the Holy Spirit living in their *heart* receives the same inheritance as the Jews did in the Old Testament. This includes every true Christian.

Does this mean that there is no value to what the Jews had been given? No. He points out that there are great advantages to being Jewish. For example, 'they have been entrusted with the very words of God' (3:2). What an amazing privilege! However, you now not only have the words of God in the Scriptures they had, you also have the words of Jesus and the whole of the rest of the New Testament. You have an even greater advantage.

Later on in Romans, he will expound this at greater length (Romans 9–11). Meanwhile, he digresses to deal with an argument his opponents have levelled against him (3:3–8). He stresses again God's faithfulness. Even when we are faithless, God remains faithful to us. It would be absurd to take advantage of this by doing evil. Rather God's faithfulness encourages us to be faithful to him.

PRAYER

Lord, fill my heart today with your Spirit, with love and compassion for every person I meet. Thank you that you have entrusted us with the very words of God. Help me to be faithful to you today.

OLD TESTAMENT READING

Amos 1:1–2:16
Harden your feet to help the poor and needy

A soft heart must lead to hard feet, with God's people prepared to act on behalf of the poor and vulnerable, to fight against injustice and stand up for the oppressed.

This was a time (760–750 BC) of great prosperity for Israel and Judah. But material prosperity is not always a sign of God's blessing. At this time, it had resulted in complacency, corruption, immorality and terrible injustice.

Amos was a prophet. But he was not a priest or an ordained minister. He stayed in his workplace – a sheep breeder, who was unimpressed by prosperity, power and position. He was a defender of the downtrodden poor and an accuser of the privileged rich who were using God's name to legitimise injustice and oppression.

Like the apostle Paul, Amos proclaims God's judgment against both non-religious and religious.

He starts with the non-religious who 'sin apart from the law'. Israel's neighbours had committed terrible sins. They are condemned for their excessive cruelty and horrible torture (1:3), for slavery and slave trading (v.6), for 'stifling all compassion' (v.11), for ripping open pregnant women (v.13) and for desecrating the dead (2:1). Amos speaks of God's wrath at such terrible sins (1:3, 6, 9, 11, 13).

Amos and Paul (Romans 1:18–20) both argue for a 'natural law'. Even if they did not have the written law of God, there is a 'natural law' – 'written on their hearts' (2:15). They know that certain things are wrong. This was effectively the basis upon which the Nazi leaders were condemned at the Nuremberg trials after World War II.

Amos, like Paul (2:12), goes on to say that God's people who have the written law will be judged by an even stricter standard. Amos turns from judgment of the Gentiles to judgment of Judah and Israel because 'they rejected GOD's revelation, refused to keep my commands' (Amos 2:4, MSG).

Although God had acted on their behalf – 'I was always on your side' (v.9, MSG) – they failed to keep his laws. In particular, the issue that matters to God is their attitude to the poor and needy. Their hearts had become hard. 'People for them are only things – ways of making money. They'd sell a poor man for a pair of shoes. They'd sell their own grandmother! They grind the penniless into the dirt, shove the luckless into the ditch' (vv.6c–7b, MSG). They are also guilty of slavery and sexual sin (v.7c).

While all this is going on, 'stuff they've extorted from the poor is piled up at the shrine of their god, while they sit around drinking wine they've conned from their victims' (v.8, MSG).

The sins of God's people are not as horrific as those of the non-religious. Yet the judgment against them is as severe (vv.13, 16) because God has blessed them so richly (vv.10–11). We are not to congratulate ourselves that our sins are less than others. Our sins may be less obvious, but they may be as great in God's sight. Thank God for the forgiveness and grace that we receive through Jesus.

PRAYER

Lord, give us soft hearts of compassion and love for the issues of extreme poverty and injustice in our world – and hard feet and courage to go out and do something about it.

16 July | Day 197
God's Game-changing Answer

'We sometimes fall into the trap of thinking we are the worst people on the face of the earth and that nobody does as many wrong things as we do. But Romans 3:23 says that *all* have sinned and fall short of the glory (excellence) of God. Every man, woman, or child who was ever born, or ever will be, has a problem with sin. But the good news is that God has provided an *answer to our dilemma,*' writes Joyce Meyer.[1]

When Saint Augustine found *the answer* in 386, 'a clear light flooded [his] heart'. Martin Luther found *the answer* and a few years later the Reformation began, in 1517. When John Wesley understood *the answer* in 1738, his heart was 'strangely warmed' and the seeds of a revival began.

In each case, their lives were radically changed through understanding '*the righteousness of God*'. It's a game changer. The moment anyone comes to understand this expression, it changes your life. It certainly changed mine.

READING FROM PSALMS

Psalm 85:8–13
God's answer gives you his peace

'I grew up in an atmosphere of strife,' writes Joyce Meyer, 'and that was all I ever knew. I had to learn an entirely new way of living. Now I am addicted to *peace*. As soon as my peace disappears, I ask myself how I lost it and start looking for ways to get it back.'[2]

God has promised 'peace' (v.8) to his people. This does not necessarily mean outward peace. The pressures, difficulties, trials, battles and busyness may not disappear. But in all this, God has promised to give you his peace. This peace comes from listening to what 'God the Lord' says (v.8).

Peace is very closely connected with righteousness. The psalmist says, '*righteousness* and *peace kiss each other*' (v.10b). In the same way that love and faithfulness go together (v.10a), so do righteousness and peace. Peace comes from living in a right relationship with God (Romans 5:1).

PRAYER

God, thank you that you make it possible for me to walk in a right relationship with you and to enjoy the peace that follows.

NEW TESTAMENT READING

Romans 3:9–31
God's answer is a gift you receive

We long for peace. We long to be in a right relationship with God and with other people. But how do you receive this 'righteousness *from God*'?

Paul continues his argument that no one is righteous on their own. 'There's nobody living right, not even one' (v.10b, MSG). 'They've all taken the wrong turn; they've all wandered down blind alleys' (v.12, MSG). Righteousness is the way to peace, but the reality is that 'the way of peace they do not know' (v.17).

Paul concludes his argument in this section: 'And it's clear enough, isn't it, that *we're sinners, every one of us*, in the same sinking boat with everybody else?' (v.20, MSG). The two little words that follow are of huge significance: '*But now...*' (v.21).

Having set out the problem, Paul now moves on to describe *God's game-changing answer* – 'a righteousness from God' (v.21). This righteousness from God cannot be achieved through the law because no one (apart from Jesus) has ever kept the entire law. The Old Testament (the Law and the Prophets) testifies about this and points towards God's answer (v.21).

'This righteousness *from God* comes through faith in Jesus Christ to all who believe' (v.22). This righteousness from God cannot be earned. It is a pure gift that you receive '*through faith in Jesus Christ*'. It is a gift '*to all who believe*' (v.22).

Paul then uses three images to describe what Jesus' death on the cross has achieved. Each is like a facet of a diamond. Each image is intertwined with the others:

1. The *penalty* of sin has been paid
Justification is an expression from *the law court*. We 'are *justified* freely by his grace' (v.24). God is a just judge. He could not ignore our guilt.

He came in the person of his son Jesus Christ to die for you and me: '...in his forbearance he had left the sins committed beforehand unpunished – he did it to demonstrate *his justice* at the present time, so as to be just and *the one who justifies* those who have faith in Jesus' (vv.25–26). He paid the penalty himself.

You are justified 'freely by his grace' (v.24). Grace means undeserved love. It is free. There is no merit on our part. You cannot earn it. It is a gift. Therefore, there is no room for boasting (vv.27–31).

Through his death on the cross, Jesus paid the penalty for our every wrong action, word and thought. The moment you put your faith in Jesus, you are justified. You have nothing to fear. The penalty has been paid. You have received the gift of righteousness from God.

2. The *power* of sin has been broken
The second image Paul uses comes from *the market-place*: 'through the *redemption* that came by Christ Jesus' (v.24).

Debt was a problem in the ancient world as well. If someone had serious debts, they might be forced to sell themselves into slavery in order to pay them off.

Suppose a person was standing in the market-place, offering themselves as a slave. Someone might have pity and pay the amount they owe, then let the person they've paid for go free. In doing so, they would be 'redeeming' them and paying a 'ransom' price.

In a similar way for us, '*redemption* ... came by Jesus Christ' (v.24). Your sins are like a debt that stands against you. Jesus, by his death on the cross, paid the ransom price (Mark 10:45). In this way, you are set free to have a relationship with God. Your relationship is restored. You receive a righteousness from God.

3. The *pollution* of sin has been removed
Paul's third image in this passage comes from *the temple*. 'God presented him as a *sacrifice of atonement*, through faith in his blood' (Romans 3:25).

In the Old Testament, very detailed laws were laid down regarding how sin should be dealt with. There was a whole sacrificial system that demonstrated the seriousness of sin and the need for cleansing from it, as sin was passed from the sinner to the animal, which was then killed.

But 'it is impossible for the blood of bulls and goats to take away sins' (Hebrews 10:4). The old sacrificial system was only a 'shadow' (v.1) of what was to come. The reality came with the sacrifice of Jesus. Only the blood of Christ, the 'once for all' (v.10) sacrifice of atonement, can wash away your sin and remove its pollution. This is because Jesus was the perfect sacrifice. He alone lived a perfect life. Through his blood you receive God's game-changing answer – a righteousness from God.

PRAYER

Lord, how can I ever thank you enough for the gift of 'the righteousness from God' by faith in Jesus? Thank you that as a result of your righteousness I can receive peace, forgiveness, freedom and cleansing through the blood of Jesus.

OLD TESTAMENT READING

Amos 3:1–4:13
God's answer challenges you to right living

Paul tells us that God's game-changing answer – 'a *righteousness* from God' is something about which 'the Law and the *Prophets* testify' (Romans 3:21). Amos is one of those prophets.

As Amos turned to speak the word of the Lord against Israel, we see God's desire for righteousness in that all their sins are punished. The Lord said, 'Out of all the families on earth, I picked you. Therefore, because of your special calling, I'm holding you responsible for all your sins' (Amos 3:2, MSG).

The people are condemned in what is almost a law court: '"Hear this and *testify* against the house of Jacob," declares the Lord' (v.13).

It is as if God calls witnesses to testify against his own people: 'You women! Mean to the poor, cruel to the down-and-out! Indolent and pampered, you demand of your husbands, "Bring us a tall, cool drink!"' (4:1, MSG). They are condemned for their superficiality, self-centred indulgence and their treatment of the poor and needy.

Over and over again, God speaks to his people in an attempt to draw them back to him: 'The fact is, GOD, the Master, does nothing without first telling his prophets the whole story' (3:7, MSG). 'Yet,' he declares, 'you have not returned to me' (4:6, 8–11).

When we understand this Old Testament background, it makes it all the more staggering that the apostle Paul writes, 'This righteousness from God comes through faith in Jesus Christ to all who believe' (Romans 3:22). God's game changer is that Jesus has paid the penalty for you; you are righteous in God's eyes, you can approach him with confidence today. Speak to him as your loving Father and know his peace deep in your heart.

PRAYER

Lord, thank you that your desire is always that we return to you and walk in a right relationship with you. Thank you that you have now made that possible through Jesus.

17 July | Day 198
As If You Had Never Sinned

In the years that I practised as a barrister I noticed that, for many people, appearing in a court of law is a terrifying experience – even if they are only appearing as a witness. Being a litigant, a person involved in the lawsuit, or a defendant in a criminal trial is an even more nerve-racking event. I saw the relief when a defendant was acquitted or a litigant was declared by a judge to be 'in the right'.

In the legal system of Ancient Israel, a dispute put both parties at risk of the judgment of the court. The court's process had a redemptive role; the judge was meant to help the party in the right to correct the wrong. At the end of the case, one party would be *declared righteous* and the other in the wrong. Successful performance of this function meant 'justice' had been done. The Hebrew word for righteous is *tsaddiq,* which some versions of the Bible translate as 'innocent' or 'just' – one whose status is right. This is the Old Testament background to being *'justified'*.

The child's definition of justified is *'just as if I'd'* never sinned. Jesus died for our sins. When you put your *faith* in him you were *justified*. You were acquitted. You are declared righteous in his sight. Sin no longer separates you from God. You can live in a right relationship with him and with others. This is *'justification'*.

READING FROM PSALMS

Psalm 86:1–10
Rumours of justification

David experienced *the blessing* of being justified by faith and being a child of God. He says, 'Pay attention, GOD, to my prayer; *bend down* and listen to my cry for help' (v.6, MSG). Like a parent lovingly bending down so that a child can whisper in their ear, God listens to the prayers of his children: 'In the day of my trouble I will call to you, for you will answer me' (v.7).

David did not have the benefit of living under the new covenant. He lived before the life, death and resurrection of Jesus. However, in one sense, the cross is not limited by time. It was effective for those who lived before Jesus, for example for Abraham and David. Indeed, Paul highlights how David had known the wonderful blessings of God's forgiveness and restoration (Romans 4:6–8; Psalm 32:1–2a).

In some way, Paul is saying David experienced 'justification by faith' even though the means by which it was accomplished had not yet occurred.

First, he understood God's love. He knew that the Lord is '*abounding in love* to all who call to [him]' (Psalm 86:5b).

Second, he knew that God was merciful and forgiving. 'Have mercy on me, O Lord ... You are *forgiving* and good ... listen to my cry for *mercy*' (vv.3a,5a,6b).

Third, although he knew that he did not deserve forgiveness and mercy – he had not earned it – he had the faith to believe that God would save him through *his faith* in him: 'You are my God; *save* your servant *who trusts in you*' (v.2b).

In other words, David understood all the elements that make up justification by faith, except for one. The one missing piece was the death of Jesus for our sins.

PRAYER

Lord, thank you for your amazing love for me. Thank you that you save those who put their trust in you.

NEW TESTAMENT READING

Romans 4:1–15
Celebration of justification

How can we, deeply flawed human beings, be 'in the right' before God? How can you be 'justified' in his sight? Is this something you simply have to work hard at all your life and hope for the best?

'No', says Paul. Something astonishing happened as a result of Jesus' life, death and resurrection. Now you can receive this *justification* as a *free gift*. You receive it, not by working really hard, but by an act of *faith* (vv.1–5).

One of the questions frequently asked on Alpha is: 'If Jesus died for our sins, what happens to those who lived before Jesus?'

Paul knows that he has to deal with the case of Abraham. His opponents might have argued that Abraham was justified as a result of his good works, giving him something to boast about (v.2). Paul points out that the Scriptures declare, 'Abraham *believed* God, and it was credited to him as *righteousness*' (v.3, Genesis 15:6). This phrase, Paul argues, implies a gift rather than something earned (Romans 4:5).

'If you're a hard worker and do a good job, you deserve your pay; we don't call your wages a gift. But if you see that the job is too big for you, that it's something only God can do, and you trust him to do it ... that ... is what gets you set right with God, by God. Sheer gift' (vv.4–5, MSG).

Paul's opponents might argue that this gift is only available for Jews (the circumcised). But Paul points out that *circumcision came later* on for Abraham (Genesis 17) and therefore, the blessing of justification by faith is for both the circumcised (the Jews) *and the uncircumcised* (the rest of human kind) (Romans 4:9–10).

Circumcision was *not the cause* of justification. Rather *it was a seal*. Abraham 'underwent circumcision as evidence and confirmation of what God had done long before to bring him into this acceptable standing with himself, an act of God he had embraced with his whole life' (vv.10–11, MSG).

The story of Abraham makes clear that his being counted righteous was not on the basis of works, circumcision or law, but by *God's grace through faith in Jesus*. If Abraham was justified by faith, he is the father of all who have faith (including those who have not been circumcised, vv.11–12).

The cross is effective throughout all time. Through what Jesus did on the cross, those who had *never heard* about him but put their trust in God were *justified by their faith*.

Do you need to understand all this in order to be justified by faith? Not at all. Justification is *by faith*, so you *don't even need a correct understanding of justification by faith to be justified by faith; you simply need faith*. 'This is why the fulfilment of God's promise depends entirely on trusting God and his way, and then simply embracing him and what he does. God's promise arrives as pure gift' (v.16, MSG).

PRAYER

Father, thank you so much for this amazing truth that I am justified and acquitted through the death of Jesus for me, and by faith in him. Help me to understand this truth more deeply and to explain it more clearly, so that many more know the great blessings of justification by faith.

OLD TESTAMENT READING

Amos 5:1–27
Communities of justification

God is not interested in how 'religious' you are. He is far more concerned about *integrity*, *justice* and *righteousness*. Without that, religiosity is sheer hypocrisy. He says:

'I can't stand your religious meetings.
I'm fed up with your conferences and conventions.
I want nothing to do with your religion projects,
your pretentious slogans and goals.
I'm sick of your fund-raising schemes,
your public relations and image making.
I've had all I can take of your noisy ego-music.
When was the last time you sang *to me*?
Do you know what I want?
I want *justice* – oceans of it.
I want fairness – rivers of it.
That's what I want. That's *all* I want' (vv.21–24, MSG).

A central outworking of justification by faith is that God's people respond by acting with righteousness and justice. John Calvin once said, '*It is therefore faith alone which justifies, and yet the faith which justifies is not alone*.'[1] Our natural response to what God has done for us should be to act in line with his will.

Righteousness and justice have a central role in this passage and in the whole book of Amos. God wants justice for the poor. God speaks through the prophet Amos:

'Because you run roughshod over the poor
and take the bread right out of their mouths,
You're never going to move into
the luxury homes you have built.
You're never going to drink wine
from the expensive vineyards you've planted.
I know precisely the extent of your violations,
the enormity of your sins. Appalling!
You bully right-living people,
taking bribes right and left and kicking the poor when they're down.
Justice is a lost cause' (vv.10–13, MSG).

God will not allow human injustice to continue for ever. He will intervene and bring about his justice. God hates injustice.

Issues of justice such as rescuing people from bonded labour or other forms of slavery, fighting against the trafficking of people for sex, and other forms of injustice, should be high on our agenda. They certainly seem to be high on God's agenda: 'Let *justice* roll on like a river, *righteousness* like a never-failing stream!' (v.24).

PRAYER

Lord, thank you that faith alone justifies, but that faith should never be alone. Help me to live out my faith by acting righteously and seeking justice for all.

18 July | Day 199
How to Feel God's Love for You

Robbie Williams' evocative lyric in the song 'Feel' echoes the deep longing of the human heart: 'I just wanna feel real love'.[1] God wants you to *feel* his love for you. He wants you to accept his love in your heart. You can receive his love in a new way today.

I remember an occasion when our grandson, aged two, wanted to feel his father's love. He raised both hands in the air and said, 'Hugga Dadda'. My son picked up his son, lifted him into his arms, embraced him, kissed him and hugged him. It is a wonderful thing to hold a parent's hand but an incomparably greater thing to have their arms wrapped around you. This is an illustration of the experience of God's love.

You *know* that God loves you through the cross: 'God demonstrated his own love for us in this: While we were still sinners, Christ died for us' (Romans 5:8). You *experience* God's love through the Holy Spirit: 'God has poured out his love into our hearts by the Holy Spirit, whom he has given us' (5:5).

'The whole Bible,' St Augustine observes, 'does nothing but tell of God's love.'[2] Father Raniero Cantalamessa writes: 'This is the message that supports and explains all the other messages. The love of God is the answer to all the "whys" in the Bible: the why of creation, the why of the incarnation, the why of redemption. If the written word of the Bible could be changed into a spoken word and become one single voice, this voice, more powerful than the roaring of the sea would cry out: "the Father loves you!" (John 16:27). Everything that God does and says in the Bible is love, even God's anger is nothing but love. God "is" love!'[3]

READING FROM PSALMS

Psalm 86:11–17
God's love is great and personal

When you know the greatness of God's love for you the response is worship: 'I will praise you, O Lord my God, with all my heart; I will glorify your name for ever' (v.12).

David knew it was the love of a personal God who cares for each individual. He writes, 'For great is your love towards me' (v.13a). Like David, you are God's 'dear, dear child!' (v.16, MSG).

It is God's nature to love. 'But you, O God, are both tender and kind, not easily angered, immense in love' (v.15, MSG). He prays, 'Make a show of how much you love me' (v.17, MSG). He prayed, in the light of God's love for him, for an 'undivided heart' (v.11b). He wanted to respond to God's love for him by committing himself totally to God.

PRAYER

Lord, you are compassionate and gracious, abounding in love and faithfulness (v.15). Thank you that your love for me is so great and so personal. Give me an undivided heart.

NEW TESTAMENT READING

Romans 4:16–5:11
God's love is demonstrated and poured out

Do you believe that God really loves you? God's love will never let you down; he will never stop loving you. His love for you is greater than your failings and he wants you to receive his love by faith.

Contrary to what many people think, God loves you and wants to give you *life*. He gives '*life* to the dead' (4:17). God raised Jesus to life from the dead. One day all who have died, in Christ, will also be given resurrection life. In the meantime, Jesus said that he came so that you might experience life, and life in all its fullness (John 10:10).

Paul continues to describe Abraham's faith. Abraham believed God's promise that he and Sarah would have a child, even though it was no longer a human possibility.

We learn of Abraham that 'no unbelief or distrust made him waver (doubtingly question) concerning the promise of God, but he grew strong and was empowered by faith as he gave praise and glory to God, fully satisfied and assured that God was able and mighty to keep His word and to do what He had promised' (Romans 4:20–21, AMP). In other words, Paul reiterates, Abraham was justified by faith.

But justification by faith was not only for Abraham, 'but also for us, to whom God will credit righteousness – for us who believe in him who raised Jesus our Lord from the dead' (v.24). You too are justified by faith. 'The sacrificed Jesus made us fit for God, *set right with God'* (v.25, MSG).

Paul moves on to speak of the staggering consequences of this fact. Because you are 'justified by faith', you have 'peace with God'. You have 'gained access' to his presence (5:1–2, MSG). You can draw near to him and speak to him each day, knowing that there is no barrier between you and him.

'There's more to come: We continue to shout our praise even when we're hemmed in with troubles' (v.3, MSG). We can rejoice in our sufferings: 'Because we know that suffering produces perseverance; perseverance, character; and character, hope. And hope does not disappoint us, because *God has poured out his love into our hearts by the Holy Spirit*, whom he has given us' (vv.3–5).

God's love has flooded your innermost heart. This experience of God's love is deep and overwhelming. It is the regular ministry of the Holy Spirit to help you feel God's love. If you have never had this experience of the Holy Spirit filling your innermost heart, I would encourage you simply to ask God to fill you now.

Paul has still more to say about God's love. He says that even when you were against him, he sent Jesus to die for you. 'But *God demonstrates his own love for us* in this: While we were still sinners, Christ died for us' (v.8).

The essence of love is giving. The more the gift costs and the less the recipient deserves it, the greater the love involved.

This is how you know God loves you. The Father allowed his only Son to be taken from his embrace and sent to the cross. Even though we did not deserve it – we were ungodly sinners – Jesus died for us. God did not spare his own Son. He loves you that much.

If God loves you so much, you can be certain that your future is secure. 'If, when we were at our worst, we were put on friendly terms with God by the sacrificial death of his Son, now that we're at our best, just think of how our lives will expand and deepen by means of his resurrection life!' (v.10, MSG).

PRAYER

Lord, thank you that you love me so much that you died for me. I ask that you would, again, pour your love into my heart by the Holy Spirit, and help me to feel your deep love for me.

OLD TESTAMENT READING

Amos 6:1–7:17
God's love and grief

Do you know that God's anger is nothing but love? Here we see an example of that. God's anger is directed towards 'complacent' leaders (6:1):

> 'Woe to those who live in luxury
> and expect everyone else to serve them!
> Woe to those who live only for today,
> indifferent to the fate of others!
> Woe to the playboys, the playgirls,
> who think life is a party held just
> for them!
> Woe to those addicted to feeling good –
> life without pain!
> those obsessed with looking good – life
> without wrinkles!
> They could not care less
> about their country going to ruin'
> (vv.4–6, MSG).

It is not so much that they enjoy the good things of life – none of which are sinful in themselves. Rather, it is because they don't care about the state of the people of God. God hates pride and arrogance (vv.6, 8) that fails to acknowledge our need of him and keeps us from experiencing his love for us and loving others as he loves them.

If the leaders had loved God's people as God loved them, they would have grieved over their country going to ruin.

Amos was an example of someone who did care and did do something. He interceded for the people (7:1–6).

Amos was an ordinary person: 'I never set up to be a preacher, never had plans to be a preacher. I raised cattle and I pruned trees. Then God took me off the farm and said, "Go preach to my people Israel"' (vv.14–15, MSG). God was not content to simply watch injustice flourish. He loves his people too much for that. He raised up Amos to warn them of the consequences of what they were doing and to call them to turn back to his ways.

Like Amos, let's pray and intercede for our nation:

PRAYER

'Sovereign Lord, forgive!' (v.2). In your great love, have mercy upon us. Thank you that you love your church and that you have power to bring life to the dead (Romans 4:24).

Lord, we pray that you would raise up more people who hear your words and speak them with courage, power and love.

19 July | Day 200

Just Grace

It has been said that the biggest problem on earth is not too little democracy, or too much poverty, or too few anti-viral AIDS medicines, but the fact that two-thirds of the world's population live outside the protection of the law. A lack of justice has a terrible effect on many of the world's poor.

The themes of justice and grace flow through the Bible. We cannot fully understand grace without understanding justice. One definition of grace is 'undeserved love'. There is a mnemonic used to explain grace: **G**od's **R**iches **A**t **C**hrist's **E**xpense. We see today how Jesus Christ makes *just grace* available for you and me.

READING FROM PROVERBS

Proverbs 17:15–24
The vital importance of justice

In numerous countries of the world, the guilty get away and often the prisons are full of innocent people, many of whom have never even been tried or convicted. '*Acquitting the guilty* and *condemning the innocent* – the LORD detests them both' (v.15). Both are terrible forms of injustice. They are abhorrent to God and have a damaging impact on society.

A great deal of the problem is caused by bribery. 'The wicked accept *bribes* in secret to pervert the course of justice' (v.23). One lawyer in a developing country told me that if you want a case to get to court faster than the usual approximately ten-year delay, you have to 'oil the wheels'; a euphemism for bribery.

The struggle for justice is a serious responsibility. It requires hard work and could easily lead to burnout. The book of Proverbs is full of balanced wisdom.

It reminds us of the need for *family* and *friends:* 'Friends love through all kinds of weather, and families stick together in all kinds of trouble' (v.17, MSG). Do all you can to avoid petty arguments. 'The one who loves a quarrel loves sin' (v.19). Unnecessary quarrelling can separate families and even close friends.

As well as *family* and *friends*, *fun* is important: 'A cheerful disposition is good for your health; gloom and doom leave you bone-tired' (v.22, MSG). Don't take yourself too seriously. We need to laugh at ourselves. Laughter is like an internal workout. It exercises your soul and keeps it healthy.

PRAYER

Lord, show us what you want us to do as individuals and as a church to make justice available to all. Help us to keep balance in our lives, taking our responsibilities seriously and still finding a place for family, friends and fun.

NEW TESTAMENT READING

Romans 5:12–21
The abundant provision of grace

How do you see yourself? What do you believe about yourself? How do you think God sees you? What do you imagine he feels about you?

Grace means God sees us as righteous – 'in the right' (v.19, MSG). Righteousness is a free gift that comes from God's grace. Our sin 'doesn't have a chance in competition with the aggressive forgiveness we call grace. When it's sin versus grace, grace wins hands down' (vv.20–21, MSG).

Paul begins to unfold more of the wonders of grace. He portrays two realms – Adam's realm and Christ's realm.

Naturally, he says we are all part of Adam's realm. Sin, death and separation from God entered the world through Adam (vv.12–14).

Yet Paul also describes a new realm that Jesus has brought into being through his death and resurrection. The amazing thing is that you are transferred from Adam's realm to Jesus' realm, not by earning your way into God's good books, but simply by accepting the gift of God's grace made available through Jesus.

Paul starts to compare the *death* that came through Adam with the *life* that came through Jesus Christ, but his key point is that 'the gift is *not* like the trespass' (v.15). Ultimately, they can only be contrasted because the gift of life is so much greater than the trespass.

The only similarity is that both affected *many.* Your choices to obey or not to obey not only affect you, but many others as well. As a result of Adam's sin, *many* died. But Jesus' obedience enabled *many* to have access to the grace in which you stand and to receive the free gift of justification. And the free gift is not like the sin. 'The verdict on that *one* sin was the death sentence; the verdict on the *many* sins that followed was this wonderful life sentence' (v.16, MSG).

As a result of Adam's sin, death reigned. But the one man, Jesus Christ, has reversed the process to bring justification as a free gift and enable you to stand in the grace of God. Instead of death reigning, you 'reign in life' (v.17).

Adam's sin means that we all stand in the dock condemned. Jesus' act of righteousness on the cross makes it possible for God to count you righteous also and to give you life. Jesus' righteousness leads to your righteousness. 'More than just getting us out of trouble, he got us into life! One man said no to God and put many people in the wrong; one man said yes to God and put many in the right' (v.19, MSG).

Jesus, through his death on the cross, has made God's grace and his gift possible (v.15). The result of our sin is judgment and condemnation (v.16). If we relied on justice and justice alone, that is what we would receive. But since Jesus died in your place you can receive the gift of justification.

God can be just and still acquit you. There is *just grace*. Jesus made possible God's abundant provision of grace and of the gift of righteousness (v.17). You receive justification that brings life (v.18). You are 'made righteous' (v.19). You receive eternal life through Jesus Christ our Lord (v.21).

All this is by grace (vv.15, 17, 20–21). Allow these truths to sink deep into your heart. See yourself as God sees you – as righteous in his sight – and believe that, because of what Jesus has done for you, when God looks at you he is pleased with you.

PRAYER

Lord, thank you so much for the death of Jesus on my behalf. Thank you that although I deserve judgment and condemnation, you have made it possible for me to be justified and to receive the righteousness from God by grace as a gift.

OLD TESTAMENT READING

Amos 8:1–9:15
The God of justice and grace

Amos again speaks out against injustice:

> 'Listen to this, you who walk all over the weak,
> you who treat poor people as less than nothing,
> Who say, "When's my next paycheck coming
> so I can go out and live it up?
> How long till the weekend
> when I can go out and have a good time?"
> Who give little and take much,
> and never do an honest day's work.
> You exploit the poor, using them –
> and then, when they're used up, you discard them' (8:4–6, MSG).

The condition of the people was not unlike the condition of the people that we see in our society today. People are dying of spiritual hunger. There is 'a famine of hearing the words of the Lord' (v.11). People are searching – they try drugs, alcohol, sex, or power. All this is an attempt to satisfy that deep hunger, but they do not find spiritual food (v.12).

The intention of the covenant law was to protect the disadvantaged. But, as is often the case today, the poor were not receiving justice. They were being trampled upon. They were being cheated. The Lord hates dishonesty because he loves us and he loves the poor. Injustice and dishonesty were at the heart of Israel's sins. As a result of all this Amos says, 'Judgment Day is coming!' (v.11, MSG). Israel will be driven into exile (9:1–10).

Yet, the book of Amos does not end on this note. It ends with the promise of restoration: 'I will restore David's house that has fallen to pieces ... Everything will be happening at once – and everywhere you look, blessings! Blessings like wine pouring off the mountains and hills. I'll make everything right again for my people Israel:

> They'll rebuild their ruined cities.
> They'll plant vineyards and drink good wine.
> They'll work their gardens and eat fresh vegetables.
> And I'll plant them, plant them on their own land.
> They'll never again be uprooted from the land I've given them'
> (vv.11–15, MSG).

The ultimate future of God's people is beyond your wildest dreams. Even sin and injustice cannot ultimately derail God's plans of blessing. It is the same dynamic as we saw in our New Testament passage. God's grace and mercy far outweigh our sins. Jesus ultimately makes it possible for both justice and forgiveness to go hand in hand.

PRAYER

Thank you, Lord, that you are a God of justice and of grace. Thank you that through the outpouring of the Holy Spirit we see an in-breaking of that future now. May justice triumph. May the new wine of your Holy Spirit and a great outpouring of grace drip from the mountains.

20 July | Day 201
Enjoy Your New Life

Bishop Taylor Smith, former Chaplain General to the Forces, once had a conversation with a young man that went like this:

> Bishop: 'When you think about the cross of Christ, what do you see?'
> Young man: 'I see Christ and two thieves crucified either side of him…'
> Bishop: 'What else do you see?'
> Young man: 'I see the soldiers gambling…'
> Bishop: 'If that is all you see, I think you will have trouble with the Christian life. When I see the cross – with all that – I see old Bishop Taylor Smith. *I* was crucified *with* Christ.'

In the New Testament passage for today, the apostle Paul expounds and explains what it means to have been 'crucified with Christ'. We are 'in Christ Jesus'. 'We were therefore buried with him through baptism into death in order that, just as Christ was raised from the dead through the glory of the Father, we too may *live a new life*' (Romans 6:4). 'We entered into the new country of grace – *a new life* in a new land!' (Romans 6:3, MSG).

Soon after encountering Jesus I wrote, 'I died in February 1974. My old life was buried. From then onwards I have walked *in newness of life*. It really does seem like that. Life before was so absolutely and completely different.'

Through the death and resurrection of Jesus Christ, you are able to live and enjoy '*a new life*'. In the passages for today, we see how this was anticipated in the Old Testament and fulfilled in the New Testament.

READING FROM PSALMS

Psalm 87:1–7
New song

This is a psalm of praise. It is hard to understand and has been described as one of the most problematic in the whole Psalter. It is written in the language of poetry.

The psalmist concludes by anticipating the future: 'As they make music they will sing, "All my fountains are in you."' (v.7). This picture of overflowing water is an image of abundant life. It was often used in the Old Testament to represent the presence of God in the temple (for instance in Ezekiel 47).

However, Jesus says that all this was fulfilled not in a place but in a person (John 7:37 onwards). Out of his innermost being flowed rivers of living water. We can now sing a new song of worship to the Lord, saying of him, 'All my fountains are in you.'

PRAYER

Lord, may your streams of living water flow into me and out of me today.

NEW TESTAMENT READING

Romans 6:1–14
New freedom

The insane but influential Russian monk, Rasputin, taught his followers that after their conversion they should go and sin more, so that in being forgiven, they would feel more of God's love. He failed to understand that grace is not an excuse to sin. Rather it is a *reason not to sin*.

Paul deals with this very issue, asking whether, if grace meets our every sin, and as sin increases grace abounds all the more, should we 'keep on sinning so God can keep on forgiving?' (v.1, MSG).

He answers, 'I should hope not! If we've left the country where sin is sovereign, how can we still live in our old house there? Or didn't you realize we packed up and left there for good?' (v.2, MSG).

Now we are free, we have a radically changed attitude to sin. How can we, who have been so radically changed – the difference between life and death – still live in sin? Once we were slaves to sin, in that we had to obey its commands, but now we are free.

In this passage, we see all three tenses of salvation:

1. You HAVE BEEN *saved* from the PENALTY of sin

Paul writes in the past tense that 'our old self was crucified with him so that the body of sin might be done away with, that we should no longer be slaves to sin – because anyone who has died has been freed from sin' (vv.6–7).

Through the death of Jesus on the cross for us the past is totally forgiven. Your guilt has been removed. The *penalty* for all your sin – past, present and future – has been paid. You have been freed.

2. You WILL BE *saved* from the PRESENCE of sin

Paul writes, 'If we have been united with him like this in his death, we will certainly also be united with him in his resurrection' (v.5).

Your salvation is not yet complete. There is a future tense to salvation. One day you will be united with him in his resurrection and you will for ever be freed from the *presence* of sin and will enjoy the uninterrupted *presence* of God for ever.

3. You ARE BEING *saved* from the POWER of sin

Paul writes, 'From now on, think of it this way: Sin speaks a dead language that means nothing to you; God speaks your mother tongue, and you hang on every word. You are dead to sin and alive to God. That's what Jesus did.

'That means you must not give sin a vote in the way you conduct your lives. Don't give it the time of day. Don't even run little errands that are connected with that old way of life. Throw yourselves wholeheartedly and full-time – remember, you've been raised from the dead! – into God's way of doing things.' (vv.11–14, MSG).

Jesus has set you free, not only from the guilt of sin but also from its addictive *power*. You do not need to sin any more – 'sin shall not be your master' (v.14). You are to count yourself dead to sin and alive to God. You do not need to obey sin's evil desires. This is the present tense of salvation. You are being set free from the power of sin as you offer the parts of your body to Jesus as instruments of righteousness.

PRAYER

Lord, thank you that you have set me free to enjoy a new life. I offer you my body today and pray that you will use me as an instrument of righteousness.

OLD TESTAMENT READING

Hosea 1:1–2:23
New love

God loves you unconditionally, wholeheartedly and continually. No matter what you have done, you can have a new beginning, a fresh start, a new life and a new love.

'Hosea is the prophet of love,' writes Eugene Peterson. 'But not love as we imagine or fantasize it. He was a parable of God's love for his people lived out as God revealed and enacted it – a lived parable. It is an astonishing story: a prophet commanded to marry a common whore and have children with her. It is an even more astonishing message: God loves us in just this way – goes after us at our worst, keeps after us until he gets us, and makes lovers of men and women who know nothing of real love.'[1]

Hosea was prophesying shortly after the time of Amos (c.750–722 BC). His marriage to Gomer was a kind of analogy for Israel's relationship with God. God spoke to Hosea and said:

> 'Find a whore and marry her.
> Make this whore the mother of your children.
> And here's why: This whole country has become a whorehouse, unfaithful to me, God' (1:2, MSG).

Israel's mistake was to chase after things (food, wine, fashion, jewellery and perfume) rather than God (2:5, 8, MSG). They failed to see it was God who provided these things. All he asks is that you should seek him first.

God's answer is to frustrate us when we chase after things rather than him, by not allowing us to obtain the things on which we have set our hearts. He says:

> 'She'll go on the hunt for her lovers
> but not bring down a single one.
> She'll look high and low
> but won't find a one' (v.7a, MSG).

God longs for you to be living in a relationship with him as close as a husband and a wife.

He says, 'I am now going to allure her' (v.14a). He takes her into a desert (this is so often the place where God's voice is heard) and speaks tenderly (v.14). '"In that day," declares the Lord, "you will call me 'my husband' … I will betroth you to me for ever"' (vv.16, 19).

This foreshadows the relationship of Jesus to his church. God promises a new love relationship between him and his people (vv.19–20). They will know (acknowledge) the Lord.

It will be a relationship of love and compassion. He says, 'I will show my love to the one I called "Not my loved one". I will say to those called "Not my people", "You are my people"; and they will say, "You are my God"' (v.23).

PRAYER

Lord, thank you that through the death and resurrection of Jesus it is possible for me to know you. Thank you that I can walk each day in a relationship of love with you. Thank you that you show your love for us and call us your people. Thank you that I can say to you, 'You are my God'.

21 July | Day 202
The Way Out of the Maze

At the age of eighteen, Billy Nolan ran away from the merchant navy. He was an alcoholic for thirty-five years. For twenty years he sat outside HTB drinking alcohol and begging for money. On 13 May 1990, he looked in the mirror and said, 'You're not the Billy Nolan I once knew.' To use his own expression, he asked the Lord Jesus Christ into his life and made a covenant with him that he would never drink alcohol again. From that day on, he didn't touch a drop. His life was transformed; he radiated the love and joy of Christ. I once said to him, 'Billy, you look happy.' He replied, 'I am happy because I am free. *Life is like a maze* and at last I have found the way out through Jesus Christ.'[1]

St Augustine wrote that God was the master 'whom to serve is perfect freedom'. This is a great paradox. Many people think that if they serve God they will lose their freedom. In fact, it is the very opposite. Living for ourselves is, in fact, a form of slavery. Serving God 'in the new way of the Spirit' (Romans 7:6) is the way to find perfect freedom – free to have a relationship with him and to be the kind of person that deep down you long to be.

READING FROM PSALMS

Psalm 88:1–9a
Cry out to God

This psalm describes a situation similar to the one that Billy Nolan had found himself in: 'I'm caught *in a maze* and can't find my way out, blinded by tears of pain and frustration' (v.8, MSG).

The psalmist is undergoing great suffering. His 'soul is full of trouble' (v.3a). He thinks he is going to die: 'I'm camped on the edge of hell … a hopeless case. Abandoned as already dead' (vv.3–5, MSG). He is 'in the darkest depths' (v.6), 'without strength' (v.4), 'confined and cannot escape' (v.8). He has even lost the support of his closest friends (v.8).

Only God can save us: 'God, you're my last chance of the day' (v.1, MSG). However bad your situation may feel, cry out to God for freedom.

PRAYER

'O Lord, the God who saves me, day and night I cry out before you. May my prayer come before you; turn your ear to my cry' (vv.1–2).

NEW TESTAMENT READING

Romans 6:15–7:6
Serve God

There is a *Thomas the Tank Engine* cartoon that pictures Thomas on his side, having fallen off the train tracks. He is shouting, 'I'm free! I'm free at last. I've fallen off the rails and I'm free!' Of course, the reality is that Thomas is far more 'free' when his wheels are on the rails and he is operating in line with how he has been created to function.

It is the same with us. We might imagine that we are freer if we have no one telling us what to do other than ourselves, but this is a delusion for we find ourselves enslaved to sin – it leads to 'a dead end' (6:21 MSG).

It has been said that 'the only exercise some people take is jumping to wrong conclusions'. The apostle Paul is worried that his readers will jump to the wrong conclusion – that some might argue that it doesn't matter if we carry on sinning. He writes, 'What then? Shall we sin because we are not under law but under grace? By no means!' (v.15).

The assurance of forgiveness is not an excuse to continue sinning. Grace is not a casual 'get out clause' for sin. It would be absurd to carry on sinning for two reasons:

1. New Lord

As a Christian you have a new Lord. You now serve God, 'one whose commands set you free to live openly in his freedom!' (v.17, MSG). Like it or not, we are all slaves to something. Sin is a form of slavery which brings only spiritual captivity and death, but serving God brings perfect freedom. For 'God's gift is *real life,* eternal life, delivered by Jesus, our Master' (v.23, MSG).

God is your new Lord. Every time you yield to sin you are going against the purpose of grace – which is to give you real life, eternal life. When you are tempted, remember that *you do not have to give in*. You are no longer a slave to sin. You are free to say 'no'.

Remember also the rewards of obedience. In serving God, 'the benefit you reap leads to holiness, and the result is eternal life' (v.22).

2. New love

It is absurd to carry on sinning because, as well as having a new Lord, you also have a new love.

Paul speaks about one aspect of marriage to illustrate this. A woman is released from the law of marriage when her husband dies. Death discharges us from the law (7:1–6).

Similarly, we as Christians have died to the law. Our old love was the law but, as Christians, 'we're no longer shackled to that domineering mate of sin' (v.6, MSG). You can now be bound to your new love, Jesus, just as a woman whose husband dies is free to marry a new love (v.4).

Now that you live under grace rather than under law, you have the Spirit living in you who fills you with both the *desire and ability* to do what is right. Connected to your new love, Jesus, you 'serve in the new way of the Spirit, and not in the old way of the written code' (v.6).

Jesus sets you free to be the person that, deep down, you long to be. This is true freedom.

PRAYER

Lord, thank you that serving you is perfect freedom. Today I offer all the parts of my body as slaves to righteousness (6:19). I want to serve you, my Lord and my love, in the way of the Spirit.

OLD TESTAMENT READING

Hosea 3:1–5:15
Seek God's freedom

Some people find 'sin' a hard concept, but 'loving something too much' (idolatry) is something most of us can understand. Our highest love is that which we serve and worship.

This Old Testament passage provides an illustration of the principle that Paul expounded in the book of Romans, that those who sin are slaves to sin and end up with their lives caught in a maze.

God loves his people (3:1). The prophet Hosea is called to give a visual aid of this by his love for his wife in spite of the fact that she has committed adultery (v.1): 'Love her the way I, God, love the Israelite people, even as they flirt and party with every god that takes their fancy' (v.1, MSG).

Hosea speaks the word of the Lord, 'There is no faithfulness, no love, no acknowledgement of God in the land. There is only cursing, lying and murder, stealing and adultery' (4:1–2). The people are guilty of adultery and prostitution (vv.13b, 15; 5:3). This is a fairly accurate description of many societies today.

The leaders were not setting a good example: 'The more the priests increased, the more they sinned against me; they exchanged their Glory for something disgraceful. They feed on the sins of my people and relish their wickedness. And it will be: Like people, like priests' (4:7–9).

Instead of finding freedom through their sin, they were dissatisfied and enslaved as a result of their sin: 'They'll eat and be as hungry as ever, have sex and get no satisfaction ... Wine and whiskey leave my people in a stupor ... Drunk on sex, they can't find their way home. They've replaced their God with their genitals' (vv.10–12, MSG). They are 'addicted to idols ... When the beer runs out, it's sex, sex, and more sex' (vv.17–18, MSG).

They found themselves unable to turn back to God: 'Their deeds do not permit them to return to their God' (5:4a). Adultery and prostitution were rife among the people (14:13b,15; 5:3). It is as if they had come under some demonic power: 'A spirit of prostitution is in their heart; they do not acknowledge the LORD' (v.4b). He withdrew himself from them (v.6).

But God's withdrawal was so that the people would come back to him. The way back is to admit their guilt and seek God's face: 'In their misery they will earnestly seek me' (v.15b).

'Exactly how do we seek God?' writes Joyce Meyer. 'One way is to think about Him and consider what matters to Him and what He says about certain situations. When we seek Him, we find out much more about His answers to our problems. We also find joy, peace, love, wisdom and everything else we need in our lives. Let me urge you to seek him in every area of your life today.'[2]

PRAYER

Lord I seek you today. I bring to you all the problems that I'm facing ... Please show me what you want me to do. Give me wisdom. Help me today to find perfect freedom in serving you wholeheartedly.

22 July | Day 203
Help, Lord!

One of my most frequent prayers is 'Help!' It is also one of the most common prayers in the Bible. It is a prayer you can pray every day, in any and every situation. You can cry out to the Lord for help. God's desire is for you to have a relationship with him that is real and from the heart.

READING FROM PSALMS

Psalm 88:9b–18
Help in broken relationships

Rejection is always hurtful – especially when it comes from someone you love or someone very close to you. Broken relationships are painful – particularly when we feel we have been 'dumped' by a 'lover', a 'neighbour' or a close friend. The psalmist feels that since 'lover and neighbor alike dump me; the only friend I have left is Darkness' (v.18, MSG).

He says, 'For as long as I remember I've been hurting' (v.15, MSG). The situation seems like one of utter hopelessness: darkness (v.12), feeling rejected by God (v.14), affliction (v.15a), terror and despair (v.15b). 'I'm bleeding, black-and-blue ... I'm nearly dead' (v.17, MSG).

Yet there is one note of hope. The hope comes from the fact that, in the midst of all this, he chooses to start *each day* by crying out to God: 'I call to you, O LORD, every day; I spread out my hands to you' (v.9b).

Perhaps today you're struggling with a relationship: in your marriage, workplace, church or with a close friend. However bad your situation may seem, there is always *hope* if you cry out to the Lord for help.

PRAYER

'I cry to you for help, O LORD; in the morning my prayer comes before you' (v.13). O Lord, I spread out my hands to you. I ask you for help...

NEW TESTAMENT READING

Romans 7:7–25
Help in the struggle with sin

Do you ever find yourself trapped in bad habits or sins that you want to break free from but find yourself unable to do so? Do you ever find yourself deciding that you will *not* do something and then doing it anyway?

Paul writes, 'I've spent a long time in sin's prison. What I don't understand about myself is that I decide one way, but then I act another, doing things I absolutely despise' (v.15, MSG).

He goes on, 'It happens so regularly that it's predictable. The moment I decide to do good, sin is there to trip me up. I truly delight in God's commands, but it's pretty obvious that not all of me joins in that delight. Parts of me covertly rebel, and just when I least expect it, they take charge' (vv.21–23, MSG).

Paul says, 'I obviously *need help*!' (v.18, MSG). He cries out: 'What a wretched man I am! Who will rescue me from this body of death?' (v.24).

Having said (in yesterday's passage) that you are free from the law (v.6), Paul anticipates the kind of questions that will be raised about what he is saying. Is he equating the law with sin? (v.7).

He shows that it is *not* the law that is sin. Quite the reverse. 'The law code itself is God's good and common sense, each command sane and holy counsel' (v.12, MSG). It is *we* who are sinful. The law shows this by revealing what sin is, and that we cannot keep the law. Indeed it even aggravates sin in us.

The next question follows from the previous ones. If the law is so good, why did it lead to my death? (v.13). 'No,' says Paul. It was not the law – but my sin – that led to death. If someone is condemned for a crime, it is not the law that causes the penalty. Rather it is the crime. All the law does is to set the standard.

Much ink has been spilled over this passage. The main debate is whether Paul is referring to his Christian or pre-Christian state. It is clearly autobiographical, but he is also talking generally about the condition of human beings living under the law.

Perhaps we should see this passage as describing the Christian not living in the fullness of the Spirit's power, even though he or she desires to do so. It can be read as the human cry to live in the Spirit, heard again in the lives of Christians through the ages.

We know that God's law is holy, righteous and good (v.12). We know that it is spiritual (v.14). Yet we find ourselves failing: 'I am unspiritual, sold as a slave to sin. I do not understand what I do. For what I want to do I do not do, but what I hate I do' (vv.14–15).

The difference between the 'before' and 'after' of becoming a Christian is not that before, I sinned, and that after, I was sinless. No – the difference is that before becoming a Christian, sin was in character; it did not really worry you or me. Whereas after becoming a Christian, it is utterly out of character; I do not want to do it. It causes me pain and regret when I do. Not so much because I have let myself down – although there is that. But because I want to be pleasing Christ – and I have failed him.

If you are like me, you know only too well this battle with sin. Please realise that that is a key mark of the genuine Christian believer.

As Paul cries out for help he already knows the answer to the question, '"Who will rescue me from this body of death?" Thanks be to God – through Jesus Christ our Lord!' (vv.24–25).

Perhaps, the key to understanding this passage lies in the two words 'I myself' (v.25b). On our own we are slaves to the law of sin but this is not the end of the story. Paul goes on to speak about the great liberation that the Holy Spirit brings to our lives.

As I look at myself as a Christian in terms of belonging to Christ, I realise that I am not free to sin. As I look at myself as a Christian in the world, I realise that I am not free from sin either. But as I look at myself as a Christian *empowered by the Spirit*, I realise that I am free to overcome sin. To paraphrase John Newton:

> 'I am not what I want to be.
> I am not what I ought to be.
> I am not what I one day will be.
> But, by the grace of God, I am not what I once was.'

PRAYER

Lord, I cry out to you for help. Please fill me with your Holy Spirit today. I really need the help of the Holy Spirit to lead the kind of life I know you want me to lead.

OLD TESTAMENT READING

Hosea 6:1–7:16
Help for healing

God wants to bring healing to our lives. The people knew that if they truly returned to God, he would heal them (6:1).

If you want God's healing, you need to cry out to him from your heart. God's complaint against his people in this passage is that, 'They do not cry out to me from their hearts' (7:14b). 'Instead of crying out to me in heart-felt prayer, they whoop it up in bed with their whores' (v.14, MSG).

The first three verses of chapter 6 appear to describe the painful process by which the Lord restores us to himself when we slip away from him. However, there is no acknowledgment of sin or deep repentance. It may be Hosea putting the people's shallow confession into words: 'Your declarations of love last no longer than morning mist and predawn dew' (6:4, MSG).

What is clear is that God is interested in the heart, not superficial action: 'I'm after love that lasts, not more religion. I want you to know GOD' (v.6, MSG). He is concerned about a relationship with him that comes from the heart.

His complaint is that 'none of them calls on me' (7:7). There is an arrogance, an independent spirit in humankind that refuses to 'return to the LORD ... or search for him' (v.10). He says, 'I long to redeem them ... but they turn away from me' (vv.13–14). You can receive healing and forgiveness from God for all the things you do wrong – but you need to cry out to him from your heart (v.14).

As Joyce Meyer writes, emotional 'healing does not come easily and can be quite painful. Sometimes we have wounds that are still infected, and before we can be thoroughly healed, those wounds must be opened and the infection removed. Only God knows how to do this properly. As you seek God for the healing from your hurts, spend time with God in His Word and wait in His presence. I guarantee you will find healing there!'[1]

PRAYER

Lord, I want not only to know you but also to press on to know you better (6:3). I cry to you from my heart for healing, restoration and revival. Help Lord!

23 July | Day 204
Know You Are Loved

Until it actually happened to me I would not have believed it was possible. But the moment I saw him, I experienced an overwhelming love. This tiny baby, who to others must have looked like any other baby, was *my son*. The moment a parent first sees their own child is unforgettable. The love a parent feels for a child is almost indescribable. Yet this is the analogy God uses of his love for you. You are a child of God. The love he has for you is even greater than that which parents feel for their own children.

Knowing who you are will have a big impact on your life. Know that you are a deeply loved child of God. This should be the basis of your confidence, security and hope.

READING FROM PROVERBS

Proverbs 17:25–18:6
Wise children

The Bible has a lot to say about human parenting and the relationship between parents and their children. The love parents have for their children is instinctive and powerful. Good parents want the very best for their children. Children have a high capacity to bring great joy to their parents. But, of course, they can also bring grief.

'Foolish children bring grief to their fathers and bitterness to those who bore them' (17:25). The writer goes on to expand on the difference between the foolish and the wise in different aspects of life.

For example, 'fools ... delight in airing their own opinions' (18:2), whereas the wise use words with *restraint*. In fact, 'Even fools are thought wise if they keep silent, and discerning if they hold their tongues' (17:28). As American historian Will Durant (1885–1981) once said, 'One of the lessons of history is that nothing is often a good thing to do and always a clever thing to say.'[1]

The writer then touches on other characteristics of the wise: friendliness (18:1), listening (v.2) and justice (v.5).

PRAYER

Lord, help us to be wise children who please you in the way we live (Romans 8:8).

NEW TESTAMENT READING

Romans 8:1–17
God's children

How do you see yourself in relation to God? Do you go around always feeling, at least slightly, guilty? Do you 'live under a continuous, low-lying black cloud'? (v.1, MSG).

This is *not* how you are meant to live as a Christian. You are a child of God, deeply loved, accepted and empowered by his unconditional love for you. He wants you to enjoy freedom from guilt and condemnation and to experience an intimacy of relationship with him, even closer than the best parent/child relationship.

The moment you receive Jesus the *past* is dealt with. You receive complete forgiveness. The barrier between you and God has been removed. Paul writes, 'There is now no condemnation for those who are in Christ Jesus' (v.1). You are set free from the law of sin and death (v.2). Although the law was good, it was powerless to save us because of our sinful nature (v.3a). So, God sent Jesus to die for us as a sin offering (v.3b). Jesus took away *all* your sins – past, present and future.

Now, in the *present,* you can enjoy life in the Spirit. You no longer live 'according to the sinful nature but according to the Spirit' (v.4). The Holy Spirit leads you to stop setting your mind on 'what that [sinful] nature desires' but rather to set your mind on 'what the Spirit desires' (v.5). This leads to 'life and peace' (v.6). Paul is not saying that you will be perfect, but rather that 'even though you still experience all the limitations of sin – you yourself will experience life on God's terms' (v.10, MSG). This is possible because right now the Spirit of God lives in you (v.9).

Furthermore, you can look forward to a *future* resurrection of your body. The same Holy Spirit who lived in Jesus and raised him from the dead dwells in you. Therefore your body, like Jesus', will be raised: 'He who raised Christ from the dead will also give life to your mortal bodies through his Spirit, who lives in you' (v.11).

It is to those who receive Jesus, to those who believe in his name, that he gives 'the right to become children of God' (John 1:12). You become a child of God not by being born, but by being born again by the Spirit.

If Romans is the 'Himalayas' of the New Testament, then Romans 8 is its Mount Everest and its summit is these verses where Paul describes how those who are led by the Spirit are the children of God (Romans 8:14–17).

1. Highest status

There is no higher status than to be a child of God (v.14). Under Roman law, if an adult wanted an heir he could either choose one of his own sons or adopt a son who would take his name. God has only one begotten Son – Jesus – but he has many adopted sons and daughters. You have been adopted into God's family. There is no status in the world that compares with the privilege of being a child of the Creator of the universe.

2. Closest intimacy

You have the closest possible intimacy with God. Paul says that by the Spirit we cry '*Abba*, Father' (v.15). This Aramaic word may well have been the first word that Paul ever spoke, and the way in which he addressed his earthly father. Jesus used '*Abba*' in speaking to God in a distinctive way. It expresses both profound respect and close intimacy, and is perhaps best thought of as 'Daddy' or 'Papa'. In large parts of the Middle East it is still the first word children are taught.

As God's child, you are no longer a slave of fear but an adopted child of God (v.15). You can enjoy the closest possible intimacy with your Father in heaven.

3. Deepest experience

The Spirit gives you the deepest possible experience of God. 'The Spirit himself testifies with our spirit that we are God's children' (v.16). In the same way that I want my children to know and experience my love for them and my relationship with them, so God wants his children to be assured of that love and of that relationship. 'God's Spirit touches our spirits and confirms who we really are' (v.16, MSG).

4. Greatest security

To be a son or daughter of God is the greatest security. For if we are children of God we are also 'heirs of God and co-heirs with Christ' (v.17a). Under Roman law an adopted son would inherit his estate.

As children of God we are heirs. The only difference is that we inherit, not on the death of our father, but on our own death. You will enjoy an eternity of love with Jesus: 'And we know we are going to get what's coming to us – an unbelievable inheritance!' (v.17, MSG).

Paul adds, 'if indeed we share in his sufferings in order that we may also share in his glory' (v.17b). In the Christian life, glory comes through suffering: 'We go through exactly what Christ goes through. If we go through the hard times with him, then we're certainly going to go through the good times with him!' (v.17, MSG). Christians identify with Jesus Christ. This means severe persecution for many Christians today. You will face some opposition, but your inheritance as child of God surpasses all these troubles.

PRAYER

Abba Father, thank you for the amazing privilege of being your child. Thank you that your Spirit living within me testifies with my spirit that I am your child. Thank you that my future is secure – that I am your heir and co-heir with Christ.

OLD TESTAMENT READING

Hosea 8:1–9:17
Faithful children

God loves you. He wants you to make the most of your life. He does not want you to waste it. He says to you, as he said to his people in the Old Testament, 'Don't waste your life' (9:1a, MSG). You waste your life when 'you walk away from your God' (v.1b, MSG).

As we have seen, Hosea uses a husband and wife analogy for Israel's relationship with God. However, he will go on to use the parent-child analogy: 'When Israel was a child, I loved him, and out of Egypt I called my son' (11:1).

We see how God's heart is broken by the unfaithfulness of his child: 'The people have broken my covenant and rebelled against my law ... Incapable of purity ... They sow the wind and reap the whirlwind ... Israel has forgotten his Maker ... You have been unfaithful to your God' (8:1, 5, 7, 14; 9:1). God longs for his people to be faithful to him and live life to the full as a result.

We have the immense privilege of living in the age of the Spirit. God has sent his Spirit to live in your heart – to enable you to live faithfully in accordance with the Spirit (Romans 8:5).

PRAYER

Lord, thank you that I am your much-loved child. Help me to be a wise and faithful child.

24 July | Day 205
A Pillow on Which to Rest Our Weary Heads

I sometimes struggle to believe that God really loves me. I can be tempted to feel a sense of failure and self-condemnation. It is relatively easy to believe that God loves everybody else, but it is much harder to believe that God loves *me*.

The love of God, Paul explains in Romans 8, starts with 'no condemnation' (v.1) and ends with no separation: nothing '*will be able to separate us from the love of God that is in Christ Jesus our Lord*' (v.39). John Stott describes the truth of this passage as 'a pillow on which to rest our weary heads'.[1]

'God loves each one of us as if there was only one of us to love,' wrote St Augustine. If you were the only person who had ever lived, Jesus would have died for you. And if it is true of you, it is also true of me. God loves me and you.

READING FROM PSALMS

Psalm 89:1–8
Tell of the great love of the Lord

The focus of both our worship and our witness is the love of God.

1. Worship
This psalm begins with worship, a hymn of praise (vv.1–18), focusing on God's love: 'I will sing of *the* L*ORD's great love* for ever' (v.1).

Think about God's greatness and glory – how amazing it is to be loved by the 'LORD God Almighty' (v.8). This is something that can never be taken away from you. The psalmist writes, 'Your love stands firm for ever' (v.2).

2. Witness
The message you pass onto others should always centre on God's love: 'I'll never quit telling *the story of your love*' (v.2, MSG).

PRAYER

Lord, thank you that I have experienced your love and faithfulness. Help me, Lord, to continue to make your love known to others.

NEW TESTAMENT READING

Romans 8:18–39
Meditate on the amazing love of Christ

Do your circumstances ever cause you to question God's love for you?

Paul suffered greatly – through beatings, imprisonment and many other hardships. But he says that these sufferings cannot come close to comparing to the glory we will see one day. There is no comparison 'between the present hard times and the coming good times' (v.18, MSG).

While you are waiting, you have the 'firstfruits of the Spirit' (v.23). The Holy Spirit is a down payment guaranteeing what is to come – the future glory. One day the whole of creation will be liberated (v.21). Here and now, your body may be 'groaning' (v.22) as it gradually deteriorates, but one day it will be totally healed and restored. Your resurrection will not be only 'spiritual', it will be physical. 'We wait eagerly for ... the redemption of *our bodies*' (v.23).

Paul uses the analogy of a pregnancy. You are feeling 'the pains of labor' (v.22, AMP).

'Meanwhile, the moment you get tired in the waiting, God's Spirit is right alongside helping you along. If you don't know how or what to pray, it doesn't matter. The Holy Spirit does our praying in and for us, making prayer out of our wordless sighs, our aching groans' (v.26, MSG). He enables you to pray in accordance with God's will (v.27). If your prayers are led by the Spirit, they will definitely be answered – because they will be in accordance with God's will.

Life is not the random mess it may sometimes appear. 'We know that *in all things* God works for the good of those who love him, who have been called according to his purpose' (v.28).

In every detail of your life, God is at work. 'All things' includes even our mistakes. God will take even your errors and work them out for your good. He reigns. He is sovereign. In everything he works for the good of those who love him. Supremely, the cross demonstrates that just as God took the very worst event in history and turned it into the very best; he can take the worst things in your life and use them for good.

This promise applies to all Christians. He elaborates in verses 29–30 – you are foreknown, predestined, called, justified, glorified. The first four events have happened, but glorification is a future event. However, Paul uses the same past tense for all of them. 'You *are ... glorified*.' This use of the aorist (completed) tense shows Paul's certainty about the future – it has already been secured.

This is astonishing. It is possibly the most daring statement of faith in the whole of the New Testament. It speaks of total security. The security of a Christian is solidly grounded on the unwavering love of God. This sure foundation is deeper than all your circumstances and feelings.

How can you be sure of God's love? Paul poses five unanswerable questions.

1. *With God on your side like this, how can you lose?*

'If God is for us, who can be against us?' (v.31b). If God is for you, what others think is not so important. You are set free from the fear of people and from caring too much about what others think.

2. *If God gave his only Son for you, is he likely to withhold anything else?*

'He who did not spare his own Son, but gave him up for us all – how will he not also, along with him, graciously give us all things?' (v.32).

3. *Who is going to dare to prosecute you?*

'Who will bring any charge against those whom God has chosen?' (v.33a).

4. *If God is the judge and Jesus your defence counsel, how can a prosecution succeed?*

'It is God who justifies. Who then can condemn?' (vv.33b–34). Jesus is your defence lawyer. He is supremely qualified. 'Christ Jesus, who died' (v.34) has already served the sentence for us. He 'was raised to life' by God (v.34). He is in the supreme place of honour 'at the right hand of God' (v.34). He is praying for you (v.34). He is sticking up for you. Jesus never stops praying for you.

5. *How can anyone drive a wedge between you and Christ's love?*

You can be separated from friends and family by circumstances or even death. But, 'Who shall separate us from the love of Christ?' (v.35a). This does not mean that life is easy. There may be trouble, hard times, hatred, hunger, homelessness, bullying threats and backstabbing. But 'not even the worst sins listed in Scripture … None of this fazes us because Jesus loves us' (vv.35b–37, MSG). In the midst of every difficulty, you can cling to God's love for you.

Paul lists seventeen possibilities involving calamities of life, superhuman agencies, time and space (vv.35–39). His list includes absolutely every possible difficultly and challenge you may face. And he concludes that he is totally convinced that nothing 'will be able to separate us from the love of God that is in Christ Jesus our Lord' (v.39). As Isaac Watts wrote, 'Love so amazing, so divine, demands my soul, my life, my all.'[2]

PRAYER

Lord, how can I ever thank you enough for your amazing love? Thank you that in all things you are working together for the good in my life, and absolutely nothing can separate me from your love.

OLD TESTAMENT READING

Hosea 10:1–11:11
Enjoy the unfailing love of God

Do you realise that God loves you more than any parent loves their own children?

Hosea continues to speak of God's love for his people in spite of their unfaithfulness. They have allowed sins, conflict and idolatry to grow up like 'poisonous weeds' (10:4) and 'thorns and thistles' (v.8). Be careful that these things do not grow up in your life. Keep weeding out the bad stuff – even the little weeds before they become big ones.

As well as weeding out the bad stuff, plant beautiful flowers. God calls them (and us) to 'sow for yourselves righteousness' and 'reap the *fruit of unfailing love* … for it is time to seek the LORD' (v.12).

He describes it here in terms of parental love: 'When Israel was a child, I loved him, and out of Egypt I called my son … It was I who taught Ephraim to walk, taking them by the arms … it was I who healed them. I led them with cords of human kindness, with ties of love; I … bent down to feed them' (11:1–4).

This is a wonderful picture of God's love and tenderness: like a parent looking after a toddler. 'I lifted him, like a baby, to my cheek' (v.4, MSG) – feeding them, teaching them to walk, taking them up in their arms.

Even though they refuse to repent and were determined to turn from him, he cannot give them up (vv.5–8). 'My heart is changed within me; all *my compassion is aroused*' (v.8b). This is the love that will not let you go.

PRAYER

Thank you, Father, for your love, compassion, tenderness and mercy. Thank you that nothing can separate me from the love of God in Christ Jesus our Lord. Thank you that your love is a pillow on which to rest our weary heads.

25 July | Day 206
What About Those Who Do Not Believe?

In February 1974, I had an encounter with Jesus Christ that totally changed my life. I understood he had died for me. I experienced his love. I knew God was real. I knew the extraordinary blessings of a relationship with Jesus. But almost immediately afterwards I experienced what Paul speaks about in this passage: 'A huge sorrow … an enormous pain deep within me' (Romans 9:2, MSG).

I longed for everyone to experience and know what I had only so recently experienced. I longed for my family and friends who were not yet Christians to know Christ.

The apostle Paul cared so passionately about his own people that he was willing to be cut off from God and the people whom he loved, if they would be saved. He writes, 'I could wish that I myself were cursed and cut off from Christ [a definition of hell] for the sake of my people, those of my own race, the people of Israel' (vv.3–4a).

Yet at the same time Paul trusted that God had the whole situation under control. God is sovereign. He rules and reigns in his universe.

How do we balance this anguish and passion for those we love, with a trust in God's ultimate sovereignty?

READING FROM PSALMS

Psalm 89:9–13
Thank God for his rule and reign

We do not know the answers to all the questions. But we do know that God is in control of his universe. This is God's world. He loves you and you can trust him not only with your future, but also with what will happen to everyone else.

'The heavens are yours, and yours also the earth; you founded the world and all that is in it' (v.11).

Not only did he create the world, but he also continues to act in history. '*You rule* over the surging sea ... Your arm is endued with power; your hand is strong, your right hand exalted' (vv.9a,13).

'And we know that in all things God works for the good for those who love him, who have been called according to his purpose' (Romans 8:28).

PRAYER

You are the Sovereign Lord. You are the creator of the world, and the author of history. Thank you that I can trust that you are in ultimate control of all the circumstances of my life.

NEW TESTAMENT READING

Romans 9:1–21
Trust in his mercy and compassion

'That's not fair' is the cry not only of children, but also of many adults considering the Christian faith.

Having reached the 'peak' of the epistle at the end of chapter 8, Paul turns to consider the race of Israel in chapters 9–11. Paul did not think of becoming a Christian as being converted from Judaism. Rather, he thought of it as becoming part of the fulfilment of true Israelites and true children of Abraham. For Paul, it was intensely personal. He calls Israel 'my people' (9:3), meaning not Christians but Jews. They were his family. He had grown up with them. He said that he suffers 'great sorrow and unceasing anguish' (v.2).

Some seem to suggest that there is no more sorrow in life after someone becomes a Christian. But for Paul, with great joy also came great sorrow and pain. It is a strange paradox. You too may feel this great sorrow about members of your family or friends who seem to be outside the kingdom, or when people reject Jesus.

Paul cared so much for their salvation that he was prepared not just to die for them but 'to be cut off from Christ' (v.3) – the ultimate terror for Paul.

Moses prayed a similar prayer when he prayed for the people who had sinned against God: 'Please forgive their sin – but if not, then blot me out of the book you have written' (Exodus 32:32). God would not accept either Moses' (vv.33–34a) or Paul's offer and sacrifice because neither of their lives could atone for the sins of his people.

It is only the life of the sinless Jesus who could do that. Jesus was willing to be 'cursed and cut off' (Romans 9:3) for us. He was not only willing; his sacrifice was accepted and effective. There is nothing that you can add to it.

Yet, to Paul's great sadness, he realises that most of his own people have rejected this extraordinary gift of redemption and forgiveness. God has offered them (and us) everything – and yet they can choose to reject it.

What makes it even sadder for Paul is that they are God's chosen people. God in his sovereignty had chosen the people of Israel: 'They had everything going for them – family, glory, covenants, revelation, worship, promises, to say nothing of being the race that produced the Messiah, the Christ, who is God over everything, always' (vv.4b–5, MSG).

With that background, he faces the burning question that must have tormented him throughout his ministry: 'Did God's promise fail?' His answer is, 'No, it did not.' What then is the explanation?

His first answer is to say, in effect, 'Have you never noticed that God never made promises to all Abraham's descendants?' He then gives two illustrations, one of Isaac as compared to his brother (vv.6–9), the other of Jacob as against Esau (vv.10–13). In both cases the promise was given to one and not to the other.

Is that fair? 'Is that grounds for complaining that God is unfair?' (v.14a, MSG). His answer is that if anyone says God is unfair, they do not know God.

The doctrine of election is based on God's mercy: '"I'm in charge of mercy. I'm in charge of compassion." Compassion doesn't originate in our bleeding hearts or moral sweat, but in God's mercy' (vv.15–16, MSG). The words 'mercy' and 'compassion' appear seven times (vv.14–18). You can trust God about your future and those you love. He is in ultimate control. It is his sovereign responsibility.

The Bible goes no further in answering the questions. It speaks of both God's great compassion and his justice. It teaches both election and free will. Free will means we are responsible for our own choices.

Very often the truth in the Bible is not at one pole *or* the other, nor in between, but at *both poles at once*. This is not a mystery that the Bible solves for us – there are some things about which we have to conclude, with the psalmist, 'Such knowledge is too wonderful for me' (Psalm 139:6). We need to hold onto the truths of election and free will at the same time.

PRAYER

Lord, thank you that you are loving and merciful, slow to anger and rich in love. Thank you that you died for us on the cross, so that all who believe in you can be set free. Help me to trust you when my understanding fails.

OLD TESTAMENT READING

Hosea 11:12–14:9
Turn from sin and return to God

God's unconditional love has the power to forgive our sins, heal our wounds and mend our broken hearts. Not because we deserve it or have earned it; he loves you freely (14:4). He wants to heal our faithlessness.

God calls us to turn from sin and return to his love: 'Therefore return to your God! Hold fast to love and mercy, to righteousness and justice, and wait expectantly for your God, continually!' (12:6, AMP). This sums up the message of Hosea.

God calls his people to repentance (14:1–2) and promises, 'I will heal their waywardness. I will love them lavishly … I will make a fresh start … Everything you need is to be found in me' (vv.4–8, MSG).

Israel's sins were not very different from the sins of the twenty-first century. For example, there was fraud in the city: 'The businessmen engage in wholesale fraud. They love to rip people off!' (12:7, MSG). People sought security in their finances. 'Ephraim boasts, "I am very rich; I have become wealthy. With all my wealth they will not find in me any iniquity or sin"' (v.8).

When God blesses we become satisfied (13:6a). When we are satisfied we become proud (v.6b). Then we forget God (v.6c). We see this cycle in our nation and in our own individual lives:

'I took care of you, took care of all your needs,
gave you everything you needed. You were spoiled. You thought you didn't need me.
You forgot me' (v.6, MSG).

In spite of their sins, God promised redemption: 'I will ransom them from the power of the grave; I will redeem them from death. Where, O death, are your plagues? Where, O grave, is your destruction?' (v.14, see also 1 Corinthians 15:55). Through Jesus, death has lost its power over our lives. When we return to God he promises we will flourish and blossom and that our fruitfulness will come from him (Hosea 14:7, 8).

PRAYER

Lord, please forgive my sins, receive me graciously, heal my waywardness and love me freely. Help me to blossom like a vine and be fruitful.

26 July | Day 207
Your Family Tree

My father never spoke to me about his life before he had come to England and married my mother. I knew virtually nothing about his background. A few years ago, I was contacted by The Judaica Museum in Berlin. They were doing some research into the Gumbel family. They sent me a copy of my family tree. I discovered that my great-great-grandfather was called Abraham Gumbel. My great-grandfather was called Isaac and his brother, Moses!

My father was Jewish. He qualified as a barrister and became a Doctor of Law at the University of Tübingen in 1927. Later he read Adolf Hitler's *Mein Kampf* and knew what was likely to happen to someone like him who was known as '*Israelitisch*'. He came to England and qualified as an English barrister as well. His sister and parents eventually came too. Most of the rest of my family, on my father's side, were murdered in Dachau, Riga and other Nazi concentration camps.

The treatment of the Jewish people through the centuries has been complex, and at times tragic. Sometimes even passages in the Bible have been misinterpreted and misapplied as a weapon of abuse against the Jewish people.

The people of God in the Old Testament were the nation of Israel. The people of God in the New Testament are all those who put their faith in Jesus Christ. We share a common history and family tree. We worship the same God and, the apostle Paul tells us, the way of salvation is the same for us all.

READING FROM PSALMS

Psalm 89:14–18
Your God is the God of Israel

The Lord, whom we worship, is *the Holy One of Israel*. 'All we are and have we owe to GOD, Holy God of Israel, our King!' (v.18, MSG).

The psalmist says of the Lord, 'The Right and Justice are the roots of your rule; Love and Truth are its fruits' (v.14, MSG). God's choice of the people of Israel does not make him unrighteous and unjust. He is a God of love and faithfulness. He loves all people. The foundation of his throne is righteousness and justice. He will act in a way that is right and his treatment of other nations will never be unjust.

God intended that all nations would be blessed through his choice of Israel (see Genesis 12:3). This has now been made possible through Jesus. You too can walk in a right relationship with God and experience the blessing that this psalm talks about: 'Blessed are those who... walk in the light of your presence, O LORD. They rejoice in your name all day long; they exult in your righteousness. For you are their glory and strength' (Psalm 89:15–17). As a result, 'We're walking on air!' (v.17, MSG).

PRAYER

Lord, help me today to walk in the light of your presence and to rejoice in your name all day long.

NEW TESTAMENT READING

Romans 9:22–10:4
Your salvation began with Israel

God's plan of salvation began with Israel. His plan for Israel (the Jews) and the rest (the Gentiles) is inextricably linked. What does this mean for you now?

God had a plan 'to make the riches of his glory known to the objects of his mercy, whom he prepared in advance for glory – even us, whom he also called, not only from the Jews but also from the Gentiles' (9:23–24). His plan of salvation is wider than just the nation of Israel.

Salvation is based on:

- faith – *not* your good works
- mercy – *not* what you deserve
- belief – *not* where you were born.

Paul goes on to demonstrate this by drawing on the words of Hosea. God had said that he would call people who were 'not my people' – that is, the Gentiles – 'my people', 'my loved one' and 'children of the living God' (vv.25–26).

It is an amazing privilege to be part of God's people, loved by God, called to be his children, the object of his mercy, prepared in advance for glory in order that he might make the riches of his glory known (vv. 23–24).

Under the new covenant, no one is excluded. Everyone can be saved. God has made possible, through Jesus, a righteousness by faith (v.30).

Jesus is the way of salvation. Some will stumble over him, but 'the one who trusts in him will never be put to shame' (v.33).

Paul loves the people of Israel. They are his people. He longs for them to be saved. He intercedes fervently for their salvation. 'Believe me, friends, all I want for Israel is what's best for Israel: salvation, nothing less. I want it with all my heart and pray to God for it all the time' (10:1, MSG).

There is only one way that they will be saved, and that is by faith, through 'the righteousness that comes from God' (v.3). This righteousness comes through Christ. '*Christ is the end of the law* so that there may be righteousness for everyone who believes' (v.4).

'*Christ is the end of the law*' is a huge, ground-breaking, life-changing, history-making statement. There has been a great deal of debate about exactly what Paul meant. However, some things are clear.

1. 'Christ is the end of the law' in that he has *fulfilled the law.* Jesus once described himself as having come to 'fulfil the law' (Matthew 5:17). The purpose of the law was to point us to Jesus (Galatians 3:24). Now Jesus has come, its role has been completed.
2. 'Christ is the end of the law' in that he has *satisfied the law.* Jesus was the only person who has ever fully kept the law, yet through the cross you receive the benefit of his obedience.
3. 'Christ is the end of the law' in *that he has set you free* from the burden and condemnation of the law. As we are constantly failing, we live life under a black cloud of condemnation. Because of Jesus, 'there is now no condemnation for those who are in Christ Jesus' (Romans 8:1).
4. Jesus has set you free from *seeking salvation through the law*. No one can be saved by the law. No one, apart from Jesus, has ever managed to keep the entire law. 'Christ is the end of the law' in that he has set you free from trying to establish your own righteousness. Instead, you are now given '*the righteousness that comes from God*' (v.3).

PRAYER

Lord, thank you that salvation is open to all through faith in Jesus. I pray today for the people of Israel: 'My heart's desire and prayer to God ... is that they may be saved' (10:1).

OLD TESTAMENT READING

1 Chronicles 1:1–2:17
Your history is bound up with Israel

In today's passage we see another family tree. This is *my* family tree. It is also *yours*.

'Names launch this story,' writes Eugene Peterson, 'hundreds and hundreds of names, lists of names, page after page of names, *personal* names ... Holy history is not constructed from impersonal forces or abstract ideas; it is woven from names – persons, each one unique. Chronicles erects a solid defense against depersonalized religion.'[1]

There is more than one way to tell a story. The two books of Chronicles cover the same period as the books of Samuel and Kings. The new writer (possibly Ezra), writing a hundred years or so later, traces the history of Israel from Adam to the return from exile.

We see in these chapters that Israel's history is our history. Our history goes back to Adam (1:1) and the beginning of the human race.

The church goes back to Abraham. 'Abraham was the father of Isaac. The sons of Isaac: Esau and *Israel*' (v.34). Both Israel and the church of Jesus Christ look to Abraham as their father.

In chapter 2, the chronicler traces the history of Israel through the *sons of Israel* right down to David (2:15). Again, Israel's history is your history. The church began with God's call to Abraham and continues right down the ages until now.

Whether the church is popular or unpopular, big or small is relatively unimportant. People talk about the church as if it is a fairly marginal phenomenon only interested in gaining popularity. The only question the media ask is whether it is popular or not.

But as Bishop Lesslie Newbigin pointed out, this is absurd. The church has outlived great empires, philosophical systems, totalitarian systems. The things that seem to occupy the whole horizon of public thinking now will be simply phantoms, half remembered from the past, twenty years from now. But the church will still be there. This given reality needs to be at the centre of our thinking as Christians.[2]

PRAYER

Thank you, Lord, for our common family tree with the people of Israel. Thank you for the extraordinary privilege of being part of the people of God, who trace our history back to the beginning of the human race, through Adam, Abraham and Israel, and right down to the present day.

27 July | Day 208
Beautiful Feet

Friends of ours had been waiting for ten years for a baby. They had been told it was impossible. One day our doorbell rang. There she was. It was written all over her face. As soon as she was in the house she started jumping up and down, stamping *her feet* with joy and delight, announcing the good news. She had conceived. Their wait was over. She was *carrying the good news in her own body*. There is nothing more exciting than being the bearer of good news.

You too are the bearer of good news. *The message of Jesus is in you*. That is why, according to the apostle Paul, you have *beautiful feet* (Romans 10:15)!

As his followers, we are all called to share the good news of Jesus. Some of us have the immense privilege of being called to do it as a full-time job. Way back in January 1978, when I was practising law, I wrote in my prayer diary:

'I long to spend my whole time preaching the gospel – telling people about the love of Jesus. But Romans 10:15 warns, "How can [people] preach unless they are sent?" I cannot and will not be able to preach the gospel unless I am sent by God to do so – it is a wonderful calling. "How *beautiful are the feet* of those who bring good news!"'

The heart of the good news is a righteousness that comes by faith (v.6). 'Everyone who calls on the name of the Lord will be saved' (v.13).

READING FROM PROVERBS

Proverbs 18:7–16
Run to the Lord

This passage in Proverbs is full of practical wisdom. We need to guard our lips: 'Fools are undone by their big mouths; their souls are crushed by their words' (v.7, MSG). 'Gossip' is very tempting but to be avoided: 'Listening to gossip is like eating cheap candy; do you really want junk like that in your belly?' (v.8, MSG).

We need to work hard and not be 'slack': 'Slack habits and sloppy work are as bad as vandalism' (v.9, MSG). It is foolish to rely on wealth: 'The rich think their wealth protects them; they imagine themselves safe behind it' (v.11, MSG). Pride leads to downfall: 'Pride first, then the crash' (v.12a, MSG). Humility leads to honour (v.12b).

There is also some very good advice to those hosting or helping on Alpha: 'Answering before listening is both stupid and rude' (v.13, MSG). 'Wise men and women are always learning, always listening for fresh insights' (v.15, MSG).

In the midst of all this practical advice, there is a verse that ties in with today's theme: 'The name of the LORD is a strong tower; the righteous *run to it* and are safe' (v.10). Not *all* are safe. Only those who run to the strong tower, which is 'the name of the LORD', will be saved.

Even here we find the roots of the teaching of the New Testament that those who call on the name of the Lord will be saved.

PRAYER

Lord, help me today to guard my lips, to be careful about what I say, to work hard and humbly depend on you. Thank you that your name is a strong tower and a place of safety for all who run to it.

NEW TESTAMENT READING

Romans 10:5–11:10
Call to the Lord

I was eighteen years old. I had been a Christian for two months when I had the privilege of telling someone the good news about Jesus in such a way that he believed. His life, like mine, was changed that day.

Do you remember the first time you understood the good news about Jesus and believed in him? Have you ever had the privilege of telling another person the message of Jesus in such a way that they believed?

The claim of the New Testament is breathtaking. The name of the Lord was so sacred in the Old Testament that no one dared take it on their lips. Now we know that the name of the Lord is *Jesus*. Not only can we take his name on our lips but when we believe in him and call on him we are 'saved' (10:9–10).

The Christian message is both *exclusive*, because Jesus is the *only* name given for our salvation, and *inclusive*, because *everyone* in this world can call upon his name.

Jesus is easily accessible to all of us. 'No precarious climb up to heaven to recruit the Messiah, no dangerous descent into hell to rescue the Messiah.' Paul continues:

> 'The word that saves is right here,
> as near as the tongue in your mouth,
> as close as the heart in your chest'
> (vv.6–8, MSG).

It is important to not only believe in your heart, but to actually say you have done so: 'If you confess with your mouth, "Jesus is Lord," and believe in your heart that God raised him from the dead, you will be saved. For it is with your heart that you believe and are justified, and it is with your mouth that you confess and are saved' (vv.9–10).

I have often noticed on Alpha, for example, that something happens to a person, a change takes place, when they 'confess' with their 'mouth' for the first time, 'I am now a Christian.'

Paul is keen to emphasise that as far as salvation is concerned, 'There is no difference between Jew and Gentile' (v.12a). It is 'the same Lord [Jesus, who] is Lord of all, and richly blesses all who call on him, for, "Everyone who calls on the name of the Lord will be saved"' (vv.12b–13).

It is of utmost importance, therefore, that we tell people the good news about Jesus. People cannot call on the name of the Lord unless they believe. They cannot believe unless they hear. They cannot hear unless someone tells them. People will not tell them unless they are sent (vv.14–15). It is an amazing privilege to be sent out to tell people. 'How beautiful are the feet of those who bring good news!' (v.15).

It is not enough simply to be a member of the race of Israel (any more than it is enough now to be born in a Christian country). Paul demonstrates this by quoting Moses and Isaiah. Not all believed. Some were disobedient and obstinate (v.21).

The answer to the question, "Has God rejected his people?", is, "No, no, no" (11:1–4). The rejection of Israel is only partial. There always has been and always will be a remnant. Paul was an example of that truth (v.1).

Paul refers to Elijah (who was depressed after Mount Carmel) saying, 'I am the only one left.' God says, in effect, 'Cheer up, I kept for myself seven thousand people who have not bowed the knee to Baal.' It is all of grace (v.6). Paul says, 'So too, at the present time there is a remnant chosen *by grace*. And if by grace, then it is no longer by works; if it were, grace would no longer be grace' (vv.5–6).

PRAYER

Lord, thank you that everyone who calls on your name will be saved. Thank you that there is no greater privilege than being sent out to tell others. Help us to raise up and send out those who bring good news to Jew and Gentile alike.

OLD TESTAMENT READING

1 Chronicles 2:18–4:8
Put your faith in the Lord

God created us to live in a relationship with him. Until we find that relationship, there will always be something missing in our lives.

God loves you and wants you to find fulfilment and purpose in that relationship. That is why worship of God is central to our lives and it is the backbone of the book of Chronicles. Faithful worship is what matters most of all.

God is faithful to you. He calls you to be faithful to him. Unfaithfulness leads to trouble.

The chronicler continues his introduction to the people of Israel. The list of the kings of Judah (3:10–16) is almost like the index to the books. Much of 1 Chronicles is devoted to King David – who is held up as an example of true worship and faithfulness to God.

One of the great themes of the book of Chronicles is the importance of this faith in the Lord. He is going to demonstrate that not all the people of Israel were faithful.

You may feel very isolated and alone at times. It may appear that there are not many believers around you. But there always remains a remnant who have faith in God.

This is one of the key messages throughout the book of Chronicles. 'Have faith in the LORD your God and you will be upheld; have faith in his prophets and you will be successful' (2 Chronicles 20:20).

PRAYER

Lord, thank you that you always keep a remnant. Help us not to be disheartened but rather to go on spreading the good news of Jesus.

28 July | Day 209
Your Calling Is Irrevocable

My father, like many Jews, never lived in Israel. The Jewish people are scattered all over the world. In 1947 the state of Israel was re-established. Around 7.5 million people live in Israel today, of whom approximately 6 million are Jews. There are many other Jews still scattered around the world today.

I like how Eugene Peterson translates the New Testament passage for today using the term 'insiders' for the Jewish people and 'outsiders' for the non-Jewish people.

Many individual Jews over the years have become Christians. In fact, all the very earliest Christians were Jewish 'insiders'. But now the vast majority of Christians are non-Jewish 'outsiders'. What does the future hold for the 'insiders'?

The key to Paul's understanding lies in Romans 11:29: 'For God's gifts and his call are irrevocable.' This is a theme that runs throughout the Bible as we see in today's passages.

READING FROM PSALMS

Psalm 89:19–29
God's covenant with his people will last for ever

We see in the covenant with David that God's gifts and his call are irrevocable.

God called 'a young man' from among his people (v.19c). He gave him gifts. He 'bestowed strength' (v.19b). He 'anointed' him (v.20b). He promised that his love would be with him (v.24a) and that he would maintain that love to him for ever: 'My covenant with him *will never fail*. I will establish his line *for ever*, his throne as long *as the heavens endure*' (vv.28b–29).

This promise was originally given to David (2 Samuel 7:12–16) and repeated many times. Then later, in the book of Isaiah, what was promised to David is promised to Israel: 'I will make an *everlasting covenant with you*, my faithful love promised to David' (Isaiah 55:3b).

Paul shows clearly that all this has been fulfilled in Jesus. He writes, 'We tell you the good news: *What God promised our ancestors he has fulfilled for us*, their children, *by raising up Jesus*' (Acts 13:32–33). He goes on to quote Isaiah 55:3, *'I will give you the holy and sure blessings promised to David'* (Acts 13:34).

God promises that he will maintain his love for *you* for ever and that, through Jesus, you inherit all the blessings promised to David. You are loved. You are anointed. He will give you strength. Your calling is irrevocable.

PRAYER

Father, thank you for your faithful love. Today, I call out to you, 'You are my Father, my God, the Rock my Saviour' (Psalm 89:26).

NEW TESTAMENT READING

Romans 11:11–32
God's promises to Israel will prevail

As we have seen, in Romans 11 Paul is answering the question, 'Has God rejected his people?' His answer is, 'No, no, no': 'God's gifts and his call are irrevocable' (v.29). 'God's gifts and God's call are under full warranty – never cancelled, never rescinded' (v.29, MSG).

Yet Paul still grapples with the apparent reality that most have not accepted Jesus. He speaks about them 'stumbling' (v.11) and experiencing a 'hardening' (v.25). They are now like olive branches that have been 'broken off' (v.17). How can this fit with the unbreakable promises that he has made to the people of God in the Old Testament?

1. This hardening was only *partial*. There has always been a *remnant*, chosen by grace (vv.11–16).
2. The hardening was *fruitful*, since it led to *riches* for the Gentiles: 'When they walked out, they left the door open and the outsiders walked in' (v.11, MSG).
3. The hardening was *temporary*. '"Are they out of this for good?" And the answer is a clear-cut No' (v.11, MSG). 'This hardness on the part of insider Israel toward God is temporary' (v.25, MSG). 'Now, if their leaving triggered this worldwide coming of non-Jewish outsiders to God's kingdom, just imagine the effect of their coming back! What a homecoming!' (v.12, MSG).

This last point is particularly important to Paul, who cares passionately about his people. He eagerly anticipates the full inclusion of the people of Israel (v.12). He goes on to say that 'all Israel will be saved' (v.26). He does not say '*if*' this happens, but '*when*' this happens. He uses an olive tree as a picture of the Jewish nation (vv.17, 24). Christ came. The nation rejected him. The tree was chopped down but the roots were left. The gardener grafts in the Gentiles (v.17).

The time is coming when the Jewish branches will be grafted back (vv.23–24, MSG). Then the whole tree will be complete. The Gentiles grow up out of the stump – they do not support the root (the Jews) but the root supports them (v.18). There are three successive stages in the fulfilment of the divine plan of salvation:

1. The unbelief of the greater part of Israel: 'some of the tree's branches were pruned' (v,17, MSG)
2. The inclusion of many outsiders through faith in Jesus: 'you wild olive shoots were grafted in' (v.17, MSG)
3. The salvation of 'all Israel' (v.26).

But, what does '*all Israel will be saved*' mean? Some have argued that it means Israel can still be saved apart from Christ. However, this position is not credible. Paul has argued throughout the letter that *Jesus* is the way of salvation.

Others have argued that it meant the whole nation of Israel, including every single member, will put their faith in Jesus. However, 'all Israel' is a recurring expression in the Old Testament and other Jewish literature, where it need not mean 'every Jew without a single exception' but '*Israel as a whole*' (for example, 1 Samuel 7:5; 28:1; 1 Kings 12:1; Daniel 9:11). This also fits with the context of what Paul is saying here in Romans.

Paul is considering God's dealing with the nation as a whole. Thus, 'their fullness' (Romans 11:12) is to be understood in the same sense as the fullness of the Gentiles. The large-scale conversion of the Gentile world is to be followed by the large-scale conversion of Israel.

Paul concludes: 'There was a time not so long ago when you were on the outs with God. But then the Jews slammed the door on him and things opened up for you. Now *they* are on the outs. But with the door held wide open for you, they have a way back in. In one way or another, God makes sure that we all experience what it means to be outside so that he can personally open the door and welcome us back in' (vv.30–32, MSG).

PRAYER

Thank you, Lord, that the gifts and call of God are irrevocable. I pray that we will soon see not only a large-scale conversion of the

Gentile world but also a large-scale conversion of the people of Israel.

OLD TESTAMENT READING

1 Chronicles 4:9–5:26
God's generous character and his blessings are unchanging

God is in ultimate control of history. His call and his gifts are irrevocable. What was fulfilled in the New Testament began in the Old. The chronicler traces the history of Israel from its very beginning. God is sovereign – 'the battle was God's' (5:22).

Does this mean that we are mere pawns? Are we simply pieces being moved around God's chessboard with no choice or freewill? Not at all.

You are involved in God's plans. Your actions make a difference – for good or evil.

1. Resist acts of *dishonour*

Our actions can cause us to lose out on God's blessing: 'Though Reuben was Israel's firstborn, after he slept with his father's concubine, a defiling act ... He *lost* his "firstborn" place in the family tree' (v.1, MSG). He lost a great inheritance because he could not control his desires.

We all need to take great care to resist temptation and not to allow the lust of the flesh or our emotions to cause us to miss out on a blessing from God.

2. Be a person of *honour*

Jabez, on the other hand, was a man of honour (4:9, MSG). Jabez's prayer made a difference. 'Jabez prayed to the God of Israel: "Bless me, O bless me! Give me land, large tracts of land. And provide your personal protection – don't let evil hurt me." God gave him what he asked' (v.10, MSG).

This is not the most altruistic prayer in the Bible! But nevertheless, God answered it. Jesus taught us to pray, among other things, 'Give us today our daily bread' (Matthew 6:11). Our first concern should be for God's glory, his kingdom and his will. But it is not wrong to ask for God's blessing, presence, protection and healing in our own lives as well.

Likewise, God gave his people victory 'because they cried out to him during the battle. He answered their prayers, because they trusted in him' (1 Chronicles 5:20).

The battle is God's (v.22). He is in ultimate control. Nevertheless, your prayers make a difference.

PRAYER

Lord, thank you that my calling is irrevocable. Thank you that the battle is yours. Thank you that my prayers make a difference. And Lord, I cry out to you for help today in the battles I face...

29 July | Day 210

Four Sacrifices That Please God

Looking back at my life, I now realise how many sacrifices my parents made out of love for my sister and me. I wish I had appreciated that more at the time. My parents came from a generation that was very familiar with the idea of sacrifice. Many of their contemporaries had sacrificed their lives for their fellow human beings and for their country. The whole idea of making sacrifices, great or small, seems more alien to our generation.

The vast majority of biblical references to 'sacrifice' are in the Old Testament. These passages prefigure Jesus' sacrificial death for us on the cross. In the New Testament, almost all the references are about Jesus' sacrifice. The death of Jesus as the one perfect and complete sacrifice fulfilling all the Old Testament preparation and prediction. We do not need to make any sacrifices for our sins. Yet the New Testament tells us that there are four sacrifices you can make that *please God*.

READING FROM PSALMS

Psalm 89:30–37
Thank God for the sacrifice of Jesus

God is holy (v.35) and loving. God loved David. He said, 'I will not take *my love* from him' (v.33).

God, in his love, made a covenant with David and his people. It was a covenant of grace, but it required a response of obedience to the law. But what would happen if they did not keep the law? If that happened – 'If his sons forsake my law and do not follow my statutes, if they violate my decrees and fail to keep my commands' (vv.30–31) – a penalty would be required (v.32).

The New Testament tells us that God came in the person of his son Jesus Christ to take that penalty by offering himself as the sacrifice for sin. Through that sacrifice, God's love and holiness were both fully expressed and satisfied and you need make no further sacrifice for sin.

PRAYER

Thank you, Lord, so much for the sacrifice of Jesus on the cross for me. Thank you that no further sacrifice is required for my sins.

NEW TESTAMENT READING

Romans 11:33–12:21
Make sacrifices that please God

In this passage, we see four sacrifices that you can make *in response* to Jesus' sacrifice for you:

1. Sacrifice of your *lips*

The writer of Hebrews says, 'Through Jesus, therefore, let us continually offer to God *a sacrifice of praise* – the fruit of *lips* that confess his name ... for *with such sacrifices God is pleased*' (Hebrews 13:15–16).

Much of the first eleven chapters of Romans are about the sacrifice of Jesus for us. Paul, having set out all that God has done for us, responds with a *sacrifice of praise* (Romans 11:33–36).

2. Sacrifice of your *life*

Paul continues, 'Therefore, I urge you, brothers and sisters, in view of God's mercy [because of all that Jesus has done for us through the sacrifice of himself on the cross], to offer your bodies as *living sacrifices*, holy and *pleasing* to God – this is your spiritual act of worship' (12:1, AMP).

God wants you to offer *all* of yourself and *all* of your lives – your time, ambitions, possessions, ears, mouths and sexuality – as well as your mind, emotions and attitudes. Paul's description of a living sacrifice also reminds us that you have to *go on* offering your life as a sacrifice to God, offering the whole of your life for the whole of your life.

As Eugene Peterson translates it in *The Message*, 'Take your every day, ordinary life – your sleeping, eating, going-to-work, and walking-around life – and place it before God as an offering' (v.1, MSG).

In Old Testament times, 'living sacrifice' would be a contradiction in terms. The whole point of the sacrifice was that it was killed. Jago Wynne writes, 'Our act of worship is no longer to bring a sacrifice, but to be one ourselves. We remain living. It is all of us that is being offered. Worship is about what I say with my tongue. It's about what I watch ... what I think ... where I go with my feet.'[1]

3. The sacrifice of your *'loot'*

Generous giving is another New Testament sacrifice. Paul encourages the sacrifice of generosity in contributing to the needs of others (v.8). '*Share* with God's people who are in need' (v.13). This is another sacrifice the writer of Hebrews says pleases God: 'to *share with others*' (Hebrews 13:16).

We are even to give generously to our enemies: 'Our Scriptures tell us that if you see your enemy hungry, go buy that person lunch, or if he's thirsty, get him a drink. Your generosity will surprise him with goodness' (Romans 12:20, MSG).

4. Sacrifice of your *love*

In this passage Paul gives many examples of the sacrifice of loving service (vv.9–21).

The writer of Hebrews says, 'do not forget to *do good* and to share with others, for with such sacrifices *God is pleased*' (Hebrews 13:16).

'Doing good' means giving up things that are not good. 'Don't let the world around you squeeze you into its own mould' (Romans 12:2, JBP). Although God only asks us to give up the bad stuff in our lives, it can feel costly to do so because that stuff is superficially attractive. Repentance is a very positive word, but at the time it may seem sacrificial.

Sacrificial love involves allowing God to transform us by a complete change. Our love must be sincere (v.9). The Greek word for 'sincere' means 'without hypocrisy' or literally 'without play acting' or 'without a mask'.

Often relationships in the world are quite superficial. We all put up fronts or masks to protect ourselves. When we see governments doing this, we call it 'spin'. When we do it ourselves, we call it 'image'; we are projecting something. In effect we're saying, 'I don't really like what I am inside, so I will pretend I am somebody different.'

If other people are doing the same then there are two 'fronts' or 'masks' meeting. The sad result is that the two real people never meet. This is the opposite of 'sincere love'. Sincere love means taking off your mask and daring to reveal who you are. When you know that God loves you as you are, you are set free to take off your mask.

This means that there is a completely new depth and authenticity in your relationships. Instead of trying to impress people with our masks, as we reveal who we truly are with all our flaws, we connect through our vulnerabilities.

Paul urges Christians to live in harmony with one another and to be generous (v.13), hospitable (v.13), forgiving (v.14), empathetic (v.15) and to live at peace with everyone (v.18). It is a glorious picture of the Christian family into which God calls us, beckoning us into an atmosphere of love, joy, patience, faithfulness, generosity, hospitality, blessing, rejoicing, harmony, humility and peace; where good is not overcome by evil, but evil is overcome with good (vv.9–21).

PRAYER

Lord, today I offer you my body as a living sacrifice. I am available to you. I give everything I have to you again – my life, time, money, ambitions, plans, hopes and desires. Show me your good, pleasing and perfect will (v.2).

OLD TESTAMENT READING

1 Chronicles 6:1–81
Understand the sacrifices in the Old Testament

In the Old Testament, the priests were the mediators between God and the people. 'Aaron and his sons offered *the sacrifices* on the Altar ... They made atonement for Israel' (v.49, MSG).

Priesthood was hereditary. The priests were descendants of Levi. The chronicler lists the 'sons of Levi' (vv.1, 16, 46). We see that all those who served in the tabernacle (later to become the temple) were regarded as being 'of Levitical descent' (vv.1–30).

The chronicler stresses the importance of the temple. The temple was a place of worship where God's spirit dwelt. David put some of the Levites in charge of the music in the house of the Lord – 'These are the persons David appointed to lead the singing in the house of God ... They were the ministers of music in the place of worship' (vv.31–32, MSG).

Other Levites were required to present sacrifices on the altar – 'making atonement' (v.49). As we saw earlier, a simplified definition of atonement is 'at-one-ment'. In other words, God providing a means through which people can be at one with him.

This was the pattern throughout the Old Testament. The need for sacrifice and the making of atonement prefigured the final, complete and sufficient sacrifice of Jesus. Such passages remind us of how amazing it is that sacrifices for sin are no longer necessary because of *the one true and perfect sacrifice of Jesus*.

PRAYER

Thank you, Lord, that all that is required of us today is a response to your sacrifice; to offer you the sacrifices of praise, of our bodies, of doing good and sharing with others. Thank you that with such sacrifices you are pleased. I pray that you would pour out your Spirit on our sacrifices.

30 July | Day 211
How to Be a Good Citizen

Politicians: how do we treat them? Governments and local councils: how do we view them? Taxes: do we really need to pay them? What about evil regimes? If you live under a Hitler or Stalin are you supposed to obey them?

'Be a good citizen,' writes the apostle Paul. 'All governments are under God. Insofar as there is peace and order, it's God's order. So live responsibly as a citizen. If you're irresponsible to the state, then you're irresponsible with God, and God will hold you responsible. Duly constituted authorities are only a threat if you're trying to get by with something. Decent citizens should have nothing to fear' (Romans 13:1–3, MSG).

This would have been a radical idea to Paul's original readers. In the ancient world most people saw religion and government as intertwined. The early church was still adjusting to the idea that the Messiah was not going to rule over his people in an earthly government. Those around them would have worshipped Rome and the Emperor as god. Yet here Paul tells them to follow Jesus as their King *and* still submit to Roman authority.

Paul's teaching in Romans 13 needs to be balanced by Revelation 13. Revelation 13 was written at the time of the persecution of Christians under the Emperor Domitian. The state is seen as the ally of the devil (pictured as a red dragon) who has given his authority to the persecuting state (pictured as a monster emerging out of the sea). At worst, government can be demonic.

Both Romans 13 and Revelation 13 are true. There is good government and there is bad government. There is a good side to human government but there can also be an evil side. As Oscar Cullmann remarks, according to whether 'the state remains within its *limits* or transgresses them, the Christian will describe it as the servant of God or as the instrument of the Devil'.[1]

How then can you live as a good citizen?

READING FROM PSALMS

Psalm 89:38–45
Pray for those in authority

Israel was a theocracy. Church and state were inextricably intertwined. The 'anointed' leader of God's people (v.38) was also the one who wore the 'crown' (v.39) and sat on the 'throne' (v.44).

The kings in the Old Testament were regarded as anointed by God. Yet many of them sinned and were unfaithful to the Lord. The psalmist writes, 'But you have rejected, you have spurned, you have been very angry with your anointed one. You have renounced the covenant with your servant and have defiled his crown in the dust' (vv.38–39).

PRAYER

Lord, I pray for my government and all the other leaders of my nation. May they never be covered with shame. May they govern well and wisely.

NEW TESTAMENT READING

Romans 13:1–14
Enjoy freedom under authority

We live in the period between the first and second comings of Jesus. When Jesus returns he will rule and reign for ever. There will be no need for human government. In the meantime, however, we do need human government. The authority of governments is properly seen, in St Peter's phrase, as a 'human authority' (1 Peter 2:13).

This does not mean that humans devised it in independence or isolation from God. Rather, it is an institution implicit in human social existence as God made it.

Yet, since it is God who sets the terms, St Paul writes that everyone must submit themselves to the governing authorities (Romans 13:1–2).

If this applies to secular authority – how much more must it apply to the authority of the church? Different churches have different structures of authority. In my experience, submitting to the authority of the leaders of our church brings great freedom.

This is the basic New Testament principle: you should obey every authority – the government, local authorities and the institutions you find yourself in. Why?

1. You do so because they are part of the authority that is instituted by God.
2. You do so because of the consequences of not obeying them: 'But if you're breaking the rules right and left, watch out. The police aren't there just to be admired in their uniforms. God also has an interest in keeping order, and he uses them to do it' (v.4, MSG).
3. '…because of conscience' (v.5). If you are not obeying the authorities, you cannot live with a clear conscience. 'That's why you must live responsibly – not just to avoid punishment but also because it's the right way to live' (v.5, MSG).

We see here a clear distinction between personal morality and the enforcement of law by government. In the field of personal morality, Paul's teaching is very similar to that of Jesus: it is one of non-retaliation and 'turning the other cheek' (12:14–21). However, he moves from there to discuss 'governing authorities' (13:1–6). He speaks of rulers as God's servants to bring punishment on the wrongdoer (v.4).

The state is concerned with the protection of others. To stand by and allow murder and violence would be unloving and unchristian. By analogy, if it is right for the authorities to use force to protect citizens against internal threats, arguably it is equally right to protect them against external ones by force, if necessary. In practice, of course, it is often extremely difficult to work out when such force is justified.

What is less controversial is that we should pay what we owe (vv.6–8). This means paying every penny of tax that you owe and all of your bills as soon as they arrive: 'Give everyone what you owe … let no debt remain outstanding' (vv.7–8).

It is not wrong to have a planned and manageable debt – mortgage, student loan or credit card. However, we are to mindfully avoid being in unplanned or unmanageable debt. If you find yourself in debt it is important not to ignore it and to get help as soon as possible, for example from one of the many Christian debt advice services.

The way to fulfil the law is by loving your neighbour as yourself. 'When you love others, you complete what the law has been after all along' (v.8b, MSG).

If we do this we will not steal because of the unhappiness of the person from whom we steal, we will not kill or even have the wrong kind of anger because of the hurt it will bring to others. We will not commit adultery because of the damage it does to marriage and relationships.

'The law code – don't sleep with another person's spouse, don't take someone's life, don't take what isn't yours, don't always be wanting what you don't have, and any other "don't" you can think of – finally adds up to this: Love other people as well as you do yourself. You can't go wrong when you love others. When you add up everything in the law code, the sum total is *love*' (vv.9–10, MSG).

The law is summed up and fulfilled by love. Love is not an excuse for breaking the commandments but a way of keeping them. The commands were given out of love for us and are fulfilled by love. Paul does not write if you love you need not obey the commands. Rather, he says if you love you will fulfil the commands.

Jesus is the supreme example of love. Paul says, 'clothe yourselves with the Lord Jesus Christ' (v.14). Pray that the character of Jesus, his love, will surround and protect you and be seen by the people you meet today.

PRAYER

Lord, I want to clothe myself with the Lord Jesus Christ and not 'think about how to gratify the desires of the sinful nature' (v.14). May the love of Jesus be seen in me today.

OLD TESTAMENT READING

1 Chronicles 7:1–9:1a
Be aware of the limits of authority

As we look around the world today we see good and bad leadership and government. The people of Israel had their share of bad government too.

As the chronicler concludes his lists and genealogies, he writes, 'This is the complete family tree for all Israel, recorded in the Royal Annals of the Kings of Israel and Judah at the time they were exiled to Babylon *because of their unbelieving and disobedient lives'* (9:1, MSG). In his list he mentions Saul, 'Kish the father of Saul, and Saul the father of Jonathan' (8:33), whom he will later highlight as an example of someone who started out as a good governor but ended up as a bad one (10:13–14).

Saul became an example of the kind of government that is spoken about in Revelation 13. Nevertheless, David sought as far as he possibly could to remain loyal and subject to his authority.

PRAYER

Lord, help me to live as a good citizen with the right attitude to all those who you put in authority over me. Help me to submit with good grace even when I disagree. Help us also to have the wisdom to know when the limits have been reached.

31 July | Day 212

How to Avoid Arguments, Deal with Disputes and Stop Fighting

The referendum on Britain's membership of the EU resulted in a 52:48 split in favour of leaving. The campaign was acrimonious, the nation was divided, and the main political parties soon descended into infighting and division. This is one example of what we see across the globe. Every news update seems to include stories of arguments, disputes and fighting.

When sin entered the world, arguments, disputes and fighting began. Adam blamed Eve. Cain murdered his brother. The history of the world ever since has been one of conflict of all kinds.

When people turn away from God, they start fighting one another. We see the breakdown of relationships wherever we look: broken marriages, broken homes, broken relationships at work, civil wars and wars between nations. Sadly, the church is not immune. Right from the start there have been arguments, disputes and in-fighting.

How should we handle conflict?

READING FROM PROVERBS

Proverbs 18:17–19:2
Avoid arguments

Proverbs is full of practical advice on how to avoid arguments.

1. Listen to both sides
There are usually two sides to an argument, and it is always worth hearing both parties. The right of cross-examination is an important one, with a vital place in any legal system. 'The first speech in a court case is always convincing – until the cross-examination starts!' (18:17, MSG).

2. Ask for the help of the Holy Spirit
We need God's guidance especially when facing 'tough decisions' (v.18, MSG). In the Old Testament, 'casting the lot' was a way of settling disputes. However, with the outpouring of the Holy Spirit there are better ways of receiving God's guidance over disputes (see 1 Corinthians 6:1–6).

3. Avoid unnecessary offence
Do everything you possibly can to avoid offending people: someone close to you who's been offended can be '…more unyielding than a fortified city' (Proverbs 18:19). Serious disputes create barriers among friends. These walls are easy to erect and extremely hard to pull down.

4. Choose your words carefully
Your words can be a life-giving force, bring great satisfaction and heal division: 'Words satisfy the mind as much as fruit does the stomach; good talk is as gratifying as a good harvest' (v.20, MSG).

Yet words can also be a destructive force: 'Words kill, words give life; they're either poison or fruit – you choose' (v.21, MSG). You can do great good or great damage by what you say.

5. Choose your companions carefully
The writer says, 'Find a good spouse, you find a good life – and even more: the favour of God!' (v.22, MSG). It is certainly true in my experience that Pippa's wisdom, advice and involvement have often helped me to avoid getting into trouble in this area. A good husband or wife will be a peacemaker.

Whether we are married or not, what we need are really close friends. The second part of this proverb reminds us that while friends come and go, 'There *is* a friend who sticks closer than a brother or sister' (v.24b). These are the sorts of friends we need in our lives. If you have friends like that, never stop thanking God for them.

Ultimately, of course, Jesus is *the* friend who sticks closer than a brother or sister.

PRAYER

Lord, may the words I speak be a source of life to those around me.

NEW TESTAMENT READING

Romans 14:1–18
Deal with disputes

This passage is so relevant to some of the disputes going on in the global church right now. If only the church in the last 2,000 years had followed Paul's instructions. As John Stott writes, Paul's purpose in these verses 'was to enable conservative-minded Christians (mostly Jewish) and liberal-minded Christians (mainly Gentiles) to coexist amicably in the Christian fellowship.'[1]

There are certain matters over which Paul was willing to fight to death – the truth of the gospel (that Christ died for us, vv.9, 15). The life, death and resurrection of Jesus (v.9) and the Lordship of Christ (v.9) are examples of what is non-negotiable.

However, there are other things that are not nearly as important. They are 'disputable matters' (v.1). They are secondary areas. He gives various examples such as vegetarianism or thinking of one day as more sacred than another.

Today some Christians abstain from alcohol. Others do not. Some Christians are pacifists. Others are not. And there are many other issues where Christians are passionately divided about disputable matters. How do we deal with these disputes?

1. Welcome those with different views
He writes 'accept' (the word means 'welcome') those 'whose faith is weak' (v.1a). 'Welcome with open arms fellow believers who don't see things the way you do ... Eventually, we're all going to end up kneeling side by side in the place of judgment, facing God' (vv.1, 10, MSG).

2. Do not be quick to judge
'Don't jump all over them every time they do or say something you don't agree with' (v.1b, MSG).

He goes on, 'Who are you to judge someone else's servants?' (v.4); 'You, then, why do you judge your brother or sister?' (v.10); 'Then let us no more criticise and blame and pass judgment on one another' (v.13, AMP). We must allow people to have different views from our own without judging them for it.

This is the heart of the matter. Four times in this passage Paul says we are *not* to judge one another.

3. Don't look down on others
We 'must not look down on' (v.3a) those who have different views from our own. God has welcomed them (v.3b). So should we.

4. Do what you think is right
On all these secondary matters 'everybody should be fully convinced in their own

minds' (v.5). 'Each person is free to follow the convictions of conscience' (v.5, MSG). 'If you eat meat ... thank God for prime rib; if you're a vegetarian ... thank God for broccoli' (v.6, MSG). Just because we may agree to disagree on these matters does not make them irrelevant. We need to be careful to do what we think is right in every situation.

5. Assume the best about other people's motives

'Those who regard one day as special, *do so to the Lord*. Those who eat meat, *eat to the Lord, for they give thanks to God;* and those who abstain, *do so to the Lord* and give thanks to God' (v.6).

Give others the benefit of the doubt and assume that they are seeking to do what is right in the eyes of the Lord (vv.7–8).

6. Be sensitive about other people's consciences

Paul says, 'Make up your mind not to put any stumbling-block or obstacle in another believer's way' (v.13). For example, if someone regards drinking alcohol as wrong, it would be insensitive to drink alcohol in front of them. We do not want to cause them distress (v.15).

7. Help and encourage one another

'So let's agree to use all our energy in getting along with each other. Help others with encouraging words; don't drag them down by finding fault' (v.19, MSG).

8. Always act in love

'If your brother or sister is distressed because of what you eat, you are no longer *acting in love*' (v.15). 'So be sensitive and courteous ... Don't eat or say or do things that might interfere with the free exchange of love' (v.21, MSG).

Disputable matters are important, but not as important as what unites us all: 'For the kingdom of God is not a matter of eating and drinking, but of righteousness, peace and joy in the Holy Spirit' (v.17). This is what really matters. Let us not get caught up in arguments about disputable matters, which divide the church and put off those outside the church.

Follow the words of the medieval writer Rupertus Meldenius: 'On the essentials, *unity*; on the non-essentials, *freedom*; in everything, *love*.'

PRAYER

Lord, I pray for a new unity in the church. Help us to focus today and each day on what the kingdom of God is really about: righteousness, peace and joy in the Holy Spirit.

OLD TESTAMENT READING

1 Chronicles 9:1b–10:14
Stop fighting

'The Philistines *fought* against Israel ... The *fighting grew fierce* around Saul' (10:1, 3). Saul was attacked by the Philistines and died as a result. We find this account in 1 Samuel 31. However, the writer of Chronicles adds an explanation: 'Saul died in disobedience, disobedient to GOD. He didn't obey GOD's words' (1 Chronicles 10:13, MSG).

As we look back at the book of Samuel we can see that the real problem was that Saul became jealous of David. David did everything he could to submit to Saul and to be on good terms with him. Saul would have none of it. He was out to get David. This internal dispute weakened Saul and made him vulnerable to an attack from outside.

We see today how internal disputes among the people of God make us vulnerable to attacks from outside. Jesus prayed that we would be one in order that the world would believe (John 17:23).

PRAYER

Lord, help us to be peacemakers, to stop the infighting and seek unity in order that the world will believe.

1 August | Day 213
Bring People Hope

Twenty-one-year-old Matthew had been homeless for three years. Mark Russell (who was appointed head of the Church Army aged only thirty-one) met him on the streets of Charing Cross in London, bought him some food and led him to Christ.

As he was getting up to leave he said, 'Matthew, over the next month I am going to be on platforms speaking to thousands of people. What piece of advice do you want me to give to the Church of England today?'

Matthew replied, 'The church's job is to stop arguing and *to bring people hope*.'

Mark Russell commented, 'I have never heard a better definition of what we should be about: Don't we have a gospel of hope? A gospel that brings hope? A gospel of life, a gospel of transformation and above all a *hope of eternal life*, *the hope of Jesus*.'

Many people see only a *hopeless end*; but with Jesus you can enjoy an *endless hope*.

Hope is one of the three great theological virtues – the others being love and faith. As Raniero Cantalamessa writes, 'They are like three sisters. Two of them are grown and the other is a small child. They go forward together hand in hand with the child hope in the middle. Looking at them it would seem that the bigger ones are pulling the child, but it is the other way around; it is the little girl who is pulling the two bigger ones. It is hope that pulls faith and love. Without hope everything would stop.'[1]

READING FROM PSALMS

Psalm 89:46–52
Know the hope of eternal life through Jesus

'To live without hope is to cease to live,' wrote Fyodor Dostoevsky. 'What oxygen is to the lungs, such is hope to the meaning of life,' wrote Emil Brunner.

This psalm ends on a note of hope, 'Praise be to the Lord for ever! Amen and Amen' (v.52). The psalmist clings on to hope in spite of the fact that he is wrestling with his own situation.

1. Hope in the midst of suffering and despair

'How long, O Lord?' (v.46a) is a rhetorical question. It is a cry of despair. Will this suffering go on for ever?

2. Hope in spite of the brevity of life and the inevitability of death

Life is so short: 'Remember how fleeting is my life' (v.47a). If death is the end then there is no ultimate meaning or purpose, 'For what futility you have created all humanity!' (v.47b). No one can raise themselves from the dead: 'Who can live and not see death, or who can escape from the power of the grave?' (v.48).

But the psalmist does not rule out the hope of the resurrection. He knows human beings cannot save themselves. He looks to the Lord: 'O Lord, where is your former great love, which in your faithfulness you swore to David ... your anointed one' (vv.49–51). What the psalmist saw only in blurry outlines is made crystal clear in the New Testament.

PRAYER

Lord, thank you that you have given us *a living hope* through the resurrection of Jesus Christ from the dead, and into an inheritance that can never perish, spoil or fade' (1 Peter 1:3–4).

NEW TESTAMENT READING

Romans 14:19–15:13
Overflow with hope through the Holy Spirit

Faith releases hope, joy and peace in our lives. Doubt steals our joy and peace. Faith means trusting in 'the God of hope'. Paul prays, 'May *the God of hope* fill you with all joy and peace as you trust in him, so that you may overflow ['bubbling over', AMP] with hope by the power of the Holy Spirit' (15:13).

The origin of hope is 'the God of hope'. The reason for hope is Jesus. The source of hope in you is the Holy Spirit. This hope is not wishful thinking. It is rooted in what God has done for us and is doing in us.

This hope is the driving force for our day-to-day living. As Erwin McManus comments, hope 'lifts us out of the rubble of our failures, our pain and our fear to rise above what at one point seemed insurmountable. Our ability to endure, to persevere, to overcome is fuelled by this one seemingly innocuous ingredient called hope.'[2]

The hope for the whole world is in Jesus. He is the hope for Israel. He is also the hope for the rest of us. Paul quotes a number of passages in the Old Testament to prove this, culminating with the words of Isaiah prophesying that Jesus would be 'Tall enough for everyone everywhere to see and *take hope!*' (v.12, MSG).

Paul helps us to see different aspects of the hope that Jesus brings to the world today including:

1. Hope for unity

Paul continues to plead that every effort is made for unity: 'Let us therefore make every effort to do what leads to peace and to mutual edification' (14:19). Guard this unity by being sensitive to your brothers and sisters in Christ and not offending them unnecessarily (14:20–15:1). Each of us should '*please our neighbours* for their good, to build them up' (v.2).

Follow the example of Jesus: 'For even Christ did not please himself' (v.3). Like Jesus, be a God-pleaser, not a self-pleaser or a people-pleaser. People-pleasers are those who try to please people even if they have to compromise their own conscience to do so. Paul tried to please people as long as pleasing them did not cause him to displease the Lord (Galatians 1:10; 1 Corinthians 10:33).

2. Hope from the Scriptures

The purpose of the Bible is to give us hope. 'For everything that was written in the past was written to teach us, so that through endurance and the encouragement of the Scriptures *we might have hope*' (Romans 15:4). It is through the Scriptures that you know about Jesus and the hope that is in him. The way to keep your hopes up is to study the Scriptures regularly.

This hope leads to 'All joy and peace as you trust in him' (v.13). I love the way that Corrie ten Boom puts it: 'Joy and peace mean going around with a smile on our faces and an empty suitcase.'

PRAYER

Lord, thank you that just as you raised Jesus from the dead, one day you will raise me with him to full and eternal life. May your Holy Spirit so fill me today that I brim over with hope.

OLD TESTAMENT READING

1 Chronicles 11:1–12:22
Put your hope in the coming of the King

Our hope is in Jesus, the King, who will one day return and establish his kingdom for ever. As we read of the kings of the Old Testament, it is important to remember that they, even at their very best, only faintly foreshadowed the ultimate king, Jesus.

In the chronicler's eyes, David was the ideal king: 'You were the one who led Israel on their military campaigns. And the Lord your God said to you, "You will shepherd my people Israel, and you will become their ruler"' (11:2). They 'anointed David king over Israel, as the LORD had promised through Samuel' (v.3). 'David became more and more powerful, because the LORD Almighty was with him' (v.9).

David did not do it all on his own. He needed a team around him. He had a group of thirty Mighty Men, which included the Big Three. I am so grateful for the mighty men and women who support and encourage Pippa and me as we try to lead. We could not begin to do what we do without an amazing team around us.

Amasai, chief of the thirty, 'moved by God's Spirit' said to David, 'We're on your side ... We're committed ... all's well with whoever helps you' (12:18–22, MSG). This must have been a huge encouragement to David.

In these scriptures, we see a direct equation of the Kingdom of Israel with the kingdom of God (see 1 Chronicles 28:5; 1 Chronicles 29:23; 2 Chronicles 13:8). There was no question about the continuity of kingship because it was guarded by God.

Yet, when the chronicler was writing this (hundreds of years later) there was no king. He wrote about the past in the hope that in the future a king like David would arise. This was the hope of Israel – a coming king. Jesus was that king. He was 'the anointed one', the 'Messiah' (Psalm 89:51).

Now our hope is in the return of Jesus. As Bishop Lesslie Newbigin put it, 'The horizon for the Christian is "He shall come again" and "we look for the coming of the Lord." It can be tomorrow or any time, but that's the horizon. That horizon is for me fundamental, and that's what makes it possible to be hopeful and therefore to find life meaningful.'

PRAYER

Father, thank you that all the hopes of Israel were fulfilled when Jesus, the anointed king, came. Thank you that we can now look forward to his coming again.

'Praise be to the LORD for ever! Amen and Amen' (Psalm 89:52).

2 August | Day 214
The Power of His Presence

The Duke of Wellington once remarked about Napoleon, 'I used to say of him that *his presence* on the field made the difference of forty thousand men.' The presence of a strong leader has a powerful effect. How much greater is the impact of the awesome power of the presence of God!

There is a deep spiritual hunger in all of our hearts that can only be satisfied by the presence of God himself. Adam and Eve lost this sense of his presence through their sin. Thereafter, the presence of God was not known as it was before.

God is holy. We cannot take his presence for granted. It is only through the cross and resurrection of Jesus that a way into his presence and the gift of the Holy Spirit living within you is made possible. Now you can know the power of his presence.

READING FROM PSALMS

Psalm 90:1–10
His presence reveals our secret sins

I remember a man in our small group on Alpha saying that he could not understand the concept of 'sin', as he 'led a good life and was not really aware of anything wrong in his life'. A few weeks later, on the Alpha Weekend, he encountered Jesus and was filled with the Holy Spirit. He had tears pouring down his face. He said he realised how sinful his life had been and how much he had been forgiven.

The light of God's presence reveals the dark places in our hearts – the sins we would like to conceal even from ourselves. The psalmist says, 'Lord, you have been our dwelling-place ... You have set our iniquities before you, our secret sins in *the light of your presence*' (vv.1a, 8).

The longer we spend in God's presence the more the light shines and highlights our sin. The apostle Paul started out by describing himself as 'the least of the apostles' (1 Corinthians 15:9). Later on he called himself 'less than the least of all God's people' (Ephesians 3:8). Finally, he described himself as 'the worst of sinners'! (1 Timothy 1:16).

It is not that he got worse; it is simply that, through the awesome power of God's presence, he became more and more aware of the light shining in his heart. That could seem very negative, but actually for Paul it was quite the opposite. His overwhelming feeling was gratitude and praise because no matter what he had done wrong, he knew that he was forgiven and could know relationship with God.

As Christians, we can look forward to that relationship lasting for ever. God is eternal, 'From everlasting to everlasting you are God' (Psalm 90:2b). Yet we know only too well the fragility of human life. The psalmist reminds us that we return to dust as mortals (v.3), we are like new grass that by the evening is dry and withered (vv.5–6), and our usual life span is seventy or eighty years (v.10).

God's everlasting nature is part of who he is. For us, eternal life is not automatic or natural. 'The wages of sin is death', but the gift from the everlasting God is 'eternal life in Christ Jesus our Lord' (Romans 6:23).

PRAYER

Lord, thank you for the blood of Jesus, which cleanses me from all sin and unrighteousness. Thank you that through him I have access to the awesome presence of God.

NEW TESTAMENT READING

Romans 15:14–33
His presence comes through the power of the Holy Spirit

The presence of God radically changes your life and the lives of others. He gives power to both your words and your actions. He makes possible signs and miracles. This is what characterised the early church. This is what should characterise our churches today.

As Paul begins to bring his great letter to the Romans to a conclusion, he talks about his own personal calling: 'This highly focused assignment God gave me, this priestly and gospel work of serving the spiritual needs of the non-Jewish outsiders so they can be presented as an acceptable offering to God, made whole and holy by God's Holy Spirit' (v.16, MSG).

Among other things, a priest is a person who goes to God on behalf of the people and goes to the people on behalf of God. In this sense, we are all now priests. You are in priestly service whenever you are taking a message from God to the world and when you go to God – interceding, praying for those outside of the church to come to know Christ. As they do so they become 'an offering acceptable to God, sanctified by the Holy Spirit' (v.16).

Paul's ambition was to preach the gospel where Jesus was not known, so that he would not be building on anyone else's foundation (vv.20–21). He did this by 'leading the Gentiles to obey God' (v.18). He 'fully proclaimed the gospel of Christ' (v.19).

His proclamation of the gospel was holistic. Like Jesus, his preaching with words was accompanied by a demonstration of the in-breaking of the kingdom of God. It involved three things:

1. Words

The gospel is the most powerful message in the world. Paul proclaimed the gospel: *'by what I have said...'* (v.18).

2. Works

Fully proclaiming the gospel involves not only words but actions: 'by what I have said *and done'* (v.18). For example, Paul *acted* on behalf of the poor as we see here. He writes, 'Take up a collection for the poor ... to relieve their poverty' (vv.26–27, MSG).

3. Wonders

Paul's proclamation of the gospel involved a demonstration of the supernatural power of the Holy Spirit: 'by the power of *signs and miracles*, through the *power of the Spirit*' (v.19).

People are more affected by what they see than by what they hear. It has been said, 'One in the eye is worth two in the ear.' Paul gives only one in the ear (words) and two in the eye (works and wonders).

The coming of the Holy Spirit on the day of Pentecost brought a great outpouring of the presence of God. God is present among his people now by the Holy Spirit. He is present in your heart. Supremely, he is present in his gathered community (for example, in Matthew 18:20).

PRAYER

Lord, I pray that you would restore to your church today the awesome power of your presence among us. Pour out your Holy Spirit upon me again. May I see lives radically changed as people come to obey you by what I say and do – by the power of signs and miracles.

OLD TESTAMENT READING

1 Chronicles 12:23–14:17
His presence requires respect

Never take God's presence for granted. The Lord is with you now, all the time, by his Spirit who lives in you.

God prepared his people for this extraordinary privilege. In the Old Testament, the ark was the symbol of God's presence. We see in this passage just how important it was.

David consulted with his leaders. 'He then said to the whole assembly of Israel, "If it seems good to you and if it is the will of the LORD our God ... let us bring *the ark of our God back to us*" ... The whole assembly agreed to do this ... [they] went ... to bring up ... *the ark of God the LORD... the ark that is called by the Name. They moved the ark of God* ... David and all the Israelites were celebrating with all their might before God, with songs and with harps, lyres, tambourines, cymbals and trumpets' (13:1–8).

The ark was a gold-covered chest that contained, among other items, the stone tablets of the Ten Commandments (see Hebrews 9:4). The ark was the most holy object in the whole system of temple-based worship. It served primarily as the symbol of *the awesome presence of God*, whose glory cloud was enthroned above it (1 Chronicles 13:6; see also Exodus 25:22; 1 Samuel 4:7).

On the one hand, God's presence brought great blessing. When the ark of God was with the family of Obed-Edom for three months, 'the LORD blessed his household and everything he had' (1 Chronicles 13:14). On the other hand, it required great respect and anything that verged on disrespect brought judgment (vv.9–10).

David had a great respect and reverence for God and his presence. As a result, 'The LORD blessed his household and everything he had' (v.14). David knew that his position of leadership came from the Lord (14:2). He regularly asked for God's guidance about what he should do (vv.10, 14). 'And God answered him' (v.14).

As a result, 'David's fame spread throughout every land, and the LORD made all the nations fear him (v.17). The word 'fear' means great *respect*. Because David respected God's presence, God honoured him and anointed him in such a way that everyone respected David.

PRAYER

Thank you, Lord, that through the blood of our Lord Jesus Christ, I can approach your throne with boldness and confidence. Thank you that through the Holy Spirit you make your presence available to me, all the time.

3 August | Day 215
Working Without Wilting

The average person will spend approximately 150,000 hours at work in their lifetime – that is to say, about 40 per cent of our waking lives are spent at work.

'Is God interested in our work? Many people do not see God as a 24/7 God, but as a withdrawn actor confined to a Sunday show with a declining audience. There is a widespread view that God and work simply don't mix: the competitive, cut-throat demands of the working world are seen as the obvious enemy of Christian compassion and love. But the God who created and sustains the world is also the God of the workplace. *If the Christian faith is not relevant in the workplace, it is not relevant at all.*'[1]

These are the words of one of my closest friends, Ken Costa, in his book *God at Work*. For over forty years, Ken has been living out his faith on the frontline of Christian ministry – in the 'secular' workplace in the City of London. And he sees that as his primary calling as a Christian.

Whatever kind of work you are called to, it will probably occupy a large proportion of your life. Work is an important part of God's 'economy'. It is part of what you were created to do, and will be part of what you do in heaven. Work has an intrinsic value. The Bible has a lot to say on the subject of our work.

READING FROM PSALMS

Psalm 90:11–17
Your work has lasting value

What are you doing now that will outlive you?

Psalm 90 is all about the brevity of life (vv.3–4, 10). However, even though your life is short and fleeting, according to this psalm it is possible for *your work* to outlive you. What you do can have lasting value. The psalm ends on a note of hope: 'May the favour of the Lord our God rest upon us; establish *the work* of our hands for us – yes, establish *the work* of our hands' (v.17).

The ultimate value of your work is a reflection of the fact that God too is a worker. The psalmist says, 'Let *Your* work [the signs of Your power] be revealed to Your servants, and Your [glorious] majesty to their children' (v.16, AMP).

In *Working Without Wilting*, Jago Wynne, formerly a management consultant, now a rector at Holy Trinity Clapham, writes, 'We tend to think that things like our work, which happen when we are on earth, are nothing more than temporary and transient.

'The Bible paints a different picture. When Jesus returns, God is not going to obliterate this earth, but he will renew it, redeem it and liberate it from its bondage to decay … Human work will be purified and redeemed, so that it is free from sin just as we will be free from sin. But work will certainly be a part of the new creation.'[2] This is why it is right to ask God to 'establish the work of our hands' (v.17b).

PRAYER

Lord, may your favour rest upon me. Establish the work of my hands for me. May my work outlive me and have a lasting impact for good.

NEW TESTAMENT READING

Romans 16:1–27
Give yourself fully to God's work

Being a Christian involves being set to work, especially in the work of the gospel. Paul's letter to the Romans ends with greetings to a list of people. In it, he places great emphasis on the *value of their work*.

Priscilla and Aquila are described as his 'co-*workers* in Christ Jesus' (v.3). Mary '*worked very hard* for you' (v.6). Urbanus was 'our *co-worker* in Christ' (v.9). Tryphena and Tryphosa were women 'who *work hard* in the Lord' (v.12). Persis is 'another woman who has *worked very hard* in the Lord' (v.12). Timothy is 'my *fellow-worker*' (v.21).

Elsewhere Paul writes, 'We were not idle when we were with you, nor did we eat anyone's food without paying for it. On the contrary, we *worked night and day*, *labouring* and *toiling* so that we would not be a burden to any of you. We did this, not because we do not have the right to such help, but in order to make ourselves a model for you to follow' (2 Thessalonians 3:7–9).

Paul was probably the most effective servant of Christ who ever lived, but he was not in 'full-time' ministry. He was a tentmaker earning his own keep.

Similarly, not everyone listed in Romans 16 was involved in 'full-time Christian ministry'. Erastus had a secular job – he was 'the city's director of public works' (v.23). He no doubt regarded his work as his primary calling and ministry. In that sense, all of us are involved in full-time ministry – whether we are called to work full-time in a church, or in the secular world.

It is also interesting to note how many women worked in the church. Phoebe (v.1) is described as *diakonos* (a servant) – the Greek word meaning deacon, or minister ('a key representative of the church', MSG). She is described as having been 'a great help to many people' including Paul himself (v.2). The Greek word for 'a great help' is the word used for a political sponsor, protector and patron. It suggests she possessed some social position, wealth and independence. She clearly had a very prominent role in the church.

Priscilla and Aquila (see also Acts 18) had a joint ministry. Priscilla is named first (v.3). This is probably due either to her having been converted first (and having led Aquila to Christ) or to her having played a more prominent role in the life and work of the church.

Ten of the people named in the list are women. They include Junia – one of the 'outstanding leaders' (v.7, MSG). Junia is almost certainly a female name. She is described as one of those who was 'outstanding among the apostles' (v.7). Since she was clearly not one of the twelve apostles, 'apostles' here has a wider sense, denoting someone sent out as a missionary. Paul includes a woman as being outstanding among these missionary leaders. It is clear from all of this that women occupied prominent places on Paul's team.

Paul ends on a note of thanks and worship: 'All our praise is focused through Jesus on this incomparably wise God! Yes!' (v.27, MSG).

PRAYER

Lord, help all of us, whatever our calling, to be those who work hard in the Lord and proclaim 'Jesus Christ' (v.27).

OLD TESTAMENT READING

1 Chronicles 15:1–16:36
Imitate God in work and rest

Work is one of the ways in which you imitate God. As God laboured in creation, so we are to do the same. The command to work was there before the Fall (see Genesis 2:15). As Ken Costa often says, 'Work was in the original God-breathed prospectus.'[3]

David set to work. He 'constructed buildings for himself' (1 Chronicles 15:1). He called together the leaders and set them to work (v.12).

There is no divide between the sacred and the secular. Worship was at the heart of all that they were to do. David gave instructions about '*the work* of worship' (v.2, MSG). They were appointed 'to minister before the ark of the LORD, to make petition, to give thanks, and to praise the LORD, the God of Israel' (16:4). King David joined in the worship 'dancing and celebrating' (15:29).

At set times during the day (16:7), they took what Joyce Meyer describes as a 'praise pause' – 'I do not think anything blesses God more than when we stop right in the middle of what we are doing and lift our hands to worship him ... Think about a businessman, for example, maybe the president of a large company. Wouldn't it be wonderful if several times a day, he closed the door to his office, turned the lock, knelt, and said, "God, I just want to take some time to worship you."

'The same is true for students, stay-at-home [parents], retired people, secretaries, flight attendees, brain surgeons, clerks, and salespeople – anyone you can think of. We all would benefit greatly from taking a "praise pause."'[4]

David praises and thanks the Lord for what 'he has done' (v.8), 'his wonderful acts' (v.9), 'the wonders he has done' (v.12). He recounts the great work of the Lord and calls the people to 'worship the Lord in the splendour of his holiness' (v.29).

God is a worker. We see this right from the start of the Bible. He was at work in creation, 'by the seventh day God had finished the work he had being doing; so on the seventh day he rested' (Genesis 2:2). He not only creates the world, he sustains and redeems it. Work really is one of the ways in which you imitate God.

PRAYER

Lord, thank you for work. Thank you that even 'hard work' is such a blessing. May my work in itself be an act of worship, as I present my body as a 'living sacrifice ... [my] spiritual act of worship' (Romans 12:1–2).

4 August | Day 216
Unity

Years ago, I was speaking to a friend of mine who is not a Christian. He said this to me:

> 'I don't understand. You Protestants and you Catholics, you look exactly the same to me. You both have church buildings that look the same. You both say the Lord's Prayer and do stuff with bread and wine. Whatever it is you disagree about (and I have no idea what it is) has absolutely nothing to do with my life. However, whilst you are fighting each other I am not interested.'

It struck me then how damaging disunity is to the church and our witness to the world. No wonder Jesus prayed for 'complete unity' (John 17:23) and the apostle Paul was passionate that we should be 'perfectly united' (1 Corinthians 1:10).

Unity is at the core of our faith. We believe in one God: Father, Son and Holy Spirit. There is unity in the Trinity. Disunity, on the other hand, has been the curse of humankind ever since Adam and Eve fell into sin.

Jesus died to bring reconciliation and unity. Thank God that today, all around the world, we are seeing a lowering of denominational barriers and a greater unity in the church.

READING FROM PSALMS

Proverbs 19:3–12
Unity in relationships

In this passage is one proverb that is of utmost importance for unity in our relationships: 'Good sense makes a man restrain his anger, and it is his glory to overlook a transgression or an offense' (v.11, AMP).

I have been challenged by this verse many times in my life. It is so easy to be offended. It is easy to hold a grudge. It is easy to seek revenge. If responded to in this way, even one small offence can lead to the breakdown of a relationship. It can end a friendship.

On the other hand, there is something glorious about overlooking an offence. This means refusing to be offended. It means refusing to hold a grudge. It means refusing to take revenge. It is hard to do. But it is of utmost importance if we are to maintain unity in our relationships.

PRAYER

Lord, forgive me when I am too easily offended. Thank you that, through the cross of our Lord Jesus Christ, you overlook my offences. Help me through that same power to overlook the offences of others.

NEW TESTAMENT READING

1 Corinthians 1:1–17
Unity around Jesus

Corinth was a large cosmopolitan city that attracted people from every nation, culture and religion. In many ways, it was similar to a city like London, Hong Kong or New York. It was a commercial centre. It was a centre for arts, recreation, literature and architecture. It was a place with many museums and theatres.

The people of Corinth were wealthy, hard drinking and sexually promiscuous, and it was notorious for immorality.

In AD 50, Paul went to Corinth to plant a church. He stayed with his friends Priscilla and Aquila. He got himself a job and started preaching the gospel. He started a church in a house and stayed eighteen months until the spring of AD 52. Then he handed the church over to Apollos and moved on to plant more churches.

Some time later, Paul received a report that in his absence all kinds of problems had developed, including division in the church. Three or four years after planting this church (c. AD 53–54), he wrote this letter to try to deal with some of the issues.

Quarrelling and disunity began very early in the church's history. In Corinth, it seems that the different factions were divided not so much by doctrine, as by mindset. Instead of being united in Christ they split into factions based purely on the leader they most respected – Paul, Apollos or Peter (Cephas) (vv.11–13).

Even before Paul starts his appeal for unity and love, we can see in his introduction and greetings how the theme of unity runs deep in Paul's thinking. The basis of our unity is the person of Jesus:

1. Relationship with Jesus
Paul writes to 'those sanctified in Christ Jesus and called to be his holy people, together with all those everywhere who call on the name of our Lord Jesus Christ – their Lord and ours' (v.2).

Every Christian in the world is someone who is sanctified in Jesus Christ and who calls on the name of our Lord Jesus Christ. Christ is not divided (v.13) and neither should we be. We share the same Lord. You are all called into 'fellowship' (*koinonia*) with Jesus (v.9). Spend time today enjoying his friendship. This is the deepest and most intimate relationship possible. *Koinonia* is the word used of the marriage relationship. We all love Jesus deeply and intimately.

2. Grace of Jesus
Paul writes, '*Grace* and peace to you from God our Father and the Lord Jesus Christ. I always thank God for you because of his *grace* given you in Christ Jesus' (vv.3–4). To be a Christian is to experience the grace of God given to you in Christ Jesus. You are loved. Grace means undeserved love. It is supremely shown in and made possible through the death of Jesus Christ for each one of us. Every Christian in the world, of every church and denomination, is someone for whom Christ died. His grace is the basis of our unity.

3. Spirit of Jesus
Paul writes to the Corinthians, 'Therefore you do not lack any spiritual gift' (v.7a). The Spirit of Jesus Christ lives in every Christian. Paul goes on to expound in this letter how each of us has spiritual gifts, because we have the Holy Spirit living in us. Every Christian in the world has the Holy Spirit living in them just as he lives in you.

4. Hope in Jesus
Paul goes on to say, 'as you eagerly wait for our Lord Jesus Christ to be revealed. He will keep you strong to the end, so that you will be blameless on the day of our Lord Jesus Christ' (vv.7b–8). We all await the return of Jesus. One day we will be completely united in him. In the meantime, we have a common hope.

Paul is passionate about this unity. He writes, 'I appeal to you, brothers and sisters, in the name of our Lord Jesus Christ, that all of you agree with one another so that there may be no divisions among you and that you may be *perfectly united* in mind and thought' (v.10).

He is not happy to settle for a superficial unity. He appeals for *perfect unity*. In our lifetime, we may not succeed in seeing the complete unity of the church. However, never settle for less. Pray for it and seek to do all you can to bring it about. Jesus prayed that we might be brought to *complete unity* (John 17:20–21).

PRAYER

Lord, I pray for unity in our local church and in the church around the world. Thank you that we see visible signs of a greater unity. May we be brought to complete unity in order that the world will believe in you.

OLD TESTAMENT READING

1 Chronicles 16:37–18:17
Unity under one King

God's desire has always been for unity among his people. Just as we see his desire for unity among his people in the New Testament, so we see in the Old Testament that he desired unity for the people of God.

Sadly, the history of the people of God in the Old Testament was also one of disunity. There was only one period in Israel's history where there was any real semblance of unity. That was the period we now read about in the Book of Chronicles. David united '*all Israel*' (18:14).

This was a period of great blessing for the people of God. Nathan said to David, 'Whatever you have in mind, do it, for God is with you' (17:2). 'The LORD gave David victory everywhere he went' (18:6b). 'David reigned over *all Israel*, doing what was just and right for all his people' (v.14).

This unity continued in the reign of Solomon. The chronicler sees the unity of this period as the ideal. Writing hundreds of years later, he is not naïve about the failings of King David, and neither is he slow to point out the temptations of Solomon that spelt the beginning of the end of this golden age – gold, horses and many wives (see Deuteronomy 17).

After hundreds of years of disunity, he hopes that one day Israel will have a king who can do what even David and Solomon could not fully do. He longs for a king who will bring, among other things, total and permanent unity to the people of God. The fulfilment came about, not through an earthly king, but through a heavenly one.

PRAYER

Lord Jesus, you are the Anointed King, who more than fulfilled the expectations of Israel. Thank you that you have the power to unite the entire human race under your lordship. Thank you that one day we will see this unity.

5 August | Day 217
Perfected in Weakness

I kept getting these phone calls. They came mostly from church leaders. They were from many different parts of the church. They were always long telephone conversations. They all wanted to know: 'How come you get so many people from outside of the church on the course?' 'What exactly is Alpha?' 'How do you run it?'

I thought perhaps the best solution was to get them together in one place and tell them all at the same time. As a result, we put on our first Alpha Conference in May 1993. To our astonishment a thousand church leaders turned up. I was relatively new to Christian ministry and was extremely daunted at the thought of a thousand church leaders, most of whom were far more experienced in ministry than I was.

The words of the apostle Paul, in today's New Testament passage, seemed to sum up exactly how I felt. I read them to the delegates at the start of the conference:

> 'When I came to you, brothers and sisters, I did not come with eloquence or superior wisdom as I proclaimed to you the testimony about God. For I resolved to know nothing while I was with you except Jesus Christ and him crucified. I came to you in *weakness* and *fear*, and with much *trembling*. My message and my preaching were not with wise and persuasive words, but with a demonstration of the Spirit's power, so that your faith might not rest on human wisdom, but on God's power' (1 Corinthians 2:1–5).

I thought once I had explained what Alpha was to this group of church leaders, I would never have to explain it to anyone again. But in fact, by the end of the conference we had been invited to do many more conferences. Over the years we have done hundreds of conferences. At every Alpha Conference I start by reading 1 Corinthians 2:1–5. It is always what I feel; I always feel nervous. There is always an element of '*weakness* and *fear*, and … much *trembling*'. But I thank God that it does not depend on wise and persuasive words but on a demonstration of the Spirit's power. And God's power is *perfected in weakness* (2 Corinthians 12:9).

There is a good side to 'weakness', 'fear' and 'trembling'. There is also a bad side. In the passages for today we see both the good and the bad sides of weakness, fear and trembling.

READING FROM PSALMS

Psalm 91:1–8
Fear and faith

'Fear nothing' (v.5, MSG) writes the psalmist. He gives the remedy for 'fear' in the bad sense of the word. He writes, '*You will not fear* the terror of night, nor the arrow that flies by day, nor the pestilence that stalks in the darkness, nor the plague that destroys at midday' (vv.5–6).

The remedy for fear is a close relationship with the Lord – to dwell 'in the shelter of the Most High' and 'rest in the shadow of the Almighty' (v.1). The opposite of fear is *trust* in God (v.2).

There is a strong connection between what you think and what you say. What you think will come out in your words. But also, your words can affect your thinking. What you say to God can change your thinking. The psalmist tells us to speak aloud about God's goodness: '*Say this*, "God you're my refuge. *I trust in you* and I'm safe!"' (v.2, MSG).

He promises to rescue you 'from hidden traps, shields you from deadly hazards. His huge outstretched arms protect you – under them you're perfectly safe; his arms fend off all harm' (vv.3–4, MSG).

Fear can destroy your enjoyment of the present. God raised Jesus from the dead. In doing so, he freed you from the fear of death and all the fears that go with it. 'Under his wings you find refuge' (v.4). You do not need to be afraid about the future and you can enjoy the present *without fear*.

PRAYER

Lord, thank you that I can dwell in your shelter and rest in your shadow. I say to you today: you are 'my refuge and my fortress' (v.2). I will trust in you.

NEW TESTAMENT READING

1 Corinthians 1:18–2:5
Power in weakness

'I was scared to death,' writes the apostle Paul (2:3, MSG). He felt totally inadequate for the task that God had called him to, 'But the Message came through anyway. God's Spirit and God's power did it' (v.4, MSG).

Moral weakness and cowardice are not virtues. However, as we see in this passage, there is a good side to weakness, fear and trembling.

God turns things upside down. The cross turned things upside down: 'For the message of the cross is foolishness to those who are perishing, but to us who are being saved it is the power of God' (1:18).

Jesus died as a state criminal. He died on a Roman instrument of torture – a death reserved for the most degraded and despised in Roman society. The cross did not become the symbol of Christianity for a hundred years. Crucifixion was about weakness, humiliation and defeat.

At this time, Corinth was the intellectual centre of the world. It was the place of debaters, travelling teachers, lecturers and philosophers. The mind and the intellect were highly rated.

The gospel message that we proclaim seems utterly foolish to many highly intelligent people: that Jesus dying on a cross two thousand years ago can totally transform your life seems 'foolishness' to the intelligentsia and is a 'stumbling-block' (v.23), even to many religious people.

Nevertheless, this simple message saves those who believe: 'For since in the wisdom of God the world through its wisdom did not know him, God was pleased through the foolishness of what was preached to save those who believe ... For the foolishness of God is wiser than human wisdom, and the weakness of God is stronger than human strength' (vv.21, 25).

As we look around we can see that it is still true today that not many of those in the church are 'the brightest and the best'. Not many are 'influential'. And not many are 'from high-society families' (v.26, MSG). But it is still true today that God 'chose the foolish things of the world to shame the wise'. He 'chose the weak things of the world to shame the strong' (v.27).

Do not be ashamed of speaking a very simple message, which seems foolishness to so many people. There is no need to try and dress it up with 'eloquence or superior wisdom' (2:1). Focus on the message of 'Jesus Christ and him crucified' (v.2). As Eugene Peterson translates, 'I deliberately kept it plain and simple; first *Jesus and who he is*; then *Jesus and what he did* – Jesus crucified' (v.2, MSG).

It is normal to experience 'weakness and fear, and ... much trembling' (v.3). What matters is not whether you use 'wise and persuasive words' but the 'demonstration of the Spirit's power' (v.4). And his power is made perfect in our weakness. It is often only when we feel weak that we are willing to rely completely on God. Paul was utterly dependent on the Holy Spirit to speak through him. However inadequate you feel, if you ask for the Holy Spirit to speak through you, he will.

PRAYER

Lord, thank you for the message of Jesus and him crucified, which is the power of God. Thank you that I do not need eloquence or superior wisdom. Although I speak in weakness, fear, and trembling, I pray that you accompany the preaching of that message with a demonstration of the Spirit's power.

OLD TESTAMENT READING

1 Chronicles 19:1–22:1
Fear and trembling

'Fear and trembling' before God is not always wrong. Indeed, it is sometimes appropriate.

The chronicler makes it clear, in a way that the earlier account did not, that it was 'Satan' who 'incited David to take a census' (21:1). Joab tried to persuade David not to do this (v.3). But David overruled him. 'And God was displeased with this (reliance on human resources)' (v.7, AMP).

It is not quite clear why this was *such a great sin*, but it obviously was as David said to God, 'I have sinned greatly by doing this. Now, I beg you, take away the guilt of your servant. I have done a very foolish thing' (v.8).

With what appears to be fear and trembling he says, 'I am in deep distress. Let me fall into the hands of the LORD, for his mercy is very great' (v.13).

When he comes to offer a sacrifice to God he says, 'I insist on paying the full price. I will not take for the LORD what is yours, or sacrifice a burnt offering that costs me nothing' (v.24). He called on the LORD and the LORD answered him 'with fire from heaven' (v.26).

PRAYER

Lord, I come to you today in weakness and with much trembling and ask that your power will be made perfect in my weakness (2 Corinthians 12:9).

6 August | Day 218
God Is With You

I wonder whether you have ever had this experience: you are talking to a friend about your faith and they are looking back at you with a blank stare. They have no idea what you are talking about. When you talk about a relationship with Jesus, to them it is like you are speaking about an 'imaginary friend'. It makes no sense to them at all.

The apostle Paul makes the point that you can only understand spiritual truths with the help of the Holy Spirit. The person 'without the Spirit does not accept the things that come from the Spirit of God but considers them foolishness, and cannot understand them because they are spiritually discerned' (1 Corinthians 2:14). When God is with us by his Holy Spirit he gives us understanding, 'that we may understand what God has freely given us' (v.12).

'God with us' (Immanuel) is one of the titles the New Testament uses for Jesus (Matthew 1:23). He is always with you. That the God who created the universe should be with you is not something to be taken lightly. It is an extraordinary and wonderful promise. To experience God with you by his Spirit is life changing.

READING FROM PSALMS

Psalm 91:9–16
With you in trouble

In the difficult times, 'in trouble' (v.15), you may sometimes feel that God has left you. In these times listen to God's promises over and above your feelings and emotions.

This psalm is all about God's protection and encourages you not to be afraid:

> 'If you make the Most High your dwelling –
> even the Lord, who is my refuge –
> then no harm will befall you,
> no disaster will come near your tent' (v.9).

This might appear to be the recipe for a trouble-free life. However, the psalmist goes on:

> '"Because you love me," says the Lord, "I will rescue you;
> I will protect you, for you acknowledge my name.
> You will call upon me, and I will answer you;
> *I will be with you in trouble*"' (vv.14–15).

It is clear from this that those who love the Lord will *not avoid trouble*. God does not promise a trouble-free life. Rather, he promises that he will rescue you, protect you and answer your prayers. More than that he promises, '*I will be with you*' in trouble. This is what makes all the difference. Even in the darkest times, he is with you. You are never alone.

PRAYER

Thank you, Lord, that you are with me in times of trouble. Thank you for your rescue, deliverance, protection and answers to my prayers.

Lord, today I call upon you again...

NEW TESTAMENT READING

1 Corinthians 2:6–16
With you by his Spirit

Through the Holy Spirit, God is with you in the most extraordinary way – he is actually *in* you. It would be impossible for God to be with you any more fully than he is through his Spirit.

In this passage Paul explains some of the extraordinary benefits of God being with you in this way: 'Spirit can be known only by spirit – God's Spirit and our spirits in open communion. Spiritually alive, we have access to everything God's Spirit is doing, and can't be judged by unspiritual critics. Isaiah's question, "Is there anyone around who knows God's Spirit, anyone who knows what he is doing?" has been answered: Christ knows, and we have Christ's Spirit' (vv.15–16, MSG).

Like the psalmist, the apostle Paul expounds on all the wonderful things that 'God has prepared for *those who love him*' (v.9, see also Psalm 91:14, '*Because you love me...*').

Paul compares God's wisdom to the 'fashionable wisdom of high-priced experts that will be out-of-date in a year or so' (1 Corinthians 2:6, MSG). God's secret wisdom has been revealed to us (vv.6–10) – the wonder of Jesus' life, death and resurrection. The rulers of the world did not understand it. If they had, they would not have crucified Jesus: 'The Lord of glory' (v.8).

God's secret wisdom is amazing. 'No eye has seen, no ear has heard, no mind has conceived what God has prepared for *those who love him*' (v.9).

In his book, *True Spirituality*, Vaughan Roberts notes that there is a four-fold process in which the Holy Spirit reveals God's wisdom to us.[1]

1. The Holy Spirit *knows*
He knows what no human being could otherwise know – the mind and thoughts of God. 'The Spirit searches all things, even the deep things of God. For who *knows* the thoughts of another human being except that person's own spirit within? In the same way, no one *knows* the thoughts of God except the Spirit of God' (vv.10b–11).

2. The Holy Spirit *reveals*
The Holy Spirit does not keep his knowledge of the wisdom of God to himself, but he *reveals* it to those in whom he dwells. 'We have not received the spirit of the world but the Spirit who is from God, that we may understand what God has freely given us' (v.12). You have received the Spirit who is from God. He is with you. He enables you to understand the secret wisdom of God, though of course we could never fathom the depths of God. As Paul says later in this letter, in this life 'we see but a poor reflection as in a mirror', not yet 'face to face' (13:12).

3. The Holy Spirit *inspires*
Paul was *inspired by the Spirit* to pass on the wisdom of the gospel to others. 'This is what we speak, not in words taught us by human wisdom but in words taught by the Spirit, expressing spiritual truths in spiritual words' (2:13). The Spirit similarly teaches you what to say so that you too can express 'spiritual truths in spiritual words', generally through the Spirit-inspired words of the apostles recorded in the New Testament. You can share words in line with Scripture that point people to Jesus.

4. The Holy Spirit *illuminates*
Without the Holy Spirit, you simply cannot understand spiritual truths: 'The person without the Spirit does not accept the things that come from the Spirit of God but considers them foolishness, and cannot understand them because they are spiritually discerned' (v.14). When God is with you by his Spirit you can actually understand the mind of the Lord. Indeed, you 'have the mind of Christ' (v.16).

PRAYER

Lord, thank you for this amazing truth that you are with me by your Spirit. Today, may I have the mind of Christ in all my decisions and conversations. I pray for spiritual words to express spiritual truths.

OLD TESTAMENT READING

1 Chronicles 22:2–23:32
With you in success

Have you ever felt disappointed or envious when others succeed in a ministry that you wanted to do? David's example (22:6–19) challenges us to pray for others to succeed and to encourage, bless and help them when they do.

David had really wanted to build the temple himself. Now David prepares for his son, Solomon, to succeed him. He gets everything ready for him. He has a great succession plan setting Solomon up for success.

Leadership is about serving the people you lead so that they will go further and do better than you. When you are faithful to bless others in doing well, God will be faithful to honour and bless you.

It was David *and* Solomon who *together* made possible the building of the temple. David himself could not carry out the work as he had 'shed much blood' (v.8). Solomon is the one who will actually build the temple.

David says, 'Now, my son, *the* Lord *be with you*, and may you have success and build the house of the LORD your God, as he said you would. May the LORD give you discretion and understanding ... Be strong and courageous. Do not be afraid or discouraged ... Now begin the work, and the LORD be with you' (vv.11–16).

The Lord wasn't only with Solomon: 'David ordered all the leaders of Israel to help his son Solomon. He said to them, "*Is not the LORD your God with you?*"' (vv.17–18a). God was with them also. He granted them 'rest on every side' (v.18b). He told them, 'Now devote your heart and soul to seeking the LORD your God' (v.19).

They had success and rest 'since the LORD, the God of Israel, [had] come to *dwell* in Jerusalem for ever' (23:25).

This is a cause for great rejoicing, thanksgiving and praise. The Levites were to 'stand every morning to thank and praise the LORD. They were to do the same in the evening' (v.30).

Long-term success comes from God being with you. Life may not be easy, but Jesus promised that if you stay close to him you will bear much fruit, and that fruit will last (John 15:1–17).

PRAYER

Lord, thank you that you promise me long-term success and rest. May I thank and praise you from first thing in the morning until last thing at night for your presence with me.

7 August | Day 219
Three Bad Attitudes That Cause Division

During my time at university, I shared rooms together with my great friend Nicky Lee who is now one of the associate vicars of HTB. We did all our own catering; I did the cooking and Nicky Lee did the dividing. He was an *expert at dividing* whatever was cooked into exactly equal portions! This is but one instance where *division* is used in a *good sense* rather than a bad one.

Divisions are a fact of life. They need not necessarily be a bad thing. Indeed, they may even be necessary. For example, placing people in different *divisions in an organisation* may be helpful and important. We see this kind of division in the Old Testament passage for today.

Then, there is the division that will take place on the day of judgment. This is a necessary division between good and evil. This kind of division can be seen in the psalm for today.

There is also a third kind of division, which is not good, helpful or necessary. Disunity and division in the church is a tragedy. This kind of division is one we must do our very best to avoid. It is this kind of division that the apostle Paul speaks against in the New Testament passage for today.

READING FROM PSALMS

Psalm 92:1–15
Division between the righteous and evildoers

The world is divided, according to the psalmist, between 'evildoers' (v.7) and the 'righteous' (v.12). Evildoers are senseless 'fools' who 'do not understand' (v.6). They are 'enemies' of God (v.9). One day, not only will they be divided from the righteous, but they will also be divided among themselves – they will be 'scattered' (v.9), and they will 'perish' (v.9). The 'righteous', on the other hand, have a secure future (vv.12–15).

Both 'evildoers' (v.7) and the 'righteous ... flourish' (vv.12–13), but in different ways. For the 'evildoers' (v.7) it is passing and temporal. They will soon be 'destroyed' (v.7). They are like the grass. But for the 'righteous' (v.12) it is a lasting and *eternal flourishing*. It is 'like a palm tree' or 'a cedar of Lebanon' (v.12). They 'will still bear fruit in old age, they will stay fresh and green' (v.14).

The difference between the success of the world – power, fame, making money and so on – and the success of a true follower of Jesus in living a holy life is like the difference between grass, which only lasts a few days, and a palm tree that stands throughout the ages.

PRAYER

Lord, when I see the lasting blessings you give to those who follow you, I want 'to proclaim your love in the morning and your faithfulness at night' (v.2).

NEW TESTAMENT READING

1 Corinthians 3:1–23
Divisions in the church

Paul's letter to the Corinthians is a sandwich. He starts with *praise and love*. He ends with *grace and love*. In the middle, he raises issues that he wants them to deal with.

This is a good model when confronting issues in an individual or a church. Start and end with a positive and encouraging note; but have the courage to deal with the issues.

One of the issues he raises is *division in the church*. He says that they are 'worldly' (v.1) and 'unspiritual' (v.1, MSG). In some ways, they were the most 'spiritual' of all the churches that Paul wrote to. They did 'not lack any spiritual gift' (1:7). However, they were 'unspiritual' because of bad attitudes, which led to division.

He points out *three bad attitudes*. These are dangers for all Christians, but particularly for Christian leaders.

1. Jealousy

He writes, 'For since there is jealousy ... among you, are you not worldly?' (3:3). It is tempting to compare ourselves with others and, when we hear about some blessing another has received, to start thinking, 'When is that going to happen to me?' But, as Joyce Meyer writes, 'We should bless others and not be afraid they will get ahead of us. We must not envy anyone else's appearance, possessions, education, social standing, marital status, gifts and talents, job, or anything else because that will only hinder our own blessing.'[1]

2. Boasting

Paul writes, 'So then, no more boasting about human leaders!' (v.21). Boasting is the temptation to compare ourselves with others, think we are doing rather well and boast about our 'success'. We need to see our part in God's economy in its proper perspective. We are first, 'mere human beings' (v.4); second, 'only servants' (v.5); third, 'neither the one who plants nor the one who waters is anything' (v.7). Therefore, there is no cause for 'boasting' (v.21).

3. Quarrelling

Paul writes that their 'quarrelling' is another reason that he sees them as 'unspiritual'. We must avoid taking sides, where 'one says, "I follow Paul" and another "I follow Apollos"' (v.4).

All of these stem from an inflated view of our own importance. These are 'unspiritual' attitudes. These sorts of attitudes are all too common in fallen humanity, infecting the world, and sadly the church too.

We need to understand that all of us are utterly dependent on God. One plants a seed, the other waters it, but *God* makes it grow (v.6). Planting and watering are important, but they are relatively easy. Only God can do the difficult bit and make plants, people and churches grow.

You do have a role to play. First, God uses you to bring people to faith. Apollos and Paul were those '*through whom* [the Corinthians] *came to believe*' (v.5). Second, God will reward you. The person who plants and the person who waters have one purpose and each will be *rewarded* according to their own labour. Third, you are 'God's *co-workers*' (v.9). God has chosen not to do it on his own. He chooses to use you.

Being used by God is a huge privilege. Not only are you God's 'co- worker' (v.9) – you are 'God's field, God's building' (v.9). People try to build their lives on many things – money, education, job titles, possessions, and so on, but Jesus is the only sure foundation (v.11).

Furthermore, Paul goes on to write, 'Don't you know that you yourselves are God's temple and that God's Spirit lives in you?' (v.16). Therefore, he writes, 'I don't want to hear any of you bragging about yourself or anyone else. Everything is already yours as a gift ... and you are privileged to be in union with Christ, who is in union with God' (vv.21–23, MSG).

PRAYER

Lord, thank you that we are fellow workers with you and that it is you who makes things grow. Keep us from pride and boasting, jealousy and quarrelling. Help us to guard the unity of the church.

OLD TESTAMENT READING

1 Chronicles 24:1–26:19
Divisions for ministry

Here we see the word 'divisions' used in a positive sense. 'These were the *divisions* of the descendants of Aaron' (24:1). 'David separated them into *divisions* for their appointed order of ministering' (v.3). 'A larger number of leaders were found ... they were *divided* accordingly' (v.4). 'They *divided* them impartially' (v.5). There were also '*divisions* of the gatekeepers' (26:1, 19). 'These *divisions* of the gatekeepers, through their leaders, had duties for ministering in the temple of the LORD' (v.12).

There are some interesting names in his list. Among the singers are the psalmists 'Asaph' (Psalm 50 and Psalms 73–83), 'Jeduthun' (Psalms 39; 62; 77) and 'Heman' (Psalm 88).

Among the *gatekeepers* (or as often translated, '*doorkeepers*') are the Korahites. Psalm 84 is attributed to 'the Sons of Korah' – and was therefore presumably written by a doorkeeper. This helps us to understand what he meant when he wrote, 'I would rather be a *doorkeeper* in the house of my God than dwell in the tents of the wicked' (v.10).

In the body of Christ, we divide up the roles. Each part of the body has a different function. As St Paul writes, 'The body is a unit, though it is made up of many parts; and though all its parts are many, they form one body ... God has combined the members of the body ... so that there should be *no division in the body*, but that its parts should have equal concern for each other' (1 Corinthians 12:12, 24–25).

The apostle Paul describes the good sense of division (the different roles of members in the body), while seeking to avoid the bad sense (there should be no division or disunity in the body).

It is a great honour to be involved in any way in serving in 'God's house' – whether we are helping with the car parking or welcoming teams, coffee or prayer ministry. Every person has great significance and honour because we are serving in God's house.

PRAYER

Lord, help us to make wise decisions in the assignment of roles in the body of Christ so that everybody gets involved. Help us, your church, to function as a unit made up of many parts in which each part cooperates with all the others with a unity brought about by the Holy Spirit.

8 August | Day 220

Money: A Blessing or a Curse?

Laurence was in charge of the finances of the church. He was also a deacon. There was a great revival taking place all around him. It was said that, 'All of Rome were becoming Christians.'

As a result, persecution broke out under the Emperor Valerian in around the year AD 250. Christians who owned property distributed all the church's money and treasures to the city's poor.

Valerian ordered all bishops, priests and deacons to be arrested and executed. He offered Laurence a way out if he would show where all the church's treasures were located.

Laurence asked for three days to gather it into one central place. He brought together the blind, poor, disabled, sick, elderly, widows and orphans. When Valerian arrived, Laurence flung open the doors and said, 'These are the treasures of the church!'

Valerian was so angry that he decided beheading was not terrifying enough for Laurence. He ordered that this courageous man be roasted on a gridiron. That is how Laurence died on 10 August AD 258. Apparently, he even joked with his executioners, 'You may turn me over. I'm done on this side.' His courage made such an impression that the revival in Rome only increased, with many people becoming Christians including several senators who witnessed his execution.

St Laurence had a profound understanding of the message of Jesus. He understood that the poor are the true *treasures of the church*.

What should our attitude be to the poor? What about the rich? Is poverty a blessing or a curse? Are riches a blessing or a curse? Does the gospel promise prosperity?

READING FROM PSALMS

Proverbs 19:13–22
Money is not everything

The book of Proverbs has a remarkably balanced understanding of wealth and poverty. Neither is seen as wholly good or wholly bad. They are understood as part of the wider fabric of life, and you are encouraged to use what you have wisely.

'Houses and wealth are inherited from parents, but a prudent wife is from the LORD' (v.14). There is nothing wrong with houses or wealth; but there are more important things in life. Finding the right marriage partner is far more important than having lots of money.

For those tempted to work too hard in pursuit of money or any other goal, it is important to remember the sovereignty of God: 'Many are the plans in a human heart, but it is the LORD's purpose that prevails' (v.21). Taking 'Sabbath rest' and holidays is a sign that you trust in God's sovereignty.

Wealth is not the most important thing in life; nor is poverty the worst thing that can happen to you: 'What a person desires is unfailing love; better to be poor than a liar' (v.22). We need love far more than we need riches. Integrity of character is far more important than money.

On the other hand, this passage does not exalt poverty as a virtue. Sometimes poverty can be self-inflicted: 'Laziness brings on deep sleep, and the shiftless go hungry' (v.15).

Whatever the reason may be for a person's poverty, be kind to the poor: 'Those who are kind to the poor lend to the LORD, and he will reward them for what they have done' (v.17).

This is an extraordinary and wonderful promise. God is no person's debtor. Every time you do something kind for a poor person, you are lending to the Lord and he will repay with interest. Often, we see amazing blessings in the lives of those who spend their time ministering with the poor, the homeless and the prisoners.

PRAYER

Lord, I entrust you with my finances and my future. Help me to live a life of generosity to all – especially the poor.

NEW TESTAMENT READING

1 Corinthians 4:1–21
The Poverty of the apostles

On the outside, people were rich, honoured and strong; but the church in Corinth was in a real mess. Paul points out that they were arrogant, proud and jealous. They tolerated sexual immorality, and they went to court against each other.

The apostle Paul starts to tackle some of these issues. He sees in their lives the arrogance of the rich. They are proud of their material wealth. Paul explains in a nutshell why no one has any cause for pride: 'Isn't everything you have and everything you are sheer gifts from God? So what's the point of all this comparing and competing? You already have all you need. You already have more access to God than you can handle' (vv.7b–8, MSG).

They are rich like kings: 'Already you have all you want! Already you have become rich! You have begun to reign – and that without us!' (v.8a). There is a hint of sarcasm here. They are not really rulers at all, 'How I wish that you really had begun to reign so that we might come to rule with you!' (v.8b)

He contrasts their material wealth with the poverty of himself and of the other apostles. 'You might be sure of yourselves, but we live in the midst of frailties and uncertainties. You might be well-thought-of by others, but we're mostly kicked around. Much of the time we don't have enough to eat, we wear patched and threadbare clothes, we get doors slammed in our faces, and we pick up odd jobs anywhere we can to eke out a living' (vv.11–12, MSG).

Paul was one of the most influential Christians ever. His ministry was possibly the most 'successful' of all time. However, it did not lead to material prosperity. Quite the opposite. He was materially poor. He did not have enough food. He did not have nice clothes. He was homeless.

His poverty did not come about as a result of laziness: 'We work hard with our own hands' (v.12a). But, like many poor people today, he was subject to abuse. He did not respond in kind: 'When we are cursed, we bless; when we are persecuted, we endure it; when we are slandered, we answer kindly. Up to this moment we have become the scum of the earth, the refuse of the world' (vv.12b–13).

Paul writes with great love – not to shame them but to warn them. He sees them as a father sees his own children (vv.14–15): 'I'm writing as a father to you, my children. I love you and want you to grow up well, not spoiled. There are a lot of people around who can't wait to tell you what you've done wrong, but there aren't many fathers willing to take the time and effort to help you grow up.

Paul's heart was like that of a good father. A father's heart is gentle, kind, nurturing, training, persevering and never gives up on people. This should be the attitude of a pastor. All human parents are less than perfect. But you are loved and nurtured by your perfect heavenly Father and can seek to be a parent to others based on his heavenly model.

PRAYER

Lord, thank you that I have received far more through Jesus than anything this world can offer. May I be willing to be a fool 'for Christ' (v.10). Help me to imitate Paul's example.

OLD TESTAMENT READING

1 Chronicles 26:20–27:34
The Riches of kings

When Paul wrote, 'Already you have become rich! You have begun to reign' (1 Corinthians 4:8), perhaps he had kings like King David in mind.

David was rich. He had great 'treasuries' (1 Chronicles 26:22), he had 'royal storehouses' (27:25), he had 'vineyards', 'wine vats' (v.27), 'olive and sycamore-fig trees' (v.28), 'supplies of olive oil' (v.28b), 'herds' (v.29), 'camels' and 'donkeys' (v.30b), 'flocks' and 'property' (v.31).

Finances are not 'unspiritual'. For example, the worship of God usually takes place in buildings. Buildings cost money. Running the financial side of a church is an important role. The 'Levites were put in charge of the financial affairs of The Temple ... They supervised the finances of the sanctuary of God' (26:20, 22, MSG). Shubael was 'the chief financial officer' (v.24, MSG).

Material wealth was often seen in the Old Testament as a sign of God's blessing. It is still true that godly character – hard work, reliability, integrity and honesty – are characteristics that often can lead to success and material prosperity. However, as we have seen in the New Testament passage for today, this is not the whole picture.

Over the years I have come across a number of very rich Christians. Some of them are among the godliest and most committed believers I have known. Their riches are not necessarily a sign of God's blessing – but neither are they something bad. The key thing is how you see your money, and what you do with it.

PRAYER

Lord, help us to get the balance right in our teaching and in our lifestyle. May we never be guilty of condemning or judging those whom you have blessed with material prosperity. May we be generous and give freely and be willing to go hungry and thirsty, in rags and homeless if necessary, in order to serve you.

9 August | Day 221

Only Holiness Leads to Happiness

Our magazines and TV screens are filled with stories of the rich, the beautiful and the strong. Our culture places these things on a pedestal and many of us aspire to achieve them. There is nothing wrong with these things – but they certainly don't always lead to happiness.

The French philosopher, Blaise Pascal, spoke of three orders of greatness. Riches, beauty and strength fall into his first category of superficial 'physical greatness'.

Above this is a higher, second level of greatness. It is the greatness of genius, science and art. The greatness of the art of Michelangelo or the music of Bach or the brilliance of Albert Einstein – these stand way above superficial physical greatness.

However, according to Pascal there is a third kind of greatness – the order of holiness. (And there is an almost infinite qualitative difference between the second and the third categories.) The fact that a holy person is strong or weak, rich or poor, highly intelligent or illiterate, does not add or subtract anything because that person's greatness is on a different and almost infinitely superior plane. It is open to every one of us to achieve true greatness in the order of holiness.[1]

The word 'holy' (hallowed, holiest, holiness) appears over 500 times in the Bible. God is holy. He gives you his Holy Spirit to sanctify you, and you are called to share in his holiness.

The word 'saints' means 'holy ones'. In the New Testament it is applied to all Christians. You are 'called to be holy' (1 Corinthians 1:2). Holiness is a gift you receive when you put your trust in Jesus, receive his righteousness and the gift of the Holy Spirit. Seek to live out a holy life in grateful response to God's gift, through the imitation of Jesus in the power of the Holy Spirit. Ultimately, only holiness leads to happiness.

READING FROM PSALMS

Psalm 93:1–5
Holy God

God is the creator of all, but he is also set apart from the world he has established. He is greater and more majestic than all creation, even the thunders of mighty waters (v.4).

The climax of the psalmist's praise focuses on God's *holiness*. He concludes, 'Your statutes stand firm; *holiness* adorns your house for endless days, O LORD' (v.5). The HCSB translates this, '*Holiness* is the beauty of your house...' The temple was a beautiful and impressive building, but the psalmist recognises that the holiness of God is the temple's true inner beauty and glory.

PRAYER

Lord, we worship you in the beauty of your holiness. You alone are holy. 'Holy, holy, holy is the LORD Almighty' (Isaiah 6:3).

NEW TESTAMENT READING

1 Corinthians 5:1–13
Holy church

There are several pitfalls in talking about holiness in the church today. First, there is the danger of an attitude that is 'holier-than-thou'. Avoid self-righteous superiority. Second, there is the danger of perfectionism. Only God is completely holy. Strive for excellence, but you will not achieve perfection in this life.

Our holiness is the appropriate response to God's holiness – and yet it is only made possible by the gift and the grace of God. Holiness in the church comes through the gift of the Holy Spirit (1 Corinthians 3:16–17).

Because the church is meant to be holy, Paul is horrified by what was going on in Corinth. There was gross sexual immorality of a kind that would not be tolerated even outside the church (5:1).

He writes, 'And you're so above it all that it doesn't even faze you! Shouldn't this break your hearts? Shouldn't it bring you to your knees in tears? Shouldn't this person and his conduct be *confronted* and *dealt with*?' (v.2, MSG).

In order for the church to be holy, discipline needs to be exercised. There are some extreme sins that should result in exclusion from the church (v.13). These sins are ones that are very obvious. For example, in the case of sexual immorality it is an extreme kind of immorality (between a man and his stepmother, v.1).

Paul writes about the need for discipline in relation to those who are 'greedy, idolaters or slanderers, drunkards or swindlers' (v.10–11). 'Greed' here probably carries the sense of avarice to the point of robbery or swindling. Other such sins include idolatry and slander (verbal abuse – maligning and reviling people).

'Drunkards' refers to those who willingly and persistently get drunk. Paul's focus here is not on those who are trying to overcome alcoholism (or any other addiction), for whom the church should be a place of healing and not of rejection. The word here is associated with other vices – violence and unseemly sexuality.

Paul makes it absolutely clear that he is not speaking about people outside of the church (v.10). We are not to dissociate ourselves from even the most extreme 'sinners'. Jesus was 'a friend of sinners'. He associated with everyone. These are exactly the people we should be reaching out to.

Rather, Paul is saying that if people continue with these extreme and obvious sins in an unrepentant manner, they have no place in the church. Unless we deal with the issue, 'A little yeast works through the whole batch of dough' (v.6) – it will affect the whole church.

Church discipline is therefore very positive in the sense that it enables the person to confront their own conduct and deal with it (v.5). It is also positive for the church as a whole in that it stops evil spreading through the whole church community (v.6).

Thankfully, forgiveness is possible: 'For Christ, our Passover lamb, has been sacrificed' (v.7). None of us are holy except through the gift of God. Jesus died as the Passover lamb in order that we can be forgiven and cleansed. Holiness is a gift from God. When we fail we need to come back to the cross without delay and receive forgiveness.

PRAYER

Today Lord, I come to you again and ask for your forgiveness and cleansing. Help me to lead a holy life. May your church be a holy place.

OLD TESTAMENT READING

1 Chronicles 28:1–29:30
Holy temple

David was called to prepare for the building of a holy temple (29:2–3). Because the temple was holy, David himself could not build it, since he had 'done too much fighting – killed too many people' (28:3, MSG).

However, God did guide David in the exact plans for building the temple. The plans were 'put into his mind' by 'the Spirit' (v.12). This is often how God guides us – he presents reasons to our minds for acting in a certain way.

David entrusted the work to his son Solomon. He called him to serve God with 'wholehearted devotion and with a willing mind, for the LORD searches every heart and understands every motive behind the thoughts' (v.9). God calls you, as he did Solomon, to a holiness that goes beyond action, to the heart, the motives and the thoughts.

David said that God is a God who tests the heart and is pleased with integrity (29:17). David was a man of 'integrity of heart' (Psalm 78:72). This is a good definition of holiness.

It has been said that everyone has three lives – a public life, a private life and a secret life. Holiness is about living an integrated life, rather than a dis-integrated one. Holiness is where there is no difference between our public, private and secret lives and no difference between what we profess and what we practise. Holiness is linked to wholeness. When God calls you to be holy, he is saying 'be wholly mine'.

David prayed, 'Give my son Solomon the wholehearted devotion to keep your commands, requirements and decrees and to do everything to build the palatial structure for which I have provided' (1 Chronicles 29:19).

It is interesting to note in passing that in order to build the temple they needed to raise a large amount of money. They achieved it because the leaders led. The overall leader gave first (v.3). The other leaders gave next (v.6). Then all the people 'gave willingly' (v.6) with 'a sense of celebration' (v.17, MSG).

God wants you to give willingly. If you are not willing, you can pray, 'Lord make me willing to be made willing'. And as Sandy Millar often says, at least you can pray, 'Lord make me willing to be willing to be made willing'!

As God's people gave willingly, they were filled with great joy. Everything you have comes from God in the first place (v.16). As you give your resources to the work of God generously and freely, you are filled with great joy.

The holy temple which David and Solomon built was only preparation for the holy temple of the church where the Holy Spirit dwells. Not only does the Spirit live in the church, he also lives in you. Your body is a temple of the Holy Spirit (1 Corinthians 6:19–20).

PRAYER

Lord, fill me today with your Holy Spirit I pray, and help me to be holy.

10 August | Day 222
Good Judgment

When I practised as a barrister most of the judges I appeared before were extremely good. However, I remember one occasion when I appeared before a judge who was not good. It was a terrible experience.

I was representing the defendant in a criminal case. It was only the second case I had ever done in front of a jury. I was young and inexperienced. Nevertheless, it seemed to me that there was something very wrong with the way in which the judge was conducting the case. She kept interrupting me whenever I was speaking. She intervened over and over again with her own questions. I ended up having what the court usher described as a 'stand-up row with the judge'.

The judge's summing up was more like a second prosecution speech; my client was duly convicted and sent to prison. We appealed, on the basis that the defendant was entitled to a fair trial and he had not been given one.

When I appeared before three very senior judges in the Court of Appeal, I was extremely nervous that they might not approve of my part in the 'stand-up row with the judge'! To my relief they were as appalled as I had been by her conduct of the trial. They overturned the original decision and my confidence in the British legal system was restored.

Good judges are scarce. In many parts of the world, judges are subject to bribery and corruption. There is no rule of law. The result is terrible injustice. The poor, in particular, tend to be the victims.

READING FROM PSALMS

Psalm 94:1–11
Judge of the earth

The Lord God is '*Judge of the earth*' (v.2). At the moment, we do not always see justice. We see wickedness (v.3), arrogance and boasting (v.4). We see people being crushed and oppressed (v.5). In particular, we see the poor – the widow, outsider and fatherless (v.6) – suffering.

The psalmist cries out for justice. God is a God of justice. He 'avenges' (v.1). This is not vindictive but the appropriate and just response to evil and wickedness. He will 'pay back to the proud what they deserve' (v.2b). The wicked will not get away with it any longer. The poor will no longer be oppressed.

God's judgment is an aspect of his love. He loves the marginalised. Therefore, he acts on their behalf to judge their oppressors.

Injustice is the cause of so much suffering in the world. In order to protect the innocent, it is an act of love to bring to justice those who, for example, traffic people for sex.

Sometimes we might be tempted to think that 'God does not notice' or 'God does not mind'. However, the reality is that God, 'who implanted the ear', hears and, 'who formed the eye', sees (v.9). This means that God's judgment will be loving and perfect. God has total knowledge for 'the LORD knows all human thoughts' (v.11a), and so he is able to, and will, administer perfect justice.

PRAYER

Lord, thank you that one day we will see perfect justice executed by a perfect Judge. In the meantime, Lord, help us to seek justice on this earth, especially for the marginalised.

NEW TESTAMENT READING

1 Corinthians 6:1–20
Judges in the church

The general rule in the New Testament is that Christians should never take each other to court.

The apostle Paul was shocked that the believers in Corinth were taking one another to court (v.1a). He writes, 'How dare you take each other to court!' (v.1a, MSG). This is a terrible witness for the church. Believers were fighting each other in front of the 'ungodly' (v.1): 'Does it make any sense to go before a court that knows nothing of God's ways instead of a family of Christians?' (v.1b, MSG).

It is better to be wronged or cheated than to get involved in lawsuits (vv.7–8). However, Paul appeals to them that if they do get involved in disputes, they should settle the matter between themselves (vv.4–6).

If it really is necessary to settle a dispute, then they should *appoint judges* from the church. Paul points out that one day the 'saints will *judge the world*' (v.2): 'The day is coming when the world is going to stand before a jury made up of followers of Jesus' (v.2, MSG). This judgment, Paul suggests, will include the judgment of fallen angels (v.3).

Paul's argument is that if one day we are to be involved in this great day of judgment, surely we are capable of judging relatively trivial cases now (vv.2–3). Do anything to avoid 'going to law' against each other in front of 'unbelievers' (v.6).

There will be a final judgment: 'The wicked will not inherit the kingdom of God' (v.9). Paul lists various types of sinners: 'Those who use and abuse each other, use and abuse sex, use and abuse the earth and everything in it, don't qualify as citizens in God's kingdom' (vv.9–10, MSG).

A number of those to whom Paul was writing would have been involved in these kinds of lifestyles in the recent past and would have been on Paul's list. But he writes, 'Since then, you've been cleaned up and given a fresh start by Jesus, our Master, our Messiah, and by our God present in us, the Spirit' (v.11, MSG).

All of us deserve to be condemned at the final judgment. We have no cause for self-righteousness or boasting. Through the death of Jesus for you, you were washed, sanctified and justified. To be justified means to be acquitted before the great court of God. The judgment is brought forward and you receive this verdict now.

You can have great confidence about the future. Death is not the end: 'By his power God raised the Lord from the dead, and he will raise us also' (v.14). Not only can you be sure that one day you will be raised to eternal life, but through Jesus you can also be assured that you can appear with confidence before the judge of all the earth 'sanctified' and 'justified' (v.11).

This does not mean that you can go off and do anything you like. Rather, the reverse. Your body is now a temple of the Holy Spirit (v.19). You were 'bought at a price' (v.20). Therefore, 'flee from sexual immorality' (v.18). 'We must not pursue the kind of sex that avoids commitment and intimacy leaving us more lonely than ever' (v.16, MSG). 'Your body is a sacred place, the place of the Holy Spirit' (v.19, MSG).

Do 'not be mastered by anything' (v.12). Your body belongs to God. Use it to honour him (v.20).

PRAYER

Lord, thank you that through the blood of Jesus, I am washed and cleansed. Thank you that I have already been acquitted. Help me to live as someone who has been set free and to honour you in everything I do.

OLD TESTAMENT READING

2 Chronicles 1:1–17
Judgment of Solomon

Do you ever feel overwhelmed by something you are supposed to be doing? I certainly do. Solomon was faced with a 'staggering task' (v.9, MSG).

Solomon's kingdom was firmly established (v.1). He spoke to all Israel including the '*judges*' (v.2).

He himself was also to act as a judge. In fact, throughout history Solomon has been known for his good judgment. The people held him 'in awe, because they saw that he had *wisdom from God to administer justice*' (1 Kings 3:28).

Where did this wisdom come from? It was an answer to his prayer. God said to him, 'Ask for whatever you want me to give to you' (2 Chronicles 1:7). He prayed as I often do, 'Give me wisdom and knowledge as I come and go among this people – for who on his own is capable of leading these, your glorious people?' (v.10, MSG).

'God answered Solomon, "This is what has come out of your heart: You didn't grasp for money, wealth, fame, and the doom of your enemies; you didn't even ask for a long life. You asked for wisdom and knowledge so you could govern well my people over whom I've made you king. Because of this, you get what you asked for – wisdom and knowledge. And I'm presenting you the rest as a bonus – money, wealth, and fame beyond anything the kings before or after you had or will have"' (vv.11–12, MSG).

As Jesus said, 'Seek first [God's] kingdom and his righteousness, and all these things will be given to you as well' (Matthew 6:33). And as the apostle James said, 'If any of you lacks wisdom, you should ask God, who gives generously to all without finding fault, and it will be given to you' (James 1:5).

PRAYER

Lord, I pray for good judgment, wisdom and knowledge for myself and for all those who are required to lead and govern. I pray also that you would raise up good judges and that there would be a transformation in the justice systems around the world.

---

11 August | Day 223
Anxiety and Peace

Anxiety can rob you of the enjoyment of life. The causes of anxiety are numerous: health issues, work (or lack of it), finances (debt, unpaid bills and so on) and much else besides. Some of the biggest causes of anxiety are those dealt with in today's New Testament passage: relationships, marriage (or lack of it), sex (or lack of it), singleness and divorce.

In our Old Testament passage, the book of Ecclesiastes suggests that much of the anxiety we experience is caused by something deeper. This could be described as the anxiety of meaninglessness. In the midst of all this, you are called to 'live in peace' (1 Corinthians 7:15).

READING FROM PSALMS

Psalm 94:12–23
Speak to God about your anxieties

Do you know what it is like to experience great anxiety (v.19a)?

The psalmist certainly did. He writes, 'You grant ... relief from days of trouble ... When I said, "My foot is slipping," your love, O LORD, supported me. *When anxiety was great within me*, your consolation brought joy to my soul' (vv.13a,18–19).

He goes on, 'But the LORD has become my fortress, and my God the rock in whom I take refuge' (v.22).

When surrounded by great anxiety, turn to the Lord for help. 'When I was upset and beside myself you calmed me down and cheered me up' (v.19, MSG). In God's love we find relief, consolation and joy. God provides 'a circle of quiet within the clamour of evil' (v.13, MSG).

PRAYER

Thank you, Lord, that you give me relief in the days of trouble. Today I come to you and bring my anxieties to you...

NEW TESTAMENT READING

1 Corinthians 7:1–16
Live at peace with your situation

Do you feel you are living a life of peace? 'God has called us to *live in peace*' (v.15c). How do you find this 'peace'? In this chapter, Paul sets out how you find peace in relationships, marriage, singleness and separation. He begins by asking the question, 'Is it a good thing to have sexual relations?' (v.1, MSG). He responds, 'Certainly – but only within a certain context' (v.2a, MSG).

Paul is dealing with two opposite dangers: those who say that 'all things are lawful' (see chapter 6) which leads to immorality, and the super spiritual ascetics, who deny the body totally. In response, Paul answers a number of questions:

1. Is marriage God's general will for his people?

Marriage is the norm for all men and women: 'It's good for a man to have a wife, and for a woman to have a husband' (v.2, MSG). God's general will is for people to get married for partnership (Genesis 2:18), procreation (Genesis 1:28) and pleasure (1 Corinthians 7:1–5). Singleness is the exception. It is a special call.

The reason Paul gives here is because there is 'so much immorality' (v.2). 'Sexual drives are strong, but marriage is strong enough to contain them and provide for a balanced and fulfilling sexual life in a world of sexual disorder' (v.2, MSG). He is dealing with his opponents on their own terms. They were reacting against immorality and arguing for no sex and no marriage.

Paul replies that, as well as all the positive reasons, the temptation towards immorality is a good reason to get married.

2. What is the Christian attitude to sex within marriage?

The route to spiritual fullness in marriage is not through abstinence. Within marriage there is sexual freedom and sexual equality: 'The marriage bed must be a place of mutuality – the husband seeking to satisfy his wife, the wife seeking to satisfy her husband' (v.3, MSG). The only reason to abstain is for short periods of prayer, if mutually agreed, and that is a concession not a command (vv.5–6).

3. Is it better to be single or married?

Paul writes that both are gifts from God. They are both good (vv.7–9). In a way, it is best (for reasons to be given later) to be single: 'Sometimes I wish everyone were single like me – a simpler life in many ways! But celibacy is not for everyone any more than marriage is' (v.7, MSG). But it is also a good thing to get married (v.9).

4. Should a Christian ever seek a divorce from another Christian?

The general principle of this passage, and the rest of the New Testament, seems to answer this question, 'No': 'If you are married, stay married ... a husband has no right to get rid of his wife' (vv.10–11, MSG). Of course, this is a very complex issue. (I have tried to look at this question in more detail in *The Jesus Lifestyle*, chapter 6.)[1]

5. What about relationships with people who are not Christians?

Paul does not encourage a Christian to marry someone who is not a Christian (2 Corinthians 6:14–7:1; 1 Corinthians 7:39). However, if they are already married that is quite different. They should not seek to dissolve any existing marriage relationship.

Paul's opponents were worried that being married to someone who was not a Christian would pollute the marriage. Paul's response is that the opposite is the case: 'The unbelieving husband shares to an extent in the holiness of his wife, and the unbelieving wife is likewise touched by the holiness of her husband. Otherwise, your children would be left out; as it is, they also are included in the spiritual purposes of God' (v.14, MSG).

If the person who is not a Christian insists on leaving, and clinging to the marriage would lead to nothing but frustration and tension, then the Christian should let them go, *not for the sake of purity*, but for the sake of '*peace*' (see v.15).

PRAYER

Lord, help us at whatever stage we find ourselves, regardless of our marital status, to live according to your standards and to know your peace.

OLD TESTAMENT READING

Ecclesiastes 1:1–3:22
Find purpose instead of meaninglessness

'What do people get for all the toil and *anxious striving* with which they labour under the sun?' (2:22). This expression 'under the sun' occurs twenty-eight times in this book. It is used to describe a search for meaning that never moves beyond this life and this world.

Ecclesiastes is a story of one person's anxious search for meaning. The writer, in the shoes of King Solomon 3,000 years ago, searches in various areas.

Joyce Meyer writes, 'Solomon was a busy man; he tried everything that could be tried and did everything there was to do, but at the end of his experience, he was unfulfilled and bitter ... exhausted, disappointed and frustrated.'[2] Ecclesiastes expresses some of these frustrations about life.

Eugene Peterson writes, 'Ecclesiastes doesn't say that much about God; the author leaves that to the other sixty-five books of the Bible. His task is to expose our total incapacity to find the meaning and completion of our lives on our own ... It is an exposé and rejection of every arrogant and ignorant expectation that we can live our lives by ourselves on our own terms.'[3]

Solomon finds that 'everything's boring, utterly boring – no one can find any meaning in it' (1:8, MSG). 'So what do you get from a life of hard labour? Pain and grief from dawn to dusk. Never a decent night's rest. Nothing but smoke' (2:23, MSG).

1. Intellectualism

He begins by chasing after 'wisdom' and 'knowledge' (1:18a), but this only leads to 'much sorrow' and 'more grief' (v.18b). 'The more you know, the more you hurt' (v.18b, MSG). Accumulating wisdom and knowledge does not deal with the ultimate cause of anxiety – meaninglessness.

2. Hedonism

Hedonism is the doctrine that pleasure is the chief good or proper aim. 'I said to myself, "Let's go for it – experiment with pleasure, have a good time!"' (2:1, MSG). He tries escapism through 'laughter' (v.2). He tries stimulants – 'cheering myself with wine' (v.3). He then turns to music, 'men and women singers' (v.8). He tries sexual pleasure, 'and a harem as well' (v.8b). Solomon in fact had 700 wives and 300 mistresses. All this still did not satisfy.

He concludes, 'Yet when I surveyed all that my hands had done and what I had toiled to achieve, everything was meaningless, a chasing after the wind' (v.11). He experiences the paradox of pleasure – the law of diminishing returns. The more people seek pleasure, the less they find it.

3. Materialism

Materialism is 'the tendency to prefer material possessions to spiritual values'. He tries various '*projects*' (v.4). He obtains *property* (vv.4–6). He has many men and women working for him (v.7). He has many *possessions* (v.7b). He acquires money: 'I amassed silver and gold for myself, and the treasure of kings and provinces' (v.8). He achieves greatness, success and fame (v.9). He has a successful job and career (v.10b). Yet death makes this entire search 'meaningless' (vv.16–18).

Ecclesiastes raises the questions that the New Testament answers. Meaning is found not 'under the sun', but in the Son.

PRAYER

Lord, thank you that in Jesus, I find the answer to the anxiety of meaninglessness. Thank you that in him I find true peace and purpose to my life.

---

12 August | Day 224
Enjoy Life in the Present

Some people see life today as the Three Witches in Shakespeare's *Macbeth* put it, 'Double, double *toil and trouble*.'[1] My own perspective on life changed when a friend wisely pointed out to me that, in a sense, this life is a series of problem-solving exercises. We will never be without problems in this life. If, in the midst of all the challenges, you cannot learn to thrive in the situation in which you find yourself, you will never find contentment.

The writer of Ecclesiastes says, 'We should make the most of what God gives, both the bounty and the capacity to enjoy it, accepting what's given and delighting in the work. It's God's gift! God deals out joy in the present, the now' (Ecclesiastes 5:19, MSG). Learn to enjoy this wonderful gift of life in the present. If you do not, life will pass you by and you will never enjoy where you are right now.

READING FROM PSALMS

Proverbs 19:23–20:4
Trust, respect and honour God

The answer to trouble, according to the writer of Proverbs is, 'The fear of the LORD' (19:23a) – that is, living in a relationship with God, trusting in him, respecting and honouring him. He writes, 'The fear of the LORD leads to *life*: Then one rests *content*, untouched by trouble' (v.23).

He goes on to speak of some of the *causes of trouble*:

1. Laziness

Laziness is highlighted in this passage as a cause of future trouble: 'A farmer too lazy to plant in the spring has nothing to harvest in the fall' (20:4, MSG; see also 19:24).

2. Cynicism
Mocking (19:25, 29) is a form of cynicism. It is very common in our culture today. It can even infect the church, but it is not a good thing. It leads to trouble.

3. Malice
Dishonesty is another cause of trouble. Robbery leads to 'shame and disgrace' (v.26). 'An unprincipled witness desecrates justice; the mouths of the wicked spew *malice*' (v.28, MSG).

4. Substance abuse
'Wine makes you mean, beer makes you troublesome – a staggering drunk is not much fun' (20:1, MSG). So much trouble is caused by people getting drunk. Many of the crimes that occur in society are committed under the influence of alcohol or drugs.

5. Quarrelling (v.3)
'It is the mark of good character to avert quarrels, but fools love to pick fights' (v.3, MSG).

PRAYER

Lord, thank you that it is a relationship with you that leads to life and contentment. Help me to avoid the causes of unnecessary trouble.

NEW TESTAMENT READING

1 Corinthians 7:17–35
Be totally devoted to the Lord

One of the key issues these days is the anxiety and listlessness which comes from constant comparison and FOMO (fear of missing out).

The answer to FOMO is found in the words with which Paul starts the passage for today: 'Don't be wishing you were someplace else or with someone else. Where you are right now is God's place for you' (v.17, MSG). Paul gives the principle from which all his application flows (vv.17–24). A new Christian should stay as they were when they were converted.

He gives three examples: marriage, circumcision and slavery. (Historically, the first Christians were a small minority and in no position to abolish slavery.)

However, this has a wider application. Unless their occupation is illegal or immoral, those who become Christians should not simply leave their job without receiving a clear call into some new occupation. God calls you *in* to things, not simply *out* of them.

Paul wants to spare people the '*many troubles in this life*' (v.28). 'Don't complicate your lives unnecessarily' (v.29, MSG). His overriding concern, as he looks at the questions of marriage and singleness, is 'undivided devotion to the Lord' (v.35) – the supreme aim of your life.

Paul writes of the advantages of singleness. Of course, Jesus himself was single and he spoke about the fact that, for some, singleness is involuntary, whereas for others it is a choice for the sake of the kingdom (Matthew 19:12). Involuntary singleness is a difficult and painful subject, but it is not what Jesus was speaking about in Matthew 19, nor is it what Paul is speaking about here. Paul is speaking about singleness for the sake of the kingdom. This can be either permanent or temporary.

The disadvantages of singleness are obvious. Perhaps the three hardest things for single Christians can be, first, missing the companionship of marriage and the loneliness that can result; second, a lack of sexual fulfilment; third, not having children.

However, the apostle Paul here also gives two reasons why it can be an advantage:

1. The brevity of life
He writes that 'there is no time to waste' (1 Corinthians 7:29, MSG), therefore 'don't complicate your lives unnecessarily. Keep it simple – in marriage, grief, joy, whatever. Even in ordinary things – your daily routines of shopping, and so on. Deal as sparingly as possible with the things the world thrusts on you' (vv.29–31, MSG).

He is not forbidding marriage any more than he is forbidding laughter, mourning or shopping. Rather he is saying that everything pales into insignificance besides the glory of serving the Lord. We need a detachment from the things of this world. This may be easier if a person is single.

2. Freedom from distraction
This applies especially in times of persecution, which provides the context for this passage, 'because of the present crisis' (v.26).

Paul writes, 'I want you to live as free of complications as possible. When you are unmarried, you are free to concentrate on simply pleasing the Master ... The time and energy that married people spend on caring for and nurturing each other, the unmarried can spend on becoming whole and holy instruments of God ... All I want is for you to be able to develop a way of life in which you can spend plenty of time together with the

Master without a lot of distractions' (vv.32–35, MSG).

We have a limited amount of time, energy and money. There is no doubt that there are many demands in marriage. Paul calls for a positive view of singleness – whether permanent or temporary. He is saying it can be fulfilling and liberating – as it was for Jesus.

Elsewhere he writes that marriage itself is only a picture of the relationship between Christ and the church (Ephesians 5). The reality is found in Christ. Both marriage and singleness are gifts. What really matters is 'undivided devotion to the Lord' (1 Corinthians 7:35). We often assume that marriage is the best and most obvious way of life to follow. This passage reminds us not to overlook the benefits of singleness. Singleness is equally valid, and can be very fruitful and fulfilling.

PRAYER

Lord, help me to find life and contentment in whatever situation I find myself – leading a life to 'please the Lord'. 'May [I] live in a right way in undivided devotion to the Lord' (v.35).

OLD TESTAMENT READING

Ecclesiastes 4:1–6:12
Enjoy the blessings of work and relationships

The writer continues his theme of the emptiness of life and its meaninglessness. He sees life as full of trouble, 'oppression' and '*toil*' (4:1–6).

He speaks of the emptiness experienced by those in high positions (vv.13–16). He also speaks of the emptiness of an acquisitive life (5:16–17) and the elusive quality of desire (6:9). In the midst of this rather pessimistic and depressing view of life, he gives keys to thriving amid *toil* and *trouble*.

1. Work

A lack of work is a bad thing: 'Fools fold their hands and ruin themselves' (4:5). On the other hand, don't work too hard: 'Working obsessively late into the night, compulsively greedy for more and more, never bothering to ask, "Why am I working like a dog, never having any fun?"' (v.8, MSG).

The optimum is moderate work: 'Better one handful with *tranquillity* than two handfuls with *toil* and chasing after the wind' (v.6). He goes on to say, 'The sleep of labourers is sweet, whether they eat little or much' (5:12).

2. Relationships

He goes on to speak of the vital importance of relationships: marriage, friendship and teams (4:9–12). First there is synergy. 'It's better to have a partner than go it alone. Share the work, share the wealth' (v.9, MSG). Working as a team can be more efficient.

Second, there is the advantage of mutual support. 'If they fall down, one can help the other up. But pity those who fall and have no friend to help them up!' (v.10).

Third, there is the advantage of physical and spiritual support: 'A cord of three strands is not quickly broken' (v.12).

The key to a strong friendship or a strong marriage is the third cord – what the other passages for today speak of as 'undivided devotion to *the Lord*' (1 Corinthians 7:35) and 'the fear of *the* LORD' (Proverbs 19:23a).

PRAYER

Lord, help me to avoid unnecessary 'toil and trouble' and in undivided devotion to the Lord, not just to survive, but to thrive and enjoy life in all its fullness.

13 August | Day 225
Who You Need to Know

We lived in Oxford for three years. I was training for ordination in the Church of England and studying for a degree in Theology at Oxford University. One of the things we noticed while we were there was that, compared to London, Oxford seemed to be relatively non-materialistic. People, on the whole, were not impressed by wealth. Success was measured differently.

The people in Oxford tended to be more impressed by brains than by money or beauty. Success was measured in starred firsts, distinctions, PhDs, professorships and published works. It made me wonder whether intelligence and 'knowledge' could be as much a false god as money and wealth.

Knowledge is, on the whole, good. The facts are your friends. Education is good – reading, learning and discovering are all good activities. However, as Lord Byron wrote, 'The Tree of

Knowledge is not that of Life."[1] We need to see 'knowledge' in perspective. Our knowledge is very limited. The more we know, the more we realise how little we know. God is our creator and he alone knows everything.

There are also different types of knowledge, and they are not all equally valuable. In French, there are two different words for 'to know'. One (*savoir*) means to know a fact, the other (*connaître*) means to know a person. God is more interested in us knowing people than facts. The most important knowledge of all is knowing God and being known by him. Even this is not the end though. It is never enough simply to have knowledge – you must also have love.

READING FROM PSALMS

Psalm 95:1–11
The most important knowledge is knowledge of God

The psalmist begins with a call to worship, praise and thanksgiving (vv.1–2). We worship, not because we necessarily feel like it, nor because things are going well. In fact, sometimes we worship *in spite* of difficult circumstances and hard times.

Neither do we worship because it necessarily makes us feel good. Although often we feel the need to worship for spiritual refreshment.

Rather we see in this psalm that we worship God because of who he is:

> 'For the LORD is the great God,
> the great King above all gods...
> Come, let us bow down in worship,
> let us kneel before the LORD our Maker;
> for he is our God and we are the people of his pasture,
> the flock under his care' (vv.3–7).

The psalmist reminds the people of what they know of God. This is the most important kind of knowledge – knowledge of God.

In the context of worship, God often speaks to us. It is not just that God has spoken in the past. God speaks today. The psalmist says, '*Today* if you hear his voice...' (v.7b).

In this psalm, we also see another important kind of knowledge. God says that people go astray because they have 'not known *my* ways' (v.10). Knowing and following God's ways is key to living life as God intended.

PRAYER

Lord, I kneel before you today and worship you. Thank you that you know me and I can know you. As I hear your voice today, help me not to harden my heart and go astray. May I know your ways and follow them and enter your rest.

NEW TESTAMENT READING

1 Corinthians 7:36–8:13
What matters most is not knowledge but love

Although knowledge is a good thing, it has inherent dangers. It can lead to pride and a 'know-it-all' superiority. 'Knowledge puffs up, but love builds up' (8:1b).

Knowledge is not in itself a bad thing. It's been said that 'Knowledge is like underwear – it is useful to have, but not necessary to show it off!' Instead of trying to impress others with what you know, always try to encourage and build other people up in love.

Knowledge can so often lead to pride and arrogance: 'Those who think they know something do not yet know as they ought to know' (v.2). What really matters in life is loving God and living a life of love: 'But whoever loves God is known by God' (v.3).

As Eugene Peterson translates, 'We sometimes tend to think we know all we need to know in answer to these kinds of questions – *but* sometimes our humble hearts can help us more than our proud minds. We never really know enough until we recognise that God alone knows it all' (vv.1b–3, MSG).

Paul uses the example of 'food sacrificed to idols' (vv.1, 4). A person with *knowledge* knows that it is fine to eat food sacrificed to idols because the idols are nothing: 'There is but one God, the Father, from whom all things came and for whom we live; and there is but one Lord, Jesus Christ, through whom all things came and through whom we live' (v.6).

'But not everyone *knows* this' (v.7a). Some people's consciences are weak. By eating food sacrificed to idols in front of someone who feels this is wrong, we may lead them astray. What matters is not our superior knowledge, but our love for others: 'But knowing isn't everything. If it becomes everything, some people end up as know-it-alls who treat others as know-nothings. Real knowledge isn't that insensitive' (v.7b, MSG).

Love recognises that 'Christ gave up his life for that person ... When you hurt your friend, you hurt Christ' (vv.11–12, MSG). Paul writes, 'Therefore, if what I eat causes my brother or sister to fall into sin, I will never eat meat again, so that I will not cause them to fall' (v.13).

Love is more important than knowledge. When God measures a person, he puts the tape round the heart, not the head. It is no good just *knowing* lots about God; get to know him *and* let him fill you with love for him and for others. In other words, it's not what you know, it's who you know.

PRAYER

Lord, thank you that, although the danger of knowledge is that it puffs up, love always builds up. Help me to do everything out of love for you and love for others.

OLD TESTAMENT READING

Ecclesiastes 7:1–9:12
Seek knowledge but know its limitations

Wisdom and knowledge go hand in hand in the book of Ecclesiastes. Wisdom and knowledge are basically good things:

'*Wisdom*, like an inheritance, is *a good thing*
and benefits those who see the sun' (7:11).

'Wisdom puts more strength in one wise person
Than ten strong men give to a city' (v.19, MSG).

'There's nothing better than being wise,
Knowing how to interpret the meaning of life.
Wisdom puts light in the eyes,
And gives gentleness to words and manners' (8:1, MSG).

An example of wisdom is that wise people keep their temper under control: 'Don't be quick to fly off the handle. Anger boomerangs' (7:9, MSG).

But, the writer of Ecclesiastes recognises the limits of wisdom and knowledge. First, however much wisdom and knowledge we have, we cannot really discover anything about the future (v.14). Second, there is a danger in being 'over-wise'. It is possible to have an unhealthy appetite for knowledge that is divorced from God, and so becomes a form of pride:

'When I determined to load up on wisdom and examine everything taking place on earth, I realised that if you keep your eyes open day and night without even blinking, you'll still never figure out the meaning of what God is doing on this earth. Search as hard as you like, you're not going to make sense of it. No matter how smart you are, you won't get to the bottom of it' (vv.16–17, MSG).

However wise, rich and powerful a person may be, 'no one has power over when death comes' (v.8). 'Life leads to death. That's it' (9:3, MSG). We never know when our lives will end. 'People do not *know* when their hour will come' (v.12).

God alone knows everything. In comparison to him our wisdom and knowledge is very limited. Ultimately we are 'in God's hands' (9:1). We should enjoy life and make the most of our time here. Seize life! ... God takes pleasure in *your* pleasure! ... Relish life with the spouse you love each and every day of your precarious life. Each day is God's gift ... Make the most of each one!' (vv.7, 9, MSG).

'Whatever your hand finds to do, do it with all your might' (v.10a). Don't waste your life, make the most of every moment and opportunity.

Jesus said, 'This is eternal life: that they may *know you*, the only true God, and Jesus Christ, whom you have sent' (John 17:3). This is the most important knowledge you can ever have. It starts now and goes on into eternity. This knowledge puts every other kind of knowledge in the right perspective.

PRAYER

Lord, thank you that knowing you is the beginning of wisdom. Help me to make the most of every opportunity in life – to do whatever I do with all my might. And help me to do it all in love.

14 August | Day 226
A Night with a Mosquito

History is in many ways a story of influence. Leadership is about influence. Everyone influences someone. Therefore, in a sense, everyone is a leader. Sociologists tell us that even the most introverted individual will influence 10,000 other people during his or her lifetime. We all influence one another in all sorts of ways – from what to have for lunch and what films to watch, to more important matters of truth and ethics.

My life has been influenced by so many people – my parents, teachers, friends and family. Just as I have been influenced by others, inevitably what I do and say will influence others for good or ill.

As the African proverb puts it, 'If you think you're too small to make a difference, you haven't spent the night with a mosquito.' The mosquito makes a difference in an annoying way, but the principle is the same. One person can stop a great injustice. One person can be a voice for truth. One person's kindness can save a life. Each person matters.

How can you maximise your influence and use that influence for good?

READING FROM PSALMS

Psalm 96:1–13
For the good of *everyone*

God chose Israel. He blessed the people of Israel in a special way. His purpose was not that they should feel proud and superior to others. Rather, it was that they should be a blessing to the whole world (Genesis 12:3). They were blessed to be a blessing. They were called to use their influence for the good of all nations.

Now, God has chosen us, the church, to be a blessing to all people. You are blessed to be a blessing.

This psalm has a multi-national focus. It proclaims the wonders and blessings of God to everyone. You are called to bless through:

1. Worship

It is interesting to note in passing that worship should be creative and include innovation: They sang '*a brand-new song*' (Psalm 96:1, MSG).

2. Witness

'Shout the news of his victory from sea to sea,
Take the news of his glory to the lost,
News of his wonders to one and all!...
Get out the message – God Rules!' (vv.2–3, 10a, MSG).

PRAYER

Help us, Lord, never to become inward looking or self-indulgent. May everything we do as individuals and as a community be outward focused in order to bring blessing to the world – proclaiming your salvation day after day.

NEW TESTAMENT READING

1 Corinthians 9:1–18
To spread the good news

Paul is deeply conscious of his influence as a Christian and, in particular, as an apostle. He is absolutely determined to maximise his influence for good and to 'put up with anything rather than hinder the gospel of Christ' (v.12b).

It appears that he sees his calling to singleness as one of the ways he can maximise his influence. He is not suggesting that there is anything wrong with marriage. It appears that the other apostles, including 'the Lord's brothers and Cephas [Peter]' were all married (v.5).

Another way he seeks to maximise his influence is by having a second job; working for a living. He is very keen to point out that he does not need to do this: 'The Lord has commanded that those who preach the gospel should receive their living from the gospel' (v.14). Or as Eugene Peterson translates, '... those who spread the Message be supported by those who believe the Message' (v.14, MSG). In other words, as Christians we should support financially those who spread the gospel full time.

Paul's point is that although he had this right, he did not make use of it: 'Our decision all along has been to put up with anything rather than to get in the way or detract from the Message of Christ' (v.12b, MSG).

Paul is absolutely passionate about the preaching of the gospel. He does not want anything to hinder its maximum impact. Hence, he does not make use of any of his rights – his mission is paramount (v.15a). He is 'compelled to preach' (v.16a). He writes, 'Woe to me if I do not preach the gospel!' (v.16b). He is simply discharging an obligation that he feels.

What he wants more than anything is that people should be able to hear the gospel 'free of charge' (v.18): 'I'd rather die than give anyone ammunition to discredit me or impugn my motives' (v.15, MSG).

This is one of the reasons why we are determined that no one should ever have to pay for doing Alpha. And, this is why we need to resist every attempt to persuade us to fundraise from guests as soon as they have finished Alpha. We do not want people to pay directly or indirectly for the privilege of hearing the gospel. Paul says, 'I would rather die...' (v.15b).

I remember when Billy Graham came to preach the gospel in London in 1989. It was suggested at one point that in order for the tickets (which were all free) not to be wasted, they should be sold for a nominal sum of one pound each. The suggestion was rejected out of hand. Billy Graham had determined that he would always preach the gospel free of charge.

PRAYER

Lord, help us always to follow this example of the apostle Paul and to maximise the impact and influence of the preaching of the gospel by making it available free of charge, and to put up with anything rather than hinder the gospel of Christ.

OLD TESTAMENT READING

Ecclesiastes 9:13–12:14
To plant good seeds

Solomon is very aware of the power of influence. This influence can be for good or evil.

One wise person can save a city (9:13–18a). On the other hand, 'one sinner destroys much good' (v.18b). Hitler, Stalin and Pol Pot are glaring examples of this principle. One human being can use their influence for evil and cause great harm.

But, the influence does not have to be as great as these tyrants in order to have a bad effect: 'Dead flies in perfume make it stink, and a little foolishness decomposes much wisdom' (10:1, MSG). If even a dead fly can have a bad influence, the least influential human being can have an influence for evil or good. We can all be the fly in the ointment!

The writer has much to say about how to be a good influence, rather than a bad one:

1. Watch your words

Solomon reminds us that 'words from the mouth of the wise are gracious' (v.12a). Respond to hot-tempered words with calmness (v.4). Avoid gossiping and bad-mouthing your leaders. Be careful what you say or even think. Don't revile people 'even in your *thoughts*' or curse them 'in your *bedroom*, because a bird of the air may carry your words, and a bird on the wing may report what you say' (v.20).

2. Take risks

To maximise your influence for good you need to take risks. 'Be generous: Invest in acts of charity. Charity yields high returns. Don't hoard your goods; spread them around. Be a blessing to others' (11:1–2, MSG). In other words, he says 'nothing ventured, nothing gained'. To love is to risk not being loved in return. To try is to risk failure. But risks must be taken, because the greatest hazard in life is to risk nothing.

If we are too cautious we will never achieve anything. 'Whoever watches the wind will not plant; whoever looks at the clouds will not reap' (v.4). We could apply this principle to church planting. It will require risk and determination. We must not be daunted by seemingly insuperable obstacles. We must not be put off due to 'wind' and 'clouds'.

3. Spread your efforts

In order to maximise influence, you might have to juggle different opportunities in your life: 'Sow your seed in the morning, and at evening let not your hands be idle, for you do not know which will succeed' (v.6).

Don't put all your eggs in one basket. Press ahead on all fronts and make the most of every opportunity. This is why as a church we try to sow seeds in every direction – through worship, prayer, leadership, discipleship, theological training, social transformation, evangelism, work in the prisons and with the poor and the marginalised.

4. Take your opportunities

Life is short. Don't waste time worrying. '... banish anxiety from your heart...' (11:10). Your opportunities are limited: 'Even if you live a long time, don't take a single day for granted. Take delight in each light-filled hour ... You who are young, make the most of your youth' (vv.8a,9, MSG).

The book finishes with a conclusion to all its searching and questioning. The meaning of life ultimately rests in your relationship with God. Revere him and keep his commandments. This is the whole duty for every person (12:13b).

PRAYER

Lord, help me to revere you and keep your commandments. Help me to use my influence for good and not for evil. Help me to make the most of every opportunity that you have put before me.

15 August | Day 227
No Sloppy Living

I love to play sport. I have never been particularly good at it, but I enjoy it enormously. Not many of the guys I play squash with play at a very high standard; it is all very friendly and relaxed, and yet we are very competitive! Even the level we play at requires 'strict training'. I have to train and play regularly. It is one of the reasons I try to be careful about what I eat and how much sleep I get.

The apostle Paul writes, 'You've all been to the stadium and seen the athletes race. Everyone runs; one wins. Run to win. All good athletes train hard. They do it for a gold medal that tarnishes and fades. You're after one that's gold eternally' (1 Corinthians 9:24–25, MSG).

If those who compete at sport go into strict training in order to achieve something that 'will not last', how much more should we go into 'strict training' in our moral and spiritual life in order to 'get a crown that will last for ever' (v.25).

Paul writes, 'I don't know about you, but I'm running hard for the finish line. *I'm giving it everything I've got. No sloppy living* for me! I'm staying alert and in top condition' (v.26, MSG). Worshipping and serving God is Paul's aim and ambition in life. He wants to do it to the very best of his ability. He wants to give it everything he's got. He is going for gold.

Worship and service are very closely connected (the same Greek word *latreuo* is used for both). All human beings are worshippers. You either worship the one true God, or someone or something else. All human beings are servants – to God, to yourself or to someone or something else.

In the passages for today, we see the importance of worshipping and serving the one true God with all of our hearts and beings – giving everything we have got – no sloppy living.

READING FROM PSALMS

Psalm 97:1–12
Why do you worship and serve?

God is in charge of his universe. 'The LORD reigns' (v.1). If the Lord did not reign, there would be no point to life – but he does and there is cause for rejoicing (v.1).

The psalmist calls for all creation to worship, 'On your knees ... worship him!' (v.7, MSG).

He praises God – first, for who he is, and second, for what he has done. It is because of who God is that he acts to bring protection, deliverance, guidance and joy to his people (vv.10–12).

1. God is your protector
He guards your life: 'Those who love him he keeps safe' (v.10b, MSG).

2. God is your deliverer
He delivers you from the hand of the wicked (v.10c). He snatches you from their grip (v.10c, MSG).

3. God is your guide
He sheds light on you. He guides and convicts, opening your eyes (v.11a).

4. God is your joy
He gives joy so you can rejoice in him and praise his holy name (vv.11b,12) – 'The irrepressible joy that comes from consciousness of His favor and protection' (v.11, AMP).

'So', he concludes, 'God's people, shout praise to GOD, Give thanks to our Holy God!' (v.12, MSG).

PRAYER

Lord, thank you that you are my protector, my deliverer, my guide and my joy.

NEW TESTAMENT READING

1 Corinthians 9:19–10:13
Whom do you worship and serve?

Until the love of God changes our perspective, most of us are slaves to ourselves (and to our own bodily appetites). Paul is the opposite. Because of Jesus Christ, Paul made *his own body his slave* and made *himself 'a slave to everyone*' (9:19a).

Paul says, 'I have become *all things to all people* so that by all possible means I might save some' (v.22b). This does not mean that he is hypocritical or uncomfortable in his own skin or not capable of being himself. Nor does it mean that he changes the message of the gospel to suit the audience. He was passionate about preaching the gospel and his purpose was 'to win as many as possible' (v.19b).

As Professor Gordon Fee writes, 'Whereas [Paul] is intransigent on matters that affect the gospel itself, whether theological or behavioural, that same concern for the saving power of the gospel is what causes him to become all things to all people in matters that don't count.'[1]

Paul writes, 'I entered their world and tried to experience things from their point of view' (v.22, MSG). This has wide application, perhaps even beyond the areas that St Paul had in mind. To take a trivial example, it might even affect the clothes you wear, in order that the people you are speaking to should not be put off and should be able to identify with you.

Whereas Paul was willing to be a slave to everyone, he was not willing to be enslaved by his bodily appetites. He regarded life as a race (v.24), seeing himself as a runner who needs to go into 'strict training' (v.25). Like an athlete he had to be ruthless with his own body. To make it his slave so that, having preached to others, he didn't himself become 'disqualified for the prize' (v.27). Self-discipline is essential. Bring your body, mind, mouth and emotions under control.

Paul knew that there were many temptations around. He could see this from the history of his own people – 'most of them were defeated by temptation during the hard times in the desert, and God was not pleased' (10:5, MSG).

They set their hearts 'on evil things' (v.6). They were 'sexually promiscuous' (v.8, MSG). They put God to the test (v.9). They grumbled (v.10). 'We must be careful not to stir up discontent; discontent destroyed them' (v.10, MSG).

'These are all warning markers – danger! – in our history books, written down so that we don't repeat their mistakes. Our positions in the story are parallel – they at the beginning, we at the end – and we are just as capable of messing it up as they were. Don't be so naïve and self-confident. You're not exempt. You could fall flat on your face as easily as anyone else. Forget about self-confidence; it's useless. Cultivate God-confidence' (vv.11–12, MSG).

You will be tempted just as they were. Yet he says, 'No test or temptation that comes your way is beyond the course of what others have had to face. All you need to remember is that God will never let you down; he'll never let you be pushed past your limit; he'll always be there to help you come through it' (v.13, MSG).

Ask yourself these two questions:

1. How can I ensure that I am not enslaved by my own desires?
2. How can I serve everyone I come into contact with today?

PRAYER

Lord, help me to go into strict training in order to win 'a crown that will last for ever'. Help me to avoid falling into temptation. Help me to worship and serve you, and you alone.

OLD TESTAMENT READING

2 Chronicles 2:1–5:1
How do you worship and serve?

One of the things I love and admire about Hillsong Church is the model they set in terms of excellence in their worship. We try to emulate the great attention to every detail of their music, welcome and recruiting and training of volunteers to ensure excellence in our worship.

I love the diversity of worship that is found in different parts of the church. Ultimately, style is not important. Our worship should be excellent. It should be a high priority in terms of the use of our resources because we do it in honour of God.

As Solomon began building 'the house of worship in honor of God' (2:1, MSG), he says, 'The house I am building has to be the best, for our God is the best ... this house I'm building is going to be absolutely stunning – a showcase temple!' (vv.5, 9, MSG).

Achieving excellence took a great deal of material, time and effort. It required extraordinary attention to detail (chapters 2–4). The smallest details must be of the highest quality in God's service.

This is why they used so much gold (4:21–22). Winners at sporting competitions receive gold medals because gold represents the very best. So, when you are worshipping and serving God, give your very best.

As Paul writes to the Colossians, 'Whatever you do, work at it with all your heart, as working for the Lord, not for human masters ... It is the Lord Christ you are serving' (Colossians 3:23–24).

The preacher, Charles Spurgeon, was once talking to a cleaner who had recently become a Christian. Spurgeon asked her what difference Jesus had made. Rather timidly she replied, 'Well Sir, I now sweep under the doormats.' She knew that in her job she was now ultimately serving and worshipping Jesus. No sloppy living.

PRAYER

Lord, help me in my worship and service of you to give attention to every detail and to ensure that everything I do is of the very highest quality.

16 August | Day 228
How to Raise Your Game

Some of the world's top squash players used to practise at the club where I play. I remember well the first time I saw at close hand a high-level game. It was the son of one of our regular group of players. At the time, he was ranked number 11 in the world. He came to practise at our club with the world number 2.

We all watched in amazement. We had never seen anything like it. In fact, if that was 'squash', what we played should be called something else!

Watching them always raised our game. Suddenly we realised that it was possible to return practically any shot your opponent could serve you, however good they were. We saw how important it was to get back to the middle of the court after each shot. We watched how deep they hit the ball. We noticed the shots that they avoided playing.

When we went on court after that, we astonished ourselves by how well we played. Of course, we did not play anywhere near as well as them. But, inspired by their example, we played a whole lot better than usual.

During my Christian life, I have found the same pattern. For example, I had the privilege of working for Sandy Millar for nineteen years. Through watching his life and hearing him preach, I was always inspired by his example. Even though reaching the level of those who are examples to us might not be possible, hopefully it inspires us to raise our game.

A Christian is someone who believes in Jesus, puts their faith in him, knows him and lives 'in Christ'. It is also someone who *follows his example*.

There is no greater example in human history than the example of Christ. Paul writes, 'Follow *my* example, as *I follow the example of Christ*' (1 Corinthians 11:1).

READING FROM PROVERBS

Proverbs 20:5–14
The example of your life

How you live affects others. You look to others for an example. Others look to you as an example. This happens whether you like it or not.

Nowhere is this more the case than with parents and children. I have noticed how many of my father's eccentricities I seem to have picked up. Of course, parents provide examples in more serious ways too: 'The righteous lead blameless lives; blessed are their children after them' (v.7).

Parents who live lives of integrity bring great blessing to their children. Billy Graham said, 'Integrity is the glue that holds our way of life together. We must constantly strive to keep our integrity intact. When wealth is lost, nothing is lost; when health is lost, something is lost; when character is lost, all is lost.'[1]

No one has ever lived a perfect life apart from Jesus: 'Who among us can be trusted to be always diligent and honest?' (v.9, MSG). Nevertheless, we can all seek to live a life that is a good example.

Parents need to demonstrate love and faithfulness to each other, treating one another with patience and respect, resolving disagreements with grace, supporting one another in hardship and not being drawn into inappropriate relationships with other people. 'Many claim to have unfailing love, but a faithful person who can find?' (v.6).

Another area where you can be an example is by drawing out other people's thoughts: 'The purposes of the human heart are deep waters, but those who have insight draw them out' (v.5).

I often think of this verse in the context of an Alpha small group host drawing out the thoughts of the people in their group. This is the art of a good conversation facilitator. It is the skill of the interviewer to draw out the 'deep waters' within the person being interviewed.

It is an extremely important task for parents with their children, and it is important for friends with one another. There are great depths to every human being. The skill is to draw out those depths.

PRAYER

Lord, help us to live lives that are a good example to others. Help us to demonstrate purity, faithfulness and dedication.

NEW TESTAMENT READING

1 Corinthians 10:14–11:1
The example of Paul

'People *do* what people *see*,' writes John Maxwell, the leadership expert. 'The more followers see and hear their leader being consistent in action and word, the greater their consistency and loyalty. *What they hear they understand. What they see, they believe!*'[2]

Paul writes, with what might seem to be great audacity, 'Follow *my* example, as I follow the example of Christ' (11:1). The first half of that sentence is dependent on the second half. Paul's example is only worth following to the extent to which he follows Christ. He is bold enough to say and believe that he does. That in itself is a wonderful example to follow.

This verse concludes a section in which he has urged the Corinthians to 'flee from idolatry' (10:14). They are to keep themselves pure as they participate (in the communion service) in the body and blood of Christ (v.16). This is the focus of our unity: 'We all partake of the one loaf' (v.17).

'When we drink the cup of blessing, aren't we taking into ourselves the blood, the very life, of Christ? And isn't it the same with the loaf of bread we break and eat? Don't we take into ourselves the body, the very life, of Christ? Because there is one loaf, our many-ness becomes one-ness – Christ doesn't become fragmented in us. Rather, we become unified in him. *We don't reduce Christ to what we are; he raises us to what he is*' (vv.16–17, MSG).

Even though you are free – 'everything is permissible' (v.23) – be very careful how you act because 'not everything is constructive' (v.23c). 'We want to live well, but our foremost efforts should be to help others live well' (v.24, MSG).

You have amazing freedom in Christ, but you are to use this freedom for the benefit of others and for the glory of God: 'So whether you eat or drink or whatever you do, do it all for the glory of God' (v.31).

Everything we do must be 'to the glory of God'. The whole aim of your life should be to use your freedom to seek God's glory and the good of others.

This is how the apostle Paul led his life, even as he tried 'to please everybody in every way': 'For I am not seeking my own good but the good of many, so that they may be saved' (v.33). This is the context in which he wrote, 'Follow my example, as I follow the example of Christ' (11:1).

PRAYER

Lord, thank you for the example of Jesus. Help me to follow your example as Paul did. Help me, Lord, in whatever I do, to do it all for the glory of God.

OLD TESTAMENT READING

2 Chronicles 5:2–7:10
The example of leaders

We are all called to be examples. However, some have a special responsibility. The people of God were called to be an example to the world. They were given special blessings by God and called to be an example to other nations who would be attracted by their good reputation. As a result, people from all over the world would come to know the Lord (6:32–33, MSG).

Jerusalem, in particular, was chosen as an example 'for my Name' (v.6). God also chose as particular examples David and Solomon to rule his people Israel (6:6–7:10).

But other leaders also had a responsibility to lead by example. The Levites had a particular leadership role in the worship of the temple (5:2 onwards). The trumpeters and singers also had a leadership role (6:13).

Solomon leads by example in worship and prayer. 'He knelt in full view of the whole congregation, stretched his hands to heaven, and prayed' (v.13, MSG).

He tells others about God's greatness and worships him with thanksgiving. Solomon's prayer of dedication shows that Israel would often fail in this role. He prayed many times that God would forgive them when they turned back (vv.21, 25, 27, 30, 39).

After Solomon prayed, 'God so filled The Temple that there was no room for the priests! When all Israel saw the fire fall from heaven and the Glory of God fill The Temple, they fell on their knees, bowed their heads, and worshipped, thanking God' (7:3, MSG).

Today, under the new covenant, we are God's temple (1 Corinthians 6:19). As Joyce Meyer writes, 'God wants to display His glory in and through us as dramatically as He did in the physical temple of Solomon's day. When God's glory is manifested in your life, others will look at you and say, "Wow, what a great God you serve," because the power of His goodness toward you is visibly evident to them.'[3]

PRAYER

Lord, thank you that you want to display your glory in and through me. Please fill me today with your Holy Spirit and enable me to follow the example of Jesus and be an example to others.

17 August | Day 229
How to Enjoy God

You and I are created to worship God. But why would God create human beings in order to receive their worship? Is this not, as some suggest, pure vanity?

Many years ago, I was helped in my understanding of worship through C. S. Lewis's explanation in his *Reflections on the Psalms*.

He wrote: 'The most obvious fact about praise ... strangely escaped me ... I had never noticed that all *enjoyment* spontaneously overflows into praise ... the world rings with praise ... walkers praising the countryside, players praising their favourite game – praise of weather, wines, dishes, actors, horses, colleges, countries, historical personages, children, flowers, mountains, rare stamps, rare books, even sometimes politicians and scholars...

'I think we delight to praise what we *enjoy* because the praise not merely expresses but *completes the enjoyment*; it is its appointed consummation. It's not out of compliment that lovers keep on telling one another how beautiful they are; the delight is incomplete till it is expressed.'[1]

In other words, worship is the consummation of joy. Our joy is not complete until it is expressed in worship. It is out of his love for you that God created you to worship. According to the *Westminster Shorter Catechism*, humankind's 'chief end is to glorify God and to *enjoy* him for ever'.

READING FROM PSALMS

Psalm 98:1–9
Singing and music

The psalmist calls people to worship God in song and music: '*Sing* to the LORD a new song ... Burst into jubilant song with *music; make music* to the LORD' (vv.1, 4–5).

This psalm is full of noise, as the people are asked to celebrate God's goodness in a whole host of different ways. There is a call to sing, shout for joy, play instruments, and even applaud in our celebration of God:

> '*Shout* your praises to God, everybody!
> Let loose and *sing*! Strike up the *band*!
> Round up an *orchestra* to play for God,
> Add on a hundred-voice *choir*.
> Feature *trumpets* and big *trombones*,
> Fill the air with *praises* to King God.
> Let the sea and its fish give a round of *applause*,
> With everything living on earth joining in' (vv.4–7, MSG).

This is all a response to what God has done for us. You are called to worship the Lord who is Saviour (vv.1–3), King (vv.4–6) and Judge (vv.7–9).

As we read this through the lens of Jesus, we can see this as a prophetic psalm. Jesus is the one at God's 'right hand' who has 'worked salvation' (v.1). He has made God's salvation known and 'revealed his righteousness to the nations' (v.2). (See also Romans 3:21.)

There is a joyful anticipation of the universal restoration of all things when the Saviour will come to judge the earth (Psalm 98:9). Then all creation will be restored (vv.7–8). As St Paul puts it, 'The creation waits in eager expectation for the children of God to be revealed ... the creation itself will be liberated from its bondage to decay and brought into the glorious freedom of the children of God' (Romans 8:19–21).

This psalm is a growing crescendo of praise – from the worshipping community of the people of God (Psalm 98:1–3), to *all* people (vv.4–6) and finally to *all* of creation (vv.7–9).

PRAYER

Lord, I worship you. Thank you for saving me. Thank you for your love and faithfulness. Thank you that I can worship you with joy, jubilant songs, music and shouting. Thank you that I can be confident in the fairness of your judgment – you will judge the world in righteousness and the people with equity.

NEW TESTAMENT READING

1 Corinthians 11:2–34
Awe and thanksgiving

Paul addresses the issue of honour and propriety in worship, and in particular he looks at the role and place of women in worship. A huge amount of ink has been spilt discussing what this passage means.

Paul's concern was that nothing should cause an offence to the gospel. There is general agreement that much of it is cultural – few churches today expect women to cover their hair, for example.

What is clear is that both men and women were expected to pray and prophesy in services (vv.4–5). It is also clear that there is an equality of the sexes and mutual dependence (vv.11–12): 'Neither man nor woman can go it alone or claim priority ... let's quit going through these "who's first" routines' (vv.11–12, MSG).

Next, Paul goes onto discuss the 'Lord's Supper' (v.20), or 'the Eucharist' as he calls it elsewhere (*Eucharistéin* is a Greek verb meaning 'to thank').

This is probably the earliest account of this element in our services of worship. It has been a vital part of Christian worship for the last 2,000 years, celebrated almost universally by the church worldwide. Again, there has been a huge amount of discussion about what exactly Paul means. However, it seems to me that from this passage a number of things are clear:

1. It is *frequent*
There is an expectation that when they 'come together' in their 'meetings' (vv.17, 20), the 'Lord's Supper' will take place.

2. It is *important*
Jesus tells us to 'do this' (v.24). The consequences of not doing it *properly* are very serious (v.27 onwards). 'Examine your motives, test your heart, come to this meal in holy awe' (v.28, MSG).

3. It is *proclamation*
It is one of the ways in which you proclaim the gospel. 'For whenever you eat this bread and drink this cup you proclaim the Lord's death until he comes' (v.26).

4. It involved both remembering Jesus (vv.24–25) and 'recognising the body of the Lord' (v.29)
Expect to encounter Jesus as you receive the bread and wine.

5. It is a *participation* in Christ's body and blood (10:14 onwards)
The Greek word used here is *koinonia*, which can also mean 'sharing' or 'fellowship'. It is a way for us to receive and share in the benefits of Jesus' death.

6. It is a form of *thanksgiving*
We drink from the 'cup of thanksgiving' (10:16).

7. It is an expression of *unity*
'Because there is one loaf, we, who are many, are one body, for we all partake in the one loaf (v.17). One of the great tragedies of church history is the way in which this great expression of unity has become a cause of division.

8. It anticipates the *Lord's return*
You are proclaiming 'the Lord's death *until he comes*' (11:26).

The bread and wine are the body and blood of Jesus (vv.24–25). This is one of the ways in which we experience his presence today. What exactly this means, of course, has been the subject of great speculation, debate and controversy. One approach might perhaps be simply to accept it as a mystery and not go behind Scripture and speculate too much about how exactly it works.

PRAYER

Lord, help me to worship you in a way that is right and appropriate and pleases you. Help me to focus on Jesus. Help me to find my true purpose in worshipping you and enjoying you for ever.

OLD TESTAMENT READING

2 Chronicles 7:11–9:31
Integrity and passion

Solomon 'succeeded in carrying out all he had in mind to do in the temple of the LORD' (7:11). He glorified God through what he carried out.

The chronicler focuses his account of the reigns of David and Solomon around the building of *the place to worship God*, the temple in Jerusalem. For him, virtually everything else in their reigns pales into insignificance. They built the place of worship and God blessed them richly.

Solomon's fame spread (as we read in chapters 8 and 9). The Queen of Sheba (probably in modern-day Yemen) came to visit and was so astonished by what she saw (9:1–7) that she herself praised the Lord (v.8). (Interestingly, in the light of the New Testament passage about women, no question is raised here about a female monarch ruling a country.)

Solomon's splendour was great. After Solomon had built the temple, the Lord appeared to him and said, '…if my people, who are called by my name, will *humble themselves and pray and seek my face and turn from their wicked ways, then will I hear from heaven and will forgive their sin and will heal their land*' (7:14).

This verse is justly famous and it is often used as a template for worship and prayer. In it we see the conditions for integrity in our worship. They are also the conditions necessary for revival. We see in this verse that we need to do four things:

1. humble ourselves
2. pray
3. seek God's face
4. turn from our wicked ways.

Then God promises that he will do three things:

1. hear from heaven
2. forgive our sin
3. heal the land.

PRAYER

Lord, today I want to humble myself and pray and seek your face and repent of my sins. I pray that you would hear from heaven and forgive our sin and heal our land. May we glorify you and enjoy you for ever.

18 August | Day 230
Intimate Relationships

In his book *All I Want is You*, Bishop Sandy Millar writes, 'When I first visited the Vineyard Church in California I discovered that one of their principal values was "intimacy with God". So when I came back I started to talk about that as being one of our values too.'

He continues, 'One of the very nice members of our congregation at that time took me to one side and said, "Please don't use the word 'intimacy' because we don't use that word in that context." So I started talking about "the closest possible relationship with God" which is quite a mouthful. But after a bit I stopped because what I really meant was "intimacy" and I think that's what the Bible means for our relationship with God too.'[1]

There is a hunger deep in our souls for an intimate relationship with God and with other human beings.

READING FROM PSALMS

Psalm 99:1–9
Intimacy with God

You and I are created for an intimate relationship with God. It is *personal*: 'The LORD *our* God' (v.9). Yet intimacy with God is not to be taken for granted. God is mighty, holy and just.

'The LORD reigns … he sits enthroned between the cherubim' (v.1). The cherubim are the symbol of God's holiness (see Genesis 3:24, Ezekiel 1:4ff,10:1ff). God's throne is pictured, 'between the two cherubim' (Numbers 7:89). This is the place from which God speaks.

This psalm highlights the holiness of God. The word 'holy' (Psalm 99:3) emphasises the distance between God and human beings. God is not only mighty and holy; he is also just: 'He loves justice' (v.4). The appropriate response is to 'worship at his footstool' (v.5).

Somehow, this gulf between God and us has been bridged. We know now that this is through Jesus and what he did for us by the cross and resurrection, and the outpouring of the Holy Spirit. This psalm anticipates the intimacy with this God of power, holiness and justice made possible through Christ.

God 'spoke to them' (v.7). He spoke to Moses, Aaron and Samuel (v.6). He spoke to individuals. He speaks to us individually. 'They prayed to GOD and he answered them' (v.6, MSG).

Not only is he a God of justice, he is a God of mercy and forgiveness – 'a forgiving God' (v.8). He is '*our* God' (vv.8–9). His majesty is undiminished, but the last word is now given to *intimacy*.

PRAYER

Lord, it is amazing that you are all-powerful, holy and just, yet you call me into an intimate, personal relationship with you. Thank you that you are *my* God.

NEW TESTAMENT READING

1 Corinthians 12:1–26
Intimacy with one another

There is so much loneliness in our society. The elderly are often marginalised, isolated and alone. Also, many, especially young people today, have no one with whom they can process their pain. They turn to alcohol, drugs, promiscuity or some other way in an attempt to deal with it.

You are not intended to live alone. God created you for community – a community as close and as interdependent as the various parts of the human body. Paul develops the analogy of the church being like the body of Christ. The Holy Spirit has given different gifts to every member of the church (vv.1–11).

'The body is a unit' but 'it is made up of many parts' (v.12). People come into the church from all different backgrounds, nationalities and positions in society – 'Jews or Greeks, slave or free' (v.13b). Yet regardless of where we have come from, 'Each of us is now a part of his resurrection body, refreshed and sustained at one fountain – his Spirit – where we all come to drink' (v.13, MSG).

We now belong to one another. Our relationships are as intimate as the different parts of a body. We are utterly dependent on each other (vv.12–13).

The more different we are, the more we need each other. The eye needs a hand more than it needs lots of other eyes (vv.16–17). Variety is essential (v.17b). This is true not just of the local church but of the global church. We should not look at the different parts of the body of Christ and say, 'They are different, there must be something wrong with them.' Rather, we should say, 'They are different, we really need them.'

'The old labels we once used to identify ourselves ... are no longer useful. We need something larger, more comprehensive' (v.13, MSG). It is time to drop the labels – describing ourselves or others as a particular type of Christian.

God has designed the body so that there will be this mutual dependence: 'I also want you to think about how this keeps your significance from getting blown up into self-importance. For no matter how significant you are, it is only because of what you are a part of' (vv.19–20, MSG).

We particularly need the parts that 'seem to be weaker' (v.22). Our internal organs 'seem to be weaker' in the sense of being more vulnerable. That is why they need protection. However, they are 'indispensable' (v.22). Likewise, those parts of the body that are 'unpresentable' are treated with 'special modesty' (v.23). No one would suggest that these parts are not important. Indeed, they are vital.

Because we need each other so much there should be 'equal concern for each other' (v.25). There should be such intimacy and love that 'if one part suffers, every part suffers with it' (v.26a). This is the community we need where people can process their pain. It is also a place where people can share their joys: 'If one part is honoured, every part rejoices with it' (v.26b). As St Augustine said, 'Take away envy and what I have is yours too. And if I banish envy all you possess is mine!'

PRAYER

Lord, help us to demonstrate such a unity, love and intimacy with our brothers and sisters that makes Christ beautiful to the world.

OLD TESTAMENT READING

Song of Songs 1:1–4:16
Intimacy in marriage

This book can be read on many different levels. It describes the joy and mutuality, beauty and power, agony and ecstasy of human sexual love. It speaks of marriage as it ought to be – the beautiful intimacy of marital love between man and woman.

Yet marriage is, in a sense, a metaphor to describe something even more beautiful – the relationship of God to his people. Supremely, it is used to describe the relationship between Christ and his church (Ephesians 5:21–33). It is a picture of God's deep and passionate love for you and your intimate relationship with Jesus, whose 'banner over [you] is love' (Song of Songs 2:4). For this reason, throughout church history, people have used this book as a metaphor to express the intimacy between God and the church.

However, it is interesting that the Bible has a whole book celebrating erotic love in marriage. It shows what a high view the Bible has of *sexual intimacy* in marriage. It speaks of delight and contentment – a love that is wholehearted and passionate – holding nothing back.

It is clear that this kind of sexual intimacy is for marriage alone. This is the love between a bride and a bridegroom. The lover refers to his love as 'my bride' (4:8–12ff). In a world of loveless sex, it proclaims that sex should never be separated from love and lifelong commitment.

There is a warning against opening this gift before marriage: 'Do not arouse or awaken love until it so desires' (2:7; 3:5). Or as *The Message* puts it, 'Don't excite love, don't stir it up, until the time is ripe – and you're ready' (2:7, MSG). You risk spoiling this beautiful gift if you open it too early.

There is also a warning about 'the little foxes' that spoil the vine (v.15). Our relationships are often destroyed not so much by big issues but by little ones – seemingly insignificant choices and compromises.

As Joyce Meyer writes, 'Watch the "little foxes" in your life; forgive even the most minor offence so that your heart stays clean, do not cut corners in your finances or on the job when you think no one will notice, do not expose yourself to ungodly influences, thinking, *It won't hurt me if I do it just this once*. Little things add up to big things, and before you know it, little foxes can ruin a strong, healthy vine.'[2]

This intimate love relationship described is both exclusive and inclusive. They have eyes only for each other: 'My lover is mine and I am his' (v.16). Yet this relationship is also, as in all the best marriages, a blessing to others. The friends say, 'We rejoice and delight in you. We will praise your love more than wine' (1:4).

PRAYER

Lord, thank you that the beautiful intimacy of marriage is ultimately a picture of the intimate love between Christ and the church. Help us to grow in this intimacy and love with you and with one another.

19 August | Day 231
Sixteen Characteristics of Love

I tried following the example of a missionary I once heard about who, each day, would read the four verses from today's New Testament passage, which lists sixteen characteristics of love. For the word 'love' she would substitute her own name. When she reached a characteristic that she knew was not true of her, she had to stop. Her aim was, one day, to get through the whole list.

The four verses (1 Corinthians 13:4–7) start with 'love is patient'. So I substituted my own name and started with 'Nicky is patient'. I do not think it will come as any surprise to those who know me well that I had to stop there!

The great evangelist D. L. Moody was once staying with friends in England. One evening they asked Henry Drummond to expound on a portion of Scripture. After some urging, Henry drew a small New Testament from his pocket, opened it at 1 Corinthians 13 and began to speak on the subject of love. D. L. Moody wrote in response: 'It seemed to me that I had never heard anything so beautiful. The one great need in our Christian life is love, more love to God and to each other. Would that we could all move into that love chapter and live there.'[1]

We get an idea of what Drummond must have said that evening in his book, *The Greatest Thing in the World.* He writes: 'What is ... the supreme good? You have life before you. Once only you can live it. What is the noblest object of desire, the supreme gift to covet?' In 1 Corinthians 13 'Paul takes us to Christianity at its source; and there we see, "The greatest of these is *love*."'[2]

God is love. We deceive ourselves if we think we can love God and hate other people (1 John 4:20). Love should be number one on your spiritual priority list. It should be the main thing in your life. It is, in the words of St Paul, 'the most excellent way' (1 Corinthians 12:31).

READING FROM PSALMS

Psalm 100:1–5
Enjoy God's love for you

The psalmist exhorts us to 'Shout for joy to the LORD ... Worship the LORD with gladness; come before him with joyful songs' (vv.1–2). He tells us to 'enter his gates with thanksgiving and his courts with praise; give thanks to him and praise his name' (v.4); 'Enter with the password: "Thank you!"' (v.4, MSG); 'Be thankful *and* say so to Him' (v.4, AMP).

Why? What is the reason for such joy, thanksgiving and praise? The psalmist gives the answer in verse 5: 'For the LORD is good and *his love* endures for ever; his faithfulness continues through all generations.'

God is good and he loves you. This pretty much sums up the message of the entire Bible. It is *his* love that is the source of *our* love: 'We *love* because *he first loved us*'

(1 John 4:19). Understand, believe and accept that he loves *you* and enjoy his love.

PRAYER

Lord, I thank and praise you for your amazing love for me. Thank you that your love endures for ever. Help me to enjoy your love today.

NEW TESTAMENT READING

1 Corinthians 12:27–13:13
Embrace a life of love

Henry Drummond explains that at the beginning of this chapter we have love *contrasted*; in the heart of it, we have love *analysed* and towards the end we have love *defended* as the supreme gift.[3]

1. Love contrasted

The description of love in 1 Corinthians 13 is one of the most beautiful and best-known passages in the entire New Testament. Many non-churchgoers would recognise it as the Bible passage that is often read at weddings. Paul places it in the middle of his teaching about the gifts of the Holy Spirit in the body of Christ.

He lists nine gifts in 1 Corinthians 12:27–30. At the start of chapter 12 he also listed nine gifts. There is an overlap of five. So, thirteen gifts of the Holy Spirit are listed in all. Paul has been describing the importance of these gifts for the body of Christ to function fully.

He is not diminishing the importance of gifts by talking about love. Rather, he is saying, 'gifts are very important but love is *even* more important'. We desperately need the gifts of the Holy Spirit to be properly exercised in the church today. However, as in Paul's day, love is even more important. It is 'the most excellent way' (v.31).

In fact, Paul says if we have all the gifts and give everything we have to the poor and die the death of a martyr but we have not love, we gain nothing (13:1–3). He is not criticising the use of the gifts, such as speaking in tongues and prophecy (vv.1–2), any more than he is criticising philanthropists or martyrs (v.3). He is simply stressing the importance that *everything* you do should be done in love.

2. Love analysed

Paul then lists sixteen characteristics of love. Every time I read this list I feel deeply challenged. I know how far short of all these characteristics – not just the first one! – I so often fall. I like *The Message* translation:

> 'Love never gives up ['Love is patient', NIV]
> Love cares more for others than for self.
> Love doesn't want what it doesn't have.
> Love doesn't strut,
> Doesn't have a swelled head,
> Doesn't force itself on others,
> Isn't always "me first",
> Doesn't fly off the handle,
> Doesn't keep score of the sins of others,
> Doesn't revel when others grovel,
> Takes pleasure in the flowering of truth,
> Puts up with anything,
> Trusts God always,
> Always looks for the best,
> Never looks back,
> But keeps going to the end' (vv.4–7, MSG).

Take any one of these: for example, 'Trusts God always'. Achieve that and it will be life-changing.

3. Love defended

Love is permanent. Everything else is temporary. All the gifts of the Spirit will one day be unnecessary. Some have argued that what Paul is saying here is that the gifts of the Spirit (such as speaking in tongues) would cease at some point in history. In fact, he is saying the very opposite. He is saying that the gifts of the Spirit *will not cease until we see Jesus 'face to face'* (v.12). As yet, we *do not* see Jesus 'face to face' and therefore the gifts of the Spirit have *not* yet ceased. We still need them desperately.

But, the greatest thing in the world is love. Faith, hope and love are a great trilogy, but 'the greatest of these is love' (v.13).

PRAYER

Lord, we desperately need this kind of love in the church today. Help me grow in love to reflect the way St Paul describes. May I make my love for you, and for others, the highest priority of my life.

OLD TESTAMENT READING

Song of Songs 5:1–8:14
Ensure that love is the main thing

The word 'love' or 'lover' appears over and over again in the Song of Songs. It is all about romantic love between a lover and his beloved. They are overcome by love for one another. The beloved says that she is 'heartsick with love for him' (5:8, MSG).

There is a strong element of physical and erotic love. Both describe the physical beauty of their marriage partner (5:10–16; 6:4–9). As one commentator put it, 'The Song of Songs is a long, lyric poem about erotic love and sexual desire – a poem in which the body is the object of desire and source of delight, and lovers engage in a continual game of seeking and finding ... sexual gratification.'

But their love goes way beyond the physical and the erotic. The beloved says, 'This is my lover, this is my friend' (5:16c). There is nothing better in marriage than having someone as your partner, your lover *and* your best friend.

In yesterday's passage the lover says, 'You are a garden fountain, a well of flowing water' (4:15). Each human being has a never-ending flow of beautiful and wonderful resources.

As the Song of Songs draws to an end, there is a beautiful description of the never-ending quality of love: 'Place me like a seal over your heart, like a seal on your arm; for love is as strong as death, its jealousy unyielding as the grave' (8:6). And now, after the resurrection of Jesus, we can say that love is *even stronger* than death: 'Love never fails' (1 Corinthians 13:8).

Again, I like *The Message* version:

'The fire of love stops at nothing –
it sweeps everything before it.
Flood waters can't drown love,
torrents of rain can't put it out.
Love can't be bought, love can't be sold –
it's not to be found in the marketplace'
(8:6c–7, MSG).

PRAYER

Thank you, Lord, that your love for me is like a fire that stops at nothing. May my love for you be the highest priority in my life. Thank you that your love cannot be bought or earned, but only gratefully and humbly received.

20 August | Day 232
How to Listen to the Holy Spirit

Will Wisbey was a successful, young estate agent. He was fiercely sceptical of Christianity. One Sunday, a friend invited him to HTB. During that service, someone had a 'word of knowledge' that went like this: 'There is a man here who is expecting a soft-top sports car to be delivered in the next two days. He has worked all his life so hard to achieve success. Work has been his life. He's got the car, the house, the lifestyle, and he's not happy. And God wants him to know that there's something more important for him to focus on.'

Subsequently Will wrote, 'I couldn't believe it. My new car was the nicest I'd bought. It was arriving in literally two days and I hadn't told anyone. I was earning £100k a year. My work was my life. That night, for the first time in my life, I really prayed.'

Will encountered Jesus Christ and was filled with the Holy Spirit. He says, 'Now I know Jesus does exist. He loves me and he is with me.'

Many of us live in a busy and noisy world. In the midst of all the noise, talk and distractions, how do you hear the voice of the Holy Spirit?

READING FROM PROVERBS

Proverbs 20:15–24
Listen to wisdom and knowledge

One of the ways in which you can hear the voice of the Holy Spirit is through the wise advice of others. Wise and knowledgeable people are invaluable. 'Gold there is, and rubies in abundance, but lips that speak knowledge are *a rare jewel*' (v.15). 'Drinking from *the beautiful chalice of knowledge* is better than adorning oneself with gold and rare gems' (v.15, MSG).

Seek help when making important decisions: 'Make plans by seeking advice' (v.18). You will still be responsible for your actions though: 'Form your purpose by asking for counsel, then carry it out using all the help you can get' (v.18, MSG).

The book of Proverbs is itself full of wise advice. It tells you to be careful of the gossips who betray confidence, and to avoid people who talk too much. 'Gossips can't keep secrets, so never confide in blabbermouths' (v.19, MSG). One well-known gossip had this maxim embroidered on her cushion: 'If you haven't got anything good to say about anyone come and sit by me.'

Another piece of wise advice is the warning against taking revenge, 'Don't ever say, "I'll get you for that!" Wait for God; he'll settle the score' (v.22, MSG).

Listening to the Holy Spirit means listening to the word of the Lord. 'A person's steps are directed *by the Lord*. How then can any understand their own way?' (v.24). Listen to the Spirit as he speaks to you through the Scriptures.

PRAYER

Lord, thank you that your Holy Spirit speaks to me through the Scriptures. Help me to hear and obey your voice.

NEW TESTAMENT READING

1 Corinthians 14:1–19
Listen through the gifts of the Holy Spirit

Exalt love; but do not in any way downplay the importance of the gifts of the Holy Spirit. Paul emphasises both: 'Follow the way of love *and* eagerly desire spiritual gifts, especially the gift of prophecy' (v.1). Some people say that we should 'desire the Giver and *not* the gifts', but *the Giver tells us to desire the gifts*.

Prophecy is one of the gifts of the Holy Spirit through which the Spirit speaks to the church. Paul emphasises the importance of this gift for the church. It is even more important than speaking in tongues: 'I would like every one of you to speak in tongues, but I would rather have you prophesy' (v.5a).

Although Paul was speaking into a situation where the gift of tongues was in danger of misuse, he was still remarkably positive about the gift. Paul says that those who pray in tongues edify themselves (v.4). It is a good gift for everyone (v.5). The gift of tongues is a way of praying in the Spirit (v.14) and is primarily thanks and praise (vv.16–17). He testifies about his own use of this gift, 'I thank God that I speak in tongues more than all of you' (v.18).

Paul makes a distinction between the use of the gift in private (which he generally encourages) and the use of the gift publicly in the church. If one speaks in tongues in church, there needs to be an interpretation (vv.5, 18–19). When it is used together with the gift of interpretation it becomes the equivalent of prophecy (v.5b).

The gift of interpretation enables the church to be edified after a tongue has been given publicly (v.5). All those with the gift of tongues should pray for this gift also, so that the church can be edified.

Prophecy is the ability to hear what God is saying and pass it on to others. It is a spiritual gift of very high importance in the church and should be eagerly desired (v.1). It is not necessarily about *foretelling* the future. Rather it is usually *forth telling* what God is saying in the current situation.

The early Christians came to see the Old Testament as, essentially, prophecy (2 Peter 1:20). The Old Testament is the prophetic witness to Jesus. The New Testament is the apostolic witness to Jesus. There is no equivalent today in terms of authority.

The words of prophets today are not of equal authority with the prophets and apostles whose words form the Scriptures. Scripture is for all Christians, in all places, at all times. A prophetic word is a particular word, inspired by God, given to a particular person or persons, at a particular moment, for a particular purpose. It is a human, and sometimes partially mistaken, report of something that the Holy Spirit has brought to someone's mind.

Nevertheless, Paul places a very high value on the gift of prophecy (1 Corinthians 14:1) because it is a gift that builds up the church (v.4) and can also have an impact on those who are 'unbelievers': 'If an unbeliever ... comes in while everybody is prophesying ... the secrets of their hearts will be laid bare. So they will fall down and worship God, exclaiming, "God is really among you!"' (vv.24–25). That is exactly what happened to Will Wisbey.

Prophecy needs to be tested: 'Two or three prophets should speak, and the others should *weigh carefully* what is said' (v.29).

1. Is it in line with the Bible?
God is not going to contradict himself.

2. What is the character of the prophet?
Are they a person of love? (v.1).

3. What is the effect of the prophecy?
Paul writes, '...those who prophesy speak to people for their *strengthening*, *encouragement* and *comfort*' (v.3). True prophetic words will always be positive in the sense that they will *strengthen*, *encourage* and *comfort* people.

On the whole, prophetic words are confirming what the Holy Spirit has already placed in our hearts. If you are unsure about a prophetic word, do not act hastily but do what Mary, the mother of Jesus, did – wait and ponder it in your heart (Luke 2:19).

PRAYER

Lord, help us as a church to create an atmosphere of expectation to hear the Holy Spirit speak to us as we listen – following the way of love and eagerly desiring the spiritual gifts.

OLD TESTAMENT READING

2 Chronicles 10:1–12:16
Listen to good advice and prophetic words

Rehoboam made a big mistake. The Holy Spirit spoke to him through the elders. They said, 'If you will *be a servant* to this people, *be considerate of their needs* and respond with *compassion*, work things out with them, *they'll end up doing anything for you*' (10:7, MSG).

Rehoboam made the mistake of rejecting the *advice of the elders* (v.8). He listened instead to some extremely bad advice from the young men he had grown up with (vv.10–11). He told *the people*, 'My father thrashed you with whips; I'll beat you bloody with chains!' (v.11b, MSG).

He 'did not listen to the people' (v.15). When all Israel saw that 'the king refused to listen to them' (v.16), they rebelled.

But God did not give up speaking to Rehoboam. The 'word of the LORD came to Shemaiah the man of God' and he was told to go and tell Rehoboam, '*This is what the LORD says...*' (11:2–4a).

This time the king and the people were unified in listening to the Lord – 'they obeyed the words of the LORD and turned back from marching against Jeroboam' (v.4b).

Later, God spoke again through the *prophet* Shemaiah: 'GOD's word: "You abandoned me; now I abandon you"' (12:5, MSG). Again, they listened. They 'humbled themselves and said, "The LORD is just."' (v.6). As a result, 'When the LORD saw that they humbled themselves, this word of the LORD came to Shemaiah: "Since they have humbled themselves, I will not destroy them but will soon give them deliverance..."' (v.7).

PRAYER

Lord, please give me wisdom in hearing your voice. Help me to learn how to listen to the Holy Spirit.

21 August | Day 233
How to Find and Keep Peace

In 1555, Nicholas Ridley, a former Bishop of London, was burned at the stake in Oxford because of his beliefs. On the night before Ridley's execution, his brother offered to remain with him in the prison chamber to be of assistance and comfort. Nicholas declined the offer and replied that he meant to go to bed and sleep as quietly as ever he did in his life. Because he knew the peace of God, he could rest in the strength of the everlasting arms of his Lord to meet his need.

Peace is a great blessing. 'Peace' is a word of huge significance in the Bible. The Hebrew word for peace, *Shalom*, translated by the Greek word *eirene*, means far more than the absence of war or hostility. It is not just an absence of certain circumstances but the presence of God and his reign. It means wholeness, soundness, well-being, oneness with God – every kind of blessing and good.

In order to bring peace to others, we first need to find and hold on to peace within ourselves.

READING FROM PSALMS

Psalm 101:1–8
Peace with God

'Peace' and 'silence' – in the good sense of the word – often go hand in hand. This psalm speaks of the slanderous and the wicked being 'put to silence' (vv.5–8).

David sings of God's 'love and justice' (v.1a). We talk a lot about God's love but not so much about his justice, which is as important. Love without concern for justice is not true love, as love cries out for justice.

Only the 'blameless' (vv.2, 6) can 'dwell' with him (v.6b), 'minister to' him (v.6c), 'stand' in his 'presence' (v.7). Slander (v.5a), pride (v.5b) and 'deceit' (v.7) are sins of the mouth, heart and action. They bring us under God's judgment.

Thank God for the cross where 'love' and 'justice' mingle – truth and mercy meet. This is where God is both 'just' and justifies the one who has faith in him (Romans 3:23–26). Without the cross, we would be cut off from the Lord (Psalm 101:8).

PRAYER

Father, thank you that through our Lord Jesus Christ I have been justified by faith and have peace with you (Romans 5:1). Help me to bring this message of love, justice and peace to the world.

NEW TESTAMENT READING

1 Corinthians 14:20–40
Peace in the church

'God is not a God of disorder but of *peace*' (v.33). The apostle Paul is clear that the creativity and spontaneity of the gifts of the Spirit, do not give licence for disorder in church meetings. 'When we worship the right way, God doesn't stir us up into confusion; he brings us into harmony' (v.33, MSG).

Paul describes the way to peaceful, harmonious and orderly meetings in the church – 'everything should be done in a fitting and orderly way' (v.40). It may involve an appropriate keeping quiet (v.28) in order to let others speak.

This gives us some sense of what church meetings were like in the early church. Clearly, there was an expectation that the gifts of the Spirit would be exercised regularly: 'When you come together, everyone has a hymn, or a word of instruction, a revelation, a tongue or an interpretation' (v.26).

Gifts need to be exercised in an orderly way. There shouldn't be anything weird or hyped up about spiritual gifts. It may surprise some that the singer Katy Perry once said, 'Speaking in tongues is as *normal* to me as "Pass the salt". It's a secret, direct prayer language to God.'

Paul's comments about prophecy and tongues being a 'sign' often cause confusion. He seems to say one thing in v.22 (tongues are a sign for unbelievers; prophecy for believers), and then the opposite in v.23! It is unlikely, though, that Paul would contradict himself.

It seems to me that Paul is saying that both the gift of tongues and the gift of prophecy should be used only in their appropriate ways. Throughout this chapter, Paul is giving instructions for the orderly use of tongues and prophecy in the church. When used inappropriately, both can be a source of chaos (vv.6–12 and vv.29–33), in which case unbelievers will think we are out of our minds.

If used appropriately within the context of church meetings, both tongues and prophecy can be an amazing indication of God's presence (vv.22–25). Prophecy can be a powerful 'sign' for unbelievers that 'God is really among you!' (v.25). We have often seen this to be the case.

Whereas singing in tongues is a corporate activity, speaking in a tongue is an individual activity that requires an interpretation. Therefore, people 'should speak one at a time and someone must interpret. If there is no interpreter, the speakers should keep quiet in the church and speak to themselves and God' (vv.27–28).

Likewise, prophecy should be taken in turns. There is no limit to the number of prophecies. The speaker is always in full control: 'The spirits of prophets are subject to the control of prophets' (v.32). In the demonic world, 'spirits' take over a person and they lose control. Not so with the Holy Spirit. A person speaking in tongues or prophesying is in full control. They can start when they choose and they can stop when they choose to do so. 'For God is not a God of disorder but of peace' (v.33).

Many explanations have been put forward for Paul's instruction that women should remain silent in the churches (v.34). It is important to remember that Paul's focus here is not on gender roles but on the conduct of public worship. He is addressing a series of specific problems that have arisen in the Corinthian church. He has already made it clear that he *did* expect women to speak in meetings. He writes, 'Every woman who prays or prophesies...' (11:5).

What is clear is that people, both men and women, did not come just as *consumers* but as *contributors*. The question we should ask is not 'What am I getting out of church?', but 'What am I *giving* out at church?' They did not come just to receive but also to help others. 'When you gather to worship, *each of you* be *prepared* with something that will be *useful for all*' (14:26, MSG). If we all come to church with this attitude of being a contributor it will totally transform our services of worship.

PRAYER

Lord, help us in all our services and other meetings to exercise the gifts of the Holy Spirit in such a way that when people come into the church they will 'fall down and worship God, exclaiming, "God is really among you!"' (v.25).

OLD TESTAMENT READING

2 Chronicles 13:1–15:19
Peace in the nation

War devastates nations (15:5, 6). It brings death, destruction and usually poverty. On the other hand, peace allows a nation to build and to become prosperous (14:7).

When Asa became King of Judah, 'The country was *at peace* for ten years' (v.1). This peace was a gift of God, 'God kept the peace' (v.6 MSG).

How does this peace and rest come about? The answer, which the chronicler gives is at least threefold:

1. Seek God wholeheartedly
It was when they 'prayed desperately to GOD' (13:14, MSG) that God 'delivered them' (v.16). Asa 'commanded Judah to seek the LORD' (14:4). He said to the people, 'We have this peaceful land because we sought GOD; he has given us rest from all troubles' (v.7, MSG).

The prophet Azariah says, 'If you seek him, he will be found by you' (15:2). 'In their distress they turned to the LORD, the God of Israel, and sought him, and he was found by them' (v.4). 'They entered into a covenant to seek the LORD, the God of their ancestors, with *all* their heart and soul' (v.12).

They sought God wholeheartedly and 'God gave them peace within and without – a most peaceable kingdom!' (v.15, MSG).

2. Obey God fully
When Asa heard the prophecy, 'he took courage' (v.8). Asa said to Judah, 'Obey [God's] laws and commands' (14:4). The prophet Azariah said, 'If you forsake him, he will forsake you' (15:2). This passage is an example of God's faithfulness to us when we do choose to obey him fully.

3. Rely on God totally
'The men of Judah were victorious because they relied on the LORD, the God of their ancestors' (13:18). 'They trusted GOD' (v.18, MSG). 'Asa called on the LORD his God and said, "LORD, there is no one like you to help the powerless against the mighty. Help us, O LORD our God, for *we rely on you*"' (14:11).

This is what it means to be 'fully committed to the LORD' (15:17). The result was that Asa's work was rewarded (v.7) and the Lord his God was with him (v.9). There was peace and rest.

PRAYER
Lord, I want to seek you wholeheartedly, obey you fully and rely on you totally. I pray for rest and peace in my own life, in the church, in our land and between nations.

22 August | Day 234
Wholehearted Living

I remember it as if it were yesterday. I got up out of my seat and went forward. I had only been a Christian for a few months. The message I responded to was to be fully, wholeheartedly committed to the Lord and to follow him with all my heart – wherever that might take me.

Of course, I have had my ups and downs since then, and my fair share of failures. All of us are far from perfect. I still do things that I wish I did not do. But I have been determined to try and follow the Lord with all my heart and be fully committed to him.

To be 'fully committed' with 'all your heart' means 100 per cent commitment. It means seeking to do what the Lord calls you to do. It means rooting out anything that is bad – ruthlessly tearing down the high places and getting rid of the other gods in the midst of life.

The Lord is looking for those whose 'hearts are *fully committed*' to him (2 Chronicles 16:9). The psalmist prayed, 'Give me an undivided heart' (Psalm 86:11). The expression '*all your heart*' appears many times throughout the Bible. For example, you are to do the following things '*with all your heart*':

- *love* the Lord (Deuteronomy 6:4–5; Matthew 22:36–38)
- *trust in* the Lord (Proverbs 3:5)
- *obey* the Lord (Psalm 119:34, 69; 1 Chronicles 29:19)
- *praise* the Lord (Psalm 111:1; 138:1)
- *work for* the Lord (Nehemiah 4:6; Colossians 3:23).

This is how to enjoy life and life in all its fullness (John 10:10). It's a life of love, trust, gratitude, joy and meaningful work. In the passages for today we see why and how we should live *wholeheartedly*.

READING FROM PSALMS

Psalm 102:1–11
The brevity of life

The psalmist is aware of how short life is: 'For my days *vanish like smoke*' (v.3a), 'My days are *like the evening shadow*; I *wither away like grass*' (v.11). He has this sense that time is running out. Life on this earth is so short. Make the most of every day.

The psalmist is suffering. He cries out, 'Hear my prayer, O Lord; let my cry of help come to you. Do not hide your face from me when I am in distress. Turn your ear to me; when I call, answer me quickly' (vv.1–2).

This is a striking example of wholehearted commitment to God even in the midst of distress. Choose to turn to God. Know that God is eternal (v.12) and that he can be trusted.

PRAYER

Lord, I thank you that, while my life is 'like the evening shadow', you are eternal and I can trust you. I lift my problems before you now ... Let my cry for help come to you.

NEW TESTAMENT READING

1 Corinthians 15:1–34
The certainty of resurrection

Paul tells us what was at the heart of his preaching, and why he followed Jesus so wholeheartedly: 'The *gospel* I preached to you, which you received and on which you have taken your stand' (v.1). This is the *gospel* whereby you are saved (v.2); hold firmly to it.

1. The message

It is a very simple message, 'that Christ *died for our sins* according to the Scriptures, that he *was buried*, that he *was raised* on the third day *according to the Scriptures*' (vv.3–4).

His death had a great purpose. It was '*for our sins*'. The penalty for sin has been paid. The power of sin is broken. And, one day, even the presence of sin will be removed.

You can be sure of this because of the resurrection. This is the certainty of your hope for the future.

Jesus died and was buried. One day, you will die and be buried. Jesus was raised from the dead. One day, you will also be raised from the dead to full and eternal life.

2. The evidence

The resurrection is a sign in this world of the future God has in store. Paul spoke of the future in light of what God had done: 'He has given *proof* of this to everyone by raising him from the dead' (Acts 17:31). Faith is not irrational. Faith is grounded on the event of the resurrection.

Paul gives some of the evidence for the resurrection:

- He highlights that Jesus was '*buried*' and '*raised according to the Scriptures*'. Jesus' life, death and resurrection were written about before he was born.
- He points to Christ's *appearances* to Peter, to the twelve, to 500 others, to James, all the apostles, and finally, to Paul himself (1 Corinthians 15:6–8).

This is not an exhaustive list of the appearances – but enough to show it is well attested. He shows that the resurrection is rooted in history, grounded in Scripture and confirmed by experience.

3. The importance

The resurrection really matters. If there is no resurrection, the consequences are dire. The resurrection was the basis of Paul's preaching. Without it 'everything we've told you is smoke and mirrors ... a string of barefaced lies' (vv.14a–15, MSG). Since that was what they based their faith on, without the resurrection 'your faith is futile' and 'you are still in your sins' (v.17). There would be no hope for the future, 'those who have fallen asleep in Christ are lost' (v.18). In fact, Paul concludes that without it Christianity is worse than nothing: 'If only for this life we have hope in Christ, we are to be pitied more than all people' (v.19).

4. The result

'But the truth is that Christ has been raised up, the first in a long legacy of those who are going to leave the cemeteries' (v.20, MSG). Therefore, the *resurrection is certain*. One day all those who are 'in Christ' *will be raised from the dead*. Then *death will be destroyed* (v.26). 'God's rule is absolutely comprehensive – a perfect ending!' (v.28, MSG).

Because the resurrection is certain, Paul writes, we endanger ourselves every hour (v.30): 'I die every day' (v.31). He is 100 per cent, wholeheartedly fully committed to the Lord. He even fought wild beasts in Ephesus (v.32). He was willing to risk his life because of the certainty of the resurrection.

This is the reason why Paul urges us to 'stop sinning' (v.34). Satan's tactics often start with unbelief. If he can make you doubt, then next he will tempt you to sin. In one sense, all sin stems from unbelief.

The message of Jesus, his death and resurrection, is good news. It is the gospel. You are to receive it and believe it. You are to take your stand on it. You are to hold it firmly. Like Paul, pass it on to others.

PRAYER

Father, thank you that Jesus died for my sins and you raised him from the dead so that I could be totally forgiven, set free and, one day, be raised with Christ. Help me, like Paul, to be wholeheartedly committed to passing this message on as of 'first importance'.

OLD TESTAMENT READING

2 Chronicles 16:1–18:27
The eyes of the Lord

'God is always on the alert, constantly on the lookout for people who are *totally committed to him*' (16:9, MSG).

Hanani the seer came to Asa, King of Judah, and said to him that he was in trouble because he had ceased to *rely fully* on the Lord (vv.7–9). 'For *the eyes of the Lord* range throughout the earth to strengthen those whose hearts are *fully committed* to him' (v.9).

God sees everything you do. He is looking for those whose '*hearts*' are '*fully committed*' to him. The 'eyes of the Lord' see into your heart. Are you living wholeheartedly for him?

Asa, who had done so well for most of his life, in the last years, 'even in his illness he did not seek help from the Lord but only from the physicians' (v.12). There is nothing wrong with getting help from the medical profession. He is not criticised for seeking help from the physicians. He is criticised for *not* seeking help *from the Lord*.

His son, Jehoshaphat's 'heart was devoted to the ways of the Lord' (17:6). Again, he started very well. 'He didn't fool around ... he was a seeker and follower of the God of his father and was obedient to him ... He was single-minded in following God; and he got rid of the local sex-and-religion shrines' (vv.3–6, MSG).

He was tested by the fact that 400 prophets all had a 'lying spirit' (18:21). Only Micaiah, son of Imlah, had the courage to speak truth to power. The devil is a deceiver. In an age when there is no shortage of voices to hear, we need the discernment of God not to be fooled by deception but to listen carefully to those who, like Micaiah, say, 'As sure as God lives, what God says, I'll say' (v.13, MSG).

PRAYER

Lord, I thank you that your eyes 'range throughout the earth to strengthen those whose hearts are fully committed' to you (16:9). Please, strengthen me as I recommit myself to serve you wholeheartedly.

23 August | Day 235
Trust God to Do It His Way

I sometimes wish I kept more of a diary. I am glad that, at least, I have recorded some of my prayers. Alongside the words of today's passage, 'We do not know what to do, but our eyes are upon you' (2 Chronicles 20:12), I have jotted down some of the seemingly insurmountable problems and situations we have faced over the years. It is amazing and wonderful to see and have a record of how God has delivered us from so many of them, in his own time and in his own way.

Being reminded of God's ability to deliver us increases our faith that he can do it again. God really is powerful. In fact, God is all-powerful; he is 'omnipotent'. You can trust him.

READING FROM PSALMS

Psalm 102:12–17
Trust God to answer prayer

'Prayer is the slender nerve that moves the muscle of omnipotence,' as Charles Spurgeon famously said.

When you see the problems in your life and in your nation, what is your first response? As the psalmist looks out at the mess that the people of God are in and the fact that his city is in ruins, his first response is to cry out to God.

The psalmist extols God for both his power and his love, declaring his greatness: 'You,

O Lord, sit enthroned for ever' (v.12a) and his 'compassion' (v.13) for Jerusalem: 'For her stones are dear to your servants; her very dust moves them to pity' (v.14).

As I look around our nation today, I see that so much of the church is in ruins. But God has the power to rebuild his people in this land.

You can be confident in the power of God to answer your prayers. It is not that you can control God's power by your prayers, but that God is always active in the life of his people and his world: 'He attends to the prayer of the wretched. He won't dismiss their prayer' (v.17, MSG).

PRAYER

Lord, I cry out to you to rebuild the church in this nation. Please send your Holy Spirit upon us again and on our nation, I pray.

NEW TESTAMENT READING

1 Corinthians 15:35–49
Trust God to resurrect

The loss of someone we love is very painful. And facing our own death can seem frightening. This passage gives us a new perspective on our grief and our fears. When the New Testament speaks of the love of God it usually points to the cross of Jesus. When it speaks of the power of God it usually points to the resurrection of Jesus. It was 'his incomparably great power' that raised Jesus from the dead (Ephesians 1:19–20).

Here the apostle Paul speaks of how that same power will raise your body also. He uses the analogy of a seed of wheat. It does not reach its full potential unless it first dies and is buried: 'What you sow does not come to life unless it dies' (1 Corinthians 15:36). There is continuity between the seed and the wheat, although the two look quite different.

Because of the resurrection of Jesus, you can trust that God will also raise you – in his own way – and that will be far better than anything you can imagine.

To the sceptic who asks, 'What does this 'resurrection body' look like?' he replies, 'If you look at this question closely, you realise how absurd it is ... We do have a parallel experience in gardening. You plant a 'dead' seed; soon there is a flourishing plant ... The dead body that we bury in the ground and the resurrection body that comes from it will be dramatically different' (vv.35–38, MSG).

He points to the huge variety of God's creation. Which, incidentally, suggests you should not try to be like anyone else. God made you uniquely you. It is all right to be different. Diversity is good.

You will notice that the variety of bodies is stunning (humans, animals, birds, fish). 'You get a hint at the diversity of resurrection glory by looking at the diversity of bodies not only on earth but in the skies – sun, moon, stars – all these varieties of beauty and brightness. And we're only looking at pre-resurrection 'seeds' – who can imagine what the resurrection 'plants' will be like!' (vv.40–41, MSG).

He goes on, 'This image of planting a dead seed and raising a live plant is a mere sketch at best, but perhaps it will help in approaching the mystery of the resurrection body – but only if you keep in mind that when we're raised, we're *raised for good*, alive forever!

'The corpse that is planted is no beauty, but when it's raised, it's glorious. Put in the ground weak, it comes up powerful. The seed sown is natural; the seed grown is supernatural – same seed, same body but what a difference from when it goes down in physical mortality to when it is raised up in spiritual immortality!' (vv.42–44, MSG).

The resurrection body and the spiritual body are the same substance, though that substance is transformed. Resurrection is creation *ex vetere* (from old), rather than *ex nihilo* (from nothing). The plant comes from the seed. Our current bodies will not be replaced with new bodies, but will be transformed into our resurrection bodies.

Jesus was still recognisable to his followers (with some help!). There was continuity and discontinuity in the resurrection body (Jesus could walk through walls, but still eat fish). What happened to Jesus will happen to you; you, like Adam, have a natural body. One day, like Jesus, the second Adam, you will have a spiritual body (vv.44–48): 'Just as we have borne the likeness of the earthly, so shall we bear the likeness of the heavenly' (v.49).

PRAYER

Lord, thank you that just as Jesus died, was buried and raised to life, so too through your power we will be raised and have a spiritual body like Jesus'.

OLD TESTAMENT READING

2 Chronicles 18:28–21:3
Trust God to fight your battles

What battles are you facing in your life? Jehoshaphat had his battles to fight. He was facing various '-ites'; 'Moabites, Amonites and Meunites'.

But with us, as Joyce Meyer writes, 'It is the 'fear-ites', 'disease-ites', 'poverty-ites', 'bad marriage-ites', 'stress-ites', 'grouchy neighbour-ites', 'insecurity-ites', 'rejection-ites' and so on.'[1]

When he fought against the King of Aram, 'Jehoshaphat cried out, and the LORD helped him' (18:31). We see in this the providence and sovereignty of God. God allowed a random arrow to kill the King of Israel, but protected Jehoshaphat who cried out to God (vv.28–34).

Jehoshaphat 'turned [the people] back to the LORD' (19:4). He appointed judges. He called them to avoid 'injustice', 'partiality' or 'bribery' (v.7). What a difference it would make to the world today if all the judges of the world were like that.

In spite of the fact that Jehoshaphat followed the Lord ('He walked in the ways of his father Asa and did not stray from them; he did what was right in the eyes of the LORD', 20:32), he continued to face battles. Just because you are facing battles in your life at the moment it does not mean you have done something wrong. Sometimes you face battles not because you are doing something wrong, but because you are doing something right.

A vast army came against him (v.2). Jehoshaphat proclaimed a nationwide fast and called together a massive prayer meeting with regional gatherings (vv.3–4).

He prayed to God. He recognised the power of God: 'You rule over the kingdoms of the nations. *Power* and *might* are in your hand, and no one can withstand you' (v.6).

He recognised that, '*We have no power* to face this vast army that is attacking us. We do not know what to do, but *our eyes are upon you*' (v.12).

God responded with the words of a prophet. The Spirit of the Lord came upon him as they waited on God (v.14).

He said, 'Do not be afraid or discouraged because of this vast army. For *the battle is not yours, but God's*' (v.15). 'You will not have to face this battle. Take up your positions; stand firm and see the deliverance the LORD will give you ... Go out to face them tomorrow, and the LORD will be with you' (v.17).

Jehoshaphat worshipped the Lord (v.18). 'They praised at the top of their lungs!' (v.19, MSG). He told the people, in a message that pretty much sums up the whole of the book of Chronicles, 'Have faith in the LORD your God and you will be upheld; have faith in his prophets and you will be successful' (v.20).

They began to praise the Lord, singing, 'Give thanks to the LORD, for his love endures for ever' (v.21). Worship is a weapon. As they praised, the Lord delivered them (v.22).

PRAYER

Lord, I trust you today with the battles I face. Thank you that they are *your* battles. I don't know what to do but my eyes are upon you.

---

24 August | Day 236
Victorious Living

Of course, he did not know where it was. He was eighty-five years of age and had written dozens of books. I was asking him if he could tell me exactly where in his books I could find the quote I was looking for. He told me that he had absolutely no idea, but gave me permission to quote it anyway. Since then I have used his quote over and over again because it seemed to me that Bishop Lesslie Newbigin had summarised a crucial insight for our understanding of Jesus and the New Testament.

'*The resurrection was not the reversal of a defeat but the manifestation of a victory.*'[1]

The cross was not a defeat. Rather, taken together, the cross and resurrection are the greatest victory to have taken place in the history of the world. It is a victory that has huge implications for our own lives, our society and the future of this world.

The idea of 'victory' can smack of imperialism and pride. Of course, triumphalism is to be avoided. However, 'victory' is not a negative word in the Bible, even in the New Testament.

The key to a right understanding of '*victory*' is to see it as *a gift* made possible '*through our Lord Jesus Christ*' (1 Corinthians 15:57). This means that the appropriate response is not pride, but thankfulness.

READING FROM PROVERBS

Proverbs 20:25–21:4
Victory in your heart

The biggest battle goes on in our hearts and minds. This is where the victory is won or lost. God is not only concerned about your actions and your words, but also about your inmost being. God watches and examines us 'inside and out' (20:27, MSG). He 'examines our motives' (21:2, MSG).

'Clean living before God and justice with our neighbors means far more to God than religious performance' (v.3, MSG). 'The lamp of the Lord *searches* the human spirit; it *searches* out the inmost being' (20:27). I try to pray regularly as the psalmist prays, '*Search me*, O God ... and see if there is any wicked way in me' (Psalm 139:23–4, RSV).

I also pray this for other people. Proverbs 20:27 is a very useful verse in prayer ministry. If someone feels that they are wrestling with something they can't quite put their finger on, I ask the Spirit of God to search their heart to reveal if there is any sin that needs to be dealt with.

God never gives a nebulous feeling of guilt. If a feeling of guilt is of the Holy Spirit, he will reveal the specific sin that needs to be dealt with. If something wrong comes to mind, repentance leads to forgiveness through Jesus.

Then I ask the 'lamp of the Lord' to shine again and reveal if there is anything else that needs to be dealt with. Because of Jesus' victory over sin on the cross, where there is repentance and faith in Jesus Christ, there can no longer be any condemnation.

Victory for a king (or we might say 'leader') comes through 'love and faithfulness': 'Love and truth form a good leader, sound leadership is founded on loving integrity' (v.28, MSG).

The leader's '*heart* is in the hand of the Lord; he directs it like a watercourse wherever he pleases' (21:1). God is in ultimate control of a leader's heart. I have trusted this promise many times in my life when praying about job interviews, dealings with the council, judges or governments. Thankfully, the heart of the leader is in the Lord's hands and he directs it whichever way he pleases.

The heart is so important: 'All your ways seem right to you, but the Lord weighs the *heart*. To do what is right and just is more acceptable to the Lord than sacrifice' (vv.2–3).

Since victory is a gift from God, it should never lead to pride: 'Haughty eyes and a proud *heart*, the lamp of the wicked, are sin!' (v.4).

PRAYER

Lord, I pray that you would shine your lamp into my heart today and search out my inner being. Thank you for the gift of forgiveness, freedom and victory through our Lord Jesus Christ.

NEW TESTAMENT READING

1 Corinthians 15:50–16:4
Victory over death

Many people think that death is the end. They believe death always has the last word – that death in the end will be victorious.

'Not so,' declares the apostle Paul. 'Death has been swallowed up in *victory*' (15:54). He taunts death: 'Where, oh death, is your *victory*?' (v.55).

Jesus, through the cross and resurrection, has defeated sin, guilt and death. As a result, one day you will be raised 'imperishable' and 'immortal' (vv.53–54).

There are three things you can give in response to this amazing *gift of victory* through our Lord Jesus Christ:

1. Give thanks

'Where, oh death, is *your sting*? The *sting of death* is sin, and the power of sin is law. But thanks be to God! He gives us the *victory* through our Lord Jesus Christ' (vv.55–57).

The evangelist, David Watson, told the story of when he was called into the garden by the frightened cries of his daughter who was being chased by a bee. He wrapped his arms around her and then she felt his body go tense. He let her go and said to her, 'You needn't worry any more, darling, the bee *has stung me*.'

On the cross, it was as though Jesus wrapped his arms around us and *took the sting of death for us*. We still die (if Jesus doesn't return first) but, for everyone trusting in Christ, 'the sting of death' has been removed through the cross and resurrection. And, as David Watson said to his daughter, '*Bees don't sting twice.*' '*Thank God*!' (v.57, MSG).

2. Give yourself

Do you sometimes wonder whether what you are doing in serving God is really making any difference? Are you tempted to think that it may all be a waste of time and effort?

Be encouraged: '*Nothing* you do for him is a waste of time or effort' (v.58, MSG). Paul writes that the appropriate response to the victory of Jesus is 'to stand firm. Let nothing move you. Always *give yourselves fully to the work of the Lord, because you know that your labour in the Lord is not in vain*' (v.58).

Get on with 'the work of the Lord' (v.58). That is, the work that the Lord has called *you* to do. Do not be worried or threatened by what others are up to in different ministries. Different people have different callings. It is not for us to judge. They are seeking to serve God, possibly in a different way. Each of us should follow God's call in our own lives.

Give yourself fully to whatever it is God has called *you* to do. Because of the resurrection you can stand firm and know that your labour in the Lord is *not in vain*.

3. Give money

Part of giving yourself to the work of the Lord is through giving your money (16:2). We see here a number of principles of Christian giving. First, it is primarily 'for God's people' (v.1) that is, the church. Second, it should be regular, 'On the first day of every week' (v.2). Third, everyone ('each one of you', v.2) should be involved. Fourth, it should be proportionate; in keeping with your income (see Deuteronomy 16:17): 'Be as generous as you can' (1 Corinthians 16:2, MSG).

PRAYER

Father, I can never thank you enough for the gift of victory through our Lord Jesus Christ over sin, the law and death. I rededicate my life, my money and everything I have, to do the work of the Lord.

OLD TESTAMENT READING

2 Chronicles 21:4–23:21
Victory over evil

The news today. Terrible events. Evil regimes. Horrific murders. Nothing new.

These chapters describe a bad period in the history of the people of God. God considered Jehoram 'an evil man' (21:6, MSG). He 'led Judah astray' (v.11). 'There were no tears when he died – it was good riddance!' (v.20, MSG).

Ahaziah was no better. His mother, Athaliah, was even worse: 'training him in evil ways' (22:3, MSG). When he died she carried on doing evil and causing destruction (v.10). She tried to kill all the princes.

However, Joash, like Moses before him and Jesus after him, was hidden and protected (vv.11–12).

God had promised to maintain a lamp for David and his descendants for ever (21:7). Evil was defeated. Joash was crowned King (23:11) and 'all the people of the land rejoiced. And the city was quiet, because Athaliah had been slain by the sword' (v.21).

This is a picture of the ultimate triumph of good over evil. Joash foreshadowed someone far greater who was to come. God protected Jesus from those who wanted to kill him as a baby. He is the anointed King who ultimately defeated evil and death.

PRAYER

Lord, we can never thank you enough. 'Thanks be to God! He gives us the victory through our Lord Jesus Christ' (1 Corinthians 15:57).

25 August | Day 237
Strong Families

A busy father was looking for a way to entertain his young daughter. He found a map of the world in a magazine and cut it into pieces. He gave the pieces to his child and suggested she try to piece the map back together.

After a very short time, she said she had finished. He was very surprised by how quickly she had done it. He asked her how she had managed to do it so fast. She replied, 'I noticed when you took the page out of the magazine that on the back of the map of the world there was a picture of a man and a woman. I thought that *if I could put the man and the woman back together, I could put the world back together*.'

Marriage and family life are hugely important. They are part of God's natural order, and are a vital part of the fabric of society. Pope John Paul II once wrote that family is the 'foundation' of society and 'nourishes' society continually.[1]

Nicky and Sila Lee have invested their lives in strengthening marriages and family life. Their courses and books such as *The Marriage Book* and *The Parenting Book* have had a profound impact on thousands of people in our own local church and now in many countries around the world. Recently a government official in one country said to Nicky and Sila, 'A strong society depends on strong families and strong families depend on strong marriages. That's why we are interested in your work.'

The Bible has a great deal to say about family life. Not only do we have a natural family but, as Christians, we are part of the church, which the New Testament sees as 'the family of God'.

READING FROM PSALMS

Psalm 102:18–28
Children and the next generation

Every generation has a responsibility *to think* about the future and *to plan* for it. We should be concerned, not just about what happens in our time but also about the next generation. The psalmist is concerned for the next generation: 'Let this be written for a future generation, that a people not yet created may praise the LORD' (v.18).

Jesus is the key for every generation. Interestingly, the writer to the Hebrews quotes verses 25–27 of this psalm and applies them to Jesus (Hebrews 1:10–12): 'Jesus is the same yesterday and today and for ever' (Hebrews 13:8). He 'laid earth's foundations a long time ago, and handcrafted the very heavens' (Psalm 102:25, MSG). Jesus will be there for ever: 'Year after year you're as good as new' (v.27, MSG).

The psalm ends with this hope for the next generation: 'Your servants' children will have a good place to live and their children will be at home with you' (v.28, MSG).

This is a hope, a prayer and, to some extent, a promise. While everyone is responsible for their own lives, there is a sense in which God treats people as families. We can hope, pray and believe that our children, grandchildren and their descendants will live in his presence and be established before him (v.28).

PRAYER

Lord, I pray for my own family and for those in the church, that we will live in your presence and that our children will grow up to know, love, serve and be established before you.

NEW TESTAMENT READING

1 Corinthians 16:5–24
Family and homes

Hillsong Church in Sydney, Australia, has a big sign outside saying: 'Welcome Home'. The vision of Brian and Bobbie Houston, the senior pastors, is that everyone who comes to the church will be welcomed, loved and given the hospitality that we would give to a guest in our own home.

We need to recapture this New Testament vision of church as a home. Of course, the early Christians did not have church buildings. They met in homes (v.19). Paul writes to the Corinthians, 'If Timothy shows up, take good care of him. Make him feel completely at *home* among you' (v.10, MSG).

The church is the family of God. God is our father. Paul sees the whole church as a family. He talks about other Christians as his 'brothers and sisters' (v.15). *Church is not an organisation you join; it is a family, where you belong, a home where you are loved and a hospital where you find healing*.

Paul, who was single and did not have his own wife or children, loves the Corinthians and sees *them* as his family. He found spiritual refreshment by spending time with them (v.17). He ends his letter, 'I love all of you' (v.24, MSG). He expects them to 'love the Lord' (v.22) and to love one another. They should express this love by greeting 'one another with a holy kiss' (v.20).

This is not just a nice theory; it is very personal. He longs to see them (v.5). He knows that they will 'help' him (v.6). He does not want to spend only a short time with them; he wants to spend much longer 'if the Lord permits' (v.7). Paul's message flows from his love and concern for the people in the church. He practised what he preached when he wrote 'do everything in love' (v.14).

The only reason Paul is not coming sooner is that 'a great door for effective work has opened to [him], and there are many who oppose [him]' (v.9). (It seems that whenever God opens 'a huge door of opportunity for good work' we should expect that there will also be 'mushrooming opposition', v.9, MSG.) Do not let such opposition deter you from making the most of great opportunities when they arise.

He goes on to talk about Timothy, whom he describes elsewhere as his son in the Lord (4:17), his 'brother Apollos' (16:12) and 'the family of Stephanas' (v.15, MSG). It appears from the New Testament that it was quite common for whole families to be converted and baptised together.

We also see in this passage an instance of a married couple having a joint ministry. Aquila and Priscilla ran a church in their home (v.19). Here, Aquila is named first. However, more commonly Priscilla is the one whom Paul names first (see Romans 16:3). It is clear that they ran the church together.

The family of the church is made up of single people like Paul, married couples like Priscilla and Aquila, and whole households like those of Stephanas. Together we make up the family of God.

What Paul writes applies to us all: 'Keep your eyes open. Hold tight to your convictions, give it all you've got, be resolute and love without stopping' (1 Corinthians 16:13–14, MSG).

PRAYER

Lord, please give us such love for one another that whether we are single or married, we all experience the riches and refreshment of being part of the family of God.

OLD TESTAMENT READING

2 Chronicles 24:1–25:28
Parents and children

Good parenting is a huge advantage in life. Joash's father died when he was a baby and he became king at the age of seven. His mother ensured that he was 'taught and trained by Johoiada the priest' (v.2, MSG). He clearly received a good education and 'did what pleased GOD throughout Jehoiada's lifetime' (v.3, MSG). Joash had a family of his own which included 'both sons and daughters' (v.3, MSG).

God had promised his blessing on David and his *family*. Kingship passed down the family line. However, although God's love was unconditional, each person was responsible for how they responded to this love. 'The Book of Moses' (probably a way of referring to 'the Law', the first five books of the Old Testament) is quoted in support of the fact that 'parents shall not be put to death for their children, nor children put to death for their parents; each of you will die for your own sins' (25:4). ('We each pay personally for our sins', MSG.)

We see this principle worked out here. Joash started out well. He 'did what was right in the eyes of the LORD' (24:2). He 'decided to restore the temple of the LORD' (v.4). Everyone joined in: 'All the officials and all the people brought their contributions gladly, dropping them into the chest until it was full' (v.10). 'They rebuilt the temple of God according to its original design' (v.13). (Buildings for worship do matter and can be restored if everyone gets involved.)

Sadly, Joash's reign did not end well (vv.17–27). It is so important not just to start well but also to finish well.

Tragically the same pattern was repeated in the life of his son, Amaziah. He started well (25:2), but did not finish well. He became 'arrogant and proud' (v.19) and 'turned away from following the LORD' (v.27).

PRAYER

Lord, help us to be good examples and to finish well. I pray that family life would once again be the foundation to nourish our society continually. May there be a reversal in the decline in marriages and a restoration of strong families.

26 August | Day 238
God's Benefit Package

I recently rediscovered one of my prayer diaries in which I recorded some of my early experiences of answered prayer.

On 26 September 1976, I wrote about a prayer for my mother: 'Prayed for the Lord to heal her insomnia.' (I did not tell her I was praying for her.) Exactly three months later, on 26 December 1976, I wrote that my mother 'says she has slept better in the last few weeks than for four years and it is no longer a problem'.

Of course, it is not possible to prove Christianity on the basis of answers to prayer, because cynics can always explain them away as coincidence. But as former Archbishop of Canterbury William Temple said, 'When I pray coincidences happen, when I don't they don't.' The cumulative effect of answered prayer is to reinforce our faith in God.

For the last twenty-five years, I have written by the New Testament passage for today some of my prayers for the year ahead. It is amazing to think back and remember the ways in which God has answered so many of these prayers. I find it very easy to forget all the answers to prayer. It is so easy to forget blessings.

David reminds himself in the psalm for today *not to forget 'all his benefits'* (Psalm 103:2). Many are conscious of the 'benefits' they can receive associated with their employment, or from the state. But what about the 'benefits' that we receive from our loving heavenly Father?

READING FROM PSALMS

Psalm 103:1–12
Remember and thank God for all his benefits

There is so much to praise God for. David appears almost to be speaking to himself and urging himself on: 'O my soul, bless God. From head to toe, I'll bless his holy name! O my soul, bless God, don't forget a single blessing!' (vv.1–2, MSG).

David had clearly faced many troubles in his life: sin, disease and 'the pit' (vv.3–4). Yet he, like the apostle Paul (2 Corinthians 1:3), begins with praise for so many of God's benefits.

1. Forgiveness
God forgives all your sins (Psalm 103:3): 'he does not treat us as our sins deserve or repay us according to our iniquities' (v.10); 'as far as the east is from the west, so far has he removed our transgressions from us' (v.12).

2. Healing
God '*heals* all your diseases'. One day we will be completely healed. We see signs of this now, when God heals us directly and supernaturally. In addition, God has put in our bodies the immune system, antibodies and the mending process.

3. Redemption
God 'redeems your life from the pit' (v.4a). There is no pit so deep that God's redemption cannot reach.

4. Love
He 'crowns you with love and compassion' (v.4b): 'for as high as the heavens are above the earth, so great is his love for those who fear him' (v.11).

5. Satisfaction
He 'satisfies your desires with good things' (v.5a).

PRAYER

I praise you, Lord, for all your benefits: for your forgiveness and healing, for redeeming me, for crowning me with love and compassion and for satisfying me with good things.

NEW TESTAMENT READING

2 Corinthians 1:1–11
See his benefits even in the midst of suffering

Have you suffered loss or bereavement? Are you facing some health issue? Are you under great pressure in your finances or some other area of your life? Are you being opposed or criticised? Are you in a time of difficulty, disappointment or hardship?

Paul was the founding pastor of the Corinthian church. In this, his most personal letter, he reveals the heart of a leader. He reveals his feelings as a man of flesh and blood who knows what it is to go through trouble (v.4), sufferings (vv.5–8), distress (v.6), hardship (v.8) and pressure (v.8) – the word Paul used means to be pushed down under great weight.

He had been in despair (v.8), he had felt 'the sentence of death' (v.9), he had faced 'deadly peril' (v.10). As well as physical persecution, he had faced criticism, ridicule, sickness, depression, bereavement, injustice, disappointments, temptations and difficult personal relationships.

Sir Winston Churchill said, 'The pessimist sees the difficulty in every opportunity; the optimist sees the opportunity in every difficulty.' By this definition Paul was definitely an optimist!

He starts the letter with praise – not for the problems but for the positive benefits that have come through them. What are these benefits? How can you and I see the benefits in every difficulty?

1. You will be comforted
'The God of all comfort, who comforts us in all our troubles' (vv.3–4). The word for comfort means to encourage, cheer and come alongside. God is the 'Father of compassion' (v.3). He is not aloof from suffering. He comes

alongside us and suffers with us. His Holy Spirit is 'the Comforter' (John 14:26, AMP).

2. You will be a help to others
If you are in a time of suffering right now it may not seem much comfort – but one day you will bring great comfort to other people: 'He comes alongside us when we go through hard times, and before you know it, he brings us alongside someone else who is going through hard times so that we can be there for that person just as God was there for us' (2 Corinthians 1:4, MSG). Those who have faced difficulty in life make the most effective ministers.

3. You will be changed
Hardship 'produces in you *patient endurance*' (v.6). Like gold refined by fire or a vine pruned to produce more fruit, difficulties lead to patience, endurance, steadfastness and perseverance. They lead to character transformation.

4. You will not be alone
Paul writes, 'Just as you *share* in our sufferings, so also you *share* in our comfort' (v.7). The word he uses for 'share' comes from the Greek word *koinonia,* which is the word used to describe the closest possible relationship. In times of difficulty we should experience an extraordinary closeness of relationship as we comfort and encourage one another, 'Your hard times are also our hard times' (v.7, MSG).

5. You will learn to trust God
When things go well it is easy to become self-reliant. But when everything goes wrong and we reach the end of our tether, we are forced to trust God. As Paul puts it, 'Instead of trusting in our own strength or wits to get out of it, we were forced to trust God totally' (v.9, MSG).

6. You will be rescued
Paul writes, 'He has delivered us from such a deadly peril, and *he will deliver us*. On him we have set our hope that *he will continue to deliver us*' (v.10). As you look back and see how God has delivered you in the past, you can be confident he will deliver you in the future.

7. Your prayers will help others
Prayer is powerful. God really does answer prayer. One of the best ways you can help other people is by praying for them: '*As you help us by your prayers*. Then many will give thanks on our behalf for the gracious favour granted us in answer to the prayers of many' (v.11). When your prayers are answered, God will be glorified.

PRAYER

Lord, help me to see the benefits in every difficulty. May I experience your comfort and learn to rely not on myself but on you. Lord, I cry out to you for help...

OLD TESTAMENT READING

2 Chronicles 26:1–28:27
Don't let his benefits make you proud

Times when things are going well can be as much a test upon our faith as the times when they are not going well. Abraham Lincoln, who as President of the USA knew all about power, said, 'Nearly all men can stand adversity, but if you want to *test* a man's character, give him power.'

Uzziah started so well. He became king aged only sixteen (26:1). 'He did what was right in the eyes of the LORD' (v.4). He 'was a loyal seeker of God' (v.5a, MSG). 'As long as he sought the LORD, God gave him success' (v.5b). 'God helped him' (v.7). He became famous and he became quite powerful (v.8). 'Everything seemed to go his way' (v.15, MSG).

While he was seeking God, God was answering his prayers, helping him and giving him success.

However, it all went horribly wrong when 'he became powerful' (v.15c). Fame, success and power are intoxicating. They carry with them the dangers of pride and arrogance.

'But then the strength and success went to his head. Arrogant and proud he fell' (v.16, MSG). He did what was specifically forbidden in Scripture (see Numbers 16:40; 18:7), in spite of the fact that many of the leaders 'confronted him' (2 Chronicles 26:18) and warned him against being 'unfaithful' (v.18). Instead of listening to them, in his pride he 'lost his temper' (v.19, MSG). This is a warning. If things go well, do not become proud. Keep trusting and obeying God.

PRAYER

Lord, help me to keep praising you, relying on you and seeking you all my life.

27 August | Day 239
Anointed by God

Do you realise that right now you are 'anointed' by God? 'Anointing' is not just for special Christian leaders or speakers. It is for all of us. Do you know that this anointing gives you power over sin, temptation and evil? Do you know that this anointing gives you access to God in prayer and worship? Do you know that this anointing enables you to proclaim God's message to other people?

All of this is possible because God has given you the Holy Spirit. The Holy Spirit not only guarantees your future; he is the down payment in advance. 'He *anointed* us, set his seal of ownership on us, and put his Spirit in our hearts as a *deposit guaranteeing* what is to come' (2 Corinthians 1:21–22).

When you exchange contracts on a house it is usually accompanied by a deposit, which not only guarantees what is to come but is also a part payment in advance. God 'by his Spirit has stamped us with an eternal pledge – a sure beginning of what he is destined to complete' (v.21, MSG). By giving you the Holy Spirit, God has already given you this deposit in advance of what one day you will receive in full. What does this anointing of the Holy Spirit mean in practice?

READING FROM PSALMS

Psalm 103:13–22
Experience now God's parental love for you

The moment our children were born, Pippa and I *felt* an overwhelming love for them – which continues to this day. This is the natural instinct of every parent. We *feel* a deep-seated love for our children, which is not based on performance or achievement, but simply on who they are.

This is how God loves you – only even more so. 'As parents *feel* for their children, GOD *feels* for those who fear him' (v.13, MSG).

Have you ever *felt* God's love for you? Do you know deep down that God loves you more than any parent loves their child? Have you experienced this love being poured into your heart by the Holy Spirit? God wants you to experience this parental love right now and to know that it will continue for ever.

David seems to get a glimpse of the fact that it is not just for this life: 'But from everlasting to everlasting the LORD's love is with those who fear him, and his righteousness with their children's children – with those who keep his covenant and remember to obey his precepts' (vv.17–18).

PRAYER

'Praise the LORD, O my soul' (v.22). Praise you, Lord, for your amazing love and compassion for me, even greater than any parent's compassion for their child. Thank you that you have anointed me and put your Spirit in my heart so that I can experience that love right now.

NEW TESTAMENT READING

2 Corinthians 1:12–22
Experience now the promises of God

Do you realise that all the promises of God are for you? 'Whatever God has promised gets stamped with the Yes of Jesus' (v.20, MSG).

By the Holy Spirit, God has put 'his Yes within us. By his Spirit he has stamped us with his eternal pledge – a sure beginning of what he is destined to complete' (vv.21–22, MSG).

As has been said, 'God makes a promise; faith believes it, hope anticipates it, patience waits for it.'

It is as though God's promises in the Old Testament have been underlined and re-affirmed in Jesus. As St Paul explains it, 'For no matter how many promises God has made, they are "Yes" in Christ' (v.20). We see the ultimate *expression* of God's love *at the cross*, and know the ultimate *experience* of God's love *through the Holy Spirit*.

What is *concealed* in the Old Testament is *revealed* in the New Testament. In Christ you will enjoy God's everlasting love for ever. As St Paul puts it, 'Now it is God who makes both us and you stand firm in Christ. He anointed us, set his seal of ownership on us, and put his Spirit in our hearts as a deposit, *guaranteeing* what is to come' (vv.21–22). It is the same God who anointed both Paul and the Corinthians.

It is not that only certain special Christians are anointed. We know that 'God *anointed* Jesus of Nazareth with the Holy Spirit and power' (Acts 10:38). What is so amazing is that the same Spirit who anointed Jesus, has *anointed* you. You are 'anointed' by the Holy

Spirit and so am I. God's Spirit who lives in you as the 'deposit' is also the one who gives you his 'anointing'. In order to understand how rich and beautiful this promise is we need to understand the background – some of which we see in our Old Testament passage today.

PRAYER

Lord, thank you so much that all the promises of God find their 'Yes' in Christ (2 Corinthians 1:20). Thank you that you have anointed me with your 'seal of ownership' (v.22) and put your Spirit in my heart 'as a deposit, guaranteeing what is to come' (v.22).

OLD TESTAMENT READING

2 Chronicles 29:1–31:1
Experience now God's anointing on your life

In the Old Testament, three groups of people were anointed: kings, priests and prophets. Through the work of the Holy Spirit in us, we are all now anointed with a *kingly anointing*, a *priestly anointing* and a *prophetic anointing*. What does this mean in practice?

1. Kingly anointing

You have *a kingly anointing* for the battle against temptation, sin and evil.

Hezekiah was the *anointed king*. The king was to lead the people in all their struggles and battles. Hezekiah 'was a good king' (29:2, MSG). He 'went to work. He got all the leaders of the city together' (v.20, MSG). They restored the temple and celebrated the Passover and got rid of all the false idols (31:1).

Hezekiah invited them, 'Don't repeat the sins of your ancestors who turned their backs on God ... Clasp God's outstretched hand. Come to his Temple of holy worship ... Your God is gracious and kind and won't snub you – come back and he'll welcome you with open arms' (30:7–10, MSG).

Fr Raniero Cantalamessa writes that *kingly anointing* means that the Holy Spirit 'urges Jesus and the Church on in [its] struggle against Satan'.[1] All of us have this *kingly anointing*. The Holy Spirit urges each of us on in our battle against temptation, sin and evil. You can call upon the Holy Spirit to help you when you are tempted, knowing that he will come alongside you and give you strength to overcome.

2. Priestly anointing

You have *a priestly anointing* to pray and worship.

The priests in the Old Testament, and in this passage in particular, were anointed to be the mediators between God and human beings. We see here that they made sacrifices of bulls, lambs, goats, and so on (29:20 onwards). They sprinkled the blood of the bulls and lambs on the altar. They laid their hands on the goats and sacrificed them. These were offerings to atone for sin.

'The Levites and priests praised God day after day, filling the air with praise sounds of percussion and brass. Hezekiah commended the Levites for the superb way in which they had led the people in the worship of God' (30:22, MSG).

Jesus fulfilled this *priestly anointing* by dying as the lamb of God whose blood was shed to take away our sins. This was a unique and final sacrifice for sin.

There is another sense in which the priestly anointing comes on us, the church. We share in Jesus' *priestly anointing*: 'You are a ... *royal priesthood*' (1 Peter 2:9). The Spirit urges Jesus and the church to pray. In your prayers, you have a priestly ministry as an intercessor for the people before God.

3. Prophetic anointing

You have *a prophetic anointing* to speak the good news about Jesus.

The chronicler refers to 'Nathan *the prophet*' (2 Chronicles 29:25) and says, 'This was God's command conveyed by his prophets' (v.26, MSG). The prophets in the Old Testament were anointed to speak the word of the Lord. The Spirit anointed Jesus at his baptism to preach good news to the poor. This same Holy Spirit anoints you to speak his words today. You have this *prophetic anointing*.

The church is God's agent to bring the good news of Jesus to the world. Each time you tell a friend about Jesus, invite them on Alpha, for example, or speak into their lives in some way, you are acting out this calling.

PRAYER

Lord, help me fulfil the kingly anointing in the battle against sin. Lead me not into temptation but deliver me from evil.

Help me also in my priestly anointing to be more faithful in praying for others.

Help me in my prophetic anointing to bring good news to the poor, to bind up the broken-hearted, to proclaim freedom to the captives and, to those in mourning and despair, bring the oil of gladness that comes from the Holy Spirit (Isaiah 61:1–3; Luke 4:18–19).

28 August | Day 240
Just Love

The prison governor was an immensely impressive, dynamic, eloquent and young African-American woman known as 'Chief Jennifer'.

Our team assembled at the start of the visit, together with those who ran the prison. Chief Jennifer welcomed us with these words: 'Greetings in the name of our Lord and Saviour Jesus Christ.'

She told us that there were 2.5 million people in prison in the USA, each costing the taxpayer $24,000 a year. Only 3 per cent will stay in prison for the rest of their lives. Ninety-seven per cent of those presently incarcerated will, at some point, be released back into society. For that reason, she continued, there was good secular motivation for wanting to see change in their lives, besides her own desire, as a Christian, for them to experience redemption.

The prison was run not only with *justice*, but also with *love*. All wrong attitudes and actions were lovingly *confronted*. There was no bad language, no graffiti and a learned respectful behaviour. We spent some time with a group of men who had recently completed Alpha there and heard their testimonies of changed lives.

God is love. He is also just. In his book *Justice in Love*, Nicholas Wolterstorff points out that justice is a necessary constituent part of any properly formed conception of love.

READING FROM PROVERBS

Proverbs 21:5–16
Justice and the poor

A society without justice and the rule of law is a terrifying place to live. Evil is unrestrained. The poor, in particular, suffer. We see the terrifying results of a lack of justice in many societies around the world.

Where the rule of law operates it has a double benefit. When justice is done, it brings 'joy to the righteous' (v.15a). It also deters evildoers. It brings 'terror to evildoers' (v.15b). 'Good people celebrate when justice triumphs, but for the workers of evil it is a bad day' (v.15, MSG).

Justice leads to a society where people feel protected and secure – especially the poor. One of the reasons our prayers might not be answered is that we have not heard the cries of the poor: 'If you shut your ears to the cry of the poor, you too will cry out and not be answered' (v.13).

PRAYER

Lord, I pray for justice in our world. I pray for those that are seeking to bring justice to parts of the world where injustice reigns.

NEW TESTAMENT READING

2 Corinthians 1:23–2:11
Justice and forgiveness

Many of us tend to avoid confrontation. I find it difficult. It is not just the fear of rejection or being unpopular, it is also the fear that I might make the situation worse by fuelling the fires of anger and resentment.

Some people seem positively to enjoy confrontation. If we look forward to confrontation, if we find it easy to put others right, to correct and to criticise, it is possible that we are not always acting out of love.

Paul loved the Corinthians deeply. Yet he did not shy away from confrontation. His love led him to confront, though it caused him 'great distress', 'anguish of heart' and 'many tears' (2:4). 'I didn't write it to cause pain; I wrote it so you would know how much I care – oh, more than care – *love* you!' (v.4, MSG).

Confronting people with the truth may be very painful. Truth, like surgery, may hurt, but it also cures. Operations like this must be carried out with love. We do not know exactly who or what Paul is referring to here. However, it may be the man that Paul had denounced in 1 Corinthians 5:1–5 (who had been living with his father's wife).

Paul had insisted that he be thrown out of the church. However, now he is saying that this man has received punishment enough. He urges them to forgive and comfort him, and to reaffirm their love for him (2 Corinthians 2:7–8). Justice had been done. Now was the time for mercy, grace and forgiveness.

Paul was very quick to forgive: 'Anyone you forgive I also forgive. And what I have forgiven – if there was anything to forgive – I have forgiven in the sight of Christ for your sake' (v.10). When Paul forgave, he forgot – hardly even remembering whether there was anything to forgive.

Clara Barton, founder of the American Red Cross, was once reminded by a friend of a cruel thing that had happened to her many years earlier. Clara seemed unable to remember the incident.

'Don't you remember the wrong that was done to you?' the friend asked insistently.

'No,' Clara answered calmly. 'I distinctly remember forgetting that.'[1]

Forgiveness is absolutely vital in the Christian church. Lack of forgiveness is one of the ways that the devil can get in – it opens a door for his schemes. Forgiveness shuts him out: 'In order that Satan might not outwit us. For we are not unaware of his schemes' (v.11).

PRAYER

Lord, help us to spot the schemes of the devil. Help us to be quick to forgive and love one another and to shut Satan out of the church.

OLD TESTAMENT READING

2 Chronicles 31:2–33:20
Justice and confrontation

God himself is not afraid of confrontation! In this passage we see how, in his love, God confronted both an essentially good leader who became proud, and an evil leader who was enabled to repent.

It is such a relief to read about a good king. Hezekiah restored the temple. He led by example – he contributed from his own possessions (31:3). The people responded generously (v.5). The Lord blessed them and they had plenty to eat with food left over (v.10).

'Everything [Hezekiah] took up ... he did well in a spirit of prayerful worship. He was a great success' (vv.20–21, MSG). He had an 'exemplary track record' (32:1, MSG).

All this did not save Hezekiah from coming under attack. But when the attack did come from Sennacherib, Hezekiah inspired the people, 'Be strong! Take courage! Don't be intimidated ... There are more on our side than on their side. He only has a bunch of mere men; we have our GOD to help us and fight for us! Morale surged. Hezekiah's words put steel in their spines' (32:7–8, MSG).

In our own lives, sometimes we face seemingly overwhelming problems. Christians in the UK, for example, seem to be like a small minority facing a vast army of secularism and hostility to God. But the good news is that there is a greater power with us, and with them there is only the 'arm of flesh'. With us is the Lord our God to 'help us and to fight our battles' (v.8).

There is always a danger that success will lead to pride. People look up to leaders. Indeed, we are supposed to honour our leaders. But all leaders need to be aware that this honour has danger written all over it. If pride creeps in, repent quickly and humble yourself.

As soon as Hezekiah was successful, arrogance crept in. When God confronted him, thankfully, 'He repented of the pride in his heart' (v.26) and God blessed him again with great riches and honour (v.27). He succeeded in everything he undertook (v.30).

Then, mysteriously, 'God left him to test him and to know everything that was in his heart' (v.31). It was a dark night of the soul.

Don't be discouraged if there are times when you do not sense God's presence. Sometimes God is silent and imperceptible. Continue to be faithful when God tests your heart. Hezekiah had a good heart – his life was full of acts of devotion (v.32) and was honoured when he died (v.33).

His son's life seems to be almost a complete reversal of his own. Manasseh started out doing evil in the eyes of the Lord (33:2). In fact, it is hard to think of anyone who did more evil than Manasseh. 'He burned his own sons in a sacrificial rite ... He practiced witchcraft and fortunetelling. He held séances and consulted spirits from the underworld. Much evil – in GOD's view a career in evil. And GOD was angry' (v.6, MSG).

But no one is beyond redemption. No matter how far we have fallen, if, like Manasseh, we repent and turn to God we can receive forgiveness.

God confronted Manasseh. 'Now that he was in trouble, he went to his knees in prayer asking for help – total repentance before the God of his ancestors. As he prayed, GOD was touched; GOD listened and brought him back to Jerusalem as king' (v.12, MSG).

This is one of the reasons why I love to visit prisons. No one is beyond redemption. Jesus has made this possible through his death on the cross where, in the words of John Eddison, 'Love and justice mingle, truth and mercy meet.'[2]

PRAYER

Lord, thank you that at the cross we see both your love and justice together. Thank you that you have mercy on me. Help me to show your love and bring your justice to the world, in Jesus' name.

29 August | Day 241
When the Holy Spirit Comes

I remember the first time I prayed 'Come, Holy Spirit' on an Alpha Weekend. I knew that the Holy Spirit had 'come' every time those who had led the Alpha Weekends before me had asked him to come. Even so, I did not think he would come in answer to *my prayers* – as I prayed 'Come, Holy Spirit' I shut my eyes, because I did not want to see him '*not* coming'!

When I opened my eyes, there was an amazing sight. The Holy Spirit *had come* in a powerful way – people were being filled. He was changing people's lives. This was the ministry of the Holy Spirit. That is why at some point in virtually every one of our services we pray 'Come, Holy Spirit.' We always try to leave time for 'ministry' – for the Holy Spirit to *minister* to us.

We often associate the word '*minister*' with *leadership*, whether by government *ministers* or by church *ministers*. In fact, the word really means '*to serve*'. Politicians are called to *serve* their countries. Pastors are called to *serve* the church. Doctors, who ad*minister* treatment to their patients, are called to *serve* the sick and the dying.

The Holy Spirit *ministers* to you. He brings authority greater than any politician, comfort deeper than any pastor, and healing more wonderful than any doctor. God *ministers* to you in the deepest part of your life by the Holy Spirit.

The apostle Paul speaks of '*the ministry of the Spirit*' (2 Corinthians 3:8). John Wimber defined this kind of ministry as 'meeting the needs of others with the resources of God'. Wonderfully, this type of ministry is now available to you and me.

READING FROM PSALMS

Psalm 104:1–18
Ministry of 'wind' and 'flames of fire'

This is a marvellous psalm praising God for his entire creation. Everything that God has created is good. I love the fact that in addition to '*oil* to make their faces shine, and *bread* that sustains their hearts', he has made '*wine* that gladdens human hearts' (v.15).

Of course, like every good gift from God, wine can be abused. The Bible often warns against drunkenness. However, wine, like oil and bread, is given by God for our enjoyment and to gladden the heart of human beings.

Earlier on the psalmist says, 'He makes *winds* his messengers, *flames of fire* his servants' (v.4). The word for 'servants' can be translated '*ministers*' (see RSV, ESV, KJV).

This passage is a fascinating Old Testament backdrop to the account of the day of Pentecost. When the Holy Spirit came, they heard 'a sound like the blowing of a violent *wind*' and they saw 'tongues *[flames]* of *fire*' that separated and came to rest on each of them (Acts 2:2–4).

'Wind' and 'flames of fire' are *God's ministers*. They symbolise the power, passion and purity of God. When you pray 'Come, Holy Spirit', expect God to send the wind and fire of the Holy Spirit and expect the ministry of the Holy Spirit to be powerful and life changing.

PRAYER

Lord, thank you for the transformation in people's lives as they experience the power, passion and purity of God. Come, Holy Spirit and fill me today.

NEW TESTAMENT READING

2 Corinthians 2:12–3:6
Ministry that gives life

How can you bring life to others? In this passage, Paul describes himself as a *minister* of a 'new covenant – not of the letter but of the Spirit; for the letter kills, but the Spirit *gives life*' (3:6).

1. *Through you*, people smell the sweet scent of Christ

'Everywhere we go, people breathe in the exquisite fragrance' (2:14b, MSG). Paul describes his ministry as being like that of a 'perpetual victory parade' (v.14a, MSG). When a king or general had won a notable victory, the whole city would turn out to welcome them home. They would bring with them the prisoners they had taken. It might well be accompanied by the 'sweet smell of incense'.

For some (the prisoners) it was 'the smell of death' (v.16a). For others (the victors) it was the 'fragrance of life' (v.16b). Similarly, 'We give off a *sweet scent* rising to God, which is recognised by those on the way of salvation ... But those on the way to destruction treat us more like the stench from a rotting corpse' (vv.14–15, MSG).

2. *Through you*, people read about Jesus

The only Bible some people will read is your life. Paul writes to the Corinthians, 'Your very lives are a letter that anyone can read by just looking at you. Christ himself wrote it – not with ink, but with God's living Spirit; not chiselled into stone, but carved into human lives – and we publish it' (3:1b–3, MSG).

Not everyone can or will read books – but everyone you encounter can, and will, read your life.

3. *Through you*, people hear about a relationship with Jesus

You should never say, 'I am useless', 'I can do nothing'. You are able, through the ministry of the Holy Spirit, to bring the good news of Jesus to others. This should give you great confidence – not self-confidence but *God*-confidence.

'Such *confidence* as this is ours through Christ before God. Not that we are competent in ourselves to claim anything for ourselves, but *our competence comes from God*' (vv.4–5).

The Holy Spirit gives you not just a new start in life, but also a new life to start with. The old covenant was the one made by God through Moses, but it did not have the power to make the people everything that God longed for them to be.

Because the people could not keep the law that was written on tablets of stone, ultimately it brought death – 'the letter kills' (v.6). On the other hand, the ministry of the Holy Spirit –written in your heart – is a ministry that 'gives life' (v.6).

The Holy Spirit brings a change in human nature. Never say, 'I can't change'. With the Holy Spirit you *can* change.

It is the difference between a religion of rules and regulations (which ultimately none of us are able to keep) and a relationship with God through Jesus, which brings life, and life in all its fullness (John 10:10).

PRAYER

Lord, thank you so much for this ministry where time and again we see the Spirit giving life to people who were spiritually dead.

OLD TESTAMENT READING

2 Chronicles 33:21–35:19
Ministers of a new covenant

Tim Keller defines a covenant as 'the solemn, permanent, whole self-giving of two parties to each other. It is a stunning blend of both law and love ... a relationship much more intimate and loving than a mere legal contract could create, yet one more enduring and binding than personal affection alone could make.'[1]

Paul writes, God has 'made us competent as ministers of a *new* covenant' (2 Corinthians 3:6). He contrasts this with the *old* covenant. Here we see something about this old covenant.

After Amon, who was an evil king who 'did not humble himself before the LORD' (2 Chronicles 33:23), Josiah became king at the age of eight (34:1). His faith came alive when he was sixteen years of age and 'he began to seek the God of his father David' (v.3). He cleansed Judah and Jerusalem of all the bad stuff and scrubbed the place clean (vv.3–7, MSG). He 'repaired and restored the temple' (v.10).

While they were doing so they 'found the Book of the Law of the Lord that had been given through Moses' (v.14). By looking at the old covenant they saw that 'they had not acted in accordance with all that is written in this book' (v.21).

God spoke to them through the prophetess Huldah (v.22). (Again, here in the Old Testament we see yet another example of a woman in a prominent position in ministry.)

In the hearing of the men of Judah, the people of Jerusalem, the priests and the Levites, Josiah read 'all the words of the Book of the Covenant, which had been found in the temple of the LORD' (v.30). He 'solemnly committed himself to *the covenant*: to follow GOD believingly and obediently; to follow his instructions, heart and soul, on what to believe and do; to confirm with his life the entire covenant' (v.31, MSG).

The old covenant was a good covenant. But, it was written on tablets of stone. Even when the people did try to keep the law, it never lasted very long. The outward reformation lasted only as long as Josiah was there to enforce it. Ultimately, they failed to keep it (see Jeremiah 11–13).

The law shows us our need for a saviour. You can only keep God's covenant when you receive forgiveness from Jesus and, by the ministry of the Holy Spirit, the law is written in your heart.

PRAYER

Lord, thank you that we are 'ministers of a new covenant' and that your law is now written in our hearts by the Spirit who enables us to walk in him and to minister in his power.

30 August | Day 242

How to Have a Spiritual Facelift

Father Raniero Cantalamessa, a Franciscan monk who is preacher to the papal household, aged eighty-one, kindly came and spoke at our Leadership Conference at the Royal Albert Hall. Many people comment on how his face and eyes shine with the radiance of God's presence. He was on a train one time in Italy when a woman, who was a total non-believer, approached him and said, '*Your face compels me to believe*.'

It has been said, 'We cannot control the beauty of our face, but we can control the expression on it.' As this story illustrates, you can tell a lot by looking at people's eyes and faces. We say, 'You should have seen *the look on their face*.' As the old Latin proverb says, 'The face is the index of the mind.'

It is also true that 'The eyes are the windows to the soul.' When we really want someone to listen to and believe us, we say to that person, '*Look into my eyes*.'

The Bible says a lot about faces and eyes.

READING FROM PSALMS

Psalm 104:19–30
God's face

There is a spiritual hunger in our hearts, which can only be satisfied by God. The psalms are full of a longing for relationship with God, and a desire to be in God's presence. This is described here using the language of human relationships – 'looking' to God and seeking his 'face': 'These all *look* to you ... When you hide *your face*, they are terrified ... When you send your Spirit, they are created' (vv.27–30).

The psalmist contrasts the satisfaction that comes from looking at God's face with the terror when he hides his face from us. Sin creates a barrier between us and God. When Adam and Eve sinned, they could no longer look God in the eye. They hid from him. They were removed from his presence. God hid his face from them. They were terrified.

When we are able to look God in the face the opposite is the case: 'All the creatures look expectantly to you to give them their meals on time ... You open your hand and they eat from it' (v.27, MSG). This is true not only of physical food, but also of the spiritual food which God gives us.

PRAYER

Lord, thank you that when I look to you, you open your hand and satisfy me with good things. Forgive my sins and do not hide your face from me.

NEW TESTAMENT READING

2 Corinthians 3:7–18
Our faces

Our faces are supposed to shine more brightly than the face of Moses. 'Moses' *face* as he delivered the tablets was so bright that day (even though it would fade soon enough) that the people of Israel could no more look right at him than stare at the sun' (v.7, MSG).

The ministry of the old covenant was itself good. It came 'engraved in letters on stone', but it also came 'with glory' (v.7). Moses had looked into *the face of God* and as a result *his face was shining* (see Exodus 34:29 onwards). Moses had to 'put a veil over his face to keep the Israelites from gazing at it while the radiance was fading away' (2 Corinthians 3:13).

Although the ministry of the old covenant was good, it actually 'brought death' (v.7). We are unable (of ourselves) to keep God's written laws. We sin, and 'the wages of sin is death' (Romans 6:23).

Paul continues to contrast the ministry of the old covenant with the ministry of the Spirit. The ministry of the old covenant in itself was good (2 Corinthians 3:7). However, the ministry of the Spirit is even more glorious and lasting (vv.9–11).

The ministry of the old covenant involved Moses wearing a veil. A veil stops people seeing. Paul says that even today people don't really see or understand, 'their minds were made dull' (v.14). Only when they turn to the Lord is the veil taken away (v.16).

This certainly was my experience – I had heard the Bible being read and I had been to talks about the Christian faith, yet I did not understand what people were talking about. It made no sense to me at all. My spiritual eyes were blind. The moment that I turned to the Lord, it was as if the veil was taken away. I could see and understand.

Paul goes on to write something absolutely amazing: 'And when God is personally present, a living Spirit, that old, constricting legislation is recognized as obsolete. We're free of it! All of us! Nothing between us and God, *our faces* shining with the brightness of *his face*. And so we are transfigured much like the Messiah, our lives gradually becoming brighter and more beautiful as God enters our lives and we become like him' (vv.17–18, MSG).

The whole Trinity is involved. The glory of God (the *Father*) is seen in the face of *Jesus* our Lord. Jesus and *the Holy Spirit* are so closely connected that Paul can write, 'The Lord is the Spirit ... the Lord, who is the Spirit' (vv.17–18). The Holy Spirit is the Spirit of Jesus (Acts 16:7).

The Spirit of the Lord brings radical freedom to our lives; freedom from legalism, guilt, shame, condemnation, self-hatred and self-rejection; freedom from the power of sin, selfishness, manipulation and control; freedom from the fear of death and fear of what others think of us; freedom from comparing ourselves with others.

You are free to know, love and serve God. You are free to use your life and energy to love others. You are free to be yourself. You can approach God with boldness (2 Corinthians 3:12). You do not need to veil your face.

As you look into the face of Jesus, he changes you into his likeness. The change is gradual, little by little, 'from one degree of glory to another' (v.18, AMP). When you spend time with another person you tend to become more like them. People gaze at celebrities and reproduce their mannerisms and their appearance. If you are captivated by Jesus, you will be transformed into *his* image.

You may see a thousand faces a day, images are everywhere, but the Spirit reveals the most important face of all to us. As you spend time in the presence of the Lord you become more and more like him. You are transformed into his likeness with ever-increasing glory.

PRAYER

Lord, thank you for this immense privilege that I can approach you with freedom and boldness. Thank you that I can look into your face and reflect your glory in the world. Help me today to fix my eyes on you.

OLD TESTAMENT READING

2 Chronicles 35:20–36:23
God's eyes

The eyes of the Lord see everything you do, say and think. We can escape from human eyes but we cannot escape from the eyes of the Lord.

The sad history of the people of God continues in today's passage. Human nature is unchanged. There were fights, battles, quarrelling, attacks and war (35:20–21). Josiah was succeeded by kings who did not follow his good example. Jehoakim, Jehoiachin (his son) and Zedekiah (Jehoiachin's uncle) all 'did evil in *the eyes of the Lord*' (36:5, 9, 12).

Zedekiah's problem, like the others, was that he was 'stiff-necked and hardened his heart and would not *turn to the Lord*' (v.13). Being stiff-necked is a powerful illustration of pride – refusing to bow the head before God. Hardening the heart is a description of how we can resist the Holy Spirit.

'God ... repeatedly sent warning messages to them. Out of compassion for both his people and his Temple he wanted to give them every chance possible. But they wouldn't listen' (2 Chronicles 36:15, MSG). Like many people today 'they poked fun at God's messengers, despised the message itself, and in general treated the prophets like idiots' (v.16, MSG). Eventually, God handed them over (v.17) to the great powers of that day – Babylon (modern day Iraq) and Persia (modern day Iran).

The book of Chronicles ends with a slight note of hope. The passage for today includes a description of the destruction of Jerusalem and the temple in 597 BC and the exile, but it ends with the hope of restoration and rebuilding that began in 538 BC.

This restoration pointed towards the greater hope of what was to happen through Jesus Christ our Lord. The ministry of the old covenant was to be far exceeded by the ministry of Jesus and the Holy Spirit. Our hope is of a totally different order. Paul writes 'since we have this *hope* we are very bold' (2 Corinthians 3:12). It is the *hope* of reflecting the Lord's glory and being transformed into his likeness with ever-increasing glory (v.18).

PRAYER

Lord, thank you for the hope that we have, which is so much greater than anyone had even thought or imagined. Thank you that I can gaze at the face of Jesus. Thank you that I can reflect the Lord's glory and be transformed into his likeness with ever-increasing glory.

31 August | Day 243
Fix Your Eyes on the Invisible

Do you ever get discouraged? Do you sometimes feel, 'Is this all worthwhile?' Are you ever tempted to 'lose heart'? If you are, you are not alone. Paul was almost certainly tempted himself to lose heart, and he wrote to other Christians who were also tempted to do so.

Yet Paul wrote, 'We do not lose heart' (2 Corinthians 4:1, 16). 'We do not throw up our hands and walk off the job' (v.1, MSG). Why not? Paul explains that it is because in Jesus we have received a 'treasure' (v.7). The treasure is the message of Jesus. It is because the message that Paul has to proclaim is so amazing that he starts and ends by saying, 'Therefore ... we do not lose heart' (vv.1, 16).

Yet the treasure is inward and unseen. Paul describes it as being in 'jars of clay' (v.7). Our culture emphasises the outward and the seen. The media is dominated by money, possessions, houses, cars, food, physical beauty and outward success. The Bible is very different. It stresses the importance of the invisible – the inward and *unseen* aspects of our character: the thoughts, beliefs and attitudes that determine our outward behaviour. 'For what is seen is temporary but what is unseen is *eternal*' (v.18). The invisible is eternal.

READING FROM PSALMS

Psalm 104:31–35
Inward and unseen thoughts

If you know how to worry, you know how to meditate! All you need to do is change what you think about and you will be practising Christian meditation.

'Meditation' (v.34) means what you think about, what you allow your mind to dwell on. Your actions and your words are vital. But it is not just your actions and words that can please the Lord or not; it is your inward and unseen *meditation* as well.

The psalmist praises God for the entire created universe. He says, 'I will sing to the LORD all my life' (v.33). Then, he prays, 'May my *meditation* be pleasing to him' (v.34).

What does this mean practically? The apostle Paul has some good advice: 'whatever is true, whatever is noble, whatever is right, whatever is pure, whatever is lovely, whatever is admirable – if anything is excellent or praiseworthy – *think* about such things' (Philippians 4:8).

PRAYER

Lord, may my actions, words *and thoughts* be pleasing to you today.

NEW TESTAMENT READING

2 Corinthians 4:1–18
Inward and unseen treasure

You have the most powerful message in the world. Faith in Jesus is utterly transformational, both now and into *eternity*. 'We know that the one who raised the Lord Jesus from the dead will also raise us with Jesus and present us with you in his presence' (v.14). You will live for ever.

This life is not the end, for what is seen is temporary, but what is unseen is *eternal*: 'The things we can't see now will last forever' (v.18, MSG).

Secularisation has led to the world – and now even the church – forgetting about 'eternity'. We focus on, and value, the things we can see and handle. '*Eternity*' is a vital part of the message.

In proclaiming the message about Jesus there are four things to which we must say 'No':

1. No secrecy

'We have renounced *secret* ... ways' (v.2). 'We refuse to wear masks' (v.2a, MSG). There needs to be openness in everything we do: 'We keep everything we do and say out in the open, the whole truth on display' (v.2b, MSG).

2. No shame

'We have renounced ... *shameful* ways' (v.2). We should not do anything that, if discovered, we might be ashamed about.

3. No deception

'We do not use *deception*' (v.2). 'We don't manoeuvre and manipulate behind the scenes' (v.2, MSG).

4. No distortion

'Nor do we *distort* the word of God' (v.2). 'We don't twist God's word to suit ourselves' (v.2, MSG). We must not change the message to make it more acceptable. On the contrary, Paul writes that he sets forth the truth 'plainly' (v.2).

Because the gospel is unseen and inward, not everyone sees it. 'It is veiled to those who are perishing. The god of this age has *blinded* the minds of unbelievers, so that *they cannot see* the light of the gospel of the glory of Christ, who is the image of God' (vv.3–4). I was like that. I heard the message, but I simply could not make head or tail of it.

It is only when God shines his light into our hearts that we can see 'the light of the knowledge of the glory of God in the face of Christ' (v.6).

The message is all about Jesus: 'Christ, who gives us the best picture of God we'll ever get' (v.4, MSG). 'Remember, our message is not about ourselves; we're proclaiming Jesus Christ, the Master' (v.5, MSG).

We are all vulnerable, fragile 'jars of clay' (v.7). Inside is the 'treasure' (v.7), which is inward and 'unseen' (v.18). Do not be surprised if, sometimes, Christian leaders fall. We, the messengers, are weak and fragile. If you received your faith from someone who has now lost theirs or has messed up in some way, understand that the message came to you in a jar of clay. It is not the jar that matters, but the message. The treasure is the message of Jesus. It is given by the mercy of God (v.1). God has deliberately put the treasure in jars of clay: 'We carry this precious message around in the unadorned clay pots of our ordinary lives. That's to prevent anyone from confusing God's incomparable power with us' (v.7, MSG).

Although the jars are wasting away, and 'on the outside it often looks like things are falling apart on us, on the inside, where God is making new life, not a day goes by without his unfolding grace' (v.16, MSG). You may be 'hard pressed' by financial and other pressures, and perplexed by things that happen to you. You may be criticised and 'persecuted' and at times 'struck down' (vv.8–9).

But 'our light and momentary troubles are achieving for us an eternal glory that far outweighs them all' (vv.16–17). 'These hard times are small potatoes compared to the coming good times, the lavish celebration prepared for us' (v.17, MSG).

'So,' Paul writes, 'we fix our eyes not on what is seen, but on what is unseen. For what is seen is temporary, but *what is unseen is eternal*' (v.18). As Father Raniero Cantalamessa said, 'A new standard of measurement has been introduced that makes crosses and trials seem light and momentary: *Eternity*.'

PRAYER

Lord, thank you that you have given us eternal life in Jesus. Help me to fix my eyes not on what is seen but on what is unseen.

OLD TESTAMENT READING

Micah 1:1–4:13
Inward and unseen power

What the prophet Micah says can be true for us all, 'As for me, *I am filled with power*, with the Spirit of the LORD, and with justice and might' (3:8a). Power comes from the inward and unseen work of the Holy Spirit.

Micah spoke with great power. He championed the cause of the underprivileged. As in the case of Jonah, Micah's warnings were heeded and disaster was avoided (see Jeremiah 26:18).

Micah spoke out against injustice and greed. Like most sin, it starts with inward and unseen plans: 'Woe to those who *plan iniquity*, to those who *plot evil* on their beds!' (Micah 2:1a).

They sow thoughts and reap actions. 'They covet fields and grab them, find homes and take them. They bully the neighbour and his family, see people only for what they can get out of them' (vv.1b–2). (This is an extraordinarily accurate description of what we would now describe as 'land grabbing'.)

Micah's words are particularly aimed at the 'leaders' (3:1a). 'Should you not know justice, you who hate good and love evil' (vv.1b–2a). He accuses them of treating the people like animals (vv.2–3). He warns them that if they treat the poor unjustly, God will not hear their prayers (v.4).

Money seems to have been at the root of the injustice. As so often, it is greed that leads to injustice:

> 'Judges sell verdicts to the highest
> bidder,
> priests mass-market their teaching,
> prophets preach for high fees,
> All the while posturing and pretending
> dependence on GOD' (v.11, MSG).

One day, God will put things right. God 'will judge between many peoples and will settle disputes' (4:3). There will be peace. Nation will not take up sword against nation, nor will they train for war any more' (v.3b). There will also be justice. There will be a fair dispersal of land: 'Everyone will sit under their own vine and under their own fig-tree' (v.4a).

Ultimately what matters is the *inward* and *unseen thoughts of God*, '...they do not know *the thoughts of the LORD*; they do not understand *his plan*' (v.12).

PRAYER

Lord, thank you that one day you will right all wrongs and bring everlasting peace. In the meantime, filled with the Spirit of the Lord, help me to fix my eyes on you.

1 September | Day 244
Find Your Purpose in Life

'What a *waste*!' said a woman to my friend. This woman was talking about Bishop Sandy Millar, who had practised very successfully as a lawyer for ten years, before leaving it all behind to become an ordained minister in the church.

'A *waste*?' exclaimed my outraged friend. 'Yes,' said the woman, 'Such a waste! He could have made a fortune and been at the very top of the legal profession. Think of what he *could have* achieved!'

'Think of what he *has* achieved!' replied my friend – who was thinking of the impact of Sandy's ministry on thousands of people around the world whose lives had been changed, marriages enriched and churches renewed; those who found faith, love, hope and peace through encountering Jesus Christ as a result of Sandy's ministry.

Many have given up a successful career, a high salary and – in the eyes of the world – all their prospects, in order to serve God in 'full-time ministry' with little or no pay. They know that theirs is a high calling and purpose that far exceeds what the world can promise them.

Of course, those called to serve God in their secular places of work have an equally high purpose and calling, if they are doing what they are doing in order to please God and for the sake of his kingdom. The key is not the job or career – but the goal you pursue.

So many people waste their lives. They have no purpose, meaning or goal. Other people do have a goal, but it is the wrong one. They end up chasing something that is ultimately meaningless. Many reach the top of the ladder of success only to find that it is leaning against the wrong wall. Purpose in life is far more important than property or possessions. Having more to live with is no substitute for having more to live *for.*

It has been said that 'the two greatest days of your life are the day you were born and the day you find out why'. God created you with a purpose in mind (2 Corinthians 5:5).

READING FROM PROVERBS

Proverbs 21:17–26
Pursue righteousness and love

Many people today lead hedonistic lives. 'Hedonism' is the pursuit of pleasure as the ultimate goal. Hedonists become addicted to the things that give them pleasure.

'You're addicted to thrills? What an empty life! The pursuit of pleasure is never satisfied' (v.17, MSG).

There is nothing wrong with pleasure (also, there is nothing wrong with saving): 'In the house of the wise are stores of choice food and oil' (v.20). But relationships are far more important than riches: 'Better to live in a tent in the wild than with a cross and petulant spouse' (v.19, MSG).

The purpose and goal of your life should never revolve around material things. Rather, 'Whoever *pursues righteousness and love* finds life, prosperity and honour' (v.21). Make this the aim of your life – to pursue a right relationship with God and a right relationship with others.

Love should be your aim: 'Sinners are always wanting what they don't have; the God-loyal are always giving what they do have' (v.26, MSG).

The irony is that those who pursue righteousness and love find what the hedonist is seeking: 'life, prosperity and honour' (v.21b). But these are by-products. They should not be your aim or purpose. Rather it should be God's kingdom and his righteousness. Jesus promises 'all these things will be given to you as well' (Matthew 6:33).

PRAYER

Lord, help me not to waste my life in pleasure-seeking but to seek your kingdom – to pursue righteousness and love in everything I do.

NEW TESTAMENT READING

2 Corinthians 5:1–10
Aim to please God

Paul's main aim and purpose in life was to please God: 'Pleasing God is the main thing, and that's what we aim to do, regardless of our conditions' (v.9, MSG).

You may face physical challenges. Your physical body will not always be able to do what you used to do. One day 'these bodies of ours' will be 'taken down like tents and folded away, they will be replaced by resurrection bodies in heaven' (vv.1–2, MSG).

When you put your faith in Jesus Christ, you are promised all the blessings of the kingdom of God. Yet we still feel weak and sinful, still experience hardship and frustration, and still live in a broken world. How much of the blessing of the kingdom must you wait for in the future, or on the last day, and how much do you experience here and now in the present?

There is a balance between what you will experience in the *future* and what you experience *now*. Now, you are 'away from the Lord. You live by faith, not by sight' (vv.6–7). In the future, you will be 'at home with the Lord' (v.8). What is mortal will be 'swallowed up by life' (v.4). You will not experience the full blessing of the kingdom yet.

Nevertheless now, in the present, you experience a foretaste of the future. God 'has made us for this very *purpose*' and has given us his Spirit as a '*deposit*, guaranteeing what is to come' (v.5). 'He puts a little of heaven in our hearts so that we'll never settle for less' (v.5b, MSG). That deposit is not just an assurance – it is a piece of the *not yet* of God's blessing, reign and rule in the *now*. That is what the Holy Spirit brings.

'That's why we live with such good cheer ... Cramped conditions here don't get us down. They only remind us of the spacious living conditions ahead' (v.6, MSG).

While we wait, 'We make it *our goal* to please him' (v.9). 'Sooner or later ... We will appear before Christ and take what's coming to us as a result of our actions, either good or bad' (v.10, MSG).

PRAYER

Lord, help me to make this goal the focus of my life. Lord, I want to please you in everything I do, say and think.

OLD TESTAMENT READING

Micah 5:1–7:20
Rise to Micah's challenge

It is possible to have a wasted soul. Through the prophet Micah, God warns against:

> 'Obscene wealth ...
> piled up by cheating and fraud ...
> shady deals and shifty scheming ...
> No matter how much you get, it will never be enough –
> hollow stomachs, empty hearts.
> No matter how hard you work, you'll have nothing to show for it –
> bankrupt lives, *wasted souls*' (6:10–14, MSG).

At times, Micah looks forward (for example, see 7:7–20). At one point he unknowingly prophesies about Jesus (Matthew 2:5–12). He sees *a ruler coming from Bethlehem*, 'Whose origins are from of old, from ancient times ... And he will be their peace' (Micah 5:2, 5a). He will be known as '*Peacemaker of the world*!' (v.4b, MSG).

At other times, Micah looks back. He looks at all that God has done for his people (see 6:3 onwards). He redeemed them. He led them (v.4). He urged them to 'remember' (v.5).

God is a God of astonishing love and mercy: 'Mercy is your specialty. That's what you love most. And compassion is on its way to us. You'll stamp out our wrongdoing. You'll sink our sins to the bottom of the ocean' (7:18–19, MSG).

Through Jesus your past is totally forgiven. Don't keep looking back with regret. God has 'hurled all [your] iniquities into the depths of the sea' (v.19), and there is 'no fishing' allowed.

What will your response be to this amazing grace? Micah presents this challenge: 'To *act justly* and to *love mercy* and to *walk humbly with your God*' (6:8c). This threefold challenge gives us the purpose and goal of our lives.

1. Act justly

Justice is very high up on God's agenda. Injustice causes so much of the world's suffering today. I have to make this a higher priority in my own life and in our community. We must do more to see that the poor, the marginalised and the voiceless receive justice.

2. Love mercy
God has shown us such mercy. Our response should be to show mercy. Don't put pressure on others to perform perfectly; love and accept them for who they are. We need to bring the message of the gospel of God's love and mercy to as many as possible, including the prisoners, the homeless, the elderly and the poor.

3. Walk humbly with God
Never see yourself as better, above, or more important than other people. A proud person overestimates their own importance. They cannot laugh at themselves. 'Don't take yourself too seriously – take God seriously' (v.8c, MSG). We cannot do any of this unless we are walking in a relationship with the Lord.

These three go together. True faith is evidenced by how you live. This is why Paul writes that 'the things done while in the body' (2 Corinthians 5:10) really matter. You will be judged by them. They are the evidence of your faith.

PRAYER

Lord, help me to act justly, to love mercy, and to walk humbly with you.

---

2 September | Day 245
Recognise Who You Are

The ambassadors I have met have always impressed me enormously. They have clearly been chosen very carefully. They have all been trained in the art of diplomacy. They are skilled at representing their country by both how they act and what they say.

To be an ambassador is an immense privilege. An ambassador is 'a minister of the highest rank sent to a foreign court to represent the ... sovereign or country'. A British Ambassador is a minister who represents Queen and country wherever they are sent.

Paul writes that we are 'Christ's ambassadors' (2 Corinthians 5:20). The Greek word translated as 'ambassador' shares the same root as 'presbyter', which is one of the words used to describe church leaders. Whether you are in a recognised leadership role in the church or not, you are an ambassador of Christ, with the extraordinary privilege and responsibility of representing Jesus in this world. You are God's representative on earth.

Through you, God makes his appeal for others to be reconciled to God; to receive his forgiveness, love and grace. Appeal to them to become friends of God and ambassadors themselves. As royal ambassadors, act with diplomacy and skill because you are representing Christ on earth.

READING FROM PSALMS

Psalm 105:1–11
Ambassadors to the whole world

We are called as ambassadors to be a blessing to all nations. Jesus called us to go out to all the world and make disciples of all nations (Matthew 28:19–20). The people of God are blessed in order to be a blessing to the whole world.

'Give thanks to the LORD, call on his name; make known among the nations what he has done' (Psalm 105:1). Today, some of us do not even need to travel to be in contact with many nations. In London, where I live, practically every nation in the world is represented.

The psalmist writes, 'Remember the wonders he has done' (v.5a), and then he goes on to do exactly that. He goes back through all the things God has done for them.

What are some of your favourite memories? Take time to remember God's blessing and to thank him. Find a diplomatic way, as an ambassador for Christ, to 'tell everyone you meet what he has done!' (v.1, MSG).

As an ambassador for Jesus, stay close to him. 'Look to the LORD and his strength, seek his face always' (v.4).

PRAYER

Lord, thank you for all the amazing wonders you have done for me. As I look to the days ahead, help me to make known among the nations what you have done.

NEW TESTAMENT READING

2 Corinthians 5:11–6:2
Ambassadors with an urgent message

We are all '*Christ's ambassadors*' (5:20). Paul, as an ambassador of Christ, seeks to 'persuade people' (v.11) about the truth of the gospel.

This is a big responsibility. It is urgent. Take it seriously: 'It's no light thing to know that we'll all one day stand in that place of Judgment. That's why we work *urgently* with everyone we meet to get them ready to face God' (v.11, MSG).

God makes his appeal through you. God could have made his appeal direct or through angels. Instead, he has chosen to do it through you and me. 'God has given *us* the task of telling everyone what he is doing' (v.19b, MSG). Paul writes, 'We implore you on Christ's behalf: Be reconciled to God' (v.20). 'Become friends with God; he's already a friend with you' (v.20, MSG).

1. Love is ... the motive

'For Christ's *love* compels us' (v.14). 'His love has the first and last word in everything we do' (v.14a, MSG). You are called to live a life of love. First, love for Jesus, who died for us so that we should no longer live for ourselves but for him (v.15). Second, love for others, because we are convinced that Jesus died for them: 'One man died for everyone' (v.14b, MSG).

2. Love is ... the message

The message is: 'God loves you.' He welcomes you with open arms. Because Jesus died for you, you can be a friend of God. You can approach him boldly and confidently as often as you choose.

The message is all about reconciliation (vv.18–19). Reconciliation is about restored friendship in a relationship of love – with God and with one another. It's a huge privilege and joy to see people reconciled to God and to one another – especially in marriages, families and other broken relationships.

It is made possible through Jesus' death and resurrection: 'God put the wrong on him who never did anything wrong, so we could be put right with God' (v.21, MSG).

Paul writes that '*God was* reconciling the world to himself *in Christ*' (v.19). Some people caricature the New Testament teaching and suggest that God is barbaric and unjust because he punished Jesus, an innocent party, instead of us. This is not what the New Testament says. Rather, Paul writes, 'God was ... in Christ.' He was himself the substitute in the person of his Son. He made it possible for us to be restored in a relationship with him.

As a result, 'If anyone is in Christ, there is a new creation: the old has gone, the new has come!' (v.17). As the New Living Translation puts it, 'Those who become Christians become new persons. They are not the same anymore, for the old life is gone. A new life has begun!' (v.17).

3. Love is ... the means

Never pressurise people. Rather, try to persuade them (v.11) because you love them. Implore them on Christ's behalf (v.20). You are Christ's representative. Jesus always acted in love and as his ambassadors you represent this love.

Paul writes, 'I hope you realise how much and deeply *we care*' (v.11, MSG). As is often said, 'People don't care how much you know until they know how much you care.'

PRAYER

Lord, help me to be a good ambassador of Christ. Help me to live a life of love. May Jesus' love compel me in everything I do.

OLD TESTAMENT READING

Isaiah 1:1–2:22
Ambassadors of holy love

'The characteristic name for God in Isaiah is "The Holy",' writes Eugene Peterson. 'Holiness is the most attractive quality, the most intensive experience we ever get of sheer life – authentic, firsthand living, not life looked at and enjoyed from a distance ... Holiness is a furnace that transforms the men and women who enter it.'[1]

Isaiah's message is about God's holy love for his people. God loves his people more than any parent loves a child.

Yet Isaiah says, 'For the LORD has spoken: "I reared children and brought them up, but they have rebelled against me"' (1:2). He goes on to speak of all the ways in which his children have rebelled – their unfaithfulness, the injustice they allow, and their failure to look after the widows and orphans (vv.21–23).

God's desire is for holiness:

> 'Sweep your lives clean of your
> evildoings
> so I don't have to look at them any
> longer.
> Say no to wrong.
> Learn to do good.
> Work for justice.
> Help the down-and-out.
> Stand up for the homeless.
> Go to bat for the defenseless'
> (vv.16–17, MSG).

But they have failed and rebelled. Further, they are full of superstitions, they practise divination, and their land is full of materialism and idols (2:6–8).

Their religiosity is not working. The Lord says, 'I have no pleasure in the blood of bulls and lambs and goats' (1:11c). 'I can't stand your trivial religious games ... I'm sick of your religion, religion, religion, while you go right on sinning' (vv.13–14, MSG).

Yet, God does not abandon them. He says, 'Come now, let us reason together' (v.18). 'If your sins are blood-red, they'll be snow-white. If they're red like crimson, they'll be like wool' (v.18, MSG).

He promises, 'Afterward you will be called the City of *Righteousness*, the Faithful City. Zion will be redeemed with justice, her penitent ones with *righteousness*' (vv.26b–27a). Like Micah, he promises justice and peace will come (2:2–4).

But how? How can we who are sinful and rebellious be made righteous? How can we, whose 'sins are like scarlet', be made 'white as snow' (1:18)? How will these remarkable promises of the Old Testament be fulfilled?

Only in Jesus do we find the solution. The Old Testament prophets foreshadow what was to come. The New Testament tells us how: in today's New Testament passage we read how 'God made him [Jesus] who had no sin to be sin for us, so that in him we might become the righteousness of God' (2 Corinthians 5:21).

Jesus, who 'had no sin', was made sin for us on the cross so that in him, though our sins are like scarlet, we could be made white as snow and become the righteousness of God. You become friends with God and an ambassador for Christ.

PRAYER

Lord, thank you for the immense privilege of being your ambassadors, able to take your message to a world that desperately needs forgiveness and hope.

---

3 September | Day 246
How Your Life Can Make a Difference

Alfred Nobel (1833–1896) is best known for the Nobel Peace Prize. Less well known is the fact that Alfred Nobel also invented dynamite. As well as a chemist, engineer and innovator, he was a weapons' manufacturer.

In 1888, Alfred's brother *Ludvig* died. A French newspaper erroneously published *Alfred's* obituary. It condemned him for his invention of dynamite, stating: 'The merchant of death is dead ... Dr Alfred Nobel, who became rich by finding ways to kill more people faster than ever before, died yesterday.'

Alfred Nobel was devastated by the foretaste of how he would be remembered. His last will and testament set aside the bulk of his estate to establish the Nobel prizes. He gave the equivalent of US $250 million to fund such prizes. Alfred Nobel had the rare opportunity to evaluate his life near its end and live long enough to change that assessment.

Have you ever wondered what difference your life might make? How can your life bring blessing to other people? How can you change the world for the better? How can your life be of ultimate lasting value? How can we lead fruitful lives?

READING FROM PSALMS

Psalm 105:12–22
Fruitfulness comes from faithfulness to God

If your life is to be fruitful you have to stay faithful to God in the difficult times. It is relatively easy to be faithful to God when all is going well in life. The test comes when you face fierce temptation and great trials.

As the psalmist gives thanks to God for *his faithfulness* to his people, he recalls the life of Joseph.

Joseph's life was immensely fruitful (see Genesis 37–50). Pharaoh 'made him master of his household, *ruler over all he possessed*, to *instruct* his princes as he pleased and *teach* his elders wisdom' (Psalm 105:21–22). As a result, 'The LORD made his people *very fruitful*' (v.24a).

But, Joseph's fruitfulness came at a price. In the early days, it did not seem like his life would be at all fruitful. He was 'sold as a slave' (v.17). 'They bruised his feet with shackles, his neck was put in irons' (v.18). Joseph went through betrayal, slavery, temptation, imprisonment and a great deal of suffering.

Yet in all this he remained faithful. The reason for Joseph's faithfulness was that he trusted that God was in control, even in the bad times (Genesis 45:5–8; 50:20). And eventually 'the word of the LORD proved him true' (v.19).

Not only did Joseph remain faithful to God despite his seeming abandonment, but he also remained faithful to his family in totally forgiving them, rather than blaming and rejecting them. Ultimately, his faithfulness led to great fruitfulness.

PRAYER

Lord, thank you for your amazing faithfulness to me. Help me to be faithful to you even in the difficult times of temptation, disappointment and discouragement. Like Joseph, may my life be fruitful.

NEW TESTAMENT READING

2 Corinthians 6:3–7:1
Fruitfulness comes from the Holy Spirit

Your life can be immensely fruitful, because the Holy Spirit lives within you. You are 'a temple in whom God lives' (6:16, MSG). Just as in the Old Testament God dwelt in the Holy of Holies, so now he dwells in you and me by his Holy Spirit. The Holy Spirit produces beautiful fruit in your life (Galatians 5:22–23).

Paul's life was arguably one of the most fruitful in the history of the world. He describes himself as a servant of God (2 Corinthians 6:4). In his lifetime he made many rich (v.10). The 'riches' for Paul were the spiritual riches of being in Christ. His life continues to make many rich. The fruit of Paul's life has lasted 2,000 years and will endure into eternity.

Like Joseph, Paul's fruitfulness came at a price. He lists some of the things he endured: 'hard times, tough times, bad times; when we're beaten up, jailed, and mobbed; working hard, working late, working without eating ... slandered ... distrusted; ignored by the world ... beaten within an inch of our lives ... immersed in tears ... living on handouts ... having nothing' (vv.4–10, MSG). As I look at Paul's life, I feel so challenged. It puts all my problems into perspective.

In all this suffering, Paul remained faithful 'in purity, understanding, patience and kindness; in the Holy Spirit and in sincere love; in truthful speech and in the power of God' (vv.6–7a). He remained 'genuine' and 'always rejoicing' (vv.8, 10). He says, 'We are penniless ... in reality we have everything worth having' (6:10b, J. B. Phillips).

Paul says to the Corinthians, 'We have spoken freely to you ... and opened wide our hearts to you. We are not withholding our affection from you' (vv.11–12a). He is open and vulnerable with the Corinthians and pleads with them to open their hearts to him in the same way. He says, 'Open up your lives. Live openly and expansively!' (v.13, MSG).

Paul had explored his own inner territory. He had taken a journey into the places in his heart and soul where buried treasures lie. He had carefully examined them and brought them out for display.

To act with integrity, you must first know who you are. You must know what you stand for, what you believe in and what you care most about.

Bear Grylls writes, 'People tend to think that they have to be funny, witty or incisive on stage. You don't. You just have to be honest. If you can be intimate and give the inside story – emotions, doubts, struggles, fears, the lot – then people will respond.'[1]

The Holy Spirit is the one who sets you free to be yourself. He is the one who produces fruitfulness in your life.

Paul does not want anything to spoil this fruitfulness in the lives of the Corinthians. He pleaded with them, 'Don't become partners with those who reject God' (v.14, MSG). He was not suggesting that they remove themselves from the world (1 Corinthians 5:9–10). Rather, he is warning of the danger of long-term partnerships with those who reject God.

Many people have ignored these warnings – for example, in terms of marriage partners – and some have ended up within months or years no longer going to church and then eventually losing their faith. It is heart-breaking to watch.

'So,' Paul writes, 'leave the corruption and compromise; leave it for good' (2 Corinthians 6:16, MSG). He goes on, 'Let's make a clean break with everything that defiles or distracts us, both within and without. Let's make our entire lives fit and holy temples for the worship of God' (7:1, MSG).

PRAYER

Lord, fill me with your power through your Holy Spirit. Enable me to be pure, patient, kind and truthful and to love sincerely with a wide-open heart.

OLD TESTAMENT READING

Isaiah 3:1–5:7
Fruitfulness comes from closeness to Jesus

God loves you. He wants you to stay close to him. He wants you to be a branch in his vine – producing fruit.

When we are unfaithful to him, it is like being cut off from the vine. We become unfruitful. Isaiah writes, 'The one I love had a vineyard, a fine, well-placed vineyard ... He looked for a vintage yield of grapes, but for all his pains he got junk grapes ... He looked for a crop of justice and saw them murdering each other. He looked for a harvest of righteousness and heard only the moans of victims' (5:1–7, MSG).

Much of the first thirty-nine chapters of Isaiah are about God's judgment: 'God enters the courtroom. He takes his place at the bench to judge his people. God calls for order in the court, hauls the leaders of his people into the dock' (3:13, MSG).

God's people have been unfaithful to him: 'You've played havoc with this country. Your houses are stuffed with what you've stolen from the poor. What is this anyway? Stomping on my people, grinding the faces of the poor into the dirt?' (vv.14–15, MSG).

They have enjoyed great material riches, which have led to pride, immorality and greed (vv.16–23).

Isaiah sees a coming judgment, and on that day 'the Branch of the LORD will be beautiful and glorious' (4:2).

This was only partially fulfilled at that time. Like many other prophecies, it points forward to what we can now see was achieved through Jesus, who was the true 'Branch of the Lord' (v.2). Jesus is *the* Branch from the vine of God. We are the branches from the vine of Jesus (see John 15:1–8).

Jesus is the true branch and the true vine. He is the one who was totally faithful and fruitful beyond any human being (even Joseph or Paul!). He now invites you to be part of his vine, to stay close to him and to bear much fruit – fruit that will last (John 15:8, 16).

PRAYER

Lord, I want my life to make a difference. Thank you that you have made that possible. Keep me close to you, faithful and filled with the Holy Spirit, bearing fruit that will last.

4 September | Day 247
How Can You Be Useful to God?

Pippa and I had just returned home from the hospital. Earlier that day, my mother had died of a heart attack while at her desk at work. She was sixty-nine.

I was in a state of shock and turmoil within. I wandered out of our home for a breath of fresh air and was thinking that the one person I really wanted to see was Sandy Millar – our pastor and friend.

At that moment, I looked up and recognised his car approaching. He had just heard our news and had driven straight round to see us. God *used Sandy's arrival* that day to bring us great comfort and encouragement.

In today's New Testament passage, we read that *Titus's arrival* was *used* by God to bring Paul great comfort and encouragement when Paul was in a state of turmoil, exhaustion, oppression, affliction, dread and fear: 'But God, Who comforts and encourages and refreshes and cheers the depressed and the sinking, comforted and encouraged and refreshed and cheered us by the *arrival of Titus*' (2 Corinthians 7:6, AMP).

Titus's arrival brought even further encouragement because he carried news of how the Corinthians were being useful to God. As a result, Paul 'rejoiced still more' (v.7, AMP).

However bleak things may appear, God always seems to raise up people who are instruments 'for noble purposes ... *useful* to the Master and prepared to do any good work' (2 Timothy 2:21). How can you and I be *useful* to God?

READING FROM PSALMS

Psalm 105:23–36
Be prepared to take the lead

Do you sometimes feel you are in a spiritual wasteland in your workplace, your city, or even in your entire nation?

The psalmist recalls one of the bleakest periods for the people of God. God had blessed them. They had become 'very fruitful' (v.24). But their success caused them to be hated (v.25a). Their foes conspired against them (v.25b). 'They abused and cheated God's servants' (v.25, MSG).

The people of God were oppressed and enslaved. They were in a 'spiritual wasteland' (v.27, MSG). But God 'sent Moses his *servant*, and Aaron, *whom he had chosen*' (v.26). God chose Moses and Aaron. They responded (admittedly very reluctantly in the case of Moses) to the call to lead. They performed miraculous signs and wonders and set God's people free: 'They worked marvels in that spiritual wasteland' (v.27, MSG).

PRAYER

Lord, as I look at our nation and see the state of the church, I cry out to you to raise up people like Moses and Aaron to lead your people out of the spiritual wasteland.

NEW TESTAMENT READING

2 Corinthians 7:2–16
Turn to God in times of trouble

Sometimes in life we hit a wall of pain and distress. It overwhelms us. It could be caused by bereavement, redundancy, sickness, disappointment, or other circumstances beyond our control. It could even, as in the case of the Corinthians, be caused by our own sin or mistakes.

What matters is *how you respond*. For some, times such as these drive them away from God. For others, like the Corinthians, it is the making of them. Their distress drove them to God. It transformed them into a people whom God was able to use powerfully.

Paul was someone whom God used greatly. But it was not a smooth ride; it was not a stress-free life. Paul did not go around bringing trouble on his own head. He writes, 'We have never hurt a soul, never exploited or taken advantage of anyone' (v.2, MSG). Nevertheless, he continues to speak of 'all our troubles' (v.4). He writes about 'fights in the church' and the 'fears in our hearts' (v.5, MSG).

Paul loved the Corinthians (vv.3–4a). Although Paul's love for them was not always reciprocated, it brought him enormous joy when it was. When he heard from Titus about their longing for him, and their deep sorrow and ardent concern for him, he said 'my joy was greater than ever' (v.7).

Paul had the courage to confront them in a letter. Initially it caused them hurt (v.8) – as this kind of confrontation often does. At first, Paul regretted writing the letter but thankfully the Corinthians had the right response. They allowed it to draw them closer to God. We all mess up at times. Godly King David sinned greatly (2 Samuel 11 and 12). Even the great apostle Peter messed up. However, what matters is how you respond.

'You let the distress bring you to God, not drive you from him ... We never regret that kind of pain. But those who let distress drive them away from God ... end up on a deathbed of regrets' (2 Corinthians 7:9–10, MSG).

The wrong kind of sorrow, typified by Saul in the Old Testament and Judas Iscariot, did not lead to repentance but rather to death: 'worldly sorrow brings death' (v.10c). The Corinthians, like King David (see Psalm 51) and the apostle Peter, responded in the right way.

'And now isn't it wonderful all the ways in which this distress has goaded you closer to God? You're more *alive*, more *concerned*, more *sensitive*, more *reverent*, more *human*, more *passionate*, more *responsible*' (v.11, MSG).

Titus witnessed the transformation in their lives as a result of their response to distress. He was exuberant about it. He was himself revived and refreshed by everything the Corinthians did for him.

He could not stop talking to Paul about them: 'Going over again and again the story of your prompt obedience, and the dignity and sensitivity of your hospitality. He was quite overwhelmed by it all! And I couldn't be more pleased – I'm so confident and proud of you' (vv.15–16, MSG).

PRAYER

Thank you, Lord, that when I turn to you in times of trouble you transform me and make me more alive, concerned, sensitive, reverent, human, passionate, responsible and more useful to you.

OLD TESTAMENT READING

Isaiah 5:8–8:10
Respond to God's call and say, 'I'll go'

As we look around the world today we see many nations in desperate times. The description in this passage is of a nation rife with injustice.

The leaders 'grab all the land ... evicting the old owners ... taking over the country, leaving everyone homeless and landless ... Those extravagant estates will be deserted. A ten-acre vineyard will produce a pint of wine' (5:8–10, MSG).

Meanwhile, the leaders make sure 'their banquets are well furnished' with music and 'plenty of wine' while the common people 'die of thirst'. Their leaders call evil good and good evil (vv.8–22, MSG).

But what authority does Isaiah have to speak to the society in this way? During a dark period in Israel's history, God called him. He describes the vision he had around 740 BC, in the year that King Uzziah died (6:1):

1. He encountered God

Isaiah describes an overwhelming sense of the presence of God – his majesty, holiness, glory and power (vv.1–4). The key words are 'I saw the Lord' (v.1). The key to his call was not just a nice experience; it was a life-changing encounter.

2. He was cleansed

Isaiah saw the holiness of God and said, 'Woe to me ... I am ruined! For I am a man of unclean lips, and I live among a people of unclean lips, and my eyes have seen the King, the LORD Almighty' (v.5). The closer you are to the light the more it reveals your sin.

But then God takes the initiative and provides a means of cleansing: 'Look. This coal has touched your lips. Gone your guilt, your sins wiped out' (v.7, MSG).

It is through the cross of Christ that your guilt is taken away and your sin atoned for. You do not need to go around loaded by guilt, but rather you can be filled with a sense of God's love for you.

3. He said to God, 'I'll go'

Isaiah responded to God's call. God asked him the question – I have done all this for you, now will you go for me? Your whole life is before you, what are you going to do with it? He said, 'Whom shall I send? And who will go for us?' (v.8a).

Isaiah responded, 'Here am I. Send me!' (v.8b). He saw there was a desperate need. He made no excuses. He did not delay. He said to God, 'I'll go' (v.8, MSG). *God used him greatly*.

This was nothing compared to the one whom Isaiah prophesied about. He says, 'The Lord himself will give you a sign: the virgin will be with child and will give birth to a son, and will call him Immanuel' (7:14). This had a historical fulfilment in the birth of Maher-Shalal-Hash-Baz (8:1). However, the ultimate fulfilment of this prophecy was in Jesus Christ, who is Immanuel, God with us (vv.8, 10 – see Matthew 1:23).

PRAYER

Lord, thank you that you say to me 'your guilt is taken away and your sin atoned for' (Isaiah 6:7). I want to respond today by saying to you: 'Here am I, send me!'

5 September | Day 248
Godly Wisdom for Your Finances

'I am so happy I could cry! I am so excited that we might have the chance to go to Focus [our church holiday]! I can't wait to see my children's faces when I tell them!' This was the reaction of a mother with two young children in our congregation when she heard she would be given a bursary (a discounted rate) to come to Focus. At the end of the week she wrote, 'It is the best holiday we have ever had as a family. I am so happy.'

I love the fact that hundreds of people come to Focus on bursaries, or even for nothing. Others give generously to make this possible.

A few months later the mother who had written to me unexpectedly inherited some money from a distant relative. She gave extraordinarily generously. The amount far more than covered the bursary she and her family had received.

This is a practical outworking of the New Testament principle that those who can afford give to help those who cannot afford – so that there might be equality: 'At the present time your plenty will supply what they need, so that in turn their plenty will supply what you need' (2 Corinthians 8:14).

So much of our world is taken up with thinking, writing and talking about money, wealth and riches. The Bible has a great deal to say about these subjects. However, the biblical position is in contrast to that of today's culture.

In today's New Testament passage, Paul tells us that the whole point of the incarnation of Jesus was that you might '*become rich*' (v.9). However, the passages for today totally redefine this world's understanding of the word 'rich'.

READING FROM PSALMS

Proverbs 21:27–22:6
Fasten on your *reputation* far more than riches

However much money you may acquire, it doesn't guarantee success in life: 'victory rests with the LORD' (v.31).

Reputation is far more important than riches. It is better to do what is right than to make more money by cutting corners, dubious practices or greed. 'A sterling reputation is better than striking it rich; a gracious spirit is better than money in the bank' (22:1, MSG).

Our culture values those on the 'rich list' far more than those dying of starvation in the poorer parts of the world. But the writer of Proverbs says, 'The rich and the poor shake hands as equals – GOD made them both!' (v.2, MSG).

The way of true riches is 'humility and the fear of the LORD' (v.4a). This brings 'riches and honor and life' (v.4b, AMP). It may sometimes bring material wealth. But the New Testament tells us that it always brings something of far more lasting value – *spiritual riches* in Christ.

Put God first in your life. His plans for you are 'good, pleasing and perfect' (Romans 12:2). And 'there is no wisdom, no insight, no plan that can succeed against the Lord' (Proverbs 21:30).

PRAYER

Lord, help me to live a life of integrity and generosity, humility and fear of the Lord.

NEW TESTAMENT READING

2 Corinthians 8:1–15
Follow the example of the one who went from *riches* to *rags*

The singer Lily Allen effortlessly reflects what many people think in her song, 'The Fear':

> 'I want to be rich and I want lots of money
> I don't care about clever I don't care about funny
> I want loads of clothes and **** loads of diamonds.'[1]

So many people want to get rich. There are many examples of people going from 'rags to riches'. However, there are few who have *deliberately chosen* to go from *riches to rags*!

Yet, right at the heart of our faith is one who chose to do exactly that: 'For you know the grace of our Lord Jesus Christ, that though he was rich, yet for your sakes he became poor, so that *you* through his poverty *might become rich*' (v.9). This is the heart of the gospel.

Jesus is the example we are to follow. Not only did he leave the riches of heaven for the poverty of an earthly life, but in that earthly life he chose to be born in poverty and died in the most extreme poverty imaginable.

He came to earth with nowhere to lay his head, and he hung, naked and in agony, on the cross. He did this in order that you might become rich – that you might have all the spiritual treasures of Christ. Jesus has shown us the supreme example of 'rich generosity' and what it means to 'become rich'.

The Macedonian churches followed his example: 'The trial exposed their true colours: They were incredibly happy, though desperately poor. The pressure triggered something totally unexpected: an outpouring of pure and generous gifts. I was there and saw it for myself. They gave offerings of whatever they could – far more than they could afford! – pleading for the privilege of helping out in the relief of poor Christians' (v.2–4, MSG).

Although they were extremely poor, they worked out how much they could give and they gave even more than that.

Paul urged the Corinthians to follow their example. There were many areas of their lives that were excellent (v.7a). Paul said, 'See that you also excel in this grace of giving' (v.7c).

Paul then expounds the New Testament principle that those who have should give to support those who have not (vv.13–15). We see this principle at work at Focus and on many other occasions, including the Alpha Weekends. We invite those who cannot afford to pay to come for nothing (or for whatever they can afford). At the Weekend, we have an offering so that those who can afford it help to pay for those who cannot.

PRAYER

Lord, help me to follow the example of Jesus' generosity and to excel in the grace of giving.

OLD TESTAMENT READING

Isaiah 8:11–10:19

Focus on the *reign* of Jesus rather than on riches

As Lily Allen sings in 'The Fear', if we focus on the wrong things we are 'taken over by the fear'. But Isaiah says, 'Don't fear what they fear. Don't take on their worries. If you're going to worry, worry about The Holy. Fear God-of-the-Angel-Armies' (8:12–13, MSG). The antidote to our irrational fears and worries is faith. Isaiah writes 'I will wait for the Lord ... I will put my trust in him' (v.17).

He warns against focusing on the occult, fortune-tellers, spiritualists and consulting the dead (v.19): 'Tell them, "No, we're going to study the Scriptures." People who try the other ways get nowhere – a dead end ... A blank wall, an empty hole. They end up in the dark with nothing' (vv.20–22, MSG).

He also warns against pride and 'arrogance of heart' (9:9). In addition, he has much to say on the subject of riches.

First, riches in themselves do not satisfy: 'Appetites insatiable, stuffing and gorging themselves left and right with people and things. But still they starved' (v.20, MSG). However much money we make, it will never satisfy the deep spiritual hunger in every human heart.

Second, he warns against making money at the expense of the poor (10:1–3). Injustice is at the heart of so much suffering in the world: 'Doom to you who legislate evil, who make laws that make victims – Laws that make misery for the poor, that rob my destitute people of dignity, exploiting defenseless widows, taking advantage of homeless children' (vv.1–2, MSG).

There are many countries in the world where we can see exactly this happening. A few people become very rich at the expense of the poor, the widows and the orphans. There are unjust laws and no justice for the people. Isaiah asks the question about the day of judgment: 'Where will you leave your riches?' (v.3d). All this money at the end of the day is utterly meaningless: 'What good will all your money do you?' (v.3d, MSG).

Into this world of injustice and inequality the prophet Isaiah sees a different kind of ruler arising – the ultimate fulfilment was, of course, in Jesus Christ: 'For to us a child is born, to us a son is given, and the government will be on his shoulders. And he will be called Wonderful Counsellor, Mighty God, Everlasting Father, Prince of Peace. Of the increase of his government and peace there will be no end' (9:6–7a).

The more you allow the rule of Jesus in your life, the more he directs your plans, decisions, conversations and thoughts – the wiser you will become and, instead of being 'taken over by the fear', the more you will experience his peace.

Peace does not come from money, riches, success, promotion, clothes or diamonds. It comes from living under the rule of Jesus in justice and righteousness, following his example of rich generosity.

PRAYER

Lord, I worship you, the Wonderful Counsellor, Mighty God, Everlasting Father and Prince of Peace. Help me to follow your example of generosity and find the path to true riches, honour and life.

6 September | Day 249
How to Love Your Lord

What was wrong with these people? Were they weird? Was it a cult? What was this strange expression they seemed to use?

Of course, I knew that God or even Jesus could be called 'Lord', but never before had I heard God referred to so often by a group of people as 'The Lord'. In the years since then, as I have studied the Bible, I have begun to understand why these Christians, whom I first met at university, used this expression so often: they loved their Lord! Now he is *my* Lord. I, too, love the Lord.

'The Lord' is the most common way of referring to God in the Old Testament. When written in capitals, this word translates the Jewish covenant name for God, *YHWH*. Out of respect for God, Jews do not use the word. Historically, we have often pronounced the word as 'Jehovah', when in fact it sounds more like 'Yahweh'. When the Old Testament was first translated into Greek (c. 250 BC) the name *YHWH* was translated as *Kurios* (the Lord). This translation is then reflected in the New Testament.

The New Testament gives us a more Trinitarian understanding of 'The Lord'. It makes the remarkable claim that *Jesus is the Lord*. In fact, whether someone can say 'Jesus is Lord' becomes the test of Christian authenticity (1 Corinthians 12:3). It also makes the claim that the Holy Spirit is Lord: 'Now *the Lord is the Spirit*, and where the Spirit of the Lord is, there is freedom' (2 Corinthians 3:17).

God the Father is Lord. God the Son is Lord. God the Holy Spirit is Lord. But there is only one Lord: 'One Lord ... one God' (Ephesians 4:5–6). The one Trinitarian God is Lord. The New Testament understanding of the Lord helps us interpret the Old Testament use of 'The Lord'. The Old Testament enriches our understanding of what the New Testament means when it speaks of 'The Lord'.

How can you love your Lord?

READING FROM PSALMS

Psalm 105:37–45
Praise your Lord in worship

'*Praise the Lord*' (v.45b) sums up this whole psalm. The psalmist worships and praises God for who he is and all he has done for his people: rescue (v.37), protection (v.39a), guidance (v.39b), answered prayer (v.40a), satisfaction (v.40b), faithfulness (v.42), joy (v.43) and hope (v.44).

He writes, 'They fell heir to what others had toiled for' (v.44). Of course, this originally referred to the exodus. However, it is so often true in our own lives that we 'fall heir' to, or take possession of, what others have toiled for.

I often think of this in relation to Alpha. So many people worked extraordinarily hard over many, many years to lay the foundations for Alpha – Charles Marnham, John Irvine, John Collins, Sandy Millar and Nicky Lee, to name but a few. Those of us involved now have fallen heir to what others have toiled for.

Are there people like this in your life? Are there parents, friends, pastors or others who you can thank God for today because you have fallen heir to what they have toiled for?

Supremely, we see this verse fulfilled in Jesus. You have fallen heir to everything that Jesus achieved for you through the cross and resurrection. He did the toiling. We are the heirs.

Don't forget to praise and thank your Lord for all his blessings.

PRAYER

I praise you, Lord Jesus Christ, that you have brought me forgiveness, peace, joy, purpose, satisfaction, fullness, hope, fellowship, freedom, love, power, guidance and light. Praise the Lord!

NEW TESTAMENT READING

2 Corinthians 8:16–9:5
Honour your Lord in giving

Money matters. It can be a curse or a blessing. It can bring honour to the Lord or dishonour.

Paul's desire is to '*honour the Lord* himself' (8:19). Here 'the Lord' seems to be referring to *Jesus Christ* (see v.23). He wants to do what is right in *the eyes of the Lord* (v.21).

In his handling of the offering (v.19) he is determined, first, to honour the Lord himself by 'taking every precaution against scandal' (vv.19–20, MSG). This includes any chance that someone might suspect him of using the money for himself (vv.20 –21).

Second, he is at pains to do what is right not only *in the eyes of the Lord* but also to be 'as careful in our reputation *with the public*' (v.21, MSG).

One way in which we can do this is to ensure that those who handle money in the church are like Titus, whom Paul describes as 'rock-solid trustworthy' (v.17, MSG). This is a good test for those involved in handling money in the church. Are they 'rock-solid trustworthy'?

Another way in which we can honour the Lord with our money is through generosity.

God has been so generous to us. Paul expects the Corinthians to be generous. He speaks of the 'generous gift you had promised ... a generous gift, not as one grudgingly given' (9:5).

The enthusiasm of one group of Christians spread to others, hundreds of miles away, even at a time without modern forms of communication. St Paul writes, '*...your enthusiasm* has stirred most of *them* to action' (v.2). How much greater is the impact that you can have now with global communication. What huge potential there is for any church to bring honour to the Lord.

PRAYER

Lord, may my generosity reflect your extraordinary generosity to me. May it bring honour to your name.

OLD TESTAMENT READING

Isaiah 10:20–13:22
Know your Lord in relationship

The astonishing truth is that, thanks to Jesus, you and I can know the Lord. We can *all* know the Lord.

God calls his people into a relationship with him. The expression 'The Lord' appears twenty times in this passage alone. The prophet Isaiah foresees a time when 'the earth will be *full* of *the knowledge* of *the Lord* as the waters cover the sea' (11:9b). The kind of relationship God calls you to is a:

1. Relationship based on faith

The prophet Isaiah looks forward to a time where his people 'will truly *rely on the* Lord, the Holy One of Israel' (10:20). He goes on to say that on that day they will say, 'Surely God is my salvation; *I will trust* and not be afraid. The Lord, the Lord, is my strength and my song; he has become my salvation' (12:2–3).

Here, at the heart of the Old Testament, we see that faith ('*I will trust*') and salvation are strongly linked. The New Testament makes it abundantly clear that you are saved by your faith in the Lord (Jesus).

2. Relationship based on respect

Isaiah speaks of 'the fear of the Lord'. Isaiah calls the people of God to fear God but says '*do not be afraid* of the Assyrians' (10:24). If you truly fear God (in the biblical sense of holy respect) you need fear *nothing* and *no one* else.

3. Relationship brought about by the Holy Spirit

Knowing the Lord involves watching and listening to the Holy Spirit, allowing him to lead you in your heart. Isaiah writes:

> 'The life-giving Spirit of God will hover over him,
> the Spirit that brings wisdom and understanding,
> The Spirit that gives direction and builds strength,
> the Spirit that instills knowledge and Fear-of-God' (11:2, MSG).

When the Holy Spirit comes to live in your life he brings you into a relationship of knowing the Lord. For me, it was only when I experienced the Holy Spirit that the expression 'the Lord' became among the most precious expressions in the world.

Isaiah's words were fulfilled in Jesus: 'A shoot will come up from the stump of Jesse; from his roots a Branch will bear fruit. The *Spirit of the Lord* will rest *on him*' (11:1–2a, see also 53:2).

Isaiah goes on to speak about how God will be the perfect judge (11:3b–5). His reign of justice and peace will reverse the results of the fall (see Romans 8:19–22). 'The wolf will live with the lamb' (Isaiah 11:6). This promise strains our imaginations in a conflict-ridden world – one day 'neither animal nor human will hurt or kill' (v.9, MSG).

God has a global vision: 'The whole earth will be brimming with *knowing* God-Alive, a *living knowledge of God* ocean-deep, ocean-wide' (v.9, MSG). So should we. William Booth, the founder of the Salvation Army, said, 'I am thinking up a plan, that when it is hatched, will bring blessing to the whole wide world.'

Jesus has made it possible for you to know God. The same Spirit of the Lord who rests on Jesus is given to you. He will give you wisdom and understanding, counsel and power so that your life can have a huge impact.

PRAYER

Lord, fill me with your Spirit that I may seek justice on behalf of the poor and needy. Help me to be a peacemaker and to play my part in spreading knowledge of the Lord until it covers the earth 'as the waters cover the sea' (v.9).

7 September | Day 250
Ten Reasons to Give Generously

Mick Hawkins was the most generous person I have ever met. He was always giving and always offering to pay for everything. We thought he must be very rich. Actually, he wasn't. He was just very generous. His life overflowed with thankfulness for God's grace. This opened his heart and his wallet in a way that inspired all who knew him.

I want to be like Mick. I long for the church of Jesus Christ to be full of people like him because, as we see in today's passage, grace, thanksgiving and generosity are very closely connected.

READING FROM PSALMS

Psalm 106:1–15
Thank God for grace by your worship

When we begin to experience God's grace, gratitude is the natural and appropriate response. The psalmist is overwhelmed by gratitude and worships God, saying, '*Praise* the Lord. Give *thanks* to the Lord, for he is good; his love endures for ever' (v.1).

He goes on to say, 'We've sinned a lot ... We've fallen short, hurt a lot of people ... forgot your great and wonderful love' (vv.6–7, MSG). They had 'rebelled' against God (v.7d).

Years ago, by this psalm, I wrote in the margin of my Bible: 'I sometimes wonder whether I sin more than any other Christian ... how can God go on forgiving?' If you feel like that sometimes, you are not alone.

But, the next verse starts with the word 'yet'. This is grace. In spite of everything:

- '*he saved them* for his name's sake' (v.8a)
- '*he led them*' (v.9b)
- '*he redeemed them*' (v.10b).

As a result of God's amazing grace, 'they believed his promises and sang his praise' (v.12). But 'they soon forgot what he had done and did not wait for his counsel' (v.13).

Again, I have written in my margin: 'This is the history of my Christian life – for a day or two, or even a week or two, I believe his promises and sing his praises ... but then I soon go out and forget what he has done and fail to wait for his counsel, or to ask his advice about everything.'

Let's not be as they were – complaining every step of the way and always wanting what they did not have (v.14). They 'lusted exceedingly' (v.14, AMP) and God 'gave them their request, but sent leanness into their souls' (v.15). Sometimes God says, 'Your will be done', and gives people what they ask for, even if it is not the best thing for them. Rather than craving after more, enjoy and thank God for what you have through his grace and kindness to you.

PRAYER

Lord, thank you for your amazing grace and forgiveness – that you have redeemed me

and you lead me. Help me to believe your promises, sing your praise and not forget what you have done for me.

NEW TESTAMENT READING

2 Corinthians 9:6–15
Thank God for grace by your giving

In this passage Paul gives us at least ten reasons to give generously:

1. Giving is the *best investment* you can make
Like the harvest, giving is planting seed. The farmer will reap far more than what was sown (v.6): 'A stingy planter gets a stingy crop; a lavish planter gets a lavish crop' (v.6, MSG).

This applies to everything in life. What you give to the Lord he multiplies – your time, gifts, ambitions and money.

2. Giving should be *fun*
Giving should never be forced or grudging, but rather voluntary and cheerful 'for God loves a cheerful giver' (v.7). The Greek word for cheerful is *hilaros*. We always quip at HTB that our giving should be *hilarious*! It should be fun to give. Generosity leads to happiness.

3. Giving *takes away the burden of financial worry*
Paul writes, 'and God is able to make all grace abound to you, so that *in all things at all times*, having *all that you need*, you will abound in every good work' (v.8). Giving does not mean handing over financial responsibility to God – but it does mean handing over the worry and the burden of it.

4. Giving *'enriches' you*
When God invites you to give, he is appealing not just to your emotions but also to your reason: 'Thus you will be enriched in all things and in every way so that you can be generous' (v.11, AMP). Materially, you will have enough to give away generously (v.11). Your character will be enriched (v.10). God will be praised (v.11).

5. Giving *transforms your character*
Paul speaks of 'the harvest of your righteousness' (v.10b). Giving purges the character from the constricting grip of materialism that destroys lives.

6. Giving *inspires others*
'...your generosity will result in *thanksgiving to God* ... Because of the service of which you approved yourselves, people will praise God...' (vv.11b–13a).

7. Giving *meets people's needs*
Generous giving blesses other people and supplies the needs of God's people – 'helping meet the bare needs of poor Christians' (v.12, MSG).

8. Giving is *evidence of real faith*
Generous giving is an act of obedience, which should accompany 'your confession of the gospel of Christ' (v.13). Giving is an act of trust – in doing it you are saying that it is God, not yourself or anyone else, who ultimately provides for your needs.

9. Giving *makes you a stakeholder* in the church
Paul speaks of 'your generosity in *sharing* with them and with everyone else' (v.13b). In the same way as when you share a flat or apartment you share in the bills, as you share in the needs of the community you reap the benefits of that community. For example, every time someone comes to know Christ through the community you share in the blessing.

10. Giving is *a response to God's gift to you*
God so loved you that he gave his one and only Son so that you might have eternal life (John 3:16). Our giving is a response to God's amazing grace. His 'indescribable gift' (2 Corinthians 9:15) is the gift of his Son. 'Thank God for this gift, his gift. No language can praise it enough!' (v.15, MSG).

PRAYER

Lord, thank you for the indescribable gift of your Son, Jesus Christ. Help me to respond with generosity and grace to your amazing grace.

OLD TESTAMENT READING

Isaiah 14:1–16:14
Thank God for his grace in your life

How do we explain the evil of Isis – beheadings, crucifixions of Christians and Yazidis, women and children sold into slavery? How do we explain, for example, the Holocaust, Stalin's exterminations or the Rwandan genocide?

This is one of the few passages in the Bible that hints at the origins of Satan and demonic powers.

The beauty of a diamond is best seen set against a black velvet cloth. The beauty of God's grace is also seen in its full glory and brilliance against the darkness of evil. The prophet Isaiah speaks of God's amazing compassion (14:1). The dark background is the evil of the nations around; in particular, Babylon's cruelty, torture, persecution and slave trade.

Isaiah describes Babylon's fall: 'You said in your heart, "I will ascend to heaven; I will raise my throne above the stars of God; I will sit enthroned on the mount of the assembly, on the utmost heights of the sacred mountain. I will ascend above the tops of the clouds; I will make myself like the Most High." But you were brought down to the grave, to the depths of the pit' (vv.12–15).

Jesus similarly describes Satan's fall (Luke 10:18). Perhaps it was pride and arrogance that led to an angelic fall before the fall of Adam and Eve.

But against this dark background there is also a hint of a beautiful diamond.

> 'The tyrant toppled,
> The killing at an end,
> all signs of these cruelties long gone,
> A new government of love will be established in the venerable David tradition. A Ruler you can depend upon
> will head this government,
> A Ruler passionate for justice,
> a Ruler quick to set things right'
> (Isaiah 16:4b–5, MSG).

Whatever the historical fulfilment may have been, there is only one person who perfectly fits this description – Jesus the Messiah, born in the line of David, who brought together God's love and his justice. Unlike the satanic '*I will*' (14:13, 14), Jesus denied himself and said, 'Not what *I will,* but what *you will*' (Matthew 26:39).

The only appropriate response to God's amazing grace revealed in Jesus Christ is to give him thanks with your worship, your giving, and your whole lives – to surrender your life to him and say, 'I am willing to do whatever you want.'

Whatever you are facing, you can trust that God's purposes will ultimately be accomplished: 'For the LORD Almighty has purposed, and who can thwart him?' (Isaiah 14:27).

PRAYER

Lord, thank you that we experience your amazing grace, love and faithfulness in Jesus. Thank you that he seeks justice and speeds the cause of righteousness. Help me, like him, to have a concern for the poorest of the poor and the needy (v.30) and to give generously.

8 September | Day 251
Winning the Spiritual Battle

A tragic image is unforgettable. Like so many people, I wept as I saw the picture of 3-year-old Alan Kurdi's little body washed up on the shoreline in Turkey. He had drowned, together with his brother and mother, as his family fled the war in Syria in 2015.

One of the biggest causes of the current European refugee crisis is warfare. Over 200,000 people have been killed in the civil war in Syria in recent years. In Iraq, Isis have murdered thousands of innocent people (many of them Christians) and displaced tens of thousands of people (again, many of them Christians). Appalling terrorist attacks around the world now occur with alarming regularity.

These atrocities are extreme and horrific instances of a violence that has always taken place at every level of society. 'Brother fight brother, neighbor fight neighbor, city fight city, kingdom fight kingdom – anarchy and chaos and killing!' (Isaiah 19:2, MSG).

Virtually every day in the media we see the horrors of warfare. We live in a world that is constantly developing even more terrible weapons of physical warfare. These weapons have the power to maim, kill and destroy. But this warfare is not purely physical. The issues that give rise to it, as many in both politics and the media acknowledge, are profoundly moral and spiritual.

Just as physical warfare is a serious global issue, so, according to the apostle Paul, is spiritual warfare (see Ephesians 6:10–20). This is unseen, but it is just as real. The great Welsh preacher, Dr Martyn Lloyd-Jones, once said, 'There is no grosser or greater misrepresentation of the Christian message than that which depicts it as offering a life of ease with no battle and struggle at all ... sooner or later every believer discovers that the Christian life is a battleground, not a playground.'[1]

In this battle, you are called not to be overcome by evil but to overcome evil with good (Romans 12:21). You are given the weapons with which to win the battle. Paul writes, 'We do not wage war as the world does. The weapons we fight with are not the weapons of the world. On the contrary, they have divine power to demolish strongholds' (2 Corinthians 10:3b–4).

What are these weapons? How do you use them?

READING FROM PSALMS

Psalm 106:16–31
The weapon of prayer

The psalmist recalls the leadership and ministry of Moses. Some became jealous about God's powerful use of Moses and Aaron: 'In the camp they grew envious of Moses and of Aaron' (v.16).

Moses' response was not to protect himself. Rather, it was to pray for them. He 'stood in the breach' before God (v.23), and interceded for them. In the account of Exodus 32:11–14 we see how, by the power of prayer, it is possible to change the course of history.

Phinehas was another who 'intervened' on behalf of the people (see Numbers 25). His intervention must have stemmed from his faith. We are told here that, as with Abraham, it was credited to him as righteousness (Psalm 106:31).

The powerful weapon of prayer is available to you. Pray for your family, friends and all those who the Spirit inspires you to pray for. 'Stand in the breach' and intercede on behalf of others. As Jeremy Jennings says at the end of every prayer meeting at HTB, 'Thank you for praying. *You have made a difference*.'

PRAYER

Lord, thank you for the power of intercessory prayer. Today, I want to stand in the breach and intercede for...

NEW TESTAMENT READING

2 Corinthians 10:1–18
The weapon of the gospel

Your mind is a battlefield. Your thoughts are at the root of your words and actions. The devil seeks to set up strongholds in your mind. Paul knew that at the heart of the spiritual battle is *the battle for the mind*. There is a sense in which each of us is involved in an individual spiritual battle in our own mind. This is a daily battle to resist the temptation of wrong thoughts and take captive every thought to obey Christ (v.5).

Although Paul alludes to the individual battle of the mind here, he was primarily thinking of something a little different. There was a cultural battle going on: a battle of ideas, philosophies and worldviews. Paul actively engaged in this battle to take on those competing ideas, philosophies and worldviews; to take them captive in obedience to Christ.

Paul wrote, 'The world is unprincipled. It's dog-eat-dog out there! The world doesn't fight fair. But we don't live or fight our battles that way – never have and never will. The tools of our trade aren't for marketing or manipulation, but they are for demolishing that entire massively corrupt *culture*.

'We use our powerful *God-tools* for smashing warped philosophies, tearing down barriers erected against the truth of God, fitting every loose thought and emotion and impulse into the structure of life shaped by Christ. Our tools are ready at hand for clearing the ground of every obstruction and building lives of obedience into maturity' (vv.3–6, MSG).

The 'weapons' Paul uses have 'divine power' to 'demolish strongholds' (v.4). His power comes from belonging to Christ (v.7), and he has been given authority by the Lord himself (v.8).

I find it encouraging that some people said of Paul, 'In person he is unimpressive and his speaking amounts to nothing' (v.10). However, he points out 'in all this comparing and grading and competing, they quite miss the point' (v.11, MSG). Comparison is corrosive. It either puffs you up to pride or drives you down to despair.

Don't compare yourself with other Christians, your gifts with their gifts, your 'success' with their 'success'. We are all on the same side. We should be trying to help, love and encourage one another as we fight the spiritual battle together.

Thankfully, you do not have to appear impressive, nor do you have to be an exceptional communicator to preach the gospel. Paul's power came from the 'gospel of Christ' (v.14). His desire was to 'preach the gospel' (v.16) to people who had never heard it.

Ultimately it is the 'message of Christ' (v.14, MSG) that will change your culture. It is the most powerful message in the world. It is life changing. It is culture changing. It is world changing.

Every time you tell a friend about Jesus, invite them to church or bring them along to Alpha, for example, you are in engaging in the spiritual battle with the powerful weapon of the gospel (see Romans 1:16).

PRAYER

Lord, help me to take every thought captive to obey you and give me the courage to use the powerful weapon of the gospel to destroy strongholds.

OLD TESTAMENT READING

Isaiah 17:1–19:25
The weapon of unity

Every year at our Leadership Conference[2] at the Royal Albert Hall in London, we have the privilege of welcoming thousands of Christian leaders from all around the world. There is something very powerful about leaders from numerous countries coming together in worship and unity of purpose. The prophet Isaiah foresees this kind of unity.

He continues to prophesy against those who have 'forgotten God your Saviour' (17:10). He declares God's judgment against Damascus, Cush and Egypt.

However, our passage today ends with a note of hope: 'In that day there will be an altar to the LORD in the heart of Egypt ... It will be a sign and witness to the LORD Almighty in the land of Egypt. When they cry out to the LORD because of their oppressors, he will send them a saviour and defender, and he will rescue them. So the LORD will make himself known to the Egyptians, and in that day they will acknowledge the LORD ... They will turn to the LORD, and he will respond to their pleas and heal them' (19:19–22).

He goes on to say that the Egyptians and Assyrians (modern-day Iraqis) will worship together: 'No longer rivals, they'll worship together, Egyptians and Assyrians!' (v.23, MSG).

The conversion of the Gentiles seems to have been foreseen by Isaiah. He sees a time when others, besides the people of Israel, will 'turn to the LORD' (v.22). He will hear their prayers and heal them. People of different nations will worship the Lord together (v.23). This unity will bring great blessing.

He foresees a time when the Lord's people from Egypt, Iraq and Israel come together for worship. Surely we see one way in which this prophecy is fulfilled when Christians from these nations and others come together in worship.

However, we can also pray for, and look forward to, the day when this prophecy will be completely fulfilled – when a multitude 'from every nation, tribe, people and language' will worship together before the throne of God (Revelation 7:9).

PRAYER

Lord, thank you for the power of the weapons you have given us for the spiritual battle. As we unite, pray and proclaim the gospel, may we see your victory in our lives and in our society in Jesus' name.

9 September | Day 252
How to Know and Love Jesus

Sophie is an only child. Her mother had fourteen miscarriages before she was born. Her parents adore her. She adores her parents. Sophie is now an adult, and still loves to spend as much time as possible with her parents.

She told me that when she was at school she and her fellow pupils were asked whether they thought their parents loved them more than they loved each other. Most of them replied that they thought that was the case. However, Sophie replied that she thought her parents loved each other far more, but that it was this very bond of love that made her feel so secure and so loved.

At the heart of the Christian faith is a relationship with God through Jesus Christ. To be a Christian is to know and love Christ.

What is this relationship like? The Bible describes it using human language, and human analogies. It is a relationship of the closest possible intimacy. It is like that of a parent and child (Luke 1; Romans 8). But Paul goes even further in terms of intimacy: he refers to Christ as our husband and the church as his bride (2 Corinthians 11:2; see also Ephesians 5:22–33). This is the closest, most important and most intimate relationship of all.

READING FROM PROVERBS

Proverbs 22:7–16
Enjoy friendship with the King

Ashley Madison is a Canadian-based online dating service marketed to people who are married or in a committed relationship. Its slogan is 'Life is short. Have an affair.'

A book recently published in the UK suggests that adultery may be good for the health of marriages. Nothing could be further from the truth.

Intimate relationships require faithfulness. The Lord 'frustrates the words of the unfaithful' (v.12). 'The mouth of an adulteress is a deep pit' (v.14a). Adultery breaks the faithfulness of marriage and is therefore a 'deep pit'.

'Whoever loves a pure heart and whose speech is gracious will have the king for a friend' (v.11). Here, the writer is referring to a human king. The combination of integrity and charm can bring people into contact with leaders of all kinds, even friendship with a king.

But, not everyone can be friends with the Royal Family. Few people know a human king. Amazingly, you are invited to be friends of the King of kings and Lord of lords: Jesus Christ.

The language used in verse 11, 'pure heart' and 'gracious', is not dissimilar to the language used in 2 Corinthians 11:3: 'Your sincere and pure devotion to Christ'.

Friendship itself requires effort. We have to keep choosing to show love and faithfulness in our actions to maintain an intimate relationship. 'The loafer says, "There's a lion on the loose! If I go out I'll be eaten alive!"' (Proverbs 22:13, MSG). In other words, the lazy person makes far-fetched excuses as to why they do not have to get up and expend any effort.

All intimate relationships, including your relationship with Jesus, require effort and time if they are to grow and flourish. Decide today to devote time and energy to your friendship with Jesus.

PRAYER

Lord, thank you that you invite me to be your friend. Help me to be pure in heart, gracious in speech, generous (v.9) and faithful.

NEW TESTAMENT READING

2 Corinthians 11:1–15
Guard your marriage to Christ

Sometimes we make life too complicated. We can make our faith too complicated. You are called to '*simplicity* that is in Christ' (v.3, KJV). Simplicity does not mean being simplistic. It means having a 'wholehearted and sincere and pure devotion to Christ' (v.3, AMP).

Paul led the Corinthians to faith in Jesus. He introduced them to their husband and called them 'the bride of Christ'. He did not want them to be led astray: 'I promised your hand in marriage to Christ, presented you as a pure virgin to her husband ... you are being lured away from the simple purity of your love for Christ' (vv.2–3, MSG).

Children have a 'simple purity' about their lives. They have an uncomplicated approach to relationships. They enjoy themselves as much as possible. They are carefree and without concern. This is the kind of simplicity you need to guard in your relationship with Jesus.

Paul loved them: 'I care about you so much – this is the passion of God burning inside me!' (v.2, MSG). 'It's not that I don't love you; God knows I do' (v.11, MSG).

Paul was determined to preach 'the gospel of God to [them] free of charge' (v.7). 'I'd die before taking your money' (v.12, MSG). This is one of the reasons why I feel so strongly that no one should ever be charged for going on Alpha. Nor should we ask for money at the end of a course. The gospel must always be 'free of charge'.

However, someone has to give funds to meet the expenses: 'My needs were always supplied by the believers from Macedonia province' (v.9, MSG). Paul was quite happy for other churches to contribute financially so that the gospel could be preached free of charge. It is not wrong to fundraise, but we should not try to raise funds from the people to whom we are preaching the gospel.

Paul is worried that 'the bride' is about to run away with the false teachers – teachers who are preaching a different gospel, a different Jesus in a different spirit (v.4). They, like Satan himself, are masquerading as angels of light (v.14).

This disguise makes spiritual discernment difficult, and also very important. You don't want to be suspicious of other people's motives, but you do need to ask for spiritual insight and wisdom.

Paul is not speaking here about other Christians who see things from a slightly different perspective, or those who have come to a different conclusion to you on secondary matters of doctrine. The people the apostle is warning against are 'money-grubbing preachers', 'pseudo-apostles', 'lying preachers', 'crooked workers', 'sham to the core' (vv.12–13, MSG).

This is not the equivalent of another Christian denomination or tradition. This is not Christian at all. It is 'another Jesus' (v.4, MSG). This is why Paul cares so passionately. To go after 'another Jesus' would be spiritual adultery. He is passionately concerned to guard their sincere and pure devotion as the bride of the true Jesus Christ.

PRAYER

Jesus, I love you. Help me to stay close to you. Keep me loving and serving you with a wholehearted, sincere and pure devotion.

OLD TESTAMENT READING

Isaiah 20:1–23:18
Fix your eyes on your Maker

God created you for an intimate relationship with him. Sadly, both the world, and sometimes even the people of God, chase after other things and fail to look to their Maker and consult him over their plans.

Isaiah announces God's judgment on those who look to or rely on anyone or anything other than God himself (20:5). He says that Tyre, the 'multinational broker ... that controlled the world markets' (23:3, 8, MSG) would crash. God would 'puncture the inflated reputations' (v.9, MSG).

He prophesies against Jerusalem: 'You looked and looked and looked, but you never *looked to him* who gave you this city, never once consulted the One who has long had plans for this city' (22:11, MSG). They were looking to their own strength and not relying on the One who made the city of David, and who ultimately made them as well.

Isaiah also prophesied about Eliakim. He was a good man, as appears from the title applied to him by God 'my servant, Eliakim' (v.20). He is made master of the palace, a post roughly equivalent to prime minister.

God says about him: 'I will clothe him with your robe and fasten your sash around him and hand your authority over to him. He will be a father to those who live in Jerusalem and to the house of Judah. I will place on his shoulder *the key* to the house of *David*; *what he opens no one can shut, and what he shuts no one can open*' (vv.21–22).

This foreshadows the '*key*' that Jesus was to give to Peter and the disciples (Matthew 16:19; 18:18). To them he gave the *keys* of the kingdom but, ultimately, Jesus is the holder of all the keys. In the book of Revelation Jesus is described as the one who 'holds the *key of David*. *What he opens, no one can shut and what he shuts no one can open*' (Revelation 3:7).

Look to him. Consult him about your plans. Do not trust in your own strength but rather to look to your maker. Fix your eyes on Jesus (Hebrews 12:2).

PRAYER

Lord, I commit to you the plans for the term ahead ... Please shut the door on any that are not right. Thank you that no one can shut the door against those plans that are of you.

Lord, most of all, help me to stay faithful in my intimate relationship with you as my friend, my king and my maker.

10 September | Day 253
Peace in the Dark Places

'Men don't come much tougher than daredevil climber and adventurer, Bear Grylls,' writes the *Sun* newspaper. A former member of the UK Special Forces, his TV adventure series *Man vs. Wild* has reached an estimated 1.2 billion viewers in over 180 countries.

Not being remotely adventurous or daring myself, as I read his autobiography, *Mud, Sweat and Tears,* I was spellbound, gripped and horrified by his sheer physical and mental endurance. He has survived the SAS, a broken back from a parachute jump, climbing Mount Everest, the French Foreign Legion and a variety of other extraordinary challenges.

One of the things I appreciated about reading Bear's autobiography was his refreshing openness about his struggles, both inward and outward. With admirable vulnerability, he reveals his anxieties, fear of heights and sense of weakness. Through it all his strong Christian faith shines through. He writes, 'Faith in Christ has been the great empowering presence in my life, helping me *walk strong* when so often I *feel so weak.*'[1]

In the midst of life's difficulties and extraordinary challenges, Christ is the empowering presence who brings us peace.

'Perfect peace' (Isaiah 26:3) makes me think of a beautiful, calm summer's day, sitting by a deserted lake with not a care in the world and no temptations, no problems and no difficulties to cope with. 'Perfect peace' in such circumstances would not be at all surprising or extraordinary. Yet as we read the Bible, it is clear that this promise of 'perfect peace' is not dependent on circumstances. God's peace comes to you even in the dark places – in the midst of your most difficult struggles and challenges.

READING FROM PSALMS

Psalm 106:32–39
Temptation

The temptations that the people of God faced in the past are, in some ways, no different from those that we face today. 'They rebelled against the Spirit of God' (v.33), 'they *mingled* with the nations and adopted *their customs*. They worshipped *their idols* which became a snare to them' (vv.35–36).

You are called to be 'in the world' but not 'of the world'. This is such a difficult tension. As you mingle with those who do not share your faith or lifestyle, the temptation is to adopt their customs and worship their idols. The idols of the twenty-first century include money, sex, power and celebrity. Their influence on us can be quite subtle.

We should be able to enjoy all the good gifts that God has given us, without ever becoming obsessed with anything, or worshipping anything other than the living God.

The second-century *Letter to Diognetus* described the Christian's lifestyle in the following way:

> They live in their own countries, but only as aliens. They have a share in everything as citizens, and endure everything as foreigners. Every foreign land is their fatherland, and yet for them every fatherland is a foreign land ... It is true that they are 'in the flesh', but they do not live 'according to the flesh'.
>
> They busy themselves on earth, but their citizenship is in heaven. They obey the established laws, but in their own lives they go far beyond what the laws require ... They are poor, and yet they make many rich ... *Christians dwell in the world, but are not of the world.'*

PRAYER

Lord, help me not to worship the idols of the culture, or take on the customs of those I spend time with outside the church. Help me to resist these temptations and experience your 'perfect peace'.

NEW TESTAMENT READING

2 Corinthians 11:16–33
Trials

Paul's opponents have fallen into the very trap warned against in Psalm 106. They have adopted the customs of the world around them and worshipped its idols. They are 'boasting in the way the world does' (v.18).

They have boasted of their achievements, they have wallowed in a culture of fame, success and showy rhetoric.

Their boasting forces Paul into a different kind of boasting. They, like the world, were boasting about their strengths. Paul says that if he must boast he 'will boast of the things that show [his] *weakness*' (v.30).

He lists some of the things that he has been through. It is not the usual list of things about which most people would boast. Rather they are, almost entirely, a list of things of which most people would be ashamed even to mention, let alone celebrate.

They include often being in prison, being flogged five times with the Jews' thirty-nine lashes, beaten by Roman rods three times, stoned with rocks once, shipwrecked, exposed to many dangers, hungry and thirsty, cold and naked (vv.23–27). The list culminates with what might appear to be a rather shameful escape from an arrest (vv.32–33).

In addition to all this, Paul lists his hard work (v.23), his travels (v.26) – 'I have laboured and toiled and often gone without sleep' (v.27) – the daily pressure of his concern (anxiety) for all the churches (v.28) and the pain he experiences when Christians are led into sin (v.29). He had plenty of anxiety, stress and challenges in his life.

Yet in spite of all this, Paul often spoke about the peace of God that he experienced and prayed for others to experience. God's 'perfect peace' does not mean that there are no trials to face. What is extraordinary about his peace is that it is promised in spite of the trials. I cannot begin to imagine how it is possible to experience perfect peace in prison, being flogged, shipwrecked, constantly in danger, and much more besides. Yet this is what the apostle Paul seems to have experienced.

He writes, 'Do not be anxious about anything, but in everything, by prayer and petition, with thanksgiving, present your requests to God. And the peace of God, [that is 'perfect peace'], which transcends all understanding, will guard your hearts and your minds in Christ Jesus' (Philippians 4:6–7).

As E. H. Bickersteth wrote, 'Peace, perfect peace, in this dark world of sin? The Blood of Jesus whispers peace within.'[2]

PRAYER

Lord, help us in our trials, criticism, bereavement, temptations, sicknesses and concern for all the churches. Even in the dark places, help me to live in such a way as to know your 'perfect peace'.

OLD TESTAMENT READING

Isaiah 24:1–26:21
Trust

Isaiah writes, 'You will keep in *perfect peace* those whose minds are steadfast ['whose mind is stayed on You', AMP] because *they trust in you*. *Trust* in the LORD for ever, for the LORD, the LORD, is the Rock eternal' (26:3–4). This is the secret of perfect peace. It comes from trust in the Lord, in spite of the trials and temptations: 'We trusted in him, and he saved us' (25:9).

When we think too much about tomorrow – the problems, challenges and responsibilities we are going to face – we can easily become worried and anxious. Yet, in all the trials and temptations of life, God promises to keep you in perfect peace if you turn your thoughts to God and keep your mind 'stayed' on him, trusting in him.

In today's reading, Isaiah seems to be foreseeing the end of the world. There is going to be a devastating judgment (chapter 24). Yet it will also be a day of triumph (chapter 25).

He foresees a heavenly banquet: 'On this mountain the LORD Almighty will prepare a feast of rich food for all peoples, a banquet of aged wine – the best of meats and the finest of wines' (25:6), 'he will swallow up death for ever. The Sovereign LORD will wipe away the tears from all faces; he will remove the disgrace of his people from all the earth' (v.8).

Isaiah appears to get a glimpse of the new heaven and the new earth spoken of in the book of Revelation when God 'will wipe every tear from their eyes. There will be no more death or mourning or crying or pain, for the old order of things has passed away' (Revelation 21:4).

The prophet goes on to say, 'Your dead will live; their bodies will rise. You who dwell in the dust, wake up and shout for joy' (Isaiah 26:19). Arguably, this is the first clear reference in the Bible to individual bodily resurrection. It points to the bodily resurrection of Jesus, who is 'the firstborn from among the dead' (Colossians 1:18).

Jesus has conquered death and thereby defeated the fear of death and with it every other fear and anxiety. Because of Jesus, your future is totally secure. You do not need to be worried or anxious about death or anything else. Trust him with your future, turn your thoughts towards him and begin to experience his constant and perfect peace.

Lord, 'my soul yearns for you in the night; in the morning my spirit longs for you ...

you establish peace for us; all that we have accomplished you have done for us ... your name alone do we honour' (Isaiah 26:9, 12–13).

PRAYER

Lord, I commit to you all the possible causes of anxiety at the moment ... and I put my trust in you.

11 September | Day 254
His Grace Is Enough for You

I first met Nick Vujicic when he came to speak at Focus, our church holiday. Nick is a remarkable man. I think that all of us who met him were inspired and challenged by his life.

Nick was born without arms or legs, yet he can write, 'I am truly blessed. I am *ridiculously* happy.'[1] Many times as a child he prayed for arms and legs. He would have settled for getting one arm or leg.

God did not answer his prayer in the way that he had hoped. Yet he writes, 'God used me to reach people in countless schools, churches, prisons, orphanages, hospitals, stadiums and meeting halls. Even better, I've hugged thousands of people in face-to-face encounters that allow me to tell them how very precious they are ... God took my unusual body and invested me with the ability to uplift hearts and encourage spirits.'[2]

The people of God depend on the grace of God. Mother Teresa wrote, 'I don't think there is anyone who needs God's help and grace as much as I do. Sometimes I feel so helpless and weak. I think that is why God uses me. Because I cannot depend on my own strength, I rely on Him twenty-four hours a day. If the day had even more hours, then I would need His help and grace during those as well.'[3]

Paul expresses this dependence when he writes about the 'thorn in his flesh'. Three times he pleaded with the Lord to take it away. But God said to him, 'My grace is sufficient for you, for my power is made perfect in weakness' (2 Corinthians 12:9). His grace is not only amazing; it is 'sufficient'. It is enough.

This is one of my favourite verses in the entire Bible. I often quote this verse to God and remind him of his promise that his power is made perfect in my weakness.

READING FROM PSALMS

Psalm 106:40–48
His grace comes from his great love

'*But*' is a key word in this passage.

The people were 'bent on rebellion' and 'wasted away in their sin' (v.43). '*But,*' says the psalmist, 'he took note of their distress when he *heard their cry ... out of his great love*' (vv.44–45).

The source of the sufficiency of God's grace is '*his great love*' (v.45). Because God loves his people so much, '*many times* he delivered them' (v.43). He 'heard their cry' (v.44).

Some years ago, I wrote in the margin alongside this psalm summing up all the blessings the psalm speaks about. When I 'disbelieve, grumble, disobey, worship the world's idols, sin, do wrong, act wickedly – what does God do? He shows me favour, he comes to my aid, he gives me joy, he is kind, he saves me. He leads me, he redeems me, he answers my prayers, he delivers me, he notes my distress and hears my cry, he shows me his great love.'

No wonder the psalmist ends by saying, 'Praise be to the LORD, the God of Israel, from everlasting to everlasting. Let all the people say, "Amen!" Praise the LORD' (v.48).

PRAYER

Lord, I praise and thank you for your great love for me. Thank you for delivering me over and over again. Thank you for hearing my cry. Thank you for the sufficiency of your grace.

NEW TESTAMENT READING

2 Corinthians 12:1–10
His grace is what you need

We think we will impress people with our strengths, but we connect with people through our vulnerabilities. Most of us want other people to see our strength and are nervous about anyone discovering our weaknesses. We do not advertise our limitations. However, Paul was not afraid of being vulnerable about his frailties.

Paul had some amazing spiritual experiences. He had 'visions and revelations from the Lord' (v.1). He had been 'caught up to the third heaven' (v.2). He had 'heard inexpressible things, things that human beings are not permitted to tell' (v.4). He had 'surpassingly great revelations' (v.7).

Yet Paul did not boast about these things. The false teachers in Corinth boasted about their spiritual experiences, but Paul did not. Rather, he told stories against himself. He *boasted* about his *weaknesses* (vv.5, 9).

He told the Corinthians how God gave him 'a thorn in [his] flesh, a messenger of Satan, to torment [him]' (v.7b). He made this confession in very general terms. Dr Paula Gooder, who wrote her PhD thesis on these verses, says that there are at least thirty-six theories about what the thorn in Paul's flesh could be. The fact that we do not know what it is enables us all to identify with Paul.

I remember our good friend, the evangelist J. John, saying that he had not just one, but three thorns in the flesh! I don't think he told us what they all were but it was encouraging for the rest of us to know that, like all of us, he had his struggles.

Whatever Paul's thorn was, three times he pleaded with the Lord to take it away. But God said to him, 'My grace is sufficient for you, for my power is made perfect in weakness' (v.9). Were it not for the thorn in his flesh, Paul might have become conceited because of the 'surpassingly great revelations' (v.7).

As it was, Paul knew he was totally dependent on the Lord. When things are going well, I am tempted to be proud and self-reliant. When I am struggling and know my weaknesses, I become utterly dependent on the Lord. Christ's power rests on us (v.9). His power is made perfect in our weakness.

Paul has written something absolutely remarkable. He says, 'It was a case of Christ's strength moving in on my weakness. Now I take limitations in stride, and with good cheer, these limitations that cut me down to size – abuse, accidents, opposition, bad breaks. I just let Christ take over! And so the weaker I get, the stronger I become' (vv.7–10, MSG).

PRAYER

Lord, help me, like Paul, to delight in my weaknesses because your power is made perfect in weakness. Thank you that your grace is enough for me.

OLD TESTAMENT READING

Isaiah 27:1–28:29
His grace comes through Jesus

God loves you. He speaks of his people being like a vine. God tends it, waters it, watches over it and cares for it (27:3–4, MSG).

God in his love, judges. He pulls out the thistles and thorn bushes and burns them up (v.4, MSG). There is much here about God's judgment. Yet this is described as 'his *strange* work' (28:21). Martin Luther, the great reformer, made the point that while judgment is Christ's '*strange work*', salvation is his '*proper work*'.

Isaiah continues to announce judgment on those whose attitude is the very opposite of the apostle Paul. Paul had reason enough for his pride (his 'surpassingly great revelations', 2 Corinthians 12:7) but he was, in fact, humble. Ephraim was proud whereas it had no reason for pride.

Isaiah speaks of '*the pride* of Ephraim's drunkards ... *the pride* of those laid low by wine!' (Isaiah 28:1). And '*the pride* of Ephraim's drunkards, will be trampled underfoot' (v.3). Although the Bible tells us that God gives wine to gladden our hearts (Psalm 104:15), it warns of the dangers of excess.

Here Isaiah describes 'the pretentious drunks ... shabby and washed out and seedy – tipsy, sloppy-fat, beer-bellied ... besotted with wine and whiskey, can't see straight, can't talk sense. Every table is covered with vomit. They *live* in vomit' (Isaiah 28:1, 7–8, MSG). He also speaks against the 'scoffers' (v.14, MSG) – in other words the sceptics and cynics.

In the middle of these prophecies of judgment, Isaiah foresees the one who will be the cornerstone of grace: 'Watch closely. I'm laying a foundation in Zion, a solid granite foundation, squared and true. And this is the meaning of the stone: A TRUSTING LIFE WON'T TOPPLE' (v.16, MSG).

Jesus is the cornerstone. He is the 'solid granite foundation' (v.16, MSG). The apostles Paul (Romans 9:33) and Peter (1 Peter 2:4–6) see these verses as referring to Jesus. He is the one on whom the church of living stones is built. He is the one chosen by God but rejected by human beings. Whoever turns to Jesus will never be put to shame (1 Peter 2:4–6). 'He himself bore our sins in his body on the tree ... by his wounds you have been healed' (1 Peter 2:24).

Jesus is your sure foundation. The one who trusts in him will never be dismayed (Isaiah 28:16). He is the source of all grace – the one who died so that you can be forgiven and experience his great love, grace and power for you. Whatever weaknesses and difficulties you may be struggling with today, his grace is enough for you.

PRAYER

Lord, thank you that I am utterly dependent on you and that as I boast of my weaknesses, your power rests on me. Thank you that 'a trusting life won't topple'. Your grace is enough.

12 September | Day 255
How to Stay on God's Paths

I remember reading, years ago, about an incident that occurred on the Italian Riviera. A young man was driving his sports car along a road near the sea. It was a beautiful and scenic route. But the road was not what it seemed.

All along the way were warning signs. Yet, to the young man, the road seemed perfectly good. Disaster awaited him. A landslide had recently created a precipice. No one should have been on that road. He continued at great speed. He ignored all the warning signs. He went straight over the cliff.

Sometimes we are not sure where a path will lead. At other times, we are well aware of where it leads but choose to follow it nevertheless.

Jesus said that there is a path that leads to life. There is also a path that leads to destruction (Matthew 7:13–14). Warning signs are not put up as a threat, but out of love. The signs on the Italian Riviera were erected to keep people safe. The words of Jesus, the New Testament and the Bible as a whole, are designed to keep us on the path that leads to life.

How do you make sure that you are on the right path? Once you are on that path, how do you stay on it?

READING FROM PSALMS

Psalm 107:1–9
Get on the 'wonderful road'

'Oh, thank God – he's so good! His love never runs out' (v.1, MSG). You cannot improve on God's purpose for you. God is good. He loves you. He wants the very best for your life. He has a 'wonderful road' for your life.

He wants you to walk on his paths: 'He put your feet on a *wonderful* road that took you straight to a *good* place to live' (v.7, MSG). He doesn't want you wandering for 'years in the desert, looking but not finding a good place to live, half starved and parched with thirst, staggering and stumbling, on the brink of exhaustion' (v.4–5, MSG).

The good news is that, wherever you are, you can 'cry out to the Lord' (v.6a). When you do so, he pours 'great draughts of water down parched throats; the starved and hungry' get 'plenty to eat' (v.9, MSG).

This is a psalm of thanksgiving for God's many occasions of deliverance of his people. Four times the psalmist says, 'Then they *cried out to the Lord* in their trouble' (vv.6, 13, 19, 28). Each time, God rescues them.

Furthermore, nothing that you have done in the past disqualifies you from being part of God's people. The only qualification is that you should call out to God and be redeemed (v.2). Redemption means to be 'set free by God'. Jesus came to make this redemption possible.

The 'redeemed of the Lord' are to 'tell their story' (v.2). Speak out and tell others your story of how the Lord has rescued you.

PRAYER

Lord, thank you so much for the many times in my life when I have cried out to you in my trouble and you have brought me out of my distress. Lead me, I pray, on a straight path.

NEW TESTAMENT READING

2 Corinthians 12:11–21
Live on the path of love

The apostle Paul was absolutely determined to do the right thing. He wanted to follow the right path (v.18).

He had been falsely accused. The 'super-apostles' (v.11) had tried to undermine him. As a result, he had been misunderstood and attacked by those who ought to have known better. Absurdly, he had been accused of not wanting to take money from the Corinthians because he didn't love them (v.13).

Paul points out that the reason he didn't take money from them was because he did not want to be a burden to them. He says, 'What I want is not your possessions but you. After all, children should not have to save up for their parents, but parents for their children' (v.14b).

It was because of his love for them that he would have gladly spent everything for them and indeed expended himself as well (v.15). Always acted in a way that is 'aboveboard' and 'honest' (v.18, MSG). Everything Paul did was for their benefit (v.19). He was not interested in their money or possessions. He was interested in their souls.

Just as Paul has done the right thing and stayed on the right course, he wants the Corinthians to do the same. He is afraid that some of them may be going off course: 'Quarrels, jealousy, flaring tempers, taking sides, angry words, vicious rumors, swelled heads, and general bedlam' (v.20, MSG).

He is afraid that when he comes to them he will find that crowd 'that keeps sinning over and over in the same *old ways*, who refuse to turn away from the pigsty of evil, sexual disorder and indecency in which they wallow' (v.21, MSG).

Turn away from these things to be sure that you are on the path that leads to life. The path that leads to life is a path of love – the kind of love that Paul has for the Corinthians.

PRAYER

Lord, help me always to act in love and out of concern for those to whom I am ministering. May I never seek my own personal gain. Rather, may my only motivation be love. Keep me, Lord, on your paths.

OLD TESTAMENT READING

Isaiah 29:1–30:18
Ask God about his plans for you

Sometimes we make our own independent plans or run straight to other people for help. We don't ask God first. As Joyce Meyer says, 'When you've got a problem: don't go to the phone, go to the throne.'[1]

The prophet Isaiah criticises God's people for the way in which they made their plans. They failed to consult God (30:1–2). As a result, they had gone off in the wrong direction. They had gone off to Egypt without so much as asking God.

The trouble is, they didn't really want to know God's plans. Their worship is a mere formality (29:13): 'These people make a big show of saying the right thing, but their hearts aren't in it. Because they act like they're worshiping me but don't mean it' (v.13, MSG).

Jesus says these words were not written simply for the people of Isaiah's day. He says to the Pharisees and the teachers of the Law, 'You hypocrites! Isaiah was right when he prophesied about you: "These people honour me with their lips, but their hearts are far from me. They worship me in vain; their teachings are merely human rules"' (Matthew 15:7–9).

Because their hearts are not right with God, they go to great depths to hide their plans from the Lord: 'You pretend to have the inside track. You shut God out and work behind the scenes, plotting the future as if you knew everything ... You treat the potter as a lump of clay. Does a book say to its author, "He didn't write a word of me"? Does a meal say to the woman who cooked it, "She had nothing to do with this"?' (Isaiah 29:15–16, MSG).

As a result, 'You make plans, but not mine. You make deals, but not in my Spirit ... *Going off to Egypt without so much as asking me*' (30:1b–2a, MSG).

They are 'unwilling to listen to the Lord's instruction. They say to the seers, "See no more visions!" and to the prophets, "Give us no more visions of what is right ... leave this *way,* get off this *path* and stop confronting us with the Holy One of Israel"' (vv.9a–11).

They did not want the prophets to give them any warnings. They ignored the warning signs. In fact, they wanted to take the warning signs off the road and for the prophets to 'leave this way, get off this path' (v.11). They said, 'We'll rush off on horseback!' (v.16, MSG).

Sometimes in my own life I have messed up by not consulting God and charging ahead with my own plans.

But this passage also contains hope that 'those who got off track will get back on track' (29:24, MSG). God says, 'Your salvation requires you to turn back to me and stop your silly efforts to save yourselves. Your strength will come from settling down in complete dependence on me (30:15, MSG).

God is actively looking to bless you: 'The Lord longs to be gracious to you' (v.18a) 'and therefore He lifts Himself up, that He may have mercy on you *and* show loving-kindness to you. For the Lord is a God of justice. Blessed (happy, fortunate, to be envied) are all those who [earnestly] wait for Him, who expect *and* look *and* long for Him [for His victory, His favor, His love, His peace, His joy, and His matchless, unbroken companionship!]' (vv.18b–18c, AMP).

PRAYER

Lord, I want to know your plans. Help me to hear your voice. Help me to come to you in 'repentance and rest', to walk in your paths 'in quietness and trust' (v.15).

13 September | Day 256
Jesus Christ Lives in You

I brought in a boxing glove as a visual aid. I dangled the glove and showed how ineffective it was without a hand in it. Then I put my hand in the glove, made a fist and punched the air so that everyone could see the difference it made to the power of the glove.

I was speaking at a prison for teenagers in Oxford. I was a theological student at the time and was given the opportunity to speak in a chapel service.

The prison chaplain at the detention centre, who was helping with my training, pointed out that it was an inappropriate illustration for a prison, since it might suggest that Jesus and violence were closely associated! Apart from that, he agreed that it was a good analogy.

What I was trying to illustrate was the difference it makes when Jesus Christ comes to live in you by his Spirit. Without him we are weak (2 Corinthians 13:4), like the glove without the hand in it. But when Jesus Christ comes to live within you, you have God's power in your life (vv.4–5).

If you 'realise' (v.5) this, it will transform the way you live your life.

READING FROM PROVERBS

Proverbs 22:17–27
Fill your heart with *God's* Wisdom

How healthy is your heart? Have you filled it with God's wisdom? Just as what you put in your mouth affects the health of your body, what you put in your heart really matters.

The writer urges you to keep the wisdom of God's word *in your heart,* to 'treasure its sweetness deep within' and to have it ready on your lips, so that your 'foundation is trust in GOD…' (vv.17–19a, MSG). As you learn the wisdom of Scripture (for example, by memorising Bible verses), your trust in the Lord is deepened (v.19).

He then lists thirty 'principles – tested guidelines to live by' (v.20, MSG). These are thirty 'truths that work' (v.21, MSG), the first few of which are in today's passage:

1. How you treat the poor and needy. Be kind. Don't exploit them. Don't crush them (vv.22–23).
2. How to avoid becoming ensnared by anger and a bad temper: 'Bad temper is contagious – don't get infected' (vv.24–25, MSG).
3. Warning against gambling and practical advice on how to avoid getting into debt. Don't put up security for other people's debts (vv.26–27).

These sayings are wise principles that help you to live well. The heart of wisdom is more than good advice. It is about putting 'your trust … in the LORD' (v.19).

In the New Testament, we learn that Jesus is '*the Wisdom*' *of God* (1 Corinthians 1:30).

Because Jesus lives in you, you have the wisdom of God in your heart.

PRAYER

Lord, thank you that you live in my heart by your Spirit. Thank you for the power of the word of God. Help me to read it, learn it, meditate on it and have your words ready on my lips that my trust may be in you, the Lord Jesus Christ.

NEW TESTAMENT READING

2 Corinthians 13:1–14
Realise that *Christ Jesus* is in you

Do you realise that Jesus Christ lives within you? The apostle Paul had no doubt that Jesus Christ was living in *him*. He realised that in the words he spoke to the Corinthians, '*Christ is speaking through me*' (v.3).

Paul had the advantage of meeting the risen Jesus. He was able to write with great confidence, 'for to be sure, he was crucified in weakness, yet he lives by God's power. Likewise, we are weak in him, yet by God's power we will live with him to serve you' (v.4).

Self-examination is important and is totally different from self-condemnation. He urged them to 'examine and test and evaluate your own selves to see whether you are holding to your faith and showing the proper fruits of it' (v.5a, AMP). The purpose of self-examination is so that you can see what is wrong in your life, admit it, turn from it and be set free by Jesus.

Paul urged the Corinthians to realise that just as Jesus Christ lived in him, so too 'Jesus Christ is in you' (v.5). Paul talks far more often of us being *in Christ* than Christ in us. Nevertheless, the passages in which he puts it the other way round are remarkable. In Colossians 1:27 Paul writes, '*Christ in you*, the hope of glory', and here too he writes about Christ being in you, and the difference it makes: '*Do you not realise that Christ Jesus is in you...?*' (2 Corinthians 13:5).

This is what turns our weakness into strength (v.9). This is why he prayed for their *perfection* (v.9), and was able to urge them to '*aim for perfection*' (v.11).

Of course, none of us will reach perfection in this life. Being a perfectionist is unhealthy. But we can all aim to live in a perfect relationship with God and with one another. He appealed to them, 'be of one mind, live in peace. And the God of love and peace will be with you' (v.11).

How is this possible? Paul ends with the words of 'the grace': 'May the grace of the Lord Jesus Christ, and the love of God, and the fellowship of the Holy Spirit be with you all' (v.14).

The whole Trinity is involved. It is the 'amazing grace' (v.14a, MSG) of *Jesus* that enables you to be constantly forgiven and cleansed. It is 'the extravagant love of God' (*the Father*) (v.14b, MSG) filling your hearts that enables you to aim for perfect love. It is 'the intimate friendship of the *Holy Spirit*' (v.14c, MSG) of Jesus living in you that enables imperfect people to grow into maturity and one day see him face to face. Only then will you reach perfection.

PRAYER

Lord, thank you that you live within me. May your amazing grace flow out of everything I do. Fill me today with the knowledge of your extravagant love and the intimate friendship of your Holy Spirit.

OLD TESTAMENT READING

Isaiah 30:19–32:20
Know God's love poured into your heart by the *Holy Spirit*

It is the result of Pentecost that the Spirit of Christ comes to live within you. God's love for you is poured into your heart by the Holy Spirit of Jesus (Romans 5:5). It is his Spirit who gives you the realisation that you are a child of God and that Christ lives in you.

In this passage, Isaiah sees six pictures of God:

1. Teacher

The Lord is your teacher. He teaches you through 'the bread of adversity and the water of affliction' (Isaiah 30:20). It is often through the hard times in our lives that we learn the most. Jesus described himself as your 'Lord' and 'Teacher' (John 13:14).

2. Guide

'Whether you turn to the right or to the left, your ears will hear a voice behind you, saying, 'This is the way; walk in it' (Isaiah 30:21). The Holy Spirit will lead and guide you along the narrow road that leads to life.

3. Healer
'The LORD binds up the bruises of his people and *heals* the wounds' (v.26). So often when people meet Jesus for the first time they experience healing of hurt and pain from the past. This healing is a lifelong process.

4. King
Jesus is the King who 'will rule in the right way, and his leaders will carry out justice' (32:1, MSG). He rules our lives through the Holy Spirit who lives within us.

5. Wisdom
He is the source of our wisdom (31:1–3). Isaiah warns against trusting in our own strength rather than looking to the Holy One of Israel and seeking help from the Lord (v.1). The Holy Spirit is the source of wisdom in our lives.

6. Mother
He is like a mother bird, who will shield Jerusalem and deliver it (31:5; see Luke 13:34). God is both a Father and a Mother to us. The Holy Spirit is often associated with the feminine side of God's nature.

The Holy Spirit is the 'Spirit of Jesus' (Acts 16:7). Through the Holy Spirit, Jesus comes to live within you.

The prophet Isaiah seems to have caught a glimpse of the day of Pentecost when 'the Spirit is *poured* down on us from above' (Isaiah 32:15a, MSG).

'The Spirit is poured upon us from on high ... justice ... righteousness ... peace ... quietness and confidence for ever ... secure ... undisturbed places of rest ... how blessed you will be' (vv.15–20).

The outpouring of the Spirit leads to great fruitfulness, righteousness and peace (quietness, confidence, security and rest). It leads to generous sowing and freedom. God promises you that if you walk by the Holy Spirit you will enjoy great blessings in this life and into eternity.

PRAYER

Lord, thank you for the privilege of living in the age of the Spirit – an age that the prophet Isaiah only glimpsed. Thank you that now I can experience it to the full – as Jesus Christ lives within me by his Spirit.

14 September | Day 257
'Are You Saved?'

I have a picture, sitting on the windowsill in my study, of Bishop Westcott. It was given to me by his great-grandson. The nineteenth-century English scholar, Bishop B. F. Westcott, was Regius Professor of Divinity at Cambridge University.

On one occasion he was approached by a zealous undergraduate who asked him, '*Are you saved?*' 'Ah,' said the Bishop, 'a very good question. But tell me: do you mean...?' And then he mentioned three passive participles of the Greek verb '*to save*', indicating that his answer would depend on which of the three the student had in mind (the English translation is given here in italics). 'I know *I have been saved*,' he said; 'I believe *I am being saved*; and I hope by the grace of God that *I shall be saved.*'

'Salvation' is a huge and comprehensive word. It means 'freedom'. As the Bishop pointed out, there are three tenses of salvation: you *have been* set free from the *penalty* of sin, you *are being* set free from the *power* of sin and you *will be* set free from the *presence* of sin.

READING FROM PSALMS

Psalm 107:10–22
Know freedom from *the past*

The psalmist continues to give thanks to God for the many times he has *saved* his people when they have cried out to him in their trouble (vv.13, 19). Each time, he set them free.

In this section we see two examples:

1. Freedom from chains of sin
Here the people are sitting in 'deepest gloom', prisoners suffering in *iron chains* (v.10). 'When they cried out to the LORD in their trouble he saved them from their distress' (v.13).

Often what happened to people physically in the Old Testament is a picture of what happens to us spiritually in the New Testament.

Sin leads to darkness and deepest gloom. It is addictive. It chains our hearts. On the cross, Jesus broke the chains. He forgives your sins and sets you free. You, like Charles Wesley, can declare, 'My chains fell off, my heart was free. I rose, went forth and followed thee.'[1]

2. Freedom from fear of death

The psalmist goes on to say that again they rebelled and drew near the gates of death. Again, they cried out to the Lord and he saved them. 'He sent forth his word and healed them; he rescued them *from the grave*' (v.20).

Again, this foreshadows what Jesus did for you. Through his death and resurrection, he rescues you from the grave and from the fear of death. You are freed from death – from the fear of death and all the fears that go with it. No wonder the psalmist wrote:

> 'So thank God for his marvelous love,
> for his miracle mercy to the children he loves;
> Offer thanksgiving sacrifices,
> tell the world what he's done – sing it out!'
> (vv.21–22, MSG).

PRAYER

Lord, how can I ever thank you enough for setting me free from the chains of sin and addiction? Thank you that I need never fear death because you, Jesus, have conquered death through your death and resurrection.

NEW TESTAMENT READING

Galatians 1:1–24
Enjoy freedom in *the present*

Your salvation was won at a great cost. Jesus 'gave himself for our sins to rescue us from the present evil age' (v.4).

Galatians is one of Paul's earliest letters, possibly written as early as AD 48. Paul is burning with indignation because the freedom of the gospel is under threat. Freedom is hard won and easily lost.

Religion can be used as a means of controlling people. That is how Saul of Tarsus had used it. Then he encountered Jesus and experienced something radically different – a freedom that comes from within.

The message of the gospel is one of freedom. You are freed from sin, guilt, shame, addiction and death. You are also set free from justification by works of the law. You do not have to be circumcised. You do not first have to become a Jew before you can become a proper Christian. Paul's passionate indignation in this letter is explained by the fact that the freedom of the gospel was at stake.

In his early travels, he had planted a series of churches in the Roman province of Galatia. He had told them about this Jesus who sets us free. They had experienced this freedom. A few years later some religious leaders had come along questioning Paul's views and authority and trying to introduce rules and regulations that would have taken away the new-found freedom of the Galatians.

They were saying it was not enough to put your faith in Jesus. You had to be circumcised as well. They were drawing the boundaries of what it meant to be a true Christian far too restrictively.

Some today try to draw these kinds of boundaries. They say it is not enough to be a Christian. You need to be 'like us'. You need to be 'evangelical' or 'Catholic' or 'Pentecostal' – you have to be like us, whatever we are. You have to be a *particular type* of Christian to be a proper Christian. But faith in Jesus is enough. You do not need to add to it by circumcision or by any other brand. Accept one another on the basis of faith in Jesus, rather than the type of Christian.

Paul testifies to his own experience of finding this freedom in Jesus and how it changed him from someone who was 'all out in persecuting God's church' and 'systematically destroying it' to 'preaching the very message he had tried to destroy' (vv.13–24, MSG). Paul's conversion reminds us that no one is beyond the reach of God.

Have you ever wondered whether God could use *you*? Have you ever thought that something you have done in the past might disqualify you? Paul's testimony is evidence that God not only forgives, he sets you free and can use you greatly – no matter what you have done in the past.

This testimony was powerful: 'Their response was to recognise and worship God because of me!' (v.24, MSG). Your testimony, even if seemingly far less spectacular than Paul's, will have an impact on those who hear it.

PRAYER

Lord, thank you that the moment we put our faith in Jesus we find true freedom. Help me today, and every day, to live in that freedom.

OLD TESTAMENT READING

Isaiah 33:1–35:10
Anticipate freedom in *the future*

Although you have been saved from the penalty of sin and you are being saved from the power of sin, you are still anticipating an even greater future freedom from the *presence* of sin – from the struggles of this life. You await the time when you will know everlasting joy and when sorrow and sighing will be removed (35:10).

Isaiah paints the picture of a scorched desert (ch.34) – but then he anticipates how the desert will be transformed into a lush garden – with bubbling springs and blossoming crocuses and grass and reeds and flowing rivers (ch.35).

For God's people, as they were being taken into exile in Babylon, they could look forward with anticipation and expectation to being rescued by God and brought back to the freedom of Jerusalem.

Yet, this picture in Isaiah 35 is of something far bigger than just a return to a physical homeland. This is a prophecy of God's people returning to their *eternal* homeland in a new heaven and a new earth.

Isaiah writes of how 'the ransomed of the LORD shall return, and come to Zion with songs and *everlasting joy* upon their heads: they shall obtain joy and gladness, and sorrow and sighing shall flee away' (v.10, KJV).

And, just like the people of Israel, as you are in anticipation of future freedom, how should you wait? In frustration? In anger? In disbelief? In denial? In rejection?

Isaiah gives us two commands as to how to wait:

1. Be strong

'Strengthen the feeble hands, steady the knees that give way. Say to those with fearful hearts, Be strong, do not fear, your God will come' (vv.3–4).

2. Be holy

'A highway will be there; it will be called the Way of Holiness. The unclean will not journey on it; it will be for those who walk in that Way; ... only the redeemed will walk there and the ransomed of the LORD will return' (vv.8–9).

Whatever the highs and lows of life are for you, try to lift up your head and look forward. You can look forward through struggles, through challenges, even through your own death, until you come in your mind's eye all the way to heaven. It is right to anticipate your freedom from your present struggles.

Having this certain future in mind will enable you to live now a strong and holy life – even in times of sorrow and sighing.

PRAYER

Lord, thank you that because of your victory on the cross, one day all creation will be liberated. As I await this day, be my strength every morning (Isaiah 33:2).

15 September | Day 258
Every Crisis Is an Opportunity

President John F. Kennedy once remarked that 'when written in Chinese, the word "crisis" is composed of two characters. One represents danger, and the other represents opportunity.'[1] Every crisis is, at the same time, an opportunity. Crises are often caused by unexpected difficulties.

All of us have problems. Many of us will face crises. How do you respond to a time of trouble, danger or unexpected difficulties in your personal life? How do we respond to unexpected difficulties in the church or in our nation? What do we do when we are '*at [our] wits' end*'? (Psalm 107:27). What do we do when the '*truth of the gospel*' is at stake? (Galatians 2:5). How do we respond to '*a black day*' in our lives? (Isaiah 37:3, MSG).

READING FROM PSALMS

Psalm 107:23–32
Cry out to the Lord in prayer

There may be times in your life when you face major storms. A 'tempest' seems to blow and the waves are 'lifted high' (v.25). Your courage melts away (v.26b) and you reach your wits' end (vv.26–27). You hit an unexpected storm and cannot work out how to get out of it.

This psalm tells you how to respond. The people:

> '...called out to God in [their] desperate condition;
> he got [them] out in the nick of time (v.28 MSG).

God is never late, never early. He is always on time!

> 'He stilled the storm to a whisper;
> the waves of the sea were hushed
> ... he guided them to their desired haven' (vv.29–30b).

When God answers your cry for help don't forget to thank him:

> 'So thank God for his marvelous love,
> for his miracle mercy to the children he loves' (vv.31–32, MSG).

PRAYER

Lord, thank you for the many times you have heard me and rescued me. I cry out to you today for help in my own life and for the church in this nation.

NEW TESTAMENT READING

Galatians 2:1–10
Use skill, diplomacy and courage

As we saw yesterday, sometimes we may be tempted to look down on other parts of the church, other denominations or other Christians and wish they were more like us! 'If only they did things more like us they would be 'proper' Christians or 'better' Christians!' In thinking like this we are, in effect, denying that faith in Jesus is enough.

This is what was happening to the churches in Galatia. They were being told that their faith in Jesus was not enough. If they wanted to be 'real' Christians, they needed to be circumcised.

The early church was facing an unexpected crisis and the apostle Paul had to use every ounce of his courage and determination, combined with skill and diplomacy, to avoid a damaging division and split in the church.

Paul wants to make clear that he acted under the guidance and activity of the Holy Spirit: 'I went in response to a revelation' (v.2). Paul was convinced of the validity of the gospel he preached, but was also concerned for unity: 'I did this *in private* with the leaders ... so that our concern would *not become a controversial public issue*' (v.2, MSG).

He took with him two friends: Barnabas and Titus. Barnabas was a Jew and Titus was a Greek (an uncircumcised Gentile). For a first-century Jew there were two kinds of people in the world: Jewish and Greek (circumcised and uncircumcised). Circumcision was a sign that marked out a Jew, in accordance with God's command (Genesis 17:9–14). It signified God's covenant with his chosen people.

Yet, Paul chose Titus as one of his companions. 'Significantly, Titus, non-Jewish though he was, was not required to be circumcised' (Galatians 2:3, MSG). Paul's point in this section is that the Jerusalem apostles (James, Peter and John) agreed that the good news of Jesus Christ was for everyone: Jew and Gentile, circumcised and uncircumcised.

Paul was forced to defend the 'freedom we have in Christ Jesus' (v.4). True freedom is only found through faith in Christ. The necessity of circumcision for justification before God would 'make us slaves' (v.4).

If they had yielded to the demands for circumcision of Gentile converts, they would have denied the very essence of the gospel. The purpose of this letter was to explain 'the *truth* of the gospel' (v.5). Paul wanted to demonstrate that Jesus' life, death and resurrection had fulfilled *all* the requirements of the Law of Moses.

The meeting in Jerusalem was to resolve the circumcision question. The ruling reached was one of the most important ever made in the history of Christianity. The decision here prevented a ruinous division within the church. The crisis had become an opportunity.

Not only was the issue resolved, but also the gospel preached by Peter and Paul was firmly established as being *one and the same* (v.6). The leaders in Jerusalem recognised that Paul's apostleship bore all the marks of God-given authority.

Peter and the others accepted Paul and agreed a division of responsibility – Paul for the non-Jews and Peter for the Jews. The same gospel would be brought to two different spheres by different people. They shook hands on it as a sign that the agreement would be honoured (vv.7–9). This was a monumental moment for the early church.

The parties had a sensible and detailed discussion about their differences. Paul refused to be overawed, although those he met were 'reputed to be pillars' (v.9). This was, after all, quite a group to take on! James had presumably already become leader of the Jerusalem church. Peter and John were both members of Jesus' inner circle.

A pleasing agreement was reached. Paul seems to have acted with respect and courtesy despite being a determined man conscious of a special task. He would not allow opposition from without, nor discouragement from within, to stop him from doing what he was called to do.

The only condition that the Jerusalem leaders stipulated caused no problem for Paul: 'to remember the poor' (v.10). The church must always prioritise the poor and disadvantaged in society.

PRAYER

Lord, please give me the skill, diplomacy and courage that the apostle Paul had. Help us, like Paul, to embrace the entire church of Jesus Christ.

OLD TESTAMENT READING

Isaiah 36:1–37:38
Bring to the Lord the 'impossible' situation

Have you ever been taunted or mocked for your faith in God? 'Do you really think that God is with you?' they say. 'Isn't it just your imaginary friend?'; 'Do you really think that trusting in God is going to do you any good?' This is the way God's people have been taunted throughout history.

The people of God faced an unexpected attack. This is such an important incident that it appears three times in the Bible (see 2 Kings 18; 2 Chronicles 32). Sennacherib, King of Assyria, was attacking Jerusalem with a huge army. His minions were *taunting* the people, 'On what are you basing this confidence of yours?' (Isaiah 36:4). They were being taunted and ridiculed for their faith in God.

It must have seemed to be an impossible situation – no one else had ever been delivered out of the 'hand of the king of Assyria' (v.18). But they did not answer the taunting. Sometimes the best response to criticism is keeping a dignified silence: 'But the people remained silent and said nothing in reply, because the king had commanded, "Do not answer him."' (v.21).

King Hezekiah responded to the crisis by tearing his clothes, putting on sackcloth and going into the temple of the Lord (37:1). He sent for the prophet Isaiah. Hezekiah said, 'This is a black day. We're *in crisis*' (v.3, MSG). Hezekiah asked Isaiah to pray (v.4).

Isaiah responded by saying that God's message was: 'Don't be upset by what you've heard ... I personally will take care of him' (vv.6–7, MSG).

When Hezekiah received a threatening letter, he went up to the house of the Lord, '*spread it out before the LORD*' and prayed: 'O LORD Almighty ... you alone are God over all the kingdoms of the earth. You have made heaven and earth. Give ear, O LORD, and hear; open your eyes, O LORD and see; listen to all the words Sennacherib has sent to insult the living God ... Now, O LORD our God, deliver us from his hand, so that all kingdoms on earth may know that you alone, O LORD, are God' (vv.14–20).

Isaiah sent him a message, 'This is what the LORD, the God of Israel, says: *Because you have prayed to me* ... I will defend this city and save it, for my sake and for the sake of David my servant!' (vv.21, 35)

God heard the prayer of Hezekiah and Isaiah and he rescued and delivered his people (vv.36–38).

PRAYER

Lord, the name of Jesus is no longer honoured in our society. Would you pour out a spirit of prayer and supplication on your people so that we may turn to you in prayer. Hear our prayer and deliver us in this time of crisis.

16 September | Day 259
God Loves Imperfect People

I am far from perfect. I sometimes find it hard to believe that God really loves me – especially when I mess up, fail or make bad decisions.

Actually, no one is perfect – apart from Jesus. But God so loved the world that he gave his one and only son to die for us (John 3:16). Therefore, God must love imperfect people. In fact, 'While we were still sinners, Christ died for us' (Romans 5:8).

God knows that perfect people do not exist. We all fail. God's love for you is bigger than your mistakes. God loves imperfect people.

Everyone knows that their marriage partner is not perfect, their children are not perfect, their parents are not perfect, and their friends are not perfect. But we love imperfect people. If we love imperfect people perhaps it shouldn't surprise us that God loves imperfect people even more.

READING FROM PSALMS

Psalm 107:33–43
Meditate on how great God's love is for you

Having rehearsed all the great things God has done for them, the psalmist concludes: '*Consider the great love of the Lord*' (v.43). 'If you are really wise, you'll think this over – it's time you appreciated God's deep love' (v.43, MSG). God has rescued his people so many times. He has answered their prayers.

God's people were far from perfect. He responds to the failures of the people with discipline. Even here though, God's love is in the foreground, as he uses that discipline to draw them back to himself. As they return, the hardships turn to blessing. The 'rivers' (v.33) begin to return: 'He turned the desert into pools of water and the parched ground into *flowing springs* ... he blessed them, and their numbers greatly increased' (vv.35, 38).

Jesus said that the Holy Spirit within you would be like these 'rivers of living water' (John 7:38). Oswald Chambers writes, 'The river of the Spirit of God overcomes all obstacles. Never focus your eyes on the obstacle or the difficulty. The obstacle will be a matter of total indifference to the river that will flow steadily through you if you will simply remember to stay focussed on the Source.'[1]

PRAYER

Lord, I meditate on your great love for me. I pray that by your Holy Spirit you will turn any deserts and dryness in my life into 'pools of water' and 'flowing springs' (Psalm 107:35).

NEW TESTAMENT READING

Galatians 2:11–3:9
Understand how personal God's love is for you

The apostle Paul was far from perfect. In fact, he describes himself as the 'chief' of sinners (1 Timothy 1:15, KJV). Yet he can write, 'I have been crucified with Christ and I no longer live, but Christ lives in me. The life I live in the body, I live by faith in the Son of God, who *loved me* and *gave himself for me*' (2:20).

This is the extent of the greatness of the love of God. The Son of God gave himself *for me ... and you*. It is not just that God loves the whole world. He loves *you*. He gave himself on the cross for you and me. He died for you. If you had been the only person in the world, Jesus would have died for you. It is as personal as that.

God's love for you is unconditional, wholehearted and continual. There is nothing you can do to make God love you more and there is nothing you can do to make God love you less.

When Paul finally understood this, it radically changed his life. His old life had come to an end. 'I have been crucified with Christ. My ego is no longer central ... The life you see me living is not "mine"' (v.20, MSG). A new life had begun, 'Christ lives in me' (v.20). The Spirit of Christ had come to live in him. This new life was a life of 'faith in the Son of God' (v.20).

In this verse, Paul sums up the message of the gospel. It is so amazing and yet so simple. By adding to it, we only detract from it.

That is why Paul was vociferous in his defence of this gospel. That is why he had a 'face-to-face confrontation' with Peter (v.11, MSG). Peter himself knew the truth of this message. Yet, because of how 'fearful he was of the conservative Jewish clique [that had] been pushing the old system of circumcision' (v.12, MSG), he began to follow and promote the old Jewish laws and customs again (vv.12–13).

By doing this, Peter gave the impression that it was not enough to be a Christian – he was saying people must also follow Jewish customs (v.14).

But *faith in Jesus Christ is all that is required*. 'We know very well that we are not set right with God by rule-keeping but only through *personal faith* in Jesus Christ' (v.16, MSG).

God, in his great love, embraces *all* who put their faith in Christ, without distinction. You are justified by faith. This results in a totally changed life. Christ comes to live within you. You no longer live your old life, but a new one by faith in the Son of God.

You receive his Spirit (3:2). Faith and receiving the Holy Spirit is not only the way to begin the Christian life, it is the way to continue to live it out (v.3).

The Galatians clearly had *an experience of the Holy Spirit*, to which Paul could point: 'Did you *receive the Spirit* by observing the law, or by believing what you heard?' (v.2). When you put your faith in Christ, you received the Holy Spirit. 'Does God *give you his Spirit* and work miracles among you because you observe the law, or because *you believe* what you heard?' (v.5).

On Alpha, I have often been asked the question, 'What about those who lived before Jesus? What happens to them?' This passage points to the answer.

The cross of Jesus works through all eternity. It works backwards, as well as forwards, in time. It was effective for Abraham: 'He believed God, and it was credited to him as righteousness' (v.6). 'The Scripture foresaw that God would justify the Gentiles by faith, and *announced the gospel in advance to Abraham*' (v.8). The cross was the defining event in world history to which the law and the sacrificial system pointed.

PRAYER

Lord Jesus, thank you that you loved me and gave yourself for me. Help me trust in your great love for all the challenges I face today.

OLD TESTAMENT READING

Isaiah 38:1–40:31
Know how lasting God's love is for you

God's love for you is everlasting. It will not let you go: '*In your love you kept me* from the pit of destruction; you have put all my sins behind your back' (38:17), wrote Hezekiah. God heard his prayer and saw his tears. He added fifteen years to his life and delivered him from the hand of the king of Assyria (vv.5–6).

The second part of Isaiah begins with the words that are quoted later by John the Baptist (40:3). The message of Isaiah 40–55 is this: 'The exile will be over soon.' When Jesus came, he was proclaiming the real end of exile. In these chapters, we get a foretaste as Isaiah proclaims the end of the physical exile Israel experienced in the sixth century BC.

Isaiah foresaw a new sense of the *presence of God* (40:3–5), a new confidence in the *word of God* (vv.6–8) and a new *vision of God* (v.9 onwards).

He saw the great love of God, and he wrote, 'He tends his flock like a shepherd: He gathers the lambs in his arms and carries them close to his heart; he gently leads those that have young' (v.11; see also John 10).

No one can compare to God in terms of greatness. He is the Creator of the universe (Isaiah 40:12–14). Compared to him 'the nations are like a drop in a bucket' (v.15). It is absurd to compare God to an idol that is made by a craftsman (vv.18–20).

Compared to God, the people of this world, even its great leaders, are 'like grasshoppers' (v.22). He is the Creator of the entire universe, including the billions upon billions of stars (v.26). This is the God who loves you personally and carries you close his heart. God doesn't come and go. God lasts.

God is also a power-sharing God. He 'energises those who get tired … those who wait upon God get fresh strength' (vv.29–31, MSG). Quietly wait on God, study his word, pray, worship and meditate on his love for you. He will restore you, re-energise you and empower you to face everything you need to do.

PRAYER

Lord, thank you for the greatness of your love. You are the Creator of this vast universe. You are all-powerful. Yet you love me, take me in your arms and hold me close to your heart. Please renew my strength as I wait on you.

17 September | Day 260
The Best Way to Lead

'*Who is the servant of the Lord?*' This was the question that the Chief Financial Officer of Ethiopia asked the evangelist Philip: 'Tell me, please, *who is the prophet talking about, himself or someone else?*' (Acts 8:34).

The title '*servant of the Lord*' is one of great dignity, reserved for leaders such as Abraham, Moses and David. But in the four 'servant songs' (Isaiah 42:1–4; 49:1–7; 50:4–9; 52:13 – 53:12) a distinct concept of 'servanthood' comes into sharper focus.

The role of this 'servant' can be illustrated with the St Andrew's cross. (St Andrew, brother of Peter, is believed to have died on a diagonally traversed cross, which the Romans sometimes used for execution. It therefore came to be called the St Andrew's cross, and is the flag of Scotland.)

Originally, God intended that all humankind should be his servant. Then, after the fall, God chose the whole nation of Israel to serve him. But even his chosen race was not faithful to him. So the focus, continuing to narrow, became a mere 'faithful remnant'. Ultimately, only one individual was completely faithful (shown by the central intersection of the cross). This was Jesus.

Jesus revealed what Israel (and indeed humankind) should have been. He was an Israelite sent to Israel, totally identifying with his nation and yet remaining distinct from it. No earthly king or prophet meets the description used in all the servant passages in Isaiah. Yet, Jesus does – perfectly.

Where Israel failed, Jesus succeeded. Furthermore, it is God's plan that the church, through the victory of Christ and the power of the Holy Spirit, can and will succeed. So, the St Andrew's cross broadens out again as the members of the church of Jesus Christ become the servants of God with a mission to call all humanity back to their original creation purpose.

READING FROM PROVERBS

Proverbs 22:28–23:9
Use all your leadership skills to serve others

The writer of the book of Proverbs warns against us spending our lives serving false gods such as food (23:1–3) or riches: 'Do not wear yourself out to get rich; have the wisdom to show restraint. Cast but a glance at riches, and they are gone, for they will surely sprout wings and fly off to the sky like an eagle' (vv.4–5). The eagle on every US Dollar is a reminder of this truth.

Rather, we are encouraged to get on with doing what we do well: 'Do you see those who are *skilled in their work*? They will *serve* before kings; they will not serve before obscure people' (22:29). I have watched over the years those who have quietly got on with serving in humble and obscure ways, but done so with great skill in their work and God has raised them up to positions of influence.

PRAYER

Lord, thank you for the example of those who have pressed on – serving you with great skill and without seeking any glory for themselves. Thank you that you have raised such people up as examples for us all.

NEW TESTAMENT READING

Galatians 3:10–25
Thank God for Jesus' ultimate act of servant leadership

Jesus said that those of us who follow him should lead in a different way to those around us. We should not throw our weight around. We should not let power go to our heads (see Mark 10:42–45, MSG). Rather we should follow his model of servant leadership. Jesus said he 'did not come to be served, but to serve, and to give his life as a ransom for many' (v.45).

In this passage, Paul explains how Jesus did exactly that. The cross is the ultimate expression of *his service*.

We have all failed to keep the law of God. According to the Law of Moses, 'Cursed is everyone who does not continue to do everything written in the Book of the Law' (Galatians 3:10b; see Deuteronomy 27:26). In order to be justified by the law, a person would have to keep the entire law (Galatians 3:12). No one has ever done this. Therefore, we were all under a curse.

On the cross, Jesus took this curse on himself. He 'redeemed us from the curse of the law by becoming a curse for us' (v.13a). Paul points out that the book of Deuteronomy says, 'cursed is everyone who is hung on a tree' (v.13b, RSV; see Deuteronomy 21:23). It was the depth of disgrace to be crucified. 'He became a curse, and at the same time dissolved the curse' (v.13, MSG). He deliberately put himself in harm's way for you and me.

You are justified through what Jesus, the servant of the Lord, did on the cross for you by becoming a curse for you. 'He redeemed us in order that the blessing given to Abraham might come to the Gentiles through Christ Jesus, so that by faith we might receive the promise of the Spirit' (v.14).

God's promise was originally given to Abraham and his seed (v.16a). Paul explains that Jesus is God's promise, since 'the Scripture does not say "and to seeds", meaning many people, but "and to your seed", meaning one person, who is Christ' (v.16b).

'What, then, was the purpose of the law?' (v.19). The law had at least two main purposes. First, it pointed us to our sin (v.19). It exposed the problem. It defined sin. It was intended to put a brake on sin.

Second, the law points us to Jesus. It is intended to lead us to Christ (vv.21–25). 'The law was like those Greek tutors ... who escort children to school and protect them from danger or distraction, making sure the children will really get to the place they set out for' (v.24, MSG). It leads us to Christ through whom we are justified by faith (v.24).

Jesus Christ, the ultimate servant of the Lord, through becoming a curse for us, has removed the curse of the law. By his death he justified many. You are set free from the law to become a servant of the Lord.

PRAYER

Lord, thank you that, in this ultimate act of service, you took upon yourself the curse that should have fallen on me. Thank you that as a result I am justified by faith in you. Thank you for setting me free to serve.

OLD TESTAMENT READING

Isaiah 41:1–42:25
Follow the model of Jesus: serve to lead

The Sandhurst motto on every cap, badge and belt is, 'Serve to lead'. This was the model of Jesus. As J. Oswald Sanders wrote, 'True leadership is achieved not by reducing people to one's service but in giving oneself in selfless service to them.'[1]

As we have seen, God originally chose Israel to be his servant, serving by his side. He promised to give them strength and help them (41:8–9).

However, the people of Israel failed and became part of the problem. It is possible to have perfect 20/20 physical vision and yet be spiritually blind:

> 'You're my servant, and you're not looking!
> You're my messenger, and you're not listening!
> The very people I depended upon, servants of God,
> *blind as a bat* – wilfully blind!' (42:19, MSG).

Isaiah foresaw another servant of the Lord:

> 'Take a good look at my *servant*.
> I'm backing him to the hilt.
> He's the one I chose,
> and I couldn't be more pleased with him.
> I've bathed him with my Spirit, my life.
> He'll set everything right among the nations.
> He won't call attention to what he does
> with loud speeches or gaudy parades.
> He won't brush aside the bruised and the hurt
> and he won't disregard the small and insignificant,
> but he'll steadily and firmly set things right.
> He won't tire out and quit. He won't be stopped
> until he's finished his work – to set things right on earth' (vv.1–4a, MSG).

Matthew points out that Jesus fulfilled these words, which were spoken through the prophet Isaiah. He directly quotes Isaiah 42:1–4 (Matthew 12:17–21).

In Jesus, this prophecy was perfectly fulfilled, just as all of the other servant passages in Isaiah were perfectly fulfilled in him

(Isaiah 49:1–7; 50:4–9; 52:13 – 53:12). Jesus would be 'a lighthouse to the nations ... opening blind eyes, releasing prisoners from dungeons, emptying the dark prisons' (42:6–7, MSG).

As a result of what Jesus has done for you, these wonderful promises now apply to you:

> 'So do not fear, for I am with you;
> do not be dismayed, for I am your God.
> I will strengthen you and help you;
> I will uphold you with my righteous
> right hand' (41:10).

He will guide you along unfamiliar paths, turn darkness into light before you and make the rough places smooth (42:16).

PRAYER

Lord Jesus, thank you that you alone fulfilled this prophecy perfectly and that you will not give your glory to another (v.8). Thank you for your model of humility and gentleness. Thank you that you call us, too, to be servants of the Lord. Help me to follow your example.

18 September | Day 261

God Is Nice and He Likes You

'This seemingly insubstantial fact revolutionised my life,' wrote Adrian Plass, author of *The Sacred Diary of Adrian Plass Aged 37¾*. He continued, 'I became a Christian when I was sixteen years old, but it wasn't until I was thirty-seven that I absorbed an essential truth. *God is nice and he likes me*.'[1]

Sadly, deep down many people think that God is not that nice, he does not like us very much and he spends most of his time being cross with us. This could not be further from the truth.

In the passages for today, we see how much more than just 'nice' God is – his goodness, amazing love and faithfulness. We also see that not only does he 'like' you, he loves you – you are his 'precious and honoured' child (Isaiah 43:4).

READING FROM PSALMS

Psalm 108:1–5
Higher than the created universe

Scientists today are discovering more of the vastness of our universe – how high the heavens are.

Yet, God's love for you is so great. It is higher than the heavens. His 'faithfulness reaches to the skies' (v.4). 'The deeper your love, the higher it goes' (v.4, MSG).

David worships God with music and singing early in the morning: 'I will awaken the dawn' (v.2b). Focus your worship today on God's love and faithfulness.

PRAYER

Lord, thank you that your love for me is higher than the heavens. Thank you that your faithfulness reaches to the skies. 'Be exalted, O God, above the heavens, and let your glory be over all the earth' (v.5).

NEW TESTAMENT READING

Galatians 3:26–4:20
Greater than any human love

Imagine the greatest human love in the world – for some people it might be the love a parent has for their child. Yet, God's love for you is even greater.

When you put your faith in Jesus, you also became a child of God: 'You are all children of God through faith in Jesus Christ' (3:26). We were baptised *into Christ*. You have clothed yourself with Christ (v.27). This is how close your relationship with Jesus has become.

In Christ, no distinction of race, rank or gender exists: 'There is neither Jew nor Greek, slave nor free, male nor female, for you are all one in Christ Jesus' (v.28). We are 'all *equal ... all in a common relationship with Jesus Christ*' (v.28, MSG).

There is no excuse for discrimination, prejudice or hatred. Paul does not say that differences do not *exist*; rather, he says these differences simply do not *matter*.

You belong to Christ, you are an heir to all the amazing promises that God made to Abraham (v.29). You have now inherited 'the whole estate' (4:1).

Paul uses an analogy from Roman law. In ancient Rome, until the age of fourteen, an heir was under the control of a tutor who had been nominated by his father. Until this age a child was treated in the same way as a slave. Usually, the heir became a free agent at the age of fourteen. Paul explains that while the people of God were under the Mosaic law, it was much like being under a tutor. They were under a form of slavery (v.3).

But now, Jesus Christ has set you free: 'Thus we have been set free to experience our rightful heritage. You can tell for sure that you are now fully adopted as his own children because God sent the Spirit of his Son into our lives crying out, "Papa! Father!" Doesn't that privilege of intimate conversation with God make it plain that you are not a slave, but a child? And if you are a child, you're also an heir, with complete access to the inheritance' (vv.5–7, MSG).

How amazing it is to have the full rights of a child of God and that God sent the Spirit of Jesus to live in you. As a result, you can address God in the same intimate way that Jesus addressed him.

Paul continued to warn the Galatians against slipping backwards, as if they were still under the law. Before, they 'did not know God' (v.8). Now, they do know him – or rather they 'are known by God' (v.9). It is even more important to be known by God than to know him. But, of course, living in a relationship with God means that both are true.

He urged them not to go back to a kind of legalism (vv.10–11). False teachers were trying to lead them astray.

Paul pleaded with them. He reminded them of their love for him when he first preached the gospel to them. They welcomed him as if he was Jesus Christ himself (v.14). When he came to them he was ill. It may have been an eye condition, because he said, 'You would have torn out your eyes and given them to me' (v.15). That is how much they loved him.

Now the false teachers were trying to alienate them from him (v.17), but Paul's love for them remained constant: 'Do you know how I feel right now, and will feel until Christ's life becomes visible in your lives? Like a mother in the pain of childbirth' (v.19, MSG).

When you know God's love for you – even greater than that of a parent for their child – and his Spirit comes to live within you, he gives you a love for others. This too is like a parent's love for a child. It was this kind of love that Paul had for the Galatians.

Sometimes not getting what you want can be the best thing that can happen. Paul felt frustrated at not being able to be with and speak face-to-face with those he loved. He did not want to be 'reduced to this blunt, letter-writing language' (v.20, MSG). If Paul had had his way, the letter to the Galatians would never have been written. As it was, he was forced to do something he did not want to do and countless millions of lives have been changed and blessed as a result.

PRAYER

Lord, thank you that you have poured your love into my heart by the Holy Spirit. Help me, like Paul, to love others in this same way, to care passionately, even if it involves 'the pains of childbirth until Christ is formed in [them]' (v.19).

OLD TESTAMENT READING

Isaiah 43:1–44:23
More valuable than anything else

All of us will face trials, tests and temptations. We will go through 'fire' and 'rough waters'. There will be times when 'you're between a rock and a hard place' (43:2, MSG). These are difficult times. Sometimes you may want to give up. You cannot understand what is going on.

God says, 'Don't be afraid ... You're mine. When you're in over your head, I'll be there with you ... it won't be a dead end' (vv.1–2, MSG).

God is shaping you (44:21, MSG). He often uses the difficulties and challenges in our life like sandpaper – to smooth the rough edges. He uses them to strengthen your character, change you and advance his purpose in your life.

He is always acting in love: 'I am God, your personal God ... I paid a huge price for you ... That's how much I love you! I'd sell off the whole world to get you back, trade the creation just for you' (43:3–4, MSG).

You are precious and honoured in his sight because he loves you (v.4). Do you realise how valuable you are to God? Your worth is what you are worth to God, and he paid a huge price for you. Jesus died for you.

In all the struggles and difficulties of life, God has a good plan for your future. He says, 'I'm about to do something brand-new ... I'm making a road through the desert, rivers in the badlands' (v.19, MSG). If you are in a 'desert' or the 'badlands' right now, trust God that he has a good plan for your future.

God's love and forgiveness are amazing. Later in the passage God says, 'I, even I, am he who blots out your transgressions, for my own sake, and remembers your sins no more' (v.25). We know that this is what was made possible through Jesus Christ and what he did for you.

Isaiah goes on to warn of the absurdity of worshipping idols (see 44:6–23). When we worship anything or anyone other than the God who made us, we are worshipping a lie. We are worshipping 'created things rather than the Creator' (Romans 1:25).

The Lord urges his people to return to him. He says, 'I've wiped the slate of all your wrongdoings. There's nothing left of your sins. Come back to me, come back. I've redeemed you' (Isaiah 44:22, MSG).

PRAYER

Lord, thank you that in your amazing love for me, you paid a huge price for me. Thank you that I am precious and honoured in your sight. In all the challenges and difficulties, help me to keep on trusting that you have a good purpose for my life.

---

19 September | Day 262

Refuse to Be Trapped by your Past

John had no one to help him become a lawyer or a politician. He was not interested in the army. He had no desire to be a doctor. Therefore, the only obvious career move in those days for a man of his background was to become a clergyman in the Church of England.

He tried to make himself acceptable to God by keeping the whole law, inwardly and outwardly. He got up early. He prayed. He denied himself. He tried to earn forgiveness and peace by increased effort. But he 'groaned under a heavy yoke'.

On 24 May 1738 at 8.45 p.m. he heard someone reading a book by the great reformer, Martin Luther. He later recalled, 'While he was describing the change which God works in the heart through faith in Christ, *I felt my heart strangely warmed*. I felt I did trust in Christ, Christ alone for salvation; and an assurance was given [to] me that He had taken away my sins, even mine, and saved me from the law of sin and death.'

John Wesley became one of the greatest preachers ever, preaching over 40,000 sermons centred on freedom through faith in Jesus Christ. He had, as he put it, '*exchanged the faith of a servant for the faith of a son*'. He was free at last.

'Freedom' is the word that best sums up the Christian life. You, too, are free. Therefore, refuse to be trapped by your past.

READING FROM PSALMS

Psalm 108:6–13
Cry out for freedom

David knew that God loved him, and he prayed that God would save and help him. 'Save us and help us with your right hand, that those you love may be delivered' (v.6). To be saved is to be *set free*.

If you are facing some difficult challenge in your life, pray like David:

> 'Give us help for the hard task;
> human help is worthless.
> In God we'll do our very best'
> (vv.12–13a, MSG).

PRAYER

Lord, thank you that you love me, help me and set me free. Lord, today I pray for your help with...

NEW TESTAMENT READING

Galatians 4:21–5:6
Live a life of freedom

In our culture, freedom is often understood as being able to do whatever you want, how you want, when you want. But when you live in that way, you don't necessarily feel truly free.

According to Paul's teaching in today's passage, freedom comes through Jesus Christ. His message is that you are not 'born free' but that in order to be free, you must be 'born again'. True freedom is found in a life of faith in Christ.

Many ideas of freedom fail because they do not realise the true nature of our captivity. A belief in freedom as the birthright of a particular group of people has often given birth to malignant nationalism and racism. It has produced some of the gravest evils of recent times, including Nazism and Apartheid.

The title of the film *Cry Freedom* expresses something we all long for. Whether it's racial and political freedom (as in the case of this film), free speech, free assembly, free worship, a free conscience, or economic freedom and individual freedom, the whole world cries out for freedom.

All of these forms of freedom are important, but you can have them all and still be in slavery. Alternatively, you can have none of them but still be free. The gospel contains within it the promise of other forms of freedom, but it begins with a freedom that is more profound than any other.

'Christ has set us free to live a free life' (5:1, MSG). Jesus sets us free to live a life of freedom, faith and love through the Spirit. Paul's opponents, 'the Judaisers', boasted about the fact that they were Abraham's children. Paul, interpreting the Old Testament figuratively, used an allegorical argument to confront them.

Paul said to his opponents that there are two ways in which we can live – in bondage, or in freedom. He explains that there are two covenants. He says in effect: 'You boast of being Abraham's children – but Abraham actually had two children – one in bondage and one in freedom.' True descent from Abraham is not physical, but spiritual. It is not enough to have Abraham as your father. The crucial question is, 'Who is your mother?'

He argued that by his opponents' insistence on the law, they were, in fact, children of Hagar. This analogy represents the old covenant, the present city of Jerusalem, Ishmael, the child of the flesh, and a life of bondage (v.25). This is the life John Wesley experienced before his conversion. It is a life of frustration and failure, confusion and defeat.

To be a Christian, on the other hand, is to be a child not only of Abraham, but also of Sarah. Sarah represents the new covenant, the new Jerusalem ('the Jerusalem that is above', v.26), Isaac (the child of promise, v.28) and the freedom that is in Christ. This is what Wesley experienced the day he trusted in Christ and Christ alone for salvation. His heart was 'strangely warmed'. This is the way of peace, joy and freedom.

Paul pointed out that just as Ishmael ridiculed Isaac (see Genesis 21:9), the Galatians who are 'born by the power of the Spirit' (Galatians 4:29) should not be surprised that they are being persecuted by these 'Judaisers'.

He concluded his argument in this section by saying, 'We are not children of the slave woman, but of the free woman' (v.31). He continued, 'It is for freedom that Christ has set us free. Stand firm, then, and do not let yourselves be burdened again by a yoke of slavery' (5:1–2). The picture is of an ox bowed down with a heavy harness.

'Circumcision' was the theological symbol standing for a religion of law (vv.2–3). Paul argued that to add circumcision is to lose Christ. To seek to be justified by works is to fall away from grace (v.4).

The Christian life is a life of faith. You cannot work for your salvation, you simply wait for it (v.5). Meanwhile, 'The only thing that counts is faith expressing itself through love' (v.6b).

PRAYER

Lord, thank you for setting me free in order that I might live a life of freedom. Thank you for the freedom the Holy Spirit brings to my life. Help me to express my faith in love today.

OLD TESTAMENT READING

Isaiah 44:24–46:13
Tell the good news of freedom

God's love extends to every person, of every nation, from the moment of conception onwards. Part of his original plan in choosing Israel was that they would bring his blessing to all people (Genesis 12:3).

God is the creator of the heavens and the earth. He is your maker. There is no other. The book of Isaiah repeats this over and over again for emphasis. Ten times this passage says, 'There is no other.'

God is your maker. He 'formed you in the womb' (Isaiah 44:24). God's love extends before birth to conception and the womb; this has profound implications for the debate about abortion and how we treat the unborn. Every human being from the moment of conception is created and sustained by God. 'I have upheld [you] *since you were conceived*' (46:3b).

God's love extends beyond Israel to all the nations as well. Since he is the creator of all, God invites *all the nations* to participate in salvation and freedom: 'So turn to me and be helped – saved! – everyone, whoever and wherever you are' (45:22a, MSG). This promises a freedom greater than any the world can offer.

Here, we get a glimpse of the entire world bowing before Jesus. 'Before me every knee will bow; by me every tongue will swear' (v.23b). Paul referred to this verse as a reference to Jesus (Philippians 2:9 onwards).

This was a foretaste too, of the fact that God will also use people who are 'Gentiles', that is, non-Jewish. Cyrus was a Persian and yet he is described here as the Lord's anointed (Isaiah 45:1). Isaiah prophesies, 'I will raise up Cyrus in my righteousness: I will make all his ways straight. He will rebuild my city and set my exiles *free*' (v.13). This prophecy was fulfilled when the exile came to an end through the hand of Cyrus.

This was God's plan. He said, 'My purpose will stand, and I will do all that I please. From the east I summon a bird of prey; from a far-off land, a man *to fulfil my purpose*. What I have said, that will I bring about; what *I have planned, that will I do*' (46:10b–11). You can be confident that nothing can thwart God's plan for you.

PRAYER

Lord, thank you that from the moment of conception, you love all people regardless of race or background. Thank you that Jesus has set us free and that, one day, every knee will bow and every tongue will confess that Jesus Christ is Lord.

20 September | Day 263
How to Deal with Conflict

'The Bible tells us to love our neighbours, and also to love our enemies; probably because they are generally the same people!'[1] wrote G.K. Chesterton.

Conflict is inescapable. Even for those of us who shy away from confrontation, it is impossible to avoid. As we go through life, we will inevitably encounter people with whom we will have conflict. Additionally, for a Christian, an internal conflict exists between the desires of our sinful nature and the Holy Spirit.

We may also experience conflict when we stand up for the truth within the church, or when we engage with the prevailing culture. Even in the UK, a country that has traditionally been seen as 'Christian', the culture is becoming increasingly hostile towards the Christian faith.

READING FROM PSALM

Psalm 109:1–20
Conflict with those who hate and attack us

David cries out to God 'whom I praise' (v.1). He is in conflict with 'wicked and deceitful people who have opened their mouths against' him (v.2) with 'lying tongues' (v.2) and 'words of hatred' (v.3): 'They repay me evil for good and hatred for my friendship' (v.5).

It is deeply distressing when people we love and consider our friends attack us. Their accusations and words of hatred cause deep pain.

David's response in this psalm is to bring his pain and struggles to God. In the midst of it all he declares, 'I am a man of prayer' (v.4), and he pours out his heart to God. In no uncertain terms he calls on God, not to remain silent, but rather, to pay them back.

Some of what he says can be difficult to read and reflects just how difficult it is to forgive without God's help. It is at odds with Jesus' call to 'love [our] enemies and pray for those who persecute [us]' (Matthew 5:44). If you are being unfairly attacked, follow David's example of prayerfulness and honesty before God. At the same time ask God to help you overcome bitterness and hatred.

PRAYER

Lord, help me when I come into conflict not to react in the flesh, but to respond in the Spirit.

NEW TESTAMENT READING

Galatians 5:7–26
Conflict with heresy and in our hearts

Conflict and confrontation are never easy, but they are a necessary part of courageous leadership. Paul finds himself in conflict with the 'agitators'. He is passionate about the truth, and uses very strong language about them because they are leading the church astray.

In effect, he says that if they are so keen on cutting that part of a man's anatomy through circumcision, they may as well 'go the whole way' and castrate themselves (v.12). It is rather surprising language to find in the New Testament! But the truth matters, and Paul is prepared to face conflict in order to defend the truth.

Paul then moves on to the conflict between the sinful nature and the Holy Spirit. The Holy Spirit and the sinful nature 'are in *conflict* with each other' (v.17).

The whole point of Paul's argument has been to stress freedom. However, freedom *from* sin does not mean freedom *to* sin.

Paul contrasts two forms of slavery: *legalism* (slavery to law) and *licence* (slavery to self). You are liberated from these. Avoid both legalism and licence: 'Just make sure that you don't use this freedom as an excuse to do whatever you want to do and destroy your freedom. Rather, use your freedom to serve one another in love' (vv.13–14, MSG).

That is true freedom – not the absence of morality, but the freedom to serve others in love: to love your neighbour as yourself (v.14). If we continue responding to conflict as the world does, 'biting and devouring each other', we will destroy each other (v.15).

Paul lists four examples of realms in which this *conflict* operates:

1. Sexual sin: 'repetitive, loveless, cheap sex; a stinking accumulation of mental and emotional garbage; frenzied and joyless grabs for happiness' (v.19, MSG)
2. Religious sin: 'trinket gods; magic-show religion; paranoid loneliness' (v.20a, MSG)
3. Societal sin: 'cutthroat competition; all-consuming-yet-never-satisfied wants; a brutal temper; an impotence to love or be loved; divided homes and divided lives; small-minded and lopsided pursuits; the vicious habit of depersonalizing everyone into a rival' (v.20b, MSG)
4. Sins of excess: 'uncontrolled and uncontrollable addictions; ugly parodies of community' (v.21, MSG)

Do not gratify these desires. Rather, live and be 'led by the Spirit' (v.18). If you choose to live by the Spirit, you will not follow the lusts of the flesh that continually tempt us. Instead, you will produce the fruit of the Spirit: 'love, joy, peace, patience, kindness, goodness, faithfulness, gentleness and self-control' (vv.22–23). As my friend, Michael Timmis, wrote to me, 'The way I define love is by using the fruit of the Spirit, which starts with love. I believe that joy is love rejoicing, peace is love at rest, patience is love waiting, kindness is love interacting, goodness is love initiating, faithfulness is love keeping its word, gentleness is love empathising, and self-control is love resisting temptation.'

These are the characteristics we see in Jesus. Paul continues, 'Those who belong to Christ Jesus have crucified the sinful nature with its passions and desires' (v.24). The temptation is always to go back. But 'since we live by the Spirit, let us keep in step with the Spirit' (v.25).

As far as possible, avoid personal conflict: 'Let us not become conceited, provoking and envying each other' (v.26).

Now that the Holy Spirit lives in you, involve him in all your decisions and follow his prompting. If you are thinking, saying or doing something that makes you feel uncomfortable inside, that may be the prompting of the Holy Spirit to stop. On the other hand, when you make a decision and feel a deep sense of peace, know that that comes from keeping in step with the Holy Spirit.

PRAYER

Lord, help me to deal with conflict wisely, to keep in step with the Holy Spirit.

OLD TESTAMENT READING

Isaiah 47:1–49:7
Conflict with culture

Like many today, the people of God often found themselves in a culture with very different standards from their own. You are not called to withdraw from the culture, but you are called to be distinctive. Live a counter-cultural life and you will have a powerful impact on the culture for good.

The people of God found themselves in a cruel society (Babylon) that 'showed them no mercy' (47:6). A very proud culture (vv.8–9) who indulged in the magic arts, astrology and horoscopes (vv.9b,12–13).

It is very hard to live a totally counter-cultural life.

Isaiah then addresses Israel. He says that if only they had paid attention to the Lord and his commands, 'Your peace would have been like a river, your righteousness like the waves of the sea' (48:18).

Despite all Israel's failings and problems, God did not give up on his plans and purposes for 'my servant Israel, in whom I will display my splendour' (49:3). We read of another 'servant of the Lord' (see BiOY Day 260, p. 549), this time an individual, who would 'bring Jacob back to him, and gather Israel to himself' (v.5). God's original purposes for his servant Israel would be revealed and fulfilled in him. This points ahead to Jesus. He was an Israelite sent to Israel. He was totally identified with his nation, yet distinct from it.

The first task of the servant is to declare the truth. His mouth is 'like a sharpened sword' (v.2). God spoke to one nation and told them to tell all the others. The second task of the servant is to make God visible, 'in whom I will display my splendour' (v.3). The third task is to be a blessing to the world: 'I'm setting you up as a light for the nations so that my salvation becomes global!' (v.6, MSG).

Isaiah then gives us a glimpse of how the servant will achieve this. In a foreshadowing of Isaiah 53, he speaks of 'him who was despised and abhorred by the nation' (49:7). The servant glorifies God (v.3). Now God glorifies the servant: 'Kings will see you and rise up, princes will see and bow down, because of the Lord, who is faithful, the Holy One of Israel, who has chosen you' (v.7).

This was fulfilled when the Magi came to worship Jesus (Matthew 2:1–12). It has been fulfilled again and again over the last 2,000 years as kings, emperors, presidents and prime ministers have bowed the knee to Jesus.

Israel did not succeed, but Jesus did. Now, it is our task to be the servant of the Lord. Paul and Barnabas quoted this verse: 'This is what the Lord has commanded us: "I have made you a light for the Gentiles, that you may bring salvation to the ends of the earth"' (Isaiah 49:6; Acts 13:47).

PRAYER

Lord, help me to engage with the culture around me, speaking the truth in love, displaying your splendour and being a light to those around me.

---

21 September | Day 264
Never Give Up

Sir Winston Churchill has been described as Britain's greatest ever leader. He lived a long, heroic life and he rallied a nation with his inspiring rhetoric. One of the most striking parts of his biography is that he had to resign from the Admiralty during WWI over the failed Dardanelles campaign. He had failed spectacularly, yet he was to learn not to give up.

I was told that once, when he returned to his old school, Harrow, to address the boys, the whole school assembled to listen to his words of wisdom. The great man arose to speak: 'Young men; never give up, never give up, never give up.'[1] The entire speech lasted only a few seconds. Then he sat down. No one present ever forgot his words.

That is, at least, the popular version of the story. Churchill did indeed say words to that effect, but as part of a longer speech. Towards the end he said, 'Never give in. Never give in. Never, never, never, never – in nothing, great or small, large or petty – never give in, except to convictions of honour and good sense. Never yield to force. Never yield to the apparently overwhelming might of the enemy.'

In today's generation, our lives have become so instantaneous that anything requiring patient perseverance can appear unattractive. We require instant returns and instant results. But sometimes the biggest pay-offs are a long time coming.

READING FROM PROVERBS

Proverbs 23:10–18
Never give up being enthusiastic

'Do *not* let your heart *envy* sinners, but always *be zealous* for the fear of the LORD. There is surely *a future hope for you*, and your hope will not be cut off' (vv.17–18).

St Paul wrote something similar: '*Never be lacking in zeal*, but keep your spiritual fervour' (Romans 12:11). We should be as enthusiastic as the day we first encountered Jesus. As Bear Grylls says, 'Be the most enthusiastic person you know. Enthusiasm sustains you when times are tough, encourages those around you and is totally infectious.'[2]

Many years ago, I wrote in the margin next to these verses: 'I am feeling rather envious of the people [my work colleagues at the time] and their work. This is the Lord's word to me – not to be envious, but instead to *be zealous for him* – and he promises "a bright future" (Proverbs 23:18, GNB). Praise the Lord for that promise to cling to for my work.'

PRAYER

Lord, help me never to be lacking in zeal, but to keep my spiritual fervour. Thank you that you promise 'a bright future'.

NEW TESTAMENT READING

Galatians 6:1–18
Never give up doing good

'Let us not become weary in doing good, for at the proper time we will reap a harvest *if we do not give up*' (v.9).

As Paul reached the end of this letter, he encouraged the Galatians to work together as a team. If someone is going off the path, seek to restore them gently (v.1a). But also watch yourself lest you be tempted (v.1b). You are responsible for your own life: 'Each one should test his own actions ... for each one should carry his own load' (vv.4–5).

We also have a responsibility for other members of the team: 'Carry each other's burdens, and in this way you will fulfil the law of Christ' (v.2).

Paul assumes we all have burdens. The word used means 'heavy burdens'. It is a wide-ranging term that includes suffering, illnesses, physical disabilities, sorrows, grief, worries, responsibilities (financial and other), temptations, errors, doubts, weaknesses and failures (moral and other). In other words, it includes any and every load that is hard to bear.

One of the ways in which Jesus bears these burdens of yours is through human friendship. This was the way in which Titus helped to bear Paul's burdens.

I like to be independent and self-sufficient, not relying on other people, but I am designed to be a burden to you and you are designed to be a burden to me: 'Carry each other's burdens, and in this way you will fulfil the law of Christ' (v.2).

I can only say that in my own life I am so grateful to those close friends with whom Pippa and I talk and pray regularly, who have helped us at times when the burdens have seemed too heavy for us to carry alone. We have been through many things together, suffered together and rejoiced together. All this has helped to spread the load.

The object of the team is to carry on sowing good seed. 'People reap what they sow. Those who sow to please their sinful nature, from that nature will reap destruction; those who sow to please the Spirit, from the Spirit will reap eternal life' (vv.7–8).

St Paul wrote to the Galatians, '...do not give up' (v.9). The temptation is to become weary in doing good. But the promise is that you will reap a harvest if you do not give up. Take every opportunity to do good to all people, 'especially to those who belong to the family of believers' (v.10).

There are many discouragements around. There are huge temptations to give up. When you sow a seed, you do not see the results immediately; it takes time. Sometimes, it's only when you look back years later that you can see that the seed you have sown has finally borne a harvest. There are also many seeds sown about which you may know nothing until you see the harvest in heaven. One of the keys to staying positive is to keep an eternal perspective.

Paul never gave up preaching the simple message of the 'cross of Christ' (v.12). He kept on going and he kept on sowing. He refused to add or subtract from the message. He also refused to preach a more popular message in order to avoid persecution (v.12). As a result, he was persecuted. He wrote, 'I bear on my body the marks of Jesus' (v.17).

PRAYER

Lord, help us all to keep on sowing, keep on doing good, and hold on to your promise that, at the proper time, we will reap a harvest if we *do not give up*.

OLD TESTAMENT READING

Isaiah 49:8–51:16
Never give up trusting in God's love

Each morning, Isaiah waited on God to speak to him and to instruct him, so that he would know the right words to 'sustain the weary' – to encourage those who were tempted to give up (50:4).

In this passage, the way he did this was by speaking to them about God's love for them. He spoke of God's compassion (49:10–13), and he used five analogies for God's love:

1. Shepherd
God loves you as a shepherd loves his sheep. God, as the shepherd of Israel, will lead his people back out of exile. In his love, he will make even obstacles serve his purpose (v.11). Jesus picks up this picture of the good shepherd and applies it to himself (John 10:3–15).

2. Mother
God's love for you is greater than any mother's love for her child. 'Can a mother forget the infant at her breast, walk away from the baby she bore? But even if mothers forget, I'd never forget you – *never*' (v.15, MSG).

3. Engraver
The Lord says, 'I have indelibly imprinted (tattooed a picture of) you on the palm of each of My hands' (v.16, AMP). The Babylonians used tattoos to remind them of the person they loved. God's love and commitment to you is demonstrated by his engraving of you on the palms of his hands.

4. Conqueror
God's love is like a conqueror (vv.25–26). He is strong enough to carry out his purposes for you and to fight against those who oppress you (v.25).

5. Husband
The people were saying God had divorced them because of their sins. God replies that although it was their weakness and their sin that caused the exile, God is able to restore them. He has not divorced them or sold them into slavery (50:1). No one is too far out of God's reach. He is married to his people. His love for you is greater than the greatest love between a husband and a wife.

Isaiah urges people to keep on trusting in the Lord: 'Those who hope in me will not be disappointed' (49:23). God will rescue them through his suffering servant: 'I did not hide my face from mocking and spitting. Because the Sovereign LORD helps me, I will not be disgraced. Therefore, have I set my face like flint' (50:6–7).

Jesus, knowing that he was going to be mocked and spat upon, set his face like flint and went to Jerusalem knowing that he would be crucified there. He was utterly determined. He did not give up. God vindicated him (v.8). The result was a great victory and a great harvest.

PRAYER

Lord, thank you that those who put their trust in you will never be disappointed. Help me to keep on trusting in your great love for me.

22 September | Day 265
Understand Your Value

Have you ever felt like a failure, or of no use to God, or thought that God wouldn't want to answer your prayers?

Until I first read Colin Urquhart's book, *In Christ Jesus*,[1] I had never realised how significant that little word *'in'* is in the New Testament. Understanding that, as a Christian, you are *'in'* Christ Jesus revolutionises how you see yourself, your self-image, your identity and how you understand your value to God.

Write your name on a piece of paper. Take hold of your Bible to represent Christ. Place the paper in the book and close it. You are in Christ. Where the book goes you go. Where the paper goes he goes. You are not part of the book, but you are now identified totally with the book.

Paul uses this expression, *'in Christ Jesus'*, over and over again. God has taken hold of you and placed you *in* Christ. In Christ, you have received *'every spiritual blessing'* (Ephesians 1:3). All of the blessings, including those that the Old Testament speaks about, are yours in Christ.

READING FROM PSALMS

Psalm 109:21–31
The blessings of God's love and healing

'*You* will bless,' writes David (v.28). All of God's blessings flow out of his love for you: 'out of the goodness of your love' (v.21; Ephesians 1:4, 5, 11; Isaiah 54:10). God's love supports you and helps you to stand, even when others 'scorn' and 'curse' you (Psalm 109:25–26). He stands at your 'right hand' (v.31a).

God saves our lives (v.31b, Isaiah 52:10). He heals our wounded hearts. David says, 'My heart is wounded within me' (Psalm 109:22). God loves to use people who have been wounded and then healed because no one can minister better than a person who has had the same wound and then been healed by God (see 2 Corinthians 1:3–4).

PRAYER

Lord, thank you for your wonderful love for me. Heal my wounded heart and help me to bring healing to others.

NEW TESTAMENT READING

Ephesians 1:1–23
The blessings of being in Christ Jesus

Many struggle with a low self-image. The New Testament answer to this problem is to know who you are in Christ Jesus: 'It's in Christ that we find out who we are and what we are living for' (v.11, MSG). Understand what your identity is *in* Christ. While you may not have every *material* blessing you want (Paul was in prison when he wrote this letter), God has blessed you 'with every *spiritual* blessing in Christ' (v.3). This passage lists many of these blessings:

1. Grace and peace

Paul starts his greetings with 'grace and peace' (v.2). Later he says, 'The riches of God's grace ... [have been] lavished on us' (vv.7–8). Grace is love that cares and stoops and rescues. You have peace with God.

2. Chosen, destined and adopted

'Even as [in His love] He chose us [actually picked us out for Himself as His own] in Christ before the foundation of the world ... He foreordained us (destined us, planned in love for us) to be adopted (revealed) as His own children' (vv.4–5, AMP; see also v.11).

3. Redeemed, forgiven and free

You are redeemed through his blood (v.7a; Isaiah 52:3, 9). 'Redeemed' was the word used for the buying back of a slave – a captive set free for a price.

Your sins are forgiven (Ephesians 1:7b). Marghanita Laski, a well-known atheist, made an amazing confession on television. She said, 'What I envy most about you Christians is your forgiveness.' She added, rather sadly, 'I have no one to forgive me.'

'We're a *free* people – *free* of penalties and punishment chalked up by all our misdeeds. And not just *barely* free, either. *Abundantly* free!' (v.7, MSG).

4. In-dwelt by the Holy Spirit

'Having believed, you were marked in him with a *seal*, the promised Holy Spirit' (v.13). The Holy Spirit has come to live within you. In the ancient world when a package was dispatched a seal was placed on it to indicate *where it had come from* and *to whom it belonged*. You have been sealed with the Holy Spirit.

5. Hope for the future

Your inheritance is guaranteed. You have 'the guarantee of our inheritance [the firstfruits, the pledge and foretaste, the down payment on our heritage], in anticipation of its full redemption *and* our acquiring [complete] possession of it' (v.14, AMP). You have 'the riches of his glorious *inheritance* in the saints' (v.18b).

6. Power and position

His 'incomparably great *power* for us who believe' is in you (v.19a). Power belongs to God, but he has come to live within you and to give you 'endless energy, boundless strength!' (v.19, MSG).

You are seated with Christ in the heavenly realms (v.20). God has placed us 'in charge of running the universe, everything from galaxies to governments' (vv.20–21, MSG).

7. Authority and responsibility

In Christ, God has placed everything under you for the sake of the church 'which is his body, the fullness of him who fills everything in every way' (vv.22–23). At her coronation when the orb (the globe under a cross) was placed in her hand, the Queen was reminded: 'When you see this orb set under the cross, remember that the whole world is subject to the power and empire of Christ our redeemer.'

God has given you great responsibility. His plans for the universe are now in the hands of the church, which is Jesus' 'body' on earth (v.23). 'The church, you see, is not peripheral to the world; the world is peripheral to the church' (vv.22–23, MSG).

PRAYER

Lord, I praise you for every spiritual blessing that you have given me in Christ. May the eyes of my heart be enlightened in order that I may know the hope to which you have called me, the riches of your glorious inheritance, and your incomparably great power living within me (vv.17–19).

OLD TESTAMENT READING

Isaiah 51:17–54:17
The blessings of the good news of Jesus

Isaiah writes, 'How beautiful are the feet of those who bring good news ... who proclaim salvation, who say to Zion, "Your God reigns!"' (52:7). God's salvation is such good news that it makes even the smelly feet of the messenger seem beautiful! This good news is Isaiah's message in the next chapter (52:13–53:12). It is the last and greatest of the four servant songs that reveal God's plan of salvation. There are five stanzas, each revealing an unexpected contrast:

1. Apparent failure and actual success (52:13–15)
The cross shatters human expectations. Here, Isaiah foretells Jesus' scourging and death, his 'ruined face, disfigured past recognition' (v.14, MSG). Yet the cross is not the end. The stanza ends in success and triumph, with an image of cleansing and forgiveness across the world; 'he will sprinkle many nations' (v.15).

2. Our view and God's view (53:1–3)
'Who would have thought God's saving power would look like this?' (v.1, MSG). Here we see a contrast between God's view and the human view. Isaiah foresees that the people would reject Jesus, even though he came to save them.

3. Our sin and his suffering (vv.4–6)
Jesus loves you so much that he died instead of you. That is the message at the heart of this passage – indeed of the whole Bible:

> 'He took the punishment, and that made us whole.
> Through his bruises we get healed.
> We're all like sheep who've wandered off and gotten lost.
> We've all done our own thing, gone our own way.
> And God has piled all our sins, everything we've done wrong, on him, on him' (v.5–6, MSG). Wow!

4. The guilty and the innocent (vv.7–9)
This stanza tells of a miscarriage of justice, but one that the innocent Jesus took upon himself voluntarily to bring salvation: 'He died without a thought for his own welfare, beaten bloody for the sins of my people' (v.8, MSG). It also predicts Jesus' death with extraordinary accuracy: foreseeing his silence at his trial (v.7); that he would die with the guilty and that he would be buried with the rich (v.9).

5. Tragedy and triumph (vv.10–13)
What looked like defeat was in fact a victory, 'what God had in mind all along' (v.10, MSG). What makes Jesus' death a triumph? First, 'he will see his offspring' (v.10) and 'make many righteous' (v.11, MSG) – the millions of transformed lives which are the fruit of his death. Second, 'he will see the light of life' (v.11) – Jesus rose again! Lastly, God exalted him, giving him 'a portion among the great' (v.12) because of all that he did for us.

As a result of what Jesus did for us, we are promised expansion and growth (54:2). You need not be afraid (v.4) because 'your Maker is your husband' (v.5). His love and compassion will never leave you (v.10). 'No weapon forged against you will prevail' (v.17).

PRAYER

Lord, thank you for the good news of the gospel; that through your suffering, I am made righteous. Help me to expect great things from you and attempt great things for you.

23 September | Day 266
What Difference Does Jesus Make?

I have interviewed hundreds of people around the world who have come to faith in Jesus. The question I ask over and over again is, 'What difference has Jesus made?' and the genuine answers given by the people I quote below are typical.

'My life has completely changed. I now look at the world through different eyes ... I feel love for everyone and an inner peace that I never imagined could exist.'

'I had been living my life in a dark hole, I was carrying a great weight on my shoulders ... that burden has gone ... and I am filled with great hope, joy, excitement and love, and all I want to do is to serve Christ in whatever form he chooses.'

'I feel like I have found love and conquered death in one day.'

The difference Jesus makes is massive, eternal, and impossible to comprehend.

READING FROM PSALMS

Psalm 110:1–7
Permanent forgiveness

Jesus made forgiveness possible through his one perfect sacrifice for our sins. He was uniquely qualified to do so as the 'King of kings' and 'Great High Priest'.

Jesus clearly saw this royal psalm of David as referring to himself (v.1, see Matthew 22:42–45; Luke 20:42–44). It is one of the most frequently quoted in the New Testament. Two lines of Old Testament prophecy come together in this psalm.

1. King of kings

Although it is about a human king, it points forward to *a divine King* who will be *King over all kings* (Psalm 110:5).

2. Great High Priest

The writer of Hebrews quotes this psalm as referring to Jesus (see Hebrews 7:17–22) as the one who is *the priest for ever* in the order of Melchizedek (Psalm 110:4). Neither Melchizedek nor Jesus were Levites. But both were priests – not on the basis of their ancestry, but on the basis of the power of an indestructible life (Hebrews 7:16).

Whereas the Old Testament priests were temporary, Jesus' priesthood is permanent: 'He sacrificed for their sins *once for all* when he offered himself (v.27). 'You're *the permanent priest*' (Psalm 110:4, MSG).

PRAYER

King Jesus, thank you that you made the one perfect sacrifice for my sins so that I can be forgiven, and my life can be utterly transformed.

NEW TESTAMENT READING

Ephesians 2:1–22
Peace and reconciliation

'Peace' is a word that sums up all the blessings Jesus brings to our lives. Christ came and preached the possibility of 'peace' to everyone (v.17).

Jesus is seated, after his resurrection, at the right hand of God, as prophesied in the psalm for today (Psalm 110:1). Being seated implies rest and peace. You died with Christ, were buried with him and have been raised with him and are now seated with him in the heavenly realms (Ephesians 2:6). You can enjoy his peace and rest as you go about your daily life.

Paul describes life *without Christ* in these terms. You were:

- 'dead in your transgressions and sins' (v.1)
- following 'the ways of the world' (v.2)
- 'gratifying the cravings of our sinful nature and following its desires and thoughts' (v.3a)
- 'objects of wrath' (v.3b)
- 'separate from Christ' (v.12a)
- 'outsiders to God's ways' (v.11, MSG)

- 'foreigners to the covenants of the promise' (v.12b)
- 'without hope' (v.12c)
- 'without God in the world' (v.12c)
- 'far away' (v.13)
- separated by the 'dividing wall of hostility' (v.14b)
- 'strangers or outsiders' (v.19, MSG).

Paul describes *the difference that Jesus makes* in these contrasting terms. You are:

- 'raised up with Christ' (v.6)
- 'seated with him in the heavenly realms' (v.6)
- 'God's masterpiece' (v.10, NLT)
- 'created in Christ Jesus to do good works which God prepared in advance for us to do' (v.10)
- 'brought near through the blood of Christ' (v.13)
- 'reconciled to God through the cross' (v.16)
- 'fellow-citizens with God's people' (v.19)
- 'members of God's household' (v.19)
- 'a dwelling in which God lives by his Spirit' (v.22).

The contrast between the prior alienation – from yourself and from God – and the peace and reconciliation that Jesus brings, could not be greater. It is Jesus who makes the difference. You are made alive *with Christ* (v.5). You are raised up *with Christ* (v.6). You are saved through faith *in* Christ (v.8). It is *in Christ Jesus* that you are brought near (v.13). It is *through Jesus* that you have access to the Father by one Spirit (v.18). *Jesus Christ himself* is the chief cornerstone of the new temple, the church.

The only command that Paul gives here is to 'remember' (vv.12–13). So often we can *forget* that being a Christian is all about what Jesus has done for us, and get caught up in what we are doing. This passage helps you to stop, *remember*, and give thanks to your amazing Saviour for all he has done for you.

PRAYER

Lord, thank you for your great love for me. Thank you for the utter transformation you bring to my life.

OLD TESTAMENT READING

Isaiah 55:1–57:13
Purpose and meaning

The Bible is one long invitation to come to God. It starts with God's call to Adam, full of love and anguish, 'Where are you?' (Genesis 3:9). It ends with the invitation from the Spirit and the Bride who say, '*Come!*' (Revelation 22:17).

Jesus often invited people: '*Come* to me' (Matthew 11:28), '*Come* to the wedding banquet' (22:4), '*Come* to me and drink' (John 7:37). In this chapter, God once again issues an invitation to come.

> 'Hey there! All who are thirsty,
> *come to the water*!
> Are you penniless?
> *Come* anyway – buy and eat!
> *Come*, buy your drinks, buy wine and milk.
> Buy without money – everything's free!' (Isaiah 55:1, MSG).

The invitation is urgent and universal. The New Testament sees it as Jesus' invitation to us (see Acts 13:34–35). Here are four reasons why you should come to him:

1. Jesus alone can satisfy the hunger in your heart

Without Jesus we are thirsty (Isaiah 55:1). We labour for what does not satisfy (v.2). The opening verses echo the cries of those selling their wares in Babylon, the centre of commerce in the ancient world. The message is this: material things do not satisfy. Without God we are always partly empty, experiencing a lack of fulfilment and a feeling of dissatisfaction.

The offer of Jesus is free. It is to 'you who have no money' (v.1). The promise is that as you come to Jesus 'your soul will delight in the richest of fare ... your soul will live' (vv.2–3). Those who come to him are deeply satisfied. God does not offer you junk food, but a feast. His words are 'life-giving' and 'life-nourishing' (v.2, MSG).

2. Jesus' love and mercy is great

Repentance is necessary in order to enjoy God's presence fully (vv.6–9). Turn away from sin: 'Let the wicked forsake their ways and the unrighteous their thoughts' (v.7a). I like the child's definition of repentance: 'being sorry enough to stop'.

Repentance also involves turning to God: 'Let them turn to the LORD, and he will have mercy on them, and to our God, for he will freely pardon' (v.7b). No matter how far you have fallen, God will forgive you. He is 'lavish with forgiveness' (v.7, MSG).

3. Jesus is the life transformer

'You will go out in joy and be led forth in peace; the mountains and hills will burst into song before you, and all the trees of the field will clap their hands. Instead of the thorn bush will grow the pine tree, and instead of briers the myrtle will grow' (vv.12–13).

The immediate application of this passage was to the departure of the Jews from Babylon. Israel was to 'go out' from Babylon and go back to Jerusalem in 'joy' and 'peace'.

However, the prophecy will not reach complete fulfilment until the return of Jesus Christ. Then, nature itself will be renewed and restored. You get a foretaste of this now, in this life, but the ultimate fulfilment of these verses will come when Jesus returns, in the new heaven and new earth.

The Bible is not only the story of the human race, but is the story of the whole of creation in which the human race plays a central and crucial role.

4. Jesus has a purpose for your life

God's blessings were never intended to be enjoyed selfishly (vv.3b–5). They were to overflow to others. You can't offer to others what you have not received yourself. But when you have enjoyed a blessing, pass it on.

As Paul puts it in today's New Testament passage, you are 'God's masterpiece'. He created you anew in Christ Jesus so that you can do the good works he planned for you long ago (see Ephesians 2:10, NLT). Your life has a purpose. Your story is important. Your dreams count. Your voice matters. You were born to make an impact.

PRAYER

Lord, thank you that you invite me to come to you to drink the water of life. Thank you for the massive difference you make to my life, both now and into eternity.

---

24 September | Day 267
Mystery

The best novelists are able to write in such a way that as you read through a story, the ending is a mystery but, when you look back from the end, the clues were there all along.

In today's New Testament passage, the apostle Paul tells us that God has revealed the mystery of Christ. He writes about 'the *mystery* made known to me by revelation ... the *mystery* of Christ, which was not made known to people in other generations as it has now been revealed by the Spirit' (Ephesians 3:3–5).

Reading the Old Testament is like going into a dark room full of furniture. We get a sense of what is inside the room by feeling the sofas, chairs and pictures. But, as we read the New Testament, it is as if a light is switched on and we see the room clearly. Jesus places the Old Testament in new light. To paraphrase St Augustine, 'In the Old the New is concealed, in the New the Old is revealed.'[1]

Jesus is the climax of God's great plan for the world. Thus, Paul writes, 'My task is to bring out in the open and make plain what God, who created all this in the first place, has been doing *in secret* and *behind the scenes* all along' (vv.8–9, MSG). The word that Paul uses (*photisai*) means 'to turn the light on so that people can see'.

The secret God reveals in Jesus is reconciliation not only with God but also with one another. Paul tells us, 'This mystery is that through the gospel the Gentiles are heirs together with Israel, members together of one body, and sharers together in the promise in Christ Jesus' (v.6). Both Jews and Gentiles can now approach God on equal terms.

If we are in Christ, we are all reconciled to God and to one another – regardless of race or social and cultural background. It must also apply to the church: Catholic, Orthodox, Protestant, Pentecostal, and so on. In the Old Testament, we see only hints of this – it was concealed to some extent. Now, however, the mystery has been revealed in Christ.

READING FROM PSALMS

Psalm 111:1–10
God's wisdom is revealed

Knowledge is good: 'GOD's works are so great, worth a lifetime of study' (v.2, MSG). Wisdom is better. Wisdom is the right use of knowledge.

The psalmist writes that, 'the fear of the LORD is *the beginning of wisdom*' (v.10a). True wisdom begins with respecting, revering, honouring and worshipping God: 'He is so personal and holy, worthy of our respect' (v.9, MSG).

Like other Old Testament writers, he caught a glimpse of this wisdom. He saw the greatness of all that God had done (v.2). He saw that the Lord is gracious and compassionate (v.4b). He realised that God loved and wanted to redeem his people (v.9). But his attitude to 'other nations' (v.6) is not yet expanded by the revelation of Christ and the gospel ('None of our ancestors understood this', Ephesians 3:2 MSG).

In Christ, these nations are included in God's love and they become part of his church. As we see in today's New Testament passage, this is how the manifold wisdom of God is revealed.

PRAYER

Lord, help us in the church to reveal the manifold wisdom of God as people are reconciled to you and to one another.

NEW TESTAMENT READING

Ephesians 3:1–21
God's power is revealed

Do you want to be useful to God? Do you want to make a difference – in your family and with your friends, in your school, university or workplace, to the nation and to the world? This passage not only reveals the mystery of Christ, but it also shows you how, as a result, your life can make an impact.

Paul concludes, 'God can do anything, you know – far more than you could ever imagine or guess or request in your wildest dreams!' (v.20, MSG). How is this possible? Paul's answer is that it is possible 'according to his power that is at work within us' (v.20). Where does this power come from?

- **The power *of the gospel***

Power does not come from your position, title or circumstances in life. Paul himself was a prisoner (v.1). It doesn't come from human greatness. Paul writes, 'I am less than the least of all God's people' (v.8). Power doesn't come from lording over people. Paul writes, 'I became a servant' (v.7). Rather, it comes from the message of the gospel, that Paul described in this passage. The gospel is 'the power of God' for the salvation of everyone who believes (Romans 1:16).

- **The power of *unity***

We are co-heirs, sons and daughters of God the Father. We are brothers and sisters, inheritors together in the promises of Christ Jesus. We are co-members, belonging to the same body of Christ (Ephesians 3:6). We are united in Jesus Christ, co-sharers of the promised Holy Spirit.

This unity is extraordinarily powerful. 'His intent was that now, through the church, the manifold wisdom of God should be made known to the rulers and authorities in the heavenly realms, according to his eternal purpose which he accomplished in Christ Jesus our Lord' (vv.10–11).

The use of 'manifold' here refers to the multi-faceted wisdom of God. It is multi-racial and multicultural. God has brought everybody together in his church. Therefore, not only is disunity (of churches and denominations) harmful to the spread of the gospel but unity is so powerful.

The battle is against 'the rulers and authorities in the heavenly realms' (v.10). These powers operate through the economic, social and political structures and institutions of human society, and beyond into the entire cosmos. Every time a person is reconciled to God and to their brothers and sisters in Christ, the demons scream and the angels rejoice. The manifold wisdom of God is revealed.

- **The power of the *Holy Spirit***

Paul prayed that 'out of his glorious riches he may *strengthen you with power through his Spirit in your inner being*, so that Christ may dwell in your hearts through faith' (vv.16–17) and that 'you may be filled to the measure of all the fullness of God' (v.19).

- **The power of *God's love***

Do you really understand the full extent of God's love for you? Paul prayed that 'with both feet planted firmly on love, you'll be able to take in with all followers of Jesus the extravagant dimensions of Christ's love. Reach out and experience the breadth! Test its length! Plumb the depths! Rise to the heights! Live full lives, full in the fullness of God' (vv.17–19, MSG).

PRAYER

Lord, today I ask that I may be filled to the measure of all the fullness of God.

OLD TESTAMENT READING

Isaiah 57:14–59:21
God's love is revealed

In the Old Testament (and particularly in Isaiah), you can see hints of the expansive love of God, and how his love extends beyond the people of Israel to all the people on earth. In this passage for today, we get a glimpse of this love.

The Lord says, 'Peace, peace, to him who is far off [*both Jew and Gentile*] and to him who is near!' (57:19, AMP; see also Ephesians 2:17). Paul seems to interpret these passages of Isaiah as anticipating the inclusion of the Gentiles in God's love (Ephesians 2:17).

Isaiah then goes on to show how God's people should reflect this amazing love in the way they treat the poor and marginalised around them. Mere religious activity is of no avail. God is looking for a love that will: 'break the chains of injustice, get rid of exploitation in the workplace, free the oppressed, cancel debts' (Isaiah 58:6, MSG).

He is looking for a love that will lead you to 'sharing your food with the hungry, inviting the homeless poor into your homes, putting clothes on the shivering ill-clad, being available to your own families' (v.7, MSG).

This is a love that will ensure that you 'spend yourself on behalf of the hungry and satisfy the needs of the oppressed' (v.10). True love for our neighbour must include a passion for social justice – 'to loose the chains of injustice' (v.6a) – and social action. Love means doing something about poverty, homelessness and hunger. These words challenge us today about how we respond to the refugee crisis that is across the whole world; especially Europe.

Isaiah promises that, 'If you get rid of unfair practices, quit blaming victims, quit gossiping about other people's sins, If you are generous with the hungry and start giving yourselves to the down-and-out, your lives will begin to glow in the darkness, your shadowed lives will be bathed in sunlight' (vv.9–10, MSG). The light will be switched on. The secret will be revealed.

PRAYER

Lord, may we be a church that reveals the manifold wisdom of God by our unity and love. Give us wisdom as to how we respond to poverty. Pour out your Spirit on us. May the mystery of Christ be revealed in us.

25 September | Day 268
Spirit-powered Living

'I felt ablaze with a desire to go through the length and breadth of Wales to tell of the Saviour: and had it been possible, I was willing to pay God for doing so,'[1] wrote Evan Roberts, the man at the centre of the Welsh revival of 1904–5. He spoke about how the Spirit of God gave him an overwhelming experience of God's love. He was filled with compassion and a desire to tell others about Jesus.

We live in the age of the Spirit. In the Old Testament, the Holy Spirit came on particular people at particular times for particular purposes. We see an example of this in today's reading, when the Holy Spirit came on Isaiah (Isaiah 61). This event was a foretaste of the Holy Spirit coming upon Jesus (Luke 4:14–18), as well as of the outpouring of the Holy Spirit on all Christians, from the day of Pentecost onwards.

The book of Proverbs anticipates what Spirit-powered living should look like. Then, in the New Testament, we see the fulfilment of Spirit-powered living.

READING FROM PROVERBS

Proverbs 23:19–28
A wise life

What does a wise lifestyle look like? How do you 'become wise' and point your life 'in the right direction' (v.19, MSG)? The Holy Spirit is the Spirit of wisdom (Isaiah 11:2, Ephesians 1:17). Living according to the Spirit of wisdom and understanding means taking care over:

1. What you eat and drink
'Don't drink *too much* wine and get drunk; don't eat *too much* food and get fat' (Proverbs 23:20, MSG). We are to be neither 'drunks' nor 'gluttons' (v.21, MSG).

2. Whom you listen to
'*Listen* with respect to the father who raised you, and when your mother grows old, don't neglect her' (v.22, MSG). Respect for parents is the mark of wisdom. Wise children should make their parents proud of them (vv.24–25, MSG).

3. How you learn
An inquisitive mind is the mark of the Spirit of wisdom: 'Buy truth ... buy wisdom, buy education, buy insight' (vv.23, MSG). The Spirit of wisdom gives you a hunger for truth and knowledge.

4. What you think about
What you think in your heart you become. 'My child, give me your heart' (v.26a) – this is where everything starts. Guard your heart and your mind.

5. What you look at
'Let your eyes keep to my ways' (v.26b). Watching what you look at is one of the ways to guard against promiscuity and immorality (vv.27–28).

PRAYER
Lord, fill me today with the Spirit of wisdom. May my life be honouring to Jesus.

NEW TESTAMENT READING

Ephesians 4:1–16
A healthy life

What are the characteristics of a healthy church? Paul tells us how the church can grow up 'healthy in God' (v.16, MSG).

1. Unity
Unity is not simply the work of the Holy Spirit but the very instrument through which the Holy Spirit works.

The Holy Spirit unites the church (v.16). The church is one: 'There is *one* body and *one* Spirit – just as you were called to *one* hope when you were called – *one* Lord, *one* faith, *one* baptism; *one* God and Father of all, who is over all and through all and in all' (vv.4–6).

Unity is relational. All Christians are sons and daughters of the 'one God and Father of all'. Therefore, we are brothers and sisters. We all love 'one Lord' Jesus. We all have the Holy Spirit living within us. Ultimately, it is our relationship to God; Father, Son and Holy Spirit that unites us.

And yet, unity is so hard in practice. It is easy to argue. It's easy to split. It's easy to start our own group with people who agree with us. Unity requires great effort. Paul urges us to '*make every effort* to keep the unity of the Spirit through the bond of peace' (v.3). We need to spare no effort to make the invisible unity of the one church visible at every level, within local churches, between churches and among all denominations.

Before he went to the cross, Jesus prayed that the church would be one in order that the world might believe (John 17:21–23). This unity is founded in God's unity, so it can never be at the expense of truth (vv.17, 23). We must continue to speak the truth in love (Ephesians 4:15). As John Stott writes, 'Truth becomes hard if it is not softened by love; love becomes soft if it is not strengthened by truth.'[2]

The visible unity of the church should always be our aim. Paul describes characteristics that help this unity: 'Be completely humble and gentle; be patient, bearing with one another in love' (v.2).

2. Diversity
Unity does not mean uniformity. The Holy Spirit brings both unity and diversity. Paul goes on to say, 'But to each one of us grace has been given as Christ apportioned it' (v.7).

Jesus has 'ascended higher than all the heavens' (v.10). But he has also returned to the earth in the person of the Holy Spirit, through whom different gifts are now given to each of us in the church (vv.10–12).

Every single person in the church is a minister (vv.11–12). You are a minister. The word for service means 'ministry'. We are all given different gifts.

3. Maturity

The purpose of these gifts is that the body of Christ may be built up until we all reach *unity* in the faith and in the knowledge of the Son of God, becoming *mature* as we attain the complete measure of the fullness of Christ.

It is not enough to get older; we need to grow in spiritual maturity.

4. Growth

Healthy children grow. Healthy churches grow in depth and in number. Church growth should be natural. This is a beautiful picture of how we each play our own part in the growth of the body of Christ: 'Speaking the truth in love, we will in all things grow up into him who is the Head, that is, Christ. From him the whole body, joined and held together by every supporting ligament, grows and builds itself up in love, as each part does its work' (vv.15–16). You have to play your 'part', and we grow as we all work at it 'together'.

PRAYER

Lord, fill me with your Spirit and help me to grow into a mature knowledge of Jesus in a healthy, united and growing church.

OLD TESTAMENT READING

Isaiah 60:1–62:12
An anointed life

Jesus announced his manifesto for his ministry and kingdom by reading from Isaiah 61. It is an audacious and revolutionary manifesto – and you have a part to play in bringing it about.

Jesus went into the synagogue in Nazareth and was handed the scroll of the prophet Isaiah. Unrolling it, he found the place in today's passage where it is written, 'The Spirit of the Lord is on me, because he has *anointed me* to preach good news to the poor. He has sent me to proclaim freedom for the prisoners and recovery of sight for the blind, to release the oppressed, to proclaim the year of the Lord's favour' (Isaiah 61:1–2; Luke 4:18–19).

He said to those there, 'Today this scripture is fulfilled in your hearing' (v.21). What does Jesus' manifesto involve?

1. Transforming lives

When you encounter Jesus, a great exchange takes place in your life. He takes your sin and gives you his righteousness. He gives freedom to the prisoners, sight to the blind and release for the oppressed (Isaiah 61:1–3). He bestows on you 'a crown of beauty instead of ashes, the oil of gladness instead of mourning, and a garment of praise instead of a spirit of despair' (v.3).

2. Transforming relationships

Jesus uses the analogy of marriage: 'As a bridegroom rejoices over his bride, so will your God rejoice over you' (62:5b). Marriage is meant to point people to the close, intimate and loving relationship God desires to have with us. A strong society is built on strong families. Strong families are built on strong marriages.

3. Transforming culture

Cities tend to be the source of culture. Isaiah declares, 'They will rebuild the ancient ruins and restore the places long devastated; they will renew the ruined *cities* that have been devastated for generations' (61:4). The manifesto of Jesus involves the transformation of the mountains of influence: the market-place, government, education, media, arts and entertainment.

4. Transforming society

A transformed society will involve dealing with issues of poverty. Jesus came to preach good news to the *poor* (v.1b). It will also involve issues of justice. So much of the world's suffering is caused by injustice. 'For I, the LORD, love *justice*; I hate robbery and iniquity' (v.8a).

5. Transforming leadership

Leadership is key in any society: 'You'll have the title "Priests of GOD," honored as ministers of our God' (v.6, MSG).

PRAYER

Lord, anoint me today with your Holy Spirit to bring good news to the poor, to bind up the broken-hearted, comfort those who mourn and to see lives transformed from ashes to beauty, from mourning to gladness and from despair to praise.

26 September | Day 269
Six Keys to Good Relationships

When she was nineteen years of age, Chiara Lubich gathered with a few friends in northern Italy. It was 1939 and, as bombs fell, they asked this question: 'Was there an ideal that bombs could not destroy?' Their answer was, 'Yes, the *love of God*'.

They had experienced God's overwhelming love and they wanted to share it with others. *They imitated God by living a life of love* (Ephesians 5:1–2). They helped those in need. They shared what little food they had. They found clothing for those who had none. They comforted the bereaved.

Such a warmth emanated from Chiara and her friends that people gave them the name 'Focolare', which means 'hearth' or 'fireplace'. Focolare now has 2 million members in 182 countries. Members of the Focolare community make it their rule of life, 24 hours a day, to live by the golden rule of Jesus: 'Do to others what you would have them do to you' (Matthew 7:12).

Love is practical. Chiara said, 'Love the other person as yourself ... Imagine how the world would be if the golden rule were put into practice not only between individuals, but also between ethnic groups, peoples and nations, if everyone *loved* the other country as their own.'

How can we imitate God and live a life of love?

READING FROM PSALMS

Psalm 112:1–10
Be filled with the Holy Spirit

It is the Holy Spirit in you who produces a life that imitates God. In this psalm, we see the kind of life God wants you to lead, and it includes all the fruit of the Spirit described by Paul in Galatians 5:22–23. It is a life of:

- love ('compassionate', Psalm 112:4)
- joy ('delight', v.1)
- peace ('they will have no fear of bad news', v.7)
- patience ('their hearts are steadfast', v.7)
- kindness ('generous and lend freely', v.5b; 'they have scattered abroad their gifts to the poor', v.9)
- goodness ('the righteous will be remembered for ever', v.6b)
- faithfulness ('their hearts are secure', v.8a)
- gentleness ('gracious', v.4b)
- self-control ('surely they will never be shaken', v.6a).

All this stems from knowing God – spending time reading and meditating on his word: 'Blessed are those who fear the LORD, who find great delight in his commands' (v.1).

PRAYER

Lord, help me today to live a life overflowing with the fruit of your Spirit.

NEW TESTAMENT READING

Ephesians 4:17–5:7
Be transformed into the likeness of Jesus

Jesus Christ set the supreme example of love by giving up his life for us. St Paul writes, '*Be imitators of God*, therefore, as dearly loved children and *live a life of love*, just as Christ loved us and gave himself up for us as a fragrant offering and sacrifice to God' (5:1–2). As St Athanasius wrote, 'God became like us in order that we might become like God.'

What does this 'life of love' look like?

Paul writes about how the Ephesians came 'to *know* Christ' (4:20), and how knowing him they were taught to 'be made new in the attitude of your minds and to put on the new self, created to be *like God* in true *righteousness* and *holiness*' (vv.23–24).

What is 'holiness'?

Paul gives six practical examples of holiness – six keys to good relationships in a holy church (4:25–5:7):

1. Authenticity

'What this adds up to, then, is this: no more lies, no more pretence. Tell your neighbour the truth. In Christ's body we're all connected to each other, after all' (4:25, MSG).

Live a life of honesty and integrity. The danger of talking about 'holiness' is that it leads to intensity. But there is a fine line between holiness and being 'holier than thou', between being pious and being poisonous! Authenticity frees us to admit we're far from perfect. We can be vulnerable with one another. This leads away from hypocrisy.

2. Passion

'Go ahead and be angry. You do well to be angry – but don't use your anger as fuel for revenge. And don't stay angry. Don't go to bed angry. Don't give the Devil that kind of foothold in your life' (vv.26–27, MSG).

Although anger is not intrinsically sinful, it often leads to sin. In anger, the devil sometimes finds a foothold in our lives that easily becomes an addiction. Anger is an emotion that we need to handle with care.

On the other hand, there is a positive side to anger. It can be a God-given emotion. God expresses anger (5:6), but of course he does so under control. Jesus' anger was a righteous anger towards sin. It was Wilberforce's *passionate* hatred of slavery that eventually led to the abolition of the slave trade.

3. Work and generosity

'Did you use to make ends meet by stealing? Well, no more! Get an honest job so that you can help others who can't work' (v.28, MSG).

Holiness is often mistakenly understood as the need to separate ourselves from those we consider unholy. Perhaps work colleagues, for example. Paul's point is very different. He sees work as part of a holy life. Work in itself is good for the satisfaction that it brings but there is also toil, struggle and effort. So why do people go to work in the morning? One answer is: in order to be holy.

Paul finds it necessary to say do not steal *any longer*, which hints that some members of the early church were ex-offenders. The church clearly welcomed and rehabilitated them.

Rather than taking from others, they should now contribute to those around them. The best way to do that is by working. Work in itself is 'doing something useful', as well as enabling them to 'share with those in need' (v.28). Work is, for everyone, a part of being holy.

4. Encouragement

'Watch the way you talk. Let nothing foul or dirty come out of your mouth. Say only what helps, each word a gift' (v.29, MSG).

Words matter. What you say is of vital importance. It can either build people up or drag them down. Use your mouth for good – for encouragement and for building others up.

Encouragement is not flattery or empty praise; it is like verbal sunshine. It costs nothing and warms other people's hearts and inspires them with hope and confidence.

5. Grace

'Make a clean break with all cutting, backbiting, profane talk. Be gentle with one another, sensitive. Forgive one another as quickly and thoroughly as God in Christ forgave you' (vv.31–32, MSG).

Paul's vision of a holy church is a community that rids itself of all bitterness, anger and slander, and that welcomes ex-offenders, those struggling with lifestyle issues, those who are divorced, those who have messed up. It is a community of people in need of forgiveness and a place where forgiveness flows freely because forgiven people forgive.

Churches are not supposed to be museums that display perfect people, walking around looking holy. They are called to be hospitals where the wounded, hurt, injured and broken find grace and healing.

6. Purity

The church welcomes everyone, because it is kind, compassionate and gracious. At the same time, you are called to a life of purity without 'even a hint of sexual immorality, or of any kind of impurity, or of greed, because these are improper for God's holy people' (5:3).

Rather than self-centred sins (vv.3–4a), you are called to God-centred thanksgiving (v.4b). There is also a strong warning here from Paul. There is forgiveness for sins, but those who end up setting their course against God's ways will not inherit his kingdom (v.5).

PRAYER

Lord, help me today to live a life of love and to become more like Jesus.

OLD TESTAMENT READING

Isaiah 63:1–65:16
Become like the compassionate father

God's love for Israel was like that of a father: 'You are our Father' (63:16; 64:8, MSG).

'You're our *living* Father, our Redeemer, famous from eternity!' (63:17, MSG).

Just as God loved the people of Israel in the Old Testament, so God loves you as a father loves his children. Isaiah speaks of the kindnesses of the Lord: 'All the LORD has done for us – yes, the many good things he has done for the house of Israel, according to his compassion and many kindnesses. He said, "Surely they are my people, children who will not be false to me"' (vv.7–8).

God loves us in spite of the fact that 'we're all sin-infected, sin-contaminated. Our best efforts are grease-stained rags' (64:6, MSG).

God, like any human father, suffers when we suffer or go astray: 'In all their troubles, he was troubled, too' (63:9a, MSG). 'In his love and mercy he *redeemed* them; he lifted them up and carried them all the days of old' (v.9b).

God has plans for you that no eye has seen, no ear has heard and no mind has conceived (Isaiah 64:4; 1 Corinthians 2:9).

PRAYER

Lord, thank you that you love me more than any human father. Thank you that because of your love for me, I am able to love those around me.

27 September | Day 270
Seven Ways You Please the Lord

You can please God. It is amazing when you really think about it: human beings – seemingly so insignificant when we look at the size and scale of the universe that God has created – have the ability to please the Lord. It is also possible to 'displease' the Lord (Isaiah 66:4c). The apostle Paul wrote, 'Find out what *pleases the Lord*' (Ephesians 5:10), or as *The Message* translation puts it, 'Figure out what will please Christ, and then do it.'

READING FROM PSALMS

Psalm 113:1–9
1. Praise the Lord

Praise is the appropriate response to God. He is worthy of all your praise. We teach our children to be thankful – not for our own sake but for *theirs*. We are pleased when they are thankful. God teaches you to praise him because it is the right response to him, and because it is good for you. Thanksgiving is an appropriate response to human generosity. Continual praise is the appropriate response to God's generosity.

The psalmist repeats over and over again that you should 'praise the LORD' (v.1). Praise him all day long: 'From the rising of the sun to the place where it sets' (v.3). Praise him throughout your life, 'now and tomorrow and always' (v.2, MSG). Praise him particularly for his love for the marginalised: the poor, the needy and the barren (vv.7–9).

PRAYER

Hallelujah! Praise the Lord...

NEW TESTAMENT READING

Ephesians 5:8–33
2. Live in the light

Ephesians 5:8–14

As Christians, we are called to be a community whose conduct shines as a beacon to others, illuminating the way that God intended life to be lived.

Paul wrote that you are 'light in the Lord' (v.8). Therefore, you should live as 'children of light' (v.8). Light produces good fruit: goodness (generosity towards others), righteousness (doing right in relation to God and humanity) and truth. These are ways you can *please the Lord* (v.10).

Light exposes evil. The best way to get rid of evil is to drag it into the light. Evil thrives in the darkness, but the moment you bring it into the light, its power diminishes.

Ask God to shine the light of the Holy Spirit into your heart. If the Holy Spirit exposes an area of darkness, deal with it through confession and repentance. The moment you do so, the power of evil is broken.

3. Make the most of every opportunity

Ephesians 5:15–17

Time is your most valuable possession. You can get more money but you cannot get more time.

Paul wrote, 'Be very careful, then, how you live – not as unwise but as wise, making the most of every opportunity, because the days are evil' (vv.15–16). Do not fritter away your life, like a fool. Life is short – live in the moment and make the most of every day.

4. Be filled with the Spirit

Ephesians 5:18–20

Paul contrasts the escapism of substance abuse (getting 'drunk on wine, which leads to debauchery') with being 'filled' (v.18) with the Holy Spirit: 'Drink the Spirit of God, huge draughts of him' (v.18, MSG). In these verses, he uses 'filled' in the present continuous tense, urging us to go on and on being filled with the Spirit.

Being filled with the Spirit leads to singing 'psalms, hymns and spiritual songs' (v.19) instead of 'drinking songs!' (v.19, MSG). It leads you to worship the Lord Jesus in your heart and to give thanks to God – the very opposite of grumbling and complaining. It is characteristic of the Spirit-filled community to be grateful to God for all things, in all places and at all times. It also leads to mutual submission as we see in the next section.

5. Submit to one another with love and respect

Ephesians 5:21–33

John Paul Getty, once the wealthiest man on the planet, who was married three times, said, 'I would gladly give all of my millions for just one lasting marital success.'[1] Mutual respect is the key to a happy marriage. The key words in verses 21–33 are '*respect*', '*love*' and '*submit*'. The overall heading for this section is that 'out of respect for Christ' (v.21, MSG), we are to 'submit to *one another*' (v.21).

The word used for submission is different from the word used for 'obey' (6:1). Submission is voluntarily yielding in love. It is a beautiful characteristic and it is clear from the overall heading, 'submit to one another' (5:21), that Paul expects mutual submission. This teaching would have been a revolutionary concept in first-century culture.

Respect is the key to a good relationship between the sexes. We are not at war. As Pope Benedict put it, 'In Christ, the rivalry, enmity and violence can be overcome and has been overcome. It is respect throughout marriage that elevates the other and gives them the dignity and increases their confidence and self worth.'[2]

The overall emphasis of the passage is on love. Although it is directed particularly at the husband, it would be absurd to suggest that the love is not mutual. Paul is saying that both love and submission are mutual. Love is self-giving; this is how a husband submits.

This kind of love is sanctifying (vv.26–27). It makes us holy. It makes us like Jesus. It is sensitive (vv.28–30). And it is sealed in marriage by sexual union (v.31).

And this is the New Testament context of sexual union. It is the most beautiful and the most romantic view of sex and marriage. As Robert Spaemann put it, 'The essence of marriage is that two lives, two whole biographies, are so tied together that they become one history.'[3]

Furthermore, these verses are precious gems to be treasured because of what they suggest about the forthcoming marriage feast of the Lamb, and the consummation of the union between Christ and his church.

PRAYER

Lord, please fill me today with the Holy Spirit so that I may shine in a way that pleases you and make the most of every hour of every day. Help us in all our relationships to submit to one another, respecting and loving each other and pleasing you.

OLD TESTAMENT READING

Isaiah 65:17–66:24

6. Be humble

Isaiah 66:2b

The Lord himself says, 'these are the ones I esteem: those who are humble and contrite in spirit, and tremble at my word' (v.2b). 'But there is something I'm looking for: a person simple and plain, reverently responsive to what I say' (v.2b, MSG).

This is another way to please the Lord. Through constant study of, and submission to, his word, God keeps us humble and contrite. It is easy to become prideful until we fall on our knees before God and his word, and see ourselves in the light of his truth.

7. Look forward to a world where everything pleases God

Isaiah 65:17 – 66:24

Isaiah encouraged the people: 'Be glad and rejoice for ever in what I will create' (65:18). God promises that he will create 'new heavens and a new earth' (v.17).

This new heaven and new earth will finally be a place where *everything* pleases God, where he can 'delight in [his] people' (v.19). In these final chapters, Isaiah sketches out a glorious vision of what this new creation will be like.

This passage also warns of the coming judgment, as all that displeases God is excluded from this new creation (66:4b).

The imagery of a new creation, which these chapters give us, is then a picture of joy and rejoicing (65:18–19a); a place where there is no more suffering and 'the sound of weeping and of crying will be heard in it no more' (v.19b, see also Revelation 21:4).

Isaiah promises that everyone will reach their full potential (Isaiah 65:20). But the New Testament goes even further, with Jesus promising eternal life. There will be no need for funerals, undertakers or cemeteries. God's people will be given immortality (1 Corinthians 15:53).

Isaiah looks forward to a time when all activity will be a blessing (Isaiah 65:21–23a). There will be no more work in vain. There will be no more labour or toil. Rather, there will be a restoration of the rule over creation with which we were originally entrusted (see Genesis 1:26; Revelation 22:5).

There will be a closeness of relationship with God (Isaiah 65:23b–24), with no more struggling or seemingly unanswered prayer. You will have an unimpaired vision of God and of Jesus.

There will be harmony and peace (v.25). All relationships will be restored – including even the animal world. There will be unity and intimacy in all our relationships. Nature will be restored as a place of stability, safety and peace. The kingdom of God will be fully established. Martin Luther wrote, 'I would not give up one moment of Heaven for all the joys and riches of the world, even if they lasted for thousands and thousands of years.'

PRAYER

Lord, may this wonderful promise of a new heaven and a new earth spur me on in my desire to live now in the ways that please you.

28 September | Day 271

Seven Life-changing Habits

For many years, Bruce Streather, a successful lawyer, was an atheist. He never went to church, even though his family did. Most weekends he played golf. Eventually, as a result of considerable persuasion from his wife and three teenage daughters, he came on Alpha. He was extremely argumentative and hostile. None of the sessions had any impact on him until, towards the end of the course, he heard the talk 'How Can I Resist Evil?' Afterwards he came up to me and said, 'In my work as a lawyer, I have seen so much evil. I have always believed in the power of evil. Tonight, it struck me that if there is a power of evil, it makes sense to believe that there is also a power of good.'

That night Bruce became a Christian. Ever since, he has been a committed member of the church with a very powerful and effective ministry affecting the lives of hundreds of people.

We struggle with the global evils of terrorism, the rise of Isis, the tragic plight of refugees, events in Syria, the Zika virus, starvation, poverty, the destruction of the environment, corrupt governments and countless other domestic, local and international issues. We also face struggles against evil in our own lives – temptation, sin and addiction.

The Bible is realistic about this struggle. In the Old Testament, we read about physical battles against the forces of evil. In the New Testament, the struggle is more often described as a spiritual battle. As St Paul puts it, 'Our struggle is not against flesh and blood, but against the rulers, against the authorities, against the powers of this dark world and against the spiritual *forces of evil* in the heavenly realms' (Ephesians 6:12).

Today's passages show us that the battle is won through the victorious power of the Lord.

READING FROM PSALMS

Psalm 114:1–8
Victory over bondage and slavery

The psalmist recalls how Israel was set free from its bondage and slavery in Egypt. The victorious power of God led them out of Egypt and across the sea, which 'looked and fled' (v.3).

The 'presence of the Lord' with his people gave the Israelites the victory (v.7). It was *his presence* that 'turned the rock into a pool, the hard rock into springs of water' (v.8).

The character of God was revealed to his people in the Exodus, when God liberated his people from oppression through his victorious power and presence, making it clear that *slavery is an evil* from which God longs *to set people free*.

This helps us address one of the big questions from today's New Testament reading in which Paul gives instructions to slaves and masters (Ephesians 6:5–9). Why did Paul never attempt to abolish slavery altogether?

We need to remember that in those days, Christians were a tiny persecuted minority and they were in no position to end what was a universal *institution* in the ancient world. In the Roman Empire alone, about 60 million people (a high percentage of the population) were slaves.

As Professor F. F. Bruce writes, 'It was better to state the principles of the gospel clearly ("in Christ there is neither slave nor free", Galatians 3:28) and leave them to have their own effect in due course on this iniquitous institution.'[1]

God wants to set people free, both from the literal bondage and oppression experienced by modern day slaves, and from our slavery to sin and addictions (such as a reliance on alcohol, drugs, violence or pornography). And in the future, when Jesus returns in victorious power, God will free everyone from *every* kind of slavery.

PRAYER

Lord, thank you that you set me free through your presence with me, and that you turn the rock into a pool and the hard rock into springs of water through your Holy Spirit dwelling within me.

NEW TESTAMENT READING

Ephesians 6:1–24
Victory over the devil's schemes

Our battle is against 'the triple alliance', writes Raniero Cantalamessa. 'The world, the flesh and the devil; the enemy around us, the enemy within us and the enemy above us.'[2]

Relying on God's victorious power does not mean that we are passive or inactive. Paul insists that, in order to win the battle, you need to take responsibility for your life and 'be strong in the Lord' (v.10).

We need to take action. Paul uses phrases like 'put on' (v.13a), 'stand your ground' (v.13b) and 'stand firm' (v.14). Be active, replacing bad habits with good habits. Paul outlines seven life-changing habits you should adopt:

1. Focus on the truth of Jesus

'With a *belt of truth* buckled around your waist' (v.14a).

Focus on truth of heart. Transparency and authenticity are the opposite of hypocrisy. We also need to focus on the truth of doctrine as revealed in Scripture. Both are personified in Jesus who said, 'I am the truth' (John 14:6).

2. Keep short accounts

'With the breastplate of righteousness in place' (Ephesians 6:14b).

Jesus died so that you might have the *righteousness* of God. When you fall, get up quickly. Keep in a right relationship with God and with others.

3. Get actively involved

'With your feet fitted with the readiness that comes from the gospel of peace' (v.15).

Here Paul may have had a verse from our Old Testament reading for today in mind: 'Look, there on the mountains, the feet of one who brings good news, who proclaims peace!' (Nahum 1:15). The devil hates the gospel – because it is God's power to change lives.

Paul asked the Ephesian Christians to pray for him: 'that whenever I open my mouth, words may be given me so that I will fearlessly make known the mystery of the gospel' (Ephesians 6:19).

4. Trust God in difficult times

'In addition to all this, take up the shield of faith, with which you can extinguish all the flaming arrows of the evil one' (v.16).

The arrows are such things as: false guilt, shame, doubt, disobedience, malice and fear.

5. Win the battle of the mind

'Take the helmet of salvation' (v.17a).

The battle is won or lost in our minds, so it is essential that we 'take captive every *thought* to make it obedient to Christ' (2 Corinthians 10:5).

6. Soak yourself in the word of God
'The sword of the Spirit, which is the *word of God*' (Ephesians 6:17b).

Use the Bible when you are under attack, just as Jesus did when he was tempted in the desert (Matthew 4:1–11).

7. Keep praying
'Pray in the Spirit on all occasions with all kinds of prayers and requests' (Ephesians 6:18)

Prayer is a powerful weapon. Mary Queen of Scots said, 'I fear John Knox's prayers more than an army of ten thousand men.'

PRAYER

Lord, thank you that although on my own I am powerless, with the armour of God, the strength of Jesus and the power of the Holy Spirit, I can experience your victory.

OLD TESTAMENT READING

Nahum 1:1–3:19
Victory over the forces of evil

We all go through tough times. Jesus told us not to be surprised by trouble (John 16:33). But you are promised that you will be more than a conqueror through Christ who loves you (Romans 8:37).

Take comfort from the promises that God made to his people then, which are still applicable to us now: 'God is good, a hiding place in *tough times*. He recognises and welcomes anyone looking for help, no matter how desperate the trouble' (Nahum 1:7, MSG).

Empires come and go. The British Empire once dominated the world. No longer. Likewise, the Roman Empire and every other Empire has come and gone.

At the time Nahum was writing, the Assyrian Empire dominated the world and seemed invincible. Yet shortly after the book of Nahum was written, in 612 BC, Nineveh, the proud capital of the Assyrian Empire, fell to the Babylonians and Medes.

Nahum assures the people of God, surrounded by powerful forces, that God is in command and no power on earth can stand against him (2:1–13). The message is: 'Don't admire or be intimidated by this enemy. They are going to be judged by the very same standards applied to us'[3] (Eugene Peterson).

The evil of Nineveh is described in chapter 3: 'Doom to murder city – full of lies, bursting with loot, addicted to violence ... luring nations to their ruin with your evil spells' (3:1, 4, MSG).

If the end of this earthly kingdom was 'good news' (1:15) bringing such relief and jubilation, how much more should the victory of Jesus over the spiritual forces of evil bring us relief and jubilation? You are still surrounded by enemies in the form of the world, the flesh and the devil, but with God on your side, you will ultimately see his victorious power.

PRAYER

Lord, thank you that you are more powerful than any spiritual force of evil. Thank you that you are a refuge in times of trouble and that you care for those who trust in you (v.7). Help me today to trust in you and your victorious power.

29 September | Day 272
A Life Worth Living

'In the future, scientists may be able to prolong life, but will it be worth living?' wrote Nigel Hawkes in *The Times*.

Apparently, one Oxford professor claims it may soon be possible to prolong many people's lives until the age of 115. But Hawkes rightly asks, 'Will it be worth living?' An increased lifespan is of little value unless it is for a life worth living.

The apostle Paul did not see the prolonging of life as a major objective: 'For to me, to live is Christ and to die is gain' (Philippians 1:21). Indeed, he regarded death as something of even greater worth. Yet for him, Jesus had made his life profoundly worth living.

READING FROM PROVERBS

Proverbs 23:29–24:4
Live in a relationship with God

Another *Times* columnist, Bernard Levin, spoke of how there is a hole inside each of us. However much you try to fill it with food, drink, relationships, possessions, 'it aches'.[1] You were created for a relationship with God through Jesus Christ. Without that relationship, we ache.

People try to fill this hole with different things. For some, it is alcohol, and although there is nothing wrong with drinking wine, it does not satisfy the deep inner thirst we have in our hearts.

It looks so attractive 'when it sparkles in the cup, when it goes down smoothly!' (23:31). However, if we follow this path and overindulge, 'in the end it bites like a snake and poisons like a viper' (v.32). The writer describes the effects of drunkenness with great vividness: the hangover, splitting headache, queasy stomach, seeing double, slurred speech (vv.34–35, MSG). It leads to sorrow, strife, complaints, needless bruises and bloodshot eyes (v.29).

By contrast, the writer speaks of the blessings of wisdom and knowledge: intelligence, strategic planning and a lot of good counsel (24:3–4, MSG). Where can we find such wisdom and knowledge? The apostle Paul spoke of knowing Christ 'in whom are hidden *all the treasures of wisdom and knowledge*' (Colossians 2:2–3).

PRAYER

Lord, I come to you today and drink so that out of my heart may flow rivers of living water.

NEW TESTAMENT READING

Philippians 1:1–26
Make a difference to the lives of others

Do you wish your circumstances were different?

If you are facing major challenges or difficulties, be encouraged by the fact that you can be useful in the midst of your struggles. God can work through you in ways you might not expect.

When Paul wrote this letter he was under house arrest in Rome, attached to a Roman soldier by a chain that was three feet long. He was imprisoned in very bad conditions, awaiting trial and possible execution. Yet, he believed that his life in Christ meant 'fruitful labour' for him (v.22).

When Paul says, 'I have you in my heart' (v.7), he is expressing his deep love for the people of Philippi. He has already spoken of their 'partnership in the gospel' (v.5) and now he speaks of sharing God's grace with them (v.7). There is such a close bond between those who work together for Jesus Christ. There is an even closer bond when one is responsible for the conversion of the others. Paul says that he longs for all of them 'with the affection of Christ Jesus' (v.8).

In an age of almost unparalleled opportunity and choice, so many people are unduly anxious about missing their destiny or taking a wrong step. But you can have confidence that because God began the good work in you, he will complete it (v.6). God always finishes what he starts.

None of us are there yet. You are a work in progress. Paul's prayer for the Philippians was that they might be even more fruitful:

1. Grow in love

Pray for others and for yourself that your 'love will flourish and that you will not only love much but well' (v.9, MSG).

2. Grow in knowledge

Pray not simply for growth in love, but that your 'love may abound more and more in knowledge and depth of insight, so that you may be able to discern what is best' (vv.9–10). Love is to be more than an emotional experience; 'sincere and intelligent, not sentimental gush' (v.10, MSG).

3. Grow in holiness

Paul prayed that they 'may be pure and blameless' (v.10). The word for 'pure' describes an inner purity in which even our motives are unmixed. The word for 'blameless' means without giving offence and refers more to the outer way of life. Pray, like Paul, that you may be holy both inwardly and outwardly – 'making Jesus Christ attractive to all' (v.11, MSG). As Dietrich Bonhoeffer put it, 'Your life as a Christian should make non-believers question their disbelief in God.'

Paul could bear his chains because they gave him an opportunity to preach the gospel and to encourage others to 'speak the word of God more courageously and fearlessly' (v.14).

Don't be concerned about other people's motives for preaching the gospel: 'Some preach

Christ out of envy and rivalry' and 'selfish ambition' (vv.15, 17). Others do it out of love (v.16). However, Paul didn't seem to think it mattered very much as long as Christ was preached (vv.17–18). Don't criticise other Christians who are preaching the gospel even if you don't like their style or you question their motives. Be glad that they are proclaiming Jesus.

Paul's whole life was centred on Christ. His desire was for Christ to be exalted in his body, 'whether by life or by death' (v.20). He felt himself 'torn between the two' (v.23). In many ways, he desired 'to depart and be with Christ, which is better by far' (v.23).

The saintly Prebendary John Collins was vicar of HTB from 1980–1985. When his wife Diana died on 16 July 2013 John wrote to me, 'I am thankful that we had fifty-eight glorious years together – getting better and better! Although strokes are horrible and death is an enemy ... like St Paul, for many years she had longed "to be with Christ, which is far better". I am deeply thankful, therefore ... that she was not afraid, because she knew where she was going and her faith in Christ's promises never wavered.'

Although Paul was longing to be with Christ, part of him also wanted to stay alive because he knew it would 'mean fruitful labour' (v.22). His desire was to see the Philippians progress in their faith and their joy in Christ Jesus overflow (v.26).

PRAYER

Lord, help me to live life to the full and take every opportunity to spread the message of Jesus.

OLD TESTAMENT READING

Zephaniah 1:1–3:20
Experience God's love for you

Do you realise how much and how deeply God loves you? No matter what happens in this life God loves you. Not only does he love you, he takes great delight in you. In fact, he sings over you with joy (3:17).

The theme of Zephaniah is 'the great day of the LORD' (1:14). This was the day that the people of God were anticipating. In popular thinking, this was the day that they expected Israel to be blessed. Zephaniah's message was that it is not simply going to be a day of blessing, but it will also be a day of judgment.

He urged repentance. Sin leads to judgment. But God loves us and longs to be merciful and to forgive: 'Seek the LORD, all you humble of the land, you who do what he commands. Seek righteousness, seek humility; perhaps you will be sheltered on the day of the LORD's anger' (2:3).

He foresaw that a remnant, who are 'meek and humble, who trust in the name of the LORD', will survive (3:12). He foresaw that God would again bless his people, 'The LORD your God is with you, he is mighty to save. He will take great delight in you, he will quiet you with his love, he will rejoice over you with singing' (v.17).

When Jesus announced the kingdom of God, he was proclaiming that the day of the Lord had broken into history. One day, when Jesus returns, there will indeed be a day of judgment and reckoning. However, some aspects of the day of the Lord can also be experienced right now in Christ. You can know God saving you, delighting in you, quieting you with his love and rejoicing over you with singing right now. You can know this, despite the reality of God's judgment, because, in Christ, 'the Lord has taken away your punishment' (v.15).

For those who are in Christ, the promises of the Lord in Zephaniah are fulfilled in *you*. As Father Raniero Cantalamessa writes, 'Everything that God does and says in the Bible is love, even God's anger is nothing but love. God is love!'[2] And that makes life worth living.

PRAYER

Lord, thank you that you take great delight in me, quiet me with your love and rejoice over me with singing. Thank you that your love makes this life worth living.

30 September | Day 273
Bounce It Back Up

It was one of the most moving and powerful testimonies I have ever encountered. A former sex worker, drug addict and dealer described how she had reached a point at which, in her own words, she was 'dead'. She said her 'blood was black' and her 'heart was black'. She described how she came on Alpha and heard that Jesus loved her so much that he died for her.

She described how this had broken 'the concrete' of her heart. She experienced God's love for her for the first time. She is now filled with love for everyone, forgiving those who abused her, and radiating the love of Christ.

After she had given her testimony to a stunned congregation, I went up to thank her and said how extraordinarily powerful it had been. She replied, 'I need to *bounce it back up*!' I didn't understand what she meant. I asked her to explain. She said, 'It's all his grace. *I need to bounce the glory back to him*.' She has a profound understanding of grace, glory and what it means to be Christ-like.

The theme of '*glory*' runs through each of today's readings (Psalm 115:1; Philippians 2:11; Jeremiah 2:11). We see why, how and when to *bounce the glory back up to God*.

READING FROM PSALMS

Psalm 115:1–11
Why glorify God?

When people praised John Wimber because of a talk he had given or a healing that had happened through his ministry, he used to say, 'I'll take the encouragement, but I'll pass the glory on.'

The psalmist gives us a great example of passing the glory on – bouncing it back up to God. He starts: '*Not to us*, O LORD, *not to us* but to *your name* be the glory, because of your love and faithfulness' (v.1). He goes on to give two reasons why you should glorify and worship God.

First, because of our experience of God's 'love and faithfulness' (v.1b). Worship is a response to what God has done for you. Give him all the glory.

Second, because you become like that which you worship: 'Those who make them will be like them, and so will all who trust in them' (v.8). So, if we worship idols, we become totally lifeless, unable to do anything of any value.

Put your trust in the Lord who is your '*help and shield*' (vv.9–11). Put your faith in the Lord and worship him, and you will become like him – you will be changed into his likeness and obtain fullness of life.

PRAYER

Lord, my help and shield, help me to experience more of your love and faithfulness, to 'bounce it back up' and to give you all the glory.

NEW TESTAMENT READING

Philippians 1:27–2:11
How to glorify God

Paul explains how you can glorify God by becoming like Jesus: 'Think of yourselves the way Christ Jesus thought of himself' (2:5, MSG). Become Christ-like in attitude because of concern for the 'name of Jesus' (v.10) and the 'glory of God' (v.11).

Live a life 'worthy of the gospel of Christ' (1:27). It is a privilege, not only to believe in Jesus, but also to suffer and struggle for him (vv.29–30).

When people or events come against you, '*stand firm*' (v.27) in unity against all the opposition and attacks that you are bound to encounter. The language Paul uses is that of a *phalanx* – the most formidable military device of antiquity. With shields together and spears out front, the soldiers stood shoulder to shoulder in files eight men deep. As long as they did not break rank, they were virtually invincible.

'Stand *united*, singular in vision, contending for people's trust in the Message, the good news, not flinching or dodging in the slightest before the opposition. Your courage and *unity* will show them what they're up against: defeat for them, victory for you – and both because of God' (vv.27–28, MSG).

A Christ-like attitude is the key to this unity. Any disunity in the church would have detracted from Paul's 'joy' (2:2). Disunity so often comes from 'selfish ambition and vain conceit' (v.3a). The key is to consider others better than yourself (v.3b), to look not only to your own interests 'but also to the interests of others' (v.4).

'Don't push your way to the front; don't sweet-talk your way to the top. Put yourself aside, and help others get ahead. Don't be obsessed with getting your own advantage. Forget yourselves long enough to lend a helping hand' (vv.3–4, MSG).

In other words, you are to have the same attitude as Jesus, who let go of his natural, legal and social status, and made himself 'nothing'. He took 'the very nature of a servant ... he humbled himself' and 'became obedient to death – even death on a cross!' (vv.7–8). He took the path of downward mobility, humble service and unselfish love. If you are ever anxious about your relative status, remember that Jesus made himself lower than we could ever imagine.

And as a result, 'God exalted him to the highest place and gave him the name that is above every name, that at the name of Jesus every knee should bow, in heaven and on earth and under the earth, and every tongue confess that Jesus Christ is Lord, *to the glory of God the Father*' (vv.9–11).

This is how you can glorify God: by following Christ in his humble service and selfless love.

PRAYER

Lord, help me to have the same attitude as Jesus. Help me to take the path that brings glory to God the Father. Help me always to bounce the glory back to you.

OLD TESTAMENT READING

Jeremiah 1:1–2:30
When to glorify God

What happens when troubles, difficulties and disruption come into your life and the lives of those around you?

Jeremiah lived in one of the troubled periods in Israel's history – the fall of Jerusalem in 587 BC and the exile in Babylon. He was given a difficult message to give to the people. He did it with great courage in the face of hostility and persecution.

The opening chapters of Jeremiah show two more ways that you can glorify God and when you can do so.

First, you glorify God when you *respond to God's call*. Age is no barrier to leadership. Jeremiah was probably a teenager when God called him, around the year 627 BC. He could be described as both a 'born leader' and a 'born prophet'. Before his birth he was set apart to be a prophet. God said, 'Before I formed you in the womb I knew [and] *approved of you* … and before you were born I separated *and* set you apart … I appointed you as a prophet to the nations' (1:5, AMP).

God knows all about you – the good and the bad. His knowing leaves nothing out. He loves you. He does not necessarily approve of everything you do, but he wants you to live, like Jeremiah, with the freedom of knowing his love and *approval*.

The Lord tells you, as he told Jeremiah, to go wherever he tells you to go and say whatever he tells you to say (v.7). This takes the ultimate responsibility off your shoulders. Glorifying God does not mean having to try to save the whole world (that is God's responsibility), but rather doing what God asks you to do. This will not be easy. God warns that there will be opposition (vv.17–19).

Second, you glorify God when you respond to God's correction. God asked Jeremiah to warn the people against worshipping worthless idols and to call them back to worshipping him.

Jeremiah said, 'My people have exchanged their Glory for worthless idols' (2:11b). Not only does this deny God the glory he deserves, it is actually self-destructive. When we turn away from God we lose the blessings of relationship with him, and replace it with something useless. God laments how 'my people have forsaken me, the spring of living water, and have dug their own cisterns, broken cisterns that cannot hold water' (v.13).

In particular, they were 'on the hunt for sex, sex, and more sex – insatiable, indiscriminate, promiscuous' (v.24, MSG). They were 'addicted' and could not 'quit' (v.25, MSG).

Again, we see that you become like whatever you worship. Those who follow 'worthless idols' become 'worthless themselves' (v.5). If you follow Jesus, you become like him. If we try to find satisfaction, meaning and purpose through our own ambitions and self-centred appetites, our lives become of no value.

Jeremiah despaired that God's people had not responded to his correction (v.30). They had forsaken his blessings, and failed to give him glory. Thank God that the remedy for all this came in the person of Jesus, who laid aside his glory in order to rescue us. To him be all the glory!

PRAYER

Lord, help me to fix my eyes on Jesus, the spring of living water, and to turn my face towards him. May I become Christ-like and give you all the glory.

1 October | Day 274
How to Be a Blessing Machine

Do you ever wonder whether you can make a difference to the lives of those around you?

I once watched an episode of the reality TV Show, *The Secret Millionaire*. Kevin Green – a covert multi-millionaire – searched for people and causes that would benefit from his financial support. He gave about $100,000 to a range of people working with the homeless, teenage addicts and disabled children. The response of all these people was deeply moving. They were so grateful, and the causes that they work for benefited greatly. They were blessed and enabled to bring greater blessing to others.

However, the most interesting aspect of the programme was the change in Kevin Green. He had experienced in a new way the joy of blessing others. His life was changed as a result. The words of Jesus are true: 'It is *more blessed to give* than to receive' (Acts 20:35).

Archie Coates, vicar of St Peter's Brighton, speaks of the church as a '*blessing machine*'. That is exactly what we as Christians are called to be, as the church and as individuals. You really can be a blessing machine.

READING FROM PSALMS

Psalm 115:12–18
God is the ultimate blessing machine

It is God's blessing on your life that enables you to make a difference to the lives of others. God is the source of *all* blessing. He loves to bless you. The psalmist repeats this over and over again. Five times in quick succession he talks about how *the Lord will bless us* (vv.13–15).

God is not just some multi-millionaire. He is 'the Maker of heaven and earth … The highest heavens belong to the LORD' (vv.15b–16a). In his extraordinary generosity, 'the earth he has given to [us]' (v.16b).

God loves to bless. The appropriate response to blessing is gratitude: 'we *bless* GOD, oh yes – *we bless him now*, *we bless him always*!' (v.18, MSG).

PRAYER

'Praise the LORD' (v.18c). Lord, I can never praise you enough – you have blessed me in Christ with every spiritual blessing (see Ephesians 1:3).

NEW TESTAMENT READING

Philippians 2:12–30
Be a blessing machine to others

How, in practice, can you make a difference to the lives of those around you?

We are 'children of God' (v.15). You are called to be like your Father in heaven, who loves to bless. You have a responsibility to work out your own salvation (to see God's grace impact every area of your life), but it is he who 'works in you to will and to act according to his good purpose' (v.13).

Many people are reluctant to trust God with their future because they fear that God will make them do something that they have no desire to do, or will make a mess of their life. Of course, both of these fears are without foundation.

If your *will* is surrendered to him, God will give you the desire to do whatever he is calling you to do. If he is calling you to a ministry with the poor, that is where your heart will be. If he is calling you to teach, he will give you a desire to teach. If you surrender to his will, he will bring about 'his good purpose' (v.13).

What he wants for your life is good. It will not necessarily be easy, but you will not be able to improve on his plan. He will also give you the energy you need: 'That energy is *God's* energy, an energy deep within you, God himself willing and working at what will give him the most pleasure' (v.13, MSG).

Paul knows the joy of being a 'blessing machine'. He writes, 'Do everything readily and cheerfully – no bickering, no second-guessing allowed! Go out into the world uncorrupted, a breath of fresh air in this squalid and polluted society. Provide people with a glimpse of good living and of the living God. Carry the light-giving Message into the night' (vv.14–16a, MSG).

You have the immense privilege of being able to give people not just money, but 'the word of life' (v.16a). There is no greater joy than seeing people who are spiritually dead come to life through Jesus.

Paul is willing to give his life with joy for this privilege: 'But even if I am being poured out like a drink offering on the sacrifice and service coming from your faith, I am glad and rejoice with all of you. So you too should be glad and rejoice with me' (vv.17–18).

Paul then gives two examples of friends of his who both demonstrated *how* to be a 'blessing machine':

1. Take a *genuine interest* in others

Timothy was one of Paul's closest friends, and is often mentioned in his letters. His loyalty and help were so great that Paul describes it as being 'like a son with his father' (v.22).

Paul pays tribute to his friend, 'He is *loyal*, and *genuinely concerned* for you' (v.20, MSG). Paul compares this to the blight of self-interest, saying, 'Most people around here are looking out for themselves' (v.21, MSG).

Timothy was a 'blessing machine' because he took a 'genuine interest' in the welfare of God's children (v.20). Timothy's interest was totally authentic: 'the real thing' (v.22, MSG). Paul says that he 'served with me in the work of the gospel' (v.22).

2. Show *courage* on behalf of others

Epaphroditus was also a loyal friend to both Paul and the Philippians. His true character comes across in both the big and little things, and often it is the little things that are most telling. Having become seriously ill, almost to the point of death, Epaphroditus is troubled, not because he is ill and close to death, but because they might have been upset by it. He was like those who, when ill, are not so much worried by the illness as by the fact that they might be a burden to their family or friends.

Paul describes Epaphroditus as a 'brother, fellow-worker and fellow-soldier' (v.25). Epaphroditus had been prepared to 'risk his life' for the sake of his friend Paul (v.30). This expression is actually more literally translated as 'gambling his life'.

In the early church, there were societies of men and women who called themselves '*the gamblers*', who ministered to the sick and those in prison. For example, Cyprian, a bishop of Carthage, showed remarkable courage during the plague, which began in AD 250. Where everyone else fled from the sick and the dead, Cyprian and other Christians buried the dead, nursed the sick and saved the city at the risk of their own lives.

Epaphroditus *gambled his life* by associating himself with Paul, who was in prison on a capital charge, thereby risking the same charge as Paul. Epaphroditus showed reckless courage on behalf of Paul. He too was a 'blessing machine'.

PRAYER

Lord, help me to do everything without complaining or arguing and to hold out the word of life to someone today.

OLD TESTAMENT READING

Jeremiah 2:31–4:9
Don't turn away from God's blessing

If you are experiencing the blessing of walking in a close relationship with God, those around you 'will get *caught up in the blessing*' (4:2, MSG).

The prophet Jeremiah urges the people to return to the Lord (v.1). God longs to bless you. 'You must get rid of your stinking sin paraphernalia and not wander away from me anymore. Then you can say words like, "As God lives..." and have them mean something true and just and right. And the godless nations will get *caught up in the blessing*' (vv.1b–2a, MSG).

God longed to bless his people and all the nations, but they turned away from this blessing. Jeremiah warned the people of the dangers of turning from God to false idols: 'You cut and hurt a lot of people to get where you are' (v.34, MSG). They have been unfaithful (3:1b).

Again and again the Lord urges them to return: 'Return, faithless Israel ... for I am merciful ... Then I will give you shepherds after my own heart, who will lead you with knowledge and with understanding ... How gladly would I treat you like my children and give you a desirable land, the most beautiful inheritance of any nation. I thought you would call me "Father" and *not turn away* from following me' (vv.12, 15, 19).

The Lord is interested in your heart more than your outward appearance. You cannot pretend with God: 'Judah did not return to me with all her heart, but only in pretence' (v.10). The Lord urges, 'Circumcise yourselves to the LORD, circumcise your hearts' (4:4). Even in the Old Testament God said it was a circumcised *heart* (a heart wholly committed to him) that he desired.

If in any way you have turned away from the Lord, return to him today with all your heart.

PRAYER

Lord, today I give to you everything I have – time, money, possessions and everything else. Thank you that you long to bless me and to bless others through me. Help me today to be a 'blessing machine'.

2 October | Day 275
Godly Ambition

Chuck Colson was a self-made man. As a student, he arrogantly turned down a scholarship to Harvard. He joined the Marines, set up his own law firm and entered politics. By the age of forty he had become one of President Nixon's closest advisers. Later, he described himself as 'a young *ambitious* political kingmaker'. He was known as Nixon's 'hatchet-man'.

He pleaded guilty to his part in the Watergate cover-up scandal and was sent to prison. By then he had encountered Jesus. When he left the court after hearing the sentence he said, 'What happened in court today ... was the court's will and the Lord's will – I have committed my life to Jesus Christ and I can work for him in prison as well as out.'

Colson did just that. After his release, he set up Prison Fellowship and became directly or indirectly responsible for leading thousands to Christ. I once heard him say, '*I was ambitious, and I am ambitious today*, but I hope it is not for Chuck Colson (though I struggle with that quite a lot as a matter of fact). But *I am ambitious for Christ*.'[1]

Ambition has been defined as the 'desire to succeed'. There are ultimately only two controlling ambitions to which all others may be reduced: one is our own glory, and the other is God's glory.

READING FROM PSALMS

Psalm 116:1–11
Be ambitious about your relationship with God

Make your relationship with God your number one priority. Like the psalmist, declare that your ambition is to walk before the Lord: 'I'm striding in the presence of GOD' (v.9, MSG). Make sure that your life is centred on a love relationship with God. This is the way to find 'rest' for your 'soul' (v.7).

This relationship is founded on the many ways in which we experience God's help. Like the psalmist, I remember how God 'heard my cry for mercy' (v.1), how 'when I was in great need he saved me' (v.6), how 'the LORD has been good to me' (v.7) and how God 'delivered my soul from death, my eyes from tears, my feet from stumbling' (v.8). This is then the basis of his ambition to 'walk before the LORD' (v.9).

PRAYER

Lord, I love you. I want to make it my ambition today, and for the rest of my life, to walk before you in the land of the living.

NEW TESTAMENT READING

Philippians 3:1–4:1
Be ambitious for Christ

Sometimes Christians wonder whether it is right to be ambitious. They associate ambition with pride and think that humility means not being ambitious.

However, Paul was fiercely ambitious. Before he was a Christian, Paul had been ambitious in his zeal for Judaism, which led to a desire to persecute the church. After his conversion, he did not lose his ambitious nature, but its direction changed. If anything, he was even more ambitious! He describes himself in this passage as being like an athlete desperate to win a race (3:13–14).

Paul contrasts his great ambition for Jesus with two wrong types of ambition. The first is his own ambition before he became a Christian. He describes how he put his confidence in the flesh ('outward privileges and physical advantages and external appearances', v.3, AMP), trusting in the different marks of his old religion (vv.3–6). But, as the great theologian Karl Barth once said, 'Jesus Christ came to destroy human religion.'

God wants you to be confident, but not 'in the flesh'. Rather your confidence should be in God alone – his love and provision. Paul's religious ambition and zeal were misdirected. He ended up 'persecuting the church' (v.6).

The second wrong type of ambition is the material and earthly focus of so many in the world around us: 'Their god is their stomach ['their appetites, their sensuality', AMP], and their glory is in their shame. Their mind is on earthly things' (v.19).

Paul now had a godly ambition. He describes the 'surpassing greatness of knowing Christ Jesus my Lord' (v.8), and the ambitions that flow from it (vv.8–11).

Paul realised he could never attain perfection. All his ambitions to attain 'a righteousness on my own', he now regards as 'rubbish' (v.9). Like Paul, enjoy the fact that, through trust in Christ, you too have now received 'the righteousness that comes from God and is by faith' (v.9).

We will never achieve perfection in this life. Our weaknesses keep us dependent on God; leaning on him and on his love and grace.

What should your ambition be?

1. To know Christ intimately

Paul's ambition was 'to know Christ' (v.10). The Greek word for 'to know' means far more than intellectual knowledge – knowing things about something. Instead, it is a personal knowledge. Like Paul, make your ambition not just to know about Christ, but to know him more intimately.

2. To experience Christ's resurrection power

Paul describes what this intimate relationship with Christ looks like. It means to know 'the power of his resurrection' (v.10), not just as a past event in history, but as a dynamic and exhilarating power at work in *your* life.

The Spirit of God brings this resurrection power to your life. By the power of his death and resurrection, Jesus disarmed Satan, broke the hold of sin and defeated death. This power is available to you to enable you to live a holy life and to minister to others with his resurrection power. Make it your ambition to know that power more and more.

3. To partner in Christ's suffering

For Paul, 'knowing Christ' involves 'the fellowship of sharing in his sufferings, becoming like him in his death' (v.10). He sees suffering as an inevitable part of knowing Christ. It is not a penalty but a privilege.

The suffering and death of Jesus is different from ours in that he died for our sins to save us from what we deserve. You will never suffer in exactly the way he did. But sometimes you will suffer for your godly ambition.

This suffering is the practical result of our Christian life. For some, this will mean severe persecution.

For all of us, it will include 'all the pangs and afflictions ... in the struggle against sin either within or without' (J. B. Lightfoot).[2] It is at these moments of suffering that we experience 'fellowship' with Christ. Make that fellowship your ambition whatever the cost.

4. To know your destination

Knowing Christ means sharing his destiny, 'somehow, to attain to the resurrection from the dead' (v.11). When Paul says 'somehow', he is not doubting this hope but acknowledging that this is a wonderful mystery.

Jackie Pullinger says that God gave her 'resurrection eyes'. She says, 'Only Jesus opens eyes ... but all who believe in the resurrection of the dead know their destination is a place of comfort, a better country, a heavenly city.'

Paul says he is not there yet but it is his aim and ambition (v.12): 'I've got my eye on the goal' (v.14, MSG). Don't focus on the past – how far you have fallen, your failures or even your successes. Rather, 'forgetting what lies behind' keep focused on Jesus, be single-minded, press forward and respond to his call.

PRAYER

Lord, help me to get my ambitions right. Help me to focus my life on 'the surpassing greatness of knowing Christ Jesus my Lord' (v.8).

OLD TESTAMENT READING

Jeremiah 4:10–5:31
Be ambitious to speak God's words

The Lord speaks through Jeremiah and says, 'My people are fools; they do not know me ... they are skilled in doing evil; they know not how to do good' (4:22). He warns that judgment is coming because the people have focused their ambitions in the wrong direction.

Jeremiah thinks that surely the leaders will know the right way: 'So I will go to the leaders and *speak to them*; surely they know the way of the LORD, the requirements of their God' (5:5). But they, like the people, 'refused to repent' (v.3c). Their ambitions were focused on the false gods of money, sex and power.

Only God can satisfy our deepest needs (v.7b, MSG). God says to them, 'I supplied all their needs, yet they committed adultery and thronged to the houses of prostitutes. They are well-fed, lusty stallions, each neighing for another man's wife' (vv.7b–8).

He goes on to say that their houses are full of deceit. They have 'become rich and powerful and have grown fat and sleek' (vv.27–28a). Although they were rich and powerful, they did not care for the poor: 'Right and wrong mean nothing to them. They stand for nothing, stand up for no one, throw orphans to the wolves, exploit the poor' (v.28, MSG).

God calls Jeremiah to a new level of powerful speaking: 'I'm putting my words as fire in your mouth' (5:14, MSG). Now you too can have this experience of speaking God's powerful life-changing words to those around you.

PRAYER

Lord, may the words in my mouth be like fire so that others may come to experience the surpassing greatness of knowing Christ Jesus, my Lord.

3 October | Day 276
The Key to Contentment

Recently I spoke with a friend who is not a Christian. He is a charming and delightful person. He is a successful businessman and has made a great deal of money. He has a wonderful wife, a good marriage and a great family. Yet he spoke to me of the deep emptiness in his life, and the lack of peace and contentment he experiences.

'Content makes poor men rich; discontent makes rich men poor,' said the American Statesman, Benjamin Franklin. Few people seem to be genuinely content. As Martin Luther once said, 'Contentment is a rare bird, but it sings sweetly in the breast.'

The Bible never promises that we will not face hard times or difficult situations. But it does promise us God's strength and grace in these times.

The apostle Paul found the key to a life of peace and contentment in times of trouble. He tells the Philippians how to find peace and shares *the secret of being content* (Philippians 4:12).

READING FROM PROVERBS

Proverbs 24:5–14
Find soul satisfaction in God's wisdom

What happens when you face a crisis in your life? How do you respond to hard times and difficult situations?

All of us are likely to face *times of trouble* in our lives. The writer of Proverbs says, 'If you falter in times of trouble, how small is your strength!' (v.10). 'If you fall to pieces in a crisis, there wasn't much to you in the first place' (v.10, MSG).

The wise person will not 'fall to pieces', for they have 'great power' and 'knowledge increases strength' (v.5). They seek guidance and have 'many advisers' (v.6).

When evil things are happening (v.11), do not close your eyes and say, 'But we knew nothing about this' (v.12).

How do you get this wisdom? The wisdom of God is like the sweet taste of honey: 'Know also that wisdom is sweet to your soul; if you find it, there is a future hope for you, and your hope will not be cut off' (v.14). This wisdom is found supremely in Christ, for he is 'the wisdom of God' (1 Corinthians 1:24).

PRAYER

Lord, thank you that in Christ, the wisdom of God, we find soul satisfaction. Please fill me today with the Spirit of Jesus – with wisdom, contentment and peace.

NEW TESTAMENT READING

Philippians 4:2–23
Find the secret in Christ Jesus

No one goes through life without difficulties and hard times. Paul is not without his troubles (v.14). He is in prison and no doubt has plenty to worry about.

However, he writes, 'Do not fret or have any anxiety about anything, but in every circumstance and in everything, by prayer and petition (definite requests), with thanksgiving, continue to make your wants known to God. And God's peace [shall be yours, that tranquil state of a soul assured of its salvation through Christ, and so fearing nothing from God and being content with its earthly lot of whatever sort that is, that peace] which transcends all understanding shall garrison and mount guard over your hearts and minds in Christ Jesus' (vv.6–7, AMP). This is a remarkable and wonderful promise, and one that I have claimed and experienced many times in my own life.

Corrie ten Boom defined worry as 'a cycle of inefficient thoughts whirling around a centre of fear'.[1] Worry can wreck our lives. Some of our worries, like Paul's, are real, and some are illusory, but in either case, a life weighed down by worry is not really living.

Paul's solution is to encourage us to turn to prayer, bringing our specific requests to God: 'Let petitions and praises shape your worries into prayers, letting God know your concerns' (v.6, MSG).

Sometimes, I find it a help to write down specific requests. This enables me to look back at the ways in which God has answered my prayers. If you do this, you can then give thanks (v.6), and your confidence in prayer will increase.

Offer your current prayers from a foundation of a life that is filled with 'thanksgiving' (v.6). The wonderful promise is that as you do this 'the peace of God, which transcends all understanding will guard your hearts and your minds in Christ Jesus' (v.7). God exchanges your worries for his peace.

The word for peace means far more than an absence of hostility. It means wholeness, soundness, well-being, oneness with God and every kind of blessing and good. It is a peace 'which transcends all understanding'. It surpasses both your ability to cope, and your anxiety about what is to come.

Paul then turns his attention to what we think about. We are surrounded by images and words from the media, conversations and events, which can so easily tempt us, almost daily, with wrong thoughts. But you can resist this. As Martin Luther said, 'You can't stop a bird flying overhead, but you can stop it nesting in your hair.'

The way to get wrong thoughts *out* is to get right thoughts *in*. Your mind cannot be unoccupied. If you don't occupy your mind with good thoughts the enemy will fill it with bad ones.

Follow Paul's advice: 'you'll do best by filling your minds and meditating on things true, noble, reputable, authentic, compelling, gracious – the best' (v.8, MSG). He realises that what you think about will affect every area of your life. Fill your mind with good things, whatever 'is excellent and praiseworthy' (v.8).

Think about what you think about. The root of our problems may be our thought life. If you change the things you allow your mind to dwell on, 'God, who makes everything work together, will work you into his most excellent harmonies' (v.9, MSG).

The hardest part is always putting all this 'into practice' (v.9). The only way of learning any skill, trade or sport is by practising. Practise avoiding quarrels, staying united with other Christians (vv.2–3) and avoiding anxiety by continual prayer. If you do, then Paul promises that 'the God of peace will be with you' (v.9).

Paul did not worry about his needs being met. He had learnt that the *secret of contentment* in every situation, in plenty or in want, was that he could 'do everything through him who gives me strength' (v.13). Whatever situation you are in, God will strengthen you to do whatever he is calling you to do.

Paul praises the Philippians for their generosity, which is a 'fragrant offering, an acceptable sacrifice, pleasing to God' (v.18). This generosity is a part of love. You can give without loving, but you cannot love without giving.

God promises that he will meet all your 'needs according to his glorious riches in Christ Jesus' (v.19), as you live a generous life free of financial worries. This includes your material *needs* – though not necessarily your *wants*. 'You can be sure that God will take care of *everything you need*, his generosity exceeding even yours in the glory that pours from Jesus' (v.19, MSG). You cannot out-give God.

PRAYER

Lord, today I bring to you my anxieties ... Thank you for the promise of your peace, which transcends all understanding.

OLD TESTAMENT READING

Jeremiah 6:1–7:29
Find soul rest on God's paths

God loves you. He wants you to find 'rest for your soul' (6:16). He wants to protect and provide for you. It is tragic when people do not listen to him.

Jeremiah continues to prophesy about times of trouble. God does not act without warning. He warned his people through the prophets, asking, 'To whom can I speak and give warning? Who will listen to me?' (v.10). The false prophets spoke of a false peace, '"Peace, peace" they say, when there is no peace' (v.14b).

On the other hand: 'Thus says the Lord: Stand by the roads and look; and ask for the eternal paths, where the good, old way is; then walk in it, and you will find *rest for your souls*' (v.16, AMP).

The problem was that they did not listen: 'Their ears are stuffed with wax' (v.12, MSG). 'They ignored everything I said' (v.19, MSG).

Jeremiah proclaimed the message courageously (7:2) and called them to repentance: 'Reform your ways and your actions' (v.3), 'change your ways and your actions and deal with each other justly' (v.5). Don't oppress the outsider, the fatherless or the widow, and don't follow other gods.

God says, 'Obey me, and I will be your God and you will be my people. Walk in all my ways I command you, that it may go well with you' (v.23). 'But do you think they listened? Not a word of it. They did just what they wanted to do' (v.24, MSG).

Resolve in your heart today to listen to God and to walk in his ways, that it may go well for you.

PRAYER

Lord, forgive me when I have not listened to you. Thank you that you promise that if I return to the eternal paths and walk in them, I will find rest and contentment for my soul.

4 October | Day 277
Attitude of Gratitude

Jean Smith told me her story. She was in her mid-sixties. She came from Cwmbran in Wales. She had been blind for sixteen years. She had a white stick, and a guide dog named Tina. An infection had eaten away at the retinas and mirrors behind her eyes – they could not be replaced. She was in constant pain.

Jean went on a local Alpha course. They had a day away to focus on the work of the Holy Spirit. During this time, the pain left. She went to church the following Sunday to thank God. The minister anointed her with oil. As she wiped the oil away she could see the communion table. God had miraculously healed Jean.

She had not seen her husband for sixteen years. She was surprised at how white his beard was! Jean had never even seen her daughter-in-law before. Her six-and-a-half-year-old grandson used to guide her around the puddles to avoid her getting her feet wet.

He said to her, 'Who done that Gran?'
She replied, 'Jesus made me better.'
'I hope you said thank you, Gran.'
'I will never stop saying thank you,' she answered.

Yesterday we read Paul's encouragement: 'In everything, by prayer and petition, with *thanksgiving*, present your requests to God' (Philippians 4:6). Today we see him putting his own instructions into practice. Like Jean, Paul was also constantly giving thanks to God. He had an attitude of gratitude.

Praise is giving glory to God for who he is. Thanksgiving is giving glory to God for what he has done for us. It is the lens through which to view our entire life. Ultimately, as we see in today's passages, the world can be divided into two categories: those who acknowledge God and give thanks to him, and those who don't.

How do you cultivate an attitude of gratitude?

READING FROM PSALMS

Psalm 116:12–19
Publicly offer a sacrifice of thanksgiving

It is not enough to thank God in the privacy of your own home. There is something significant about coming together and publicly thanking God 'in the presence of all his people' (v.14). The psalmist asks the rhetorical question, 'What can I give back to God for the blessings he's poured out on me?' (v.12, MSG).

God has been so good to him. He is thankful that his future is secure, that 'when they arrive at the gates of death God welcomes those who love him' (v.15, MSG). He gives thanks for what God has done in the past, declaring that 'you have freed me from my chains!' (v.16).

Sometimes thanksgiving is easy. At other times, it is more of a sacrifice (v.17). St John of Avila (1500–1569) wrote, 'One act of thanksgiving when things go wrong with us is worth a thousand thanks when things are agreeable to our inclination.'

The psalmist says, 'I'm ready to offer the *thanksgiving sacrifice* and pray in the name of God. I'll complete what I promised God I'd do, and I'll do it in company with his people, in the place of worship, in God's house, in Jerusalem, God's city, Hallelujah!' (vv.17–19, MSG). 'Hallelujah' is one of the few Hebrew words to have entered the English language – it is a call to praise the Lord.

He remembers his anguish (vv.1–4). He remembers God's mercy (vv.5–11) and now he ends with great gratitude (vv.12–19).

PRAYER

Lord, how can I ever thank you enough? Thank you that you have saved me. For all your goodness to me, I will give thanks to you in 'the house of the Lord' (v.19).

NEW TESTAMENT READING

Colossians 1:1–23
Continually give thanks to God

Most people, even today in secular societies, would recognise that Jesus was a great historical figure. They might rank him alongside Moses, Buddha, Socrates and other great religious leaders.

But is Jesus the unique and universal Saviour of the world? This was an issue in the first century just as much as it is now in the twenty-first century. For those in Colossae some cosmic forces were being put on an equal footing with Jesus.

In this letter, Paul, with great humility and gentleness, declares that Jesus is the unique and universal Saviour of the world. It is the God and 'Father of our Lord Jesus Christ' (v.3) who is the one who is worthy of all our worship, praise and thanksgiving.

As he prays for the Colossians, he gives *thanks to God* for their faith and love springing from the hope that is stored up for them in heaven (v.5).

He prays that they may, in turn, be *thankful to God*. He summarises the ways in which he prays for their faith to develop – asking for 'spiritual wisdom and understanding', fruitfulness and 'knowledge of God', 'endurance and patience'. The list builds to a crescendo as each quality feeds into the next, ending on the note of 'joyfully *giving thanks* to the Father' (vv.9–12).

Paul is praying that they will give thanks to the Father for transferring them 'from the dominion of darkness' to the kingdom of light – for his redemption, the forgiveness of sins (vv.13–14): 'God rescued us from dead-end alleys and dark dungeons. He's set us up in the kingdom of the Son he loves so much, the Son who got us out of the pit we were in, got rid of the sins we were doomed to keep repeating' (vv.13–14, MSG).

The one you are to thank is 'the image of the invisible God' (v.15) – 'We look at this Son and see the God who cannot be seen' (v.15, MSG). Jesus is the one by whom all things were created. Everything was created by Jesus and for Jesus. It all 'got started in him and finds its purpose in him' (v.16, MSG). Jesus is the head of the church (v.18). All the fullness of God dwells in him (v.19).

Jesus has made peace with God 'through his blood, shed on the cross' (v.20). He has reconciled you to God (v.22a). You are now holy in his sight, without blemish and free from accusation (v.22b).

This is the gospel for which we give thanks: Jesus 'was supreme in the beginning and – leading the resurrection parade – he is supreme in the end. From beginning to end he's there, towering far above everything, everyone ... Every creature under heaven gets this same Message' (vv.17–23, MSG).

PRAYER

Lord Jesus, thank you for peace and reconciliation with God through your blood shed on the cross for me. Thank you for giving us the immense privilege of proclaiming this gospel and seeing other people set free.

OLD TESTAMENT READING

Jeremiah 7:30–9:16
Beware of neglecting thanksgiving

Paul's words in Romans 1 could be seen as a summary of this passage: 'For although they knew God, they neither glorified him as God *nor gave thanks to him*' (Romans 1:21).

In Jeremiah, we see God's warning of his judgment on his people. They have *done evil* in the eyes of the Lord (Jeremiah 7:30). They 'just keep on going – *backward*! ... Not a single "I'm sorry" did I hear' (8:5–6, MSG). 'They have no shame ... they don't even know how to blush' (v.12, MSG). 'They go from one sin to another; they *do not acknowledge me*' (9:3). 'In their deceit they *refuse to acknowledge me*' (v.6).

'Their tongue is a deadly arrow; it speaks with deceit. With their mouths they all speak cordially to their neighbours, but in their hearts they set traps for them' (v.8). At the root of all their sin was a failure to acknowledge God and give him thanks; they 'refuse to know me' (v.6, MSG).

God had given them so much, yet they failed to acknowledge him or thank him for it. Therefore, he says, 'What I have given them will be taken away from them' (8:13d). 'I will take away their harvest ... there will be no grapes on the vine ... no figs on the tree' (v.13).

This judgment is painful for Jeremiah: 'Are there no healing ointments in Gilead? Isn't there a doctor in the house? So why can't something be done to heal and save my dear, dear people?' (vv.21–22, MSG).

All our passages today call on us to give thanks and praise to God. One way we could respond is by drawing all our thoughts and prayers together in the words of one of the Anglican communion services:

PRAYER

Let us give thanks to the Lord our God.
It is right to give thanks and praise.

It is indeed right,
it is our duty and our joy,
at all times and in all places
to give you thanks and praise,
holy Father, heavenly King,
almighty and eternal God,
through Jesus Christ your Son our Lord...

Therefore with angels and archangels,
and with all the company of heaven,
we proclaim your great and glorious name,
for ever praising you and saying:

Holy, holy, holy Lord,
God of power and might,
heaven and earth are full of your glory.
Hosanna in the highest.[1]

5 October | Day 278
What Is the Meaning of Life?

Jonathan Gabay, a thirty-one-year-old professional writer, was facing employment challenges and stress when he hit rock bottom. He began to ask questions about the meaning of life. He wrote to people in all walks of life: world leaders, the homeless, Oscar-winning actors, philosophers, comedians, taxi-drivers, teachers, explorers and prisoners on death row. He even wrote to me!

To each one he asked, 'What is the meaning of life?' Gabay compiled a book of our responses, together with others who had attempted, over time, to answer this question. They include the following:

> Richard Nixon: 'Life is one crisis after another.'
> John Lennon: 'Life is what happens to you while you're busy making other plans.'
> Dennis the Menace: 'Life is what you make it – and I can make it UNBEARABLE!'
> Albert Einstein: 'The man who regards his life and that of his fellow creatures as meaningless is not merely unhappy but hardly fit for life.'[1]

Numerous people replied that the meaning and purpose of life was to be found in Jesus Christ. Not only Mother Teresa and Billy Graham, but actors, scientists and the then Lord Chancellor. The Chief Cashier of the Bank of England, Graham Kentfield (whose signature was on every banknote at the time) said, 'I am clear that the meaning of life can only be properly understood in the context of our *relationship with God*.'

READING FROM PSALMS

Psalm 117:1–2
Life is about love and worship

This short psalm says so much about what life is all about. The key is your relationship with God. You should 'praise' and 'extol' the Lord (v.1) because of his great 'love' for you and 'faithfulness' towards you (v.2). The psalmist gives us a beautiful summary of God's attitude to you, and what your attitude to him should be.

PRAYER

Lord, thank you that Jesus laid down his life for me. Thank you that I am a child of God. Thank you that the love of God is poured into my heart by the Holy Spirit who has been given to me (Romans 5:5). Thank you, Lord, that through an experience of your love for me, I find the very meaning of my life.

NEW TESTAMENT READING

Colossians 1:24–2:5
The meaning of life is found in Jesus Christ

The meaning of your life is found in Jesus Christ. Christianity is Christ. This passage highlights how Paul's entire life, thinking and preaching are focused on Jesus Christ.

Paul is in prison suffering for the sake of Christ's body: that is, the church (1:24). Paul is a servant of Christ, commissioned to disclose the mystery that was kept hidden for ages and generations but is now revealed (v.26). God has 'chosen to make known among the Gentiles the glorious riches of this mystery, which is *Christ in you*, the hope of glory' (v.27).

There will always be an emptiness in your heart until it is filled by Christ living within you. The moment you put your faith in him, he came to live within you by his Spirit. You experience, right now, 'the glorious riches of this mystery' and you have 'the hope of glory' (v.27).

Jesus Christ should be at the centre of all our teaching and preaching in the church. Paul writes, 'We proclaim *him*, admonishing and teaching everyone with all wisdom, so that we may present everyone perfect in Christ' (v.28).

Not only is Christ in you, but you are also 'in Christ'. Paul's desire is that everyone should grow and mature in this relationship. This is what drives him: 'To this end I labour, struggling with all his energy, which so powerfully works in me' (v.29).

This provides an excellent model for pastoral care, discipleship and mentoring:

1. The aim

Paul's aim was to bring 'each person to maturity' in Christ (v.28, MSG).

- Our concern should be for *each person*. As a good pastor, Paul did not want to lose any of his sheep.
- Aim for *spiritual maturity*. This does not happen overnight. It takes a lifetime.
- Aim for maturity *in Christ*. We do not want to attach people to ourselves, but to Christ. In the same way that good parents encourage their children to be independent, Paul encouraged the independence of believers – not to be dependent upon him, but strengthened to cling to Christ.

2. The method

Our method should be to proclaim Jesus. Paul wrote, 'We proclaim him, admonishing and teaching everyone with all wisdom' (v.28). Jesus Christ is the key to spiritual maturity. As your knowledge of and intimacy with Jesus increases, you grow in maturity.

That is why it is so important to prioritise the things in your life that feed that knowledge and intimacy – such as worship, prayer and Bible reading.

3. The commitment

Paul writes, 'To this end I labour, struggling with all his energy, which so powerfully works in me' (v.29). In Paul's ministry, there was a balance between God's grace and his own responsibility. There was an element of 'toiling' and 'striving', which all effective Christian ministry involves. It requires time and effort, overcoming disappointments and difficulties.

On the other hand, you can only do it through God's grace. You do not 'labour' and 'struggle' on your own. You do it with 'all his energy, which so powerfully works in [you]'. You need his help and his power for each and every task.

What delights Paul is to see 'how firm' the Colossians 'faith in Christ is' (2:5). The whole purpose of Paul's life revolved around Jesus: 'I want you woven into a tapestry of love, in touch with everything there is to know of God. Then you will have minds confident and at rest, focused on Christ, God's great mystery. All the richest treasures of wisdom and knowledge are embedded in that mystery and nowhere else' (vv.2–3, MSG).

PRAYER

Lord, thank you that I found the meaning of life in Christ. Thank you that you came to live within me by your Spirit. Thank you that in Jesus I find all the treasures of wisdom and knowledge. Help me to proclaim Jesus Christ and to present everyone fully mature in Christ.

OLD TESTAMENT READING

Jeremiah 9:17–11:17
Knowing God is what it is all about

Today, some people still literally worship idols. Others worship a different type of 'idol'. We are tempted to worship success, intelligence, money, power, celebrity or sensual indulgence. Personally, I have never met anyone made happy by these things alone. Yet, advertisers consistently play on our desire for these things, even though they fail to bring us true happiness.

Jeremiah proclaims that God's judgment is coming on his people because they have missed the very purpose of their lives. They are worshipping idols who cannot speak and can do neither harm nor good (10:5).

Yet this is what the Lord says: 'Let not the wise boast of their wisdom or the strong boast of their strength or the rich boast of their riches, but let those who boast boast about this: that they understand and know me, that I am the Lord' (9:23–24a).

In other words, Jeremiah says that what matters in life is not your brains (wisdom), nor your body (strength), nor your bank account (riches). None of these provide the purpose of your life. The purpose of your life is to understand and know God (v.24a). If you know God and his kindness, justice and righteousness, then you will imitate him and bring him delight (v.24b).

God's concern is for your heart. It is not true that the Old Testament was concerned with physical circumcision and the New Testament with circumcision of the heart. God has always looked at the heart and regarded it as far more important than the outward sign (vv.25–26).

God is always looking for leaders of his people who know him and listen to him: 'It's because our leaders are stupid. They never asked God for counsel' (10:21, MSG). They didn't realise that 'mere mortals can't run their own lives' (v.23, MSG).

Jeremiah on the other hand *did listen* to the Lord, constantly proclaiming: 'The word that came to Jeremiah from the Lord' (11:1).

The great strength of Jeremiah, and of all-powerful preachers, is that they wait on the Lord and speak what the Lord tells them to, rather than simply relying on human understanding. God speaks in public through those who first speak to him in private. As the papal preacher, Raniero Cantalamessa, says, 'The more you are called to speak, the more you are called to listen.'

PRAYER

Father, help me to grow into maturity in my knowledge of you and to hear the words of Jesus speaking to me clearly. Help me to proclaim Jesus with authority and power, so that many will put their faith in Christ and find the purpose and meaning of their lives.

6 October | Day 279

Can a Leopard Change Its Spots?

Brian Emmett was a career criminal in south London – a drug smuggler and gangster and contemporary of the notorious Kray twins, whom he knew well.

Brian had a son called Michael, who joined 'the family business' at a young age. Father and son worked together as international drug smugglers. Their activities were very successful until, one night, they were arrested as part of a massive police operation involving twelve armed officers and sixty regulars in a small Devon fishing port, where a hoard of four metric tonnes of cannabis with a street value of £13 million was being landed.

At the time, it was the largest ever known importation of cannabis to the UK and they were each sentenced to twelve and a half years.

In 1994, Brian and Michael heard about Alpha while in Exeter Prison and decided to give it a try. They were filled with the Holy Spirit and their lives were completely transformed.

As father and son continued to serve their sentences, they were regularly transferred from prison to prison throughout England as is the normal practice. On arrival in each one, they introduced Alpha and more and more prisoners experienced the love of God for the first time.

From those beginnings, Alpha in Prison has grown. In 2016 (the last year for which we have the statistics) over 45,000 men and women did Alpha in prisons in dozens of countries around the world.

When I interviewed Michael, I asked him what difference Jesus has made. He replied, 'I was a drug addict for years, entrenched with crime. I looked the part but inside I was very broken. There was a hole inside of me that I tried to fill with things that didn't work. Jesus is real. He did an inside job on me. The change is dramatic – healing and changing, transforming my mind and heart. The curse has been broken over my family.'

Brian and Michael's lives were changed because Jesus set them free from their addictions and the sin that was destroying their lives. After lives of crime and lawlessness, they never went to prison again.

Is it possible for you too to change? One of the most difficult things in the world is to break a bad habit or to give up sin. In one of today's passages Jeremiah asks, '*Can a leopard change its spots?*' (Jeremiah 13:23).

READING FROM PSALMS

Psalm 118:1–16
Changed by God's help

Are you fearful about what other people think or say about you? Are you worried about what they might do to you – that they might treat you unfairly or reject you?

Realise how big God is and how small our problems are in comparison with his power. The psalmist gives thanks to the Lord because of his great love (vv.1–4). He writes, 'In my anguish I cried to the LORD, and he answered by *setting me free*' (v.5).

Freedom gives us a new perspective on life. The psalmist turns to God, knowing he can be relied on no matter what: 'GOD's now at my side and I'm not afraid: who would dare lay a hand on me? GOD's my strong champion; I flick off my enemies like flies' (vv.6–7, MSG).

Praise God today that, like the psalmist, you can say: 'The LORD is my strength and my song, he has become my salvation' (v.14).

PRAYER

Lord, thank you that you are always with me, and that you are my helper, my strength, my salvation and my song.

NEW TESTAMENT READING

Colossians 2:6–23
Changed by Jesus

Sometimes we overcomplicate our faith. It can appear that if you want to be part of the 'spiritual elite', there are various extra things you need to understand or do. Paul challenges this kind of false teaching head on.

All you need is Jesus. It is not a matter of adding anything to Jesus, but rather of living out what you already have in him: 'You received Christ Jesus, the Master; now *live* him. You're deeply rooted in him. You're well constructed upon him. You know your way around the faith. Now *do* what you've been taught' (vv.6–7a, MSG).

Paul warns the Colossians against the false teachers who try to dazzle them with their 'big words and intellectual double-talk' (v.8, MSG). 'You don't need a telescope, a microscope or a horoscope to realize the fullness of Christ and the emptiness of the universe without him. When you come to him, that fullness comes together for you, too. His power extends over everything' (vv.9–10, MSG).

In the immediate context, Paul was telling his readers that they had no need to be circumcised. He explains that they have already been circumcised – not 'by human hands' but 'with the circumcision done by Christ' (v.11). Those who have been baptised do not need to be circumcised (v.12). Baptism symbolises something even more amazing than circumcision: death and resurrection.

You are *in* Christ. Therefore, when Jesus died, *you died in him*. When Jesus was buried, *you were buried with him* – and when he rose from the dead, *you rose with him* (v.12). This is how you got rid of your sinful nature – 'putting off of the sinful nature' (v.11). It died with Christ and was buried with him. 'When you were stuck in your old sin-dead life, you were incapable of responding to God. God brought you alive – right along with Christ!' (v.13, MSG).

In the ancient world, triumphs over hated enemies were celebrated with public spectacles (v.15). The spoils of war were brought back, often consisting of a long line of prisoners whom they had disarmed.

Understand and think about the amazing victory of Jesus on the cross: 'All sins forgiven, the slate wiped clean, that old arrest warrant canceled and nailed to Christ's cross. He stripped all the spiritual tyrants in the universe of their sham authority at the Cross and marched them naked through the streets' (vv.13–15, MSG).

Jesus has done it all. You don't need to add anything: 'So don't put up with anyone pressuring you in details of diet, worship services or holy days' (v.16, MSG). All you need is Christ 'who puts us together in one piece, whose very breath and blood flow through us. He is the Head and we are the body. We can grow up healthy in God only as he nourishes us' (v.19 MSG).

PRAYER

Lord Jesus, thank you that as you hung on the cross for me and for the entire human race, in your apparent defeat you actually triumphed over all the powers and authorities of this dark world. Thank you that you set me free from sin, addiction and death. Help me never again to allow anyone or anything to take me captive.

OLD TESTAMENT READING

Jeremiah 11:18–13:27
Changed by testing

Don't be afraid of pressure. Pressure is what transforms a lump of coal into a diamond. Life can be seen as a series of tests. We test things by putting them under pressure. Physical muscles grow through being put under pressure. God is more interested in how your heart and mind grow when they are tested; he tests 'the heart and mind' (11:20).

God is not impressed by what *we say* that we will do – he is impressed by what *we do* when we are put under pressure. Progress in life and in ministry happens when you are tried and tested, and you pass the test. Jeremiah was tested. He had the unenviable task of warning people that they were about to go into exile – 'the LORD's flock will be taken captive' (13:17).

As a result, he was very unpopular and under constant attack. God revealed one of the plots against him: '...the LORD revealed their plot to me, I knew it, for at that time he showed me what they were doing (11:18).

He turned to God for help: '...to you I have committed my cause ... I bring a case before you' (11:20; 12:1).

God warned him that even worse was to come: 'So, Jeremiah, if you're worn out with this footrace with men, what makes you think you can race against horses?' (v.5, MSG).

Jeremiah calls the people to change their ways. He says, *'Can a leopard get rid of its spots*? So what are the odds on you doing good, you who are so long-practiced in evil?' (13:23, MSG).

It is hard to change. It is difficult to pass the test. But the New Testament tells us that change is possible through Jesus. Brian and Michael Emmett are examples of how this is still being worked out today. *A leopard can change its spots*.

PRAYER

Lord, help me when I am tried and tested to rise to the challenge. Thank you that it is possible to change through your help and by the power of the victory of Jesus on the cross. May my life be transformed and may I continue to proclaim Jesus and his power to change me.

7 October | Day 280
New Clothes

I tend to wear very similar clothes every day. I cannot claim to have much 'dress sense'. Yet, believe it or not, before Pippa and I got married it was even worse.

When I got married, my flared trousers, misshapen sweaters with holes, string vests, ties (inherited from an uncle) and dilapidated trousers had to go. I hate getting rid of things – especially clothes to which I am attached. They feel like old friends. But alas, the time had come to be re-clothed.

As well as the outer clothing, our hearts and minds have an inner clothing. When you come into a relationship with God through Jesus, the old clothes have to go and you need a new set of clothes for your heart and mind.

READING FROM PROVERBS

Proverbs 24:15–22
Control your heart and mind regarding other people

Have you been wronged or hurt in some way by someone and then found out that they got into trouble?

This passage warns us against *thinking* that they are getting what they deserve and rejoicing over their problems: 'Do not gloat when your enemies fall; when they stumble, do not let your heart rejoice, or the LORD will see and disapprove' (vv.17–18a).

It is so easy to gloat when those who have been causing us problems and opposing us mess up and fall. It is rather tempting to enjoy the moment. But this is the wrong response. Watch *your heart* and resist these *thoughts*.

As Joyce Meyer writes, 'It takes a lot of "heart work" for us not to be at least a little bit glad to see that person get what is coming to [them] ... We should always remember that "hurting people hurt people". Those who hurt us are usually hurting within themselves, and their pain may be so strong that they are not even aware they are hurting us.'[1]

PRAYER

Lord, forgive us for the times when we have gloated, and help us to resist the temptation to do so. Help me to control my heart and my mind with the help of the Holy Spirit.

NEW TESTAMENT READING

Colossians 3:1–4:1
Clothe your heart and mind with love

As a Christian, you are 'in Christ'. You are united with him in his death and resurrection. Therefore, Paul can write that 'you died' (3:3). And he can also write, 'you have been raised with Christ ... your life is now hidden with Christ in God' (vv.1, 3). In the future, 'When Christ, who is your life, appears, then you also will appear with him in glory' (v.4).

Because of all that Jesus has done for you and made possible, you need to re-clothe your heart and mind.

1. Change what you think about (vv.1–12)

Right action begins with right thinking. You can now live this resurrection life, made possible by Jesus, Paul writes: 'Set your *hearts* on things above ... Set your *minds* on things above, not on earthly things' (vv.1–2).

This is not easy because you are surrounded by 'earthly things' (v.2) and temptations. Take radical action. Paul writes, 'That means killing off everything connected with that way of death: sexual promiscuity, impurity, lust, doing whatever you feel like whenever you feel like it, and grabbing whatever attracts your fancy' (v.5, MSG). This is what we used to do *before we were Christians*.

'Strip off' the old clothes (v.9, AMP). You must '*rid yourselves*' (v.8) of the bad stuff: 'anger, rage, malice, slander, and filthy language from your lips. Do not lie to each other, since you have *taken off* your old self with its practices and have put on ['*clothed yourselves* with', AMP] the new self, which is being renewed in knowledge in the image of its Creator' (vv.8–10).

Put on the new clothes. You are one of God's chosen people and therefore, you are called to live as such. This means a radical change of your position in the world. Don't be passive; be active. Instead of the bad stuff, you are called to clothe yourself with 'compassion, kindness, humility, gentleness, and patience' (v.12).

2. Change your reaction to others (vv.13–15)

Jesus lives in every Christian, regardless of background. In Christ there is no racial barrier ('no Greek or Jew'), no religious barrier ('circumcised or uncircumcised'), no national barrier ('barbarian, Scythian') and no class barrier ('slave or free') but 'Christ is all, and *in all*' (v.11).

Paul goes on, 'bear with each other' (v.13). In the world, if someone lets you down, that is often the end of the relationship. But you are to 'forgive whatever grievances you may have against one another. Forgive as the Lord forgave you' (v.13).

This kind of forgiveness is a uniquely Christian virtue. Others may forgive, but only Christians have such a solid basis for forgiveness. As C. S. Lewis says, 'To be a Christian means to forgive the inexcusable because God has forgiven the inexcusable in you.'[2]

One word sums up your new set of clothes: 'love'. Paul writes, 'And over all these virtues *put on* love, which binds them all together in perfect unity' (v.14). Love is not just an emotion; it is an action. It is something you 'put on'. As you put on your physical clothes, so you are *to put on love*.

This is the beauty of the Christian community – Christ brings about a radical change in your relationships. The way Christians relate is so different from the world and should be so attractive.

How is it possible? You must set your heart and mind in the right place and, as Paul goes on to write, 'Let the peace of Christ rule in *your hearts*, since as members of one body you were called to peace' (v.15).

God's peace acts like a referee in your heart – telling you what is in and what is out. One of the questions you should ask about any decision is: 'Do I sense God's peace about what I am about to do?'

3. Change your attitude to Jesus (vv.16–17)
Be constantly guided by 'the word of Christ' (v.16). Paul says, 'Let the word of Christ – the message – have the run of the house. Give it plenty of room in your lives. Instruct and direct one another using good common sense. And sing, sing your hearts out to God!' (v.16, MSG).

This kind of community will be centred on the worship of God and listening to the word of Christ in the Scriptures. It will be a community of love, 'sincerity of heart and reverence for the Lord' (v.22).

It will also be one of hard work. Whether you are an employer or an employee, you are serving Christ. Do your job well and with a good attitude in your heart and mind: 'Whatever you do, work at it with *all your heart*, as working for the Lord ... It is the Lord Christ you are serving' (vv.23–24).

PRAYER

Lord, help me today to live a life of compassion, kindness, humility, gentleness and patience. Help me to forgive as you have forgiven me. May your peace rule in my heart.

OLD TESTAMENT READING

Jeremiah 14:1–15:21
Change the direction of your heart and mind towards God

The book of Jeremiah is a call to repentance that begins with Jeremiah's own heart: 'Therefore, this is what the LORD says: "*If you repent*, I will restore you that you may serve me; if you utter worthy, not worthless, words, you will be my spokesman..."' (15:19). Repentance means changing *your heart and mind* and turning back to God.

Jeremiah was God's spokesperson. He turned his heart and mind to listening to the word of the Lord. This was in stark contrast to the false prophets of the day: the Lord says about them, 'These preachers are liars, and they use my name to cover their lies. I never sent them, I never commanded them, and I don't talk with them. The sermons they've been handing out are sheer illusion, tissues of lies, whistlings in the dark' (14:14, MSG).

On the other hand, Jeremiah's heart and mind was set on *listening to the Lord*: 'This is the word of the LORD to Jeremiah' (v.1); 'Then the LORD said to me...' (15:1). He knew how amazing it was to hear the words of the Lord: 'When your words came, I ate them; they were my joy and my heart's delight' (v.16). Ultimately, this is the only thing that will satisfy the deepest longings of your heart and mind.

Resolve to continue to read God's words every day and to meditate on them in your heart and mind. Once you have heard the word of the Lord, pass on the life-changing message unchanged: 'Let your words change them. Don't change your words to suit them' (v.19, MSG).

PRAYER

God be in my head, and in my understanding;
God be in my eyes, and in my looking;
God be in my mouth, and in my speaking;
God be in my heart, and in my thinking;
God be at my end, and at my departing
(*Sarum Missal*).

8 October | Day 281
Glorified in Defeat

I will never forget a conversation I had with Father Raniero Cantalamessa, Franciscan monk and preacher to the Papal Household. He was about to be involved in a public debate with one of the 'New Atheists' in Italy.

I asked him whether he thought he would win the debate. He replied that he did not know. He said he might lose. 'But,' he added, '*the Lord can be glorified in defeat.*'

Jesus turned the world upside down. He reversed the values of the world. Supremely on the cross, Jesus turned the world upside down. In an act of ultimate humiliation and *apparent* defeat he brought the greatest victory the world has ever known.

It was said of his followers that they were 'turning the world upside down' (Acts 17:6, NRSV). In each of today's passages we see how this works, and how the Lord can be glorified in defeat.

READING FROM PSALMS

Psalm 118:17–29
God can bring success out of apparent failure

As I look back on my life, God seems to have used the difficulties and defeats more than any apparent success.

The psalmist has clearly been through a difficult time. He writes, 'God tested me, he pushed me hard' (v.18a, MSG). Yet he is full of thanksgiving, praise and rejoicing: 'I will ... give *thanks* to the Lord' (v.19). 'This is the day the Lord has made; let us *rejoice* and be *glad* in it' (v.24).

He is full of thanksgiving because he sees that God is able to bring success out of apparent defeat. He writes, 'The stone which the builders rejected has become the chief cornerstone' (v.22, AMP).

Jesus is the supreme example of God bringing success out of apparent failure. He is the stone that the builders rejected, which has now become the cornerstone of the church. Jesus quotes this verse in Psalm 118 as referring to himself (Mark 12:10). Peter too makes this application (1 Peter 2), pointing out that Jesus is 'the living stone – rejected by human beings but chosen by God' (v.4). Jesus is now the chief cornerstone on which the whole church rests.

Respond like the psalmist: 'Give thanks to the Lord, for he is good; his love endures for ever' (Psalm 118:29).

PRAYER

Lord, thank you so much for the way in which you bring success out of apparent defeat. 'You are my God, and I will give you thanks; you are my God, and I will exalt you' (v.28).

NEW TESTAMENT READING

Colossians 4:2–18
God can use you in spite of your circumstances

At times, we are distracted by many *'if onlys'*. *If only* we were married. *If only* we were not married to the wrong person. *If only* we were in the right job. *If only* we didn't have to go to work. *If only* we had children. *If only* we didn't have so many children. *If only* we lived in the right place ... But God used Paul in spite of his circumstances, and even because of them!

Paul writes, 'Make the most of every opportunity' (v.5, MSG). We cannot all be 'successful' but we can all do our best in whatever situation we find ourselves. Paul writes that they are to tell Archippus, 'Do your best in the job you received from the Master. *Do your very best*' (v.17, MSG).

Paul was extraordinarily gifted. He had a vital message to proclaim to the world. He might have expected that God would place him in a position of authority and power so that he could best use his gifts and proclaim his message.

However, God allowed him to end up in prison. He ends the letter, 'Remember I am still *in prison* and *in chains*' (v.18, AMP). Yet the Lord was glorified in his apparent defeat. God turned Paul's situation upside down. Almost 2,000 years later you are still reading the words Paul wrote while in prison. God used his words to change the world.

Your words are powerful. Paul writes, 'Let your speech at all times be gracious (pleasant and winsome), seasoned [as it were] with salt, [so that you may never be at a loss] to know how you ought to answer anyone [who puts a question to you]' (v.6, AMP). For example, if you are hosting on Alpha, pray for wisdom to know when to speak, what to say and how to say it.

God also used Paul's prayers to change the world. Here is another challenge to our priorities. He writes, 'Devote yourselves to prayer' (v.2). The world considers prayer a complete waste of time. Paul saw it as the highest priority of our lives. He commends Epaphras because he is 'always *wrestling in prayer* for you, that you may stand firm in all the will of God, mature and fully assured' (v.12).

He wants his readers *to pray* that 'God may open a door for our message, so that we may proclaim the mystery of Christ, for which I am in chains. *Pray* that I may proclaim it clearly, as I should' (vv.3–4).

Here is yet another challenge to our priorities. Paul does not want them to pray for large crowds to come and hear him – rather he prays that he may proclaim the message clearly.

Paul doesn't want them to pray for an open door to the prison, but an open door for the message of the gospel to be proclaimed. Rather than looking to the future when you might be in a better situation in which to serve God, focus on how you can serve God in the present, whatever your situation.

PRAYER

Lord, help me to get my priorities right – to devote myself to prayer and proclamation whatever my circumstances. Give me wisdom today to know when to speak, what to say and how to say it.

OLD TESTAMENT READING

Jeremiah 16:1–17:27

God can make the 'worst of times' the 'best of times'

'It was the best of times, it was the worst of times.'[1] These are the opening words of Charles Dickens' novel *A Tale of Two Cities* (1859), set in London and Paris before and during the French Revolution.

Again, we can see that God can be glorified in apparent defeat. A 'year of drought' can become a 'year of bearing fruit' (17:8). Bad times can be good times for the church. The good news shines brighter as society gets darker.

Rick Warren pointed out, 'In the 1930s [recession] there were two things that increased: theatre attendance and church attendance. People were looking for escapism and they were looking for meaning. The economy is very tough right now. This really is a good thing. This is the time for us to expand and push out, not for us to retreat.'[2] The worst of times can be the best of times.

Something like this is expressed in this passage. Jeremiah continues to warn of the coming judgment because the people have followed the stubbornness of their evil hearts instead of obeying God (16:12). He cautions us against the danger of deceiving ourselves: 'The heart is deceitful above all things' (17:9).

We can easily deceive ourselves. If we want something, our minds can present a variety of reasons why we should have it. We can easily justify ourselves even when we are in the wrong.

This is one of the reasons you need to stick close to God (v.7, MSG). Constantly check yourself with the word of God and the wisdom of the Christian community, or else your trust can end up in the wrong place. The Lord says, 'Cursed are those who trust in mortals, who depend on flesh for their strength and whose hearts *turn away from the Lord*' (v.5).

On the other hand, he says, 'But blessed are those who *trust in the Lord*, whose confidence is in him. They will be like a tree planted by the water that sends out its roots by the stream. It does *not fear* when *heat comes*; its leaves are always green. It has *no worries* in a year of drought and never fails to bear fruit' (vv.7–8).

Again, God turns things upside down. 'When heat comes' we would expect the leaves of the tree to dry out and turn brown. Yet because the tree is planted by the water it sends out roots by the stream and the leaves are always green. The psalmist likens this to the person who trusts in the Lord, whose confidence is in him. That person will neither fear nor worry when heat comes.

There are times in your life when the 'heat' increases. You are tested by difficult circumstances and challenges. If you stay close to the Lord, trusting in him, God is able to turn things upside down. 'Blessed are those who trust in the Lord, whose confidence is in him' (v.7).

PRAYER

Lord Jesus, you brought success out of apparent defeat. Thank you that I can trust you even when circumstances seem to be against me. I put my trust and confidence in you today.

9 October | Day 282
Life-changing Words

Earl had far too much money. He did not need to work. He took all kinds of drugs, including heroin. At the age of thirty he ended up in hospital.

Someone came to visit him in hospital and gave him a New Testament. He was thrilled. The paper was very thin and was ideal for rolling joints. He rolled his way through Matthew, Mark and Luke. When he came to John's Gospel, he started reading. As a result of reading the words of John's Gospel, he encountered Jesus. He was filled with joy.

The psychologist in charge of his case was a very beautiful young woman, who had been a model. One day she said to Earl, 'Look, I have it all – success, beauty and endless qualifications – yet I am not fulfilled. Your life is a mess yet you seem to have something – a peace and a joy. What is it?'

Then he led her to faith in Jesus Christ. Later they were married. Earl and his wife, Thommy, were great friends of ours at theological college in Oxford. His life had been radically changed by the words of God in the Bible.

READING FROM PSALMS

Psalm 119:1–8
Words of blessing

If you want a 'blessed' life – one without any regrets – then you need God's words. This, the longest of all the psalms, is all about the blessings of aligning your conduct and conversation with God's words.

'You're blessed when you stay on course, walking steadily on the road revealed by GOD. You're blessed when you follow his directions, doing your best to find him' (vv.1–2, MSG).

God loves you and wants to bless you. Through God's words in Scripture, discover the blessings of life in relationship with God. Seek him with all your heart (v.2), walk in his ways (v.3), learn his words (v.7) and you will never be put to shame (v.6).

PRAYER

Lord, thank you that your words bring such blessing to my life. Help me to 'read, mark, learn and inwardly digest' them.

NEW TESTAMENT READING

1 Thessalonians 1:1–2:16
Words of power

No church is perfect. If you find the perfect church, don't join it. The moment you or I join the church it will become imperfect! Nevertheless, there is such a thing as a *model* church – a church that is a good example and an inspiration to others. People will travel from all over the world to learn from this kind of church.

The church in Thessalonica was a model church (1:7): 'Believers look up to you ... all over the place' (vv.7–8, MSG). It was a church full of faith, love and, especially, hope: 'They marvel at how expectantly you await the arrival of ... Jesus, who rescued us from certain doom' (v.10, MSG). The church was loved by God (v.4). It was a suffering church (v.6), boldly proclaiming the words of God. The Lord's message rang out from them, not only in Macedonia and Achaia but everywhere (v.8).

This should be our aim and our prayer – to be a church worthy of imitation, where the gospel rings out not only in our own local area, but everywhere. The aim is not empire building, but gospel spreading. Paul does not commend the Thessalonians for the size of their church (we do not know how big it was). Instead, he commends them, 'you're the message!' (v.8, MSG).

The message came 'not simply with words but also in power, with the Holy Spirit and with deep conviction' (v.5):

1. Words

There is a time to speak. It is not enough simply to live out the Christian life. Tell people about Jesus and what he has done.

2. Power

Words in themselves are not enough; you also need power. The power of God speaks through you; the Holy Spirit bringing deep conviction to the heart of the hearer.

3. Lives

Paul goes on, 'You know how we *lived* among you for your sake' (v.5). Even powerful words will not have a lasting effect unless your life is consistent with the message. It is not life *or* lips, but life *and* lips.

You, like the apostle Paul, have been 'entrusted with the gospel' (2:4). It is an immense privilege. Proclaim faithfully the words of God, 'not after crowd approval – only God approval' (v.4, MSG). Don't misuse words: 'We never used words to butter you up ... And God knows we never used words as a smoke screen to take advantage of you' (vv.4–5, MSG).

The task of proclaiming the gospel is a wonderful privilege as well as a great responsibility. God has entrusted the work to us. Ultimately you are accountable to him and to him alone. Don't be concerned primarily with whether the preaching of the gospel pleases other people – in all probability it will not – but be concerned that it pleases God (v.6).

Paul did not simply throw words at the Thessalonians. He was 'never patronizing, never condescending' (v.7, MSG). He loved them like a parent – caring for them and sharing his whole life with them (vv.7–8), and setting them an example and encouraging them to live for God (v.12): 'Like a father with his child, holding your hand, whispering encouragement, showing you step by step how to live well before God' (v.12, MSG).

Speaking the words of God is not always easy. Paul writes, 'Surely you will remember, brothers and sisters, our toil and hardship; we worked night and day in order not to be a burden to anyone while we preached the gospel of God to you' (v.9).

1.'Toil'

Preaching the gospel involves hard work; 'working our fingers to the bone' (v.9, MSG). Some of the work may appear tedious. I think of our amazing 'A' team on Alpha, who work from 5 p.m. until 11 p.m. – cooking, cleaning, serving and scrubbing saucepans.

2. 'Hardship'

The 'revival' came at a cost. There was insult, strong opposition, suffering (v.2) and hostility (v.15). But in spite of this there was great joy, 'You welcomed the message with the *joy* given by the Holy Spirit' (1:6). Suffering and joy go hand in hand in the New Testament. Do not expect one without the other. Many around the world are suffering great hardship for their preaching of the gospel.

3. 'Working day and night'

Not only is there an intensity about the work, there is also a huge amount to do. In Paul's case, like most Christians today, he was not a full-time evangelist. He was doing two jobs at once. He was preaching during the day and earning a living at night.

The Thessalonians recognised that the words of the gospel spoken by Paul were not just human words, but *the very words of God* (2:13). They had a life-changing impact – so that the Thessalonians were willing to pass the message on, in spite of all the suffering and hostility they faced.

PRAYER

Lord, thank you for the life-changing power of the gospel. Give me the strength, energy and enthusiasm to keep on telling people the good news about Jesus.

OLD TESTAMENT READING

Jeremiah 18:1–20:18
Words of fire

The insults, opposition, hostility and ridicule that we in the West experience in the media, online, and even in personal attacks, are minor in comparison with the persecution of Paul, the Thessalonians, Jeremiah and many around the world today.

Jeremiah was a true prophet. *He listened* to the word of God: 'This is the word that came to Jeremiah from the LORD' (18:1), 'The word of the LORD came to me' (v.5). God spoke to Jeremiah through the visual aid of a potter and his pots. This powerful image was picked up and used by Paul (Romans 9:21). You are spiritual clay in the hands of God who is shaping you for the purpose he has for your life.

Having heard the Lord's word, Jeremiah *spoke it out*: 'This is what the LORD says' (Jeremiah 19:1). He proclaimed the words that God had told him. He said, 'Hear the word of the LORD ... this is what the LORD Almighty, the God of Israel says: Listen!' (vv.3, 15a).

However, they would not listen (v.15b). Jeremiah was beaten and put in stocks (20:2). He was ridiculed and mocked (v.7). It was not easy for him. Sometimes it is tempting to give up speaking the words of God because it is so painful. However, Jeremiah concludes:

> 'The words are fire in my belly,
> a burning in my bones.
> I'm worn out trying to hold it in.
> I can't do it any longer!' (v.7, MSG)

The fire of God's word burned so powerfully within him that he had to go on speaking it. As you follow Jeremiah's courageous example, you can say like him, 'But the LORD is with me like a mighty warrior' (v.11a).

PRAYER

Lord, help me to listen carefully to you and not to be put off by opposition, insults, hostility or ridicule. Thank you that your word in my heart is like a fire, which I cannot hold in. Help me to speak the message with your love and power.

10 October | Day 283
Surprised by Joy

'Surprised by joy' is how C. S. Lewis described his conversion from atheism to faith in Jesus Christ. He had never expected that there was any connection between *God* and *joy*. If anything, he had thought it would be the opposite: 'For all I knew, the total rejection of what I called Joy might be one of the demands.'[1]

Convinced that it was true, Lewis 'admitted that God was God'. At that moment, he was 'the most dejected and reluctant convert in all England'. To his great surprise he found that following Jesus was the very opposite to what he expected. He experienced great joy through his new-found faith. He discovered that 'the heart of reality' is to be found in a Person. He was *surprised by joy*.

Many people confuse pleasure, contentment and joy. 'Pleasure' can come from a good holiday, a pay rise or a bar of chocolate. People can become pleasure addicts – always seeking the next fix. But these experiences of pleasure come and go.

'Contentment' is longer term – being satisfied with your life, your home, your job and your relationships.

But there is another kind of happiness that we call 'joy'. It is not a fleeting emotion, but a deep way of being – a state of mind that is available to everybody. It is not found in things, but in a Person.

READING FROM PSALMS

Psalm 119:9–16
Joy in studying the Bible

Neither Pippa nor I have a very good sense of direction. We often get lost on car journeys (even with a satnav or Google Maps!). There is great joy when we find someone who is able to give us good directions.

The Bible gives you the best directions for life. It helps you to avoid straying (v.10) and getting lost. There is such great joy in finding directions to abundant life.

Reading the Bible is the last place in the world that most people would expect to find joy. Yet, as the psalmist points out, God's wisdom and his promises are a source of *delight*, *rejoicing* and *great riches*. He writes, 'I *rejoice* in following your statutes as one *rejoices* in *great riches* ... I *delight* in your decrees' (vv.14, 16a).

In the Bible we find the path to purity: 'How can the young keep their way pure? By living according to your word' (v.9). He writes, 'I have hidden your word in my heart that I might not sin against you' (v.11). Learn verses, meditate on them (v.15) and speak them out (v.13). These are some of the ways in which you can avoid straying and getting lost (v.10).

As you sense the Holy Spirit speaking to you through a particular verse or passage, you are able to say with the second-century Church Father, Origen, 'This is my scripture.' You have the joy of hearing God's voice and rejoicing in following his statutes (v.14).

PRAYER

Lord, thank you that your words bring me such joy. Help me to hide your words in my heart and to recount them with my lips.

NEW TESTAMENT READING

1 Thessalonians 2:17–3:13
Joy in leading others to faith in Jesus

Paul had led the Thessalonians to encounter Jesus Christ. There is great joy in seeing people come to faith in Christ. I think this is one of the reasons people love to help on Alpha. They have the joy of seeing people come to Christ, being filled with the Spirit and getting excited about Jesus.

The Thessalonians were Paul's 'pride and *joy*' (2:20, MSG). There was such a close bond with them. He had an intense longing to see them (v.17). He writes, 'For what is *our hope*, *our joy*, or *the crown* in which we will glory in the presence of our Lord Jesus Christ when he comes? Is it not you? Indeed, you are *our glory* and *joy*' (vv.19–20).

Rewards are not wrong in principle and seeing others put their faith in Jesus is a great reward ('crown'). How different is our glory from that of the world; the world glories in money, success and power. But we *glory* in Jesus and in those we have been privileged to see drawn to him through our words and our prayers.

Paul's joy had nothing to do with his own circumstances. He was in the middle of trouble and hard times: 'stress and crushing difficulties' (3:7, AMP). Paul's concern, amazingly, was not about his own situation, but about the effect the trials and persecution might have on the faith of the Thessalonians (v.3).

Paul's joy came from their joy. It really is true that the secret of happiness is making someone else happy.

Paul writes, 'For now we really live, since you are standing firm in the Lord' (v.8). His quality of life is deeply affected by the relationship that they have with the Lord. He is filled with joy: 'How can we thank God enough for you in return for *all the joy* we have in the presence of our God *because of you*?' (v.9).

This joy flowed out of the depth of relationship that Paul had with the Thessalonians. His love and concern for them is so clear. That love and concern continued after he left. He longed to return to them (2:18; 3:10–11), sent Timothy to help them (even though it meant his being alone for a while, 3:1–2), and prayed 'most earnestly' for them 'night and day' (v.10).

Committing deeply to the lives of those around you can seem daunting and it may involve hard work. Yet, as Paul's example shows, it is also a source of joy and celebration. It was joy 'in the presence of God'. As Paul was praying, his heart must have been filled with joy as he thought about them. So much of Paul's letters are filled with thanksgiving and joy. As we enter God's presence, our hearts are unburdened and we see things as God sees them: 'You will fill me with joy in your presence' (Psalm 16:11).

PRAYER

Lord, thank you so much for the joy of seeing people come to Christ. May I increase and overflow with love, and be infused with strength and purity, filled with confidence in the presence of God our Father.

OLD TESTAMENT READING

Jeremiah 21:1–23:8
Joy in the friendship of Jesus

As you stay close to Jesus, his joy flows into you and your joy is complete. As Gordon Fee writes, 'Unmitigated, untrammelled joy is – or at least should be – the distinctive mark of the believer in Christ Jesus.'[2] The 'righteous Branch' which Jeremiah speaks about in this passage (23:5) is going to be the source of complete joy.

The Lord says to his people through Jeremiah, 'I am setting before you the way of life and the way of death' (21:8).

He calls them to 'administer justice' (v.12). He says, 'Attend to matters of justice. Set things right between people. Rescue victims from their exploiters. Don't take advantage of the homeless, the orphans, the widows. Stop the murdering!' (22:3, MSG).

The kings should have acted like Josiah: '"He defended the cause of the poor and needy, and so all went well. Is that not what it means to *know me*?" declares the LORD' (v.16).

Here we see God's concerns, both then and now. He is concerned about justice; about the poor and the homeless; about widows and orphans; about victims of injustice. How we treat the marginalised in our society matters to God.

The people of God were under his judgment for failing in these areas. They had become an 'evil regime' (21:14, MSG). They were about to go into exile. Yet, in the midst of these prophecies of doom and exile, there was a ray of hope.

'"The days are coming," declares the LORD, "when I will raise up to David a righteous Branch, a King who will reign wisely and do what is just and right in the land. In his days Judah will be saved and Israel will live in safety. This is the name by which he will be called: The LORD Our Righteousness"' (23:5–6).

Through the lens of the New Testament we see how Jesus fulfilled this prophecy about the 'righteous Branch' (23:5, see also Isaiah 11, Ezekiel 17 and Jeremiah 33:15 onwards). He was descended from David, King of the Jews, a Saviour, The Lord Our Righteousness.

Jesus is the one in whom we find complete joy. He is the 'righteous Branch' (v.5) out of which every other branch should come. The 'righteous Branch' is linked to a vine (Ezekiel 17). Jesus said, 'I am the true vine, and my Father is the gardener' (John 15:1), 'I have told you this so that *my joy* may be in you and that *your joy may be complete*' (v.11).

PRAYER

Lord, thank you for the joy that comes from being close to Jesus. Help me each day to stay close to the 'righteous Branch' so that the joy of Jesus may be in me and my joy may be complete.

---

11 October | Day 284
More

More Please is the title of the autobiography of comedian and actor Barry Humphries (best known for playing his alter ego Dame Edna Everage). He writes that these two words, 'More please', were his first coherent utterance.

He went on to say, 'I have always *wanted more*. I *never had enough* milk or money or socks or sex or holidays or first editions or solitude or gramophone records or free meals or real friends or guiltless pleasure or neckties or applause or unquestioning love or persimmons. Of course, I have always *had more* than my share of most of these commodities but it always left me with a vague feeling of unfulfillment: *where was the rest?*'[1]

Seeking pleasure for ourselves will always leave us with 'a vague feeling of unfulfillment'. In the passages for today, you can see what really *will* satisfy your spiritual hunger and thirst, and the things that you should seek *more and more*. Paul highlights two things in particular: living to 'please God more and more' (1 Thessalonians 4:1), and 'loving each other ... more and more' (vv.9–10).

READING FROM PROVERBS

Proverbs 24:23–34
More wisdom from God

'Wisdom' comes from God and is very practical. The 'Sayings of the Wise' (v.23) cover many different aspects of our lives. Here we see some examples:

1. Judge impartially

'To show partiality in judging is not good' (v.23b). For those who judge justly, 'rich blessing will come upon them' (v.25).

2. Speak honestly

'An honest answer is like a kiss on the lips' (v.26). Sometimes it is hard to speak the truth in love, but we need to be honest with one another. The best answer you can give to *any* question asked (for example, by a guest on Alpha) is an *honest* one!

3. Stay loyal
'Don't talk about your neighbours behind their backs – no slander or gossip, please' (v.28, MSG). Anyone can stay true to your face but it is the people who stay true behind your back that really count.

4. Show restraint
The temptation to pay back those who have done us harm is very great. However, the writer of Proverbs warns against taking revenge: 'Do not say, "I'll do to them as they have done to me; I'll pay them back for what they did"' (v.29).

5. Work hard
The book of Proverbs often warns against laziness. 'A little sleep, a little slumber, a little folding of the hands to rest – and poverty will come on you like a bandit and scarcity like an armed man' (vv.33–34).

PRAYER

Lord, help me to grow in wisdom – in impartiality, honesty, faithfulness, restraint and industry – so that *more and more* I may live a life that pleases you.

NEW TESTAMENT READING

1 Thessalonians 4:1–18
More pleasing to God

Instead of just 'looking out for number one', we are called to live lives that please God more and more (v.1). Rather than '*more, please*' we should live lives that are '*more pleasing*' to God. You are called to love God 'more and more' and to love others 'more and more' (v.10). How do you do this?

1. Give dignity to your body
God is concerned about your body as well as your soul: 'Learn to appreciate and give dignity to your body' (v.4, MSG). Paul writes, 'You should avoid sexual immorality: each of you should learn to control your own body in a way that is holy and honourable, not in passionate lust like the heathen, who do not know God' (vv.3–5).

2. Live a beautiful life
'God did not call us to be impure but to live a holy life' (v.7) – 'holy and beautiful – as beautiful on the inside as the outside' (v.7, MSG). True beauty has nothing to do with looks. It is about how you are on the inside. The process of being made holy takes place through the work of the 'Holy' Spirit. God 'gives you his Holy Spirit' (v.8) for this purpose.

3. Love each other
Paul writes, 'About your mutual love we do not need to write to you, for you yourselves have been taught by God to love each other' (v.9). 'Get better and better at it' (v.10, MSG).

4. Mind your own business
Paul writes that we are not just to be ambitious – but we are to be ambitious to live a quiet life and to be industrious. This is surprising to read, particularly given the great things Paul did for God, but it seems there is a deep significance in the apparently small things of life. Paul specifically writes 'mind your own business' (v.11). Gossip is when you are sharing information and you are neither part of the problem, nor part of the solution. Of course, there is a time when we need to get involved and help other people, but we are not to go around interfering in other people's business.

5. Get a job, if you can
Paul writes, '...work with your hands, just as we told you, so that your daily life may win the respect of outsiders and so that you will not be dependent on anybody' (vv.11–12). For some, such as stay-at-home parents, their work is in the home. Others work outside the home earning money to support their family. The general rule is that we should try to get a job if we can and *not* be dependent on others for our support. Some may be dependent on the body of Christ for support – such as those in certain types of unpaid full-time ministry. But this is the exception rather than the rule.

6. Enjoy an endless hope
No one can live well until they can die well. Death is another subject on which you are called to have a different attitude. Of course, we grieve when someone dies. But Paul says we should not 'grieve like the rest, who have no hope' (v.13) because 'since Jesus died and broke loose from the grave, God will most

certainly bring back to life those who died in Jesus' (v.14, MSG).

Death is not the end. Paul is saying that just as Jesus died and rose again, in the same way we believe that in the resurrection God will bring with him all those who have *fallen asleep*. Paul uses a different word here – whereas Jesus *died* for you, you will never die, you only 'fall asleep' (vv.13, 15).

You will be reunited with Jesus 'to meet the Lord' (v.17a) and we will be reunited with each other: 'caught up together with them' (v.17a) – 'one huge family reunion' (MSG). Not only will you be with the Lord for ever (v.17b), but you will also be with all those 'who have fallen asleep in him' (v.14). Many people see only a *hopeless end*, but you have an *endless hope*. Remind and 'encourage each other with these words' (v.18).

PRAYER

Lord, thank you for your Holy Spirit who is at work within me, and who helps me to live a life that pleases you more and more. Help me in my weakness to live a holy life: of love, sexual purity, right ambition, hope and encouragement.

OLD TESTAMENT READING

Jeremiah 23:9–25:14
More listening to God

God speaks. You and I can listen to the words of God. This is what makes the Bible so powerful '"Is not my word like fire," declares the LORD, "and like a hammer that breaks a rock in pieces?"' (23:29).

Jeremiah spoke 'holy words' (v.9) to the people of God and rebuked their leaders for a failure to lead holy lives: 'The land is full of adulterers' and leaders who 'use their power unjustly' (v.10). He accuses them of being sex-driven, living a lie (v.14, MSG). He calls them to repentance (25:5–6).

At the root of their problem is a failure to listen to God, 'You refused to listen' (v.7, MSG).

The Lord asks through Jeremiah, 'But which of [the prophets] has stood in the council of the LORD to see or hear his word? *Who has listened* and heard his word?' (23:18). 'I never sent these prophets, but they ran away. I never spoke to them, but they preached away. If they'd have bothered to sit down and meet with me, they'd have preached my Message to my people...' (vv.21–22, MSG).

If you hear the words of God and speak them out, they will have a very powerful impact: 'But you prophets who have a message from me – tell it truly and faithfully ... Isn't my Message like fire? ... Isn't it like a sledgehammer busting a rock?' (vv.28–29, MSG) The words of the Bible are so powerful – like fire and like a hammer that breaks a rock to pieces. The more I study it, the more it breaks the rock of my heart, and the Holy Spirit works a process of transformation and sanctification.

PRAYER

Lord, help me to spend more and more time listening to and hearing your words, and to live a life more and more loving, holy and pleasing to you.

12 October | Day 285
Dare to Be Different

I once had the privilege of meeting and interviewing Pastor Nadarkhani. Youcef Nadarkhani encountered Jesus Christ at the age of nineteen. He went on to become an ordained pastor and lead a church in Iran.

In 2010, aged thirty-two, married with two young children, he was arrested and sentenced to death for 'apostasy' (converting to Christianity from Islam). Thankfully, two years later, after sustained international pressure, the decision was reversed.

During his trial, Pastor Nadarkhani refused to recant his belief despite facing a death sentence. He told the judge, 'I am resolute in my faith and Christianity and have no wish to recant.' The then UK Foreign Secretary, William Hague, paid tribute to his courage.[1] The

Guardian newspaper described him as 'an inspiringly brave Christian'.[2] Pastor Nadarkhani, like many Christians around the world today, still faces persecution for his faith.

Jesus gives us a picture of true humanity. Dare to be different, by being like him. Don't follow what the world tells you is desirable, but follow God by becoming more Christ-like.

READING FROM PSALMS

Psalm 119:17–24
Be a 'stranger' on earth

Do you ever feel like you don't quite fit in with those around you at work or in your neighbourhood? Do your values and lifestyle seem to be a little different? Do you sometimes face 'scorn' and 'contempt' (v.22)?

The psalmist says, 'I am a *stranger* on earth' (v.19). All the great men and women in the Old Testament were '*strangers* on earth' (Hebrews 11:13). The apostle Peter writes, 'Live your lives as *strangers* here' (1 Peter 1:17). Like the psalmist, as servants of God, we are called to be different from those around us.

Unlike those around him, the psalmist writes, 'My soul is consumed with longing for your laws at all times' (Psalm 119:20). As he reads the Scriptures, he prays, 'Open my eyes that I may see wonderful things in your law' (v.18). This is a great prayer to pray when you study the Bible. We only understand what is revealed by the Spirit.

Some of those around him are 'bad neighbors' who 'maliciously gossip' (v.23a, MSG). But God's words are to him like 'good neighbors' (v.24, MSG). He writes, 'I'm absorbed in pondering your wise counsel. Yes, your sayings on life are what give me delight; I listen to them as to good neighbors!' (vv.23b–24, MSG).

PRAYER

Lord, give me courage to live as a stranger on earth. Help me to be consumed with longing for your word, to meditate on what you say. Open my eyes that I may see wonderful things in your word.

NEW TESTAMENT READING

1 Thessalonians 5:1–28
Live differently

Called to be different from the world around us, we are given practical instructions on how to do this. Paul writes, 'Let us *not be like others*' (v.6). Dare to be different. Paul uses four metaphors to describe the difference:

1. *Light* not darkness

The world around is living in darkness (v.4). Don't run away from the darkness, rather, shine in it. 'You are all children of the light' (v.5a). Darkness implies ignorance and sin. You were in darkness. Jesus shines his light into your life. You are a child of the light. To be a child of something is to be characterised by that thing. When Christians are spoken of as 'children of the light', it means that 'light' is your distinguishing characteristic.

2. *Day* not night

Paul writes, 'You are ... children of the day. You do not belong to the night' (v.5). As well as the previous point about light and darkness, this also refers back to 'the day of the Lord' (v.2). We are children of the day of the Lord, with all that this means in terms of anticipation and participation in the triumph of that great day when Jesus returns.

3. *Awake* not asleep

Paul writes, 'Let us not be like others, who are *asleep* ... For those who sleep, sleep at night' (vv.6–7). He goes on, 'Whether we are awake or asleep, we may live together with him' (v.10). Jesus is with you now. Jesus himself used this same language of keeping watch and being awake (Matthew 24:42; 25:13). Don't go to sleep spiritually. Be prepared for the Lord's coming – awake and watchful.

4. *Sober* not drunk

Paul writes, 'Let us be self-controlled' (1 Thessalonians 5:8). This word literally means 'not intoxicated by wine'. Like the other metaphors it speaks of both a physical state and a spiritual reality. Drunkenness arises from a lack of self-control and an indulgence of the senses in order to escape reality. Seek to be self-controlled in every area of your life. Put on the clothing of faith, love and hope (v.8).

Your lifestyle is to be totally different from those around you. You are to honour your leaders: 'We ask you to honor those leaders who work so hard for you, who have been given the responsibility of urging and guiding you along in your obedience. Overwhelm them with appreciation and love!' (vv.12–13a, MSG).

You are called to a life of respect (v.12). Always treat people with respect. Always stay peaceful (v.13): 'Gently encourage the stragglers, and reach out for the exhausted, pulling them to their feet. Be patient with each person, attentive to individual needs. And be careful that when you get on each other's nerves you don't snap at each other. Look for the best in each other, and always do your best to bring it out' (vv.14–15, MSG). If you want to bring out the best in people you must see the best in them.

Be kind to everyone. Kindness should be a distinguishing feature of your life: 'Always try to be kind to each other and to everyone else' (v.15). Even little acts of kindness are so powerful that they can change the world around you.

You are a citizen of a different world. You have to learn a new language. What Paul describes here is effectively the grammar of a new language: 'Be joyful always; pray continually; give thanks in all circumstances' (v.16). Prayer should be like breathing – something we do continually, but often unconsciously. Instead of always complaining 'give thanks in all circumstances' – expressing your thanks to God and other people – in little things as well as big things.

'Do not put out the Spirit's fire; do not treat prophecies with contempt. Test everything. Hold on to the good. Avoid every kind of evil' (vv.19–22).

All this can seem a very daunting prospect. But you are not on your own. Paul prays, 'May God himself, the God of peace, sanctify you through and through' (v.23), and he finishes on a resounding note of hope and help – 'He who calls you is faithful, and *he* will do it' (v.25).

PRAYER

Lord, help me to dare to be different. Thank you that you died for me that I may live together with you (v.10). Help me to avoid every kind of evil (v.22) and live a life of love, kindness, joy and peace.

OLD TESTAMENT READING

Jeremiah 25:15–26:24
Speak differently

People do not always want to hear God's views. It takes courage to speak God's words to a society that has its own views, which may be very different to God's.

Jeremiah's ministry required great courage. He had to dare to be different from the prophets around. They were all prophesying peace, but Jeremiah knew that the exile was coming. He was warning the people about the coming disaster.

God said to him, 'Tell them everything I command you; do not omit a word. Perhaps they will listen and each will turn from their evil ways' (26:2–3).

However, 'As soon as Jeremiah finished telling all the people everything the Lord had commanded him to say, the priests, the prophets and all the people seized him and said, "You must die!"' (v.8).

Jeremiah's response was again very courageous. He said, 'Change the way you're living, change your behavior. Listen obediently to the Message of your God. Maybe God will reconsider the disaster he has threatened ... If you kill me, you're killing an innocent man ... God sent me and told me what to say. You've been listening to God speak, not Jeremiah' (vv.13–15, MSG).

In fact, like Youcef Nadarkhani, Jeremiah escaped the death sentence – but both men were willing to pay the ultimate price to stay true to God. We may not face the same pressure, but the world around us will often dislike us for being different. Do not be surprised or dismayed by such opposition – as Jesus told his disciples, 'In this world you will have trouble. But,' Jesus continued, 'take heart! I have overcome the world' (John 16:33).

PRAYER

Lord, thank you for the examples of Pastor Nadarkhani, Jeremiah, Paul and, ultimately, Jesus himself, who were willing to dare to be different from those around them, even to the point of being sentenced to death. Give me courage to dare to be different and to speak the words you tell me to say.

13 October | Day 286
God's Good Plans for Your Future

Futurologists make predictions about the future. One prediction is that some babies born now are likely to live to the ripe old age of 150. *Wired* magazine, not long ago, predicted that meal replacement patches (taking nicotine replacement patches a step further) would be in existence by 2018, and that by 2020 there would be a new financial currency introduced for purchases in space!

Some look to futurologists to know what is coming. Others go further. Some people read their horoscopes because they want to know what their future holds. However, Jeremiah warns in the passage for today: 'Don't for a minute listen to ... spiritualists and fortunetellers, who *claim to know the future*' (Jeremiah 27:9, MSG).

The study of history helps us to predict the future. As Winston Churchill once said, 'To understand the future we need to understand the past.'

But as the one who holds the past, present and future in his hands, only God truly knows the future. Much of it is hidden from us. However, there are certain things about your future that God tells you.

READING FROM PSALMS

Psalm 119:25–32
Your future is freedom

I love the psalms. There is an honesty, reality and authenticity about them.

We all face temptation, sin, difficulties, sorrows, fears, hopes and desires. How does the psalmist respond to all these challenges?

He does not disguise his feelings. He speaks openly and vulnerably about them: 'I am feeling terrible – I couldn't feel worse!' (v.25a, MSG).

You too can be real with God and say, 'I recounted my ways and you answered me' (v.26a). Spread your case before the Lord, opening your heart with sincerity to him. There are times of deep sorrow: 'My soul is weary with sorrow' (v.28a).

Pray like the psalmist, 'Preserve my life according to your word' (v.25b). Meditate on God's word (v.27b) and pray, 'Strengthen me according to your word. Keep me from deceitful ways; be gracious to me through your law' (vv.28b–29).

Resolve to follow God's ways in everything, but not out of a sense of obligation or guilt. Choose to run in the path of God's commands, *for he has set your heart free* (v.32).

PRAYER

Lord, thank you that you have a path of freedom for me and that, in times of struggle, I can turn to you. I turn to you now and speak honestly with you.

NEW TESTAMENT READING

2 Thessalonians 1:1–12
Your future is secure

Jesus is coming back. His second coming is the most important thing to know and believe about the future. It changes everything about how you live your life now, and infuses every moment of the present with hope. No one knows exactly when it will happen, but live every day as if he were returning today – doing what he would want you to be doing.

Paul begins this letter with the assertion that 'our God gives you everything you need, makes you everything you're to be' (v.2, MSG). He thanks God for their growth: 'Your faith is growing phenomenally; your love for each other is developing wonderfully ... We're so proud of you' (vv.3–4, MSG).

There is a great deal of emphasis in the New Testament on spiritual growth. You are not meant to stand still. Your faith and love should grow. God is trying to increase the muscles of your faith. Is your faith getting stronger? Is your love increasing? Do you react differently from two or three years ago?

So often, it is our struggles rather than our 'successes' that make us stronger. The Thessalonians' faith and love were growing in spite of – maybe even because of – the persecution and trials that they were enduring (v.4).

Paul tells them that in the future God will put things right (vv.6–7). 'Justice is on the way' (v.6, MSG). When Jesus returns he will execute a perfectly just judgment: 'This will happen when the Lord Jesus is revealed from heaven in blazing fire with his powerful angels' (v.7).

God desires that all people repent and come to a knowledge of the truth (1 Timothy 2:4). But he warns those who consistently reject the knowledge of God throughout their life, and do not obey the gospel of our Lord Jesus Christ (2 Thessalonians 1:8) – as was the case with those who were persecuting the Thessalonians – that there is a judgment to come. They will miss out on the possibility of eternal life.

The opposite of eternal life is 'destruction' and being 'shut out from the presence of the Lord' (v.9). Those who know God and obey the gospel will experience his presence and his majesty into eternity 'on the day he comes to be glorified in his holy people and to be marvelled at among all those who have believed' (v.10a). Paul says this includes the Thessalonians: 'because *you believed* our testimony to you' (v.10b). Their long-term future is totally secure.

Their response to the gospel determined their future. The gospel message is urgent. The gospel is only good news if it gets there in time.

As far as their short-term future is concerned, Paul writes, 'We constantly pray for you, that our God may count you worthy of his calling, and that by his power he may fulfil every good purpose of yours and every act prompted by your faith' (v.11).

Do not simply sit around waiting for Jesus to return. God has a '*good purpose*' for your life. He has called you. He puts ideas into your heart. He works in you both to will and to act according to his *good purpose* (Philippians 2:13).

In all this, Paul prays that the name of Jesus will be glorified: 'If your life honors the name of Jesus, he will honor you' (2 Thessalonians 1:12, MSG).

PRAYER

Lord, thank you so much that my long-term future is secure. Help me to make the most of my life here – to grow in faith and love, fulfil the purpose you have for me and bring honour to your name.

OLD TESTAMENT READING

Jeremiah 27:1–29:23
Your future is hopeful

This passage contains one of the most wonderful and often quoted promises of God about his future plans for our lives. Jeremiah was a true prophet. He heard the word of the Lord.

But there were false prophets around, like Hananiah. Jeremiah says, 'The prophet who prophesies peace will be recognised as one truly sent by the Lord only if his prediction comes true' (28:9). Hananiah's predictions did not come true because the Lord had not sent him (v.15).

Jeremiah's prophecies *did* come true. The people of God did go into exile as he had warned.

Jeremiah speaks the message from the Lord to his people in exile. He tells them, 'Seek the peace and prosperity of the city to which I have carried you into exile. Pray to the Lord for it, because if it prospers, you too will prosper' (29:7).

There is an important principle here. Generally, you should seek the peace and prosperity of the place in which God has put you and pray for it. This includes places where you may work, your local church, your city and your nation.

There is an expression: 'Bloom where you're planted.' This passage encourages you to make roots even where you feel uncomfortable or isolated (like in exile). Sometimes the place where you find yourself is not where you want to be but if God has led you there, then that place must be fertile ground for God's work in you to thrive.

God promises his people that the exile will come to an end: 'When seventy years are completed for Babylon, I will come to you and fulfil my gracious promise to bring you back to this place' (v.10).

This is the context of the wonderful promises: 'For I know *the plans I have for you … plans to prosper you and not to harm you, plans to give you hope and a future.* Then you will call upon me and come and pray to me, and I will listen to you. You will seek me and find me when you seek me with all your heart. I will be found by you' (vv.11–14a).

God has good plans for you. They are not plans for your failure or defeat. They are plans to 'prosper you'. They are not average or mediocre plans. They are 'good, pleasing and perfect' (Romans 12:2).

But God will not force his plans on you. He requires your cooperation. If you want his plans to be fulfilled in your life, you need to seek him. He promises that, if you do so, he will be found by you (Jeremiah 29:13–14b). As you spend time with him, you will become like him and he will lead you into the good plans he has for your life.

PRAYER

Lord, today I want to seek you with all my heart. Thank you that you have great plans for me. Help me to walk in your paths and fulfil the purpose you have for me.

14 October | Day 287
How to Avoid Backsliding

As a young man, Philip was kidnapped and held hostage in Greece. There he remained for several years. During this time he received a military education. Then he returned to his homeland, which had conceded many defeats and had lost much land during the war with Greece. Within five years he had become king.

Philip II of Macedon desperately needed his army to stand firm. He is remembered for two major innovations. First is the *sarissa*, a very long spear. Second is the re-development of a rectangular military formation used by ancient armies (known as a *phalanx*). A core of highly-trained infantrymen, armed with Philip's longer spears, *stood shoulder to shoulder* in files normally eight men deep.

As long as they *stood firm* and did not break rank they were virtually invincible and struck fear into the hearts of their enemies. Using this tactic, Philip united the city-states of Greece and took the city of Philippi (that is named after him) in 356 BC.

Sometimes, it seems that the Christian life is like facing a powerful enemy. It feels like an intense struggle in which another army is attempting to push us back and break down our ranks. If we don't stand firm, we fall on our backs and slide in the mud in the wrong direction. We have seen how Jeremiah warned the people many times against *backsliding* (Jeremiah 2:19; 3:22; 5:6; 14:7; 15:6).

It is not a matter of us standing firm on our own. We are part of a community. In today's New Testament passage, Paul invokes the image of the *phalanx* with which Philip II of Macedonia once conquered the city of Philippi (Philippians 1:27). Shoulder to shoulder, the church can stand firm. This is one of many occasions that Paul exhorts the church to 'stand firm' (2 Thessalonians 2:15).

READING FROM PSALMS

Psalm 119:33–40
Get a firm grip on your heart and your eyes

It has been said that 'a great oak is only a little nut that held its ground'. The temptation to fall away and backslide usually begins with our hearts and eyes. The psalmist clearly experienced a battle within himself. He wrote, 'Turn *my heart* towards your statutes and not towards selfish gain. Turn *my eyes* away from worthless things' (vv.36–37a).

So often, backsliding begins by setting our hearts on what's in it for us, or allowing our eyes to wander onto 'worthless things' (v.37). Turn your heart and eyes to God's word and you can stand firm.

God's word is the place to find delight (v.35) and be enabled to persevere (vv.37, 40). This is because God's 'laws are good' (v.39). Pray like the psalmist, 'Teach me, O LORD, to follow your decrees; then I will keep them *to the end*' (v.33). Jesus said, 'Whoever *stands firm to the end* will be saved' (Matthew 24:13).

PRAYER

Lord, help me to find delight in your words. Turn my heart away from 'selfish gain' and my eyes from 'worthless things'.

NEW TESTAMENT READING

2 Thessalonians 2:1–17
Hold firmly to the truth of the gospel

Paul urges his readers to persevere and *stand firm*, holding firmly to the truth of the gospel.

He warns the Thessalonians, 'Don't let anyone deceive you in any way' (v.3). '[Don't] become easily unsettled or alarmed' (v.2).

Satan is a deceiver. Paul warns about 'the coming of the lawless one' that 'will be in accordance with the work of Satan displayed in all kinds of counterfeit miracles, signs and wonders, and in every sort of evil that deceives' (v.9). Those who 'refuse' to 'love the truth' will be taken in by 'a powerful delusion so that they will believe the lie' (vv.10–11).

Don't be taken in by those 'saying that the day of the Lord has already come' (v.2). I know of at least one dangerous and deceptive cult today that is saying exactly that. But when Jesus returns, it will be obvious to everyone. There will be great darkness before the dawn (vv.3–7), but the powers of evil will be revealed.

These powers are absolutely nothing compared with Jesus who will 'overthrow' the 'lawless one' with the 'breath of his mouth and destroy by the splendour of his coming' (v.8).

The early church lived in daily expectation of the second coming of Jesus. So should we. Martin Luther said, 'I live as though Jesus Christ had been crucified yesterday, had risen this morning and was coming again tomorrow.'

While you wait for Jesus' return, *stand firm*. Paul had every confidence that the Thessalonians would do so. What is true of them is true of you – you are 'loved by the Lord, because from the beginning God chose you to be saved by the sanctifying work of the Spirit and through belief in the truth. He called you to this through our gospel, that you might share in the glory of our Lord Jesus Christ' (vv.13–14).

You have your part to play. You have to '*stand firm* and hold to the teachings' (v.15) of the New Testament. However, the reason that you can be so confident in standing firm to the end is because of the love of God, 'the sanctifying work of the Spirit' and the power of the gospel, which enables you to share in the glory of Jesus Christ (vv.13–14).

So Paul writes, 'May our Lord Jesus Christ himself and God our Father, who loved us and by his grace gave us eternal encouragement and good hope, encourage your hearts and strengthen you in every good deed and word' (vv.16–17).

Encouragement is like verbal sunshine. It warms hearts and brings light to people. God himself has given you 'eternal encouragement' (v.16) and wants to encourage your heart.

God encourages you so that you may encourage and help others 'in every good deed and word' (v.17). You are encouraged to live like Jesus 'who went around doing good' (Acts 10:38).

PRAYER

Father, thank you that I am loved by the Lord and that, one day, I will share in the glory of the Lord Jesus Christ. Help me to stand firm, holding onto the truth of the gospel despite opposition.

OLD TESTAMENT READING

Jeremiah 29:24–31:14
Stand firm together as a strong community

You are not on your own. God never intended you to fight your battles alone. He called you to be a part of a strong, healthy, vibrant, growing community of his people. Together you can stand firm, not only resisting backsliding but moving forward.

Jeremiah warned the people against being deceived by false prophets: 'This is what the LORD says ... Shemaiah has prophesied to you, even though I did not send him, and has led you to believe a lie ... he has preached rebellion against me' (29:31–32).

Yet, although Israel had *backslidden* – 'your guilt is so great and your sins so many' (30:14) – God promises that he will restore them: 'But I will restore you to health and heal your wounds ... I will restore the fortunes of Jacob's tents and have compassion on his dwellings; the city will be rebuilt' (vv.17–18). He promises at least four things:

1. Joyful worship

There will be 'songs of thanksgiving and the sound of rejoicing' (v.19a). There will be shouts of joy, 'they will rejoice in the bounty of the

Lord ... They will be like a well-watered garden ... they will sorrow no more' (31:12): 'I will turn their mourning into gladness; I will give them comfort and joy instead of sorrow' (v.13).

2. Numerical growth

There will be growth: 'I will *add to their numbers*, and they will not be decreased' (30:19b). Numerical growth is a blessing from God. Pray for it, plan for it and prepare for it.

3. Strong community

Their 'community will be established' (v.20), 'a community in which I take pride' (v.20, MSG) – something strong and immovable. You are not on your own. We need one another to help and support each other and enable us together to stand firm.

4. Good leadership

The leader will be one of their own: 'Their ruler will come from their own ranks' (v.21, MSG). Someone with the same vision and who walks in a close relationship with God: 'I will bring him near and he will come close to me, for who is he who will devote himself to be close to me?' (v.21b). This is the challenge for all of us as individuals and as the church. Devote yourself to getting close to the Lord.

God loves you with an 'everlasting love' (31:3). God told his people, 'I've never quit loving you and never will. Expect love, love, and more love!' (v.3, MSG). He promises to rebuild and restore (v.4). He '"will watch over his flock like a shepherd." For the Lord will ransom Jacob and *redeem* them from the hand of those stronger than they' (vv.10–11).

PRAYER

Lord, may we not backslide but stand firm to the end with joy and thanksgiving. May our love and numbers increase. I devote myself today to being close to you.

15 October | Day 288
Never Tire of Doing What Is Right

Martin Luther King said, 'On some positions, Cowardice asks the question, "Is it safe?" Expediency asks the question, "Is it politic?" And Vanity comes along and asks the question, "Is it popular?" But Conscience asks the question, "Is it right?" The ultimate measure of a person is not where they stand in moments of convenience, but where they stand in moments of challenge, moments of great crisis and controversy.'[1]

Doing what is right in difficult situations in the workplace is a huge challenge. In his book, *God at Work,* Ken Costa writes, 'There are right and wrong choices ... all the invented terms such as "inappropriate" and "counterproductive" are efforts to avoid the simple ethical fact that there is a right and wrong course of action.'[2]

When facing a difficult pastoral situation those of us in the leadership of the church need to remind ourselves that the first question we have to ask is, 'What is the right thing to do?' And only then move to the second question, 'What is the most pastoral way to do it?'

Of course, none of us get it right all the time. We all make mistakes. As Ken Costa writes, 'We only grow in wisdom if we learn from our mistakes. Siegmund Warburg (Ken's first boss) said on this subject: "Some name it disappointment and become poorer, others name it experience and become richer."'[3]

In today's New Testament passage, Paul writes to the Thessalonians, 'Never tire of *doing what is right*' (2 Thessalonians 3:13). Jesus did not go for the easy or popular solution, but he always did the right thing. This is an important principle that runs throughout the entire Bible.

READING FROM PROVERBS

Proverbs 25:1–10
Doing right is very practical

Doing what is right means getting rid of everything that is not right in our lives: '*Remove the dross* from the silver, and out comes material for the silversmith; remove the wicked from the king's presence, and his throne will be established through *righteousness*' (vv.4–5). Here are some practical examples of what living righteously looks like:

1. Act with humility
You do not need to push yourself forward. The right thing to do is to act with humility: 'Don't work yourself into the spotlight; don't push your way into the place of prominence. It's better to be promoted to a place of honour than face humiliation by being demoted' (vv.6–7, MSG).

This is exactly the point that Jesus expounded in one of his parables (Luke 14:8–11).

2. Always assume the best
'Don't jump to conclusions – there may be a perfectly good explanation for what you just saw' (Proverbs 25:8, MSG).

3. Never betray a confidence
Do the right thing in relation to your neighbour. Do not go hastily to court (v.8). If you do end up in court, always do and say the right thing. 'In the heat of an argument, *don't betray confidences'* (v.9, MSG).

PRAYER

Lord, help us in our church community to get rid of the dross in our hearts, to act with humility towards one another and to seek always to do the right thing.

NEW TESTAMENT READING

2 Thessalonians 3:1–18
Doing right spreads the message

Paul's overriding concern was that the gospel should get out to as many people as quickly as possible – that it would 'simply take off and race through the country to a ground-swell of response' (v.1, MSG).

For this to happen, he prays that they will continue to do the right things: 'We have confidence in the Lord that you are doing and will continue to do the things we command' (v.4). He tells them, 'you ought to follow our example' (v.7). Paul lived in such a way that provided 'a model for you to follow' (v.9). He urges, 'never tire of *doing what is right*' (v.13).

1. Pray for your leaders
Leaders need your prayers: 'And pray that we may be delivered from wicked and evil people, for not everyone has faith. But the Lord is faithful, and he will strengthen and protect you from the evil one' (vv.2–3).

2. Follow the way of love
Paul prays, 'May the Lord direct your hearts into God's love' (v.5a).

3. Never give up
He prays that the Lord will direct their hearts into God's love and 'Christ's *perseverance*' (v.5).

It's not enough to do the right thing occasionally or when you feel like it. Persist, endure and continue all the way to the end.

4. Pull your weight
Do not do anything to bring the gospel into disrepute. Do not sit idly and watch life pass by. Paul sets an example of hard work: 'We showed you how to *pull your weight* when we were with you, so get on with it. We didn't sit around on our hands expecting others to take care of us. In fact, we worked our fingers to the bone … we simply wanted to provide an example of diligence, hoping it would prove contagious' (vv.7–9, MSG).

We are to exercise discipline. If people are not doing the right thing they should not be regarded as enemies but warned as brothers and sisters (v.15).

PRAYER

Lord, give me wisdom and perseverance so that I may always do the right thing. May the peace and grace of our Lord Jesus Christ be with us all (vv.16, 18).

OLD TESTAMENT READING

Jeremiah 31:15–32:25
The Spirit helps you to do right

In one of the greatest prophecies of the Old Testament, Jeremiah foresees the new covenant (31:31). The new covenant will be different from the old one (v.32).

> '"This is the covenant that I will make
> with the people of Israel
> after that time," declares the LORD.
> "I will put my law in their minds
> and write it on their hearts.
> I will be their God,
> and they will be my people.
> No longer will they teach their
> neighbour,
> or say to one another, 'Know the LORD,'
> because they will all know me,
> from the least of them to the greatest,"
> declares the LORD.
> "For I will forgive their wickedness
> and will remember their sins no
> more."' (vv.33–34).

These few verses are alluded to again and again in the New Testament (see, for instance, Luke 22:20; 2 Corinthians 3:5–18 and Hebrews 8:8–12). They highlight a series of wonderful promises about this 'new covenant', which pointed forward to Jesus:

1. God forgives your failure to do the right things

This new covenant was made possible by the blood of Jesus Christ. At the Last Supper, before he was crucified, 'he took the cup, saying, "This cup is the new covenant in my blood, which is poured out for you"' (Luke 22:20).

The new covenant between God and humans that Jeremiah spoke about enables you to be in right relationship with God. It came about through Jesus' blood shed on the cross.

All of your sins have been forgiven, 'the slate wiped clean' (Jeremiah 31:34, MSG), through the blood of Christ. As Joyce Meyer says, 'Whatever your sin or failure, you need to confess it to God and then let it go. Stop punishing yourself for something that is in the past. Refuse to remember something God has chosen to forget.'[4]

2. God's Spirit helps you to do the right thing

We have the extraordinary privilege of living in the age of the Spirit. God's law is not simply written on tablets of stone. Rather, God works in you, by his Spirit, to give you a passion to please him ('I will put my law in their minds and write it on their hearts,' v.33b), and to give you the experience of a personal relationship with him ('I will be their God and they will be my people,' v.33c). We can all *know* the Lord (v.34).

God calls you to do the right thing even when it's not easy. Doing what is right does not necessarily lead to an easy life. Jeremiah was shut up in jail in the royal palace. Zedekiah locked him up for choosing to do the right thing (32:1–3).

We see another example of Jeremiah doing the right thing in spite of the circumstances (vv.6–8). God tells him to buy a field, even though the Babylonians were about to take over Jerusalem. The field itself would become utterly worthless. But Jeremiah was not concerned about money. Doing the right thing is more important than financial gain or the likelihood of success.

Jeremiah's obedience in doing the right thing was remembered for all time. In Matthew's Gospel, we read that the purchase of the 'potter's field' with the money paid to Judas for his betrayal of Jesus was a fulfilment of Jeremiah's prophetic action (Matthew 27:5–10).

PRAYER

Lord, help me to do the right thing regardless of circumstances. Thank you that the past is forgiven and forgotten. Thank you that I can know you. Thank you that you have put your Spirit into my heart. Guide me to do the right thing today and into the future.

16 October | Day 289
The Biggest Decision of My Life

In early February 1974, I was facing the biggest decision of my life. I was convinced through reading the New Testament that Jesus really is the Son of God. But I did not want to be a Christian as I feared that I would lose my freedom. The last things that I associated with faith were love and freedom. I associated faith with *losing* my freedom. I thought that God would want me to stop doing all the things that were fun and that I enjoyed.

In fact, I have discovered over the last forty years that true faith *leads to* freedom and love. Love, faith and freedom are inextricably entwined.

READING FROM PSALMS

Psalm 119:41–48
Trust in God's word

'May *your unfailing love* come to me, O Lord' (v.41a), the psalmist cries out as he begins this section of Psalm 119. 'Let *your love*, God, shape my life' (v.41a MSG). It ends with a response of love: 'I cherish your commandments – oh, *how I love* them! – relishing every fragment of your counsel' (vv.47b–48, MSG).

In between, he speaks of his *faith* in God's word declaring, 'then I will answer the one who taunts me, for *I trust* in your word' (v.42). Trust and faith are almost synonyms.

People of faith are taunted today as they always have been. But, whatever happens, keep on trusting in God's word. This trust enables you to respond even to taunting with confidence.

Ask God to reveal to you more and more his unfailing love (v.41). Respond in love (vv.47–48), trust, hope and obedience (vv.42–44). Seek God's ways through the Bible, and you will discover true freedom and be able to say, 'I'll stride freely through wide open spaces as I look for your truth and your wisdom' (v.45, MSG).

PRAYER

Lord, today may I experience your unfailing love and respond with love to all those I meet and with whom I speak. As I put my trust in you and your word, may I walk in freedom.

NEW TESTAMENT READING

1 Timothy 1:1–20
Hold on to your sincere faith

The apostle Paul was responsible for leading Timothy to faith in Jesus and, in this way, is Timothy's spiritual father. Like any good father, Paul is concerned about Timothy and wants the very best for him. He describes Timothy, to whom this letter is written, as his 'true son *in the faith*' (v.2).

Timothy has also become a leader, pastor and teacher. Paul gives him instructions on leadership and how to deal with problems in the church. These are of great relevance to all of us today.

God's work is *by faith* (v.4): 'The goal of this command is *love*, which comes from a pure heart and a good conscience and *a sincere faith*' (v.5). Love and faith should always go together.

Paul lists various sins that are to be avoided at all costs (vv.8–11). Among these is slave trading (v.10). Slavery is the opposite of freedom and trafficking people is an abomination.

Paul goes on to give his own testimony in which faith, love and freedom are intertwined. He was 'once a blasphemer and a persecutor and a violent man' (v.13). He describes himself as 'the worst of sinners' (v.16).

I find it fascinating to see the progression in the way in which the apostle Paul describes himself:

- Much earlier, he described himself as '*the least of the apostles*' who does not 'even deserve to be called an apostle' (1 Corinthians 15:9).
- Later on, he says, '*I am less than the least of all God's people*' (Ephesians 3:8).
- Now, he describes himself as '*the worst of sinners*' (1 Timothy 1:16).

It seems that the more he has grown in his relationship with the Lord and the closer he has come to the light of Christ, the more he sees his own unworthiness. I think it is often true that as we go on in the Christian life, our conviction of sin increases and our appreciation of God's forgiveness, love and mercy grows.

True guilt is *not* an unhealthy emotion – provided it is followed by repentance and forgiveness. The Scottish theologian P. T. Forsyth (1848–1921) once said, 'Our churches are full of the nicest, kindest people who have never known the despair of guilt or the *breathless wonder of forgiveness*.'[1]

Jesus Christ sets us free: 'Christ Jesus came into the world to save sinners – of whom I am the worst' (v.15). Salvation means freedom; it came about as a result of grace. Do not wallow in your past. Rather celebrate your present freedom and the grace that brought it about: 'Grace mixed with faith and love poured over me and into me. And all because of Jesus' (v.14, MSG).

Christian love flows out of God's love for you, which is poured into your heart by the Holy Spirit (Romans 5:5). Yet it is far more than an emotion. Christian love is not the victim of your emotions but the servant of your will. Arguably, love is 10 per cent emotion, 20 per cent understanding, 70 per cent will.

Paul became an example for others who would believe in Jesus Christ and receive eternal life (1 Timothy 1:16). 'To believe on him' is the act of faith.

This initial act of faith needs to be followed by a life of faith. Thus, Paul urges Timothy to 'fight the good fight, holding on to *faith*' (vv.18–19). He warns of others who have 'shipwrecked *their faith*' (v.19). This advice is a reminder of the importance for all of us to 'pursue a Paul' and 'train a Timothy'.

PRAYER

Lord, thank you that although Paul was the 'worst of sinners', you set him free to live a life of love. Thank you that you can also do it for me and for everyone who puts their faith in Jesus.

OLD TESTAMENT READING

Jeremiah 32:26–34:22
Put your faith in Jesus

'Whatever you love most, be it sports, pleasure, business, or God, that is your god!'[2] wrote Billy Graham. The constant temptation of the world is to divide our hearts. But God is looking for those who are single-minded. God himself rejoices in doing good to us with *all his heart and soul* (32:41). Surely we can return his love by serving him with *all* our heart and soul – with singleness of heart and action?

God's love endures for ever (33:11). He loves you. He longs for you to walk in a close relationship with him. He was desperately disappointed that his people 'turned their backs on me – won't even look me in the face!' (32:33, MSG). He longed for a time when they would relate to him in 'singleness of heart and action' (v.39).

In his love for you God wants to communicate with you: 'Call to me and I will answer you and tell you great and unsearchable things you do not know' (33:3). He wants to bring you health and healing (v.6a). He wants you to enjoy peace and security (v.6b). He wants to cleanse you from all the sins you have committed and forgive you completely (v.8).

He wants you to enjoy freedom from captivity (v.7). He wants to bring you joy and gladness (v.11). All this will result in renown, joy, praise and honour for God (v.9). It will lead to thanksgiving: 'Give thanks to the Lord Almighty, for the Lord is good; his love endures for ever' (v.11).

God wants his people to be free. Jeremiah was being held in captivity (v.1), which was contrary to God's purpose for his people. God wants to set his people free from the captivity of the exile into which they are about to go. In New Testament terms, this restoration, this redemption from exile, is ultimately fulfilled through faith in Jesus and the freedom he brings from the captivity of sin.

God continues to have a concern about physical captivity. That is why slavery is such a terrible evil. In the Old Testament we see some hints of God's disapproval of slavery. He tells Jeremiah 'to proclaim *freedom for the slaves*' (34:8). Initially, the people responded by setting their slaves free, but afterwards they changed their minds and took them back (vv.10–11). God strongly disapproved of their actions.

The Lord says, 'You have not proclaimed freedom for your own people. So I now proclaim "freedom" for you ... "freedom" to fall by the sword, plague and famine' (v.17). This 'freedom' is the false freedom that we so often see experienced in the world today. The freedom to sin leads to destruction. The freedom that God wants to bring in your life leads to a life of faith and love. This is true freedom.

PRAYER

Lord, thank you for the freedom you bring to my life. Today I turn my face toward you. I want to call on you and hear your voice – to understand great and unsearchable things. Help me to serve you today with singleness of heart and action, to give thanks to you for all your goodness and for your love, which endures for ever.

---

17 October | Day 290

How to Pray

Prayer is the most important activity of your life. It is the main way in which you develop a relationship with your Father in heaven. If you love someone, naturally you will want to spend time in their presence communicating with them. Like any relationship, communication can take many different forms.

Lancelot Andrewes (1555–1626), was one of the great theologians and preachers of his day. After he died, his private notebook on prayer was discovered and published. In it he had written two lists:

First, he wrote a list of *times* of prayer in the Bible:

'Always...
Without ceasing...
At all times...
Three times a day...
Evening, and morning, and at noon...
Seven times a day...
In the morning, a great while before day...
At daybreak...
The third hour of the day...
About the sixth hour...
The hour of prayer, the ninth...
The evening...
By night...
At midnight...'

Next, he wrote a list of *places* of prayer in the Bible:

'In the assembly ... and in the congregation...
Your closet...
An upper room...
A housetop...
The temple...
On the shore...
A garden...
On their beds...
A desert place...
In every place...'[1]

There is no limit to the times, places and different ways in which you can pray.

READING FROM PSALMS

Psalm 119:49–56
The word of God, song and prayer in the night

Prayer is *two-way* communication. Prayer involves listening to God as well as speaking to him. The main way in which we hear God today is through his word. Jesus is the Word of God (John 1:1) and the Bible is all about him. As you study the Bible, pray that God will speak to you through it.

This will give you 'hope' (Psalm 119:49) in the midst of all the difficulties of life: 'These words held me up in bad times; yes, your promises rejuvenate me' (v.50, MSG). You will find comfort in God's words to you (v.52).

These words also inspire our worship of God: 'Your decrees are the theme of my song' (v.54). So many of the greatest hymns and worship songs are based on the words of the Bible.

You do not need to confine your prayers to daytime. 'In the night I remember your name, O LORD' (v.55a): this is one of the best ways to use times of wakefulness in the night. It may even be a way to cure insomnia!

PRAYER

Lord, please speak to me today through your word and bring me hope and comfort. Help me to pray.

NEW TESTAMENT READING

1 Timothy 2:1–15
Requests, prayers, intercession, thanksgiving and raising hands

What is your first priority? Paul writes, 'The first thing I want you to do is *pray*. Pray every way you know how, for everyone you know' (v.1, MSG).

Do you ever complain about your government or your politicians? If you want good government you must *pray for it*. Paul prioritises prayer 'for kings and for those in authority, that we may live peaceful and quiet lives in all godliness and holiness' (v.2).

If you live in a country with relatively stable government, thank God and pray for continued stability. In much of the world, people suffer due to unstable governments and tyranny. The rule of law was a high priority in the prayers of the apostle Paul.

When there is good and peaceful government it can make it easier to spread the gospel and for as many people as possible to hear the message. 'This is good and pleases God our Saviour, who wants *all people* to be saved and to come to a knowledge of the truth' (vv.3–4). God loves every human being. No one is destined by God to be lost. He wants everyone to be saved.

Jesus died for us all. He 'gave himself as a ransom for *all*' (v.6). This is a beautiful summary of the work of Jesus. Through his mediation and the ransom he paid, it is possible for everyone to experience an intimate relationship with the Father.

Pray 'for everyone you know' (v.1, MSG). This will include your family, friends, neighbours and anyone for whom the Holy Spirit is prompting you to pray.

It is interesting to note in passing that there was an expectation that people would lift up their hands in prayer. 'Not shaking angry fists at enemies but *raising holy hands to God*' (v.8, MSG). It was taken for granted that Christians, like Jews, would lift up their hands in prayer (v.8).

This was the *traditional form of prayer*. I often jest that 'if you go into a church and see everyone with their hands in the air say, "This is a traditional church practising *ancient* forms of worship." If they all have their hands down by their sides that is fine also. Just say, "This is a modern, trendy church experimenting with *new forms of worship*!"'

There is a difficult section to expound at the end of today's passage (vv.9–15). Many of the interpretations of this passage do not really fit with the rest of the New Testament where it is clear that women had roles of leadership within the church. Paul speaks of women as apostles and deacons (Romans 16). He expects them to be praying and prophesying in the assembly (1 Corinthians 11).

Paul also writes that Christ has brought an end to disunity and prejudice on the basis of gender – in Christ 'there is neither ... male nor female' (Galatians 3:28). In Jesus' ministry, we read of Mary of Bethany sitting at Jesus' feet. In other words, she joined the men in becoming a disciple and a learner (Luke 10:38–42).

Paul's basic point is to insist that women too must be allowed to learn (1 Timothy 2:11) and study as Christians. In order to do that they needed to exercise humility and not dominate proceedings. The word Paul uses here for 'authority' (*authentein*) is used elsewhere for brutal or domineering forms of leadership – so this probably refers to particular issues in this congregation, rather than being a more general comment on the leadership of women.

As *The Message* translation puts it, 'I want women to get in there with the men in humility before God ... doing something beautiful for God and becoming beautiful doing it' (vv.9–10, MSG).

PRAYER

Lord, I pray especially today for those in authority, that the rule of law may be established and that people will be able to live peacefully in all godliness and holiness.

OLD TESTAMENT READING

Jeremiah 35:1–37:21
Listening to God and praying for others

Do you ever get discouraged by the fact that many people do not seem to be interested in listening to God's words and obeying them?

God *spoke* to Jeremiah. Jeremiah said that God, 'began speaking to [him] in the reign of Josiah' (36:2). Jeremiah dictated to Baruch, 'all the words the LORD had *spoken* to him' (v.4).

Over and over again 'the *word* came to Jeremiah *from the LORD*' (for example, in today's passage 35:1, 12; 36:1, 27; 37:6). Presumably, Jeremiah heard the word of the Lord as he was praying.

Jeremiah urged the people to *listen* to God. God had spoken 'again and again' (35:14). He said, 'Listen! ... I spoke to them and they did not listen' (v.17).

In spite of the fact that the Lord was speaking through his prophet Jeremiah, King Jehoiakim refused to listen to his advisers' warnings (36:25). Jeremiah had had the words of God painstakingly written on a scroll with quill and ink. But Jehoiakim, who was sitting in front of a charcoal fire warming himself, cut up the entire scroll and burned it piece by piece (v.23).

Jeremiah must have been devastated to hear what the king had done with all his hard work. God tells Jeremiah to 'do it all over again' (v.28, MSG). He was not put off by personal rejection. Like Jeremiah, we must be willing to keep going even if our message is rejected: 'do it all over again'.

Disaster came, 'Because they have not *listened*' (v.31). When Zedekiah was made king, 'Neither he nor his attendants nor the people of the land paid any attention to the words the LORD had *spoken* through Jeremiah the prophet' (37:2). They ill-treated Jeremiah and rejected his word. Yet, despite this refusal to listen, the authorities recognised the power of Jeremiah's prayers. King Zedekiah sent a message to Jeremiah the prophet: 'Please pray to the LORD our God for us' (v.3).

Later he was arrested, beaten and imprisoned (vv.14–15). He 'was put into a vaulted cell in a dungeon, where he remained a long time' (v.16). Yet when he was taken from his high-security cell in a dungeon to see the king and was asked, 'Is there any word from the LORD?' (v.17), he had the courage to speak out again. He was at the king's mercy and yet he was completely fearless.

PRAYER

Lord, help me in my prayers to listen attentively to your words and to have the courage to speak them regardless of the consequences.

18 October | Day 291
The Life of a Leader

Good leadership is vital at all times, in all places and in all areas of life. But what *is* good leadership?

'Leadership is a potent combination of strategy and character. But if you must be without one, be without the strategy.'[1] These are the words of General Norman Schwarzkopf, commander of the coalition forces in the Gulf War of 1991. Character is what really matters. It is the only thing that counts in the end.

We make a distinction in our church between those in positions of leadership and those 'on their way in'. We welcome everyone regardless of their lifestyle. We have a big front door. Everyone is welcome. The church is not a museum displaying perfect people. It is a hospital in the traditional sense of the word – a place of hospitality and restoration. It is a place where the wounded, hurt, broken and injured find healing. It is a community of sinners.

On the other hand, we do not put people in positions of leadership if their lifestyle is in direct contrast to the New Testament. Leadership is not only functional, but also involves a responsibility to live *as an example* to others. Leaders are models for the rest of the congregation. Of course, no one is perfect. You do not have to be perfect to be an example. However, we try to ensure that the lifestyle and character of our leaders is in line with the New Testament.

READING FROM PSALMS

Psalm 119:57–64
Worship leaders

'The real test, in these days', as John Wimber put it, 'will not be the writing and producing of new and great worship music. The real test will be the *godliness and character* of those who deliver it.'

The psalmist was a worship leader who walked in a close relationship with the Lord: 'Because you have satisfied me, GOD, I promise to do everything you say' (v.57, MSG).

The worship leader who has sought the face of the Lord with all their heart is in a position to lead the congregation in praise of God. The psalmist is really careful to keep to God's ways, 'I have considered my ways and have turned my steps to your statutes' (v.59).

Even in real difficulties, do not forget God's law: 'Though the wicked bind me with ropes, I will not forget your law' (v.61).

Inspiration sometimes comes in the middle of the night: 'I get up in the middle of the night to thank you; your decisions are so right, so true – I can't wait till morning!' (v.62, MSG). It is vital to be part of a worshipping community: 'I'm a friend and companion to all who fear you, of those committed to living by your rules' (v.63, MSG).

Here is a worship leader who has a deep appreciation of God's love: 'The earth is filled with your love, O LORD' (v.64). God's love for you should be right at the heart of your worship.

PRAYER

Lord, I seek your face today with all my heart. Be gracious to me just as you have promised (v.58).

NEW TESTAMENT READING

1 Timothy 3:1–16
Church leaders

In one sense of the word, every Christian is a leader. If leadership is about influence, all of us have influence in the workplace, at home and in community. But this passage is specifically about leadership in the church.

The church should be like a home. It is 'God's household' (v.15). Leading a church is like leading a big family. Paul asks how anyone can lead a church if they can't lead their own family (v.5).

Good leaders should be capable of running their own *households* (vv.4, 12) (the same Greek word is used as for *God's household* – the church). They should be capable of guiding and nurturing their own family with wisdom, love and faithfulness.

It is interesting that almost all of the qualities needed to be an overseer are just the same as those encouraged in terms of godliness for all Christians. The Scottish minister, Robert Murray M'Cheyne, once said, 'My people's greatest need is my own personal holiness.'[2]

The list of characteristics is extensive (v.2). Leaders should be 'well thought of'. They should live in such a way that no one can find good grounds to accuse them of wrongdoing.

If they are married they need to be faithful to their marriage partners. Faithfulness, loyalty, trustworthiness is key to leadership and it starts with faithfulness in marriage.

They need to be 'sensible' (v.2, AMP). Being a Christian does not mean abandoning common sense. Quite the opposite. Much day-to-day decision-making simply involves godly, spirit-filled leaders prayerfully using their common sense.

The word for 'overseer' is sometimes translated 'bishop'. It is not wrong to desire to be a bishop, 'Whoever aspires to be an overseer desires a noble task' (v.1).

I find it interesting that one of the differences between a bishop and a deacon is that the bishop 'must not be a recent convert' (v.6). This does not apply to deacons. Sometimes people criticise putting those who are new to faith into positions of leadership – such as leading small groups on Alpha. My reply, always, is that we are not asking them to be bishops, only to serve as hosts in an Alpha small group!

The reason Paul gives for why an overseer must not be a recent convert, is that they 'may become conceited and fall under the same judgment as the devil' (vv.4–6). The devil fell through pride. There is a danger for all Christian leaders of falling into spiritual pride.

The test for deacons is very similar to overseers. A deacon literally means 'a servant'. Originally, they were people set aside to serve at tables (Acts 6:1–7). Jesus provided the model for servant leadership (Mark 10:35–45). Albert Einstein once said, 'Only a life lived in the service to others is worth living.'[13] If service is beneath you, then leadership is beyond you.

These servant leaders *and their marriage partners* (v.11) need to be people of strong and proven character. This is why any good selection process for married church leaders should involve both partners. They should be worthy of respect, sincere, not prone to drunkenness, honest, full of faith, trustworthy, and faithful in marriage (1 Timothy 3:8–12).

Above all, leaders are to be people of godly character. In fact, the sole quality in the list that is not directly linked to our character is being 'able to teach' (v.2). Church leaders are to be Christians of good character who are able to teach.

Mark Twain quipped, 'To do what is right is wonderful. To teach what is right is even more wonderful – and much easier.'[14] The task of Christian leadership is to align our life and character with our teaching. That is a challenge for all of us and will be a lifelong process of becoming like Jesus who is the model of 'godliness' (v.16).

Of course, before anyone (bishop or deacon) is put in a major position of leadership they need to be 'tried and investigated and proved' (v.10, AMP). A faith that has not been tested cannot be trusted. We are tested by difficulties, disappointments and desert times. Hopefully these mature us, develop our character and make us ready for leadership.

PRAYER

Lord, help me by your Spirit to live up to your high standards and be above reproach.

OLD TESTAMENT READING

Jeremiah 38:1–40:6
Prophetic leaders

Faithfulness to God and good character do not guarantee prosperity and a pain-free life. In fact, for Jeremiah, the opposite was the case.

Jeremiah was a prophet whose life and character is a fine example for us. He remained faithful to God. He continued to hear God's word and to speak it out. This was in spite of the fact that he suffered a great deal for his pains.

Over and over again, he was threatened, beaten, locked up, put in an underground dungeon and then thrown into a muddy cistern to be left to starve to death. Yet he continued to listen to God's message and spoke it out courageously.

On the whole, the people were unresponsive. He was completely misunderstood (38:4). He was condemned for destroying morale and actually causing harm to the people he was trying to save. You should not be surprised if you receive the same treatment.

Once rescued from the cistern, Jeremiah was brought before King Zedekiah for the fourth time. Zedekiah was a man with a wishbone rather than a backbone. It was out of cowardice that Zedekiah disobeyed the law (v.19). He was afraid of the people – rather like Pontius Pilate who condemned Jesus.

Four times God had spoken to Zedekiah to try and save him from the consequences of his actions. Each time he had weakly refused to obey. In chapter 39, we read of the consequences. Jeremiah is finally vindicated (40:1–6).

PRAYER

Lord, please bless and strengthen the leaders of our churches today. May their lifestyles and characters inspire us all to lead good and fruitful lives.

19 October | Day 292

Words, the Word of God and 'Words'

Actor David Suchet, well known for his title role in *Poirot*, tells how a few years ago he was lying in his bath in a hotel in America, when he had a sudden and impulsive desire to read the Bible. He managed to find a Gideon Bible and started to read the New Testament. As he read, he encountered Jesus Christ. He said:

> From somewhere I got this desire to read the Bible again. That's the most important part of my conversion. I started with the Acts of the Apostles and then moved to Paul's Letters – Romans and Corinthians. And it was only after that I came to the Gospels. In the New Testament I suddenly discovered the way that life should be followed.'[1]

The most powerful words ever written are in the Bible. Words are an important theme in it, and the word 'word' is used in different senses in today's passages.

- First, it is used in the sense of *our words*. The things we say can be good or bad (Proverbs 25:11–20).
- Second, it is also used in the sense of the *Word of God*. This is supremely Jesus Christ (John 1:1; Hebrews 1:2), but also refers to the Word of God in the Scriptures and in preaching and teaching (1 Timothy 4:1–16).
- Third, the Bible also uses the phrase '*word of the Lord*' in the sense of prophecy (Jeremiah 42:7). God continues to speak to the church through prophetic messages (1 Timothy 4:14). Of course, we need to distinguish the Old Testament prophets, whose 'words' were definitely 'the word of the Lord' and are now part of Scripture, from prophetic 'words' today, which need testing against Scripture.

READING FROM PROVERBS

Proverbs 25:11–20
Use your words to good effect

1. Good words

The words we speak really matter. Sometimes, they have a very good effect. When someone finds the right words for the right occasion there is something very beautiful about it: 'The right word at the right time is like a custom-made piece of jewelry' (v.11, MSG).

Something less easy to hear, but equally valuable is 'a wise rebuke to a listening ear' (v.12b). Receiving criticism is always hard but, as the writer of Proverbs says, 'a wise friend's timely reprimand is like a gold ring slipped on your finger' (v.12, MSG). Friends who love us enough to challenge us are highly valuable.

Likewise, trustworthy friends or messengers who keep to their word 'are like cool drinks in sweltering heat – refreshing!' (v.13, MSG).

The tongue is so powerful: 'Through patience a ruler can be persuaded, and a gentle tongue can break a bone' (v.15). Or as *The Message* puts it, 'gentle speech breaks down rigid defences'.

2. Bad words

There are some uses of words that the writer of Proverbs warns us against. Empty promises lead to disappointment: 'Like clouds and wind without rain is one who boasts of gifts never given' (v.14).

On the whole, it is not good to spend too much time talking to any one person or group of people: 'When you find a friend, don't outwear your welcome; show up at all hours and he'll soon get fed up' (v.17, MSG). We need a balance in our relationships. Words need to be spread wisely.

Another bad use of words is 'false testimony' (v.18) – saying what is untrue. This could be in court or simply in our conversation or online: 'Anyone who tells lies against their neighbours in court or on the street is a loose cannon' (v.18, MSG). It is very painful to read or hear things that are simply untrue.

PRAYER

Lord, thank you for the power of words to bring blessing. Today, put a guard over my lips and watch over my tongue that I might speak only good words.

NEW TESTAMENT READING

1 Timothy 4:1–16
Devote yourself to the word of God

It is sad and disappointing when professing Christians stray from their faith. Paul writes that some are giving up on their faith and chasing after 'demonic illusions put forth by professional liars' (v.1, MSG).

Guard yourself against deception by studying the truth – which is revealed by the Holy Spirit in the word of God.

Paul warns against false teaching that tells us 'not to get married' or 'not to eat this or that food' (v.3, MSG). He writes, 'The Spirit clearly *says*...' (v.1) and 'everything God created is good, and is to be received with thanks. Nothing is to be sneered at and thrown out. God's word and our prayers make every item in creation holy' (vv.4–5, MSG).

Paul urges Timothy to pass on the '*good teaching*' he has received (v.6). An example of the good teaching is 'a trustworthy *saying*' (v.9) – that God 'is the Saviour of all people, and especially of those who believe' (v.10).

Timothy is called to 'Get the word out. *Teach* all these things' (v.11, MSG). He is to be an example to the believers in *speech* (as well as in life, in love, in faith and in purity). Paul urges him to devote himself to the public *reading of Scripture*, of *preaching* and *teaching* (v.13). This must always be a high priority for Christian leaders (see 5:17).

All this is part of training 'yourself to be godly' (4:7). It is good to exercise and keep fit: 'Physical training is of some value' (v.8a), but training in 'godliness' is far more important than physical training. 'Exercise daily in God – no spiritual flabbiness ... making you fit both today and forever' (v.8b, MSG).

In the Christian life, your age does not define your maturity. Paul writes, 'Don't let anyone put you down because you're young' (v.11, MSG). Whatever your age, you can set an example by your life. Furthermore, age is no bar to teaching the word of God.

Paul urges Timothy to watch his *life* and *doctrine* closely (v.16). Watch your *life* and your *lips*. 'Keep a firm grasp on both your character and your teaching' (v.16, MSG).

He also refers to a gift that was given to Timothy through a prophetic message when the body of elders laid hands on him. This is a New Testament example of a 'word' from the Lord given through the gift of prophecy.

PRAYER

Lord, help me to train myself in godliness (v.7b), to devote myself to the Scriptures and to set an example in every area of my life (vv.12–13).

OLD TESTAMENT READING

Jeremiah 40:7–42:22
Listen carefully to the 'words' of the prophets

Have you ever been in a situation where you decided what you were going to do and then looked for a word from God to confirm what you had already decided in your heart to do?

I've been there. It is not a good place to be. This is what happened here. The people of God had decided they wanted to go down to Egypt and they wanted Jeremiah to give them a message from God confirming it was the right thing to do. It led to disaster.

Jeremiah was an Old Testament prophet who had a reputation for being able to hear 'the word of the Lord' (42:1–7).

Israel had reached one of the lowest points in its history. Gedaliah, who had been appointed as governor over the remnant of the people who had not gone into exile (40:7), had been murdered (40:7 – 41:15). Since the water supply was so precious in Palestine, the fouling of the system was a particularly irresponsible act of vandalism (41:9).

Johanan was thoroughly competent to deal with the situation involving military skill. But his only thought was to escape to Egypt from what he imagined to be the inevitable Babylonian reprisals. In this policy, he was to clash with Jeremiah.

Johanan and all the army officers came to Jeremiah and asked him to 'pray that the Lord your God will tell us where we should go and what we should do' (42:3).

Jeremiah's response was 'I will certainly pray to the Lord your God as requested; I will tell you everything the Lord says and will keep nothing back from you' (v.4).

They promise, 'Whether it is favourable or unfavourable, we will obey the Lord our God' (v.6).

It is interesting to note that, even for Jeremiah, guidance did not come instantly on the spur of the moment. Instead, 'Ten days later the word of the LORD came to Jeremiah' (v.7).

He faithfully passed it on: 'This is what the LORD ... says ...' (v.9). He promises blessing if they stay in the land (vv.10–12) and judgment if they go in to Egypt (v.13 onwards).

It turned out that they had already decided what they would do and merely wanted the Lord to confirm it. They made the mistake of not obeying the word of the Lord (v.21). How vital it is to ask the Lord before we make our decisions rather than after!

PRAYER

Lord, thank you that you speak to us through the Scriptures and the prophets. Help me to listen carefully to your words and to obey them.

20 October | Day 293

Hard Times

Smith Wigglesworth was born on 8 June 1859 to an impoverished family in Yorkshire. As a small child he worked in the fields pulling turnips alongside his mother. He was illiterate until, at the age of twenty-three, he married Polly, who taught him to read. He often said that the Bible was the only book he ever read.

He was a plumber by trade but had to abandon it after he became too busy with an amazing ministry of preaching and healing. There are even accounts of people being raised from the dead through his ministry. Yet, he said on one occasion that he would rather see one person saved through his preaching than 10,000 healed.

Life was not always easy for Smith Wigglesworth. He went through some very hard times. He wrote, 'Great faith is a product of great fights. Great testimonies are the outcome of great tests. Great triumphs can only come out of great trials.'

The Bible is very realistic. We live in a fallen world. Everyone goes through hard times and some people find themselves in circumstances that make life hard all of the time.

READING FROM PSALMS

Psalm 119:65–72
See hard times as God's training school

Suffering is never good in itself, but God is able to use it for good (Romans 8:28). Sometimes God uses our suffering to train us. Just as a gardener prunes the vine (John 15:2), parents discipline their children (Hebrews 12:10) and a metal worker refines silver and gold in the fire (1 Peter 1:6–7).

The psalmist writes, '*Train me* in good common sense ... Before I learned to answer you, I wandered all over the place, but now I'm in step with your Word ... *train me* in your *goodness'* (Psalm 119:66–68, MSG). The fact that he was going through hard times did not make him doubt God's goodness. Instead, he saw it as God's training school.

Unfair criticism is hard to receive. The psalmist writes, 'The godless spread lies about me, but I focus my attention on what you are saying' (v.69, MSG). Attack may come from those whose 'hearts are callous and unfeeling'. Yet, in the midst of this, you, too, can find 'delight' in God's words (v.70).

He is able to see that God has actually used his troubles, affliction and suffering: 'My troubles *turned out all for the best* – they forced me to learn from your textbook. Truth from your mouth means more to me than striking it rich in a gold mine' (vv.71–72, MSG).

PRAYER

Lord, 'Teach me ... good judgment' (v.66). Thank you that as I look back on my life I can often see the ways in which you have used the hard times. Thank you that the words of your mouth are more precious than thousands of pieces of silver and gold.

NEW TESTAMENT READING

1 Timothy 5:1–6:2
Take care of those going through hard times

The Bible is a very practical book. Paul gives Timothy sensible and practical instructions on how to look after those in the congregation who are going through hard times.

1. Take care of the old and young
Paul says that we are to treat those who are older than us with the respect we would show to our parents, and to treat those younger than us as our brothers and sisters (vv.1–2). Someone once observed that many men should have this verse as a screensaver on their computers: 'Treat younger women as sisters, with absolute purity' (v.2).

2. Take care of the needy
For example, the church is to provide for widows who don't have any family to support them: 'Give proper recognition to those widows who are *really in need*' (v.3). Those who do have family should be supported by them if at all possible (v.4).

3. Take care of your extended family
Paul makes a point that still has great relevance today. Not only do we have a duty to provide for our own spouse and children, but we must also provide for our 'extended family', our parents and grandparents (vv.7–8).

4. Take care of leaders
Church is also to provide for the leaders 'who direct the affairs of the church' (v.17). 'Those who work deserve their pay!' (v.18, NLT). Their position of responsibility means that we should not easily entertain a complaint against them: 'Don't listen to a complaint against a leader that isn't backed up by two or three responsible witnesses' (v.19, MSG). But, at the same time, the consequences of sin are greater for those in a position of leadership (v.20). Paul warns 'keep a close check on yourself' (v.21, MSG).

5. Take care of yourself
Timothy himself clearly had stomach problems and 'frequent illnesses' (v.23). Paul does not reproach him for his sickness. Rather, he gives him some practical advice (which may sound strange to our modern ears): 'Stop drinking only water, and use a little wine because of your stomach and your frequent illnesses' (v.23).

6. Take care in the workplace
This letter was written at a time when Christians were in no position to lead the fight against slavery. They were a tiny minority in an empire where a high proportion of the population were slaves. Paul is not endorsing slavery. Rather, he is giving practical advice on how to live when we find ourselves in circumstances that are far from ideal. Whatever circumstances you find yourself in, however hard life is, your concern should be for 'God's name' (6:1).

PRAYER
Lord, help us as a church to look after those who are going through hard times. May we be a community that looks after the needy, the sick and the oppressed – following in the footsteps of Jesus.

OLD TESTAMENT READING

Jeremiah 43:1–45:5
Stay faithful to God in hard times

Mother Teresa said, 'I am not called to be successful but to be faithful.'[1]

At this point in his ministry, Jeremiah was probably in his mid-sixties. He had been a prophet for forty-seven years. During this time, he had seen Jerusalem reduced to ruins. He had *faithfully* spoken the word of God, but his message had been consistently ignored and rejected by those to whom he was sent. He had also suffered a great deal due to their opposition and disobedience. All this must have been very disappointing and discouraging for Jeremiah.

Even after all that happened, and though his earlier prophecies had been fulfilled, the people *still refused* to listen to him. Jeremiah was telling them 'everything the LORD had sent him to tell them' (43:1). He was telling the truth. But he had to put up with what must have been the very hurtful slander of arrogant people saying to him, 'you are lying' (v.2).

In spite of Jeremiah's warning, they 'disobeyed the LORD's command' (v.4). They 'entered Egypt in disobedience to the LORD' (v.7). Although the Lord warned them 'again and again' (44:4), 'they did not listen or pay attention' (v.5). They said to Jeremiah, 'We will not listen to the message you have spoken to us in the name of the LORD!' (v.16). Jeremiah's message was flatly contradicted by those who heard it.

Jeremiah's ministry must have appeared to be a *failure*; once again full of *discouragement* and *disappointment*. Even so, he remained true to the task that God had given him and *faithfully* delivered God's words to the people.

In chapter 45, we encounter another person's discouragement and disappointment – Jeremiah's associate Baruch. Baruch, despite being of high birth, had to play second fiddle to Jeremiah. His role was to record Jeremiah's prophecies. He despaired of the fruitlessness of his efforts. He said 'Woe to me! The LORD has added sorrow to my pain;
I am worn out with groaning and find no rest' (45:3).

But the Lord says, 'Should you then seek great things for yourself? Seek them not' (v.5).

It is always a temptation to be self-centred and to seek great things for ourselves – whether through money, success, position, fame, reputation or respectability – but we must never seek any of these things for ourselves. At the end of the day, it does not matter if our life appears to have been a failure and ends in disappointment. What matters is faithfulness to the Lord. God will reward each person according to their faithfulness, not according to their apparent success (see Matthew 25:14–30).

When you are faithful to God, you allow him to work and to achieve his plans through your life. Jeremiah and Baruch must have felt like failures, and yet few people in history have had a greater impact than they. The prophecies they recorded are a key part of God's revelation to the world, and contain some of the most important prophecies about Jesus in the Old Testament – and how many authors can claim a readership of billions over 2,500 years after their death?

PRAYER

Lord, help me to be faithful in following you regardless of hard times: afflictions, smears and difficulties. May I never seek great things for myself but rather seek to see your name glorified.

21 October | Day 294
Living Content

Her hands were full of rings, bracelets, necklaces, chains and other treasures. Torrents of lava were erupting and pouring down from Mount Vesuvius in AD 79. As she fled, this woman was not prepared to leave behind her valuable jewels. Encumbered by her treasures, she was overwhelmed by the rain of ashes from the volcano and was buried under it.

During the course of modern building operations, her petrified body was found outside the area of the buried city of Pompeii, an ancient Roman port. Her body was unearthed in a sea of jewels. She lost her life in an attempt to save her treasures.

Jesus warned us that ultimately you have to choose between money and God (Matthew 6:24). In the New Testament, there is no ban on private property or making money, or even enjoying the good things in life. The command to the rich, however, is that they do not 'put their *hope* in wealth' (1 Timothy 6:17). A selfish accumulation of wealth and an unhealthy obsession with material things will never bring contentment. What promises security leads to perpetual insecurity.

Ultimately, contentment only comes from putting your hope in God: 'godliness with contentment is great gain' (v.6). The promise of God's word is that those who 'put their hope in God' (v.17) find 'a firm foundation' and 'take hold of the life that is truly life' (v.19).

READING FROM PSALMS

Psalm 119:73–80
Hope in God's word and invest your time in it

Time is your most valuable possession. You can make more money but you cannot create more time. How you spend your time is evidence of where your hope lies. If your hope is in God and his word, then you will invest time in them.

The psalmist places his hope firmly in God's word: 'For I have put *my hope in your word*' (v.74b). What does this mean in practice?

Spend time seeking to understand God's word (vv.73, 79), meditate on it (v.78), delight in it (v.77) and learn it off by heart (v.73).

When you are going through difficult times, continue to trust God's word: 'Your testing has taught me what's true and right' (v.75, MSG). Trust in God's faithfulness, 'unfailing love' (v.76) and 'compassion' (v.77).

Spending time with God is the way in which God breathes his wisdom into you (v.73, MSG). He comforts you so that you can live, 'really live ... live whole and holy, soul and body' (vv.77, 80a, MSG), and always walk with your 'head held high' (v.80b, MSG).

If you live like this, it will encourage others to do the same: 'May those who fear you rejoice when they see me' (v.74a). Likewise, it is encouraging for us to see other people who are hoping in God's word.

PRAYER

Lord, as I put my hope in your word today, may I be an encouragement to others: 'May those who fear you rejoice when they see me' (v.74a).

NEW TESTAMENT READING

1 Timothy 6:3–21
Hope in God and not in wealth

The apostle Paul begins this passage by warning against those who teach false doctrines – rejecting godly teaching and the 'sound instruction of our Lord Jesus Christ' (v.3). These people have an unhealthy interest in controversies and disputes (v.4).

These false teachers cause 'constant friction between people of corrupt mind, who have been robbed of the truth and who think that godliness is a means to financial gain' (v.5).

Paul's words about wealth in this passage apply to everyone – especially to those of us who live in the West, where we are rich in comparison to so much of the world. Paul writes, 'Command those who are rich in the present world not to be arrogant *nor to put their hope in wealth*, which is so uncertain, but *to put their hope in God*, who richly provides us with everything for our enjoyment' (v.17).

Don't be tempted to think that you would be more content if you had more money (provided that you have food and clothing, v.8). Be content with what you have materially: '...godliness with *contentment* is great gain' (v.6).

Contentment is worth more than all the wealth you could possibly accumulate. People who want to get rich 'fall into temptation and a trap and into many foolish and harmful desires that plunge people into ruin and destruction' (v.9).

Paul is often misquoted as saying, 'Money is the root of all evil.' What he actually says is, 'The *love of* money is a root of all kinds of evil' (v.10a). Money can do a lot of good. But the *love of* money is extremely dangerous. 'Lust for money brings trouble and nothing but trouble. Going down that path, some lose their footing in the faith completely and live to regret it bitterly ever after' (v.10, MSG).

Whether you are very wealthy or have scarcely any money, the danger is the same – to love money. The temptation is there, whether it is to love money you already have, or money you would dearly love to have.

Instead of loving and pursuing money, love and pursue: 'a righteous life – a life of wonder, faith, love, steadiness, courtesy' (v.11, MSG). He urges Timothy to 'fight the good fight of the faith' (v.12a). The 'fight' starts with our hearts and minds focused on Jesus (vv.13–14).

He does not command them to give all their money away, but not to put their hope in it. If you get your attitude towards money sorted out, it will help sort out almost every other area of your life. Paul gives five ways to sort out your attitude to money (vv.17–18):

1. Don't be full of yourself

One of the dangers attached to wealth is arrogance: 'Tell those rich in this world's wealth to quit being so full of themselves' (v.17, MSG).

2. Don't put your security in wealth
'We enter the world penniless and we will leave it penniless' (v.7, MSG). Wealth provides only a false security. 'Quit ... being so obsessed with money, which is here today and gone tomorrow' (v.17, MSG). The real measure of our wealth is how much we would be worth if we lost all our money.

3. Put God first
Put your hope in God, who richly provides you with everything for your enjoyment (v.17). There is nothing wrong with enjoying the good things of life. God provides all good things for our enjoyment. But recognise that it all comes from him and it all belongs to him.

4. Do all the good you can
Paul urges the wealthy to 'do good' and to 'be rich in helping others' (v.18, MSG). Don't focus on how much money you can make, but how much good you can do. It is possible to be materially rich but spiritually poor. Equally it is possible to be materially poor but 'rich in good deeds' (v.18).

5. Share your resources
John Wesley said, 'When I have money, I get rid of it quickly, lest it find a way into my heart.' Generosity is the way to break the hold of money in our lives. 'Be extravagantly generous' (v.18, MSG).

Everything you own ultimately comes from God. Therefore, be willing to share it with others. Francis Bacon said, 'Money is like manure. It's not good unless it is spread around.'[1]

PRAYER

Lord, help us not to put our hope in wealth but to be content and to put our hope in you. Help me to do good, to be rich in good deeds and to be generous and willing to share.

OLD TESTAMENT READING

Jeremiah 46:1–47:7
Hope in the Lord and not in powerful people

Some people put their hope in riches. This is what the Moabites and Ammonites did (48:7; 49:4). Others put their hope in powerful people – as the Egyptians did.

The prophet Jeremiah realised that the Lord (Yahweh) was not just the national God of Israel but was Lord over all the nations of the world. He was given a message by the Lord for Egypt and the other nations.

He warned against relying on Pharaoh in spite of the fact that he was one of the most powerful people in the world. Those who trust in 'Pharaoh' are heading for trouble (46:25).

By contrast, he promises those who serve him: 'But you ... my servant, you have *nothing to fear ... there's no need to worry* ... Depend on it, *I'm on your side* ... I'm not finished with you yet' (vv.27–28, MSG). In Christ, he promises to you also peace, security and contentment. He is with you. You do not need to be afraid.

Ultimately, it is the Lord alone who is our hope. As Pope John Paul II put it, 'Christ is the source of hope for the whole world ... Jesus Christ is our hope.'

PRAYER

Lord, I will not be afraid because you are with me. Help me always to put my hope in you and serve you only. May my trust never be in money, powerful people or anything else. May my trust and contentment always be in you.

22 October | Day 295
Your Most Important Task

'Great leaders all have one thing in common. They know that acquiring and keeping good people is a leader's *most important task,*' writes John Maxwell in his book, *Developing the Leaders Around You*. He urges his readers, 'Find the best people you can, then develop them into the best leaders they can be.'[1]

Paul is condemned and in a dark, dank dungeon with just a hole in the ceiling for light and air. He is in 'chains' (2 Timothy 1:16), 'like a criminal' (2:9). He is lonely, bored and cold (4:9–13). Death is inevitable. According to tradition, he was condemned to die by beheading under Nero's persecution.

This (2 Timothy) is probably his last letter. Paul chose to write to an individual rather than to a church. Timothy was a leader whom Paul had found, trained and developed. Paul was probably in his sixties and Timothy in his early thirties.

As Paul becomes aware that he is handing on the gospel to the next generation, his greatest concern is that Timothy should guard it (1:11–14). The older I get, the more I appreciate the wisdom of the generations before me and the more I realise the responsibility we *all* have to pass the baton on to the next generation.

READING FROM PSALMS

Psalm 119:81–88
The right foundation for the next generation

This psalm is both a personal reflection on life and also a resource produced by the psalmist to help others build their lives and leadership on the right foundation.

In particular, he sets an example of faith in God's word: 'I have put my hope in your word ... All your commands are trustworthy ... I have not forsaken your precepts' (vv.81b, 86a, 87b).

PRAYER

Lord, help me to be faithful in spite of all the 'pitfalls' (v.85) and persecutions (v.86). Help me to do all I can to train up the next generation of leaders.

NEW TESTAMENT READING

2 Timothy 1:1–18
The way to develop the next generation

All of us can have *spiritual children*.

Paul probably had no natural children but he had *spiritual children*. He describes Timothy as 'my dear *son*' (v.2). He had led him to faith in the Lord (Acts 16:1–2). For fifteen years Timothy had been Paul's companion and had accompanied him on his second and third missionary journeys (Romans 16:21; 1 Thessalonians 3:2 and Philippians 2:19–20). Now Timothy is in a position of leadership in Ephesus.

Paul mentored, trained and discipled Timothy and passed wisdom on to him. He sets a model and example of how to develop the next generation of leaders.

1. Love them

'The son *I love so much'* is how Paul describes Timothy (2 Timothy 1:2, MSG). Paul constantly thanked God for him (v.3). Paul was a passionate and emotional man – when people said goodbye to him there were often tears of emotion: 'I miss you a lot, especially when I remember that last tearful goodbye, and look forward to a joy-packed reunion' (v.4, MSG).

2. Pray for them

'Night and day I constantly remember you in my prayers' (v.3). Praying for other people is not a waste of time, it makes a difference. Intercessory prayer is an act of love.

3. Believe in them

'I have been reminded of *your sincere faith*, which first lived in your grandmother Lois and in your mother Eunice and, *I am persuaded*, *now lives in you also*' (v.5). Paul trusted Timothy with responsibility at a young age. The people who influence us are the people who believe in us.

4. Minister to them

'I remind you to fan into flame the gift of God, which is in you through the laying on of my hands' (v.6). Previously Paul had written, 'Do not neglect your gift, which was given you through a prophetic message when the body of elders laid their hands on you' (1 Timothy 4:14).

They may have prayed for him for the gift of evangelism or ordination to leadership in the church. It may have been to be filled with the Spirit and possibly to receive the gift of speaking in tongues or prophecy. We do not know exactly what it was, but it shows the importance of prayer ministry. This is why we lay our hands on people, for example, in the ministry time at the end of practically every church service at HTB.

5. Encourage them

Timothy needed encouragement. Encouragement is like oxygen to the soul. Timothy was young. He had physical weaknesses ('frequent illnesses', 1 Timothy 5:23), and he was possibly a shy and introverted character.

Paul writes, 'God did not give us a spirit of timidity (of cowardice, of craven and cringing and fawning fear)' (2 Timothy 1:7, AMP). We are not cowards if we feel afraid. In fact, there can be no courage unless you are scared. Courage is doing what you are afraid to do, and not allowing fear to rule your decisions.

To overcome your fears, God has equipped you with the Holy Spirit and with 'power, love and self-discipline' (v.7b).

6. Challenge them

Paul urged Timothy to 'stir up' (v.6, KJV), to 'fan into flame' (v.6) the gift that he had been given. Other people can help you but at the end of the day you are responsible for your own spiritual development. Stir *yourself* up. Fan the flames of your faith through worship, prayer, Bible reading, community – or whatever it takes.

7. Trust them

'Guard the good deposit that was *entrusted* to you' (v.14). The good deposit is the gospel of which Paul has been appointed a herald, apostle and teacher (v.11).

The gospel is all about Jesus ('our Lord', v.8). It is about a relationship with him: 'I know whom I have believed' (v.12). We have been saved by grace, 'not because of anything we have done' (v.9). Jesus, our Saviour, through the cross and resurrection, 'destroyed death and has brought life and immortality to light' (v.10).

Paul urged Timothy not to be ashamed of their friendship, nor to be ashamed to testify about the Lord (v.8). They had the gospel to proclaim and to guard (vv.9–14). Paul was confident that he had chosen the right person to pass it on to the next generation 'with the help of the Holy Spirit who lives in us' (v.14).

8. Share with them

'Join with me in suffering for the gospel' (v.8). Even though Paul served God 'with a clear conscience' (v.3), he did not escape suffering. He was in 'chains' (v.16). He had been badly let down by other Christians: 'You know that everyone in the province of Asia has *deserted* me, including Phygelus and Hermogenes' (v.15).

Yet one person stood out. Don't run away from those who are suffering, but be like Onesiphorus who, Paul says, 'often refreshed me and was not ashamed of my chains' (v.16).

PRAYER

Lord, help me to pass on the baton to the next generation – to pray for them, love them, believe in them, minister to them, encourage them, entrust them and share with them.

OLD TESTAMENT READING

Jeremiah 48:1–49:6
The importance of developing the next generation

One of the problems highlighted again and again in Jeremiah is the weakness and wickedness of the people's leaders. Here we see the awful consequences of how wrong things can go without the right leadership.

'Doesn't Israel have any children, no one to step into her inheritance?' (49:1, MSG). The inheritance was open but there was no one who grew into it.

The antithesis of God's way of leadership is pride and arrogance – the great sins of Moab, 'the extremely proud one – his loftiness, his arrogance, his conceit, and the haughtiness of his heart' (48:29, AMP).

Pride and independence are often regarded as good qualities by the world – but they are a great sin in the eyes of the Lord because they lead us away from him. Pride and independence say, 'I don't need you.'

Proclaiming judgment against Moab and Ammon, Jeremiah says, 'A curse on those who are lax in doing the LORD's work!' (v.10). 'Moab has always taken it easy – lazy as a dog in the sun, never had to work for a living, never faced any trouble, never had to grow up, never once worked up a sweat' (v.11, MSG).

Hard work is more important than innate talent. As Thomas Edison famously said, 'Genius is one percent inspiration, ninety-nine per cent perspiration.'[2]

Developing the next generation will involve hard work.

There is an important principle. We should apply the same standard to the Lord's work as we do, for example, to our secular jobs (provided we are committed to them!). In most secular jobs, there is a requirement of 100 per cent efficiency and commitment. I am always so impressed by our volunteers who turn up with such regularity, love and commitment. It is amazing to see their dedication year after year. For many, it is a lifelong commitment to service.

PRAYER

Lord, may I never be lax in doing your work. May our generation be a generation that guards the gospel, develops leaders and passes it on to the next generation.

23 October | Day 296
Twenty-five Ways to Be Useful to God

He is one of my great heroes of faith. He was a model of godliness, faith and humility. God used him greatly. When he died in 1982, his executors were unable to trace a single member of his family still living. No one came forward claiming to be even a distant relation.

Yet, *The Times* obituary about him rightly noted that his influence within the Church of England during the previous fifty years was probably greater than any of his contemporaries. John Stott, who was one of the numerous influential Christian leaders whom he led to faith in Christ, said of him: 'Those who knew him well and those who worked with him never expect to see his like again; for rarely can anyone have meant so much to so many as this quietly spoken, modest and deeply spiritual man.'[1]

Why was this man – Reverend E. J. H. Nash – so useful to God? How can you be useful to God?

St Paul writes, 'Become the kind of container *God can use* to present any and every kind of gift to his guests for their blessing' (2 Timothy 2:20–21, MSG).

John Stott writes, 'No higher honour could be imagined than to be an instrument in the hand of Jesus Christ, to be at his disposal for the furtherance of his purposes, to be available whenever wanted for his service.'[2] Being 'useful to the Master' and 'instruments for noble purposes' (v.21) starts with *dedicating* your life to him and re-dedicating it regularly to his service.

READING FROM PROVERBS

Proverbs 25:21–26:2

1. Love your enemy

> 'If you see your enemy hungry, go buy him lunch;
> if he's thirsty, bring him a drink.
> Your generosity will surprise him with goodness,
> and God will look after you' (25:21–22, MSG; see also Romans 12:20).

2. Watch your tongue

> 'A north wind brings stormy weather,
> and a gossipy tongue stormy looks' (Proverbs 25:23, MSG).

If you want to change your actions, start with your thoughts and words. 'Avoid godless chatter, because those who indulge in it will become more and more ungodly' (2 Timothy 2:16).

3. Avoid quarrelling

'Better to live on the corner of the roof than to share a house with a quarrelsome wife' (Proverbs 25:24).

On the same theme Paul writes, 'Warn them before God against *quarrelling about words*; it is of no value, and only ruins those who listen' (2 Timothy 2:14). He goes on to say, 'Don't have anything to do with foolish and stupid arguments, because you know they produce quarrels. And the Lord's servants *must not quarrel*' (vv.23–24).

4. Bring good news

'Like cold water to a weary soul is good news from a distant land' (Proverbs 25:25). We are so privileged to be able to bring the good news of Jesus. It is like 'cold water to a weary soul'.

5. Stand your ground

'Like a muddied spring or a polluted well are the righteous who give way to the wicked' (v.26). Sometimes it is important to stand your ground.

6. Do not seek honour

If you seek your own honour, you will find that true honour eludes you: 'It is not good to eat too much honey, nor is it honourable to seek one's own honour' (v.27).

7. Be self-controlled

'A person without self-control is like a house with its doors and windows knocked out' (v.28, MSG). Don't try to control others. The only person you should try to control is yourself. Self-control is one of the characteristics that make up the fruit of the Spirit (Galatians 5:22–23).

8. Don't worry about what others say

You do not need to fear bad publicity or slander: 'Like a fluttering sparrow or a darting swallow, an underserved curse does not come to rest' (Proverbs 26:2).

NEW TESTAMENT READING

2 Timothy 2:1–26
9. Pass it on

It is so important to pass on the message and invest in others. Paul lays out four stages of investing in others in 2 Timothy 2:2:

1. 'what I said'
2. 'and you heard'
3. 'entrust to reliable people'
4. 'who teach others.'

10. Endure hardship

Paul uses the analogy of being a soldier (v.4). Soldiers have to endure hardship. He explains, 'therefore I *endure everything* for the sake of the elect, that they too may obtain the salvation that is in Christ Jesus' (v.10). Paul encourages us by going on to say that 'if *we endure*, we will also reign with him' (v.12).

11. Avoid distractions

'No one serving as a soldier gets involved in civilian affairs' (v.4a). Keep a clear focus and avoid distractions that waste time. As a soldier, you need to keep your focus and seek to please your commanding officer (v.4b).

12. Keep to the rules

Paul moves from the analogy of a soldier to that of an athlete: 'An athlete who refuses to play by the rules will never get anywhere' (v.5, MSG).

13. Work hard

From the soldier and athlete, Paul moves to the analogy of a farmer: 'The *hardworking* farmer should be the first to receive a share of the crops' (v.6).

14. Meditate on God's words

Only God can give understanding, but you have your part to play. Paul writes, '*Reflect* on what I am saying, for the Lord will give you insight into all this' (v.7).

15. Focus on Jesus

'Remember *Jesus Christ*, raised from the dead, descended from David. This is my gospel' (v.8). The gospel is all about Jesus. Salvation 'is in Christ Jesus' (v.10).

16. Correctly handle God's word

'Do your best to present yourself to God as one approved, a worker who does not need to be ashamed and who *correctly handles the word of truth*' (v.15).

17. Turn away from evil

'Everyone who confesses the name of the Lord must turn away from wickedness' (v.19). Repentance is not a one-off act; it is a continuing attitude. It involves *turning away from wickedness* (v.19) and fleeing 'the evil desires of youth' (v.22a).

18. Be a peacemaker

Paul urges Timothy among other things to 'pursue ... peace' (v.22). 'Refuse to get involved in inane discussions; they always end up in fights. God's servant must not be argumentative' (v.23, MSG).

Joyce Meyer writes, 'Strife is bickering, arguing, heated disagreement, and an angry undercurrent. Strife is dangerous and destructive.' Keeping strife out of our lives 'requires willingness to constantly communicate and confront issues ... ask for the Holy Spirit's help to be a person who avoids strife and restores peace everywhere you go.'[3]

19. Be kind to everyone

'The Lord's servant ... must be *kind to everyone*' (v.24). Everyone includes *everyone* – not just your friends, or the people you like, but all the people you come into contact with during the day (especially those who are often unappreciated, such as the person on the supermarket checkout, the person driving the bus, the person on reception, the person who helps you on the phone...).

20. Learn to teach

'The Lord's servants must be ... able *to teach*' and 'opponents must be gently instructed' (vv.24–25). Teaching is a specialist ministry but it is also the task of every Christian. A key characteristic is gentleness. 'God's servant must ... [be] a gentle listener and a teacher who keeps cool, working firmly but patiently with those who refuse to obey' (vv.24–25, MSG).

21. Don't be resentful

'The Lord's servant must ... *not* [be] *resentful*' (v.24). Resentment poisons relationships.

OLD TESTAMENT READING

Jeremiah 49:7–50:10

22. Hear the word of the Lord

Jeremiah was greatly used by God because as he said, '*I have heard a message from the Lord*' (49:14).

23. Allow God to speak through you

Jeremiah not only heard the word of the Lord, he was prepared to speak it out and God spoke through him. 'This is the word *the Lord spoke through Jeremiah...*' (50:1).

24. Walk closely with the Lord

Jeremiah foretold of the days when 'the people of Israel and the people of Judah together will go in tears *to seek the Lord their God*' (v.4).

This is the type of relationship God wants us to have with him – bound together, walking closely with him all the time (v.5). 'Hold tight to God' (v.5, MSG).

25. Find rest in the Lord

'My people have been lost sheep; their shepherds have led them astray and caused them to roam on the mountains. They wandered over mountain and hill and forgot their *own resting place*' (v.6). The Lord is described as your 'own resting place' (v.6), the place where you find rest for your soul (see also 6:16).

PRAYER

Lord, I want to be useful to you, the Master – an instrument for noble purposes, prepared to do any good work. I want to seek your face, to bind myself to you. I dedicate myself to you again today.

May we as a church be useful to you, Lord. May we be a community where people find kindness, faith, love and peace. May we bring the good news of Jesus to all those around, transforming society and changing our world in the power of the Holy Spirit.

24 October | Day 297
How God Speaks to You

Fyodor was a wild young man. His life revolved around eating, drinking, talking, music, theatre and the company of women. He dreamt of fame. He was caught up in a movement for political and social reform in Russia during the repressive reign of Tsar Nicholas I. He was arrested, tried and condemned to be executed.

On a bitterly cold morning, the prisoners were taken out to be shot. The prison guards raised their muskets to their shoulders and took aim. At the last moment, a white flag was raised to announce that the Tsar had commuted their sentence to life imprisonment in Siberia.

On his arrival in Siberia on Christmas Eve 1849, at the age of twenty-eight, two women slipped him a New Testament. When the guard turned away momentarily, they suggested he should search the pages thoroughly. He did.

While in prison, Fyodor Dostoyevsky, the great Russian novelist, read the New Testament from cover to cover and learnt much of it by heart. He wrote, 'I believe that there is no one lovelier, deeper, more sympathetic and more perfect than Jesus. I say to myself with jealous love not only is there no one else like him, but there never could be anyone like him.'[1] It was through the Bible that he had encountered Jesus Christ.

The apostle Paul describes all Scripture as '*God-breathed*' (2 Timothy 3:16). The Bible is not just inspired in the way that artists, poets, composers and musical performers can be said to be inspired. It actually has God's breath, his Spirit, in it. Through the Bible, God speaks to you.

READING FROM PSALMS

Psalm 119:89–96
Enjoy reading the Bible

The eighteenth-century philosopher and critic of Christianity, Voltaire, said, 'Within a hundred years the Bible will be obsolete and will have gone out of circulation altogether.' A hundred years later the Bible was more popular than ever. His own house in Paris was converted into a Bible factory, churning out Bibles by the hour! When you hear attacks on the Bible, it is good to remember that this is nothing new.

God's word is 'eternal' (v.90). In spite of all the attacks on the Bible it has survived. 'What you say goes, God, and *stays*, as permanent as the heavens. Your truth never goes out of fashion; it's as up-to-date as the earth when the sun comes up. Your Word and truth are dependable as ever' (vv.89–90, MSG).

The Bible is a delight. The psalmist describes the Scriptures he has read as 'my delight' (v.92).

It is fitting that this, the longest psalm in the psalter, should be all about the Scriptures.

When you are under attack, meditate on God's word: 'The wicked lie in ambush to destroy me, but I'm only concerned with *your plans for me*. I see the limits to everything human, but the horizons can't contain your commands!' (vv.95–96, MSG). God's commands are there to protect you, and remembering God's words will help keep you from harm: 'I will never forget your precepts, for by them you have preserved my life' (v.93).

PRAYER

Lord, help me each day to meditate on your eternal words and find delight in reading the Bible.

NEW TESTAMENT READING

2 Timothy 3:1–17
Look for Jesus as you read

The Bible is all about Jesus: 'There's nothing like the written Word of God for showing you the way to salvation through *faith in Christ Jesus*' (v.15, MSG).

Paul was writing to a society not unlike our own. He wrote:

'There are difficult times ahead. As the end approaches, people are going to be self-absorbed, money-hungry, self-promoting, stuck-up, profane, contemptuous of parents, crude, coarse, dog-eat-dog, unbending, slanderers, impulsively wild, savage, cynical, treacherous, ruthless, bloated windbags, addicted to lust, and allergic to God' (vv.1–4, MSG).

Paul describes them as 'having a form of godliness while denying its power' (v.5). It describes both a secular world and a kind of nominalism that has a form of godliness (people would say, if asked their religion, that they are Christian), but denying its power. There are also some who go to great lengths to oppose the truth (v.8).

You are called to be different. The pressure of the world is strong. Paul writes, 'But as for you…' (v.14). He points to his teaching, his way of life, his purpose, faith, patience, love, endurance, persecutions, sufferings (vv.10–11). He warns that 'anyone who wants to live all out for Christ is in for a lot of trouble; there's no getting around it' (v.12, MSG). Do not be surprised by opposition. Take a rock-like stand on the 'holy Scriptures' (v.15).

Some books inform, and even reform. The Bible transforms. A man complained to his pastor that he didn't read his Bible because it interfered with his work. When asked what his work was he replied, 'I'm a pickpocket'! The Bible was not given simply to increase your knowledge. It was given to change your life.

The Bible's aim is to point you to Christ. The Scriptures are able to make you 'wise for salvation through *faith in Christ Jesus*' (v.15). Jesus said, 'the Scriptures … testify about me' (John 5:40). As Martin Luther, the great reformer, put it, 'The Bible is the cradle in which Jesus lies … Every word rings of Christ.'[2]

Like many others, I first encountered Jesus through reading the Bible. It was as if he emerged from the pages of the New Testament.

But it is not just initial faith that comes through the Bible. It is your continuing faith and growth, *because* 'every part of Scripture is God-breathed and useful one way or another – showing us truth, exposing our rebellion, correcting our mistakes, training us to live God's way. Through the Word we are put together and shaped up for the tasks God has for us' (2 Timothy 3:16–17, MSG). As the *Catechism of the Catholic Church* puts it, Scripture is 'written under the inspiration of the Holy Spirit, [with] God as [its] author'.

The Bible is our authority in all matters of faith and life. You find out what God says (and what you should, therefore, believe) about suffering, about Jesus, about the cross, and so on. It is also in the Bible that you find out what is wrong in God's eyes and how you can live a righteous life. Feeding on the Bible is the way to be 'thoroughly equipped for every good work' (v.17).

PRAYER

Lord, thank you that you equip me for each day as I study your words, ponder them, meditate on them, and listen to your Spirit. May I grow closer to Jesus and be transformed into his likeness as I spend time in his presence.

OLD TESTAMENT READING

Jeremiah 50:11–51:14
Hear God's words and put them into practice

We all put our trust and security somewhere. The temptation is to place your trust and security in your money, education, job, health, family or friends. There is nothing wrong with these things, but ultimately there is only one absolutely secure place in which to put your trust, and that is in the Lord.

Throughout these closing chapters of Jeremiah, we have seen how all the nations had put their security and trust in things that could not ultimately deliver. Today we read how Babylon trusted in its rivers and its wealth: 'You who live by many waters and are rich in treasures…' (51:13). One by one, Jeremiah dismantles these false hopes.

Again and again, Jeremiah calls on his readers to listen to the words and promises of God rather than the things of the world. Two phrases that are repeated continuously are: 'this is what the LORD Almighty says' (50:18, 33; 51:1), and 'declares the LORD' (50:21, 30, 40).

We are encouraged to *listen to his words*, to '*do what I tell you*' (v.21, MSG), and to 'tell the good news' (51:10, MSG). You can build your life on the promises of his word. You are to hear God's words and put them into practice (see Matthew 7:24–27).

There are two great things that the Lord promises to those who hear his words, put their trust in him and put his words into practice.

First, he promises *satisfaction*. Your spiritual appetite can only be satisfied by a relationship with God (Jeremiah 50:19), which Jesus came to make possible.

Second, he promises complete forgiveness of your sins and removal of your guilt: 'They'll look high and low for a sign of Israel's guilt – nothing; search nook and cranny for a trace of Judah's sin – nothing. These people that I've saved will start out with a clean slate' (v.20, MSG). What God promised to Israel and Judah was fulfilled through Jesus on the cross. However careful a search is made, no one will be able to find any sin or guilt in you because of what Jesus has done.

PRAYER

Lord, I put my trust in you. Help me each day to listen to your words, put them into practice and find satisfaction in your presence and your love.

25 October | Day 298

Your Most Valuable Possession

As the novelist, historian and poet, Sir Walter Scott (1771–1832), lay dying, he turned to his great friend and son-in-law, J. G. Lockhart – the man who was later to write his life story – and said, 'Will you read to me from the Book?' Lockhart wondered which of his many books he meant – for he knew he was a great writer. So he asked, 'Which book?'

'Which book?' replied Scott, 'There is but one book; bring the Bible.' In his last moments on earth, he was comforted and encouraged by what God had to say to him. His last words were about his most valuable possession.[1]

In the case of the apostle Paul, we don't exactly know what his last words were. However, we do have his last *recorded* words; they are in our passage for today. As he comes to the end of this letter he writes, 'The time has come for my departure. I have fought the good fight, I have finished the race, I have kept the faith' (2 Timothy 4:7). We see his passion for Jesus Christ and his word. His whole life has been about telling others the good news of Jesus. His last words urge Timothy to do the same.

READING FROM PSALMS

Psalm 119:97–104
Love God's words

Without God, our lives make no sense. As we read his word we understand the meaning and purpose of our lives: 'With your instruction I understand life' (v.104, MSG). Nothing could be more important or more valuable than this.

At her coronation, the Queen was handed a copy of the Bible with these words, 'We present you with this Book, the most valuable thing that this world affords.'

The psalmist writes, 'Oh, how I love your law!' (v.97a). He says, 'I reverently ponder it all the day long' (v.97b, MSG). He writes, 'Your words are so choice, so tasty; I prefer them to the best home cooking' (v.103, MSG).

The effect of loving God's word, and meditating on it, is to give you wisdom (v.98), insight (v.99) and understanding (vv.100, 104): 'I've even become smarter than my teachers' (v.99, MSG). It makes you determined to keep your feet from every evil and wrong path (vv.101, 104).

PRAYER

Lord, thank you that your words give me wisdom, insight and understanding. Help me to love them, to meditate on them and to obey them.

NEW TESTAMENT READING

2 Timothy 4:1–22
Proclaim God's words

The apostle Paul urges, 'proclaim the Message' (v.2a, MSG). This passage is then full of practical advice on how to go about doing this.

1. Get involved
Paul writes to Timothy, 'I give you this charge' (v.1). His charge to Timothy is to be an evangelist and a preacher. According to the New Testament this is also the task of *every Christian*.

2. Speak about Jesus
Paul says preach 'the Word' (v.2a). The Greek word here is 'logos', which was used to describe Jesus in John 1:1. The good news is all about *Jesus*.

When we hear the word 'preach' we often think of a person in robes addressing a group of convinced believers within the precinct of the church. The word Paul uses here means a herald who delivers a message that has been given to them by the king. It is an 'up-to-the-minute' relevant message. You may not be a 'preacher' in the narrowest sense, but you can be a herald of the good news about Jesus.

3. Be prepared
It is important to be prepared and ready to take advantage of every opportunity God gives you to speak about your faith. Paul writes, '*be prepared* in season and out of season' (2 Timothy 4:2) – that is, when it is convenient and when it is not. The word he uses for 'prepared' has military connotations. He is saying, *stay at your post*. Be on duty. On guard. Be ready. Be at hand.

4. Speak to the whole person
Paul's message is holistic:

- It appeals to *the mind* (v.5). He says 'correct' (v.2), which could be translated as 'prove'. We are to teach the gospel with 'careful instruction' (v.2). Our presentation of the gospel should never be devoid of content. Paul's message is based on evidence and reason. Indeed, Paul says to Timothy, 'keep *your head*' (v.5).
- It is also an appeal to *the heart* and *conscience*. He says, 'rebuke' (v.2). Reason is not enough – a change of heart is required.
- Finally, it is an appeal to *the will*: 'encourage'. We need to get alongside people and help them with 'great patience' (v.2). This is a spirit that never gets irritated, never despairs and never regards a person as beyond salvation.

5. Keep speaking the truth
You may be tempted to change the content to what your hearers want to hear, or to what you think they are more likely to respond to, but keep passing on the same message that has been handed down to you. In spite of the fact that some people may prefer 'spiritual junk food – catchy opinions that tickle their fancy' to 'solid teaching' (v.3, MSG) – keep proclaiming the truth of the gospel.

6. Keep going
Paul writes to Timothy, 'do the work of an evangelist, discharge all the duties of your ministry' (v.5c). Telling others is your responsibility before God. Jesus is coming back to judge and reign (v.1). What you do now has eternal consequences. You are going to have to give an account.

Therefore, be willing to endure hardship (v.5). If you pass on the message, you will be misunderstood, misrepresented and misinterpreted. Paul has been deserted by Demas (v.10). He has been strongly opposed by Alexander, the metal worker who did him a great deal of harm (v.14). No one stood up for Paul in his hour of greatest need (v.16).

Never give up. Listen to Paul's words to Timothy as if they were addressed to you: 'make the spreading of the good news your life work' (v.5, JBP). This is what Paul did. He was willing to be poured out like a drink offering (v.6).

Now he says to Timothy, 'You take over. I'm about to die, my life an offering on God's altar. This is the only race worth running. I've run hard right to the finish, believed all the way. All that's left now is the shouting – God's applause! Depend on it, he's an honest judge. He'll do right not only by me, but by everyone eager for his coming' (vv.6–8, MSG).

7. Know that the Lord is on your side
In spite of all the opposition and difficulties, one thing makes all the difference: 'The Lord *stood at my side and gave me strength*' (v.17). This is so that 'the message might be fully proclaimed and all Gentiles might hear it' (v.17). Paul is confident about his future, even though he is facing the immediate threat of death (v.18). His greatest desire for Timothy and the other believers with him is that they are intimately connected to Jesus. His final words are, 'The Lord be with your spirit. Grace be with you' (v.22).

PRAYER

Lord, thank you that I am not on my own as I tell others the good news about Jesus – you go with me by your Spirit. Help me to do it faithfully, to fight the good fight, to finish the race and keep the faith.

OLD TESTAMENT READING

Jeremiah 51:15–64
Declare God's words

Do you ever feel powerless to do anything about your situation? Sometimes it appears that the forces raging against God and his people are so much more powerful than us. This was the situation in Jeremiah's day when the people of God were confronted by the most powerful empire of its time – Babylon.

Into this time of difficulty, Jeremiah kept on declaring the word of the Lord – right to the end of his life (vv.25–26, 39, 48, 52–53, 57–58). We have read the apostle Paul's last words. Now we come to Jeremiah's last words: 'The words of Jeremiah end here' (v.64).

Jeremiah's message was this: God is all-powerful. 'By his power he made earth. His wisdom gave shape to the world. He crafted the cosmos' (v.15, MSG). This all-powerful God is on your side: 'I'm on your side, taking up your cause' (v.36, MSG). Therefore, he says, 'Don't lose hope. Don't ever give up' (v.46, MSG).

The Babylonian empire, which seemed so powerful at the time, was about to collapse – like every other empire before or since. But God's people not only survived, they continued to grow and flourish.

Jeremiah wrote down the message on a scroll. He commanded, 'see that you read all these words aloud' (v.61). Jeremiah was a faithful prophet who heard the word of the Lord and kept on telling others the messages throughout his life.

PRAYER

Lord, thank you that the message about Jesus has changed my life and thank you that I have the privilege of seeing it change so many people's lives. Help me to keep on speaking your words boldly right to the end of my life.

26 October | Day 299

If It's Not All Right, Then It's Not the End

There is a line in the film *The Best Exotic Marigold Hotel*: 'Everything will be all right in the end ... If it's not all right, then it is not the end.'[1] Way beyond its context in the film, these words convey a profound theological truth.

READING FROM PSALMS

Psalm 119:105–112
Run the race to the end

Be determined, like the psalmist, to stay faithful to the Lord *to the very end of your life*. Say, 'My heart is set on keeping your decrees *to the very end*' (v.112).

In some ways, your life is like an obstacle race. There are snares along the path (v.110a). There is a temptation to stray (v.110b), and there is suffering (v.107).

How are you to avoid stumbling or making a mess of life? Wandering around in the dark is frightening and dangerous. The psalmist's answer is that, in the darkness of the world around, the word of God provides:

1. Guidance

The word of God sheds light in the darkness: 'Your word is a *lamp to my feet* and a *light to my path*' (v.105). It enables you to see the obstacles in your path, and hopefully to avoid stumbling over them. Study God's word regularly and he will guide you one step at a time: 'By your words I can see where I'm going; they throw a beam of light on my dark path' (v.105, MSG).

2. Sustenance

You need spiritual sustenance to keep going and God's word is 'sweeter than honey to my mouth' (v.103).

3. Wisdom
You need wisdom when you face stressful situations and decisions, and God's word provides 'understanding from your precepts' (v.104).

4. Encouragement
It is not easy. He writes, 'I constantly take my life in my hands' (v.109). You need encouragement to keep going and God's word is 'my heritage for ever' and 'the joy of my heart' (v.111).

God is faithful and will help you. The psalmist writes, 'Accept, O LORD, the willing praise of my mouth' (v.108). He is determined with God's help to keep going 'to the very end' (v.112b).

PRAYER

Lord, there is so much to praise you for. Accept the willing praise of my mouth. Your words are the 'joy of my heart' (v.111). I set my heart on keeping them to the very end.

NEW TESTAMENT READING

Titus 1:1–16
Pass on the baton to the next generation

In some ways leadership is like being in a relay race. Succession is key. Pass on the baton to the next generation because your part in the race is not the end.

The apostle Paul's life changed when he met Jesus on the road to Damascus. He realised in that moment that God had raised Jesus from the dead, and therefore death (the ending of this life) is not the end.

He sees himself as 'Christ's agent for promoting the faith' (v.1a, MSG). Jesus has sent him out to proclaim the message 'getting out the accurate word of God and how to respond rightly to it' (v.1b, MSG).

One day, Jesus will return and that will be the end of the world as we know it. However, even that will not be the end. Paul's aim is to 'raise hopes by pointing the way to life *without end'* (v.2, MSG). This amazing good news is the message that inspired and drove Paul's ministry.

This is the foundation of your faith. This is the truth. You can be absolutely confident about your future because of this hope of eternal life. This is a hope that was promised by God from the beginning of time (v.2), and which you can be sure of because 'God ... doesn't break promises!' (v.2, MSG). This is the message that Paul has 'been entrusted to proclaim ... by order of our Savior' (v.4, MSG).

In the end, you have the sure hope of eternal life. In the meantime, your task is *'unfinished'* (v.5). Paul gives instructions to Titus whom, like Timothy, he seems to have led to Christ (v.4).

Paul is coming to the end of his part of the race. But the end of his part is not the end of the race. He is passing on the baton to Titus, 'so you could complete what I left half-done' (v.5, MSG). At the same time, he is urging Titus to pass on the baton to others by appointing 'leaders in every town' (v.5, MSG).

The key to succession is finding the right leaders. Paul gives a similar list of qualifications to the ones we have already looked at in Timothy (vv.5–9).

He contrasts these high-calibre, godly leaders with those who 'claim to know God but by their actions deny him' (v.16). These people, under the guise of being 'religious teachers', ruin whole households. They do it for dishonest gain. They are not convicted by their sin. They do not understand that what they do is evil (vv.10–16).

The task of a good church leader is not only to 'encourage others by sound doctrine', but also to 'refute those who oppose it' (v.9). This should not be an excuse for criticising and judging other Christians, or churches, who are slightly different from us. Rather, verses 10–16 show us the types of behaviour that church leaders are called to refute – for example, those 'disrupting entire families with their teaching, and all for the sake of a fast buck' (v.11, MSG).

The ultimate purpose of this strong leadership is to protect the people of God from being blown off course. Paul's opening vision of eternal life should still be in our minds here as it shows us why it is so important to remain 'sound in the faith' (v.13). The hope of eternal life is our goal, our message and our motivation.

PRAYER

Lord, thank you that this life is not the end because of all that Jesus has done for us on the cross and through the resurrection. Help me to lead well and pass on the baton to good leaders for the future.

OLD TESTAMENT READING

Jeremiah 52:1–34
Never give up hope

Sometimes the circumstances of our lives can seem very bleak. Everything has gone wrong. Darkness has set in. And yet ... God never leaves us without a ray of hope. If it is not all right, then it is not the end.

Jeremiah had the unenviable task of proclaiming judgment. His name has passed into the English language as meaning 'a person given to lamentation or woeful complaining, a denouncer of the times, a dismal prophet.'[2] And yet ... even the book of Jeremiah ends with a hint of hope.

Jeremiah's words were fulfilled in the fall of Jerusalem. This was one of the most terrible times for the people of God. Their king, Zedekiah, was captured, blinded and imprisoned (v.11). 'The summary murder of his sons was the *last thing* Zedekiah saw, for they blinded him ... The king of Babylon threw him in prison, where he stayed until the day he died' (vv.10–11, MSG). The temple was destroyed by fire, as was the royal palace and every important building (vv.13–14). Many of the people went into exile.

Then, in 562 BC, in the thirty-seventh year of the exile of Jehoiachin king of Judah, a new king arose in Babylon who released Jehoiachin and freed him from prison (v.31).

'The king treated him most courteously and gave him preferential treatment beyond anything experienced by the political prisoners held in Babylon. Jehoiachin took off his prison garb and from then on ate his meals in company with the king. The king provided everything he needed to live comfortably for the *rest of his life*' (vv.32–34, MSG).

This is the slight hint of hope with which the book of Jeremiah ends. It is not all over for the people of God. This restoration had actually been prophesied by Jeremiah (chapter 24), along with a prophecy that the exiles would one day return to the land. With this first sign of restoration, the book comes to an end on a note of hope. This is a foretaste of the return from exile, which was to take place in 537 BC.

This in itself was only a foreshadowing of the restoration and renewal that would come through the kingdom of God, with the coming of Jesus and the outpouring of the Holy Spirit.

Even in Jeremiah *the end* (the fall of Jerusalem and the exile) *was not the end*. The people of God survived and would return to the land, rebuild the temple and restore the city. But this is also a picture of something far greater. Jesus proclaimed the end of the exile. In him, we have a new temple and a new Jerusalem. God raised Jesus from the dead. You have a new hope beyond the grave.

PRAYER

Father, thank you for the hope of the return of Jesus and for eternal life. Thank you for the hope of a new earth and a new heaven. Thank you that the end is not the end.

27 October | Day 300
Challenging Contradictions

I have often heard it said that 'the Bible is full of contradictions'. It is certainly true that there are many *apparent* contradictions.

When faced with challenging contradictions:

- seek to harmonise the apparent contradictions within the message of the Bible as a whole
- avoid artificial means of harmonisation
- be patient – be prepared to wait and live with unresolved questions.

READING FROM PROVERBS

Proverbs 26:3–12
To answer or not to answer?

The words 'fool', 'foolish', 'folly' occur ninety-six times in the book of Proverbs. The fool is the opposite of the wise person commended by the writer of Proverbs.

He says,

- '*Do not answer fools* according to their folly, or you will be like them yourself' (v.4).
- '*Answer fools* according to their folly, or they will be wise in their own eyes' (v.5).

This couldn't be a clearer apparent contradiction. If the two verses appeared in different sections of the Bible, it would be hailed as an obvious contradiction. However, the fact that they appear right after each other suggests that in the author's eyes there is no actual contradiction.

Criticism can often be extremely helpful and we can learn from it. However, sometimes criticism comes from ignorance (from 'fools'). How do we respond? There is a tension: on the one hand, we do not want to reply because, in a sense, it is descending to the level of the critic (the fool, v.4).

On the other hand, we want to reply because otherwise the critic may feel they are right and they 'will be wise in their own eyes' (v.5).

It may well be that the writer of the Proverbs is using the dilemma to make a humorous point, that when it comes to talking with fools – whether you respond or stay silent – you can't win.

It is very tempting to think that the fool is someone else and not me. If we think this, then we are 'wise in our own eyes': 'Do you see a person *wise in their own eyes*? There is more hope for fools than for them' (v.12)! This is the sting in the tail. After making us smile by showing how silly fools can be, we are reminded that when we think we are wise we are even worse off than a fool!

PRAYER

Lord, preserve me from being wise in my own eyes. Give me wisdom in all my decisions and how I answer my critics.

NEW TESTAMENT READING

Titus 2:1–15
'Boring' or 'attractive'?

If Christianity is to be credible and attractive to the world, Christians must live authentic and attractive lives.

Paul writes to Titus that in every way we should 'make the teaching about God our Saviour *attractive*' (v.10). The instructions he gives about teaching women to be reverent, self-controlled, pure, kind and so on, are so that 'no one will malign the word of God' (v.5).

Similarly, the instructions he gives to Titus about self-control, integrity and so on, are so that 'they have nothing bad to say about us' (v.8).

However, as we read his instructions, they are the very opposite of what our twenty-first century culture would think is attractive. He speaks of 'sound doctrine' (v.1), being temperate (v.2), self-controlled (v.2), sound in faith (v.2), reverent (v.3), not addicted to too much wine (v.3), virtuous and pure (v.5, MSG), living disciplined lives (v.5, MSG), showing integrity, seriousness and soundness of speech (vv.7–8), saying 'No' to ungodliness and worldly passions, and living self-controlled, upright and godly lives (v.12).

All this sounds very unattractive to modern ears. Yet when we actually see someone living like this – Mother Teresa or Pope Francis, to name but two – it is very attractive. Our culture dislikes the idea of holiness, but when people see a holy life they are captivated by it. True 'holiness' is when you leave every person more alive than when you found them.

As Simone Weil put it: 'Imaginary evil is romantic and varied; real evil is gloomy, monotonous, barren, boring. Imaginary good is boring; real good is always new, marvellous, intoxicating.'[1]

There is something beautiful about lives of 'dignity and wisdom', 'healthy faith' and 'love' (v.2, MSG); people who are 'models of goodness' and 'virtuous and pure' (vv.3, 5, MSG); lives of good character shining through action; 'God-filled, God-honouring lives' (v.12, MSG).

Jesus died for you and me 'to free us from a dark, rebellious life into this good, pure life, making us a people he can be proud of, energetic in goodness' (v.14, MSG).

PRAYER

Lord, help me by my life and by my love to make the teaching about you attractive.

OLD TESTAMENT READING

Habakkuk 1:1–3:19
Faith *and* doubt?

Are doubts, questioning and fears compatible with faith? Are you facing problems with your marriage (or lack of marriage), your family, your job, your health, your finances or a combination of all of these? Does this make you doubt the existence of God? Should you stop believing?

Many people regard faith as unquestioning. They think faith and doubt are opposites. In fact, faith and doubt are *two sides of the same coin*. There is no doubt that 2 + 2 = 4. However, it does not take any faith to believe it. On the other hand, to believe that someone loves you is open to an element of doubt. To put your faith in God is similar to loving a person. There is always the possibility of doubt. Without doubt, faith would not be faith.

Likewise, it is not wrong to question God within the context of faith. The book of Habakkuk starts with a man who believes, yet questions. It ends with a towering expression of faith, scarcely equalled anywhere else in the Old Testament.

Habakkuk looked at the world and was perplexed and fearful. He saw 'violence' (1:2), 'injustice' (v.3a), 'destruction' (v.3c), 'strife' and 'conflict' (v.3d). Yet the Lord did not seem, to him, to be doing anything about it (vv.2–4). He saw pain and suffering and asked, *'How long, O Lord...? Why...?'* (vv.2–3).

He took the problem to God and asked genuinely heartfelt questions. God replied that he was going to do something amazing, but not what Habakkuk expected (v.5). He was raising up the Babylonians (v.6). Consequently, Israel was to be overwhelmed and would go into exile.

Habakkuk was perplexed. Surely God was in control of history and all-powerful (v.12)? How could a pure God use the cruel and idolatrous Babylonians to punish a godly nation? 'God, you chose *Babylonians* for your judgment work? ... You can't be serious. *You* can't condone evil!' (vv.12–13, MSG). Habakkuk didn't seem to get a direct answer. However, he took his puzzled complaints and problems to God and left them with him as he waited (2:1).

God told him first to write down the vision (v.2). When you sense God speaking to you and giving you a vision, it is good to write it down so that you can refer back to it and hold on to it. Second, God told him that he may have to wait for the answer: 'Wait for it; it will certainly come and not delay' (v.3).

God wants you to bring your doubts and questions to him. You may not always get immediate answers to all your questions. While you wait for answers you are called to trust in God, even when you don't fully understand what he is doing.

Faith involves believing what God has said in spite of the difficulties you face: 'The righteous will live by their faith' (v.4). Habakkuk foresaw that judgment was coming on the ungodly Babylonians. He also foresaw that, one day, the outlaws would be destroyed and 'the earth will be filled with the knowledge of the glory of the Lord, as the waters cover the sea' (v.14). He foresaw the ultimate triumph of good over evil.

Until that time, he resolved to stay close to God whatever happened.

Like Habakkuk, commit yourself to praise and not complaint. Resolve to take the long-term view and be patient. Resolve to rejoice whatever the circumstances. Commit yourself to faith, even when there was no fruit (3:17–19).

God is concerned, not so much about the harvest as about your heart. Even if you can find nothing else, you can rejoice over your relationship with the Lord. Habakkuk says, 'I will rejoice in the Lord, I will be joyful in God my Saviour' (v.18). God made him sure-footed and light-hearted: 'The Sovereign Lord is my strength; he makes my feet like the feet of a deer, he enables me to go on the heights' (v.19).

As Joyce Meyer writes, 'We need to allow our difficulties to help us develop "hinds' feet". When we have hinds' feet ... we will walk and make progress through our trouble, suffering, responsibility, or whatever is trying to hold us back.'[2]

PRAYER

Lord, help me trust completely in you as I honestly express my doubts and questions to you, and to rejoice in you even when I do not immediately see an answer.

28 October | Day 301
Do Good

There are some people in our church community who never seem to stop doing good. Whenever I see them, they are serving or washing up, praying for someone, encouraging others, offering to take food to the sick, or doing some other kind act. They give generously to the work of the church. They do all these things with such grace and enthusiasm. I am always encouraged and challenged by their example. They never seem to tire of doing good.

In our society, the term 'do-gooder' has become pejorative; it is used as an insult. But doing good should not be seen in this way. Jesus, 'went around *doing good*' (Acts 10:38).

St Paul writes to Titus, 'Remind the people ... to be ready to *do whatever is good*' (Titus 3:1). His desire is that those who have trusted in God 'devote themselves to *doing what is good*' (vv.8, 14).

To quote John Wesley, 'Do all the good you can, by all the means you can, in all the ways you can, in all the places you can, at all the times you can, to all the people you can, as long as ever you can.'

READING FROM PSALMS

Psalm 119:113–120
Do good, not evil

The opposite of doing good is doing evil. The psalmist is determined to do good. That is why he says, 'Away from me, you *evildoers*' (v.115a). The evildoers are 'double-minded' (v.113). They stray from God's decrees and are deceitful (v.118).

Choose to avoid evil and do good. Love God's words (vv.113, 119). God is your refuge and shield (v.114a). Put your hope in his word (v.114b): 'I'll give total allegiance to your definitions of life' (v.117, MSG).

The psalmist writes, 'Sustain me according to your promise, and I shall live; do not let my hopes be dashed' (v.116). Our hope being deferred is bad enough. The book of Proverbs says, 'Hope deferred makes the heart sick' (Proverbs 13:12). Bring your hopes before God today and pray, like the psalmist, that your hopes will not be dashed.

PRAYER

Lord, I love your words. Help me to live by them, to stay away from doing evil and to do good. Today I bring my hopes to you again ... Do not let my hopes be dashed

NEW TESTAMENT READING

Titus 3:1–15
Always be ready to do good

There is such a striking contrast between Paul's life before he experienced a relationship with Jesus Christ and his life afterwards (and I relate to this in my own experience). Paul writes, 'We too were foolish, disobedient, deceived and enslaved by all kinds of passions and pleasures. We lived in malice and envy, being hated and hating one another' (v.3).

However, Jesus utterly transforms us: 'when the *kindness* and love of God our Saviour appeared, he saved us, not because of righteous things we had done, but because of his mercy' (vv.4–5). Doing good is a response to God's kindness and love for you. We often think of the kindness of our family and friends, but God is infinitely more kind than that. If God has been so kind to you, it is a natural response for you to be kind to others.

Out of his kindness and love, God has not only forgiven you, he has also given you the Holy Spirit: 'He gave us a good bath, and we came out of it new people, washed inside and out by the Holy Spirit. Our Savior Jesus poured out new life so generously. God's gift has restored our relationship with him and given us back our lives' (vv.5–7, MSG). It is the Holy Spirit who enables you and empowers you to do good.

Therefore, Paul can write of the kind of lives we are now to lead: 'Remind the people to respect the government and be law-abiding' (v.1, MSG). This is our civil responsibility – to obey the laws of the country – unless they are contrary to God's law.

But obedience and submission to rulers and authorities is not enough. We must 'be ready to *do whatever is good*, to slander no one, to be peaceable and considerate, and to show true humility towards everyone' (vv.1–2). He urges them twice more to devote themselves to *doing what is good* (vv.8, 14).

It is striking that Paul's focus here seems to be on their relationships with other people. Paul is encouraging an 'other-focused' mindset, rooted in humility, truthfulness and consideration for others. While you are to be motivated by love, sometimes it is by actually serving others that you learn to love them.

Even after you have been reborn and renewed by the Holy Spirit, there will be temptations to get sidetracked and become unproductive. Don't get involved in incessant arguments. Paul writes, 'Avoid foolish controversies and genealogies and arguments and quarrels about the law, because these are unprofitable and useless' (v.9).

Paul is concerned that the Christians in Crete be distinct and different from the culture in which they live. He writes, 'Our people must learn to devote themselves to *doing what is good*, in order that they may provide for daily necessities and not live unproductive lives' (3:14).

You live out what you believe in front of a watching world. If we are lazy and unproductive, it will be noticed. You are to reflect 'the kindness and love of God our Saviour' (v.4) as you 'do good'.

Doing good and living a productive life does not necessarily mean that you need to change your job. When I was practising as a lawyer, I remember considering whether God was calling us to ordination in the Church of England. I was very struck by the mention of '*Zenas the lawyer*' (v.13). It reminded me that if I were to stop practising as a barrister, it was not because there was anything wrong with being a Christian lawyer. Wherever you are in life and whatever your job or ministry, it is possible to go around doing good.

PRAYER

Lord, thank you so much for the way in which you have transformed my life. Help me to lead a productive life and, like Jesus, to go around doing good.

OLD TESTAMENT READING

Lamentations 1:1–2:6
Stay close to the one who went around doing good

'To be human is to suffer. No one gets an exemption. Lamentations keeps company with the extensive biblical witness that gives dignity to suffering by insisting that God enters our suffering and is companion to our suffering,' writes Eugene Peterson in his introduction to the book of Lamentations.[1]

The book, as the name suggests, focuses on the sorrow, sadness, grief, pain, loss and tragedy that the people of God experienced during the exile. Our circumstances may be different, but our suffering is just as real.

The writer laments how the once great nation of Israel has gone into exile because of her many sins: 'she's stuck between a rock and a hard place' (1:3, MSG), '...lost everything' (v.7, MSG), '...Massacres in the streets, starvation in the houses' (v.20, MSG).

As we read today's passage there seems to be very little hope. It is all about judgment and suffering. The writer says, 'Is any suffering like my suffering...?' (v.12). That is often how we feel when going through difficulties and trials.

He writes, 'My sins have been bound *into a yoke*; by his hands they were woven together. They have come upon my neck and the Lord has sapped my strength. He has handed me over to those I cannot withstand' (v.14).

The picture is of his sins being like a great heavy yoke around his neck, weighing him down. He is weary and burdened by them.

This is the experience of exile, judgment and immense suffering. The physical exile lasted approximately seventy years, but there was a sense in which the spiritual experience of exile continued.

Thank God that Jesus came to announce that the exile was well and truly over, and that you need no longer go around weary and burdened by sins. Jesus said, 'Come to me, all you who are weary and burdened, and I will give you rest. *Take my yoke* upon you and learn from me, for I am gentle and humble in heart, and you will find rest for your souls. For my yoke is easy and my burden is light' (Matthew 11:28–30).

This is the secret of doing good: stay close to the one who went around doing good. Hand over your burdens to Jesus and receive his rest. Take his yoke upon you as you learn from him – from his gentle, humble heart – because he is the source of doing good.

PRAYER

Thank you, my Lord and my Saviour, that you take the yoke of sin from me and remove its heavy burden. Thank you that when I am yoked to you, my yoke is easy and my burden is light. Help me today to stay close to you, to minister in the power of your Holy Spirit and, like you, to go around doing good.

29 October | Day 302

How to Refresh Your Mind, Heart and Soul

The former televangelist, Jim Bakker, in his autobiography *I Was Wrong*, tells of his descent into ignominy, impoverishment and imprisonment for accounting fraud. He lost his freedom, his sanity, his dignity, his confidence in his faith and, eventually, even his wife. Inmate 07407-058, one-time friend and advisor of presidents, had hit rock bottom.

At his very lowest point, a prison official told him, 'Billy Graham is here to see you!' He thought, '*Billy Graham has come here ... to this place ... to see me*.' When he walked into the room, Billy Graham turned towards him and opened his arms wide.

At that moment, Jim Bakker felt total acceptance and love: 'I will never forget that the man who had just been voted one of the most influential men in the world and who has ministered to millions of people took time out of his busy schedule to come minister to one prisoner.' He describes how in the midst of his depression, flu, filth and hopelessness, Billy Graham's visit *refreshed his heart* and boosted his spirit. 'I felt as though Jesus Himself had come to visit me.'[1]

Refreshment means restoring strength, energy and vigour. A light snack is sometimes referred to as a 'refreshment'. Physical refreshment can also come, for example, from sleep, rest, or exercise.

Paul tells Philemon that he has '*refreshed the hearts* of the saints' (Philemon 7). Later on in the letter, Paul asks him to '*refresh my heart* in Christ' (v.20). But how do you refresh your mind, heart and soul?

READING FROM PSALMS

Psalm 119:121–128
The words of God

Gold is the most valuable thing this world affords. It cannot be tarnished. It shines with a glow like no other metal.

Yet God's words are far more valuable than even the finest gold. The psalmist writes: 'I love your commands *more than gold*, *more than pure gold*' (v.127).

The source of the psalmist's soul refreshment is God's words. Earlier in the psalm he said, 'My soul is consumed with longing for your laws at all times ... My soul is weary with sorrow; strengthen me according to your word' (vv.20, 28). Allow God's words to refresh your mind, heart and soul.

PRAYER

Lord, thank you so much for how amazing it is to be refreshed emotionally and spiritually by reading your words, meditating on them and absorbing them in my mind, heart and soul.

NEW TESTAMENT READING

Philemon 1–25
The people of God

Paul writes to his friend Philemon to ask for a favour (v.1). Philemon had a slave called Onesimus who had escaped. While Onesimus was on the run, Paul had led him to Christ (v.10).

The normal fate of a runaway slave was death or flogging and branding on the forehead. Now, in this letter, which is full of grace, humility, genuine love and charm, Paul writes to persuade Philemon to take Onesimus back – not as a slave, but as a friend and brother (v.16). Centuries later, the ripple effect of these words contributed to massive social change. Local history became global history.

It is a request that Paul expects will receive a positive answer. He is absolutely confident that Philemon will do what he has asked him to do (v.21). This is an example and a challenge to bring love, forgiveness and reconciliation everywhere you go.

Philemon is a close friend. He leads a church that meets in his home (v.2) and he is a man of faith and love (v.5).

Paul prays that Philemon may be 'active in sharing his faith' (v.6). It is interesting to note that Paul thinks that this is the way that he will receive 'a full understanding of every good thing we have in Christ' (v.6). For example, I have often noticed on Alpha how quickly people grow in their understanding as they become small group helpers and hosts on the course. The way to grow is to be active in sharing your faith.

He then goes on to say, 'Your love has given me great joy and encouragement because you have *refreshed the hearts* of the saints' (v.7). And he asks Philemon to *refresh his heart* in Christ by another act of love (v.20). His whole appeal for Onesimus is 'on the basis of love' (v.9).

Clearly, Philemon was a man known for his love: 'I keep hearing of the love and faith you have for the Master Jesus, which brims over to other believers' (v.5, MSG).

Paul makes 'a very personal request' (vv.8, 9, MSG), asking Philemon to welcome Onesimus back as 'no mere slave this time, but a true Christian brother ... welcome him back as you would me. If he damaged anything or owes you anything, chalk it up to my account' (vv.16–18, MSG). He writes, 'You'll be doing it for Christ' (v.20, MSG), but it will also 'refresh my heart' (v.20).

Forgiveness involves extending love and mercy to someone who has wronged or hurt you. It clears the way to reconciliation and restoration of a relationship.

Paul is longing to see Philemon. He writes, 'Prepare a guest room for me, because I hope to be restored to you in answer to your prayers' (v.22). Spending time with people you love and who love you, whether it is family or friends, refreshes your heart and soul.

PRAYER

Lord, thank you so much for the church and the love of brothers and sisters in Christ. Thank you for how they refresh my heart and soul.

OLD TESTAMENT READING

Lamentations 2:7–3:39
The presence of God

The prophet's heart is in great need of refreshment. As Jeremiah looks out at the devastation of Jerusalem, he is surrounded by the most appalling suffering. There is destruction all around. The people are starving. It has reached such a nadir that there is the horrific possibility of women eating their own children (2:20).

It is not just that the suffering is all around Jeremiah. It is also in his own heart and soul. He writes, 'My eyes fail from weeping, I am in *torment* within, *my heart is poured out* on the ground' (v.11). His heart is pierced (3:13). He feels besieged and surrounded by 'bitterness and hardship' (v.5). He is dwelling in darkness (v.6).

He feels he has been 'left ... without help' (v.11). He is laughed at and mocked (v.14). On top of all this, he has 'been deprived of peace' (v.17).

Like Jeremiah, sometimes our prayers do not seem to have been answered: 'Even when I call out or cry for help, he shuts out my prayer. He has barred my way with blocks of stone; he has made my paths crooked' (vv.8–9).

The answer lies '*in the presence of the Lord*'. He writes, 'Arise, cry out in the night, as the watches of the night begin; pour out your heart like water in *the presence of the Lord*' (2:19).

He goes on, 'My soul is downcast within me.
Yet this I call to mind and therefore I have hope:
Because of the LORD's great love we are not consumed, for his compassions never fail.
They are new every morning; great is your faithfulness.

I say to myself, "The LORD is my portion;
therefore I will wait for him."
The LORD is good to those whose hope is in him,
to the one who seeks him…
Though he brings grief, he will show compassion, so great is his unfailing love' (3:20–25, 32).

Times of refreshing come from 'the presence of the Lord' (Acts 3:19, AMP). You can receive this refreshing every day.

God's mercy is new every morning. You can make a fresh, new start every single day. Every day you can seek him, wait for him quietly, hope in him and be refreshed by his presence.

When you realise how much God has forgiven you and how great is his mercy, you can more easily forgive those who have hurt you and extend mercy to them. This is the key to great relationships.

These are not naïve or superficial words of encouragement. They are realistic about the depth and extent of suffering and struggles without and within. Yet in the midst of all this, you can hang on to the goodness and love of God: 'Because of the LORD's great love we are not consumed' (Lamentations 3:22).

We see here a hint of how this love is made possible. The prophet writes, 'Let them offer their *cheeks* to one who would strike them, and let them be filled with *disgrace*' (v.30). Jesus offered his *cheek* to the ones who struck him (John 19:3; see also Matthew 5:39) and bore our *disgrace* on the cross. It is the blood of Christ that cleanses you from all sin (1 John 1:9) and through his death you can be forgiven, cleansed, renewed and refreshed in your heart and soul every day.

PRAYER

Lord, I pour out my heart to you today. Refresh me with your presence. Thank you for your great faithfulness and unfailing compassion – made available to me, new every morning, through Jesus Christ my Lord.

30 October | Day 303
Your Key to Life

- Madonna said, 'When I was growing up … Jesus Christ was like a movie star, my favourite idol of all.'[1]
- Napoleon Bonaparte said, 'I know men and I tell you that Jesus Christ is no mere man.'[2]
- Novelist H. G. Wells said, 'I am an historian, I am not a believer. But this *penniless preacher* from Galilee is irresistibly the centre of history.'[3]

Even people who would not describe themselves as followers of the 'penniless preacher' recognise that there is something extraordinary about Jesus.

No one, not even angels, can compare to Jesus (Hebrews 1:1–14). If you want to know what God is like, look at Jesus. He said, 'Anyone who has seen me has seen the Father' (John 14:9). Everything you read and understand about God through the Bible needs to be read through the lens of Jesus. He is the ultimate revelation of God.

Your key to getting your life sorted out is Jesus. Your key to understanding the Bible is Jesus. Your key to understanding God's character is Jesus. Your key to life is Jesus.

READING FROM PSALMS

Psalm 119:129–136
Jesus provides cleansing from our sins

Reading the Bible is, in some ways, like looking in a mirror with a very bright light: 'The unfolding of your words gives light' (v.130a). The light reveals what is wrong with our life and what we need to have cleaned up. It reveals the things that cause a barrier between us and God.

This barrier was removed when Jesus provided cleansing for your sins. Through Jesus, you can be confident that God's face will shine upon you (v.135).

Pray like the psalmist:

'Turn to me and have mercy on me,
as you always do to those who love your name.

Direct my footsteps according to
your word;
let no sin rule over me.
Redeem me from human
oppression,
that I may obey your precepts.
Make your face shine upon your
servant' (vv.132–135a).

The psalmist's prayer foreshadows the great act of Jesus in providing purification for sins. Through Jesus always turn to God with confidence knowing that he will have mercy, 'as you always do to those who love your name' (v.132).

PRAYER

Lord, thank you for Jesus. Thank you for your mercy. May no sin rule over me. Keep me from pride, anger, lust, greed, envy, prayerlessness, rivalry and all the other temptations of life. I pray that you would make your face shine upon me today.

NEW TESTAMENT READING

Hebrews 1:1–14
Jesus is superior to angels

Jesus is unique and he is all you need. As Eugene Peterson points out, you do not need Jesus-and-angels. You do not need Jesus-and-Moses. You do not need Jesus-and-priesthood. 'This letter deletes the hyphens, the add-ons.' *All you need is Jesus*.

The book of Hebrews is all about who Jesus is and how he is better and greater than any other being, teaching, or religious system. It opens with a comparison between Jesus and the Old Testament prophets. It explains the wonderful truth of how God spoke through the prophets, but then describes how Jesus is *even better* (vv.1–3). He is 'the heir of all things', he was involved in creation, he is the ultimate revelation of God, he is your sustainer, and he is your redeemer. The reason for all of this lies in who Jesus is.

Jesus 'is the radiance of God's glory and the exact representation of his being' (v.3). As *The Message* puts it, he 'perfectly mirrors God, and is stamped with God's nature.'

Jesus came to sort out our lives. 'After he had provided purification for sins, he sat down at the right hand of the Majesty in heaven' (v.3b). Sitting down symbolises the fact that his work was finished (see also John 19:30).

There have always been people who can't accept this truth. Today, some argue that Jesus was 'just a great religious teacher', and nothing more. In a similar way, at the time of this letter, some people were arguing that Jesus was 'just an angel'. The writer of Hebrews says: 'So he became as much superior to the angels as the name he has inherited is superior to theirs' (Hebrews 1:4). He then goes on to argue the superiority of Jesus over the angels.

There are nearly 300 references to angels in the Bible. What do we know about them?

In this passage we see that angels worship and serve God (vv.6–7). They are God's messengers (v.7, MSG). They are spiritual beings who serve Christians (v.14). They 'are sent to serve those who will inherit salvation' (v.14).

Angels are nearer than you think. They guard and protect you (Psalm 91:11): God has given 'his angels charge of you to guard you in all your ways' (Psalm 91:11). For example, an angel strengthened Jesus at Gethsemane (Luke 22:43). Each church has one (Revelation 1–3).

But Jesus is far greater. The writer of Hebrews sets out seven passages from Old Testament Scriptures to show the superiority of Jesus over the angels (Psalm 2:7; 2 Samuel 7:14; Deuteronomy 32:43; Psalms 45:6–7; 102:25–27; 104:4; 110:1).

All these passages are the answer to anyone who says that Jesus was only an angel or (more likely today) a 'great religious teacher'. The peak of the argument is in Hebrews 1:8, 'About *the Son* he says, "Your throne, *O God*..."' This is an outright ascription of *divinity to Jesus*. Jesus is the one whose identity is God.

PRAYER

Lord, thank you that you send angels to guard and protect us. Thank you that they serve us. But thank you even more for Jesus, who is far superior to all angels.

OLD TESTAMENT READING

Lamentations 3:40–5:22
Jesus is the anointed Messiah

The writer of Lamentations says, 'Let us lift up our hearts and our hands' (3:41).

The lifting of hearts and hands seem to go together in prayer. Raising hands in prayer is not eccentric or weird, it is the traditional form of prayer in both the Old Testament and New Testament.

The writer calls the people to pray and says, 'Let's take a good look at the way we're living and reorder our lives under God' (v.40, MSG). This is an important discipline in a life of faith. Ask God to reveal if there are any areas of your life that you need to change.

If there are, then return to God in confession and repentance (v.42 onwards). Now you know that you will be forgiven and your relationship with God will be restored because of what Jesus has done for you. This passage, like so many others in the Old Testament, points forward to Jesus.

The writer of Lamentations says, 'You, O Lord, reign *for ever*; *your throne* endures from generation to generation' (5:19).

The writer of Hebrews says of Jesus: '"*Your throne*, O God, will last *for ever* … therefore God, your God, has set you above your companions by *anointing you* with the oil of joy"' (Hebrews 1:8–9). Jesus is God's anointed one – the Christ, the Messiah.

He is the one to whom all the Scriptures point. The people of God were expecting the Lord's anointed. The writer of Lamentations speaks of '*the Lord's anointed*' (Lamentations 4:20). The Hebrew word for anointed one is 'Mashiach' from which we get the word Massiah. He goes on to say, 'to you also the cup will be passed' (v.21). Jesus spoke of the cup he would drink (Mark 10:38; John 18:11). Jesus was alluding to the cup of God's wrath against sin.

God's anger is not like ours. It contains no element of spite, pettiness or hypocrisy. It is the reaction of a holy and loving God towards sin. Passages like this help us to understand how serious our sin is in God's sight and how amazing it is that, on the cross, Jesus bore the wrath of God for you and me.

The prophet sees that they are cut off from God by their sin: 'You have covered yourself with a cloud so that no prayer can get through' (Lamentations 3:44). This is the barrier that Jesus removed when he drank the cup of God's wrath and provided purification for sins. This is the answer to the prayer of the writer of Lamentations when he prayed, 'Restore us to yourself, O Lord, that we may return; renew our days as of old' (5:21).

Because of Jesus, the Anointed One and the one who drank the cup, God's presence is no longer covered with a cloud, and your prayers can get through to him. You can lift up your heart and your hands to God. He will restore you and renew you.

Although there are many words about judgment in the Bible, they can be read through the lens of Jesus who revealed the true character of God and provided purification for your sins.

PRAYER

Father, thank you for Jesus. Thank you that I can know and understand who you are through Jesus. Thank you that the key to life is in Jesus.

31 October | Day 304
The Surprising Secret of Freedom

'I have on my table a violin string,' wrote Rabindranath Tagore. 'It is free to move in any direction I like. If I twist one end it responds; it is free. But it is not free to sing. So I take it and fix it into my violin. I bind it and *when it is bound*, it is free for the first time to sing.'[1]

True freedom comes when we *bind ourselves* to Jesus and fix our eyes on him. As the violin string comes alive when bound into the violin, so we come alive in Christ. Jesus is the great liberator. He sets us free.

At the heart of Christianity is a relationship with Jesus. Jesus died for you. He was raised to life and he is alive today. You cannot see him physically, but you can see him with the eyes of faith.

In today's passage, the writer of Hebrews says, '*we see Jesus*' (Hebrews 2:9). Later, he writes, 'let us *fix our eyes* on Jesus, the *author* and *perfecter* of our faith' (12:2). He is both the *author* of our faith and the *author* of our salvation (2:10), described earlier as such a '*great salvation*' (v.3).

What does this salvation involve? What are we freed from?

READING FROM PROVERBS

Proverbs 26:13–22
Freedom from fear

As Christians, we should be fearless. We should never allow fear of the enemy to slow us down.

The writer of Proverbs says, 'A sluggard says, "There is a lion in the road, a fierce lion roaming the streets!"' (v.13). Every Christian ministry faces 'fierce lions'. Don't be put off by fear, which leads to inertia and lack of activity (vv.14–15). Jesus sets us free to advance without fear of the opposition.

Freedom is the antithesis of apathy. The writer goes on to warn against every kind of laziness. He warns us not to get involved with other people's arguments (v.17). He warns also against jokes that involve telling lies (v.19).

The best way to heal a quarrel is to stop gossiping. Without gossip a quarrel dies down just as without wood a fire goes out (v.20). It is so tempting to listen to gossip because 'the words of a gossip are like choice morsels; they go down to the inmost parts' (v.22). But listening to gossip is as bad as gossiping – rather like receiving stolen goods is as bad as theft.

Here is wisdom about how to heal a quarrel: never add fuel to the fire but rather be a peacemaker.

PRAYER

Lord, thank you that through Jesus I can be set free from my fears. Help me to be bold in the face of opposition and never allow fear to slow me down.

NEW TESTAMENT READING

Hebrews 2:1–18
Freedom from sin and death

The letter of Hebrews is written to warn against drifting away (v.1). Most people do not suddenly give up being Christians, but we can *drift*. The author of Hebrews includes himself in this warning: 'We must pay careful attention, therefore, to what we have heard, so that we *do not drift away*. For if the message spoken by angels was binding, and every violation and disobedience received its just punishment, how shall we escape if we ignore such a great salvation?' (vv.1–3a).

In the first chapter of Hebrews, the writer establishes the divinity of Jesus. In this chapter, he establishes his humanity: 'he had to enter into every detail of human life' (v.17, MSG).

Jesus became like us in that he:

- became, for a while, lower than the angels (v.9)
- is of the same family (v.11)
- calls us brothers and sisters (v.11)
- shares in our humanity (v.14)
- was made like us in every way (v.17)
- suffered when he was tempted (v.18).

But, he adds, although Jesus was tempted in every way *just as we are*, he was 'without sin' (4:15). This shows that temptation is not sin. Do not allow the devil to condemn you just because you are tempted. The fact that Jesus himself was tempted means that he is able to help you when you are tempted (v.17).

He was like us but *different from us* in regard to sin. It is so encouraging to know that Jesus has experienced the full range of human experience and emotion – he understands and sympathises with you. Yet it is also important that he was sinless. We do not just need a friend who can sympathise with us; we need a saviour.

Jesus was both fully divine and fully human. This is what made it possible for him to achieve such a great salvation through his death and resurrection. He is able to bridge the gap between you and God.

In this passage, the writer tells us a number of things about the death of Jesus. On the cross, he:

- tasted death for everyone (2:9)
- destroyed the devil (v.14)
- freed us from the fear of death (v.15)
- made atonement for our sins (v.17)
- pioneered our salvation (v.10)
- was made perfect through suffering (v.10).

A free person is not afraid to think about death. It has been suggested that ultimately all our fears are related to the fear of death. In setting you free from death and the fear of death, Jesus has enabled you to be set free from all your other fears.

The writer of Hebrews says that Jesus tasted 'death for everyone' (v.9) so that by 'embracing death, taking it into himself, he destroyed the devil's hold on death and freed all who cower through life, scared to death of death' (vv.14–15, MSG).

God testified to what Jesus had done – this great salvation – by 'signs, wonders and various miracles, and gifts of the Holy Spirit distributed according to his will' (v.4). If the gifts of the Holy Spirit are for those other than the apostles, surely signs, wonders and miracles are also. And we should still expect them today to accompany the preaching of the message of Jesus and his great salvation.

PRAYER

Thank you, Jesus, that you were willing to suffer and taste death for me. Thank you for setting me free and making it possible to enjoy freedom from the results of sin and the fear of death.

OLD TESTAMENT READING

Obadiah 1–21
Freedom from injustice

We live in a world of terrible injustice. To take one example – there are still over 24 million people in forced labour worldwide. Two million children are trafficked every year.[2] There are more people in slavery today than in the 350-year history of the transatlantic slave trade.

The book of Obadiah promises that the world will not always be like this. One day, when God's kingdom comes in its fullness, there will be justice for all.

The name Obadiah means 'one who serves and worships Yahweh'. In this, the shortest Old Testament book, Obadiah, about whom we know virtually nothing, foretells the downfall of one of the enemies of God's people.

The people of Edom were descended from Esau, Jacob's twin. They were always felt to have a real kinship with the people of Israel. However, this often showed itself – not so much in mutual assistance – as in hostile recriminations and charges of treachery. The two neighbouring peoples – Israel and Edom – had a long history of war and rivalry.

Pride was the downfall of Edom: 'You thought you were so great ... Thinking to yourself, "Nobody can get to me! Nobody can touch me!"' (vv.2–3, MSG). Pride is the opposite of love. Love is not proud. It does not boast (1 Corinthians 13:4).

Obadiah suggests that when Jerusalem fell to the Babylonian army in 587 BC the Edomites did nothing to help and they may even have taken advantage of Judah's fate.

He writes, 'You shouldn't have gloated over your brother when he was down-and-out' (Obadiah v.12, MSG). He goes on to say, 'As you have done, it will be done to you; your deeds will return upon your own head' (v.15). We should never gloat when an enemy falls. Rather, we should extend the same compassion as God extends to us.

Obadiah speaks of the great deliverance (vv.17, 21) that will take place on the day of the Lord (vv.8, 15). He writes, 'The day of the LORD is near' (v.15). On that day the great deliverance will take place:

> 'The remnant of the saved in Mount Zion
> will go into the mountains of Esau
> And *rule justly and fairly,*
> *a rule that honours God's kingdom'*
> (v.21, MSG).

One day, God's people will take on the reins of government and administer God's justice. They will represent God's rule in God's kingdom.

With the coming of Jesus the kingdom of God has broken into history. When Jesus returns, we will see the kingdom of God in all its fullness. On that day, all the prophecies of Obadiah and others will be fulfilled. We will be freed from all injustice.

PRAYER

Lord, thank you that, one day, justice will come for all. In the meantime, help us to fight injustice wherever we see it.

1 November | Day 305
Fix Your Thoughts

When the British people are asked who the greatest Briton of all time was, Sir Winston Churchill usually tops the poll. If you were to ask an American who the greatest American was, they might reply George Washington or Abraham Lincoln. If you asked a Jew at the start of the first century AD who the greatest Jew was, without a doubt they would have said 'Moses'. Moses was the supreme figure of their history. He had rescued them from slavery and given them the Law.

The writer of Hebrews describes to Jewish Christians how *Jesus* is greater than Moses. His argument is that, in spite of the greatness of Moses, Jesus is in a completely different league. Jesus is the 'centrepiece of everything we believe' (Hebrews 3:1, MSG); 'he has been found worthy of honour greater than Moses, just as the builder of a house has greater honour than the house itself' (v.3). 'Moses was faithful as a servant' (v.5); 'Christ is faithful as a Son over God's house' (v.6).

The themes for today's passages are trouble and distress, testing times, and trials and tribulations. However, you can see in these same scriptures that the secret to dealing with these is to '*fix your thoughts* on Jesus' (v.1).

READING FROM PSALMS

Psalm 119:137–144
Trouble and distress

At any given point in our life there is usually some area that causes us trouble and distress. It may be something you yourself are going through, or a family member, or a close friend, or something to do with your work or ministry.

I remember hearing the American pastor, Rick Warren, say how he used to think that life was a series of battles, followed by times of blessing. Now, he thinks of life as being on two tracks – one track is blessing, the other is battle. They run concurrently.

The psalmist certainly went through times of battle: 'Trouble and distress have come upon me' (v.143a).

How do we respond? The psalmist's answer is to keep trusting in the Lord. He keeps on believing that God's words are 'fully trustworthy (v.138): 'your servant loves them ... your commands are my delight' (vv.140, 143).

He fixes his thoughts upon the Lord: 'Righteous are you, O LORD' (v.137a). The great revelation of the New Testament is that 'Jesus is the Lord' (Romans 10:9). He is the one on whom you are to fix your thoughts.

PRAYER

Lord, thank you that in times of trouble and distress I can fix my thoughts on you and trust in your promises.

NEW TESTAMENT READING

Hebrews 3:1–19
Times of testing

A faith that has not been tested cannot be trusted. Sooner or later all of us go through times of testing. In these times, the challenge is to *stay faithful* to God – not to harden our hearts but to keep them soft and tender towards God – to keep on trusting in spite of all the difficulties and challenges to our faith.

During these times of testing, every time you feel like doing the wrong thing but choose to do right, you grow in spiritual maturity, wisdom, character and faithfulness.

'Moses was faithful' (v.2). But Jesus, of course, is our supreme example of faithfulness. He went through years of training and times of powerful temptation. Yet he was '*faithful* in everything God gave him to do' (v.2, MSG).

This letter was written to a group of people who were going through a time of testing and persecution. It was written to encourage them to hold on to their 'courage' and 'hope' (v.6), inspired by Jesus: 'Fix your thoughts on Jesus' (v.1).

In this passage, the writer quotes Psalm 95:7–11 (Hebrews 3:7–11). Interestingly, he does not write, 'as the Holy Spirit *said*' but, 'as the Holy Spirit *says*' (v.7). He clearly believes that the Holy Spirit continues to speak through the Scriptures in a contemporary way to the readers. As you read the Bible, *expect the Holy Spirit to speak to you today*.

In spite of the great high moment of deliverance from Egypt, the people of God had fallen away in *a time of testing* in the desert (v.17). This is a warning for us: 'See to it, brothers and sisters, that none of you has a sinful, unbelieving heart that turns away from the living God. But encourage one another daily ... so that none of you may be hardened by sin's deceitfulness' (vv.12–13).

One of the remedies to unbelief that the writer highlights here is *community*. He tells them to 'encourage one another daily' (v.13). This is why it is so important to be part of Christian community, spending time with other Christians, encouraging one another and building up your faith.

'Sin's deceitfulness' is an interesting expression. Sin is deceptive. If it were not, we would not sin. Sin is usually accompanied with a deceptive label: 'This isn't really sin, and it won't do you any harm anyway.' But, when we enter in to sin, bad patterns form, our conscience is seared and our hearts become hardened.

At the heart of sin is unbelief. Ever since the Garden of Eden, the deceitfulness of sin has caused us to doubt God's goodness, his love for us and his word – 'Did God really say?' (Genesis 3:1), 'You will not surely die' (3:4). You always swallow a lie about God before you swallow forbidden fruit. For us today, it is still the same. If we really believed God's love for us, his goodness and his word, then we would not fall for sin's deceitfulness.

Because the people of God kept on complaining, they never entered God's rest – which was the one thing they wanted. They did not trust God to provide. They were 'unbelieving' (Hebrews 3:12). They were not able to enter God's rest 'because of their unbelief' (v.19). When we do not trust God, we lose the peace of God. Find peace by fixing your thoughts on Jesus, trusting him and listening to him as he continues to speak to you through the Scriptures.

PRAYER

Lord, help me today to fix my thoughts on Jesus. Help me not to live in fear and unbelief but in trust and peace.

OLD TESTAMENT READING

Joel 1:1–2:17
When disaster strikes

'When disaster strikes, understanding of God is at risk', writes Eugene Peterson. There are times when we face unexpected illness or death of someone we love, national catastrophe, social disruption, personal loss, economic uncertainty or the devastation of natural disasters. Peterson continues: 'It is the task of the prophet to stand up at such moments of catastrophe and clarify who God is and how he acts.'[1]

The prophet Joel describes a time when disaster struck – the great devastation caused by a plague of locusts. This may have been a real event or a vision. There was a plague of locusts that hit Jerusalem in 915 BC. The devastation they caused was extraordinary.

The army of locusts is (without insecticide) unswerving, unstoppable and invincible. It ruins the vineyards, strips the orchards and, as a result, all the crops fail. The livestock then has nothing to eat. The locusts are like a tornado that moves through the land.

'What a day! Doomsday! God's Judgment Day has come' (1:15, MSG). This image of the locusts is picked up in the book of Revelation and used as a description of the tribulations of the final judgment (Revelation 9:7–11).

Jesus himself used the language from Joel 2, 'The sun and moon are darkened, and the stars no longer shine' (Joel 2:10; see also Matthew 24:29), in his description of the coming judgment.

What should our response to all this be? None of us like half-hearted apologies – nor does God. He seeks for genuine repentance:

> 'It's not too late –
>   GOD's personal message! –
> "Come back to me and really mean it!
>   Come fasting and weeping, sorry for
>   your sins!"
> Change your life, not just your clothes.
>   Come back to GOD, your God.
> And here's why: God is kind and
>   merciful.
>   He takes a deep breath, puts up with
>   a lot,
> This most patient God, extravagant in
>   love' (Joel 2:12–13, MSG).

In the midst of these prophecies of judgment, there is hope. When you turn to God and seek his forgiveness, you no longer have to fear this final judgment. Joel uses the image of a trumpet being blown to herald this day of judgment (v.1).

In the New Testament though, Paul uses this same image to describe how Jesus has conquered death, and made forgiveness and salvation possible – 'In a flash, in the twinkling of an eye, at the *last trumpet*. For the trumpet will sound, the dead will be raised imperishable and we will all be changed ... Death has been swallowed up in victory ... Thanks be to God! He gives us the victory through our Lord Jesus Christ' (1 Corinthians 15:52–57).

PRAYER

Father, thank you that you are gracious and compassionate, kind and merciful. Help me, as I await with confidence the day of his return, to fix my thoughts on Jesus.

2 November | Day 306
Destiny-defining Decisions

Every day we make decisions – what to wear, what to eat and what to do. There are little decisions and big decisions. Perhaps, for most people, the biggest decisions in life are about relationships, marriage (whether to marry and whom to marry) and work.

But these decisions pale into insignificance beside the great decision. The great decision is how you respond to God. Bernard Levin, perhaps the most influential *Times* columnist of the twentieth century, described his experience of trying to decide about the Christian faith in these terms: 'People such as me who hover on the edge of the swimming pool, simultaneously longing and fearing to jump...'[1]

All the way through the Bible, the importance of this destiny-defining decision is stressed. We can see it in all of today's passages. There is a division of destiny between those who are far and those who are near (Psalm 119). There is a division of destiny between those who hear the gospel and respond with faith, and those who do not combine it with faith (Hebrews 4:2). In the book of Joel, there is a division of destiny between those who call on the name of the Lord and those who do not (Joel 2:32).

Joel goes on to say, 'Multitudes, multitudes in the *valley of decision*! For the day of the Lord is near in the *valley of decision*' (3:14).

READING FROM PSALMS

Psalm 119:145–152
Decide to meet with God first

I love this verse: 'I rise before dawn and cry for help' (v.147). Nearly forty years ago I wrote next to it in my Bible, 'How vital it is to meet with the Lord before the day starts – "before dawn". From now on I intend always to read and pray immediately when I get up in order to be prepared for the battles each day brings.' I have not always succeeded in doing this. However, that *decision* has made a huge difference to my life.

There is a distinction, according to the psalmist, between those who are far from God and those who are near to him. The psalmist writes, 'Those who devise wicked schemes are near, but *they are far* from your law. Yet *you are near*, O Lord' (vv.150–151).

The psalmist has made a decision to 'call [to God] with all my heart ... I call out to you; save me' (vv.145–146).

As those who are out to get him come closer and closer, the psalmist is able to say: 'But you're the closest of all to me, God' (v.151, MSG).

PRAYER

Lord, thank you that you are near when I call upon you. Today, I cry out to you for help...

NEW TESTAMENT READING

Hebrews 4:1–13
Decide to believe God's promises

Are you experiencing 'God's rest' in your life? Or are you worn out trying to control everything and everyone around you? Maybe it is time to resign as general manager of the universe and start believing God's promises and trusting God to do what only he can do.

The way to find 'rest' for your soul is to listen to God's promises, believe them and show that you believe them by living in obedience to the word of God.

Many people hear the gospel. When you hear the gospel you have to make the most important decision of your life. Do you respond with faith and believe? Or do you respond by hardening your heart and disobeying?

The writer of Hebrews says, 'We received the same promises as those people in the wilderness, but the promises didn't do them a bit of good because they didn't receive the promises with faith' (v.2, MSG). He urges them not to harden their hearts (v.7) or to fall through disobedience (v.11).

God's promise to everyone who believes in the gospel is that they will enter his rest (v.1): 'If we believe ... we'll experience that state of resting' (v.3, MSG).

In this life, there will always be trials and testing. It is never going to be without times of turmoil. However, the moment that you believe the gospel, you have the promise of God's eventual and eternal rest: 'And at the end of the journey we'll surely rest with God' (v.10, MSG).

One day, every human being will have to give an account before God: 'Nothing in all creation is hidden from God's sight. Everything is uncovered and laid bare before the eyes of him to whom we must give account' (v.13).

In the meantime, you have an amazing opportunity to experience a foretaste of that 'rest' as you open your heart to the word of God, for 'the word of God is living and active. Sharper than any double-edged sword ... it judges the thoughts and attitudes of the heart' (v.12).

As you open yourself day by day, the word of God penetrates your inner being, revealing areas of your life ('the thoughts and attitudes of the heart') that you need to sort out. At times, this may seem painful and challenging. However, the purpose is to prepare you for entering God's rest.

Today, you can enjoy God's rest and peace as you trust in him and his word believing that he will take care of you and provide for all your needs.

PRAYER

Lord, I believe your promises. Thank you that I can look forward to entering into an eternity of your rest. Thank you that even now I get a foretaste of that rest.

OLD TESTAMENT READING

Joel 2:18–3:21
Decide to enjoy life in the Spirit

The prophet Joel instructs the people: 'Be glad ... Rejoice in the LORD your God' (2:23). As Joyce Meyer writes: 'Joy is the fruit of the Holy Spirit. However, it is released only by making *the decision* not to allow adverse circumstances to rule your emotional and mental attitudes. Through joy, you can receive strength to do things that would otherwise be impossible.'[2]

God makes a remarkable promise that is recalled in the New Testament: 'Everyone who calls on the name of the Lord will be saved' (2:32; see Acts 2:21; Romans 10:13).

This comes at the end of the great prophecy that Peter quoted on the day of Pentecost: 'And afterwards, I will pour out my Spirit on all people. Your sons and daughters will prophesy, your *old* men will dream dreams, your *young* men will see visions. Even on my *servants*, both *men* and *women*, I will pour out my Spirit in those days ... And everyone who calls on the name of the Lord will be saved' (Joel 2:28–32; see also Acts 2:16–21).

Others may have discriminated against you, but God does not discriminate on the basis of your age, gender or situation in life. The promise of salvation and the outpouring of the Holy Spirit is for everyone – male *and* female, young *and* old. We see this on the Alpha weekends when countless people's lives are transformed by this promised outpouring of the Holy Spirit.

There are many still in the 'valley of decision' (Joel 3:14). The decision of whether or not to call on the name of the Lord has far reaching implications. The New Testament makes absolutely clear that the name of the Lord is Jesus: 'If you confess with your mouth, "Jesus is Lord," and believe in your heart that God raised him from the dead, you will be saved ... for, "Everyone who calls on the name of the Lord will be saved"' (Romans 10:9, 13).

Joel promises those who do this that 'the Lord will be a refuge for his people' (Joel 3:16). He promises wonderful blessings. He also warns that there is a winepress of God's judgment (v.13; see Mark 4:29; Matthew 13:39). The book of Revelation refers to the wine press as a description of the judgment of Jesus on the last day.

God's hope in this passage is that the people will hear this call to make a decision and turn to him. 'It's not too late' (Joel 2:12, MSG). The Lord will 'take pity on his people' (v.18): 'I am sending you grain, new wine and oil, enough to satisfy you fully' (v.19). He promises, 'I will repay you for the years the locusts have eaten' (v.25). This is a wonderful promise, especially for those who feel that much of their life has been 'devoured by locusts'.

As Joyce Meyer puts it, God promises us 'double for our trouble'.[3] He restores, redeems, renews and revives us by his Spirit. He promises, 'In that day the mountains will drip with new wine, and the hills will flow with milk; all the ravines of Judah will run with water. A fountain will flow out of the Lord's house' (3:18, see also John 7:37–39).

This is all astonishing, good news that you can bring to those who are in the valley of decision.

PRAYER

Lord, thank you that you promise to restore the years the locusts have eaten and to pour out your Holy Spirit on me. Please fill me with your Spirit again today.

3 November | Day 307

How Can You Approach God?

The more I study it, the more I love it. The Book of Hebrews appears to be addressed to Jewish Christians. It is written in a way that seems strange to our modern ears – the language is steeped in the Old Testament. It deals with this vital question: *How can you approach God?*

The author's answer is: through Jesus, our Great High Priest. The high priesthood of Jesus is the pinnacle of the letter. It is the only New Testament document that expressly calls Jesus a Priest. The priestly work of Jesus is hinted at elsewhere, for example, the 'high priestly' prayer of Jesus in John's Gospel (John 17) and the 'beloved disciple's' description of Jesus as 'advocate with the Father' (1 John 2:1). But it is here in the book of Hebrews that the theme is taken up and expounded.

READING FROM PSALMS

Psalm 119:153–160

Approach God knowing he is loving and compassionate

God's love for humanity has always been great. 'Your compassion is great, O Lord' (v.156). The psalmist knew God's love: 'Preserve my life, O Lord, according to your love' (v.159). He knew God was a deliverer (v.153). He speaks of redemption (v.154) and salvation (v.155).

He knew God would deliver, redeem and save, and it was because of this that he knew he could approach God with confidence. What he did not know was *how* God would save him.

As we read the whole Old Testament, including this psalm, through the lens of the New Testament, we can see that what the psalmist described is made possible through the high priesthood of Jesus.

PRAYER

Lord, thank you for your great love and compassion. Thank you that through Jesus you have made it possible for me to be delivered, redeemed and saved.

NEW TESTAMENT READING

Hebrews 4:14–5:10

Approach God through Jesus, your Great High Priest

It is quite astonishing that you and I can approach the Creator of the universe with confidence and boldness. Of course, we must be respectful but we do not need to be timid or fearful. How is this possible?

As the writer introduces the central theme of his letter, the high priesthood of Jesus, he makes the point that the main purpose of his letter is to encourage them to 'hold firmly to the faith we profess' (4:14). Learning more about who Jesus is enables *you* to stand firm in *your* faith through the storms and temptations of life.

Jesus is unique. The Great High Priest is both 'the Son of God' (v.14) and fully human. He is able to *sympathise* with our weaknesses and he 'has been *tempted in every way, just as we are* – yet was without sin' (v.15).

Jesus had all the same feelings you have. There were times when he felt like doing the wrong thing, but always chose to do the right thing. As you speak to him in prayer you can know that he knows how you are feeling.

There were three necessary qualifications for the priesthood:

- humanity ('selected from among human beings', Hebrews 5:1)
- compassion ('able to deal gently', v.2)
- divine appointment ('called by God', v.4).

Jesus exactly fits the role.

But Jesus belonged to the tribe of Judah, not Levi, and therefore he lacked qualification for the normal priesthood, which was made up of descendants of Moses' brother Aaron (who was a Levite). Thus, the writer identifies him with a *new* order of priests, identified with the Old Testament character Melchizedek, who was a priest of 'God most High' and ministered to Abraham (Genesis 14:18–20).

The book of Hebrews shows how in every way the priesthood of Melchizedek was superior to that of Aaron (see Hebrews 7). Because Jesus' priesthood is like Melchizedek, it is *eternal* (5:6). It is therefore effective for all time. It affects those who lived before Jesus, as well as everyone who lives after him.

Jesus is our representative (v.1). He is both the model priest and far superior to any other priest.

Jesus gained experience through the things he suffered (v.9). God uses everything in your path, however painful, for you to gain experience. You can learn to use your pain for someone else's gain.

Rick Warren writes, 'God loves to turn crucifixions into resurrections. The things you wish were most removed from your life are often the very things that God is using to shape you and make you into the believer he wants you to be. He wants to use that problem for good in your life. There's something more important than your pain. It's what you're learning from that pain.'[1]

Like us, Jesus gained experience through what he suffered. However, unlike us, he is without sin. Therefore, he did not need to offer sacrifices for his own sins. He is 'the source of eternal salvation for all who obey him' (v.9).

You can '*approach the throne of grace with confidence*, so that [you] may receive mercy and find grace to help [you] in [your] time of need' (v.16). As you ask for forgiveness for the past – you can know that you will receive '*mercy*'. As you ask for help for the future you can know that you will receive '*grace to help*' you in whatever your needs are and whatever difficulties you are facing at the moment.

The image of the throne is a way of emphasising the majesty and glory of the one who sits on it – God. Yet *through Jesus* you can approach God in prayer and worship no matter how you are feeling or what you have done.

PRAYER

Lord Jesus Christ, thank you that through your sacrifice I can approach the throne of grace with confidence, receive mercy and find grace to help me in my time of need.

OLD TESTAMENT READING

Ezekiel 1:1–3:27
Approach the throne of grace with confidence

What an amazing thing to be told that we can approach the heavenly throne at all – let alone 'with confidence' (Hebrews 4:16)! The prophet Ezekiel (whose name means 'God is strong') caught a glimpse of this throne: 'There was something that looked like a *throne*, sky-blue like a sapphire, with a *humanlike figure towering above the throne* ... from the waist up he looked like burnished bronze and from the waist down like a blazing fire. Brightness everywhere! ... It turned out to be the Glory of God! When I saw all this, I fell to my knees, my face to the ground. Then I heard a voice' (Ezekiel 1:26–28, MSG).

Ezekiel was called by God (in 593 BC) at the age of 30 (v.1). He was a priest (v.3). He was a Jewish exile in Babylonia (whereas Jeremiah was in Jerusalem). He was taken captive with the young king Jehoiachin in 597 BC (2 Kings 24:8–17). Like Jeremiah he called the people to repentance and foretold the eventual rebuilding of Jerusalem.

Ezekiel's call begins with a vision of God. In the vision he sees four strange creatures (Ezekiel 1:10). Each one is a witness to part of the character of God.

The first has the face of a *human being*, the second a *lion*, representing strength and courage, the third an *ox*, representing fertility, and the fourth an *eagle*, representing speed. Together they point to the awesome majesty and greatness of God (v.10).

In this vision, Ezekiel catches a glimpse of a man – who we now know was *Jesus* (Revelation 4:1–10).

Ezekiel's response to the vision of the throne of grace is to fall flat on his face (Ezekiel 1:28). This was not an unusual response to the presence of God (see, for example, Revelation 4:10).

God speaks to him (Ezekiel 2:1). The Holy Spirit enters Ezekiel (v.2). He is given the words of God to devour (3:1): 'So I ate it, and it tasted as sweet as honey in my mouth' (v.3b). He is told to go and speak the message that God has given.

He is to face great opposition but is told, '*Do not be afraid* of them or terrified by them' (v.9). It is not his responsibility 'whether they listen or fail to listen' (v.11b). Your responsibility, like Ezekiel, is simply to speak the message that God gives you.

You are not responsible for the reaction of others (vv.18–21) but you will be held accountable for whether or not you obey God and speak the words that God has given you (vv.18, 20). Sometimes you don't know what the outcome will be in a certain situation, but you can trust and obey God no matter what.

Later on, the glory of the Lord appears to Ezekiel again and he falls face down (v.23). Again, the Spirit enters him (v.24). God promises, 'When I speak to you, I will open your mouth and you shall say to them, "This is what the Sovereign LORD says"' (v.27).

PRAYER

Lord, thank you for this immense privilege: that I can approach the throne of grace with confidence, talk with you and hear your message. Help me to speak your words today.

4 November | Day 308
Warnings

These days, practically everything you buy seems to carry some kind of *warning* on it. Some of these warnings can seem a little ridiculous. For example:

Sainsbury's *peanuts*: 'Warning – Contains *nuts*'
Nytol Nighttime *Sleep-Aid*: 'Warning – May cause *drowsiness*'
On a household *DIY drill*: 'Not intended for use as *dentist drill*'[1]

Because so many warnings seem almost absurd, the danger is that we ignore them. But not all warnings are so ridiculous.

A foggy day, on 13 March 1991, led to one of Britain's worst road accidents. Ten people died and twenty-five people were injured in a disaster on the M4 motorway. In the midst of the accident, one man was hailed as a hero. Alan Bateman climbed out of his damaged car and ran along the central reservation to try to *warn* oncoming vehicles of the wreckage ahead. Not all appreciated the warnings. Some drivers sounded their horns at him and drove on towards the crash.

Alan's warnings to the other drivers were not only heroic; they were an *act of love*. Jesus himself often warned of dangers ahead (see for example Matthew 7:13, 19, 26–27). Jesus knew that in the long run it is more loving to warn people by telling them the truth.

God loves you. He does not want you to get hurt. There are many warnings in the Bible and they all stem from God's love for you.

READING FROM PROVERBS

Proverbs 26:23–27:4
Warnings about human nature

It is an almost invariable principle of life that what you sow now, you reap later. Much of the teaching in this section of Proverbs is summed up by the verse: 'If you dig a pit, you will fall into it; if you roll a stone, it will roll back on you' (26:27). In other words, you reap what you sow.

The writer warns against malice: 'Malice backfires; spite boomerangs' (v.27, MSG). However much we try to conceal our desire to hurt other people, it will eventually be exposed: and we will reap the consequences.

Next, he warns against 'a lying tongue' (v.28). Be very careful that you only speak the truth about others. It is sometimes tempting to tell exaggerated stories about our opponents. But the writer warns, 'A lying tongue *hates* those it *hurts*' (v.28).

He goes on to warn about boasting (27:1). Don't boast about what you are going to achieve, as you don't know what the future will hold. It is all right to receive praise from others but it should not come from your own lips (v.2).

Then, he warns against provoking people: 'Stone is heavy and sand a burden, but provocation by a fool is heavier than both' (v.3).

Finally, in this passage, he warns about jealousy, which Shakespeare described as 'the green-eyed monster' that mocks 'the meat it feeds on'.[2] Jealousy is an even more powerful and dangerous force than anger and fury (v.4): 'We're blasted by anger and swamped by rage, but who can survive jealousy?' (v.4, MSG).

PRAYER

Lord, guard my heart. Forgive me my sins as I forgive those who sin against me. Lead me not into temptation but deliver me from evil.

NEW TESTAMENT READING

Hebrews 5:11–6:12
Warnings about immaturity

God's desire for you is that you 'grow up in Christ' (v.11, MSG) into a healthy, strong, spiritually mature follower of Jesus.

Maturity requires a listening attitude. The Christians addressed here have 'picked up the bad habit of not listening' (v.11, MSG). God is continually speaking to us (Matthew 4:4). Develop a regular habit of listening to him as he speaks to you, primarily through the Bible.

The writer of Hebrews warns his readers against *spiritual immaturity*. They 'ought to be teachers' (5:12). This does not mean a specialised group. Anyone instructed in the faith was expected to teach others (1 Peter 3:15). One of the best ways to start growing in your faith is to pass it on to others. This is why we often invite those who have encountered Jesus on Alpha to come back and help on the next course.

He wants them to move on from milk to solid food. Teaching is part of Christian maturity. He encourages them to move on from the elementary teachings about Christ: repentance, faith, baptism, laying on of hands, the resurrection and judgment (Hebrews 6:1–2).

This is a striking list of what the writer considers to be the basics, and it is a challenge to all of us who teach in the church. We need to ensure that we are indeed training all people in these things, and then moving them on to 'solid food' (5:14). You feed yourself through, for example, worship, church community, Bible study, reading inspiring books and listening to good teaching.

He says, 'Solid food is for the mature, who by constant *use* have trained themselves to distinguish good from evil' (v.14). In other words, maturity comes through practice – applying God's words to our lives. As John Wimber used to say, 'The meat is on the street.' Maturity is not just about head knowledge. You learn as you live out your faith. You learn discernment 'on the street', and that enables you to receive the 'meat'.

He then warns them of the *danger of* abandoning, or renouncing, their faith (6:4–8). This is a very difficult passage, as at first sight it seems to suggest both that a Christian *can* fall away, and that there is a group of people for whom repentance is impossible. These are two things that the rest of the New Testament makes clear are *not* the case (see especially Romans 5–8).

His main aim is to encourage perseverance. The severity of these warnings (Hebrews 6:4–8) makes clear how important this is. However, the point about falling away is not developed because he is confident that they will *not* do so – 'I'm sure that won't happen to you, friends' (v.9, MSG).

He then congratulates them for the fruit they are showing in their lives. Their acts of kindness are already reckoned by God as if they were done to himself (v.10). He will reward them.

They have started well and now he encourages them to finish well – 'to show this same diligence to the very end' (v.11).

Generally, in life, it is much easier to start things than to finish them. When the initial enthusiasm wears off, follow-through requires hard work, patience and courage. Success, fruitfulness and reward come to those 'who stay the course with committed faith and then get everything promised to them' (v.12, MSG).

PRAYER

Lord, help me to grow into spiritual maturity. Help me to imitate those who through faith and patience inherit what has been promised' (v.12).

OLD TESTAMENT READING

Ezekiel 4:1–6:14
Warnings about judgment

From the start, it is clear that warning people is never an easy job! This passage is all about God *warning* his people about what is going to happen to them. Furthermore, what is about to happen to Israel is intended to be 'a *warning* ... to the nations' (5:15).

Ezekiel is asked to enact visual aids to show the seriousness of sin and the warning of the impending judgment that will happen if the people do not repent.

Ezekiel must have appeared to be rather eccentric. Lying on his side for a total of 430 days (4:5–6) must have seemed a little odd – but it was a powerful visual aid. (It has probably *always* been the case that people are more likely to remember what they see than what they hear.) Judgment was coming because the people of God had 'not even conformed to the standards of the nations around [them]' (5:7).

God never issues empty threats: 'I did not threaten in vain' (6:10). God's warnings are always acts of love. He desires that all people should repent and 'come to the knowledge of truth' (1 Timothy 2:4).

Today, we are so worried about sounding negative or judgmental that there is a danger of us being unloving by not being sufficiently bold in warning people of the dangers ahead.

It was love for God *and* for God's people that caused Ezekiel to carry out these visual demonstrations warning of God's judgment ahead. Ezekiel was told to 'bear the sin' of the people (Ezekiel 4:4–6). This visual aid was also a sign of what was to come. Jesus did what Ezekiel was only able to foreshadow. Jesus bore your sins on the cross (1 Peter 2:24). He took the judgment of God upon himself and enabled you and me to receive all the wonderful promises of blessing for those in Christ.

The life, death and resurrection of Jesus changed everything, yet the warnings for us are still real and serious. Indeed, these warnings make the reality of salvation and the many blessings available in Christ all the more amazing. The gospel is great news.

PRAYER

Lord, give me wisdom in how I communicate the good news of Jesus with sensitivity and faithfulness. Give me courage to proclaim the whole counsel of God.

5 November | Day 309
The Promises of God

Billy Bray, born in 1794, was a miner from Cornwall. He was an alcoholic. He was always getting involved with fights and arguments at home. At the age of twenty-nine he encountered Jesus. He went home and told his wife, 'You will never see me drunk again, by the help of the Lord.' She never did.

His words, his tone of voice and his looks all had magnetic power. It was as if he was charged with divine electricity. Crowds of miners would come and hear him preach. Many were converted and there were some remarkable healings. He loved the Bible and said, '*The promises of God* are just as good as ready money any day.'

God is the God of promise. Faith involves trusting the promises of God. God makes a promise; faith believes it, hope anticipates it, patience quietly waits for it.

READING FROM PSALMS

Psalm 119:161–168
Find joy, satisfaction and peace in God's promises

The psalmist says, '*Great peace* have they who love your law, and nothing can make them stumble' (v.165). I remember one young atheist who came on Alpha speaking of the feeling of emptiness and a void in her life. What she noticed about Christians was that they had great *peace*. She recognised that this came from faith.

The last place many people would expect to find peace, satisfaction and joy is through the words of the Bible. Yet the psalmist says,

'I *rejoice* in your *promise* like one who finds great spoil' (v.162).

The writer describes the words of God using many different expressions. He speaks of 'your word' (v.161), 'your law' (vv.163, 165), 'your commands' (v.166), 'your statutes' (vv.167, 168) and 'your precepts' (v.168). But here he describes the word of God as 'your *promise*' (v.162).

The words of God are his promises to you. Discovering them is like discovering a great treasure trove. As you keep digging into it you will find more and more amazing and beautiful treasures. This leads the psalmist on to say, 'Seven times a day I praise you' (v.164).

PRAYER

Lord, I praise you for the great treasures that are in your words. Please give me peace today as I trust in your promises.

NEW TESTAMENT READING

Hebrews 6:13–7:10
Trust in God's promises and wait patiently

Abraham waited for 25 years. Joseph waited 13 years. Moses waited 25 years. Jesus waited 30 years. If God makes you wait you are in good company.

I have often found the gap between the promise of God and its fulfilment to be much longer than I had anticipated. I am learning to be more patient. God's promises to us are the anchor of our souls (6:19). They are solid and secure. He keeps his word, even when it seems impossible, even when the circumstances seem to point to the opposite. Delay does not negate the promises of God.

Abraham is described as, 'him who had *the promises*' (7:6). When Abraham and Sarah were called by God, he *promised* that from them would come a great nation. He *promised* them children. But they had to wait many years before the promise was fulfilled. They waited and waited. They went down wrong paths to try to fulfil God's promise through human means. However, eventually, 'The Lord did for Sarah what he had *promised*' (Genesis 21:1). Abraham was a hundred years old! Finally, God fulfilled his *promise:* 'After waiting *patiently*, Abraham received what was *promised*' (Hebrews 6:15).

God's promises are absolutely certain: 'When people make promises, they guarantee them by appeal to some authority above them ... When God wanted to guarantee his promises, he gave his word, a rock-solid guarantee' (vv.16–17, MSG).

Your hope is not based on some vague optimism or wishful thinking. It is *trust in the unbreakable promises of God*. It centres on *Jesus*, who is 'a high priest for ever, in the order of Melchizedek' (v.20). Melchizedek appears from nowhere in Genesis and we know nothing about what happens to him afterwards. He foreshadowed Jesus: 'Resembling the Son of God, he continues to be a priest without interruption and without successor' (7:3, AMP).

The writer demonstrates the superiority of Jesus (Melchizedek's priesthood) to that of any other priest (of Levi) (vv.1–10).

Jesus, a priest in the order of Melchizedek, is a righteous king of peace. Melchizedek's name means '*king of righteousness*' and he was also 'king of Salem', which means '*king of peace*' (v.2).

Jesus' priesthood is *permanent*. No 'end of life' is recorded for Melchizedek (vv.3, 8). Likewise, Jesus is a living priest for ever. Psalm 110 also declares that the Lord is a 'priest for ever in the order of Melchizedek' (v.4).

Jesus (Melchizedek) received a tithe from Abraham (Hebrews 7:4). This spontaneous gift from Abraham showed that he realised his own inferiority to Melchizedek. Levi was Abraham's great-grandson. An ancestor is regarded in biblical thought as containing within himself all his descendants (vv.9–10). Therefore, the priesthood of Jesus (Melchizedek) enjoys a higher status than that of the Levitical priesthood.

Melchizedek gave Abraham a blessing (vv.6–7). God had promised that in Abraham all the nations of the world would be blessed (Genesis 22:18). Therefore, if Melchizedek could bless Abraham, Melchizedek's status must be superior to the Levitical order (Hebrews 7:7).

Jesus' priesthood, 'in the order of Melchizedek', reminds us that we can trust that the promises of God are totally secure. Jesus guaranteed them for us by going where we could not, 'on our behalf'. He is your 'high priest for ever, in the order of Melchizedek' (6:20).

PRAYER

Lord, thank you that even though I sometimes have to wait patiently, you always fulfil your promises – they are firm and secure – an anchor for my soul.

OLD TESTAMENT READING

Ezekiel 7:1–9:11
Listen to God's promises and feed on them

Those who feed on God's promises will never spiritually starve. But many people put their trust in the wrong things. Some put their trust in money for security. However, God says that 'their silver and gold will not be able to save them' (7:19a). Their wealth 'will not satisfy their hunger' (v.19b).

Aristotle Onassis, one of the richest people in the world, said at the end of his life: 'Millions do not always add up to what a man needs out of life.'[1] Many people try to fill the emptiness deep inside of them in ways that ultimately do not satisfy. They are looking for joy in the wrong places.

Wealth, far from bringing satisfaction and joy, can often lead us into pride, sin and idolatry (vv.1–11). Furthermore, wealth will never provide total security. A downturn in the market and rampant inflation can lead to even a whole country becoming bankrupt (vv.12–20).

On the other hand, the promises of God are rock solid. What God says, *he promises*. Ezekiel declared the *promises of God* saying: 'The word of the Lord came to me: "Son of man, this is what the Sovereign Lord says…"' (vv.1–2). His message is 'the end of business as usual' (v.2, MSG).

Ezekiel promises God's judgment. It will be absolutely just: 'I will deal with them according to their conduct, and *by their own standards* I will judge them' (v.27; see also Romans 2:1). This will take place 'on the day when God will judge everyone's secrets through Jesus Christ' (Romans 2:16).

Ezekiel caught a glimpse of the one who will judge the world: 'I looked, and I saw a figure like that of a man. From what appeared to be his waist down he was like fire, and from there up his appearance was as bright as glowing metal' (Ezekiel 8:2). This description is close to the description of Jesus in Revelation 1:10–16.

The only way to escape the judgment is to have a mark on the forehead (Ezekiel 9:4). The Lord said, 'Go throughout the city of Jerusalem and put a mark on the foreheads of those who grieve and lament over all the detestable things that are done in it … do not touch anyone who has the mark' (vv.4, 6).

The person with a mark on their forehead had a mark of protection as the impending judgment drew near. The word for 'mark' is the Hebrew letter *tav*. This is the last letter of the Hebrew alphabet. At the time, the letter would have been written X – a cross. Is this a coincidence? Or is there some significance in the fact that those who were protected were those who had the sign of the cross on their foreheads?

In Revelation, we read of the angel calling out, 'Do not harm the land or the sea or the trees until we put a seal on the foreheads of the servants of our God' (Revelation 7:3; see also Revelation 9:4; 14:1).

PRAYER

Lord, thank you that you bore my sin and judgment on the cross. Thank you that you put a mark on my forehead. Thank you that I can trust in your promises for the future and have this hope as the anchor for my soul.

6 November | Day 310
It's Who You Know

During the American Civil War, as a result of a family tragedy, a soldier was granted permission to seek a hearing from the President. He wanted to request exemption from military service. However, when he arrived at the White House, he was refused entry and sent away. He went and sat in a nearby park.

A young boy came across him and remarked how unhappy he looked. The soldier found himself telling the young boy everything. Eventually the boy said, 'Come with me.' He led the dejected soldier back to the White House. They went around the back, none of the guards stopped them. Even the generals and high-ranking government officials stood to attention and let them pass through.

The soldier was amazed. Finally, they came to the presidential office. Without knocking, the young boy opened the door and walked straight in. Abraham Lincoln, standing there, turned from his conversation with the Secretary of State and said, 'What can I do for you, Tad?' Tad said, '*Dad*, this soldier needs to talk to you.'[1]

The soldier had *access* to the President *'through the son'*. According to the New Testament, in an even more amazing way, you have *access* to *God 'through the son'* – Jesus.

Many people pray, but not all prayer is Christian. Christian prayer is distinctive – it is Trinitarian. St Paul writes, '*Through him* [Jesus] we have *access to the Father by one Spirit*' (Ephesians 2:18).

This is why prayer is such an immense privilege. You are able to speak to God, the creator of the universe, *as your Father*. You come to him *through Jesus*, the man who is God, our Lord, brother and friend. Your prayers are inspired by *the Holy Spirit of God,* who lives within your heart.

READING FROM PSALMS

Psalm 119:169–176
***Access* ... to the Father**

When I first encountered Jesus, I was taught a model for prayer using the mnemonic 'A.C.T.S.': Adoration, Confession, Thanksgiving and Supplication (see also BiOY Day 61, p.127). Each of these is represented in this passage.

The psalmist's prayer is addressed to God. Jesus teaches us to address God as our Father. As Psalm 119 draws to a close, the psalmist prays a variety of prayers, which include 'A.C.T.S.':

A Adoration
Praise God for who he is and what he has done.
'Let me live *that I may praise You*' (v.175, AMP).

C Confession
Ask God's forgiveness for anything that you have done wrong.
'*I have gone astray* like a lost sheep' (v.176, AMP).

T Thanksgiving
Thank God for health, family, friends and so on.
'My lips shall pour forth praise (with *thanksgiving* and renewed trust)' (v.171, AMP).

S Supplication
Pray for yourself, for your friends and for others.
'May my *supplication* come before you' (v.170).

PRAYER

A – Lord God our Father, I adore you. I love you Lord. I praise you that I have access to you, the Creator of the universe.
C – I confess my sins to you and ask for your forgiveness...
T – Thank you so much for all the blessings in my life. Thank you for my family and friends. Thank you for so many wonderful answers to prayer. Thank you for...
S – Lord, I pray today for...

NEW TESTAMENT READING

Hebrews 7:11–28
***Access* ... through Jesus**

Jesus 'brings us right into the presence of God' (v.19, MSG). Access to the Father is made possible through Jesus. You can '*draw near to God*' (v.19). Jesus is the great high priest who makes it possible for you to '*come to God through him*' (v.25).

Jesus is the Son, 'who has been made perfect for ever' (v.28). He provides you with a 'better' hope (v.19). The word 'better' appears numerous times in the book of Hebrews. The writer is constantly contrasting; not something bad with something good, but something good with something 'perfect' and therefore far 'better'.

Jesus' priesthood is based on a superior *promise*. The writer quotes Psalm 110:4 to show how Jesus' priesthood was established through *a promise of God*. Unlike the temporary former priests, Jesus' priesthood was confirmed by God's *promise* (Hebrews 7:20–21). Jesus perfectly meets all your needs (v.26).

1. Jesus has defeated death for you
It is 'by the sheer force of resurrection life – he lives!' (v.16). Unlike the former priests, Jesus lives for ever, and his priesthood is permanent (vv.23–24).

2. Jesus is constantly praying for you
Jesus continually intercedes for those who come to God through him: 'He is always living to make petition to God and

intercede with him and intervene for them' (v.25b, AMP).

Robert Murray M'Cheyne (1813–1843) wrote: 'If I could hear Christ praying for me in the next room, I would not fear a million enemies. Yet distance makes no difference. He is praying for me.'[2]

3. Jesus is uniquely able to represent you

The priests had to offer sacrifices for their sin first, but Jesus was 'completely holy, uncompromised by sin, with authority extending as high as God's presence in heaven itself' (v.26, MSG). He is the unique mediator who is fully God and fully human.

4. Jesus offered the perfect sacrifice for your sins

'Unlike the other high priests he does not need to offer sacrifices day after day, first for his own sins, and then for the sins of the people' (v.27). When Jesus offered himself on the cross, it was only necessary for this sacrifice to be offered once, since it was totally effective: 'He sacrificed for their sins *once for all* when he offered *himself*' (v.27).

Jesus' qualities of a superior life, a superior promise, a superior 'offerer' and a superior offering, all demonstrate that his priesthood is totally effective in providing you *access to the Father*. As a result of Jesus' permanent and perfect priesthood, you can 'draw near to God' (v.19). You can, 'come to God *through him*' (v.25).

PRAYER

Father, thank you that I can draw near to you today through Jesus and that I can know that he is constantly praying for me.

OLD TESTAMENT READING

Ezekiel 10:1–12:28
***Access*... by the Holy Spirit**

As you pray, the Holy Spirit, who lives in you, helps you to pray. It is an extraordinary privilege to be living in this time when every Christian has the Holy Spirit living within them. Before the day of Pentecost (which we read about in Acts 2), the Holy Spirit only came on particular people at particular times for particular tasks.

Ezekiel was one of those particular people. Extraordinary visions of God were given to him *by the Spirit* who lifted him up. Twice in this passage he says, 'Then *the Spirit lifted me up*...' (11:1, 24). It was 'the *Spirit of the* LORD' who 'came upon' him and 'told' him what 'to say': 'This is what the LORD says...' (v.5).

Ezekiel went on to prophesy that one day the Spirit of God would not only be in him, but will be in *all the people*: 'I will give them an undivided heart and *put a new spirit in them*; I will remove from them their *heart of stone* and give them a *heart of flesh*' (v.19).

God has given every human being a conscience. However, if we rebel against our conscience too often we become hard-hearted. If, for example, we have been hurt by others, we can harden our hearts in an attempt to block further emotional pain.

It is almost impossible to change your heart simply through a decision of the will. But God promises to give you a 'soft heart' – 'a heart of flesh' (v.19). He does this by putting a new Spirit in you (this is the Holy Spirit, see Ezekiel 36:26–27). The Holy Spirit now lives in you. He changes your heart. He replaces a heart of stone with a heart of flesh.

The Holy Spirit pours God's love into your heart (Romans 5:5). He heals your hurts and wounds and makes your heart tender. He gives you a 'soft heart' that is responsive to his gentle touch and filled with love and sensitivity to the needs of others.

These prophecies of Ezekiel were fulfilled on the day of Pentecost. In the book of Acts, the apostle Peter explains that the promises (including those in Ezekiel) have been fulfilled: 'Exalted to the right hand of God, he has received from the Father *the promised Holy Spirit* and poured out what you now see and hear' (Acts 2:33).

From that moment onwards, everyone who puts their faith in Jesus has the Holy Spirit living within them. This remains the same for all Christians today. He promises you an undivided heart, a new spirit and a heart of flesh. He says therefore, you will obey and you will be part of God's people and he will be your God. It is by the same Holy Spirit that you have access to the Father through Jesus (Ephesians 2:18).

PRAYER

Lord, give me an undivided heart. Help me today to be careful to follow your decrees and to keep your laws. Thank you that you help me to pray – to the Father, through Jesus, by the Holy Spirit.

7 November | Day 311
The Answer to Loneliness

I remember reading an article in *The Big Issue* (the magazine sold by, and in aid of, the homeless) called 'Single Lives'. It pointed out that most people's image of loneliness in London is of a frail old lady stuck on the twenty-fourth floor of a block of flats. In reality, it could equally be a young, fashionably dressed guy trying desperately to make conversation with a girl standing next to him in a crowded bar. Being surrounded by so many people only compounds the feeling of isolation.

Mother Teresa said, 'Loneliness and the feeling of being uncared for and unwanted are the greatest poverty.'[1] Loneliness is one of the greatest problems facing humanity today.

'The solitary human being is a contradiction in terms,' writes Desmond Tutu. He continues, 'We are made for complementarity. We are created for a delicate network of relationships, of interdependence with our fellow human beings ... We belong in one family – God's family, the human family ... the greatest good is communal harmony.'[2]

God does not intend for you to be lonely and isolated. Loneliness has been described as 'a homesickness for God'. God created you for community – calling you into a loving relationship with him and with other human beings.

READING FROM PSALMS

Psalm 120:1–7
A peaceful community

We live in a world full of aggression, division and broken relationships.

One of the main reasons for loneliness is 'quarrelling' (v.6, MSG), which leads to the breakdown of relationships. We see this wherever we look – broken marriages, family bust-ups, fall-outs between friends, work colleagues and neighbours.

Adam and Eve's friendship with God was broken. This led to a separation between Adam and Eve themselves. Cain and Abel quarrelled, and the rest is history.

The psalmist is feeling isolated as though living in a foreign land (v.5). Do you ever feel like him? He is surrounded by lying lips and deceitful tongues (v.2). The people he lives among hate peace (v.6) and are for war (v.7). Do you ever feel doomed to live your life among 'quarrelling neighbours'? (v.6, MSG).

In your distress, call out to the Lord to save you and the Lord will answer you (v.1). In contrast to those around you, be a person of peace (v.7). This is the characteristic of the people of God: Jesus said, 'Blessed are the peacemakers, for they will be called children of God' (Matthew 5:9).

PRAYER

Lord, help me to avoid unnecessary quarrelling and to be a peacemaker in my family, workplace and community.

NEW TESTAMENT READING

Hebrews 8:1–13
A 'new' community

The local church is 'the world's hope'.[3] The church in the New Testament is described as 'the people of God'. The people of God gather in local churches all over the world. The writer of Hebrews quotes the book of Jeremiah saying, 'I will be their God, and they will be *my people*' (v.10). No longer isolated and alone, you are part of the most amazing community.

In the Old Testament, God made a covenant with his people. However, the people did not 'keep their part of the bargain' (v.9, MSG). God promised that one day he would make a new covenant whereby he would have a new relationship with his people: 'I will be their God, and they will be *my people*' (v.10).

You are far better off now than they were under the old covenant. The writer goes on to say, 'The ministry Jesus has received is as *superior* to theirs as the covenant of which he is mediator is *superior* to the old one, and it is founded on *better promises*' (v.6).

There was a problem with the old covenant, for 'if there had been nothing wrong with that first covenant, no place would have been sought for another' (v.7). The problem with the old covenant was that the people were unable to keep the law. They 'did not remain faithful' (v.9).

God promised a new covenant that would be superior to the old one and founded on better promises. The writer quotes the promises from the book of Jeremiah (Hebrews 31:31–34).

What were these promises? They are fourfold:

1. New thinking
God promises to implant his laws in your heart. This does not mean simply committing the law to memory (as per Deuteronomy 6:6–9). It means having a renewed heart, 'I will put my laws in their minds and write them on their hearts' (Hebrews 8:10b).

2. Firsthand knowledge
He promises that the knowledge of God will be a matter of personal experience. 'No longer will they teach their neighbours, or say to one another, "Know the Lord," because they will all know me' (v.11). It is possible for you to know God in the way that Jeremiah knew God: 'They'll all get to know me firsthand' (v.11, MSG).

3. Universal scope
'They will *all* know me, from the least of them to the greatest' (v.11b). This was a fulfilment of the promise in the Old Testament that the promise would no longer be confined to Israel and Judah but would extend to all nations (Isaiah 42:6; 49:6; 19:24).

4. Total forgiveness
'For I will forgive their wickedness and will remember their sins no more' (Hebrews 8:12). For the Hebrews, the word 'remembering' meant more than mental effort; it carried with it the sense of doing something to the advantage or disadvantage of the person who remembered. If your sins are not remembered, it means that God is determined to forgive and that the 'slate' of your sins is 'forever wiped clean' (v.12, MSG). All this is possible because Jesus offered his life for you (v.13).

This new covenant is far superior and 'has made the first one obsolete; and what is obsolete and ageing will soon disappear' (v.13).

The new covenant is the basis of the new community into which God calls you. This new covenant is the answer to loneliness. The covenant is with God's people together and not solely with each individual person. The promises are all in the plural. You have the immense privilege of belonging to the new community of God's people. You know God personally. Your sins are forgiven. The Holy Spirit has come to live within you and given you a renewed heart. You are never alone.

PRAYER

Father, thank you that I am never alone. Thank you that I can experience a personal relationship with you and be part of the most wonderful community of the people of God.

OLD TESTAMENT READING

Ezekiel 13:1–15:8
A faithful community

The great idols of our age are money, sex and power. But an idol can be anything we worship by giving it more attention and treating it as more important than God in our lives. It could be your home, car or possessions but it could also be your work or ministry. When we make an idol out of any of these things, it takes us away from God (14:14).

God is looking for people who are faithful to him. The problem under the old covenant was that 'they *did not remain faithful*' (Hebrews 8:9). God spoke through Ezekiel about a country that 'sins against me by being *unfaithful*... they have been *unfaithful*, declares the Sovereign Lord' (Ezekiel 14:13; 15:8).

Ezekiel, the prophet, saw ahead to what we have read about in our New Testament passage for today. He foresaw a time when the people 'will not defile themselves any more with all their sins. They will be *my people*, and I will be their God, declares the Sovereign Lord' (14:11).

God's people were ensnared by lies. As we read in the psalm about 'lying lips' (Psalm 120:2), so we read here about lying prophets 'who prophesy out of their own imagination' (Ezekiel 13:2). 'Their visions are false and their divinations a lie' (v.6). Using 'magic charms' they 'ensnare people' (v.18). They lie 'to my people, who listen to lies' (v.19). They dishearten the righteous with their lies (v.22).

How had they been unfaithful? The Lord said that they 'set up idols in their hearts and put wicked stumbling-blocks before their faces' (14:3). Even in the Old Testament, the Lord was not concerned only about physical idols – but also about the idols in people's hearts. God's longing is for us to be a faithful vine bearing good fruit (chapter 15; see also Isaiah 5:1–7).

You are called to be part of a faithful community who know and love God. Welcome everyone 'from the least of them to the greatest' (Hebrews 8:11). We are called to be a community where many lonely, isolated people find love and forgiveness – a community of the people of God – a people of peace who know and love the Lord and are faithful to him in every way. This is the answer to loneliness.

PRAYER

Lord, help me to be faithful to you. Help us to be a loving, peaceful and faithful community where many isolated and lonely people come to know you and find, in the community of God's people, the answer to loneliness.

8 November | Day 312
Meet Your Blood Donor

Our god-daughter's second child, Hazy, was diagnosed with leukaemia in 2015. Medically, her only hope was a matching donor. A young German man, who has to remain anonymous, sacrificially gave his bone marrow. Wonderfully, his donation saved Hazy's life. Can you imagine what it would be like for Hazy to meet her donor?[1]

In an even more remarkable way, *you* can meet *your* blood donor. Jesus came 'to *give his life* as a ransom for many' (Mark 10:45). At the Last Supper, when Jesus took the cup, he said: '*This is my blood* of the covenant' (Matthew 26:28; Mark 14:24). The '*precious blood of Christ*' (1 Peter 1:19) is stressed throughout the whole New Testament:

- it makes *forgiveness* possible (Colossians 1:14)
- it *purifies* you from every sin (1 John 1:7)
- through it, you *draw near to God* (Ephesians 2:13)
- it brings *peace and reconciliation* (Colossians 1:20)
- it *gives life* (John 6:53)
- it enables you to *overcome Satan* (Revelation 12:11).

In today's passages, we see different aspects of what all of this means.

READING FROM PROVERBS

Proverbs 27:5–14
The ultimate act of friendship

It is such a privilege to have good friends. The greatest privilege of all is the friendship of Jesus. He calls you his friend and shed his blood as the ultimate act of friendship. Jesus said, 'Greater love has no one than this, to lay down one's life for one's *friends*' (John 15:13).

This section of Proverbs is all about the importance of friendship: 'Better a nearby friend than a distant relative' (Proverbs 27:10, MSG). The advice of a friend is a great blessing: 'Just as lotions and fragrance give sensual delight, a sweet friendship *refreshes the soul*' (v.9, MSG). Loyalty to your friends is very important: 'Do not forsake your *friend* and the *friend* of your parent' (v.10).

A good friend will not only say nice things: 'Better is open rebuke than hidden love' (v.5). The writer of Proverbs goes on to say, 'Wounds from a friend can be trusted' (v.6). True friendship involves more than unquestioning approval. I am so grateful to my good friends who have confronted me with painful truth from time to time – always out of love and with great sensitivity and grace.

'Wounds' is used here figuratively, in the sense of causing emotional pain or grief to a friend for their good, out of love. However, I cannot help thinking, in the light of today's theme, of the fact that 'wounding', in the literal understanding of the word, means 'shedding blood'. In the case of Jesus, he did not shed our blood, but his own. 'He was *wounded* for our transgressions' (Isaiah 53:5). His blood was shed for you in the ultimate act of friendship.

PRAYER

Lord, thank you so much for friends and, most of all, for your great friendship. Thank you that you were willing to lay down your life and shed your blood for me.

NEW TESTAMENT READING

Hebrews 9:1–15
A clear conscience

'Most people, most of the time, have something which hangs heavy on their hearts, something they have done or said which they wish they hadn't, something which haunts them and makes them afraid of being found out,' writes Bishop Tom Wright. 'How wonderful to know that the sacrifice of Jesus and *the sprinkled blood* which results from it has the power as we accept it in faith and trust, to wash every stain from the conscience so that we can come to God without any shadow falling across our relationship.'[2]

The book of Hebrews explains how under the old covenant, only the high priest could enter the Most Holy Place 'only once a year [on the day of atonement], and never *without blood'* (v.7). The blood of a sacrifice represented the life of the animal that had been killed ('the life is in the blood', Leviticus 17:11). Their life was given in exchange for that of the person making the sacrifice.

The priests were not allowed to enter the Most Holy Place. Their work was done in the outer tent. Except on the annual occasion, the way into the throne room of God was barred to all, even to the high priest himself.

When the high priest did receive permission to enter, his entry was safeguarded *by sacrificial blood*. However, this sacrificial blood was not totally effective. Fresh blood had to be shed and fresh entry made into the Holy of Holies each year. Further, although they might have brought about outward cleansing (Hebrews 9:13), they were *not able to cleanse 'the conscience* of the worshipper' (v.9).

In reality, it was only an 'illustration' (v.9), 'a visible parable ... a temporary arrangement until the complete overhaul could be made' (vv.8–10, MSG). It pointed beyond itself. It was fulfilled through the blood of Christ.

When Jesus came, he 'bypassed the sacrifices consisting of goat and calf blood, instead using *his own blood* as the price to set us free once and for all' (vv.11–12, MSG). By doing this 'he brought together God and his people in this new way' (v.17, MSG).

What does this mean?

1. You are clean inside and out

Jesus makes it possible for your conscience to be cleansed: '*The blood of Christ cleans up our whole lives*, inside and out ... through the Spirit' (v.14, MSG).

2. You have been set free

'Christ offered himself as an unblemished sacrifice, *freeing us* from all those dead-end efforts to make ourselves respectable, so that we can live all out for God' (v.15, MSG).

The Holy Spirit and the blood of Christ go together. Joyce Meyer writes, 'The Spirit could not be poured out on the Day of Pentecost until the blood was poured out on the cross of Calvary.'[3]

PRAYER

Lord Jesus, thank you that you make it possible for me to have a clear conscience and to live all-out for God. Thank you that you paid the ransom price, setting me free by shedding your blood for me.

OLD TESTAMENT READING

Ezekiel 16:1–63
Restored fortunes

God loves you. Everything God does stems from his love for you. In this prophetic allegory, God's love for his people is described as being like a husband's for his wife: 'I took care of you ... and protected you. I promised you my love and entered the covenant of marriage with you' (v.8, MSG).

The Lord's blessing involves cleansing (v.9), clothing with fine linen (v.10), giving of beauty (vv.11–13), food to satisfy (v.13), fame (v.14) and splendour (v.14).

The tragic words that follow can apply to us as individuals or as a nation: '*But you'* (v.15). In spite of all that God had done, they turned around and rejected him. Instead they trusted in their beauty and used their fame in an unfaithful way (v.15).

Sin often starts with unbelief, trusting in something other than the Lord. It leads to idolatry – worshipping something other than the Lord, and then to increasing sin (v.26), often from our weak wills (v.30).

The results of sin are dissatisfaction (vv.28–29) and God's judgment (vv.30–34). Jerusalem has been like an unfaithful wife, serving idols and giving them '[their] children's blood' (v.36). Because she has shed blood, her own blood will be shed (v.38). The word 'blood' occurs seven times in this passage (vv.6, 9, 22, 36, 38).

He compares their sin to the sin of Sodom. What he speaks about are not the sexual sins normally associated with Sodom; rather, he writes, 'She lived with her daughters in the lap of luxury – proud, gluttonous, and lazy. They ignored the oppressed and the poor. They put on airs and lived obscene lives' (vv.49–50, MSG).

They are the common sins of any prosperous society – arrogance, overeating and a lack of concern for the poor and needy. When people do not have any needs they frequently turn away from God. Their worst sin was not to help the poor and needy.

Yet in spite of all of this, God promises to restore the fortunes of Sodom and the fortunes of his people (v.53). He promises an everlasting covenant (v.60) and that he will make *atonement* (v.63).

This word '*atonement*' is also found in today's passage from Hebrews – the '*atonement* cover' on the Ark of the Covenant, a symbol of the mercy of God (Hebrews 9:5).

Atonement points to the need for something to be done to wash away your sins. It speaks of two great realities.

First, the reality and seriousness of God's reaction against sin. Second, the reality and greatness of his love, which provided the sacrifice through the blood of Jesus. St Paul wrote, 'The Son of God ... loved me and gave himself for me' (Galatians 2:20). It is as personal as that. His blood was given for you. He bore your sins. He died your death. His blood atoned for your sin. He is your blood donor.

PRAYER

Thank you, Lord, that in your great love, you shed your blood. Thank you that today I can know that I am loved, forgiven and can live with a clear conscience.

9 November | Day 313
Once for All

Once, on 7 January 1978, I stood as the bridegroom at the front of HTB. The bride, Pippa Hislop, walked down the aisle with her father and joined me at the front of the church. We made our vows to each other before God and we were united in marriage. We left the church as 'Mr and Mrs Gumbel'. It was a '*once*' event, but it has had huge implications for our lives. It stemmed from our love for each other and we committed ourselves to love one another until the end of our lives.

Almost four years before that, on 16 February 1974, I had encountered Jesus Christ for the first time. A love relationship began, which has utterly transformed my life. It was another '*once*' event, but the implications and effect of that '*once*' event are ongoing and all-encompassing. I experienced God's love for me and committed myself to love him for ever.

In today's New Testament passage, the writer of Hebrews speaks of the greatest '*once*' *event* of all time. It changed the course of history and has the potential to change all of our lives. Jesus has appeared '*once for all*' (Hebrews 9:26). 'Christ was sacrificed *once*' (v.28). Jesus entered the Most Holy Place '*once for all* by his own blood' (v.12). 'We have been made holy through the sacrifice of the body of Jesus Christ *once for all*' (10:10). This '*once*' event stemmed from God's great love for us and has huge implications for your life and mine.

READING FROM PSALMS

Psalm 121:1–8
God will guard and protect you

Where is the *first* place you look when you are in trouble or don't know what to do? Do you look to friends, family or the medical profession? There is nothing wrong in looking for help in all these directions. But the *first place* the psalmist looks is upwards.

Regret looks back. Fear looks around. Worry looks in. Faith looks up.

The psalmist *looks up*, 'I lift up my eyes to the hills – where does my help come from?' (v.1). Your help, strength and protection come from the maker of the universe: 'My strength comes from God, who made heaven, and earth, and mountains' (v.2, MSG). 'He will not let your foot slip – he who watches over you will not slumber' (v.3).

This beautiful psalm speaks of the Lord's love for you and his protection over your life.

> 'God's your Guardian,
> right at your side to protect you...
> God guards you from every evil,
> he guards your very life.
> He guards you when you leave and when you return,
> he guards you now, he guards you always' (vv.5–8, MSG).

I have sometimes used this psalm as a prayer for our family or friends who are facing difficulties in their lives.

The promise of this psalm is that the Lord will protect you from all ultimate harm. The psalmist could not have known that this is made possible through the 'once for all' sacrifice of Jesus, which means that one day he will come 'to bring salvation for those who are waiting for him' (Hebrews 9:28).

PRAYER

Lord, thank you that you watch over me day and night. Thank you that you watch over my coming and going both now and for evermore.

NEW TESTAMENT READING

Hebrews 9:16–28
Jesus sacrificed himself for you

Do you realise how much God loves you? Do you know that Jesus shed his blood so that you could receive total forgiveness? Do you understand that he has already paid the price for every sin you have committed in the past and every sin you will ever commit in the future?

Why was the death of Jesus necessary? The author points out that, both in the case of *a will* and a *covenant* (the same Greek word is used for both), they do not come into effect without a *death* taking place. The death leads to an inheritance for others.

'The first covenant was not put into effect *without blood*' (v.18). He goes on to describe in detail 'the blood of the [old] covenant' and concludes that 'without the *shedding of blood* there is *no forgiveness*' (vv.19–22).

The writer then makes three statements contrasting the sacrifice of Jesus with the inferior sacrifices under the law:

1. Jesus was dealing with *the real thing*
'For Christ *didn't* enter the earthly version of the Holy Place; he entered the *Place Itself*, and offered himself to God as the sacrifice for our sins' (v.24, MSG).

2. Jesus' sacrifice was '*once, for all*'
'*Nor* did he enter heaven to offer himself again and again, the way the high priest enters the Most Holy Place every year' (v.25). Rather, 'Everyone has to die *once*, then face the consequences. Christ's death was also a *one-time event*, but it was a sacrifice that *took care of sins forever*' (vv.27–28, MSG).

3. Jesus shed *his own blood*
Jesus did *not* offer 'blood that is not his own' (v.25). Unlike the High Priest it was *his own blood* that was shed (v.12).

No further sacrifice is now required: 'These animal sacrifices aren't needed anymore, having served their purpose' (v.23, MSG). As the Book of Common Prayer puts it, the once for all sacrifice of Jesus was 'a full, perfect and sufficient sacrifice, oblation and satisfaction for the sins of the whole world'.[1] As Jesus cried out on the cross, 'It is finished' (John 19:30).

When Jesus comes again, it will not be 'to bear sin' but rather, 'to bring salvation to those who are waiting for him' (Hebrews 9:28).

PRAYER

Thank you, Lord, for Jesus. Thank you for his once for all sacrifice for me so that I might receive total forgiveness. Help me to remember today that 'it is finished'.

OLD TESTAMENT READING

Ezekiel 17:1–18:32
Make a clean break!

Although Jesus' death for us was a 'once' event, God, in his love, was preparing his people for that event for hundreds of years. He was teaching them about the serious consequences of sin and pointing ahead to a Saviour.

God's word to his people was through an allegory and parable (17:1). The immediate context of the allegory was the 'great eagle' (v.3) of Babylon, taking King Jehoiakim from Judah to Babylon in 597 BC, but its application is far wider.

There are two types of shoots, two types of vines and two types of kingdom. There is the kingdom of this world – human-made, apparently very strong, using all the best resources, appearing to flourish, but that will ultimately shrivel and die and be completely useless. On the other hand, there is the kingdom of God, which, from a very small beginning, against all the odds, will flourish and bear permanent fruit (see Matthew 13:31–32 and Revelation 22).

As we read this passage through the lens of Jesus, we see hints of his 'once for all' sacrifice for sin. The 'shoot' (Ezekiel 17:22) is the language that the prophet Isaiah uses in what is clearly a messianic passage, foretelling the coming of Jesus (Isaiah 53:2). This is the one who was pierced for our transgressions (v.5) upon whom the Lord laid the iniquity of us all (v.6). He is the one who made the 'once for all' sacrifice of himself for our sins.

Ezekiel goes on to say, 'You die for your own sin, not another's' (Ezekiel 18:4, MSG). 'The soul who sins is the one who will die' (v.20). Earlier, Ezekiel spoke of corporate responsibility (17:12). Now he speaks of individual responsibility. We will all have to take responsibility for our own lives. You will not be judged for your parents' or your children's sins (18:20), but for your own sins.

God loves everyone. He does not want anyone to fall under his judgment: '"Do I take any pleasure in the death of the wicked?" declares the Sovereign Lord. "Rather, am I not pleased when they turn from their ways and live?"' (v.23).

He concludes this passage, 'I'll judge each of you according to the way you live. So turn around! Turn your backs on your rebellious living so that sin won't drag you down. Clean house ... Get a new heart! Get a new spirit!' (vv.30–31, MSG). The passage then finishes with a final reminder of how that is possible – 'Repent and live!' (v.32).

This is the wonderful news. However far you have fallen – whatever mess you've made with your life – you can make a clean break with the past. Simply 'repent' – turn from the bad ways and turn to Jesus. You receive total forgiveness, a new heart and a new spirit and can enjoy the relationship with God made possible by his once for all sacrifice for your sins.

PRAYER

Lord, thank you that I can 'repent and live'. Thank you that you promise me a new heart and a new spirit. Help me to make a clean break and to enjoy the relationship with God that you have made possible, by your 'once-for-all' sacrifice for my sins.

10 November | Day 314
Beauty

'The serene beauty of a holy life is *the most powerful influence in the world* next to the power of God,' according to Blaise Pascal. Holiness is beautiful and it has nothing to do with outward beauty. It is a beauty that radiates from within. This is the way the world will be changed. It starts with you and me. St Francis of Assisi said, 'Sanctify yourself and you will sanctify society.'

Holiness is not an optional extra. It is not just for saints and special Christians. It should be something we all aspire to in this life. Holiness is not the same thing as intensity. Intensity is not a fruit of the Holy Spirit! The ability to laugh at yourself is key to holiness. Take Jesus seriously but don't take yourself too seriously. A sense of *humour* is the link between *holiness* and *humility*.

Holiness is not boring. As C. S. Lewis wrote, 'How little people know who think that holiness is dull. When one meets the real thing ... it is *irresistible*.'[1]

READING FROM PSALMS

Psalm 122:1–9
Where do you find holiness?

For the psalmist, the source of his joy was the chance to worship God in the temple. This was the place where the people went 'to praise the name of the Lord' (v.4b). This is why Jerusalem was of such great importance for the people of God and why the psalmist was so passionate about the peace and security of the city (vv.6–9).

Jerusalem was the *holy city*. It is described in our Old Testament passage for today as 'my *holy* mountain' (Ezekiel 20:40). The temple was God's home. This is what made it holy.

Now, the church is God's home. It is the new *holy place* 'with Christ Jesus as the cornerstone that holds all the parts together. We see it taking shape day after day ... *a holy temple* built by God, all of us built into it, a temple in which God is quite at home' (Ephesians 2:20–22, MSG).

The people are the new place. Through Jesus, you are a new house of God – you are a temple of the Holy Spirit.

PRAYER

Lord, I long for your holy presence. I long to praise the name of the Lord. Thank you

for the peace and security that comes from your presence in the house of God.

NEW TESTAMENT READING

Hebrews 10:1–18
When do you become holy?

Holiness is now possible for you through the sacrifice of Jesus and the gift of the Holy Spirit who comes to live within you. In one sense, you can experience 'instant holiness'. But, in another sense, holiness is a very long process that will never be complete in this life.

One of the questions frequently asked in an Alpha small group is, 'What happens to all the people who lived *before* Jesus? Isn't it unfair that Jesus came at a particular point in history and made forgiveness possible?' The assumption behind the questions is that the cross can only work forward in time and cannot be effective for those who lived before Jesus.

However, the writer of Hebrews says, 'But when this priest [Jesus] had offered *for all time* one sacrifice for sins, he sat down at the right hand of God' (v.12). The sacrifice of Jesus is effective *for all time*. The cross is effective for those who lived before Jesus and for those who live after him.

'The old plan was only a hint of the good things in the new plan' (v.1a, MSG). In other words, it only foreshadowed something superior that was to come.

The law could not perfect (v.1b). The proof that it could not perfect people is that the sacrifices had to go on being offered (v.2). People continued to feel guilty for their sins (v.2c) 'Because the blood of bulls and goats is powerless to take sins away' (v.4, AMP). Only the blood of Christ can take away your sin. He alone was the perfect sacrifice, since he alone lived a perfect life.

His voluntary sacrifice brought an end to the old order and established the new one (vv.5–9). The result of his sacrifice is that you '*have been made holy* through the sacrifice of the body of Jesus Christ once for all' (v.10).

This is in stark contrast to the law: 'Christ made a single sacrifice for sins, and that was it! ... It was a perfect sacrifice by a perfect person *to perfect some very imperfect people*' (vv.12–14, MSG).

The expression 'he sat down' is very significant. The Aaronic priests never sat down to rest in the sanctuary (v.11). Their sacrifices were never complete. On the other hand, Jesus '*sat down* at the right hand of God' (v.12). It showed that his work had been completed: 'By one sacrifice he has made perfect for ever those who are being made holy' (v.14).

Here you can see how holiness takes place in your life:

1. Immediate holiness
As far as the past is concerned, the *penalty for sin has been paid*: '*We have been made holy* ... he has made [us] perfect for ever' (vv.10, 14). This is justification. Jesus' sacrifice has made possible total forgiveness and a perfect relationship with God. You are totally forgiven. Therefore, forgive others and, most difficult of all, *forgive yourself*. There is no need for any further sacrifice for sins (v.18).

2. Process holiness
In the present, the *power of sin is being broken*. Sanctification is a *process* of '*being made holy*' (v.14). In my case at least, it seems to be a very slow and challenging process. Jesus is setting me free from the power of sin. Holiness is the work of the Holy Spirit who 'testifies to us about this' (v.15). Through the Holy Spirit coming to live in you, God's laws will be in your heart and on your mind (v.16).

3. Perfect holiness
In the future, even the *presence of sin will be removed*. One day it will be seen that evil has been totally defeated. Jesus 'waits for his enemies to be made his footstool' (v.13a) and the process of our 'being made holy' will be complete (see also 1 John 3:2).

PRAYER

Lord, thank you that by your sacrifice you bring me into a holy relationship with God. Thank you that through your Holy Spirit I am in the process of being made holy and that, one day, there will be perfect holiness for ever.

OLD TESTAMENT READING

Ezekiel 19:1–20:44
How do you become holy?

The key to holiness is found in your relationship with God. God says, '*I am The Holy*' (20:40, MSG). Through your relationship with him, he wants you to become like him. He says, 'I, God, am in the business of making them holy' (v.12, MSG).

This was the reason for the 'holy rest days', the Sabbath (v.20, MSG). It was to give the people time to develop their relationship with God. Giving God the first day of the week symbolised giving God priority over everything.

God's desire has always been for a holy people. In this passage, we see once again his frustration with the lack of holiness of his people. God's people are intended to be a reflection of God's holy character.

Today's passage begins with a lament for the last kings of Judah (19:1). The 'lioness' refers to Judah and the last kings are described as her lion cubs.

The image changes to that of an uprooted vineyard (19:10–14), but the message of the lament is constant. Any empire we build for ourselves may seem strong, but it will be easily and quickly destroyed.

The rest of the passage then goes on to explain why Israel was uprooted and judged, and what their actions should have been. God describes how the people have 'defiled' and 'profaned' his holiness, but looks forward to a time when that will no longer be the case.

The key factor in what makes the people holy or not seems to lie in their relationship with God. His complaint against them centres on their following other gods, and the way in which they defiled themselves by the images they looked at (20:16; see also vv.7, 24, 28, 30). This is in stark contrast to what should have been a close relationship with God, in which 'I the LORD made them holy' (v.12).

All the way through, we can see that God's longing is for a holy people who will reflect his character. He had a plan to make this kind of holiness possible. That moment only came with the sacrifice of Jesus and the outpouring of the Holy Spirit on the day of Pentecost.

You have been made holy. The Holy Spirit lives in you. Put God first in your life and avoid anything that spoils your relationship with him. The serene *beauty* of your holy life will be influential and irresistible.

PRAYER

Father, I want to put you first in my life and to avoid anything that spoils my relationship with you. Help me to lead a holy life.

11 November | Day 315
Stick At It

Maryam and Marziyeh were arrested in Iran in 2009. Their crime: being Christians. They were blindfolded, interrogated and became ill during their time in prison. They were taken to court. Mr Haddad, the prosecuting lawyer, asked the two women if they were Christians. 'We love Jesus,' they replied. He repeated his question and they responded, 'Yes, we are Christians.'

Mr Haddad asked whether they regretted becoming Christians, to which they replied, 'We have no regrets.' Then he stated emphatically, 'You should renounce your faith verbally and in written form.' They stood firm and replied, 'We will not deny our faith.'

When Mr Haddad told the women to return to prison to think about their options and come back to him when they were ready (to comply), Maryam and Marziyeh responded, 'We have already done our thinking.'[1]

The author of Hebrews writes to Christians who are the subject of persecution: 'You stood your ground in a great contest in the face of suffering' (Hebrews 10:32) – as Maryam and Marziyeh did before their prosecutors. (Thank God they have been released – we interviewed them as part of the Alpha Film Series.[2])

The will to persevere is often the difference between success and failure. This is true of learning a new skill or sport, or achieving success at work. As has been said, 'Observe the postage stamp; its usefulness depends on the ability to stick to one thing till it gets there.'[3] 'Stickability' is also a key to the Christian life. If you want to learn to read the Bible, pray, resist evil or whatever else, learn to persevere. The writer of Hebrews encourages his readers not to be 'quitters' but 'to stick it out' (vv.34–39, MSG).

READING FROM PSALMS

Psalm 123:1–4
Look to God for help

'I look to you ... God, look up to you for help' (v.1, MSG). Like the psalmist, wait patiently for God to help. Stick at it in the face of opposition: 'We have *endured* much contempt. We have *endured* much ridicule from the proud, much contempt from the arrogant' (vv.3b–4).

His response to this opposition is to turn his focus on to God. He writes, 'I lift my eyes to *you* ... our eyes look to the *Lord our God*' (vv.1–2). This focus is built upon a recognition of who God is – the one 'whose throne is in heaven' (v.1) – and also on his relationship with God.

God is 'the Lord *our* God'. Look to him to help you: 'like servants alert to their master's commands, like a maiden attending her lady, we're watching and waiting, holding our breath, awaiting your word of mercy' (v.2–3, MSG).

PRAYER

Lord, whatever happens, help me to endure, persevere and keep my eyes fixed on you.

NEW TESTAMENT READING

Hebrews 10:19–39
Stand your ground

Millions of Christians around the world today are still being persecuted for their faith. The letter of Hebrews is written to Christians who were the subject of persecution (possibly at the hands of Nero in Rome). One of the main purposes of the book is to encourage the readers to *persevere*. The writer has finished his doctrinal exposition. He now begins a prolonged call to *perseverance*. Here he gives reasons, incentives and encouragements to stick at it.

1. You can be confident

Persevere because of what Christ did and does for you. You have a new freedom, boldness and confidence. You are welcomed into God's presence through the sacrifice of Jesus: You 'can now – without hesitation – walk right up to God into "the Holy Place". Jesus has cleared the way by the blood of his sacrifice' (vv.19–20, MSG).

2. You are not on your own

We are to persevere because we have one another to help. As the writer urges us to '*hold unswervingly* to the hope that we profess' (v.23), he does so in the context of community. Gather together often: 'consider how we may spur one another on towards love and good deeds. Let us not give up meeting together, as some are in the habit of doing, but let us encourage one another' (vv.24–25).

3. This really matters

He warns against deliberately continuing to sin (v.26). This means something like sinning 'defiantly'. He warns of 'a mighty fierce judgment ... if you turn on God's Son, spit on the sacrifice that made you whole ... God has warned us that he'll hold us to account and make us pay ... Nobody's getting by with anything' (vv.26–31, MSG).

This is often applied to people outside of the church but actually it was written in the context of the Lord judging his own people. This is not something his readers have fallen into. He reminds them of the time when 'you *stood your ground*' (v.32).

4. The rewards are great

He encourages them to 'Remember those early days when you first saw the light? Those were the hard times! Kicked around in public, targets of every kind of abuse – some days it was you, other days your friends. If some friends went to prison, you stuck by them. If some enemies broke in and seized your goods, you let them go with a smile, knowing that they couldn't touch your *real treasure*' (vv.32–34, MSG).

5. Be patient

Life is long and life is short. On the one hand, life is long. In the course of a lifetime there will be tests, trials and difficulties that require 'stickability': patience, endurance and perseverance: 'Patient endurance is what you need now, so that you will continue to do God's will. Then you will receive all that he has promised' (v.36, NLT).

On the other hand, life is short. In a short time, we will either have died or Jesus will have returned:

> 'For in just a little while,
> the Coming One will come and not delay'
> (v.37, NLT).

The writer has full confidence that his readers will persevere: 'But we are not of those who shrink back and are destroyed, but of those who believe and are saved' (v.39).

PRAYER

Lord, help me to persevere and to encourage others towards love and good deeds as we meet together.

OLD TESTAMENT READING

Ezekiel 20:45–22:22
Confront evil

Personally, I find that confrontation is never easy, but it is sometimes necessary. Ezekiel is told to *confront evil* (22:2).

He was called to preach and prophesy (20:46). His was not an easy task. His message was a difficult one. It was counter-cultural. Yet he *persevered*. He did not give up. He stuck at it. He kept on preaching. The word of the Lord came to him time and time again and he faithfully proclaimed it.

God knew that it was not easy. He encouraged Ezekiel, '*set your face*' (20:46; 21:2): 'Set your face *against* Jerusalem and preach *against* the sanctuary. Prophesy *against* the land of Israel and say to her: "This is what the LORD says: I am *against* you"' (vv.2–3). It must have been really hard.

The sins that he speaks against are as relevant to us as they were to the people of Israel: treating parents with contempt, ill-treatment of the poor and marginalised (including immigrants, widows, and orphans), sexual abuse, incest, rape, bribery, greed and extortion (22:7–12).

They have forgotten God: 'And *you have forgotten me*, declares the Sovereign LORD' (v.12). Those of us who live in the West live in a society that is in danger of forgetting God. As we look around us at a world where there is so much wrong, it can be easy to think that God must have forgotten us. Paradoxically though, passages of judgment like this one actually show us how much God cares for us. God cares passionately about injustice and suffering – that is why he is so angry with those who inflict them on others, and why he refuses to ignore those who suffer.

There is a spiritual dimension to all this too. Our concern isn't just to oppose injustice, but also to turn people back to God. The wonderful message of the second half of Ezekiel (and indeed of the whole Bible) is that this judgment is not the last word. God will also act in grace, to redeem and save his people.

It is this passionate concern of God for the poor, the downtrodden and the lost that inspired Ezekiel, and that has inspired Christians down the centuries. General William Booth, founder of the Salvation Army, modelled remarkable 'stickability'. He said, 'While women weep as they do now, I'll fight; while little children go hungry as they do now, I'll fight; while men go to prison, in and out, in and out, I'll fight; while there is a poor lost girl upon the street, I'll fight; while there remains one dark soul without the light of God, I'll fight – I'll fight to the very end.'[14]

PRAYER

Lord, help me to set my face with determination not to be put off by opposition, contempt and ridicule. Help me to stick at it; confronting evil and proclaiming the good news about Jesus to the very end.

12 November | Day 316
What Is Faith?

I studied law at university and practised as a barrister for a number of years. I was involved in many criminal trials where the judge told the jury that they had to reach a verdict – but they could not find the defendant guilty unless they were 'satisfied so that they *felt sure*'. Every such verdict was an act of faith. The jury was not there at the time the crime was committed. They had to believe the evidence.

Faith and '*being sure*' are not opposed. The writer of Hebrews says, 'Now *faith* is *being sure* of what we hope for and assurance about what we do not see' (Hebrews 11:1). St Augustine wrote, 'God does not expect us to submit our faith to him without reason, but the very limits of our reason make faith a necessity.'

READING FROM PROVERBS

Proverbs 27:15–22
Faith is the way to true satisfaction

'I can't get no satisfaction,' sang Mick Jagger in 1965.[1] The Rolling Stones' song echoes the cry of the human heart; we try and we try and we try, but human eyes are 'never satisfied' (v.20). Where is satisfaction to be found?

This passage contains a wealth of practical wisdom. It warns against being quarrelsome (vv.15–16). It points out how friendship can improve our effectiveness: 'As iron sharpens iron, so a friend sharpens a friend' (v.17, NLT).

Faith means serving the Lord – looking after our master: 'Those who tend a fig-tree will eat its fruit, and those who look after their masters will be honoured' (v.18).

The writer goes on, 'Death and Destruction are *never satisfied*, and neither are human eyes' (v.20) 'Hell has a voracious appetite, and lust just never quits' (v.20, MSG). True satisfaction comes through faith in Jesus, who said, 'I have come that [you] may have life, and have it to the full' (John 10:10).

The writer then makes an interesting point about the importance of how we deal with compliments: 'The crucible for silver and the furnace for gold, but people are *tested by the praise they receive*' (Proverbs 27:21).

The person of faith recognises that God is always the primary cause of any success we have. He created you, and gives you the gifts and opportunities that come your way.

When people praise you, don't let it go to your head. When they criticise you, don't let it get to your heart (see v.19).

PRAYER

Lord, help me to live a life of faith, looking to you as my Lord, giving you all the glory and serving you each day.

NEW TESTAMENT READING

Hebrews 11:1–16
Faith is trust in God

'The fundamental fact of existence is that this *trust in God*, this faith, is *the firm foundation under everything that makes life worth living*. It's our handle on what we can't see. The act of faith is what distinguished our ancestors, set them above the crowd' (vv.1–2, MSG).

What does this faith look like in practice?

1. Faith leads to understanding

By faith we *understand* that the universe was formed at God's command, so that what is seen was not made out of what was visible' (v.3). St Augustine pointed out, 'Faith is the first step to understanding; understanding is the reward of faith. Therefore, seek not to understand that you may believe, but believe that you may understand.'

2. Faith pleases God

Enoch *pleased God*. As a result, he 'skipped death completely' (v.5, MSG). The writer goes on to explain, 'It's impossible to *please God* apart from faith. And why? Because anyone who wants to approach God must believe both that he exists and that he cares enough to respond to those who seek him' (v.6, MSG).

3. Faith leads to intimacy with God

'By faith, Noah built a ship in the middle of dry land. He was warned about something he couldn't see, and acted on what he was told ... As a result, Noah became *intimate with God*' (v.7, MSG).

4. Faith means saying 'Yes' to God

'By an act of faith, Abraham said *yes to God's call* to travel to an unknown place that would become his home. When he left he had no idea where he was going' (v.8, MSG). True faith commits us to obedience.

Abraham left Ur of the Chaldeans at the height of its prosperity (2006–1950 BC). He heard God's call and 'obeyed and went' (v.8). He did not 'know *where* he was going' (v.8). But he knew *with whom* he was going. His faith brought blessing to him, his family, his nation and to you and me.

He trusted God even when the evidence pointed in the opposite direction. Abraham's one great disappointment was that his wife couldn't have children to continue the long family line (Genesis 11). We read that Abraham's family was 'as good as dead' (Hebrews 11:12).

Abraham believed God (see Romans 4). It was not that he never had any doubts. In fact, he got fed up with waiting and tried to fulfil God's promises by human means. Thankfully, God does not judge us on the basis of our lapses, failures or mess-ups. He saw Abraham's settled attitude of faith (Romans 4:3, 18).

5. Faith sees beyond this life

Abraham took a long-term view. We live in an 'instant' culture. Everything is about instant satisfaction. Abraham was in it for the long haul. He was 'a stranger in a foreign country' (v.9). He lived in tents. Yet he knew where God had called him.

He did not look back to what he had left behind through his step of faith. Rather, 'he was *looking forward* to the city with foundations, whose architect and builder is God' (v.10).

Abel's faith also had a lasting impact: '...by faith he still speaks, even though he is dead' (v.4).

The writer concludes: 'Each one of these people of faith died not yet having in hand what was promised, but still believing ... You can see why God is so proud of them, and has a City waiting for them' (vv.13, 16, MSG).

PRAYER

Lord, I want to please you today. I earnestly seek you.

OLD TESTAMENT READING

Ezekiel 22:23–23:49
Faith means staying faithful

What are you to do if you live in a society that turns its back on God? How do you remain faithful to God when all around you people are faithless? Do you give up and join them? Do you judge and condemn them? Or is there another way for the people of God?

The word of the Lord came to Ezekiel again. God's concern was typical: 'Extortion is rife, robbery is epidemic, the poor and needy are abused, outsiders are kicked around at will, with no access to justice' (22:29, MSG).

He describes the sin of Jerusalem and Samaria as being like those of two prostitutes who become 'more and more promiscuous' (23:19); 'Crazy with lust' (v.12, MSG).

The nature of sin and addiction means that because it does not satisfy, the practices become more and more extreme. People were meant to love God and be *faithful* to him. Instead we have lusted after the wrong things.

It is surprising to see such shocking and explicit language in the Bible, but God uses these disgusting images to help the people to grasp the full reality of their sin, and how much it pains him to see it.

The root of the problem is their unfaithfulness to the Lord. 'Therefore this is what the Sovereign LORD says: Since you have *forgotten me* and thrust me behind your back, you must bear the consequences of your lewdness and prostitution' (v.35).

Forgetting God is the opposite of faith. It leads to the terrible consequences described in this passage.

But Ezekiel remained faithful to God. He continues to proclaim God's message. What God was looking for was someone to intercede for them, and to 'stand before me in the gap on behalf of the land' (v.30). This is the way of faithfulness for the people of God.

I am so grateful to the many people who have told me over the years that they pray for us regularly. We also have a 24-7 Prayer room at our church, and I am thrilled by the way in which it has galvanised people to pray and intercede.

Prayer really does make a difference. Intercession is one of the most important things you can do. Make prayer and intercession a high priority in your life.

Sexual craving, being at its root a craving for intimacy, can only be satisfied through our relationship with God. The Ezekiel passage is extraordinarily contemporary with the large number of people today with some form of sexual addiction. Prayer, believing that God 'rewards those who earnestly seek him' (Hebrews 11:6), is an important part of the answer.

Keep your eyes fixed on Jesus. Trust in him. Abide in him. Serve him with all your heart. Live a life of faith. Stay faithful to him and pray faithfully for others. This is the way of true satisfaction. Faith pleases God.

PRAYER

Lord, increase my faith.

13 November | Day 317

Three Ways You Can Exercise Faith

The islanders were cannibals. Nobody trusted anybody else. His life was in constant danger. He had come to tell them the good news about Jesus. He wanted to translate John's Gospel into their language, but he discovered that there was no word in their language for 'trust', 'belief' or 'faith'.

John Paton (1824–1907), a Scot, had travelled to the New Hebrides (a group of islands in the south-west Pacific) determined to tell the tribal people about Jesus, but he struggled to find the right word for 'faith'. One day, when his indigenous servant came in, Paton raised both feet off the floor, sat back in his chair and asked, 'What am I doing now?' In reply, the servant used a word that means, '*to lean your whole weight upon*'. This became the expression that Paton used. Faith is *leaning our whole weight upon Jesus*.

READING FROM PSALMS

Psalm 124:1–8
Faith as trust when under attack

'Faith is *the bird* that sings when the dawn is still dark,' wrote Sir Rabindranath Tagore.

There are times in all of our lives when our faith is tested. We come under 'attack': 'When everyone went against us' (v.2, MSG) and there seems to be a 'torrent' (v.4) of 'raging waters' (v.5) – temptations, doubts, fears, and so on.

These things could overwhelm you, but for the fact that the Maker of heaven and earth is on your side (v.1). Faith means trusting that he won't leave you defenceless. He frees you from the traps: 'Their grip is broken; we're free as a bird in flight' (v.7, MSG).

David is one of the most tried and tested figures in the Bible. Like David, remain faithful to God. Trust in the Lord. He will protect you from raging torrents and from being 'swallowed alive' (v.3). Your 'help is in the name of the LORD, the Maker of heaven and earth' (v.8).

PRAYER

Lord, help...

NEW TESTAMENT READING

Hebrews 11:17–40
Faith as choice, perseverance and expectancy

What does heroic faith look like? Moses was the supreme figure in Israel's history. He rescued them from slavery. He gave them the Law. In today's passage, the writer shows that Moses was pre-eminently a *man of faith*.

As we have seen, the word *'faith'* carries a number of meanings. It describes our whole relationship with God – trusting in him, leaning our whole weight on Jesus, and having the courage to act on our belief. Through the example of Moses, we see three ways in which you too can exercise faith:

1. Faith as a *choice*

Moses was 'no ordinary child' (v.23). He was brought up in the Egyptian royal household and received a first-class education and training. He was also physically good looking (Exodus 2:2). So many people strive today, as they did then, for money, sex and power. Moses could have had them all in abundance.

Moses had another great advantage – the faith of his parents (Hebrews 11:23). Pharaoh's daughter gave Moses' mother the job of bringing him up. However, at the end of the day, Moses himself, like you and I, needed to make a choice.

He could have *chosen* 'to enjoy the pleasures of sin for a short time' (v.25). However, 'he *chose* to be ill-treated along with the people of God' (v.25). Moses *chose* to be identified with a group of people that those with an upbringing like his regarded with contempt – a slave nation, the people of God. By identifying with them he brought upon himself danger, scorn and suffering.

He made this choice because 'he regarded disgrace for the sake of Christ as of greater value than the treasures of Egypt' (v.26). Compared to the pleasures of the world, which are fleeting, God offers you an *everlasting* reward.

Faith as choice is the faith that justifies. This initial act of faith can be summarised with the mnemonic:

Forsaking All I Take Him (FAITH)

2. Faith as *perseverance*

Moses left Egypt twice. The first time he was fleeing as a criminal after killing an Egyptian. The second time, he left as leader of the people of God. In between, he persevered with courage and determination. He 'persevered because he saw him who is invisible' (v.27). His eyes were opened to the whole spiritual realm.

From the moment of choice to the moment of triumph, there will be many battles. This is the pattern in the Bible. First comes the call, then the problems. Finally, there is the fulfilment. In between, keep persevering and trusting.

This kind of faith can be summarised in another mnemonic:

Feeling Afraid I Trust Him (FAITH)

This aspect of faith is one that is particularly stressed by the author of Hebrews. It is also probably what Paul has in mind when he lists *faithfulness* as a fruit of the Spirit (Galatians 5:22).

3. Faith as *expectancy*

When I interviewed Rick Warren at the HTB Leadership Conference, he asked rhetorically: 'Why does God use me?' And he gave the answer: 'Because I *expect* him to use me.' Joyce Meyer defines *expectancy* as 'a joy-filled looking forward to receiving a desired result'.[1]

Moses heard God. He did what God told him to do. He knew that God had the power to kill, but he believed he would pass over the Israelite homes that were sprinkled with blood (Hebrews 11:28). He believed in God's power to perform signs and wonders, such as the crossing of the Red Sea (v.29).

Expectancy is that mysterious surge of confidence that God will perform a mighty work. In the first three Gospels, nearly two-thirds of the references to faith occur in relation to miracles. Faith here must be understood to be *trusting* in God's power.

The writer goes on to give many other examples of faith in the Old Testament, including those 'who through faith conquered kingdoms, administered justice, and gained what was promised; who shut the mouths of lions, quenched the fury of the flames, and escaped the edge of the sword; whose weakness was turned into strength' (vv.33–34). I particularly love the fact that God turns your, and my, weaknesses into strengths.

He concludes this sweep of history by saying something quite extraordinary: 'God had a better plan for us' (v.40, MSG). He is saying *you are better off* than Noah, Abraham, Moses, Joshua, Samson, David, and all the others. 'Not one of these people, even though their lives of faith were exemplary, got their hands on what was promised' (v.39, MSG). While they could only look forward to something better, you live in the age of the Spirit and have *received* this better and fuller revelation in Christ.

PRAYER

Lord, help me to trust you, to persevere and have an expectant faith in you to perform healings and wonders.

OLD TESTAMENT READING

Ezekiel 24:1–25:17
Faith in times of tragedy

'Faith is not shelter against difficulties, but belief in the face of all contradictions,' wrote Paul Tournier.

Ezekiel's faith is remarkable. His message is a very tough one. God is saying to his people that he has tried to cleanse them from their impurities, but they would not be clean and therefore his judgment is coming: 'You will be judged according to your conduct and your actions' (24:14). If we refuse to accept God's forgiveness (which we now know is made possible through the cross of Christ), we will be judged on our own conduct and actions.

Ezekiel's faith survives the tragic loss of his wife ('*the delight of [his] eyes*', v.16). God says he is going to take away Israel's sanctuary – which is the *delight of their eyes*, the object of their affection (v.21). He is foretelling the terrible destruction of Jerusalem by the Babylonians.

He warns the other nations not to rejoice with malice in their hearts (25:6, 15). God strongly disapproves of that feeling of secret glee (by which we can be tempted) when we see other people getting into trouble – it is the opposite of love.

When people hurt you, do not take vengeance into your own hands. Trust in God who promised that, in the end, he will ensure that justice is done (vv.15–17).

In the midst of the darkness in this passage, there is one ray of light. As the messenger arrives with news of Jerusalem's destruction, Ezekiel's enforced silence (see Ezekiel 3:24–27) comes to an end. This heralds a remarkable shift in his ministry. When his focus returns to the nation of Israel (chapter 33), the prophet of doom is transformed into a messenger of hope. The God of justice will also be revealed as a God of grace and salvation.

Jesus has taken the judgment on himself. The blood of Jesus cleanses you from all sin. The Holy Spirit lives in you. Expect him to do great things through you – as you lean your whole weight on him.

PRAYER

Lord I bring to you today all my fears, anxieties and the challenges that lie ahead. I put my trust in you. I lean my whole weight on you today.

14 November | Day 318
The Race Marked Out for You

I have made many mistakes in life and have quite a few regrets. When I was nineteen, I took part, on a whim, without any training, in 'The Boundary Run'. It was slightly longer than a marathon and involved running around the boundary of the city of Cambridge, with much of it across ploughed fields.

For the first 14 miles, I was fine. After that, various bits of my body started to seize up. Although I completed the race in a reasonable time, it took me weeks to recover. Running a marathon without training is not a wise thing to do.

The writer of Hebrews says that the Christian life is like running a race. It is more like a marathon than a sprint. We are 'long-distance runners' (Hebrews 12:13, MSG). It requires *training*, *endurance* and *discipline* 'if we are not to grow weary and lose heart' (v.3). In each of the passages for today, you see what you need to do in order to run 'the race marked out for [you]' (v.1), as well as some of the results of doing so.

READING FROM PSALMS

Psalm 125:1–5
Stay on track and keep going

'Nothing great was ever done without much enduring,' wrote St Catherine of Siena.

The key to *endurance* lies in trusting God: 'Those who *trust* in God are like Mount Zion, which cannot be shaken but *endures for ever*' (v.1). This is not based on wishful thinking, but on the character and protection of the God in whom we trust.

God is *with* you. He is *for* you. He is *above* you. He is *in* you. He *surrounds* you: 'the LORD *surrounds* his people' (v.2). This protection is something you can rely on 'both now, and for evermore' (v.2).

Faith ('trust in the Lord', v.1) leads to righteousness (Romans 3:22), and the rest of this psalm focuses on the long-term outlook for both the righteous and the wicked. Regardless of how things may seem at the moment, 'the sceptre of the wicked will not remain over the land allotted to the *righteous*' (Psalm 125:3a).

The psalmist warns against turning off the track: 'Those who turn to crooked ways the LORD will banish with the evildoers' (v.5). When we wander off the path we lose our peace. The psalmist's prayer is '*peace* be upon Israel' (v.5b).

PRAYER

Lord, thank you that you surround those who trust in you. I trust you with my life again today. Please protect me and give me your peace.

NEW TESTAMENT READING

Hebrews 12:1–13
Run the race with perseverance

There is a race 'marked out' for you that you are urged to 'run with perseverance' (v.1). In this race, you have great encouragement. You are 'surrounded by a great cloud of witnesses' (v.1). These are the men and women of faith. Those listed in Hebrews 11 have all died, but the witnesses that surround us also include those still alive who are living examples of faith: 'all those pioneers who blazed the way, all those veterans cheering us on' (v.1, MSG).

Running your race is not going to be without its obstacles, difficulties, opposition and challenges. There are things that can trip you up along the way: 'throw off everything that hinders and the sin that so easily entangles' (v.1).

In the ancient world, *contestants* stripped down to a loincloth for the race. Don't be a *spectator*. Get in the race as a *contestant*.

Too many clothes would hinder an athlete. This is an analogy of getting rid not only of sin but also of other hindrances and distractions. Today, for example, social media can be good but it may also be a distraction.

The key to running the race successfully is to 'fix our eyes on Jesus' (v.2). Where an athlete looks is key to their success. Good athletes keep their eyes fixed on the finish line.

Jesus 'never lost sight of where he was headed – that exhilarating finish in and with God' (v.2, MSG). The only way to make 'straight paths for your feet' (v.13, KJV) is to be looking ahead at the goal rather than looking down at your feet. Keep your eyes fixed on Jesus. For every one look *within*, take ten looks at *him*.

As a follower of Christ, you will receive a lot of opposition, criticism and negative publicity, but it is absolutely nothing compared to what Jesus endured for you.

Jesus is 'the author ['leader', 'originator', 'pioneer'] and perfecter ['completer', 'finisher'] of our faith, who for the joy set before Him endured the cross, scorning its shame, and sat down at the right hand of the throne of God' (v.2, AMP). The key to your endurance is to 'consider him who endured such opposition from sinners, so that you will not grow weary and lose heart' (v.3).

Keeping your eyes fixed on Jesus should help you to put it all in perspective. For most of us, in our struggle against sin (like the readers of this letter) we have not yet resisted to the point of shedding our blood (v.4).

Running a successful race requires training. Training is hard work; it requires discipline and can even be quite painful.

Here the writer uses the image of parents disciplining their children. It is done out of love: 'the Lord disciplines those he loves' (v.6a). Discipline is the proof 'that God regards you as his children' (v.6, MSG).

He goes on, 'God is educating you; that's why you must never drop out. He's treating you as dear children. This trouble you're in isn't punishment; it's training, the normal experience of children' (vv.7–8, MSG).

'We respect our own parents for training and not spoiling us, so why not embrace God's training so we can truly live?' (v.9, MSG). God is training you for your own good that you may 'share in his holiness' (v.10). It may be painful at the time but, 'later, of course, it pays off handsomely, for it's the *well-trained* who find themselves mature in their relationship with God' (v.11, MSG).

Keep running the race: 'So don't sit around on your hands! No more dragging your feet! Clear the path for long-distance runners so no one will trip and fall, so no one will step in a hole and sprain an ankle. Help each other out. And run for it!' (vv.12–13, MSG).

PRAYER

Lord, help me to endure hardship as discipline, knowing that you are treating me as your child (v.7). May I come to share in your holiness and produce a harvest of righteousness and peace.

OLD TESTAMENT READING

Ezekiel 26:1–27:36
Throw off anything that slows you down

Western society is in danger of going in the same direction as Tyre. It was wealthy and powerful. It was a nation of successful business and global trading. This has a contemporary feel. As Ken Costa describes in his book, *God at Work*, 'Tyre was at the corner of all financial and commercial transactions in the region. Tyre could so easily be the City of London or Wall Street or Tokyo.'

Tyre is an example of society organised to fulfil itself without God. It is attractive (27:3), and that is what makes it so seductive. Money-making, empire building and luxury *are* attractive.

We are supposed to *love people* and *use things*. We go wrong when we start *loving things* and *using people*. Consumerism is a great danger in the modern world, but it is nothing new. Tyre was a nation that had ended up loving things and using people – even trading slaves (v.14).

To run the race successfully we have to 'throw off everything that *hinders* and the *sin* that *so easily entangles*' (Hebrews 12:1).

The sins of Tyre were pride, revelling and self-sufficiency (Isaiah 23; Ezekiel 27:3). There was treachery and slave trading (Amos 1:9; Ezekiel 27:13). Ezekiel warns that God's judgment will fall on the nation (Ezekiel 26:1–6). Its pride will be its downfall. Tyre boasted, 'I am perfect in beauty' (27:3).

But God warns, 'Everything sinks – your rich goods and products, sailors and crew, ship's carpenters and soldiers, sink to the bottom of the sea. Total shipwreck' (v.27, MSG).

This prophecy was partially fulfilled in 586–573 BC, when Nebuchadnezzar, King of Babylon, laid siege to Tyre for thirteen years. Nebuchadnezzar did not completely destroy Tyre, but Alexander the Great fulfilled these verses in 332 BC.

The focus on trading, money and consumer goods seems eerily similar to some aspects of modern consumerism (especially in this season as we lead up to Christmas). We need to remember that, however enticing these things may seem, they are transitory and fleeting.

Don't get entangled. Keep your eyes fixed on Jesus the author and perfecter of your faith (Hebrews 12:1–2). Throw off everything that hinders and the sin that so easily entangles. Run with perseverance the race marked out for you.

PRAYER

Lord, help me to run with perseverance the race marked out for me, to fix my eyes on Jesus and never to grow weary nor lose heart.

15 November | Day 319
Why and How to Worship

Why is worship important? What are you doing when you worship God?

The writer of Hebrews urges us to 'worship God acceptably with reverence and awe, for your "God is a consuming fire"' (Hebrews 12:28–29).

The common theme in all three passages for today is *Mount Zion* (Psalm 126:1), '*the heavenly Jerusalem*, the city of the living God' (Hebrews 12:22), '*the holy mount of God*' (Ezekiel 28:14, 16). This is the place of the presence of God, where God is worshipped both in the old and new covenant. However, there is a difference between the two.

You no longer have to go to a specific physical place to experience the presence of God. Because of Jesus, the 'mediator of a *new covenant*' (Hebrews 12:24a), you can worship *anywhere*. Jesus is the one who has made this new relationship with God possible through his death on the cross for you and me.

Your 'holy mountain', where you can worship Jesus, is the whole earth, and this anticipates the 'heavenly Jerusalem' we read about in our passage from Hebrews, and which is described in Revelation 21 – the new heaven and new earth.

As you draw close to Jesus in worship there are, as C.H. Spurgeon pointed out, 'three results of nearness to Jesus' – happiness, holiness and humility.[1]

READING FROM PSALMS

Psalm 126:1–6
1. Happiness

Children laugh, on average, 150 times a day. Adults laugh, on average, only six times a day. Jesus tells us to be more like children.

The Christian faith uniquely combines laughter and tears, joy and solemnity. 'We laughed, we sang ... God was wonderful to us; we are one happy people' (vv.2–3, MSG). This psalm celebrates the return to Zion of the people who had been in captivity. They are so happy: 'When the Lord brought back the captives to Zion, we were like those who dreamed' (v.1).

They had returned to the holy mountain – Mount Zion. This was the place of the temple of God. This earthly salvation foreshadows the even greater salvation that you experience through Jesus.

Like them, your response should be one of worship: 'Our mouths were filled with laughter, our tongues with *songs of joy*. Then it was said among the nations, "The Lord has done great things for them." The Lord has done great things for us, and we are filled with joy' (vv.2–3).

There are plenty of tears in the Christian life. If life is tough for you at the moment, pray that God will restore your fortunes. If you are sowing in tears right now, there will come a time when you will begin to reap with songs of joy (vv.5–6).

PRAYER

Restore my fortunes, O Lord. May I find happiness, laughter and joy in your presence.

NEW TESTAMENT READING

Hebrews 12:14–29
2. Holiness

'More spiritual progress can be made in one short moment of speechless silence in *the awesome presence of God* than in years of mere study,'[2] wrote A. W. Tozer.

Worship is coming into '*the awesome presence*' of a holy God on his holy mountain. Our God is 'a consuming fire' (v.29). You are called to be like him: 'Make every effort ... to be holy; without holiness no one will see the Lord' (v.14b). Holiness involves effort. As Mother Teresa said, 'Our progress in holiness depends on God and ourselves – on God's grace and on our *will* to be holy.' You can decide to let Jesus make you holy.

Relationships really matter: 'Make every effort to live in peace with everyone' (v.14a). Don't do anything that could cause you to miss out on the grace of God (to miss out on his holy presence). 'Keep a sharp eye out for weeds of bitter discontent. A thistle or two gone to seed can ruin a whole garden in no time' (v.15, MSG). Pull out the roots of bitterness as soon as you detect them.

We have a responsibility for ourselves and for each other: 'see that no-one is sexually immoral' or 'godless like Esau', who, in a moment of madness, threw away so much for instant gratification: 'trading away God's lifelong gift in order to satisfy a short-term appetite' (v.16, MSG).

Look at the contrast between the *physical mountain* where the law was given in the Old Testament, and the *heavenly Mount Zion* where you now come to worship God. Think about the extraordinary display of God's holiness, which accompanied the giving of the law and which left even Moses terrified (vv.18–21).

Every time you worship, you are surrounded by thousands upon thousands of angels (v.22b) and the very presence of the living God (v.23b). All those who have died in Christ join in the heavenly worship (v.23c). You join with billions of Christians alive now and those in heaven.

Supremely, every time you worship 'you've come to Jesus' (v.23, MSG) who makes all this possible (v.24b). 'The murder of Jesus, unlike Abel's – a homicide that cried out for vengeance – became a proclamation of grace' (v.24, MSG). The blood of Christ brings a message of cleansing, forgiveness and peace with God to all who place their faith in him.

As you come to worship Jesus, 'do you see how thankful we must be? Not only thankful, but brimming with worship, deeply reverent before God' (v.28, MSG).

PRAYER

Lord Jesus, thank you that I can come into your presence through your blood shed for me on the cross. Help me to be holy and to worship God acceptably with reverence and awe.

OLD TESTAMENT READING

Ezekiel 28:1–29:21
3. Humility

Holiness and humility are inextricably linked. Jesus showed us that at the heart of holiness is humility. On the other hand, pride is at the root of all sin. It was pride that led to Satan's downfall.

According to the biblical world-view, behind the evil in the world there lies the devil. The Greek word for devil, *diabolos*, translates the Hebrew word *satan*. We are not told very much about the origins of Satan in the Bible. But this passage is one of the few that might give some hint of the origin of Satan.

Although the original context is the fall of the King of Tyre, it seems that Satan, the ruler of this world (2 Corinthians 4:4), was behind the ruler of Tyre.

Read alongside Isaiah 14:12–23 and Revelation 12, it appears that both humans and Satan were created good: 'You were the model of perfection, full of wisdom and perfect in beauty. You were in Eden, the garden of God' (Ezekiel 28:12–13). It appears that Satan was an angel: 'You were anointed as a guardian cherub, for so I ordained you. You were on the *holy mount of God*' (v.14). Satan had access to the throne of grace and to the presence of the Lord. He was blameless in his ways (v.15).

Instead of worshipping God on the mountain of God 'his heart became proud, going around saying, "I'm a god. I sit on God's divine throne, ruling the sea"' (v.2, MSG). He was 'trying to be a god' (v.2, MSG). 'By your great skill in trading you have increased your wealth, and because of your wealth your heart has grown proud' (v.5).

Just as great skills and wealth can lead to pride, so can good looks: 'Your heart became proud on account of your beauty, and you corrupted your wisdom because of your splendour' (v.17).

This is a description of self-worship, which happens when we put our success down to our own wisdom, skill and abilities (v.4), without realising that these things come from God and that we should worship him alone. Instead of worshipping the Sovereign Lord, the temptation is to worship success, wealth and beauty – the gods of our culture – they are 'god-pretentions' (v.7, MSG).

God brings down the proud and exalts the humble. As a result of his pride and sin, Satan was expelled from the presence of God: 'you sinned. So I drove you in disgrace *from the mount of God*, and I expelled you' (v.16), 'So I threw you to the earth' (v.17; see Isaiah 14:12; Luke 10:18). Satan's final destruction is assured (Ezekiel 28:18b–19). Jesus defeated Satan by his death and resurrection.

The attitude of Jesus is the complete opposite to that of Satan. He took the opposite path: 'Who, being in very nature God ... made himself nothing ... he *humbled himself* and became obedient to death – even death on a cross! Therefore God exalted him to the highest place and gave him the name that is above every name, that at the name of Jesus every knee should bow, in heaven and on earth and under the earth, and every tongue confess that Jesus Christ is Lord, to the glory of God the Father' (Philippians 2:6–11).

Worship Jesus today. As you draw close to him throughout your lifetime you will experience these benefits – happiness, holiness and humility.

PRAYER

Lord Jesus, today I bow my knee to worship you and confess that you are Lord, to the glory of God the Father.

16 November | Day 320

Eight Characteristics of Christian Community

Former England football captain, David Beckham, recounts being sent off in the 1998 World Cup Finals: 'It was probably the longest walk in my life ... looking back I'm not sure what thoughts were going through my mind: it was a swirl of fear, guilt, anger, worry and confusion. My head was spinning ... I walked into the dressing room. The rules stated that I had to stay in there for the remainder of the match. England lost. We were out of the World Cup.

'When the England players came back into the dressing room, no one breathed a word to me. There was almost complete silence. I could feel my stomach tightening even more. I gulped, breathed in, and gulped again. I was in a packed changing room but I had never felt so *lonely* in my life. I was *isolated* and afraid ... I was trapped in my own sense of guilt and anxiety.'[1]

God does not intend for you to be *lonely* and *isolated* God created you for community – calling you into relationship with him and with other human beings.

The Christian community, the church, is the community of our Lord Jesus, the 'great Shepherd of the sheep' (Hebrews 13:20). Every local church is called to be a community of the great Shepherd.

READING FROM PROVERBS

Proverbs 27:23–28:6
A community of pastoral care

At the end of the day it is people that count. 'Know your sheep by name; carefully attend to your flocks' (27:23, MSG).

The Bible often uses this same image of a shepherd and their flock to describe God's care of his people, and the role of leaders within the people of God (e.g. Psalm 78:70–71; 1 Peter 5:2–4). Take great care of those entrusted to you. Know their condition and give careful attention to them. In fact, we should be so proximate to the people that as Pope Francis puts it, the shepherd should 'smell of the sheep'.[2]

These verses point to three characteristics of the kind of community we should build:

1. A bold community

Be bold in your faith: 'The wicked are edgy with guilt, ready to run off even when no one's after them; Honest people are relaxed and confident, *bold as lions*' (Proverbs 28:1, MSG).

2. A well-led community

Where there is chaos everyone has a plan to fix it, 'but it takes a leader of real understanding to straighten things out' (v.2, MSG).

3. A just community

'The wicked ... oppress the poor ... Justice makes no sense to the evilminded; those who seek God know it inside and out' (vv.3, 5, MSG).

PRAYER

Lord, help us to follow the example of Jesus, the great Shepherd of the sheep. May we be a bold community, well led, seeking you and your justice and caring for the poor.

NEW TESTAMENT READING

Hebrews 13:1–25
A community of Jesus

The community of Jesus, the great Shepherd of the sheep (v.20), is the most wonderful community on earth. It is 'held together by love' (v.1, MSG). This love is not just about feelings. It makes a difference to the way you act. If you want to know what loving each other 'as brothers and sisters' (v.1) looks like in practice, the writer of Hebrews emphasises five further defining traits that should be characteristics of Christian community:

1. Extend hospitality

'Be ready with a meal or a bed when it's needed. Why, some have extended hospitality to angels without ever knowing it!' (v.2, MSG) – as did Abraham and Sarah (Genesis 18).

Shared meals are central to hospitality and mission. When you eat together you let down your guard, welcome strangers and become friends.

2. Help those in need

'Regard prisoners as if you were in prison with them. Look on victims of abuse as if what happened to them had happened to you' (Hebrews 13:3, MSG). When you minister to those in prison, or to victims of abuse, you encounter Jesus (Matthew 25:40).

3. Honour marriage

'Honour marriage, and guard the sacredness of sexual intimacy between wife and husband. God draws a firm line against casual and illicit sex' (Hebrews 13:4, MSG).

4. Be content

'Don't be obsessed with getting more material things. Be relaxed with what you have. Since God assured us, "I'll never let you down, never walk off and leave you"' (v.5, MSG). You don't need to have your mind set on money, because God has promised that as you set your mind on him, he will take care of these things for you. He will never leave you nor forsake you (v.5).

5. Please God

'Through Jesus, therefore, let us continually offer to God a *sacrifice of praise* – the fruit of lips that confess his name. And do not forget to *do good* and to *share with others*, for with such sacrifices *God is pleased*' (vv.15–16). These three things please God: *praying* (especially praising), *serving* (doing good) and *giving* (sharing with others).

The writer also emphasises the importance of leadership in the Christian community. We are all under our Lord Jesus, 'that great Shepherd of the sheep' (v.20). However, there are human leaders as well. There are five things he says about leaders:

1. Appreciate them

'Appreciate' *all* your leaders and especially those who first brought the good news to you and first looked after you (v.7a, MSG).

2. Imitate them

'Consider the outcome of their way of life and *imitate their faith*' (v.7b). This is a huge challenge for any involved in Christian leadership. Others are watching and are called to imitate. A good example is worth twice as much as good advice.

3. Be responsive to them

'Be responsive to your pastoral leaders. Listen to their counsel. They are alert to the condition of your lives and work under the strict supervision of God. Contribute to the joy of their leadership, not its drudgery. Why would you want to make things harder for them?' (v.17, MSG).

4. Pray for them

The writer himself was presumably one of their leaders and he urges, '*Pray for us*. We have no doubts about what we're doing or why, but it's hard going and we need your prayers' (v.18, MSG).

5. Welcome them

'*Greet* all your leaders and all God's people' (v.24). Presumably they are to be greeted with the words with which the letter ends. 'Grace be with you all' (v.25). 'Grace' is the word that sums up the letter and the kind of community that we are to be. It is in the community of grace where all people will find love, meaning and hope.

PRAYER

Lord, help us to be a community of love, hospitality, help, faithfulness and contentment. May we please you by our worship, serving and giving.

OLD TESTAMENT READING

Ezekiel 30:1–31:18
A community that knows the Shepherd

God's intention for his community is that we should be a place where the lost, the broken and the lonely find hope, healing and love.

Later on, Ezekiel speaks about the shepherd who is a national ruler (Ezekiel 34). In a prophecy about Jesus he says, 'I will place over them *one shepherd* ... he will tend them and *be their shepherd*' (v.23).

However, in today's passage, Ezekiel speaks of the community that does *not* know the Lord. He predicts the judgment day when 'they *will* know that I am LORD' (30:8, 19, 26). This passage is a warning about the kind of attitudes to avoid. They relied on their wealth (v.4) and their 'proud strength' (v.6). They were arrogant (v.10, MSG). They were complacent (v.9) and they displaced God with idols (v.13).

The cedar of Lebanon (chapter 31) contrasts with the kind of community Jesus describes. This great cedar started off towering higher than all the trees of the field, with all the birds of the air nesting in its boughs (vv.5–6). All the great nations lived in its shade. It was majestic and beautiful. Its roots went down to abundant waters (v.7). However, it was cut down and came to nothing (v.10 onwards).

The kingdom of God is the very opposite. It starts off 'like a mustard seed, which is the smallest seed you plant in the ground. Yet when planted, it grows and becomes the largest of all garden plants, with such big branches that the birds of the air can perch in [our] shade' (Mark 4:31–32).

Let's seek to be a community that grows like the mustard seed and becomes a place where the lost, the broken and the lonely can perch in its shade – a community that knows the Lord, where people really matter, and where we enjoy the leadership of our Lord Jesus, the great Shepherd of the sheep.

PRAYER

'May the God of peace, who through the blood of the eternal covenant brought back from the dead our Lord Jesus, *that great Shepherd of the sheep*, equip [us] with everything good for doing his will, and may he work in us what is pleasing to him, through Jesus Christ, to whom be glory for ever and ever. Amen' (Hebrews 13:20–21).

---

17 November | Day 321
Five Ts of the Christian Life

The Christian life is multi-faceted. At any given moment, I find there are a number of different things going on at the same time. In the passages for today we see five of these aspects, which all begin with the letter T.

READING FROM PSALMS

Psalm 127:1–5
1. Trust

The Christian life is not meant to be one of self-dependent toil, but of dependent trust. With trust comes *peace* and *sleep*.

'Unless the LORD builds the house, its builders labour in vain. Unless the LORD watches over the city, the guards stand watch in vain. In vain you rise early and stay up late, toiling for food to eat – for *he grants sleep to those he loves*' (vv.1–2). As Victor Hugo wrote, 'When you have ... accomplished your daily task, go to sleep in peace; God is awake.'

It is easy to get caught up with our own plans for our lives, families and ministries. This psalm is a wonderful reminder that ultimately you are totally dependent on the Lord.

This is a message of great comfort, but it is also a challenge. Is God part of everything you do? Are there any areas of your life where you are going it alone, and therefore 'labouring in vain'?

God wants to be involved in every area of your life. If you want your work to have lasting value, you need to make sure you are partnering with the Lord and not going it alone. Trust God with your children as well. Children are a blessing (vv.3–5) and you have to trust God for them and for their future.

PRAYER

Lord, I commit my life, my family, our church, and everything I am involved in into your hands. I trust in you.

NEW TESTAMENT READING

James 1:1–27
2. Trials

One of the things that you have in common with all Christians everywhere, is that we all face '*trials of many kinds*' (v.2b). The letter of James is written to the twelve tribes scattered among the nations (that is, to all Christians everywhere).

In one of the strangest verses of the New Testament, James says, 'consider it *pure joy* ... whenever you face trials' (v.2). Rejoice in difficult situations. This turns the world's view upside-down. 'Trials' are the challenges of life that test your faith and develop perseverance (vv.3–4).

As has been said, 'Every storm is a school. Every trial is a test. Every experience is an education. Every difficulty is for your development.'

Joyce Meyer writes, 'I finally realised that God was not going to do things my way. He placed people and situations in my life that caused me to want to quit this whole process, and he did not want an argument from me. He only wanted to hear, "Yes, Lord. Your will be done."'[1]

In the midst of your trials you need wisdom. As Eugene Peterson says: 'Wisdom is not primarily about knowing the truth, although it certainly includes that; it is skill in living.' James says, 'If any of you lacks wisdom, you should ask God, who gives generously to all without finding fault, and *it will be given to you*' (v.5).[2]

There are two ways to handle a problem. One is to go it alone – that is the natural way. The other is to ask God for divine wisdom to help you to know what to do.

James speaks of 'the *testing* of your faith' (v.3). He goes on, 'blessed are those who persevere under trial, because when they have stood the *test*, they will receive the crown of life that God has promised to those who love him' (v.12). It is almost as if James is saying that the whole of life is a test. After you have stood the test, you will receive the crown of life that God has promised to those who love him.

PRAYER

Lord, please give me wisdom for all the decisions I have to take and all the trials that I face.

3. Temptation

'Temptation', wrote William Shakespeare, is 'the fiend at mine elbow.'[3] Somebody else said: 'Opportunity may knock only once, but temptation leans on the doorbell.' Temptation is when we feel like doing the wrong thing. Temptation itself is not a sin. Rather, it is a call to battle.

Where does temptation come from? Certainly not from God. James says, 'when tempted, no one should say, "God is tempting me." For God *cannot be tempted* by evil, *nor does he tempt anyone*' (v.13).

Often, in the Bible, temptation is seen as coming from the devil. Jesus was tempted by the devil. Adam and Eve were tempted by the serpent. Job was attacked by Satan.

However, the devil works on our own evil desires: 'Each of you is tempted when, by your own evil desire, you are dragged away and enticed. Then, after desire has conceived, it gives birth to sin; and sin, when it is full-grown, gives birth to death' (vv.14–15).

Sin is always a deception. James writes, 'Don't be deceived, my dear brothers and sisters' (v.16). Good things come from God: 'Every good and perfect gift is from above, coming down from the Father of the heavenly lights, who does not change like shifting shadows' (v.17).

You are deceived when you think that you need things that are not good. The deception in the Garden of Eden was that Adam and Eve thought that they needed to experience evil as well as good. God only wants you to experience good. Every time you feel like doing the wrong thing and choose to do the right thing, you grow in maturity, strength and wisdom.

PRAYER

Lord, thank you that every good and perfect gift is from you. May I not be deceived into wanting to experience things that are not good.

4. Tongue

One of the tests of your character is your tongue. James has a great deal to say on the subject of the tongue. Keep a tight rein on the tongue. Get your mouth under control (v.26).

He writes, 'Everyone should be *quick to listen*, *slow to speak* and slow to become angry, for human anger does not bring about the righteous life that God desires. Therefore, get rid of all moral filth and the evil that is so prevalent, and humbly accept the word planted in you, which can save you' (vv.19–21).

The word of God has the power to transform you. You need to allow time for God's word to be planted firmly in you, to hear it and then do what it says. Rather than speaking too much, listen to God's word and get rid of all the bad stuff in your life.

Listening in itself, though, is not enough. 'Do not merely listen to the word, and so deceive yourselves. Do what it says' (v.22). If you do what it says, you will 'be blessed' (v.25). This includes looking after orphans and widows and keeping yourself from being polluted by the world (v.27).

PRAYER

Lord, help me today to keep a tight rein on my tongue. Help me to listen, especially to the word of God.

OLD TESTAMENT READING

Ezekiel 32:1–33:20
5. Turn

God's will is for 'all people to be saved and to come to a knowledge of the truth' (1 Timothy 2:4).

The word '*turn*' or '*turns*' appears seven times in Ezekiel 33. God appointed Ezekiel as a watchman. He was to be held accountable. God told him to 'warn the wicked to *turn* from their ways' (Ezekiel 33:9).

Provided you speak the message God gives you, you are not responsible for the results. Ezekiel was only responsible if he failed to give the warning (vv.8–9).

This is an important reminder about family, friends and those you know who are not followers of Jesus, for example, guests on Alpha. Your responsibility is to love them, encourage them and give them the opportunity to hear the gospel. It is hugely disappointing when they do not respond positively. However, do not take the burden of their decisions on your own shoulders.

The message Ezekiel was told to give was this: if a righteous person leaves the path and *turns* to wickedness, their former righteousness will not help them. Yet, however 'wicked' a person has been, if they *turn to the Lord, they will be forgiven* (v.12).

God says, 'I take no pleasure from the death of the wicked. I want the wicked to *change their ways* and live. *Turn your life around!* Reverse your evil ways!' (v.11, MSG).

God wants everyone to repent of their sins and start 'living a righteous and just life – being generous to the down-and-out, restoring what [was] stolen, cultivating life-nourishing ways that don't hurt others ... living a just and righteous life' (vv.15–19, MSG).

PRAYER

Lord, help me to turn from evil and find life, and then to see others doing that in their lives – on Alpha, in our church and in churches all around the world – that many, many people may turn to you and find life.

18 November | Day 322
How Now Shall We Live?

How Now Shall We Live? is the title of a book by Chuck Colson, former 'hatchet-man' of President Nixon, founder of Prison Fellowship, whose life was completely changed as a result of an encounter with Jesus Christ.

Centuries ago, when the people of God were in exile and despair, they cried out to God, "*How should we then live?*" (Ezekiel 33:10, KJV). The same question rings down through the ages. As 'believers in our glorious Lord Jesus Christ' (James 2:1), *how now shall we live?*

READING FROM PSALMS

Psalm 128:1–6
Bask in blessings

God promises blessing on families, peace, prosperity and long life for those who walk in his ways: 'Blessed are all who fear the LORD, who *walk in his ways*' (v.1).

You will eat the fruit of your labour (v.2). Some people slave away for money and success but never enjoy what they have earned.

But, 'all you who fear GOD, how blessed you are! How happily you walk on his smooth straight road! ... Enjoy the blessing! Revel in the goodness! ... Stand in awe of God's Yes. Oh, how he *blesses* the one who fears GOD! Enjoy the good life...' (vv.1–6, MSG).

These promises are superseded by Jesus' promise of 'life in all its fullness' (John 10:10, GNT). Our life on this earth may be short and, for many, full of trouble and difficulty. But the blessings are even greater and eternal (17:3). Eternal life is a quality of life that starts now and goes on for ever.

Bask in his blessings. Walk in his ways and lead others to do the same.

PRAYER

Lord, thank you for these amazing promises. Help me to bask in your blessings today.

NEW TESTAMENT READING

James 2:1–26
Live with love

The poor come to all of us in many forms. Mother Teresa said, 'Never turn your back to the poor, for in turning your back to the poor, you are turning it to Christ.'[1]

Love for the poor is not an optional extra. It is at the heart of the New Testament. It is evidence of living faith: 'If you really keep the royal law found in Scripture, "*Love* your neighbour as yourself," you are doing right' (v.8). Your love is shown especially in what you do for the poor (vv.2–7), the hungry (v.15) and the needy (v.16). 'Kind mercy wins over harsh judgment every time' (v.13, MSG).

Treat the rich and the poor equally. If we discriminate against the poor, then we have 'become judges with evil thoughts' (v.4). God's bias, if anything, is in favour of the poor (v.5).

James goes on to say, 'Suppose a brother or sister is without clothes and daily food. If one of you says to him, "Go, I wish you well; keep warm and well fed," but does nothing about his physical needs, what good is it?' (vv.15–16).

As believers in Jesus, we are called to live differently. Your faith must be evidenced by your deeds. All the way through the New Testament, these two go together. As do words and actions; proclamation and demonstration; the conversion of individuals and the transformation of society.

James writes, 'What good is it, my brothers and sisters, if people claim to have *faith* but have no *deeds*? Can such faith save them? ... Faith by itself, if it is not accompanied by action, is dead' (vv.14, 17): 'Isn't it obvious that *God-talk* without *God-action* is outrageous nonsense?' (v.17, MSG). In other words, if your faith does not change how you live, it is not real faith at all.

James continues, 'You can no more show me your works apart from your faith than I can show you my faith apart from my works. Faith and works, works and faith, fit together hand in glove' (v.18, MSG).

He proves that mere intellectual belief in God is not enough: 'You believe that there is one God. Good! Even the demons believe that – and shudder' (v.19).

Interestingly, like Paul, James uses the example of Abraham. Paul used the example of Abraham to show that justification comes by faith. James uses his life to show that 'his faith and his actions were working together, and his faith was made complete by what he did' (v.22).

James' second example of this 'seamless unity' is a more unusual one. He looks at the actions of the prostitute Rahab. She demonstrated her faith in God by helping out two Israelite spies (see Joshua 2) and was 'considered righteous' as a result – though she can hardly be described as a model citizen!

By using her as an example, James makes clear that he is not talking about earning our way to God by being good people. Rather, he is demonstrating that there is a 'seamless unity of *believing* and *doing*' (James 2:25, MSG). Rahab acted on what she believed. James concludes, 'As the body without the spirit is dead, so faith without deeds is dead' (v.26).

As John Calvin put it, 'Faith alone justifies, but faith which justifies is never alone.' You cannot earn your salvation. You are not saved by your good works, but you are saved in order to do good works (Ephesians 2:9–10). The book of James does *not* contradict the apostle Paul (as some have suggested). James' point is not that you can earn your salvation by good deeds. Rather, he is saying that genuine faith will be *evidenced* by how you live.

PRAYER

Lord, help me to live a life of love and to act urgently on behalf of the poor – locally and globally.

OLD TESTAMENT READING

Ezekiel 33:21–35:15
Shepherd the sheep

The Lord spoke out against the leaders of Israel – 'the shepherds of Israel' (34:2). He accused them of only taking care of themselves and not taking care of the flock (v.8). 'You have not *strengthened the weak* or *healed the sick* or *bound up the injured*. You have not *brought back the strays* or *searched for the lost*' (v.4).

The Lord said, 'I myself will search for my sheep and look after them ... I myself will tend my sheep ... I will *search for the lost* and *bring back the strays*. I will *bind up the injured* and *strengthen the weak*, but the sleek and the strong I will destroy. I will *shepherd the flock with justice*' (vv.11, 15–16).

God's message to his people through Ezekiel had a very similar theme to that of James. The Lord said to Ezekiel, 'They listen to you speak, but don't do a thing you say ... They love to hear you talk, but nothing comes of it' (33:31–32, MSG).

How now shall we live? When we compare the good shepherd to those who have failed to look after the flock, it is clear that there are a number of things that we are called to do:

1. Strengthen the weak
We do this through good teaching, encouragement, prayer and building community.

2. Heal the sick
Honour all those in the medical profession and all those involved in the healing of the sick. You can lay hands on the sick and pray for them in Jesus' name.

3. Bind up the injured
There are so many broken people in our society – in the prisons, homeless on the streets and even in the boardrooms of companies. The Spirit of the Lord enables you to bind up the broken-hearted as you pray for them, embrace them, listen to them and care for them in your community.

4. Go after the strays
There are many prodigal sons and daughters who have strayed from the Father, like lost sheep. Help them come back to the Father's arms.

5. Search for the lost
At times, you may have to leave the other sheep to search for the one who is lost, to bring them back to repentance and cause more joy in heaven. (Luke 15:1–7).

6. Shepherd with justice
Seek justice on behalf of the oppressed, the needy and the poor. We should rescue children, women and men from slavery, bring the perpetrators to justice, set the captives free and care for them.

God's promises to tend his flock become intertwined with the promise of a new shepherd, 'my servant David' (Ezekiel 34:23). This promise points back to the historical king David, who was Israel's best shepherd to date, but it also points forwards to an even greater 'David' who will fulfil all these promises – Jesus, our King and Shepherd.

Jesus said, 'I am the good shepherd' (John 10:14). Through him you receive the 'showers of blessing' (Ezekiel 34:26) and salvation (v.27). He says, 'You my sheep, the sheep of my pasture, are people, and I am your God.' (v.31).

Bask in his blessings. Live a life of love. Strengthen the weak, heal the sick, bind up the injured, bring back the strays, search for the lost and look after people with justice. This is how you should live today.

PRAYER

Lord, let me not just hear your words, but put them into practice.

19 November | Day 323
Divine Connections

God has divine connections lined up for your life. There is power in connection. Connections lead to life. When a husband and a wife *come together*, babies are born. When the spirit of a person and the Spirit of God *come together*, new birth takes place. When brothers and sisters *come together* in unity, God commands his blessing (Psalm 133). When the disciples *came together* on the day of Pentecost, there was an outpouring of the Holy Spirit.

The devil fears connection. His ultimate aim is to cut you off from God. He tries to split marriages, to split friendships, to divide churches, to divide denominations and to isolate people. Although our culture is more connected than ever before through the internet, phones and social media, people are more isolated and lonely than ever.

In 586 BC, Ezekiel had a vision of a battle scene; he saw Death Valley. The valley was full of bones; bones that were very dry because they had separated. They were scattered, fragmented, divided, cut-off, 'abandoned' and therefore dried up. The people of God were in exile and had been scattered by the enemy. They were saying, 'Our bones are dried up and our hope is gone; we are cut off' (Ezekiel 37:11). God asks Ezekiel, *'Can these bones live?'* (v.3). The answer is yes, yes, yes.

READING FROM PSALMS

Psalm 129:1–8
Divine connection to God

Do you sometimes feel kicked around by the enemy? Everything seems to be going wrong. You seem to be losing. You are experiencing the oppression of the enemy (v.1).

But victory rests with the Lord. The psalmist says, 'They've kicked me around ever since I was young ... Their plowmen plowed long furrows up and down my back; then God ripped the harnesses of the evil plowmen to shreds' (vv.1–4, MSG).

Jesus has made victory possible for you through his death and resurrection, which connects you to God.

PRAYER

Lord, help me to stay connected to you in spite of all the attacks.

NEW TESTAMENT READING

James 3:1–18
Divine connection in a healthy community

Dry bones can live again as the bones reconnect. 'You can develop a healthy, robust community that lives right with God and enjoy the results' (v.18, MSG). However, there are conditions, which the apostle James sets out.

He continues to warn about the tongue – especially for those of us who teach: 'Teaching is highly responsible work. Teachers are held to the strictest standards' (v.1, MSG). It is consoling that he adds, 'we all stumble in many ways' (v.2) – certainly I do.

The tongue is a powerful little instrument that can do so much good, and yet so much harm. It can unite or divide: 'By our speech we can ruin the world, turn harmony to chaos, throw mud on a reputation, send the whole world up in smoke and go up in smoke with it, smoke right from the pit of hell' (v.8, MSG).

Relationships, even marriages, often end because of things that have been said or not said. People lose their jobs, their reputation, start arguments or even wars by their words.

Harsh, unjust words have destructive power: 'With the tongue we praise our Lord and Father, and with it we curse people, who have been made in God's likeness' (v.9). To curse means to speak evil. To bless means to speak well. Don't speak negatively. Learn to control the tongue so that you speak words of blessing to people and about people.

Speak words of life. Your words have tremendous power for connection. You can bring healing, encouragement and edification. Your words can change a person's day or even their life.

The apostle James goes on to speak of 'the wisdom that comes from heaven' (v.17). He writes, 'Do you want to be counted wise, to build a reputation for wisdom? Here's what you do: Live well, live wisely, live humbly. It's the way you live, not the way you talk, that counts' (v.13, MSG).

Get rid of all bitter envy and selfish ambition (v.14). They are unspiritual, from the devil and cause all kinds of disorder and evil practice (vv.14–15).

However, wisdom from heaven 'is first of all pure; then peace-loving, considerate, submissive, full of mercy and good fruit, impartial and sincere. Peacemakers who sow in peace raise a harvest of righteousness' (vv.17–18).

If you live like this, your life will have great influence. This is 'the hard work of getting along with each other, treating each other with dignity and honour' (v.18, MSG). If you work hard at your relationships with those around you, then you will 'reap a harvest of righteousness', and you will have a huge impact on society.

PRAYER

Lord, help me to be a peacemaker who brings about connection; sowing peace and producing a harvest of righteousness.

OLD TESTAMENT READING

Ezekiel 36:1–37:28
Divine connection through the Holy Spirit

Hope at last! Dry bones can live! We have read so many prophecies of judgment. But God is about to act. God speaks to his people and says, you are 'coming home': 'I'm on your side'. Instead of death, there is going to be 'life, life and more life' (36:8–11, MSG). How is this to happen? In this passage we see three divine connectors – the world's greatest wireless connectors:

1. The word of God

The word of God gives you connection with God and transforms your relationships: 'Prophesy to these bones and say to them, "Dry bones hear the word of the LORD!"' (37:4). In my own life, I was spiritually dry. In fact, I was dead. I had lots of friends but there wasn't a deep connection. But then I read the New Testament. I heard the word of the Lord. I connected with God and I experienced a far deeper connection with other people. God's promise of restoration is so powerful: 'I will give you a *new heart* and put a *new spirit in you*; I will remove from you your heart of stone and give you a heart of flesh. And I will put my Spirit in you and move you to follow my decrees and be careful to keep my laws' (36:26–27).

God can revive things that have been dry and even dead. When the word of God and the Spirit of God come together, there is resurrection life and the knowledge of God. What is impossible with human beings becomes possible with the power of God. Without God, the church would indeed crumble away as the world tells us. But *with* God, these dry bones *will* live again.

2. The body of Christ

The unity of the church is so important. We need visible signs of this unity, divine connections between different parts of the church and within each local church. This is what Jesus prayed for in John 17. Here the Lord gives Ezekiel a visual aid, using two sticks to communicate the unity God is going to establish: 'Join them together into one stick so that they will become one in your hand ... *one king over all of them ... one shepherd*' (Ezekiel 37:17, 22, 24).

This is a foretaste of the unity of the body of Christ (Ephesians 4:4–6). God promises, '*I will be their God, and they will be my people*' (Ezekiel 37:27). The unity of the church will also lead to the restoration of the city (36:33–38): '*So will the ruined cities be filled with flocks of people*' (v.38). This vision of restored unity gives me such hope for the church in our city, in our nation, and across the world. God never abandons his people, and his plans are always ultimately to restore and save us.

3. The Holy Spirit

The dry bones had 'no breath in them' (37:8), but the Lord said '"Prophesy to the breath ... 'Come ... O breath, and breathe into these slain, that they may live.'" So I prophesied as he commanded me, and breath entered them; they came to life and stood up on their feet – a vast army' (vv.9–10). No English translation can do justice to the Hebrew word *ruach*. It occurs 400 times in the Old Testament (and is translated as different English words in this passage – 'breath' (vv.8–9), 'wind' (v.9), and 'spirit' (vv.1, 14). This Spirit brings new life: 'I am going to open your graves and bring you from them ... I will put my Spirit in you and you will live' (vv.12, 14). This resurrection power lives in you, bringing you new life: 'the Spirit of him who raised Jesus from the dead is living in you' (Romans 8:11).

There is a rattling sound as bones come together. The sound of divine connections forming once again. The sound of God breathing new life into his church by his Spirit. The church is a rising giant, a vast army of Spirit-filled people, full of power, unified in purpose.

PRAYER

Lord, would you breathe new life into your people. From dry bones, raise up a mighty army so that all nations come to know that Jesus Christ is Lord.

20 November | Day 324
You Can Resist Evil

With the rise of global terrorism, world leaders have spoken a great deal about vanquishing evil. But, as one writer in the *Guardian* pointed out, 'Their rhetoric reveals a failure to accept that cruelty and conflict are basic human traits.'[1] As Albert Einstein said, 'I do not fear the explosive power of the atom bomb. What I fear is the explosive power of *evil* in the human heart.'

Why is there so much evil in the world? Why is there such a battle with evil in our own lives? How can you resist the devil? What will happen to the devil at the end of time?

READING FROM PROVERBS

Proverbs 28:7–17
Confess and renounce evil

Here is the answer to evil in our own lives: 'Those who conceal their sins do not prosper, but those who *confess* and *renounce* them find mercy' (v.13).

The writer of Proverbs speaks of different types of evil: murder (v.17), leading the upright along an evil path (v.10), turning a deaf ear to the law (v.9), charging exorbitant interest (v.8) and hard-heartedness (v.14).

He also speaks about evil rulers: 'When good people are promoted, everything is great, but when the bad are in charge, watch out!' (v.12, MSG). 'Among leaders who lack insight, *abuse abounds*' (v.16a, MSG). We've seen this in recent years in, for example, Syria, Libya, Iraq, Zimbabwe, North Korea, Sudan and so on. Good leadership is so important.

He says that an evil leader is 'like *a roaring lion* or a charging bear' ruling over a helpless people (v.15). The apostle Peter describes the devil as '*a roaring lion* looking for someone to devour' (1 Peter 5:8).

When you confess your sins, God offers mercy. 'You can't whitewash your sins and get by with it; you find mercy by admitting and leaving them' (Proverbs 28:13, MSG). Or as St John puts it, 'If we confess our sins, he is faithful and just and will forgive us our sins and purify us from all unrighteousness' (1 John 1:9).

PRAYER

Lord, thank you for this wonderful promise that when I confess my sins and renounce them, I find mercy.

NEW TESTAMENT READING

James 4:1–17
Resist the devil

Why is there so much division in the world? James gives us an uncomfortable answer: 'Where do you think all these appalling wars and quarrels come from? Do you think they just happen? Think again. They come about because *you want your own way*, and fight for it deep inside yourselves' (v.1, MSG). The Bible acknowledges the human sources of evil, but also points to a deeper source.

All human beings have evil tendencies. This chapter is focused on the key battle ground in the fight against evil – *ourselves.* Evil must be resisted. How can you win this battle?

The first problem that James identifies is that when we want something, we go out there and fight for it, rather than asking God: 'You lust for what you don't have and are willing to kill to get it. You want what isn't yours and will risk violence to get your hands on it' (v.2, MSG).

The lure of the pleasures of this world is so strong. But God wants us to be faithful to him. When we pursue the pleasures of this world we become adulterous in our relationship with God: 'When you ask, you do not receive, because you ask with wrong motives, that you may spend what you get on your pleasures' (v.3).

He goes on to say, 'You're cheating on God. If all you want is your own way, flirting with the world every chance you get, you end up enemies of God and his way' (v.4, MSG). This upsets the Holy Spirit: 'Or do you think Scripture says without reason that the spirit he caused to live in us envies intensely?' (v.5). We grieve the Holy Spirit when we go after other gods.

It is also possible to sin by *not* doing something. Sin is not just doing what we know is wrong, it is also failing to do what we know is right: 'In fact, if you know the right thing to do and don't do it, that, for you, is evil' (v.17, MSG).

You cannot overcome evil on your own. Yet, here is the remarkable thing: 'he gives us *more grace*' (v.6a). God does not condemn you. 'God opposes the proud but *gives grace* to the humble' (v.6b). He gives you more grace to overcome evil.

Submit yourself humbly to God: '*Resist the devil*, and he will flee from you. *Come near to God* and he will come near to you' (vv.7–8a). These are wonderful promises worth learning by heart. 'Yell a loud *no* to the Devil and watch him scamper. Say a quiet *yes* to God and he'll be there in no time' (v.7–8a, MSG).

How do you do this? He goes on to explain, 'Quit dabbling in sin' (v.8, MSG). It is no good thinking you can live a holy life and hang on to just *a little bit of sin* in your life. 'Purify your inner life. Quit playing the field ... Get down on your knees before the Master.' God does not leave us there. Getting down on our knees is the way to get back on our feet! (vv.8b–10, MSG).

As we recognise our own shortcomings, we realise we are in no position to judge anyone else. The best way to forget the faults of others is to remember our own. As we ourselves are law-breakers, who are we to sit around judging other people (v.11)? There is only one who is qualified to be the judge: 'the one who is able to save and destroy. But you – who are you to judge your neighbour?' (v.12).

Another evil is self-importance, to be 'full of your grandiose selves' (v.16, MSG). We 'brashly announce, "Today – at the latest, tomorrow – we're off to such and such a city for the year. We're going to start a business and make a lot of money"' (v.13, MSG).

It is good to plan ahead but, at the end of the day, 'You don't know the first thing about tomorrow' (v.14, MSG). You are totally dependent on God. 'Instead, make it a habit to say, "If the Master *wills* it and we're still alive, we'll do this or that."' (vv.15, MSG). The expression '*God-willing*' should not be a formality. Rather, it should express the reality of a heart that recognises that God is ultimately in control, and you are not. The prayer of your heart should be, 'your will be done'.

PRAYER

Lord, forgive us our sins as we forgive those who sin against us. Lead us not into temptation but deliver us from the evil one.

OLD TESTAMENT READING

Ezekiel 38:1–39:29
Be confident in the triumph of good

Evil will not have the last word. Good will ultimately triumph. God is sovereign. As St Thomas Aquinas put it, 'God is so powerful that he can direct any evil to a good end.'

Ezekiel prophesies against 'Gog, of the land of Magog ... I am against you, O Gog' (38:2–3). The identities of Gog and Magog seem to be deliberately mysterious, but Ezekiel uses them to represent the archetypal enemies who 'cook up an evil plot' against God's people (v.10, MSG).

This identification becomes clearer in the book of Revelation (Revelation 19:11 – 20:10), which describes the end of the world and the destruction of Satan. Gog and Magog are identified with Satan and used to represent all the evil forces and people of the earth. The message of both Revelation and Ezekiel is clear: God wins!

This is essentially a message of hope. God says, 'I will execute judgment [on Satan] ... so I will show my greatness and my holiness, and I will make myself known in the sight of many nations. Then they will know that I am the LORD' (Ezekiel 38:22–23).

The context in Ezekiel is that the people were exiled because they were unfaithful to God. So he hid his face from them and handed them over to their enemies (39:23–24). Now he promises that a day will come when evil will fall (vv.4–5). God will be glorified: 'The day I am glorified will be a *memorable day* for them' (v.13).

He promises that he will have compassion on them: 'I'll be compassionate with all the people of Israel ... I'll use them to demonstrate my holiness with all the nations watching ... After I've poured my Spirit on Israel, filled them with my life, I'll no longer turn away. I'll look them full in the face' (vv.25–29, MSG).

These are amazing promises. Satan is a defeated foe. His end will come. You can begin to experience that victory right now. You can resist evil.

PRAYER

Lord, thank you that the powers of evil have been defeated. May there be a great outpouring of your Spirit, so that everyone will know that you are the Lord our God.

21 November | Day 325
How to Pray with Power

I received a call from someone in our church. He wanted me to go and pray for his wife who had suddenly been admitted to hospital for an operation.

As it happened, I myself had an appointment nearby to have an injection in my shoulder. I'd had a 'frozen shoulder' for almost two years. However, in the previous couple of days, it had suddenly got better. I explained what had happened to the consultant. He looked at me and said, 'It's a miracle!' I said, 'Don't frozen shoulders suddenly get better?' Over and over again, he repeated, 'No, it is a miracle.' Here was a secular doctor trying to persuade a rather faithless pastor that what had happened could only be explained by the supernatural power of God!

I thanked him very much for raising my faith, as I was about to go and pray in the hospital. As I walked through the corridors, I passed a hospital porter who was singing (quite loudly!), 'Lay your hands on the sick and they will be healed.' I said, 'That is exactly what I am about to go and do.' He looked deeply shocked and surprised. He obviously didn't think I looked like the sort of person who could possibly believe that!

I went upstairs to pray for the woman and explained why my faith was riding high. She then said she had been reading James 5 (our passage for today), which says, 'Is any one of you sick? Call the elders of the church to pray over you ... And the prayer offered in faith will make you well' (James 5:14–15). By now the Lord had given (even me!) enough signs to pray in faith. The Holy Spirit came upon her with great power. She was not immediately healed (although she is better now), but it gave me a greater understanding of 'the prayer of faith'.

Watchman Nee wrote, 'Our prayers lay the track down which God's power can come. Like a mighty locomotive, his power is irresistible, but it cannot reach us without rails.'

How then can you pray with power?

READING FROM PSALMS

Psalm 130:1–8
Pray honestly

Have you ever felt like you were in the depths of despair? Have you felt that 'the bottom has fallen out of [your] life' (v.1, MSG)? The psalmist says, '*Out of the depths I cry to you*, O Lord; O Lord, hear my voice. Let your ears be attentive to my cry for mercy' (vv.1–2).

Your prayers and God's mercy are like two buckets in a well. When one goes up, the other comes down.[1]

There is an honest desperation about this prayer. Don't try to gloss over the difficulties of your situation, but instead recognise your dependence on God for help.

Trust in God's mercy and forgiveness:

> 'If you, God, kept records on wrong-doings,
> who would stand a chance?
> As it turns out, forgiveness is your habit' (v.3–4a, MSG).

If God does not keep a record of your wrongdoings, you should not keep 'lists' of other people's offences against you. Love 'keeps no record of wrongs' (1 Corinthians 13:5).

You do not need to get your life sorted out before you approach God. He wants to hear the cry of your heart.

However desperate the situation, you can be confident that help will come from God (Psalm 130:6). Bring your request to God. Wait patiently (v.5) and trust in his unfailing love (v.7).

PRAYER

Lord, out of the depths I cry to you for mercy and help. Thank you that with you there is forgiveness and unfailing love.

NEW TESTAMENT READING

James 5:1–20
Pray in all circumstances

One of the obstacles to the power of God in our life can be trusting in things other than God. In some ways, faith and wealth are like oil and water. They are hard to mix and do not often go together.

There is nothing wrong with having money in itself. But there are great spiritual dangers inherent in having wealth – arrogance, greed, self-indulgence and disregard for the needs of others (vv.1–6).

The greatest danger for the wealthy (which probably includes most of us in the West today) is that we put our trust in wealth, rather than in God (1 Timothy 6:17). Why is it that there seem to be far more miracles of healing in some of the poorer parts of the world? Perhaps wealth is a potential barrier to faith, leading us to put our faith in the wrong place. You are called to put your hope in him who provides for all your needs and to pray in all circumstances.

The readers of this letter are clearly going through difficult times. James encourages them to 'be patient and to stand firm' (James 5:8). He points to Job as an example of someone who was patient in the face of suffering, and persevered (v.11a). He reminds them that 'the Lord is full of compassion and mercy' (v.11b).

Pray in all circumstances:

1. If you are hurting

'Is any one of you in trouble? You should pray' (v.13a).

It has been said that 'most of us have much trouble praying when we are in little trouble, but little trouble praying when we're in much trouble.'

2. If you are feeling great

'Is anyone happy? Sing songs of praise' (v.13b).

St Augustine said that 'the thought of you stirs [a person] so deeply that [they] cannot be content unless [they] praise you.'

3. If you are sick

'Is any one of you sick? Call the elders...' (v.14).

Of course, God often heals with the cooperation of the medical profession. But also expect God to heal miraculously today.

4. If you have sinned

There is no automatic link between sin and sickness. However, we cannot rule out the possibility. James says here, 'If you have sinned, you will be forgiven. Therefore confess your sins to each other and pray for each other so that you may be healed' (vv.15b–16).

Confessing our sins to each other and praying for each other helps in the process of healing and restoration. When things in our lives are kept hidden in the dark they can have a destructive power. When we bring them out into the light, we are set free. This does not necessarily mean that you have to tell the whole world. But, you need to find at least one person you can trust and with whom you can be totally honest, vulnerable and unburden yourself.

Prayer is powerful and effective. James makes this point forcefully by looking at the example of Elijah. He famously managed to control the weather through his prayers, causing and ending a drought, and yet James declares that 'he was a man just like us' (v.17). In other words, whatever Elijah could do, you can do!

PRAYER

Lord, thank you that you hear *my* prayers. Today, I pray...

OLD TESTAMENT READING

Ezekiel 40:1–49

Pray with eyes open and ears attentive

Prayer is not a monologue. It is a dialogue. God speaks to you as you pray.

Ezekiel says, 'The hand of the LORD was upon me' (v.1). He was called to be a prophet and a preacher. To a greater or lesser extent, this is the task of every believer in Jesus. We see what is involved:

1. See: *'look with your eyes'*

Look at everything going on around you with the eyes of the Spirit. As D.L. Moody said, 'The Christian on his knees sees more than the philosopher on tiptoe.'

2. Listen: *'hear with your ears'*

Listen to what the Lord says about it all. In your two-way communication with God, what he says to you is more important than what you say to him.

3. Attend: *'pay attention'*

'Attention is the rarest and purest form of generosity,' wrote Simone Weil.[2] This applies to all relationships including your relationship with God.

4. Tell: *'tell ... everything'*

It is not enough just to see and hear. We must obey. Be willing to say what God tells you to say.

Ezekiel receives a vision of a new temple. It is a visionary temple intended to be symbolic. In this, it is like the city described in Revelation (Revelation 21:16). There is a symmetry and perfection about it.

At the heart of the temple is a room where the priests 'draw near to the LORD to minister before him' (Ezekiel 40:46). To 'draw near to the LORD' was restricted to a small number of a small tribe in the Old Testament.

Now, through the blood of Christ, you may *draw near* to the Lord to minister before him (Ephesians 2:13). What a great and wonderful privilege this is. Keep your eyes open and your ears attentive to hear what God is saying to you. Have the courage to speak and the faith to pray the prayer of faith. You are a much-loved child of God. Your prayers are powerful.

PRAYER

Lord, thank you for the extraordinary power of prayer. Please speak to me today as I draw near to you.

22 November | Day 326
How to Grow Up Spiritually

I remember that first night so well. Every time we heard the slightest sound, we leapt out of bed and picked him up. He was so tiny – not that much bigger than a hand. This was a new life. Our first child had been born. We were so proud. Three or four times a night, he would wake craving milk. Pippa would feed him regularly. Of course, he grew up. Now as I look at him, almost twice the size of Pippa, it is hard to believe that he was once so small.

New birth is an exciting moment. So is new spiritual birth. Jesus said, 'No one can see the kingdom of God without being *born again*' (John 3:3). In our passage for today, Peter writes about '*a new birth*' (1 Peter 1:3). 'Because Jesus was raised from the dead, we've been given *a brand-new life* and have everything to live for' (v.3, MSG).

This spiritual birth is contrasted with natural birth, which led only to a 'dead-end, empty-headed life you grew up in' (v.18, MSG).

New birth means you can now call God your Father (v.17). In fact, the whole Trinity is involved: '*God the Father* has his eye on each of you, and has determined by the *work of the Spirit* to keep you obedient through the *sacrifice of Jesus*' (v.2, MSG).

Physical birth will one day end with physical death. But spiritual birth leads to eternal life – 'a future in heaven – and the future starts now!' (v.3, MSG). Physical life is like grass that withers. But this brand new life is conceived by God himself and goes on and on for ever (vv.23–25, MSG).

In today's passages, we see the implications of this new birth, the various stages of spiritual growth as a son or daughter of God and how 'you may grow up in your salvation' (2:2).

READING FROM PSALMS

Psalm 131:1–3
Trust like a baby

Sometimes I get worried, anxious and even fearful. That is why I love this psalm. It is a beautiful picture of total trust: 'Like a baby content in its mother's arms' (v.2, MSG). When I look at any of our baby grandchildren in their parents' arms, I see a picture of total trust and security.

How does this total trust happen? First, resign as managing director of the universe. Stop trying to control everyone and everything. The psalmist writes, 'I'm not trying to rule the roost, I don't want to be king of the mountain. I haven't meddled where I have no business or fantasized grandiose plans' (v.1, MSG).

Second, put your trust in God in the same way that a baby has total trust in a parent: 'I've kept my feet on the ground, I've cultivated a quiet heart. Like a baby content in its mother's arms, my soul is a baby content' (v.2, MSG).

PRAYER

Lord, please give me your peace today like that of a weaned child with its mother.

NEW TESTAMENT READING

1 Peter 1:1–2:3
Grow like a child

Life as a child of God is exciting. The apostle Peter writes about being 'filled with an inexpressible and glorious joy' (1:8). It comes as a result of '*new birth*' (v.3). Peter tells us that '*new birth*' leads to:

1. Security in spite of ageing

Your future is certain because it is based on the resurrection of Jesus. Jesus was buried. God raised him from the dead (v.21). One day, the same will happen to you.

You are an heir to the greatest inheritance. Nothing in this life is perfect – all earthly possessions will ultimately decay or be destroyed. But your inheritance will 'never perish': it will never 'spoil', it will never 'fade' (v.4). It is guaranteed, 'kept in heaven for you, who through faith are shielded by God's power until the coming of the salvation that is ready to be revealed in the last time' (vv.4–5). It has your name on it.

C. S. Lewis wrote: 'As we grow older, we become like old cars – more and more repairs and replacements are necessary. We must just look forward to the fine new machines (latest Resurrection model) which are waiting for us, we hope, in the Divine garage.'[1]

2. Rejoicing in spite of suffering
Rejoicing is not dependent on circumstances (vv.6–7). Life is not always easy: 'In this you greatly rejoice, though now for a little while you may have to suffer grief in all kinds of trials' (v.6). This letter was probably written from Rome, around AD 62–64, in the days immediately before the persecution by Nero. The Christians were already suffering. My suffering may be very small compared to theirs, but we all suffer bereavements, disappointments, opposition, temptation and all the struggles in life.

Peter says, 'you greatly rejoice' (v.6, see also James 1:2) for three reasons:

- the *relative shortness* of the trials ('for a little while', 1 Peter 1:6) compared to what lies in the future
- because there is a *purpose behind them*: our 'faith – of greater worth than gold' (v.7) is being refined
- *their result* is 'praise, glory and honour' (v.7) when Jesus Christ is revealed.

3. Intimacy in spite of invisibility
Peter had actually seen Jesus. Those to whom Peter is writing had not, yet: 'Though you have not seen him, *you love him*; and even though you do not see him now, you believe in him and are filled with an inexpressible and glorious joy' (v.8). Like them, you have never seen Jesus – but also like them, you too can experience a personal and daily relationship with Jesus, and receive the goal of your faith – the salvation of your soul (v.9).

It is an extraordinary privilege to live in a time after the first coming of Jesus. You live in the age of the Spirit. You have received the grace to which the whole Old Testament pointed. The 'Spirit of the Messiah' was at work in the prophets, pointing to Jesus' suffering and glory. Jesus was active in the Old Testament, but they had to wait for his full revelation.

He is coming back. Be prepared.

In the meantime, grow up: 'As obedient children, let yourselves be pulled into a way of life shaped by God's life, a life energetic and blazing with holiness. God said, "I am holy; you be holy"' (vv.14–16, MSG). Only the Holy Spirit, who brings about this new birth and now lives in you, can make you holy.

Leave behind the empty way of life and, instead, live a life of 'sincere love', loving one another deeply from the heart (v.22). This is the ultimate goal of the Christian life: love for Jesus who died to make all this possible (vv.19–20) and a passionate love for one another (v.22).

'So,' the apostle Peter writes, 'clean house! Make a clean sweep of malice and pretence, envy and hurtful talk. You've had a taste of God. Now, like infants at the breast, drink deep of God's pure kindness. Then you'll grow up mature and whole in God' (2:1–3, MSG).

PRAYER

Lord Jesus, I have not seen you, but I love you. Help me to grow up and become a strong, healthy child of God, loving others deeply from my heart.

OLD TESTAMENT READING

Ezekiel 41:1–42:20
Bear fruit into old age

Some people never lose their beauty. It moves from their faces to their hearts. There is an old English proverb, 'the older the fiddle, the sweeter the tune.' At the age of ninety-eight, Titian painted his magnificent picture of the Battle of Lepanto. Old age can be a time of great fruitfulness.

Ezekiel continues his description of the new temple. As he describes the 'Most Holy Place' (41:4), he seems to focus on 'cherubim' and 'palm trees' (v.18). We may assume that their function was merely decorative, but actually they are richly symbolic.

Since we know from our New Testament passage that these words were inspired by the 'Spirit of Christ' (1 Peter 1:11), perhaps it is not too much to see significance in the two faces of each cherub; one of a man and one of a lion, pointing forward to the one who was both fully human being and 'the Lion of the tribe of Judah' (Revelation 5:5) – that is, Jesus Christ.

The psalmist writes, 'the righteous will flourish like a *palm tree* ... They will still *bear fruit* in old age, they will stay fresh and green' (Psalm 92:12–14).

The palm trees were probably date palms – one of the world's oldest food-producing plants. Dates provide energy, vitamins, minerals, fat, fibre, protein, sugar, riboflavin and niacin. The palm trees speak of strength, nourishment and endurance.

PRAYER

Lord, thank you that you take me through all the stages of life, from new birth to being a new born baby craving pure spiritual milk, to an obedient child growing up in my salvation, right the way through to bearing fruit even in old age. May I be like a palm tree – a source of strength, nourishment and endurance.

23 November | Day 327
Where Is God?

Elie Wiesel was born into a Jewish family in Romania. He was only a teenager when he and his family were rounded up by the Nazis and taken first to Auschwitz, and then to Buchenwald. In his book, *Night*, he gives a terrifying and intimate account of the increasing horrors he endured – the death of his parents and eight-year-old sister, and the loss of his innocence by barbaric hands.

In the foreword to the book, François Mauriac writes of his encounter with Elie Wiesel: 'On that most horrible day, even among all those other bad days, when the child witnessed the hanging (yes!) of another child who, he tells us, had the face of a sad angel, he heard someone behind him groan: "For God's sake, *where is God*?" And from within me, I heard a voice answer: "*Where He is*? This is where – hanging here from this gallows."'

François Mauriac goes on, 'And I, who believe that God is love, what answer was there to give my young interlocutor ... What did I say to him? Did I speak to him of that other Jew, this crucified brother who perhaps resembled him and whose cross conquered the world?

'Did I explain to him that what had been a *stumbling block* for his faith had become a *cornerstone* for mine? And that the connection between the cross and human suffering remains, in my view, the key to the unfathomable mystery in which the faith of his childhood was lost ... That is what I should have said to the Jewish child. But all I could do was embrace him and weep.'[1]

His words point to the most profound answer to the question, 'Where is God?' *God is in Christ*. He was on the cross bearing our sins in his body. Now the crucified is among his people. Not only has he suffered *for* you, but he now suffers *with* you.

In the Old Testament, the tabernacle (and later the temple) was the place where people went to meet with God. This was God's home as we see in our Old Testament passage for today (Ezekiel 43:5).

The message of our New Testament passage though is that the glory and presence of God is to be found supremely in Jesus. It is at the very moment that Jesus is rejected and crucified that God's presence among people is finally and fully realised. From that point on there is no need for a physical temple. The only church building the New Testament speaks about is a building made of people (Ephesians 2:20–22), founded and built upon Jesus, the chief cornerstone. The holy temple in the New Testament is one made of 'living stones' (1 Peter 2:5) – in other words, people like you and me. This is God's new home.

READING FROM PSALMS

Psalm 132:1–18
Find God's home

The desire of David's heart was to honour God and to put him above all material comfort: 'I'm not going home, and I'm not going to bed, I'm not going to sleep, not even take time to rest, until I find a *home for God*' (vv.3–5, MSG).

The people said, 'Let us go to *his dwelling-place*; let us worship at his footstool – arise, O LORD, and come to your resting place ... For the Lord has chosen Zion, he has desired it for *his dwelling*' (vv.7–8). God said, '...this will always be *my home*' (v.14, MSG).

PRAYER

Lord, I long for your presence. It is so good to worship at your footstool. Thank you that on the day of Pentecost, when the Spirit of God was poured out, your presence came to live in and among your people.

NEW TESTAMENT READING

1 Peter 2:4–25
Find God in Jesus

Jesus changed everything.

He is the cornerstone of the new home, which is made up of people: 'As you come to him, the living Stone – rejected by human beings but chosen by God and precious to him – you also, like living stones, are being built into *a spiritual house'* (vv.4–5a).

Jesus is either the chief cornerstone or he is the stumbling-block (vv.7–8). Many today still find Jesus a stumbling-block. But if you make him the cornerstone of your life and put your trust in him, you 'will never be put to shame' (v.6)

Peter is saying, to all who believe, that we are called to be the living stones that make up the *spiritual house* that is built around Jesus. I have been struck recently by this image of the church as the *household* of God. When you encounter Jesus, you come *home*.

These verses have a whole string of descriptions of this transition: 'But you are the ones chosen by God, chosen for the high calling of priestly work, chosen to be a holy people, God's instruments to do his work and speak out for him, to tell others of the night-and-day difference he made for you – from nothing to something, from rejected to accepted' (v.9, MSG).'

In light of this, live differently to the world around you – 'friends, this world is not your home, so don't make yourselves cozy in it' (v.11, MSG).

We are the people of God. You have received mercy (v.10). Now you have a battle on your hands. It is very real. You have to abstain from sinful desires that *war* against your soul (v.11).

Do not be surprised at the accusation of wrongdoing (v.12). Seek to live a life that glorifies God. This will include respect for authority (v.13, MSG), doing good (v.15), treating everyone you meet with dignity (v.17, MSG), love for your spiritual family (v.17, MSG), non-retaliation (v.23), suffering for doing good (v.20) and trusting 'in him who judges justly' (v.23).

How is this possible when we are sinful human beings? Peter's answer is to point to Jesus: 'He used his servant body to carry our sins to the Cross so we could be rid of sin, free to live the right way. His wounds became your healing' (vv.24, MSG).

Jesus changes everything. Peter draws from Isaiah 53, which prophesies the way in which the Messiah will die in place of his people. This is what it meant for the cornerstone to be rejected, this is the foundation stone of your faith, and this is how you are brought back into the presence of God. At the cross, the place of suffering has become the place of salvation.

PRAYER

Lord, thank you for the new spiritual house you are building where I can experience the presence of God.

OLD TESTAMENT READING

Ezekiel 43:1–44:31
Find God in 'the house' of the Lord

The Spirit of God makes Jesus real to you: 'Then the Spirit lifted me up and brought me into the inner court, and *the glory of the LORD filled the temple'* (43:5).

Jesus Christ is the glory of God: 'The Word became flesh and made his dwelling among us. We have seen his glory, the glory of the One and Only, who came from the Father, full of grace and truth' (John 1:14).

In his vision, Ezekiel sees Jesus, 'the glory of the God of Israel' (Ezekiel 43:2). 'His voice was like the roar of the rushing waters and the land was radiant with his glory' (v.2). Where Jesus is, everything around becomes radiant. *In Jesus' presence, all we can do is fall down and worship* (v.3): 'I looked, and behold, the glory of the Lord filled the house of the Lord, and I fell upon my face' (Ezekiel 44:4, AMP).

Every time God's people gather in worship, for example at a Sunday service, expect 'the glory of the Lord' *to fill the house*. This is why church should be exciting, powerful and life changing.

As you read in the Old Testament of all the sacrifices they had to make for their sins, remember that the book of Hebrews tells us that this is an illustration (Hebrews 9). These were 'copies' of the heavenly things (v.23). They were a 'shadow' of what was to come (10:1). They had to make a sin offering (Ezekiel 43:19) with blood (v.20) to purify and make atonement (v.20). The goat had to be without defect (v.22).

This all foreshadows Jesus' perfect sacrifice for your sins (1 Peter 2:24).

The holy priesthood of Ezekiel 44 foreshadows the holy priesthood described in

1 Peter 2:5. This now is the task of every Christian. Your first duty as a 'priest' is to be holy yourself, to keep yourself pure so that you can be used by the Lord. Your second duty is to help others to do the same by your teaching and by your example (Ezekiel 44:23).

Where is God now? He lives in you by his Spirit. He is there when we gather in his name and fall before him in worship, adoration and praise.

PRAYER

Lord, thank you that I am a holy temple in which you live by your Spirit. I desperately need your help to live a holy life.

24 November | Day 328
Your Example

Pope Francis paused for a moment after one of his general audiences to pray, embrace and lay hands on a man with neurofibromatosis, a severely disfiguring disease. The man's face was covered in tumours. The image of the Pope's embrace in St Peter's Square went viral on social media, inspiring millions by his poignant example of the love of Christ.

There is great power in example. It is hard to improve if we have no other model than ourselves to follow. A good example is not only inspirational, it also gives us a pattern to copy and learn from.

Not only do you benefit most from following the example of others, but your example is vital if you are to have any influence on other people. Albert Schweitzer, the French theologian, philosopher and physician said, 'Example is not the main thing in influencing others – it is the only thing.' More depends on your walk than on your talk, what you practise than what you preach, what you do than what you say.

What people see is far more important than what they hear. People do what people see. As John Maxwell writes, 'Eighty-nine per cent of what people learn comes through visual stimulation; ten per cent through audible stimulation and one per cent through other senses ... *What they hear they understand. What they see they believe!*'[1]

As we read yesterday, you are called to follow Jesus' example in your life (1 Peter 2:21). Today we see some of the implications of this.

READING FROM PROVERBS

Proverbs 28:18–28
Walk in wisdom

Knowledge is horizontal. Wisdom is vertical – it comes down from above. To follow the example of Jesus means to walk in wisdom. Jesus walked in wisdom from his earliest days: 'He was filled with *wisdom*' (Luke 2:40). 'People remarked, 'What's this *wisdom* that has been given him...?' (Mark 6:2).

What does it mean to walk in wisdom? The writer of Proverbs says, 'Walk straight – live well and be saved; a devious life is a doomed life' (Proverbs 28:18, MSG). He goes on to say, 'If you think you know it all, you're a fool for sure; real survivors *learn wisdom from others*' (v.26, MSG).

It is wise to work hard rather than to 'chase fantasies' (v.19): 'Work your garden – you'll end up with plenty of food; play and party – you'll end up with an empty plate' (v.19, MSG).

Faithfulness is better than the 'get rich quick' attitude (v.20). It is wise to be generous: 'The stingy are eager to get rich and are unaware that poverty awaits them ... Those who give to the poor will lack nothing, but those who close their eyes to them receive many curses' (vv.22, 27).

Sometimes confrontation is necessary. 'Whoever rebukes a person will in the end gain more favour than one who has a flattering tongue' (v.23). Jesus was never afraid of confrontation. 'In the end, serious reprimand is appreciated far more than bootlicking flattery' (v.23, MSG).

Keep trusting in the Lord. The person who trusts in the Lord will prosper (v.25b) and 'those who *walk in wisdom* are kept safe' (v.26b).

PRAYER

Lord, help me to walk in wisdom, trusting in you.

NEW TESTAMENT READING

1 Peter 3:1–22
Win over, with or without words

Living out the Christian life is the most appropriate way of passing on the good news to those who live in very close proximity to you. This certainly applies to your family, work colleagues and those you live with. Often you can preach a better sermon with your life than with your lips.

This is of great importance if your husband or wife is not a Christian. Peter encourages Christian wives that if any of them have husbands who do not believe the word, they may be won over *without words,* when they see the purity and reverence of their lives (v.2).

They may be indifferent to any words about God but they will be 'captivated by your life of holy beauty. What matters is not your outer appearance ... but your inner disposition' (vv.3–4, MSG). There is a beauty greater than outer beauty, 'that of your inner self, the unfading beauty of a gentle and quiet spirit, which is of great worth in God's sight' (v.4).

The teaching of Jesus, and of the apostles, about the way in which husbands should behave is revolutionary. In a society where only wives had duties and only husbands had rights, Peter says here that both have duties towards each other.

Just as he tells the wives to be 'good wives' (v.1, MSG), he tells the husbands to be 'good husbands' (v.6, MSG). 'Honour them, delight in them ... treat your wives, then, as equals so your prayers don't run aground' (v.7, MSG). He says husbands should be considerate and show respect. Unless you get this relationship right your prayers will not be effective (v.7).

What is the lifestyle that will win people over without words? It is one of living in harmony with one another, of sympathetic love, compassion and humility; where evil is not repaid with evil, nor insult with insult, but with blessing (vv.8–9): 'No retaliation. No sharp-tongued sarcasm. Instead, bless – that's your job, to bless. You'll be a blessing and also get a blessing' (v.9, MSG).

This involves controlling your tongue, 'Say nothing evil or hurtful' (v.10, MSG). Train yourself always to speak positively and truthfully. You are to 'snub evil and cultivate good; run after peace for all you're worth' (v.11, MSG). This will lead to a life without fear (v.14), where Jesus is set apart in your heart as Lord (v.15).

'Without words' may be the best initial way to win over those in close proximity to you. However, words are also very important. Do not be ashamed to speak: 'Always be prepared to give an answer to everyone who asks you to give the reason for the hope that you have. But do this with *gentleness* and *respect*' (v.15).

Arrogance and rudeness will seldom win people over. As well as a verbal defence, you need a moral defence – a clear conscience, so that people can say what they like about you and it does not matter because God knows the truth: 'Keep a clear conscience before God so that when people throw mud at you, none of it will stick' (v.16, MSG).

As Rick Warren says, 'You cannot control the lies that people may speak about you, but you can control the truth ... Live so that people have to make up stuff in order to accuse you.' It is the cross and resurrection that makes a clear conscience possible. Jesus died for sins, once for all ... to bring you to God (v.18).

This is what baptism symbolises: 'not the removal of dirt from the body but the pledge of a good conscience towards God.' (v.21).

PRAYER

Lord, help me to live with a clear conscience.

OLD TESTAMENT READING

Ezekiel 45:1–46:24
Worship in the way of the Lord

In his vision, Ezekiel sees a 'sacred space for GOD' (45:1, MSG). The entire area was holy (v.1), and included a sanctuary where priests minister before the Lord (vv.2–4), and property for the Levites, princes and all the people. It is a vision of a people at peace with itself, in which all the different sections and levels of society live harmoniously and fairly with one another.

But it is not just about people living well together – it is a place for 'the people of the land ... to worship in the presence of the LORD' (46:3). The harmony between people stems from God, and at the heart of everything is *worship*.

Two things are required to *worship in the way of the Lord*. The first is repentance. God's message to the leaders (the 'princes of Israel') is, 'Quit bullying and taking advantage of my people. Do what's just and right for a change. Use honest scales – honest weights and honest measures' (45:9–10, MSG).

The second is atonement (vv.15, 17). The 'Passover' symbolises that God passes over your sin because of the sacrifice of Jesus. Blood had to be put on the doorposts prefiguring the blood of Christ.

The number seven is the perfect number: 'The *seventh* day ... A feast lasting *seven* days ... during the *seven* days of the Feast he is to provide *seven* bulls and *seven* rams without defect ... during the *seven* days ... which begins in the *seventh* month...' (vv.20, 21, 23, 25).

It points to the one *perfect* and sufficient sacrifice and atonement made by Jesus for you, which enables you to come into the presence of the Lord and live a life of worship.

Walk in the way of the cross and resurrection of Jesus. Live a life that will win people over. Keep a clear conscience and live without fear. Follow Jesus' perfect example and your life will be an example to others.

PRAYER

Lord, thank you that you died, the righteous for the unrighteous, to bring me to God. Help me to live a life of worship, following your perfect example.

25 November | Day 329
Know When to Kneel

Father Raniero Cantalamessa is a Franciscan monk. In 1977, he was sent by the Vatican to be an observer at a conference in Kansas City, USA where there were 20,000 Catholics and 20,000 other Christians. On the last day of the conference, after someone had spoken about the tragedy of all the divisions in the body of Christ (the church), 40,000 people *knelt* in repentance. As Father Raniero looked out, he saw the words 'JESUS IS LORD' on a big neon sign over the conference venue. He describes how, at that moment, he caught a glimpse of what Christian *unity* is all about – 40,000 people *kneeling in repentance* under the Lordship of Jesus.

He asked 'a lay Protestant' to pray for him to experience more of the Holy Spirit. *The Holy Spirit* filled him. He experienced *God's love* for him in a new way. He found himself speaking 'in a manner like speaking in tongues'. The Bible came alive in a new way. He received a new ministry. In 1980, he was invited by Pope John Paul II to be the preacher to the Papal Household. This is what he has been ever since. Three themes dominate his remarkable ministry: unity, love and the Holy Spirit. They are distinct, but closely linked.

READING FROM PSALMS

Psalm 133:1–3
Live together in unity

God blesses 'unity' (v.1). I have seen that over and over again. He blesses unity in marriage, families, teams, communities, nations and in the church. When Christians from different churches, traditions and denominations come together in unity, 'that's where God commands the blessing' (v.3, MSG).

The psalmist writes, 'How wonderful, how beautiful when brothers and sisters get along!' (v.1, MSG). There is a proverb: 'weak things united become strong.' The same is true of people: weak people united become strong.

The psalmist describes this unity as being 'like precious oil' (v.2, using an image from Leviticus 8:12). It is like 'the dew of Hermon' (Psalm 133:3). Mount Hermon is a vast area. It is usually snow-capped. It rises 9,100 feet above sea level. Its dew is thought to keep the whole land fresh.

These images of oil and dew are images of blessing. Where there is unity, 'there the Lord *bestows his blessing*' (v.3).

PRAYER

Lord, thank you that you bless unity so much. May there be unity in our church and between the churches around the world.

NEW TESTAMENT READING

1 Peter 4:1–19
Love each other deeply

'Love each other deeply,' writes the apostle Peter (v.8a). The Greek word used for 'deeply' is the word used for a horse at full gallop. It means 'stretched out' and is sometimes translated 'fervently'.

This kind of love 'covers a multitude of sins (forgives and disregards the offenses of others)' (v.8b, AMP). Love forgives faults in others because you know the loving, forgiving grace of God in your own life.

This is key to maintaining good relationships and avoiding falling out with others too easily. You know in your own life how much God loves you and has forgiven your own sins. Be willing to overlook offences and sins in others.

This does not mean that sin does not matter. On the contrary, Peter urges us to be 'done with sin' (v.1). Break with the old life of evil human desires and live for the will of God (v.2).

I remember well the reaction of some of my friends when I first encountered Jesus. They were surprised at the change and thought it strange. Peter writes, 'You've already put in your time in that God-ignorant way of life, partying night after night, a drunken and profligate life. Now it's time to be done with it for good. Of course, your old friends don't understand why you don't join in with the old gang anymore' (vv.3–4, MSG).

You are called to live differently: to be clear-minded and self-controlled so that you can pray (v.7); above all, to *love* (v.8), to be hospitable and to use your gifts (vv.9–10). 'Most of all, *love each other as if your life depended on it*. Love makes up for practically anything. Be quick to give a meal to the hungry, a bed to the homeless – cheerfully' (vv.8–9, MSG).

Like the apostle Paul, Peter sets the use of the gifts of the Holy Spirit in the context of love (vv.10–11; also see 1 Corinthians 12–14). The purpose of the gifts is love.

Even if you love fervently, that love will not always be returned. Expect opposition. Do not be surprised by it: 'When life gets really difficult, don't jump to the conclusion that God isn't on the job. Instead, be glad that you are in the very thick of what Christ experienced. This is a spiritual refining process with glory just around the corner' (1 Peter 4:12–13, MSG).

This is a type of suffering all Christians are called to. Suffering is part of the purifying process. God uses suffering to refine you and get rid of the sin in your life (vv.1–2). Insults are actually a blessing: 'If you're abused because of Christ, count yourself fortunate. It's the Spirit of God and his glory in you that brought you to the notice of others' (v.14, MSG).

Although insults are hurtful, all criticism is, ultimately, a blessing. In so far as it is true, it is a blessing because you can learn from it. If it is not true and you are 'insulted because of the name of Christ, you are *blessed*' (v.14). It is such an honour to be associated with Jesus that even sharing in his suffering is a blessing. Either way, once you grasp this, you should be able to see all criticism, however painful, as a blessing!

Sometimes we suffer because of our own sin (v.15), but suffering for *being a Christian* is not a cause for shame – it is a cause for rejoicing and praising God (vv.13, 16). It should not put you off, rather keep on doing what is good: 'So if you find life difficult because you're doing what God said, take it in stride. Trust him. He knows what he's doing, and he'll keep on doing it' (v.19, MSG). Martin Luther King said, 'I have decided to *stick with love*. Hate is too great a burden to bear.'

PRAYER

Lord, help us to be a community that loves each other deeply, and where love covers over a multitude of sins.

OLD TESTAMENT READING

Ezekiel 47:1–48:35
Long for the outpouring of the Holy Spirit

When the love of God is poured into your heart by the Holy Spirit (Romans 5:5), the Spirit of God brings abundant life, spiritual growth, increasing fruitfulness and healing to your life.

Ezekiel sees a picture of this when he sees water pouring out from under the temple. It *gushes* out and becomes a river that is first ankle deep, then knee deep, then waist deep and eventually 'it was a river over my head, water to swim in, water no one could possibly walk through' (Ezekiel 47:5, MSG). There are lots of trees on both sides of the river (v.7). Wherever the river flows, the Sea becomes fresh (v.8).

'Wherever the river flows, *life will flourish* – great schools of fish – because the river is turning the salt sea into fresh water. Where the river flows, *life abounds*. Fishermen ... casting their nets. The sea will teem with fish of all kinds...

'But the river itself, on both banks, will grow fruit trees of all kinds. Their leaves won't wither, *the fruit won't fail*. Every month they'll bear fresh fruit because the river from the Sanctuary flows to them. Their *fruit will be for food* and their *leaves for healing*' (vv.8–12, MSG).

Jesus said that these promises of Ezekiel would be fulfilled not in a place, but in a *person* – Jesus himself (John 7:37–39). Through the Holy Spirit, the streams of living water will flow from you also. Jesus said, 'Whoever believes in me, as the Scripture has said, will have *streams of living water* flowing from within' (v.38).

This river of living water is therefore a picture of the work of the Spirit, who brings life and abundance and blessing to you, and then flows out of you to have a positive impact on others. All the imagery points to life, growth, fruitfulness and healing. It is a picture of the church of Jesus Christ growing and bringing life wherever the river flows.

Ultimately, the river foreshadows and anticipates the new Jerusalem – *the city* where God lives. The name of the city is, 'The Lord Is There' (Ezekiel 48:35). This foreshadows the new heaven and the new earth (see Revelation 22:1–2), which Jesus will bring about when he returns.

PRAYER

Lord, thank you for the Holy Spirit and the promise that rivers of living water will flow out of my innermost being. Please fill me today with the Holy Spirit so that I may bring life, love, unity and healing wherever I go.

26 November | Day 330
God's Great Grace

Seeing a crowd of condemned criminals being led up to execution, John Bradford (c.1510–1555), the English reformer, is said to have remarked: 'There, but for *the grace of God*, goes John Bradford.'

In 1807, John Newton, best known as composer of the hymn 'Amazing Grace', encapsulated the amazing grace of God in some of his last words as he lay dying. He declared: 'I am a great sinner but Christ is a great Saviour.'

In today's New Testament passage, Peter speaks of '*the God of all grace*' (1 Peter 5:10). How should you respond to God's great grace?

READING FROM PSALMS

Psalm 134:1–3
Thank and praise the God of all grace

Grace is a gift, and the appropriate response to a gift is *thanksgiving*. Praise is the supreme form of thanksgiving, and therefore praise and worship is the appropriate response to the God of all grace.

The psalmist writes, 'Praise the Lord, all you servants of the Lord who minister by night in the house of the Lord. Lift up your hands in the sanctuary and praise the Lord' (vv.1–2).

PRAYER

Lord, thank you so much that you are the God of all grace. Thank you that you, 'the Maker of heaven and earth, bless' me (v.3).

NEW TESTAMENT READING

1 Peter 5:1–14
Humble yourselves before the God of all grace

Leaders are called to be 'examples to the flock' (v.3). Humility should be the mark of the Christian leader. Don't boss others around, telling them what to do: 'not lording it over those entrusted to you' (v.3); 'Not bossily telling others what to do, but tenderly showing them the way' (v.3, MSG).

Leaders in the church are called to be shepherds. Pope Francis says that pastors should 'smell of the sheep'. Shepherds love their sheep, look after them and stay close to them. A leader watches over the pastoral work of others, encouraging them to use their gifts.

Peter says this is not something that should be regarded as a duty, but something that we really want to do (v.2). It should not be done out of a desire for personal gain – 'not greedy for money' (v.2) – but out of a desire to serve others – being 'eager to serve' (v.2).

Peter then says that 'you who are younger must follow your leaders' (v.5, MSG). Leaders should lead with grace and followers should follow with grace.

He closes his letter with three instructions for 'all of you' (v.5). They are a response to the 'God of all grace' (v.10). Grace permeates the New Testament and it permeates this passage: 'This is the true grace' (v.12).

1. Humble yourselves

Peter writes, *'Clothe yourselves with humility* towards one another' (v.5). Whereas 'God opposes the proud', he 'gives *grace* to the humble' (v.5b). Humility is a choice. It is something you are required to do to yourself: 'Humble yourselves' (v.6). Humility is an act of the will.

Humility is not thinking less of yourself; it is thinking of yourself less.[1] There is a strong link between humility and grace. Because grace is free, the only appropriate response to grace is humility.

2. Live carefree before God

Peter writes, 'Cast all your anxiety on him because he cares for you' (v.7). He ends with the words, *'Peace* to all of you who are in Christ' (v.14). God loves you. He is a God of all grace. You can cast *all* your cares on him. There is nothing too big or too small to hand over to him. Thomas à Kempis wrote, 'They travel lightly whom God's grace carries.'

Staying peaceful is evidence that you have humbled yourself before God, and that you trust him to do what needs to be done.

3. Stay alert

'Keep a cool head. *Stay alert*. The devil is poised to pounce, and would like nothing better than to catch you napping. Keep your guard up' (v.8, MSG). Peter reminds his readers that they are 'not the only ones' suffering and that it 'won't last forever', saying, God 'gets the last word' (vv.9–11, MSG).

The qualities commended in this passage are very different from the values of our culture. The cult of youth and beauty is replaced with an emphasis on valuing and submitting to the elderly and wise. Self-aggrandisement is replaced by humility. You are promised God's help in dealing with the struggles of stress and worry. Instead of pursuing instant gratification, you are called on to be 'self-controlled and alert'. These are not easy things to do – but if you do them, you will stand firm and resist the devil.

PRAYER

Lord, help me to be submissive, humble, self-controlled and alert. Help me to spot the work of the devil and resist him.

Today I want to cast all my anxiety on you ... Thank you that you are the God of all grace.

OLD TESTAMENT READING

Daniel 1:1–2:23
Put your trust in the God of all grace

Do you work in a secular environment where those around you have very different standards to your own?

The book of Daniel charts the lives and careers of Daniel and three other young men, who were able to flourish in the Babylonian Civil Service. Their example gives you a great model for how to work in a godly way, in a context where God is not acknowledged or followed. This mirrors the situation in most 'secular' workplaces. These chapters are therefore a goldmine of practical examples and help.

We see the four friends *co-operating* with their employers, but *without compromise*. They *refuse to conform*, but they throw themselves wholeheartedly into their new situation and career. They undergo three years of leadership training and preparation. They allow their names to be changed to reflect that they are now part of the Babylonian administration, and subsequently they all seem to pursue successful careers.

At the same time, they resolved *not to compromise* their beliefs or defile themselves. You can defile yourself today by the kind of films and TV you watch, the internet sites you visit, or the things you listen to. 'Daniel resolved *not to defile himself* with the royal food and wine' (1:8). (This was perhaps because the royal food had been a sacrificial offering to the Babylonian gods.) They never allowed their commitment to their new careers to trump their higher allegiance to God.

However, Daniel was wise enough not just to disobey – he tried to work with those in authority over him. He asked for permission and then God, in his grace, caused the official to show favour and sympathy to Daniel (v.9).

'God gave knowledge and understanding of all kinds of literature and learning. And

Daniel could understand visions and dreams of all kinds' (v.17). Although these young men had outstanding natural ability – they were 'handsome, showing aptitude for every kind of learning ... well informed, quick to understand and qualified to serve' (v.4) – Daniel's real power came from God's supernatural wisdom.

Like Daniel you are called to live a life of purity and be totally at peace. Follow Daniel's example and be comfortable in your own skin and walk in a close relationship with God.

On the other hand, Nebuchadnezzar had enormous power and wealth. He was popular, respected and feared. There was no real threat to his security and yet he was very insecure and fearful. Be aware that beneath the façade of self-sufficiency can hide a deep-rooted insecurity.

He was so haunted by his dreams that he couldn't sleep. In this crisis, he knew in his heart that the magicians did not have the power they claimed but were just playing games. They virtually admitted they had no supernatural wisdom (2:9–11).

Daniel recognised that God alone is the source of all power and wisdom (v.20). In a wonderful way, God, in his grace, will not only reveal things to you, but also give you the wisdom and power to understand and deal with your situation. You can learn from Daniel's example:

1. Have faith in God
He believed that God would speak to him (v.16). God will speak to you as well.

2. Know the power of prayer
He requested a little time and then he asked his friends to '*pray* to the God of heaven for mercy in solving this mystery' (v.18, MSG).

3. Combine prayer with action
He went to see Nebuchadnezzar and 'spoke to him with *wisdom and tact*' (v.14).

4. Learn to recognise God's voice
When God spoke to him in a vision, he was so completely certain he was able to thank and praise him in advance of sharing it with the king: 'Praise be to the name of God for ever and ever; wisdom and power are his ... I thank and praise you, O God' (vv.20, 23).

PRAYER

God of all grace, praise you that you are the Maker of heaven and earth who blesses me. Help me to live a life of purity in a close relationship with you. Please give me wisdom. Help me to hear your voice and speak it with confidence.

27 November | Day 331
There Is a God and He Is Great

I studied and practised law for nearly ten years. In every legal case, evidence is vital. Evidence matters to me. I could not be a Christian if I did not believe that our faith is based on compelling evidence. There is good evidence for the life, death and resurrection of Jesus Christ.

Over recent years, there has been a spate of books by the 'new atheists' suggesting that there is no evidence for God; that God is a 'delusion' ('*The God Delusion*') and that '*God is Not Great*' (the title of another of these books). While of course, the Bible does not try to provide a scientific proof for the existence of God, it does point to the evidence of '*eyewitnesses*' (2 Peter 1:16) and proclaims that '*there is a God in heaven*' (Daniel 2:28) and that '*the Lord is great*' (Psalm 135:5).

There is good reason to put your trust in God. You will grow in faith as you study the truth of God's word and boldly proclaim that 'there is a God' and 'he is great'.

READING FROM PSALMS

Psalm 135:1–12
Proclaim the greatness of God

'God's so good' (v.3, MSG). This is the claim of the psalmist: 'The Lord is great' (v.5). He remembers God's relationship with his people (v.4). He sees the world that God created and sustains (vv.6–7), and he testifies to God's wonderful protection (vv.8–11). This range of experience and evidence underpins his belief in the greatness of God.

Respond to God's greatness in worship. Again and again the psalmist calls us to 'praise the LORD' – a call that is repeated, in various forms, five times in the first three verses. Praise the Lord!

PRAYER

Lord, today I want to praise you and worship you. I trust you with my life again today.

NEW TESTAMENT READING

2 Peter 1:1–21
Proclaim the truth of God's word

If you want a closer relationship with God, put time aside to develop that relationship. Spend time with him. As you study his word, your faith grows and your life is changed. The strength of all relationships, including your relationship with God, depends on communication.

In his letter, 'Simon Peter, a servant and apostle of Jesus Christ' (v.1), writes about his 'faith' and the faith of his readers 'whose experience with God is as *life-changing* as ours' (v.1, MSG).

Your faith is precious (v.1). 'Grace' and 'peace' (v.2) are two of the most precious gifts you can ever experience in life. Peter says that they are yours 'in abundance through the knowledge of God and of Jesus our Lord' (v.2).

Your faith is not irrational. It is 'the truth' (v.12). Some people today think that the Bible is full of 'cleverly invented stories' (v.16). But Peter writes, 'We did *not* follow *cleverly invented stories* when we told you about the power and coming of our Lord Jesus Christ, but we were *eyewitnesses* of his majesty' (v.16). Peter is talking particularly about the transfiguration (vv.17–18), when he witnessed the revelation of Jesus' glory and identity (see Mark 9; Matthew 17; Luke 9). He testifies, 'We saw it with our own eyes' (v.16, MSG).

A witness is a word used for someone who gives evidence in a court of law. The evidence about Jesus is more akin to legal evidence than mathematical or scientific proof. There is evidence from eyewitnesses. Faith is not irrational; it is based on what they saw. Peter asserts, 'We couldn't be *more sure* of what we saw and heard' (2 Peter 1:19, MSG). There are good reasons to believe.

Peter also reminds them of the power and trustworthiness of Scripture: 'The main thing to keep in mind here is that no prophecy of Scripture is a matter of private opinion. And why? Because it's not something concocted in the human heart. Prophecy resulted when the Holy Spirit prompted men and women to speak God's word' (v.21, MSG). The Holy Spirit still speaks through these words of Scripture. As you experience his presence and power through them, they reinforce the truth of your faith.

Faith is not just a set of ideas – it changes the way you live your life. Peter explains that through the Holy Spirit '[God's] divine power has given us everything we need for life and godliness' (v.3).

In light of this he explains that you need to 'complement your basic faith'. Then Peter lists various qualities you need to seek to develop – 'good character, spiritual understanding, alert discipline, passionate patience, reverent wonder, warm friendliness, and generous love, each dimension fitting into and developing the others' (vv.5–7, MSG). These things will keep you from being an ineffective Christian (v.8), and help you to remain strong in your faith until the end (vv.10–11).

PRAYER

God, thank you that our faith is based upon the solid testimony of eyewitnesses and upon our experience of a relationship with you. Help me to grow in that relationship as I trust the truth of your word.

OLD TESTAMENT READING

Daniel 2:24–3:12
Proclaim that 'there is a God'

Refuse to conform to the standards of the world. Have the courage to proclaim that '*there is a God*' in spite of what others may be saying and doing.

I once knew a godly man nicknamed 'Gibbo' who, when he was young, worked as a clerk at Selfridges, the London department store. One day, when the owner Gordon Selfridge was there, the telephone rang and Gibbo answered it. The caller asked to speak to Gordon Selfridge. Gibbo passed on the message and Selfridge replied, 'Tell him I'm out.' Gibbo held out the receiver to him and said, 'You tell him you're out.' Gordon Selfridge took the call, but was furious with him. Gibbo said to him afterwards, 'If I can lie for you, I can lie to you.' From that moment onwards, Gordon Selfridge had the highest regard for and trust in Gibbo.

Daniel and his three friends believed that 'there is a God', and therefore they refused to compromise. By their lives and their lips, they boldly proclaimed, 'there is a God'.

Daniel was convinced that '*there is a God* in heaven' (2:28), and this conviction underpins both of the stories in today's Old Testament passage. In chapter 2 we read of Daniel's conviction that this God 'reveals mysteries' (v.28), and his willingness to act on that belief. In chapter 3, we see his three friends willing to risk death because of their conviction that God exists, and their commitment to worship him alone.

Daniel was humble enough to recognise that the interpretation had been given, not because of his wisdom, but because of the grace of God (v.30).

God told Nebuchadnezzar three things, which are true for *you* also (vv.36–38): First, all you have has been given to you by God. Second, God has placed you in the position that you are in. Third, God has made you who you are.

Therefore, there is no cause for pride, arrogance or self-satisfaction. Your abilities, gifts and resources are all given to you by God.

Daniel continued to interpret the dream: There will be a succession of kingdoms. (probably Babylonian, Medo-Persian, Greek under Alexander the Great and Roman). The key point though is that all the empires of the world – be they Babylonian, Roman, British, Soviet, American or Chinese – all come to an end. *None are eternal*.

Daniel then spoke of a kingdom that will never be destroyed but *will endure for ever* (v.44). This kingdom is based on the rock cut out of a mountain not of human hands (v.34), a rock that broke the iron, the clay, the bronze, the silver and the gold to pieces (v.35).

This rock 'struck the statue' and 'became a huge mountain and filled the whole earth' (v.35). Now, through the lens of Jesus, we see that the rock is Christ (see Isaiah 28:16; 1 Peter 2:4–8; Psalm 118:22–23). He has divine origin. He is the Son of God ('a rock was cut out, but not by human hands', Daniel 2:34). His kingdom has seen phenomenal growth ('filled the whole earth', v.35).

There are now well over two billion people in the world who profess the name of Jesus. His kingdom has an eternal quality (v.44). It is, 'The eternal kingdom of our Lord and Saviour Jesus Christ' (2 Peter 1:11).

Daniel's own position was achieved, not by worldly ambition but by divine intervention on behalf of someone whose aim was simply to obey God rather than human beings. He didn't seek or crave human affirmation like the magicians of Nebuchadnezzar's court, but knew his Father and sought his pleasure.

Daniel, Shadrach, Meshach and Abednego remained committed to God and were ready to die for their beliefs (Daniel 3). They were willing to stake everything on the fact that *there really is a God and he is great.*

PRAYER

Lord, help me to proclaim to the world, by my life and my lips, that there is a God and that you are great.

---

28 November | Day 332
How to Be Inspired

In successive weeks at HTB, I interviewed two people of courage and faith. One, Ben Freeth, inspired by his faith in Jesus Christ, had taken a courageous stance against the unjust regime in Zimbabwe. As a result, he was beaten, tortured and forced to watch his elderly mother-in-law and father-in-law undergo torture, from which the latter eventually died. Yet in the midst of his suffering, he chose to love and bless the torturers.

The second was a pastor from one of the sixty countries around the world where physical persecution of Christians still takes place. He had been imprisoned and, at one stage, sentenced to death for no other reason than his faith in Jesus Christ. Yet in the face of extreme suffering he refused to deny his faith.

The lives of men and women like this are hugely inspiring, challenging and motivational.

READING FROM PROVERBS

Proverbs 29:1–9
Inspirational champions of justice

I am inspired by the examples of churches, individuals and organisations that care deeply about justice for the poor. There is so much in the Bible about issues of poverty and justice. The *Poverty and Justice Bible*[1] highlights over two thousand verses that wake us up to these issues.

Justice really matters. 'By *justice* a king gives a country stability, but one who is greedy for bribes tears it down' (v.4). It is terrible to live in a place where bribery of judges and politicians is normal. 'A leader of good judgment gives stability; an exploiting leader leaves a trail of waste' (v.4, MSG).

No justice system is perfect. However, it is a privilege to live in a country that has a good justice system.

'When the righteous thrive, the people rejoice; when the wicked rule, the people groan' (v.2). In other words: 'When good people run things, everyone is glad, but when the ruler is bad, everyone groans' (v.2, MSG).

The righteous person has a clear conscience and can sing and be glad, whereas an evil person is snared by their own sin (v.6).

Caring about '*justice* for *the poor*' (v.7) is the mark of a righteous life: 'The good-hearted understand what it's like to be poor; the hardhearted haven't the faintest idea' (v.7, MSG).

PRAYER

Lord, help us to make a real difference to this world in seeking to bring justice to the poor, the homeless, the prisoners and the hungry.

NEW TESTAMENT READING

2 Peter 2:1–22
Inspirational godly lives

I am so thankful for the examples of those around us today like Bishop Sandy Millar, Father Raniero Cantalamessa and many lesser known others who inspire us by their example and godliness.

The New Testament warns about deceptive and potentially dangerous cult leaders who '*secretly* introduce *destructive* heresies' (v.1). In very recent times, one such cult, called Shincheonji, tried to infiltrate churches in London and around the world, posing as a 'Bible study' for new believers. The leaders of this 'Bible study' teach their followers to lie and deceive. This chapter is a strongly worded attack on *lying* prophets and immoral teachers. Peter contrasts the lives of Noah and Lot with the 'false teachers' (v.1).

Noah, 'the sole voice of righteousness' (v.5, MSG), lived among 'ungodly people' but was 'a preacher of righteousness' (v.5). Lot also was a 'good man' (v.8, MSG). He was 'a righteous man, who was distressed by the filthy lives of the lawless' (v.7).

Peter holds out Noah and Lot as examples to those to whom he is writing, as they contend with false teachers who 'introduce destructive heresies' and follow 'shameful ways' that 'bring the way of truth into disrepute' (vv.1–2).

These false teachers are not simply other Christian leaders with whom Peter disagrees. Their lives and teachings are at complete odds with the Christian faith: 'With eyes full of adultery, they never stop sinning ... They have left the straight way' (vv.14–15). They appeal 'to the lustful desires of sinful human nature' (v.18). 'They promise ... freedom, while they themselves are slaves of depravity – for people are slaves to whatever has mastered them' (v.19).

The things that Peter describes here can seem very tempting – which is why he is so concerned about these leaders. His descriptions of pleasure seeking (v.13), sexual freedom (vv.14, 18–19) and the pursuit of money (v.15), all strike a chord today.

The false teachers are slaves to these things, yet they entice others (especially new believers) into the same way of life, leading them astray by promising freedom (vv.18–19). However, true freedom is only found in God's ways, not in any of these enticements that promise so much but actually result in emptiness. Those who pursue and recommend them are 'springs without water and mists driven by a storm' (v.17).

This is a terrible warning: 'If they have escaped the corruption of the world by knowing our Lord and Saviour Jesus Christ and are again entangled in it and overcome, they are worse off at the end than they were at the beginning. It would have been better for them not to have known the way of righteousness, than to have known it and then to turn their backs' (vv.20–21).

PRAYER

Lord, the pull of the world is strong. Help me never to turn my back on you, my Lord and Saviour, Jesus Christ.

OLD TESTAMENT READING

Daniel 3:13–4:18
Inspirational faith and courage

I am always inspired by people of courage and faith who refuse to be frightened or intimidated.

Shadrach, Meshach and Abednego are inspiring examples of absolute trust in God. They refused to bow down and worship the image of gold, in spite of the threat of being thrown into a fiery furnace. They were determined to do the right thing, however great the cost might be, because they believed in God and his power to vindicate them if he so desired.

They said to the king, 'Your threat means nothing to us. If you throw us in the fire, the God we serve can rescue us from your roaring furnace and anything else you might cook up, O king. But even if he doesn't, it wouldn't make a bit of difference, O king. We still wouldn't serve your gods or worship the gold statue you set up' (3:16b–18, MSG).

It would have been easy for Shadrach, Meshach and Abednego to have tried to find a way out. They could have sought to negotiate a settlement with Nebuchadnezzar that involved some compromise but not too much. But they had complete confidence in the power of God to deliver them if he wanted to, and if he did not, they were still going to trust in him and obey him.

This is an inspiring example. When faced with difficult decisions ask, as they did, 'What is the right thing to do?' Then do it regardless of the consequences.

Their absolute trust in God was a tremendous witness to Nebuchadnezzar. As he looks into the fiery furnace he sees four men walking around in the fire, unbound and unharmed, and the fourth looks 'like a Son of God' (v.25, KJV). Reading this through the lens of the New Testament, it is possible to see the fourth man as a vision of Jesus himself, with them in their time of trial.

They came out 'not a hair singed, not a scorch mark on their clothes, not even the smell of fire on them!' (v.27, MSG). If you are facing trials in your life that might seem like the fiery furnace, you can be assured that Jesus is right there with you in whatever situation you are facing.

Even Nebuchadnezzar himself is inspired by their example (v.28). A change of heart began in him as a result. However, it took a long time for God to get the message through to him. In spite of Daniel's example in chapter 2, Nebuchadnezzar was not converted. Shadrach, Meshach and Abednego's absolute trust in God had a big impact on him. However, his conversion was not complete.

In chapter 4 we read his remarkable testimony of how he did eventually come to acknowledge God. Giving a testimony brings great pleasure: 'It is *my pleasure* to tell you about the miraculous signs and wonders that the Most High God has performed for me' (4:2). By this stage, his attitude had completely changed and the glory was all given to God (v.3).

He begins by saying that, in one sense, he had all he wanted. 'I, Nebuchadnezzar, was at home in my palace, contented and prosperous' (v.4). But underneath the prosperity and contentment there was a deep fear (v.5).

One of the main points of the book of Daniel is that God uses inspiring examples like Daniel, Shadrach, Meshach and Abednego and their absolute trust in God to change a king's life – and as a result, to change a nation.

PRAYER

Lord, help me to do the right thing, however great the cost appears to be. Thank you for inspiring examples of men and women who raise my sights and show me what is possible.

29 November | Day 333
God's Perfect Timing

God has his own sense of timing: 'With the Lord a day is like a thousand years, and a thousand years are like a day' (2 Peter 3:8). He has perfect timing: never early, never late. God is never in a hurry, but he is always on time.

We see in today's passages that the Lord is sovereign over the future (Daniel 4:32). 'We are looking forward to a new heaven and a new earth' (2 Peter 3:13). God is going to vindicate his people (Psalm 135:14).

But what do you do while you are waiting for God to do what he has promised to do?

READING FROM PSALMS

Psalm 135:13–21
Trust in the Lord

When your prayers don't seem to be answered, you may be tempted to stop trusting the Lord and start chasing other 'gods'.

Trusting in the Lord may seem a little old fashioned. But the psalmist says, 'God, your name is eternal, God, *you'll never be out-of-date*' (v.13, MSG).

The great biblical truth is that you become like that in which you put your trust. If you put your trust in 'gods' of silver or gold, then you will be like them – spiritually lifeless, blind and deaf (vv.16–18). If you trust in God, you will be filled with life and joy as you become like him.

Keep trusting God, 'For the Lord will *vindicate his people* and have compassion on his servants' (v.14). 'God stands up for his people, God holds the hands of his people' (v.14, MSG). Hence, you are called to praise and honour the Lord (vv.19–21).

Remain totally dependent on God and look for him to vindicate you. When things aren't working out as you wish, be patient. Stop trying to move ahead of God. His timing is perfect. Trust him.

PRAYER

Lord, I trust in you alone. Help me become like you – full of love, joy and peace.

NEW TESTAMENT READING

2 Peter 3:1–18
Turn to the Lord

When you look at all the evil in the world – all the wars, violence, institutional torture, horrific crimes and the amount of suffering – you might wonder why Jesus does not come back now and sort it all out.

Why does God delay? Why has the Lord not returned already?

Peter warns us that people will mock us and say, 'So what's happened to the promise of his Coming?' (v.4, MSG). He says there is a very good reason for the delay. The reason that the Lord has not come already is to give people more time to repent.

God is not in a hurry. 'With the Lord a day is like a thousand years, and a thousand years are like a day' (v.8).

God is not being slow in keeping his promise. Rather, the delay comes from his patience: 'He is patient with you, not wanting anyone to perish, but everyone to come to repentance' (v.9). 'God isn't late with his promise as some measure lateness. He is restraining himself on account of you, holding back the End because he doesn't want anyone lost. He's giving everyone space and time to change' (v.9, MSG).

Repentance is all about a change of direction in your life. It is *turning* away from all the bad stuff and *turning* to Jesus. By giving people time to repent God is lovingly holding the door open for their salvation. 'Interpret our Master's *patient restraint* for what it is: salvation' (v.15, MSG).

This theme of *salvation* is one of the great themes of Paul's letters, and so at this point Peter refers to them. I find it encouraging that he describes them as sometimes 'hard to understand' (v.16) – if you struggle to understand them, you are in good company!

Significantly, Peter then goes on to compare them with the Old Testament ('the other scriptures', v.16). In doing so, he demonstrates that the early church and apostles understood the New Testament writings as having the same divine authority as those of the Old Testament.

The Lord will come at a time when we don't expect him ('like a thief', v.10). The world as we know it will be 'laid bare' (v.10). There will be 'a new heaven and a *new earth*' (v.13). The New Testament vision of the future is not so much of people 'going up to heaven' – rather it is that there will be '*a new heaven and a new earth*' (v.13).

Again and again, Peter points out that God is faithful to his word and his promises (vv.2, 5, 7, 9, 13). The truth is that what God says will definitely happen.

The way to prepare for this certain, but delayed, future is 'to live a holy life' and 'daily expect the Day of God, eager for its arrival' (v.11, MSG), and 'be found living at your best, in purity and peace' (v.14, MSG), and to 'grow in grace and understanding of our Master and Saviour, Jesus Christ' (v.18, MSG).

Grace is undeserved love. You grow in grace as you turn to the Lord, dependent on him in every situation you face, bringing your needs to him day by day, as you eagerly expect his return.

PRAYER

Lord, as I await your coming, help me to live a holy and godly life – 'to be found spotless, blameless and at peace with [you]' (2 Peter 3:14).

OLD TESTAMENT READING

Daniel 4:19–5:16
Thank the Lord

Pride comes before a fall – as I have discovered many times in my own life. Everything we have comes from God. We are dependent upon him for our next breath. He is in control of the past, present and future. Thanksgiving prompts humility.

'When it comes to life, the critical thing is whether you take things for granted or take them with gratitude,'[1] wrote G.K. Chesterton.

It is relatively easy to pass on a message of encouragement from the Lord. It is less easy to convey a message of rebuke. Daniel found it perplexing and alarming, but he was obedient to the Lord (4:19 onwards).

The mistake Nebuchadnezzar made, and that all of us possibly make from time to time, is to think that what he had achieved was all his own doing: 'Is not this the great Babylon *I* have built as the royal residence, by *my* mighty power and for the glory of *my* majesty?' (v.30). Be wary of using 'I' and 'my' in this way!

The lesson that God had to teach Nebuchadnezzar, and sometimes has to teach us, is that *everything you have is a gift from God* – 'the Most High is sovereign over the kingdoms on earth and gives them to anyone he wishes' (v.32).

Our spiritual gifts, bodies, families, homes, intellect, looks, money, sporting abilities – are all gifts from God. Your reaction to any success should not be one of pride, self-importance or self-congratulation, but one of praise and *thanks to God* – honouring him and exalting him for what he has given you (vv.34–37).

Nebuchadnezzar took things for granted and failed to give thanks and glory to the Lord for what the Lord had done for him. Rather, he saw it all as the work of his own hands.

When Nebuchadnezzar was restored he realised that everything he had came from God. Instead of taking the glory himself, he thanked and glorified God, 'singing and praising the King of Heaven' (vv.34–37, MSG).

Humility does not mean pretending that you do not have what you have, but rather it means recognising the source of what you have, and giving the praise where it is due: 'Now I, Nebuchadnezzar, praise and exalt and glorify the King of heaven, because everything *he* does is right and all *his* ways are just' (v.37).

His testimony is summed up with these words, 'He knows how to turn a proud person into a humble man or woman' (v.37b, MSG).

Daniel says to Nebuchadnezzar, 'So, king, take my advice: Make a clean break with your sins and start *living for others*. Quit your wicked life and look after the needs of the down-and-out. Then you will continue to have a good life' (v.27, MSG).

The next generation did not learn the lessons of the past. King Belshazzar broke the command to worship God alone, and 'praised the gods of gold and silver, of bronze, iron, wood and stone' (5:4).

As with Nebuchadnezzar, beneath the surface there was a deep-rooted fear in Belshazzar's life – he did not have peace with God. Both were warned by God and told what to do. The difference is that Nebuchadnezzar repented, humbled himself, acknowledged and thanked God, whereas Belshazzar did not.

Daniel himself was 'well known for his intellectual brilliance and spiritual wisdom' (v.11, MSG). He was full of the Holy Spirit. There must have been a great temptation to pride. Yet Daniel remained humbly dependent on God, giving him all the glory and honour and thanksgiving.

PRAYER

Lord, thank you that you are in charge of this universe and everything I have comes from you. I want to give you all the praise, honour and glory.

30 November | Day 334
Intimate Connection

Fellowship – it's a wonderful word. It's what you were made for. It satisfies the deepest longings of your heart. It is the answer to loneliness. Nothing in this life compares with it. It starts now and goes on for ever.

There is no greater joy in life than fellowship. John wants his readers to enjoy the same fellowship he has: 'We want you to enjoy this, too. Your joy will double our joy!' (1 John 1:3, MSG).

Koinonia, the Greek word used for fellowship, is almost untranslatable. It expresses 'a relationship of great intimacy and depth ... it even became the favourite expression for the marital relationship – the most intimate between human beings'.[1] It is a rich word that describes a life together in which everything is shared. This is the word that John uses of our intimate relationship with God (v.3).

It also describes our relationship with one another. You can have deep genuine friendships and honest communication. There is no need for masks or 'spin' or 'image'. You can be real before God and before others. The result is a level of authenticity, vulnerability and intimate connection with one another that is best summed up in this beautiful word, 'fellowship'.

READING FROM PSALMS

Psalm 136:1–12
Thank God

God loves you. We need to be constantly reminded of God's love for us. Twenty-six times in this psalm the psalmist repeats, 'His love endures for ever'. Your intimate connection with the Lord is based on his enduring love for you.

Respond by giving 'thanks' to God for:

1. Who he is
He is the 'God of gods' and 'Lord of lords' (vv.2–3). He is good (v.1).

2. What he has made
He does great wonders. He made the heavens and spread out the earth; he made the sun, the moon and the stars (vv.4–9).

3. What he has done for you
His hand is strong and his arm is outstretched towards you (v.12).

PRAYER
Lord, thank you that your love for me endures for ever.

NEW TESTAMENT READING

1 John 1:1–2:11
Talk to God

John knew who he was talking about. He knew Jesus Christ personally. He was the disciple whom Jesus loved in a special way (John 13:23), and with whom he had spent a great deal of his time.

John, now an old man, writes that he had 'heard', 'seen', 'looked at' and 'touched' Jesus (1 John 1:1). What he had 'seen' he wanted to 'testify' to and 'proclaim', in order that his readers also might have an intimate connection with the Father and his Son, Jesus Christ (vv.2–3).

Astonishingly, you too can experience this intimate connection: 'we saw it, we heard it, and now we're telling you so you can experience it along with us, this experience of communion with the Father and his Son, Jesus Christ' (v.3, MSG).

How can you have this intimate connection with the Father and the Son?

You are enabled to 'walk in the light' because of 'the blood of Jesus', which 'purifies us from all sin' (v.7). Because of this, even though we are still sinners (v.8), we are offered continual forgiveness for our sins. You are called to this intimate relationship with him, where you can talk to him about your sins and be assured of forgiveness: 'If we confess our sins, he is faithful and just and will forgive us our sins and purify us from all unrighteousness' (v.9).

The blood of Jesus continually cleanses you in the same way that the combination of your liver and your physical blood continually cleanses your physical body.

The only requirement is that you admit that you have sinned and confess your sins.

Keep short accounts with God. When you sin, quickly confess, repent and receive God's cleansing. Get up and keep going.

There is an extraordinary balance here. We are not supposed to sin, but rather to walk in the light. However, we have all sinned and, 'if we claim we have not sinned, we make him out to be a liar and his word has no place in our lives' (v.10).

This leads to a wonderful combination: John both encourages his readers *not* to sin, while at the same time assuring them of God's grace and mercy if they do (2:1). This balance of a call to holiness alongside grace is right at the heart of the Christian life.

Amazingly, when we mess up, Jesus is our 'advocate' (KJV), our divine defence lawyer: 'we have one who speaks to the Father in our defence – Jesus Christ, the Righteous One' (v.1).

It is the sacrifice of Jesus on the cross for you that makes it possible for you to be able to talk to the Father and the Son in the intimate relationship of 'fellowship' (1:3). You are called to know God (2:4) and to experience his love for you (v.5). 'Anyone who claims to be intimate with God ought to live the same kind of life Jesus lived' (v.6, MSG).

Part of this is seen in our connection with one another in the Christian community. 'If we walk in the light ... we have *fellowship* with one another' (1:7). A clear conscience, love, obedience, intimacy with God and intimacy with one another all go hand in hand.

PRAYER

Lord, thank you for the amazing privilege of being able to have fellowship with you and with one another through your blood shed for us on the cross.

OLD TESTAMENT READING

Daniel 5:17–6:28
Trust God

Daniel enjoyed close intimate connection with God. He is a wonderful example of someone who had total and complete trust in the Lord. He refuses to accept Belshazzar's gifts (5:17). Be careful about simply accepting gifts from anyone. Daniel did not want to compromise his position.

Belshazzar's sins were: first, pride (v.20) – he did not humble himself (v.22); second, arrogance (v.20) – he set himself up against the Lord of heaven (v.23); and third, idol worship – praising gods of silver and gold (v.23).

Daniel is a superb example of a Christian politician. It is not just that his intelligence completely outclassed the others. What really made him stand out was his integrity. When they tried to find an old scandal or skeleton they could not find anything: 'He was totally exemplary and trustworthy. They could find no evidence of negligence or misconduct' (6:4, MSG).

Not all of us can distinguish ourselves as Daniel did (v.3), but we can all have an 'excellent spirit' (v.3, AMP). Seek to be trustworthy in your work, and to be honest and careful, 'neither corrupt nor negligent' (v.4). Be faithful in your work and most importantly be faithful in your relationship with God.

Daniel was one of the top three men in the country and he had great responsibility. He had an extremely busy, time-consuming job. Yet he managed to find the time to pray three times a day.

Daniel had lived in Babylon for many years by this stage and his attitude to the state is very interesting. He played his full part. He obeyed all the laws. His accusers knew this. They realised that the only way to attack him was to make up a law that went against God – so they made it illegal to pray (vv.5–7). Daniel had no hesitation in disobeying that command openly (v.10).

Talking to God is inextricably linked with trusting in him. Fellowship with God was the number one priority in Daniel's life. He continued to pray just as he always had done. He refused to compromise. He did not even try to hide the fact he was praying. He kept the windows open as he had done before – so that all could see.

Daniel was thrown into the lion's den. The whole story seems to foreshadow the last period of *Jesus' life*:

- Jealousy led to false accusations against him.
- His enemies were unable to find any basis for a charge.
- In the end they resorted to a religious charge.
- A reluctant and weak king was persuaded to take some action he did not really want to take.
- The great courage of Daniel foreshadowed the supreme courage of Jesus.
- The rescue by God foreshadowed the resurrection.
- Even the empty tomb seems to be foreshadowed: 'A stone was brought and placed over the mouth of the den, and the king sealed it ... At the first light of dawn, the king got up and hurried to the lions' den' (vv.17, 19).

The key to the whole story is Daniel's complete trust in God. This made him fearless. It is said that the lions did not eat Daniel 'because he was grit and backbone'! He served God continually (vv.16, 20), and was recognised and thought of as a servant of the living God (v.20). He was at God's disposal every moment of the day.

Resist the pressure to compromise. Keep trusting God even when everything seems to go wrong. Have the courage to be different.

PRAYER

Lord, help me to keep walking in an intimate relationship of connection with you – thanking you, talking to you and trusting in you.

1 December | Day 335
How to Avoid Spiritual Infections

Joseph Lister, the nineteenth-century medic, is known as 'the father of antiseptic surgery'. Lister was disturbed by the high proportion of patients who died from post-operative infections.

He became convinced that infinitesimal microbes, invisible to the naked eye, were causing the infections. He began to develop a number of antiseptic solutions with which to treat the wounds. Sure enough, the proportion of patients dying from infections decreased.[1]

In a similar way, there are evil spiritual forces at work in our world today. They cannot be seen, but they wreak havoc in people's lives, causing them to fall into temptation, moving evil people into positions of national power, manipulating people's emotions, tearing them apart and destroying them.

But just as Lister's contemporaries dismissed his theory of destructive microbes, many people today are ignorant or dismissive of spiritual realities. Yet you have the powerful spiritual 'antiseptic' to use against these destructive forces. It is vital that you learn to do so.

READING FROM PSALMS

Psalm 136:13–26
Thank God continually

Do you ever feel 'under attack' – from powerful temptations, overwhelming fears, major anxieties or from some other form of attack?

The 'enemies' in the Old Testament were often *physical attacks*, whereas in the New Testament they are usually *spiritual attacks*. But the outcome is the same – God promises to rescue you from *all* your enemies.

The psalmist *gives thanks* for what God has done. In particular, he *thanks God* for freeing us from *our enemies* (v.24):

'God remembered us when we were down ... *Rescued* us from the trampling boot ... Takes care of everyone in time of need ... *Thank God* who did it all!' (vv.23–26, MSG).

The final verse summarises the psalm: '*Give thanks to the God of heaven. His love endures for ever*' (v.26).

PRAYER

Lord, thank you that you have rescued me through the cross and resurrection of Jesus Christ. Thank you that your love endures for ever.

NEW TESTAMENT READING

1 John 2:12–27
Stay close to Jesus

Pippa and I were very young when we got married. We had no money to pay for our honeymoon. A friend kindly lent us a cottage in Scotland and another friend called Micky lent us his car.

On the way home, we crashed the car right outside Micky's house. We rang his doorbell. Micky could see that we were both very upset. Immediately he said, 'Oh, don't worry about my car, it's only a piece of metal!' Micky loved God and he loved people. He did not love things; he held them lightly.

Do not love the things of the world (v.15). Don't use people and love things. Love people and use things.

Your struggle is against the enemy *within* – sin (v.12), the enemy *around* – the world (vv.16–17), and the enemy *above* – the devil (v.14). You have already been rescued from these enemies.

1. The enemy within (sin)

Jesus has rescued you from your sins: 'I write to you, dear children, because your sins *have been forgiven* on account of his name' (v.12).

2. The enemy around (the world)
Jesus has rescued you from needing to be intimately attached to the world. John writes, 'Practically everything that goes on in the world – wanting your own way, wanting everything for yourself, wanting to appear important – has nothing to do with the Father. It just isolates you from him. The world and all its wanting, wanting, wanting is on the way out – but whoever does what God wants is set for eternity' (vv.16–17, MSG).

3. The enemy above (the devil)
Jesus has given you the power to be free from the devil – the evil one: 'I write to you, young people, because ... the word of God lives in you, and you have overcome the evil one' (v.14b). The victory comes from staying close to God: 'Your fellowship with God enables you to gain a victory over the evil one' (v.14, MSG).

John then goes on to warn his readers against false teachers who would seek to shake them from this firm foundation (vv.18–23). He encourages them to steer well clear of such false teaching. He highlights some of the marks of the false teachers, which you can use to identify them:

1. 'Lies' about Jesus
Lies and deceit are the mark of false teachers, 'no lie comes from the truth' (v.21). John explains that 'whoever denies that Jesus is the Christ' (v.22) is a 'liar' and an 'antichrist', opposed to both the Father and the Son (v.23).

2. Leaving the fellowship
These false teachers were individuals who '*went out from us*', which was an indication that 'they *did not really belong to us*' (v.19). They often leave the fellowship because they leave the apostolic teaching.

3. Leading people astray
'I am writing these things to you about those who are trying to *lead you astray*' (v.26). Have nothing to do with such false teachers, but instead root yourself in the truth of the gospel. 'Stay with what you heard from the beginning, the original message. Let it sink into your life' (v.25, MSG). If you do this, then you have nothing to fear.

You have the Holy Spirit living within you to lead and guide you; 'the anointing you received from him remains in you' (v.27).

Immerse yourself in Scripture (v.14), and in the fellowship of the church (v.19). This will protect and strengthen you. The key is to stay close to Jesus: 'If what you heard from the beginning lives deeply in you, you will live deeply in both Son and Father. This is exactly what Christ promised: eternal life, real life!' (vv.24–25, MSG).

PRAYER

Lord, thank you that you have rescued me from sin, the world and the devil; and anointed me with the Holy Spirit to lead and guide me.

OLD TESTAMENT READING

Daniel 7:1–8:14
Remember his victory is complete

Jesus came to destroy the works of the devil. Jesus lives within you. Through him you have the victory. When it comes to understanding who Jesus is and what he came to do, this is one of the most important passages in the entire Bible.

God spoke to Daniel through dreams and visions while he was lying on his bed. 'He wrote down the substance of his dream' (7:1). (When God speaks, it is wise to write it down so you don't forget.) Daniel had a vivid dream all about spiritual warfare: 'making war on God's holy people' (v.21, MSG).

There was an immediate historical fulfilment of the vision and dream. The four beasts, for example, represent four kingdoms – the Babylonian Empire, the Medo-Persian Empire; the Greek Empire and the Colossus of the Roman Empire.[2]

But this dream and vision had a far greater fulfilment. Daniel foresaw that there will come a time when evil is completely destroyed and eradicated from the earth (vv.11, 26), and when God will reign supreme and eternally over the whole universe (v.14).

He also foresaw a great victory for the people of God: 'the horn will be stripped of its power and totally destroyed. Then the royal rule and the authority and the glory of all the kingdoms under heaven will be handed over to the people of the High God. Their royal rule will last for ever. All other rulers will serve and obey them' (vv.26–27, MSG).

More than that, Daniel foresaw that the victory would be won by a messianic figure in the form of a '*son of man*' (v.13).

'I saw a human form, a son of man,
arriving in a whirl of *clouds*...
He was given *power* to rule – all the *glory* of royalty.
Everyone – race, colour, and creed – had to serve him.
His rule would be forever, never ending.
His kingly rule would never be replaced' (vv.13–14, MSG).

Jesus spoke of 'the *Son of Man* ... coming on the *clouds of heaven*' (Mark 14:62), and 'the *Son of Man* coming in *clouds* with *great power and glory*' (13:26; see also Matthew 24:30; 26:64).

This passage clearly had a profound impact on Jesus and his own understanding of himself. He often described himself as the 'Son of Man'. The expression appears eighty-two times in the Gospels, all in the sayings of Jesus.

Jesus chose a title that did not have the same political overtones as some of the other Messianic titles. It spoke of a representative figure who would identify with human beings and 'give his life as a ransom for many' (Mark 10:45). It carried with it the idea of suffering (Daniel 7).

In his great love for you and me, Jesus, the Son of Man, suffered as a representative of the entire human race, so that you could be rescued from all the spiritual forces of evil in the world. One day, Jesus will return 'with the clouds of heaven' (v.13) as he promised, and victory will be complete (Matthew 24:30–31).

PRAYER

Lord, thank you for this amazing victory of Jesus over all the forces of evil. Thank you that all the powers of evil have been defeated and one day will be utterly destroyed.

2 December | Day 336

From Vision to Action

Jackie Pullinger has spent her life working with the poor and destitute, triad gang members, heroin and opium addicts. She has helped thousands to come off drugs through the power of the Holy Spirit. She has seen transformation in numerous lives and has made a huge impact on the city of Hong Kong.

Jackie wrote, 'I have spent over half my life in a dark, foul smelling place because I had a "*vision*" of another city ablaze with light, it was my dream. There was no more crying, no more death or pain. The sick were healed, addicts set free, the hungry filled. There were families for orphans, homes for the homeless, and new dignity for those who lived in shame. I had no idea how to bring this about but with "*visionary zeal*" imagined introducing the Walled City people to the one who could change it all: Jesus.'[1]

Vision is a 'holy discontent' – a deep dissatisfaction with what *is,* combined with a clear grasp of what *could be.* It is a picture – 'a mental sight' – of the future that inspires hope.

Vision without action is merely a dream. Action without vision is a nightmare! But *vision combined with action* can change the world.[2]

READING FROM PROVERBS

Proverbs 29:10–18
The importance of vision

'Where there is no *vision*, the people perish' (v.18, KJV).

The Hebrew word used can be translated as 'revelation' (NIV) or 'vision' (KJV). It refers to God's communication to his prophets. Where there is no revelatory vision from God, there is often spiritual and political anarchy – 'the people cast off restraint' (v.18).

Vision and restraint should go together. The passion and moral outrage that drives vision can lead to 'uncontrolled anger'. But, says the writer, 'Fools give vent to their anger, but the wise keep themselves under control' (v.11). Jackie Pullinger, alongside Martin Luther King, William Wilberforce and many others, is a superb example of a leader holding together the tension between vision and restraint.

In the rest of the passage we see the results of both good and bad leadership. 'When degenerates take charge, crime runs wild' (v.16, MSG), whereas 'leadership gains authority and respect when the voiceless poor are treated fairly' (v.14, MSG).

PRAYER

Lord, please help me to hear your voice. Give me a fresh revelation of who you are today.

NEW TESTAMENT READING

1 John 2:28–3:10
The power of vision

Jesus had a very clear vision for his life and he combined that vision with action: 'he appeared *so that he might take away our sins*' (3:5).

John goes on to say, '*The reason* the Son of God appeared was *to destroy the devil's work*' (v.8). Through his death and resurrection, Jesus has taken away your sins and destroyed the devil's work.

Do you realise how much God loves you? 'How great is the love the Father has lavished on us, that we should be called children of God! And that is what we are! (v.1).

God had a very clear vision in sending his Son to die for you. He wants to lavish his love on you. His vision for you is that, one day, you will become *like Jesus* and *see Jesus* '*as he is*' (v.2).

God has a vision for your life. You too should have a vision for your life. Your overarching vision should be to become as much like Jesus now as possible: 'All of us who look forward to his Coming stay ready, with the glistening purity of Jesus' life as a model for our own' (v.3, MSG).

The test of whether you are a child of God is this: 'It's not in the nature of the God-begotten to practice and parade sin ... The one who won't *practice righteous ways* isn't from God, nor is the one who won't *love brother or sister*. A simple test' (vv.9–10, MSG). Love and right living are the two indicators that you are a child of God.

Joyce Meyer writes, 'I used to be a full-time sinner, and once in a while I "accidentally" did something right. But now that I have spent many years developing a deep, personal relationship with God ... I still make mistakes, but not nearly as many as I once did, I am not where I need to be, but thank God, I am not where I used to be. I do not do everything right, but I do know that the attitude of my heart is right.'[3]

Your vision should be to stay close to Jesus: 'stay with Christ. Live deeply in Christ ... with no cause for red-faced guilt or lame excuses when he arrives' (2:28, MSG).

This should be your primary vision for your life. It is possible to focus on specific things that we (usually rightly) believe God has called us to do, and yet neglect this overarching vision for our lives. God is much more concerned about how you live your life than what you achieve. Our individual callings are good and important – but our primary vision for life should always be to draw nearer to Jesus.

PRAYER

Lord, thank you for your amazing vision for me – that one day I will be like Jesus and I will see him as he is.

OLD TESTAMENT READING

Daniel 8:15–9:19
The fulfilment of vision

Daniel was a 'visionary' in both senses of the word. He received divine revelation ('*vision*' – a word that appears seven times in Daniel 8:15–27) and had *visionary goals* for his life.

In the first half of today's passage, Daniel is given the interpretation of his vision (divine revelation) by the angel Gabriel (v.16, this is the first place in Scripture where an angel is mentioned by name). Gabriel explains to Daniel that the vision he has seen 'concerns the time of the end' (v.17). 'This vision ... is accurate ... It refers to the far future' (v.26, MSG).

There is both a historical fulfilment of this vision and a long-term fulfilment. The historical fulfilment is probably to be found in a particularly dark period in Jewish history. Between 175 and 164 BC they were ruled by a foreign king, Antiochus IV Epiphanes. He persecuted the Jews, outlawing the worship of God, desecrating the temple and killing thousands. But the spirit that possessed Antiochus and allowed him to achieve earthly success (vv.23–25) is the same spirit that will inspire the final antichrist in the last days (see 2 Thessalonians 2:3–8; Romans 13:11, 14).

Daniel prophesied that '*he will be destroyed, but not by human power*' (Daniel 8:25). Antiochus's troops marched into Jerusalem and massacred 80,000 Jews and enforced the worship of Zeus. He died suddenly and unexpectedly in 164 BC from an unknown disease. This prophecy will find its final fulfilment when Jesus returns and destroys the devil 'with the breath of his mouth' (2 Thessalonians 2:8).

Daniel was also a visionary in the other sense. He understood 'from the Scriptures': 'I, Daniel, was *meditating on the Scriptures* ... according to the word of God to the prophet Jeremiah' (Daniel 9:2, MSG; see also Jeremiah 25:11–12; 29:10), that the exile would last seventy years (that is, from 587 BC to the rebuilding of the temple in 516 BC).

If you want God to give you a specific vision for your life, we see in this passage that there are two essential keys. First, all godly vision needs to come from, and be earthed in, our understanding 'from *the Scriptures*'. Second, fulfilment of vision begins with *prayer*. Daniel turned to the Lord in prayer. He was conscious of the greatness of the God to whom he was praying (Daniel 9:4).

Daniel's prayer was a free-flowing outpouring of his heart to God. He was conscious throughout of God's greatness and mercy and his own unworthiness. But he was also confident of God's ability to answer his prayer.

God longs for you to talk to him about what is on your heart. You don't need to hold back or censor what you talk to him about or try to come across as something you are not. He already knows everything about you; he wants to hear it from you and to talk it through with you. Be yourself with God when you pray – not the way you think you should be.

Daniel confesses that they have sinned in every way imaginable, ignoring God and doing what they please. They are filled with guilt and shame (vv.3–16, MSG).

Yet Daniel knew that God would never give up on those who love him (v.4, MSG) and that 'compassion is our only hope' (v.9, MSG).

On that basis, he prayed for his city and his nation (vv.17–19). Daniel's prayer was answered. You too can cry out to God for your city and nation, and believe that God will answer your prayers and fulfil the vision he gives you.

PRAYER

Lord, give me a vision for my city and my nation: For the sake of your Name have mercy on us, O Lord. Revive us and heal us. Glorify your Name.

3 December | Day 337
How to Be Confident

To describe someone as 'confident' is usually meant as a compliment. But, there is a right and wrong form of confidence. The wrong form of confidence involves valuing yourself over and against God. This is arrogance. The right form of confidence involves valuing yourself *in* and *through* Christ. 'Confidence in the natural world is self-reliance. In the spiritual world, it is God-reliance.'[1] Supremely, it involves confidence in the presence of God.

READING FROM PSALMS

Psalm 137:1–9
Confidence lost

There is something very comforting about the raw anger that is expressed in this psalm. It is a reminder that you can be real and honest with God, and that you don't need to censor your prayers. He can cope with even your darkest thoughts.

The people of God had lost their confidence in the presence of God. The psalmist is in exile, in Babylon, away from Jerusalem and the temple of God's presence. The worst thing about the exile for God's people was this sense of being away from God's presence: 'By the rivers of Babylon we sat and *wept* when we remembered Zion' (v.1).

Their violent response and desire for revenge – 'treat them as they treated us' (vv.8–9) – is a far cry from the New Testament command to love your enemies (see Matthew 5:44). But it is a cry within a lament of people tormented (Psalm 137:3), and desperate for God's presence.

PRAYER

Lord, I long for your presence today.

NEW TESTAMENT READING

1 John 3:11–4:6
Confidence restored

Confidence and love go hand in hand. If you know God's love for you, you love him and you love others, then you will live confidently before God and before your fellow human beings.

Love is not just a feeling. It involves action: 'This is how we know what love is: Jesus Christ laid down his life for us. And we ought to lay down our lives for one another. If anyone of you has material possessions and sees a brother or sister in need but has no pity on them, how can the love of God be in you?' (3:16–17).

It is important to tell people that God loves them and that you love them. However, words are not enough: 'My dear children, let's not just talk about love; let's practice real love' (v.18, MSG). Demonstrate your love in the way that Jesus did – by actions, especially towards the poor.

This is a hugely challenging command in a world where many of our brothers and sisters are in desperate need. We must take action on issues of global poverty, injustice and preventable disease. Also, in the context of the local church, show your love, not just with words, but also with actions and in truth.

God wants you to be confident before him (v.21). He wants you to be 'bold and free before God!' (v.21, MSG).

Confidence is the opposite of condemnation. Condemnation never comes from God: 'There is now *no condemnation* for those who are in Christ Jesus' (Romans 8:1). Condemnation comes either from the devil – who is the accuser – or from our own hearts (1 John 3:20).

There is a big difference between condemnation – 'debilitating self-criticism' (v.20, MSG) – and conviction of sin, which comes from the Holy Spirit (John 16:8). When the Holy Spirit convinces me about my sins it is very specific. I know what I have done wrong. The purpose is to help me repent, be restored and lifted up again.

On the other hand, condemnation is more of a nebulous feeling of guilt and shame that makes us feel bad about ourselves – even after we've repented and asked for forgiveness. It steals our confidence before God.

The wonderful reassurance is that 'God is greater than our worried hearts and knows more about us than we do ourselves' (1 John 3:20, MSG). No one is perfect. But even imperfect love is evidence of the Spirit at work in your life. When you recognise the failings in your heart, your hunger for a more perfect Christ-like love should not shake your assurance, but rather confirm it.

God does not condemn you, but he accepts you, in spite of your failures, weaknesses and imperfections. Indeed, he promises that you will receive from him anything you ask, because you obey his commands and do what pleases him (v.22).

What does it mean to obey his commands and do what pleases him? It is very simple. Two things are required: first, to believe in Jesus, and second, to love one another. If you do these two things, you can be assured that you live in him and that he lives in you: 'This is how we experience his deep and abiding presence in us: by the Spirit he gave us' (v.24, MSG).

How do we know that it is God's Spirit and not some other spirit who lives in us? 'Every spirit that acknowledges that Jesus Christ has come in the flesh is from God' (4:2).

We will fight many battles. We will be hated by the world (3:13). There will be many false prophets: 'Not everyone who talks about God comes from God' (4:1, MSG). But you can be confident because 'the one who is in you is greater than the one who is in the world' (v.4).

PRAYER

Lord, thank you that I can know your presence through your Spirit, and that I can have *confidence before you*. Help me today to love in the way that Jesus loved – to be willing to lay down my life for others.

OLD TESTAMENT READING

Daniel 9:20–11:1
Confidence given

It is encouraging to me that Daniel was not perfect. Up to now, most of what we have read about Daniel suggests he was faultless. However, here we read: 'I was pouring out my heart, baring *my sins and the sins of my people*' (9:20, MSG). Yet, as soon as he began to pray an answer was given and he is called '*highly esteemed*' (v.23; 10:11): 'You are much loved!' (9:23, MSG).

The vision and the prophecy, like so many prophecies, have different layers of fulfilment. There is the immediate historical fulfilment and there is a long-term fulfilment.

The long-term fulfilment was in the death of Jesus. He is the one 'to finish transgression, to put an end to sin, to atone for wickedness, to bring in everlasting righteousness' (v.24). He is the anointed one (Luke 4:18). He is the one who will return and the end will come like a flood.

Jesus echoed these words to his disciples when speaking about the struggles that his followers would face after he had gone, and until his final return (see Matthew 24:6, 8, 15–16). They are partly fulfilled whenever someone sets themselves up against God, from Roman Emperors to Stalin, and will one day be fulfilled in Jesus' final victory over evil.

Daniel has a vision, which, when read through the lens of the New Testament, we understand to be a vision of Jesus: 'I looked up and to my surprise saw a man dressed in linen with a belt of pure gold around his waist. His body was hard and glistening, as if sculpted from a precious stone, his face radiant, his eyes bright and penetrating like torches, his arms and feet glistening like polished bronze, and his voice, deep and resonant, sounded like a huge choir of voices' (Daniel 10:5–6, MSG).

This is very similar to the description of Jesus in Revelation 1:12–18. When Daniel sees this vision of Jesus he 'went weak in the knees, the blood drained from [his] face' (Daniel 10:8, MSG).

As Daniel humbles himself he receives reassurance. A voice tells him, 'Relax, Daniel ... don't be afraid. From the moment you decided to humble yourself to receive understanding, your prayer was heard' (v.12, MSG).

The vision continues and Daniel describes how he 'was surprised by something like a human hand that touched [his] lips.' He goes on, 'I opened my mouth and started talking ... this humanlike figure touched me again and gave me strength. He said, "Don't be afraid, friend. Peace. Everything is going to be all right. Take courage. Be strong." Even as he spoke, courage surged up within me. I said, "Go ahead, let my master speak. You've given me courage"' (vv.15–19, MSG).

When Jesus touches your lips, you are given the confidence and ability to speak (v.16). When Jesus touches your body, you are given the confidence and strength to act (v.18).

The message given to Daniel is, 'Do not be afraid ... Peace! Be strong' (v.19). This confidence comes to you because Jesus gives you boldness, peace and strength.

PRAYER

Lord, I desperately need the presence of Jesus with me. Help me to understand your word and to humble myself before you (v.12). Give me confidence in your presence. Please touch my lips and give me the confidence and ability to speak your words. Please touch my body and give me the confidence and strength to act. Take away my fears and give me your peace.

4 December | Day 338
Four Keys to Overcoming Fear

Alex Buchanan was well known as a 'pastor to the pastors'. He was profoundly deaf in one ear, with only 5 per cent hearing in the other, and one side of his face was paralysed after he suffered nerve damage during major surgery. I remember hearing him speak about God's love and he kept repeating the words, 'God loves you *unconditionally*, *wholeheartedly* and *continually*.'

When he finished his talk he came up to me and said, 'Do you believe that God approves of you?' I said, 'Actually, I really struggle with that because I know things about myself that mean I find it difficult to believe that God approves of me.' He replied, 'We all struggle with that. But God wants you to know that he approves of you. He wants you to know he loves you *unconditionally*, *wholeheartedly* and *continually*.'

If I were asked to summarise what I thought the Bible was all about in one word – apart from the word 'Jesus' – I would choose the word 'love'. Twice in today's New Testament passage John writes, 'God is love' (1 John 4:8, 16). The word 'love' is used widely in our society. Nowhere in the Bible does it say, 'Love is God'. In other words, it is God who defines what love is rather than the other way around. God is love.

This is the message you need to understand yourself, meditate on constantly and speak about to the world: 'God is love.'

Here is the answer to the greatest longing of the world today. People are looking for love. Their hearts are searching. When you really know God's love for you, your life is transformed. As we will see in the New Testament passage for today, God's love is at the heart of each of the four keys to overcoming unhealthy fear in your life: 'There is no fear in love. But perfect love drives out fear' (v.18).

READING FROM PSALMS

Psalm 138:1–8
Thank God for his love

'Thank you! Everything in me says "Thank *you!*"', *writes the psalmist, 'Thank you for your love*, thank you for your faithfulness' (vv.1–2, MSG).

God is loving and faithful in answering our prayers: 'When I called, you answered me; you made me bold and stout-hearted' (v.3).

In this life we face many 'troubles' (v.7b) – sickness, opposition, temptation, exhaustion, trials and attacks. God, in his love and faithfulness, preserves us. 'Though I walk in the midst of trouble, you preserve my life' (v.7a).

I think verse 8 is one of the most encouraging verses in the entire Bible: '*The Lord will fulfil his purpose for me*' (v.8a). God, in his love and faithfulness, has a purpose for your life and he will fulfil that purpose.

Human love can be fleeting, but '*your love*, O Lord, endures for ever' (v.8b). As God's love and faithfulness go hand in hand, so should our love for one another – in marriage, and in all our other relationships.

PRAYER

Lord, thank you so much for your amazing love and faithfulness towards me. Thank you that you promise to fulfil your purpose for me. Help me to live a life of love and faithfulness.

NEW TESTAMENT READING

1 John 4:7–21
Live in the love of God

'God is love. When we take up permanent residence in a life of love, we live in God and God lives in us' (v.17, MSG).

The words 'love', 'loves' and 'loved' appear twenty-seven times in this short passage. Here is the heart of the New Testament. Here is the heart of the Bible. Here is God's heart.

Love is the antidote to fear: 'Perfect love drives out fear' (v.18). Or, 'perfect love turns fear out of doors and expels every trace of terror' (v.18, AMP). Love is the opposite of fear. They are like oil and water. Love is something everyone wants. Fear is something everybody wants to get rid of. We see in this passage four keys to overcome unhealthy fear in your life.

1. Understand God's Love

'This is love: not that we loved God, but that he loved us and sent his Son as an atoning sacrifice for our sins ... so that we will have confidence on the day of judgment ... there is no fear in love. But perfect love drives out fear, because fear has to do with punishment. The one who fears is not made perfect in love' (vv.10, 17–18).

Unhealthy fear entered the world when Adam and Eve sinned. They hid from God. When God asked, 'Where are you?' Adam replied, '*I was afraid* ... so I hid' (Genesis 3:10). Adam was afraid that God would punish him.

The deepest root of fear is condemnation – the feeling that God is cross with you. But God 'sent his Son as an atoning sacrifice for our sins' (1 John 4:10). Jesus took your condemnation. God wants you to have confidence before him.

2. Experience God's Love

'We know that we live in him and he in us, because he has given us of *his spirit* ... we know and rely on the love God has for us' (vv.13, 16).

You truly start living when you know you are unconditionally loved by God. The Holy Spirit gives us the experience of God's love for us. When Pippa was a little girl, whenever she was frightened, her father would pick her up in his arms and sing, 'Daddy's got you now'. This is the work of the Holy Spirit – God picks us up in his arms and reassures us of his love for us.

3. Believe God's Love

'We know and *rely on* the love God has for us' (v.16). The Greek word used for 'rely' is the same word as for believe. Even when we know and have experienced God's love, we need to *keep on believing*.

'Object permanence' is an expression used by psychologists of a child's ability to understand that objects still exist even if they are no longer visible.

Up to about four months old, babies don't have the capacity to believe something exists if they can't see it. If you hide a toy it no longer exists as far as they are concerned. They reach a stage where if you hide a toy, they will keep on looking for it. They realise that objects exist even when you don't see them.

This is a sign of Christian maturity: when we continue to believe in God's love *even when we don't see it or feel it*. We remember and recall. As we believe in the sun even when it is not shining, we *continue to believe* in God's love even in times of darkness when we don't feel his love.

4. Complete God's Love

'No-one has ever seen God; but if we love one another, God lives in us and his love is made complete in us' (v.12). 'Perfect love drives out all fear' (v.18).

The more you love him and demonstrate that reality by loving one another – the less you are prey to fear. Develop a culture of love – giving and receiving love. This is the opposite of competition and gossip. The more love you give to others – the more fear disappears.

PRAYER

Lord, thank you that you love me unconditionally, wholeheartedly and continually. Thank you that perfect love casts out all fear.

OLD TESTAMENT READING

Daniel 11:2–35
Stand firm in the love of God

People who know their God (v.32) are people of love. Love is not weak. The people who really know God resist evil leaders. Dietrich Bonhoeffer was a man who knew God and firmly resisted Adolf Hitler, while praying, 'Give me such love for God and men, as will blot out all hatred and bitterness.'[1] Over the centuries many people who have known their God have stood firm and resisted evil.

Once again, this prophecy (vv.2–35) has different levels of fulfilment. The immediate historical fulfilment concerns the various kings and rulers who reigned between 530–150 BC, many of whom were evil and ungodly in their actions.

However, there is also a long-term fulfilment. As we saw yesterday, Jesus referred to the abomination that causes destruction (9:27; 11:31; Matthew 24:15). He was probably referring to the destruction of Jerusalem in AD 70, which was a foreshadowing of the end times.

In the midst of all this evil 'the people who know their God will firmly resist [the evil one]' (Daniel 11:32b). As the RSV puts it, they will 'stand firm and take action'. Or as *The Message* puts it, 'those who stay courageously loyal to their God will take a strong stand' (v.32b). It goes on, 'those who keep their heads on straight will teach the crowds right from wrong by their example ... The testing will refine, cleanse, and purify those who keep their heads on straight and stay true' (vv.33, 35, MSG).

Today, thank God for his love, live in the love of God, overcome your fears, stand firm and resist evil.

PRAYER

Lord, help us to be a people of love who know their God and stand firm, overcome our fears, resist evil and take action.

5 December | Day 339
God's Purpose for You

Purpose in life is far more important than property or possessions. Having more to live with is no substitute for having more to live for. 'The two greatest days of your life are the day you were born and the day you find out why.'[1]

God has *a specific purpose* for you. In addition, God's *general will* for all of us is revealed in the Bible. In the passages for today we see what God wants for you and for everyone.

READING FROM PSALMS

Psalm 139:1–10
To be known and to know him

God's calling for all of us is to be known by him and to know him. 'Oh LORD, you have searched me and *you know me'* (v.1).

Perhaps this is David reflecting in his old age on how God has guided him throughout his life. 'You hem me in – behind and before; you have laid your hand upon me' (v.5): this speaks of God's loving and gentle hand pressing him along the path of his choosing.

You cannot escape God's presence. He knows everything (v.2) and he is everywhere (vv.7–10). Look to him for guidance: 'your hand will guide me, your right hand will hold me fast' (v.10).

PRAYER

Lord, I desperately need your guidance. Thank you for the promise here that your hand will guide me – your right hand will hold me fast.

NEW TESTAMENT READING

1 John 5:1–21
To be loved and to love for ever

The moment you put your faith in Jesus Christ, you were 'born of God' (v.1). You become the much-loved child of God who 'is love'. God loves you far more than human parents love their own children.

We love our Father in heaven and, therefore, we should love *all* his children. Over the years, Pippa and I have noticed that, from the moment they are born, we have a special love for the children of our friends. This is because of the love we have for their parents. John writes, 'everyone who loves the father loves his child as well' (v.1).

Just as parents who love their children want them to be confident about their future, God wants you to be confident about your future.

The moment you put your faith in Jesus Christ you are 'born of God' (v.1) and receive 'eternal life' (v.12) – but how can you be confident of this? St John tells us that this is the purpose of his letter: 'I write these things to you who believe in the name of the Son of God *so that you may know that you have eternal life*' (v.13).

In this passage we see three tests of a true Christian:

1. Faith

'Everyone who *believes* that Jesus is the Christ is born of God ... This is the victory that has overcome the world, even our *faith*. Who is it that overcomes the world? Only the one who *believes* that Jesus is the Son of God' (vv.1a,4–5).

A Christian is a person who puts their faith in Jesus. In doing so, you become a child of God.

2. Love

'Everyone who *loves* the father *loves* his child as well' (v.1b).

The evidence of true faith is love – love for God, love for Jesus, love for others. Faith expresses itself in love.

3. Obedience

'This is how we know that we love the children of God: by loving God and *carrying out his commands*. This is love for God: to *obey his commands*' (vv.2–3).

This love is not just a feeling. It involves action – obedience to God's commands.

John goes on to speak about three witnesses. How can you be sure that Jesus is the Christ, the Son of God? God has three witnesses (vv.6–8):

1. Water

At the baptism of Jesus, God testified, 'This is my Son, whom I love; with him I am well pleased' (Matthew 3:17). The sacrament of *baptism* focuses on '*the water*'.

2. Blood

The blood Jesus shed on the cross for you is the second witness. Jesus 'came by water *and blood* ... he did not come by water only, but by water *and blood*' (1 John 5:6). The sacrament of *Holy Communion* focuses on '*the blood*'.

3. Spirit

The Holy Spirit testifies in our hearts that Jesus is the Son of God (vv.6, 10). The Spirit is the Spirit of truth (v.6). 'And we are in him who is *true* – even in his Son Jesus Christ. He is the *true* God and eternal life' (v.20).

On the Alpha Weekend, for example, there is a chance for each of the guests to be prayed for, and to ask to be filled with the Holy Spirit. For many people this is the key moment on Alpha – as they are filled with the Holy Spirit, they experience the reality of a relationship with God and assurance of his love for them. It is this experience of God that confirms and establishes their faith.[2]

God wants you to be confident that Jesus really is the Christ, the Son of God. He wants you to know that you have life in his Son (v.11). Indeed, you have 'eternal life' (v.13).

He wants you to have confidence in approaching God: 'This is the confidence we have in approaching God: that if we ask anything according to his will, he hears us. And if we know that he hears us – whatever we ask – we know that we have what we asked of him' (vv.14–15).

Sometimes you know what God's will is – it is clearly spelt out in the Scriptures. At other times, you may not be so sure. In whatever situation, you can add to your prayers, 'Your will be done.'

If the answer is 'yes' he may be increasing your faith. If the answer is 'wait' he may be increasing your patience. If the answer is 'no', he may have something better in mind. Trust that his will is 'good, pleasing and perfect' (Romans 12:2).

John challenges us that those 'born of God [Christian believers] do not continue to sin' (1 John 5:18a). In other words, we must not wilfully carry on sinning just as we did before we turned to Christ. However, he also reminds us of God's wonderful promise that 'the one who was born of God [Jesus] keeps [you] safe, and the evil one cannot harm [you]' (v.18b). You are safe in Jesus' arms of love.

PRAYER

Father, thank you that you love me and keep me safe in Jesus' arms of love. Help me to love all your children.

OLD TESTAMENT READING

Daniel 11:36–12:13
To be blessed and to bless

God blesses you in order that you may be a blessing to others.

By the start of this passage, the mind of the writer has already turned from the time of Antiochus IV Epiphanes (215–164 BC, who was the king who will do as he pleases, 11:36a) to the end times.

We have here one of the great Old Testament affirmations of life beyond the grave: 'But at that time your people – everyone whose name is found written in the book – will be delivered. Multitudes who sleep in the dust of the earth will awake: some to *everlasting life*, others to shame and everlasting contempt. Those who are wise *will shine like the brightness of the heavens*, and those who lead many to righteousness, *like the stars for ever and ever*' (12:1b–3).

You have everlasting life. One day *you* will shine like the stars for ever and ever. In the meantime, a purification process needs to take place. 'Many will be purified, made spotless and refined' (v.10). As well as leading yourself, lead others 'on the right path to life' (v.3, MSG). God's purpose for you is not that you should sit around waiting for Jesus' return to redeem the world. He wants your life to make a difference now. You are called to be a blessing to those around you.

We are called to help each other in our discipleship. I am very grateful for the encouragement, support and challenge over the years of close Christian friends, as well as of older, wiser mentors. It is so helpful to have mentors, and to be willing in turn to help those younger in faith than us. As we challenge and help each other we all grow in our discipleship.

Daniel was told, 'And you? Go about your business without fretting or worrying. Relax. When it's all over, you will be on your feet to receive your reward' (v.13, MSG). What a wonderful promise this must have been for Daniel. He had worked so hard both in his business life and in his work as a prophet. Now rest would come and God had allotted to him an inheritance.

You too have this promise of everlasting life and you will shine like the stars for ever and ever.

PRAYER

Lord, thank you that you have blessed me so much. Help me to bring blessing to others as I lead them on the right path to life.

6 December | Day 340
Find Your Balance

My body is so inflexible. I was told once by a professional fitness trainer, who happened to notice the way I was walking, that I was one of the worst cases of stiffness he had ever come across. I am now trying to do more stretching!

I had considered myself reasonably fit (for my age!), as a result of still playing squash and biking everywhere. But in other ways, I realised I am not. Physical fitness is a balance of strength, flexibility, aerobic and anaerobic fitness. Some people are exceptionally strong but cannot even run to catch a bus. Others are aerobically very fit (they could run a marathon), but are not very strong.

However, spiritual fitness is far more important than physical fitness. It also involves balancing a number of areas of your life.

READING FROM PROVERBS

Proverbs 29:19–27
Humility and confidence

I find it very hard to maintain the balance between humility and confidence. There have been times in my life when I have been humbled (perhaps by some failure) and not felt very confident. At other times, I have felt great confidence but, perhaps, lacked humility.

There is much to ponder in today's passage in Proverbs about not speaking before we think (v.20), controlling anger and hot-temperedness (v.22), and trusting God as being the ultimate source of justice (v.26).

In particular, I notice this balance between humility and confidence: 'Pride lands you flat on your face; humility prepares you for honors' (v.23, MSG). This is a constant theme in Proverbs (11:2; 18:12; 21:4; 22:4).

Be confident in the Lord. Do not live in fear of what others may think or do. 'To fear anyone will prove to be a snare, but whoever trusts in the LORD is kept safe' (29:25).

The key to keeping this balance is to avoid self-confidence and to practise humble God-confidence, ensuring that your confidence comes not from your own abilities or successes, but from trusting in the Lord.

PRAYER

Lord, help me to have a confidence that comes from trusting in you, to avoid fearing anyone and to walk humbly before you.

NEW TESTAMENT READING

2 John 1–13
Truth and love

Here is another difficult balance to maintain. Love becomes soft if it is not strengthened by truth. Truth becomes hard if it is not softened by love.[1] Sometimes in my life I have been passionate about 'the truth', but perhaps have not been very loving. Other times I have tried to be very loving but perhaps have failed to care enough about 'the truth'.

In this second letter of John (probably written to a church referred to as 'the chosen lady', v.1), he warns them of the danger of false teaching that denied the fact that Jesus had come to this earth in bodily form and was therefore both fully divine *and* fully human. John urges this beautiful balance of 'truth and love' (v.2). Indeed, he intermingles the two, even in the greeting.

He writes, 'I, your pastor, *love* you in very *truth*. And I'm not alone – everyone who knows the *Truth* that has taken up permanent residence in us *loves* you' (v.1, MSG).

Because he loves them, he wants to see them in person and 'have a heart-to-heart talk' (v.12, MSG). Letter writing, emails, texts, phone calls, WhatsApp and even Skype or FaceTime are no substitute for being with someone 'face to face' (v.12) and talking heart to heart.

He urges them to 'love one another' (v.5) and to '*walk in love*' (v.6). Love should be the aim of our lives. Study love, talk about it and practise it.

The test of love is obedience to Jesus: 'Love means following his commandments, and his unifying commandment is that you conduct your lives in love' (v.6, MSG).

Truth and love are not opposed to each other. Indeed, they complement one another. John is delighted to find this church 'living out the Truth' (v.4, MSG). Truth really matters. Truth is found in a person. Jesus said, 'I am ... the Truth' (John 14:6). Listen to the truth. Teach the truth. Love the truth.

There are many deceivers out there (2 John 7–8). Cling to the truth and do not be deceived or you will lose out.

Only by knowing the truth and holding fast to it and continuing in the teaching will we have 'both the Father and the Son' (v.9).

The next verse does not sound very loving – 'If anyone shows up who doesn't hold to this teaching, don't invite him in and give him the run of the place. That would just give him a platform to perpetuate his evil ways, making you his partner' (v.10, MSG). But actually, John's passion for the truth stems from his love for this church. Because he loves them, he is not willing to tolerate falsehood. False teachers may seek to lead you astray, but 'do not lose what you have worked for' (v.8).

PRAYER

Lord, help me to maintain this balance between truth and love and always 'speak the truth in love' (Ephesians 4:15).

OLD TESTAMENT READING

Haggai 1:1–2:23
Vision and action

A top management consultant once told me that 'no chief executive was ever fired for lack of vision'. But many are unable to put their vision into action.

Visions don't work unless you do. In this little book of Haggai, we see a wonderful balance between vision and action.

Five times, the Lord Almighty said through the prophet Haggai: 'Give careful *thought*' (1:5, 7; 2:15 and twice in 2:18). Vision starts with thinking – grasping in our *minds* a picture of what could be.

Get your *priorities* sorted out. Haggai challenged God's people about their *priorities*. They were living in comfortable homes while the house of the Lord remained a ruin (1:4). Yet they were saying, 'The time has not yet come for the Lord's house to be built' (v.2).

The people had decided to rebuild the temple. They had good intentions, but they had not done it because it was not their *priority*.

The prophet Haggai urged them to think carefully about their ways (v.5). Their primary concern should be to see God's name honoured (v.8), yet they left God's house as a 'ruin' (vv.4, 9).

Eugene Peterson writes that there are 'times in our lives when repairing the building where we worship is an act of obedience every bit as important as praying in that place of worship.'[1]

Some of the people were dismayed that the new temple was not as splendid as the old had been: '"Who of you is left who saw this house in its former glory? How does it look to you now? Does it not seem to you like nothing? But now be strong ... For I am with you ... And my Spirit remains among you. The glory of this present house will be greater than the glory of the former house ... And in this place I will grant peace"' (2:3–5, 9).

These are the verses through which God spoke to Sandy Millar, and others, about HTB Onslow Square in July 1981, when the church building was about to be closed and sold to a property developer. It was the theme of our 2010 thanksgiving service celebrating the 150th anniversary of the church, and the official reopening after three years of restoration work.

Now it is a thriving centre for The Marriage Course and other family-life courses and hundreds of young people worship Jesus there every Sunday. Our prayer and hope for the future is that 'the glory of this present house will be greater than the glory of the former house' (v.9).

In the book of Haggai, having seen this vision, they had to 'Get to work, all you people! – God is speaking ... *Put into action*' (v.4, MSG). And so the work began (1:14).

As you look around at the church in your own nation give careful thought to your ways. It is not right to live in comfort while God's house remains a 'ruin'. God wants people in your nation to come to know him and be part of his church. Visualise how God could be even more glorified in his church today than he was in the past (2:9).

First, 'be strong' (v.4). Do not weaken in your resolve because of attack, criticism or discouragement. Second, 'work' (1:14; 2:4). It is hard work but there is nothing wrong with that. There are times when you need to work exceedingly hard. Third, 'do not fear' (v.5). This suggests that there *will* be things that could cause fear.

You can trust God with the finances. The Lord declares, 'The silver is mine and the gold is mine' (v.8).

The key is that the Lord says, 'I am with you ... And my Spirit remains among you' (1:13; 2:5). You can overcome all your fears because you know that God is with you.

PRAYER

Lord, help me to balance humility and confidence, love and truth, vision and action, to trust that you are with us and to work hard to see your name glorified.

7 December | Day 341

Is God Really in Control?

Do you sometimes wonder whether God is really in control? Maybe something has gone wrong with your health, relationships, job or some other situation in your life, and you wonder: Does God know? Does God care? Is there anything he can do about it anyway?

One of the things that I remember so well about Bishop Sandy Millar's time as vicar of HTB is that whenever things seemed to have gone wrong, or we were facing some kind of crisis, he would always remind us: '*The Lord reigns.*' God not only loves you, but he is also the sovereign Lord who is ultimately in control of your life. He is also in control of events and history.

As A. W. Tozer wrote, 'God is love and God is sovereign. His love disposes Him to desire our everlasting welfare, and His sovereignty enables Him to secure it.'[1] The Lord reigns!

READING FROM PSALMS

Psalm 139:11–16

The Lord reigns from *conception to death*

You do not need to worry about or fear death. God has a good plan and purpose for your life. Even before you were born, he planned *all* the days of your life (v.16). You are 'fearfully and wonderfully made' (v.14).

Human life begins at the moment of conception. God's sovereign love extends to those in the womb. This is where our personal history began:

> 'You watched me grow from conception to birth;
> all the stages of my life were spread out before you,
> The days of my life all prepared before I'd even lived one day' (v.16, MSG).

God is in control from the moment of your conception to the moment of your death and beyond. Put your trust in him.

PRAYER

Lord, thank you for your sovereign love for every human being. Help us to extend that same love and protection to all.

NEW TESTAMENT READING

3 John 1–14
The Lord reigns *over every area of your life*

God wants to bring restoration to every area of your life today. The apostle John prays for his dear friend Gaius in a holistic way: 'I pray for ... everything you do, and for your good health – that your everyday affairs prosper, as well as your soul!' (v.2, MSG).

John was thrilled to hear that Gaius was making spiritual progress: 'I have *no greater joy* than to hear that my children are *walking in the truth* ... They have told the church about *your love*' (vv.4, 6).

However, John's prayer extends beyond the 'spiritual' to the physical needs of Gaius. There is nothing wrong with praying for friends to enjoy 'good health' and that 'all may go well with [them]' (v.2).

Faith is made visible by love. Love is practical. Hospitality is an act of love. In providing 'meals and a bed we become companions in spreading the Truth' (v.8, MSG).

When you show hospitality, you are part of a long Christian tradition that goes back to the New Testament.

John warns Gaius about Diotrephes who 'not only refuses hospitality to travelling Christians but tries to stop others from welcoming them' (v.10, MSG). He 'loves to be in charge' and will have nothing to do with John, but spreads 'vicious rumours' about him (vv.9–10, MSG). Even the holy and loving apostle John did not win everyone's approval.

He urges Gaius, 'don't go along with evil. Model the good' (v.11, MSG) and he prays: 'peace to you' (v.14).

John deliberately does not put everything down on paper (vv.13–14, MSG). Some things are best reserved for face-to-face meetings.

PRAYER

Lord, today I pray for my family and friends ... that they will enjoy good health and that all may go well with them.

OLD TESTAMENT READING

Zechariah 1:1–4:14
The Lord reigns *over events and history*

It is not just in your own life that things can go wrong and you can wonder whether God is really in control. Sometimes, as we look at world events and history, we wonder what on earth is going on. Does the Lord really 'reign' in all the chaos?

Zechariah's original audience needed to be reminded that 'the Lord reigns'. He was a priest and prophet, who prophesied to the people who had returned to Jerusalem devastated after many years in exile. Zechariah lifts their gaze to God with messages of hope and salvation. God reigns – and he has not finished with his people!

At the heart of this renewed hope are promises of renewed relationship with God, which are ultimately fulfilled through Jesus. Again and again in these visions we see glimpses of Jesus:

1. God will *return* (chapter 1)

The book opens with a call to repentance, as God calls the people to return to him. Alongside the call there is a promise – '"return to me," declares the LORD Almighty, "and *I will return to you*"' (1:3). Returning to God means repenting and admitting our guilt (v.6).

God's promise to return is illustrated by a vision of a man riding a red horse (v.8). God promises: *'Everything's under control'* (v.11, MSG). *He cares about them* (v.14, MSG). The Lord reigns, and he loves you. It seems that the myrtle trees are a picture of the people of God then and the church now, and so it symbolises Jesus (the man riding the red horse) who stands among his church.

If this is the case, then it is Jesus who intercedes for the church (v.12). His intercession was answered: 'I'll see to it that my Temple is rebuilt' (v.16, MSG). This had a literal, historical fulfilment in the rebuilding of the temple in Jerusalem but it also applies to the church.

2. God will *protect* (chapter 2)

Next, Zechariah saw a man with a measuring line in his hand (2:1). Again, could this be Jesus? God promises that Jerusalem will be a city without walls but he will be a wall of fire around it and its glory within. The church is the new Jerusalem – a city without walls (v.4). It is the 'apple of his eye' (v.8). God's Spirit lives among us (v.10).

He assures them, 'Anyone who hits you, hits me' (v.8, MSG). He promises: 'I'm moving into your neighbourhood!' (v.10, MSG).

3. God will *forgive* (chapter 3)
I have a habit of putting pens in my back trouser pocket and then sitting on them, leaving a stain that seems impossible to remove however often the trousers are washed.

You cannot remove the stain of sin in your life. But Jesus can.

The angel of the Lord appears to foreshadow Jesus. Standing before Jesus, Zechariah saw Joshua the high priest and Satan, standing at his right to accuse him (3:1). The name 'Satan' means accuser (see Revelation 12:10).

But Jesus is more powerful than Satan. The Lord rebuked Satan and said of Joshua, 'Is not this man a burning stick snatched from the fire?' (Zechariah 3:2). This is an image that applies to all who have been rescued by Jesus.

Joshua was dressed in 'filthy clothes' standing before Jesus (v.3) who said, 'Take off his filthy clothes ... I have taken away your sin and I will put rich garments on you' (v.4). Jesus cleanses and re-clothes you through the cross.

The Lord Almighty says, 'I am going to bring my servant, the Branch' (v.8; see Jeremiah 23:5f). It continues, 'and I will remove the sin of this land in a single day' (Zechariah 3:9) – this points to the first Good Friday, when Jesus removed all our sin in a single day.

The result is: 'In that day each of you will invite your neighbour to sit under your vine and fig-tree' (v.10). This is a symbol of peace, security and prosperity.

4. God will *give you his Spirit* (chapter 4)
God's word came to Zerubbabel: 'Not by might nor by power, but by my Spirit' (4:6). Neither the temple nor the church is built by might or power: 'You can't force these things. They only come about through my Spirit' (v.6, MSG).

Are you facing a seemingly impossible situation? You cannot overcome by sheer willpower. Ask for the help of the Holy Spirit.

Do not despise 'the day of small things' (v.10). Don't look at seemingly minor accomplishments as unimportant. Don't despise apparently insignificant, humble, 'small beginnings'. The kingdom of God starts with a mustard seed, which grows into a big tree. Small numbers make no difference to God. There is nothing small if God is in it. Everything big has to start small. Nothing you do for God goes unnoticed or unrewarded. You may not see the fruits but you are accomplishing God's purposes. Don't give up on your dream.

The Lord reigns. He is in charge of events and history. In his sovereign love, by his Spirit, from a day of small beginnings, the temple was rebuilt. Now you can trust him to keep building and rebuilding his church from small beginnings by his Spirit.

PRAYER

Lord, thank you that you have removed my sin and given me peace, security and spiritual prosperity. I pray that you will pour out your Spirit and rebuild your church.

8 December | Day 342
Desperate

You were created for an intimate relationship with God. Jesus came to make that possible. Sometimes I find I get distracted, caught up with other things – even my work *for* God can distract me from my relationship *with* him. At other times, I am absolutely desperate for God's presence, his mercy and grace. When we find ourselves in this place of desperation, nothing but the presence of God will satisfy.

READING FROM PSALMS

Psalm 139:17–24
Desperate for God's *thoughts*

It is an amazing blessing to be able to wake up each morning and know that God is with you and that he wants to speak to you: 'Oh, let me rise in the morning and live always with you!' (v.18, MSG). This is why I love to read the Bible first thing in the morning. I am desperate to know God's thoughts.

David is *desperate for God*. He wants to know God's *thoughts*: 'How precious to me are *your thoughts*, O God! How vast is the sum of them! Were I to count them, they would outnumber the grains of sand *When I awake, I am still with you*' (vv.17–18).

David is also *desperate not to offend God* in any way:

> Search me, O God, and know my heart;
> test me and know my anxious thoughts.
> See if there is any offensive way in me,
> and lead me in the way everlasting (vv.23–24).

PRAYER

Lord, I am desperate to know your thoughts and to hear your voice. Lead me into your presence, I pray. Draw me close to you.

NEW TESTAMENT READING

Jude 1–25
Desperate for God's *truth*

Not long ago, I discovered that a dishonest and deceptive South Korean cult called Shincheonji had been trying to infiltrate our church and churches all over the world. These false teachers invite young people to a 'Bible study', lead them astray and teach them to deceive other people.

Jude is desperate for his readers to hold on to God's *truth* and not to be led astray by false teaching: 'I have to write insisting – *begging*! – that you fight with everything you have in you for this faith entrusted to us as a gift to guard and cherish' (v.3, MSG).

Jude encourages his readers to stick to the teaching they were originally given, and to 'contend for the faith' (v.3). The truth really matters. You have been entrusted with it (v.3). You must contend for the truth – against false teachers and false teaching. Why?

First, because we know that God's judgment is on them – and that is serious (vv.5–10). Second, because we know the harm they can do, which is also serious (vv.11–16): '[They] split churches, thinking only of themselves' (v.19, MSG).

Jude gives a description of the characteristics of false teachers and false teaching. Typically, cults will display at least one of these:

- They are deceptive. They 'have secretly slipped in among you' (v.4).
- They reject authority. They want to replace 'sheer grace' with 'sheer license' (v.4, MSG).
- They deny Jesus Christ 'as our one and only Master' (v.4, MSG).
- They look down on and 'sneer at anything they can't understand' (v.10, MSG).
- They 'do whatever they feel like doing' (v.10, MSG).
- They are immoral: 'carousing shamelessly' (v.12, MSG).
- They grumble, complain and find fault (v.16).
- They grab for themselves 'the biggest piece of the pie' (v.16, MSG).
- They are ambitious, 'saying anything they think will get them ahead' (v.16, MSG).

God's people are encouraged to be desperate for God's truth. The beginning and the end of the letter speak of an intimacy with God and how to live as those desperate for God's truth.

I love the way that Jude begins this letter. He sees himself as 'a servant of Jesus Christ' (v.1). There is no higher calling or a more liberating job than to see every day as an opportunity to *serve* Jesus Christ.

He then reassures his readers that they are '*called*' and '*loved*' by God the Father 'and *kept* by Jesus Christ' (v.1). This is true of every Christian. What he wants for his readers is '*mercy*', '*peace*' and '*love in abundance*' (v.2). If these were the only verses we had in the whole Bible, we could meditate on them for the rest of our lives.

He ends by urging them to:

- study the truth: 'Build yourselves up in your most holy faith' (v.20)
- pray: 'Pray in the Holy Spirit' (v.20). The Holy Spirit will guide you into the truth
- stay close to God: 'Keep yourselves in God's love' (v.21)
- be merciful: 'Be tender with sinners, but not soft on sin' (v.23, MSG).

PRAYER

Lord, help us to be desperate to hold on to your truth and to contend for the faith (v.3).

OLD TESTAMENT READING

Zechariah 5:1–8:23
Desperate for God's *Justice* and God's *Blessing*

Zechariah warns of God's judgment and the need for God's justice (chapter 5). There is also great hope here as the prophet foresees the rebuilding of the temple and the restoration of God's presence at the heart of his people.

Joshua the high priest foreshadows Christ. He has a crown on his head (6:11) and he is named 'the Branch' (v.12). He will rebuild the temple of the Lord and be clothed with majesty and will sit and rule on his throne. He will be a priest on his throne (v.13). Like Melchizedek, he combines the kingly and the priestly role, which was ultimately fulfilled in Jesus, the King of kings (Revelation 17:14) and our Great High Priest (Hebrews 4:14).

You, like God's people back then, are called to clean up your act and enable justice for all: 'This is what the Lord Almighty says: "Administer true justice; show mercy and compassion to one another. Do not oppress the widow or the fatherless, the alien or the poor. In your hearts do not *think* evil of each other"' (Zechariah 7:9–10).

There is such a passion in the heart of God that it could almost be said that it *verges on desperation* in his own heart: 'The Lord Almighty says: "I am very jealous for Zion; *I am burning* with jealousy for her ... I will return to Zion and dwell in Jerusalem. Then Jerusalem will be called the City of Truth, and the mountain of the Lord Almighty will be called the Holy Mountain"' (8:2–3).

The Lord Almighty speaks of an amazing future for God's people. There is peace, harmony, prosperity, joy and truth. Both for the people back then, and for us now, some of these blessings are for now, and some are not yet. God says, '*now* I will not deal with the remnant of the people as I did in the past' (v.11), and '*now* I have determined to do good again to Jerusalem and Judah' (v.15).

You experience many *blessings* now through your connection to Christ, but some blessings you will only experience in full measure in the future, in the new heaven and the new earth.

However, right now we are to work to bring this blessing into being: 'O Judah and Israel, so will I save you, and you will be a blessing. Do not be afraid, but let your hands be strong' (v.13).

For example, God is concerned for everyone whatever their age. We too should be concerned for both old and young: 'Once again men and women of ripe old age will sit in the streets of Jerusalem, each of them with a cane in hand because of their age. The city streets will be filled with boys and girls playing there' (vv.4–5).

Again, God is concerned for truth and peace, and so we too must be concerned for these things: 'These are the things you are to do: Speak the truth to each other, and render true and sound judgments in your courts; do not plot evil against your neighbour, and do not love to swear falsely ... Therefore love truth and peace' (vv.16–19).

Above all, God is concerned that as many people as possible experience the blessing of his presence. You are to be a blessing to those around you who do not yet know God through Christ, and a pointer to God through your actions and your words. When others see the difference that God makes, they will be drawn to him. 'This is what the Lord Almighty says: "In those days ten people from all languages and nations will take firm hold of one Jew by the hem of his robe and say, 'Let us go with you, because we have heard that God is with you.'"' (v.23).

When you are desperate to be a channel of God's love, justice and blessing, then others will come to know God's presence.

PRAYER

Lord, we are desperate for you. Please fill your church with your presence. Help us to be a place that ministers to the poor and needy, and a place of truth and peace, where people bring their friends and family because they have heard that 'God is with you'.

9 December | Day 343
Unlocking Revelation

It stars Martin Sheen and Marlon Brando. Set in the Vietnam War, *Apocalypse Now* is a 1979 epic war film. The use of the word '*apocalypse*' is based on the popular misunderstanding of the word as 'destruction'.

The Greek word *apokalupsis*, translated 'revelation' (Revelation 1:1), is made up of two Greek words – *apo* ('out of') and *kalupsis* ('hiding'). The word actually means '*disclosure*'. In the book of Revelation, the veil is taken off. The mystery is unlocked.

'The revelation of Jesus Christ' (v.1) has a double meaning. First, it is the revelation that is given by Jesus. Second, it is the revealing of Jesus, who lies hidden in the Old Testament and is *revealed* in the New Testament. In the book of Revelation, Jesus is further unveiled. We get a clearer disclosure of his great love for us, and his victory over evil.

READING FROM PSALMS

Psalm 140:1–5
Revelation of the righteousness of God

David prays to be rescued from evil people. He speaks of evil *thoughts* (v.2a), evil *words* (v.3) and evil *deeds* (v.4).

Evil is not just about other people. It is about me. All of us have had bad thoughts, said hurtful things and done wrong. All of us have failed to be righteous.

The apostle Paul writes, 'There is no one righteous, *not even one*' (Romans 3:10), and then goes on to illustrate his point using a verse from our psalm – 'the poison of vipers is on their lips' (Psalm 140:3 and Romans 3:13).

But Paul explains that now a righteousness from God has been '*revealed*' (Romans 3:21, GNB). This righteousness from God comes through faith in *Jesus Christ* to all who believe' (v.22).

PRAYER

Lord, thank you for the revelation of your righteousness that comes to us through faith in Jesus Christ.

NEW TESTAMENT READING

Revelation 1:1–20
Revelation of Jesus Christ

This book is a record of the apostle John's revelation of Jesus, which came to him *as he was worshipping*. Eugene Peterson writes that 'we are enlisted as participants in a multidimensional act of Christian worship'.[1] John 'has worship on his mind and is pre-eminently concerned with worship'. God speaks to John as he is worshipping and Jesus is revealed.

The book of Revelation was written to seven churches in Asia minor (v.11), which were pastored by the apostle John who was in exile on the island of Patmos 'because of the word of God and the testimony of Jesus' (v.9). John sees 'seven golden lampstands' (v.12), which he tells us represent the 'seven churches' (v.20).

Seven in the Bible is the number of completeness and perfection. So, this can be taken to mean the whole church. It is written for you and me. Jesus calls John to write down what he sees. He begins to unlock the 'mystery': 'The *seven* stars are the angels of the *seven* churches, and the *seven* lampstands are the *seven* churches' (v.20). This suggests that every church, including yours, has its own angel. Jesus holds all the churches in his hands.

John, in revealing the nature of spiritual reality, uses poetry, songs, metaphors, visions, symbols and pictures. Parts of the book of Revelation are extremely difficult to understand. But it is worth persevering. This is the only book in the Bible where we are specifically told that those who read it will be blessed: 'How *blessed* the reader! How *blessed* the hearers and keepers of these oracle words' (v.3, MSG).

It seems that the early Christians had already changed their day of rest and worship from Saturday (the Sabbath) to Sunday. The revelation began 'On the Lord's Day…' (v.10) – the day the Lord was resurrected, in other words, Sunday.

The book of Revelation, like the Bible as a whole, centres on Jesus: 'Jesus Christ, who is the faithful witness, the firstborn from the dead, and the ruler of the kings of the earth' (v.5). It is very easy to get bogged down in the details of Revelation, but the key is to remain focused on Jesus. The general message of the book is clear – Jesus wins!

Jesus is the one 'who *loves us* and has *freed us* from our sins by his blood, and has *made us to be a kingdom* and *priests* to serve his God and Father' (vv.5b–6). Through Jesus you are *loved*, *loosed* from your chains and *lifted up*.

Your sense of worth is not based on what you do or look like, nor on what others think about you. You are of great value and worth because Jesus loves you so much that he shed his blood for you.

Jesus is going to come again. It will not happen secretly. Everyone will see it: 'Look, he is coming with the clouds, and *every eye will see him*, even those who pierced him' (v.7). You are on the winning team. Jesus is coming back and you will enjoy eternity with him.

John sees 'someone "like *a son of man*"' (v.13). This was Jesus' favourite way of referring to himself. He sees Jesus in all his majesty and glory, 'dressed in a robe reaching down to his feet and with a golden sash round his chest' (v.13). He sees him in all his purity and timelessness: 'His head and hair were … as white as snow, and his eyes were like blazing fire. His feet were like bronze glowing in a furnace, and his voice was like the sound of rushing waters' (vv.14–15).

He sees the total splendour of his appearance: 'In his right hand he held seven stars, and out of his mouth came a sharp double-edged sword. His *face was like the sun shining in all its brilliance*' (v.16). Sometimes, when people spend time in the presence of Jesus, their faces seem to shine. This gives us a taste of what Jesus himself looks like.

John's response to the revelation of Jesus is worship: to fall 'at his feet as though dead' (v.17). Jesus places his hand on him saying, '*Don't fear*: I am First, I am Last, I'm Alive. I died, but I came to life, and my life is now forever. See these keys in my hand? They open and lock Death's doors, they open and lock Hell's gates' (vv.17–18, MSG).

PRAYER

Lord Jesus Christ, I want to fall at your feet and worship you today. I give you my fears today. Thank you that, ultimately, I am safe in your hands.

OLD TESTAMENT READING

Zechariah 9:1–11:17
Revelation of the Saviour

Why are some people so relentlessly positive? It all stems from a little word: 'hope'. Jesus, as revealed in this passage, sets the prisoners free from 'their hopeless cells' (9:11, MSG).

Jesus fills you with hope. However bad your current situation, never give up hope. We are 'prisoners of hope' (v.12). Joyce Meyer writes, 'Real hope is a constant positive attitude that no matter what is happening currently, things will change for the better.'[2]

The words of Zechariah have several levels of fulfilment. Far greater than the historical fulfilment of chapter 9 (through Alexander the Great and the Maccabees), was the fulfilment revealed in Jesus.

'See, *your king comes* to you *righteous* and *having salvation*, *gentle* and *riding on a donkey*, on a colt, the foal of a donkey' (v.9). These words were fulfilled on the first Palm Sunday, as Jesus entered Jerusalem on a donkey (Matthew 21:1–5; Mark 11:1–11).

Zechariah foresees that a humble, righteous king will come bringing *salvation*. He is meek, humble and externally poor. His kingdom would not come by traditional methods of battle. He is not a military king (Zechariah 9:10).

He will bring peace to Jews and Gentiles (v.10, see also Ephesians 2:17). His rule will extend from sea to sea (Zechariah 9:10). You will experience great blessings 'because of *the blood of my covenant with you*' (v.11).

He brings *freedom* for the prisoners (v.11; see also Isaiah 61:1; Luke 4:18). He brings you *security*: 'Return to your fortress, O prisoners of hope' (Zechariah 9:12). He brings you great *blessing*: 'I will restore twice as much to you' (v.12). He is invincible 'like a warrior's sword' (v.13; see Revelation 1:16). He brings you *salvation* (Zechariah 10:16; see also Luke 12:32; John 10:1–16).

There are many other wonderful promises in these prophecies of Zechariah including Jesus as 'the cornerstone' (Zechariah 10:4) and the 'Good Shepherd' who will pastor the flock with 'Favour' and 'Union' (11:7). In sharp contrast to the 'foolish' shepherd described here (v.15), you are called to 'care for the lost', 'seek the young', 'heal the injured' and 'feed the healthy' (v.16).

We also see in this passage a foreshadowing of the betrayal of Judas. The 'thirty pieces of silver' (v.12) is the price that was put on Jesus' head (see Matthew 26:15).

Almost every detail of Jesus' life, character, mission, death, resurrection and victory was foreshadowed in some way in the Old Testament and revealed in the New Testament.

PRAYER

Father, thank you for the revelation of Jesus Christ, our Saviour and Lord.

10 December | Day 344
How to Find Jesus

The whole of the Bible is about Jesus. Martin Luther said, 'Scripture is the manger in which the Christ lies.' As a parent goes to a cot to find their baby, so the Christian goes to the Bible to *find Jesus*. Don't inspect the cot and forget to worship the baby.

In today's passages, we see how Jesus Christ is revealed not only in the New Testament, in the book of Revelation, but also in the Old Testament – in Proverbs and Zechariah.

READING FROM PROVERBS

Proverbs 30:1–10
The name of Jesus

Is there any evidence for God?

> 'The skeptic swore, "There is no God!
> No God! – I can do anything I want!...
> I see no evidence of a holy God"' (vv.1–3, MSG).

The sceptic goes on to ask five questions (v.4):

1. Who has gone up to heaven and come down?
2. Whose hands have gathered up the wind?
3. Who has wrapped up the waters in a cloak?
4. Who has established all the ends of the earth?
5. What is that person's *name*, and what is *the name* of that person's son?

The New Testament reveals that the answer to each of these five questions is Jesus, Jesus, Jesus, Jesus, Jesus. It is Jesus who ascended on high (see, for example, Ephesians 4:8–10). It is through Jesus that the whole world came into being (John 1:1–3). He is *the name above every name* (Philippians 2:9). The evidence for God is found in Jesus.

The New Testament reveals that the name of God is Jesus. The writer of Proverbs cares deeply about 'the name of [his] God' (Proverbs 30:9). He asks for 'neither poverty nor riches' (v.8). He fears that riches may make him disown the Lord and poverty might make him steal and thereby 'dishonour *the name* of [his] God' (v.9).

PRAYER

I worship you, Jesus, the name above every name. I bow my knee before you. Be my shield today as I take refuge in you (v.5). May I never bring dishonour to your name.

NEW TESTAMENT READING

Revelation 2:1–17
The words of Jesus

These words of Jesus ('The First and the Last, who died and came to life again', v.8) to the seven churches are hugely challenging. The risen, ascended, glorified Jesus reveals what kind of church he wants:

1. Don't lose your first love

Jesus is looking for a church that is famous, above all, for its love.

Do you remember what you felt when you first encountered Jesus? Perhaps you experienced joy, peace, a new sense of meaning and purpose, and an excitement. Did you 'fall in love'? Was there a 'honeymoon period'?

As life goes on it is easy to lose your 'first love' (v.4). Other things creep in. Work, the busyness of life, or even your ministry can lead you away from the passion of your first love.

Jesus commends their service: 'I know your deeds, your hard work' (v.2). But there have been times in my life when I've been working so hard for the kingdom that I have neglected the King.

Jesus commends their patience in suffering and perseverance: 'you have ... endured hardship for my name' (v.3). But there have been times when I have been so focused on my own problems and suffering that I have lost my enthusiasm.

He commends the orthodoxy of their beliefs – they have not tolerated evil (v.2). But there have been times when I have been so concerned about orthodoxy that I have forgotten to love.

Jesus challenges: 'You have forsaken *your first love*' (v.4). These are haunting words. What are you to do if this has happened?

- *Remember* your first love – to remember the height from which you have fallen (v.5). Never lose your first love, enthusiasm and excitement about Jesus.
- *Repent* and clean up your act. If you have slipped into complacency or compromise, you may need to get rid of the dross. As we read in Zechariah, 'I will refine them like silver and test them like gold. They will call on my name and I will answer them; I will say, "They are my people", and they will say, "The LORD is our God"' (Zechariah 13:9).

  If you are in a time of testing and trial in your life, God will use the heat of the fire to refine you.
- *Return* to doing the things you did when you first encountered Jesus. 'Do the things you did at first' (Revelation 2:5).

2. Stand firm in the face of persecution
Pastor Youcef Nadarkhani was imprisoned in Iran for no other reason than his faith in Jesus Christ. He was sentenced to death. As a result of international pressure he was released and reunited with his family. I had the privilege of interviewing him at HTB. We were all inspired by his faithfulness and courage.

Only two of the seven churches are not faulted by Jesus – Smyrna and Philadelphia. Smyrna is spiritually rich in spite of the persecutions and material poverty: 'I know your afflictions and your poverty – yet you are rich!' (v.9).

Jesus' words to the church are not 'repent' (as so often was the case with the other churches), but rather, 'Do not be afraid' (v.10). Like the persecuted church today, they faced prison, persecution and even death. But God has set a limit ('for ten days') and promises, 'I will give you the crown of life' (v.10b).

3. Fight for the truth
The church in Pergamum was living in the most godless place on earth – 'where Satan has his throne' (v.13). Yet Jesus says, 'You remain *true* to my name' (v.13). They have not renounced their faith in Jesus in spite of persecution.

Nevertheless, Jesus challenges them about holding to false teaching and committing sexual immorality (v.14). Truth matters. He calls them to repent (v.16), and promises that if they overcome, he will give them food that feeds the soul ('the hidden manna', v.17) and eternal security in Christ.

PRAYER

Lord, may I never lose my first love for you. Help me to *remember* the height from which I have fallen and return to you. Thank you for the inspiring courage of the persecuted church in the face of great trial. Help me to hold to your truth in spite of our culture. Keep me faithful to you.

OLD TESTAMENT READING

Zechariah 12:1–14:21
The grace of Jesus

God promises his people: 'I will pour out ... a spirit of *grace* and supplication' (12:10). The Holy Spirit is the Spirit of grace and supplication. He pours into your heart God's grace (his undeserved love for us) and helps you to pray (see Romans 8:26–27). The Holy Spirit is at work in your thoughts – prompting you to pray for people and situations.

How is all this possible? Zechariah continues, 'They will look on me, *the one they have pierced*' (Zechariah 12:10). Who is *the one they have pierced*? The apostle John gives us the answer: 'One of the soldiers *pierced Jesus'* side with a spear ... These things happened so that the Scripture would be fulfilled ... "They will look on *the one they have pierced*"' (John 19:34–37).

What is the result? 'On that day a fountain will be opened to the house of David and the inhabitants of Jerusalem, to *cleanse* them from sin and impurity' (Zechariah 13:1). This is the grace of our Lord Jesus Christ. Through his death, through him being pierced for you, he made it possible for you to be cleansed from every sin and all impurity.

Jesus seemed to have this passage in mind when he was thinking about his own death. He quoted Zechariah 13:7 when predicting that, upon his arrest, the disciples would desert him: 'Strike the shepherd, and the sheep will be scattered' (v.7; see Matthew 26:31, 56).

The words of Zechariah 14 can be seen as looking forward to the life, death and resurrection of Jesus, and also to his return:

1. Jesus is the one whose feet would stand on the Mount of Olives (Zechariah 14:4; Matthew 21:1).
2. Jesus is the one to go out and fight against the nations in the day of battle (Zechariah 14:3; Revelation 20).
3. Jesus is the one out of whom living water would flow (Zechariah 14:8; John 7:37–39).
4. Jesus is the one who will be worshipped as king (Zechariah 14:16; Revelation 5).
5. Jesus is the one who makes it possible for 'HOLY TO THE LORD' to be inscribed on everything (Zechariah 14:20).
6. Jesus abolishes the distinction between the secular and the sacred. The cooking pots were the most common household vessels, yet they too had the words 'HOLY TO THE LORD' inscribed on them.

PRAYER

Lord, thank you that you promise to pour out a spirit of grace and supplication on me. Thank you that you opened a fountain to cleanse me from sin and impurity. Cleanse me today and fill me again with your Holy Spirit. Help me to love with all the enthusiasm of my first love for Jesus and to bring honour to the name of Jesus.

11 December | Day 345
How You Can Make a Difference

In an interview in *Time* magazine, the great Swiss theologian Karl Barth recounted that he advised young theologians to 'take your Bible and take your newspaper and read both. But interpret newspapers from your Bible.'[1]

When we read, watch or listen to the news it could be easy to get depressed. It sometimes seems that evil is triumphing over good. The plans of 'the wicked' seem to succeed, while others are subject to the ravages of terrorism, war, poverty and injustice.

This is why we desperately need to hear the voice of the Holy Spirit and listen to the word of God. As we study the Scriptures, we see the triumph of good over evil. In each of the passages for today we see that evil will *not* ultimately triumph. At the end of the day, good wins. Furthermore, in this struggle between good and evil, you *can* make a difference.

READING FROM PSALMS

Psalm 140:6–13
Cry out to God for good to triumph

In a world with so much injustice towards the poor and needy, God will secure justice for the poor and uphold the cause of the needy. We know ultimately that the righteous will praise God's name and the upright will live before him for ever (vv.12–13).

David is surrounded by 'trouble makers' (v.9, MSG). They are 'slanderers' and people of violence (v.11). Some deal in physical blows, others deal in words. Both can be equally damaging. In the midst of this David cries out, 'O LORD; *do not let their plans succeed*' (v.8).

He ends this psalm on a note of trust: 'I know that you, God, are on the side of victims, that you care for the rights of the poor. And I know that the righteous personally thank you, that good people are secure in your presence' (vv.12–13, MSG).

PRAYER

Lord, I cry out: '"You are my God." Hear, O LORD, my cry for mercy' (v.6). Do not let those who slander your name succeed. Thank you that you are our strong deliverer and our shield (v.7).

NEW TESTAMENT READING

Revelation 2:18–3:6
Be someone who overcomes evil with good

As we continue today to read Jesus' words to the seven churches, we see that the battle between good and evil is not only something that occurs between the church and the world, but also inside the church itself. Jesus makes extraordinary and wonderful promises to those who overcome evil.

1. Live a holy life

The church in Thyatira is praised for its love, faith, service, perseverance and personal growth: 'I know your deeds, your love and faith, your service and perseverance, and that you are now doing more than you did at first' (2:19).

However, Jesus challenges the church about its so-called 'tolerance'. Today, the word 'tolerance' is regarded as one of the great virtues and only seen in a positive light. Tolerance is an extremely important quality. But, there are limits to tolerance and some forms of tolerance are not good.

Jesus criticises the church in Thyatira for their tolerance of sexual immorality in the church: 'You *tolerate* that woman Jezebel, who calls herself a prophetess. By her teaching she misleads my servants into sexual immorality and the eating of food sacrificed to idols. I have given her time to repent of her immorality, but she is unwilling' (vv.20–21).

We live in a sex-saturated culture in which we are encouraged and expected to be sexually active and seek personal 'sexual fulfilment'. The Bible has an extremely high view of sex, delighting in and encouraging it in the right context – that of a loving marriage. But anything beyond this, such as promiscuity or pornography, is exposed as destructive and unhelpful. We do not know what Jezebel's sexual immorality was – but these verses are a reminder of the importance of sexual purity.

Jesus warns that unless they repent of Jezebel's ways, disaster will follow (v.22b). The Son of God, 'whose eyes are like blazing fire and whose feet are like burnished bronze' (v.18), 'searches hearts and minds', and will repay each according to their deeds (v.23).

These aren't simply words of condemnation, as they are accompanied by a call to 'repentance'. In fact, even 'Jezebel' has been given a chance to repent (v.21). Where we have sinned sexually, it is so important to remember that we can be forgiven – our response to passages like this should not be despair, but repentance and gratitude.

The church is called to holiness. Jesus promises, 'To those who overcome and do my will to the end, I will give authority over the nations ... just as I have received authority from my Father' (vv.26–27). Jesus will share his authority with his faithful overcoming people.

You will also share his glory: 'I will also give them the morning star' (v.28). If you turn your back on the darkness of sin, you will see the light of the glory of God in the face of Jesus Christ. However great your current struggles in your battle for holiness, one day with this star, Jesus, you will remain absolutely and eternally content.

2. Be authentic

Holiness does not mean being perfect. It means living a life of integrity. It's the opposite of hypocrisy. It means being real, honest and authentic.

The church in Sardis had the reputation for being alive, but was in fact dead (3:1). It looked active. It sounded like a good church to go to. Yet it had become complacent. Jesus calls them to repent: 'Remember, therefore, what you have received and heard; obey it, and repent' (v.3). They had heard the gospel and received the Holy Spirit. Remember what extraordinary and wonderful privileges these are, and do not take them for granted and become complacent.

The charge against Sardis is hypocrisy and inauthenticity. The call is to reality and authenticity. There were a few in the church 'who have not soiled their clothes' (v.4a). 'They will walk with [Jesus], dressed in white, for they are worthy' (v.4b).

Again, Jesus makes amazing promises to those who overcome: 'Those who overcome will, like them, be dressed in white. I will never blot out their names from the book of life, but will acknowledge their names before my Father and his angels' (v.5).

PRAYER

Lord, give me wisdom to know the limits of toleration. Help me to overcome sin in my own life. May I never become complacent about your great love. Help me to obey you and overcome evil with good. May my name be indelibly inscribed in the 'book of life' (v.5).

OLD TESTAMENT READING

Esther 1:1–2:18
Watch God turn the tables on evil

One person *can* make a difference. Esther was one of the saviours of the Jewish nation. She was an orphan (2:7). She was beautiful (v.7) and charming: 'Esther won the favour of everyone who saw her' (v.15). She was obedient to her adopted parents: 'She continued to follow Mordecai's instruction as she had done when he was bringing her up' (v.20). Her call was so significant that it needed a long period of preparation.

Esther is one of the two books in the Old Testament named after a woman (the other being Ruth). It is also one of two books in the Old Testament that does not mention God by name (the other being Song of Songs). It contains the account of the origin of the annual Jewish holiday and feast of Purim. It is set during the reign of Xerxes, King of Persia (486–465 BC).

At about the age of thirty-five, Xerxes inherited a massive empire, which included modern-day Iran, Iraq, Egypt and Ethiopia, as well as parts of India (1:1).

The book of Esther is the account of a moment in the history of the Jewish people when they were able to *turn the tables* on those who wanted to destroy them.

As Eugene Peterson writes, 'No matter how many of them you kill, you can't get rid of the communities of God-honouring, God-serving, God-worshipping people scattered all over the earth. This is still the final and definitive word.'[2]

In the next few days we will read more about Esther's extraordinary qualities. However, in today's passage we see how God's hand was upon her. He was preparing the ground to use her to turn the tables and bring about the triumph of good over evil.

Joyce Meyer writes, 'I believe that God has a great call and purpose for your life as he did for Esther's. Your assignment may not be the deliverance of a nation, but whatever God has called you to is extremely significant. Whatever it is, be diligent to embrace the preparation process it requires so that you will be well-equipped when the time comes for you to act.'[3]

PRAYER

Sovereign Lord, thank you that you are in ultimate control of my life and of history. Thank you that through Jesus, I am assured of the ultimate triumph of good over evil. Help me to make a difference in your plans to overcome evil with good.

12 December | Day 346

The Benefits of Being Rebuked

I never enjoy being rebuked by someone else, but over time I have come to see the faithful rebuke of a friend as something of great value. The Scriptures tell us that the right kind of rebuke is an important way in which God cares for us, and in which we can care for each other.

READING FROM PSALMS

Psalm 141:1–10
The kind rebuke

There have been times in my life when people have rebuked me out of kindness. It is never easy at the time. But, on reflection, I am so grateful to them. David regards *the rebuke* of the righteous person *as kindness* – like 'oil on my head' (v.5), because his desire is that not only his head, but *every part of his body* and his life, should honour God:

1. *Lift your hands*

'May the lifting of *my hands* be like the evening sacrifice' (v.2). The lifting of hands to God symbolises an opening of the whole body to God.

2. *Guard your lips*

'Set a guard over *my mouth*, O LORD; keep watch over the door of *my lips*' (v.3). I often pray this before I give a talk or go into a meeting – that God will protect me from saying anything unhelpful, and that my words will be an encouragement and a blessing.

3. *Watch your heart*

'Let not *my heart* be drawn to what is evil' (v.4a). Your thoughts become your actions. Your actions become your habits. Your habits become your character. Your character becomes your life. It all starts in your heart.

4. *Fix your eyes*
'*My eyes* are fixed on you, O Sovereign LORD' (v.8a). We are urged to 'fix our eyes on Jesus' (Hebrews 12:2).

PRAYER

Lord, I lift my *hands* and *voice* to you in worship, and fix my *eyes* upon you. Set a guard over my *mouth* and *lips*, and keep my *heart* from evil.

NEW TESTAMENT READING

Revelation 3:7–22
The loving rebuke

Jesus loves you. When he allows you to go through the fire of rebuke, testing or discipline, he does so out of love. He says to the church in Philadelphia: 'it's you that *I've loved* ... I'll keep you safe in the time of *testing'* (vv.9–10, MSG). He says to the church in Laodicea: '*Those whom I love I rebuke* and *discipline'* (v.19). How should you respond?

1. Make the most of every opportunity
Jesus is holy and true and he '*holds the key* ... What he opens no one can shut, and what he shuts no one can open' (v.7). If you are unsure about, for example, a job or relationship, ask God to shut the door if it is not right, or to open the door if it is.

On at least two occasions in my life God has closed the door on something that I very much wanted, and which I believed at the time was God's will. Praying and struggling, I tried to force the doors open – but they remained shut. I was bitterly disappointed. But, years later, I am very grateful and now understand why he closed those doors. (However, I'm not sure I will ever know, this side of heaven, why God has closed other doors in my life).

The Spirit continues, 'See, I have placed before you an open door that no one can shut' (v.8). Sometimes God places before you a door of opportunity. If he opens the door, no human being can shut it. You may come under great attack but, if Jesus opens the door, you can be confident that he is in control.

This does not mean passively waiting for the doors to open. Often, we have to take the first steps in faith. It is rather like approaching automatic doors – you have to take a step forward before you see whether or not the doors open.

This church in Philadelphia has little strength, yet it has kept Jesus' word and not denied his name (v.8). They have endured patiently and Jesus promises to keep them from the hour of trial (v.10).

Humanly speaking, this church does not appear to have been particularly impressive. Yet Jesus has no words of criticism for it. His perspective can often be very different from ours, and faithfulness to him matters far more than outward signs of size or strength.

His message is simply: *hold on to what you have*. He promises that those who overcome will be made pillars in the temple of God. His name will be written on them (v.12). Your future is utterly secure.

2. Open your heart to Jesus
The harshest words of Jesus are reserved for the church at Laodicea (vv.15–17). The church in Laodicea was like so much of the church in the West. At one level, it was 'successful' – Laodicea was a place famous for its banks and industry. But spiritually they were proud, 'lukewarm', 'wretched', 'pitiful', spiritually 'poor, blind and naked' (v.17). I find these words deeply challenging.

Yet, there is hope here. We are still loved by the Lord (v.19). He urges us to acquire real treasure, refined in the fire, so that we may become spiritually rich (v.18a). The only way to cover our shameful nakedness is with his robes of righteousness (v.18b). We need his salve on our eyes to remove our spiritual blindness (v.18c).

As we go through the refiner's fire it is a form of discipline (v.19). It has a purpose. He wants us to 'be earnest, and repent' (v.19).

It is in this context that this wonderful and famous verse is found: 'Here I am! I stand at the door and knock. If anyone hears my voice and opens the door, I will come in and eat with them, and they with me' (v.20). Eating together is a sign of the intimate friendship that Jesus offers to all those who open the door of their lives to him.

There is only one handle and it is on the inside of the door.[1] In other words, you have to open the door to let Jesus into your heart. Jesus will never force his way in. He gives you the freedom to choose. It is up to you whether or not you open the door to him. If you do, he promises, 'I will come in and eat with them and they with me.'

PRAYER

Lord, I repent of the times when I have been lukewarm, half-hearted, complacent and spiritually poor. I long for a greater intimacy with you. Come and fill me today with your Holy Spirit.

OLD TESTAMENT READING

Esther 2:19–5:14
The wise rebuke

My father was Jewish and many of my Jewish family perished in the concentration camps during the holocaust.

But anti-Semitism is not a recent phenomenon. Here in the book of Esther, set in the fifth century BC, we read of appalling anti-Semitism. Esther had to keep her background a secret (2:20). Haman wanted to 'annihilate all the Jews – young and old, women and little children – on a single day ... and to plunder their goods' (3:13).

Mordecai's response was to tear his clothes, put on sackcloth and ashes, and wail loudly and bitterly (4:1). Effectively, he was calling on God for help.

Mordecai realised that Esther, his adopted daughter, was in a position to make a difference. Esther pointed out the problems of her situation, and how it would be very difficult for her to help (vv.9–11).

Mordecai's response was in effect the wise rebuke of a parent: 'Do not think that because you are in the king's house you alone of all the Jews will escape. For if you remain silent at this time, relief and deliverance for the Jews will arise from another place, but you and your father's family will perish. And who knows but that you have come to royal position *for such a time as this*?' (vv.13–14).

Esther realised that God had put her in that position for a purpose. You too have a purpose. Many people go through life without meaning or ultimate purpose, trying to pursue their own agenda – not realising that God's purposes are so much better. You are alive today in order to fulfil God's purposes for this generation. Whatever position you are in, believe that you are there '*for such a time as this*'.

Esther listened to Mordecai's wise words. She asked the people to fast for her and said, 'I will go to the king, even though it is against the law. And if I perish, I perish' (v.16). There is risk involved. We only have one life. We have to go for it. If we perish, we perish. But better to take the risk than never to have tried. May we rather be like Esther – utterly dependent on God and willing to risk our lives to save the lives of others.

PRAYER

Lord, help me to listen to wise and kind rebukes. As I go through the refiner's fire, purify my heart, that I may love you more fully, seize every opportunity of life and serve you wholeheartedly.

13 December | Day 347
How to Celebrate

It will be a 'joyous celebration' – a time of 'happiness and joy, gladness and honour' (see Esther 8:16–17).

Pippa and I love our annual Leadership Conference held at the Royal Albert Hall (which was built in central London to display 'the greatness and power and glory and victory and the majesty of God'). Thousands of people gather together. There are times of *great celebration* with heavenly worship and powerful life-changing teaching. People are inspired, refreshed and equipped to make a difference to the world around them.

The Bible has much to say about celebration. There is a *celebration* in heaven every time one person turns to Christ. When the prodigal son returned to the father, the father said, 'Let's have a feast and *celebrate*' (Luke 15:23).

In our Old Testament passage for today, we read that 'the city of Susa held a joyous *celebration*' (Esther 8:15). It '... exploded with joy' (MSG). What were they celebrating? What should you celebrate now? How should you celebrate?

READING FROM PSALMS

Psalm 142:1–7
Celebrate answered prayer

For many years, as I've read this psalm, I have written down a list of 'troubles' and situations for which I am crying out to God for mercy and help. As I look back, it is amazing to see the way in which he has answered these prayers.

The context of this psalm is that David is imprisoned in a cave (1 Samuel 22:1–2) and fearing for his life. He cries out loudly to God, spelling out his troubles and pleading for mercy (Psalm 142:1–2, MSG). He prays:

> 'Get me out of this dungeon
> so I can *thank you in public*.
> Your people will form a circle around me
> and you'll bring me *showers of blessing*!' (v.7, MSG).

David longs to be able to praise God for answering his prayers and rescuing him. He promises that if he is rescued he will turn it back to worship and gather others together to celebrate God's goodness.

It is important to remember to celebrate answered prayers – to praise God's name and celebrate his goodness. It will build your faith and increase your love for God.

PRAYER
Lord, thank you for the many times you have rescued me. Again, today, I cry out to you...

NEW TESTAMENT READING

Revelation 4:1–11
Celebrate before the throne in heaven

We have a 24-7 Prayer Room at our church. There is worship and prayer twenty-four hours a day, seven days a week: 'night and day, never taking a break' (v.8, MSG).

You do not need to wait until heaven to experience 'heavenly' worship. This worship is happening now – 24-7 – in heaven. In this passage, we get a glimpse of what it looks like. Every time you worship, you join in with the worship of heaven.

John's eyes turn from the church on earth to the church in heaven. John looks through an open door in heaven (v.1). Accompany John as he is invited to 'Ascend and enter. I'll show you what happens next' (v.1, MSG).

What follows is an extraordinary vision of the greatness and glory of God. God is at the centre of the universe, surrounded here by images of who he is and what he has done. The 'throne' suggests the highest authority, the 'rainbow' is the rainbow of promise, the 'lightning, rumblings and peals of thunder' point to the power of God, and the 'sea of glass, clear as crystal' suggests peace and security (vv.2–6).

'Seven fire-blazing torches fronted the throne (these are the Sevenfold Spirit of God)' (v.5, MSG). There is one Holy Spirit but the fire-blazing torches represent all the different ways in which he expresses himself and in which you experience his fullness in your life.

Around the throne are twenty-four elders seated on thrones, probably representing the twelve tribes of the Old Testament and the twelve apostles of the New Testament. This is the completed and perfect church of Jesus Christ. You are included (1 Peter 2:9–10).

As those around the throne contemplate the wonder of God the natural response is to turn to worship – and this is the first thing that John finds going on in heaven. There are five worship songs in the next two chapters.

'Day and night they never stop saying: "Holy, holy, holy is the Lord God Almighty, who was, and is, and is to come"' (v.8). (Those of us who find repetition hard may have to get used to a lot of it!)

'Whenever the living creatures give *glory, honour and thanks* to him who sits on the throne and who lives for ever and ever, the twenty-four elders fall down before him who sits on the throne, and *worship him* who lives for ever and ever. They *lay their crowns before the throne* and give him all the glory' (vv.9–11).

The church, the angels and all created things bow down and worship God. The eternal Father sits on the throne surrounded by the worshipping community.

As John Stott wrote, one day you will 'join the church triumphant, the great multitude that no one will be able to count, drawn from every nation, tribe, people and language, and you will stand with them before God's throne. The King of the universe will give you refuge in the shelter of his throne. You will see him and worship him day and night. The Lamb turned Shepherd will lead you with the rest of his sheep to fountains of living water. You will satisfy your thirst forever at his eternal springs.'[1]

PRAYER

My Lord and my God, I thank you that I don't have to wait until the new heaven and the new earth to worship you. You are worthy to receive glory, honour and power today and every day.

OLD TESTAMENT READING

Esther 6:1–8:17
Celebrate the great acts of God

Sometimes as we look at the world it seems that evil is triumphing. Good people suffer and are even being persecuted for their faith. Will things ever be put right?

Yes, they will. God has come to earth in the person of his Son, Jesus (the incarnation, which we celebrate at Christmas). He has defeated evil through the cross and resurrection (which we celebrate at Easter). The final victory will take place when Jesus comes again. In the meantime, he has given you the Holy Spirit so that you can experience a foretaste of that final victory right now (this we celebrate at Pentecost).

God was preparing his people for these great events. In the book of Esther, we see a prefiguring and a picture of what was to come in Jesus.

In a dramatic turnaround, Haman's plot fails. Mordecai 'the Jew' is honoured. Judgment falls on the evil and arrogant Haman. Esther is used by God to save the people.

This is the origin of the great Jewish *celebration* of Purim. The providential hand of God rescued his people from 'destruction and slaughter and annihilation' (7:4).

Events began to turn when 'the king could not sleep; so he ordered the book of the chronicles – the record of his reign – to be brought in and read to him' (6:1). He was reminded of the heroic loyalty of Mordecai (v.2).

Have you ever achieved something for which other people have taken the credit? Haman tried to take the honour that belonged to Mordecai. Mordecai's response is a model of humility and trust in God. Other people may not see what you have done, but God sees and he will reward you.

Instead of being hanged, Mordecai receives honour and recognition. The king issues an edict granting the Jews in every city 'the right to assemble and protect themselves' (8:11).

The city of Susa held a '*joyous celebration*' (v.15). It was 'a time of *happiness* and *joy*, *gladness* and *honour*' (v.16) 'with *feasting* and *celebrating*' (v.17).

'Many people of other nationalities became Jews because fear of the Jews had seized them' (v.17). This is the earliest reference to many non-Hebrews putting their faith in the Lord. There had been cases of individuals coming to faith (for example, Ruth and Uriah the Hittite), but nowhere before had there been a mass movement like this.

When the Jewish festival of Purim is celebrated, the book of Esther is read. It is now one of the three great Jewish celebrations.

The church also has three great celebratory festivals: Christmas, Easter and Pentecost. These should be joyous celebrations of happiness, gladness, honour and feasting – celebrating the great acts of God in history: the incarnation, the resurrection of Jesus who died for us on the cross, and the outpouring of the Holy Spirit. As well as the annual celebrations, celebrate these great events daily in your heart.

PRAYER

Lord, thank you that you have given us so much to celebrate. Thank you that you have delivered us through Jesus Christ. Thank you for the birth, death and resurrection of Jesus and the outpouring of the Holy Spirit. Help me to celebrate these great events, annually in our church festivals and daily in my heart.

14 December | Day 348
Doing Hard Things the Right Way

Doing hard things requires us to be lion-like – bold, steely and courageous. Doing things the right way means being like a lamb – gentle, meek and submissive. We are supposed to be a godly mixture of the qualities of both the lion and the lamb.

But how can one person be both 'the Lion' and 'the Lamb'?

In C. S. Lewis's Narnia books, the lion, Aslan, represents Jesus. In the most famous of these books, *The Lion, the Witch and the Wardrobe*, Aslan is slain:

'"Bind him, I say!" repeated the White Witch ... "Let him first be shaved" ... the shorn face of Aslan looked ... braver, and more beautiful, and more patient than ever. "Muzzle him!" said the Witch ... the whole crowd of creatures kicking him, hitting him, spitting on him, jeering at him ... They began to drag the bound and muzzled *Lion* to the Stone Table.'

Later, 'they heard from behind them a loud noise – a great cracking, deafening noise ... The Stone Table was broken into two pieces by a great crack that ran down it from end to end ... There, shining in the sunrise, larger than they had seen him before, shaking his mane (for it had apparently grown again) stood Aslan himself.' Aslan tells them that 'when a willing victim who had committed no treachery was killed in a traitor's stead, the Table would crack and Death itself would start working backwards.'[1]

In the book of Revelation, we see Jesus is standing at the centre of the throne of heaven. He is the Lion and the Lamb. He is both triumphant ('has triumphed', 5:5) and slain ('you were slain', v.9). In an imaginative and powerful way, C. S. Lewis shows how Jesus can be both 'the *Lion* of the tribe of Judah' (Revelation 5:5) and 'a *Lamb [that] had been slain*' (v.6).

READING FROM PROVERBS

Proverbs 30:11–23
Be cleansed by the Lamb who was slain

We need to be cleansed from our sin – our 'filth', as the writer of Proverbs describes it (v.12). This 'filth' of sin comes in many guises and disguises:

- failure to give sufficient blessing and obedience to our parents (vv.11–12, 17)
- pride, which can come in the form of 'haughty' eyes and 'disdainful' looks (v.13). 'Don't be stuck-up and think you're better than everyone else' (v.13, MSG)
- failure to look after 'the poor' and 'the needy' (v.14)
- sexual sin, which justifies itself by saying, 'I've done nothing wrong' (v.20).

The worst state to be in is not to recognise the need to be cleansed (v.12). It is a wonderful thing to be cleansed of our sins.

In the New Testament passage for today we see the whole of creation worshipping the Lamb that had been slain, because 'with your blood you "purchased for God" members of every tribe and language and people and nation' (Revelation 5:9). It is the blood of Jesus that 'purifies us from all sin' (1 John 1:7).

PRAYER

Lord, may I not just be 'pure' in my 'own eyes' (v.12). Please cleanse me by the blood of the Lamb, who purchased me for God.

NEW TESTAMENT READING

Revelation 5:1–14
Worship the Lamb who is also a Lion

Sometimes I find myself acting like a lamb when I should be a lion. I act meekly when I should be bold, steely and courageous. At other times, I act like a lion when I should be more lamb-like. I am too fierce when I should be gentle, meek and submissive.

Jesus took on powerful opponents with lion-like courage: for example, throwing out the money-changers from the temple. On the other hand, with the woman caught in adultery (John 8:1–11), he could have been steely, but instead he was gracious and gentle as a lamb. The challenge for us is to follow the example of the one we worship.

What is going on in heaven right now? John tells us that when he glimpses into heaven he sees millions worshipping Jesus: 'the Lion' who is also 'a Lamb'. Jesus is the key to understanding history and salvation.

On earth, we find it so hard to understand what is going on. What are God's plans and purposes for history and salvation? What are his plans and purposes for your life and my life? The scroll 'sealed with seven seals' (Revelation 5:1) probably represents God's plans and purposes.

No one in heaven or on earth, or under the earth, is found worthy to open the scroll or even to look inside it, except for Jesus: 'The Lion of the tribe of Judah' who 'has triumphed' (vv.2–5).

Here stands Jesus in all his majesty and kingship. Only Jesus can open the secrets of history, God's plan of salvation and his purpose for each of our lives.

The Lion is also a Lamb: '*A Lamb*, slaughtered but standing tall ... He came to the One Seated on the Throne and took the scroll from his right hand. The moment he took the scroll, the Four Animals and Twenty-four Elders fell down and worshiped *the Lamb* (vv.6–7, MSG).

The Lamb is worshipped by the whole created order and the entire church falls down before him.

Here is an amazing fact. Your prayers on earth affect the worship of heaven: 'Each had a harp and each had a bowl, a gold bowl filled with incense, *the prayers of God's holy people*' (v.8, MSG). Your prayers fill the golden bowls of heaven. Your prayers really do make a difference.

'They sang a new song ... "with *your blood you purchased for God* members of every *tribe* and *language* and *people* and *nation*. You have made them to be a kingdom and priests to serve our God, and they will reign on the earth"' (vv.9–10).

'Then I looked and heard the voice of many angels, numbering *thousands upon thousands*, and *ten thousand times ten thousand*' (v.11a). There are more than a hundred million angels worshipping Jesus:

'"The slain Lamb is worthy!
Take the power, the wealth, the wisdom, the strength!
Take the honor, the glory, the blessing!"'
(v.12, MSG)

There is something extraordinarily powerful about large crowds worshipping Jesus together.

This is one of the reasons I love the Leadership Conference and Alpha Global Week, when people from over a hundred nations and numerous languages – peoples and tribes all together – worship Jesus. This is a foretaste of heaven.

Here we see that the activity of heaven is the worship of Jesus. You will sing songs of redemption. The whole of heaven bursts with praise (v.13). There is a great orchestra and a magnificent choir and all types of music in harmony. You were created for the worship of God's glory, which was revealed in Jesus Christ – the Lion who is also the Lamb.

PRAYER

Lord, I worship you as *the Lion* of the tribe of Judah who has triumphed, and *the Lamb* that was slain. Lord, I want to become more like Jesus and know when to be bold and courageous like a lion, and when to be meek and gentle as a lamb.

OLD TESTAMENT READING

Esther 9:1–10:3
Celebrate the triumph of the Lion of the tribe of Judah

Jesus is the Lion who *turns the tables* on your spiritual enemies. He is the one against whom no one can stand. He is the cause of feasting and joy and celebration. Ultimately, he is the reason we give presents on Christmas day, to celebrate his coming and his triumph.

Esther is a 'type' of Christ – that is to say, her life prefigured and foreshadowed Jesus. Humanly speaking, if it were not for her intervention, the Jewish nation would have been destroyed. Her action brought defeat to the evil one – Haman – and brought freedom, joy and triumph to the people of God. The '*tables were turned* and ... No one could stand against them' (9:1–2).

Trust God that, in the end, whatever evil is planned against you will come to nothing. God has promised, in Jesus, to give you the ultimate victory.

In the meantime, have the lion-like courage of Esther and Mordecai, and their lamb-like willingness to sacrifice their lives in obedience to God's purpose.

This led to God's people 'freeing themselves from oppression'. They 'celebrated with much food and laughter ... laughing and feasting ... their day for parties and the exchange of gifts' (vv.17–19, MSG).

These events foreshadowed the great event of the triumph of the 'Lion of the tribe of Judah, the Root of David' (Revelation 5:5) – through the life, death and resurrection of Jesus.

He brought about: 'sorrow turned to joy, mourning somersaulted into a holiday for parties and fun and laughter, the sending and receiving of presents and of giving gifts to the poor' (Esther 9:22, MSG). This too should be part of our celebration.

PRAYER

Lord, thank you for the ultimate triumph of the Lion, who is also the Lamb who was slain. 'To him who sits on the throne and to the Lamb, be praise and honour and glory and power, for ever and ever!' (Revelation 5:13).

15 December | Day 349

What is Going on Behind the Scenes of History?

In the West, many people assume history is aimless: 'Full of sound and fury, signifying nothing' (as Shakespeare put it in *Macbeth*). Many Eastern religions tend to regard history as either circular or illusory, while Marxists understand history in terms of class struggle.

In contrast to all these views, the New Testament sees history as moving towards a climax. The ultimate struggle is between *good and evil* – ending with the *triumph of good and God*.

The kingdom of God will not fail. God is working his purposes out in history. Jesus is the centrepiece. All lines in history converge on him. As someone has said, 'the hinge of history is on the door of a Bethlehem stable.'

History is 'His story'. As you hear the news and read history books you get some of the details. As you read the Bible you get the big picture. In particular, the book of Revelation unveils what is going on behind the scenes of history.

God is the Sovereign Lord of history. But we are not mere robots. You are not being moved around like a piece on a chessboard. Rather, you have a part to play. God involves you in his plans. God works out his purposes in co-operation with his people.

READING FROM PSALMS

Psalm 143:1–12
Be guided by the God of history

We need God's guidance. You have the potential to change the events of history for good. But there are many challenges to be faced.

David was depressed. He was in 'a black hole' – a 'dungeon': 'I sat there in despair, my spirit draining away, my heart heavy, like lead' (v.4, MSG). How do you begin to get yourself out of a situation like this?

1. Remember the good things

David chose to think about the positive: 'I remembered the old days, went over all you've done, pondered the ways you've worked' (v.5, MSG).

2. Keep worshipping

Worship can be an oasis in difficult times. David says, 'I ... stretched out my hands to you, as thirsty for you as a desert thirsty for rain' (v.6, MSG).

3. Cry out to God for help

He prays, 'Hurry with your answer, God! I'm nearly at the end of my rope. Don't turn away; don't ignore me!' (v.7, MSG).

4. Listen for God's guidance

Year after year I have written next to the verse, 'Show me the way I should go' (v.8a), a list of areas in which I have desperately needed God's guidance. It is so encouraging to look back and see the way he has guided me – sometimes in ways beyond anything I could have asked or even imagined.

PRAYER

'O Lord, hear my prayer ... my soul thirsts for you like a parched land ... Show me the way I should go ... I hide myself in you ... For your name's sake, O Lord ... bring me out of trouble.'

NEW TESTAMENT READING

Revelation 6:1–17
See behind the scenes of history

In spite of all the terrible things that you see going on in the world around you and read about in history, you have great hope. The good news centres on Jesus. Jesus, the Lamb of God, opens *the seals* of history (v.1). He reveals what is going on behind the scenes of the events you read and hear about.

1. The gospel preached to all nations

The first rider was given 'a victory garland. He rode off victorious, conquering right and left' (v.2, MSG).

This sounds like Jesus himself, the conqueror of death, the crowned King of the universe going out to proclaim good news to the nations.

2. Wars and military power

The second rider 'was given power *to take peace from the earth* and to *make people slay each other*. To him was given *a large sword*' (v.4).

History has been full of violence and warfare, as people have sought to dominate and control each other.

3. Injustice and inequality

The third rider 'was holding a pair of black scales in his hand' (v.5).

Prices had been inflated (v.6). There was an economic disaster. As is the case today, while some live in terrible poverty, others live in luxury (v.6), untouched by the needs of the poor.

4. The curse of death

The fourth rider 'was named Death, and Hades was following close behind him' (v.8a).

Death takes its toll in history. As we read the history of this world it is one of violence ('kill by sword'), starvation ('famine') and disease ('plague'), as well as other random causes of death ('the wild beasts of the earth') (v.8b).

5. The persecuted church

'...those who had been slain *because of the word of God and the testimony they had maintained*' (v.9).

Persecution of Christians continues to the present day throughout the world, with millions of Christians living in fear of being caught, beaten, imprisoned or even put to death because of their faith in Jesus.

6. The beginning of the end

Jesus predicted similar upheavals to the ones described here – 'these are the beginning of birth-pains' (Matthew 24:8). These will no doubt include social and political upheavals, as well as natural disasters.

The six seals give a general view of history between the first and second coming of Jesus.

PRAYER

Lord, may we be peacemakers who feed the hungry, fight against injustice, stand with the persecuted and bring good news as we anticipate your return and the beginning of a new heaven and a new earth that will last for ever.

OLD TESTAMENT READING

Malachi 1:1–2:16
Look at God's love in history

'Look at history' (v.2, MSG) God says through the prophet Malachi (c.450 BC), whose name means 'my messenger'. If you want to know how much God loves you, look at history. The message of the God of history is 'I love you' (v.2, MSG): 'Take a good look. Then you'll see how faithfully I've loved you and you'll want even more' (v.5, MSG).

The background is that, even after the rebuilding of the temple, there is 'shoddy, sloppy, defiling worship ... worship of God is no longer a priority' (vv.6–7, MSG): there is a failure to give generously and a breakdown of family life.

The words of this book are hugely challenging to those involved in any kind of leadership of God's people (v.6).

The priests were the leaders of God's people. Like the prophets, they were supposed to be the ones through whom God spoke: 'For the lips of a priest ought to preserve knowledge, and from his mouth people should seek instruction – because he is the messenger of the LORD Almighty' (2:7).

The challenge to us all is:

1. Single-minded determination to see God's name honoured

'Set your heart to honour my name' (v.2).

2. Receive 'life and peace'

God has covenanted (promised) to give 'life and peace' (v.5) – these are two of the greatest blessings you can ever receive.

3. Worship God with reverence and awe

This should be our response to God's extraordinary generosity and kindness: 'This called for reverence and [Levi] revered me and stood in awe of my name' (v.5).

4. Teach the truth

'True instruction was in his mouth and nothing false was found on his lips' (v.6a).

5. Live a righteous life

'He walked with me in peace and uprightness' (v.6b). Christian leaders must set an example by living holy lives.

6. Lead a life of helping others to find a relationship with God

'...and turned many from sin' (v.6b).

Next, Malachi turns to relationships. He criticises them for marrying non-believers (v.11). This is also discouraged elsewhere in Scripture (see 2 Corinthians 6:14). We might find this challenging. The imagery Malachi uses here can help us understand why it is not a good idea. He describes non-believers as 'the daughter of a foreign god' (Malachi 2:11), a phrase which highlights their competing religious views.

All of us have religious ideas and beliefs, even if they are the belief that there is no God. Giving ourselves to someone who holds a different belief may ultimately pull us away from God.

God wanted children to be brought up in the security of the marriage relationship: 'Has not the LORD made them one? In flesh and spirit they are his. And why one? Because he was *seeking godly offspring*. So guard yourself in your spirit, and *do not break faith with the wife of your youth*. "I hate divorce," says the LORD God of Israel ... So guard yourself *in your spirit*, and do not break faith' (vv.15–16).

These words can seem harsh, but actually they are a reminder of how much God loves and values marriage. It is because marriage is so wonderful that God is so utterly opposed to anything that would undermine it.[1]

Unfaithfulness begins in our hearts: 'Therefore, keep a watch upon your spirit (that it may be controlled by My Spirit), that you deal not treacherously and faithlessly (with your marriage mate)' (v.16, AMP).

PRAYER

Lord, thank you for Jesus who came to make forgiveness possible. May we guard ourselves in our hearts and in our spirits and not break faith.

16 December | Day 350

Who Is Lord of Your Life?

Polycarp (AD 70–156) was a bishop during a time of bitter attack against the Christians. At the age of eighty-six, he was arrested for no other crime than being a Christian. All he had to do to avoid torture and death was to proclaim, 'Caesar is Lord.'

Polycarp responded, 'Eighty-six years I have served Christ, and he never did me any wrong. How can I blaspheme my King who saved me?' For Polycarp, the fact that '*Jesus is Lord*' meant that he could not say, 'Caesar is Lord.' Steadfast in his stand for Christ, Polycarp refused to compromise his beliefs and was burnt alive at the stake on 22 February AD 156.

God is described in the Old Testament as 'the LORD'. In the New Testament passage for today, we see the background to the extraordinary claim that 'Jesus is Lord!'

READING FROM PSALMS

Psalm 144:1–8

Jesus – the Lord who has come down from heaven

What battles are you fighting in your life? Temptation? Anxiety? Fear? Depression? Financial battles? Health battles? Work or relationship battles?

This psalm is a plea for help before battle. The original context was probably a physical battle. However, through the lens of the New Testament, you can see it in terms of a spiritual battle. There are times when we seem to be losing ground in a spiritual battle, for example, for our nation. But, never give up!

Perhaps you are facing a frightening battle in your own life. David praises the Lord: 'my

Rock', 'fortress', 'stronghold', 'deliverer', 'my shield in whom I take refuge' (vv.1–2).

The Lord is powerful. He is also 'my *loving* God'. He involves you in his plan; 'he trains me to fight fair and well' (v.1, MSG). You are a partner with God. God, of course, is the major partner but you have a part to play as well.

David goes on to say, 'Part your heavens, *O Lord*, and come down ... reach down your hand from on high; deliver me and rescue me' (vv.5a,7). This is exactly what God did, which we celebrate at Christmas. The Lord Jesus *came down* from heaven and delivered and rescued us.

Whatever battles you are fighting today, spend time with Jesus praising him for who he is, calling on him for help and trusting him to deliver you.

PRAYER

Lord, I cry out to you, my loving God – my fortress, my stronghold, my deliverer, my shield, my rescuer. Help, Lord!

NEW TESTAMENT READING

Revelation 7:1–17
Jesus – the Lord at the centre of worship

One of the highlights of every Olympics Games is the opening ceremony, involving 225 nations coming together for a joyful celebration. Yet this pales in significance compared to what is described in this passage, where we see a great multitude from every nation, tribe, people and language coming together before the throne of God.

The six seals we looked at yesterday gave a general view of history between the first and second comings of Jesus. Tomorrow, we will read of the breaking of the seventh seal.

In the interlude of Revelation 7, there is significant reassurance given to God's people: 'Do not harm the land or the sea or the trees until we put a seal on the foreheads of the servants of our God' (v.3). Whatever may take place around you, your eternal security is not in doubt, for you have been given 'the seal of the living God' (v.2).

The 144,000 referred to in verses 1–8 and the unnumbered multitude in verses 9–17 are probably *not* two distinct groups, but pictures of *the same group* from two different angles. In the first, God's people are assembled on earth, and, in the second, they are assembled before God in heaven with their struggles and battles behind them in the past.

The people of God are described as those who have washed their clothes and made them white 'in the blood of the Lamb' (v.14). This is an example of non-literal metaphorical language of the apocalyptic literature in the book of Revelation and this chapter in particular. Robes would not be made white by being washed in blood! However, metaphorically, you are washed clean by the blood of Jesus.

The number 144,000 is therefore not literal but is symbolic of the entire people of God throughout history. John sees them as 'a great multitude that no one could count, from every nation, tribe, people and language, standing before the throne and in front of the Lamb' (v.9).

The multitude 'were wearing white robes and were holding palm branches in their hands' (v.9). They are singing songs of worship to the Lord (v.10). The angels join the multitude and worship God (vv.11–12). Finally, the whole church, together with the angelic hosts, worships Jesus. Earthly choirs and orchestras are rehearsing for the heavenly concert.

'The Lamb at the centre of the throne will be their shepherd' (v.17a). This is an extraordinary reversal of roles. The Lamb has become the shepherd! You will never again be hungry or thirsty. You will be satisfied by 'springs of living water, and God will wipe away every tear' from your eyes (v.17b). There will be no more pain or suffering or bereavement or tragedy.

PRAYER

Lord, thank you that I can look forward to an eternity in the presence of Jesus. Thank you that you will satisfy my hunger and quench my thirst and wipe away every tear from my eyes.

OLD TESTAMENT READING

Malachi 2:17–4:6
Jesus – the Lord who refines and blesses

The book of Malachi ends with the expectation of the coming of the one who will prepare the way for the Lord: 'I will send you the prophet Elijah before that great and dreadful day of the LORD comes. He will turn the hearts of the parents to their children, and the hearts of the children to their parents' (4:5–6).

This is how John the Baptist is described (Luke 1:17). Jesus said that he is the Elijah who was to come (Matthew 11:14; see also Matthew 17:12–13; Mark 9:12–13).

In the Christian Bible, the last book of the Old Testament is the book of Malachi. It ends with an expectation of the coming of the Lord and of the one who will prepare the way for the Lord.

The people are called to prepare for the day of the Lord's coming, which will be 'like a refiner's fire' (Malachi 3:2). God wants to change our attitudes, desires, thoughts and conversations so that we will rid ourselves of selfishness and self-centredness. As Joyce Meyer writes, 'Believe me, getting rid of selfishness takes some fire (difficult times) – and usually a lot of it – but it is worth it in the end.'[1]

Listen to the call to return to the Lord (v.7). In particular, get your giving sorted out (vv.8–12). Your attitude towards money is a barometer of your whole outlook on life.

The 'tithe' was a kind of ecclesiastical income tax that went to the maintenance of the temple and its staff. In addition, people gave in a variety of other ways – through hospitality, gifts to the poor, and 'free will' offerings.

The prophet accuses them of robbing God by their failure to get their giving sorted out. He urges them, '"Bring the whole tithe into the storehouse, that there may be food in my house. Test me in this," says the LORD Almighty, "and see if I do not throw open the floodgates of heaven and pour out so much blessing that you will not have room enough for it"' (v.10).

This shows how important your giving is in God's eyes. Prioritise giving to the church you attend – which is our equivalent of the temple. If you fail to give generously, you are 'robbing God'. If as a church community all give generously, then you can expect that God will 'throw open the floodgates of heaven and pour out so much blessing that [we] will not have room enough for it' (v.10).

It appears that they did get their priorities sorted out: 'Then those who feared the LORD *talked with each other*, and the LORD *listened and heard*. A scroll of remembrance was written in his presence concerning those who feared the LORD and *honoured his name*' (v.16). I love this verse. Sometimes, when you meet together you may not even get around to praying, but still 'the LORD listened and heard' because they 'feared the LORD and honoured his name' (v.16).

He promises, 'for you who *revere my name*, the sun of righteousness will rise with healing in its wings. And you will go out and leap like calves released from the stall' (4:2). Whatever your wounds, hurts and brokenness, God promises to bring healing, restoration and wholeness to your life.

PRAYER

Lord, help us to be a generous community. Thank you that you are with us in our daily battles and that one day we will worship you for ever as part of the great multitude, declaring 'Jesus is Lord'!

---

17 December | Day 351
How to Read and Understand the Bible

When reading and trying to understand the Bible, you have three helpers. First, you have the *Holy Spirit* living in you (1 Corinthians 2:2–16). Second, you have the help of the church. It would be arrogant to think that the Holy Spirit only speaks to me. He has spoken to others in history and he continues to speak to his people. Paul prays that 'you may have power to comprehend, *with all the saints*' (Ephesians 3:18, NRSV). Third, you have the benefit of reason – your *mind*. Paul encourages each person to be 'fully convinced in their *own minds*' (Romans 14:5).

In interpreting the Bible, there are three main questions you need to ask:

1. What does it actually say?

The Old Testament is written in Hebrew (and Aramaic), and the New Testament in Greek. But you can be confident that most modern translations are trustworthy and accurate.

2. What does it mean?

In order to answer this question, you have to ask: What sort of literature is it? Is it historical writing? Poetry? Prophecy? Apocalyptic? Law? Wisdom? Gospel? The passages for today are each different types of literature (poetry, apocalyptic and history), and therefore we read them in different ways.

Next, ask what it meant to the person who first wrote it, and to those who first read or heard it. Then ask, 'Has anything happened subsequently to alter our understanding?' For example, what difference does the coming of Jesus make to our understanding of Old Testament passages? Ultimately the Bible is all about Jesus (see John 5:39–40).

3. How does this apply to my life?

To avoid it becoming a mere intellectual exercise, you must think through how it applies to your daily living.

READING FROM PSALMS

Psalm 144:9–15
Be real with God (poetry)

God wants us to be real with him. The Psalms are not prayers from nice people using polite language. They are often raw, earthy and rough; they are an honest, true and personal response to God.

The Psalms are written in the language of poetry. The poet, Robert Burns, wrote, 'My love is *like* a red, red rose.' He did not mean it *literally.*

Much of the language of theology involves comparison. When two things are compared it does not mean they are alike in all respects.

For example:

'Make our sons in their prime
like sturdy oak trees,
Our daughters as shapely and bright
as fields of wildflowers' (v.12, MSG).

The Psalms also express very human sentiments. For example, in our passage for today the psalmist writes, 'Deliver me and rescue me from the hands of foreigners whose mouths are full of lies, whose right hands are deceitful' (v.11).

Obviously, it is not true that all foreigners are liars and deceivers. But the Psalms sometimes express anger towards God and vindictiveness towards others. It does not mean that these feelings are right, but they are candid responses, which many of us also feel at different times in our lives.

David was in the midst of war and was being attacked regularly by foreign city states. Armed conflict was a fact of life for him, and it is against this backdrop that he thanks God for training his hands for war. Yet this does not imply that we should emulate these sentiments. Both in the New Testament and in the Old Testament we are supposed to have a special love for foreigners and outsiders.

However, there are other sentiments that you can be inspired to follow. For example, David's words in verse 9 inspire us to worship. He goes on to speak of his longing for God's blessing on his family, his work and the security of his nation. He ends, 'Blessed are the people of whom this is true; blessed are the people whose God is the LORD' (v.15).

PRAYER

Lord, thank you that your blessing is on the church – the people whose God is the Lord. I worship you today and pray for your blessing on my family, work, ministry, city and nation.

NEW TESTAMENT READING

Revelation 8:1–9:12
Make a difference by your prayers (apocalyptic)

Apocalyptic literature is the literature of dreams and visions, of divine mysteries and the end of history. It is full of symbols that need to be decoded. In it we are given glimpses of things that are often at the very limits of human understanding; the complicated and fantastic imagery can help us begin to grasp things that are beyond comprehension.

Apocalyptic literature is notoriously difficult to interpret. Within the Bible it is found in several places – especially the books of Daniel and Revelation.

Typically, the reading from the apocalyptic writing for today is not easy to understand. It appears to be Christ calling the world to repentance and his warning of the coming judgment.

Before the judgment: 'Heaven fell quiet – complete silence for about half an hour' (8:1, MSG). During this period of trembling suspense, all of heaven is silenced, possibly symbolising the opportunity for the prayers of God's people to be presented to and heard by God.

The seven trumpets (v.2) suggest he is doing everything in his power to bring us to repentance. God's desire is to warn us of the inevitable consequences of our ways. The first four trumpets herald damage to nature (vv.6–13). There is environmental disaster (v.7), chaos in creation (vv.8–9), human tragedy (vv.10–11) and harm to the cosmos (v.12). Then the fifth and sixth angels herald damage to human beings (9:1–21).

In the midst of this, you can see the importance of your prayers. 'Another angel ... was given much incense to offer, with *the prayers of all the saints* ... The smoke of the incense, *together with the prayers of the saints*, went up before God from the angel's hand' (8:3–4). The exact effect of the prayers is not clear, but what is clear is that *your prayers are heard by God*. Your prayers matter. They make a difference.

We live in the time between the first and the second coming of Christ. We see evidence of much of what is written about in these chapters happening in our world. Our response should be repentance and prayer.

PRAYER

Lord, I want to examine my own life and repent of any known sins. Thank you that you hear my prayers and that they make a difference.

OLD TESTAMENT READING

Ezra 1:1–2:67
Fulfil God's purpose for your life (history)

God has a purpose for your life. You are called to do something special for him. The book of Ezra shows us that even when it is God's plan, there will be plenty of opposition and resistance. But God is with you (1:3) and God's plans will ultimately succeed.

In the book of Ezra, we find ourselves in the more familiar territory of history. The historical books of the Bible are not simply records of what happened, they also provide interpretations of the events they describe. Historical writing was seen as a *prophetic* activity, both recording the facts and explaining or revealing how God was at work through the events that are described.

The opening verse of Ezra is an excellent example of this bringing together of fact and interpretation: 'In the first year of Cyrus king of Persia, *in order to fulfil the word of the LORD spoken by Jeremiah*, the LORD moved the heart of Cyrus king of Persia to make a proclamation throughout his realm and to put it in writing' (v.1). (Contemporary inscriptions show that Cyrus king of Persia allowed other captive nations to return home as well.)

At the same time the writer explains the *significance* of these *historical* events. He highlights how they fulfilled the earlier prophecy of Jeremiah that the exile would last approximately seventy years (Jeremiah 25:12 and 29:10). This is not just a lesson in ancient history; it is a revelation of God. It shows us God's faithfulness to his people; it reminds us that he is a saving God, and it demonstrates how he is in command and control of history.

The events Ezra describes in these chapters took place in 536 BC. After seventy years of decline, defeat and exile there was a new beginning as God's people were allowed to return home.

Cyrus's decree allowed the Jews to return and to rebuild the temple in Jerusalem. Ezra focuses on rebuilding the temple, and Nehemiah on the rebuilding of the walls of Jerusalem. However, their underlying motives were exactly the same. They were concerned for God's glory and God's people. Both, in their different ways fulfilled God's purpose for their lives.

Today, it is the same for you. You have a unique purpose for your life. We all have different projects, depending on our different jobs, passions and giftings, but your underlying motive should be the same – a concern for God's glory and God's people. God will fulfil his purpose for you.

PRAYER

Lord, I want to be available for you to fulfil your purpose for me. May my life bring glory to your name.

18 December | Day 352

How to Honour the Lord

One billion people watched the rescue. On 13 October 2010 at 10pm (GMT) Jose Henriquez Gonzalez emerged from 2,300 feet underground after being trapped for sixty-nine days when the San Jose mine collapsed in northern Chile.

It was originally thought that no one had survived the collapse, or that the thirty-three trapped underground would starve to death before they were found.

Many of them had been atheists, agnostics, un-believers or semi-believers. Jose Henriquez Gonzalez was known as the 'evangelist' because he led so many of the others to faith in Jesus Christ. He formed and led a prayer group. With thirty-three tiny Bibles sent down by friends, he led devotions twice a day.

They testified to the presence of a thirty-fourth person. Nineteen-year-old miner, Jimmy Sanchez, said, 'There are actually thirty-four of us, because God has never left us down here.' Jesus was there with them. When they emerged out of the mine the rescued men were all wearing similar t-shirts. The shirts said on the front, 'Thank you, Lord', and on the back it said, '*To him be the glory and honour*'.

I had the privilege of interviewing Jose Henriquez at HTB. 'The true hero is Jesus Christ,' he said. 'He is the only hero that should be mentioned. Apart from what man may have done both inside and outside that mine, he is the one who deserves the honour and the glory.'

Jesus taught us to pray that God's name should be honoured (Matthew 6:9). My greatest fear is that I might do or say something that will bring dishonour to his name. My deepest longing is to see the name of the Lord honoured again in our society.

How should you act in order to see his name honoured?

READING FROM PROVERBS

Proverbs 30:24–33
Stir up good, not evil

Our whole lives should be devoted to exalting the name of Jesus and *not ourselves*. The writer of Proverbs says, 'If you have played the fool and *exalted yourself*, or if you have planned evil, clap your hand over your mouth! For as churning the milk produces butter, and as twisting the nose produces blood, so *stirring up* anger produces strife' (vv.32–33). We call people 'stirrers' if they stir up arguments, conflict and anger.

The opposite is stirring up *good* things. Seek to be someone who never stirs up anger but, rather, good. Never seek to exalt yourself, but only Jesus. Always seek to honour the name of the Lord.

PRAYER

'*Stir up*, O Lord, the wills of your faithful people, that they, bringing forth the fruit of good works, may by you be richly rewarded: through Jesus Christ our Lord'.[1]

NEW TESTAMENT READING

Revelation 9:13–10:11
Speak the message of Jesus

You honour the name of Jesus when you tell the world about him. Not everyone will be interested, but some will. To those who believe, the message will be 'sweet as honey' (10:9), and their lives will be transformed by Jesus.

The terrible warnings of judgment continued with the sixth angel sounding his trumpet. There was horrible warfare ('The number of the mounted troops was two hundred million', 9:16), violent death and injury.

The twentieth century was probably the most violent in history and the first in which those kinds of numbers were involved in warfare. Yet, there has been little repentance.

'The remaining men and women who weren't killed by these weapons went on their merry way – didn't change their way of life ... There wasn't a sign of a change of heart. They plunged right on in their murderous, occult, promiscuous, and thieving ways' (vv.20–21, MSG). You only have to watch the news to see that these words are also being fulfilled in our time.

Then John saw 'another mighty angel coming down from heaven' (10:1). This sounds like Jesus Christ himself. He is robed in a cloud, which symbolises the presence of God. There is a rainbow above his head symbolising the promise of God. 'His face was like the sun, and his legs were like fiery pillars' (v.1). This is very similar to the description of Jesus in the first chapter of Revelation (1:12–16).

'He gave a loud shout like the roar of a lion' (10:3) – Jesus is '*the Lion* of the tribe of Judah' (5:5). (In our passage for today from Proverbs, the lion is described as 'king of the beasts, deferring to none', Proverbs 30:30, MSG).

Jesus gave the little scroll to John and told him to take it and eat it: 'It will turn your stomach sour, but in your mouth it will be as sweet as honey' (Revelation 10:9). The message of the gospel will have a sour taste for some who reject it, but to all who accept it, it is 'as sweet as honey' (v.9).

Then, John was told to take this message out: 'Then I was told, "You must prophesy again about many peoples, nations, languages and kings"' (v.11).

PRAYER

Lord, in the midst of all the troubles around us, help us to proclaim the gospel faithfully and to see the name of Jesus honoured again.

OLD TESTAMENT READING

Ezra 2:68–4:5
Sacrifice for the Lord's honour

We should not expect a trouble-free life. Jesus warned us that in this life we would experience trouble (John 16:33). Faith does not keep you from trouble but it helps you get through trouble. Don't focus on your troubles but focus on the one who carries you through them, and be willing to sacrifice in order to bring honour to his name.

The people of God had been longing to rebuild the temple in Jerusalem. God's name was *dishonoured* when the temple was destroyed by the Babylonians. Now it was their opportunity to rebuild and see God's name *honoured* again.

They appointed Levites *twenty years old* and older to supervise the building of the house of the Lord (Ezra 3:8) – a good example of appointing young leaders. They were *willing to sacrifice* their money and possessions. *According to their ability they gave* to the treasury for this work 61,000 drachmas of gold, 5,000 minas of silver and 100 priestly garments' (Ezra 2:68–69).

Giving is an essential part of your worship and service to God. Your gifts should not be grudging or forced, but generous 'freewill offerings'. Do not compare your giving to that of others, but give what you can afford. The wonderful thing about this offering was that as each gave according to their ability, they raised all the money that was needed.

If everyone in the church gives sacrificially, generously, each according to their ability, God's kingdom will advance rapidly and his name will be honoured.

In spite of all the opposition around ('despite their fear of the peoples around them', 3:3a), they began to worship the Lord again and offer him sacrifices. Today, worship God by offering him your body as a living sacrifice (Romans 12:2) – that is, offer everything you have, and everything you are, to be used to bring honour to his name.

They did not wait for the temple to be completed before they began their worship. As soon as the foundations were laid, 'with praise and thanksgiving they sang to the LORD: "He is good; his love to Israel endures for ever." And all the people gave a great shout of praise to the LORD, because the foundation of the house of the LORD was laid' (Ezra 3:11).

Exuberant worship is not only a contemporary phenomenon! 'The people made *so much noise*. And the sound was *heard far away*' (vv.12b–13). And yet, while many shouted for joy, the older members of the community 'wept aloud when they saw the foundation of this temple being laid' (v.12a).

This was possibly because the stones used were smaller than for the original temple and it was not as grand. It is a reminder that this temple was not the answer but only a foreshadowing of the temple of the Holy Spirit – the people of God, with Jesus as the chief cornerstone (Ephesians 2:19–22).

The building of the temple was not unopposed: '...the peoples around them set out to *discourage* the people of Judah and make them afraid to go on building. *They hired counsellors* to work against them and *frustrate their plans* during the entire reign of

Cyrus king of Persia and down to the reign of Darius king of Persia' (Ezra 4:4–5).

When you set out to bring honour to the Lord, you may be opposed. Whether it is the rebuilding of churches today, or any other work of the kingdom of God, there is bound to be opposition. The opposition succeeded in *delaying* them, but *not defeating* them altogether.

PRAYER

Lord, may the temple of your Holy Spirit, the church – the people of God – be rebuilt in our generation. May we see the church buildings that are empty and derelict today filled again with people worshipping you. May your name be honoured again in our generation.

19 December | Day 353
Your King

The birth of Prince George of Cambridge in July 2013 brought great joy and celebration. He is the son of a future king of England and is himself third in line of succession to the British throne.

The United *Kingdom* has been ruled by kings and queens for centuries, and our royal family are an important part of our national life. However, most modern monarchs only have limited power. By contrast, in the ancient world, kingship was much more all-encompassing, and the king was the final authority in all aspects of national affairs. In our Old Testament passage, we read of the reigns of the kings of Persia and Israel. But alongside this, each of our passages also points us to an even greater *King* – God.

The central theme in the teaching of Jesus was the *kingdom of God*. It not only refers to kingdom in a political or geographical sense, but it also conveys the notion of activity – the activity of ruling and reigning. The *kingdom of God* means '*the rule and reign of God*'.

READING FROM PSALMS

Psalm 145:1–7
Worship your King

'O my King!' David exclaims, 'I'll bless your name into eternity' (v.1, MSG).

David worships the King of the universe: 'I lift you high in praise' (v.1, MSG). He goes on to speak of the 'splendour of *your majesty*' (v.5a) and, 'the glory of *your kingdom*' (v.11), 'the glorious splendour of *your kingdom*' (v.12) and '*your kingdom* is an everlasting kingdom, and your dominion endures through all generations' (v.13).

He worships his King every day: 'Every day I will praise you' (v.2a), and says he is going to keep on worshipping 'from now to eternity' (v.2, MSG). He can 'never be praised enough' (v.3, MSG). David writes songs of worship: 'I compose songs on your wonders' (v.5, MSG).

Praise God for his power and rule, and for his 'abundant goodness and ... righteousness' (v.7). The joy and exultation of the Psalms stem from these twin truths that God is King *and* God is good. You can trust that he is in control – and that is good news!

PRAYER

Lord, you reign. You are King of the entire universe. You are worthy of my praise. Every day I will praise you.

NEW TESTAMENT READING

Revelation 11:1–19
Hope in your King

Why is life such a struggle? Why do the innocent continue to suffer? Will it always be like this? Will our suffering ever come to an end? Is there any hope? What will the future look like?

In today's passage, we get a glimpse of what the future will be like when Jesus returns: the *kingdom* of the world is transformed into the *Kingdom* of our God and his Messiah who 'will *rule* forever and ever!' (v.15, MSG).

Jesus came proclaiming the kingdom of God. There is a sense in which it was 'now', and a sense in which it was 'not yet'.

The present reality of the kingdom of God was shown by all that Jesus did in his ministry. God's rule and reign is shown by the suppression of evil. The inauguration of the kingdom of God is seen by, for example, the forgiveness of sins, casting out demons and healing the sick.

On the other hand, the future aspect of the kingdom of God was made apparent by Jesus. He taught his disciples to pray, 'your kingdom come' (Matthew 6:10). He speaks of a harvest at 'the end of the age' (13:39). It appears that the kingdom of God will not be fully realised until Jesus returns.

Today's passage from Revelation describes what will happen *just before* the kingdom of God comes in its fullness. The people of God are simultaneously *persecuted* and *protected*.

There will be two witnesses (Revelation 11:3). The Old Testament legal system always required at least two witnesses (Deuteronomy 19:15; John 8:17). Jesus always sent his witnesses out two by two.

The two witnesses here are probably Moses (who turned 'the waters into blood', Revelation 11:6) and Elijah ('who shut up the sky', v.6), 'for these two prophets pricked the conscience of all the people on earth, made it impossible for them to enjoy their sins' (v.10, MSG).

The two witnesses prophesied for 1,260 days (forty-two months or three-and-a-half years). This is probably symbolic of the period between the first and the second coming of Jesus.

Just before the end, they are killed by the beast. Their bodies lie in 'the street of the great city' (v.8) – that is Babylon or Rome – with the symbolic names of 'Sodom and Egypt', and 'where also their Lord was crucified' (v.8), that is Jerusalem.

For a very short time ('three and a half days', v.9), everyone gloats over their death (v.10). Then God raises them up: 'the Living Spirit of God will enter them – they're on their feet! – and all those gloating spectators will be scared to death' (v.11, MSG), and they are taken to heaven as the time for the final judgment approaches (vv.12–13).

This is the moment that the seventh trumpet sounds. There is a three-fold sequence. First, the kingdom of God finally arrives in all its fullness (v.15). Second, the completed church ('the twenty-four elders', v.16) worships the King. Falling on their faces they worship God saying:

> 'We thank you, O God, Sovereign-Strong,
> Who Is and Who Was.
> You took your great power
> and took over—reigned!' (v.17, MSG).

Third, the final judgment begins (v.18). The destroyers will be destroyed. God will reward his 'prophets and saints' – both 'small and great' will be rewarded.

As ever in Revelation, these scenes are symbolic. Moses and Elijah, the two witnesses to God, are figures of great courage and great power, who encounter opposition and suffering before their final vindication.

This is the reality of what you are to expect in this period between the first and second comings of Jesus – the period in which you now live. There is a struggle between the kingdom of God and the kingdom of the 'beast'. But it is a struggle in which you know the final outcome.

Your struggles will come to an end. The innocent will no longer suffer. There is great hope for the future. Jesus will return. He will reign for ever and ever.

PRAYER

Lord, thank you that one day the kingdom of this world will become the kingdom of our Lord and of his Christ, and that you will reign for ever and ever.

OLD TESTAMENT READING

Ezra 4:6–5:17
Trust in your King

Have you ever been unjustly accused or criticised to your boss or to someone else in authority in a way that is very unfair?

Have you ever felt that the work of God was being hampered or even stopped by opposition, by a local council, by your boss at work or by others in authority?

Human leaders are powerful and they can use their power for good or evil. Artaxerxes was king of Persia (4:7). He received what could be described as one of those 'dreaded letters'. It was a letter from those who oppose the work of God. It was full of flattery, half-truths and even lies.

The writers tried to make it sound as if they were being really helpful to the king: 'the king should know...' (vv.12–13). It describes Jerusalem as a rebellious and wicked city. Then, as now, money had a disproportionate power and the threat that 'no more taxes, tribute or duty will be paid, and the royal revenues will suffer' (v.13) was a powerful one, as was the suggestion that the king would be 'dishonoured' (v.14) by this rebellious and troublesome city. The result was that the work of rebuilding the temple and Jerusalem was brought to a standstill (v.24).

If you are on the receiving end of such hostility, it is encouraging to know that you are not the only one to receive letters of 'accusation' (v.6) from people who feel threatened (v.22) and who would like to stop the work (v.21). We know that in the end no one can succeed in such opposition if God is behind the plans. However, it can hold things up and temporarily bring the work to a standstill.

Ultimately these accusers do not succeed. Another king arose and we are told, 'But God had his eye on the leaders' (5:5, MSG).

A favourable report was sent to King Darius. It mentioned a great king of Israel who built and finished the temple (v.11) and the permission given by Cyrus king of Babylon (v.13).

Ultimately you can trust the sovereign rule of God: 'the king's heart is in the hand of the LORD; he directs it like a watercourse wherever he pleases' (Proverbs 21:1). Don't put your ultimate trust in human leaders; trust in God your King.

Human leaders come and go. Some are good. Some are evil. But the Lord is in ultimate control of history.

PRAYER

Lord, thank you that all true kingship points ultimately to your kingship. You are my God, my King. May I see your kingdom come in my community, city and nation.

20 December | Day 354
Three Ways to Overcome Evil

In the last speech he ever made, on 31 March 1968, Martin Luther King repeated the phrase '*we shall overcome*' over and over again. He was echoing the words of folksinger Joan Baez, who in 1963 led a crowd of 300,000 people in singing '*We shall overcome*'. The song speaks of overcoming and of discovering hope and a future amid adversity.

Throughout this year, as we have studied the entire Bible, we have seen that we should not expect an easy life. The Bible is true to *real* life. Life involves many struggles, trials, tests, temptations, difficulties and battles. Yet, in Christ you can be an *overcomer*.

READING FROM PSALMS

Psalm 145:8–13a
God's love overcomes everything

Love is the most powerful force in the world. We overcome through love. This was the message of Martin Luther King who said, 'Darkness cannot drive out darkness, only light can do that. Hate cannot drive out hate, only love can do that.'

God is the source of love. He is 'compassionate', 'rich in love' (v.8). 'He has compassion on all he has made' (v.9). It is God's love that overcomes evil.

In all your relationships – especially when you encounter great difficulties – imitate God. Be 'gracious and compassionate, slow to anger and rich in love' (v.8).

God's love is not a weak or feeble love. It is backed up by his power and might. God's people will 'tell of the glory of your kingdom and speak of your might, so that all people may know of your mighty acts...' (vv.11–12). This is something you can rely on 'through all generations', for God's kingdom is 'an everlasting kingdom' (v.13).

As he declares God's love and power together, it is no wonder that David turns to praise: 'All you have made will praise you, O LORD; your saints will extol you' (v.10).

PRAYER

Lord, thank you that, although the battles in this life may be great, we will overcome and enjoy the glorious splendour of your kingdom for ever.

NEW TESTAMENT READING

Revelation 12:1–13:1a
Jesus overcomes the devil

Do you sometimes feel guilty, even after you've confessed your sin and asked for forgiveness? Do you sometimes feel bad about yourself for no apparent reason? Do you ever experience a vague, nebulous feeling of condemnation?

This is one of the ways in which the devil operates. He is 'the accuser' (12:10). The Hebrew word for Satan means 'accuser' or 'slanderer'. He *accuses* God before people. God gets the blame for everything. God, he says, is not to be trusted.

He also *accuses* Christians before God. He denies the power of the death of Jesus. He condemns you and makes you feel guilty – not necessarily for any particular sin, but with a general and vague feeling of guilt. In contrast, when the Holy Spirit convinces us of our sin he is always specific.

This passage tells us how the devil can be overcome. The book of Revelation opens up what is happening behind the events of history and reveals what is ahead. Over and over again, John recapitulates the story from the first coming of Christ to his second coming. Each time there is conflict and persecution, but ultimately there is victory and celebration.

There are three main protagonists in chapter 12:

1. The Son

Jesus is the 'Son who will shepherd all nations' (v.5a, MSG). He is 'placed safely before God on his Throne' (v.5b, MSG).

2. The devil

The devil is described as the 'red dragon' (v.3). His identity is revealed in verse 9: 'The great dragon was hurled down – that ancient serpent called the devil, or Satan, who leads the whole world astray' (v.9). He is the *accuser* (v.10).

3. The woman

Perhaps the most obvious interpretation is that the woman is Mary, the mother of Jesus. Other suggestions are that she is personified wisdom, the heavenly Jerusalem, personified Israel, or the church. Given the nature of apocalyptic writing and its many layers of interpretation, she may represent all of these.

The woman is 'clothed with the sun, with the moon under her feet and a crown of twelve stars on her head' (v.1b). 'She was giving birth to a Child' (v.2, MSG). After her child was snatched up to God and to his throne, the woman 'fled into the desert to a place prepared for her by God, where she might be taken care of for 1,260 days [that is, three-and-a-half years]' (v.6).

Later on, we read that the serpent tries to sweep the woman away: 'But the earth helped the woman by opening its mouth and swallowing the river that the dragon had spewed out of his mouth' (v.16).

What is clear in this passage is that, in the end, Jesus overcomes the devil and his allies. Behind the scenes of human history are great, intelligent forces of good and evil: 'And there was war in heaven. Michael and his angels fought against the dragon, and the dragon and his angels fought back' (v.7).

In the end, good overcomes evil: 'But he was not strong enough, and they lost their place in heaven. The great dragon was hurled down ... to the earth, and his angels with him' (vv.8–9). He attempts to lead 'the whole world astray' (v.9).

Right now, you are at war with the demonic forces of evil. But victory is secure: 'They overcame him' (v.11a). 'They' are the church – the people of God – who are in Christ. 'Him' is Satan, the devil, the accuser, the serpent, who will ultimately be destroyed. You overcome him in three ways:

1. Trust in *the blood*

The cross of Jesus – '*the blood of the lamb*' (v.11a) – is the supreme victory over the devil. You can be sure of your standing before God. 'There is now no condemnation for those who are in Christ Jesus' (Romans 8:1). You do not need to wake up feeling guilty, or go to bed feeling guilty. As Corrie ten Boom pointed out, 'The blood of Christ is like tears in the eyes, it washes away the specks of dirt.'

2. Tell your story

They overcame '*by the word of their testimony*' (Revelation 12:11b). Your testimony is the most powerful way of overcoming opposition to faith. It is hard to argue with your story. No one can deny your personal experience.

3. Take risks for Jesus

'*They did not love their lives so much as to shrink from death*' (v.11c).

> 'They weren't in love with themselves; they were willing to die for Christ' (v.11c, MSG).

You can be absolutely sure of your future. Therefore, you can take the risk of betting your life on Jesus, safe in his arms.

PRAYER

Lord, thank you that, the moment we side with Jesus, we are on the winning side. Help me overcome the enemy by the blood of the Lamb, by the word of my testimony and by being willing to risk my life for you.

OLD TESTAMENT READING

Ezra 6:1–7:10
The people of God overcome opposition

Mark Twain once said, 'The dictionary is the only place where *success* comes before *work*!' Vision without work is just hallucination. The church will not be rebuilt without God's hand (7:6). But equally it will not be rebuilt without *hard work*, *commitment* and *application*.

Although work on the temple was held up because of opposition, eventually King Darius 'issued an order' (6:1). They found the original decree of King Cyrus ordering that the temple be rebuilt (vv.1–3). Darius then reissued the order that construction should continue on the house of God and that no one should interfere (vv.6–12).

The temple was completed (vv.14–15) in 515 BC. This was a cause of enormous celebration and joy (v.16). '*They celebrated with joy* ... because the Lord had *filled them with joy*' (v.22).

There was then a long period of silence between the end of chapter 6 and the beginning of chapter 7 (possibly 458 BC). Ezra is introduced as the one who, above all others, was responsible for the establishment of the law for the religious and social life of the community of the people of God after they returned from many years of exile in Babylon.

Ezra was a teacher and 'the hand of the Lord his God was on him' (7:6). 'Ezra had committed himself to *studying* the Revelation of God, to *living it*, and to *teaching* Israel to live its truths and ways' (v.10, MSG). Study of God's words without action is worthless.

Ezra's example gives a wonderful model to follow. Immerse yourself in God's word, committing time and effort to studying it. Realise that, on its own, this is not enough. Allow God's word to shape and change your life as well; put it into action, and teach others to do the same.

PRAYER

Lord, thank you that you give me ultimate victory over *all* obstacles and opposition, and you fill me with great joy. Help me to study the revelation of God, to live it out and to teach others to live its truths and ways.

21 December | Day 355
God's Hand Is On You

Hands are very important. On her wedding day, I took hold of our daughter's *hand* and passed it over to the minister (who happened to be our son). *His hand* (for these purposes) represented *God's hand*. He, in turn, joined *her hand* to that of her husband. Symbolically, I gave her to God and God gave her to her husband. A key part of the marriage ceremony is the *joining of hands.*

At one level, your hand is simply your palm, fingers, and thumb. But when we use the word 'hand' we often mean it in more than just a physical sense. The '*hand*' can be used as a metaphor for *action*, *care* and *possession*.

God uses hands. We read of Jesus *healing* through *laying his hands* on sick people, or even just touching them *with his hands* (for example, Mark 6:5; 8:23). At other times, he put *his hands* on people *to bless them* (10:16). He told his disciples that *their hands* would be used to *heal the sick* (16:18). Indeed, people were *healed* through the *laying on of their hands* (for example, Acts 8:17–18). Others were *filled with the Holy Spirit* (9:17; 19:6), or *received gifts* through the *laying on of hands* (2 Timothy 1:6).

What about '*the hand of God*'? What does that mean? In the Bible, '*the hand of God*' means something very profound. Ezra said, 'Because *the hand of the Lord my God was on me*, I took courage…' (Ezra 7:28). God's invisible and intangible hand is also on you: leading, guiding, encouraging, protecting, strengthening and giving you courage.

READING FROM PSALMS

Psalm 145:13b–21
God's hand is open and generous

'You open *your hand* and satisfy the desires of every living thing' (v.16). This metaphor of the extraordinary generosity of God, who opens his hand to you to satisfy your desires, comes in the middle of a section of the psalm that describes God's great love and faithfulness.

The poet, Robert Browning, wrote, 'I have lived, seen *God's hand through a lifetime*, and *all was for best*.'[1] 'God gives *a hand* to those who are down on their luck' (v.14a, MSG). 'The trademark on all his works is love' (v.17b, MSG).

'The Lord is faithful to all his promises' (v.13b). This psalm is full of wonderful promises. The Lord will uphold you (v.14). 'The Lord is near' to you (v.18), he fulfils your desires (v.19), he watches over you (v.20). All this inspires praise: 'My mouth will speak in praise of the Lord. Let every creature praise his holy name for ever and ever' (v.21).

PRAYER

'Father, let me hold your hand, and like a child walk with you down all my days, secure in your love and strength' (Prayer of Thomas à Kempis, c.1380–1471).

NEW TESTAMENT READING

Revelation 13:1b–18
God's hand writes your name in the book of life

What an amazing privilege to have *God's hand* write *your name* in 'the book of life' belonging to Jesus (v.8b). In the face of persecution 'God's holy people passionately and faithfully stand their ground' (v.10b, MSG).

The first 'beast' (v.1b) appears to be a persecuting power. This chapter contains a description of human government at its worst – a demonic power. It needs to be read alongside Romans 13, in which human government is seen at its best – a godly authority. All human government is a mixture of Revelation 13 and Romans 13. Some governments are more like Romans 13, and some more like the description here. Do not be surprised, therefore, by governments making anti-Christian laws and even persecuting the church.

Perhaps the 'seven heads' (Revelation 13:1b) represent the seven hills on which Rome was built (see 17:9). The prophet Daniel saw beasts that look like the leopard, the bear and the lion, representing three successive *world powers* (Daniel 7:3). Here they are all rolled into one (Revelation 13:2).

'The fatal wound' that 'has been healed' (v.3) may refer to Nero (notorious for his persecution of Christians), who attempted suicide in AD 68 and was believed to have survived or come alive again (according to legend). This could be seen as a parody of the death and resurrection of Jesus.

The beast attacks God's people for forty-two months or three and a half years (this is typically the period that represents the time between the first and second coming of Jesus – that is, the age of the church). The beast persecutes the church. He makes 'war against the saints' (v.7). He has a large following.

The only ones who do not follow him are all those whose names are written in the book of life belonging to the Lamb, who was slain from the creation of the world (v.8b).

The second beast is a pseudo-Christ figure. He performs 'great and miraculous signs' (v.13). He is a deceiver. He forces everyone to have his mark on their *right hands* or on their foreheads (v.16). His number is 666 (v.18).

The number 666 at one level may again represent Nero, since the Hebrew letters for 'Nero Caesar' when converted into numbers total 666. On another level, numbers in Revelation are normally symbolic. Six is the number of imperfection (since seven is the number of perfection). 666 is therefore the number of triple imperfection, or complete sinfulness.

'This calls for wisdom' (v.18a). Satan himself masquerades as an angel of light and his servants masquerade as servants of righteousness (see 2 Corinthians 11:13–14). The first beast has a 'mouth like that of a lion' (Revelation 13:2). The second beast has two horns 'like a lamb' (v.11). It is as if they are trying to appear to look like Jesus (who is the Lion and the Lamb, see Revelation 5:5–6).

Later, we will read of a third beast – Babylon (see Revelation 14:8 and chapters 17–18). The three beasts together seem to masquerade as a diabolical parody of the Trinity.[2] They seem great and deceive many people. We need wisdom to discern the good from the evil.

Thank God that by his hand he has written your name in the Lamb's book of life.

PRAYER

Lord, please give me wisdom, faithfulness and patient endurance. Help me to overcome evil with good.

OLD TESTAMENT READING

Ezra 7:11–8:14
God's hand is on those who look to him

God's hand was on Ezra. The book of Ezra is about a community making a fresh start. It is not about one man. However, God did use Ezra in a special way.

Ezra knew that the *Lord's hand was on him*: '*Because the hand of the* Lord *my God was on me, I took courage* and gathered leaders from Israel to go up with me' (7:28). Ezra takes a further 1,500 men – probably about 5,000 people in all – with him (8:1–14).

In tomorrow's passage, we also read: 'the gracious *hand of our God* was on us' (v.18); 'the gracious *hand of our God* is on everyone *who looks to him*' (v.22); '*the hand of our God* was on us, and he protected us from enemies and bandits along the way' (v.31). As you look to God, you can be sure that God's hand is on you as well.

Ezra was a priest and a teacher who had studied the Scriptures very closely – 'priest and scholar, expert in matters involving the truths and ways of God' (7:11, MSG).

God worked through a secular leader (Artaxerxes) to bring about his good purposes. Again, we are reminded that 'the king's heart is *in the hand of the* Lord; he directs it like a watercourse wherever he pleases' (Proverbs 21:1). Artaxerxes wrote a letter ordering provision for Ezra (Ezra 7:12 onwards).

Here we see an example of secular government that is more like Romans 13 than Revelation 13. Artaxerxes writes, 'You are sent by the king ... to enquire about Judah and Jerusalem with regard to the Law of your God which is in *your hand*' (Ezra 7:14). He continues, 'I authorize you, Ezra, exercising the wisdom of God that you have *in your hands*, to appoint magistrates and judges so they can administer justice ... Anyone who does not know the Teaching, you teach them' (v.25, MSG).

Ezra says, 'Praise be to the Lord, the God of our ancestors, who has *put it into the king's heart* to bring honour to the house of the Lord in Jerusalem in this way and who has *extended his good favour* to me before the king and his advisers and all the king's powerful officials' (vv.27–28).

When God's hand is on you, you are like a light on a hill (Matthew 5:15). His light shines out of you and it will attract people to him. He will use you as a leader, equipping you with all the courage and authority you need.

PRAYER

Lord, thank you that your gracious hand is on everyone who looks to you. Thank you for your love, mercy and protection. Because your gracious hand is on me I look to you today and take courage.

22 December | Day 356
Purity and Power

At our Christmas services, I sit right by our orchestra and choir. There are usually around fifty musicians in the orchestra and ninety in the choir – all members of the congregation volunteering their time and gifts. I'm not at all musical. In fact, I'm virtually tone deaf. However, I am always stunned by the beauty of the marvellous music and singing. It is a foretaste of heaven.

The apostle John writes, 'And I heard a sound from heaven like the roar of rushing waters and like a loud peal of thunder. The sound I heard was like that of harpists playing their harps. And they sang a new song before the throne' (Revelation 14:2–3). The heavenly orchestra and choir will sing a new song before a heavenly audience.

John goes on to describe the completed church in heaven – their *purity* and their *power*. The two are connected. As Pastor Rick Warren has tweeted, 'In ministry, *private purity* is the source of *public power*.'

READING FROM PROVERBS

Proverbs 31:1–9
Purity and the powerless

'Leaders can't afford to make fools of themselves' (v.4, MSG). King Lemuel was a leader who had been given wise teaching by his mother. She had warned him against impurity (v.3) and intoxication (vv.4–7).

These can ruin (v.3) your life. They can leave you forgetting what you should be doing (v.5a) and deprive the powerless of their rights (v.5b).

Instead of using your power to indulge in self-gratification, use it for good: '*Speak up* for those who *cannot speak for themselves*, for the rights of all who are destitute. Speak up and judge fairly; defend the rights of the *poor* and *needy*' (vv.8–9).

Who are the voiceless in our society who 'cannot speak for themselves'? Who are the people that you and I should be speaking up for? They will surely include the following:

1. The poor

About 10 per cent of the world's population go to bed hungry every night. Every few seconds, poverty takes a child's life. Today, and every day until we act, thousands of children die of avoidable diseases or because they live in poverty. Millions under the age of five die every year. Over half of these early child deaths are due to conditions that could be prevented or treated with access to simple, affordable interventions. They are the 'poor and destitute' (v.9, MSG).

2. The enslaved

There are probably now more slaves globally than at the height of the transatlantic slave trade. Human trafficking enslaves millions of people around the globe, many of them under the age of eighteen. Slavery is a terrible injustice. 'Speak up for justice' (v.9a, MSG).

3. The unborn

Those in the womb have no voice of their own. The journalist, Nigella Lawson, who describes herself as 'pro-abortion', has written, 'If anecdotal evidence is anything to go by (and I suspect it is), [abortion] is becoming more and more a value-free, post-facto alternative to contraception.'[1] Yet few people have the courage to speak up for the unborn today – who have 'no voice' (v.8a, MSG).

4. The prisoners

Many around the world are in prison unjustly and even those who are in prison justly are often treated inhumanely. But the vast majority are in no position to 'speak for themselves' (v.8a).

PRAYER

Lord, help me to speak up for the voiceless, judge fairly and defend the rights of the destitute, the poor and the needy.

NEW TESTAMENT READING

Revelation 14:1–13
Purity and proclamation

'It took my breath away!' (v.1, MSG). Jesus (the Lamb of God) stands on Mount Zion with his 144,000 followers 'with him, his Name and the Name of his Father inscribed on their foreheads' (v.1, MSG). They represent the completed church worshipping together.

The five-fold description is one of complete purity. They:

1. are redeemed from the earth by the blood of the Lamb (v.3)
2. have kept themselves pure and undefiled – 'lived without compromise' (v.4a, MSG)
3. follow Jesus wherever he goes (v.4b)
4. are purchased and offered as firstfruits to God and the Lamb (v.4c). As St Paul writes, 'We were bought at a price' (1 Corinthians 6:20)
5. are people of integrity: 'No lie was found in their mouths; they are blameless' (Revelation 14:5).

It is not coincidental that the vision of the *pure* church is followed by a vision of the *proclamation* of the eternal gospel: 'to those who live on the earth – to every nation, tribe, language and people' (v.6). This is the calling of the church – to proclaim the good news of Jesus. This is represented by the first angel.

The second and third angels show what humanity needs to be rescued from. Everyone needs to be rescued from the corrupting influence of 'Babylon the Great', 'which made all the nations drink the maddening wine of her adulteries' (v.8). They also need to be rescued from 'the beast', who wants to put his mark on *the forehead* (v.11) and see them tormented.

The good news is that no one needs to have this mark on *their forehead*. We, the people of God, need to proclaim the good news that every person can have the name of Jesus and the Father's name written on *their forehead* (v.1). You are called to patient endurance, obedience to God's commandments and faithfulness to Jesus (v.12).

Get the message out. So many people lack peace. There is '*no rest day or night* for those who worship the beast and his image' (v.11). On the other hand, there is no greater blessing than following the Lamb: 'Then I heard a voice from heaven say, "Write: *Blessed* are the dead who die in the Lord from now on." "Yes," says the Spirit, "*they will rest* from their labour, for their deeds will follow them"' (v.13).

PRAYER

Lord Jesus, help us to be pure and undefiled followers of you, people of integrity, who know that we have been redeemed and bought at a price. Help us to proclaim the eternal gospel to every nation, tribe, language and people.

OLD TESTAMENT READING

Ezra 8:15–9:15
Purity and prayer

Are you facing challenges ahead in your life? Ezra was facing the huge challenge of leading the return journey to Jerusalem and the rebuilding of the temple.

He had to lead a company of 5,000 people, including women and children, on a four-month hazardous trek through uninhabited regions – while carrying vast quantities of money and precious objects (8:15–27).

Ezra wisely began with the leaders: 'So I summoned ... leaders and ... men of learning' (v.16). Leadership was a key to the fulfilment of Ezra's vision for return and rebuilding.

The fulfilment of almost every God-given vision requires these three things:

1. *Everyone* praying

Ezra was a man of prayer. Before he set out on the journey he proclaimed a fast. They all humbled themselves and asked God for a safe journey (v.21). God heard their prayer: 'So we fasted and petitioned our God about this, and he *answered our prayer*' (v.23).

2. *Everyone* giving

'I weighed out to them the offering of *silver* and *gold* and the articles that the king, his advisers, his officials and *all* Israel present there *had donated for the house of our God*' (v.25).

3. *Everyone* serving

'Then the exiles who had returned from captivity sacrificed ... They also delivered the king's orders to the royal satraps and to the governors of Trans-Euphrates who then *gave assistance* to the people and to the house of God' (vv.35–36).

God blessed them in every way in the rebuilding of the house of God. But in spite of God's faithfulness to them, the people were not faithful to God. They did not keep themselves pure. It was not so much the fact that they had intermarried, but the fact that they had '*polluted*' themselves (9:11) with the 'detestable practices' (v.1) of the nations around. The leaders and officials had led the way in their unfaithfulness (v.2).

Ezra, by contrast, gives us a great example of not taking sin lightly. He is absolutely devastated: 'When I heard all this, I ripped my clothes and my cape ... I slumped to the ground, appalled' (v.3, MSG).

He fell on his knees with his hands spread out to the Lord and prayed a prayer, which it may be good to pray for ourselves and for the church today: 'O my God, I am too ashamed and disgraced to lift up my face to you, my God, because our sins are higher than our heads and our guilt has reached to the heavens. From the days of our ancestors until now, our guilt has been great. Because of our sins, we ... have been subjected to ... humiliation' (vv.6–7).

Yet, as with the people in Ezra's time, so it is for the church today: '... our God *has not deserted us*' (v.9).

PRAYER

Lord, help us to be pure, cleansed by the blood of Jesus, to speak up for the voiceless, proclaim the eternal gospel to the nations, and rebuild the church in our cities and nations.

23 December | Day 357
How to Live in Hope

In July 1999, Ralph Crathorne spoke at our church about the recent death of his eight-year-old daughter, Sasha, from a brain tumour.

I remember so well going to visit Sasha in hospital. On the way, in the taxi, I was desperately trying to think and pray about what God would want me to say. Only one word came into my mind: hope.

In his talk Ralph said, 'That one word exploded in my spirit. It was as though I suddenly saw the fullness of what God has meant us to understand about "living in hope". It's not the kind of wishy-washy, "I hope this will happen, but it probably won't happen." It's the sure, confident, positive hope – the way God designed us to live.

'Our hope was placed not in an outcome but in the Lord.

'Sasha, too, held onto hope – not necessarily to be healed, although that was included, but a deeper hope, the hope that comes from the certainty of being in the palm of the hand of an all-loving God.'

In the final two weeks of her life, she went blind. Ralph said, 'I remember lying in the bed saying to her, "Sasha do you ever see angels?"

'She didn't have much energy to speak. She said, "No dad."

'I was a bit disappointed. So, I thought, we'll go for the big one. "Do you ever see Jesus?" I asked.

'"Of course, I do. He holds my hand."'

'The dream that she would be healed was shattered, but we're not disappointed with God. He hasn't changed. He still loves us. We don't understand her death. I doubt we really ever will. One day we'll know ... These are the foundational principles of living in hope.'

READING FROM PSALMS

Psalm 146:1–10
Put your hope in the right place

Many today put their hope in the wrong place. They trust in wealth, or a successful career, or a long-term relationship, or in their image or status. There is nothing necessarily wrong with any of these things – but none of them are a firm enough foundation upon which to build your life.

It really matters where you put your hope: 'Do *not* put your trust in princes, in human beings, who cannot save. When their spirit departs, they return to the ground; on that very day their plans come to nothing' (vv.3–4).

The psalmist proclaims *the right place to put your hope*: 'Blessed are those whose help is the God of Jacob, *whose hope is in the* LORD their God' (v.5). If you put your hope in the Lord, this hope is 'an anchor for the soul, firm and secure' (Hebrews 6:19).

The psalmist has this firm hope in the Lord. He praises God continuously (Psalm 146:1–2). He recognises that he is 'the Maker of heaven and earth, the sea, and everything in them' and that he 'remains faithful for ever' (v.6).

The God of hope gives new hope to those who seem to have little hope, and he calls you and me to do the same.

The psalmist lists some of those to whom God especially gives hope: the oppressed (v.7a), hungry (v.7b), prisoners (v.7c), blind (v.8a), marginalised (v.9a) and bereaved (v.9b).

PRAYER

Lord, thank you that I can put my hope in you. Thank you that this is a sure and steadfast anchor for my soul. Help me to give hope to those who need it most.

NEW TESTAMENT READING

Revelation 14:14–15:8
Look forward with hope

Hope is powerful. It is not just a feeling or an emotion. It is not dependent on circumstances. Real hope is a constant positive attitude that, no matter what the circumstances, things will change for the better.

'Hope has a thick skin and will endure many a blow,' wrote John Bunyan (1628–1688). 'It will endure all things if it be of the right kind, for the joy that is set before it ... it is hope that makes the soul exercise patience and long-suffering under the cross, until the time comes to enjoy the crown.'

When we look around at the world we see so much injustice. Bad things happen to good people. Evil often seems to thrive. There may be injustice now, but one day there will be justice for all. God will put everything right.

As Bishop Lesslie Newbigin put it, 'The horizon for the Christian is, "he shall come again" and "we look for the coming of the Lord". It can be tomorrow, or any time, but that is the horizon. That horizon for me is fundamental, and that is what makes it possible to be *hopeful* and therefore to find life meaningful.'[1]

In this passage, John gets a glimpse of what the final 'putting things right' will look like. Jesus will be the judge. 'I looked, and there before me was a white cloud, and seated on the cloud was one "like a son of man" with a crown of gold on his head and a sharp sickle in his hand' (14:14).

Jesus said that, in this life, the wheat and the weeds grow up together until the harvest (Matthew 13:30), and that 'the harvest is the end of the age, and the harvesters are angels' (v.39). He speaks of the weeds being pulled up and destroyed and how 'the righteous will shine like the sun in the kingdom of their Father' (v.43).

There is a radical judgment where every vestige of evil is destroyed 'in the great winepress of God's wrath' (Revelation 14:19).

As you read this, remember that Jesus drank the cup of God's wrath for you on the cross, and so you are saved from these judgments. In this passage, we see what it looks like when God's judgment is completed (15:1). John sees 'what looked like a sea of glass mixed with fire' (v.2) – an image which combines burning purity and serenity. Peace and righteousness go together.

God's judgment purifies the world, destroying evil and corruption, and rescuing his people from those who persecute and oppose them ('the beast and his image' v.2).

Just as after the Exodus a great cry of praise went up from the people of God who had crossed the Red Sea, so now a great cry of praise goes up to God:

> 'Great and marvellous are your deeds,
> Lord God Almighty.
> Just and true are your ways,
> King of the ages...
> All nations will come and worship
> before you,
> for your righteous acts have been
> revealed' (vv.3–4).

PRAYER

Thank you, Lord, that one day you will put everything right. Thank you that I have such a great future hope, made possible through the cross of Jesus.

OLD TESTAMENT READING

Ezra 10:1–44
Never give up hope

Do you ever feel that you have gone too far, done something too often, or failed too badly for God to forgive you? This passage is an encouragement that, however much you have messed up, 'there is still hope' for you: 'But *in spite of* this, there is still *hope* for Israel' (v.2), says Shecaniah to Ezra.

Ezra was 'praying and confessing, weeping and throwing himself down before the house of God' (v.1a). He was joined by 'a large crowd of Israelites – men, women and children... They too *wept bitterly*' (v.1b).

Ezra fasted and mourned over the unfaithfulness of the people of God. In total, there were 113 people guilty of this unfaithfulness. Eighty-six were 'laity' and twenty-seven were 'clergy' (Levites). A call to full-time ordained Christian ministry does not make us immune from temptation.

The particular issue highlighted in this passage was that of Israelites marrying non-believers. By this time there was probably an official ceremony by which non-Jews could convert (see 6:21), and it seems that these people were the ones who had refused to do so.

Ezra was concerned that they would draw their spouses (many of whom were part of Israel's leadership) away from God. The Bible encourages you to think hard about whom you marry, and to avoid marrying someone who will draw you away from God (see 2 Corinthians 6:14 and commentary for 3 September).

Nevertheless, divorcing their wives (Ezra 10:19) can seem in a way to make the unfaithfulness worse, and this is a difficult passage for us to read. It is interesting that it was not unanimous (v.15). Once the unfaithfulness had occurred, the solution was bound to be less than ideal. When the same issue was addressed by the church in the New Testament, those married to non-believers were given very different instructions – they were told to remain married, and be an example and blessing to their spouses (see 1 Corinthians 7; 1 Peter 3).

PRAYER

Lord Jesus, help us to take our own sin and the sin of the community seriously – to pray, confess, weep, throw ourselves down before you in repentance and resolve to be radical and ruthless about avoiding unfaithfulness in the future. Thank you that there is *still* hope for the people of God. Thank you that our hope is in the Lord, 'who remains faithful for ever' (Psalm 146:6).

24 December | Day 358
Look Up

In *A Christmas Carol*, by Charles Dickens, the central character, Ebenezer Scrooge, was a miserable, mean, miserly old businessman who is shown his past, present and future. He eventually *repents and starts to give generously*.

Dickens captures the transformation in his character: 'He went to church, and walked about the streets ... and found that everything could yield him pleasure. He had never dreamed that any walk – that anything – could give him *so much happiness*.'[1]

'Repentance' is a *very positive word* in the Bible. The Greek word 'metanoia' means 'change of mind'. That means, first, *turning away from the bad stuff*. This is the stuff that spoils your life and breaks your relationship with God. Repentance means to be sorry enough to quit. Getting rid of the bad stuff only enhances your life. But, that is only the first part.

The change of heart and mind means not only turning *away* from the bad things, but also *turning towards God and good*. The word 'repent' rarely appears on its own in the Bible. *Genuine repentance* is shown by its *fruit*. Remorse is not enough. A change of mind, heart and life is required. It is nearly always, 'repent *and...*'. Repent *and believe*. Repent *and put your faith in Jesus Christ*. It is not just a case of looking back, but also looking up. Faith looks up.

READING FROM PSALMS

Psalm 147:1–11
Repent *and* rejoice

The context of this psalm may well be the rebuilding of Jerusalem under Nehemiah: 'God's the one who *rebuilds* Jerusalem, who re-gathers Israel's scattered exiles' (v.2, MSG). This started (as we see today in Nehemiah 1–2) with a genuine repentance by Nehemiah on behalf of himself and all the people.

Genuine repentance starts with being 'broken-hearted' (Psalm 147:3). The wonderful news is that God heals the broken-hearted and binds up their wounds (v.3; see also Isaiah 61:1).

'Repentance' involves humbling yourself before God. Whereas he 'casts the wicked to the ground' (Psalm 147:6b), 'the Lord sustains the humble' (v.6a). But God does not leave you there. He wants you not only to *look back with repentance*, but also to *look up with rejoicing*.

God's 'delight' is not in 'the legs of a man' (v.10). He is not reliant on (or impressed by) physical strength: 'He's not impressed with horsepower; the size of our muscles means little to him' (v.10, MSG). Instead, 'the Lord delights in those who fear him, who put their hope in his unfailing love' (v.11).

This whole psalm is about rejoicing in the Lord. It starts with a call to 'Praise the Lord', and a reminder of how 'good ... pleasant and fitting' (v.1) it is to do so. Worship brings joy and pleasure, and it is an appropriate response to such an amazing God.

PRAYER

Lord, today I want not only to repent, but also to rejoice in you. Thank you that you promise that if I fear you, I need not fear anything else.

NEW TESTAMENT READING

Revelation 16:1–21
Repent *and* respond

This must be one of the most terrifying chapters in the entire Bible. It describes God's final judgment. These are the seven last plagues (see Exodus 7–10). It all ends in 'Armageddon'. In the midst of the awful judgment, there are four things that should bring you comfort:

1. Jesus is coming back

'Keep watch! I come unannounced, like a thief. You're blessed if, awake and dressed, you're ready for me' (Revelation 16:15, MSG). Later on in Revelation, we will see all the blessings that the second coming of Jesus will bring to you and to the whole creation.

2. Jesus took your judgment

The words, 'It is done!' (v.17) tell us that once this final judgment has taken place, 'It is finished' – echoing the last words of Jesus on the cross (John 19:30). They remind us of what Jesus achieved on the cross for you. God so loved the world that he sent his one and only Son to die for you so that you might not come under God's final judgment, but rather receive all the blessings of eternal life (see John 3:16–17).

3. Judgment is delayed

The judgment only falls on those who '*refused to repent* and glorify him' (Revelation 16:9). God gives them, like Pharaoh, so many opportunities to repent, 'but they *refused to repent* of what they had done' (v.11). God's desire is that everyone should come to repentance (2 Peter 3:9). He gives many, many opportunities. It is only those who absolutely *refuse* to repent that come under his judgment.

4. Judgment will be totally just

Many people worry, understandably, about passages like this in the Bible. However, God's judgments are going to be absolutely 'true' and 'just' (v.7). As the former vicar of HTB, John Collins, always says, 'We will all say on that day, "That is absolutely right."'

Look up as you wait for Jesus' return. Get your life sorted out now. Make sure there is no refusal to repent in your own heart. Respond in the right way to these warnings and help everyone else to do the same.

PRAYER

Lord, thank you that on the cross you bore my sins for me so that I need never face the judgment described here. Thank you that you are coming back and that you will put everything right. In everything I do, may I glorify you.

OLD TESTAMENT READING

Nehemiah 1:1–2:20
Repent *and* rebuild

Nehemiah's situation was not dissimilar to our own. The church in many parts of the world is in great 'trouble and disgrace' (1:3). It seems to have been devastated, and is regarded either as irrelevant or as an object of scorn.

In 445 BC, Nehemiah was also devastated by the fact that God's name was not being honoured. God's people were in 'bad shape. Conditions [were] appalling' (v.3, MSG): 'The wall of Jerusalem is still rubble; the city gates are still cinders' (v.3, MSG).

Nehemiah was a government worker who had risen to high office in the Persian administration. He was cupbearer to the king (v.11b). This was an important office involving responsibility for tasting the king's wine and for guarding the royal apartment.

Nehemiah's response is a great model for us to follow. He was a man of action, but he began by looking up in prayer. His response was to weep, mourn, fast and pray (v.4). His prayer begins with reminding God of his love (v.5). He goes on to *repent* of his sins and the sins of the people: 'I confess the sins we Israelites, including myself and my family, have committed against you. We have acted very wickedly towards you' (v.6b).

He ends the prayer by asking God to give him success (v.11). As so often happens, the answer to his prayer involved something he himself was going to do. He saw the problem and he acted. He gave up a brilliant career for a life of danger, struggle and self-sacrifice. In doing so, he became the answer to his own prayer.

Artaxerxes noticed his 'sadness of heart' (2:2). When he asked, 'What is it you want?' (v.4), again Nehemiah's 'arrow' prayer ('praying under my breath', v.4, MSG) is a good example to follow. In any situation you find yourself in, where you only have a split second to decide what to do, pray: 'Then I prayed to the God of heaven, and I answered the king' (vv.4–5). He had already done the serious length of prayer. Now he only had time to glance upwards before he had to give an answer.

The moment that he looked up, his request was granted and he was allowed to go to Jerusalem to rebuild (v.8). After inspecting the walls in secret (wisely keeping his plans confidential while he assessed the situation), he gathered the people and announced his plans (vv.11–18). He followed up his prayer with action.

Throughout the whole process, he retained his focus on God and, again and again, acknowledged that it is God who had inspired and enabled him to do this – '*Because the gracious hand of my God was upon me*, the king granted my requests' (v.8; see also vv.12, 18). It can be so easy to pray about something, but then forget to acknowledge God when things start to go well. However, Nehemiah was always conscious of his reliance on God, and quick to attribute his success to God.

Trust in God that he will give you the confidence to continue with his plans, even when you encounter opposition. In good times and hard times, Nehemiah looked up to God: 'The God of heaven will give us success. We his servants will start *rebuilding*' (v.20). Don't allow opposition to deflect you from your God-given task – trust God and get on with the job. Look up and trust God to give *you* success.

PRAYER

Lord, your church lies in ruins. The walls are broken down. You call us to rebuild. As we look up to you and start rebuilding, may the God of heaven give us success.

25 December | Day 359
Why Christmas?

Today we celebrate the 'central event in the history of the earth, the very thing the whole story has been about' (C. S. Lewis).[1] We celebrate the birth of Jesus. It is a day of great joy and celebration around the world.

And yet, in the midst of all the trappings and celebrations of Christmas, it can be easy to miss *why* Jesus' birth is so significant. The key to Christmas lies, not in the details of the shepherds' visit or the wise men's journey, but in the identity of the one whom they came to worship. In Jesus, God became 'flesh' and 'made his dwelling among us' (John 1:14). Christmas is about Jesus!

Our New Testament passage for today helps us to grasp something of the enormity of what that means. In it we are reminded that 'baby Jesus' is also the 'Lord of lords and King of kings' (Revelation 17:14b). We are given a glimpse of the cosmic struggle between good and evil, as a vast array of powers and authorities line up against God. Yet we are reminded that, in the end, it is through the humility and self-sacrifice of 'the Lamb' that they are overcome.

Jesus puts aside the glories of heaven for a humble stall. As the carol, *Hark! The Herald Angels Sing,* puts it:

Christ, by highest heaven adored;
Christ, the everlasting Lord;
late in time behold him come,
offspring of a virgin's womb.
Veiled in flesh the Godhead see;
hail the incarnate Deity,
pleased as man with man to dwell,
Jesus, our Emmanuel.
Hark! The herald angels sing,
'Glory to the new born King!'[2]

In each of today's passages we see the blessings of following this 'new born King'.

READING FROM PSALMS

Psalm 147:12–20
Blessing, peace and satisfaction

All the promises of God were fulfilled when Jesus came. God promised his people blessing, peace and satisfaction ('the best bread on your tables', v.14, MSG). He 'launches his promises earthward' (v.15, MSG).

When the birth of Jesus was announced to the shepherds, the angel described it as 'good news of great joy for all the people' (Luke 2:10). The heavenly hosts praise God for 'peace on earth' (v.14). Jesus had been born in Bethlehem (meaning 'the house of bread'). He is the one who satisfies the spiritual hunger in the heart of every human being.

PRAYER
Lord, thank you for the way in which you bless your people. Thank you that 'we have peace with God through our Lord Jesus Christ' (Romans 5:1). Thank you that you satisfy the deepest longings of my heart.

NEW TESTAMENT READING

Revelation 17:1–18
Called, chosen and faithful

Christmas is not only a nice story, but a decisive moment in human history. In the cosmic battle between good and evil, God and the devil, Jesus is the decisive figure. That battle, and Jesus' centrality and victory in it, is the focus of our New Testament passage for today.

Sometimes, the church appears to be fighting a losing battle. In Western Europe today, church attendance has been in decline for some time. Secularism *appears* to be winning. The book of Revelation reveals what is happening behind the scenes, and how things will ultimately turn out.

As we look around at our world, it is immensely powerful, attractive and seductive at one level. Yet, beneath the surface we see so much evil and so much opposition to the Lamb.

The opposition to Jesus is personified in 'Babylon the Great, the mother of prostitutes and of the abominations of the earth' (v.5), which is written on the woman who rides on a beast.

In the original context, the identity of 'Babylon' is ancient Rome. As we have seen, the 'seven hills on which the woman sits' (v.9) are the seven hills around Rome.

Superficially, there was something very attractive about the Roman Empire, representing all that the world offers. She is 'dressed in purple and scarlet, and was glittering with gold, precious stones and pearls' (v.4).

But beneath the superficial attraction lay violence and vice: 'With her the kings of the earth committed adultery and the inhabitants of the earth were intoxicated with the wine of her adulteries' (v.2).

It gradually becomes apparent that despite appearances to the contrary, this violence and vice was not random, but specifically targeted against God and his people. The array of characters that appear in the first half of the passage 'have one purpose ... they will make war against the Lamb' (vv.13–14).

The wonderful news of this passage is that the Lamb wins. He doesn't only win, but he also includes you in his victory: 'They will make war against the Lamb, but the Lamb will overcome them because he is Lord of lords and King of kings – and with him will be his *called*, *chosen* and *faithful* followers' (v.14). As the church often comes under great attack and the forces of darkness sometimes seem to be in the ascendency, I find this verse to be a great comfort and encouragement.

As Mother Teresa said, 'God has not called me to be successful. He called me to be *faithful*.'[3] If you are faithful to Jesus you will ultimately be successful, because Jesus will ultimately succeed.

Celebrate today the privilege of being one of those *called*, *chosen* and *faithful* followers of Jesus. Jesus, the baby, born that first Christmas day, grew up, died as the Lamb of God and was raised to life.

Ultimately the Lamb will overcome all evil 'because he is Lord of lords and King of kings' (v.14). That is wonderful news to celebrate this Christmas. As one of the great Christian carols puts it, we have a saviour 'to free all those who trust in Him from Satan's power and might. O tidings of comfort and joy!'

PRAYER

Lord, thank you that you are Lord of lords and King of kings. Thank you that you rule and reign. Thank you that ultimately the Lamb will overcome all the forces of evil. Help me to stick close to Jesus and be among his faithful followers.

OLD TESTAMENT READING

Nehemiah 3:1–4:23
Rebuilding, restoring and repairing

Christmas Day especially, is a day when, all over the world, the name of Jesus should be honoured. Sadly, it is so often not the case. What can you contribute to seeing the name of Jesus honoured in our world?

Jerusalem was the city of God where God dwelt. God had called Nehemiah and the people to rebuild the walls of Jerusalem. This is a wonderful visual illustration of the task of the church today. We are called to rebuild and repair so that the name of Jesus may be honoured again in our society.

Do you ever wonder 'Am I needed?'; 'Do I have anything to offer?'; 'Is what I do of any value or significance?'.

In this passage, we see that *everyone* was needed. *Everyone* went to work shoulder to shoulder, side by side, rebuilding, restoring and repairing. Each was given a portion of different lengths. The key is not to compare, but simply to get on with whatever God calls you to do.

God notices what you do and values what you do. 2,500 years later, we are still reading what the people of God did here. Their names are listed.

They were all volunteers. None of them appear to have been professional builders by trade. They were businesspeople, entrepreneurs, rulers, nobles, goldsmiths and perfume-makers. Yet they were willing to offer themselves for the task of rebuilding. All ages were involved (3:12).

They might have been tempted to think that what they were doing did not seem very significant. Malkijah the ruler was asked to repair the *Dung* Gate! He did not complain that it was beneath him. He simply got on with it. Together they were part of something very significant. They were rebuilding Jerusalem. They were bringing honour to God's name.

Opposition and ridicule came from the outside (4:1–8) and discouragement from within (vv.10, 12). The same was true for Jesus. His birth was not welcomed by all. Herod tried to kill him. The opposition to Jesus and his church continues today.

You do not need to be afraid (v.14). Through a combination of prayer and action, success is possible. When opposition comes, respond like Nehemiah (v.9) with increased prayer and extra vigilance. They never dropped their guard (v.23).

The key: 'Our God will fight for us!' (v.10). With God fighting for us, a nation can be changed, churches can be filled, family life strengthened, marriage honoured, the crime rate can fall and society can be transformed. Most important of all, the name of Jesus can be honoured again.

As you look around at the state of the church, get involved in this task of rebuilding. Be willing to work hard and not to be put off by opposition.

PRAYER

Lord, thank you that the Lamb always wins – that the one whose birth we celebrate today will ultimately be victorious because he is 'King of kings and Lord of lords'.

26 December | Day 360
How to Handle Money

The day after Christmas, many of us may feel rather out of pocket. But this issue does not only arise around Christmas time. Most of us have to deal with money in some way every day of our lives. But we prefer not to talk about it in church. However, Jesus talked about money a great deal. The Bible has a lot to say about it. Money matters. It matters to us and it matters to God. How should you handle money?

READING FROM PROVERBS

Proverbs 31:10–20
Prioritise relationships over money

Relationships matter far more than money. For example, all the money in the world cannot compensate for an unhappy marriage. On the other hand, anyone who has a happy marriage 'lacks nothing of value' (v.11): 'A wife of noble character who can find? She is *worth far more than rubies*. Her husband has full confidence in her and lacks nothing *of value*' (vv.10–11).

As the writer of Proverbs extols the virtues of 'a wife of noble character', he begins with a number of areas of her life that relate directly or indirectly to finance. She is a great example of someone who has the right attitude to money. As John Wesley said, '*Earn* all you can. *Save* all you can. *Give* all you can.'[1]

1. '*Earn* all you can'
She is hardworking and diligent in earning a living: 'She gets up early and provides food for her family' (vv.12–15a). She is a good steward. She invests her money wisely. She trades profitably (vv.16–18a).

2. '*Save* all you can'
She enjoys her work and the good things of life (v.13). She saves some of her earnings. She puts money aside (v.16, MSG).

3. '*Give* all you can'
She is generous. 'She opens her arms to the poor and extends her hands to the needy' (v.20). Generous giving is the appropriate response to God's generosity and to the needs of others. It is the way to break materialism.

PRAYER

Lord, help me to be a good steward of everything you entrust to me. May I always be generous, especially to the poor and needy.

NEW TESTAMENT READING

Revelation 18:1–17a
Do not put your trust in money

In the Bible, there is no ban on making money, saving it and enjoying the good things of life. What is warned against is selfish accumulation, an unhealthy obsession with money, or putting your *trust in riches*. This leads to perpetual insecurity and takes you away from God.

Money is not a neutral, impersonal medium of exchange. Jesus said you cannot serve both God and *mammon* (Matthew 6:24). 'Mammon' was the god of wealth in Carthage. Money has all the characteristics of *a god*. It seems to offer security, freedom, power, influence, status and prestige. It is capable of inspiring devotion and single-minded preoccupation. Yet, as Dietrich Bonhoeffer put it, 'Our hearts have room *only for one* all-embracing devotion, and we can only cleave to *one* Lord.'[2]

In this passage, John is given a vision of an event that must have seemed inconceivable to his readers – the fall of 'Babylon the Great' (Revelation 18:2). In the immediate context, this is a prophecy of an event that will not take place for another 320 years – the overthrow of the Roman Empire in AD 410.

When John was writing, the empire seemed invulnerable. It was at the height of its power. It was enjoying peace and security. Yet, John sees that the characteristics of the city were the seeds of its own downfall.

'Babylon' here also represents any power that sets itself up apart from God. John highlights a series of fatal weaknesses that lie behind any society's downfall:

1. Rampant evil
'She has become a home for *demons* and a haunt for every *evil spirit*' (v.2).

2. Endemic promiscuity
'All the nations have drunk the maddening wine of her adulteries. The kings of the earth committed adultery with her' (v.3a).

3. Excessive luxuries
'The merchants of the earth grew rich from her *excessive luxuries*' (v.3b, see also v.7 and v.9). It is probably her great riches that led to arrogance (v.7b).

4. Human trafficking
'And slaves – their terrible traffic in human lives' (v.13, MSG). John appears to be pointing out that slaves are not mere carcasses to be bought and sold as property, but are human beings. In this emphatic position at the end of the list (vv.11–13), this is more than just a comment on the slave trade. It is a comment on the whole list of cargoes. It suggests the inhuman brutality, the contempt for human life, on which the whole empire's prosperity and luxury rested. Today, human trafficking and the resurgence of slavery – with millions of modern-day slaves – points to something desperately wrong with our society.

Riches, splendour and luxury are transient. They come and they go. John warns the people of God not to be contaminated by the sins of Babylon: 'Come out of her, my people, so that you will not share in her sins' (v.4). The glories of ancient Rome may have long passed, but this challenge and message are as relevant to us today as they were then.

PRAYER

Lord, keep my heart from arrogance and all the other evils that so often can go with relative wealth. Help us as the church to do all we can to fight against human trafficking and modern-day slavery. Thank you that while great empires come and go, the word of the Lord endures for ever.

OLD TESTAMENT READING

Nehemiah 5:1–7:3
Set an example in handling money

Nehemiah was a leader who set a superb example in handling money. Sooner or later, most of us will go through times of financial difficulty and lack of resources, either in our personal lives or in our churches. What do you do in these situations?

Nehemiah was facing such a situation. Some of the people did not have enough food to stay alive (5:2). Others had to mortgage their fields and homes (v.3). Still others had to borrow money to pay their taxes (v.4). What can we learn from Nehemiah's example?

First, he *thought about it very carefully*: 'I *pondered* ... in my mind' (v.7a). When facing a financial crisis, it is not wise to rush into hasty solutions. It needs careful thought.

Second, he *called a meeting* (v.7b). Some meetings are at best a waste of time, and at worst counter-productive. However, some meetings are important and necessary. Nehemiah had the wisdom to know the difference between these two kinds of meetings. He refused to meet with his opponents who were 'scheming to harm him' (6:2), despite being asked five times.

However, here Nehemiah calls a meeting. He tells the people that what they are doing is not right. They should not be charging interest. 'Let the exacting of usury stop!' (5:10). He orders them to give back the 'fields, vineyards, olive groves and houses, and also the usury you are charging them' (v.11).

The meeting was successful. '"We will give it back," they said. "And we will not demand anything more from them. We will do as you say"' (v.12). The people did as they promised (v.13).

Third, and most important, he *set an example in his own life*:

1. Personal integrity
Out of his reverence for God, Nehemiah did not act like the earlier governors who had placed heavy burdens of taxation on the people and allowed their assistants to lord it over them (v.15).

2. Modest lifestyle
'Neither I nor my brothers ate the food allotted to the governor' (v.14).

3. No personal gain
'All my men were assembled there for the work; we did not acquire any land ... I never demanded the food allotted to the governor, because the demands were heavy on these people' (vv.16, 18).

4. Generosity to others
'Furthermore, a hundred and fifty Jews and officials ate at my table, as well as those who came to us from the surrounding nations' (vv.17–18).

5. Single-minded hard work
'I devoted myself to the work on this wall' (v.16a). He refused to be put off by the threats of his opponents who were trying to frighten him. Instead he prayed, 'Now strengthen my hands' (6:9).

Nehemiah finished what he had started (v.15). Many people know how to start things. But often they lack what Pippa's father used to call 'carry-through'. Nehemiah had the stickability to complete what he had begun.

The success of the project was the perfect answer to the critics: 'So the wall was completed on the twenty-fifth of Elul, in fifty-two days. When all our enemies heard about this, all the surrounding nations were afraid and lost their self-confidence, because they realised that this work had been done with the help of our God' (vv.15–16).

PRAYER

Lord, give me wisdom in how to handle money. Help me to set an example in my own personal life – to live a life of integrity, with no preoccupation with personal gain, and a modest lifestyle, hard work and generosity to others.

27 December | Day 361
Hallelujah

Over 50 million people have now watched a YouTube clip of unsuspecting shoppers who get a surprise while eating lunch. A young woman, seemingly enjoying her lunch in a food court, stands up. She appears to be on her mobile phone. She begins singing the 'Hallelujah' chorus. All around her, over 100 (clearly prearranged) opera singers stand one by one and join in.[1]

Messiah is George Frederick Handel's most famous work. It tells the story of Jesus – the Messiah. Part Two is about his death on the cross, his resurrection and his ascension into heaven. It ends with the 'Hallelujah' chorus. In the spring of 1742, King George II rose to his feet as the first notes of the triumphant 'Hallelujah' chorus rang out. Royal protocol has always demanded that, whenever the monarch stands, so too does everyone in the monarch's presence. Thus, the entire audience and orchestra stood. King George II had accepted that he too was subject to the Lord of lords and King of kings.

The word 'Hallelujah' is an invitation to worship – it literally means 'Praise (Hallal) the Lord' (Yahweh). It occurs twenty-four times in the Old Testament (mainly in the Psalms) and it occurs four times in the New Testament – each of them in our passage for today.

READING FROM PSALMS

Psalm 148:1–6
The Hallelujah psalms

At rock concerts, football matches and other big sporting events, we see extraordinary scenes of exuberant enthusiasm. Yet all these should pale into insignificance compared to our exuberant worship of God.

The opening words of this psalm are, '*Hallelujah*! Praise God from heaven' (v.1, MSG). The last five psalms (Psalm 146–150) each begin and end with 'Hallelujah'. The Psalms, as with the New Testament and the whole Bible, end with exuberant praise, blessing and delight.

'Hallelujah! Praise the Lord from the heavens; praise him in the heights. Praise him, all his angels' (vv.1b–2a, HCSB).

Even the angels praise God. As we will see in our New Testament passage for today, John, when he saw one of the angels, fell at his feet to worship him (the angel). But the angel said to him, 'Do not do it! I am a fellow-servant with you and with your brothers and sisters who hold to the testimony of Jesus. Worship *God*!' (Revelation 19:10).

As with all the psalms, it can naturally turn into your own prayer and praise:

PRAYER

'Praise him, all his heavenly hosts. Praise him, sun and moon, praise him, all you shining stars. Praise him, you highest heavens and you waters above the skies. Let them praise the name of the Lord' (Psalm 148:2b–5a).

NEW TESTAMENT READING

Revelation 18:17b–19:10
The Hallelujah party

My father was a German Jew. Many of his family suffered and died in concentration camps under the evil empire of the Third Reich. That empire came to an end. Not long after, another evil empire arose. In Stalin's Soviet Russia at least 20 million people were murdered. The people of God were imprisoned, tortured and killed. Today there is Isis, North Korea, and other evil regimes around the world.

The New Testament passage for today starts with the complete destruction of the great city of 'Babylon'. We have seen that this is a way of describing, not only the destruction of the Roman Empire, which the writer has in mind, but also the destruction of every 'Babylon' that has flourished throughout history.

'Babylon' stands for the Roman Empire, the Third Reich, Stalin's Russia, Isis and all the other evil empires, totalitarian and philosophical systems. Whole nations were led astray (18:23) and the people of God persecuted: 'In her was found the blood of prophets and of the saints' (v.24a).

This is why there is such relief when their power is brought to an end. The mass choirs of heaven sing 'Hallelujah':

'After this I heard what sounded like the roar of a great multitude in heaven shouting: "*Hallelujah*!"' (19:1). They praise God that justice has been done. God's judgments are true and just: 'O Heaven, celebrate! ... God has judged her; every wrong you suffered from her has been judged' (v.20, MSG).

'*Hallelujah*!' is repeated (v.3). The whole church and all creation falls down and worships God who is seated on the throne (v.4). And they cry for a third time, 'Amen, *Hallelujah*!' (v.4).

Finally, a fourth time: 'Then I heard the sound of massed choirs, the sound of a mighty cataract, the sound of strong thunder: *Hallelujah*!' (v.6, MSG).

Then the *party* begins:

> 'Let us celebrate, let us rejoice,
> let us give him the glory!
> The Marriage of the Lamb has come;
> his Wife has made herself ready.
> She was given a bridal gown
> of bright and shining linen.
> The linen is the righteousness of the
> saints (vv.7–8, MSG).

A human wedding is a whisper of the gospel. Our earthly marriages point to something even more amazing and eternal – your relationship with Christ Jesus.

The wedding of the Lamb is the marriage of Christ and his church (see Ephesians 5:32; Revelation 21:2). In contrast to the gaudy clothes of the adulterous and promiscuous Babylon (18:16), the church is dressed simply in 'fine linen, bright and clean' (19:8). You are clothed in the righteousness of Christ and every righteous act (v.8b) is remembered, valued and celebrated.

This is the great and eternal party of the 'wedding supper of the Lamb' (v.9). To be 'invited' (v.9) is the greatest blessing of all. The rest of the New Testament tells us that you are invited, but you have to choose to accept the invitation.

It is not surprising that John wants to fall at the feet of the angel and worship him. But you are not to worship the messenger, only the one whom the message is about: 'Worship God!' (v.10). And you are to go and tell others: 'For the testimony of Jesus is the spirit of prophecy' (v.10).

PRAYER

Lord, thank you that the story of this universe is going to end with 'Hallelujah!' – praise, thanksgiving and worship. Thank you that we can look forward to the wedding of the Lamb. 'Let us rejoice and be glad and give him glory!' (v.7).

OLD TESTAMENT READING

Nehemiah 7:4–8:18
The Hallelujah people

As we have seen, just as God called Nehemiah and his people to the rebuilding of the walls of Jerusalem, he calls us to build and rebuild the church. One of the ways God guides you is that he puts ideas into your heart. Nehemiah said, 'God put it in my heart to gather the nobles, the officials, and the people in general to be registered' (7:5, MSG). Nehemiah listed the exiles who had returned (vv.6–73).

When the rebuilding of the walls of Jerusalem was completed, the people gathered to hear the Scriptures being expounded by Ezra. 'And all the people listened – they were all ears – to the Book of The Revelation' (8:3, MSG). 'As he opened the book everyone stood' (8:5, MSG). They *stood* out of respect for the word of God.

'Then Ezra praised God, the great God and all the people responded "Oh Yes! Yes!" with *hands raised high*. And then *they fell to their knees* in worship of God, their *faces to the ground*' (v.6, MSG).

Our bodies express our hearts. That is why, when I'm on my own, I like to kneel as I read the Bible as a mark of reverence and respect for God. I have come to listen to him and worship him.

To raise hands in worship was the common practice of both the Jewish people and the early Christians ('hands raised high', v.6). 'The oldest gesture of prayer in Christendom is prayer with arms extended' writes Pope Benedict. This gesture is 'the radical form of worship'. It expresses opening ourselves to God and at the same time opening ourselves in love to others.

All of our gatherings to praise and worship God are an anticipation of, and participation in, the great worship of heaven – the eternal Hallelujah chorus. In this passage in Nehemiah we see an example of this. It echoes and anticipates the great worship of Revelation 19.

Nehemiah the governor, Ezra the priest and scribe and the Levites instructed the people. They wept as they listened to the words of the Law (v.9).

But Nehemiah told them that it was a time for *joy* and *celebration*: 'Go and enjoy choice food and sweet drinks ... Do not grieve, for the joy of the Lord is your strength' (v.10). There was a time of *celebration* and *great joy* (v.12).

As Joyce Meyer writes, 'Each day that God gives us is holy and a precious gift from him. We should enjoy it fully. Joy is powerful. Nothing releases supernatural joy in our lives more than being a blessing to other people.'[2]

PRAYER

Lord, I praise you for the coming of Christ on the first Christmas Day. Thank you that we anticipate now his coming again, the marriage feast of the Lamb that will take place, and the great praise and worship of heaven that will go on for ever. Hallelujah!

28 December | Day 362
Covenant of Love

When my daughter got married, I walked her down the aisle. At the front of the church, before all their family and friends, in their overflowing love for each other, she and her husband promised exclusive loyalty. They made a *covenant of love*. It was a love-filled occasion.

A covenant is two people, or two parties, entering into a formal agreement. The making of covenants was a common feature in the ancient world. A covenant would often be made with a solemn action, such as a blood sacrifice.

The idea of covenant is so important in the Christian Bible that the two parts came to be called the Old and the New *Testaments* ('*Testamentum*' being the Latin word for *covenant*). Although the new covenant was different from the old one, both covenants come from God's abounding love for you.

READING FROM PSALMS

Psalm 148:7–14
***Praise* God for his intimate friendship**

Do you know that you can be an 'intimate friend' of God? This is what it means to be part of 'his very own people' who 'love GOD' (v.14, MSG). This is what God's covenant of love is all about.

As a result of God's love for him, the psalmist's heart is bursting with praise. He calls the whole created world to praise God, as well as the whole of humankind (vv.7–12): 'Let them praise the name of the LORD, for his name alone is exalted' (v.13).

The psalm reaches its climax: 'He has raised up for his people *a horn*, the praise of all his saints, of Israel, the people *close to his heart' – 'intimate friends of GOD'* (v.14, MSG).

A *'horn'* symbolises the strength of the Lord (see Deuteronomy 33:17) and found fulfilment in Jesus: 'He has raised up *a horn of salvation* for us in the house of his servant David' (Luke 1:69). He did this out of his great love for us; he made a covenant of love because he wants a people close to his heart. No wonder the psalmist finishes with a shout of 'Praise the LORD!' (Psalm 148:14).

PRAYER

Lord, thank you that you make a covenant with me, that you draw me close to your heart and call me your intimate friend.

NEW TESTAMENT READING

Revelation 19:11–21
Thank* Jesus for paying the *price

God's covenant comes at a price. But the price is paid, not by us but by God himself in the person of Jesus, whose blood was shed for you. John sees Jesus riding a white horse. He describes him with four names:

1. Faithful and True
'With justice he judges' (v.11). He pierces the secrets of our hearts ('his eyes are like blazing fire', v.12a). He has universal authority ('on his head are many crowns', v.12b). Yet in spite of our unfaithfulness, he is '*Faithful and True*' (v.11).

Throughout the Bible we read of the faithfulness of God to his covenant and promises. Supremely the faithfulness of God is seen in *Jesus* – the one who is 'faithful and true'.

2. The name only Jesus knows
'...he has *a name written on him that no one knows* but he himself' (v.12c). God's revelation of himself in *Jesus* will not be completed until we see him face to face (1 Corinthians 13:12).

3. The Word of God
'...his name is the *Word of God*' (Revelation 19:13). The Word of God is how God communicates with us. The supreme revelation of God is in the person of *Jesus* – the Word of God (John 1:1).

'He is dressed in a robe soaked with blood' (Revelation 19:13a, MSG). This is the evidence of his abounding love for you. This is 'the blood of the covenant' (Matthew 26:28). The blood of *Jesus* was shed for you.

4. King of kings and Lord of lords
He is '*King of kings and Lord of lords*' (Revelation 19:16). This is the name written on his robe and on his thigh. He leads the church 'dressed in fine linen, white and clean' (v.14). This is the one before whom every knee will bow and every tongue confess that *Jesus* Christ is Lord (Philippians 2:9–11).

No evil can stand before Jesus. Ultimately, all evil will be destroyed. The final battle (Revelation 19:17–21) will not be a battle at all. The demonic powers will be thrown into 'the fiery lake of burning sulphur' (v.20), and God's enemies that opposed Christ will be stripped of their power once and for all (v.21). The dramatic imagery is there to show us how total the victory of Jesus will be.

The great victory has already been won by him who is faithful and true. Through the cross and resurrection, he has already defeated all the powers of evil (Colossians 2:15). The victory we read of here is a forgone conclusion when Jesus arrives on the scene.

PRAYER

Lord, thank you for your sacrificial covenant of love and that you are faithful and true – abounding in love – and that one day we will see you face to face.

OLD TESTAMENT READING

Nehemiah 9:1–37
***Trust* God for his provision**

Do you ever find yourself in a desperate situation, crying to God for help and making all kinds of promises of what you will do if he answers your prayer? Then, when God does answer, you forget and begin to drift away from him again?

The history of the people of God is very similar. When God blesses us, we can become complacent, start to compromise and fall into sin. Then we cry out to God and he delivers us and has mercy on us. Then we become lax again. Certainly, I have sometimes found this to be a pattern in my own life. But this is not how we are meant to live.

God made a covenant with his people – starting with Abraham (v.8). It was a *covenant of love* (v.32). He promised to provide 'bread from heaven for their hunger' and 'water from the rock for their thirst' (v.15, MSG). He wanted them to live by faith in his provision.

God wants you to trust in him. Make a decision today not to worry about tomorrow. Trust him to provide for you every day, one day at a time. God does not just love you; he *abounds* in love for you. He loves you as if there were only you to love.

The walls have been rebuilt. The Law has been read. Now the people recognise the abounding love of God and his covenant of love with them. They realise that God has blessed them in an extraordinary way. Yet, when they think about their own lives, they see how undeserved it is.

They come together with fasting and prayer. They stand and confess their sins and wickedness (v.2). They 'read from the Book of the Law of the Lord their God for a quarter of the day' (v.3). No doubt, as they hear the words, their sins are brought to light. They 'spent another quarter in confession and in worshipping the LORD their God' (v.3).

Their prayer is a model prayer. It starts with worship. Having praised God for his abounding love in creation (vv.5–6), they praise him for his abounding love in history (v.8). They recall his covenant of love and faithfulness to Abraham, Moses and the people (vv.7–15).

They recall that in spite of all God's abounding love and generosity, the people were 'arrogant' and 'bull-headed' and 'wouldn't obey' (v.16, MSG). Sometimes, like them, I fail to remember the miracles God has performed among us (v.17).

Yet God's love abounds: 'a forgiving God, gracious and compassionate, incredibly patient, with tons of love ... amazing compassion ... showed them the right way to go. You gave them your good Spirit to teach them ... You never stinted ... You supported them ... they revelled in your bountiful goodness' (vv.17–25, MSG).

As they rehearse their history, the same pattern is repeated over and over again. God blesses them, 'But then they ... rebelled ... You ... made life rough for them. But when they called out for help in their troubles you listened from heaven ... But as soon as they had it easy again they were right back at it – more evil ... They cried out to you again; in your great compassion you heard and helped them again ... You didn't walk out and leave them for good; yes, you *are* a God of grace and compassion ... loyal in *covenant* and love' (vv.26–32, MSG).

It was because the people were unable to keep *their* side of the covenant that God promised he would make *a new covenant.* The new covenant is sealed by the blood of Jesus and involves the Holy Spirit coming to live within you to help you to keep your side of the covenant, and to abound in love for God and for others.

PRAYER

Father, thank you that you have made a covenant of love with me, which was sealed by the blood of Jesus. Thank you that you have given me your Holy Spirit to help me to abound in love for you and for others.

29 December | Day 363
Your Crown Is Coming

Queen Elizabeth II acceded to the throne in 1952. At her coronation in Westminster Abbey, she was handed a Bible, anointed and then crowned by the Archbishop of Canterbury.

Her Diamond Jubilee was a multinational celebration marking the sixtieth anniversary of her accession to the throne. The climax was a weekend in June 2012 filled with street parties and concerts, a special service of thanksgiving and the largest river-pageant for 300 years. The whole country came together to celebrate. On 6 February 2017, she became the first British monarch to celebrate a Sapphire Jubilee, commemorating sixty-five years on the throne.

According to the New Testament, every Christian will be crowned and will reign even longer and there will be an even bigger cause for celebration and rejoicing than that of any earthly ruler. You will reign *with Christ* (Revelation 20:4, 6). What does this mean? Who reigns with him? When does this reign begin?

READING FROM PSALMS

Psalm 149:1–9
Enjoy the honour of being crowned by the Lord

The people of God are called to celebrate their *sovereign* Creator, their *King* (v.2, MSG), to praise him with dancing and make music to him (vv.2–3).

The reason given is that 'the LORD takes delight in his people; he *crowns* the humble with salvation. Let the saints *rejoice* in this honour and sing for joy on their beds' (vv.4–5). 'All who love God' are 'in the seat of honor' (v.9, MSG). There is a hint here, in the crowning of his people, of reigning with Christ.

God delights in sharing his blessings with you, and these verses are a reminder of how much you have already received from him. You can delight in the 'crown' of salvation, and rejoice in the honour of being in relationship with him.

The psalmist goes on to say that God's people will execute judgment ('a double-edged sword in their hands', v.6b). In our New Testament passage for today, we see that God's people will accompany Christ in judgment (Revelation 19:11 onwards). The weapons are not literal swords, but the double-edged sword of the word of God (Hebrews 4:12).

This awesome responsibility and *honour* could easily make for pride. However, he 'crowns the *humble*' (Psalm 149:4). We have not earned our salvation. It is a gift. We have not earned the right to reign with Christ. This also is an extraordinary gift, privilege and honour.

PRAYER

Lord, thank you that you crown me with salvation. Thank you that you call me to reign with you. Thank you that you are my King, and that you call me to be a co-heir with Christ.

NEW TESTAMENT READING

Revelation 20:1–15
Experience your reign with Christ now

However we interpret the specifics of this passage, it is clearly wonderful news: Christ will return, Satan will be overthrown, and you will *reign with Jesus* and experience eternal life. This is something worth celebrating!

This is a notoriously difficult passage in the book of Revelation. Many books, commentaries and novels have been written about 'millennialism' and when 'the rapture' will take place. There are passionately held views on this subject and, sadly, divisions in the church over it. It is, therefore, with some trepidation that I express here my tentative views on the subject.

A millennium (plural millennia) is a period of time equal to 1,000 years. It derives from the Latin *mille*, thousand, and *annus*, year. Several times 'a thousand year' period is mentioned (vv.2–7). When is this thousand-year period? Broadly speaking, there have been three views:

1. Postmillennialism
This is the view that the return of Christ would not occur until the kingdom of God had been established by the church in human history for a thousand years.

2. Premillennialism
This is the view that the coming of Christ will be followed by the binding of Satan and the resurrection of the saints who will be 'raptured' and will join him in a temporal kingdom where he reigns over the earth for

a thousand years. This millennial kingdom will end with a final rebellion and the last judgment.

3. Amillennialism

This is the view that the thousand years is the period between the first and second coming of Christ. This position holds that the period of a thousand years is metaphorical, not literal and that the rapture will occur when Christ returns.

No doubt there is room for difference of opinion between Christians on this matter. Personally, I think there are difficulties with all three views. However, when we read this passage in the context of the rest of the New Testament and the Bible as a whole, I take the view that in spite of all the arguments to the contrary, 'amillennialism' fits best with the evidence.

As we have seen, much of the language of the book of Revelation is apocalyptic language and not intended to be interpreted literally. The 'one thousand years' stands for a very long but unspecified period of time. What is the evidence that the one-thousand-year period has already begun?

First, Satan is bound (v.2). The devil is described as 'the dragon, that ancient serpent, who is the devil, or Satan' (v.2). By his coming, Jesus defeated Satan. He bound the 'strong man' (Mark 3:27; Matthew 12:29). On the cross, Satan was defeated – thrown 'into the Abyss', which was 'locked and sealed' over him (Revelation 20:3).

Second, the nations are not deceived any more during this period: 'to keep him from deceiving the nations any more until the thousand years were ended' (v.3). This is the era of the church, when the gospel is preached to all nations. Millions, and now billions, profess the name of Christ. Their eyes are being opened to the good news of Jesus.

Third, according to the apostle Paul, we are already reigning with Christ. The resurrected martyrs and people of God reign with Christ for a thousand years. 'I saw thrones on which were seated those who had been given authority to judge ... they reigned with Christ for a thousand years' (v.4). As St Paul put it, 'God raised us up with Christ and seated us with him in the heavenly realms in Christ Jesus' (Ephesians 2:6).

Fourth, you are called to reign as 'priests of God and of Christ' (Revelation 20:6). This priesthood of all believers has already begun. We are called to be 'a holy priesthood' (1 Peter 2:5). Indeed, Peter refers to us as 'a *royal* priesthood' (v.9).

At the end of this period, Satan will be 'released from his prison' (Revelation 20:7), and the final conflict will take place. Once again, we see here that it will not really be a conflict at all. Rather, it will be the outworking of the victory that Jesus has already achieved. The destruction of evil will be complete (vv.8–10). Then the final judgment will take place (vv.11–15).

PRAYER

Lord, thank you that you have raised us up with Christ and seated us along with him in the heavenly realms. Help me to make the most of every opportunity to bring the good news to the nations.

OLD TESTAMENT READING

Nehemiah 9:38–11:21
Exercise your God-given authority responsibly

As in so many Old Testament passages, here we get a foretaste of the future. God delights in his people. He puts us in positions of authority to rule and to reign. However, we are called to exercise this authority with *obedience and responsibility* (10:35).

The people of God made a binding agreement, putting it in writing. The leaders, Levites and priests affixed their seals to it (9:38). They promised to keep the Law and 'bind themselves with a curse and an oath to follow the Law of God' (10:29).

Their problem, like ours, was an inability to keep the laws. We would therefore be under God's curse but for the fact that Jesus bore it for us on the cross (Galatians 3:13).

We are called to a balanced rhythm of life that includes work and rest.

The people of God had to keep to the Sabbath and, every seventh year, forgo working the land and cancel all debts (Nehemiah 10:31). They had to offer sacrifices to make atonement for their sins (v.33).

The leaders settled in Jerusalem (11:1), but it is clear from this passage that the pledge was by the community – the keeping of the law was plainly made the *responsibility of everyone*, not just the kings and princes.

PRAYER

Lord, thank you that I am called to take responsibility for my own life and for serving you and obeying your commands. Thank you that I need no longer make sacrifices in order to make atonement for my sins. Thank you that, through the death and resurrection of Jesus, not only has Satan been defeated but you have raised me with Christ to reign with him in the heavenly realms, far above all rule and authority, power and dominion, and every title that can be given, not only in the present age, but also in the one to come (Ephesians 1:20–21).

30 December | Day 364
The Bride

I often get very emotional at weddings. When I was conducting the marriage of my goddaughter, as the vicar, tears were pouring down my face. My great friend, her father, said in his speech afterwards that when you are taking your daughter down the aisle, you expect the vicar to be '*a rock*', but instead he found that I was '*a wreck*'!

When it came to my own daughter's wedding, I was determined to hold it together. I was doing well until half-an-hour *before* the wedding! Then I went upstairs and saw her in her wedding dress. At that point, I lost it.

This powerful and beautiful metaphor of '*the bride*' is one that is used to describe the church in the New Testament (Ephesians 5:22–32). It is used in today's New Testament passage of the church of the future, which comes down out of heaven from God, 'prepared as *a bride* beautifully dressed for her husband' (Revelation 21:2). This picture of the bride, the new Jerusalem, is prefigured in different ways in both our Old and New Testament passages.

READING FROM PROVERBS

Proverbs 31:21–31
The bride to be *proud* of

As you read the characteristics of 'a good wife' (MSG), realise that much of this applies not only to wives, nor even only to women. As we are the bride of Christ, it applies to us all; men and women, married and unmarried. This is what the church *should* be like – and through Jesus, one day, *will* be like.

This description of 'the wife of noble character' is the model human bride. She keeps her family warm (v.21); she is well dressed (v.22b). Her husband is respected because of her (v.23a). Her business flourishes (v.24). She is clothed with strength and dignity (v.25a). She can face the future with confidence and joy (v.25b).

Her words are full of wisdom (v.26). 'When she speaks she has something worthwhile to say and she always says it kindly' (v.26, MSG). What a great model! Avoid words that are full of hatred, anger, resentment and distrust. Only speak kind words.

She watches over the affairs of her household and 'does not eat the bread of idleness (gossip, discontent, and self-pity)' (v.27, AMP).

Her children 'arise and call her blessed' (v.28a). Abraham Lincoln said, 'No man is poor who has had *a godly mother*.' Not only is she appreciated by her children, her husband also praises her and says, 'Many women do noble things, but you surpass them all' (vv.28b–29).

The last verses focus on all women: 'Charm can mislead and beauty soon fades. The woman to be admired and praised is the woman who lives in the Fear-of-GOD. Give her everything she deserves! Festoon her life with praises!' (vv.30–31, MSG).

PRAYER

Father, thank you for this picture of what the church should be like – the bride of Christ. Help us to be the kind of church in which Jesus can take pride.

NEW TESTAMENT READING

Revelation 21:1–27
The bride *prepared*

What does the future hold? What will 'heaven' be like? The New Testament answer is that it will not just be 'heaven' but 'a *new heaven and a new earth*' (v.1a). The *new* heaven and the *new* earth are very real and solid.

This passage has within it a paradox concerning the new creation. There will be '*a new heaven* and *a new earth*', but Christ says, '*I make all things new*' (v.5, NKJV) – not, 'I make all new things'. *This is an indication of the continuity* with this creation. That is why Martin Luther said, 'If I knew the world was ending tomorrow, I would plant a tree today.' This has huge implications for our understanding of the resurrection (and also for how we treat the environment now).

In this new heaven and the new earth, John sees the church – us – as we will be. He sees the 'Holy City, the new Jerusalem, coming down out of heaven from God, prepared as *a bride beautifully dressed for her husband*' (v.2). One of the angels says, 'Come, I will show you *the bride, the wife of the Lamb*' (v.9).

Jesus will satisfy your thirst for God: 'He said to me: "It is done. I am the Alpha and the Omega, the Beginning and the End. To those who are thirsty I will give to drink without cost from the spring of the water of life."' (v.6).

There will be a new relationship with God. You experience a foretaste of this today through the indwelling presence of God in the church by his Spirit. On this great day, you will be brought into a place of complete intimacy with Jesus. Take the most beautiful relationship you have ever seen, multiply it a million times, and you will get some idea of the sheer beauty of the relationship you will experience with God in eternity.

The church will not just be in a perfect relationship with God, she will be *made perfect*. The description of this 'bride' is *dazzlingly beautiful*: 'It shone with the glory of God, and its brilliance was like that of a very precious jewel, like a jasper, as clear as crystal' (v.11).

This is the place for the completed church (the 'twelve apostles of the Lamb'), with its roots in the Old Testament (the 'twelve tribes of Israel', vv.12–14). The city is a perfect cube (vv.15–16). It is absolutely beautiful, peaceful and totally secure (vv.17–21).

There are six notable absences:

1. No suffering
God himself will be with you and he will wipe away every tear from your eyes (vv.3b–4a). There will be no more suffering, sickness or sadness.

2. No death
There will be no more death, or mourning, or crying, or pain (v.4b). There will be no more hospitals, no walking sticks, no funerals and no cemeteries.

3. No temple
There is no sign of a temple, 'because the Lord God Almighty and the Lamb are its temple' (v.22).

4. No sun
It does not need the sun or moon to shine, 'for the glory of God gives it light, and the Lamb is its lamp' (v.23). The nations will walk by its light and the kings of the earth will bring their splendour into it.

5. No night
There is no night there: 'On no day will its gates ever be shut, for there will be *no night there*' (v.25).

6. No impurity
Those who choose to carry on living lives that destroy others have no place in this inheritance (vv.7–8): 'Nothing impure will ever enter it, nor will anyone who does what is shameful or deceitful, but only those whose names are written in the Lamb's book of life' (v.27). Nothing will be ruined by sin. It will be totally perfect.

Are you going through a difficult time right now? One day your troubles will come to an end. In the meantime, *God is with you* and will give you a foretaste of the future – his strength for today and hope for tomorrow.

This hope is a comfort and strength to those going through hardship and difficulty in the present (for instance, Romans 8:18), and an inspiration to live holy lives in anticipation of what is to come (for instance, 1 John 2:28).

St Augustine explains how you should respond to this hope for the future: 'He who loves the coming of the Lord is not he who affirms that it is far off, nor is it he who says it is near, but rather he who, whether it be far off or near, awaits it with *sincere faith*, *steadfast hope*, and *fervent love*.'

PRAYER

Lord, thank you for the amazing hope for the future. Help me to wait for it with sincere faith, steadfast hope and fervent love.

OLD TESTAMENT READING

Nehemiah 11:22–12:47
The bride *prefigured*

Celebrations are important. One day there will be a massive eternal celebration. When the church comes together, our celebration is an anticipation of the great celebration that is to come. All this is prefigured in the Old Testament.

The city of Jerusalem anticipates and prefigures what is to come. The *new Jerusalem* is the church, glorified and triumphant; 'The bride, the wife of the Lamb' (Revelation 21:9–10).

Much attention is given to Jerusalem in the Old Testament. This is why there was such *joy* and *celebration* when Jerusalem was rebuilt. A great celebration took place, with 'thanksgiving hymns, songs, cymbals, harps, and lutes' (Nehemiah 12:27, MSG).

The joy of the new Jerusalem is also anticipated in the great celebratory worship led by two large choirs (Nehemiah 12:31 onwards): 'an *exuberant celebration* because God had filled them with *great joy*. The women and children raised their happy voices with all the rest. *Jerusalem's jubilation was heard far and wide*' (v.43, MSG).

PRAYER

Lord, thank you for the great joy, worship and celebration that we will enjoy into all eternity in the new Jerusalem, that will come down out of heaven from God, prepared as a bride beautifully dressed for her husband (Revelation 21:2).

31 December | Day 365
How to Begin and End

One young woman asked me the following questions: 'What will it be like in heaven? What will our heavenly bodies look like? Will we be able to fly? Will we be sexless? Will we be able to see the Garden of Eden? Will we recognise family and friends? What sort of friendships will we have? What will we do? Will there be Bible studies and Alpha? Who is the congregation?'

The Bible does not give the answers to all our questions.

I have a book on my bookshelf entitled, *50 Remarkable events pointing to THE END*.[1] Written in 1997, it predicted that Jesus could return by AD 2000. This is one of many attempts to predict the timing of 'the End' that have turned out to be false. That is why Tony Campolo wisely says he wants to be 'on the welcoming committee' rather than the 'planning committee'!

We are *not* told *when* the end will come, but we *are* told about the *how* and the *who*. The key is the *who*. Jesus says, 'I am ... *the Beginning* and *the End*' (Revelation 22:13). Of course, 'the End' and 'the Beginning' appear very different. However, there can be significant similarities to both the beginning and the end.

READING FROM PSALMS

Psalm 150:1–6
Begin and end with worship

In the end, God's 'servants will offer God service – *worshiping*, they'll look on his face, their foreheads mirroring God' (Revelation 22:3, MSG). Our response to seeing God face to face will be eternal worship.

The book of Psalms ends with 'Hallelujah', translated here 'Praise the LORD' (Psalm 150:6b). Psalm 150 itself begins and ends with 'Hallelujah' ('Praise the LORD', vv.1, 6). All of us are called to worship: 'Let every living, breathing creature praise GOD!' (v.6, MSG).

1. Worship everywhere
The worship of God should fill the universe: 'Praise God in his holy house of worship, praise him under the open skies' (v.1b, MSG).

2. Worship him for everything
Praise God for *who he is* ('his surpassing greatness') and *what he has done* ('his acts of power', v.2).

3. Worship in every way
Praise God with everything you have, including every type of music and dancing (vv.3–5).

PRAYER

Lord, I praise you for your surpassing greatness and your acts of power. I worship you as the creator of the entire universe, yet you love me personally.

NEW TESTAMENT READING

Revelation 22:1–21
Begin and end with Jesus

In the end, it is all about Jesus. It always has been about Jesus. It always will be about Jesus. Begin now to focus your life, your thoughts, your ministry, your evangelism and everything else on Jesus.

The Bible begins with Jesus. The creation of the universe (Genesis 1–2) was actually through Jesus. 'In the *beginning* was the Word, and the Word was with God, and the Word was God ... *Through him all things were made*' (John 1:1, 3).

The Bible also ends with Jesus: 'Amen. Come, *Lord Jesus*. The grace of the *Lord Jesus* be with God's people. Amen' (Revelation 22:20b–21). He is 'the Alpha and the Omega, the First and the Last, the Beginning and the End' (v.13).

We see how the world will be in the end. The language is figurative. It is not an exact description, but it is full of images of life and blessing. The Bible begins and ends with 'the tree of life', symbolising God's life of blessing and his 'good' plan for his people.

In the new heaven and the new earth, there will be 'the river of the water of life' (v.1). This will fulfil the prophecy in Ezekiel 47, which Jesus related to 'rivers of living water' flowing from the Holy Spirit (John 7:37–39). It will bring 'healing of the nations' (Revelation 22:2). How desperately that is needed, both within countries and between nations. How wonderful it will be when the 'United Nations' becomes a reality.

The '*tree* of life bearing fruit continually' (v.2), which was there at the beginning (from which humankind was barred because of sin), will be available again for all. The curse of Eden will be revoked (v.3). The word for 'tree' (*xylos*) is sometimes used in the New Testament to describe the cross (for example, Acts 5:30).

In the end, you will see God's face. No one could see God and live (Exodus 33:20), but in the new heaven and the new earth, you will see his face and his name will be on your forehead (Revelation 22:4). 'There will be no more night. They will not need the light of a lamp or the light of the sun, for the Lord God will give them light' (v.5a). And you will reign with him for ever and ever (v.5b).

There is so much to look forward to in the new heaven and the new earth. Jesus promises, 'I am coming soon' (vv.7, 12, 20).

No wonder that 'the Spirit and the bride [the church] say, "Come!" And let those who hear say, "Come!" Let those who are thirsty come; and let all who wish take the free gift of the water of life' (v.17).

The Bible is one long invitation to come to Jesus. In him, you find the meaning and purpose of your life. Part of that purpose is to invite others to come, so that they too will find refreshment and fulfilment in the water of life that Jesus pours out on all who come to him.

The Holy Spirit and the church invite people to come and to receive the amazing gifts God has for them, rather than missing out on the wonders of the holy city (as with vv.11a,15, 19). They pray too for the return of Jesus – 'Come, Lord Jesus' (v.20).

PRAYER

Lord, thank you that one day I will drink the water of life to my heart's content. Thank you that I will see you face to face and I will reign with you for ever and ever. Come, Lord Jesus.

OLD TESTAMENT READING

Nehemiah 13:1–31
Begin and end with love

The book of Nehemiah, like the Bible as a whole, begins and ends with *love*. Nehemiah began by praying, 'O LORD, God of heaven, the great and awesome God, who keeps his covenant of *love*...' (Nehemiah 1:5).

As the book of Nehemiah draws to an end, he prays, 'Remember me for this also, O my God, and show mercy to me according to your great *love*' (13:22).

In this last chapter, we read of Nehemiah's final reforms. They read from the 'Book of Moses' (v.1) how 'Our God ... turned the curse into a blessing' (v.2). This is the pattern throughout the Bible. 'In *all things* God works for the good of those who *love him*' (Romans 8:28). What you are facing in your life right now may seem like a curse – a health issue, a battle in a relationship, a difficult boss, or whatever. It may seem like a curse but God can turn the curse into a blessing.

As a good leader, Nehemiah chose to delegate to people considered 'trustworthy' (v.13) and 'faithful' (AMP) – 'those who had a reputation for honesty and hard work' (MSG).

Sometimes God tests our faithfulness. Have you ever found yourself in a situation where you are asked to do something that you really don't want to do, or to submit to authority when everything in your being wants to resist it?

But these challenges are opportunities to do something, not because it's fun or exciting, but in faithfulness, with a good attitude and with integrity. And God rewards such faithfulness (Luke 16:12).

Nehemiah achieved so much, but he could not change the hearts of the people. They had promised wholehearted commitment to the Lord, but they were unable to deliver (compare Nehemiah 10:30 with 13:23; 10:31 with 13:16; 10:39 with 13:11). The problem of human sin still remained.

Nehemiah warns them (13:15, 21). He rebukes them (vv.17, 25). He wants them to be pure (vv.22,30), but it is in vain. Nehemiah's frustration points us forward to Jesus, the only one who could deal with the problem of the human heart, and deal with our sin.

Again and again Nehemiah asks to be remembered (vv.14, 22, 31) with favour because he had faithfully served God. But ultimately, he trusts in God's mercy and love: 'Remember me for this also, O my God, and show mercy to me according *to your great love*' (v.22).

Nehemiah, like all of us, needed to be the recipient of God's mercy and love, which was displayed supremely as Jesus died in our place. As Paul wrote to the Romans, 'God demonstrates his own love for us in this: While we were still sinners, Christ died for us' (Romans 5:8).

PRAYER

Lord, thank you that in the new heaven and the new earth I will enjoy your great love for ever and ever. Thank you that right now I know your love, through the death and resurrection of Jesus, and I experience your love, poured into my heart by the Holy Spirit. Lord Jesus, I will praise your name for ever and ever!

Notes

Preface
1 Rick Warren, *Purpose Driven Life* (Zondervan, 2004) p. 170.
2 Lesslie Newbigin, *The Gospel in a Pluralist Society* (SPCK, 2004).

3 January | Day 3
1 *Chariots of Fire* (Dir. Hugh Hudson, 20th Century Fox, 1981).

4 January | Day 4
1 Joyce Meyer, *100 Ways to Simplify Your Life* (Faithwords, 1987), p. 152.

5 January | Day 5
1 St Augustine, *Confessions: Book 1* (Penguin, 1961), p. 21.
2 Joyce Meyer, *The Everyday Life Bible* (Faithwords, 2018) p. 1483.
3 C. S. Lewis, *The Weight of Glory* (William Collins, 2013). Used by permisson copyright © C. S. Lewis Pte Ltd 1949.
4 For a more detailed explanation and application of 'The Sermon on the Mount' (Matthew 5–7) see Nicky Gumbel's book *The Jesus Lifestyle* (Hodder & Stoughton, 2018).

7 January | Day 7
1 Dietrich Bonhoeffer, *The Cost of Discipleship* (SCM Press, 2015) p. 153.

8 January | Day 8
1 Corrie ten Boom, *Clippings from My Notebook* (Triangle, 1983).

9 January | Day 9
1 Miroslav Volf, *Exclusion and Embrace*, (Abingdon Press, 1994), pp. 303–4.

11 January | Day 11
1 *How to Be a Huge Success* (Lagoon Books, 2003).
2 Alpha is a series of sessions exploring the Christian faith. Typically run over ten weeks, each session explores a different question of faith that inspires conversation in small groups. To find out more or to find an Alpha near you, visit alpha.org/try, or if you are interested in running Alpha, visit alpha.org/run.

14 January | Day 14
1 Joyce Meyer, 'Just Relax and Let God Be God', 1 January 2013 https://twitter.com/joycemeyer/status/286320915329994752 [last accessed March 2018].

16 January | Day 16
1 Joyce Meyer, *Love Out Loud* (Hodder & Stoughton, 2011).

17 January | Day 17
1 Abbot Christopher Jamison, *Finding Happiness: Monastic Steps for a Fulfilling Life* (Phoenix, 2009).
2 Joyce Meyer, *The Everyday Life Bible* (Faithwords, 2018), p. 59.
3 Rick Warren, @RickWarren, 10 December 2010, https://twitter.com/rickwarren/status/13199824941752321

18 January | Day 18
1 Queen Elizabeth II's Christmas Day speech, https://www.bbc.co.uk/news/av/uk-46680354/the-queen-s-christmas-message-2018-in-full [accessed 14 March 2019].
2 ibid. 2016 Christmas speech https://www.gov.uk/government/speeches/queens-speech-2016 [accessed 14 March 2019].
3 C. Peter Wagner, *Strategies for Church Growth* (Regal, 1987), p. 168.

20 January | Day 20

1 'Smith Wigglesworth' *Relevant*, https://relevantmagazine.com/god/13-smith-wigglesworth-quotes-will-challenge-your-faith [accessed 25 March 2019].

21 January | Day 21

1 Joyce Meyer, *The Everyday Life Bible* (Faithwords, 2018), p. 72.

23 January | Day 23

1 Alexandre Dumas, *The Count of Monte Cristo* (Wordsworth editions, 1997).
2 R. T. Kendall, *Total Forgiveness* (Hodder & Stoughton, 2003).

25 January | Day 25

1 R. T. Kendall, *God Meant it for Good* (Paternoster Press, 2003), p. 62.
2 For a wider discussion about suffering, see 'Why Does God Allow Suffering?' in *Searching Issues* by Nicky Gumbel (Hodder & Stoughton, 2018), pp. 4-21.

26 January | Day 26

1 C. S. Lewis, *Mere Christianity* (William Collins, 2012), p. 12. Used by permission copyright © C. S. Lewis Pte Ltd 1942, 1943, 1944, 1952.
2 For a wider discussion about suffering, see 'Why Does God Allow Suffering?' in *Searching Issues* by Nicky Gumbel (Hodder & Stoughton, 2018), pp. 4-21.

28 January | Day 28

1 Norman Vincent Peale, *The Power of Positive Thinking* (Prentice-Hall, 1952).

29 January | Day 29

1 C. S. Lewis, *A Grief Observed* (Faber & Faber, 2013). Used by permission © C. S. Lewis Pte Ltd 1961.

30 January | Day 30

1 John Stott, *Essential Living: The Sermon on the Mount* (IVP, 1988) p. 189.
2 Rick Warren, PastorRick.com, 'Four Ways God Answers Your Prayers', 26 October 2018, https://pastorrick.com/four-ways-god-answers-your-prayers/

4 February | Day 35

1 John C. Maxwell, *Developing the Leader Within You* (Thomas Nelson, 2005).

5 February | Day 36

1 Joyce Meyer, *The Everyday Life Bible* (Faithwords, 2018), p. 1536.

7 February | Day 38

1 The writings of Mother Teresa of Calcutta copyright © by the Mother Teresa Center, exclusive Licensee throughout the world of the Missionaries of Charity for the works of Mother Teresa. Used with permission.
2 Joyce Meyer, *The Everyday Life Bible* (Faithwords, 2018), p. 812.

8 February | Day 39

1 Francis Collins, *The Language of God* (Simon & Schuster UK, 2007), p. 67.

9 February | Day 40

1 Frank Sinatra, 'My Way', lyrics © Warner/Chappell Music Publishing.

11 February | Day 42

1 Solomon Northup, *Twelve Years a Slave* (Sampson Low, Son & Company, 1853).
2 Cardinal Joseph Ratzinger, *Joseph Ratzinger: Collected Works – Theology of the Liturgy* (Ignatius Press, 2014).

13 February | Day 44

1 John Stott, *The Cross of Christ* (IVP, 2012).

14 February | Day 45
1 Corrie ten Boom, *Clippings From My Notebook*, (Triangle, 1983).

15 February | Day 46
1 The Alpha Weekend takes place just over half way through Alpha, usually between sessions 7 and 8. It provides an opportunity for small groups get to know each other better and to hear teaching focused on the person and work of the Holy Spirit. For many guests this is the most transformative moment on Alpha.

17 February | Day 48
1 Further practical suggestions for how to avoid sexual temptation in particular can be found in *The Jesus Lifestyle*, chapter 5: 'How to Understand Sex in the 21st Century' (Hodder & Stoughton, 2018), p. 56.
2 Joyce Meyer, *The Everyday Life Bible* (Faithwords, 2018), p. 965.
3 C. S. Lewis, *Mere Christianity* (William Collins, 2012), p. 53. Used by permission copyright © C. S. Lewis Pte Ltd 1942, 1943, 1944, 1952.

20 February | Day 51
1 Duncan Campbell, *The Price and Power of Revival* (Faith Mission, 2000).

21 February | Day 52
1 Nicky & Sila Lee have been married for over forty years and have four children. They are on the staff at HTB, London, UK. They have spoken to thousands on the subject of marriage and family life, authored *The Marriage Book* and *The Parenting Book*, and created The Marriage Course, The Marriage Preparation Course, The Parenting Children Course and The Parenting Teenagers Course. For more information visit www.themarriagecourses.org
2 Jago Wynne, *Working Without Wilting* (IVP, 2009).
3 Henry F. Lyte, 'Praise, My Soul, the King of Heaven', 1834.

23 February | Day 54
1 John Calvin (translated by John King), *Commentaries: Volume 32, Matthew, Mark and Luke, Part II*, (Edinburgh, Calvin Translation Society, 1847–1850) p. 268.
2 ibid.

24 February | Day 55
1 Hattie May Wiatt illustration from sermon by Russell H Conwell, 'The History of the 57 Cents', Sunday morning, December 1, 1912.

25 February | Day 56
1 Shane Claiborne, *Irresistible Revolution* (Zondervan, 2006), p. 121.

27 February | Day 58
1 Eugene Peterson, *The Message:* 'Introduction to Leviticus' (NavPress, 2007).
2 F. M. Dostoevsky, *Polnoe sobranie sochinenii*, Vol. 28-2 (Nauka, 1985), p. 251.
3 Peterson, *The Message*.

1 March | Day 60
1 Prayer from the Anglican collect for the Fourth Sunday of Lent. *Common Worship: Services and Prayers for the Church of England*, copyright © The Archbishops' Council 2000.
2 Adapted from the Prayer of St Richard of Chichester (1197–1253), http://www.spck.org.uk/classic-prayers/st-richard-of-chichester/, copyright © SPCK 2015 [last accessed February 2015].

2 March | Day 61
1 Copyright © Sharon Feinstein. Freelance journalist and writer. Used by permission.
2 Joyce Meyer, *The Everyday Life Bible* (Faithwords, 2018), p. 1583.

5 March | Day 64

1 American Heart Association, 'Life's Simple 7', http://www.heart.org/HEARTORG/Conditions/My-Life-Check---Lifes-Simple-7_UCM_471453_Article.jsp#.VqvcnbSp8Rk [last accessed March 2019]

9 March | Day 68

1 Aleksandr Isaevich Solzhenitsyn, *The Gulag Archipelago*, Parts 1 & 2, (Harper Row, 1974).
2 Joyce Meyer, *The Everyday Life Bible* (Faithwords, 2018), p. 1593.

10 March | Day 69

1 The introductory illustration was taken from http://www.cbn.com/special/BlackHistory/Harry_Burleigh_Spirituals.aspx

11 March | Day 70

1 C. S. Lewis, *The Weight of Glory* (Harper Collins, 2001; Originally published 1949), p. 158. Used by permission copyright © C. S. Lewis Pte Ltd 1949.
2 C. S. Lewis, *Collected Letters of C. S. Lewis* (Zondervan, 2007), p. 1591. Used by permission copyright © C. S. Lewis Pte Ltd 2000.

12 March | Day 71

1 Hunter Davies, *The Beatles: The Authorized Biography* (McGraw-Hill Book Co., 1968), p. 131.
2 Jack Schofield, 'Ken Olson Obituary', The *Guardian*, 9 February 2011: https://www.theguardian.com/technology/2011/feb/09/ken-olsen-obituary
3 Tim Keller, *King's Cross: The Story of the World in the Life of Jesus* (Hodder & Stoughton, 2011), p. 222.
4 Joyce Meyer, *The Everyday Life Bible*, (Faithwords, 2018) p. 199.

14 March | Day 73

1 Raniero Cantalamessa, *Come, Creator Spirit: Meditations on the Veni Creator* (Liturgical Press, 2002), p. 287.
2 *The Book of Common Prayer* (Cambridge University Press), p. 89.
3 Cantalamessa, *Come, Creator Spirit*.
4 Eugene Peterson, *The Message* (NavPress, 2002), p. 169.

15 March | Day 74

1 C. S. Lewis, *Reflections on the Psalms* (Fount, 1993), pp. 94–95. Used by permission copyright © C. S. Lewis Pte Ltd 1958.
2 Corrie ten Boom, *Jesus is Victor* (Fleming H. Revell Company, 1984).

17 March | Day 76

1 The writings of Mother Teresa of Calcutta copyright © by the Mother Teresa Center, exclusive licensee throughout the world of the Missionaries of Charity for the works of Mother Teresa. Used with permission.

18 March | Day 77

1 Lights, 'Saviour', from The Listening, Songwriters Salter, Thomas / Poxleitner, Valerie. Lyrics © Sony/ATV Music Publishing LLC.
2 Lecrae, @lecrae on Twitter, 23 August 2012, https://twitter.com/lecrae/status/238677876927504386 [last accessed February 2016].
3 Reuben Morgan, Ben Fielding, 'Mighty to Save', Music and lyrics by Reuben Morgan and Ben Fielding, © Hillsong Music Publishing.
4 Ben Cantelon, 'Saviour of the World' from Everything in Colour, 2010 Thankyou Music/Adm. by Capitol CMG Publishing excl. UK & Europe, adm. By Integrity Music, part of the David C Cook family, songs@integritymusic.com.

19 March | Day 78

1 John Wimber, *Healing Clinic Notes* (Fuller Seminary, 1988), 9.05.

20 March | Day 79

1 Researchers have been unable to find these precise words in the oeuvre of John Wesley who died in 1791; however, there is evidence that he delivered sermons containing passages providing a partial match and from which the popularised version of the quote has emerged. https://quoteinvestigator.com/2016/09/24/all-good/

21 March | Day 80

1 C. S. Lewis, 'True humility is not thinking less of yourself. It is thinking of yourself less.' C. S. Lewis may not have used these exact words but he did say something similar in *Mere Christianity*, which has inspired the evolution of this quote. Used by permission copyright © C. S. Lewis Pte Ltd 1942, 1943, 1944, 1952.

22 March | Day 81

1 Colin Barras, BBC earth, 'The abominable mystery of how flowers conquered the earth' (16 October 2014) http://www.bbc.co.uk/earth/story/20141017-how-flowers-conquered-the-world
2 Joyce Meyer, *The Everyday Life Bible* (Faithwords, 2018), p. 233.

24 March | Day 83

1 Joyce Meyer, *The Everyday Life Bible* (Faithwords, 2018) p. 1615.
2 Heinrich Heine (1856) cited in Sigmund Freud, *The Joke and Its Relation to the Unconscious* (Penguin Classics, 2003), p. 111.
3 *Oxford English Dictionary* (Oxford University Press). Copyright © 2019.

26 March | Day 85

1 Interview with Mother Teresa of Calcutta, *Hello*, Issue 324, 1 October 1994.
2 Used by permission. Copyright © C. S. Lewis Pte Ltd.
3 Nelson Mandela cited in Phil Cousineau, *Beyond Forgiveness: Reflections on Atonement* (Jossey-Bass, 2011) p. 139.
4 Lewis A. Drummond, *Spurgeon: Prince of Preachers* (Kregal Publications, 1992), p. 23.

27 March | Day 86

1 A Prayer of Saint Francis of Assisi (1181–1226).

29 March | Day 88

1 Quoted in Kim Lachance Shandrow, Entrepreneur.com, '3 Inspiring Business Lessons from Billionaire Media Mogul Oprah Winfrey', 2 August 2016, via https://www.entrepreneur.com/article/280148

30 March | Day 89

1 The Leadership Conference is a yearly event that takes place in the Royal Albert Hall in London, in May. It unites people from every corner of the world for two days with world class speakers, worship and encouragement. It is an opportunity for any leader, whether you are a senior church leader or a small group leader to enhance your expertise, cultivate connections and be part of God-breathed moments with creative thinkers, church builders, influencers and entrepreneurs. See htb.org/events for more information.

31 March | Day 90

1 Lily Allen, 'The Fear' from It's Not Me, It's You (2008), Songwriters: Allen, Lily Rose / Kurstin, Greg. Lyrics © Universal Music Publishing Group, EMI Music Publishing.

1 April | Day 91

1 Corrie ten Boom, *The Hiding Place* (Hodder & Stoughton, 2004), p. 196.

2 April | Day 92
1 Stoeber, Joachim; Childs, Julian H. (2010). 'The Assessment of Self-Oriented and Socially Prescribed Perfectionism: Subscales Make a Difference' (PDF). *Journal of Personality Assessment*. 92 (6): pp. 577–585.
2 'The Alternative Jesus: Psychedelic Christ', *TIME*, 21 June 1971. © Time inc.

3 April | Day 93
1 John Eddison, 'At the Cross of Jesus', copyright © Scripture Union.
2 Miroslav Volf, *Exclusion & Embrace* (Abingdon 1996), p. 304.

4 April | Day 94
1 General George Smith Patton, *War As I Knew It* (Houghton Miffin Harcourt, 1995), p. 357.

7 April | Day 97
1 Raniero Cantalamessa, *The Mystery of Easter* (The Liturgical Press, 1994), p. 105.

11 April | Day 101
1 Nelson Mandela, *The Long Walk to Freedom* (Abacus, 1995), p. 748.

13 April | Day 103
1 Oliver O'Donovan, *Measure for Measure: Justice in Punishment and the Sentence of Death, Grove Booklet on Ethics No. 19* (Grove Books, 1977), p. 8.

14 April | Day 104
1 James Rampton, 'James Cameron: My Titanic obsession', The *Independent*, Monday 8 August 2005.
2 Rick Warren, *Daily Hope with Rick Warren*, 'Take the First Step to Integrity' November 2014, accessed via: http://rickwarren.org/devotional/english/take-the-first-step-to-integrity [last accessed March 2016]
3 Dietrich Bonhoeffer, *The Cost of Discipleship* (Macmillan Books, 1970) p. 196.

16 April | Day 106
1 Joyce Meyer, *How to Hear from God* (Faithwords, 2003), p. 222.

17 April | Day 107
1 William Temple, *Readings in St John's Gospel* (Macmillian, 1952).
2 Corrie ten Boom, *Clippings from My Notebook* (Triangle, 1983).

20 April | Day 110
1 Sailor/rock illustration taken from Washington Jarvis, *With Love and Prayers* (David R. Godine Publishers, 2004), p. 286.

22 April | Day 112
1 Joyce Meyer, *The Everyday Life Bible* (Faithwords, 2018), p. 337.

23 April | Day 113
1 Eugene Peterson, *The Contemplative Pastor* (William B Eerdmans Publishing Co, 1993), pp. 91–93.

24 April | Day 114
1 Aleksandr Solzhenitsyn, *The Templeton Address*, 'Men have forgotten God', world copyright © 1983 by Aleksandr Solzhenitsyn.

25 April | Day 115
1 Introductory illustration from David Wiles, *Stories from the Edge* (Monarch, 2010).

27 April | Day 117

1 Lesslie Newbigin, *The Open Secret* (Eerdmans B Publishing, 1995), p. 36.

28 April | Day 118

1 John Stott, *Issues facing Christians Today* (Zondervan, 2006), p. 368.

29 April | Day 119

1 Raniero Cantalamessa, *Faith Which Overcomes the World* (Alpha International, 2006), p. 9.
2 Cited in Josh McDowell, *The New Evidence That Demands a Verdict* (Thomas Nelson, 1999), p. 317.
3 Jean Vanier, *Drawn into the Mystery of Jesus through the Gospel of John* (Darton, Longman & Todd Ltd, 2004). I have recently been reading *Drawn into the Mystery of Jesus though the Gospel of John* by Jean Vanier. It's a wonderful book which I thoroughly recommend. I am deeply indebted to him for some of the material that I have added to the New Testament section of this commentary.

30 April | Day 120

1 William Temple, *Readings in St. John's Gospel*, (MacMillan, 1939) p. 29.

1 May | Day 121

1 *Surprised by Joy* is the title of a semi-autobiographical book by C. S. Lewis which looks at his early life and his conversion to Christianity. (William Collins, 2012) copyright © C. S. Lewis Pte Ltd 1955.

2 May | Day 122

1 Martin Luther King Jr, *Strength to Love* (Fortress Press, 2010 gift edition), p. 47.

4 May | Day 124

1 The writings of Mother Teresa of Calcutta copyright © by the Mother Teresa Center, exclusive licensee throughout the world of the Missionaries of Charity for the works of Mother Teresa. Used with permission.
2 John Stott, *Issues Facing Christians Today*, Fourth edition (Zondervan, 2006), p. 331.
3 Cardinal Joseph Ratzinger, 'Letter to the Bishops of the Catholic Church on the Collaboration of Men and Women in the Church and in the World' (2004) from The Offices of the Congregation for the Doctrine of the Faith, http://www.vatican.va/roman_curia/congregations/cfaith/documents/rc_con_cfaith_doc_20040731_collaboration_en.html.

5 May | Day 125

1 Jackie Pullinger has been in ministry in Hong Kong since 1966. Her work has resulted in thousands of addicts being set free from their addictions. I will talk more about Jackie on Day 336. To read her full story see, *Chasing the Dragon* by Jackie Pullinger (Hodder & Stoughton, 2006).

6 May | Day 126

1 My friend, Pete Greig, has written an excellent book on this subject called *God on Mute* (Kingsway Publications, 1st Paperback Edition, 2007).
2 Joyce Meyer, *The Everyday Life Bible* (Faithwords, 2018), p. 1685.
3 ibid. p. 380

9 May | Day 129

1 Copyright © Charles Laurence / Telegraph Media Group Limited 2003. Used by permission.
2 http://www.who.int/mediacentre/news/releases/2017/world-hunger-report/en/

10 May | Day 130

1 John Stott, *Calling Christian Leaders* (IVP, 2013), p. 57.
2 Marghanita Laski, quoted in John Stott, *The Contemporary Christian* (IVP, 1995), p. 48.

11 May | Day 131

1 Alice Cooper quoted in http://www.newsreleasetoday.com/artistdetail.php?artist_id=3421 [accessed June 2019].

12 May | Day 132

1 Robbie Williams, 'Feel', from *Escapology* (EMI, 2002). Songwriters: Williams, Robert Peter / Chambers, Guy Antony. Lyrics © Kobolt and Farrell Music Limited.
2 C. S. Lewis, *Mere Christianity* copyright © C. S. Lewis Pte Ltd 1942, 1943, 1944, 1952.

14 May | Day 134

1 Romeo Dallaire, *Shake Hands with the Devil: The Failure of Humanity in Rwanda* (Random House, 2003), Preface p. xviii.
2 Martin Luther King Jr, *Strength to Love* (Fortress Press, 2010 gift edition), p. 47.

15 May | Day 135

1 Sandy Millar, *All I Want is You* (Alpha International, 2005), p. 21.
2 Nelson Mandela quote from Jean Vanier, *Finding Peace* (Continuum IPG, 2003), p. 24.

17 May | Day 137

1 J. I. Packer, *Knowing God* (Hodder & Stoughton, 1973), p. 31.

18 May | Day 138

1 Bernhard Langer, http://www.thegoal.com/players/golf/langer_bernhard/langer_bernhard.html [last accessed June 2019].
2 Cardinal Joseph Ratzinger, *The Spirit of the Liturgy* (Ignatius Press, 2000), pp. 203–4.

19 May | Day 139

1 Callum G. Brown, *The Death of Christian Britain: Understanding Secularisation 1800–2000* (Routledge, 2009).
2 Divorce Statistics from Office of National Statistics, accessed via: https://www.ons.gov.uk/peoplepopulationandcommunity/birthsdeathsandmarriages/divorce/bulletins/divorcesinenglandandwales/2016
3 Samaritans statistic from Samaritans.org, accessed via: http://www.samaritans.org/news/samaritans-volunt-heroes-give-more-5-million-hours-year-save-lives
4 Interview with Mother Teresa of Calcutta, *Hello*, Issue 324, 1 October 1994.

21 May | Day 141

1 https://en.wikipedia.org/wiki/Government
2 Sir Winston Churchill, *Churchill Speaks: Winston S. Churchill in Peace and War: Collected Speeches, 1899–1963* (Atheneum, 1981) (Speech in the House of Commons, 11 November 1947).

23 May | Day 143

1 Festo Kivengere, *I Love Idi Amin* (Marshall, Morgan and Scott, 1977).

24 May | Day 144

1 Jim Collins, *How the Mighty Fall* (Random House Business, 2009).
2 Henry Cloud, *Integrity* (HarperBusiness, 2009).

25 May | Day 145

1 http://www.globalissues.org/issue/2/causes-of-poverty; http://www.unwater.org
2 A. W. Tozer, *The Knowledge of the Holy* (HarperCollins, 1978).
3 Joyce Meyer, *The Everyday Life Bible* (Faithwords, 2018), p. 448.

26 May | Day 146

1 Joyce Meyer, *The Everyday Life Bible*, (Faithwords, 2018), p. 451.

28 May | Day 148

1 Joyce Meyer, *New Day, New You* (Faithwords, 2007), p. 365.

29 May | Day 149

1 Winston Churchill, *Amid These Storms: Thoughts and Adventures* (C. Scribner's Sons, 1932), p. 113.
2 Oliver James, *Affluenza* (Vermillion, 2007), p. 35.

30 May | Day 150

1 Paul Rincon, 'Apollo 13: From Disaster to Triumph' [online] http://news.bbc.co.uk/1/hi/sci/tech/8613766.stm [last accessed June 2019].

31 May | Day 151

1 William Temple (ed), *Readings in St John's Gospel: First and Second Series* (MacMillan, 1963), p. 360.

2 June | Day 153

1 Francis Chan, *Crazy Love* (David C Cook, first edition, 2009) pp. 54–55, 179.

3 June | Day 154

1 John Skinner, *The Confession of Saint Patrick: The Classic Text in New Translation* (Penguin Random House, 1998), p. 11.

4 June | Day 155

1 Rick Warren in conversation with Nicky Gumbel at the Leadership Conference 2012, https://www.htb.org/media/rick-warren-interview-1

8 June | Day 159

1 The Monkees, 'Shades of Gray' (1965), from Headquarters. Songwriters: Mann, Barry / Weil, Cynthia. Lyrics © EMI Music Publishing.

15 June | Day 166

1 St John of the Cross (tr. Mirabai Starr), *The Dark Night of the Soul* (Riverhead Books, 2003).

16 June | Day 167

1 Eugene Peterson, *The Message*, 'Introduction 1–2 Kings' (NavPress, 2007), p. 406.

17 June | Day 168

1 St John Chrysostom, quoted in Leonard Ravenhill, *Why Revival Tarries* (Bethany Fellowship, 1959), p. 156

20 June | Day 171

1 Joyce Meyer, *The Everyday Life Bible* (Faithwords, 2018), p. 530.

21 June | Day 172

1 Acts of Paul 3, 'The Acts of Paul and Thecia', Paragraph 2, in J. K. Elliot, *The Apocryphal New Testament* (Clarendon, 1993), p. 364.

23 June | Day 174

1 C. S. Lewis, *The Four Loves* (William Collins, 2012) copyright © C. S. Lewis Pte Ltd 1960. Used by permission.

2 The writings of Mother Teresa of Calcutta copyright © by the Mother Teresa Center, exclusive licensee throughout the world of the Missionaries of Charity for the works of Mother Teresa. Used with permission.
3 John Stott, *The Message of Acts* (IVP, 1991).

24 June | Day 175
1 Juan Carlos Ortiz, *Disciple* (Charisma House, 2001), pp. 101–102.
2 Julie Schwietert Collazo, Lisa Rogak (eds), *Pope Francis in His Own Words* (New World Library, 2013), p. 46.

25 June | Day 176
1 Spurgeon's Sermons Volume 12: 1866: 'The Ravens' Cry', delivered on Sunday evening, 14 January 1866 by C. H. Spurgeon at the Metropolitan Tabernacle, Newington.

26 June | Day 177
1 Corrie ten Boom (in a letter, 1974).

1 July | Day 182
1 https://www.thecatholictelegraph.com/pope-francis-priests-should-be-shepherds-living-with-the-smell-of-the-sheep/13439

4 July | Day 185
1 Stephen Lungu, *Out of the Black Shadows: The Amazing Transformation of Stephen Lungu* (Monarch Books, 2006).
2 Gustave Flaubert, letter to Louise Colet, 14 June 1853.

5 July | Day 186
1 The writings of Mother Teresa of Calcutta copyright © by the Mother Teresa Center, exclusive licensee throughout the world of the Missionaries of Charity for the works of Mother Teresa. Used with permission.

6 July | Day 187
1 John F. Kennedy, Address of Senator John F. Kennedy Accepting the Democratic Party Nomination for the Presidency of the United States, Memorial Coliseum, Los Angeles, 15 July 1960.
2 C. S. Lewis, *Mere Christianity* copyright © C. S. Lewis Pte Ltd 1942, 1943, 1944, 1952.

9 July | Day 190
1 Corrie ten Boom, *The Hiding Place* (Hodder & Stoughton, 2004).

11 July | Day 192
1 Alan Whiticker, *Speeches that Shaped the Modern World* (New Holland Publishers, 2005).
2 Northumbria Community's Morning Prayer from Celtic Daily Prayer

12 July | Day 193
1 Graham Tomlin, *Luther and His World* (Lion Books, 2012), p. 58.

13 July | Day 194
1 Pete Greig, *The Vision and the Vow* (Kingsway Publications, 2005), pp. 17–18.

14 July | Day 195
1 Second Life quotation from Robert M. Geraci, *Virtually Sacred: Myth and Meaning in World of Warcraft and Second Life* (OUP USA, 2014), p. 101.
2 Eugene Peterson, *The Message*: 'Introduction to Jonah', (NavPress, 1993), p. 1265.

15 July | Day 196
1 Jackie Pullinger, *Crack in the Wall* (Hodder & Stoughton, 1993), pp. 15–16.

16 July | Day 197
1 Joyce Meyer, *The Everyday Life Bible* (Faithwords, 2018), p. 1804.
2 ibid., p. 1805.

17 July | Day 198
1 John Calvin, 'Acts of the Council of Trent with the Antidote Canon 11' (1547), http://www.monergism.com/thethreshold/sdg/calvin_trentantidote.html

18 July | Day 199
1 Robbie Williams and Guy Chambers, 'Feel', from *Escapology* (Chrysalis, 2002).
2 St Augustine, *De Catechizandis Rudibus* 1, 8, 4; PL 40, 319, quoted in Raniero Cantalamessa, *Life in Christ* (Liturgical Press, 2002), p. 7.
3 Raniero Cantalamessa, *Life in Christ* (Liturgical Press, 2002), p. 7.

20 July | Day 201
1 Eugene Peterson, *The Message*: 'Introduction to Hosea' (NavPress, 1993), p. 1221.

21 July | Day 202
1 Nicky Gumbel, *Questions of Life* (Alpha International, 2011), p. 47.
2 Joyce Meyer, *The Everyday Life Bible* (Faithwords, 2018), p. 1368.

22 July | Day 203
1 Joyce Meyer, *The Everyday Life Bible* (Faithwords, 2018), p. 1370.

23 July | Day 204
1 Will Durant, *The Mansions of Philosophy: A Survey of Human Life and Destiny* (Garden City Publishing Company, 1929).

24 July | Day 205
1 John Stott, *The Message of Romans* (IVP, 1994), p. 246.
2 Isaac Watts, 'When I Survey the Wondrous Cross' (1707).

26 July | Day 207
1 Eugene Peterson, *The Message*: 'Introduction to 1 and 2 Chronicles' (NavPress, 1993), p. 484.
2 Lesslie Newbigin, *Discovering Truth in a Changing World* (Alpha International, 2012), p. 96.

29 July | Day 210
1 Jago Wynne, *Working Without Wilting* (IVP, 2009).

30 July | Day 211
1 Oscar Cullmann, *The State in the New Testament* (SCM, 1957), p. 86.

31 July | Day 212
1 John Stott, *The Message of Romans* (IVP, 2001), p. 357.

1 August | Day 213
1 Raniero Cantalamessa, *Life in Christ* (Liturgical Press, 2002), p. 81.
2 Erwin McManus, *Soul Cravings* (Thomas Nelson, 2008), p. 2.
3 Corrie ten Boom, *Clippings from my Notebook* (Triangle, 1983).

3 August | Day 215
1 Ken Costa, *God at Work* (Alpha International, 2013).
2 Jago Wynne, *Working Without Wilting* (IVP, 2009).

3 Costa, *God at Work*.
4 Joyce Meyer, *The Everyday Life Bible* (Faithwords, 2018), p. 635.

6 August | Day 218
1 Vaughan Roberts, *True Spirituality* (IVP, 2011).

7 August | Day 219
1 Joyce Meyer, *The Everyday Life Bible* (Faithwords, 2018), p. 1849.

9 August | Day 221
1 Blaise Pascal, *Pensées* (Penguin Classics, 1995).

11 August | Day 223
1 Nicky Gumbel, *The Jesus Lifestyle* (Hodder & Stoughton, 2018), pp. 75–92.
2 Joyce Meyer, *The Everyday Life Bible* (Faithwords, 2018), p. 1017.
3 Eugene Peterson, *The Message*: 'Introduction to Ecclesiastes' (NavPress, 1993), p. 882.

12 August | Day 224
1 William Shakespeare, *Macbeth*, Act IV Scene I, first published 1623.

13 August | Day 225
1 Lord Byron, *Manfred: A Dramatic Poem*, 1816–17.

15 August | Day 227
1 Gordon D. Fee, *The First Epistle to the Corinthians* (William B. Eerdmans Publishing Co., 1987), p. 431.

16 August | Day 228
1 Billy Graham, quoted in John C. Maxwell, *Developing the Leader Within You* (Thomas Nelson Publishing, 2012), p. 45.
2 John C. Maxwell, *Developing the Leader Within You* (Thomas Nelson Publishing, 2012), p. 38.
3 Joyce Meyer, *The Everyday Life Bible* (Faithwords, 2018), p. 663.

17 August | Day 229
1 C. S. Lewis, *Selected Books* copyright © C. S. Lewis Pte Ltd 1999.

18 August | Day 230
1 Sandy Millar, *All I Want is You* (Alpha International, 2005).
2 Joyce Meyer, *The Everyday Life Bible* (Faithwords, 2018), p. 1036.

19 August | Day 231
1 D. L. Moody Foreword to Henry Drummond, *The Greatest Thing in the World* (Revell, 2011), p. 10.
2 Henry Drummond, *The Greatest Thing in the World* (Revell, 2011), p. 13.
3 ibid., p. 13.

23 August | Day 235
1 Joyce Meyer, *The Everyday Life Bible* (Faithwords, 2018), p. 681.

24 August | Day 236
1 Lesslie Newbigin, *The Open Secret* (William B. Eerdmans Publishing Co., 1995), p. 36.

25 August | Day 237
1 Pope Jean Paul II, *Familiaris Consortio* © Copyright 1981 Libreria Editrice Vaticana: http://w2.vatican.va/content/john-paul-ii/en/apostexhortations/documents/hfjp-iiexh19811122 familiaris-consortio.html

27 August | Day 239
1 Raniero Cantalamessa, *The Holy Spirit in the Life of Jesus* (Liturgical Press, 1994).

28 August | Day 240
1 The Clara Barton illustration is taken from John C. Maxwell, *Developing the Leader Within You* (Thomas Nelson Publishing, 2012), p. 105.
2 John Eddison (1916–2011), 'At the Cross of Jesus'.

29 August | Day 241
1 Timothy Keller, *Preaching: Communicating Faith in an Age of Scepticism* (Hodder & Stoughton, 2015), p. 104.

2 September | Day 245
1 Eugene Peterson, *The Message*: 'Introduction to Isaiah', (NavPress, 1993).

3 September | Day 246
1 Bear Grylls, *Mud, Sweat and Tears* (Channel 4, 2012).

5 September | Day 248
1 Lily Allen, 'The Fear', From *It's Not Me, It's You* (Regal, 2009).

8 September | Day 251
1 Dr Martyn Lloyd-Jones, *The Christian Warfare: An Exposition of Ephesians* 6:10–13 (Baker Books, 1998), p. 20.
2 For more information about the Leadership Conference, visit: https://alpha.org/lc

10 September | Day 253
1 Bear Grylls, *Mud, Sweat and Tears* (Channel 4, 2012).
2 E. H. Bickersteth, 'Peace, Perfect Peace' (1875).

11 September | Day 254
1 Nick Vujicic, *Life Without Limits* (Waterbrook, 2012), p. viii.
2 ibid., p. 21.
3 Mother Teresa, quoted in *The Power of Prayer* (MJF Books, 1998), p. 3, taken from *United States Catholic Catechism for Adults* (USCCB, 2006) pp. 479–80.

12 September | Day 255
1 Joyce Meyer, @JoyceMeyer: https://twitter.com/joycemeyer/status/367322178749857792 [last accessed: September 2015]

14 September | Day 257
1 Charles Wesley, 'And Can it Be' (1738).

15 September | Day 258
1 John F. Kennedy in a speech to the Convocation of the United Negro College Fund on April 12, 1959.

16 September | Day 259
1 Oswald Chambers, *My Utmost for His Highest*: 'March 19' (Discovery Books, 1992).

17 September | Day 260
1 J. Oswald Sanders, *Spiritual Leadership* (Moody Publishers, 2007), p. 13.

18 September | Day 261
1 Adrian Plass, *Clearing Away the Rubbish* (HarperCollins, 2000).

20 September | Day 263
1 G. K. Chesterton, *Illustrated London News*, 16 July 1910.

21 September | Day 264
1 Winston Churchill excerpt from his address to Harrow School, 29 October 1941: https://www.nationalchurchillmuseum.org/never-give-in-never-never-never.html
2 Bear Grylls, *A Survival Guide for Life* (Corgi, 2013), p. 29.

22 September | Day 265
1 Colin Urquhart, *In Christ Jesus* (Hodder & Stoughton, 1981).

24 September | Day 267
1 Philip Schaff (ed.), NPNF1-05, St Augustine: Anti-Pelagian Writings (CCEL, 1886).

25 September | Day 268
1 Quoted in Nicky Gumbel, *Heart of Revival*, (Alpha International, 1997), p. 151.
2 John Stott, *God's New Society: The Message of Ephesians* (IVP, 1980), p. 156–7.

27 September | Day 270
1 John Paul Getty, quoted in Linda and Charlie Bloom, 'The Price of Success', *Psychology Today*, 24 April 2012: https://www.psychologytoday.com/blog/stronger-the-broken-places/201204/the-price-success
2 Cardinal Joseph Ratzinger, Letter to the Bishops of the Catholic Church on the Collaboration of Men and Women in the Church and in the World, 31 May 2004. http://www.vatican.va/roman_curia/congregations/cfaith/documents/rc_con_cfaith_doc_20040731_collaboration_en.html [accessed June 2019].
3 Robert Spaemann, *Persons: The Difference between 'Someone' and 'Something', Oxford Studies in Theological Ethics* (Oxford University Press, 2007), p. 227.

28 September | Day 271
1 F. F. Bruce, *The Epistle to the Galatians, The New International Greek Testament Commentary* (William B. Eerdmans Publishing Co.; reprint edition, 2014), p. 190.
2 Raniero Cantalamessa, *Come, Creator Spirit* (Liturgical Press, 2002), p. 187.
3 Eugene Peterson, *The Message*: 'Introduction to Nahum' (NavPress, 2004), p. 1271.

29 September | Day 272
1 Bernard Levin (1928–2004), British columnist.
2 Raniero Cantalamessa, *Life in Christ* (Liturgical Press, 2002), p. 7.

2 October | Day 275
1 Charles W. Colson, *Born Again* (Chosen Books, 2008), p. 37.
2 J. B. Lightfoot, *Saint Paul's Epistle to the Philippians* (Macmillan, 1896), p. 151.

3 October | Day 276
1 Corrie ten Boom, *Clippings from My Notebook* (Triangle, 1983).

4 October | Day 277
1 Eucharistic Prayer A for use in Order One, *Common Worship* (Church House Publishing, 2000), pp. 184–5, © The Archbishops' Council.

5 October | Day 278
1 Jonathan Gabay, *The Meaning of Life: Revelations, Reflections and Insights from All Walks of Life* (Virgin Books, 1995).

7 October | Day 280

1 Joyce Meyer, *The Everyday Life Bible* (Faithwords, 2018), p. 1002.
2 C. S. Lewis, *The Weight of Glory* (William Collins, 2013) copyright © C. S. Lewis Pte Ltd 1949.

8 October | Day 281

1 Charles Dickens, *A Tale of Two Cities* (Penguin Classics, 2003).
2 Rick Warren interviewed by Nicky Gumbel at the Leadership Conference 2012 in the Royal Albert Hall. www.alpha.org/lc

10 October | Day 283

1 C. S. Lewis, *Surprised by Joy* (William Collins, 2012) copyright © C. S. Lewis Pte Ltd 1955.
2 Gordon Fee, Paul's Letter to the Philippians, *The New International Commentary on the New Testament* (William B. Eerdmans Publishing Co., 1995), p. 404.

11 October | Day 284

1 Barry Humphries, *More Please: An Autobiography* (Penguin Books, 1993).

12 October | Day 285

1 Tim Marshall, Sky News foreign affairs editor, news.sky.com, 13:57pm, Thursday 29 September 2011: http://news.sky.com/story/iran-christian-convert-may-still-be-hanged-10485456 [last accessed August 2016]
2 The *Guardian*, 'Iran: live free – and die', 29 September 2011: https://www.theguardian.com/commentisfree/2011/sep/29/iran-live-free-die-editorial [last accessed August 2016].

15 October | Day 288

1 Martin Luther King, 6 February 1968, Washington DC, quoted in Gordon Brown, *Courage – Eight Portraits* (Bloomsbury, 2008), p. 113.
2 Ken Costa, *God at Work* (Alpha International, 2013), pp. 69–70, 85.
3 ibid.
4 Joyce Meyer, *The Everyday Life Bible* (Faithwords, 2018), p. 1199.

16 October | Day 289

1 P. T. Forsyth, quoted in David Pawson, *A Commentary on Acts* (Anchor Recordings Ltd, 2014), p. 47.
2 Billy Graham, *The Quotable Billy Graham* (Droke House, 1966).

17 October | Day 290

1 Alexander Whyte (ed.), *Lancelot Andrewes and His Private Devotions* (Apocryphile Press, 2008).

18 October | Day 291

1 James Charlton (ed.), *The Military Quotation Book* (St Martin's Press, 2002), p. 83.
2 Robert Murray M'Cheyne, quoted in Tony Sargent, *The Sacred Anointing* (Crossway Books, 1994), p. 128.
3 Quoted in John C. Maxwell, *Developing the Leaders Around You* (Thomas Nelson, 2005), p. 62.
4 Mark Twain, quoted in John C. Maxwell, *The 5 Levels of Leadership: Proven Steps to Maximize Your Potential* (Center Street, 1960).

19 October | Day 292

1 Bill Bradfield, *On Reading the Bible: Thoughts and Reflections of Over 500 Men and Women* (Dover Publications, 2005), p. 121.

20 October | Day 293

1 The writings of Mother Teresa of Calcutta copyright © by the Mother of Teresa Center, exclusive licensee throughout the world of the Missionaries of Charity for the works of Mother Teresa. Used with permission.

21 October | Day 294

1 Francis Bacon, 1625, *The Essayes or Counsels, Ciuill and Morall, of Francis Lo. Verulam, Viscount St Alban* (printed by John Haviland, Early English Books Online 2), p. 85.

22 October | Day 295

1 John C. Maxwell, *Developing the Leaders Around You* (Thomas Nelson Publishing, 2012), pp. 2–3.
2 Frank Lewis Dyer and Thomas Commerford Martin, *Edison: His Life and Inventions*, Vol. 2 (Harper & Brothers, 1910), p. 607.

23 October | Day 296

1 John Eddison, *A Study in Spiritual Power* (Highland,1982).
2 John Stott, *The Message of 2 Timothy* (IVP, 1973).
3 Joyce Meyer, *The Everyday Life Bible* (Faithwords, 2018), p. 2012.

24 October | Day 297

1 Letter to Mme. N. D. Fonvisin, 1854, as published in *Letters of Fyodor Michailovitch Dostoevsky to His Family and Friends* (1914), tr. Ethel Golburn Mayne, Letter XXI, p. 71.
2 Martin Luther, E. Theodore Bachmann (ed.), *Luther's Works, Volume 35: Word and Sacrament I* (Fortress Press, 1960), p. 236.

25 October | Day 298

1 David M. Atkinson, *Leadership – By the Book* (Xulon Press, 2007), p. xiv.

26 October | Day 299

1 *The Best Exotic Marigold Hotel* (20th Century Fox, 2012).
2 Jeremiah: 'a person given to lamentation or woeful complaining, a denouncer of the times, a dismal prophet' (*New Shorter Oxford English Dictionary*).

27 October | Day 300

1 Simone Weil, *Gravity and Grace* (Routledge, 2002), p. 70.
2 Joyce Meyer, *The Everyday Life Bible* (Faithwords, 2018), p. 1434.

28 October | Day 301

1 Eugene Peterson, *The Message*, 'Introduction to Lamentations', (NavPress, 1993) p. 1110.

29 October | Day 302

1 Jim Bakker, *I Was Wrong* (Thomas Nelson, 2010), pp. 282–4.

30 October | Day 303

1 Madonna, SPIN, May 1985.
2 Josh McDowell, *Evidence That Demands a Verdict* (Here's Life Publishers, 1986) p. 127.
3 Robert P. Vande Kappelle, *Truth Revealed: The Message of the Gospel of John – Then and Now* (Wipf and Stock, 2014) p. xii.

31 October | Day 304

1 Charles Allen, *Raj: A Scrapbook of British India 1877–1947*, (Penguin Books, 1979).
2 Child Trafficking stats: Accessed via, https://www.stopthetraffik.org/the-scale-of-human-traffiking [last accessed October 2017]; https://www.globalslaveryindex.org/ [last accessed for research: June 2019]

1 November | Day 305
1 Eugene Peterson, *The Message*: 'Introduction to Joel' (NavPress, 1993), p. 1225.

2 November | Day 306
1 Bernard Levin, 'Clodhoppers on Crusade', *The Times*, 27 January 1992.
2 Joyce Meyer, *The Everyday Life Bible* (Faithwords, 2018), p. 1384.
3 ibid., p. 1385.

3 November | Day 307
1 Rick Warren, 'God Uses Your Problems for Good', *Daily Hope*, 22 September 2015. Accessed via: https://www.oneplace.com/ministries/daily-hope/read/devotionals/daily-hope-with-rick-warren/god-uses-your-problems-for-good-daily-hope-with-rick-warren-sep-22-2015-11744838.html

4 November | Day 308
1 Will Pavia, 'Warning: Department of Labelling May Contain Nuts', *Times Online*, 6 January 2006.
2 William Shakespeare, *Othello*, Act III, Scene III.

5 November | Day 309
1 Peter Evans, *Ari: Life and Times of Aristotle Socrates Onassis* (Summit Books, 1986), p. 283.

6 November | Day 310
1 Abraham Lincoln story from Graham H. Twelftree, *Your Point Being?* (Monarch Books, 2003), p. 97.
2 Andrew Bonar, *Robert Murray M'Cheyne* (Banner of Truth, 1960), p. 179.

7 November | Day 311
1 The writings of Mother Teresa of Calcutta copyright © by the Mother of Teresa Center, exclusive licensee throughout the world of the Missionaries of Charity for the works of Mother Teresa. Used with permission.
2 Desmond Tutu, *God is Not a Christian* (Ridder, 2013), pp. 21–24.
3 'The Church the World's Hope': a sermon delivered by C. H. Spurgeon in the Metropolitan Tabernacle in 1863.

8 November | Day 312
1 Read more about Hazy's remarkable story at: https://www.anthonynolan.org/news/2017/06/19/courageous-hazel-face-new-charity-campaign-after-recovering-two-stem-cell or listen to Alice Richardson (Hazy's mother) at https://www.htb.org/sunday-talks-archive/2017-12-10/how-does-this-display-gods-glory
2 Tom Wright, *Hebrews for Everyone* (SPCK Publishing, 2003), p. 116.
3 Joyce Meyer, *The Everyday Life Bible* (Faithwords, 2018), p. 2045.

9 November | Day 313
1 Text from *The Book of Common Prayer*, the rights in which are vested in the Crown, is reproduced by permission of the Crown's Patentee, Cambridge University Press.

10 November | Day 314
1 C. S. Lewis, *Letters to an American Lady* copyright © C. S. Lewis Pte Ltd 1967.

11 November | Day 315
1 Maryam Rostampour and Marziyeh Amirizadeh with John Perry (ed.), *Captive in Iran* (Tyndale, 2014).
2 *The Alpha Film Series* features the original content of Alpha reimagined for a new global generation of guests and features interviews and stories from around the world. Watch the first episode at https://alpha.org/watch/alpha-film-series/

3 Josh Billings, quoted in *The Salt Lake Herald*, 17 May 1895, Untitled filler item, Quote Page 4, Column 1, Salt Lake City, Utah, via Quote Investigator: https://quoteinvestigator.com/2017/12/22/postage/
4 William Booth, Cyril Barnes (ed.), *The Founder Speaks Again* (Salvation Army, 1960).

12 November | Day 316
1 Rolling Stones, '(I Can't Get No) Satisfaction', (Decca Records, 1965), lyrics by Keith Richards and Mick Jagger, published by ABKCO Music and Records Inc.

13 November | Day 317
1 Joyce Meyer, *The Everyday Life Bible* (Faithwords, 2018), p. 2051.

14 November | Day 318
1 Ken Costa, *God at Work* (Alpha International, 2013), p. 174.

15 November | Day 319
1 C. H. Spurgeon, *Morning and Evening Daily Readings*, 'Morning reading 12 May' (Wilder Publications, 2009).
2 A. W. Tozer, compiled by Marilynne E. Foster, *Tozer on the Holy Spirit: A 365-Day Devotional* (Wingspread: Reissue edition), p. 337.

16 November | Day 320
1 David Beckham, *David Beckham* (Headline, 2013), pp. 40–41.
2 https://www.thecatholictelegraph.com/pope-francis-priests-should-be-shepherds-living-with-the-smell-of-the-sheep/13439

17 November | Day 321
1 Joyce Meyer, *The Everyday Life Bible* (Faithwords, 2018), p. 2060.
2 Eugene Peterson, *The Message*: 'Introduction to James' (NavPress, 1993), p. 1669.
3 William Shakespeare, *The Merchant of Venice*, Act II, Scene II.

18 November | Day 322
1 Mother Teresa in her Nobel Peace Prize Acceptance Speech on 10 December 1979.

20 November | Day 324
1 John Gray, 'The Truth about Evil', *Guardian*, 21 October 2014: http://www.theguardian.com/news/2014/oct/21/-sp-the-truth-about-evil-john-gray [last accessed November 2015]

21 November | Day 325
1 Ezekiel Hopkins, *The Works of the Right Reverend and Learned Ezekiel Hopkins* (Published 1701), p. 756.
2 Simone Weil & Joë Bousquet, *Correspondance* (Editions l'Age d'Homme, c, 1982) p. 18.

22 November | Day 326
1 C. S. Lewis, *Letters to an American Lady* copyright © C. S. Lewis Pte Ltd 1967.

23 November | Day 327
1 Elie Wiesel, *Night* (Penguin, 1985), p. xxi.

24 November | Day 328
1 John C. Maxwell, *Developing the Leader Within You* (Thomas Nelson Publishing, 2012), p. 38.

26 November | Day 330
1 C. S. Lewis, copyright © C. S. Lewis Pte Ltd.

28 November | Day 332
1 *The Poverty and Justice Bible* (American Bible Society, 2008).

29 November | Day 333
1 G.K. Chesterton, *Irish Impressions* (London: Collins, 1919), p. 24.

30 November | Day 334
1 William F. Arndt and F. Wilbur Gingrich (eds) *A Greek-English Lexicon of the New Testament and Other Early Christian Literature* (University of Chicago Press, 1957), p. 439.

1 December | Day 335
1 Stephen Gaukroger and Nick Mercer, *Frogs in Cream* (Scripture Union, 1990), p. 113.
2 For more detail on this, see commentaries on the book of Daniel, for example, Ronald S. Wallace, *The Lord is King: The Message of Daniel* (IVP, 1979).

2 December | Day 336
1 Jackie Pullinger, *Crack in the Wall* (Hodder & Stoughton, 1997), p. 15
2 Tricia Neill, *From Vision to Action* (Alpha International, 2013).
3 Joyce Meyer, *The Everyday Life Bible* (Faithwords, 2018), p. 2101.

3 December | Day 337
1 Oswald Chambers, *If You Will Ask: Reflections on the Power of Prayer* (Discovery Books, 1994), p. 30.

4 December | Day 338
1 Dietrich Bonhoeffer, *Letters and Papers from Prison* (Pocket Books, 1997), p. 140.

5 December | Day 339
1 This is often attributed to Mark Twain but probably not one of his original quotes. It appears that the origin is anonymous.
2 The work of the Holy Spirit in confirming and strengthening our faith is also recognised in the more liturgical traditions of the church. In the Anglican Church, among other churches, the service of Confirmation focuses on the Holy Spirit.

6 December | Day 340
1 This is a combination of excerpts from two of John Stott's writings: *God's New Society: The Message of Ephesians* (IVP, 1980) p. 172 and *Epistles of John: An Introduction and Commentary* (Tyndale, 1964), p. 205.
2 Eugene Peterson, *The Message*: 'Introduction to Haggai' (NavPress, 2007), p. 1300.

7 December | Day 341
1 A. W. Tozer, *Knowledge of the Holy* (HarperOne, 2009), p. 99.

9 December | Day 343
1 Eugene Peterson, *The Message*: 'Introduction to Revelation' (NavPress, 1996), p. 1674.
2 Joyce Meyer, *The Everyday Life Bible* (Faithwords, 2018), p. 1459.

11 December | Day 345
1 Karl Barth in *Time* Magazine, Friday 31 May 1963.
2 Eugene Peterson, *The Message:* 'Introduction to Esther', (NavPress, 2006) p. 618
3 Joyce Meyer, *The Everyday Life Bible* (Faithwords, 2018), p. 752.

12 December | Day 346
1 The pre-Raphaelite artist Holman Hunt (1827–1910) inspired by this verse, painted 'Light of the World'. He painted three versions in all – the most famous still hangs in St Paul's Cathedral. Jesus, the Light of the World, stands at a door which is overgrown with ivy and weeds. The door clearly represents the door of someone's life. This person has never invited Jesus to come into his or her life. Jesus is standing at the door and knocking. He is awaiting a response. He wants to come in and be part of that person's life. Apparently, someone said to Holman Hunt that he had made a mistake. They told him, 'You have forgotten to paint a handle on the door.'

'Oh no,' replied Hunt, 'that is deliberate. There is only one handle and that is on the inside.'

13 December | Day 347
1 John Stott, *What Christ Thinks of the Church* (Candle Books, 2000), p. 127.

14 December | Day 348
1 C. S. Lewis, *The Lion, the Witch and the Wardrobe* copyright © C. S. Lewis Pte Ltd 1950.

15 December | Day 349
1 For more in-depth exploration of the subject of divorce, see Nicky Gumbel, *The Jesus Lifestyle*, chapter 6, 'How to view marriage and divorce': https://shop.alpha.org/departments/books/the-jesus-lifestyle.

16 December | Day 350
1 Joyce Meyer, *The Everyday Life Bible* (Faithwords, 2018), p. 1471.

18 December | Day 352
1 Anglican collect for the last Sunday before Advent.

21 December | Day 355
1 Hiram Corson, *Introduction to Robert Browning* (IndyPublish, 2002), p. 306.
2 John Stott describes this as seeming 'to masquerade a diabolical parody of the Trinity' (*The Incomparable Christ*, IVP, 2014, p. 200).

22 December | Day 356
1 Nigella Lawson, *The Times*, 28 May 1997.

23 December | Day 357
1 Lesslie Newbigin in an interview with Andrew G. Walker, 1988, transcript in: Andrew G Walker, *Note from a Wayward Son: A Miscellany* (Cascade Books, 2015), p. 268.

24 December | Day 358
1 Charles Dickens, *A Christmas Carol and Other Christmas Books* (Oxford University Press, 1988), p. 88.

25 December | Day 359
1 C. S. Lewis, *The Joyful Christian* copyright © C. S. Lewis Pte Ltd 1977.
2 Charles Wesley, 'Hark the Herald Angels Sing', 1739.
3 The writings of Mother Teresa of Calcutta copyright © by the Mother of Teresa Center, exclusive licensee throughout the world of the Missionaries of Charity for the works of Mother Teresa. Used with permission.

26 December | Day 360
1 John Emory (ed.), Sermon 50 'The Use of Money' in *The Works of the Reverend John Wesley*, A.M. (1840), Vol. I, p. 446.
2 Dietrich Bonhoeffer, *The Cost of Discipleship* (SMG, 1959; Pocket Books: 1st Touchstone edition, 1995), p. 176.

27 December | Day 361
1 YouTube, 'Christmas Food Court Flash Mob, Hallelujah Chorus': http://www.youtube.com/watch?v=SXh7JR9oKVE&feature=youtubegdataplayer
2 Joyce Meyer, *The Everyday Life Bible* (Faithwords, 2018), p. 741.

31 December | Day 365
1 Ed Dobson, *50 Remarkable Events Pointing to The End: Why Jesus Could Return by AD 2000* (Zondervan, 1997).

Alpha is a series of interactive sessions exploring the Christian faith.

Each talk looks at a different question around faith and is designed to create conversation. Alpha is run all around the globe, and everyone's welcome.

It runs in cafés, churches, universities, homes - you name it.